Georgia Edition

GLENCOE
Writer's Choice

Grammar and Composition
Grade 9

Glencoe McGraw-Hill

New York, New York   Columbus, Ohio   Chicago, Illinois   Peoria, Illinois   Woodland Hills, California

ACKNOWLEDGMENTS

Grateful acknowledgment is given authors, publishers, photographers, museums, and agents for permission to reprint the following copyrighted material. Every effort has been made to determine copyright owners. In case of any omissions, the Publisher will be pleased to make suitable acknowledgments in future editions.

Acknowledgments continued on page 958.

The Standardized Test Practice pages in this book were written by The Princeton Review, the nation's leader in test preparation. Through its association with McGraw-Hill, The Princeton Review offers the best way to help students excel on standardized assessments.

The Princeton Review is not affiliated with Princeton University or Educational Testing Service.

The **Facing the Blank Page** feature in this book was prepared in collaboration with the writers and editors of *TIME* magazine.

Copyright © 2004 by The McGraw-Hill Companies, Inc. All rights reserved. Except as permitted under the United States Copyright Act of 1976, no part of this publication may be reproduced or distributed in any form or means, or stored in a database or retrieval system, without the prior written permission of the publisher.

PRINTED IN THE UNITED STATES OF AMERICA

Send all inquiries to:
GLENCOE/MCGRAW-HILL
8787 Orion Place
Columbus, OH 43240-4027

ISBN 0-07-861345-0
(Student Edition)
ISBN 0-07-861349-3
(Teacher's Wraparound Edition)

1 2 3 4 5 6 7 8 9 10 027/043 07 06 05 04 03

Letter to Students

Dear Student,

You are about to learn how to use one of the world's most valuable tools. It organizes; it informs; it instructs; it delights. It tells stories. It shares ideas. It keeps people in touch. It persuades them to act. It is the foundation for all kinds of products that matter in people's lives—commercial Web sites, news broadcasts, presidential speeches, as well as laws that protect citizens and help governments run. What is this tool? *Writing.* **Glencoe Writer's Choice: Grammar and Composition** puts that tool in your hands and helps you to fully develop as a writer, so that you will succeed in whatever path you choose to follow in life.

Your book is divided into three parts. **Part 1: Composition** will teach you how to write in a variety of genres—from journal entries to research papers—and according to each stage in the writing process. Fellow students and well-known authors model each writing genre. The writers and editors of *TIME* magazine and other real-world writers share their insights into the writing process. Lesson by lesson in each writing unit, you will hone your skills in genre writing. At the end of a unit, you will put those skills to use in an extended piece of writing that you can add to a portfolio of your favorite work.

Part 2: Grammar, Usage, and Mechanics will help you master the conventions of English from the word-level to the sentence-level. The brief lessons here provide clear illustrations of fundamental grammar topics and plenty of exercises to check your understanding. Grammar Reviews at the end of each unit tie the grammar topics to models of literary writing.

Part 3: Resources and Skills will help to round you out as a writer. Through the lessons in Part 3, you will increase your knowledge of words, learn tips on how to find and retrieve information, and practice effective studying and test-taking techniques. You will also learn techniques in speaking and listening and in using visual and electronic media.

To guide you in your classwork and to help prepare you for the real world, the Georgia Department of Education has created content and performance standards for you—**Quality Core Curriculum (QCC) Standards for Language Arts: Core Skills and the Ninth Grade Principles of Literature and Composition.** We have included these standards on pages GA 5–GA 8. Take time to read them over with your teacher and family. Then outline steps that you can take to help you achieve the standards both in and outside the classroom.

We hope that you enjoy *Writer's Choice* and find it helpful in mastering the QCC standards. We think you'll soon agree how useful a tool your own writing can be.

                                                        Sincerely,

                                                        The Editors

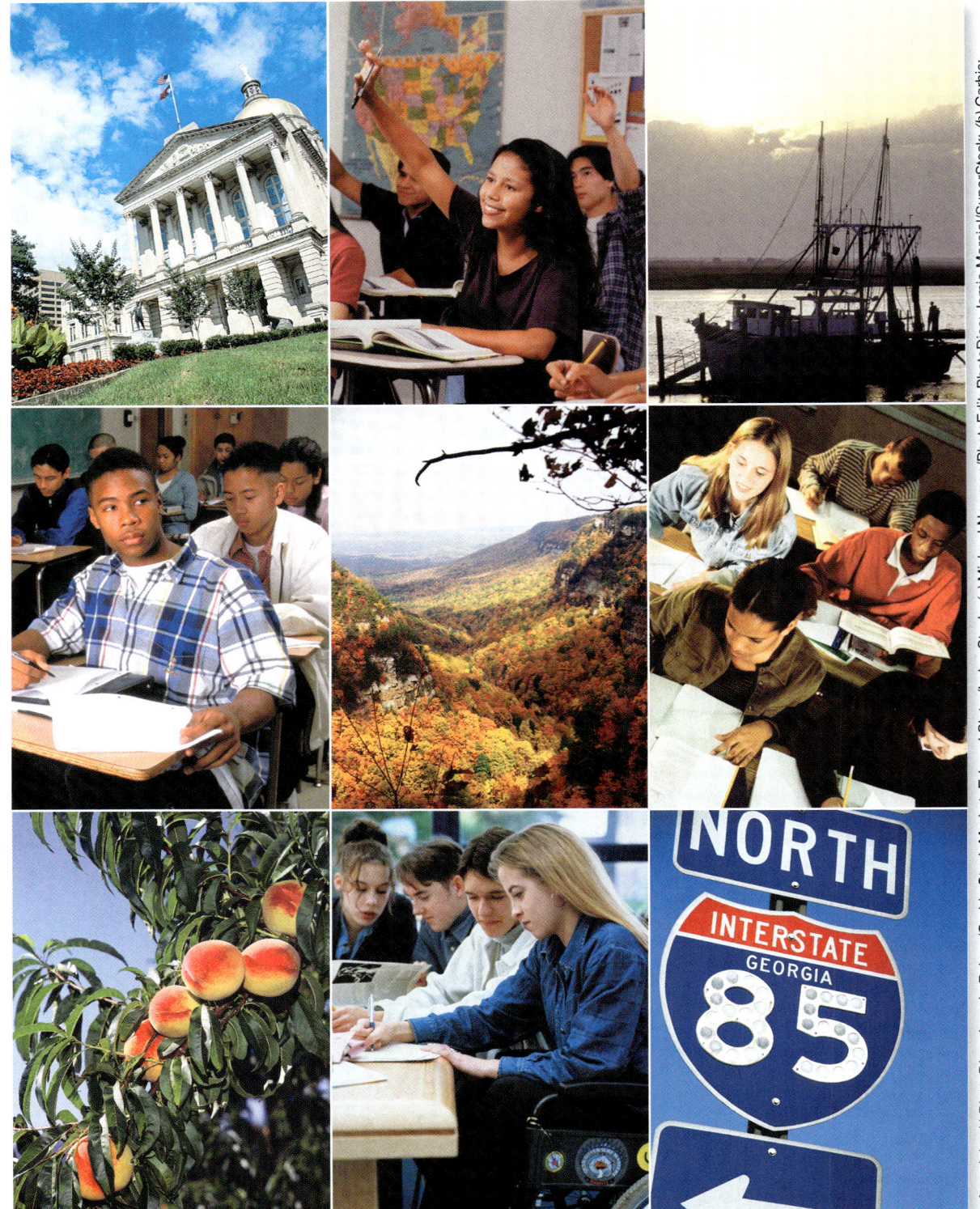

Left to right: (t) PhotoDisc; Jose L. Pelaez/Corbis Stock Market; Edward Slater/Index Stock; *(c)* Michael Newman/PhotoEdit; PhotoDisc; Jamie Marcial/SuperStock; *(b)* Corbis; Ian Shaw/Stone; Comstock.

GEORGIA
Quality Core Curriculum Language Arts

Topic: Core Skills

Standard 1: Reads poems, short stories, essays, novels, magazines, newspapers, charts, graphs, and technical documents for pleasure and self-improvement.

Standard 2: Reads critically, asks pertinent questions, recognizes assumptions and implications, and evaluates ideas.

Standard 3: Takes notes on the main and subordinate ideas in lectures and discussions and reports accurately what others have said.

Standard 4: Uses research process: selecting topic, formulating questions, identifying key words, choosing sources, skimming, paraphrasing, note-taking, organizing, summarizing, and presenting.

Standard 5: Identifies, comprehends, and summarizes the main and subordinate ideas in a written work.

Standard 6: Learns that words gather meaning from their context and carry connotation and denotation.

Standard 7: Distinguishes between fact and opinion.

Standard 8: Comprehends, develops, and uses specifics and generalizations.

Standard 9: Acquires new vocabulary through reading and listening; demonstrates progress through speaking and writing.

Standard 10: Uses literal comprehension skills (e.g., sequencing, explicitly stated main idea).

Standard 11: Uses inferential comprehension skills (e.g., predictions, comparisons, conclusions, implicitly stated main idea).

Standard 12: Defines unfamiliar words by using appropriate structural analysis skills including prefixes, suffixes, root words, and context clues.

Standard 13: Uses a variety of print and nonprint resources (e.g., films, recordings, theater, computer databases) as parts of the study of literature.

Standard 14: Draws reasoned conclusions from various sources.

Standard 15: Writes Standard American English sentences with correct verb forms, punctuation, capitalization, possessives, plural forms and other mechanics, word choice, and spelling.

Standard 16: Recognizes speaker's purpose and identifies verbal and nonverbal components of communication (body language, facial expression, gestures).

Standard 17: Uses language appropriate to situation and audience.

Standard 18: Participates in the writing process: prewriting, drafting, revising, editing, proofreading, and publishing.

Standard 19: Writes for many purposes including, but not limited to, personal (journals, diaries, stories, poems), social (friendly letters, thank-you notes, invitations), academic (themes, reports, essays, analyses, critiques), and business (letters, memos, and applications) writing.

Standard 20: Gains insight into human behavior from the study of literature.

Standard 21: Creates hypotheses and predicts outcomes.

Standard 22: Defends conclusions rationally.

Standard 23: Speaks so others can hear and understand.

Standard 24: Works as a team member to solve problems.

Standard 25: Composes and revises on a computer.

Topic: Critical Thinking

Standard 26: Solves word analogy problems.

Topic: Reading/Literature

Standard 27: Uses the features of print materials appropriately (e.g., table of contents, preface, introduction, titles and subtitles, index, glossary, appendix, and bibliography).

Standard 28: Varies reading speed and methods according to the type of material and purpose of reading.

Standard 29: Identifies the structural elements of literature (e.g., plot, characterization, setting, mood, tone, and point of view).

Standard 30: Reads and responds to mythology.

Standard 31: Reads, discusses, and analyzes technical literature and general exposition.

Standard 32: Experiences a variety of print and nonprint resources (e.g., films, recordings, theater, and computer databases) as a part of the study of literature and technical/vocational writings.

Standard 33: Expands reading vocabulary.

Standard 34: Applies word recognition strategies through the use of the graphophonic, semantic, syntactic, and orthographic cueing systems.

Standard 35: Interprets literal and nonliteral meaning of words and phrases.

Standard 36: Adjusts reading speed according to purpose and rereads for comprehension.

Standard 37: Analyzes explicit and implicit main ideas, details, sequence of events, and cause/effect relationships.

Standard 38: Makes comparisons, predictions, generalizations, and draws conclusions.

Standard 39: Analyzes fact and opinion, persuasion, bias, and stereotyping.

Standard 40: Recognizes different contextual structures and adapts vocabulary and comprehension strategies appropriately.

Topic: Speaking/Listening

Standard 41: Engages critically and constructively in discussions by speaking and listening.

Standard 42: Follows multipart instructions and asks questions for clarification.

Standard 43: Adapts words and statements to various situations and audiences.

Standard 44: Conceives and develops ideas about a topic for the purpose of speaking to a group, chooses and organizes related ideas, presents them clearly in standard American English, and evaluates similar presentations by others.

Standard 45: Evaluates the messages and effects of mass media.

Standard 46: Identifies verbal and nonverbal components of interpersonal communications.

Topic: Writing/Usage/Grammar

Standard 47: Writes well-developed paragraphs with clear, controlling ideas.

Standard 48: Writes in narrative, descriptive, persuasive, and expository modes of writing.

Standard 49: Uses precise punctuation, capitalization, spelling, and other elements of manuscript form.

Standard 50: Writes for a variety of purposes including, but not limited to, technical (process, explanation), business (letters of order, request, application, complaint), personal (journal, diaries, stories), social (friendly letters, thank-you notes, invitations), and academic (themes, reports, essays, analyses, critiques).

GLENCOE
Writer's Choice
Grammar and Composition
Grade 9

Glencoe McGraw-Hill

New York, New York   Columbus, Ohio   Chicago, Illinois   Peoria, Illinois   Woodland Hills, California

ACKNOWLEDGMENTS

Grateful acknowledgment is given authors, publishers, photographers, museums, and agents for permission to reprint the following copyrighted material. Every effort has been made to determine copyright owners. In case of any omissions, the Publisher will be pleased to make suitable acknowledgments in future editions.

Acknowledgments continued on page 958.

The Standardized Test Practice pages in this book were written by The Princeton Review, the nation's leader in test preparation. Through its association with McGraw-Hill, The Princeton Review offers the best way to help students excel on standardized assessments.

The Princeton Review is not affiliated with Princeton University or Educational Testing Service.

The **Facing the Blank Page** feature in this book was prepared in collaboration with the writers and editors of *TIME* magazine.

PROGRAM CONSULTANTS

Mark Lester is Professor of English at Eastern Washington University. He formerly served as Chair of the Department of English as a Second Language, University of Hawaii. He is the author of *Grammar in the Classroom* (Macmillan, 1990) and of numerous other professional books and articles.

Sharon O'Neal is Assistant Professor at the College of Education, Southwest Texas State University, where she teaches courses in reading instruction. She formerly served as Director of Reading and Language Arts of the Texas Education Agency and has authored, and contributed to, numerous articles and books on reading instruction and teacher education.

Jacqueline Jones Royster is Associate Professor of English at The Ohio State University. She is also on the faculty at the Bread Loaf School of English at Middlebury College in Middlebury, Vermont. In addition to the teaching of writing, Dr. Royster's professional interests include the rhetorical history of African American women and the social and cultural implications of literate practices.

William Strong is Professor of Secondary Education at Utah State University, Director of the Utah Writing Project, and a member of the National Writing Project Advisory Board. A nationally known authority on the teaching of composition, he is the author of many volumes, including *Writing Incisively: Do-It-Yourself Prose Surgery* (McGraw-Hill, 1991).

Jeffrey Wilhelm, a former English and reading teacher, is currently an assistant professor at the University of Maine, where he teaches courses in middle and secondary level literacy. Author of several books and articles on the teaching of reading and the use of technology, he also works with local schools as part of the Adolescent Literacy Project.

Denny Wolfe, a former high school English teacher and department chair, is Professor of English Education, Director of the Tidewater Virginia Writing Project, and Director of the Center for Urban Education at Old Dominion University in Norfolk, Virginia. Author of more than seventy-five articles and books on teaching English, Dr. Wolfe is a frequent consultant to schools and colleges on the teaching of English language arts.

Advisors

Michael Angelotti
Head of Division of Teacher Education
College of Education
University of Oklahoma

Larry Beason
Assistant Professor of English
Eastern Washington University

Charles Duke
Dean of the College of Education and Human Services
Clarion University

Carol Booth Olson
Director
University of California, Irvine, Writing Project

Willis L. Pitkin
Professor of English
Utah State University

Judith Summerfield
Associate Professor of English
Queens College, City University of New York

Bonnie S. Sunstein
Associate Professor of English and Director, Master of Arts in Teaching Program
Rivier College

Educational Reviewers

Janice Brown
Houston ISD
Houston, Texas

Lenore Croudy
Flint Community School
Flint, Michigan

John A. Grant
St. Louis Public Schools
St. Louis, Missouri

Vicki Haker
Mead Junior High School
Mead, Washington

Frederick G. Johnson
Georgia Department of Education
Atlanta, Georgia

Sterling C. Jones Jr.
Detroit Public Schools
Detroit, Michigan

Barry Kincaid
Raytown School District
Kansas City, Missouri

Evelyn G. Lewis
Newark Public Schools
Newark, New Jersey

M. DeAnn Morris
Crescenta Valley High School
La Crescenta, California

Anita Moss
University of North Carolina
Charlotte, North Carolina

Ann S. O'Toole
Chesterfield County Schools
Richmond, Virginia

Suzanne Owens
Glendale High School
Glendale, California

Sally P. Pfeifer
Lewis and Clark High School
Spokane, Washington

Marie Rogers
Independence High School
Charlotte, North Carolina

Barbara Schubert
Santa Clara County Office of Education
San Jose, California

Ronnie Spilton
Chattahoochee High School
Alpharetta, Georgia

Robert Stolte
Huntington Beach High School
Huntington Beach, California

Student Advisory Board

The Student Advisory Board was formed in an effort to ensure student involvement in the development of *Writer's Choice*. The editors wish to thank members of the board for their enthusiasm and dedication to the project. The editors also wish to thank the many student writers whose models appear in this book.

BOOK OVERVIEW

Part 1 Composition

Unit 1	Personal Writing	2
Unit 2	The Writing Process	52
TIME	Facing the Blank Page	121
Unit 3	Descriptive Writing	132
Unit 4	Narrative Writing	174
Unit 5	Expository Writing	222
Unit 6	Persuasive Writing	282
Unit 7	Research Paper Writing	322
Unit 8	Sentence Combining	358
Unit 9	Troubleshooter	386
	Business and Technical Writing	412

Part 2 Grammar, Usage, and Mechanics

Unit 10	Parts of Speech	438
Unit 11	Parts of the Sentence	494
Unit 12	Phrases	518
Unit 13	Clauses and Sentence Structure	538
Unit 14	Diagraming Sentences	570
Unit 15	Verb Tenses and Voice	580
Unit 16	Subject-Verb Agreement	608
Unit 17	Using Pronouns Correctly	632
Unit 18	Using Modifiers Correctly	658
Unit 19	Usage Glossary	686
Unit 20	Capitalization	710
Unit 21	Punctuation, Abbreviations, and Numbers	730

Part 3 Resources and Skills

Unit 22	Sources of English Words	782
Unit 23	Library Resources	798
Unit 24	Using Dictionaries	811
Unit 25	Vocabulary	818
Unit 26	Spelling	827
Unit 27	Study Skills	836
Unit 28	Taking Tests	847
Unit 29	Listening and Speaking	884
Unit 30	Viewing and Representing	893
Unit 31	Electronic Resources	905

Writing and Language Glossary 918
Spanish Glossary 928
Index 938
Acknowledgments 954

CONTENTS

Part 1 Composition

UNIT 1 Personal Writing 2

Writing in the Real World 4

A Letter to Gwendolyn Brooks
Personal letter by Sandra Cisneros

Instruction and Practice

1.1 Writing to Discover 8
Freewrite About Yourself; Cross-Curricular Activity;
Viewing and Representing; Grammar Link

1.2 Keeping a Journal 12
Write a Journal Entry; Listening and Speaking;
Cross-Curricular Activity; Grammar Link

1.3 Writing a Personal Essay 16
Write a Personal Essay; Viewing and Representing;
Cross-Curricular Activity; Grammar Link

1.4 Writing Autobiography 20
Write an Autobiographical Sketch; Using Computers;
Viewing and Representing; Grammar Link

1.5 Writing a Poem 24
Write Your Own Poem; Listening and Speaking;
Cross-Curricular Activity; Grammar Link

Writing About Literature

1.6 Keeping a Reader-Response Journal 28
Write a Reader-Response Journal Entry; Viewing and
Representing; Using Computers; Grammar Link

Writing About Literature

1.7 Writing About Biography 32
Write a Response to a Biography; Listening and
Speaking; Spelling; Grammar Link

vi

Writing Process in Action

Personal Writing Project **36**
Write about an event or relationship that had
a positive effect on your life.
• Prewriting • Drafting • Revising
• Editing/Proofreading • Publishing/Presenting

Literature Model

from *I Know Why the Caged Bird Sings*
by Maya Angelou **40**

Linking Writing and Literature

Examining the style of Maya Angelou's writing and its appeal **50**

UNIT 1 Review

Reflecting on the Unit
Adding to Your Portfolio
Writing Across the Curriculum **51**

UNIT 2 The Writing Process 52

Writing in the Real World 54

The Quest for Hispanic Roots
Magazine article by Lorenzo Chavez

Instruction and Practice

2.1 Overview of the Writing Process **58**
Write a Comparison; Using Computers; Viewing and
Representing; Grammar Link

2.2 Prewriting: Getting Started **62**
Generate Story Ideas; Using Computers; Listening and
Speaking; Grammar Link

2.3 Prewriting: Identifying Purpose and Audience .. **68**
Identify Purpose and Audience; Using Computers; Listening
and Speaking; Grammar Link

2.4 Prewriting: Gathering Information **72**
Gather Information About Your Topic; Using Computers;
Listening and Speaking; Grammar Link

2.5 Drafting: Turning Notes into Paragraphs **76**
Write a Confirming Draft; Listening and Speaking;
Using Computers; Grammar Link

2.6 Drafting: Writing Unified Paragraphs **80**
Check Your Paragraphs; Cross-Curricular Activity; Viewing
and Representing; Grammar Link

vii

	2.7	**Drafting: Ordering the Details** **84**
		Check Organization; Cross-Curricular Activity; Listening and Speaking; Grammar Link
	2.8	**Drafting: Writing Coherent Paragraphs** **88**
		Check Your Paragraphs for Coherence; Viewing and Representing; Cross-Curricular Activity; Grammar Link
	2.9	**Revising: Improving Paragraphs** **92**
		Revise Your Draft; Cross-Curricular Activity; Listening and Speaking; Grammar Link
	2.10	**Editing/Proofreading: Final Checking** **96**
		Edit Your Human-Interest Story; Using Computers; Viewing and Representing; Grammar Link
	2.11	**Publishing/Presenting: Sharing Writing** **100**
		Present Your Human-Interest Story; Using Computers; Viewing and Representing; Grammar Link

Vincent van Gogh, *The Starry Night*, 1889

Writing About Literature

	2.12	**Explaining Theme** **104**
		Write an Analysis; Viewing and Representing; Cross-Curricular Activity; Grammar Link

Writing Process in Action

Writing Process Project **108**
Retell a story a family member has told you.
- Prewriting • Drafting • Revising
- Editing/Proofreading • Publishing/Presenting

Literature Model

Linking Writing and Literature

from **The Kitchen God's Wife** by Amy Tan **112**

Examining how Amy Tan uses details to develop her theme **119**

UNIT **2** Review

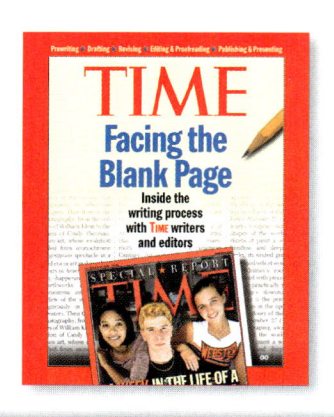

Reflecting on the Unit

Adding to Your Portfolio

Writing Across the Curriculum **120**

Facing the Blank Page **121**

Writing for *TIME* • Prewriting • Drafting • Revising
• Editing/Proofreading • Publishing/Presenting

viii

UNIT 3 Descriptive Writing 132

Writing in the Real World 134
from *Big*
Screenplay by Gary Ross and Anne Spielberg

Instruction and Practice

3.1 Writing a Descriptive Paragraph 138
Write a Descriptive Paragraph; Cross-Curricular Activity; Viewing and Representing; Grammar Link

3.2 Using Descriptive Language 144
Write a Vivid Paragraph; Using Computers; Viewing and Representing; Grammar Link

3.3 Describing an Imaginary Place 148
Describe a Scene; Cross-Curricular Activity; Listening and Speaking; Grammar Link

3.4 Describing an Imaginary Person 152
Write About an Imaginary Person; Cross-Curricular Activity; Listening and Speaking; Grammar Link

Writing About Literature

3.5 Analyzing Character Descriptions 156
Write a Character Analysis; Using Computers; Viewing and Representing; Grammar Link

Writing Process in Action

Descriptive Writing Project 160
Write about an imagined place.
- Prewriting • Drafting • Revising
- Editing/Proofreading • Publishing/Presenting

Literature Model
Linking Writing and Literature

from ***The Crystal Cave*** by Mary Stewart 164

Analyzing Mary Stewart's use of description 172

UNIT 3 Review

Reflecting on the Unit
Adding to Your Portfolio

Writing Across the Curriculum 173

ix

UNIT 4 Narrative Writing 174

Writing in the Real World 176
Salute to an Amazing Ironman
Sports Writing by Lisa Twyman Bessone

Instruction and Practice

4.1 Writing Simple Narratives 180
Write a Personal Narrative; Listening and Speaking; Using Computers; Grammar Link

4.2 Developing Conflict in Narrative 184
Write a Narrative About a Conflict; Viewing and Representing; Cross-Curricular Activity; Grammar Link

4.3 Writing Dialogue 188
Write a Dialogue; Viewing and Representing; Cross-Curricular Activity; Grammar Link

4.4 Using Anecdotes 192
Write an Anecdote; Cross-Curricular Activity; Listening and Speaking; Grammar Link

4.5 Writing a Sports Narrative 196
Write a Sports Narrative; Listening and Speaking; Cross-Curricular Activity; Grammar Link

Writing About Literature

4.6 Writing About Suspense 200
Write to Analyze Setting; Cross-Curricular Activity; Listening and Speaking; Grammar Link

Writing About Literature

4.7 Analyzing Point of View in a Narrative 204
Write to Analyze Point of View in a Story; Using Computers; Viewing and Representing; Grammar Link

Writing Process in Action

Narrative Writing Project 208
Write a narrative based on conflict and resolution.
- Prewriting • Drafting • Revising
- Editing/Proofreading • Publishing/Presenting

Literature Model

from ***How the García Girls Lost Their Accents***
by Julia Alvarez 212

Linking Writing and Literature

Examining Julia Alvarez's use of character and conflict 220

UNIT 4 Review

Reflecting on the Unit
Adding to Your Portfolio
Writing Across the Curriculum 221

UNIT 5 Expository Writing 222

Writing in the Real World 224
Counting Cacti
Magazine Article by Suzanne Winckler

Instruction and Practice

5.1 Explaining and Informing 228
Write an Expository Paragraph; Cross-Curricular Activity; Using Computers; **Grammar Link**

5.2 Going into Detail 232
Write a Background Information Article; Viewing and Representing; Cross-Curricular Activity; **Grammar Link**

5.3 Explaining How To… 236
Write a "How To" Paper; Cross-Curricular Activity; Listening and Speaking; **Grammar Link**

5.4 Explaining Cause and Effect 240
Write a Cause-and-Effect Paragraph; Viewing and Representing; Cross-Curricular Activity; **Grammar Link**

5.5 Classifying a Subject 244
Write a Classification; Using Computers; Viewing and Representing; **Grammar Link**

5.6 Comparing and Contrasting 248
Write a Comparison-Contrast Paper; Cross-Curricular Activity; Listening and Speaking; **Grammar Link**

5.7 Writing with Graphics 252
Write a Paragraph with a Graphic; Using Computers; Viewing and Representing; **Grammar Link**

5.8 Writing a Feature Article 256
Write a Feature Story; Viewing and Representing; Using Computers; **Grammar Link**

5.9 Answering an Essay Question 262
Write an Essay Answer; Cross-Curricular Activity; Listening and Speaking; **Grammar Link**

Writing About Literature

5.10 Comparing and Contrasting Two Myths 268
Write a Comparison-Contrast Essay; Listening and Speaking; Using Computers; **Grammar Link**

xi

Writing Process in Action

Expository Writing Project. 272
Write to inform the reader about a repellent insect or other animal.
- Prewriting • Drafting • Revising
- Editing/Proofreading • Publishing/Presenting

Literature Model
Linking Writing and Literature

from *Of Wolves and Men* by Barry Holstun Lopez 276

Learning how Barry Holstun Lopez conveys in-depth information in a lively and appealing way 280

UNIT 5 Review

Reflecting on the Unit
Adding to Your Portfolio
Writing Across the Curriculum 281

UNIT 6 Persuasive Writing 282

Writing in the Real World 284

Petrie's "Toy Soldiers" Has Glitches
Movie Review by Melanie McFarland

Instruction and Practice

6.1 **Writing Persuasively** 288
Write a Letter to the Editor; Cross-Curricular Activity; Listening and Speaking; **Grammar Link**

6.2 **Using Evidence Effectively** 292
Evaluate an Editorial; Using Computers; Viewing and Representing; **Grammar Link**

6.3 **Checking Reasoning** 296
Write a Persuasive Argument; Viewing and Representing; Using Computers; **Grammar Link**

6.4 **Using Language to Advantage** 300
Write a Positive Description; Cross-Curricular Activity; Using Computers; **Grammar Link**

6.5 **Writing an Editorial** 304
Write an Editorial for a TV Program; Using Computers; Listening and Speaking; **Grammar Link**

Writing About Literature

6.6 **Writing a Movie Review** 308
Write a Movie Review; Cross-Curricular Activity; Using Computers; **Grammar Link**

xii

Writing Process in Action

Persuasive Writing Project 312
Write a persuasive editorial about a problem in your school or community.
- Prewriting • Drafting • Revising
- Editing/Proofreading • Publishing/Presenting

Literature Model

Linking Writing and Literature

"Skeletons in the Attic" by Clara Spotted Elk 316

Analyzing how Clara Spotted Elk makes her argument effective. . . 320

UNIT 6 Review

Reflecting on the Unit

Adding to Your Portfolio

Writing Across the Curriculum 321

UNIT 7 Research Paper Writing 322

Instruction and Practice

7.1 Prewriting: Planning and Researching 324
What is a Research Paper?; Choose a Good Topic; Find Information on Your Topic; Take Notes

7.2 Prewriting: Outlining 330
Create an Outline; Develop a Thesis Statement

7.3 Drafting 334
Use Your Outline and Notes; Prepare the First Draft; Write the Introduction and Conclusion

7.4 Citing Sources 338
Document Information; Format Citations Properly; Format Your List of Works Cited

7.5 Revising 344
Improve Your Paper; Revise Your Paper

7.6 Editing and Presenting: A Model Paper 348
Prepare the Final Copy; Present the Complete Paper

Student Model

George W. G. Ferris: The Man Who Reinvented the Wheel by Britta C. Waller 350

UNIT 7 Review

Reflecting on the Unit

Adding to Your Portfolio

Writing Across the Curriculum 357

xiii

UNIT 8 Sentence Combining......358

Instruction and Practice

Style Through Sentence Combining............360
Varying Sentence Length and Structure; Using Parallelism, Interrupting Phrases, and Unusual Patterns for Emphasis

- 8.1 Description......365
- 8.2 Narration......369
- 8.3 Exposition......373
- 8.4 Persuasion......377
- 8.5 Literature Exercises......381

UNIT 9 Troubleshooter......386

Problems and Solutions

- 9.1 Sentence Fragment......388
- 9.2 Run-on Sentence......390
- 9.3 Lack of Subject-Verb Agreement......392
- 9.4 Lack of Pronoun-Antecedent Agreement......396
- 9.5 Lack of Clear Pronoun Reference......398
- 9.6 Shift in Pronoun......400
- 9.7 Shift in Verb Tense......401
- 9.8 Incorrect Verb Tense or Form......402
- 9.9 Misplaced or Dangling Modifier......404
- 9.10 Missing or Misplaced Possessive Apostrophe......406
- 9.11 Missing Commas with Nonessential Element......408
- 9.12 Missing Commas in a Series......410

Keith Haring, *Untitled*, 1985

Business and Technical Writing......412

Instruction and Practice

- Business Letters......413
- Memos, E-mail, and Applications......421
- Using the Computer as a Writing Tool......425
- Technical Writing......431
- Collaborative Writing in the Business World......434

Part 2 Grammar, Usage, and Mechanics

UNIT 10 **Parts of Speech** 438

Instruction and Practice
- 10.1 Nouns 439
- 10.2 Pronouns 446
- 10.3 Verbs 452
- 10.4 Adjectives 461
- 10.5 Adverbs 467
- 10.6 Prepositions 473
- 10.7 Conjunctions 475
- 10.8 Interjections 481

Grammar Review Parts of Speech 482

Literature Model from *Housekeeping* by Marilynne Robinson

Writing Application Nouns in Writing; Techniques with Nouns; Practice 493

xv

UNIT 11 Parts of the Sentence 494

Instruction and Practice
- 11.1 Simple Subjects and Simple Predicates 495
- 11.2 Complete Subjects and Complete Predicates   496
- 11.3 Compound Subjects and Compound Predicates 498
- 11.4 Order of Subject and Predicate 501
- 11.5 Complements 504

Grammar Review
Parts of the Sentence 510

Literature Model
from *Things Fall Apart* by Chinua Achebe

Writing Application
Sentence Elements in Writing; Techniques with Sentence Elements; Practice 517

UNIT 12 Phrases 518

Instruction and Practice
- 12.1 Prepositional Phrases 519
- 12.2 Appositives and Appositive Phrases 521
- 12.3 Verbals and Verbal Phrases 523

Grammar Review
Phrases 528

Literature Model
from *Picture Bride* by Yoshiko Uchida

Writing Application
Phrases in Writing; Techniques with Phrases; Practice 537

UNIT 13 Clauses and Sentence Structure 538

Instruction and Practice
- 13.1 Main Clauses 539
- 13.2 Subordinate Clauses 540
- 13.3 Simple and Compound Sentences 541

xvi

13.4	Complex and Compound-Complex Sentences	543
13.5	Adjective Clauses	545
13.6	Adverb Clauses	548
13.7	Noun Clauses	550
13.8	Four Kinds of Sentences	552
13.9	Sentence Fragments	553
13.10	Run-on Sentences	555

Grammar Review Clauses and Sentence Structure 558

Literature Model from *Delta Wedding* by Eudora Welty

Writing Application Clauses and Sentence Structure in Writing; Techniques with Clauses and Sentence Structure; Practice 569

UNIT 14 Diagraming Sentences 570

Instruction and Practice

14.1	Diagraming Simple Sentences	571
14.2	Diagraming Simple Sentences with Phrases	574
14.3	Diagraming Sentences with Clauses	577

UNIT 15 Verb Tenses and Voice 580

Instruction and Practice

15.1	Principal Parts of Verbs	581
15.2	Regular and Irregular Verbs	582
15.3	Tenses of Verbs	586
15.4	Perfect Tenses	589
15.5	Progressive and Emphatic Forms	592
15.6	Compatibility of Tenses	594
15.7	Voice of Verbs	596

xvii

Grammar Review	Verb Tenses and Voice	598
Literature Model	from *Black Boy: A Record of Childhood and Youth* by Richard Wright	
Writing Application	Verbs in Writing; Techniques with Verbs; Practice	607

UNIT 16 Subject-Verb Agreement ... 608

Instruction and Practice
- 16.1 Intervening Prepositional Phrases ... 609
- 16.2 Agreement with Linking Verbs ... 611
- 16.3 Agreement in Inverted Sentences ... 612
- 16.4 Agreement with Special Subjects ... 614
- 16.5 Agreement with Compound Subjects ... 616
- 16.6 Intervening Expressions ... 618
- 16.7 Indefinite Pronouns as Subjects ... 619

Grammar Review	Subject-Verb Agreement	622
Literature Model	from *Savushun* by Simin Daneshvar	
Writing Application	Subject-Verb Agreement; Techniques with Subject-Verb Agreement; Practice	631

UNIT 17 Using Pronouns Correctly ... 632

Instruction and Practice
- 17.1 Case of Personal Pronouns ... 633
- 17.2 Pronouns with and as Appositives ... 635
- 17.3 Pronouns After *Than* and *As* ... 637
- 17.4 *Who* and *Whom* in Questions and Subordinate Clauses ... 638
- 17.5 Pronoun-Antecedent Agreement ... 640
- 17.6 Clear Pronoun Reference ... 645

Grammar Review	Using Pronouns Correctly	648
Literature Model	from *The Old Man and the Sea* by Ernest Hemingway	
Writing Application	Pronouns in Writing; Techniques with Pronouns; Practice	657

UNIT 18 Using Modifiers Correctly 658

Instruction and Practice
- 18.1 The Three Degrees of Comparison 659
- 18.2 Irregular Comparisons 661
- 18.3 Double Comparisons 663
- 18.4 Incomplete Comparisons 665
- 18.5 *Good* or *Well*; *Bad* or *Badly* 666
- 18.6 Double Negatives 668
- 18.7 Misplaced and Dangling Modifiers 670

Grammar Review	Using Modifiers Correctly	676
Literature Model	from *An American Childhood* by Annie Dillard	
Writing Application	Modifiers in Writing; Techniques with Modifiers; Practice	685

UNIT 19 Usage Glossary 686

Problems and Solutions
- 19.0 Usage Glossary 687

Grammar Review	Usage Glossary	702
Literature Model	Quotations About Friendship and Love	
Writing Application	Usage of *Lie* in Writing; Techniques with Usage of *Lie*; Practice	709

xix

UNIT 20 Capitalization 710

Instruction and Practice
- 20.1 Capitalization of Sentences 711
- 20.2 Capitalization of Proper Nouns 713
- 20.3 Capitalization of Proper Adjectives 720

Grammar Review Capitalization 724

Literature Model from *Lake Wobegon Days* by Garrison Keillor

Writing Application Capitalization in Writing; Techniques with Capitalization; Practice 729

UNIT 21 Punctuation, Abbreviations, and Numbers 730

Instruction and Practice
- 21.1 The Period 731
- 21.2 The Exclamation Point 732
- 21.3 The Question Mark 732
- 21.4 The Colon 733
- 21.5 The Semicolon 735
- 21.6 The Comma 738
- 21.7 The Dash 749
- 21.8 Parentheses 750
- 21.9 Quotation Marks 752
- 21.10 Italics (Underlining) 757
- 21.11 The Apostrophe 759
- 21.12 The Hyphen 762
- 21.13 Abbreviations 765
- 21.14 Numbers and Numerals 768

Grammar Review Punctuation, Abbreviations, and Numbers 772

Literature Model from *Arctic Dreams* by Barry Holstun Lopez

Writing Application Commas and Parentheses in Writing; Techniques with Commas and Parentheses; Practice 779

Part 3 Resources and Skills

UNIT 22 Sources of English Words 782

Instruction and Practice

22.1 English in Our Time 783
   wordworks EPONYMS
22.2 Conquest and Conversion 786
   wordworks SPOONERISMS
22.3 A Conqueror from France 789
   wordworks PUNS AND TOM SWIFTIES
22.4 Commerce, Culture, and Settlement 792
   wordworks EUPHEMISMS
22.5 New Technology and Ideas 795
   wordworks SLANG

UNIT 23 Library Resources 798

Instruction and Practice

23.1 Library Arrangement 799
23.2 Locating Books and Other Resources 801
23.3 How to Search for Periodicals 806
23.4 Using Reference Sources 808

xxi

UNIT 24 Using Dictionaries 811

Instruction and Practice
- 24.1 General Dictionaries 812
- 24.2 Thesauruses 816

UNIT 25 Vocabulary 818

Instruction and Practice
- 25.1 Building Vocabulary 819
- 25.2 Recognizing Parts of a Word 823

UNIT 26 Spelling 827

Instruction and Practice
- 26.1 Improving Your Spelling 828
- 26.2 Spelling Difficult Words 833

UNIT 27 Study Skills 836

Instruction and Practice
- 27.1 Taking Notes in Class 837
- 27.2 Studying Outside of Class 838
- 27.3 Learning from Graphics 843

UNIT 28 Taking Tests 847

Instruction and Practice

The Princeton Review

28.1 Classroom Tests. 848
28.2 Standardized Tests. 853
28.3 FCAT Test Practice. 859

UNIT 29 Listening and Speaking 884

Instruction and Practice

29.1 Listening Effectively 885
29.2 Speaking Effectively 888
29.3 Participating in Groups 891
29.4 Conducting Interviews. 892

xxiii

Unit 30 Viewing and Representing 893

Instruction and Practice
- 30.1 Examining Visual Messages 894
- 30.2 Evaluating Media Messages 899
- 30.3 Producing Media Messages 902

Unit 31 Electronic Resources 905

Instruction and Practice
- 31.1 Word Processing and the Writing Process 906
- 31.2 Learning with Technology 909
- 31.3 Communicating Visually 912
- 31.4 Producing in Multimedia 915

Writing and Language Glossary 918
Spanish Glossary 928
Index 940
Acknowledgments 958

LITERATURE MODELS

Composition Models

Each literature selection is an extended example of the mode of writing taught in the unit.

Maya Angelou, *I Know Why the Caged Bird Sings*   40
Amy Tan, *The Kitchen God's Wife*   112
Mary Stewart, *The Crystal Cave*   164
Julia Alvarez, *How the García Girls Lost Their Accents*   212
Barry Holstun Lopez, *Of Wolves and Men*   276
Clara Spotted Elk, "Skeletons in the Attic"   316

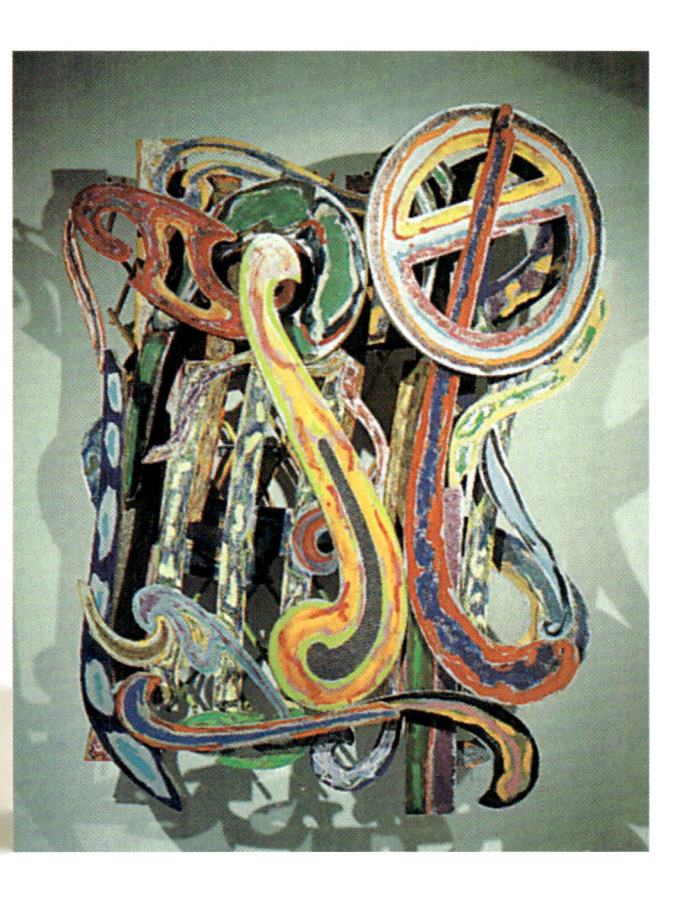

Skill Models

Excerpts from outstanding works of fiction and nonfiction exemplify specific writing skills.

N. Scott Momaday, *The Names*   8
Anne Frank, *Anne Frank: The Diary of a Young Girl*   12
Robert Fulghum, *It Was on Fire When I Lay Down on It*   16
Kareem Abdul-Jabbar with Mignon McCarthy, *Kareem*   22, 37
Langston Hughes, "My People"   24
Ogden Nash, "Song of the Open Road"   25
Soseki, *Cricket Songs*   26
Shel Silverstein, "Reflection"   30
Gwendolyn Brooks, "Old Mary"   31
Alice Walker, *In Search of Our Mothers' Gardens*   60
Yoshiko Uchida, *Desert Exile*   69
Dorothy Gallagher, *Hannah's Daughters*   74
Flannery O'Connor, "A View of the Woods"   78
Sandra Cisneros, *The House on Mango Street*   80
Jim Barnes, "On Native Ground"   85
N. Scott Momaday, *House Made of Dawn*   90, 109
J. R. R. Tolkien, *The Return of the King*   138
Mary Stewart, *The Crystal Cave*   142
Madeleine L'Engle, *A Wrinkle in Time*   144
Ray Bradbury, *The Martian Chronicles*   148
Ursula K. LeGuin, *Tehanu: The Last Book of Earthsea*   153
T. H. White, *The Once and Future King*   161

xxv

LITERATURE MODELS

Skill Models *continued*

Jamaica Kincaid, "The Circling Hand" 180
Russell Baker, *Growing Up* 186
Arnold Rampersad, *The Life of Langston Hughes, Volume II: 1941–1967* 192
Roger Angell, *Season Ticket* 198
Mario Vargas Llosa, "Sunday" 201
Edgar Allan Poe, "The Pit and the Pendulum" 203
Eugenia Collier, "Marigolds" 205
John Updike, "Man and Daughter in the Cold" 206
Julia Alvarez, *How the García Girls Lost Their Accents* 209
David Bodanis, *The Secret House* 228
Judith Stone, *Light Elements* 232
Patrick McManus, *Rubber Legs and White Tail-Hairs* 236
Carl Sagan and Ann Druyan, *Comet* 240
Sue Hubbell, "For the Love of Loons" 244
David Day, *The Doomsday Book of Animals* 248
"Another Crude Year," *Discover*, January 1991 252
Donald Dale Jackson, "Searching for Medicinal Wealth in Amazonia" 257, 260
Cecil Adams, *The Straight Dope* 262
Barry Holstun Lopez, *Of Wolves and Men* 274
Anthony Lewis, "Merchants of Death" 294
Yona Zeldis McDonough, "Sisters Under the Skin" 298
"Winking at Steroids in Sports," *New York Times* 304
Clara Spotted Elk, "Skeletons in the Attic" 314

Language Models

Each Grammar Review uses excerpts to link grammar, usage, or mechanics to literature.

Marilynne Robinson, *Housekeeping* 482
Chinua Achebe, *Things Fall Apart* 510
Yoshiko Uchida, *Picture Bride* 528
Eudora Welty, *Delta Wedding* 558
Richard Wright, *Black Boy: A Record of Childhood and Youth* 598
Simin Daneshvar, *Savushun,* translated from the Persian by M. R. Ghanoonparvar 622
Ernest Hemingway, *The Old Man and the Sea* 648
Annie Dillard, *An American Childhood* 676
Ali Ibn-Abi-Talib, *Sentences* 702
William Shakespeare, "Sonnet 104" 702
Henry Wadsworth Longfellow, "The Arrow and the Song" 702
Charles Dickens, *Oliver Twist* 702
Christina Rossetti, "Goblin Market" 702
Sarah Orne Jewett, *The Country of the Pointed Firs* 702
Willa Cather, *Shadows on the Rock* 703
Hugo von Hofmannsthal, *The Book of Friends* 703
W. H. Auden, *The Dyer's Hand* 703
Ved Mehta, *The Ledge Between the Streams* 703
Garrison Keillor, *Lake Wobegon Days* 724
Barry Holstun Lopez, *Arctic Dreams* 772

FINE ART

Fine art—paintings, drawings, photos, and sculpture—is used to teach as well as to stimulate writing ideas.

Vincent van Gogh, *The Starry Night* viii
Keith Haring, *Untitled*, xiv
Deborah Butterfield, *Twig Sculpture* xxviii
John Lennon, *Self Portrait* 8
Allan Crite, *Harriet and Leon* 19
Rufino Tamayo, *Hombre Ante el Infinito (Man Contemplates Infinity)* 27
Harriet Powers, *Pictorial Quilt* 41
Beverly Buchanan, *Bogart, Georgia* 43
Charles Alston, *Girl in a Red Dress* 45
Wilmer Angier Jennings, *Landscape* 47
Eastman Johnson, *The Hatch Family* 78
Romare Bearden, *Blue Interior, Morning* 79
Georges Seurat, *Bathers at Asnières* 81
Henri Matisse, *The Painter's Family* 85
Artist Unknown, Iranian glazed ceramic bowl 87
Aaron Douglas, *Building More Stately Mansions* 91
Tomie Arai, *Laundryman's Daughter* 114
Ch'ing dynasty, porcelain teapot and beaker 117
Nancy Thill, *Untitled* 142
Claude Monet, *Arbres En Fleurs* 144
Marc Chagall, *Paris Through the Window* 147
Nam June Paik, *Family of Robot: Grandfather* 152
John James Audubon, *Labrador Falcon* 167
Peter Paul Rubens, *Portrait of an Old Man* 170
César A. Martinez, *Mestizo* 187
Joan Brown, *After the Alcatraz Swim #3* 195
Grant Wood, *Death on the Ridge Road* 200
Diego Rivera, *Tina Modotti* 215
Adrián Luis González, Painted pottery typewriter 218
Pablita Velarde, *Old Father Storyteller* 247
Katsushika Hokusai, *The Great Wave off Kanagawa* 251
Alexander Calder, *Flamingo* 261
Nancy Schutt, *Encroachment* 277
Artist Unknown, Makah wolf mask 279
Artist Unknown, Benin bronze plaque 291
Leonardo da Vinci, *Mona Lisa* 302
Pablo Picasso, *Two Acrobats with a Dog* 303
Howling Wolf, Untitled drawing 318
Decorative Jugs for Water in Ghana 436
Anna Mary Robertson ("Grandma") Moses, *Early Skating* 491
Artist Unknown, Ijo Shrine, Nigeria 515
Andō Hiroshige, *The Compound of the Tenjin Shrine at Kameido* 535
Artist Unknown, *Nike of Samothrace* 553
Robert Duncan, *Mandy's Sunhat* 567
William H. Johnson, *Jim* 605
Habib Allah, from *Mantiq at-Tayr (Language of the Birds)* 629
Winslow Homer, *Palm Trees, Nassau* 655
Georgia O'Keeffe, *The White Place in Shadow* 683
John Singer Sargent, *Carnation, Lily, Lily, Rose* 707
Georgia O'Keeffe, *New York Night* 723
Grant Wood, *Stone City, Iowa* 727
Rockwell Kent, *The Trapper* 777
Paul Klee, *AD Parnassum* 780
François Boucher, *Madame de Pompadour* 785

xxvii

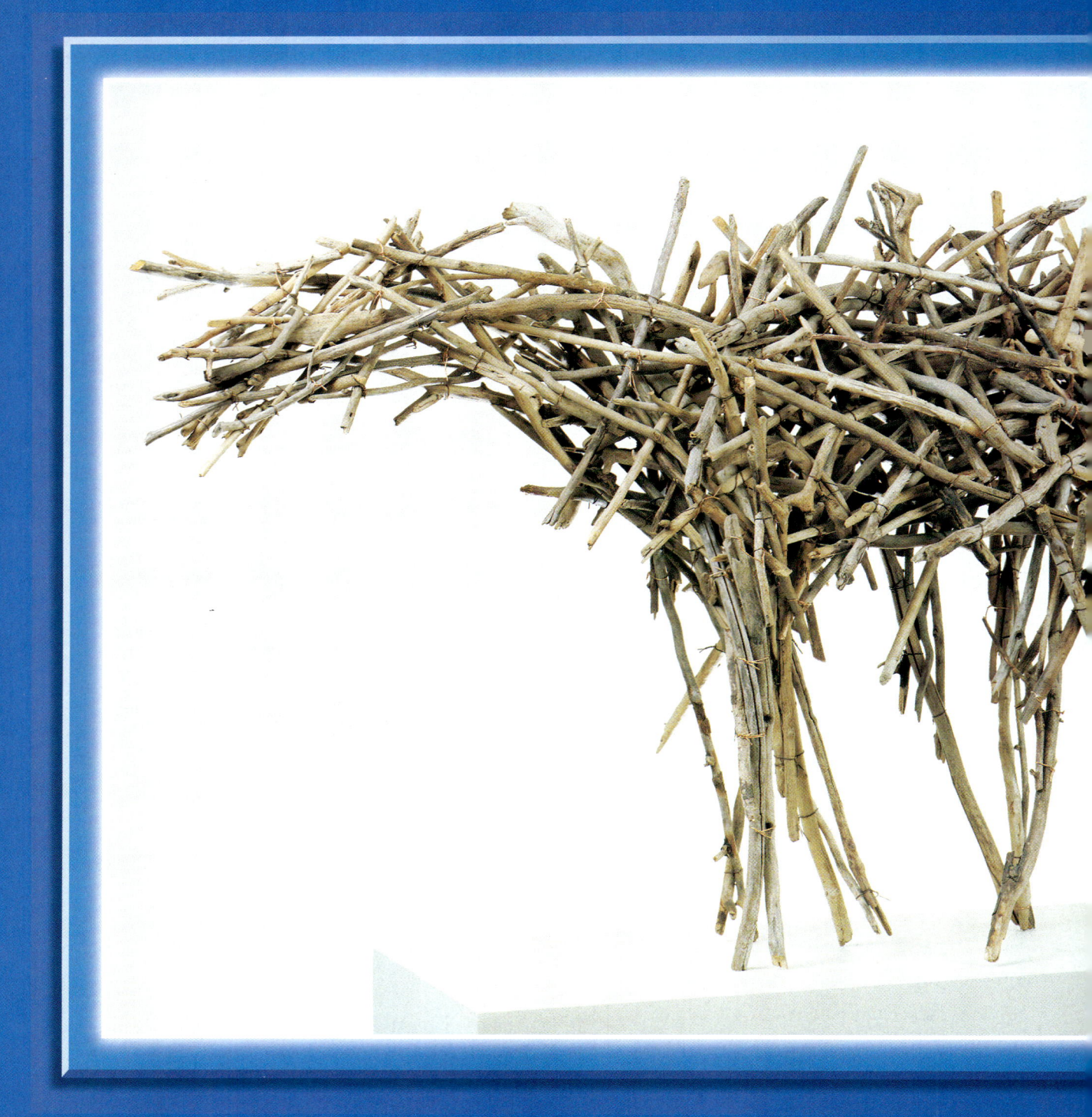

"What perils that tangle of trees and underbrush might hold for him did not concern Rainsford just then."

Richard Connell

PART 1

Composition

Unit 1   **Personal Writing**   2

Unit 2   **The Writing Process**   52

TIME Facing the Blank Page   121

Unit 3   **Descriptive Writing**   132

Unit 4   **Narrative Writing**   174

Unit 5   **Expository Writing**   222

Unit 6   **Persuasive Writing**   282

Unit 7   **Research Paper Writing**   322

Unit 8   **Sentence Combining**   358

Unit 9   **Troubleshooter**   386

Business and Technical Writing   412

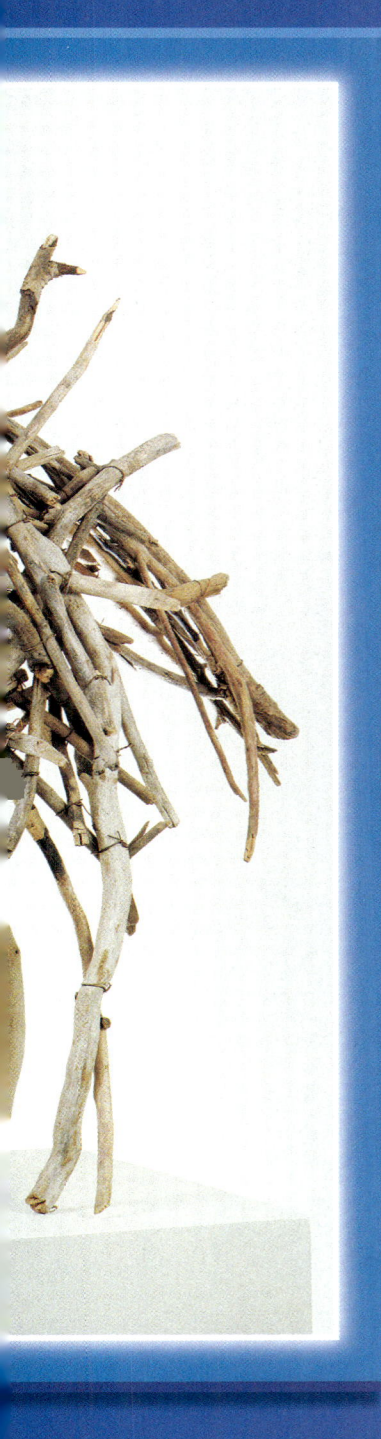

Deborah Butterfield,
Twig Sculpture

"I chose a heavy, compact one that was wrapped in shiny silver foil and a red satin ribbon."

—Amy Tan, "Rules of the Game"

UNIT 1 Personal Writing

Writing in the Real World: Sandra Cisneros 4

Lesson **1.1** Writing to Discover 8

Lesson **1.2** Keeping a Journal 12

Lesson **1.3** Writing a Personal Essay 16

Lesson **1.4** Writing Autobiography 20

Lesson **1.5** Writing a Poem 24

Lesson **1.6** Writing About Literature: Keeping a Reader-Response Journal 28

Lesson **1.7** Writing About Literature: Writing About Biography 32

Writing Process in Action 36

Literature Model: from *I Know Why the Caged Bird Sings* by Maya Angelou 40

Unit 1 Review 51

Writing in the Real World

A letter to Gwendolyn Brooks by Sandra Cisneros

Writing about your own thoughts, feelings, and experiences is called personal writing. Personal writing can either be kept confidential or be shared. Personal letters can help you communicate with someone, teach you something about yourself, and stimulate new ideas. Novelist Sandra Cisneros wrote the letter shown on the next page to her friend Gwendolyn Brooks, Pulitzer Prize winner and poet laureate of Illinois.

Author Sandra Cisneros

Cisneros begins her letter by describing the wind over the mesa.

Writing in the Real World

A Writer's Process

Prewriting
Getting the Idea

The letter to Gwendolyn Brooks was written by Sandra Cisneros as she was about to go on a book tour to promote her new book *Woman Hollering Creek.* She says, "For some reason, I always tour with Brooks's book *Maud Martha.* That morning I'd read one of the stories. I thought, 'I should tell Ms. Brooks how much I like her book.'" Cisneros had not written to Brooks for a long time, but she says, "I wanted her to know how happy her book made me at this moment and how important it's been to me."

Everyone who sits down to do some personal writing approaches it in his or her own personal style. For Cisneros, being free to be herself is important. The author says her letters are "not the kind of conversations you have when you're dressed in your suit, but the kind you have sitting at your kitchen table wearing your pajamas, talking to someone who's very dear to you."

Even the writing tools that Cisneros uses set a cozy mood for her writing. She says she often writes her letters on "pretty paper, that delicious creamy kind with texture. Not intimidating paper, but paper you can do anything on. I'm very fussy about my pens and my papers."

March 5th, 1991

Dear Ms. Brooks,

It is what Winnie the Pooh would call a blustery day here. Or what Miss Emily would designate a wind like a bugle. From over and over the mesas, snapping dust and terrifying trees.

I am in my pajamas though it's past mid-day but I like my leisure to dream a little longer when I am asleep, and continue dreaming on paper when I am awake. I am rereading your wonderful MAUD MARTHA again, a copy you gave me, and which I am very grateful to have. I remember when I first discovered that book, in the American library in Sarajevo, across from the famous river where the archduke was shot that started a world war. And it was there too that I read T.S. Eliot's collected poems. If you go to Sarajevo, and look at the chapter on PRACTICAL CATS you'll see a cherry stain on one of the pages--because I was reading the book on the opposite bank of the river, under a row of cherry trees in front of my American friend Ana's apartment house, and at the moment I was reading about one of Eliot's cats--the Rum Tum Tigger?--a wind shook a cherry loose that landed with a startled plop on the page. And my heart gave a little jump too because the book wasn't mine. A wine-colored stain against the thick creamy pages.

I mean to teach it one day along with other books that use a series of short inter-related stories. Perhaps with Ermilo Abreu Gomez's CANEK and Nellie Campobello's CARTUCHO albeit the translation of both is crooked. The form fascinates. And I'd done as much with MANGO STREET, though I hadn't met your MAUD yet. Perhaps I was "recollecting the things to come."

Ms. Brooks, please know I haven't quite disappeared altogether from the land. I've been migrant professor these past years, guest writer-in-residence at UC Berkeley, UC Irvine, the Univ. of Michigan at Ann Arbor and now here for one semester. All for the sake of protecting my writer self. Some years dipped low and some reeled to high heaven. But now the days are good to me. I have a new book due out from Random (see enclosed reviews) and I have sold my little house on Mango to the big house of Vintage. Both books slated for this April. And it seems my life is in a whirl like the wind outside my window today. Everything shook and snapped and wind-washed and fresh, and, yes, that is how it should be.

I only wanted to say this to you today. That your book gives me such pleasure. That I admire it terribly. I think of you often, Ms. Brooks, and your spirit is with me always.

un abrazo fuerte, fuerte,

Sandra Cisneros

Writing in the Real World

Drafting
Fresh Discoveries

When you write a letter to a dear friend, says Cisneros, "You are blessing your recipient with your confidence, allowing [her or him] to follow your inner meanderings and showing a part of you that perhaps no one else has seen."

Cisneros had recently moved to New Mexico when she began her letter to Gwendolyn Brooks. "When I get to a new place, I like to sift through the events that are affecting me. I don't know how I feel about them until I write letters. Now, [people] talk about the sky in New Mexico, but they never mention the wind. The wind here just rolls out and bangs porch doors open. I've never seen anything like it."

So Cisneros opened her letter to Gwendolyn Brooks by talking about the wind in New Mexico. As Cisneros says, "People don't realize that you can start a letter from whatever comes into your head."

In the course of drafting a letter, Cisneros may discover deeper, hidden aspects of herself. She calls letter writing her "way of meditating, of listening inside my heart to how I'm being affected by the outside world. The heart of who you are comes out when you truly write."

This writer considers her letters to be a much more accurate reflection of her life than any other kind of record, including her journal, which she uses primarily as a place to write "shorthand" notes to herself.

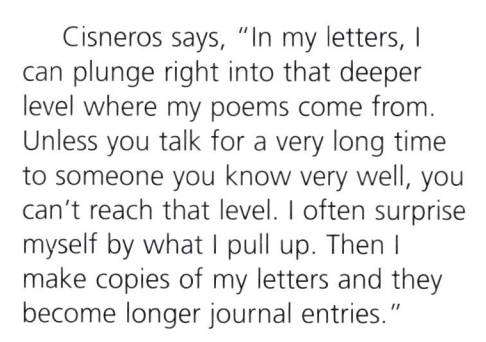

Cisneros says, "In my letters, I can plunge right into that deeper level where my poems come from. Unless you talk for a very long time to someone you know very well, you can't reach that level. I often surprise myself by what I pull up. Then I make copies of my letters and they become longer journal entries."

Revising/Editing
Runways

Although Cisneros often writes her drafts by hand, she says, "Then I need to get to a typewriter, I need to see it typed to do the editing."

Even after she mails a letter, Cisneros keeps marking the copy she makes for herself. She says she often uses a letter as a "runway" to the creative writing process.

She says, "Sometimes I'll go through copies of my letters and I'll underline with a marker some nugget I'm going to save to reuse. When I'm stuck with a story, I might go through all my old letters and just read. I'll ask, 'Where can I put this?' Sometimes I start by writing a letter and then realize I've got a story. Other times, as I'm writing a story, I'll have a character rant or rave or whine or howl or laugh or swoon, and I'll realize that was really a letter to someone, but it's not going to get sent and it doesn't matter."

She continues, "I might use part of this letter to Gwendolyn Brooks in an essay that would include the anecdote of the cherry stain. What this letter particularly sparked for me was how I would like [to teach] the book *Maud Martha* in a course."

Cisneros often revises her letters.

Examining Writing in the Real World

Analyzing the Media Connection

Discuss these questions about the letter on page 5.

1. How does Cisneros's language signal that she is writing a friendly letter rather than a formal one?
2. What words does Cisneros use to place the reader by the river in Sarajevo?
3. How does Cisneros's language create a vivid sense of the place where she currently lives?
4. What images in her letter might contribute to a story Cisneros might later write?
5. How well do you think Sandra Cisneros knows Gwendolyn Brooks? Use evidence in the letter to support your answer.

Analyzing a Writer's Process

Discuss these questions about Sandra Cisneros's writing process.

1. What inspired Cisneros to write to Gwendolyn Brooks?
2. How might Cisneros's choice of writing materials influence her writing process? Would the letter be the same if she did all of the writing on her computer?
3. In what way does Cisneros feel that writing a personal letter helps her learn about herself?
4. How does Cisneros use her letters as a source of ideas for her other writing?
5. In her letter to Gwendolyn Brooks, what details does Cisneros include that help you understand her feelings?

Grammar Link

Use subordinate clauses to create variety in sentence structure.

A **subordinate clause** has a subject and a predicate, but it cannot stand alone as a sentence. It must be attached to a main clause to make sense.

I am in my pajamas **though it's past mid-day.** . . .

Use each subordinate clause below in a sentence. Start by thinking whom or what the clause might describe.

1. who moved away last year
2. after I had finished supper
3. although I have a desk in my room
4. before I was halfway through
5. when I get a chance

See Lesson 13.2, page 540.

LESSON 1.1

Writing to Discover

Self-discovery can happen in many ways. Former Beatle John Lennon expressed his identity in this self-portrait. N. Scott Momaday, in the model below, writes to discover something about himself.

John Lennon, *Self Portrait*

Literature Model

Oh I feel so dumb . . . I don't know how to be a Kiowa Indian my grandmother lives in a house . . . only it doesn't have lights . . . and you have to carry wood in from the wood pile . . . but that isn't what makes it Indian its my grandma the way she is the way she looks her hair in braids the clothes somehow yes the way she talks she doesn't speak English so well . . . wait I know why it's an Indian house because . . . there is Indian stuff all around blankets and shawls bows and arrows everyone there . . . talks Kiowa and the old people wear Indian clothes . . . and there is laughing Indians laugh a lot and they sing oh yes they love to sing . . . there are drums too and it goes on through the night *that's* Indian . . .

N. Scott Momaday, *The Names*

> What uncertainties does Momaday give voice to here? In your opinion, for whom is this written?

> Recalling specific details of sights and sounds helps Momaday deal with his uncertainties.

Learn by Writing

Asking personal questions is one way to get started writing about yourself. In the model on page 8, Momaday probably began with questions about his Kiowa heritage and then found answers as he recalled experiences, feelings, and observations. You can review elements of your own life to learn more about who you are, as the diagram below illustrates.

Personal Questions Chart (with Sample Answers)

Q. What are some of the central things that make me *me*?
A. African American, teenager, oldest kid in my family, member of soccer team

Q. How do I feel as a typical day goes on?
A. I usually feel pretty good; too much homework gets me down, though. I feel warm and secure at home but free and more myself with my friends.

Q. What kinds of lessons have I learned recently?
A. I've learned about friendship, about dating, and about being a good sport in soccer.

Q. What do I enjoy most?
A. I like hanging out with friends, playing soccer, watching TV, and, believe it or not, my world history class.

Some sources for personal writing

Observations
Our dog, Sparky, is getting pretty old. He sleeps most of the time and doesn't play catch anymore.

Reactions
I get so angry when Mom expects me to babysit my little sister, Mandy.

Memories
Oatmeal always reminds me of breakfasts with my grandmother.

Experiences
The first time Alissa and I went downtown alone, we got lost.

Feelings
I feel completely in control when I strike out a batter.

Journal Writing

John Lennon's self-portrait on page 8 emphasizes three features: his hair, his nose, and his eyeglasses. In your journal, draw a simple sketch of yourself. Emphasize three simple attributes, either physical characteristics or personality traits. Then write to answer this question: What does your self-portrait reveal about who you are?

Write About Yourself

Whatever your sources, often the easiest way to begin personal writing is simply to begin—let your thoughts run free and write whatever comes to mind. Don't worry about spelling or grammar. Set a definite time limit—say, ten minutes—and keep writing until the time is up. If you get stuck, write anything, even "I'm stuck!" Just keep going. Before you know it, a word will spark a memory or another idea, and you'll be on your way. In the process, you may clarify your thoughts and even discover something about yourself. The chart below shows how this might happen.

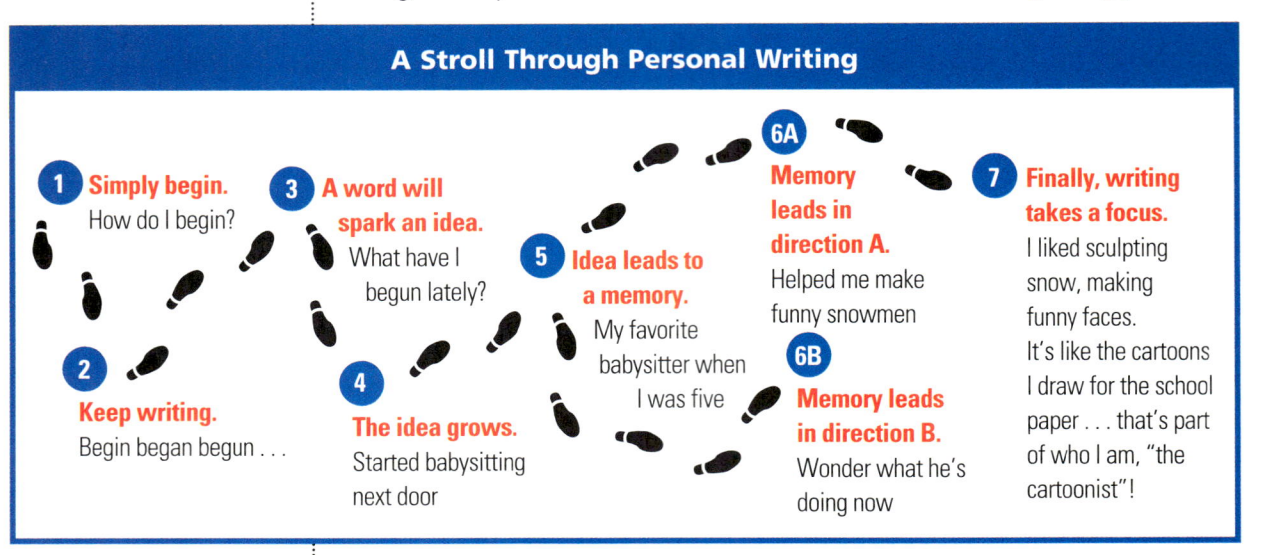

A Stroll Through Personal Writing

1 Simply begin. How do I begin?

2 Keep writing. Begin began begun . . .

3 A word will spark an idea. What have I begun lately?

4 The idea grows. Started babysitting next door

5 Idea leads to a memory. My favorite babysitter when I was five

6A Memory leads in direction A. Helped me make funny snowmen

6B Memory leads in direction B. Wonder what he's doing now

7 Finally, writing takes a focus. I liked sculpting snow, making funny faces. It's like the cartoons I draw for the school paper . . . that's part of who I am, "the cartoonist"!

Your experiences, feelings, memories, observations, and reactions are your best sources for personal writing. See what student Vallery McCann learned about herself.

> How would you assess the honesty of Vallery's writing? Does it sound authentic?

> This journal entry helps Vallery think about plans for her future. What plans might you write about?

Student Model

Well, today is a milestone in my life. Yeehah. Three years ago today I was ending an old life and beginning a new one, & I didn't even know it. The freedom I have today is incredible. I am not ashamed of me. I have gotten to know myself. I was thinking on my way to school today maybe the difference between a romantic relationship & a friendship is that in a friendship the only commitment is unconditional love. I'm getting ready to graduate. Life looms ahead. I'm finding myself believing in education. I want to teach and give that opportunity of freedom to others. So today is my third anniversary drug free! I will not back down! I am free!

Vallery McCann, Hamilton Heights High School, Arcadia, Indiana

1.1 Writing Activities

Freewrite About Yourself

Choose one of the following opening phrases, or use one of your own, to write about freely for five minutes. Remember, keep writing. If you get stuck, repeat a word over and over until something else comes to you.

- If only I could . . .
- The one word that best describes me is . . .
- I would never give up my . . .
- No one knows that I . . .
- The one thing I would like to change about myself is . . .

PURPOSE Self-discovery
AUDIENCE Yourself
LENGTH 3–4 paragraphs

WRITING RUBRICS To freewrite effectively about yourself, you should

- let your thoughts run free and simply begin writing whatever comes to mind
- write without stopping to reread, rephrase, or rethink what you are saying
- set a definite time limit

Cross-Curricular Activity

SOCIAL STUDIES Spend several minutes writing a paragraph or two about your community. Include answers to some of the following questions:

- How does the size of your community affect you?
- Do your friends and neighbors share a similar cultural background, or is the neighborhood very mixed? What have you learned from the neighborhood's culture?
- How have the schools and other institutions in your neighborhood affected you?
- How do the characteristics of your community contribute to making you the kind of person you are?

Grammar Link

When you write, avoid shifting verb tenses for no reason.

Revise each sentence below to make the verb tenses consistent.

1. We went to the movies yesterday, and we see a double feature.
2. Sam's birthday party will be next week; it was a bowling party.
3. That school bus goes along Main Street and turned right on Linden.
4. When I got to school, I meet my friend before science class.
5. Pat likes this book because she enjoyed the author's style.

See Lesson 15.6, page 594.

Viewing and Representing

CREATING A MAP Draw a map of your neighborhood, placing your home at the center of the image. Illustrate the map with images that identify places important in your life. In a paragraph or two, explain what your map illustrates about who you are and how the place you live has shaped you.

LESSON 1.2

Keeping a Journal

A writer's journal can be a place to examine feelings, record daily events, or try out new ideas. During World War II, thirteen-year-old Anne Frank and her family were forced to hide in a cramped attic to avoid capture by the Nazis. Frank's journal became her refuge during those terrible times.

> **Literature Model**
>
> Friday, 24 December 1943
>
> When someone comes in from outside, with the wind in their clothes and the cold on their faces, then I could bury my head in the blankets to stop myself thinking: "When will we be granted the privilege of smelling fresh air?" And because I must not bury my head in the blankets, but the reverse—I must keep my head high and be brave, the thoughts will come not once, but oh, countless times. Believe me, if you have been shut up for a year and a half, it can get too much for you some days . . . . Cycling, dancing, whistling, looking out into the world, feeling young, to know that I'm free—that's what I long for; still, I mustn't show it. . . . I sometimes ask myself, "Would anyone, either Jew or non-Jew understand this about me, that I am simply a young girl badly in need of some rollicking fun?" I don't know, and I couldn't talk about it to anyone.
>
> from *Anne Frank: The Diary of a Young Girl*

- Notice that Frank dates the journal entry.
- Frank is first inspired to write by thoughts of sensory details—"cold on their faces," "smelling fresh air."
- Frank uses this brief journal entry to ask important questions, give herself advice, and vent her feelings. In your opinion, what is the value of such expression?

Why Keep a Journal?

Keeping a journal is like thinking out loud—on paper. In your journal, you might record daily events, but you also are free to follow an idea wherever it leads. By writing about your experiences, reactions, and observations, you can make discoveries about yourself and the world.

Student Model

It just dawned on me! In only five days my sister will be nineteen years old! The last year of teen-agism. What happened to the little girl who would play Barbies with me, to my best friend who had been by my side for the last sixteen years? I miss her so much! Growing up can really hurt. It really is painful how everyone must part and make their separate way.

Kimberly Daniel, Jefferson Davis High School, Montgomery, Alabama

Freewriting can go wherever the writer's mind goes. Notice how Kimberly even makes up a word—"teen-agism."

Kimberly expresses an important lesson about growing up and moving on. Perhaps she'll develop this idea more fully later.

You can choose from a number of different kinds of journals, each with a different purpose. A diary, for example, is a personal record of daily events that the writer doesn't usually plan to share. A student may also keep a learning log to record thoughts and impressions of classes.

A journal can also serve as a writer's journal—that is, a source for ideas to inspire your writing. These might be brief notes on writing ideas, a collection of words or phrases, even news clippings, jokes, or photographs. Here's a story idea that came from one student's journal.

Student Model

I was thinking about something rather funny the other day. I wondered what it would be like to have grown old overnight and pass up all the hardships of life (develop this as the opening of my story). I would already be retired and I wouldn't have to worry about finishing school or getting a job . . . I would be able to go places and do things without having to worry about getting somewhere on time (give examples and go into more detail) . . . (All of this could be developed into a story about a boy who has grown old and finds out . . . that he has missed the best parts of life.)

Matthew Porter, Jefferson Davis High School, Montgomery, Alabama

Do you find Matthew's idea for writing interesting?

Notice how Matthew uses his writing to come up with a concrete idea for a story. This can work for you too.

Journal Writing

Compare the two student models on this page. What do they reveal about their writers? What kinds of materials are included in each? Record your reactions in your own journal.

1.2 Keeping a Journal 13

How Do You Keep a Journal?

Journal writing has no set rules. You just need to find a system that works for you. Here are some tips that might help you get started on your own journal.

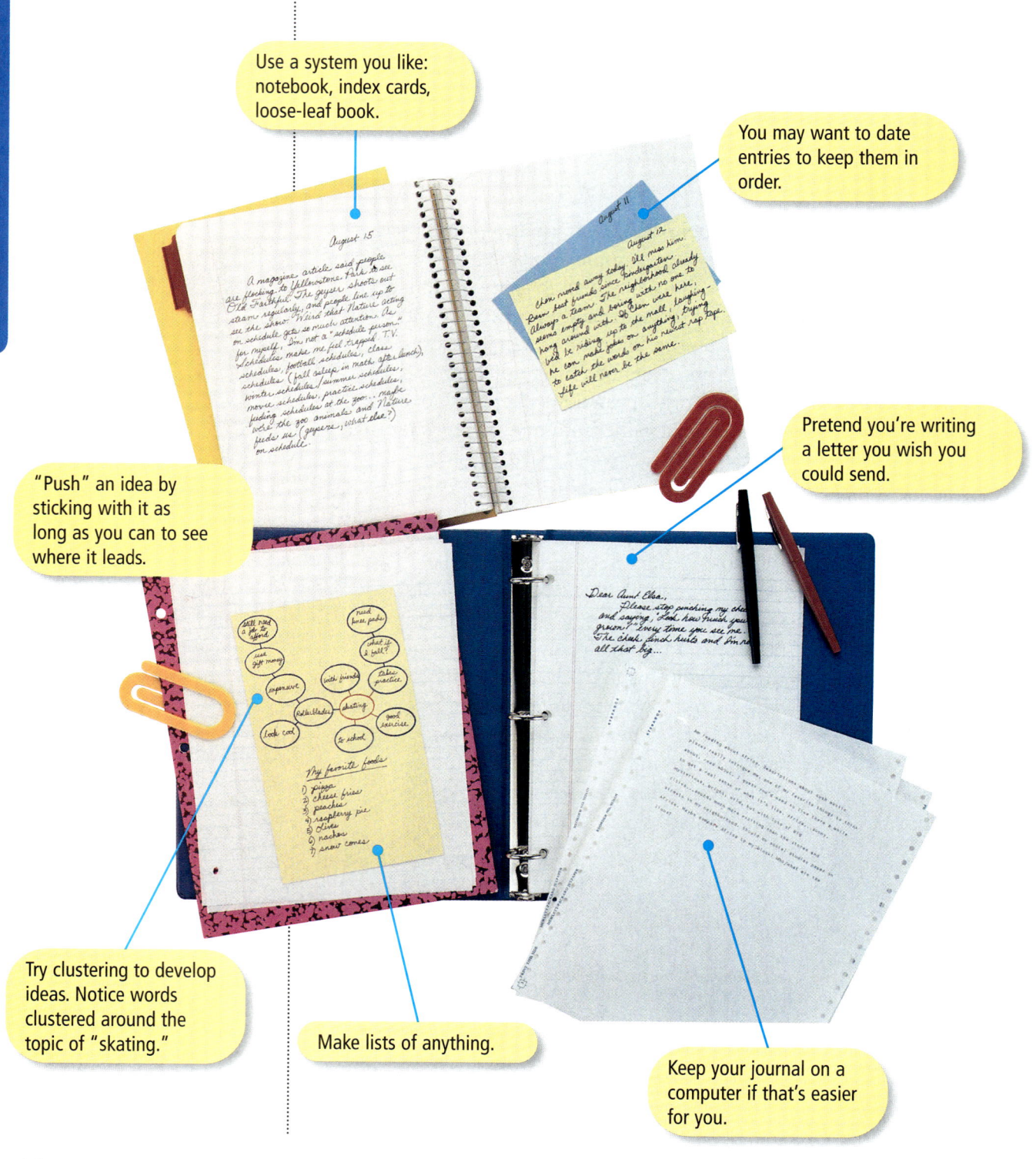

- Use a system you like: notebook, index cards, loose-leaf book.
- You may want to date entries to keep them in order.
- Pretend you're writing a letter you wish you could send.
- "Push" an idea by sticking with it as long as you can to see where it leads.
- Try clustering to develop ideas. Notice words clustered around the topic of "skating."
- Make lists of anything.
- Keep your journal on a computer if that's easier for you.

1.2 Writing Activities

Write a Journal Entry

Look through this book to find a painting that interests you. Create a journal entry based on that painting. Write, for example, about what you see in the painting. Does it evoke any memories? Any feelings or ideas for writing?

PURPOSE To free-associate from a painting
AUDIENCE Yourself
LENGTH 1–3 paragraphs

WRITING RUBRICS To write an effective journal entry, you should

- let one idea lead to another
- date your entry
- write about experiences, reactions, observations

Listening and Speaking

From a published journal, log, or diary of your choice, select a passage that describes an event that was important to the writer. Read the passage aloud with as much feeling as you can. Record your reading, and replay the passage several times. Then, in your journal, describe your impressions of the reading. Consider the following questions:

- How did the writer convey the importance of the experience?
- How well were you able to interpret the passage as the author might have?
- If you were an actor playing the writer, would the audience understand the meaning and importance of the passage?

Grammar Link

In personal writing, be sure you use the correct pronoun, *I* or *me*, in a compound subject or object.

Use *I* or *me* to complete each sentence below.

1. Dan and _____ are working on a history project.
2. His grandfather has sent some old family documents for him and _____ to use.
3. My sister drove Dan and _____ to the main library on Saturday.
4. He and _____ each used the computer and microfiche to locate information.
5. Our adviser told Dan and _____ that we can exhibit our project in the media center.

See Lesson 17.1, page 633.

Cross-Curricular Activity

SOCIAL STUDIES In a small group, brainstorm about travel experiences that have helped you discover something about yourself. Talk about places you have seen, people you have met, and other cultures you have experienced. Write a journal entry about how such experiences have changed you and, in general, how experiencing other cultures can change a person.

LESSON 1.3

Writing a Personal Essay

A personal essay offers opinions about something the writer has experienced or takes a personal interest in. In the model below, Robert Fulghum tells why he thinks certain household experiences are crucial to growing up.

Literature Model

After the dishes are washed and the sink rinsed out, there remains in the strainer at the bottom of the sink what I will call, momentarily, some "stuff." A rational, intelligent, objective person would say that this is simply a mixture of food particles too big to go down the drain.... But any teenager who has been dragooned into washing dishes knows this explanation is a lie. That stuff in the bottom of the strainer is toxic waste—deadly poison—a danger to health. In other words, about as icky as icky gets.

One of the . . . reasons I had . . . respect for my mother when I was thirteen was because she would reach into the sink with her bare hands—BARE HANDS—and pick up that lethal gunk and drop it into the garbage....

Never mind what any parent or objective adult might tell me, I knew that the stuff in the sink drainer was lethal....

But now. Now, I am a grown-up. And have been for some time. And I imagine making a speech to a high school graduating class.... I would give them this list of things that grown-ups do: clean the sink strainer . . . clean up the floor when the baby throws strained spinach, clean ovens and grease traps and roasting pans.... I'd tell the graduates that when they can do these things, they will be adults. Some of the students might not want to go on at this point. But they may as well face the truth . . . Being an adult *is* dirty work.

But someone has to do it.

Robert Fulghum, *It Was on Fire When I Lay Down on It*

> **What effect do words like "toxic" and "icky" have on you? What other words contribute to Fulghum's vivid, humorous picture?**

> **Why do you suppose Fulghum saved the main point for the end of his piece?**

16 Unit 1 Personal Writing

What Is a Personal Essay?

A personal essay expresses your viewpoint about a subject you have experienced—a subject other than yourself. The personal essay is not directly about you. You may write your personal essay in a traditional essay format—introduction, body paragraphs, and conclusion—or you may write it in a freer way, following your own train of thought. As you write your essay, you can follow Fulghum's example and use humorous anecdotes and exaggeration to express your views.

What Can I Write About?

If you have an assigned topic, explore the aspects that especially intrigue you. Otherwise, write about whatever interests you.

Select a Topic Your journal, newspapers, and magazines are sources of essay ideas. Here are two other ways to find a topic.

Freewriting

Write freely to find a topic. Write on whatever we want...write on write on write on...right on! Old slang phrase. Not totally awesome or even groovy--more tubular? Slang words mean different things. "Bad" means good (drove Dad crazy with that one!) Where did all those words come from? (requires research) What does slang do for me? Why slang? with friends? with adults? It'S LANG uage isn't it? TOPIC!

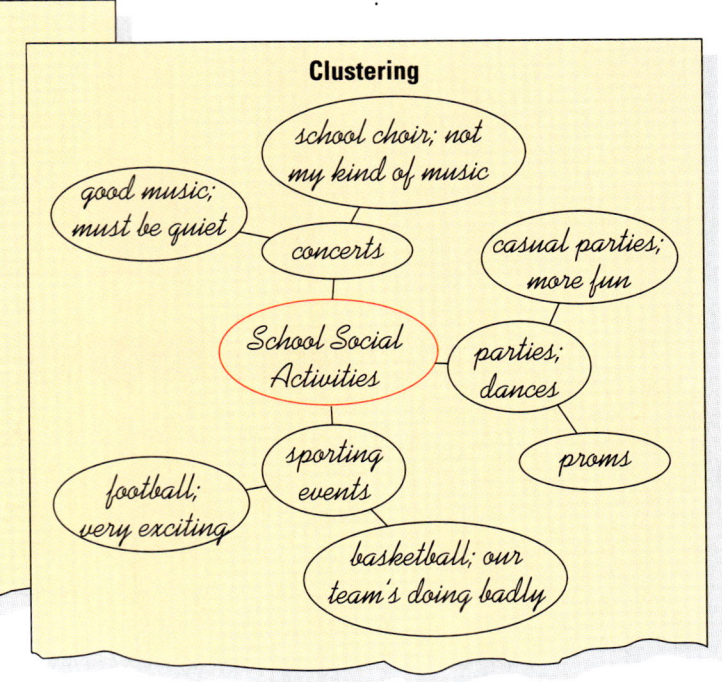

Clustering

- good music; must be quiet
- school choir; not my kind of music
- concerts
- casual parties; more fun
- *School Social Activities*
- parties; dances
- proms
- football; very exciting
- sporting events
- basketball; our team's doing badly

Journal Writing

In your journal, try creating a cluster diagram to help you think of an essay topic. Begin with a base word about something that interests you and see where you end up. If you need help getting started, look around the room, and write the name of an object.

Compose a Thesis Statement A thesis statement conveys your main point. It may also explain how you intend to support your main point. To develop a thesis statement, ask yourself questions about your topic. Focus on a specific aspect of the subject; then condense the subject to a basic statement. Consider Fulghum's thesis statement: "Being an adult *is* dirty work."

How Can I Make My Essay Come to Life?

By letting your enthusiasm for your topic influence your choice of words and details, you can make your essay lively. Support your thesis statement with vivid details and examples. Use these tips and model.

How Can I Make My Essay Interesting?

TIP	EXAMPLE
Answer offbeat questions about the subject.	What might views on this subject have been a hundred years ago? A hundred years ago, people might have thought that . . .
Include personal anecdotes.	I won my first carnival goldfish when . . .
Pretend to be a reporter covering a news story.	We are at the local video arcade to . . .
Compare your topic to something familiar and fun.	Doing algebra problems is a little like working out crossword puzzles.

Student Model

> Don't You Know Me?
> Our smiles are simple smiles. As we both sit down next to each other we realize that smile that was shared will probably be the first and last between us. Even though we go to the same school and have the same classes, we're two different people with two different images to uphold. Hers is the jet set world of witty conversation, the latest styles, and dates. The purse, the walk, and the friends she keeps tell her lifestyle and identity. The buzzing in the halls, the shared glances between them let you know you are the outsider looking in.
>
> As we step off the bus we put on our "masks" for the stage we'll be on. One's mask is a little bit brighter, the other one's dull, but each a character just the same.
>
> Keshia White, Hyde Park Career Academy, Chicago, Illinois

Notice how Keshia expresses herself by following her own train of thought instead of using traditional essay form.

Like Fulghum, Keshia presents her main point at the end of the essay.

1.3 Writing Activities

Write a Personal Essay

On a topic of your own choosing, write a personal essay that could be published in your school or hometown newspaper.

PURPOSE To express your viewpoint on a topic that interests you
AUDIENCE Adult and teenage newspaper readers
LENGTH 3–4 paragraphs

WRITING RUBRICS To write an effective personal essay, you should
- include a thesis statement
- use vivid details and examples
- compose complete and logical sentences

Viewing and Representing

In a small group, study and discuss the painting below. Consider how the same artist might have painted your street if he had used you or your neighbors as subjects, and write an essay about this topic.

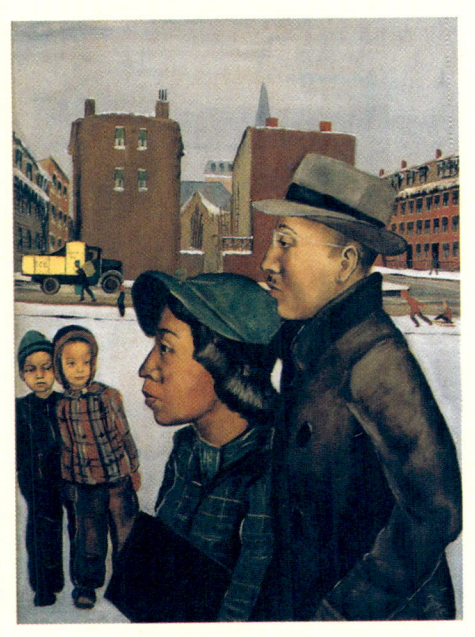

Allan Crite, *Harriet and Leon*, 1941

Grammar Link

Use strong, specific verbs to make your personal writing clear and effective.

In each sentence, replace the general verb with one that is more precise.
1. The student volunteers worked all day at the new community center.
2. Some cleaned floors and windows.
3. Others moved lumber and cinder blocks from the yard into the meeting room.
4. Most of the students like the results of the day's efforts.
5. Only a few spoke about the difficulty of the work.

See Lesson 10.3, pages 452–460.

Cross-Curricular Activity

GOVERNMENT Attend a meeting of the student council, school board, city council, or other local governing body. Obtain a copy of the agenda and use it as a guide to the issues under discussion. Listen to ways in which participants on all sides of the issues frame their arguments. Divide a sheet of paper into two columns. Write statements "for" a position in one column and "against" in the other.

After the meeting, look over your lists. Choose a potential thesis and rewrite it so that you could develop it to reflect your personal approach to the issue.

LESSON 1.4

Writing Autobiography

Autobiographies are first-person accounts of important moments in an individual's life. In the model below, Lynn Griffey describes a personal experience.

Student Model

Ever since I was a child, I've been fascinated with space. So in the fall of my junior year my parents sent me to the United States Space Camp. I was so excited; I thought this was going to be the beginning of great things to come. This was my dream come true. I always had dreams of me in space, and I always knew I could do it.

Immediately after I got there, I looked around. I saw how every one of those kids had the same dreams and feelings I had. It was incredible.

After sitting through lecture after lecture, and going through experiment after experiment, I realized that I wasn't sure of my feelings anymore. I knew I was having a great time learning and exploring, but I also knew that I didn't have the same look in my eye that one boy did. He was having more than just a "good time"; he lived to be doing this.

I began feeling guilty because I started thinking of all the money my parents had spent for me to go there. Then I realized they want me to be happy. That's why they spent all the money, to see if this was what I wanted to do for the rest of my life.

I think I learned a lot about myself that week. I discovered that at sixteen it's not necessary to know precisely what the future holds. Maybe I'll still want to be in space some day. However, right now I just want to be sixteen and explore all the exciting careers I have to choose from.

Lynn Griffey,
Hamilton Heights High School, Arcadia, Indiana

> Notice how Lynn introduces the subject, setting, and main idea early on. Where do you first sense what might happen? Which words help to create this sense?

> Lynn concludes by relating how her experience changed her perception of herself as well as her goals and expectations.

Unit 1 Personal Writing

What Is an Autobiography?

An autobiography is a person's written account of his or her own life—experiences, thoughts, feelings. An autobiographical sketch, like Lynn's, is personal writing about a significant event or period in the writer's life. It should give readers a sense of who the author is, how the author came to be that way, and what the author has experienced.

How Do You Find Autobiographical Material?

Your autobiographical material comes from your life—anything you have done, felt, thought, dreamed, experienced, or learned. We all have mental files of our experiences. Each of us uses a variety of different filing systems. We file events by emotional content—happy, sad, exhilarating. We file them according to the time in our lives they occurred—before school age, during elementary school. We even file them according to the areas in our lives to which they relate—school, family, friends.

To search through your mental files, start by making a list of general categories, or file labels, you might find in each of the filing systems listed below. Then brainstorm, freewrite, or use other prewriting techniques to retrieve some of the specific experiences you have stored in these files. Refer to Lesson 2.2, pages 62–67, for other prewriting techniques.

Your Autobiographical Files

FILING SYSTEM	SAMPLE FILE LABELS	SAMPLE EXPERIENCE
By emotional content	Happy, sad, afraid, angry	Getting a new bicycle
By time they occurred	Early childhood, junior high	Beginning junior high school
By area in life they relate to	Family, friends	Taking car trips with my family

Journal Writing

In your journal, create a "life map." From left to right, draw or write important events from your life in chronological order. Shape your map any way—straight line, peaks and valleys, loops.

How Do You Present Your Material?

There are many ways to present autobiographical material. You can begin with "I remember" and then recount a particular event. You can structure your story as an interview or you can use one of the methods shown in the chart. You may need to explain the significance of an event, as Kareem Abdul-Jabbar does in the model.

Two Ways to Present Your Material

	PRESENT	PAST	PRESENT
Flashback	Shopping with Gloria—we both loved the same clothes.	Even as four-year-olds, she and I wanted the same toys.	I hope that we don't start to like the same boys now.
	FEB. 8	**FEB. 9**	**FEB. 10**
Successive Journal Entries	Nelsons asked me to go skiing with them—sort of scared.	Best day ever! I skied quite well—for my first time out.	Couldn't get out of bed. It hurt to walk.

Literature Model

Abdul-Jabbar sets the scene and presents the main idea immediately.

What kind of words does Abdul-Jabbar use to create a vivid picture of the event?

In the final sentences of this autobiographical sketch, Abdul-Jabbar sums up the significance of this event.

It was that summer [after seventh grade] that I grew so many inches and started at least to *look* like a basketball player. I started to be able to do things like palm a basketball and touch the rim, and it was soon obvious that the long frame could be put to use in places other than the baseball diamond. Around this same time, one event changed my view of basketball and how to play it dramatically. I went to see a high school all-star game at the Brownsville Boys Club in Brooklyn. Guys like Connie Hawkins, Roger Brown, Billy Burwell, and other All-City players were on the court doing their thing, and I was awestruck. I had never seen people dunk and soar and change direction in midstride the way these guys did. . . . The warm-up was awe-inspiring, and I feel that evening in Brooklyn changed my concept forever of what is possible on the court. Baseball would remain close to my heart, but here was a game that was best played by individuals with *my* physical attributes. The possibilities seemed endless.

Kareem Abdul-Jabbar with Mignon McCarthy, *Kareem*

1.4 Writing Activities

Write an Autobiographical Sketch

Think of an event or period in your life that you feel had an impact on the kind of person you are now. You might remember making or losing a friend, visiting a new place, or learning a new skill or sport. Once you have chosen a topic, decide on the most effective technique to tell your story.

PURPOSE To tell about an important event in your life
AUDIENCE Classmates and teacher
LENGTH 5–6 paragraphs

WRITING RUBRICS To write an effective autobiographical sketch, you should

- provide all the information your readers will need
- explain why the episode you are describing had such an effect on you
- tell what happened; don't just comment on it
- write in complete sentences

Using Computers

You may wish to present your autobiographical sketch to family members or friends. Word processing, presentation, and Web page design software offer abundant options for composing documents and presentations. Such software allows you to import scanned photographs, sound clips, and even video.

Grammar Link

In general, avoid sentence fragments in your writing.

A **sentence fragment** is an incomplete sentence that is punctuated as a complete sentence.

Ever since I was a child. (fragment)
I've been fascinated with space.
Ever since I was a child, I've been fascinated with space. (complete sentence)

Change each sentence fragment below to form a complete sentence.

I want to make my career in music. [1]Because I love playing trumpet. I play in the band and orchestra. [2]And the jazz band too. Next I want to learn to play the French horn. [3]Maybe during summer vacation. [4]If my job leaves me enough time to practice. My parents say I should plan a different career. [5]Something dependable, like accounting or teaching. We'll see.

See Lesson 13.9, pages 553–554.

Viewing and Representing

CREATING A TIMELINE Imagine you will live to be one hundred years old. On drawing paper, create a fictional timeline that charts those hundred years. Highlight the important events.

LESSON 1.5

Writing a Poem

Whether rhymed or unrhymed, poems often convey personal feelings through the use of strong, precise language.

Langston Hughes wanted to express his feelings about his people, African Americans. Notice how powerfully he does so—and with so few words—in this brief poem.

> **Literature Model**
>
> ### My People
>
> The night is beautiful,
> So the faces of my people.
>
> The stars are beautiful,
> So the eyes of my people.
>
> Beautiful, also, is the sun.
> Beautiful, also, are the souls of my people.
>
>   Langston Hughes

> This free-verse poem does not have regular rhyme or rhythm patterns, but the repetition gives it a rhythmic feeling.

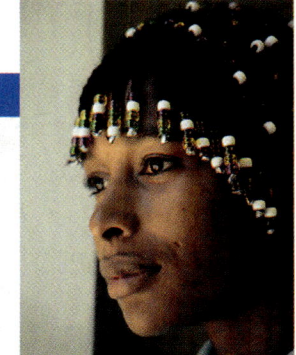

Poetry as Self-Expression

Effective poets like Hughes put together words to create sounds and images that express much more than what the words alone actually say. Such sounds and images help poets actively engage their readers' memories, emotions, and imaginations.

Traditional and Free Verse

In free verse such as Hughes's poem, there are no set patterns of rhyme or rhythm. More traditional poems, however, do follow set rhyme and rhythm patterns. Compare the following humorous poem with Hughes's poem. Read each poem aloud. Notice the regular rhyming and rhythmic patterns in "Song of the Open Road" and the freer form and style of "My People."

24 Unit 1 Personal Writing

Literature Model

Song of the Open Road

I think that I shall never see
A billboard lovely as a tree.
Indeed, unless the billboards fall
I'll never see a tree at all.

Ogden Nash

The Special Language of Poetry

The language of poetry is one of vivid sounds and images. Just think of how Langston Hughes's images of night, stars, and sun linger and overlap with the images of his people's faces, eyes, and souls. Poets create such memorable pictures with a variety of techniques such as those explained in this chart.

Some Poetic Devices

Device	Definition	Example
Sensory detail	A detail that appeals to one of the senses: sight, touch, taste, smell, or hearing	Slivers of frosty grass crunched underfoot.
Simile	A comparison between two unlike things, using the words *like* or *as*	Sleep, like a soft, dark blanket, comforted him.
Metaphor	A comparison between two unlike things, without using the words *like* or *as*	Her dress was a pink cloud of crepe.
Personification	The giving of human qualities to objects, animals, or things	Flowers saluted the morning sun.
Sound effect	A pattern of sound (e.g., rhyme, rhythm, repetition) used to help create an image	The raspy snarl of a motorcycle awakened him.

Journal Writing

Find a single word in one of the poems in this lesson or in the list of examples above and use it as the center for brainstorming. Generate associations, in the form of words or phrases, with this word as fast as you can. Then use some of your associations to create a brief poem.

Forms of Poetry

Literature Model

There was a young person from Perth
Who was born on the day of his birth.
He was married, they say,
On his wife's wedding day
And died when he quitted this earth.

Anonymous

Like most limericks, this one begins "There was a . . ." and ends with a funny or unusual rhyming line.

Literature Model

Butterfly, these words
from my brush are not flowers,
only their shadows.

Soseki

Like most traditional haiku, this one has five syllables in lines 1 and 3 and seven in line 2.

With a partner, read these poems aloud. Notice the limerick's rhyming pattern and the haiku's syllable pattern. Following is a free verse poem.

Student Model

Intimate Calm

There—
With the soft rays of the lamp
Resting on the pallid walls
And the earthen carpet—
With the falling leaves and the dark, dewy dusk
Enveloping me
Like my grandmother's familiar afghan—
With the comforting sounds of the television
Capturing my attention with its witty charm—
With the beautiful willowing wisps
Of my brother's laughter in the kitchen
With my body
Propped against my favorite pillow
Sunken into the billowing cushions
Curled like the kitten
Asleep in my lap
Underneath that familiar yarn
Which conceals the memories of my mother's mother—
I lay
With a peaceful mind—
Eating refried beans

Heather Robertson,
Jefferson Davis High School, Montgomery, Alabama

Why do you suppose Heather chose to repeat the word "with" at the beginning of several lines?

The repetition of the k and hard c sound provides a rhythm to these two lines.

1.5 Writing Activities

Write Your Own Poem

Try freewriting to come up with an idea for a poem. Begin by focusing on a subject about which you have strong feelings. Underline any words or phrases that are especially descriptive of your topic or your feelings about it. Use some or all of the underlined items as you write your poem.

PURPOSE To write an original poem
AUDIENCE Students and teachers
LENGTH 5–15 lines

WRITING RUBRICS To write an effective poem, you should

- use poetic devices such as those listed on the chart on page 25
- decide whether rhyme or free verse will be more effective
- use sensory detail and clear language to convey your feelings

Listening and Speaking

READING POETRY ALOUD In a small group, select two favorite poems. Practice reading them aloud, paying attention to the patterns of sound, where the emphasis falls in each line, and the mood created by the poet. Discuss afterward why the poems you chose are important to you.

Cross-Curricular Activity

ART In a small group, brainstorm to create a list of ideas for a poem about what you see in the painting on this page. Use some of the poetic techniques discussed in this lesson (similes, metaphors, personification). Imagine that you are the central figure in the painting. What do you see? What are you thinking about? Write your own poem; then, meet again as a group to share and discuss your poems.

Rufino Tamayo, *Hombre Ante el Infinito* (*Man Contemplates Infinity*), 1950

Grammar Link

Use precise adjectives to bring your sentences to life.

Notice how Heather Robertson, in her poem "Intimate Calm," uses precise *adjectives* to create vivid images:

pallid walls; **billowing** cushions

Revise the lines below by adding vivid adjectives to modify nouns.

1. two people standing on a hillside overlooking a lake
2. a baby sleeping in its stroller
3. the chair in the dentist's office, surrounded by tools and equipment
4. wind in the trees outside the cabin
5. a potted plant on the table near the window

See Lesson 10.4, pages 461–466.

LESSON 1.6

WRITING ABOUT LITERATURE

Keeping a Reader-Response Journal

A reader-response journal is a place where you can record your reactions to what you are reading.

When Mitchell Kittlaus, a student from Illinois, finished reading Katherine Mansfield's story "The Doll's House," he was prompted to write in his reader-response log. Read the "letter-to-the-character" letter Mitchell wrote. See what it was that impressed him about the character Kezia.

Student Model

Dear Kezia,

I admire you greatly for the courage you displayed.... You took a big risk by inviting the Kelvey girls into your courtyard to see the doll house. Do not be intimidated by your aunt's punishment. Although you should obey your elders, it was right of you to question their negative opinion of the Kelveys. If you do not understand their attitude, take the initiative to talk with your parents and relatives, so that together you can discuss their views. You may not agree with what they believe, but it is important that you fully comprehend their feelings.

I also respect you for the kindness that you showed to Lil and Else Kelvey. It is always easier to hurt someone's feelings by acting in an inconsiderate way, especially when such thoughtless behavior is encouraged by one's peers....

I encourage you to continue to keep an open mind in your relations with others. People should only be judged by the content of their character. Hopefully, you can set a positive example for others to follow.

Mitchell Kittlaus,
Evanston Township High School, Evanston, Illinois

What word choices in Mitchell's letter suggest the degree of his involvement in the story?

Mitchell expresses his personal feelings about the story's main incident.

Respond Personally

A reader-response journal can be a special section in a larger personal journal or a journal in itself. In a reader-response journal, you can write about what interests, puzzles, angers, or even bores you about your reading. The journal can help you keep track of what's going on in the work you are reading. More importantly it can help you relate your reading to your own life. For example, you might write about similarities you find between a character's view of life and your own.

Respond Creatively

Think of new ways to respond to your reading. You might write a letter of encouragement (or complaint) to the main character. You could rewrite a scene from a play to make it take place in your home town. Some of these ideas may inspire you to write your own creative pieces.

Responding to What You Read

IDEA	SAMPLE
1. Write a news flash.	Flash! Three local children disappeared last night from their backyard. Relatives say the three had been talking about time travel just prior to their disappearance. (response to *A Wrinkle in Time* by Madeleine L'Engle)
2. Imagine yourself as a main character.	Here I am shipwrecked on a deserted island with just a bunch of other boys my own age. I'd better make a plan for survival. (response to *Lord of the Flies* by William Golding; the photo on the right is from a movie based on that novel)
3. Write about the character visiting your home.	As Mrs. Luella Bates Washington Jones came through the door, she filled our living room with her powerful presence. (response to "Thank You, M'am" by Langston Hughes)

In your reader-response journal, you could suggest what might have happened if two characters had never met or if one event hadn't taken place. What if the setting were changed? Be creative in finding ways to write about your reading.

Journal Writing

Choose a book or story you have read recently. In your journal, respond to the story in any way you wish.

Respond to Learn About Yourself

An important part of any story, novel, play, essay, or poem is what you, the reader, bring to it. When you reflect on it in light of your personal experiences and impressions, literature can actually change you.

Keeping a reader-response journal gives you a chance to think more about a work of literature—to consider the relevance of the story or poem to your own life. What do you think about . . . ? How would you change it to make it more real? What if . . . ? Would you have done what the characters did?

By considering these kinds of questions, you come to a new, deeper understanding of the story. Michelle Kalski learns about herself by responding to Shel Silverstein's poem "Reflection" in two different ways.

Reflection
Each time I see the Upside-Down Man
Standing in the water,
I look at him and start to laugh,
Although I shouldn't oughtter.
For maybe in another world
Another time
Another town,
Maybe HE is right side up
And I am upside down.

Shel Silverstein

Student Model

Just a reflection of myself.
Or so it seems.
What stares back is a person
Full of peace and at ease.
A backward image of me.

Dear Mr. Silverstein,
    Finally, someone has managed to step into the world of a reflection. As a curious youngster, I was always fascinated with reflections and looked for ways to prove that the person in the pool of water or the mirror was somehow different than me. I thought it was wonderful of you to reveal the idea of a reflection being in the world right side up.

Michelle Kalski,
Evanston Township High School, Evanston, Illinois

> Notice how Michelle relates Silverstein's poem to her own life by telling of a childhood fascination of hers.

1.6 Writing Activities

Write a Reader-Response Journal Entry

Read the poem below and the Langston Hughes poem on page 24. Then choose one of them or a poem of your own choosing. Respond to the poem you select in a creative way as you would in a reader-response journal.

Old Mary

My last defense
Is the present tense.

It little hurts me now to know
I shall not go

Cathedral-hunting in Spain
Nor cherrying in Michigan or Maine.

Gwendolyn Brooks

PURPOSE To explore your reactions to a poem
AUDIENCE Yourself
LENGTH 1–3 paragraphs

WRITING RUBRICS To write a memorable reader-response journal entry, you should

- explain how the literature selection relates to your life
- describe the feelings and new ideas it evokes
- express yourself in complete, logical sentences

Viewing and Representing

CREATING A COMIC STRIP In your reader response journal, respond to a favorite story by drawing a multipaneled comic strip. Illustrate key scenes from the story. Draw yourself as a character in the story. Present your comic strip to a group of classmates and discuss its effectiveness.

Using Computers

If you are entering your reader-response entries into a computer file, you will need some way to identify your entries for retrieval. A good plan is to date each entry. Or you might add a code word, such as *poems* or the author's name. Then you can use the Search function to retrieve a particular entry.

Grammar Link

When using pronouns, do not shift person or number without a good reason.

Supply appropriate pronouns in the following sentences.

1. I especially like reading science fiction, where _____ appreciate the combination of fact and fantasy.
2. When one reads a play, _____ must visualize the action of the characters.
3. We enjoyed his poetry because _____ can clearly understand his feelings.
4. If you don't like the major characters in a book, it is hard for _____ to take much interest in what happens to _____.
5. They love Agatha Christie's stories because _____ never tire of her characters.

See Lesson 17.5, pages 640–641.

1.6 Keeping a Reader-Response Journal **31**

LESSON 1.7

WRITING ABOUT LITERATURE
Writing About Biography

When you are reading a biography, one way to respond is to relate events in the subject's life to your own life. Shella Calamba does this in the model below.

Student Model

I never thought Amelia Earhart and I could have so much in common. Although, as a little girl, I was outfitted in frilly doll dresses and constantly reminded to be "ladylike," I, like Amelia, preferred to do things that were branded as "tomboy" activities, such as climbing trees, which was hard, but feasible, while wearing a pink dress. Amelia's roller coaster project reminded me of my own skateboard dashes down a hill in sledding fashion. As Amelia did, I, too, often employ the phrase "because I want to," to justify actions that may seem inane or highly psychotic to others.

Not only did Amelia's childhood remind me of mine, she also made me think of a friend from grammar school who dreams of becoming a pilot. She will undoubtedly be forced to deal with sexism in pursuing her goal, but I think reading Amelia's biography would prevent her from being discouraged in achieving her ambitions. Even by today's standards, what Amelia accomplished was remarkable and unprecedented by any man or woman. However, Amelia is not someone to be admired exclusively by pilots. Her courage, determination, and persistence set an inspiring example for anyone with a dream.

Shella Calamba,
Lincoln Park High School, Chicago, Illinois

Amelia Earhart, 1933

What words signal the many comparisons between Shella and Amelia in the first paragraph?

Shella shows the relevance of the biography to others in today's world, moving from personal meanings to more general ones.

Respond Personally to a Biography

When you respond personally to a biography, you are responding to the subject of the biography and to his or her world. You can try to get to know the subject by focusing your reader-response journal entries on the subject's attitudes, values, and behavior. What does the subject care about? What motivates her or him in life? Relate your discoveries to your own life. Do you care about the same kinds of things as the subject? What qualities does the subject have that you admire? What do the subject's accomplishments teach you about your own life?

The chart below shows some ways you can respond personally to a biography. Try any of the following suggestions or come up with other ways of thinking about a biography's subject.

Some Formats for Responding to Biography

FORMAT	EXAMPLE
Write a skit showing how the person might act in a new and unusual situation.	Ben Franklin at an electrical plant
Write an encouraging letter helping the subject with a problem.	To Mohandas Gandhi encouraging his efforts to win independence for India
Write an editorial endorsing the person for public office.	Michael Jordan for mayor of your town
Bring a historical figure into the modern day world.	Queen Isabella visiting NASA and learning about space exploration
Write a diary entry from a crucial day in the person's life.	Amelia Earhart's diary from the day her plane was lost over the Pacific Ocean
Rewrite an incident from the subject's life, changing one part slightly.	Abraham Lincoln not going to the theater where he was assassinated
Enact an on-the-spot news story with your subject.	A news interview with Clara Barton immediately after a Civil War battle

Journal Writing

In your journal, respond to a biography you have read or seen. Use one of the ideas from the chart on this page.

1.7 Writing About Biography

Interview Your Subject

One way to get to know the subject of a biography is through an imaginary interview. To develop such an interview, work with a classmate and role-play. One of you should take the role of the interviewer and the other should portray the subject of the biography. Ask questions that get at the whys and hows of the person's life. Tailor your questions to your particular subject. Base the subject's responses on what you know from your reading.

Feel free to be creative and have fun with the interview. For example, you might choose the form of a late-night talk show discussion, such as Jay Leno interviewing Leonardo da Vinci. You might pretend that a historical character is visiting the present-day world, as Elizabeth Chen did an imaginary interview with Dr. Martin Luther King Jr. for a fictional newspaper, the *Chronicle*.

Sample Interview Questions

- What was the accomplishment you were most proud of?
- What was your greatest challenge?
- What surprises you most about today's world?
- If you could tell the people of today one thing, what would it be?

Student Model

Chronicle: Dr. King, what you did for the civil rights movement in the 1950s and 1960s obviously had an enormous impact then, but do you think it affects society today?

MLK: What the people did then, promoting the cause of civil rights through peaceful means, has led the way toward a day of equal rights for all people.

Chronicle: Do you think there is equality now?

MLK: Under the law, yes, but in the hearts and minds of some Americans, no. I cannot say there is equality when I hear of racial violence every day. There will not be equality until everyone is treated the same in practice as well as under the law.

Chronicle: But how can we change that?

MLK: Through education. Through the help of all people—black, white, red, and yellow—to show that the only difference between us is skin color. By showing that all people can achieve the same success if given an equal opportunity.

Elizabeth Chen,
Downers Grove North High School, Downers Grove, Illinois

1.7 Writing Activities

Write a Response to a Biography

Choose a major event or decision in the life of a person whose biography you have read. Write a response to share with your classmates. You can use one of the formats suggested in the chart on page 33, you can write an imaginary interview, or you can write a more personal response.

PURPOSE To explore a section of a biography
AUDIENCE Your classmates
LENGTH 2–4 paragraphs

WRITING RUBRICS To write an effective response to a biography, you should

- show that you understand your subject
- make your response interesting to your audience
- write in clear, complete sentences

Listening and Speaking

RESEARCH AND REPORT In a small group, select a famous scientist, artist, or author whose work is familiar to everyone in the group. Divide up the task of researching the person's life, one member of the group taking the person's childhood, another the person's early career, and so on. Prepare a brief oral report on the area you researched; then combine the reports and give a group presentation for the class.

Spelling

COOPERATIVE LEARNING Exchange your response to a biography with a partner. Work together to identify spelling problems and develop a strategy for resolving them.

Grammar Link

When the subject of a sentence is a compound joined by *and* that refers to two or more different things, the verb that agrees with it must be plural.

Notice subject and verb in this sentence:
Her courage, determination, **and** persistence **set** an inspiring example. . . .

Add the correct verb form.

1. Washington and Adams _____ the first two presidents of the United States.
2. John Adams and his son, John Quincy Adams, _____ both presidents.
3. Both the House of Representatives and the Senate _____ in the Capitol.
4. The Declaration of Independence, the Constitution, and the Emancipation Proclamation _____ kept in the U.S. Archives.
5. The secretary of state and the attorney general _____ members of the president's cabinet.
6. Ulysses Grant and Dwight Eisenhower _____ generals.
7. John Quincy Adams and Andrew Jackson _____ born in 1767.
8. Kennedy, F. D. Roosevelt, and Wilson _____ students at Harvard.
9. Dwight Eisenhower and Lyndon Johnson _____ born in Texas.
10. Gerald Ford and Richard Nixon _____ born in 1913.

See Lesson 16.5, pages 616–617.

UNIT 1
Writing Process in Action

Personal Writing

In preceding lessons you've learned about using personal writing for a variety of purposes. Now it's time to make use of what you learned. In this lesson you're invited to write an autobiographical sketch about an incident or a personal interaction that made a positive difference in your life—an event or a relationship that provided a good "lesson in living."

Assignment

Context

Everyday People magazine plans a special issue featuring autobiographical sketches by students. You are invited to write an uplifting story about a person or an incident that made a real difference in your life. Focus on your personal feelings and on why the event or person was so important to you.

Purpose

To write a vivid personal account that will allow readers to understand the impact of this event

Audience

"Everyday" people—students, parents, teachers, other townspeople

Length

1–2 pages

The following pages can help you plan and write your autobiographical sketch. Read through them and then refer to them as you need to, but don't feel limited by them. You are in charge of your own writing process.

WRITING Online

Visit the *Writer's Choice* Web site at **writerschoice.glencoe.com** for additional writing prompts.

36 Unit 1 Personal Writing

Writing Process in Action

Prewriting

Begin by choosing an incident to write about. It might be from any period in your life. It might have taken place over several weeks or months, or it may have happened quickly. It may have been dramatic or quiet, serious or humorous. If you can't think of an incident, use some of the prewriting options listed here to help you get started. Once you have an idea in mind, try to recall what happened as fully as possible. You might begin by writing your answers to *who*, *what*, *when*, *where*, and *why* questions.

Part of your goal is to explain the significance of the event. One way to do this:

- List things that describe yourself, your attitudes, and your circumstances *before* the event or interaction took place.
- Then note the ways in which things were different afterward. Write a statement that summarizes what the experience meant to you, how it changed you, or what you learned from it.

Notice how these lines from Kareem Abdul-Jabbar's autobiography vividly describe the life-changing effect of his seeing a particular basketball game when he was young.

Prewriting Options

- Read over your journal entries.
- Make a list of important people in your life.
- Look through scrapbooks and photographs at home.
- Search your mental files for possible topics.
- Freewrite to discover your thoughts.

Literature Model

I was awestruck. I had never seen people dunk and soar and change direction in midstride the way these guys did. . . . The warmup was awe-inspiring, and I feel that evening in Brooklyn changed my concept forever of what is possible on the court. Baseball would remain close to my heart, but here was a game that was best played by individuals with *my* physical attributes. The possibilities seemed endless.

Kareem Abdul-Jabbar with Mignon McCarthy, *Kareem*

Writing Process in Action

> **Drafting Tip**
>
> For more information about enlivening your personal writing, see Lesson 1.3, page 18.

Drafting

Start with your summary statement about the significance of the event. This will help you focus your thoughts as you write. It will also prepare your readers for what follows. Then add sentences and paragraphs to tell your story. Write freely, referring to your prewriting notes, but try to organize your thoughts in some logical way. If your experience involves a clear sequence of events, you might present the details in straight chronological order—the order in which they occurred.

As you write, look for ways to make your sketch come to life. What anecdotes, descriptions, comparisons, or other details can make your story vivid? Consider using dialogue to help bring your characters to life. To be sure the dialogue sounds natural, read your draft aloud.

Revising

To begin revising, look back at the assignment; then read your draft to see if you have met the goals. Next, have a **writing conference.** Read your draft to a partner or small group. Use your audience's reactions to help you evaluate your work so far. The following questions can help you and your listeners:

- Does my writing qualify as an autobiographical sketch?
- Is my sketch easy to follow?
- Is my sketch vivid and accurate?
- Is my tone natural? Does it sound like me talking?
- Does my writing show how this incident or interaction changed my life for the better?
- Is my writing appropriate for my audience?

> **Revising Tip**
>
> For help with adding significant details and finding a suitable structure for your sketch, see Lesson 1.4, pp. 20–23.

TIME
For more about drafting and revising, see **TIME Facing the Blank Page**, pp. 126-129.

Personal Writing

38 Unit 1 Personal Writing

Writing Process in Action

Editing/Proofreading

Once you are happy with the basic content and set-up of your autobiographical sketch, **proofread** it carefully for errors in grammar, usage, mechanics, and spelling. Use the questions at the right as a guide.

In addition to proofreading, use the self-evaluation list below to make sure your autobiographical sketch does everything you want it to do. When you're satisfied, make a clean copy of your sketch, and proofread it one more time.

Editing Checklist

- Have I avoided sentence fragments?
- Are all my verb forms and tenses correct?
- Have I used I and me correctly in compounds?
- Are my pronoun references clear?
- Have I checked spellings of any words I'm unsure of?

Self-Evaluation

Make sure your autobiographical sketch—

✔ Focuses on an incident or interaction that improved your life
✔ Conveys the significance of this incident or interaction
✔ Answers the *who, what, where, when, why,* and *how* questions
✔ Reflects your spoken rhythms and phrases
✔ Follows correct grammar, usage, and mechanics

Publishing/Presenting

You can use the autobiographical sketches you and your classmates have written to produce an issue of *Everyday People.* Create a cover and a table of contents. Add illustrations if you wish. Make it available for others to read. If you feel your sketch is too personal to share publicly, keep it with your journal so that you can refer to it later.

Proofreading Tip

For proofreading symbols, see page 411.

Journal Writing

Reflect on your writing process experience. Answer these questions in your journal: What do you like best about your personal writing? What was the hardest part of writing it? What did you learn in your writing conference? What new things have you learned as a writer?

UNIT 1
Literature Model

Personal Writing

from

I Know Why the Caged Bird Sings

by Maya Angelou

Maya Angelou, best known for her autobiographies I Know Why the Caged Bird Sings *and* Gather Together in My Name, *has also been a poet laureate, playwright, movie and television writer, journalist, dancer, actress, director, composer, and civil rights worker. As you read this autobiographical sketch, see if the turning point she describes reminds you of any significant event in your own life. Then try the activities in Linking Writing and Literature on page 50.*

Literature Model

For nearly a year, I sopped around the house, the Store, the school and the church, like an old biscuit, dirty and inedible. Then I met, or rather got to know, the lady who threw me my first life line.

Mrs. Bertha Flowers was the aristocrat of Black Stamps. She had the grace of control to appear warm in the coldest weather, and on the Arkansas summer days it seemed she had a private breeze which swirled around, cooling her. She was thin without the taut look of wiry people, and her printed voile[1] dresses and flowered hats were as right for her as denim overalls for a farmer. She was our side's answer to the richest white woman in town.

Her skin was a rich black that would have peeled like a plum if snagged, but then no one would have thought of getting close enough to Mrs. Flowers to ruffle her dress, let alone snag her skin. She didn't encourage familiarity. She wore gloves too.

I don't think I ever saw Mrs. Flowers laugh, but she smiled often. A slow widening of her thin black lips to show even, small white teeth, then the slow effortless closing. When she chose to smile on me, I

---

[1] **voile** (voil) a thin, sheer fabric; often made of cotton

Harriet Powers, *Pictorial Quilt*, c. 1895–1898

Literature Model

always wanted to thank her. The action was so graceful and inclusively benign.[2]

She was one of the few gentlewomen I have ever known, and has remained throughout my life the measure of what a human being can be.

Momma had a strange relationship with her. Most often when she passed on the road in front of the Store, she spoke to Momma in that soft yet carrying voice, "Good day, Mrs. Henderson." Momma responded with "How you, Sister Flowers?"

Mrs. Flowers didn't belong to our church, nor was she Momma's familiar. Why on earth did she insist on calling her Sister Flowers? Shame made me want to hide my face. Mrs. Flowers deserved better than to be called Sister. Then, Momma left out the verb. Why not ask, "How *are* you, *Mrs.* Flowers?" With the unbalanced passion of the young, I hated her for showing her ignorance to Mrs. Flowers. It didn't occur to me for many years that they were as alike as sisters, separated only by formal education.

Although I was upset, neither of the women was in the least shaken by what I thought an unceremonious[3] greeting. Mrs. Flowers would continue her easy gait up the hill to her little bungalow,[4] and Momma kept on shelling peas or doing whatever had brought her to the front porch.

Occasionally, though, Mrs. Flowers would drift off the road and down to the Store and Momma would say to me, "Sister, you go on and play." As I left I would hear the beginning of an intimate conversation. Momma persistently using the wrong verb, or none at all.

"Brother and Sister Wilcox is sho'ly the meanest—" "Is," Momma? "Is"? Oh, please, not "is," Momma, for two or more. But they talked, and from the side of the building where I waited for the ground to open up and swallow me, I heard the soft-voiced Mrs. Flowers and the textured voice of my grandmother merging and melting. They were interrupted from time to time by giggles that must have come from Mrs. Flowers (Momma never giggled in her life). Then she was gone.

> *They were interrupted from time to time by giggles that must have come from Mrs. Flowers . . .*

She appealed to me because she was like people I had never met personally. Like women in English novels who walked the moors (whatever they were) with their loyal dogs racing at a respectful distance. Like the women who sat in front of roaring fireplaces, drinking tea incessantly from silver trays full of scones and crumpets. Women who walked over the "heath"[5] and read morocco-bound[6] books and had two last names divided by a hyphen. It would be safe to say that she

---

2 benign (bi nīn′) good-natured
3 unceremonious (un′ ser ə mo′ nē əs) impolite
4 bungalow (bung′ gə lō′) a small house, usually one story high plus an attic
5 heath (hēth) an expanse of wasteland, especially in Britain, covered with heather and shrubs
6 morocco-bound (mə rä′ kō) having a leather cover

42   Unit 1 Personal Writing

Literature Model

Beverly Buchanan, *Bogart, Georgia*, 1989

made me proud to be Negro, just by being herself.

She acted just as refined as whitefolks in the movies and books and she was more beautiful, for none of them could have come near that warm color without looking gray by comparison.

It was fortunate that I never saw her in the company of powhitefolks. For since they tend to think of their whiteness as an evenizer, I'm certain that I would have had to hear her spoken to commonly as Bertha, and my image of her would have been shattered like the unmendable Humpty-Dumpty.

One summer afternoon, sweet-milk fresh in my memory, she stopped at the Store to buy provisions. Another Negro woman of her health and age would have been expected to carry the paper sacks home in one hand, but Momma said, "Sister Flowers, I'll send Bailey up to your house with these things."

She smiled that slow dragging smile, "Thank you, Mrs. Henderson. I'd prefer Marguerite, though." My name was

Literature Model

beautiful when she said it. "I've been meaning to talk to her, anyway." They gave each other age-group looks.

Momma said, "Well, that's all right then. Sister, go and change your dress. You going to Sister Flowers's."

The chifforobe[7] was a maze. What on earth did one put on to go to Mrs. Flowers' house? I knew I shouldn't put on a Sunday dress. It might be sacrilegious.[8] Certainly not a house dress, since I was already wearing a fresh one. I chose a school dress, naturally. It was formal without suggesting that going to Mrs. Flowers' house was equivalent to attending church.

I trusted myself back into the Store.

"Now, don't you look nice." I had chosen the right thing, for once.

"Mrs. Henderson, you make most of the children's clothes, don't you?"

"Yes, ma'am. Sure do. Store-bought clothes ain't hardly worth the thread it take to stitch them."

"I'll say you do a lovely job, though, so neat. That dress looks professional."

Momma was enjoying the seldom-received compliments. Since everyone we knew (except Mrs. Flowers, of course) could sew competently, praise was rarely handed out for the commonly practiced craft.

"I try, with the help of the Lord, Sister Flowers, to finish the inside just like I does the outside. Come here, Sister."

I had buttoned up the collar and tied the belt, apronlike, in back. Momma told me to turn around. With one hand she pulled the strings and the belt fell free at both sides of my waist. Then her large hands were at my neck, opening the button loops. I was terrified. What was happening?

"Take it off, Sister." She had her hands on the hem of the dress.

"I don't need to see the inside, Mrs. Henderson, I can tell . . ." But the dress was over my head and my arms were stuck in the sleeves. Momma said, "That'll do. See here, Sister Flowers, I French-seams around the armholes." Through the cloth film, I saw the shadow approach. "That makes it last longer. Children these days would bust out of sheet-metal clothes. They so rough."

> *I had buttoned up the collar and tied the belt, apronlike, in back. Momma told me to turn around.*

"That is a very good job, Mrs. Henderson. You should be proud. You can put your dress back on, Marguerite."

"No ma'am. Pride is a sin. And 'cording to the Good Book, it goeth before a fall."

"That's right. So the Bible says. It's a good thing to keep in mind."

I wouldn't look at either of them. Momma hadn't thought that taking off my dress in front of Mrs. Flowers would kill me stone dead. If I had refused, she would have thought I was trying to be "womanish" and might have remembered St. Louis. Mrs. Flowers had known that I would be embarrassed and that was even worse. I picked up the groceries and went out to wait in the

---

7 chifforobe (shif′ ə rōb′) a combination of wardrobe and chest of drawers
8 sacrilegious (sak′ rə lij′ əs) involving the violation of something holy

44 Unit 1 Personal Writing

Literature Model

Charles Alston, *Girl in a Red Dress*, 1934

Literature Model

hot sunshine. It would be fitting if I got a sunstroke and died before they came outside. Just dropped dead on the slanting porch.

There was a little path beside the rocky road, and Mrs. Flowers walked in front swinging her arms and picking her way over the stones.

She said, without turning her head, to me, "I hear you're doing very good school work, Marguerite, but that it's all written. The teachers report that they have trouble getting you to talk in class." We passed the triangular farm on our left and the path widened to allow us to walk together. I hung back in the separate unasked and unanswerable questions.

"Come and walk along with me, Marguerite." I couldn't have refused even if I wanted to. She pronounced my name so nicely. Or more correctly, she spoke each word with such clarity that I was certain a foreigner who didn't understand English could have understood her.

"Now no one is going to make you talk—possibly no one can. But bear in mind, language is man's way of communicating with his fellow man and it is language alone which separates him from the lower animals." That was a totally new idea to me, and I would need time to think about it.

"Your grandmother says you read a lot. Every chance you get. That's good, but not good enough. Words mean more than what is set down on paper. It takes the human voice to infuse them with the shades of deeper meaning."

I memorized the part about the human voice infusing words. It seemed so valid and poetic.

She said she was going to give me some books and that I not only must read them, I must read them aloud. She suggested that I try to make a sentence sound in as many different ways as possible.

"I'll accept no excuse if you return a book to me that has been badly handled." My imagination boggled at the punishment I would deserve if in fact I did abuse a book of Mrs. Flowers's. Death would be too kind and brief.

The odors in the house surprised me. Somehow I had never connected Mrs. Flowers with food or eating or any other common experience of common people. There must have been an outhouse, too, but my mind never recorded it.

The sweet scent of vanilla had met us as she opened the door.

"I made tea cookies this morning. You see, I had planned to invite you for cookies and lemonade so we could have this little chat. The lemonade is in the icebox."

It followed that Mrs. Flowers would have ice on an ordinary day, when most families in our town bought ice late on Saturdays only a few times during the summer to be used in the wooden ice-cream freezers.

She took the bags from me and disappeared through the kitchen door. I looked around the room that I had never in my wildest fantasies imagined I would see.

> *She said she was going to give me some books and that I not only must read them, I must read them aloud.*

Literature Model

Wilmer Angier Jennings, *Landscape,* 1945

Browned photographs leered or threatened from the walls and the white, freshly done curtains pushed against themselves and against the wind. I wanted to gobble up the room entire and take it to Bailey, who would help me analyze and enjoy it.

"Have a seat, Marguerite. Over there by the table." She carried a platter covered with a tea towel. Although she warned that she hadn't tried her hand at baking sweets for some time, I was certain that like everything else about her the cookies would be perfect.

Literature Model

They were flat round wafers, slightly browned on the edges and butter-yellow in the center. With the cold lemonade they were sufficient for childhood's lifelong diet. Remembering my manners, I took nice little lady-like bites off the edges. She said she had made them expressly for me and that she had a few in the kitchen that I could take home to my brother. So I jammed one whole cake in my mouth and the rough crumbs scratched the inside of my jaws, and if I hadn't had to swallow, it would have been a dream come true.

As I ate she began the first of what we later called "my lessons in living." She said that I must always be intolerant of ignorance but understanding of illiteracy. That some people, unable to go to school, were more educated and even more intelligent than college professors. She encouraged me to listen carefully to what country people called mother wit. That in those homely sayings was couched the collective wisdom of generations.

When I finished the cookies she brushed off the table and brought a thick, small book from the bookcase. I had read *A Tale of Two Cities* and found it up to my standards as a romantic novel. She opened the first page and I heard poetry for the first time in my life.

"It was the best of times and the worst of times . . ." Her voice slid in and curved down through and over the words. She was nearly singing. I wanted to look at the pages. Were they the same that I had read? Or were there notes, music, lined on the pages, as in a hymn book? Her sounds began cascading gently. I knew from listening to a thousand preachers that she was nearing the end of her reading, and I hadn't really heard, heard to understand, a single word.

"How do you like that?"

It occurred to me that she expected a response. The sweet vanilla flavor was still on my tongue and her reading was a wonder in my ears. I had to speak.

I said, "Yes, ma'am." It was the least I could do, but it was the most also.

> **"** *There's one more thing. Take this book of poems and memorize one for me. Next time you pay me a visit, I want you to recite.* **"**

"There's one more thing. Take this book of poems and memorize one for me. Next time you pay me a visit, I want you to recite."

I have tried often to search behind the sophistication of years for the enchantment I so easily found in those gifts. The essence[9] escapes but its aura[10] remains. To be allowed, no, invited, into the private lives of strangers, and to share their joys and fears, was a chance to exchange the Southern bitter wormwood[11] for a cup of mead[12] with Beowulf or a hot cup of tea and milk with Oliver Twist. When I said aloud, "It is a far,

---

[9] **essence** (es′ əns) the basic nature or most important quality
[10] **aura** (ôr′ ə) the atmosphere or feeling that seems to surround a certain person or thing
[11] **wormwood** (wurm′ wood′) a bitter oil
[12] **mead** (mēd) a drink made of honey and water

Literature Model

far better thing that I do, than I have ever done . . ." tears of love filled my eyes at my selflessness.

On that first day, I ran down the hill and into the road (few cars ever came along it) and had the good sense to stop running before I reached the Store.

I was liked, and what a difference it made. I was respected not as Mrs. Henderson's grandchild or Bailey's sister but for just being Marguerite Johnson.

Childhood's logic never asks to be proved (all conclusions are absolute). I didn't question why Mrs. Flowers had singled me out for attention, nor did it occur to me that Momma might have asked her to give me a little talking to. All I cared about was that she had made tea cookies for *me* and read to *me* from her favorite book. It was enough to prove that she liked me.

Literature Model

Linking Writing and Literature

Readers Respond to the Model

What makes Maya Angelou's autobiographical account appealing?

Explore Maya Angelou's personal writing by answering these questions. Then read what other students liked about Angelou's autobiographical story.

1. Do you share Marguerite's admiration for Mrs. Flowers? Explain.
2. How does Maya Angelou's use of imagery make her writing intensely personal? Name some specific images that you found memorable.
3. Do you find a connection with your own life in this description of a special childhood relationship?
4. How might reading this selection affect your personal writing? Does it give you any specific ideas? Explain.

What Students Say

"This selection from *I Know Why the Caged Bird Sings* was about a special relationship a young girl has with a woman whom she looks up to and admires. What I liked best about the passage was Mrs. Flowers' poetic words of advice about how the human voice can express words better than paper can. What I remember best was a small part about ice: Marguerite was thinking about how it figured that Mrs. Flowers had ice on any ordinary day, when most people just had it on Saturdays. In a few short sentences the author described how special Mrs. Flowers was to Marguerite.

The story made me realize more about how it was to grow up then, and I think this would be a good selection for anyone to read."

Claire Monty

"I liked the fact that Mrs. Flowers opened Marguerite's eyes to speech and literature. I would recommend this selection to a friend because I think there's a point in everyone's life when someone they like has taken them aside to teach them something good."

David Ojeda

UNIT 1 Review

Reflecting on the Unit

Summarize what you have learned in this unit by answering the following questions.

1. In what ways can personal writing help you make discoveries about yourself?
2. What can you keep in a personal journal and how can it serve as a valuable source of writing ideas?
3. What strategies can you use to explore ideas for personal essays?
4. What are some of the different methods you can use to present autobiographical materials?
5. What are some devices poets use to create memorable word pictures?
6. What is the purpose of a reader-response journal and how can it help you learn?

Adding to Your Portfolio

CHOOSE A SELECTION FOR YOUR PORTFOLIO Look over the personal writing you have done during this unit. Select a piece of writing to put into your portfolio. The piece should demonstrate that you have worked with one or more of the concepts listed above. In other words, look for a piece of writing that shows some or all of the following:

- a valuable self-discovery, or something special that makes you *you*
- an idea source for a future personal essay
- ideas generated by freewriting, clustering, or creating an idea map
- your own personal thoughts and feelings in poetic form

REFLECT ON YOUR CHOICE Attach a note to the piece you chose, explaining briefly why you chose it and what you learned from writing it.

SET GOALS How can you improve your writing? What skill will you focus on the next time you write?

Writing Across the Curriculum

MAKE A CIVICS CONNECTION Think about an experience you had with someone quite different from yourself—in age, culture, or economic status. Make brief notes about how the person was different from you and what you learned from the encounter. Then, using those notes, write a paragraph demonstrating how encountering this new person affected your life or beliefs.

Review 51

"The afternoon sun penetrated the mass of honeysuckle that covered the porch, and fell on my upturned face."

—Helen Keller, *The Story of My Life*

UNIT 2 The Writing Process

Writing in the Real World: *Lorenzo Chavez* — 54

Lesson 2.1	Overview of the Writing Process	58
Lesson 2.2	Prewriting: Getting Started	62
Lesson 2.3	Prewriting: Identifying Purpose and Audience	68
Lesson 2.4	Prewriting: Gathering Information	72
Lesson 2.5	Drafting: Turning Notes into Paragraphs	76
Lesson 2.6	Drafting: Writing Unified Paragraphs	80
Lesson 2.7	Drafting: Ordering the Details	84
Lesson 2.8	Drafting: Writing Coherent Paragraphs	88
Lesson 2.9	Revising: Improving Paragraphs	92
Lesson 2.10	Editing/Proofreading: Final Checking	96
Lesson 2.11	Publishing/Presenting: Sharing Writing	100
Lesson 2.12	Writing About Literature: Explaining Theme	104

Writing Process in Action — 108

Literature Model: from *The Kitchen God's Wife* by Amy Tan — 112

Unit 2 Review — 120

Writing in the Real World

MEDIA Connection — Magazine Article

As both a freelance writer and writing teacher, Lorenzo Chavez has lots of experience with the writing process. Chavez writes feature stories, or "human interest" stories, that cover a large range of topics. Below is an excerpt from a feature he wrote for *Vista,* a magazine for Hispanic readers inserted in about twenty Sunday newspapers nationwide.

The Quest for Hispanic Roots

by Lorenzo Chavez

For 15 years, Mickey Garcia has searched quietly for clues to a lost treasure buried in history books, church records and dusty family albums. The Texan's "treasure" is her family history: a unique link with the past that may help her gain a better understanding of her Latin roots.

"Some of my Mexican cousins think I'm crazy," she says from her suburban Houston home. "They think: 'What in the world does she want with all these dead people?'"

Whether out of cultural pride, simple curiosity or legal necessity, Latinos like Garcia are actively tracing their ancestral roots for clues to their Hispanic identity.

Garcia's success challenges the notion that genealogy is reserved for university academicians and librarians . . . "It's my hobby and I enjoy it," says the working mother of three. "You don't have to have a college degree. I've always been interested in history."

Since the 1977 telecast of Alex Haley's *Roots* sparked interest in family history, Hispanics have enthusiastically joined other Americans in the rush to the libraries.

Mexican Americans in particular, especially in the Southwest, are tracing generations of family roots. The historical records of immigrants from Cuba, Puerto Rico and South America—more recent, by comparison—are still evolving.

Genealogical societies, libraries and universities in southern Texas eagerly compile church and civil records relating to pioneers who explored and settled the border between the United States and Mexico.

The sense of *familia* is a powerful unifying force. On July 7, 1984, approximately 1,500 Vela family members descended on Reynaldo Vela's ranch in McAllen, Texas, in what may have been the largest and most successful Hispanic family reunion ever held in the United States.

Through that warm summer weekend, they gathered at the 5,000-acre Laguna Seca ranch to celebrate their surname and to honor Salvador Vela and Leonor Zamora, who carried their children across the Rio Grande from Reynosa, Mexico, to McAllen in the late 1800s.

A book published last December, "Four Generations of Velas," was the result of ten years of research by those immigrants' descendants. . . .

Spanish surnames are more accessible than non-Spanish surnames, [George Ryskamp, a California genealogist] explains, thanks to the extensive records kept by the Spanish monarchy. The Archives of the Indies, a repository in Seville, houses more than 40 million documents dealing with Spain's conquest of the New

Writing in the Real World

World from the 15th to the 19th centuries.

Amateur and professional researchers should be grateful for that bureaucratic system, which required three copies of every document. . . . The copies were kept by the local officials, the regional governor and the Crown. Catholic church records also helped unify the Hispanic world, says Ryskamp.

"Most people who get interested in genealogy are two or three generations removed from their mother country," Ryskamp notes. "Economically, they are middle-class or above. I expect the interest to grow in the next 10 to 20 years as the Hispanic population makes greater economic gains. . . ."

Meanwhile, Mickey Garcia continues searching for names and dates. She has traced her mother's family to the early 1700's, but remains "stuck" in the 1880's with the paternal branch of the tree.

"You have to be interested," Garcia explains. "One of my ancestors was married three times and ended up with 21 children. And in 1833 a lot of my relatives died of cholera. That makes for a lot of added research."

"To be a good genealogist you have to be a good detective," sums up Ryskamp, the California lawyer. "You never know what you are going to find."

A Writer's Process

Prewriting
Collecting the Facts

Chavez will tell you that ideas for feature stories are everywhere, in fact, there are "just too many," laughed Chavez. And, of course, you have to be alert and open to ideas. The idea for Chavez's story on family histories, "The Quest for Hispanic Roots," came from *Vista* readers. Over the years, hundreds of *Vista* readers had written in to "Rootsearch," a popular genealogy column devoted to tracing family histories. With so many readers writing in to the column, the *Vista* staff decided to run an article that could help people do family research on their own. They commissioned Chavez to write the article.

Before Chavez could start researching the article, he had to narrow the original idea to a few key points—no more than he could cover in the allotted space of 1,500 words, or about six pages in *Vista* magazine. Chavez then gathered the facts by looking for answers to these questions: Why do people search for their pasts? What libraries or associations can help?

It took Chavez about a week to get the answers. Some information came from newspaper clippings, but most of it came through the thirty or forty phone calls he made to libraries and researchers.

Vela family reunion

Writing in the Real World

Drafting
Telling the Story

After his interviews, Chavez had twenty pages of notes, several taped conversations, a few newspaper clips, and a head full of ideas. Before sitting down at the computer, Chavez reminded himself of the people he was writing for. His audience was a "middle-aged to older generation, people of Mexican descent, mostly retirees, who have spare time and an interest in history and politics." To engage his readers, Chavez had to put himself in their shoes and anticipate questions they might ask.

Now Chavez was ready to write. To grab the reader, he used an anecdote about Mickey Garcia, a Texas genealogist who researches family histories. He portrayed Garcia as a treasure hunter. "She's searching for a valuable thing—not gold, but a family history," Chavez said. "I used that [approach] because I didn't want to frighten the reader by saying this was a long, time-consuming, arduous task."

From there Chavez stitched the story together using quotes, descriptions, and explanations about what sparked people's interest in genealogy. He introduced top researchers, described huge family reunions, and explained how to find family records.

Revising
Making Necessary Changes

Chavez wrote a rough draft in three days. "It was messy, but I knew I had everything I wanted there," he said. Now he was ready to revise.

At this stage, Chavez began working on a printout of his story instead of working at the computer. On hard copy, he could spot problems more clearly. "If the lead is too long, you can see it—the paragraph is all gray. No one is going to get through that first paragraph," he explains.

Editing
Bringing in Style

Chavez began editing his story by checking his facts, spelling, and grammar. "If you have poor spelling and grammar or the facts are wrong, the reader will ask, 'Why should I read this guy? He doesn't know what he's talking about.'"

After that, Chavez worked to improve his style. He rewrote dull sentences to make them bold and active. He varied sentence lengths to create rhythm, so the story sounded interesting, not monotonous. Finally, he checked to be sure the story had some mystery. "You can't put all the information at the top or the reader doesn't have anything to look forward to," Lorenzo said. "You have to have some suspense, something pushing the reader forward."

Finally, Chavez turned his copy over to staff editors who reviewed his work before publication. His editors, he said, catch mistakes and other problems because they have a fresh point of view.

Examining Writing in the Real World

Analyzing the Media Connection

Discuss the following questions about the article on pages 54–55.

1. For what audience did Chavez write his feature story?
2. In what ways does Chavez direct the article to the interests of his readers?
3. Chavez describes the Vela family reunion that 1,500 family members attended. How effective was this anecdote?
4. Why do you think Chavez opens the story by focusing on the family search of one woman, Mickey Garcia? Why does he return to Garcia at the closing?
5. Chavez includes some history about Spanish and Mexican migration. What do you think his reason is for including this information?

Analyzing A Writer's Process

Discuss these questions about Lorenzo Chavez's writing process.

1. How was the topic for Chavez's article selected?
2. What sources of facts did Chavez use for his story? What are some other possible sources he might have used?
3. Before he started to draft his story, what did Chavez need to know about his audience?
4. Why did Chavez revise on a printout rather than on the computer?
5. Why does Chavez take extra care to check his spelling and grammar?

Grammar Link

Vary sentence lengths.

Lorenzo Chavez writes that he varied sentence lengths to create rhythm, so the story sounded interesting, not monotonous. You can vary sentence lengths by using a variety of sentence patterns: simple, compound, complex, and compound-complex.

Revise each item below by combining each pair of simple sentences in two different ways. Add or change words or phrases as needed.

1. Feature story ideas are everywhere. Ideas often come from news articles.
2. Chavez writes for *Vista* magazine. *Vista* is targeted to Hispanic readers.
3. Chavez interviewed genealogists. He collected taped conversations.
4. Chavez improved his draft. He changed words and sentences.
5. Genealogists share their research findings. There are many genealogical societies.

See Lessons 13.3 and 13.4, pages 541–544.

LESSON 2.1

Overview of the Writing Process

Writing is a way for you to explore your thoughts and mental images. It is also a way to discover more about yourself and the people and experiences that helped make you who you are.

Discover the Stages in the Process

After Michelangelo had begun painting the Sistine Chapel in Rome in the sixteenth century, he thought of new ideas and decided to resketch and repaint based on those new ideas. His finished painting is thus a product of many false starts and stops—a composite of all the different ideas that occurred to Michelangelo during the painting process.

A writer works in much the same way, exploring ideas in a rough draft, refining the draft, or even discarding it and starting again. Although no two writers approach the writing process in exactly the same way, most writers go through five stages: prewriting, drafting, revising, editing/proofreading, and publishing/presenting.

Michelangelo, detail of the Sistine Chapel ceiling, 1508–1512

Prewriting During prewriting, you decide what you want to write about by exploring ideas, feelings, and memories. You also begin to think about your audience and your purpose. Your audience is the people who will read your work. Your purpose is what you hope to accomplish through your writing.

Drafting Writing a draft, or turning your ideas into paragraphs, is a stage in the writing process and a tool in itself. As you compose your draft, you explore and develop your ideas.

58 Unit 2 The Writing Process

Revising The purposes of revising are to make sure that your writing is clear and well organized, that it accomplishes your objectives, and that it reaches your audience. To achieve these goals, you may need to cut or add to your writing. Mark these changes right on your draft and then incorporate them. Compare the writer's revised draft with her earlier draft to see what changes she incorporated during revising.

Editing/Proofreading The purposes of editing are to make sure that you've chosen the best possible words to communicate your ideas and that your sentences are grammatically correct. Finally, you proofread your writing and correct mistakes in capitalization, punctuation, and spelling. Note the editorial changes this writer has marked on her revised copy.

Publishing/Presenting This is the stage at which you share your work with others. You might read what you've written aloud in class, submit it to the school newspaper, or give it to a friend to read. There are many avenues for presenting your work.

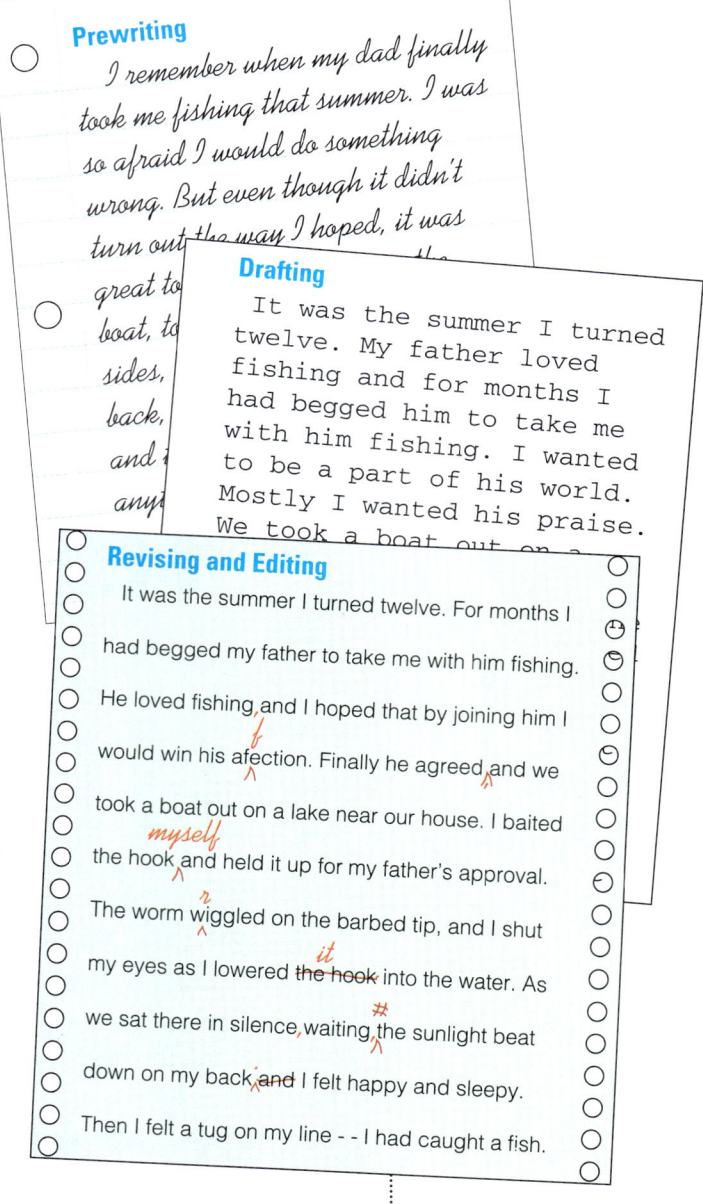

Prewriting
I remember when my dad finally took me fishing that summer. I was so afraid I would do something wrong. But even though it didn't turn out the way I hoped, it was great to...

Drafting
It was the summer I turned twelve. My father loved fishing and for months I had begged him to take me with him fishing. I wanted to be a part of his world. Mostly I wanted his praise. We took a boat out on a...

Revising and Editing
It was the summer I turned twelve. For months I had begged my father to take me with him fishing. He loved fishing, and I hoped that by joining him I would win his afection. Finally he agreed, and we took a boat out on a lake near our house. I baited the hook *myself* and held it up for my father's approval. The worm wiggled on the barbed tip, and I shut my eyes as I lowered ~~the hook~~ *it* into the water. As we sat there in silence, waiting, the sunlight beat down on my back, ~~and~~ I felt happy and sleepy. Then I felt a tug on my line - - I had caught a fish.

Journal Writing

In your journal, explain the stages you went through on a recent writing assignment. How do they compare with the five stages described above?

2.1 Overview of the Writing Process **59**

Follow the Process

At any point in the writing process, you may return to any of the preceding stages. For example, if you're having trouble drafting a paragraph, you may go back to the prewriting stage and outline it first. If you get stuck as you revise, you may redraft some of your writing. You may even need to gather more information or reevaluate your purpose.

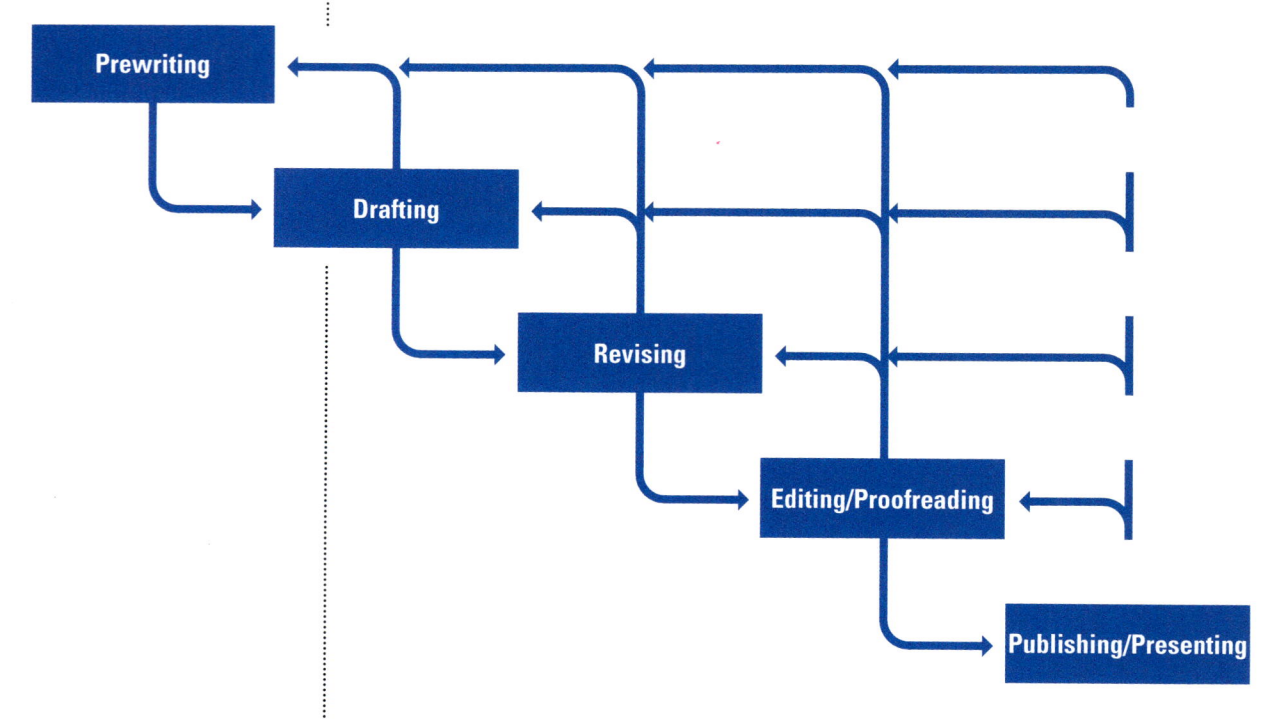

The Writing Process

Prewriting → Drafting → Revising → Editing/Proofreading → Publishing/Presenting

Remember, too, that because writing is a process of discovery, you may be surprised by what you find when you write. Like Alice Walker in the model below, you may discover something new about yourself, your world, and the forces that have shaped your life.

Literature Model

> Through her writing, what did Walker discover about her mother?

> After years of listening to her mother's stories, Walker decides she wants to write about them.

So many of the stories that I write . . . are my mother's stories. Only recently did I fully realize this: that through years of listening to my mother's stories of her life, I have absorbed not only the stories themselves, but something of the manner in which she spoke, something of the urgency that involves the knowledge that her stories—like her life—must be recorded.

Alice Walker, *In Search of Our Mothers' Gardens*

2.1 Writing Activities

Write a Comparison

Writer Lawrence Osgood noted that "writing is like exploring. . . . As an explorer makes maps of the country he has explored, so a writer's works are maps of the country he has explored." Use Osgood's analogy to suggest how writing is like another process, such as producing a school play, making a dress, or constructing a birdhouse.

PURPOSE To compare two processes
AUDIENCE Your classmates
LENGTH 1–2 paragraphs

WRITING RUBRICS To write a comparison of two processes, you should

- explain the actions that should occur at each stage of each process
- point out similarities and differences in the two processes
- give at least three reasons one might repeat one or more of the steps in either process

Using Computers

A diagram can often help you compare two things or two processes. Create a table using a word processing program. (Often "Table" is listed in the menu bar.) Use the table you construct to list the steps of the two processes you described in the writing activity. Compare the steps for each process and analyze which steps are repeated and why.

Grammar Link

Add commas to avoid run-on sentences.

The worm wriggled on the barbed tip, and I shut my eyes . . .

Revise the sentences below, correcting the run-on sentences by adding commas where needed.

1. It was the summer I turned thirteen and I longed to be independent.
2. My parents said the highway was too dangerous so they wouldn't let me ride my bike to the mall.
3. One day temptation grew too strong and the lure of my bike became irresistible.
4. Gasoline fumes made me feel queasy and the noise gave me a headache.
5. I got really tired and I thought I would never get there!

See Lesson 13.10, pages 555–557.

Viewing and Representing

CREATE A MEDIA PRODUCT With a partner, create a video demonstrating the two processes you compared for the writing activity. To illustrate the writing process, use the materials from a recent writing assignment, including drafts and revisions. As you demonstrate each stage of the writing process, orally describe your objectives and actions. Follow this procedure for the other process you have chosen as well. Then tell how the processes are similar and different.

LESSON 2.2
Prewriting: Getting Started

Ideas for writing are everywhere. In prewriting you can use a variety of techniques to find and focus on a writing topic.

Prewriting is the stage during which you generate ideas. During prewriting you unleash your imagination to allow promising writing topics to emerge. Among the techniques that writers find useful for generating writing ideas are freewriting and collecting.

Begin with Ideas

Freewriting To freewrite, choose a topic and a time limit and then just start writing your ideas as they come to you. Don't worry about grammar, spelling, punctuation, or logic. If you run out of ideas, repeat the same word over and over until a new idea occurs to you. When the time is up, review what you've written. The ideas that most interest you are likely to be the ones that will be most worth writing about.

Take a look at the freewriting model generated by one writer. Note how many ideas she came up with in just a few minutes.

> Is the writer more interested in the quick flow of ideas or in following grammar or punctuation rules? How do you know?

> The writer has discovered an idea for a possible writing project: her uncle's early experiences.

Model

I love spending time with my uncle Edward. He always has stories to tell—like how he used to roller-skate to work when he first got out of college. And stories about my father—his little brother—that make me laugh but that seem like they're about somebody else because I can't imagine my dad as a kid but I can imagine Uncle Edward as a kid, even though he's a lot older than my dad. Probably because he's so easy to talk to—he's more like my friend than my uncle. I told him that I wanted to be a writer someday, but he didn't laugh—he said I should start now. I wonder if I could write a story about Uncle Edward on skates.

Collecting Books, magazines, newspapers, movies, and even conversations with other people are valuable sources of ideas and information. A good source of raw material is your journal. Based on a journal entry, Moses Thomas Greene II wrote the following reaction to a TV show.

Student Model

As a young person in America, I think of death as something that will occur when I am in my eighties or older. However, an episode of a TV show made me realize that I can't take this longevity for granted anymore.

In this episode, a group of college students in a public speaking class were given a unique assignment: they were asked to deliver their own eulogy. Although most of the students gave humorous speeches, one student took the assignment more seriously because she had Acquired Immune Deficiency Syndrome, or AIDS. Up until then, the student had kept her condition a secret, but she decided to tell her classmates the truth when she delivered her eulogy. As a result, the rest of the students began avoiding the young woman and didn't want to hear about how she was dealing with her condition.

What I liked best about the episode was that it handled the issue realistically. The students' reactions reflected the attitude of many "real" people toward the disease—ignore it and it will go away. However, the episode made me see that AIDS is a problem that needs to be dealt with and that can't be ignored.

Moses Thomas Greene II
Brentwood High School, Brentwood, New York

> How does Moses "hook" you in the first paragraph of his essay?

> Writing about this difficult subject helped Moses sort out his feelings about it.

Journal Writing

Pick one idea you find interesting from your own collection of raw material and freewrite about it for five minutes. What new ideas did your freewriting generate? Note these in your journal.

Explore Your Ideas

Explore your ideas to clarify your thinking and find a focus for your writing. Two useful techniques for exploring ideas are making lists and asking questions.

Making Lists Start with a key word or idea and list other ideas as they occur to you. Don't worry about the order; just let your ideas flow freely from one to the next. This kind of free-association activity is also often referred to as brainstorming.

One writer used the technique of list making to generate the ideas shown below. What other ideas come to mind as you read through each list?

Memorable Events
- Eighth-grade graduation
- Visiting my dad last summer
- When I got my first bicycle
- Mom's graduation from college
- Grandfather in the hospital

Favorite Places
- My grandmother's house
- The mall
- The park down by the waterfront
- My room
- The basketball court behind the school

Embarrassing Moments
- When I forgot my lines in the school play
- When I struck out in the playoff game
- When I marched the wrong way during the band's halftime performance
- When I tripped on my dress at my sister's wedding

Earliest Memories
- Falling down the basement stairs when I was three
- A family trip to Yellowstone Park
- Fingerpainting in kindergarten
- Building a snow fort with my best friend in first grade
- Listening to my grandfather tell stories

Once you've finished your lists, look them over and underline the ideas that seem most interesting to you. Draw lines between related ideas. Did any unexpected ideas appear? Did you recall events you had not thought about for a long time? Did you learn something new about yourself? These ideas may be worthwhile writing topics.

Asking Questions To explore a topic by asking and answering questions about it, begin with six basic questions: *who? what? where? when? why?* and *how?* In the chart below, the writer explored an idea generated through list making by asking and answering questions based on these six questions.

Questions to Explore Ideas

Who
- **Q.** Who or what do I want to write about?
- **A.** My 73-year-old grandfather, who grew up in Vietnam and came to the United States after the Vietnam War.

What
- **Q.** What happened to my subject?
- **A.** During the war he was separated from his family. He finally escaped from Vietnam. He spent a long time in a refugee camp, until family members in the United States could arrange for him to come here.

Where
- **Q.** Where did this happen?
- **A.** In a small village in Vietnam and later in a refugee camp just across the border of Thailand.

When
- **Q.** When did this happen?
- **A.** He escaped in 1973 and lived in a makeshift tent in Thailand until 1978.

Why
- **Q.** Why did this happen?
- **A.** He escaped from Vietnam because of the war. Many people left Vietnam because they were afraid of the new Communist leaders. They fled to nearby Thailand because it wasn't under Communist rule.

How
- **Q.** How did this happen?
- **A.** He was able to escape from Vietnam and start a new life in the United States partly because of his determination to see his family again and partly because of luck.

Journal Writing

Choose a family member you might like to write about. In your journal, pose *who, what, where, when, why,* and *how* questions to explore your subject. Think of possible answers and record them in your journal.

2.2 Prewriting: Getting Started   **65**

Narrow Your Topic

Once you've chosen a general topic to write about, you need to narrow its scope. You can use a network tree to help you narrow your writing topic. Start by listing your general topic at the top of the tree. Then use the same free-association technique that you used in list making to generate ideas to fill out the tree. Notice in the network tree below how many ideas the writer identified by using the questions on page 65 to explore an idea generated during list making.

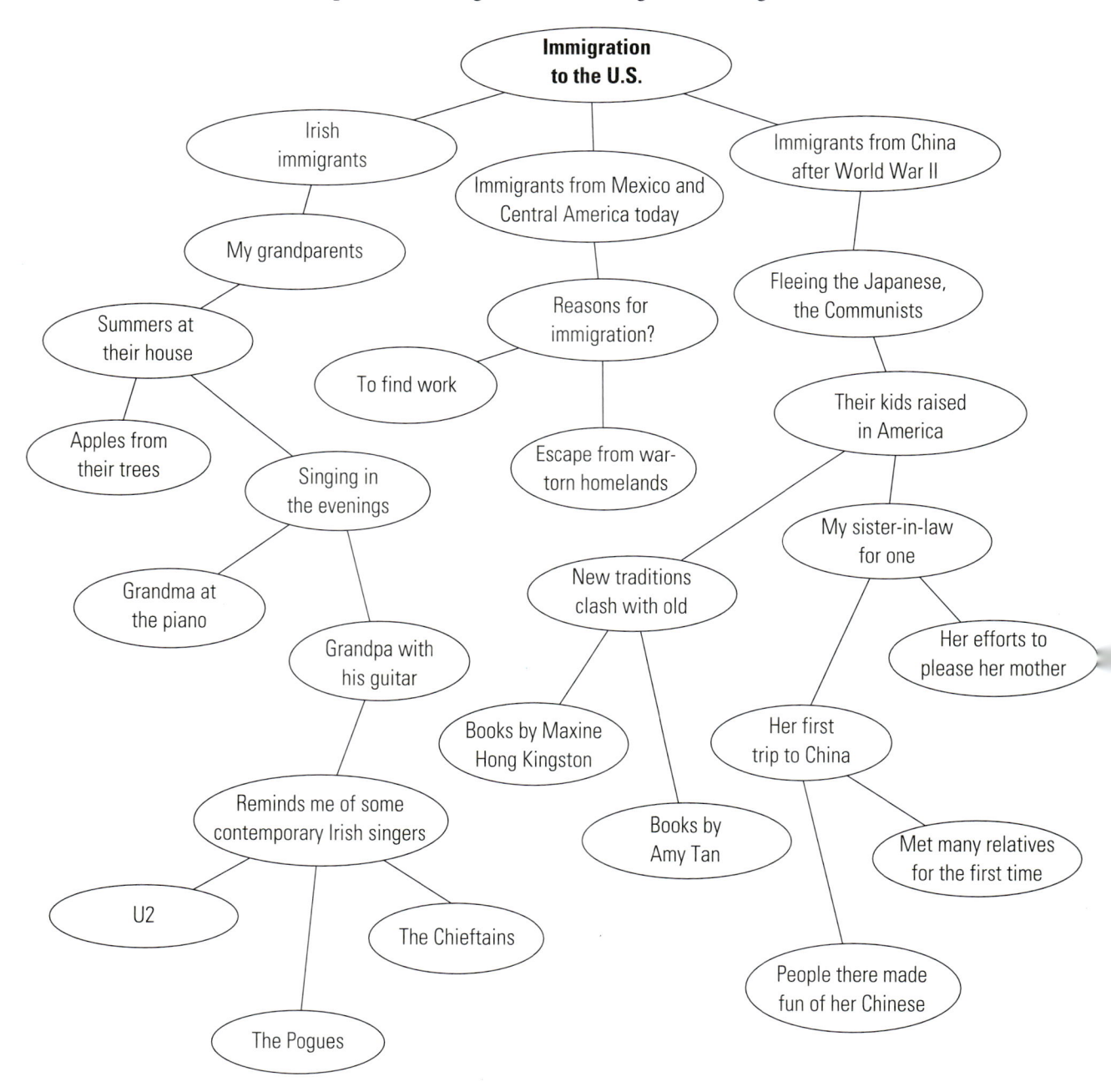

Immigration to the U.S.
- Irish immigrants
  - My grandparents
    - Summers at their house
      - Apples from their trees
    - Singing in the evenings
      - Grandma at the piano
      - Grandpa with his guitar
        - Reminds me of some contemporary Irish singers
          - U2
          - The Chieftains
          - The Pogues
- Immigrants from Mexico and Central America today
  - Reasons for immigration?
    - To find work
    - Escape from war-torn homelands
  - New traditions clash with old
    - Books by Maxine Hong Kingston
    - Books by Amy Tan
- Immigrants from China after World War II
  - Fleeing the Japanese, the Communists
  - Their kids raised in America
    - My sister-in-law for one
      - Her efforts to please her mother
      - Her first trip to China
        - Met many relatives for the first time
        - People there made fun of her Chinese

2.2 Writing Activities

Generate Story Ideas

In this unit you will be writing a human-interest feature story. Use the prewriting methods discussed in this lesson to choose three possible topics for your story.

PURPOSE To explore story ideas
AUDIENCE Yourself
LENGTH 1–2 pages

WRITING RUBRICS To effectively prewrite, you should

- freewrite or collect ideas from other sources
- list ideas and see how they relate to each other
- ask questions to explore and clarify ideas
- create a network tree to narrow a topic

Using Computers

Explore human-interest stories by checking the Web pages of newsmagazines on the Internet. Read the topics highlighted in the tables of contents of the issues. Use these topic ideas to help generate your own topic ideas for a human-interest feature story.

Listening and Speaking

COOPERATIVE LEARNING In a small group, study and discuss a painting in this book that features a person. What do the details in the painting reveal about the life of this person? Then brainstorm to develop a list of possible topics for human-interest stories suggested by the painting. Choose a group member to record the topics so that they can be shared with the entire class.

Grammar Link

Make collective nouns and verbs agree.

A *collective noun* takes a plural verb when it refers to individual members of a group and a singular verb when it refers to the group as a whole. In the second paragraph of the student model on page 63, Moses uses a plural verb, *were given*, with the collective noun, *group*.

Find the subject in each sentence and write it on your paper. Then write the verb in parentheses that agrees with the subject.

1. A group in English class (is/are) interested in brainstorming to gather ideas related to writing a family history.
2. The committee (is/are) quick to agree among themselves on several topics.
3. The class (agree/agrees) to pursue two or three of the suggested ideas.
4. The majority (enjoy/enjoys) writing stories about their families.
5. A panel (is chosen/are chosen) to evaluate the essays.

See Lesson 16.4, page 614.

LESSON 2.3
Prewriting: Identifying Purpose and Audience

You can focus your ideas by defining the reason for your writing (your purpose) and determining the people for whom you are writing (your audience).

The earlier you determine the audience and purpose for your writing, the more focused your final product will be. Here is how one writer narrowed her topic to establish a purpose. How will her choice of audience focus her topic still further?

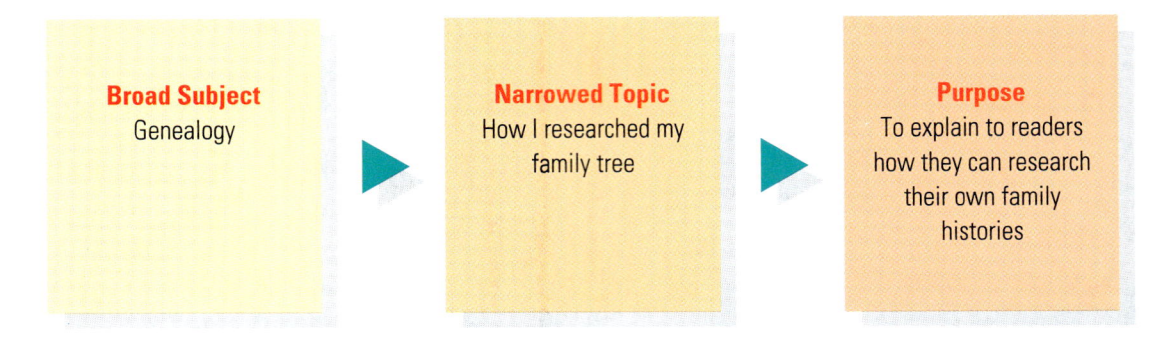

Broad Subject	Narrowed Topic	Purpose
Genealogy	How I researched my family tree	To explain to readers how they can research their own family histories

Determine a Purpose

Consider the primary purpose for your writing: to inform or explain, to persuade, to amuse or entertain, to narrate, or to describe. Sometimes, however, you may write to accomplish more than one purpose. For instance, if you write a letter to the editor of your school newspaper praising a campaign to raise money for a shelter for the homeless, your primary purpose might be to inform your fellow students about the campaign and the shelter. Your secondary purpose might be to persuade students to help with the campaign. To determine the primary purpose of your writing, answer the questions on page 69.

68 Unit 2 The Writing Process

Questions for Determining Your Purpose

1. Do I want to narrate, or tell, a story?
2. Do I want to describe someone or something?
3. Do I want to inform my readers about the topic or to explain something about it?
4. Do I want to persuade my readers to change their minds about something or take some action?

In the following paragraphs, writer Yoshiko Uchida explains her purpose in writing about the lives of Japanese Americans during World War II. At that time, the United States was at war with Japan. Many Japanese American families were forced to leave their homes and live in camps run by the U.S. government. Uchida often speaks to schoolchildren about her own experiences in one of the camps.

Literature Model

I always ask the children why they think I wrote *Journey to Topaz* and *Journey Home,* in which I tell of the wartime experiences of the Japanese Americans. "To tell about the camps?" they ask. "To tell how you felt? To tell what happened to the Japanese people?"

"Yes," I answer, but I continue the discussion until finally one of them will say, "You wrote those books so it won't ever happen again."

And that is why I wrote [*Desert Exile*]. I wrote it for the young Japanese Americans who seek a sense of continuity with their past. But I wrote it as well for all Americans, with the hope that through knowledge of the past, they will never allow another group of people in America to be sent into a desert exile ever again.

Yoshiko Uchida, *Desert Exile*

> What is Uchida's primary purpose? Do you think Uchida believes that "the pen is mightier than the sword"?

> Uchida considers the needs of her two audiences: Japanese Americans and all other Americans.

Journal Writing

Choose a topic that appeals to you. How might you approach that topic if your purpose were to inform? To persuade? To entertain? To narrate? To describe? In your journal, jot down ideas about different ways to approach the same topic.

Address Your Audience

To best communicate with your audience, put yourself in their place. Think about what your readers need or want to know about the subject. Consider also the language that would best communicate your ideas to them.

Find the Right Level Identify the various aspects of the subject that will most interest your readers. For example, an audience of tennis enthusiasts may enjoy reading about the specific shots a player used to win a game. However, an audience that is less familiar with the sport may be more interested in reading about the player's personality.

Then consider how much your audience already knows about the topic you've chosen. This will help you avoid explaining something most of your readers already know or writing about something they don't understand.

Find the Right Language Choose words that are appropriate to your audience and purpose. For a research paper or a letter to the principal, you would use formal English, paying attention to rules of standard grammar and usage. For a letter to a friend, conversational English would be more appropriate.

To make sure that your writing will reach its intended audience, you can ask yourself several questions. The questions below helped one writer determine how to address his audience. The writer chose to write on the following topic: "How My Sister Ann Drives Me Crazy." His basic purpose was to entertain.

Questions to Help You Address Your Audience

1. Whom am I writing for?	My English class, other ninth graders
2. How much do they know about Ann?	Not much. I'll have to present a vivid description and character sketch of my sister.
3. What writing style should I use?	I'll use a humorous, informal, conversational style to help keep them interested in what I'm saying.
4. What vocabulary is appropriate?	Words they understand, especially some contractions and slang to get across the way my sister talks.

2.3 Writing Activities

Identify Purpose and Audience

For each of the possible topics you listed in the Generate Story Ideas activity, page 67 of Lesson 2.2, ask yourself the questions on page 69 to define your purpose for writing. Likewise, use the questions on page 70 to identify your audience and determine how to address that audience. Then select a final topic for your human-interest story.

PURPOSE To choose a final topic
AUDIENCE Yourself
LENGTH 1–2 pages

WRITING RUBRICS To choose a final topic, you should

- determine if your purpose is to inform, persuade, entertain, or describe
- consider the aspects of a topic suitable for your audience

Using Computers

Write e-mails to three friends, describing your final topic. Ask each to comment on your topic, to share ideas on how he or she would make the topic more specific or interesting, and to offer suggestions for developing the topic into a story. Make a list or printout of their suggestions and keep it handy as you work on the story.

Listening and Speaking

COOPERATIVE LEARNING In a small group, prepare and give a short presentation describing an event from your history textbook. Each group member should choose a different purpose and audience for his or her presentation. For example, one student might describe the event as if he or she were talking to a kindergarten class, with the purpose of illustrating courageous behavior. Another student might describe the event as if talking to a history class, with the purpose of analyzing the factors that led up to the event. After the presentations, discuss how vocabulary, sentence structure, content, and other elements vary with differences in purpose and audience.

Grammar Link

Revise sentences to suit an audience.

Revise each complex sentence into two simple sentences to make it more suitable for a young audience.

1. When our big family reunion took place last August, we all looked forward to a good time.
2. Because we had planned so many special events, there was scarcely time to visit with everybody.
3. Despite the fact that some of the younger cousins ate too much, no one became ill.
4. We tried to include a picture of everyone in the big photo album that we made to record the event.

See Lesson 13.3, pages 541–542.

LESSON 2.4

Prewriting: Gathering Information

Whatever your writing project is, you will need some type of information. Using the library and interviewing people can usually provide you with the information you need.

Use the Library

If your writing project requires information that you do not already have, your school or public library is the best place to find the information you need. Use these tips to make your research more efficient.

- Search for books by title, subject, or author, using either the card catalog or the online computer system.
- Use the subject headings for each listing as cross-references to related material.
- Browse among other books in the section in which you locate a useful book.
- Jot down the author, title, and call number of each book you think you will use.
- Record books that *don't* provide help (so you won't search for them again).
- Examine each book's bibliography for related titles.
- Try to be an independent researcher, but ask a librarian for help if you cannot locate much information on your topic.

See Unit 23, pages 798–810, for more information on using library resources.

Conduct Interviews

Some of your best sources for information may be people. Use interviews to find out about a person's ideas, feelings, and experiences.

Informational Interviews In an informational interview, you ask a person to speak about a subject he or she knows well. The interview may be informal (that is, a casual conversation) or formal (that is, one for which you need to make an appointment).

Whether your interview will be formal or informal, prepare for it carefully. Learn as much as you can about your subject and about the person you are going to interview. Think about what your readers will want to know. Then write down at least four or five major questions that will help you get at this material. Use *who, what, where, when, why,* and *how* questions so that you get answers that provide information, not just a yes or no response.

During the interview, listen carefully so that you can ask intelligent follow-up questions. Often the most interesting information emerges in response to a question you had not planned to ask. Take notes or tape-record the interview.

As soon as possible after the interview, write up a full account of it, based on your notes or your tapes. Write down everything you remember. If necessary, contact the person you interviewed to clarify any confusing ideas or questionable facts.

Before the Interview	During the Interview	After the Interview
• Make the appointment. • Research your topic and find out about your source. • Write out four or five basic questions.	• Ask informational questions (*who, what, where, when, why,* and *how*). • Listen carefully. • Ask follow-up questions. • Take accurate notes (or tape-record).	• Write a more detailed account of the interview. • Contact source for any needed clarification or to double-check facts.

Journal Writing

You are researching services for senior citizens in your community for a class assignment. In your journal, write down four or five informational questions you might ask a senior citizens' program director during an interview.

2.4 Prewriting: Gathering Information **73**

Oral Histories To obtain information about an event in recent history, you might interview someone who lived through the event. For example, if you want information about your family history, interview a relative who can tell you about the lives of other family members. Such "spoken memories" are called oral history.

Family stories can tell you a great deal about both the storyteller and life in the past. The excerpt below is from the oral history *Hannah's Daughters*, which was compiled by Dorothy Gallagher. In this excerpt, Hannah Lambertson Nesbitt, who lived from 1876 to 1974, describes life on her grandfather's farm.

Literature Model

In my grandaddy's time it was different than it is now. It was all hand labor, and men could support their families. . . . We had poorhouses, yes. A lot of men lived on a poor farm. I used to know a portion of a song about a son who persuaded his parents to deed him their farm. Well, they yielded to him and he turned them out. They had to go "over the hills to the poorhouse." That's what the song was called. There's many children did that to their folks. But I'm talking about what *my* folks done. They looked after those that needed help. If a man took sick or died, they looked after his family. Grandaddy sent Grandma to different places; she had several families she used to keep. She'd clothe them and everything else. She'd just go to visit and see what they had to have. . . . And if they needed a barrel of flour, they got it. . . . The farmers just did it. They helped those that needed it. Not like it is today.

Dorothy Gallagher, *Hannah's Daughters*

Observation

One tool that newswriters use is observation—witnessing an event and recording it. Trials, ball games, and congressional debates are examples of events that are described for millions by people observing the events. Careful observation requires the use of the observer's five senses to gather information. The observer takes notes, writing down the important points so that nothing is forgotten or overlooked. The notes then are the basis for the written report of the event—perhaps in a newspaper or magazine article.

2.4 Writing Activities

Gather Information About Your Topic

Think carefully about your topic. What kind of information do you need? What is the most effective method of gathering that information? Using the method you have chosen, start making informational notes that you might include in your paper.

PURPOSE To gather information
AUDIENCE Yourself
LENGTH Varies

WRITING RUBRICS To gather information for your topic, you should

- locate the best sources of information
- make arrangements to interview sources
- prepare a list of questions you will ask in an interview
- include enough information in your notes

Using Computers

Your computer can be an excellent tool to save valuable information for research projects. You can use it when compiling a family history or any research project for which you will gather information over a long period of time. Establish a classification system, and use it to list the information you've obtained, the source, and the date. As you gather additional data, create subheads to classify, store, change, and retrieve information as needed.

Grammar Link

Use quotation marks to indicate speech.

Rewrite each of the sentences below, adding quotation marks wherever they are necessary.

1. When I first began teaching, said my former teacher Mrs. Moody, things were very different.
2. Can you tell me about some of those differences? I asked.
3. Well, she said, for one thing, many classes were bigger.
4. We really didn't do much group work, she added.
5. I also remember, she continued, that there was time for physical education as well as art and music.

See Lesson 21.9, pages 752–756.

Listening and Speaking

PREPARING TO INTERVIEW In a small group, plan questions you might ask a subject in order to explore your topic. Write your questions legibly on note cards or notebook paper. Then role-play an interview with one member of the group. Invite other group members to share suggestions for improving your interview. Repeat the process so that all group members participate.

LESSON 2.5
Drafting: Turning Notes into Paragraphs

When you draft, you use your prewriting notes to create a piece of writing.

Family ties, sometimes I feel like I've got so many responsibilities to my family I don't have a life of my own. Babysitting my brothers. If I have to do that again next weekend I'll just scream. And when they do something wrong, I get the blame. Can't Mom see I need to have some time to myself? Wasn't she ever my age? Life must have been so different when she was growing up.

Prewriting Notes

Swimming

First experience—nearly drowned when I fell into a pond when I was four years old

Learning to swim was a nightmare for me

If we were meant to swim, we'd have gills and fins

The time my uncle taught me how to tread water— he was so patient, didn't laugh at me

Overcame fears

Wonder what a wave-action pool is like . . .

Prewriting Notes

Your first draft will not be perfect. It's your first try at presenting your ideas in an order that makes sense and shaping them into paragraphs.

Put Your Ideas in Order

One way to put your ideas in order is to sort them into categories. If an idea doesn't seem to fit anywhere, leave it out. If a new idea occurs to you while you are sorting, include the idea if it fits. Look at the way one writer organized her ideas on the topic "I always liked my aunt Alicia best."

Organizing Ideas

- My aunt Alicia
- Her mysterious apartment in the city
- Apartment filled with books and the little clay animals she found in Mexico
- I got lost once on my way there
- Her embroidered jeans jacket
- Her flashy jewelry
- Long dark hair, held up with a comb
- Treated me like a person, not just her niece
- Listening to her old rock-and-roll records

Introductory Material
- My aunt Alicia
- Her flashy jewelry
- Her embroidered jeans jacket
- Long dark hair, held up with a comb

Body
- Her mysterious apartment in the city
- Listening to her old rock-and-roll records
- Apartment filled with books and the little clay animals she found in Mexico

Concluding Material
- Treated me like a person, not just her niece
- One place in the world I felt at home

Write Paragraphs

Each paragraph in your draft should be organized around one main, controlling idea. Often the main idea is stated in a topic sentence. The supporting details develop the main idea by proving, clarifying, or expanding upon it. Like building blocks, the supporting ideas provide the foundation on which the main idea rests.

There is no magic formula for writing a paragraph. One approach is to write supporting sentences first to help determine a main idea and then write a topic sentence to express that idea. An alternative approach is to write the topic sentence first. Keep in mind that you can revise any part of your paragraph at any point in the writing process.

Journal Writing

Look through your journal for possible main ideas for paragraphs. Pick one idea and list supporting details that you might use to develop that idea in a paragraph.

A topic sentence may be a statement or a question. Whatever its form, a good topic sentence expresses the main idea clearly and makes the reader want to keep reading. Your choice of topic sentence also helps determine how you will develop the paragraph.

Try out several possible topic sentences before choosing the one that best expresses your main idea. Each of the following topic sentences is based on the painting shown here. Note how each would take a paragraph in a different direction.

- Just a century ago, several generations of a family often lived together under one roof.
- Although a frail man, my grandfather still ruled the family.
- The dark wood paneling glowed in the firelight.

Eastman Johnson, *The Hatch Family*, 1871

Notice how the writer in the model below relates every detail to the idea stated in the topic sentence.

Literature Model

Why do you suppose O'Connor puts a topic sentence up front and reinforces it at the paragraph's conclusion?

Details reveal physical resemblance and point out similarities in personality traits.

No one was particularly glad that Mary Fortune looked like her grandfather except the old man himself. He thought it added greatly to her attractiveness. He thought she was the smartest and the prettiest child he had ever seen and he let the rest of them know that if—IF that was—he left anything to anybody, it would be Mary Fortune he left it to. She was now nine, short and broad like himself, with his very light blue eyes, his wide prominent forehead, his steady penetrating scowl and his rich florid complexion; but she was like him on the inside too. She had, to a singular degree, his intelligence, his strong will, and his push and drive. Though there was seventy years' difference in their ages, the spiritual distance between them was slight. She was the only member of the family he had any respect for.

Flannery O'Connor, "A View of the Woods"

2.5 Writing Activities

Write a First Draft

Use your prewriting notes to get your ideas down on paper. Do not worry about spelling, grammar, or correct usage at this point.

PURPOSE To write a first draft
AUDIENCE Yourself
LENGTH 1–2 pages

WRITING RUBRICS To write an effective first draft, you should

- arrange your ideas in an order that makes sense
- organize your draft into paragraphs
- make sure that each paragraph is organized around one main idea

Listening and Speaking

COOPERATIVE LEARNING In a small group, discuss the collage shown below. Then individually write a topic sentence focusing on some aspect of the picture. List details to support the topic sentence. Draft a paragraph, using the topic sentence and details.

Romare Bearden, *Blue Interior, Morning,* 1968

Grammar Link

Use apostrophes with possessive indefinite pronouns.

Indefinite pronouns, such as *everyone* and *no one,* use apostrophes to form the possessive. *Personal pronouns,* such as *his* and *hers,* do not.

Rewrite the following sentences, underlining each personal and indefinite pronoun. Add apostrophes where they are needed.

1. Someones idea was to make a list of everybodys names and special skills for a school directory.
2. You and your classmates think about each others unique talents and strengths.
3. While you compile your list, others are working on theirs.
4. Your friend Carol says that no ones list is exactly like hers.

See Lesson 17.1, page 633, and Lesson 21.11, page 759.

Using Computers

In the draft you write for the Listening and Speaking activity, boldface the topic sentence of each paragraph. Underline the supporting sentences. Then check your draft's content and organization. Evaluate your topic sentences. Check that your main ideas are well supported.

2.5 Drafting: Turning Notes into Paragraphs

LESSON 2.6

Drafting: Writing Unified Paragraphs

While every paragraph in your draft should be about one main idea, not every paragraph needs a topic sentence. What is the main idea of each paragraph in the model below?

Literature Model

My great-grandmother. I would've liked to have known her, a wild horse of a woman, so wild she wouldn't marry until my great-grandfather threw a sack over her head and carried her off. Just like that, as if she were a fancy chandelier. That's the way he did it.

And the story goes she never forgave him. She looked out the window all her life, the way so many women sit their sadness on an elbow. I wonder if she made the best with what she got or was she sorry because she couldn't be all the things she wanted to be. Esperanza. I have inherited her name, but I don't want to inherit her place by the window.

Sandra Cisneros, *The House on Mango Street*

> The narrator, Esperanza, uses details from her great-grandmother's life to support the selection's main idea.

> Do you like the way Cisneros has delayed stating the main idea until the last sentence? Why or why not?

Keep to the Main Idea

You can express a paragraph's main idea in a direct statement—that is, in a topic sentence. Or you can imply the main idea by suggesting it indirectly through your choice of supporting details.

Main Idea Stated in a Topic Sentence There are several advantages to stating your main idea in a topic sentence. First, providing a clear statement of what the paragraph is about helps give your writing direction. Second, the sentence tells the reader what to focus on.

A topic sentence may appear anywhere in the paragraph. A topic sentence that appears at the beginning of a paragraph lets the reader know what's to come. A topic sentence that appears at the end summarizes the preceding supporting details and ensures that the reader has understood the main idea.

Implied Main Idea In some paragraphs, particularly descriptive or narrative paragraphs, the main idea is implied, or stated indirectly. In these types of writing, the supporting details are so strongly linked by a main idea that this main idea shines through without having to be stated directly. Instead of saying "I was happy to be home," a narrative writer might use details to *show* he or she was happy.

Include Supporting Details

In a unified paragraph, each sentence provides one or more details that support the main idea. The supporting details can be sensory details, examples or incidents, facts, statistics, and reasons. Your purpose in writing will help you determine which kinds of supporting details to use.

Georges Seurat, *Bathers at Asnières*, 1883–1884

Sensory Details Vivid sensory words describe how things look, sound, smell, feel, or taste. They draw your readers in and help them experience the scene or subject. To develop sensory details, try to visualize the scene you are describing and think about each of the senses in turn. For example, how would you use sensory details to describe the scene in the painting above? First, think about what you would see, hear, smell, feel, and taste if you could step inside it. Then decide what words you would use to make the scene come alive for your readers.

> ## Journal Writing
>
> Pick a place that's important to you or your family. Close your eyes and try to "see" it. Now listen for the sounds you hear there. Work your way through each of the other senses. In your journal, jot down the sensory details that come to mind.

2.6 Drafting: Writing Unified Paragraphs **81**

Examples or Incidents Sometimes the best way to develop a main idea is through describing examples or incidents. For example, to develop the main idea that "starting high school was one of the hardest things I've ever done," you might tell about something that happened when you started high school. Then, to explore a specific incident, ask yourself *who*, *what*, *where*, *when*, *why*, and *how* questions.

Facts and Statistics Another way to support a main idea is to use facts and statistics. A fact is a statement that has been proved by observation, experience, or study—for example, "Washington, D.C., is the capital of the United States." Statistics are facts that involve numbers—for example, "The average person sees three hundred ads a day."

Suppose you wanted to write a paragraph with the following topic sentence: "There's not enough free time in the average high school student's life." Here's how one student used a time line to organize facts and statistics that could help support this topic sentence.

Facts and Statistics Organized on a Time Line

1 P.M.	2 P.M.	3 P.M.	4 P.M.	5 P.M.	6 P.M.	7 P.M.	8 P.M.	9 P.M.

Above the line:
- Algebra: 25 word problems due tomorrow. (1–3 P.M.)
- Track practice: 1 hour. (3–4 P.M.)
- Eat dinner: 30 minutes. Then spend 30 minutes cleaning up, taking out the garbage. (5–7 P.M.)
- Begin practicing lines for drama club play. (9 P.M.)

Below the line:
- English: essay assigned. Get 85% on quiz. (2–3 P.M.)
- Go home. Take care of brother until Mom gets home in 1.5 hours. (4–5 P.M.)
- Start homework. (6–8 P.M.)

Reasons If your topic sentence expresses an opinion or gives an explanation, you can back it up with reasons. For example, if the topic sentence of your paragraph is "Husbands and wives should undertake an equal share of the housework and child care," you might use a graphic organizer like the one below to help you develop and outline reasons that document your topic sentence.

Why should husbands and wives undertake an equal share of the housework and child care?

- The notion that taking care of the home and children is "women's work" is sexist.
- An equal relationship between parents presents a good model for their children.
- Spending more time together benefits both fathers and their children.
- It is unfair to expect women employed outside the home to shoulder all of the domestic responsibilities as well.

82 Unit 2 The Writing Process

2.6 Writing Activities

Check Your Paragraphs

Look over your draft to make sure that your paragraphs are unified.

PURPOSE To check paragraphs for unity
AUDIENCE Yourself
LENGTH 1–2 pages

WRITING RUBRICS To check paragraphs for unity, ask yourself whether

- every paragraph has an implied or a stated topic sentence
- you have used sensory details
- examples or incidents help make your point
- facts help support your main idea

Cross-Curricular Activity

SCIENCE Perform this simple experiment:

1. Fill two identical glasses nearly to the top with water.
2. Guess how many paper clips you will have to drop into each glass before the water overflows if you drop the paper clips one at a time into one glass and ten at a time into the other.
3. Explain whether you think there will be a difference and why.
4. Now drop one paper clip at a time into one glass and ten paper clips at a time into the other glass. Take notes as you observe what happens.
5. Was your guess correct?

Draft a paragraph, using your guess or theory as your topic sentence. Use your observations to support or refute your topic sentence. Include any reasons you can provide for your results.

Grammar Link

Make sure subjects agree with verbs.

Rewrite the following paragraph. Choose the form of the verb in parentheses that agrees with each statistical subject.

[1]When 100 percent of the world's population (is/are) considered, more than 56 percent of the people (live/lives) in rural areas. [2]In the United States, however, the opposite is true; nearly 80 percent (live/lives) in metropolitan areas. [3]More than 971,000 people now (live/lives) in Las Vegas, Nevada, making it the fastest-growing area in the country. [4]In actual numbers, more than 500,000 people (was added/were added) to the population of Los Angeles from 1990 to 1992; 231,000 (was/were) the increase in Houston. [5]Only 20 of the 268 metropolitan areas in the United States (has/have) lost population since 1990.

See Lesson 16.4, page 614.

Viewing and Representing

ANALYZING DESIGN With a partner, select a painting from this book. View the painting in terms of its elements of design: check the use of shape, color, and texture in the painting. Keep a list of your impressions. Then use your list and refer to the painting. Do all the elements of design work together to achieve one effect or to give one message to the viewer?

LESSON 2.7

Drafting: Ordering the Details

The way you organize details will depend on your purpose—whether you are narrating, explaining, persuading, or describing.

The computer screen below lists various methods of organizing supporting details and the most common purposes for which these methods are used. However, do not feel that you have to limit the organization of your writing to just what is shown here.

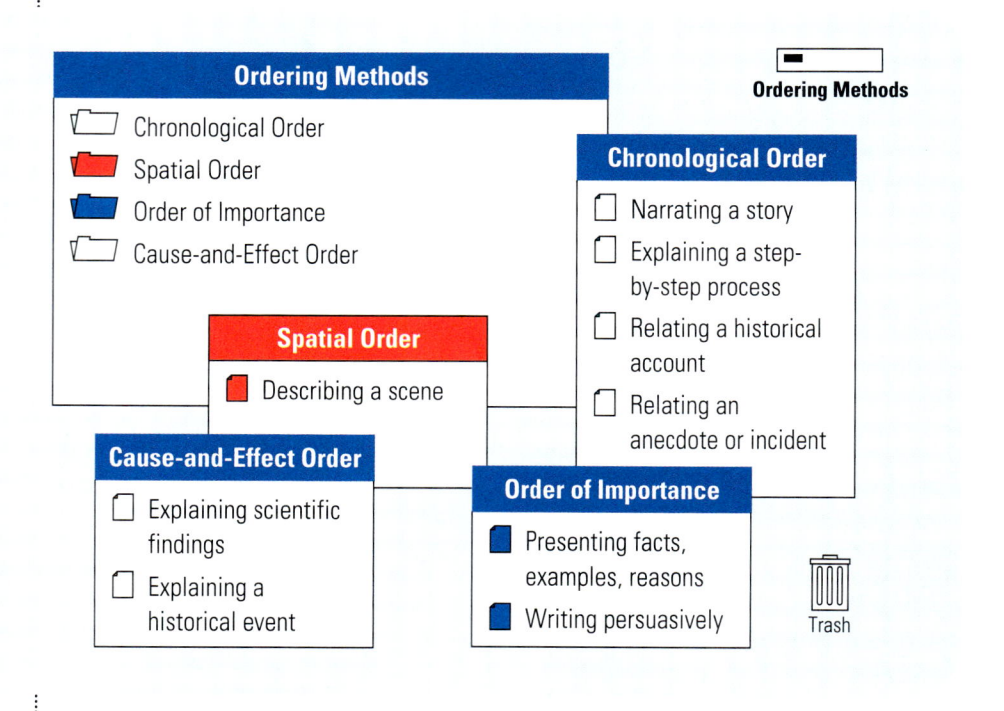

Ordering Methods
- Chronological Order
- Spatial Order
- Order of Importance
- Cause-and-Effect Order

Chronological Order
- Narrating a story
- Explaining a step-by-step process
- Relating a historical account
- Relating an anecdote or incident

Spatial Order
- Describing a scene

Cause-and-Effect Order
- Explaining scientific findings
- Explaining a historical event

Order of Importance
- Presenting facts, examples, reasons
- Writing persuasively

Chronological Order

Chronological order—presenting events in the order in which they happened—is often used to organize narrative writing. Study the model on page 85. Notice how writer Jim Barnes uses chronological order to narrate the details of a frightening incident.

Literature Model

A deep, low moan—ghostly but unmistakably human—rolled up from the bowels of the black earth. There was for a moment, my brother recalls, a stillness like doom upon all of them. Then everybody was running, running. . . .
A great shadow passed beside my brother. It was a horse. The moan persisted, even over the sound of thumping boots and racing hoofs. Now my brother passed the horse, and burst through the barbed wire fence at the edge of the field with one wild bound. He flung himself down the lane and plunged through the doorway of our house and hugged himself close to the dying coals in the fireplace. An hour passed before he began to cry.

Jim Barnes, "On Native Ground"

> How many major events are signaled by transitions like "then," "now," and "an hour passed"?

> Because Barnes describes the action almost minute by minute, the reader feels drawn into the events.

Spatial Order

Spatial order—the order in which objects appear in a physical place—is often used to organize descriptive writing. To use spatial order, describe items as they appear from left to right, from top to bottom, from back to front, or in any other logical combination. Use words like *above, below, behind,* and *next to* to help readers "see" the scene you are describing.

For example, to describe the scene shown, you might begin by identifying the checkerboard in the middle of the room. From that starting point, you might go on to describe the two men on either side of the checkerboard. Then you might move behind the men to the fireplace against the wall. Finally, you could describe the women.

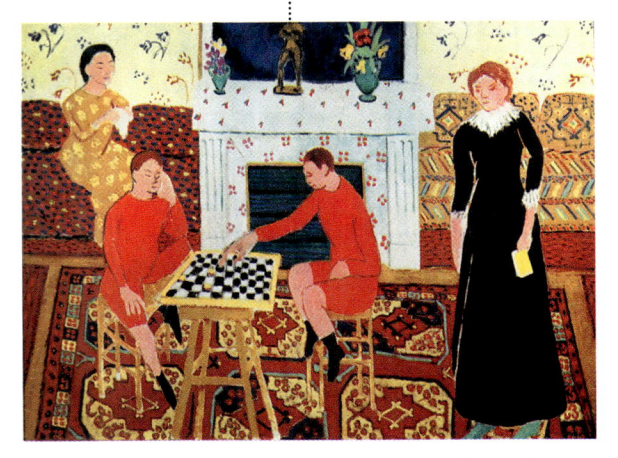

Henri Matisse, *The Painter's Family*, 1911

Journal Writing

Use spatial order to describe your favorite room. Identify a starting point in the room and use words like *next to* and *above* to indicate clearly the placement of each object in the room.

2.7 Drafting: Ordering the Details **85**

Order of Importance

Order of importance is an appropriate method to use when your supporting details are facts, statistics, incidents, or examples. For example, if you want to make an immediate impact on your reader, start with your most important detail. If you want to leave your reader thinking about your strongest point, build up to the most important detail.

Cause-and-Effect Order

When you want to show that one event took place because of another, you can use cause-and-effect order. In a cause-and-effect paragraph, the topic sentence may state the cause and the supporting details identify the effects. Conversely, the topic sentence may state the effect and the supporting details present the causes. This method works well when you write about science, history, or even about yourself. In the paragraph below, Ginger Lumpkin uses cause-and-effect order.

> **Student Model**
>
> A teacher who once doubted me ironically became a source of inspiration. In the seventh grade, I wrote a poem entitled "Lost on a Desert." After my teacher read my poem, she asked me who I had copied it from—she didn't believe that I had written it. Her remarks hurt me, but the experience made me feel determined to prove my creative writing abilities. As a result, I began to write a variety of poems, short stories, and plays, all of which my teacher praised. In the end, I not only showed my teacher that I could write well, but through my writing, I also gained a better understanding of myself.
>
> Ginger Lumpkin, Hyde Park Career Academy, Chicago, Illinois

The topic sentence prepares the reader for a cause-and-effect ordering of the supporting details.

How do these details support the topic sentence?

The graphic below shows the cause-and-effect relationships presented in the paragraph. Note that most of the effects in turn act as causes.

- I wrote a poem for my seventh-grade teacher.
- My teacher read the poem but didn't believe I had written it.
- Hurt but determined to prove my abilities, I continued to write.
- The teacher liked my new work; I gained new self-knowledge.

2.7 Writing Activities

Check Organization

Read over your draft to make sure that the details in your paragraph are ordered. Remember that not all your paragraphs will be organized in the same way.

PURPOSE To check order of details
AUDIENCE Yourself
LENGTH 1–2 pages

WRITING RUBRICS To evaluate the order of details in your paragraphs, you should
- describe the type of order you have used
- decide how to organize supporting details
- decide whether to change your order

Grammar Link

Use commas to separate three or more words, phrases, or clauses in a series.

Answer each question in one complete sentence. Remember to write commas where they are needed.

1. What three pizza toppings do you like?
2. Who are your four favorite singers?
3. What four TV programs do you watch?

See Lesson 21.6, page 739.

Cross-Curricular Activity

ART Use the glazed ceramic bowl pictured on this page as a source of details for a paragraph. Decide on a topic sentence and then write your paragraph. Use chronological order, spatial order, order of importance, or cause-and-effect order to organize your supporting details.

Listening and Speaking

PEER REVIEW Read your draft aloud to a partner. Ask your partner if your ideas make sense, if they flow logically from one to another, and if the method of organization you have chosen fits well with the topic of your draft.

Iranian glazed ceramic bowl, c. 1200

LESSON 2.8

Drafting: Writing Coherent Paragraphs

In a coherent paragraph, all the sentences are clearly and logically connected to one another. Transition words and phrases, repeated words, synonyms, and pronouns are the "glue" or "mortar" you can use to link together sentences and build a better paragraph.

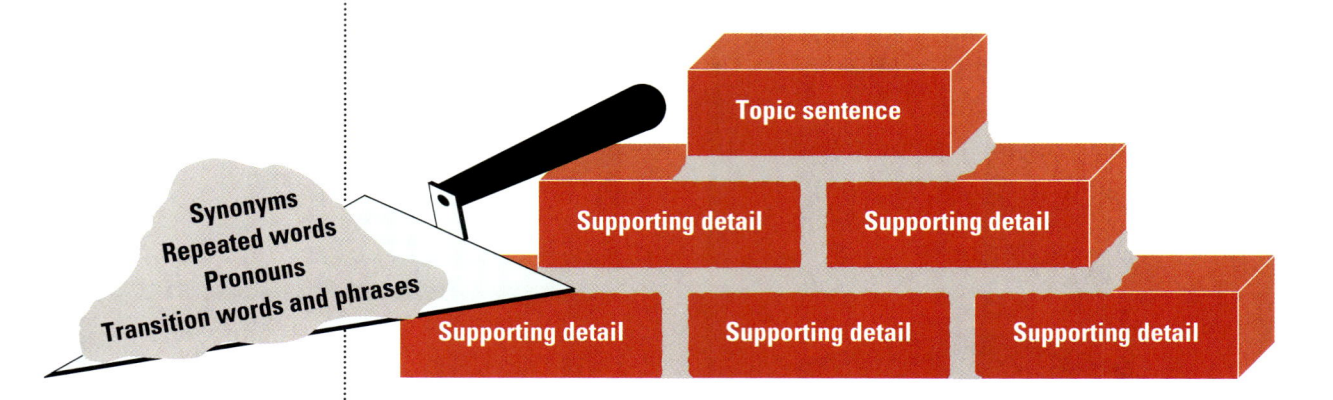

Build a Coherent Paragraph

Use the following checklist to help make sure your paragraphs are coherent.

Checklist for Writing Coherently

1. Are all the sentences linked clearly and logically to one another?
2. Can I repeat any words to help show the connections between ideas?
3. Have I used synonyms that my readers will be able to understand?
4. Does each pronoun have an antecedent?
5. Are there any transitions I can use to link the sentences?

88 Unit 2 The Writing Process

Use Transition Words and Phrases

Use transitions—words or phrases that show relationships between ideas—to help you write coherent paragraphs. Transitions create logical links between sentences in a paragraph and help the reader follow your train of thought. The chart below shows some common transitions.

Transitions

Kinds	Examples			
Time	after first	before meanwhile	finally then	next when
Place	above below	beside here	next to near	there opposite
Importance	first primary	second mainly	more important last	most important least important
Cause and effect	as a result so	consequently therefore	for that reason on account	because due to
Comparison and contrast	although similarly	in contrast however	on the other hand like	in the same way unlike
Example	for example together with	for instance along with	namely likewise	that is such as

You can also use transitions to link paragraphs in a longer piece of writing. Transitions such as *first*, *second*, and *most important* can help readers understand the relative importance of each paragraph. Other transitions can help the reader understand relationships between paragraphs. Transitions such as *finally* and *therefore* often create a successful link to the concluding paragraph.

Journal Writing

Look through your journal, and select a paragraph. Then use the list of questions on page 88 to make sure the paragraph is coherent. Insert transitions listed in the chart above to create links between your sentences.

2.8 Drafting: Writing Coherent Paragraphs

Use Repetition and Synonyms

Another way to link sentences is to repeat the same word from sentence to sentence. But be careful: too much repetition will bore your readers. One way to avoid too much repetition is to read your work aloud. If you hear the same word too often, it's probably time to use synonyms—words that have similar meanings. Keep your audience in mind, however. Unfamiliar synonyms may make your ideas more difficult to follow.

In the paragraph below, N. Scott Momaday repeats words and phrases and uses synonyms to link his sentences.

Literature Model

> My grandmother lived in a house near the place where Rainy Mountain Creek runs into the Washita River. Once there was a lot of sound in the house, a lot of coming and going, feasting and talk. The summers there were full of excitement and reunion. The Kiowas are a summer people; they abide the cold and keep to themselves, but when the season turns and the land becomes warm and vital they cannot hold still; an old love of going returns upon them. The old people have a fine sense of pageantry and a wonderful notion of decorum. The aged visitors who came to my grandmother's house when I was a child were men of immense character, full of wisdom and disdain. They dealt in a kind of infallible quiet and gave but one face away; it was enough. They were made of lean and leather, and they bore themselves upright. They wore great black hats and bright ample shirts that shook in the wind. They rubbed fat upon their hair and wound their braids with strips of colored cloth. Some of them painted their faces and carried the scars of old and cherished enmities. They were an old council of war lords, come to remind and be reminded of who they were.
>
> N. Scott Momaday, *House Made of Dawn*

Repetition of words such as "they" and "there" helps link sentences.

What effect does the use of synonyms have?

Effective repetition of "they" results in parallel structure.

Use Pronouns

To avoid the boring repetition of specific nouns, substitute pronouns for a word, a group of words, or an idea that appears in a preceding sentence. Note the use of pronouns in the literature model above. As an experiment, mentally substitute nouns for the pronouns. How does the selection read?

2.8 Writing Activities

Check Your Paragraphs for Coherence

Make any changes to your paragraphs that will make them more coherent.

PURPOSE To make paragraphs coherent
AUDIENCE Yourself
LENGTH 1–2 pages

WRITING RUBRICS To make paragraphs coherent, you should
- use transition words and phrases
- use repeated words or synonyms to link sentences and paragraphs
- use pronouns to avoid unnecessary repetition

Viewing and Representing

DESIGN What might artist Aaron Douglas be saying about the creation of historically significant structures? How does the design help communicate this message? Write a paragraph about the theme and style of the painting and the use of color and shape to express the theme.

Aaron Douglas, *Building More Stately Mansions*, 1944

Grammar Link

Use conjunctive adverbs to show relationships.

The following words are conjunctive adverbs: *so, consequently, therefore, similarly, however,* and *likewise.* They are preceded by semicolons and followed by commas.

Use a conjunctive adverb to join each pair of sentences below into one.

1. When she grew older, Amy Tan decided to become a writer. Her parents did not encourage her in this pursuit.
2. As time passed, she sold several stories she had written. She decided to become a full-time writer.
3. Today Amy Tan is the author of two best-selling novels. She is researching a third book.

See Lesson 10.7, page 479.

Cross-Curricular Activity

ART Investigate historical murals created for the WPA (Works Progress Administration) during the 1930s. What themes are presented? How does each artist achieve unity in presenting his or her message? Share your findings with the class.

LESSON 2.9

Revising: Improving Paragraphs

Revising is the stage of the writing process in which you step back and take a new look at your work. You evaluate it, get the reaction of others, and then rewrite your draft to solve any problems.

As you revise, you may learn something new about your piece of writing. You may clarify its meaning, find a way to say it more effectively, or even discover entirely new ideas. Sometimes you don't get the words quite right the first time. For instance, it may have taken General MacArthur several tries before he came up with his memorable farewell line: "I shall return."

Revise in Stages

One useful strategy for revising is to break the process down into three parts. First, put yourself in the place of your readers and go through the draft quickly, checking to make sure that your meaning is clear. Make any necessary changes.

Next, read your draft aloud to a partner or small group. Often ideas that seem clear to you will need to be rephrased for an audience. Take notes on the questions your peer reviewers ask and on their suggestions.

Finally, go back to your draft and read it carefully one final time. Look at the notes from your writing conference. Now is the time to decide what changes you want to make.

Check for Meaning

After you finish your first draft, set it aside for a while. Then when you pick it up to revise it, you'll see it with fresh eyes.

Read it through once quickly and jot down notes or ideas in the margins. Don't worry about word choices, grammar, spelling, or punctuation. Use the checklist below to help you focus on the big picture—the meaning.

Meaning Checklist

1. Have I presented the main idea clearly? What is the main idea? (Hint: If you cannot easily answer this question after reading your writing, chances are you have not presented the main idea clearly.)
2. Have I achieved my purpose through my writing?
3. Who is my audience? Have I written this piece with their needs in mind?
4. Do I need to give my readers more information?

If you have trouble answering any of these questions, you may need to return to the prewriting or drafting stages to rework your ideas. Don't be discouraged. Going back and forth between the stages is part of the writing process. Even writers like Joan Didion rework their ideas: "My writing is a process of rewriting, of going back and changing and filling in. In the rewriting process you discover what's going on."

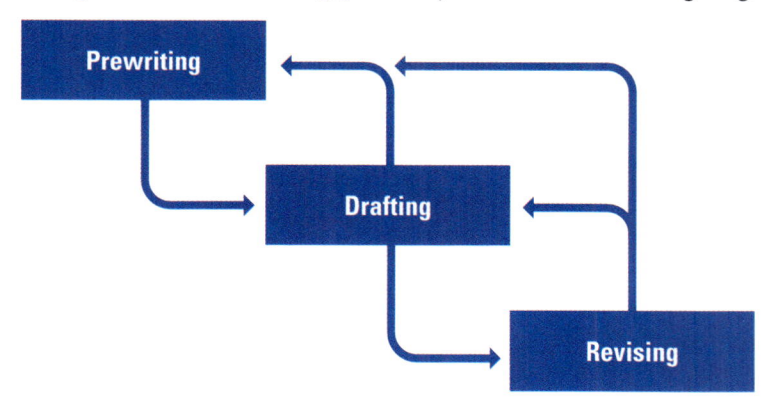

Prewriting → Drafting → Revising

Journal Writing

Review an entry in your journal that you have not looked at recently. Using the checklist above, write any suggestions you now have for clarifying the main idea in the space below your entry.

Have a Writing Conference

Read your draft to a peer reviewer or reviewers. Ask them to read the checklist below and keep it in mind as they listen.

Unity Checklist

1. Does every detail I have selected support the main idea?
2. Have I organized the supporting details in the most logical way?
3. Have I included any sentences that are unnecessary because they simply restate the main point without adding any new information or meaning?
4. Have I made the relationships among my ideas clear?

After you have read your draft aloud, ask your listeners these questions:

- What was the strongest part of my writing?
- What, if anything, was not clear?

Then go over the questions in the checklist with your listeners. They may ask you to read your draft again as they listen carefully.

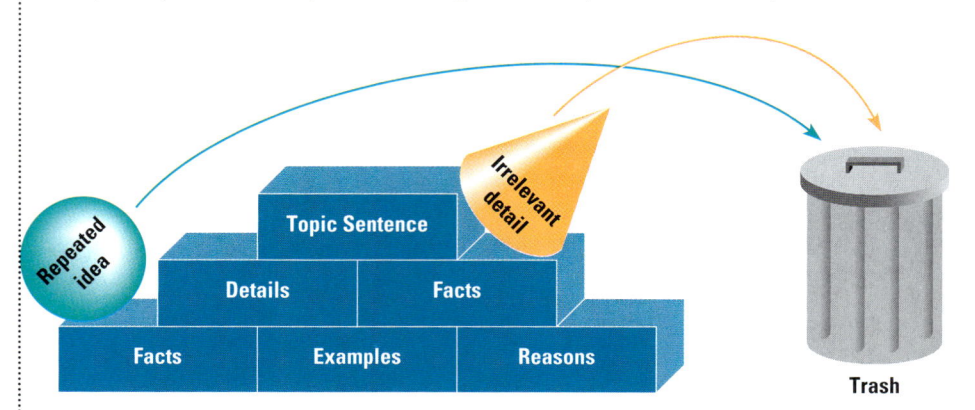

Do a Final Reading and Revise

Use the checklist below for your final reading. Make your revisions, using your notes from the writing conference and from your own checking of your draft.

Coherence Checklist

1. Have I written sentences that flow logically and clearly?
2. Would pronouns, synonyms, repeated words, or transitions improve the flow of my writing?
3. Have I made appropriate word choices?
4. Have I used specific nouns and active verbs?
5. Have I deleted all unnecessary words?

Revising Tip

Parallelism To help keep the relationships among your ideas clear, use parallel construction.

2.9 Writing Activities

Revise Your Draft

To revise, use circles and arrows, taped-on additions, or cross-outs to mark your changes.

PURPOSE To revise your draft
AUDIENCE Yourself, peer reviewers
LENGTH 1–2 pages

WRITING RUBRICS To revise your draft, you should

- read your draft over once for meaning
- have a writing conference and take notes
- do a final reading and make changes

Cross-Curricular Activity

SOCIAL STUDIES Revise the following paragraph about families in western Sumatra in Indonesia. Use the checklists presented in this lesson to help you.

The society is matrilineal. All inherited property and family names are handed down from mother to daughter. Most of the people are rice farmers. The grandmother is the most powerful member of the family. Children are given the name of their mother's family. All the descendants of one grandmother live together in one big house. Up to thirty family members live in one house. A woman marries and the husband moves in with his wife's family.

Listening and Speaking

PEER REVIEW Follow the writing process to revise your draft. Read the draft quickly to yourself for meaning. Then have a writing conference, and read your draft aloud to a partner. Take notes on your reviewer's comments in the margins of your draft. Look over the comments and make any changes you find valid.

Grammar Link

Use active and passive voice.

Rewrite each sentence below that you think should be in the active voice. If you think a sentence belongs in the passive voice, write *passive*.

1. Great tennis talent is being developed by a young Californian named Venus Ebonistarr Williams, trained by her father to become a tennis star.
2. At the age of ten, Venus was ranked by some tennis experts as number one in southern California in the girls' twelve-and-under division.
3. This ranking was attained only after a great deal of hard work.
4. As part of her routine, she is coached by her father at the tennis courts every day.
5. Great discipline is required to practice tennis skills on a daily basis.
6. Net shots, as well as forehand and backhand drills, are some of the skills practiced by this rising star.
7. Tennis is played by Venus's entire family.
8. In the family's life, an important role is played by tennis.
9. A journal has been kept by Venus's father of the important events in her life.
10. A winning future is predicted by coaches and pros for this young player.

See Lesson 15.7, page 596.

LESSON 2.10

Editing/Proofreading: Final Checking

During the editing stage, you make sure that you've used words correctly. Check your writing for errors in grammar, word usage, punctuation, capitalization, and spelling. The goal of editing, as in the other stages in the writing process, is to communicate your ideas clearly to your readers.

COMPLAINTS ABOUT NBA REFEREES GROWING UGLY

It is bad manners to break your bread and roll in your soup.

Plunging 1,000 feet into the gorge, we saw Yosemite Falls.

GRANDMOTHER OF EIGHT MAKES HOLE IN ONE

TUNA BITING OFF WASHINGTON COAST

No bear feet allowed.

Edit Your Draft for Sense

To edit for sense, make sure that your words and sentences say what you want them to say. For example, check for and correct any unclear or misplaced modifiers like those shown in the examples above. Use the checklist on page 97 to help identify and correct errors in your writing.

Editing Checklist

Question	Example
1. Are all words used correctly?	She could ~~of~~ *have* waited.
2. Do subjects and verbs agree?	Each of my brothers drive*s* a truck.
3. Are verb tenses correct?	If you wanted it, you should ~~say~~ *have said* so.
4. Are pronoun references clear and correct?	~~Ann~~ *She* called her mother every day*,* when ~~she~~ *Ann* was away at camp.
5. Have I corrected all run-ons and fragments?	She turned on the radio*, but* she heard only static*,* ~~W~~hich was annoying.

Self-Editing To edit your own writing, you need to approach your work objectively and critically. Reading your work aloud is crucial. Note the changes Rachelle Netkow chose to make in the model below.

Student Model

My family is *a* typical ~~of a~~ family ~~in~~ *of* the times. Both of my parents work, which means many of the household responsibiliti*e*s are left to my brother and ~~I~~ *me*. We do them, of course, *the extra work* even though we don't like ~~it~~. Since *everyone in* my family is busy with *various* activities, it is unusual for all of us to be home at the same time. ~~But~~ *O*ccasionally, though, we try to do special things *together*. My family is very close even if we don't see each other ~~all that~~ *very* often.

Rachelle Netkow, Centennial High School, Pueblo, Colorado

> Change makes pronoun reference grammatically correct.

> Why did Rachelle add "everyone in" here?

Journal Writing

How can you make sure that your changes in one sentence do not alter the meaning of the following sentence? Write down a few general tips that will help you edit any writing project.

2.10 Editing/Proofreading: Final Checking   **97**

Peer Editing To edit another's writing, focus on the ideas and organization of a piece of writing rather than on its grammar and mechanics. Be honest, but respect the writer's feelings. Identify strengths as well as weaknesses. Offer suggestions for improvement, not just criticisms. Note the peer editor's comments on the paragraph below.

Avoid repetition of pronouns.
Good transition!
Expand—tell us what she talked about.
Rearrange sentences.

Last fall, my family drove my older sister Shana to college. It was her freshman year, and even though she didn't say so, I could tell ~~she~~ *Shana* was scared and sad to leave home. For one thing, she talked more during the drive than she has for the past three years. She didn't even yell at me when I helped carry her stereo equipment to her room. Normally, ~~She~~ *Shana* has a fit if I so much as touch one of her things. It really was a day full of surprises. When it was time to go, she even hugged me.

Proofread and Mark Your Draft

Proofreading is reading closely to find errors in spelling, punctuation, and capitalization. For marking corrections, use a set of basic proofreading symbols. The chart below shows a few.

Proofreading Marks

Mark	Meaning	Example
∧	Insert	My granmother is eighty-six years old.
⁊	Delete	She grew up on a dairry farm.
#∧	Insert space	She milked cows every morning.
⌒	Close up space	She fed the chickens in the barn yard.
≡	Capitalize	times have changed.
/	Make lowercase	Machines now do the Milking.
⊙ sp	Check spelling	Chickens are fed automatically.
∼	Switch order	Modern farms are like more factories.
¶	New paragraph	Last year I returned to the farm.

98 Unit 2 The Writing Process

2.10 Writing Activities

Edit Your Human-Interest Story

After you have prewritten, drafted, and revised your story, you must edit it. Check to make sure your story makes sense (see the checklist on page 97). Then proofread your draft for spelling, grammar, and usage errors. Use proofreading symbols (see the chart on page 98).

PURPOSE To polish your paper
AUDIENCE Yourself
LENGTH 1–2 pages

WRITING RUBRICS To polish your paper, you should

- edit your sentences so they make sense
- be objective when editing your own work
- proofread closely to find errors

Using Computers

A useful proofreading tool is the spelling checker in your word processing program. The spelling checker will probably identify your name as a spelling error until you enter your first and last names into the computer's spelling dictionary.

Remember that the spelling checker feature on your personal computer cannot be relied on as the only method of proofreading your work. For example, the computer will not tell you when you typed *form* but meant *from*.

Grammar Link

Correct dangling and misplaced modifiers.

Dangling modifiers modify no word at all; misplaced modifiers modify the wrong word.

Rewrite the following sentences, correcting the misplaced or dangling modifiers in each.

1. The large mural attracts the visitor's eye on the wall.
2. Working out too long, the volleyball practice session made me feel stiff and sore.
3. We bought souvenirs at the main lodge that only cost $5.50.
4. Tacos and enchiladas were served at the buffet covered with salsa.
5. The air was released from the balloon with a hissing sound.

See Lesson 18.7, pages 670–675.

Viewing and Representing

COOPERATIVE LEARNING Evaluate the presentation of one human-interest story that has been covered in the daily newspaper, in a newsmagazine, and on the television news (recorded on a video recording). How are the media presentations alike and different? What techniques are particularly effective for each type of media? Display the media coverages you have gathered, and share your conclusions with the class.

LESSON 2.11 Publishing/Presenting: Sharing Writing

The last stage in the writing process is sharing or presenting your work. A school newspaper, such as that shown below, is just one of the many places, or forums, in which you can present your writing.

---

10 SPORTS The Peninsula Outlook November 20, 1990

Forever a Seahawk: Erstwhile PHS football great shines with Seattle Seahawks

by Cain Claxton

Twelve years have passed since Paul Skansi played split end for Peninsula High School.

Since Skansi played football in high school, he has gone on to play the sport for the University of Washington Huskies, the Pittsburgh Steelers, and the Seattle Seahawks. Along the way he impressed many people: his coaches, his friends and relatives, and even people who have never met him.

"In the sixth grade you could see that he was a blue chipper," Key Peninsula Middle School teacher John Leverett said. Leverett, who taught Skansi in the sixth grade at Goodman Middle School, threw passes to him before any professional quarterbacks did.

"That was one of the funnest years I've had growing up," Skansi said, adding that Leverett "was a teacher that I'll never forget. We did a lot of math, a lot of social studies, and played a lot of football."

Skansi's small size worried his parents, Nick and Patti Skansi. They were concerned that he might get injured playing against larger players. They didn't let Skansi play his freshman and sophomore years, and were reluctant to let him play his junior year.

"He was engaged in all the other athletic events

Photos courtesy of Corry Trewin (Seattle Seahawks)
CATCH AND CELEBRATION—Seattle Seahawk Paul Skansi (#82) in the end zone after catching the game-tying touchdown pass from teammate Dave Krieg between Kansas City Chief players Pearson (#24) and Martin (#57). Seahawk John L. Williams (#32) looks on. After Seahawk kicker Norm Johnson lifted Seattle over the Chiefs, 17-16, Skansi and Krieg (#17) revel over the come-from-behind win.

that were offered," Skansi's father said. "I just thought that was enough."

When Skansi finally got a chance to play his junior year, 1977, former Head Football Coach Larry Lunke, now coaching Anacortes High School, already had Mike Bos, a star receiver in his senior year. Lunke needed Skansi to play in other areas and placed him at

Skansi's Collegiate Records
Paul Skansi

---

100   Unit 2 The Writing Process

Publish or Present Your Writing

Because presentation often depends on your particular audience, you should begin thinking during the prewriting stage about where and how you'd like your writing to appear. You have many options for presenting your work to others: at school, in your community, and in the wider world.

School Forums The diagram below shows some of the presenting options that may be available at your school. Consider the nature of your writing project to help you determine its forum. For example, a short story or poem might be ideal for a class anthology. A movie review might appear in a school newspaper.

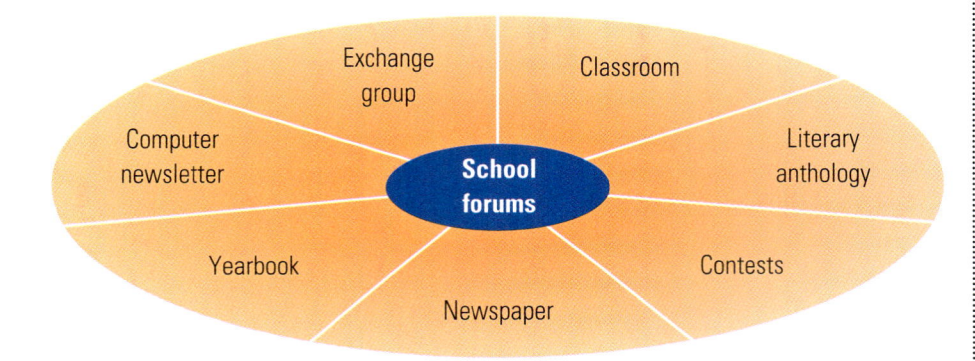

School forums: Exchange group, Classroom, Literary anthology, Contests, Newspaper, Yearbook, Computer newsletter

Community Forums If you'd like to reach a wider audience, find out what's being published in your community. Community newspapers may print feature stories about local people and events. Community groups, too, may publish newsletters that accept student work.

Contests Magazines, such as *Redbook*, *Seventeen*, and *Merlyn's Pen*, and organizations, such as the National Council of Teachers of English (NCTE), often sponsor writing contests. The winners may receive prizes and have their work published.

Journal Writing

In your journal, create a diagram like the one shown above. Put a check mark next to each of the school forums in which you currently present your work. Circle those to which you would like to submit your work. Find out more about each new forum you have circled.

Open-Market Forums If you're interested in writing for periodicals, you might target magazines aimed at teenagers, such as *Seventeen*, *Sassy*, or *'Teen*. You also might choose special-interest magazines, such as *Bicycling* or *American Photo*.

Start with something you've already written and try to find a market for it. Or do the reverse: find a magazine first and then write a piece for that publication. *Writer's Market* and the *Market Guide for Young Writers* list publications that accept material from young writers, describe the type of material each publication accepts, explain how to prepare a manuscript for submission, and often tell about writing contests.

> The first paragraph lists the name of the publication, the publisher's name and address, and a description of the publication and its audience

* **PURPLE COW,** Signa Publications, 3423 Piedmont Road N.E., Ivy Place Suite 320, Atlanta, GA 30305. Monthly tabloid (ten issues) covering any subject of interest to 13 to 18 year olds.

Publishes: General articles of interest to teens; book, movie, and record reviews; humor; interview/profile; sports (general and anecdotal—no "How to Play Soccer"); personal experience: coping with problems . . . ; and seasonal interest material.

Submission Info: All manuscripts must be typed and accompanied by SASE. Articles should be 500–3,000 words. Pays $5–$40. Maximum length for fillers is 150 words. Pays $5–$10 for fillers and photos. Send complete manuscript or query with published clips of published work.

> The second paragraph describes the type of material published.

> The third paragraph explains how to submit material. Note that "SASE" stands for "self-addressed, stamped envelope."

Give Oral Presentations

The most common forum for oral presentation is the classroom, where you may give an oral report or your teacher may read your writing aloud. Other opportunities in your school may include

- a drama club (for presenting your original play)
- a competitive tournament (for presenting a speech)
- a school radio station

2.11 Writing Activities

Present Your Human-Interest Story

You have followed all the steps in the first four stages of the writing process: prewriting, drafting, revising, and editing. You are through with the actual writing of your piece. Now you must decide how to present your story. You might submit it to a newspaper or magazine, or decide to present it orally to a group. If you have made any of these decisions, then the paper must be prepared in a way that best fits the requirements of the presentation.

PURPOSE To make a final version of a human-interest story for presentation
AUDIENCE Varies with the type of presentation
LENGTH 1–2 pages

WRITING RUBRICS To prepare for presentation, you should

- decide the best way to share your writing, considering all the options, written and oral
- prepare a final, legible version suited to your audience, which might be a school, community, open-market, forum, or contest
- check that your draft meets the requirements of the presentation

Using Computers

When appropriate, use your computer program function to italicize, underline, or boldface words, phrases, and sentences. For example, italicize stage directions to distinguish them from dialogue in a script. To emphasize words or phrases in a speech, use bold-faced type.

Grammar Link

Italicize or underline titles.

Titles of books, newspapers, magazines, lengthy poems, plays, and films should always be italicized. If you are typing or handwriting a paper, indicate italics by underlining.

Rewrite the sentences below, underlining the parts that should be italicized.

1. I have submitted my story to Reader's Digest.
2. Who is the book editor of the Boston Globe?
3. I have just finished reading Palace Walk by Naguib Mahfouz.
4. Her poems have been published in The Norton Anthology of American Literature.
5. That was a very interesting Time magazine article.

See Lesson 21.10, pages 757–758.

Viewing and Representing

WEB SITE As a class project, create your own school electronic literary magazine and publish your human-interest stories on the World Wide Web. Check several electronic magazines to get a sense of what they contain. Assign appropriate tasks (design, editing, inputting) to class members and publish your stories. Be sure to consult your school's Internet policy to ensure your magazine conforms to school requirements.

LESSON 2.12

WRITING ABOUT LITERATURE
Explaining Theme

To analyze a piece of literature, you must first identify a theme, or underlying meaning, in the work. In the model below, Tad Burton identifies a theme in Louise Erdrich's poem "Indian Boarding School"—the meaning of freedom—and uses that theme to analyze the piece.

Student Model

In Louise Erdrich's poem "Indian Boarding School," the poet suggests that freedom is a state of mind. Although the Native American girls who live in the boarding school are subjected to physical abuse and are forced to deny their heritage, their will is not crushed. The girls imagine what a real home would be like and visit it in their dreams. In addition, even though they really have no chance to escape from their captors, some of the boarding school's inmates feel free when they hide out for a brief time in the enclosed boxcar of a train.

The idea that freedom is in one's mind is also extended to encompass a broader scope. In the last line of the poem, speaking about "the old injuries of the past," Erdrich compares the girls' situation with the experience of the Native American people at the hands of the early settlers. Like the girls in the school, the Native Americans underwent much suffering. They were taken away from their homes and placed on reservations. Nonetheless, the poet believes that the Native American people ultimately remained free because no one could manipulate their thoughts.

Tad Burton, Rangeview High School, Aurora, Colorado

- Tad states Erdrich's theme in his topic sentence: freedom does not depend upon physical restrictions for it is a state of mind.

- Tad uses specific details as well as lines from the poem to support his main idea.

- How does Tad broaden his theme? How does he link this theme to his original one?

Identify a Theme

A theme is a generalization about life or human nature that the writer communicates through the piece of literature. For example, one theme in Shakespeare's play *Romeo and Juliet* is that love can triumph over hate.

To discover themes in a piece of literature, you need to see what messages the writer is trying to communicate. One way to discover a theme is to use prewriting techniques such as freewriting. For example, begin with the line "What [title of work] tells me" and freewrite for five minutes. Another way to close in on a theme is to brainstorm. For example, in a small group, take turns completing the following: "I think one of the author's messages is . . . " Discuss each group member's answer.

Freewriting

What *Romeo and Juliet* tells me is that love can spring up in the most unlikely circumstances, that love can triumph over hate, that love and hate are closely related, that strong emotions can lead to violent ends.

Brainstorming

Maria: I think one of Shakespeare's messages is that hatred can destroy lives.

Jamal: I think one of Shakespeare's messages is that even though hatred can destroy lives, love can triumph over hatred.

Journal Writing

What other strategies—besides the freewriting and brainstorming techniques described above—might you use for discovering the themes in a piece of literature? Write your ideas in your journal.

2.12 Explaining Theme 105

Support the Theme with Evidence

Once you have identified a theme, look to the piece of literature for details that reflect or support that theme. You need to provide evidence to convince your readers that the message you have discovered is indeed one that the author was trying to convey.

The basic elements of any piece of narrative literature are character, setting, and plot. Use prewriting techniques to examine each of these elements as you seek details to support the theme you have found. Your evidence may include quotations, descriptions, summaries of key events, and explanations of passages in the text.

Characters To support your analysis of a theme, study the characters' physical descriptions, thoughts, actions, words, and relationships with other characters. For example, to show that one of Shakespeare's themes in *Romeo and Juliet* is that love can triumph over hate, you might describe Romeo's impulsive behavior at the masked ball.

Setting The setting—time of day, place, mood, and other details—can also help develop a theme. Try to determine what message the author is conveying through the choice of setting. For example, Romeo and Juliet first meet at a masked ball. Perhaps, in choosing this setting, Shakespeare is saying something about the senselessness of a feud based only on appearances and one's last name.

Plot The plot—the sequence of events in the story being told—can also reveal the theme. Generally, the plot begins with a central conflict and develops to its climax and resolution. Romeo and Juliet's meeting at the ball triggers the central conflict—that is, the conflict between their love and the hatred between their families.

A scene from the movie *Romeo and Juliet*

Write About the Theme

Once you have identified a theme and have gathered the details to support it, you're ready to draft your paragraph. Like any other paragraph you write, your analysis should be unified and coherent. Generally, you will want to state the theme in your topic sentence and then present the supporting details in a logical order—perhaps in order of importance. As you revise your work, be sure to use transitions to help the reader understand relationships between ideas.

2.12 Writing Activities

Write an Analysis

Choose a piece of literature with which you are familiar. Freewrite for five minutes to try to discover a theme that you can then write about. Use quotations, descriptions, and summaries of events in the story to support your analysis. Use the five stages of the writing process to write a paragraph based on the theme.

PURPOSE To analyze literature
AUDIENCE Your teacher
LENGTH 1 paragraph

WRITING RUBRICS To write an analysis of literature, you should

- look for a generalization about life or human nature
- support the theme with details of character, setting, and plot
- check that your paragraph is unified and coherent

Viewing and Representing

ILLUSTRATING THEME Create a book jacket that expresses the theme of the story you have recalled for the writing activity. Select an image that visually expresses a generalization about life or human nature that the story communicates. Draw your book jacket on poster board or create it on the computer using drawing software.

Grammar Link

Capitalize proper nouns.

Rewrite the following paragraph, correcting errors in capitalization.

[1]In william shakespeare's play *macbeth*, the writer suggests that the lust for power corrupts people. [2]Witches tell macbeth that he will eventually become king of scotland. [3]Convinced that the witches have told the truth, he and his wife, lady macbeth, murder king duncan. [4]Macbeth then becomes involved in other murders, including those of the wife and son of macduff. [5]By the time macbeth is killed by the scots, the desire for power has corrupted him completely.

See Lesson 20.2, pages 713–719.

Cross-Curricular Activity

ART Identify features of a painting from this book that attract your interest or attention or that evoke memories or mental images. Freewrite for five minutes or use a cluster map to define the painting's theme. To find details that support the theme, look for elements of character, setting, and plot. Use the theme and details to write one or two paragraphs analyzing the painting.

UNIT 2
Writing Process in Action

The Writing Process

In the preceding lessons, you've learned about the stages of the writing process. Now it's time to make use of what you learned. In this lesson, you are invited to retell a story a family member has told you—whether the story has been in your family for generations or is a new addition to your family's collection of favorites.

Assignment

Context

Your cousin has decided to create a written collection of memorable family stories so that future generations will be able to know about their ancestors and their past. You have been asked to contribute your favorite family tale to the collection.

Purpose

To write a story that captures something of your family members and their experiences.

Audience

Family members, friends, and future generations

Length

1–2 pages

The following pages can help you plan and write your family story. Read through them and then refer to them as you need to. But don't be tied down by them. You're in charge of your own writing process.

Prewriting

Where will you get your story idea? Talk with your family, look through old pictures, and think about your own memories. Once you've identified a story, use freewriting, list making, or questioning to brainstorm for details.

To bring your story into sharper focus, think about your purpose and audience and keep them in mind as you gather details to provide

WRITING Online

Visit the *Writer's Choice* Web site at **writerschoice.glencoe.com** for additional writing prompts.

TIME

For more about the writing process, see **TIME Facing the Blank Page**, 121-131.

108 Unit 2 The Writing Process

a full and accurate account. In the literature model below, notice how the author uses story details to reinforce the theme of the writing.

> **Literature Model**
>
> The aged visitors who came to my grandmother's house when I was a child were men of immense character, full of wisdom and disdain. . . . They were made of lean and leather, and they bore themselves upright. They wore great black hats and bright ample shirts that shook in the wind. They rubbed fat upon their hair and wound their braids with strips of colored cloth. . . . They were an old council of war lords, come to remind and be reminded of who they were.
>
> N. Scott Momaday, *House Made of Dawn*

Now that you have a story in mind, think about your purpose. You want to tell a memorable story, but is there anything else you want to accomplish? Do you want to make your readers laugh? Persuade them to be proud of their roots? If you do have a secondary purpose, identify it so that you can keep it in mind as you draft.

Next, consider your audience. Friends and future generations might lack your and your family's current familiarity with your subject. So you might add to your prewriting notes any information these readers would need to understand your story.

Finally, gather any remaining details you may need to tell your story effectively. You want to provide a full and accurate account of your chosen tale.

Prewriting Options

- Check your journal. What have you already written about family members or personal experiences?
- Talk with your family. What family stories have they especially enjoyed?
- Look at family albums. What clues do faces and places provide?

Writing Process in Action **109**

Writing Process in Action

Drafting

A good way to start drafting is to just jump in. Let the story tell itself, flowing naturally from beginning to end. As you draft, refer to your prewriting notes for details that will make your story stick in the reader's mind.

If you have trouble starting your story, think about the main idea you're trying to communicate and write it as a topic sentence. Then try to develop your idea by describing incidents that support it. Ask yourself *who, what, where, when, why,* and *how* questions to help you think of details about the event.

If you're telling the story in chronological order, consider ordering the details in the same way. Sometimes, however, using cause-and-effect order works well too. Do not be too concerned with spelling and grammar at this point. Your goal at this stage is to get the story and supporting details down on paper.

Once you've finished your draft, put it away for a while. You will return to it later with a fresh perspective.

Drafting Tip
For help writing coherent paragraphs, see Lesson 2.8, pages 88–91.

Revising

To begin revising, read over your draft to make sure that what you have written fits your purpose and your audience. Then have a **writing conference.** Read your draft to a partner or small group. You might also ask a family member who is familiar with the story to read your draft to help you identify whether any important details are missing or whether you have told anything incorrectly. Then revise the story to strengthen it. You can use the questions on this checklist to help you.

Revising Tip
To check the paragraphs in your story for unity and coherence, use the checklists in Lesson 2.9, page 94.

Revising Checklist
- Does this story match the one in my head?
- Does the story have a clear beginning and end?
- Does the story capture something of the essence of the people in my family and our experiences?
- Does the "flavor" of the people and their experiences come through?

Writing Process in Action

Editing/Proofreading

After you're satisfied with the basic content and flow of your story, **proofread** it carefully to correct errors in grammar, usage, mechanics, and spelling. Use the Editing/Proofreading Questions as a guide. You'll also need to consider the following special questions:

- If you used any foreign words or names, did you spell and capitalize them correctly?
- If you used any family expressions, dialect, or slang, did you include enough explanation so that readers will be able to understand them?

Editing/Proofreading Questions

- Have I used commas to avoid run-ons with "and"?
- Have I used quotation marks to enclose all direct quotes in the dialogue?
- Have I punctuated possessive pronouns correctly?
- Have I capitalized names, groups, and places correctly?
- Have I used my spelling checker or checked the spelling of any unfamiliar words?

Self-Evaluation

Make sure your family story—

- ✔ focuses on a tale about a family member or experience
- ✔ hooks interest early on by establishing relevance to the reader
- ✔ uses vivid sensory details and realistic dialogue
- ✔ provides any needed explanations
- ✔ follows correct grammar, usage, mechanics, and spelling

Publishing/Presenting

You can use your story to start your own family collection. Send your story along with a request to members of your family, asking them to send you *their* favorite family tales in return. You can also tell your story at your next family gathering.

Proofreading Tip

For proofreading symbols, see page 411.

Journal Writing

In your journal, write down the names of three or four characters from your story. Under each name, list as many words and phrases as you can that describe that character.

UNIT 2
Literature Model

from

The KITCHEN God's WIFE

by Amy Tan

Amy Tan, who was born of Chinese parents in the United States, uses incidents from her own family history as the raw material of her writing process. In this excerpt, Tan depicts the differences between the narrator, Pearl, and Pearl's mother, while at the same time emphasizing the ties that bind them together. Pay special attention to how the author uses detail in the dialogue to bring the characters to life. When you finish the excerpt, try the activities in Linking Writing and Literature on page 119.

Literature Model

My mother is standing outside the house when we return. "I tried to chase you, but you were too fast," she says as soon as I get out of the car. "And then I knew you would remember and come back." Tessa and Cleo are already racing up the stairs.

"Remember what?"

"Grand Auntie's farewell gift. Remember? Two, three days ago I told you not to forget. Yesterday I said, Don't forget. You forgot?"

"No, no," I say. "Where is it?"

"In back, in the laundry room," she says. "Very heavy, though. Better ask your husband to carry it." I can just imagine what it must be: the old vinyl ottoman Grand Auntie used to rest her feet on, or perhaps the set of chip-proof Melmac dishes. As we wait for Phil to come back with the girls, my mother hands me a cup of tea, waving off my protests. "Already made. If you can't drink it, I only have to throw it away."

I take a few quick sips. "This is really good." And I mean it. I have never tasted tea like this. It is smooth, pungent, and instantly addicting.

"This is from Grand Auntie," my mother explains. "A few years ago she bought it for herself. One hundred dollars a pound."

"You're kidding." I take another sip. It tastes even better.

"She told me, 'If I buy myself the cheap tea, then I am saying my whole life has not been worth something better.' So she decided to buy herself the best tea, so she could drink it and feel like a rich person inside."

I laugh.

My mother looks encouraged by my laughter. "But then she thought, If I buy just a little, then I am saying my lifetime is almost over. So she bought enough tea for another lifetime. Three pounds! Can you imagine?"

"That's three hundred dollars!" I exclaim. Grand Auntie was the most frugal[1] person I knew. "Remember how she used to keep all the boxes of See's candies we gave her for Christmas, telling us they were too good to eat? And then one year, she gave a box back to us for Thanksgiving or something. Only it was so old—"

My mother was nodding, already laughing.

"—all the candies were white with mold!"

"Bugs, too!" my mother adds.

"So she left you the tea in her will?" I say.

"Already gave it to me a few months ago. She was thinking she was going to die soon. She didn't say, but she started to give things away, good things, not just junk. And one time we were visiting, drinking tea. I said, 'Ah, good tea!' same as always. This time, Grand Auntie went to her kitchen, brought back the tea. She told me, '*Syau ning*, you take this tea now.' That's what she called me, *syau ning*, 'little person,' from the old days when we first knew each other.

> "*She told me, 'If I buy myself the cheap tea, then I am saying my whole life has not been worth something better.' So she decided to buy herself the best tea, so she could drink it and feel like a rich person inside.*"

---

[1] **frugal** (froo′ gəl) thrifty

Literature Model

Tomie Arai, *Laundryman's Daughter*, 1988

"I said, 'No, no! I wasn't saying this to hint.' And she said, '*Syau ning,* you take this now so I can see how happy you are to receive it while I am still alive. Some things can't wait until I'm dead.' How could I refuse? Of course, every time I came to visit, I brought back her tea."

Phil returns with Cleo, Tessa is right behind. And now I am actually sorry we have to leave.

"We better hit the road," says Phil. I put the teacup down.

"Don't forget," my mother says to Phil. "Grand Auntie's present in the laundry room."

"A present?" Cleo says. "Do I have a present too?"

Phil throws me a look of surprise.

"Remember?" I lie. "I told you—what Grand Auntie left us in her will."

He shrugs, and we all follow my mother to the back.

Literature Model

"Of course it's just old things," says my mother. She turns on the light, and then I see it, sitting on the clothes dryer. It is the altar for Grand Auntie's good-luck god, the Chinese crèche.[2]

"Wow!" Tessa exclaims. "A Chinese dollhouse."

"I can't see! I can't see!" Cleo says, and Phil lifts the altar off the dryer and carries it into the kitchen.

The altar is about the size of a small upturned drawer, painted in red lacquer. In a way, it resembles a miniature stage for a Chinese play. There are two ornate[3] columns in front, as well as two ceremonial electric candles made out of gold and red plastic and topped by red Christmas tree bulbs for flames. Running down the sides are wooden panels decorated with gold Chinese characters.

"What does that say?" I ask my mother.

She traces her finger down one, then the other. "*Jye shiang ru yi.* This first word is 'luck,' this other is another kind of luck, and these two mean 'all that you wish.' All kinds of luck, all that you wish."

"And who is this on the inside, this man in the picture frame?" The picture is almost cartoonlike. The man is rather large and is seated in regal splendor, holding a quill[4] in one hand, a tablet in the other. He has two long whiskers, shaped like smooth, tapered black whips.

"Oh, this we call Kitchen God. To my way of thinking, he was not too important. Not like Buddha, not like Kwan Yin, goddess of mercy—not that high level, not even the same level as the Money God. Maybe he was like a store manager, important, but still many, many bosses above him."

Phil chuckles at my mother's Americanized explanation of the hierarchy of Chinese deities.[5] I wonder if that's how she really thinks of them, or if she's used this metaphor[6] for our benefit.

"What's a kitchen god?" says Tessa. "Can I have one?"

"He is only a story," answers my mother.

"A story!" exclaims Cleo. "I want one."

My mother's face brightens. She pats Cleo's head. "You want another story from Ha-bu? Last night, you did not get enough stories?"

"When we get home," Phil says to Cleo. "Ha-bu is too tired to tell you a story now."

But my mother acts as if she has not heard Phil's excuses. "It is a very simple story," she says to Cleo in a soothing voice, "how he became Kitchen God. It is this way."

> *The altar is about the size of a small upturned drawer, painted in red lacquer. In a way, it resembles a miniature stage for a Chinese play.*

---

2 **crèche** (kresh) a display representing the birth of Jesus

3 **ornate** (ôr nāt′) heavily decorated and ornamented

4 **quill** (kwil) a pen made from the stem of a feather

5 **the hierarchy of Chinese deities** (hī′ ə rär′ kē) (dē′ ə tēz) the order of importance of all the Chinese gods

6 **metaphor** (met′ ə fôr) a comparison of two unlike things used to clarify the meaning of the less familiar one

Literature Model

And as my mother begins, I am struck by a familiar feeling, as if I am Cleo, again three years old, still eager to believe everything my mother has to say.

"In China long time ago," I hear my mother say, "there was a rich farmer named Zhang, such a lucky man. Fish jumped in his river, pigs grazed his land, ducks flew around his yard as thick as clouds. And that was because he was blessed with a hardworking wife named Guo. She caught his fish and herded his pigs. She fattened his ducks, doubled all his riches, year after year. Zhang had everything he could ask for—from the water, the earth, and the heavens above.

"But Zhang was not satisfied. He wanted to play with a pretty, carefree woman named Lady Li. One day he brought this pretty woman home to his house, made his good wife cook for her. When Lady Li later chased his wife out of the house, Zhang did not run out and call to her, 'Come back, my good wife, come back.'

"Now he and Lady Li were free to swim in each other's arms. They threw money away like dirty water. They slaughtered ducks just to eat a plate of their tongues. And in two years' time, all of Zhang's land was empty, and so was his heart. His money was gone, and so was pretty Lady Li, run off with another man.

"Zhang became a beggar, so poor he wore more patches than whole cloth on his pants. He crawled from the gate of one household to another, crying, 'Give me your moldy grain!'

"One day, he fell over and faced the sky, ready to die. He fainted, dreaming of eating the winter clouds blowing above him. When he opened his eyes again, he found the clouds had turned to smoke. At first he was afraid he had fallen down into a place far below the earth. But when he sat up, he saw he was in a kitchen, near a warm fireplace. The girl tending the fire explained that the lady of the house had taken pity on him—she always did this, with all kinds of people, poor or old, sick or in trouble.

"'What a good lady!' cried Zhang. 'Where is she, so I can thank her?' The girl pointed to the window, and the man saw a woman walking up the path. Ai-ya! That lady was none other than his good wife Guo!

"Zhang began leaping about the kitchen looking for some place to hide, then jumped into the kitchen fireplace just as his wife walked into the room.

"Good Wife Guo poured out many tears to try to put the fire out. No use! Zhang was burning with shame and, of course, because of the hot roaring fire below. She watched her husband's ashes fly up to heaven in three puffs of smoke. Wah!

"In heaven, the Jade Emperor heard the whole story from his new arrival. 'For having the courage to admit you were wrong,' the Emperor declared, 'I make you Kitchen God, watching over everyone's behavior. Every year, you let me know who deserves good luck, who deserves bad.'

> **"And once a year, seven days before the new year, Kitchen God flew back up the fireplace to report whose fate deserved to be changed, better for worse, or worse for better."**

Literature Model

Ch'ing dynasty, porcelain teapot and beaker, c. 1700

"From then on, people in China knew Kitchen God was watching them. From his corner in every house and every shop, he saw all kinds of good and bad habits spill out: generosity or greediness, a harmonious nature or a complaining one. And once a year, seven days before the new year, Kitchen God flew back up the fireplace to report whose fate deserved to be changed, better for worse, or worse for better."

"The end!" shouts Cleo, completely satisfied.

"Sounds like Santa Claus," says Phil cheerfully.

"Hnh!" my mother huffs in a tone that implies Phil is stupid beyond words. "He is not Santa Claus. More like a spy—FBI agent, CIA, Mafia, worse than IRS, that kind of person! And he does not give *you* gifts, you must give *him* things. All year long you have to show him respect—give him tea and oranges. When Chinese New Year's time comes, you must give him even better things—maybe whiskey to drink, cigarettes to smoke, candy to eat, that kind of thing. You are hoping all the time his tongue will be sweet, his head a little drunk, so when he has his meeting with the big boss, maybe he reports good things about you. This family has been good, you hope he says. Please give them good luck next year."

"Well, that's a pretty inexpensive way to get some luck," I say. "Cheaper than the lottery."

"No!" my mother exclaims, and startles us all. "You never know. Sometimes he is in a bad mood. Sometimes he says, I don't like this family, give them bad luck. Then you're in trouble, nothing you can do about it. Why should I want that kind of person to judge me, a man who cheated his wife? His wife was the good one, not him."

Literature Model

"Then why did Grand Auntie keep him?" I ask.

My mother frowns, considering this. "It is this way, I think. Once you get started, you are afraid to stop. Grand Auntie worshiped him since she was a little girl. Her family started it many generations before, in China."

"Great!" says Phil. "So now she passes along this curse to us. Thanks, Grand Auntie, but no thanks." He looks at his watch and I can tell he's impatient to go.

"It was Grand Auntie's gift to you," my mother says to me in a mournful voice. "How could she know this was not so good? She only wanted to leave you something good, her best things."

"Maybe the girls can use the altar as a dollhouse," I suggest. Tessa nods, Cleo follows suit. My mother stares at the altar, not saying anything.

"I'm thinking about it this way," she finally announces, her mouth set in an expression of thoughtfulness. "You take this altar. I can find you another kind of lucky god to put inside, not this one." She removes the picture of the Kitchen God.

"This one, I take it. Grand Auntie will understand. This kind of luck, you don't want. Then you don't have to worry."

"Deal!" Phil says right away. "Let's pack 'er up."

But now I'm worried. "Are you sure?" I ask my mother. She's already stuffing the plastic candlesticks into a used paper bag. I'm not exactly superstitious. I've always been the kind who hates getting chain letters—Mary used to send them to me all the time. And while I never sent the duplicate letters out as instructed, I never threw the originals away either.

Phil is carrying the altar. Tessa has the bag of candlesticks. My mother has taken Cleo upstairs to find a plastic neon bracelet she left in the bathroom. And now my mother comes back with Cleo and hands me a heavy grocery sack, the usual care package, what feels like oranges and Chinese candy, that sort of thing.

"Grand Auntie's tea, I gave you some," my mother says. "Don't need to use too much. Just keep adding water. The flavor always comes back."

> *"It was Grand Auntie's gift to you," my mother says to me in a mournful voice. "How could she know this was not so good?"*

Literature Model

Linking Writing and Literature

Readers Respond to the Model

How does Amy Tan use details to develop her theme?

Explore Amy Tan's use of detail to develop her theme and bring her characters to life. Then read what other students liked in Tan's story.

1. What terms might you use to describe Pearl's mother? Which details in the story led you to select those terms?
2. How do the details in the dialogue point out the differences between the mother's and daughter's generations?
3. The theme of this story deals with relationships between generations and between cultures. Freewrite or list some details Amy Tan has used to develop this theme.
4. The story of the Kitchen God's Wife is a detail within the larger story. How has Tan related this tale to her overarching theme?

What Students Say

"The scene that I remember most clearly was when Zhang went before the Jade Emperor, who decided that Zhang should be Kitchen God to look over people's households and to see whether they were decent people. The writer kept my attention because of the interesting story of the Kitchen God and the wonderful detail in the story.

I enjoyed the portrayal of the Chinese American family, where the husband was Caucasian and his wife and her family were Chinese and very loyal to their culture. The story showed how cultures relate and clash at the same time."

Rachel Hansen

"I enjoyed the story because it informed me of another religion and culture. I thought the facts and details surrounding the story of the Kitchen God's origin, however, seemed very far-fetched. I would have made Phil's doubts of the grandmother's story more critical so that there would have been a logical response to a story that seems illogical."

Michael Kim

Literature Model   119

UNIT 2 Review

Reflecting on the Unit

Summarize what you learned in this unit by answering the following questions:

1. What are the five stages of the writing process?
2. What are the important elements of each stage of the process?
3. What strategies and techniques can help you at each stage of the writing process?
4. What are some ways to analyze theme in a piece of literature?

Adding to Your Portfolio

CHOOSE A SELECTION FOR YOUR PORTFOLIO Look over the writing you did for this unit. Select a completed piece for your portfolio. The writing you choose should show some or all of the following:

- ideas generated by using such techniques as freewriting or listing
- words and ideas chosen with a particular audience in mind
- a clear topic sentence that controls appropriate supporting details
- careful revising and editing
- development through all five stages of the writing process, including presenting

REFLECT ON YOUR CHOICE Attach a note to the piece you chose, explaining briefly why you chose it and what you learned from writing it.

SET GOALS How can you improve your writing? What skill will you focus on the next time you write?

Writing Across the Curriculum

MAKE A SOCIAL STUDIES CONNECTION Choose a family member who lived either in another country or who lived in the United States during the early twentieth century. Write a paragraph comparing one or two important aspects of this person's daily life with your daily life today.

Prewriting ✱ Drafting ✱ Revising ✱ Editing & Proofreading ✱ Publishing & Presenting

TIME

Facing the Blank Page

Inside the writing process with TIME writers and editors

121

Writing for TIME

Every story published in TIME is the work of experienced professionals. The writing is strong; the facts are accurate; the grammar, spelling, and punctuation are error-free (or close!). Behind the scenes, however, there is another story to be told. As these pages reveal, TIME staffers struggle with many of the same challenges that students face in the messy, trial-and-error process that is writing: selecting among topics; finding information; getting organized; starting to draft; and then revising, revising, and revising some more.

What is the secret to the quality of writing in TIME? Beyond experience and hard work, the key lies in collaboration. As the chart on these pages illustrates, TIME stories are created through a form of "group journalism" that has become the magazine's hallmark. The writers and editors teach and learn from one another at every step in the writing process; student writers can do the same. Try out and adapt the writing and collaboration strategies presented in "Facing the Blank Page" to discover what works for you.

PREWRITING

Senior Editor in New York
Staff Writer in New York
Correspondent in the field

Story idea is proposed and assigned

Writer takes assignment, refines topic, sends "query" to correspondents and researchers

Research begins

Correspondents investigate, conduct interviews

Researchers gather material from reliable sources: "clips" from articles, studies, statistics

DRAFTING

Correspondents send their reporting or "files" to writer

Researchers compile and submit research files

Writer reads and organizes information, drafts the story

TIME Facing the Blank Page

REVISING

Editor reads draft, asks for revisions

Correspondents
check interpretation,
make suggestions
⬅ ┄┄┄┄ ➡
Writer revises, resubmits for comments
⬅ ┄┄┄┄ ➡
Researchers
check accuracy,
details

Writer and editor revise again, "green" (edit for length)

EDITING AND PROOFREADING

Checks for conformity to TIME
style and conventions
⬅ ┄┄┄┄ ➡
Copy Desk
⬅ ┄┄┄┄ ➡
Checks and corrects grammar,
mechanics, spelling

PUBLISHING AND PRESENTING

Managing Editor chooses to print, hold, or "kill" (omit) story

Circulation of TIME
rises or falls
⬅ ┄┄┄┄ ➡
Readers respond to published story
⬅ ┄┄┄┄ ➡
E-mail and letters
to the editor

123

Prewriting
Finding an Angle

At TIME, story ideas can be proposed by any member of the editorial staff. But once a story is assigned, it is the staff writer's job to develop the idea and find the most compelling way to approach and tell it.

Senior Editor Janice Simpson:

"In magazine or feature writing, you need to determine what we call the angle on a subject. Imagine asking a random group of people, 'What was the best thing about the movie *Titanic*?' Some people might say Leo DiCaprio right off the bat. Leo DiCaprio is a story. We can do a feature story on this young actor. Someone else might say, 'The special effects. The way they made that ship crack in half and go down.' We could do a story on the special effects in the movie. That's the difference between a subject and a story. The *subject* is the movie *Titanic*. The *story* is either the career of Leonardo DiCaprio or the amazing special effects. Those are stories, something I can tell you about what happened. We take a subject—a movie, a presidential campaign—and we look for the stories within it.

One of the best exercises for people learning to be journalists is to send a whole bunch of people to the same event, and have them come back and write about it. You'll get as many different stories or angles as there are writers!"

Janice Simpson: Looking for the story within the subject.

LEARNING FROM THE EDITOR

DISCUSSION
In your own words, explain the distinction that Janice Simpson makes between a subject and a story. Brainstorm a list of several subjects as a class. Then, working in smaller groups, come up with several different story ideas for each subject.

TRY IT OUT
Try the exercise Simpson recommends. In pairs or groups, "cover" an event at school: an assembly, a sports or arts event, a daily ritual such as eating in the cafeteria. Write a page or two about what you witness, and then switch papers or read them aloud. What do you hear?

HOW I WRITE
Look through your writing portfolio. For each piece, identify the subject and the story. Then look through your journal or learning log and make a list of possible subjects and stories that could be developed from these entries you have written. See Lesson 2.2, "Explore Your Ideas."

124 TIME Facing the Blank Page

Refining a Topic: "Simplicity in Conception"

Assistant Managing Editor Howard Chua-Eoan:

"When we sit down and talk about story ideas, we'll say, 'This is an important subject.' But it can't be just a subject without anything to hold onto. There has to be something controversial or a pressing question. Then we try to investigate that, to provide an answer. You want to be sure you focus on the part that will make people say, 'Yes, that's an important subject for me, and that's an important point. I want to find out more about it.' Don't make the subject too broad: you'll start in one place but lose sight of where you are going. Simplicity in conception is the best starting point, and then you can elaborate as you go on, piling on the detail until you have a really ornate and detailed story."

LEARNING FROM THE EDITOR

Read this excerpt from one of Howard Chua-Eoan's stories in TIME:

Her Serena Highness

What am I doing here? Serena Williams asked herself in the middle of the championship tie breaker that would help her make history, allow her to fulfill her father's predictions and alter her relationship with her older sister. It was a moment of doubt. But being 17, she dismissed it quickly—just as swiftly as she recovered from the nervousness that tripped up two earlier chances to win the title outright in her match against Martina Hingis. Serena's prevailing ethos reasserted itself: she doesn't lose tie breakers. She hasn't lost one all year. The rule held. She won.

And so Serena Williams was transformed. On Saturday evening in New York City, she became the first African American to win a tennis Grand Slam singles title since Arthur Ashe won Wimbledon in 1975, and the first African-American woman to win the U.S. Open since Althea Gibson in 1958. As a historymaker, Serena transfigured her family as well. She, her sister Venus and their father Richard were no longer the loudest mouths on the tennis circuit. She had shown the world that her father was not just some voice crying in the wilderness but a true prophet. He had long predicted his daughters would dominate the world of women's tennis. Daddy did know best.

—Howard Chua-Eoan

DISCUSSION

1. What does Chua-Eoan mean by the phrase "simplicity in conception"? Do you agree that this is a helpful idea to use when drafting?

2. Read the excerpt above from one of Chua-Eoan's own pieces. What is the focus of his article on tennis champion Serena Williams? Does he follow his own advice: start out simply and then elaborate? Refer to specific lines in his text.

TRY IT OUT

Write a feature story. Begin by reading the tips and strategies presented in Lesson 5.8, "Writing a Feature Article." Then choose and refine your own subject and story. What is the concept you will begin with? What story will you tell? How do you plan to "pile on the detail"?

TIME Facing the Blank Page

Drafting

Starting Strong: Leads and Billboards

You don't have to write the opening paragraph of a story or article first, but at some point in the writing process you must decide how your piece will begin. At TIME, writers call the opening paragraphs of a piece *leads* and *billboards*.

From *Writing for TIME*, a stylebook distributed to staff.

Lead: It hardly needs saying that the lead is the toughest part of a story to get right. It is an invitation into the piece, so it must tantalize. It states the theme, so it must touch on the essentials of the story. It is a road map for the journey ahead, so it must provide a guide that will steer the reader through to the end.

A group of TIME writers discusses the importance of strong leads and billboards.

Senior Editor Nancy Gibbs:
"The hardest part, the most fun part, and the most important part is the first paragraph. I think that's true of every kind of writing. No matter how brilliant your information or elegant your argument, if you lose the reader at the beginning of a piece, then you've lost the reader forever. It doesn't matter what comes next. It's really a free ride for the writer: you have permission to do almost anything that's going to provoke or intrigue your reader. It doesn't necessarily have to include any information. It can just be a bewitching little sentence that says, 'This is why you're going to read this story.' It can be some fantastic illustration of an issue you're going to raise three pages later. It can be a quote that's like an explosive. It can be anything captivating."

Senior Reporter Andrea Sachs:
"A good lead draws the reader in quickly. You lose people really fast. People glance at a story and decide in a few seconds whether it's worth reading. So you've got to find something catchy to draw them in. The common wisdom is that anecdotal leads do very well. If you break it down to the level of one person, it's easier to understand. I think that's true. That's what I like when I'm reading."

What needs to follow an attention-grabbing lead?

Senior Editor Janice Simpson:
"After your lead, you need to reach out and pull the readers in, and you need to tell them why they're there. We call that the *billboard*. It's the place where you very briefly let the reader know what the rest of

126   TIME Facing the Blank Page

your story is going to say. Then you go through the story, developing your arguments, giving examples, using quotes to bolster and support the argument or information you're trying to impart."

Writing a good billboard paragraph can help focus and structure the rest of the draft.

Assistant Managing Editor Howard Chua-Eoan:
"Sometimes the best way to start is by writing the billboard paragraph, so you know exactly what the story is about. It's the flag you're waving, the advertisement for more that comes toward the middle and end of the story."

Nancy Gibbs:
"The billboard is hard to do well, because those few paragraphs have to do a lot of heavy lifting. Ideally, it has to touch on the important points that the story is going to raise. It has to signal why the story is important. Why are you writing about this in the first place? It has to foreshadow where you're going to go.

Ideally, a billboard ought to answer these questions in a way that is rather seamless, so that it isn't saying: 'The first point I'm going to make is X, and then I'm going to argue Y, and then I'm going to argue Z.' You want it to be a little more organic than that, to serve almost as a table of contents to your story. After that, the story starts to unfold itself."

LEARNING FROM THE WRITERS

DISCUSSION
1. What is a *billboard* as defined by TIME writers? What is a *lead*? Why do you think they use these names? Note how similarly each writer defines and describes the process of writing leads and billboards. What do you think accounts for this similarity?

2. There are conventional ways to open the pieces of expository writing you do in school (reports, essays, and research papers, for example). Read Lesson 2.5 on topic sentences and Lesson 7.2 on developing a thesis statement for a research paper. How is a journalistic lead similar to a topic sentence? How is a billboard like a thesis statement?

3. What genres of writing (short stories, novels, poetry, autobiographies, journals, memoirs) lend themselves to the kind of lead and billboard strategies used by TIME writers? How can the advice from these writers help make the opening paragraphs of school papers more interesting?

TRY IT OUT
What is an anecdote? What do you think Andrea Sachs means by an "anecdotal lead"? Find one in a current newspaper or magazine article, or in one of the Literature Models in this textbook. Do you think anecdotal leads are effective? Why or why not? Try using one for your next writing assignment.

HOW I WRITE
At what point in your writing do you usually write your lead paragraph? Do you tend to write the lead first, last, or at some other point in the drafting process? Next time you're writing a paper, try the opposite approach. Is the new method better?

Revising

Incorporating Quotes

Howard Chua-Eoan: Get close to the subject.

Revising (literally, "looking again") is an essential part of the writing process. First drafts can always be improved, and one way of strengthening a piece of writing is to incorporate direct quotations. These may be written quotes from a book or another source of information, or spoken quotes from an interview or conversation. They are always set off with quotation marks. TIME writers share their thoughts on the importance of using direct quotations, and the process of refining and editing them.

Assistant Managing Editor Howard Chua-Eoan explains why well-selected quotations add value to a story:

"Using quotations is always important. It gives a sense that your reporters have talked to the people involved. Quotations give a sense that the writer—and the reader—are as close to the subject as they can get. Quotes impart a sense of immediacy to the story. Unlike television, where quotes are basically sound bites, in a newsmagazine you can stop and analyze the quote, and you can give it background. You can say what the speaker looked like, that he paused, that he was uncomfortable when he said something."

Senior Reporter Andrea Sachs knows an effective quote when she "hears" it on the page:

"Some quotes sing, and some people are naturally articulate. Using quotes can be a way of compressing the central idea. It could be a way of illustrating something about the personality of the speaker. It juices up the story.

You rarely get anything surprising from well-known people because what they say tends to be rehearsed. They've been through it before. It's people who are new to the process who sometimes say things that make you gasp, because they don't know they're not supposed to."

Do writers go back to their interview subjects to verify quotes?
Andrea Sachs:

"At TIME, we never read quotes back to people. Some magazines do. Certainly you want to get it right the first time, but if you read quotes back, people start changing what they've said: 'Did I say that? I can't say that!' Sometimes people beg you to read them their quotes, but we don't do it. It's the policy here not to. Get it right the first time."

Andrea Sachs: Some quotes sing.

128 TIME Facing the Blank Page

Can writers and editors change and polish quotes for readability?

Judy Paul, Deputy Copy Chief at TIME, explains the policy that her department follows:

"We try to clean up people's quotes. If someone speaks ungrammatically, we'll fix it (unless the writer is trying to show that this is how the speaker really talks). Of course, you can't change written quotes, but with spoken quotes, we generally delete words such as *um* and *like*, which occur frequently in speech but are distracting in print."

LEARNING FROM THE WRITER

Read this excerpt from a cover story based on an interview conducted by Andrea Sachs:

Author Tom Wolfe Writes Again

The megayield critical and commercial success of *The Bonfire of the Vanities* in 1987 made Tom Wolfe a rich and very gratified author indeed. After *Bonfire*, though, came the inevitable question. What next? Topping his first novel would be hard, the risk of failure and I-told-you-so reviews high. But Wolfe found the challenge irresistible. "I was 57," he says, "and I thought the eight or nine years I'd spent on *Bonfire* had taught me what not to do the second time. So, I proceeded to make every blunder a beginning writer could stumble into."

As he lists them, it becomes clear why readers have had to wait 11 years for *A Man in Full*. "First, I tried to take the easy way out by setting most of the new novel in Manhattan, the same locale I'd used in *Bonfire*. I didn't realize until 1995 that this approach wasn't working and that I was repeating myself. Second, I always recommend to people that they start with an outline. Naturally, I didn't take my own advice and do an outline until I was years into this project.

"A third mistake," he adds, "was feeling that the new book had to raise the stakes and include more than *Bonfire*, that I was obligated to write the biggest book in the world. I have bales of discarded manuscripts."

—Paul Gray

DISCUSSION
1. According to these TIME writers, what do direct quotations add to a story?
2. Why did Paul Gray use so many direct quotes in the excerpt above?
3. Do you agree with TIME's policy not to read quotes back to people who have been interviewed? Have you ever had the experience of being interviewed and then quoted—or misquoted? How did you feel? What policy for quotes do you think student publications should set?

TRY IT OUT
1. **Interview a friend or family member** about a topic of your choice and take notes as you do so, using the tips in Lesson 2.4. Then write a paragraph incorporating your interview subject's words as direct quotes. Units 5, 20, and 21 explain more about using and punctuating quotations.

2. **Quoting accurately.** Did you find you needed to edit the quotes? Show your revised quotes to your interview subject. Does he or she feel the quotes are accurate?

TIME Facing the Blank Page

Editing and Proofreading

Refining Style: The Voice of Verbs

The following memo, drafted for the benefit of TIME correspondents and writers, offers general advice on matters of style and usage.

Memo to Correspondents:

Though much of the ornamentation that marked the old TIME style has been abandoned, the essentials remain the same: we still prize, among other things, clarity, vitality, surprise and viewpoint. Sure, we do keep a few conventions and frequently used devices. Yet nowadays a hundred stylistic flowers bloom in our pages. Read the magazine closely; you'll be able to figure out what style and tone are appropriate for a particular story. Moreover, as you have no doubt found, different senior editors have different tastes. A particular rhetorical flourish of yours may be praised one week and edited out of your copy the next. Do not despair...

Deputy Copy Chief Judy Paul is always on the lookout for sentences written in the passive voice. In most instances, Paul and her colleagues will change this construction before the story runs in the magazine.

Judy Paul:
"We always try to shoot for the active voice. We're trying to make writing punchy and clear, and the passive voice just stops that."

WRITING TIP

Verbs: an active verb gives vitality to a sentence; a passive verb puts a sentence to sleep.
—from *Writing for TIME*, a style handbook for TIME staff

LEARNING FROM THE EDITOR

DISCUSSION

1. Review Lesson 15.7, "The Voice of Verbs." How can you tell if a verb is active or passive? Why do writers generally prefer to write in the active voice? How does the active voice make writing "punchy and clear"? Under what circumstances might you choose to use the passive voice?

2. Choose one of the Literature Models in *Writer's Choice* and read a page, noting which verb forms are active and which are passive. What overall effect does the writer's decision to use active or passive voice have on the story?

3. Read the "Memo to Correspondents" above. What message is conveyed to TIME writers? Is there good advice here for student writers, as well? Which points?

TRY IT OUT

1. Using passive verbs, rewrite the *Writing for TIME* entry on verbs. Compare your entry with those of your classmates.

2. Identify a passive verb used in the "Memo to Correspondents," above. Why do you think the writer composed the sentence in this way, ignoring the advice in the TIME style handbook?

TIME Facing the Blank Page

Publishing and Presenting
A Measure of Success

The final phase of the writing process is publishing and presenting your work—sharing your writing with friends, family, school, or community. How do you measure success? First, you must be clear about what your purpose is. What are you trying to communicate? What do you hope your readers will learn? Then listen to your readers' responses.

Senior Editor Bruce Nelan explains his criteria for successful news writing:

"Objective standards of writing don't have much to do with style. They have to do with how well the writer achieves what he or she sets out to do. If it's a news story, it should be accurate, it should be clear, and it should be relatively concise. It should include interesting and important material.

News writing is a craft. It's not short story or poetry writing. It's using the writer's tools for another purpose: to deliver information. If there's a little style in there, so much the better. But the central purpose of news writing is to get people to understand what happened and why.

Henry Luce, the founder of TIME, said that what mattered was not what you got on to the printed page. What mattered was what you got *off* the printed page and into the minds of the people who were reading the magazine. I think that's right. I think that what really matters is what people get out of it, and how well you deliver it to them."

When he can give his readers the information they need, Nelan derives real satisfaction from the hard work of writing:

"I do view writing in the same way I suspect that people who have the calling to teach feel about teaching. To me, what I do is a form of education, in the sense that we are explaining things, teaching people. I like that feeling. I find it very rewarding. If I've done a good job on a story and someone says, 'That really told me something,' then that's my reward."

LEARNING FROM THE WRITER

DISCUSSION

1. What is Bruce Nelan's definition of good news writing? How do you define success for the genre of writing you like best?

2. Do you agree with Henry Luce that what matters is not what writers put on to the printed page, but what readers get off it? Nelan makes a distinction between the purpose of news writing and imaginative genres such as short story and poetry writing. Does Luce's notion apply to these genres, as well?

3. Have you ever had a writing experience that brought you satisfaction? What made it rewarding? Did your readers respond favorably to your writing? What did they say?

TRY IT OUT
Defining success. Look at a piece of your writing in progress. What is the purpose of this piece? How will you know if this is a successful work of writing? Remind yourself of the composition's purpose as you continue to develop the piece.

"On this day the faded dry petals of the sunflower were swept across the land."

—Linda Hogan, "Walking"

UNIT 3　Descriptive Writing

Writing in the Real World:
Gary Ross **and** ***Anne Spielberg***　　134

Lesson 3.1　**Writing a Descriptive Paragraph**　138

Lesson 3.2　**Using Descriptive Language**　144

Lesson 3.3　**Describing an Imaginary Place**　148

Lesson 3.4　**Describing an Imaginary Person**　152

Lesson 3.5　**Writing About Literature: Analyzing Character Descriptions**　156

Writing Process in Action　160

Literature Model: from *The Crystal Cave* by Mary Stewart　164

Unit 3 Review　173

Writing in the Real World

MEDIA Connection: Screenplay

Writing a screenplay, or movie script, involves more than creating dialogue and a plot. Description is important too. Actors and directors need a script that conveys a real sense of mood so that they can visualize the movie they are about to make. The following excerpts are from Gary Ross's screenplay *Big*, which he wrote with his friend Anne Spielberg. The story tells of a boy who wishes he were bigger and suddenly gets his wish.

from *Big* by Gary Ross and Anne Spielberg

JOSH AND SUSAN
They look at it awkwardly for a moment, then glance at each other. It seems like each of them is about to say something, but neither one does. They stay like that for a second, when Susan cocks her head to the side.

           SUSAN
      You hear that?

           JOSH
      What?

           SUSAN
      Music.

EXT. BOARDWALK
The sounds of Big Band Music drift out of the old dance Pavilion. Built near the turn of the century, it is part Mosque, part Opera Hall, part Seaside Pleasure Palace. All the obelisks have flagpoles for the banners that have long since gone away. The sound of Moonlight Serenade echoes up the boardwalk as the ocean pounds in the distance.

EXT. ARCADE
Josh and Susan walk out of the arcade onto the nearly deserted boardwalk. Towering above them i̶s̶ ̶t̶h̶e̶ hulk of a roller coaster ̶.̶.̶.̶ on is the lat̶e̶s̶t̶

EXT. BASEBALL FIELD
It's late afternoon as the sun turns the field a light gold. Two boys stand alone on the grass, shagging flies in the faded light. There is silence, then the crack of a bat, then the distant pop of a ball hitting leather. Josh watches silently from the side of the field leaning back in his business suit. There is no conversation as the ritual continues between them—just the swing of the bat and the long lazy arc of a fly ball as it goes from one boy to another. Josh loosens the knot of his tie as he stares at the boys in front of him. A light breeze ruffles his hair.

Screenwriter Gary Ross

134 Unit 3 Descriptive Writing

Writing in the Real World

A Writer's Process

Prewriting
Getting Ideas and Getting Started

When Gary Ross is asked how he came to write *Big*, he replies, "Every child says, 'I wish I were a grown-up.' The screenplay for *Big* came out of wondering what would happen if that wish were ultimately fulfilled."

The inspiration for different scenes came in various ways. One of Ross's favorite scenes takes place at a seaside carnival (see excerpt on page 134). Josh has been transformed to an adult at this stage. As he and his girlfriend stand on the boardwalk, they hear music coming from an old dance pavilion. Ross says, "I was inspired by something I'd read in an F. Scott Fitzgerald book, about life on the French Riviera. We wanted to evoke the same romance and magic but also the decline and the sadness that's coming."

Ross worked on the *Big* script with fellow screenwriter Anne Spielberg. Describing their process, he says, "First, we outlined the whole movie. We planned out every scene in detail, and we each wrote our own scenes. Then we'd rewrite each other's scenes until the script was unified into one voice."

Even in the early stage of outlining the movie, Ross and Spielberg were aware of the mood they wanted the finished film to evoke. This awareness helped them select dramatic details and develop them into descriptive paragraphs in the script.

Drafting
Writing the Scenes

Descriptive details are especially important in describing a setting. As Ross and Spielberg draft scenes, they look for just the right setting to underscore the character's experience and feelings. The baseball scene in *Big* needed to be nostalgic. Ross says, "We knew if we wrote this scene poetically, the director would end up putting the poetry into the film. Usually you have to write lean for the screen, but this time we really pulled out all the stops and went for it. We even used

Descriptive Writing

Writing in the Real World 135

Writing in the Real World

a poetic device, alliteration, to describe the 'long, lazy arc' of the fly ball."

The baseball field scene takes place in what Ross calls "that mystical, magical, temporal instance between night and day. The sun turns the field gold for only a few minutes a day, so there's a fragile, fleeting quality of something that's there for only an instant and then is lost." Ross continues, "The fact that the two boys stand alone gives the scene a beautiful, isolated quality. There's nothing in the world except them."

Ross and Spielberg empower their descriptions with language that appeals to the senses. They enhance the "fragile, fleeting quality" of the baseball scene by emphasizing how quiet the world seems at this moment. They use sensory language that appeals to the senses of sight, touch, and—especially—sound.

Revising/Editing
Choosing the Right Details

As Ross and Spielberg revise and edit, they focus on getting the right details. Small, well-chosen details can create a powerful impact. In the baseball scene, Josh watches kids playing ball. Ross says, "Josh is privy to this scene, but he's lost the beauty of it because of his wish to be big. Showing Josh in a business suit emphasizes that he's constrained by being an adult. And when he loosens his tie, he shows that being big is constricting him. That's what I mean by writing description that bolsters a point. When the light breeze ruffles his hair, it harkens back to the magical wind that blew when he first wished to be big. This time the wind shows he's drawn back to the world of childhood."

Crafting a revised script requires close attention to these sorts of details. A loosened tie and a slight breeze are small elements that contribute hugely to both an understanding of the main character and the development of the story.

Presenting
Turning the Screenplay into a Film

Once Ross and Spielberg are satisfied with their last draft, they make copies for the director, producers, and others involved in turning the screenplay into a film. As the movie is shot, the writers are often asked to make further changes. At this point in the process, the collaboration widens.

A scene from the movie *Big*

Examining Writing in the Real World

Analyzing the Media Connection

Discuss these questions about the excerpts from the screenplay on page 134.

1. What is the mood of the baseball scene? How does the use of alliteration contribute to that mood?
2. How does the time of day contribute to the mood of the baseball scene? How might the mood shift if the action were to take place earlier in the day or later in the evening?
3. What sensory details enhance the mood of the baseball scene?
4. From whose perspective is the baseball scene described in the first three sentences? In the last four sentences? What is the effect of that shift in perspective?
5. What is the mood of the old dance pavilion scene? Which words and phrases contribute to this mood?

Analyzing a Writer's Process

Discuss these questions about Ross and Spielberg's writing process.

1. How is writing a screenplay similar to writing a feature story? How do the two processes differ?
2. Who is the audience for the screenplay? How does that audience differ from the audience for a feature story?
3. What difficulties might you expect when two or more writers collaborate on a screenplay or story? How did Ross and Spielberg collaborate?
4. How closely do you think a finished movie resembles the screenplay from which it was made? Explain.
5. To what extent does Ross imagine specific locations in creating settings and characters for his work? How might thinking about real places and people influence the writing process?

Grammar Link

A **participle** is a verb form used as an adjective. A **participial phrase** is a participle with its complements and modifiers.

Standing on the platform, the mayor waved to the crowd.

Use each participial phrase below in a sentence. Start by thinking of a noun or pronoun for each phrase to modify.

1. wandering in the neighborhood
2. blowing wildly through the bare-limbed trees
3. nervously clutching her purse
4. scratching against the darkened window
5. whispering fearfully behind the broken gate

See Lesson 12.3, page 523.

LESSON 3.1

Writing a Descriptive Paragraph

In the model below author J. R. R. Tolkien uses his descriptive skills to transport you to an eerie scene. Notice how Tolkien creates a mood in his topic sentence and then uses well-ordered details to paint a vivid picture that reinforces the mood.

Literature Model

Hard and cruel and bitter was the land that met his gaze. Before his feet the highest ridge of Ephel Dúath fell steeply in great cliffs down into a dark trough, on the further side of which there rose another ridge, much lower, its edge notched and jagged with crags like fangs that stood out black against the red light behind them: it was the grim Morgai, the inner ring of the fences of the land. Far beyond it, but almost straight ahead, across a wide lake of darkness dotted with tiny fires, there was a great burning glow, and from it rose in huge columns a swirling smoke, dusky red at the roots, black above where it merged into the billowing canopy that roofed in all the accursed land.

> Tolkien's first sentence conveys the overall impression of the scene.

> What is Tolkien's writing strategy, as indicated by words like "before his feet," "on the further side," and "far beyond it"?

> Sam was looking at Orodruin, the Mountain of Fire. Ever and anon the furnaces far below its ashen cone would grow hot and with a great surging and throbbing pour forth rivers of molten rock from chasms in its sides. Some would flow blazing toward Barad-dûr down great channels; some would wind their way into the stone plain, until they cooled and lay like twisted dragon-shapes vomited from the tormented earth. In such an hour of labor Sam beheld Mount Doom, and the light of it, cut off by the high screen of the Ephel Dúath from those who climbed up the path from the West, now glared against the stark rock faces, so that they seemed to be drenched with blood.
>
> J. R. R. Tolkien, *The Return of the King*

Create an Overall Impression

There are many ways to begin putting together a description. One way is to think of the overall impression, or mood, you want to communicate. Then, in your topic sentence, use words and phrases that will help convey this mood to your reader.

Mood Your descriptive paragraph will have greater impact if it evokes a particular mood rather than just presenting details that aren't unified. Perhaps you want to express horror or inspire fear, as Tolkien does. Maybe you intend to communicate a happy, light-hearted feeling or a sad, nostalgic one. Whatever impression you choose, carefully write your paragraph to present that impression clearly.

Concentrate on conveying a single, effective picture to the reader. In the Tolkien model, for example, the author creates a picture of a forbidding, polluted, "accursed land." He appeals to the reader's senses with images of dull fires, smoke, jagged rocks like fangs, and a "lake of darkness." The overall impression in the reader's mind is of a grim, tormented, and frightening landscape.

> **Grammar Tip**
>
> When you revise your writing, you can add vivid adjectives to help create a mood and draw a picture. Refer to Lesson 10.4, page 461.

Journal Writing

Think of a powerful scene in a book or movie—one that was incredibly beautiful, scary, or hilarious. In your journal jot down the overall impression, or mood, the scene conveyed. Make a list of the details in the scene that supported the overall impression.

3.1 Writing a Descriptive Paragraph

Vocabulary Tip

In the revising stage of your work, check to make sure the details you have used actually support your topic sentence.

Topic Sentence In a descriptive paragraph, the topic sentence should "overview" the scene and summarize the content of the paragraph. In doing so, it can also help establish the paragraph's mood. The rest of the paragraph should contain details that support the topic sentence. You might want to envision the parts of your paragraph like this.

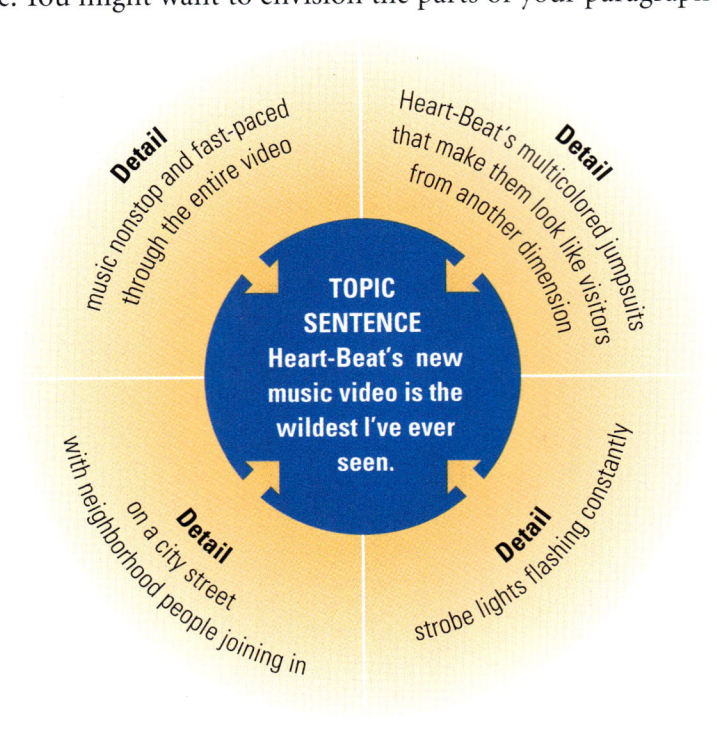

TOPIC SENTENCE
Heart-Beat's new music video is the wildest I've ever seen.

- **Detail**: music nonstop and fast-paced through the entire video
- **Detail**: Heart-Beat's multicolored jumpsuits that make them look like visitors from another dimension
- **Detail**: on a city street with neighborhood people joining in
- **Detail**: strobe lights flashing constantly

Notice that the topic sentence of the literature model on page 138 is at the very beginning of the paragraph. A topic sentence at or near the beginning of the paragraph lets the reader know what's coming. On the other hand, a topic sentence at or near the end of a paragraph, as in the model below, can summarize what you have just described.

Model

Ambassador Aleesa Aguilar entered the control room of the Galavian spacecraft, guided wordlessly by two of the craft's security officers. As the first earthling to meet the Galavians and to see a Galavian craft, she instinctively did a quick scan of her surroundings. A whirring sound directed her eyes to the far left of the brightly lit, cavernous white room. There she saw the "pilots," actually two androids—robots—who monitored the ship's course. Her experienced eyes next followed a series of about fifteen "space windows," computer screens that simulated the view off into space in fifteen directions. At five of these "windows" sat groups of

Galavians, as expressionless as the androids, rapidly making calculations and plotting courses. Then a sharp voice to her right blared "All rise," as the craft's commander entered. In these few seconds, the savvy Ambassador Aguilar learned much about these hard-working, severe, highly regimented aliens.

The topic sentence at the end summarizes the importance of this brief description.

Orient the Reader

In writing a descriptive paragraph, your goal is to transport the reader to the scene. Yet you must also help to orient the reader by providing a sense of direction and of where things are. Describing items in spatial order is one way to help orient the reader.

Spatial Order There are many kinds of spatial orders. For example, the Tolkien model on pages 138–139 uses near-to-far spatial order. The author begins by describing what lies nearest the character and proceeds to describe things farther and farther away. In fact, he follows the order your own eyes might follow if you were looking at the scene. Other ways your eyes might move include left to right (or right to left), as in the model on pages 140–141, and top to bottom (or bottom to top).

Prewriting Tip
Before you begin drafting, decide how you want to arrange the details in your description.

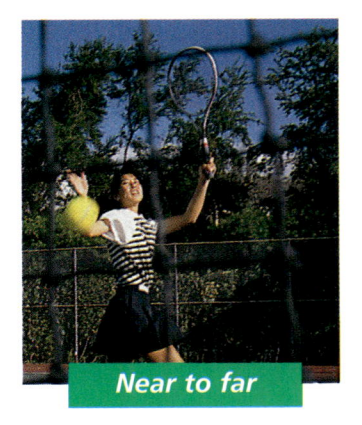

Near to far   **Left to right**   **Top to bottom**

Journal Writing

What are some other ways to look at and describe a scene? In your journal suggest two alternatives to spatial order. Then write a brief description of your room, the street you live on, or your school, using spatial order or one of your alternative suggestions.

3.1 Writing a Descriptive Paragraph   **141**

Grammar Tip

Many transitions begin with prepositions. To write more precisely as you draft, refer to the list of common prepositions in Lesson 10.6, page 473.

Transitions Transitions are words that connect one sentence or idea to the next and help show the relationship between the two—words like *before, then, next, under, in front of, to the right of,* and *inside.* In descriptive writing, transitions can help the reader keep track of where things are. What transitions might you use in describing the scene pictured below?

Nancy Thill

The model below, by Mary Stewart, is from a story about Merlin, teacher and friend of the legendary King Arthur. Notice how the author ties together her description with spatial-order transitions.

Literature Model

Stewart uses the following spatial-order transitions: "behind," "against," "over," "around," "in front," "a few paces away," "between," "above," "beyond," "to the peak," "at," "where we had seen."

At first, after the blaze of the guard-room, I could see nothing. I shut the door behind me and leaned back against the damp wall, while the night air poured over me like a river. Then things took shape around me. In front and a few paces away was a battlemented wall, waist high, the outer wall of the castle. Between this wall and where I stood was a level platform, and above me a wall rising again to a battlement, and beyond this the soaring cliff and the walls climbing it, and the shape of the fortress rising above me step by step to the peak of the promontory. At the very head of the rise, where we had seen the lighted window, the tower now showed black and lightless against the sky.

Mary Stewart, *The Crystal Cave*

3.1 Writing Activities

Write a Descriptive Paragraph

Imagine your school gymnasium or some other sports arena at night, after a game is over and the crowd has left. Write a one-paragraph description that gives the reader a clear visual picture of the place.

PURPOSE To describe a place and evoke a mood
AUDIENCE Other students
LENGTH 1 paragraph

WRITING RUBRICS To write a descriptive paragraph, you should

- decide what mood you want to create in the paragraph
- write a strong topic sentence
- orient the reader by presenting details in a logical order
- select precise transition words

Cross-Curricular Activity

ART Look closely at a painting in this textbook. How do the colors and form of the landscape or figures contribute to the painting's mood? Identify specific details in the painting, and write a paragraph that vividly describes the scene.

Grammar Link

Use prepositional phrases to show spatial relationships.

A **prepositional phrase** is made up of a preposition such as *under, over,* and *above* plus an object.

Revise the following sentences by adding at least one prepositional phrase to each sentence to clarify a spatial relationship.

1. The vase fell.
2. A flock of Canada geese flew.
3. There was a bright flash of lightning.
4. The artist painted.
5. The sun set and the moon rose.

See Lesson 12.1, page 519.

Viewing and Representing

COOPERATIVE LEARNING Complete the assignment outlined in the Cross-Curricular Activity. Then exchange papers within a small group. Try to sketch the painting a classmate has written about. How difficult is it to figure out exactly how the scene should look? What words or phrases help you? Next, look at the painting in the textbook together. What words or phrases would you now add to the description?

LESSON 3.2

Using Descriptive Language

In the model below, Madeleine L'Engle seems to choose just the right words to convey a feeling or a vision. Notice how she uses precise nouns and vivid modifiers to capture your attention and help you picture the experience she is describing.

Literature Model

She looked around rather wildly. They were standing in a sunlit field, and the air about them was moving with the delicious fragrance that comes only on the rarest of spring days when the sun's touch is gentle and the apple blossoms are beginning to unfold. She pushed her glasses up on her nose to reassure herself that what she was seeing was real.

They had left the silver glint of a biting autumn evening; and now around them everything was golden with light. The grasses of the field were a tender new green, and scattered about were tiny, multicolored flowers. Meg turned slowly to face a mountain reaching so high into the sky that its peak was lost in a crown of puffy white clouds. From the trees at the base of the mountain came a sudden singing of birds. There was an air of such ineffable peace and joy all around her that her heart's wild thumping slowed.

Madeleine L'Engle, *A Wrinkle in Time*

What is the combined effect of such phrases as "delicious fragrance," "when the sun's touch is gentle," and "golden with light"?

With the words "tender," "new," and "tiny," L'Engle suggests that the world she describes is innocent, unsullied, and young.

Claude Monet (1840–1926), *Arbres En Fleurs*

Choose Words for Their Connotations

Connotations are the feelings and the values readers usually associate with any given words—associations that go beyond the simple dictionary definition of the word. In her first paragraph, L'Engle writes of a "delicious fragrance." Why didn't she use the word *odor*, since *odor* and *fragrance* have the same basic meaning—smell? The answer is simple: most readers associate *odor* with an unpleasant smell and *fragrance* with an appealing one.

In choosing words for your descriptive writing, remember that many words come loaded with such connotations. Just as L'Engle chose "delicious fragrance," you should choose the best words you can find to re-create your vision.

Use Precise Nouns

Precise, vivid nouns are an important tool for re-creating your vision and making your writing more lively. By choosing nouns that are specific (*cloak*, for example) instead of general (*clothes*), you convey a clearer, more complete picture to your reader. The chart below shows some examples of nouns going from general to specific.

Nouns		
General	**Specific**	**More Specific**
monster	vampire	Count Dracula
animal	amphibian	bullfrog
rain	storm	hurricane

Grammar Tip

When drafting a description, you can refer to the material about concrete nouns in Lesson 10.1, page 439.

Journal Writing

How specific can you get? In your journal write the words *plant, machine, person, music, art, sport,* and *game* down the left side of one page. Next to each word, write as many nouns as you can think of that are increasingly specific examples of the general word.

3.2 Using Descriptive Language   **145**

Vocabulary Tip

When revising your writing, you can use a thesaurus to help you find more colorful and appropriate modifiers. A thesaurus lists words with their synonyms and antonyms.

Select Vivid Adjectives and Adverbs

Vivid modifiers—that is, adjectives and adverbs—can bring your descriptions to life. Make sure each word's connotation fits the impression you want to create. For example, a *shining* sword gives a different impression from a *blazing* one.

Don't settle for dull, overused modifiers, like *good* or *bad*. Select more colorful and original modifiers, such as *honorable* and *wicked*. Sometimes you may even want to use exaggeration to make your description more colorful. You might say, for example, "My date last night was horrendous—everything went wrong." For help finding more colorful and appropriate words, you can check the listings in a thesaurus.

Making Your Modifiers More Lively

funny	amusing	hilarious
heavy	weighty	ponderous
well	adequately	expertly

Here's how one student used precise nouns and lively modifiers in her writing. Notice how the carefully chosen words re-create an eerie scene from her imagination.

> Notice the dramatic effect created by "nightmarish," "looming shadow," and the narrator "flattened . . . against the far wall."

> What is the effect of the words "massive claws"? What impact does this effect have on the ending?

Student Model

It was after me again. I kept on running, my heart beating wildly. But it kept on coming, more determined than ever to catch me. I ran into a small hut near the end of the village, hoping I could find protection there; but the hut was empty and that horrible, nightmarish creature grew closer with every step. When I saw its looming shadow in the doorway, I flattened myself against the far wall. It came toward me, my screams for help growing louder with every step it took. Finally, it was but mere inches from my face. I closed my eyes and prayed for a quick demise. It reached slowly with its massive claws toward me and said, "You're it!"

Nikki Phipps,
Hamilton Heights High School, Arcadia, Indiana

3.2 Writing Activities

Write a Vivid Paragraph

Imagine you will write a story in which you wake up one day in an imaginary world. Write a paragraph describing the place. Perhaps you are inside a television or in your own house but you are only one inch tall.

PURPOSE To write a vivid description of a fantasy world
AUDIENCE Readers of a journal
LENGTH 1 paragraph

WRITING RUBRICS To write a vivid paragraph, you should

- use precise nouns
- select vivid modifiers
- choose words with connotations that help you express your meaning
- proofread for spelling, punctuation, and grammar

Using Computers

Use a word processing program to compose your descriptive paragraphs. Use its thesaurus feature to add lively modifiers as you revise your work.

Viewing and Representing

COOPERATIVE LEARNING In a small group, discuss the painting at the right. Identify specific details, such as the heart in the man's palm. Work together to come up with vivid and specific nouns and modifiers to describe these details. Then write individual paragraph descriptions of the scene. As a group, decide how best to present the paragraphs to the class.

Grammar Link

Use specific language to write effective descriptions.

Revise this descriptive paragraph, using precise nouns and adding vivid modifiers.

[1]They entered the woods at night. [2]Trees stood all around and blocked out the sky. [3]The air smelled. [4]As they walked farther, they could hear noises behind and beside them. [5]The ground under their feet felt soft. [6]Lights flickered ahead of them, then died. [7]Something flew into one girl's face. [8]Then they heard another sound and tried to run out of the woods.

See Lesson 10.1, page 439, Lesson 10.4, page 461, and Lesson 10.5, page 467.

Marc Chagall, *Paris Through the Window,* 1913

3.2 Using Descriptive Language **147**

LESSON 3.3

Describing an Imaginary Place

In the model below Ray Bradbury orders details to create a mood and allow the reader to picture an imaginary place.

Literature Model

They had a house of crystal pillars on the planet Mars by the edge of an empty sea, and every morning you could see Mrs. K eating the golden fruits that grew from the crystal walls, or cleaning the house with handfuls of magnetic dust which, taking all the dirt with it, blew away on the hot wind. Afternoons, when the fossil sea was warm and motionless, and the wine trees stood stiff in the yard, and the little distant Martian bone town was all enclosed, and no one drifted out of their doors, you could see Mr. K himself in his room, reading from a metal book with raised hieroglyphs over which he brushed his hand, as one might play a harp. And from the book, as his fingers stroked, a voice sang, a soft ancient voice, which told tales of when the sea was red steam on the shore and ancient men had carried clouds of metal insects and electrical spiders into battle.

Mr. and Mrs. K had lived by the dead sea for twenty years, and their ancestors had lived in the same house, which turned and followed the sun, flower-like, for ten centuries.

Mr. and Mrs. K were not old. They had the fair, brownish skin of the true Martian, the yellow coin eyes, the soft musical voices. Once they had liked painting pictures with chemical fire, swimming in the canals in the seasons when the wine trees filled them with green liquors, and talking into the dawn together by the blue phosphorus portraits in the speaking room.

Ray Bradbury, *The Martian Chronicles*

"Fossil sea," "motionless," "stiff," "bone town"—what is the overall feeling created by this description?

How does the order in which various activities are described contribute to the overall effect of the description?

Create Your Own Imaginary Place

You might already have an idea for an imaginary place. If not, try brainstorming, freewriting, or clustering to come up with an idea. A few words that might help you focus on imaginary places include *beneath, beyond, inside, before,* and *after.* Let your mind wander or simply let yourself wonder, "What would it be like there?" Look at something familiar, like your school, from a different point of view—such as through the eyes of a bug. Maybe one of the following topics will start you on the way to your own imaginary place:

fantasy lands	future societies	glacial caves
under the sea	behind the wall	a laboratory
an ancient castle	inside a chrysanthemum	alien planets

> **Grammar Tip**
>
> To explore the details of your imaginary place, think about vivid adjectives and adverbs that help evoke clear images. See Lessons 10.4 and 10.5, pages 461–472.

Explore Your Imaginary Place

Mentally exploring your imaginary place will help you see it in greater detail, and these details will enable you to describe the place to your reader. One good way to explore a place in detail is by asking and answering questions about it. What are its inhabitants like, if there are any? What can I see, hear, smell, feel, and taste here? What, if anything, does this place resemble? Don't be afraid to ask creative questions, such as the ones below.

Creative Questions and Answers

Q: What colors do I see here?
A: Neon-green atmosphere, acid-yellow swampland, and orange vines

Q: What do the inhabitants do for fun?
A: March stiffly in long lines around the main swamp

Q: What presents the greatest danger here?
A: Deadly purple vapors from the swamp

Q: What do the inhabitants eat?
A: Yellow vapors that spray from the swamp vines

Journal Writing

In your journal, list questions you could use to explore any imaginary place. Try to come up with questions about specific, even unusual, details of the place. Keep the list. You can use it when you begin planning and creating your own imaginary world or place.

> **Vocabulary Tip**
>
> As you revise, eliminate details that detract from the mood of your description. Do the sounds of your words help create the feeling you want? To review how to create mood, see Lesson 3.1, page 138.

Determine the Mood of Your Place

The description you write of your imaginary place will be more effective if it conveys a strong mood. Create a chart like the one below to help you come up with sensory details that will help you create a mood. Some of the most effective details are those that appeal to a reader's senses. What details can you add to the ones below?

Using Details to Create a Mood	
FEELING	**SAMPLE DETAILS**
loneliness	utter silence, dusty furniture, ticking clock, dead air, musty odors
mystery, horror	secret passages, distant moaning, creaking floors
excitement	fast pace, lively music, bright colors, laughter
warmth, safety	glowing lights, crackling fire, steaming tea kettle, soft cushions

Organize the Details of Your Place

After you've decided on what details you want to use to create a mood, the next step is to choose the method of organization that will best convey your description to the reader. What is the most important feature of the scene—a castle, a tree, clouds of purple mist? How does that feature relate to other details?

As you draft your description, follow the spatial order that works best for your scene. If, for example, a tree or tall building dominates the picture, top-to-bottom spatial order might work best. What kind of organization would you choose to describe the place pictured below?

3.3 Writing Activities

Describe a Scene

Write a paragraph describing a backyard barbecue from the point of view of a fly. In your description, include details that appeal to each of the five senses—sight, hearing, touch, taste, and smell. Taken together, the details should convey a single, specific mood or idea.

PURPOSE To write a description of a place from an unusual perspective
AUDIENCE Your classmates
LENGTH 1–2 paragraphs

WRITING RUBRICS To describe a scene, you should
- decide on the mood you wish to evoke
- select sensory details to convey the information
- use appropriate spatial order

Cross-Curricular Activity

MUSIC Music can evoke a scene or setting in one's imagination. Listen to a piece of classical or other instrumental music with your eyes closed. Then write a paragraph describing the setting the music evokes for you. Use specific sensory details in your description. You may wish to exchange papers with a classmate for peer review.

Listening and Speaking

COOPERATIVE LEARNING Working with a partner, choose a setting from real life or a book, movie, or TV show. Describe the scene to classmates. Then play a piece of music appropriate to the mood of the scene. Ask your classmates to identify the mood you tried to evoke. Discuss how important rhythm and repetition were to establishing the mood. What other elements do composers use to convey a mood?

Grammar Link

Use appositives to clarify.

An **appositive** is a noun or pronoun that follows another noun or pronoun to identify or give additional information:

*a house of crystal pillars on the planet **Mars***

Expand each of the following sentences. Add an appositive or an appositive phrase—an appositive plus a modifier or modifiers—to follow each italicized term. Remember to add commas where necessary—when the appositive is not essential to the meaning.

1. An excerpt from Ray Bradbury's *book* can be found on page 148.
2. Although the description is imagined, the reader can almost see the *place*.
3. The description of the place includes a description of some of its *inhabitants*.
4. The way the *author* arranges details that appeal to the senses helps evoke a mood.
5. One *character* liked to read.
6. His *wife* cleaned house with magnetic dust.
7. The inhabitants had lived by the dead sea a *long time*.
8. They used to have a *shared interest*.
9. The *book* is science fiction.
10. *Ray Bradbury* has a rich imagination.

See Lesson 12.2, page 521.

LESSON 3.4

Describing an Imaginary Person

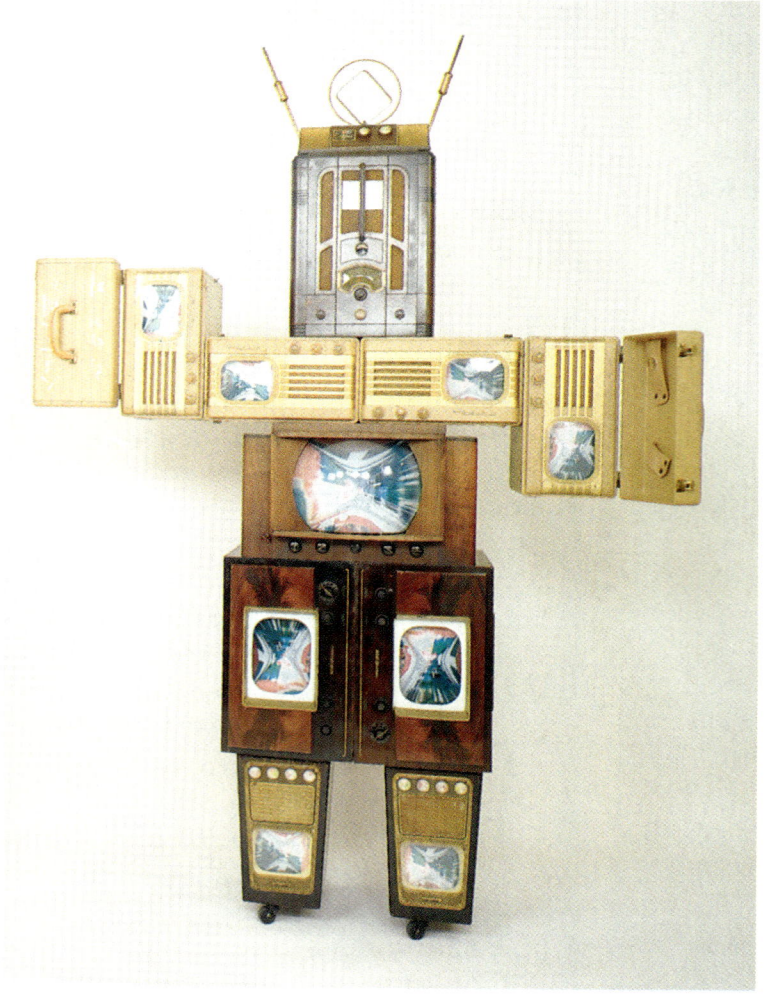

To describe a fictional character, first imagine the character. Then think up details of appearance, movement, or personality that will help bring that character to life.

Imagine a Character

To create an imaginary character, begin by deciding on the type of character you want to create. Your own imaginary character can be based on just about anything—from your wildest fantasy to someone you observe on the bus. Then ask yourself some creative questions to help develop details about your character. Questions like those in the chart below might help.

Nam June Paik, *Family of Robot: Grandfather*, 1986

Questions for Developing Character Details

1. What are my character's most prominent features?
2. How does my character move and communicate?
3. What trait or traits set my character apart from others?
4. Does my character's appearance fit his, her, or its personality?

152 Unit 3 Descriptive Writing

In the model below an aged woman from the imaginary town of Gont is trying to help a child. The observer, Tenar, has doubts about this woman.

Literature Model

Tenar was not at all sure what she wanted Aunty Moss to be, finding her unpredictable, unreliable, incomprehensible, passionate, ignorant, sly, and dirty. But Moss got on with the burned child. Perhaps it was Moss who was working this change, this slight easing, in Therru. With her, Therru behaved as with everyone—blank, unanswering, docile, in the way an inanimate thing, a stone, is docile. But the old woman had kept at her, offering her little sweets and treasures, bribing, coaxing, wheedling. "Come with Aunty Moss now, dearie! Come along and Aunty Moss'll show you the prettiest sight you ever saw. . . ."

Moss's nose leaned out over her toothless jaws and thin lips; there was a wart on her cheek the size of a cherry pit; her hair was a gray-black tangle of charm-knots and wisps; and she had a smell as strong and broad and deep and complicated as the smell of a fox's den. "Come into the forest with me, dearie!" said the old witches in the tales told to the children of Gont. "Come with me and I'll show you such a pretty sight!" And then the witch shut the child in her oven and baked it brown and ate it, or dropped it into her well, where it hopped and croaked dismally forever, or put it to sleep for a hundred years inside a great stone, till the King's son should come, the Mage Prince, to shatter the stone with a word, wake the maiden with a kiss, and slay the wicked witch. . . .

"Come with me, dearie!" And she took the child into the fields and showed her a lark's nest in the green hay, or into the marshes to gather white hallows, wild mint, and blueberries.

Ursula K. LeGuin, *Tehanu: The Last Book of Earthsea*

> LeGuin contrasts unpleasant aspects of Moss's appearance with her good side, both here and later in the selection.

> What is the picture of Aunty Moss created by such details as "toothless jaws," "thin lips," and "gray-black tangle"?

> By contrasting Moss's behavior with that typically attributed to witches, LeGuin helps us to see her more as an individual than as a stereotype.

Journal Writing

In your journal describe a fantasy or science-fiction character with whom you are familiar. Explain how the character's personality does or does not fit his or her appearance.

Make a Character Come to Life

If you were to describe your best friend, you would probably mention your friend's looks and personality. You might also note some of your friend's unique quirks, strengths, or habits. Such details would help other people to see your friend as you do.

When describing an imaginary character, use these same kinds of details to make your character come to life. The details that are most unusual or most inconsistent with the rest of the description will do the most to make your character real. Such details will help give your character a three-dimensional quality. In addition, inconsistencies will tend to arouse your reader's curiosity. Aunty Moss, in the model on page 153, is interesting because she seems to look like a witch, but she does not behave as we might expect a witch to behave.

Here's a character description from the imagination of student Todd Crusey. How does he bring life to his character? Think about what inconsistencies you might add to make the character more interesting, yet still believable.

> **Grammar Tip**
>
> When editing a character sketch, make sure you have used pronouns correctly. See Lessons 17.5 and 17.6, pages 640–647.

> How would you describe the overall impression created by sensory details such as sweat rolling down his forehead "like an avalanche" and "the carved stones he called hands"?

> Crusey holds our interest by describing the character but waiting until the very end to reveal his identity.

Student Model

Sweat rolled like an avalanche down his broad, sloping forehead. It collected on the ledge of his square jutting brow and was then absorbed by the dense brown forest of his eyebrows. Slowly the perspiration dripped down into the large sockets that housed his squinting onyx eyes. From his hollow temples ran a flood of exhaustion that made his whole face glisten in the dark amber light of the prison wall. His nose was a wide, flat wedge, beaten down by the fists of over a hundred men. From his broad shoulders to the carved stones he called hands, he was a warrior. He had done battle in countless brawls and riots and had the scars to show for it. His only reward was his heartbeat; he had survived. This mean and relentless beast of a man always prevailed and was feared by all sane men. That's why they brought him here. Within these prison walls he reigned. He was truly a giant; he made the rules and he had the power to enforce them. That's why they called him warden.

Todd Crusey, Jefferson Davis High School,
Montgomery, Alabama

154 Unit 3 Descriptive Writing

3.4 Writing Activities

Write About an Imaginary Person

Observe someone while you are riding on a bus, looking out your window, or from another location of your choice. Take notes on the person's appearance, and use your notes to create a description of an imaginary person you could later include in a short story.

PURPOSE To create an imaginary person based on a real one
AUDIENCE Your teacher and classmates
LENGTH 1–2 paragraphs

WRITING RUBRICS To describe an imaginary person, you should

- list unique physical traits
- create possible personality quirks
- describe inconsistencies between appearance and personality

Cross-Curricular Activity

HISTORY Choose a historical work of art from your history book. In a group, brainstorm to come up with details that describe the character in the painting. What does the environment add to your perceptions of the character? After each person writes a one-paragraph description, combine the paragraphs into a group description.

Grammar Link

Use correct forms of verbs.

Write the correct form of the verb in parentheses to complete each sentence.

1. When you edit your character sketch, make sure that you have (do) all you can to bring the character to life.
2. The details Ursula K. LeGuin used in writing about Aunty Moss (bring) the character to life.
3. I have (feel) that I've known many of the characters I've read about.
4. I also have (write) about characters I have created myself.
5. Some of these imaginary characters (begin) to seem like friends as I wrote about them.

See Lesson 15.2, page 582.

Listening and Speaking

SPELLING Homophones are words that sound the same but have different meanings and usually different spellings. The spelling checker feature on your computer will not detect a wrong word choice. Common homophones include *allowed* and *aloud*, *band* and *banned*, *cent* and *scent*, *council* and *counsel*. Create a strategy for checking to be sure that you have used the correct homophone. One idea is to exchange papers with a peer and have your writings read aloud. The reader is likely to notice the difference between what is written and what is meant.

LESSON 3.5

WRITING ABOUT LITERATURE
Analyzing Character Descriptions

When you write to analyze a character in literature, pay attention to what you can learn from the character's physical appearance, thoughts, words, and actions.

One student writer chose a dragon to describe. The dragon is a character from "The Rule of Names" by science-fiction writer Ursula K. LeGuin. As you read the model below, notice the aspects of the dragon that Arthur Housinger focuses on.

Student Model

One common desire links one living being to another, to be happy. Some find happiness with friends and money. In this respect, the dragon in "The Rule of Names," Yevaud, was no different from a man. He was a slightly egocentric being who just wanted some friends and some treasure.

Yevaud showed his egocentricity several times. As Blackbeard told Birt, Yevaud attacked the island of Pendor and killed many men just so he could have a treasure all for himself. After one hundred years, he ran away from the island with the treasure. He locked it in his inner chamber at Sattins Island.

Yevaud knew that this would not be enough to ensure happiness, but he had a few more tricks up his sleeve. First, he changed his appearance. Yevaud knew the unfortunate truth that people often judge a book by its cover; therefore, he changed his cover to a "little fat man of fifty who waddled along with his toes turned in." By changing his appearance, Yevaud, also known as Mr. Underhill, not only made a few friends, but he covered his tracks as the thief of the treasure.

> Housinger notes the importance of this character's change in appearance.

Blackbeard accurately called him a "wise, cunning monster, full of strength and subtlety."

Yevaud's tricks lacked perfection, though, just as many of his elixirs did. Since Yevaud was constantly showing a false front, a barrier came between him and the villagers. His smiles were even false and made the village girls feel nervous. Yet since he was such a bumbling wizard, the townspeople simply treated Mr. Underhill as a fellow villager. This too was a falsehood, as was shown when Yevaud used his great powers to fight Blackbeard.

Yevaud tried to be something he wasn't, a friendly, inept wizard called Mr. Underhill. Once this barrier of deceit disappeared, Yevaud's true self, along with his true name, could spread its wings. Although Blackbeard's description of Yevaud was accurate, it was not complete. Yevaud was also a friendly being who found a home where he felt comfortable, one who wanted friends and treasure.

Arthur Housinger, Rich East High School,
Park Forest, Illinois

> Here Housinger shows the villagers' reactions to Yevaud/Underhill.

> Housinger next analyzes Yevaud/Underhill's actions and how these actions affected other characters.

Consider a Character's Appearance

A character's physical appearance can suggest a great deal about the nature and background of the person. In "The Rule of Names," for example, the details of the main character's appearance are especially significant, because they hint at his true nature and background.

The order and way in which these physical details are presented may also be important. An author may put the most important facts about a character first, or describe them in the greatest detail so as to impress them upon you. In *Robin Hood: Prince of Thieves,* for example, novelist Simon Green first describes Robin Hood's friend Azeem as follows: "Tall and heavily muscled, he had dark skin covered with intricate tattoos. Even his shaved head was ornamented with them." Thus, Green emphasizes Azeem's strength and his exotic quality, suggesting that these are important features. As the story unfolds, readers learn that these are, in fact, among the most important things to know and remember about Azeem.

Presenting Tip

When you present your description orally, you can create or emphasize a mood with vocal techniques such as lowering your voice, or drawing out a phrase or word.

Journal Writing

In your journal jot phrases to describe someone you know. Circle the most significant details.

Note Thoughts, Words, and Actions

Because a character's thoughts, words, and actions might not always be consistent with his or her appearance, you should consider all information you have about the character. For example, although Azeem looks like a powerful and exotic person, his thoughts, words, and actions reveal him also to be a loyal, honorable, and loving friend.

Thoughts	Words	Actions	Conclusion
"Not for the first time, Azeem realized he was a long way from home, and those he had loved."	"It is because I love them so dearly that I cannot dishonor them by breaking my vow."	"Azeem examined Fanny's swollen belly… and then looked at her compassionately." He then delivered Fanny's baby.	These thoughts, words, and actions indicate that Azeem is a loving, loyal, and compassionate man.

Revising Tip

When you revise, look for places where you might strengthen your draft by adding details about a character's appearance, thoughts, words, and/or actions. Use quotations from the literature to support your ideas.

When you analyze a character's thoughts, words, and actions, you may want to ask yourself how you feel about what the character says and does. You might also ask such questions as these: How would I feel around this person? What qualities does this character have that I admire or dislike? Asking and answering such questions will help you get to "know" the character personally and will help make your writing about the character fresh and stimulating.

Think About Reactions of Other Characters

An author can also reveal much about a character by showing how other people react to that character. Be aware of these reactions as you analyze a character, but be sure to consider the nature of each person who is doing the reacting too. For example, the character's enemies would naturally dislike him or her, while the character's friends would be biased in his or her favor. The reactions of either group should be analyzed. The chart below shows two reactions to Azeem. Which do you think shows the truer picture?

Reaction A
Robin Hood tells his men his opinion of Azeem: "I trust him."

Reactions to Azeem

Reaction B
Friar Tuck and the others distrust Azeem because his ways are so different from their own.

158 Unit 3 Descriptive Writing

3.5 Writing Activities

Write a Character Analysis

Select a character from one of the books or stories mentioned in this unit, or from another work you know and like. Imagine that the character was a dinner guest in your home last night. Write in your journal about your family's reactions to the character as well as any discussions or activities that may have happened during the evening.

PURPOSE To analyze a character from literature who has been put in another setting
AUDIENCE Yourself
LENGTH 3–4 paragraphs

WRITING RUBRICS To write a character analysis, you should

- describe the character's appearance
- analyze his or her words and actions
- describe the reactions of others to the character

Using Computers

You can help organize the details for your character analysis with the help of your word processor. Type in each significant detail you discover about the character. Hit the return key after each note you type. Then you can later rearrange your details without having to retype the pieces of information into your file. You can use each detail wherever you want as you develop your writing structure.

Grammar Link

Make pronoun references clear.

When you write to analyze a character, use clear, consistent, and unambiguous pronoun references.

Rewrite the sentences below to correct each unclear pronoun reference.

1. Arthur writes about Yevaud and Blackbeard, and he says that he called him a "wise, cunning monster."
2. Yevaud and Mr. Underhill are really the same character, because he turns himself into him.
3. When writers describe characters, they should make them come alive.
4. Azeem, who was a friend of Robin Hood, had an exotic appearance, and he told his men his opinion of him.
5. It is important to write clearly when you analyze a character one has read about.

See Lesson 17.6, page 645.

Viewing and Representing

EVALUATING A CHARACTER Create a poster of a favorite character who undergoes a physical transformation. Create a before-and-after illustration. For both pictures, identify distinctive physical features of the character. Write two or three sentences that describe the character's thoughts and actions and note any changes that they undergo. Compare your illustration with an illustration of the character in a book or on a Web site.

UNIT 3
Writing Process in Action

Descriptive Writing

In preceding lessons you've learned about describing imaginary places and characters and about the kinds of words and details that can make descriptions effective. You've also had a chance to write your own descriptive paragraphs. Now it's time to make use of what you have learned. In this lesson you're invited to create a place in your imagination and then describe it. This place may be one that could actually exist in this world or it may be an entirely fantastical place—one that's out of this world.

WRITING Online

Visit the *Writer's Choice* Web site at **writerschoice. glencoe.com**, and click on additional writing prompts.

Assignment

Context

You are a staff writer for *Vicarious Voyager,* a magazine filled with descriptive writing that lets "even dedicated couch potatoes expand their horizons." You have been asked to write an article describing an imagined place. Focus on describing personal impressions and sensations.

Purpose

To write a description of a place you've imagined that is so vivid that it helps readers feel transported there

Audience

Teenagers who want the experience of visiting new places

Length

1–2 pages

The following pages can help you plan and write your description. Read through them and then refer to them as you need to—but don't be tied down by them. You're in charge of your own writing process.

Writing Process in Action

Prewriting

What kind of place will you be describing—an exotic country, an alien wilderness, a landscape that might exist on the head of a pin? Use a place that you think up yourself, or review the literature models in this unit for possible ideas. Then start exploring your place by mentally wandering through it. The prewriting questions shown here may help you get started.

As you wander, write down your impressions, using as many sensory details as you can. Think, too, about the mood you want to create and what details you could accentuate to convey this mood. In the model below, T. H. White creates a sense of nostalgia in his description of an imaginary castle by using details that describe not only the ruins, but also the living things that still inhabit them.

Prewriting Questions
- What type of place is it?
- Who or what lives here, if anything?
- What do the inhabitants do?
- Do natural laws as we know them hold here?
- What is the overall mood of the place?

Literature Model

The castle of the Forest Sauvage is still standing, and you can see its lovely ruined walls with ivy on them, standing broached to the sun and wind. Some lizards live there now, and the starving sparrows keep warm on summer nights in the ivy, and a barn owl drives it methodically, hovering outside the frightened congregations and beating the ivy with its wings, to make them fly out. Most of the curtain wall is down, though you can trace the foundations of the twelve round towers which guarded it....

T. H. White, *The Once and Future King*

TIME For more about the writing process, see **TIME Facing the Blank Page**, pp. 121–131.

Drafting

To begin drafting, think of a likely place of entry to your scene. One approach is to choose a spot from which you could easily orient your readers to the surroundings. For example, you could be crouched behind a door, or you might be up on a hill, with an overview of a whole scene below.

Writing Process in Action

Drafting Tip

For more information about using spatial order, see Lesson 3.1, page 138.

Now visualize your place from your chosen point of entry and, using your prewriting notes, begin drafting. Don't stop writing just to find the absolutely "right word." For now, just keep your ideas flowing.

As you may have done in prewriting, you can let your "journey" be guided by your reaction to various sensations, or you can use one of these methods of organization:

- **Spatial order** To organize details spatially, describe all of the elements in a place by their location as you perceive them—top to bottom, left to right, or front to back.
- **Order of importance** Start by describing key details and then move on to less important ones. This method works well if your readers need to grasp certain basic elements of your world first.

Once you have everything down on paper, even if you're not totally happy with how you said it, put your draft aside. A few hours' or even a day's time away from it can help you see its strengths and weaknesses more clearly.

Revising

To begin revising, read over your draft to make sure that what you've written fits your purpose and audience. Then have a **writing conference.** Read your draft to a partner or small group. Use your audience's reactions to help you evaluate your work.

Revising Tip

For help with transitions and word choice, see Lesson 3.1 and Lesson 3.2, pages 138–147.

Revising Checklist

- Have I used details consistently to establish and maintain a believable reality and mood?
- Do I keep to the same kind of order throughout the description?
- Would adding transitional words and phrases help orient my readers?
- Are my nouns and modifiers carefully and precisely chosen?

Writing Process in Action

Editing/Proofreading

Once you are happy with the basic content and set-up of your description, **proofread** it carefully for errors in grammar, usage, mechanics, and spelling. Use the questions at the right as a guide.

In addition to proofreading, use the self-evaluation list below to make sure your description does all the things you want it to do. When you're satisfied, make a clean copy of your description and proofread it one more time.

Editing/Proofreading Checklist

- Have I used appositives and phrases correctly?
- Have I used precise nouns and modifiers?
- Are my pronoun references clear?
- Are all my verb forms and tenses correct?
- Have I checked spellings of any words I'm unsure of?

Self-Evaluation

Make sure your description—

✔ focuses on an imagined place
✔ orients readers by presenting details in logical order
✔ uses vivid sensory details and appropriate figurative language
✔ uses first-person point of view consistently
✔ follows correct grammar, usage, mechanics, and spelling

Publishing/Presenting

You can use the descriptions that you and your classmates have written to create your own magazine of travel writing. Form an editorial board to select the best descriptions based on the criteria in the text; then create a cover, a table of contents, and an introduction for your collection, and make it available for others to read.

Proofreading Tip

For proofreading symbols, see page 411. Use the spelling checker and grammar checker features on the computer to catch and correct errors.

Journal Writing

Reflect on your writing process experience. Answer these questions in your journal: What do you like best about your description? What was the hardest part of writing it? What did you learn in your writing conference? What new things have you learned as a writer?

UNIT 3

Literature Model

Descriptive Writing

from

The Crystal Cave

by Mary Stewart

In The Crystal Cave, *Mary Stewart vividly describes the world of King Arthur's sixth-century England through the eyes of the magician Merlin. She calls these imaginative stories "somewhere between legend and truth and fairy tale and known history." As you read, pay special attention to Stewart's effective use of descriptive language. Then try the activities in Linking Writing and Literature on page 172.*

Literature Model

This was bigger than had appeared from outside. Only a couple of paces inside the archway—and my paces were very short—the cave opened out into a seemingly vast chamber whose top was lost in shadow. It was dark, but—though at first I neither noticed this nor looked for its cause—with some source of extra light that gave a vague illumination, showing the floor smooth and clear of obstacles. I made my way slowly forward, straining my eyes, with deep inside me the beginning of that surge of excitement that caves have always started in me. Some men experience this with water; some, I know, on high places; some create fire for the same pleasure: with me it has always been the depths of the forest, or the depths of the earth. Now, I know why; but then, I only knew that I was a boy who had found somewhere new, something he could perhaps make his own in a world where he owned nothing.

Next moment I stopped short, brought up by a shock which spilled the excitement through my bowels like water. Something had moved in the murk, just to my right.

I froze still, straining my eyes to see. There was no movement. I held my breath, listening. There was no sound. I flared my nostrils, testing the air cautiously round me. There was no smell, animal or human; the cave smelt, I thought, of smoke and damp rock and the earth itself, and of a queer musty scent I couldn't identify. I knew, without putting it into words, that had there been any other creature near me the air would have felt different, less empty. There was no one there.

I tried a word, softly, in Welsh. "Greetings." The whisper came straight back at me in an echo so quick that I knew I was very near the wall of the cave, then it lost itself, hissing, in the roof.

There was movement there—at first, I thought, only an intensifying of the echoed whisper, then the rustling grew and grew like the rustling of a woman's dress, or a curtain stirring in the draft. Something went past my cheek, with a shrill, bloodless cry just on the edge of sound. Another followed, and after them flake after flake of shrill shadow, pouring down from the roof like leaves down a stream of wind, or fish down a fall. It was the bats, disturbed from their lodging in the top of the cave, streaming out now into the daylight valley. They would be pouring out of the low archway like a plume of smoke.

I stood quite still, wondering if it was these that had made the curious musty smell. I thought I could smell them as they passed, but it wasn't the same. I had no fear that they would touch me; in darkness or light, whatever their speed, bats will touch nothing. They are so much creatures of the air, I believe, that as the air parts in front of an obstacle the bat is swept aside with it, like a petal carried downstream. They poured past, a shrill tide of them between me and the wall. Childlike, to see what the stream would do—how it would divert itself—I took a step nearer to the wall. Nothing touched me. The stream divided

> *Something went past my cheek, with a shrill, bloodless cry just on the edge of sound.*

Literature Model **165**

Literature Model

and poured on, the shrill air brushing both my cheeks. It was as if I did not exist. But at the same moment when I moved, the creature that I had seen moved, too. Then my outstretched hand met, not rock, but metal, and I knew what the creature was. It was my own reflection.

Hanging against the wall was a sheet of metal, burnished[1] to a dull sheen. This, then, was the source of the diffused[2] light within the cave; the mirror's silky surface caught, obliquely,[3] the light from the cave's mouth, and sent it on into the darkness. I could see myself moving in it like a ghost, as I recoiled[4] and let fall the hand which had leapt to the knife at my hip.

Behind me the flow of bats had ceased, and the cave was still. Reassured, I stayed where I was, studying myself with interest in the mirror. My mother had had one once, an antique from Egypt, but then, deeming such things to be vanity, she had locked it away. Of course I had often seen my face reflected in water, but never my body mirrored, till now. I saw a dark boy, wary, all eyes with curiosity, nerves, and excitement. In that light my eyes looked quite black; my hair was black, too, thick and clean, but worse cut and groomed than my pony's; my tunic and sandals were a disgrace. I grinned, and the mirror flashed a sudden smile that changed the picture completely and at once, from a sullen young animal poised to run or fight, to something quick and gentle and approachable; something, I knew even then, that few people had ever seen.

Then it vanished, and the wary animal was back, as I leaned forward to run a hand over the metal. It was cold and smooth and freshly burnished. Whoever had hung it—and he must be the same person who used the cup of horn[5] outside—had either been here very recently, or he still lived here, and might come back at any moment to find me.

I was not particularly frightened. I had pricked to caution when I saw the cup, but one learns very young to take care of oneself, and the times I had been brought up in were peaceful enough, at any rate in our valley; but there are always wild men and rough men and the lawless and vagabonds to be reckoned with, and any boy who likes his own company, as I did, must be prepared to defend his skin. I was wiry, and strong for my age, and I had my dagger. That I was barely seven years old never entered my head; I was Merlin, and, bastard or not, the King's grandson. I went on exploring.

The next thing I found, a pace along the wall, was a box, and on top of it shapes which my hands identified immediately as flint and iron and tinderbox,[6] and a big, roughly made candle of what smelled like

I grinned, and the mirror flashed a sudden smile that changed the picture completely and at once . . .

---

1 **burnished** (bur′ nisht) polished
2 **diffused** (di fūsd′) spread out in every direction
3 **obliquely** (ə blēk′ lē) indirectly
4 **recoiled** (ri koild′) fell back
5 **cup of horn** a cup made from an animal's horn
6 **tinderbox** (tin′ dər boks′) a metal box holding the materials to make a fire

Literature Model

sheep's tallow.[7] Beside these objects lay a shape which—incredulously and inch by inch—I identified as the skull of a horned sheep. There were nails driven into the top of the box here and there, apparently holding down fragments of leather. But when I felt these, carefully, I found in the withered leather frameworks of delicate bone; they were dead bats, stretched and nailed on the wood.

This was a treasure cave indeed. No find of gold or weapons could have excited me more. Full of curiosity, I reached for the tinderbox.

Then I heard him coming back.

My first thought was that he must have seen my pony, then I realized he was coming from further up the hill. I could hear the rattling and scaling of small stones as he came down the scree[8] above the cave. One of them splashed into the spring outside, and then it was too late. I heard him jump down on the flat grass beside the water.

It was time for the ring-dove again; the falcon was forgotten.[9] I ran deeper into the cave. As he swept aside the boughs[10] that

---

7 tallow (tal′ ō) animal fat used to make candles

8 scree (skrē) a slope covered with rock fragments

9 It was time for the ring-dove again; the falcon was forgotten. Unlike the ferocious falcon, the ring-dove was a bird that kept quiet and knew when to run away. While Young Merlin was often called "falcon," one character had told him that he was still a ring-dove.

10 boughs (bouz) tree branches

John James Audubon (1785–1851), *Labrador Falcon*

Literature Model **167**

Literature Model

darkened the entrance, the light grew momentarily, enough to show me my way. At the back of the cave was a slope and jut of rock, and, at twice my height, a widish ledge. A quick flash of sunlight from the mirror caught a wedge of shadow in the rock above the ledge, big enough to hide me. Soundless in my scuffed sandals, I swarmed on to the ledge, and crammed my body into that wedge of shadow, to find it was in fact a gap in the rock, giving apparently on to another, smaller cave. I slithered in through the gap like an otter into the river-bank.

It seemed that he had heard nothing. The light was cut off again as the boughs sprang back into place behind him, and he came into the cave. It was a man's tread, measured and slow.

If I had thought about it at all, I suppose I would have assumed that the cave would be uninhabited at least until sunset, that whoever owned the place would be away hunting, or about his other business, and would return only at nightfall. There was no point in wasting candles when the sun was blazing outside. Perhaps he was here now only to bring home his kill, and he would go again and leave me the chance to get out. I hoped he would not see my pony tethered[11] in the hawthorn brake.[12]

Then I heard him moving, with the sure tread of someone who knows his way blindfold, towards the candle and the tinderbox.

Even now I had no room for apprehension,[13] no room, indeed, for any but the one thought or sensation—the extreme discomfort of the cave into which I had crawled. It was apparently small, not much bigger than the large round vats they use for dyeing, and much the same shape. Floor, wall and ceiling hugged me round in a continuous curve. It was like being inside a large globe; moreover, a globe studded with nails, or with its inner surface stuck all over with small pieces of jagged stone. There seemed no inch of surface not bristling like a bed of strewn flints, and it was only my light weight, I think, that saved me from being cut, as I quested about blindly to find some clear space to lie on. I found a place smoother than the rest and curled there, as small as I could, watching the faintly defined opening, and inching my dagger silently from its sheath into my hand.

Light poured and flashed, crimson, golden, white, red, intolerable into my cave.

I heard the quick hiss and chime of flint and iron, and then the flare of light, intense in the darkness, as the tinder caught hold. Then the steady, waxing[14] glow as he lit the candle.

Or rather, it should have been the slow-growing beam of a candle flame that I saw, but instead there was a flash, a sparkle, a conflagration[15] as if a whole pitch-soaked beacon was roaring up in flames. Light poured and flashed, crimson, golden, white, red, intolerable into my cave. I winced back from it, frightened now, heedless of pain and cut flesh as I shrank against the sharp

---

11 tethered (teth′ ərd) tied with a rope or chain
12 brake (brāk) a thicket
13 apprehension (ap′ ri hen′ shən) dread
14 waxing (waks′ ing) slowly growing larger
15 conflagration (kän′ flə grā′ shən) an enormous fire

Literature Model

walls. The whole globe where I lay seemed to be full of flame.

It was indeed a globe, a round chamber floored, roofed, lined with crystals. They were fine as glass, and smooth as glass, but clearer than any glass I had ever seen, brilliant as diamonds. This, in fact, to my childish mind, was what they first seemed to be. I was in a globe lined with diamonds, a million burning diamonds, each face of each gem wincing with the light, shooting it to and fro, diamond to diamond and back again, with rainbows and rivers and bursting stars and a shape like a crimson dragon clawing up the wall, while below it a girl's face swam faintly with closed eyes, and the light drove right into my body as if it would break me open.

I shut my eyes. When I opened them again I saw that the golden light had shrunk and was concentrated on one part of the wall no bigger than my head, and from this, empty of visions, rayed the broken, brilliant beams.

There was silence from the cave below. He had not stirred. I had not even heard the rustle of his clothes.

Then the light moved. The flashing disc began to slide, slowly, across the crystal wall. I was shaking. I huddled closer to the sharp stones, trying to escape it. There was nowhere to go. It advanced slowly round the curve. It touched my shoulder, my head, and I ducked, cringing. The shadow of my movement rushed across the globe, like a wind-eddy[16] over a pool.

The light stopped, retreated, fixed

> *The light stopped, retreated, fixed glittering in its place. Then it went out.*

glittering in its place. Then it went out. But the glow of the candle, strangely, remained; an ordinary steady yellow glow beyond the gap in the wall of my refuge.

"Come out." The man's voice, not loud, not raised with shouted orders like my grandfather's, was clear and brief with all the mystery of command. It never occurred to me to disobey. I crept forward over the sharp crystals, and through the gap. Then I slowly pulled myself upright on the ledge, my back against the wall of the outer cave, the dagger ready in my right hand, and looked down.

He stood between me and the candle, a hugely tall figure (or so it seemed to me) in a long robe of some brown homespun stuff. The candle made a nimbus[17] of his hair, which seemed to be grey, and he was bearded. I could not see his expression, and his right hand was hidden in the folds of his robe.

I waited, poised warily.

He spoke again, in the same tone. "Put up your dagger and come down."

"When I see your right hand," I said.

He showed it, palm up. It was empty. He said gravely: "I am unarmed."

"Then stand out of my way," I said, and jumped. The cave was wide, and he was standing to one side of it. My leap carried me three or four paces down the cave, and I was past him and near the entrance before he could have moved more than a step. But in fact he never moved at all. As I reached

---

16 wind-eddy (wind ed′ ē) a current of wind
17 nimbus (nim′ bəs) a bright cloud or aura surrounding a person or object

Literature Model

Peter Paul Rubens (1577–1640), *Portrait of an Old Man*

the mouth of the cave and swept aside the hanging branches I heard him laughing.

    The sound brought me up short. I turned. From here, in the light which now filled the cave, I saw him clearly. He was old, with grey hair thinning on top and hanging lank over his ears, and a straight growth of grey beard, roughly trimmed. His hands were calloused and grained with dirt, but had been fine, with long fingers. Now the

Literature Model

old man's veins crawled and knotted on them, distended[18] like worms. But it was his face which held me; it was thin, cavernous almost as a skull, with a high domed forehead and bushy grey brows which came down jutting over eyes where I could see no trace of age at all. These were closely set, large, and of a curiously clear and swimming grey. His nose was a thin beak; his mouth, lipless now, stretched wide with his laughter over astonishingly good teeth.

"Come back. There's no need to be afraid."

"I'm not afraid." I dropped the boughs back into place, and not without bravado[19] walked towards him. I stopped a few paces away. "Why should I be afraid of you? Do you know who I am?"

> "Come back. There's no need to be afraid."

He regarded me for a moment, seeming to muse. "Let me see you. Dark hair, dark eyes, the body of a dancer and the manners of a young wolf . . . or should I say a young falcon?"

My dagger sank to my side. "Then you do know me?"

"Shall I say I knew you would come some day, and today I knew there was someone here. What do you think brought me back so early?"

---

18 distended (dis tend′ əd) swollen
19 bravado (brə vä′ dō) pretended confidence or courage

Literature Model

Linking Writing and Literature

Readers Respond to the Model

What makes Mary Stewart's descriptions effective?

Explore Mary Stewart's descriptions by answering these questions. Then read what other students liked about Stewart's descriptions.

1. Mary Stewart's description of a child's experience is told from an adult character's memories of that experience. How does that perspective affect the telling of the story?
2. How did you react when you read the line "Then I heard him coming back"? What descriptive words caused you to have this reaction?
3. Choose a descriptive paragraph from the selection that you particularly like. What specific words or images make this description work?

What Students Say

"I always enjoy exploration type scenes, so the scene during which the boy explores the cave was the one I liked most. The dominant mood was one of curiosity and suspicion. The writer created that mood by making all things very odd or at least out of the ordinary. The meeting of the old man and the boy seemed for a second to be the end for one of them.

The old man is the sort of character I usually enjoy. He laughs at the over-inventive and imaginative people. He is quite likely a cynic. The scene in which the boy, Merlin, met the old man was by far the most memorable."

Charles Dayton

"The owner of the cave had an easy-going, relaxed feeling about him. He laughed when he saw the kid running out instead of being angry for his being there. Stewart made the old man seem real by giving such a detailed description of his face and of what he did each moment. I also liked the description Stewart gave of the moment when the man lit the candle and the "diamonds" were sparkling brightly."

Yahna Awazu

UNIT 3 Review

Reflecting on the Unit

Summarize what you learned in this unit by answering the following questions.

1. What are the important elements of a well-written descriptive paragraph?
2. In what ways does word choice affect the quality of descriptive writing?
3. What are the important aspects of describing an imaginary place? Of creating a convincing character?
4. What are some things to keep in mind when you analyze a fictional character?

Adding to Your Portfolio

Follow this procedure to choose selections for your portfolio. Look over the descriptive writing you have done during this unit. Select a completed piece of writing to put into your portfolio. The writing you choose should show some or all of the following:

- descriptive details that contain a strong overall impression
- precise, vivid language that has the appropriate connotations
- a well-defined mood
- attributes that convey a character's uniqueness

REFLECT ON YOUR CHOICE Attach a note to the piece you chose, explaining briefly why you chose it and what you learned from it.

SET GOALS How can you improve your writing? What skill will you focus on the next time you write?

Writing Across the Curriculum

MAKE A GEOGRAPHY CONNECTION Decide on a real country in which you'd like to situate the imaginary place you just wrote about. Choose the country because of such things as its climate and terrain, its political system, or any other factors you think are relevant. Then write a paragraph explaining some of the attributes of the country that made you think your imaginary place belongs there.

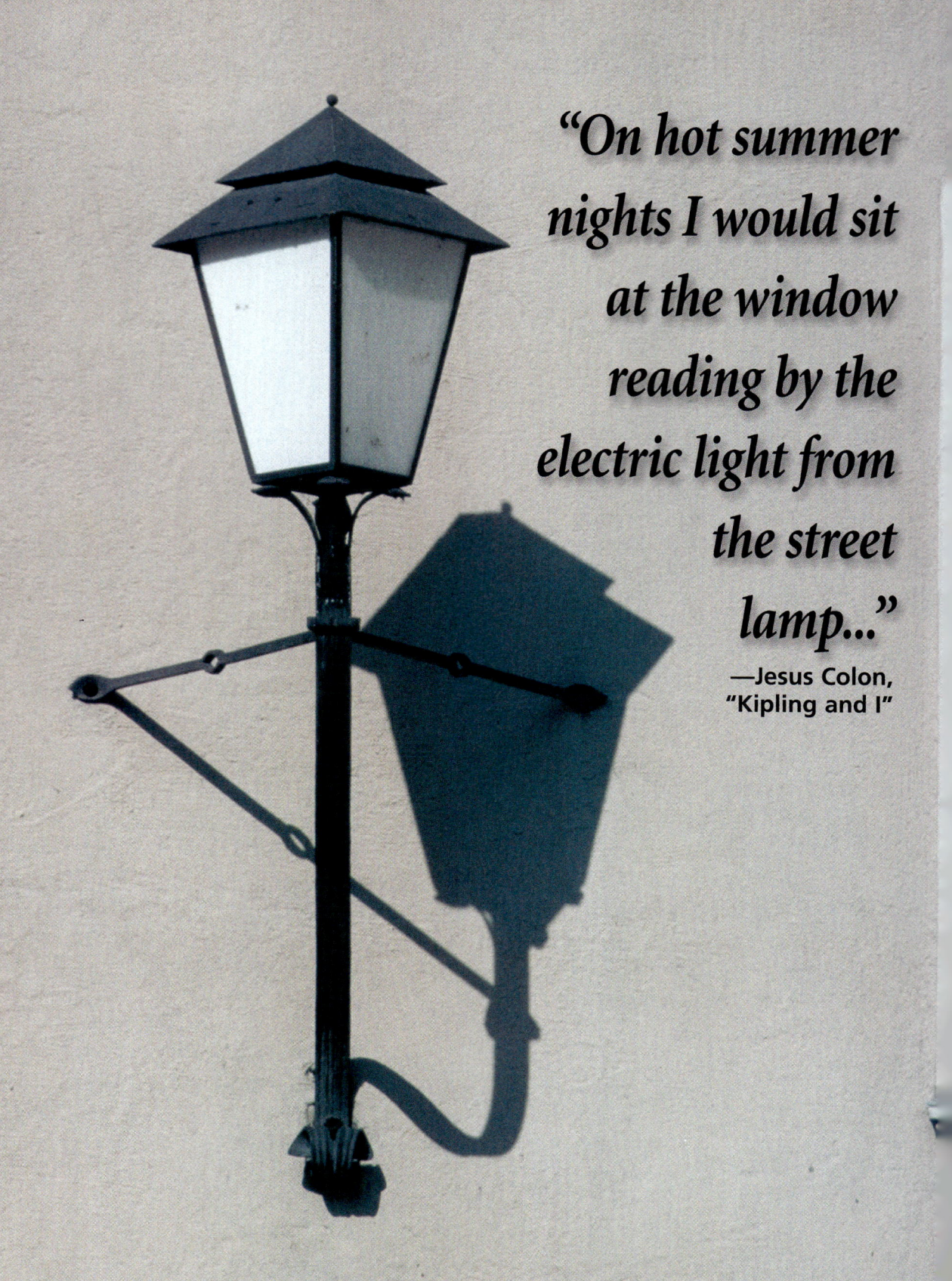

"On hot summer nights I would sit at the window reading by the electric light from the street lamp…"

—Jesus Colon, "Kipling and I"

UNIT 4 Narrative Writing

Writing in the Real World:
Lisa Twyman Bessone ... 176

Lesson 4.1 **Writing Simple Narratives** ... 180

Lesson 4.2 **Developing Conflict in Narrative** ... 184

Lesson 4.3 **Writing Dialogue** ... 188

Lesson 4.4 **Using Anecdotes** ... 192

Lesson 4.5 **Writing a Sports Narrative** ... 196

Lesson 4.6 **Writing About Literature: Writing About Suspense** ... 200

Lesson 4.7 **Writing About Literature: Analyzing Point of View in a Narrative** ... 204

Writing Process in Action ... 208

Literature Model: From *How the García Girls Lost Their Accents* by Julia Alvarez ... 212

Unit 4 Review ... 221

Writing in the Real World

MEDIA Sportswriting Connection

The mass media, such as newspapers and magazines, are terrific sources for narrative writing. For example, most sports stories focus on character and conflict—conflict between players or between teams, or an individual's struggle to overcome physical limitations. The following is an excerpt from a narrative article about triathlete Jim MacLaren. It was written by Lisa Twyman Bessone, a writer for *Sports Illustrated.*

Salute to an Amazing Ironman

By Lisa Twyman Bessone

In the marathon leg of the . . . Ironman Triathlon in Hawaii, Jim MacLaren, a 27-year-old professional triathlete and a former linebacker for Yale, fell in step with 41-year-old Ken Mitchell, who played the same position for the Atlanta Falcons from 1972 to '75. Given the demands of the race (a 2.4-mile swim, a marathon run and a 112-mile bike ride), conversation had to be minimal, but the two did talk a bit about Mitchell's 11 knee operations, the result of his football career. After about a mile MacLaren decided to pull ahead. "I'm saying a little prayer for you, Jimmy," Mitchell called out as he dropped farther and farther behind. MacLaren, you see, was running with a prosthesis on his left leg.

. . . The challenges in that [Ironman] event are "enormous," MacLaren says. "To do well, you need some sense of humor and some sense of your own mortality." MacLaren qualifies on both counts—especially the latter. MacLaren, who is also an actor, lost his leg in a traffic accident on Oct. 20, 1985. He was riding his motorcycle down Fifth Avenue in New York City. . . . A westbound city bus weighing 40,000 pounds roared into the intersection and hit MacLaren. According to the police report, the bus threw MacLaren, who was still at his football weight of 290 pounds, 89 feet.

The force of the impact sent MacLaren's helmet flying. His unprotected head hit the pavement first, and his skull split open across the forehead. A lung was punctured, his spleen was ruptured, his kidneys were lacerated, and all his ribs were broken. He was bleeding profusely, both externally and internally. His left leg, which the bus had mashed into the engine of his bike, was burned and crushed.

MacLaren was pronounced dead on arrival at Bellevue Hospital, but doctors were able to restart his heart—twice. They then had to restrain him when he tried to get off the operating table. . . .

MacLaren awoke from a coma six days later to the sound

Writing in the Real World

of a respirator pumping air into his lungs. His left leg had been amputated just below the knee. . . . "My leg was gone," he says, "but I felt extremely lucky to be around." . . .

About the only person who isn't especially impressed with MacLaren is MacLaren himself. But even he admits that the '89 Ironman was a high note in his career.

"You know, we all have our own dramas in life," MacLaren adds. "Not everyone has to do a triathlon to push themselves. Maybe your challenge is simply getting along with your father. Everything is relative. I don't want to sound like I have all the answers; I just believe that there are no limits on any of us."

A Writer's Process

Prewriting
Finding and Researching the Narrative

While watching a triathlon, Lisa Bessone knew she'd found a great story. She recalls, "A couple of my friends were running. Along comes this guy running with a prosthesis [artificial leg] and doing incredibly well. We all remarked on how amazing it was. A small feature appeared in the paper the next day about this football player, Jim MacLaren, who had lost his leg in a motorcycle accident and was now running triathlons in excellent times." So Bessone's idea for the nonfiction narrative came from her observation of MacLaren running in the triathlon and from reading the newspaper feature story about him later.

Once she got the idea for the narrative, Bessone was ready to do the research. Armed with a tape recorder, she flew to New England to interview Jim MacLaren. Before an interview Bessone always writes down questions. She calls her notes "touchstones to remind myself of the direction I want to go. Usually one question will spark a half-hour discussion."

At first, MacLaren didn't want to talk about the injury that destroyed his leg and nearly took his life. Bessone was willing to wait. "As a sportswriter, you learn the art of hanging out. The more people know you, the more they trust you. After a while Jim told me about the accident. . . . It was obviously traumatic that he'd lost his leg, but most of the other aspects of his story were really upbeat."

In addition to interviewing MacLaren, his mother, and several of his friends, Bessone sought statistics from the Triathlon Federation: "You need that kind of stuff to give your story a factual basis." Even as she was collecting information, Bessone considered how best to arrange those crucial elements of character and conflict into a compelling narrative.

Writing in the Real World

Drafting
Getting the Story Down

To select the information for her draft, Lisa Bessone listened to her tapes. She noted all the things she wanted to include in the narrative.

The next step was organizing the material. Bessone notes that a sportswriter usually has some idea of the organization she's going to use. "That's like a road map you're following the whole time," she says. Bessone's "road map" for this narrative was MacLaren's progression from his accident and rehabilitation to competing in races.

Revising/Editing
Making Necessary Changes

After Bessone had completed her draft, MacLaren ran the Ironman Triathlon. At this triathlon, held annually in Hawaii, MacLaren bested the previous amputee record by almost two hours. Bessone decided to revise her original draft to include the event.

When MacLaren told her about an incident that occurred during the marathon leg of the triathlon, Bessone decided to use his anecdote in her opening paragraph. This new lead sets a scene that arouses curiosity, creates drama, and then reels the reader in with the last sentence. Bessone comments, "At first you don't know why you're reading; then you find out. It's like holding a card back."

Presenting
Sharing with the World

In response to her article about MacLaren, Bessone says she got many telephone calls, including one from someone who wanted to do a movie about Jim MacLaren. "He's a heroic figure," says Bessone. "It was a happy story."

178 Unit 4 Narrative Writing

Examining Writing in the Real World

Analyzing the Media Connection

Discuss these questions about the article on pages 176–177.

1. What does Lisa Bessone reveal about Jim MacLaren in the excerpt?
2. What is the conflict in the story?
3. How does Bessone use concrete details to establish the enormity of MacLaren's accident?
4. Why do you think Bessone began her article with a conversation between MacLaren and Ken Mitchell? What does the anecdote reveal about MacLaren as a character? About the conflict?
5. How does Bessone reel the reader in with the last sentence in her opening paragraph?

Analyzing a Writer's Process

Discuss these questions about Lisa Bessone's writing process.

1. What prompted Lisa Bessone to write a story about Jim MacLaren?
2. How did Bessone research her article?
3. What did Bessone use as her "road map" for the story?
4. What influenced Bessone to revise her article?
5. How did Bessone arrange her character and conflict to create a compelling narrative?

Grammar Link

Capitalize proper nouns.

In her writing, Lisa Bessone uses many proper nouns naming athletes, places, and teams. Correct the following sentences, capitalizing proper nouns as necessary.

1. The ironman triathlon, the grandfather of all triathlons, is held annually in hawaii.
2. The contestants run more than twenty-six miles after bicycling on hot lava flats and swimming miles in the pacific.
3. Famous marathons are held each year in new york city and boston, massachusetts.
4. The marine corps marathon in washington, d.c., passes the lincoln memorial and the capitol.
5. Patrick Ewing of the new york knicks helped the United States win the Olympic basketball gold medal in 1992.

See Lesson 20.2, pages 713–719.

LESSON 4.1
Writing Simple Narratives

A narrative is a story that relates a sequence of events. The story may be true (nonfiction) or imagined (fiction). A successful narrative involves realistic characters and situations brought to life with specific details. In the following narrative, Jamaica Kincaid tells the true story of how her mother came to live on the island of Antigua.

Literature Model

When my mother, at sixteen, after quarreling with her father, left his house on Dominica and came to Antigua, she packed all her things in an enormous wooden trunk that she had bought in Roseau for almost six shillings. She painted the trunk yellow and green outside, and she lined the inside with wallpaper that had a cream background with pink roses printed all over it. Two days after she left her father's house, she boarded a boat and sailed for Antigua. It was a small boat, and the trip would have taken a day and a half ordinarily, but a hurricane blew up and the boat was lost at sea for almost five days. By the time it got to Antigua, the boat was practically in splinters, and though two or three of the passengers were lost overboard, along with some of the cargo, my mother and her trunk were safe.

Jamaica Kincaid, "The Circling Hand"

> Notice that the story has a beginning—the departure from Dominica; a middle—the journey; and an end—the safe arrival in Antigua.

> What vivid images help you "see" Kincaid's story?

Understand the Basics of Narrative

All narratives contain characters, setting, and plot. Characters are the individuals in a story. In the narrative above, the characters include Kincaid's mother and grandfather. Setting establishes a story's time and place, such as the boat bound for Antigua. Finally, the events that occur in a story make up its plot.

Narratives may contain a conflict, or a struggle that triggers the action. The conflict in Kincaid's story relates to the mother and the hurricane.

180   Unit 4 Narrative Writing

Generate Ideas for Writing

The best narratives contain believable characters and situations. Therefore, it's a good rule of thumb to base the narratives you write on what you know, drawing on the ordinary and not-so-ordinary experiences that shape your life. A family trip, for example, probably contains all the basic elements of a narrative. Here are some ways to get started.

Talking Talking about what you've done and where you've been can help you discover what you want to say in writing. In addition, reaction to your stories can help you gauge their audience appeal. Listening to other people's stories might also trigger writing ideas.

Freewriting You can also freewrite as a way to generate a topic for a story. Then, when you come up with an idea that interests you, use freewriting again to explore it. Write down whatever comes into your mind about your topic for about five minutes. In the following model of freewriting, a writer decided to explore an everyday experience: a routine trip to the dentist.

> **Grammar Tip**
>
> Use personal pronouns correctly when you write a personal narrative. See Lesson 17.1, page 633.

Model

Terror. Anticipation. What else do I feel when I go to the dentist? Sitting in that waiting room, trying to read a magazine. Wondering whether I'll need a filling. I wish my tooth didn't hurt. I wish my gums didn't bleed. If only I'd flossed regularly, not just two or three days before this appointment. That doesn't fool anybody. Certainly not my dentist. Does he enjoy poking around in my mouth, making me squirm? I picture him putting on his gloves, snapping the elastic loudly and watching me jump. Then, he'll grin like the dentist in *Little Shop of Horrors*. He'll say the words that frighten me most: "Open wide."

This example of freewriting contains some narrative elements. Can you identify them?

Journal Writing

Look through your journal to find story ideas. Underline any incidents that seem significant or interesting to you. Freewrite about each incident for five minutes to generate more story ideas.

4.1 Writing Simple Narratives **181**

> **Prewriting Tip**
>
> Jot down ideas for possible narratives in your journal. Anything can serve as inspiration: talking to people, reading, or even watching television.

Build on Your Ideas

You can build on your ideas by answering questions about your story's basic elements and by constructing a framework of your story's events. Remember, however, that you may not even discover your story until you begin writing it. As writer Flannery O'Connor once said, "I write because I don't know what I think until I read what I say."

Answering Questions If you want to flesh out the basic elements in your narrative before you begin drafting, try answering the questions in the chart below. If you would prefer to just begin drafting, you may want to refer to these questions as you write your draft.

Questions to Flesh Out the Basic Narrative Elements

1. Who are my characters? About whom do I want to write?
2. What conflict(s) will my characters be involved in?
3. When does my story take place?
4. Where does my story take place?
5. Why do my characters get involved in their conflict(s)?
6. How does the setting affect my characters? How do they overcome their conflict(s)?
7. Do my characters change in any way during the course of the story? If so, in what ways and why?

Constructing a Framework Most narratives are organized in chronological order, the order in which the events happened. Try plotting the events in your narrative in chronological order along a time line. Keep asking yourself the question, *What happened next?* This will help you keep track of the events and write them down in order.

1:30 P.M. First Event	4:45 P.M. Second Event	9:00 P.M. Third Event	7:00 A.M. Fourth Event	8:00 A.M. Final Event
Paul and Carlos set off to ride their mountain bikes through the woods near their home.	They become confused by the many trails and take a wrong turn. As night falls, they are hopelessly lost.	They try to keep warm and build a shelter with branches. They spend a miserable night in the woods.	The next day, they continue to try to find their way back home. They came upon old railroad tracks.	By following the tracks, they reach town and safety.

182 Unit 4 Narrative Writing

4.1 Writing Activities

Write a Personal Narrative

You've decided to enter a writing contest sponsored by a national teen magazine. The contest rules state that you must write a one-page narrative about an experience that did not turn out as you expected. Use the prewriting techniques described in this lesson to help you explore your topic and build on your narrative's basic elements. Refer to your prewriting samples as you draft your narrative, but don't feel limited by the ideas you came up with at that stage in the writing process.

PURPOSE To write a personal narrative for a contest
AUDIENCE Editors of a teen magazine
LENGTH 2–4 paragraphs

WRITING RUBRICS To write an effective personal narrative, you should

- test your ideas by talking them through or by freewriting
- ask yourself questions to fill out details of the narrative
- construct a time line or other graphic organizer for your narrative
- include believable characters, setting, and plot

Listening and Speaking

COOPERATIVE LEARNING Interview a classmate about an important experience in his or her life. Formulate questions beforehand that will elicit details of the setting, people, and events involved. Record the interview on audiotape or videotape; then review it. Take notes on the details you will include in your narrative. Use the steps in the writing process to create a narrative about your classmate's experience.

Using Computers

If your word processor has an outlining feature, you can use it to outline your personal narrative. As you create your outline, this feature simultaneously creates a skeleton draft of your writing. In addition, as you come up with new ideas and enter the changes on your outline, the draft also changes. After you have completed your outline, "flesh out" your skeleton draft. Then use the cut-and-paste feature on your computer to help you revise and edit the draft.

Grammar Link

Use strong adverbs to make writing more precise.

Note how the writer on page 181 pictures the dentist "putting on his gloves, snapping the elastic loudly."

Revise the following sentences by adding at least one strong adverb to each.

1. I wish I had flossed my teeth.
2. I imagine that the dentist has told someone to "open wide."
3. My own teeth begin to vibrate as the buzz of the drill reaches my ears.
4. I can feel the pull and push of an instrument in my mouth.
5. I remember that I'm waiting for my brother to have his teeth checked.

See Lesson 10.5, page 467.

LESSON 4.2

Developing Conflict in Narrative

In a narrative, as in a movie, it is often the conflict, or struggle, that keeps the audience interested. There are several types of conflict. Choose the one that works best with your characters and situations.

Use Events to Develop Conflict

The conflict, or struggle, in a story is what sets events in motion and makes the audience want to find out what happens. In the movie *Jaws*, for example, the uncertain outcome in the struggle between people and shark creates a gripping story.

Conflict plays the same role in a narrative that a main idea plays in other types of writing. Just as all supporting details help develop a main idea, all events in a narrative help develop its conflict.

As a character grapples with the conflict, the plot builds to a climax, the high point of the story. The resolution, in which the aftermath of the climax is revealed, brings the narrative to an end. The graph on page 185 shows how the development and eventual resolution of a conflict form the basis for the plot.

The Progression of Conflict in a Narrative

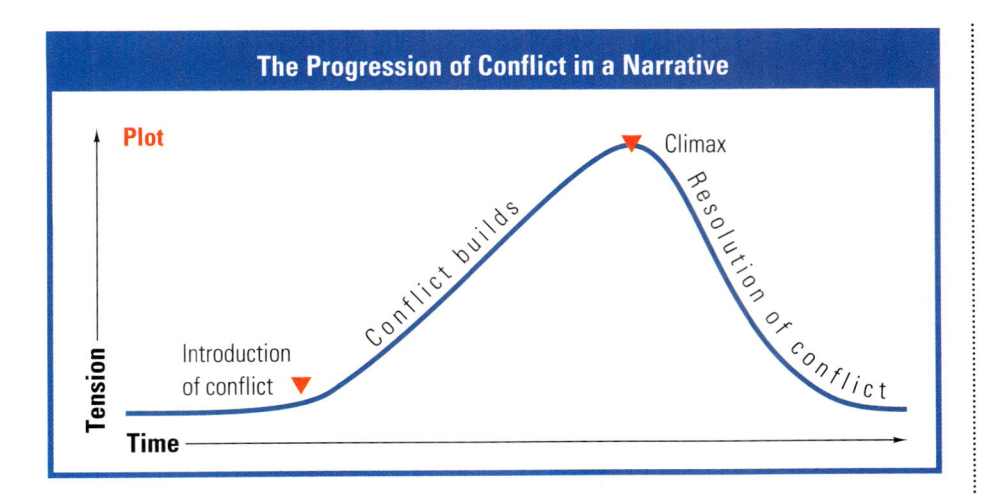

Plot — Tension vs. Time: Introduction of conflict → Conflict builds → Climax → Resolution of conflict

Drafting Tip

As you draft the conflict in your narrative, remember that a conflict with a less predictable climax and resolution is more likely to involve your readers.

Learn the Types of Conflict

Conflicts can be internal or external. External conflicts involve one or more characters and an outside force. Internal conflicts occur within a character. The chart below lists four types of conflicts—three external and one internal.

Four Types of Conflict

CONFLICT	EXAMPLES
Person Against Person The narrative pits one character against another.	One character exposes a flaw in another. One character attempts to harm another. One character opposes the beliefs of another.
Person Against Nature A character struggles against a dangerous animal, place, or condition.	A character is attacked by a rampaging elephant. A character tries to scale a dangerous peak. A character is threatened by a hurricane.
Person Against Society Society or tradition stands in the way of a character's desires.	Society prevents a character from doing something. A group tries to impose its beliefs and ideas on a character.
Person Against Self The conflict is within the character's mind.	A character struggles with a lack of ambition. A character seeks to achieve an unrealistic goal. A character tries to overcome a fear of flying.

Journal Writing

Think about a narrative you've read in which a character (or characters) faces a particular conflict. How is the conflict resolved? Write your answer in your journal.

4.2 Developing Conflict in Narrative

Develop Conflict

To identify a conflict for a narrative, start with what you want to write about and use prewriting techniques to develop conflict. For example, freewrite to discover the types of conflicts that would most challenge your main characters.

Once you have identified a main conflict, use prewriting techniques to generate a list of events that might be used to develop or resolve such a conflict. If you think an event might affect the characters or forces involved, try listing some of its possible effects. As you write, keep pushing yourself to answer the question *What happens next?* until your story is complete. See how writer Russell Baker presents two conflicts in the following model.

Literature Model

On the first day in the pool a [Navy] instructor with a voice like a bullhorn ordered fifty of us to climb a high board and jump in feet first.... A line was formed to mount the ladder and jump. I drifted to the end of the line, then stepped out when the splashing started and introduced myself to the instructor.

"I'm a nonswimmer," I said. "You want me to go to the shallow end of the pool?" At City College I'd spent four years in the shallow end of the pool.

"This pool doesn't have a shallow end," the instructor said.

"Well, what am I going to do?"

"Get up on that platform and jump," he said.

The pool depth was marked as fifteen feet at that point.

"I'm not kidding. I can't swim a stroke."

"Up! Up!" he shouted.

"But I'll drown."

"This pool's got the best lifesaving equipment in the Navy," he said. "Don't worry about it."

"Come on."

"I'm giving you an order, mister. Up!"...

I stepped to the edge, closed my eyes, and walked into space. The impact of the water was like being smacked on the bottom by a two-by-four, then I was sinking, then—my God!—I was rising irresistibly to the surface. My head broke water. The water was actually supporting me, just as everybody had always said it would.

Russell Baker, *Growing Up*

> Baker sets up two types of conflict: Baker versus his own fear of deep water, and Baker versus the Navy instructor.

> Baker uses dialogue to develop the conflict between himself and the Navy instructor.

> What is the climax of each conflict? How are the conflicts resolved?

4.2 Writing Activities

Write a Narrative About a Conflict

You've decided to contribute a one-page narrative to a booklet prepared by and designed for students at your school.

Choose one of these topics if you wish: a student is afraid to speak out when her friend is jeered at by classmates; a shy student wants to try out for a part in the school play; a student feels pressured by her friends to stay at a party after her curfew.

PURPOSE To write a narrative
AUDIENCE Students at your school
LENGTH 3–4 paragraphs

WRITING RUBRICS To write an effective narrative, you should

- include events that develop the conflict
- build your plot to a climax
- create a resolution to the conflict

Viewing and Representing

CREATING A POSTER Use one of your favorite narratives—fiction or nonfiction—to create a poster mapping the central conflict in the story. Show how the conflict builds, what occurs at the climax, and how the conflict is resolved. Include an illustration of the climax.

César A. Martinez, *Mestizo*, 1987

Grammar Link

Avoid sentence fragments.

Each item below contains a *sentence fragment,* or incomplete sentence. Rewrite the item to eliminate the fragment. Change words as necessary.

1. The conflict in a narrative engages a reader's interest. Because a reader wants to find out how the conflict will be resolved.
2. The plot is set in motion by the conflict. Which can be an internal conflict or an external one.
3. The plot building to a climax, the high point of the story. After the climax, the resolution ends the narrative.
4. A conflict within the character's mind. Internal conflict pits the character against himself or herself.
5. Much of the conflict in young adult literature is internal. Adolescents experiencing the pains of growing up.

See Lesson 13.9, page 553–554.

Cross-Curricular Activity

FINE ART The drawing at left is a self-portrait by César A. Martinez. Entitled *Mestizo*, it shows the artist flanked by a jaguar, native to the Americas, and a Spanish bull, which represents Europe. The drawing reflects Martinez's struggle to come to terms with his own cultural identity, rooted in both North America and Spain. Generate a list of events that might be used to develop and eventually resolve the conflict. Then write a brief narrative based on the drawing.

LESSON 4.3 Writing Dialogue

Dialogue, or conversation between characters, brings the characters in a story to life. Like the cartoon below, a story would be hard to follow without the dialogue.

"Mom, can I drive on the way back?"

"Of course not, Calvin."

"Can I just steer then? I promise I won't crash."

"No, Calvin."

"Can I work the gas and brakes while you steer?"

"No, Calvin."

"You never let me do anything."

Discover the Uses of Dialogue

You can use dialogue to help advance a narrative's plot. For example, if the plot involves an argument between two characters, you can let the characters speak for themselves rather than summarizing their dispute.

You can also use dialogue to reveal your characters' personality traits or to show relationships between characters. For instance, instead of telling the reader, "Robert was shy," use Robert's actions and words to reveal his shyness: "Robert shuffled uneasily, looked at his feet, and mumbled, 'Nice to meet you.'"

Additionally, you can use dialogue to make the reader feel closer to the action, to help the reader "see" the story as it unfolds rather than to hear about it from a narrator. Dialogue can also help establish character and conflict, and it can make a conflict more powerful and real to the reader.

Think About Real People to Develop Dialogue

When you're writing dialogue for a story about something that really happened, try to remember as closely as possible what each person said. If your story is fictional, you'll need to invent dialogue. To do

188 Unit 4 Narrative Writing

so, you might try to imagine that you are one of the characters and freewrite about the conflict from that character's point of view. Keep in mind the character's age, background, and personality and how those qualities may be reflected in speech.

> *Sometimes my mother makes me want to scream. Why won't she let me get an after-school job? All my friends are working and making their own money. Why does Mom still treat me like a kid?*

> **Grammar Tip**
> When you edit your dialogue, be sure to use quotation marks to enclose direct quotations. For help see Lesson 21.9, pages 752–756.

If the conflict involves two characters, you might try freewriting a letter from one character to the other. Each letter should reflect the letter writer's point of view and feelings about the conflict.

Dear Angela,
I know you're angry with me because I won't let you work after school. But I'm afraid a job would interfere with your studies. You know you won't get into a good college if your grades are poor. Besides, I'd worry when you'd be coming home after dark.

Dear Mom,
I promise you a job won't hurt my grades. I'll be home every day by 7:00, which gives me tons of time to do my homework. And Carla's already said she can give me a lift home after work. Best of all, I'll be able to buy that winter jacket I saw at the mall with my own money.

Dialogue should sound like real speech. In real speech, people often interrupt each other, ignore each other's comments, speak in fragments, and break the rules of grammar. To test whether your dialogue sounds natural, read it aloud.

Journal Writing

In your journal write down three pieces of dialogue that you have overheard and that struck you as interesting. Why do you think you remembered these particular conversations? What made them interesting? Write your ideas in your journal.

Develop Your Story with Dialogue

Dialogue can bring your writing to life. In Matthew Cheney's short story "The Nauga Hunters," Hank invites his younger brother Chucky to hunt for a nauga, an imaginary beast. Note how Cheney uses dialogue to develop his characters and advance the story.

Prewriting Tip

To develop your ability to write realistic dialogue, watch a favorite television show. Note how the dialogue reflects the ages, backgrounds, and personalities of the characters.

Student Model

Chucky stood next to his brother without saying anything. Then he asked quietly, "Is it about Mom and Dad?"

"Jus' beat it!"

"What's gonna happen? Is Dad gonna leave?"

"You wanna know? You really wanna know, you little jerk? Las' night I heard Mom and Dad talkin'."

"Fightin'?"

"Nope, jus' talkin'. Dad said he's gonna leave and go ta New York and take me, and Mom can have you. So I brought you out here jus' ta be nice 'cause I may never really be able ta do anythin' like this again. Okay? Satisfied?"

"You sure yer tellin' the truth?"

Hank stood up and jumped on his brother; they fell to the damp ground. His eyes were sparkling and his lips were unfirm. "Would I lie about that, you little . . ." His voice faded as he pulled his arm up to punch Chucky. Chucky was crying now. Hank stood up. "Forget it," he said. "Supper'll be almost ready." Chucky was still on the ground. "You comin'?"

Chucky pulled himself up and brushed off his rear end. His face was streaked with tears. "Yup," he said softly.

Matthew Cheney, New Hampton School, New Hampton, New Hampshire. First appeared in *Merlyn's Pen: The National Magazine of Student Writing*

> **Dialogue effectively reveals the story's central conflict and its climax: the boys' parents are getting a divorce.**

> **How does Cheney use dialogue to convey Hank's anger and confusion?**

Try to make your dialogue as realistic as possible. As you write it, keep the following guidelines in mind.

Dialogue Guidelines

- Use language that reflects the age, background, and personality of each character.
- Make sure your dialogue has a purpose—to advance the action, to reveal a character's personality or relationships between characters, or to show the conflict.
- Begin a direct quotation with a capital letter, and enclose it in quotation marks.
- Begin a new paragraph each time the speaker changes.

4.3 Writing Activities

Write a Dialogue

You've been chosen to write the dialogue for a skit for your school's theater group. Use the information below to develop the dialogue.

Chen and Kirby are best friends, but their personalities are very different. Chen is an optimist, always able to see the bright side. Kirby is a pessimist, always assuming the worst. Both are on the track team. For the first time in years, the team has a chance to win the state title. As they warm up before the final relay, Kirby admits to Chen that he wants to withdraw. He's afraid he'll cause the team to lose. Chen inspires Kirby with his own enthusiasm. By the time the starting signal sounds, both friends are ready to give their personal best.

As you develop your dialogue, read it aloud to find out how it sounds. Try to imagine yourself in each character's place.

PURPOSE To write dialogue for a skit to be performed by your school's theater group
AUDIENCE Your school's student body
LENGTH 1 page

WRITING RUBRICS To write effective dialogue, you should

- let the characters speak for themselves
- use dialogue for a purpose
- use language that sounds real and appropriate to the characters
- use quotation marks appropriately

Viewing and Representing

DRAW A CARTOON Using a favorite comic strip as a guide, draw a four-panel cartoon. Leave enough space for dialogue balloons. Be sure your dialogue is appropriate to your characters and advances the plot.

Grammar Link

Know when and how to use quotation marks.

Dialogue, the exact words of a speaker, is written with quotation marks.

Rewrite the sentences below, using quotation marks to enclose every direct quotation. Make other changes in capitalization and punctuation as necessary.

1. My little sister stamped her right foot and exclaimed I'm so mad.
2. Nibbling at the cuticle of her right thumb, my older sister whispered why is Alicia so mad?
3. Don't ask me I answered, lowering my voice.
4. People who have something to say my angry sister hissed should have the courage to say it so that other people can hear.
5. This is a new idea I murmured in return.

See Lesson 21.9, pages 752–756.

Cross-Curricular Activity

AMERICAN HISTORY In a small group, choose a scene from American history to dramatize. First discuss the personalities and backgrounds of the characters. Then meet with your group to write dialogue that develops the action and accurately reflects each character's personality and background. After all the dialogue has been written, present your group scene to the rest of the class.

LESSON 4.4

Using Anecdotes

An anecdote is a short narrative used to illustrate a point or reveal character. In the model below the writer uses an anecdote to demonstrate poet Langston Hughes's scorn for the so-called "Jim Crow" laws.

Most anecdotes instruct or entertain, and they often contain dialogue. Although anecdotes can stand on their own, they are frequently used as supporting details in longer pieces of writing.

> **Literature Model**
>
> By this time he unquestionably had become bolder in confronting Jim Crow. Always now he entered the dining car at the first call, instead of shrinking back and waiting for the last as blacks were supposed to do.
>
> Picking a center table, he usually tried to brazen it out before incredulous but discreetly supportive black waiters and often indignant, but often yielding, white stewards. "Are you a Puerto Rican?" a steward demanded in Alabama. "No, hungry!" The man handed over a menu. "Are you Cuban?" a curious white Navy officer then asked. "No, American," Langston coolly replied. "Are you Cuban?"
>
> Arnold Rampersad, *The Life of Langston Hughes, Volume II: 1941–1967*

This anecdote contains a plot—Hughes is trying to get served dinner; characters—Hughes, the steward, the naval officer; and a setting—a train's dining car.

How is dialogue used to reveal Hughes's attitude toward the Jim Crow laws?

Generate Anecdotes

You can generate anecdotes by drawing on real-life experiences or by using prewriting techniques to invent them. Keep in mind that you will use the anecdote to illustrate a point in a longer piece of writing.

Anecdotes Based on Fact Some anecdotes are based on incidents that actually happened. To generate true-life anecdotes, think about significant or entertaining incidents from your own life. You might want to look through your journal for ideas. Then think about the point each anecdote could make in a longer piece of writing.

Factual Anecdotes

ANECDOTE	POINT
The time I stood up for myself even though my friends disagreed	To show that you should voice your opinions, even if they are unpopular
The time my brother first went away to college	To show that life is a process of change
The time I struck out and my team lost the game	To show that true friends stand by you when you fail

Invented Anecdotes When you're writing a fictional narrative, you can invent anecdotes. First decide on the point you want to make. Then freewrite to come up with an anecdote that could illustrate that point.

Invented Anecdotes

ANECDOTE	POINT
A character thinks only of himself or herself at the expense of others	To show a character's selfishness
An argument between two characters	To show that two characters have different values
A character confronts his or her fear of heights by climbing a mountain	To show that you have to confront a fear to overcome it

> **Vocabulary Tip**
> When you draft your anecdote, be sure to present the events of the story in chronological order. Helpful transition words include *after, before, as soon as, first, next, now, soon, finally, meanwhile,* and *then.*

> **Presenting Tip**
> One effective method to present an anecdote is to read it aloud.

Journal Writing

Look through your journal for incidents that could be written up as possible anecdotes. Then list the incidents, and identify the point each could make in a longer piece of writing.

4.4 Using Anecdotes **193**

Prewriting Tip

If you are writing about yourself, you might ask family members to discuss their early memories of you. Their stories could supply you with useful anecdotes.

Decide Where and How to Use Anecdotes

Once you have an anecdote, you need to consider whether or not to use it to make a specific point in a longer piece of writing. To help you decide, ask yourself the questions in the chart below.

Questions to Determine the Usefulness of an Anecdote
1. Does this anecdote make the point I want to make?
2. Does the anecdote advance the narrative?
3. Is the anecdote brief, yet meaningful?
4. Does the anecdote instruct or entertain?

In Jennifer Tuck's short story "My Grandmother's House," the narrator dreads returning to her grandmother's house after her grandmother dies. As a little girl, she had been afraid of the house because it was so large and dark. As this anecdote reveals, however, on one particular occasion her grandmother helped her overcome her fears.

Student Model

What does the anecdote reveal about the narrator's grandmother?

I had been sitting on the porch for nearly an hour when my grandmother came out, quietly letting the screen door creak on its old rusty hinges and then sigh as it came to rest against the crooked door frame Grandpa was always saying he would fix.

"Why don't you come inside?" she said. "We are going to eat dinner soon and I would hate to think of sitting at the table without you."

"I'm afraid." I barely whispered this shameful feeling, and stared straight down at my untied shoes.

"That's OK. I was afraid when we first moved here, too. You just have to remember that this house is a lot like your house, only there's love from many families here instead of just our own. Did you ever stop to wonder who could have lived here before? There must be so many memories within these walls!"

Notice that the anecdote could stand on its own as a brief narrative, complete with plot, setting, and characters.

We talked on and on and gradually my fear began to fade. When my mother called us inside, I didn't hesitate for an instant before following my grandmother inside.

Jennifer Tuck, Central High School,
Manchester, New Hampshire
First appeared in *Merlyn's Pen:
The National Magazine of Student Writing*

4.4 Writing Activities

Write an Anecdote

Your English class is collecting an anecdote from each class member for a get-to-know-your-classmates project. The collection will be distributed to all of the students in the class. Write an anecdote that reveals something about your personality. You may choose to write about a time when you made a fool of yourself in front of someone you wanted to impress, or a time when your sense of humor helped relieve an unpleasant situation. You might choose to reveal another aspect of your personality.

PURPOSE To write an anecdote that reveals something about yourself.
AUDIENCE The members of your class
LENGTH 3–4 paragraphs

WRITING RUBRICS To write an effective anecdote, you should

- be sure your anecdote supports your point
- include significant details regarding character, setting, and plot

Cross-Curricular Activity

FINE ART Look at the painting. What ideas for anecdotes does it suggest? Freewrite or list to generate ideas for anecdotes and for the points they could illustrate.

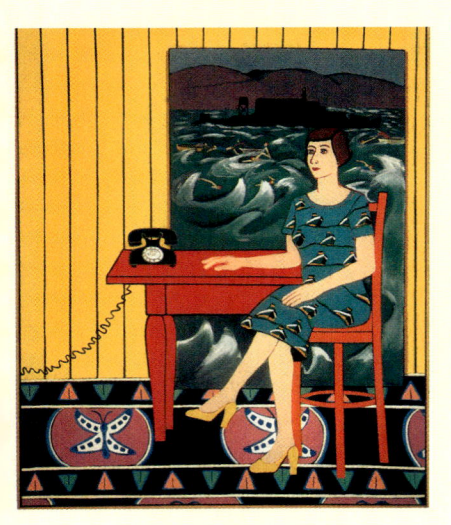

Joan Brown, *After the Alcatraz Swim #3*, 1976

Grammar Link

Use comparative and superlative forms of adjectives and adverbs correctly.

Comparative adjectives and adverbs compare two things—for example, Langston Hughes's becoming "bolder" in confronting Jim Crow. *Superlative forms* of adjectives and adverbs compare more than two things.

Complete each sentence below with the correct form of the word in parentheses.

1. After some time, Langston Hughes entered the dining car _____ than he first had. (courageously)
2. Who were _____ (amazed): the white stewards or the black waiters?
3. Perhaps _____ of all were the fellow passengers Hughes encountered in the dining cars. (surprised)
4. Some passengers moved to the _____ corner of the dining car when they saw the poet approach. (far)
5. They showed _____ what they thought than did those passengers who just ignored Hughes. (clearly)

See Lessons 18.1–18.3, pages 659–664.

Listening and Speaking

COOPERATIVE LEARNING With a classmate, create a dialogue based on your responses to the painting to the left and present it to the class as a dramatic reading.

LESSON 4.5

Writing a Sports Narrative

A good sports narrative, such as the model below, contains all the elements of any good narrative: character, setting, and conflict that builds to a climax and resolution.

Student Model

The pop of the gun sets the swimmers' legs in motion and arms flawlessly scooping pockets of water. Their heads bob rhythmically, each straining to reach the end of the pool. At the end of each lane, fellow swimmers stand and cheer their teammates, with a single exception. One blond-haired swimmer receives cries from teammates who lean close to the water, straining to show the swimmer their enthusiasm and their lips. The swimmer is deaf, and the encouraging motions of her friends urge her to go faster.

The race is close. The blond head edges out in front, neck and neck, with another swimmer beside her. However, with a last, powerful stroke, the blond swimmer breaks the tie and hits the timer seconds before her competitor. As she rests against the wall of the pool, accepting the congratulations of her teammates, an ear-to-ear grin appears across her face.

Charissa Adelman, Quartz Hill High School,
Quartz Hill, California

> The conflict in a sports narrative is often person against person, as each athlete struggles to win the sports event.

> What is the climax in this sports narrative? How is it resolved?

Begin with Intensifying Action

You'll want to begin your sports narrative at the point in the event when conflict starts to build. Usually this is the moment when the action intensifies. For example, to tell the story of a team's dramatic, come-from-behind victory, you might begin at the point in the game in which the team seized control and began its push for victory.

Include Supporting Details

Like other narratives, most sports narratives develop a conflict to its climax and resolution. You may want to chart the action that develops the conflict. This technique can help you identify the important events —the supporting details—that you'll want to include.

Development of Conflict in a Sports Narrative

Starting Point:
A baseball game is tied in the bottom of the ninth inning, with two outs. A runner on third represents the winning run.

Conflict:
The pitcher stares at third base. The base runner, determined to break the record for stolen bases, boldly stares back.

Climax:
As the pitcher fires the ball, the base runner makes a dash for home and plows into the catcher.

Resolution:
When the dust clears, the umpire waves his arms and yells, "Safe!" The crowd roars with delight.

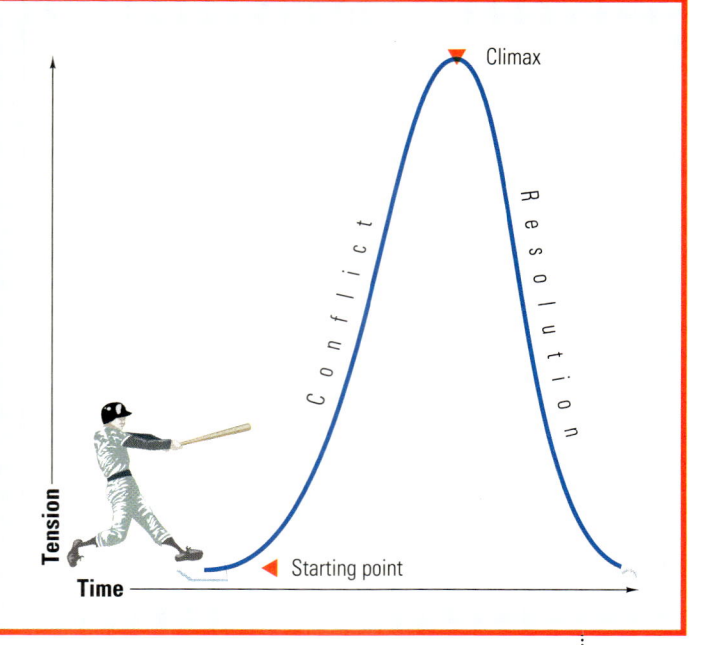

Journal Writing

Watch a sports event at school or on television. Use it as the basis for preparing a sports narrative. Choose a starting point, graph the development of the conflict to its climax and resolution, and then write a brief summary of each point in the plot.

4.5 Writing a Sports Narrative **197**

Prewriting Tip
When prewriting about a sports event, try list-making to generate details. Use the significant details to develop your narrative.

Vocabulary Tip
When revising your writing, use a thesaurus to help you find more precise, vivid verbs. A thesaurus lists words with their synonyms and, if applicable, their antonyms.

Build a Memorable Story

After you've chosen a sports event, determined your starting point, and charted the action, you're ready to draft your sports narrative. Begin by considering your lead. A **lead** is a strong opening sentence that grabs the reader's attention and gets the story moving. Examine your story's starting point. Is there anything dramatic, amusing, or surprising about it? If so, you might use that for your lead. Remember, however, that a narration of the event will only make up part of your article. (For tips on how to write a sports feature, see the Unit 4 Media Connection on pages 176–178.)

State the Facts Clearly Be sure that you have presented the sequence of events and all the facts clearly. Double-check quotations for accuracy, and make sure each source is identified.

Use Vivid Language Wherever possible, show the action rather than tell about it. Vivid action verbs and sensory details can bring your story to life and hold your readers' interest.

Read the following selection from baseball writer Roger Angell's book *Season Ticket*. Notice how Angell makes even a seemingly action-less stretch of a game interesting.

Literature Model

What verbs does Angell use to help the reader "see" the action in the ballpark?

A base runner leads cautiously away from first, then trots back as the pitcher steps off the rubber. The third-base ump walks seven steps out toward left field, turns, and strolls back again. Another foul ball, bounced softly past first base. "Throw it *straight*," somebody in the press box mutters. There are spatters of applause in the stands, but they die away for lack of hope. . . . I can see some fans getting up, in twos and threes, and heading up the aisles for home and dinner. The park is half empty by now. Out in the sloping right-field sector of the seats, there is a thin, a-cappella rendering of "Happy Birthday," for somebody—her name is Ella, it turns out—and other fans around the park join in on the last "happy birthday to you-ooo!" and Ella gets a little round of applause, too. But that ends as well (a coach is out talking to the pitcher now), and even the everyday noises of the baseball park—the hum of voices, the undercurrent of talk and cheers and laughter and vender cries—drop and fade, and Fenway Park is almost silent, just for a minute.

Roger Angell, *Season Ticket*

4.5 Writing Activities

Write a Sports Narrative

The editor of your school newspaper has asked you to write a sports narrative based on an important basketball game. Use the following information to write the narrative.

> West High and East High, long-standing rivals, meet in the state basketball finals. The game is close until the fourth quarter, when East High pulls ahead, 78–70. Finally, West High rallies to win the game 82–80, on a last-second basket.

PURPOSE To narrate an exciting sports event for a school newspaper
AUDIENCE Student and teacher sports fans
LENGTH 3–6 paragraphs

WRITING RUBRICS To write an effective sports narrative, you should

- provide essential background information
- bring your conflict to a climax and provide a resolution
- state the facts clearly in vivid language

Listening and Speaking

COOPERATIVE LEARNING Work in small groups to brainstorm ideas for a sports narrative. Chart the action. Then have one group member begin the story, someone else write the next section, and so on until everyone has written a section and the story is brought to a conclusion.

Grammar Link

Use vivid verbs in your narratives.

Effective sports stories contain verbs that let the reader "see" what is happening. Rewrite the sentences below, replacing all bold-faced words with more vivid action verbs.

1. The Phoenix Suns **went** out onto the basketball court as the overflow hometown crowd **clapped.**
2. The power forward **got** the tip and immediately **ran** to the basket.
3. The crowd **applauded** as he moved around the opposing center to score.
4. When the point guard **made** 6 of 13 three-point shots, the arena **shook.**
5. After the center **took** the ball from an opposing player and scored to win the game for Phoenix, the Phoenix coach **got up** from the bench.

See Lesson 10.3, page 452.

Cross-Curricular Activity

BROADCAST JOURNALISM With a partner, write a script describing a crucial moment in an actual sports event, such as a football game or a soccer match. Using television or radio sportscasts as your guide, create a narrative of the moment that builds to a dramatic climax, sets the scene, and provides a detailed, colorful analysis of the contest and the players. Record your script on audiotape, being sure to perform your parts with the proper enthusiasm.

LESSON 4.6

WRITING ABOUT LITERATURE
Writing About Suspense

Two of the most common ways to build suspense in a narrative are to use foreshadowing and to withhold information from the reader. In this painting the artist effectively creates suspense, or anxiety about what will happen next.

Grant Wood, *Death on the Ridge Road*, 1935

Ways to Create Suspense

- **Foreshadowing** Foreshadowing gives clues about what is going to happen later in the story. Writers often use this technique to prepare the reader for an ominous turn of events. The clues may include details of setting, characters, or plot. In the example on page 201, note how writer Mario Vargas Llosa uses a character's fearful imaginings to foreshadow events to come.

- **Withholding Information** In withholding information from the reader, a writer creates a puzzle with a few pieces missing and leaves a mystery to be solved. Curious to find out what will happen, the reader reads on. Mystery writers often withhold some key piece of information until the final scene when the mystery is solved.

Literature Model

After swimming for a few minutes Miguel felt the cold that had momentarily vanished coming over him again, and he speeded up his strokes because it was in his legs, especially in his calves, that the water had a greater effect, first making them insensitive, then stiffening them. He was swimming with his face in the water, and each time his right arm rose out of it, he turned his head to expel air and breathe in another supply, at which he submerged his face and chin once more, just barely, so as not to hinder his own progress but, on the contrary, to split the water like a prow and make his forward movement easier. With each stroke he glanced at Rubén swimming smoothly, effortlessly on the surface, not splashing now, with the delicacy and ease of a seagull gliding. Miguel tried to forget Rubén and the sea and the breakers, which must still be far off, for the water was clear and calm, and they were swimming only through newly risen surf. He wanted to remember nothing but Flora's face and the down on her arms that sparkled on sunny days like a little forest of golden threads. But he could not prevent another image from succeeding to that of the girl—the image of a mountain of raging water . . . in a real ocean stirred by inner cataclysms in which were thrown up unusual waves that could have swamped an entire ship and upset it with astonishing rapidity, hurling passengers, lifeboats, masts, sails, sailors, porthole covers, and flags into the air.

Mario Vargas Llosa, "Sunday"

> The writer builds suspense by describing Miguel's progress, stroke by stroke. As a result, the reader feels the character's weariness and fear.

> What image does the author use to foreshadow the possible dangers ahead for Miguel?

Journal Writing

Sometimes a writer withholds information from the character(s) in a story but reveals it to the readers. What effect does this have on the reader? How does it create suspense? Write your ideas about this technique in your journal.

4.6 Writing About Suspense

Drafting Tip

Sensory details can add immediacy to your suspense writing and draw the reader into your story. See Lesson 2.6 on page 81 to help you develop these details.

Grammar Tip

When you edit your writing, check to see that you have formed all possessive nouns, such as *General Zaroff's* island, correctly. You may want to refer to Lesson 9.10, pages 406–407, and Lesson 21.11, pages 759–761, for help.

Write About a Suspenseful Story

When you analyze a suspenseful story, focus on the ways in which the writer creates suspense. Provide examples from the text to support your ideas. As you read, ask yourself the questions in the chart below.

Questions to Determine How a Writer Creates Suspense

1. What details in the descriptions of the characters help build suspense?
2. Which events in the plot help build suspense?
3. What aspects of the setting build suspense?
4. What are the characters' reactions as suspense builds?
5. What atmosphere or mood does the writer create? How does the mood change?
6. In what ways does the writer foreshadow events to come?
7. What information does the writer withhold from the characters?

By exploring your answers to these questions through freewriting or brainstorming, you can develop a focus for an analysis of a suspense story. In the model below, Elizabeth Chen analyzes some of the techniques writer Richard Connell uses to build suspense in his short story "The Most Dangerous Game."

Student Model

Richard Connell uses foreshadowing to heighten suspense in "The Most Dangerous Game." When Rainsford falls off his yacht and swims to General Zaroff's island, he is relieved to reach its "dense jungle." However, the narrator states, "What perils that tangle of trees and underbrush might hold for him did not concern Rainsford just then." This statement suggests that the character will soon be in danger. By foreshadowing this future event, the author creates a sense of anticipation in the reader and compels him to read on.

Connell also draws the reader into the story by withholding information. When Zaroff asserts that he hunts "the biggest" game on his island, he does not at first reveal what that game might be. As a result, Rainsford and the reader are forced to guess. The diabolical answer, which directs the course of the rest of the story, becomes clear to both at about the same time.

Elizabeth Chen, Downers Grove North
High School, Downers Grove, Illinois

Chen uses specific examples from the story to develop the focus of her essay.

At the end of her essay, how does Chen herself withhold information in order to pique the reader's interest in the story?

4.6 Writing Activities

Write to Analyze Setting

Read the following excerpt from Edgar Allan Poe's short story "The Pit and the Pendulum." Then use the questions from page 202 to help you write an analysis.

> So far, I had not opened my eyes. I felt that I lay upon my back, unbound. I reached out my hand, and it fell heavily upon something damp and hard. There I suffered it to remain for many minutes, while I strove to imagine where and *what* I could be. I longed, yet dared not to employ my vision. I dreaded the first glance at objects around me. It was not that I feared to look upon things horrible, but that I grew aghast lest there should be *nothing* to see.

PURPOSE To identify the details in a story's setting that help create suspense
AUDIENCE Your classmates
LENGTH 1–2 paragraphs

WRITING RUBRICS To write an effective analysis of a setting, you should
- identify the mood of the passage
- identify the physical details that contribute to the mood of the passage
- explain how the passage foreshadows events or creates mystery or suspense

Cross-Curricular Activity

MEDIA STUDIES In two or three paragraphs, analyze how your favorite suspenseful movie uses foreshadowing, withholds information, and creates mood through lighting, camera angles, music, and sound.

Grammar Link

Use possessive nouns correctly.

Words like *Flora's* and *General Zaroff's* are *possessive nouns*.

Possessive nouns can be singular or plural. Revise the following sentences about the student model on page 202 by creating possessives using the words in boldface.

1. **The story of Richard Connell** uses foreshadowing to heighten suspense.
2. **The conflict of Rainsford and General Zaroff** is a serious one.
3. Only one man can win **the contest of the two men.**
4. The suspense of the situation grabs **the interest of the readers.**
5. **The analysis of Elizabeth Chen** does not reveal the outcome of the contest.

See Lesson 21.11, pages 759–761.

Listening and Speaking

CREATING A STORY Introduce a story by describing a scene in a way that creates mystery. Then turn to a classmate and ask him or her to continue the story. When he or she reaches a turning point, ask another classmate to pick up the story. Continue in this manner until the story reaches a satisfying close.

LESSON 4.7

WRITING ABOUT LITERATURE
Analyzing Point of View in a Narrative

Just as a performer on the stage and a person in the audience would describe a rock concert differently, so would different narrators tell a story differently. The author's choice of narrator determines how a particular story is told and how, in turn, a reader understands the story.

Identify the Point of View

The writer of a narrative selects a point of view, or a perspective, from which to tell the story. The author usually chooses from among three basic points of view.

In a story told from a first-person point of view, the narrator is a character in the story. This type of narrator uses first-person pronouns, such as *I* and *we*, in telling the story. A first-person narrator knows only what he or she is thinking and describes only the events he or she witnesses.

In a story told from a third-person limited point of view, the narrator stands outside the story. This type of narrator uses third-person pronouns such as *he, she, it,* and *they*. The third-person limited narrator describes the actions and words of all the characters but the thoughts and feelings of only one character.

In a story told from a third-person omniscient point of view, the narrator stands outside the action but knows all and sees all. A third-person omniscient narrator can relate everything that happens in the story, including the thoughts and feelings of all the characters.

Examine the Effect of Point of View

After identifying the point of view of a narrative, notice what effect the choice of point of view has on the presentation of the story. Then use examples from the text to support your opinion.

- **First-Person Narrator** Stories told by a first-person narrator tend to draw the reader into the action because the reader identifies with the "I" who is telling the story. As you evaluate the effect of point of view of a narrative, remember that the first-person narrator may be a biased or unreliable witness. In the following selection from Eugenia Collier's short story "Marigolds," the first-person narrator recalls how she felt after hearing her father cry for the first time.

> **Grammar Tip**
> When writing about point of view, be sure to refer to the narrator rather than the author of the narrative. As you edit your writing, check that all pronoun references are clear. See Lessons 9.5–9.6, pages 398–400.

Literature Model

The world had lost its boundary lines. My mother, who was small and soft, was now the strength of the family; my father, who was the rock on which the family had been built, was sobbing like the tiniest child. Everything was suddenly out of tune, like a broken accordion. Where did I fit into this crazy picture? I do not now remember my thoughts, only a feeling of great bewilderment and fear.

Eugenia Collier, "Marigolds"

> Notice that the first-person narrator only reports her own pain and confusion. She does not consider how her father must be feeling.

> Do you identify with the child telling the story? Why?

- **Third-Person Limited Narrator** A third-person limited narrator stands outside the story but relates events as if he or she were looking over the shoulder of one of the characters. Because the narrator is so close to this one character, the reader tends to identify with and sympathize with the character. Be aware, however, that this narrator may withhold information or tell more than the character would tell.

Journal Writing

Choose a piece of narrative writing told by a third-person limited narrator. Now imagine the same piece told by a first-person narrator. What effect might the change in point of view have on the story? Write down your ideas in your journal.

4.7 Analyzing Point of View in a Narrative

In the following example, Mathew Isaac analyzes the effect of a third-person limited narrator in O. Henry's "The Gift of the Magi."

Student Model

> Isaac maintains that O. Henry uses a third-person limited narrator to make the story's ironic ending more effective.

In O. Henry's "The Gift of the Magi," a third-person limited narrator primarily relates the actions, thoughts, and feelings of the character Della. The narrator withholds information from the reader about her husband, Jim, and thereby sets up the story's final, ironic twist.

> What specific examples and quotations from the story does Isaac use to support his opinion?

The story's narrator is also used to comment ironically on the characters themselves. For example, when Della cries because she doesn't have enough money to buy Jim a present, the narrator remarks that "life is made up of sobs, sniffles, and smiles, with sniffles predominating." . . .

Although we are encouraged to laugh at Della and Jim, at the story's end, the reader is the object of the narrator's irony. There it is implied that the reader who only laughs at the pair, without recognizing their deep love, is the real fool.

Mathew Isaac, Rich East High School, Park Forest, Illinois

- **Third-Person Omniscient Narrator** The third-person omniscient narrator stands outside the action of the story but relates the thoughts, feelings, words, and actions of all the characters. Although this narrator seems objective, keep in mind that he or she still tells only as much or as little as the author wants to reveal.

In the selection below, Ethan and his daughter Becky ride a ski lift. Consider what the narrator tells about the story's events and characters.

Literature Model

> The narrator doesn't reveal what happens to the out-of-control skier. What effect does this have on the reader?

A dark figure with spreading legs veered out of control beneath them, fell forward, and vanished. Ethan cried out, astonished, scandalized; he imagined the man had buried himself alive. Becky was barely amused, and looked away before the dark spots struggling in the drift were lost from sight. As if she might know, Ethan asked, "Who was that?"

> What words and phrases suggest that the narrator may not be telling the reader everything about the characters' thoughts?

"Some kid." Kids, her tone suggested, were in plentiful supply; one could be spared.

John Updike, "Man and Daughter in the Cold"

4.7 Writing Activities

Write to Analyze Point of View in a Story

Write a letter to a friend in which you discuss a short story you have read recently. Give the story's title and author, and tell about the story by analyzing its point of view. What effect does the story's viewpoint have on the conflict? What effect does its point of view have on the resolution? How would the story be different if it had been written from another point of view? Close your letter by telling whether or not you recommend the story.

PURPOSE To analyze the effect of point of view on a short story
AUDIENCE Your friend
LENGTH 1–2 paragraphs

WRITING RUBRICS To write an effective analysis of point of view, you should

- clearly identify the point of view as first person, third-person limited, or third-person omniscient
- use examples from the text to discuss the effect of the point of view

Using Computers

When you're ready to edit your analysis, use the spelling checker on your computer to help you proofread your work. Remember that the checker can't catch correctly spelled words that are used incorrectly. If you write *their* when you mean to say *there*, for example, the checker won't recognize the error. Therefore, it's a good idea to proofread your work yourself line by line to find the less obvious mistakes.

Grammar Link

Avoid incorrect pronoun shift.

When you write, avoid shifting pronouns from one person to another.
Incorrect: If one *works hard,* you *can succeed.*

Revise the sentences below to avoid incorrect pronoun shifts.

1. One's point of view is reflected in your understanding of an event.
2. They enjoy first-person narration because you feel close to the action.
3. I use a third-person omniscient narrator so you can relate everything that happens in a story.
4. An author entertains me best by capturing your interest.
5. One's interest will most likely be captured if their curiosity is aroused.

See Lesson 17.5, page 640.

Viewing and Representing

COOPERATIVE LEARNING In groups of three or four, use your school's video equipment to make a brief video of a journey from your classroom to the school office. Review the video and have each group member write a narration from the first-person point of view describing the journey. Use elements of setting, character, and plot to shape the narrative. Then present your video to the class and share the various narratives to demonstrate how the same event might elicit different responses and descriptions.

UNIT 4
Writing Process in Action

Narrative Writing

In preceding lessons you've learned the basics of narrative—characters, setting, plot, and conflict. You've also had the chance to analyze anecdotes and elements of suspense and to create dialogue. Now it's time to put into practice what you've learned. You're invited to write a narrative that is based on a central conflict and its resolution.

Assignment

Context

You have been asked to contribute to an anthology of student writing called *Resolutions,* a book of stories about various kinds of conflicts. Your story, which can be happy or serious, may be based on a real incident or may be wholly imaginary. It may be told in the first or the third person.

Purpose

To write a true or fictionalized narrative about a conflict.

Audience

High school students and teachers throughout the nation

Length

1–2 pages.

WRITING Online

Visit the *Writer's Choice* Web site at **writerschoice.glencoe.com** for additional writing prompts.

You will find the next few pages helpful for planning and writing your narrative. Begin by reading through the pages, but don't feel you have to remember everything on them. You can refer to the pages when you need to. Use the suggestions, but don't feel limited by them. Remember, you're in charge of your own writing process.

Writing Process in Action

Prewriting

What to write about—something imaginary or something that has actually happened to you or someone you know? Something amusing, suspenseful, or unusual? Your first task is choosing a problem or incident in which a character faces a conflict that needs to be resolved. The prewriting options may help you think of a conflict you can use.

Once you have selected an incident, map out the sequence of events involved in it. Next, arrange these details on a time line, even though you don't have to tell your story in strictly chronological order. Finally, decide what point of view you will use: first-person, third-person limited, or third-person omniscient narrator.

Prewriting Options
- List events that you remember.
- Skim your journal for ideas.
- Brainstorm imaginary conflict situations.
- Freewrite about an issue or topic you feel strongly about.
- Narrow your choices to conflicts your characters can resolve.

Drafting

To begin drafting, envision the scene in which the conflict of your story reaches its crisis point. If you've chosen to write from a particular character's point of view, get inside that character's head. Then begin writing about that crisis moment. Use vivid action verbs and strong sensory details to describe what is going on. Notice the language Julia Alvarez uses to convey how a crisis erupts in the model below.

Prewriting Tip
If you want to review information about third-person narration, see Lesson 4.7, pages 204–207.

Drafting Tip
To find out more about developing conflict in a narrative, see Lesson 4.2, pages 184–187.

Literature Model

The expression on his face shocked both mother and daughter. Carlos's toothless mouth had collapsed into a dark zero. His eyes bored into Yoyo, then shifted to Laura. In barely audible Spanish, as if secret microphones or informers were all about, he whispered to his wife, "You will permit her to read *that*?"

Julia Alvarez, *How the García Girls Lost Their Accents*

Writing Process in Action

Drafting Tip

To help you identify where to add dialogue and anecdotes, see Lessons 4.3 and 4.4, pages 188–195.

Revising Tip

To review ideas that can help you create suspense, see Lesson 4.6, pages 200–203.

TIME

For more about revising, see **TIME Facing the Blank Page**, pp. 128–129.

Next, work backward from your central paragraph. Try to fill in the information about characters, setting, and events the reader needs to know to understand what leads up to this scene.

- Who appears in the scene?
- Why are these characters there?
- How did these characters get there?
- Where does this scene take place?
- Why does it take place in this particular setting?

Then work forward from your central scene. Write about the events that resolve the complication. If you get stuck, focus on answering "What happens next?" Once you have drafted the pieces of your story, refer to your time line to arrange them. Finally, look for good places to add dialogue or anecdotes.

Revising

To begin revising, read over your draft to make sure that what you've written fits your purpose and audience. Then have a **writing conference.** Read your draft to a partner or small group. Use your audience's reactions to help you evaluate your work.

Revising Checklist

- Did I select and develop a conflict that can hold my readers' attention?
- Did I present background events and details that explain the basis of the conflict?
- Do my characters believably resolve the conflict?
- Does my narration present a clear and consistent point of view?
- Does the order in which I presented the events in the narrative make sense?
- Did I use dialogue and anecdotes correctly?

Writing Process in Action

Editing

When you are satisfied with your narrative, **proofread** it carefully for errors in grammar, usage, mechanics, and spelling. Use the questions in the Editing Checklist as a guide.

In addition to proofreading, use the self-evaluation list below to make sure your narrative does all the things you want it to do. When you feel that it does, make a clean copy of your story and proofread it one more time.

Self-Evaluation
Make sure your conflict narrative—

- ✔ focuses on an interesting conflict
- ✔ hooks interest by establishing setting, characters, and conflict early
- ✔ uses dialogue, anecdotes, and figurative language effectively
- ✔ uses point of view consistently
- ✔ follows correct grammar, usage, mechanics, and spelling

Editing Checklist
- Have I capitalized all proper nouns?
- Have I avoided sentence fragments?
- Have I correctly punctuated direct quotations?
- Have I avoided pronoun shifts?
- Have I used vivid verbs and strong adverbs?
- Have I checked spellings of any words I'm unsure of?

Presenting

Although for this assignment you have written a narrative for a fictitious anthology, there's no reason you can't submit it to a real anthology. You might have your story published in your school literary magazine. If you want to submit it for publication for a wider audience, ask your teacher or librarian to suggest suitable journals.

Proofreading Tip

For proofreading symbols, see Lesson 9.12, page 411.

Journal Writing

Reflect on your writing process experience. Answer these questions in your journal: What do you like best about your narrative? What was the hardest part about writing it? What did you learn in your writing conference? What new things have you learned as a writer?

UNIT 4
Literature Model

Narrative Writing

from

How the García Girls Lost Their Accents

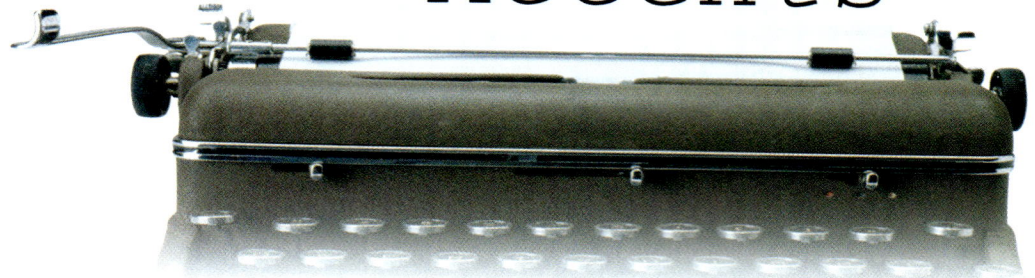

by Julia Alvarez

Born in the Dominican Republic, Julia Alvarez came to the United States with her family when she was ten years old. In this selection from "Daughter of Invention," one of the short stories in Alvarez's first book of fiction, How the García Girls Lost Their Accents, *the author presents a simply structured narrative about her family. As you read, focus on characters and conflict. Then respond in the activities in Linking Writing and Literature on page 220.*

Literature Model

The weekend before the assembly Monday morning Yoyo went into a panic. Her mother would just have to call in tomorrow and say Yoyo was in the hospital, in a coma.

Laura tried to calm her down. "Just remember how Mister Lincoln couldn't think of anything to say at the Gettysburg, but then, bang! *Four score and once upon a time ago,*" she began reciting. "Something is going to come if you just relax. You'll see, like the Americans say, *Necessity is the daughter of invention.* I'll help you."

That weekend, her mother turned all her energy towards helping Yoyo write her speech. "Please, Mami, just leave me alone, please," Yoyo pleaded with her. But Yoyo would get rid of the goose only to have to contend with the gander. Her father kept poking his head in the door just to see if Yoyo had "fulfilled your obligations," a phrase he had used when the girls were younger and he'd check to see whether they had gone to the bathroom before a car trip. Several times that weekend around the supper table, he recited his own high school valedictorian speech. He gave Yoyo pointers on delivery, notes on the great orators and their tricks. (Humbleness and praise and falling silent with great emotion were his favorites.)

Laura sat across the table, the only one who seemed to be listening to him. Yoyo and her sisters were forgetting a lot of their Spanish, and their father's formal, florid diction was hard to understand. But Laura smiled softly to herself, and turned the lazy Susan at the center of the table around and around as if it were the prime mover, the first gear of her attention.

That Sunday evening, Yoyo was reading some poetry to get herself inspired: Whitman's poems in an old book with an engraved cover her father had picked up in a thrift shop next to his office. *I celebrate myself and sing myself.... He most honors my style who learns under it to destroy the teacher.* The poet's words shocked and thrilled her. She had gotten used to the nuns, a literature of appropriate sentiments, poems with a message, expurgated[1] texts. But here was a flesh and blood man, belching and laughing and sweating in poems. *Who touches this book touches a man.*

That night, at last, she started to write, recklessly, three, five pages, looking up once only to see her father passing by the hall on tiptoe. When Yoyo was done, she read over her words, and her eyes filled. She finally sounded like herself in English!

As soon as she had finished that first draft, she called her mother to her room. Laura listened attentively while Yoyo read the speech out loud, and in the end, her eyes were glistening too. Her face was soft and warm and proud. "*Ay,* Yoyo, you are going to be the one to bring our name to the headlights in this country! That is a beautiful, beautiful speech. I want

> *The poet's words shocked and thrilled her. She had gotten used to the nuns . . . But here was a flesh and blood man . . .*

---

[1] **expurgated** (eks′ pər gāt′ əd) with objectionable passages removed

Literature Model

for your father to hear it before he goes to sleep. Then I will type it for you, all right?"

Down the hall they went, mother and daughter, faces flushed with accomplishment. Into the master bedroom where Carlos was propped up on his pillows, still awake, reading the Dominican papers, already days old. Now that the dictatorship had been toppled, he had become interested in his country's fate again. The interim government was going to hold the first free elections in thirty years. History was in the making, freedom and hope were in the air again! There was still some question in his mind whether or not he might move his family back. But Laura had gotten used to the life here. She did not want to go back to the old country where, de la Torre or not, she was only a wife and a mother (and a failed one at that, since she had never provided the required son). Better an independent nobody than a high-class houseslave. She did not come straight out and disagree with her husband's plans. Instead, she fussed with him about reading the papers in bed, soiling their sheets with those poorly printed, foreign tabloids. "*The Times* is not that bad!" she'd claim if her husband tried to humor her by saying they shared the same dirty habit.

The minute Carlos saw his wife and daughter filing in, he put his paper down, and his face brightened as if at long last his wife had delivered the son, and that was the news she was bringing him. His teeth were already grinning from the glass of water next to his bedside lamp, so he lisped when he said, "Eh-speech, eh-speech!"

"It is so beautiful, Cuco," Laura coached him, turning the sound on his TV off. She sat down at the foot of the bed. Yoyo stood before both of them, blocking their view of the soldiers in helicopters landing amid silenced gun reports and explosions. A few weeks ago it had been the shores of the Dominican Republic. Now it was the jungles of Southeast Asia they were saving. Her mother gave her the nod to begin reading.

Yoyo didn't need much encouragement. She put her nose to the fire, as her mother would have said, and read from start to finish without looking up. When she concluded, she was a little embarrassed at the pride she took in her own words. She pretended to quibble with a phrase or two, then looked questioningly to her mother. Laura's face was radiant. Yoyo turned to share her pride with her father.

The expression on his face shocked both mother and daughter. Carlos's toothless mouth had collapsed into a dark zero. His eyes bored into Yoyo, then shifted to Laura. In barely audible Spanish, as if secret microphones or informers were all about, he whispered to his wife, "You will permit her to read *that*?"

Laura's eyebrows shot up, her mouth fell open. In the old country, any whisper of a challenge to authority could bring the secret police in their black V.W.'s. But this was America. People could say what they

> *In the old country, any whisper of a challenge to authority could bring the secret police in their black V.W.'s. But this was America.*

214 Unit 4 Narrative Writing

Literature Model

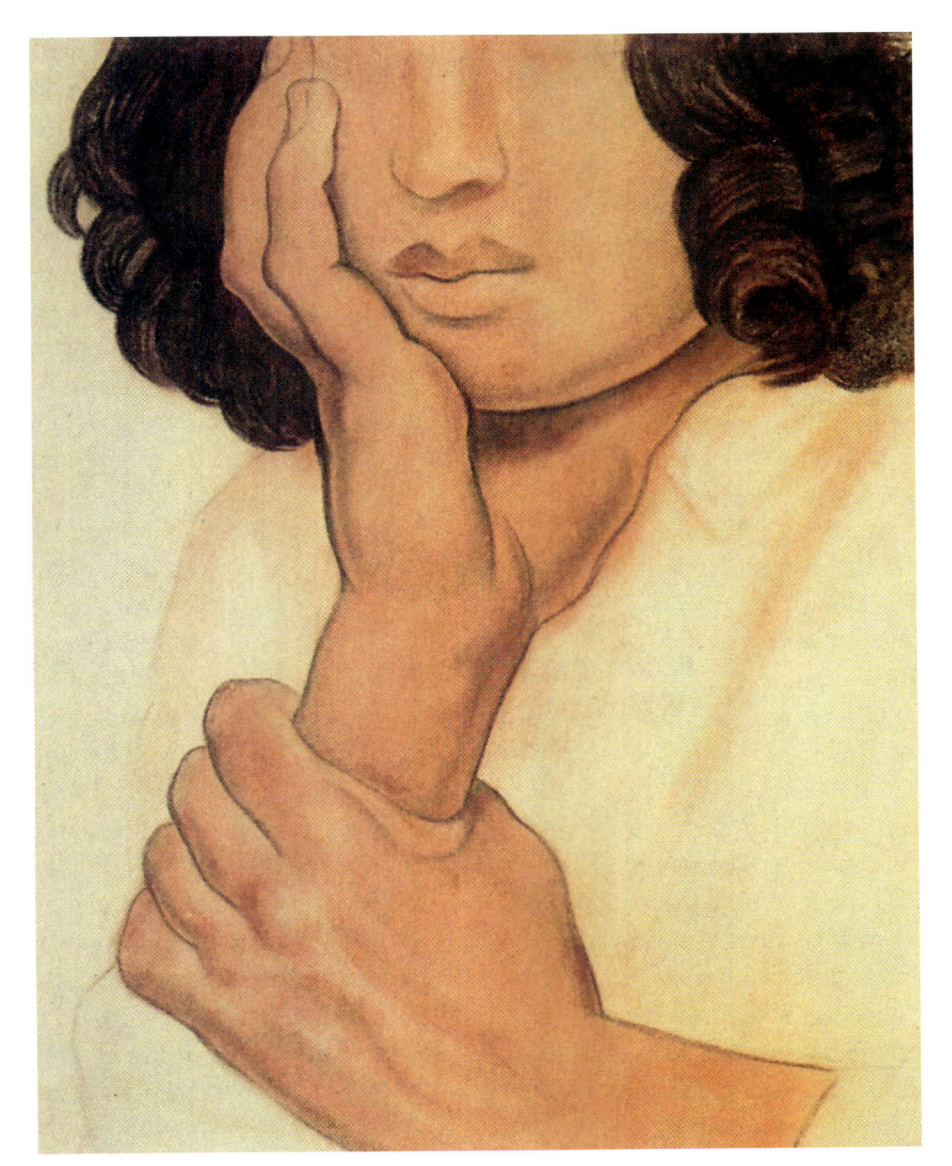

Diego Rivera, *Tina Modotti*, 1927

thought. "What is wrong with her speech?" Laura questioned him.

"What ees wrrrong with her eh-speech?" Carlos wagged his head at her. His anger was always more frightening in his broken English. As if he had mutilated the language in his fury—and now there was nothing to stand between them and his raw, dumb anger. "What is wrong? I will tell you what is wrong. It show no gratitude. It is boastful. *I celebrate myself*? *The best student learns to destroy the teacher*?" He mocked Yoyo's pla-

Literature Model

giarized words. "That is insubordinate.[2] It is improper. It is disrespecting of her teachers—" In his anger he had forgotten his fear of lurking spies: each wrong he voiced was a decibel[3] higher than the last outrage. Finally, he shouted at Yoyo, "As your father, I forbid you to make that eh-speech!"

Laura leapt to her feet, a sign that *she* was about to deliver her own speech. She was a small woman, and she spoke all her pronouncements standing up, either for more projection or as a carry-over from her girlhood in convent schools where one asked for, and literally, took the floor in order to speak. She stood by Yoyo's side, shoulder to shoulder. They looked down at Carlos. "That is no tone of voice—" she began.

But now, Carlos was truly furious. It was bad enough that his daughter was rebelling, but here was his own wife joining forces with her. Soon he would be surrounded by a houseful of independent American women. He too leapt from the bed, throwing off his covers. The Spanish newspapers flew across the room. He snatched the speech out of Yoyo's hands, held it before the girl's wide eyes, a vengeful, mad look in his own, and then once, twice, three, four, countless times, he tore the speech into shreds.

"Are you crazy?" Laura lunged at him. "Have you gone mad? That is her speech for tomorrow you have torn up!"

"Have *you* gone mad?" He shook her away. "You were going to let her read that . . . that insult to her teachers?"

"Insult to her teachers!" Laura's face had crumpled up like a piece of paper. On it was written a love note to her husband, an unhappy, haunted man. "This is America, Papi, America! You are not in a savage country anymore!"

Meanwhile, Yoyo was on her knees, weeping wildly, collecting all the little pieces of her speech, hoping that she could put it back together before the assembly tomorrow morning. But not even a sibyl[4] could have made sense of those tiny scraps of paper. All hope was lost. "He broke it, he broke it," Yoyo moaned as she picked up a handful of pieces.

> *Yoyo was on her knees, weeping wildly, collecting all the little pieces of her speech . . .*

Probably, if she had thought a moment about it, she would not have done what she did next. She would have realized her father had lost brothers and friends to the dictator Trujillo. For the rest of his life, he would be haunted by blood in the streets and late night disappearances. Even after all these years, he cringed if a black Volkswagen passed him on the street. He feared anyone in uniform: the meter maid giving out parking tickets, a museum guard approaching to tell him not to get too close to his favorite Goya.

---

2 insubordinate (in′ sə bôrd′ ən it) disobedient
3 decibel (des′ ə bel′) a numerical measure of the loudness of sound
4 sibyl (sib′ əl) a fortune teller

Literature Model

On her knees, Yoyo thought of the worst thing she could say to her father. She gathered a handful of scraps, stood up, and hurled them in his face. In a low, ugly whisper, she pronounced Trujillo's hated nickname: "Chapita! You're just another Chapita!"

It took Yoyo's father only a moment to register the loathsome nickname before he came after her. Down the halls they raced, but Yoyo was quicker than he and made it into her room just in time to lock the door as her father threw his weight against it. He called down curses on her head, ordered her on his authority as her father to open that door! He throttled that doorknob, but all to no avail. Her mother's love of gadgets saved Yoyo's hide that night. Laura had hired a locksmith to install good locks on all the bedroom doors after the house had been broken into once while they were away. Now if burglars broke in again, and the family were at home, there would be a second round of locks for the thieves to contend with.

"Lolo," she said, trying to calm him down. "Don't you ruin my new locks."

Finally he did calm down, his anger spent. Yoyo heard their footsteps retreating down the hall. Their door clicked shut. Then, muffled voices, her mother's rising in anger, in persuasion, her father's deeper murmurs of explanation and self-defense. The house fell silent a moment, before Yoyo heard, far off, the gun blasts and explosions, the serious, self-important voices of newscasters reporting their TV war.

A little while later, there was a quiet knock at Yoyo's door, followed by a tentative attempt at the doorknob. "Cuquita?" her mother whispered. "Open up, Cuquita."

"Go away," Yoyo wailed, but they both knew she was glad her mother was there, and needed only a moment's protest to save face.

> *Down the halls they raced, but Yoyo was quicker than he and made it into her room just in time to lock the door as her father threw his weight against it.*

Together they concocted a speech: two brief pages of stale compliments and the polite commonplaces on teachers, a speech wrought by necessity and without much invention by mother and daughter late into the night on one of the pads of paper Laura had once used for her own inventions. After it was drafted, Laura typed it up while Yoyo stood by, correcting her mother's misnomers[5] and mis-sayings.

Yoyo came home the next day with the success story of the assembly. The nuns had been flattered, the audience had stood up and given "our devoted teachers a standing ovation," what Laura had suggested they do at the end of the speech.

She clapped her hands together as Yoyo recreated the moment. "I stole that from your father's speech, remember? Remember how he put that in at the end?" She quoted him in Spanish, then translated for Yoyo into English.

That night, Yoyo watched him from the upstairs hall window, where she'd retreated

---

5 misnomers (mis nō′ mərz) errors in naming persons or places

Literature Model

the minute she heard his car pull up in front of the house. Slowly, her father came up the driveway, a grim expression on his face as he grappled with a large, heavy cardboard box. At the front door, he set the package down carefully and patted all his pockets for his house keys. (If only he'd had Laura's ticking key chain!) Yoyo heard the snapping open of locks downstairs. She listened as he struggled to maneuver the box through the narrow doorway. He called her name several times, but she did not answer him.

"My daughter, your father, he love you very much," he explained from the bottom

Adrián Luis González, Painted pottery typewriter, c. 1980

Literature Model

of the stairs. "He just want to protect you." Finally, her mother came up and pleaded with Yoyo to go down and reconcile[6] with him. "Your father did not mean to harm. You must pardon him. Always it is better to let bygones be forgotten, no?"

Downstairs, Yoyo found her father setting up a brand new electric typewriter on the kitchen table. It was even better than her mother's. He had outdone himself with all the extra features: a plastic carrying case with Yoyo's initials decaled below the handle, a brace to lift the paper upright while she typed, an erase cartridge, an automatic margin tab, a plastic hood like a toaster cover to keep the dust away. Not even her mother could have invented such a machine!

But Laura's inventing days were over just as Yoyo's were starting up with her school-wide success. Rather than the rolling suitcase everyone else in the family remembers, Yoyo thinks of the speech her mother wrote as her last invention. It was as if, after that, her mother had passed on to Yoyo her pencil and pad and said, "Okay, Cuquita, here's the buck. You give it a shot."

> *But Laura's inventing days were over just as Yoyo's were starting up with her school-wide success. . . . Yoyo thinks of the speech her mother wrote as her last invention.*

---

[6] **reconcile** (rek′ ən sīl′) to make up; to settle a disagreement

Narrative Writing

Literature Model

Linking Writing and Literature

Readers Respond to the Model

How does Julia Alvarez use characters and conflict to make her narrative effective?

Explore Julia Alvarez's story by answering these questions. Then read what other students liked about Alvarez's narrative.

1. What is the basic conflict in Alvarez's narrative? What background information does the author provide to set up this conflict and make it appear more realistic?

2. Choose a character that you particularly liked in the story. Explain how Alvarez's description of this character contributes to the narrative.

3. Alvarez wrote this story using a third-person omniscient narrator. Analyze how this point of view affects the story. How would the story have changed if the author had told it in the first person?

What Students Say

"My favorite character was Laura. I really enjoyed her enthusiasm for her daughter's speech and how she stood up to her husband, a forbidden act in the Dominican Republic. The author set up the conflict by telling how the family's life had been in the Dominican Republic and then contrasting that culture with the American culture.

I would have written the story in first person. Maybe the author wrote it in third person because it was based on a personal experience and brought back too many memories, so she had to distance herself by writing in third person."

Rachel Hansen

"My favorite character was Laura, the mother, because she was kind-hearted and open-minded. She reminded me of my mother. The writer made Yoyo's mother seem real by making her passionate. The scene I remembered most clearly was when the father ripped up Yoyo's speech. His reaction seemed so unjust and unfair."

Maritza Pagán

UNIT 4 Review

Reflecting on the Unit

Summarize what you learned in this unit by answering the following questions.

1. What are the basic elements of narrative writing?
2. What is the role of conflict in a plot?
3. What purposes do dialogue and anecdotes serve in a narrative?
4. What are the three narrative points of view and the characteristics of each?
5. What are some important elements and techniques in writing a sports narrative? In writing about suspense?

Adding to Your Portfolio

CHOOSE A SELECTION FOR YOUR PORTFOLIO Look over the narrative writing you have done during this unit. Select a completed piece of writing to put into your portfolio. The piece that you choose should show some or all of the following:

- believable situations and characters
- clear, realistic dialogue
- a clear sequence of events

REFLECT ON YOUR CHOICE Attach a note to the piece you chose, explaining briefly why you chose it and what you learned from writing it.

SET GOALS How can you improve your writing? What skill will you focus on the next time you write?

Writing Across the Curriculum

MAKE A LITERATURE CONNECTION Think about Julia Alvarez's story from *How the García Girls Lost Their Accents*. What other short stories have you recently read and enjoyed that involved conflict? Choose one of these stories and write a paragraph or two about it, narrating the basic conflict and explaining how the conflict was resolved.

You may wish to share your completed piece with a small group or with the whole class. Consider setting up a book and story display so that students can read each other's recommended stories.

"No matter how hard teams work to perfect their signaling system or crack the enemy's code, there's always the chance something will get lost in translation."

—Tim Kurkjian, "Sign Language: The Game Within the Game of Baseball"

UNIT 5
Expository Writing

Writing in the Real World: *Suzanne Winckler*	224
Lesson 5.1 Explaining and Informing	228
Lesson 5.2 Going into Detail	232
Lesson 5.3 Explaining How To . . .	236
Lesson 5.4 Explaining Cause and Effect	240
Lesson 5.5 Classifying a Subject	244
Lesson 5.6 Comparing and Contrasting	248
Lesson 5.7 Writing with Graphics	252
Lesson 5.8 Writing a Feature Article	256
Lesson 5.9 Answering an Essay Question	262
Lesson 5.10 Writing About Literature: Comparing and Contrasting Two Myths	268
Writing Process in Action	272
Literature Model: from *Of Wolves and Men* by Barry Holstun Lopez	276
Unit 5 Review	281

Writing in the Real World

Suzanne Winckler wrote the following expository article about the first big day in cactus hunting. Big day? Winckler got this idea from a tradition in the bird world. In bird watching, a "big day" means spotting as many birds as possible in twenty-four hours. In her article, which appeared in *Audubon* magazine, Winckler conveys technical information about cacti, yet she makes the subject lively through her first-person point of view and informal style.

MEDIA Magazine Article Connection

Counting Cacti

By Suzanne Winckler

Whenever I look back on the world's first cactus big day I will remember the Cassin's kingbirds. They started yapping in the trees over my tent at 4:30 in the morning. I lay there thinking how they sounded like a pack of overindulged miniature poodles, an analogy that distressed me, since as a birdwatcher I don't really like to disparage the objects of my esteem. They also seemed to be taunting me, as kingbirds have a way of doing, reminding me that I know more about birds than cacti, but it was too late now.

Five of us had converged the night before in the Davis Mountains, a little chip off the Rockies in far west Texas, having agreed some weeks earlier that it was time to expand the parameters of the big day. . . . We were going to crisscross west Texas in search of opuntias, chollas, hedgehogs, horse cripplers, barrel cacti, and even give a stab at finding *Coryphantha minima,* which is the smallest cactus in the world.

Large expanses of west Texas are flat and empty, and as scenery an acquired taste. The awesome monotony is broken in places by island ranges like the Davis and Chisos mountains, which by contrast are gorgeous each in its own way. . . . We were going to be operating on several hundred miles of road in and between these two mountain ranges.

There are about sixty species of cactus in west Texas out of a family total of two or three thousand. Some of them, like the chollas, which grow out on the desert like enormous candelabras, are quite common and widespread, while other species exhibit a fierce partiality to small and scattered plots of certain soils. Needless to say these finicky ones are, first, rare and, second, highly prized by cactus fanciers . . .

One complaint I have about birds is that too few of them are pink. This is not the situation with cactus flowers. They occur in many lurid and neon shades of that color, and although I could have faked a loftier purpose, it was the possibility of encountering a lot of tawdry pink flowers glowing in the desert that motivated me to participate in the cactus big day. . . .

When I found *Echinomastus intertextus* my heart leapt. I'm certain I had the look on my face that my dog does when she brings back her stick. (It is a gaze of contentment and pride in excess

Expository Writing

224 Unit 5 Expository Writing

Writing in the Real World

of the accomplishment.) The time was 9:15 A.M., and we were milling about in a grassy mountain pasture just south of the town of Fort Davis. We had already driven something like sixty miles to find an odd little lime-green prickly-pear (*Opuntia polyacantha* var. *rufispina*), but for two hours' effort the list was small—only four species. I had to remind myself that while the early morning hours are best for birds, cacti do not fly away when it gets hot.

E. intertextus was number five. I didn't know what it was, of course. I had simply stumbled upon a cactus that fit Allan [Zimmerman's] description: "Look for something that resembles a brown tennis ball."

A Writer's Process

Prewriting
Getting the Idea

Suzanne Winckler, a freelance writer and passionate bird watcher, had participated in several big days while birding. She wanted to take the big day tradition—finding as many species as possible in twenty-four hours—and apply it to another organism, in this case cactus.

Winckler's first step was to contact Dr. Allan Zimmerman, an expert taxonomist, to see if he would participate. She then got the go-ahead from an editor at *Audubon*, who gave her a two-thousand-word limit and a deadline. Winckler then readied herself for the field.

While the research for some expository writing is done by reading texts, it sometimes requires field research. In this case, Winckler went to Big Bend, a vast desert area in southwest Texas, to conduct her big day of cacti hunting. Her team, which included Zimmerman and three other biologists, started before daylight and worked intensely until after dark.

For Winckler, the day was a juggling act—stalking rare cacti with the team, then stepping back to record the experience as a writer. She jotted information in a hard-bound record book. She also sketched all the cacti and asked Zimmerman to tell her their scientific names.

At home, she interviewed several more cactus experts by phone. She then organized her notes, transcribed tapes that were made during the hunt, and mapped out a rough structure for the piece.

Suzanne Winckler, Freelance writer

Writing in the Real World

Drafting
Crafting the Story

With her plan in mind, it took Winckler about five mornings at the computer to craft the story.

She began with noisy kingbirds. "I wanted to emphasize that what I was picking up on in the landscape was birds—not cacti—and the sense that it was an incredible experience in the tent." From there, Winckler tried to teach readers about Big Bend and rare cacti, and leave them caring about the place and its garden of obscure plants.

Winckler kept her audience in mind as she wrote. She knew that most readers would be unfamiliar with cacti, so she compared these plants to everyday things. She wrote that one cactus smelled like "floor polish" while another looked like a "candelabra."

With all her descriptions, Winckler resisted the urge to "be too flowery." As a nature writer, she stressed the importance of grounding the article with solid and interesting facts. "You can use description to get readers involved in an expository article. But you can't just ride on that. You have to introduce the science of nature so people will understand how things function."

Revising/Editing
Playing With Sentences

Once Winckler finished her first draft, she began to revise—adding some details, deleting other information. She also worked on her sentence structure. "I spend a lot of time writing a sentence and then turning it on its head, putting something in the middle. I play at it a lot."

Once Winckler's editor read the story, she had relatively few changes to suggest. Most of Winckler's larger pieces do take more editing—something she appreciates. "I wish I were edited more heavily," Winckler observed. "The world needs more editors. I'm aware of how much other people can help your writing."

An elf owlet sits on a saguaro cactus.

Examining Writing in the Real World

Analyzing the Media Connection

Discuss these questions about the article on pages 224–225.

1. Suzanne Winckler wrote her article in the first-person point of view. If written in the third person, how would the article have been different?
2. How does Winckler use comparison and contrast in the excerpt of her article?
3. What is the effect of Winckler's use of informal speech?
4. How does Winckler employ both vivid description and factual information when she tells about different types of cacti?
5. What effect is Winckler trying to achieve with the opening sentences of her paragraphs?

Analyzing a Writer's Process

Discuss these questions about Suzanne Winckler's writing process.

1. How did Winckler gather information for her expository article about hunting cacti?
2. What were Winckler's purposes in writing the article?
3. How did Winckler help her readers over the hurdle of understanding an unfamiliar subject?
4. As she drafted her article, how did Winckler strike a balance between description and technical information?
5. How does Winckler value collaboration in the writing process?

Grammar Link

Make subject and verb agree in an inverted sentence.

In inverted sentences, the subject follows the verb:

> There **are** about sixty **species** of cactus in west Texas. . . .

An inverted sentence may also begin with a prepositional phrase:

> On a saguaro cactus **sits** an **elf owlet**.

Find the simple subject in each sentence below. Then write the verb that agrees with the subject.

1. Outside Winckler's tent (scream, screams) the annoying kingbirds.
2. Here (come, comes) Zimmerman.
3. In southwestern Texas (grow, grows) many kinds of cacti.
4. There (was, were) cactuses Zimmerman had never heard of before.
5. There (is, are) similarities between bird watching and cactus watching.

See Lesson 16.3, pages 612–613.

LESSON 5.1

Explaining and Informing

Expository writing is writing that explains and informs. In the model below, a science writer explains what really happens when a person gets out of bed.

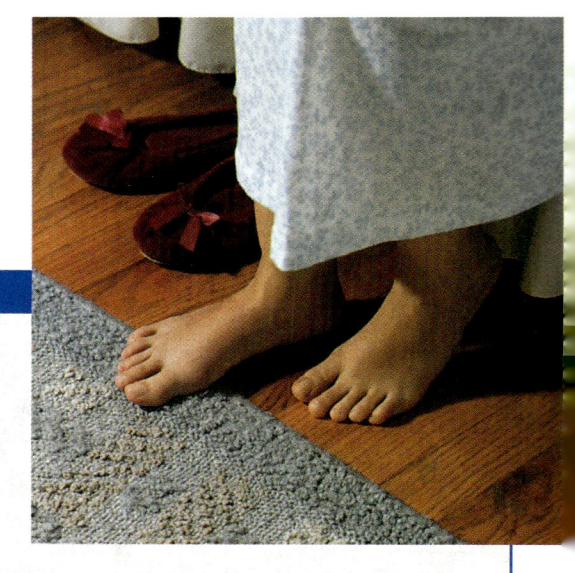

Literature Model

> Whack thump bam! The man's foot extends out of bed and lands on the floor. The floorboards jam down and their vibrations travel sideways like pond waves to the wall. The whole house compresses in the new loading—bricks where the floor fits into the wall shrinking smaller by 1/100,000 inch from the weight.
>
> Any impact that doesn't get lost in the walls stays quivering in the floor. The chest of drawers starts lifting up and down, as does the bed, the chair, the table with its plant on top, the stack of magazines and Sunday papers in the corner, and even the old coffee cup left down on the floor. All lift up and bounce down, rebound up and crash down again as the floor reverberates to get rid of its buzzing energy. In a particularly energetic leap out of bed this bouncing of furniture can be seen (lampshades especially are prone to being knocked over in such moments), but even with a softer landing the furniture shaking takes place.
>
> Then the second foot touches down, the waker stands up, and he steps to the double-glazed window to see what is happening outside.
>
> David Bodanis, *The Secret House*

Bodanis introduces the cause of the surprising chain of tiny, imperceptible events that follows the simple act of getting out of bed.

The writer uses examples to make his point memorable.

228 Unit 5 Expository Writing

The Nature of Expository Writing

Bodanis's explanation of the strange and jarring events caused by stepping out of bed is an example of expository writing. The student model below shows another type of expository writing. It describes the step-by-step process of a flower sprouting, growing, and blooming. Although there are different kinds of expository writing, all writers of exposition share one goal: to present a clear, concise explanation that readers will find interesting and informative.

> **Vocabulary Tip**
>
> As you revise, make your explanations livelier and more informative by replacing general verbs with more precise action verbs. Bodanis, for example, uses *bounce, rebound,* and *reverberates,* in his explanation. See Lesson 10.3, pages 452–460.

Student Model

The flower, one of nature's many miracles, is created through a series of complex steps. With an embryo, a supply of stored food, and a protective covering, the seed begins the process. Most seeds remain dormant at first, usually because conditions are not favorable for growth. Seeds have been known to stay dormant from one week to fifty years and still germinate properly. Germination occurs when there is an abundant supply of water, an adequate amount of oxygen, and the proper temperatures. Crucial to the plant's life, water begins the next step in the process. The seed absorbs large amounts of water, causing the protective coating to soften. The internal tissues then swell and break through the coating. This new life, this plant, immediately begins to burn food, and it produces the energy necessary for growth. The vulnerable plant now becomes susceptible to sunlight. Too much or too little can harm it. However, the sun helps make the food for the plant to burn and receive energy. This process continues even after the first leaves develop. The plant grows stronger and more mature each day. Finally, the full-grown plant is ready to receive its crowning glory—the flower.

Billy McKnight,
Jefferson Davis High School, Montgomery, Alabama

McKnight introduces this paragraph with a clear statement of what he will explain.

McKnight ties his process explanation together with transitions that show chronological order. What are some transitions that he uses?

Journal Writing

Look through some books and magazines for three expository paragraphs on different topics—for example, the development of a frog or the construction of a house. In your journal, briefly explain why each is an expository paragraph.

The Varieties of Expository Writing

The essay is one of the most common forms of expository writing. Usually, it consists of an introduction, body, and conclusion. The **introduction** includes a thesis statement—a one-sentence summary of your purpose for writing. The **body** consists of one or more paragraphs of details that support the thesis. The **conclusion** summarizes or gives the implications of what you've said in your essay.

You probably use other forms of expository writing quite often without even realizing it. You are using expository writing if you write out instructions for a neighbor on taking care of your cat while you are on vacation, or if you jot down directions for a friend.

The chart below presents the various kinds of expository writing, the basic purpose of each kind, and an example of each. While each variety has a distinct purpose, you can use two or more varieties in combination to explain and inform.

Kinds of Expository Writing		
Kind	**Basic Purpose**	**Example**
Definition	To define a term or give the basic tenets of a theory	A supernova is a star that explodes, becoming extremely bright before fading and leaving a huge cloud of dust and gas.
Process	To give the steps in a process or explain a sequence of events	To locate their prey, bats use a process called echolocation, in which they send out high-pitched sound waves. These waves bounce off insects and echo back to the bat.
Cause and Effect	To explain how or why one or more events or actions cause other things to happen	The rubbing and grinding of the Earth's crustal plates against one another causes earthquakes.
Classification	To break down a broad topic into narrower categories	There are two main types of whales: toothed whales and baleen whales.
Comparison-Contrast	To discuss similarities in and differences between two related phenomena or events	Venus's-flytraps and pitcher plants are both meat-eating plants. Venus's-flytraps trap insects in their leaves. Pitcher plants capture insects that drown in their jug-shaped leaves.

5.1 Writing Activities

Write an Expository Paragraph

Pick a simple process or event to explain or define. Be sure that you are familiar enough with the parts of it to explain it clearly. Write a paragraph or two about it.

PURPOSE To explain the details of a process or event
AUDIENCE Your teacher and classmates
LENGTH 1–2 paragraphs

WRITING RUBRICS To write an effective expository paragraph, you should
- give a clear, concise explanation
- include a clear opening and conclusion
- use details to support your thesis in the body

Cross-Curricular Activity

ART Find a painting or a photograph that conveys a message or illustrates a process in a visual way. Then write a short paper explaining the message or process. Let other students read your paper before you show them the picture, to see whether your explanation is clear. Organize your explanation so readers can see the connections to specific parts of the picture.

Grammar Link

Use precise verbs.

In both models the writers use precise action verbs to make their explanations vivid as well as informative. Use precise verbs to revise the sentences below.

1. The Aries spacecraft is off the Cape Canaveral launch pad.
2. Crowds look at the craft atop its pillar of flame.
3. In the third booster stage, the capsule leaves Earth's orbit.
4. Through their porthole, the astronauts see the red planet Mars.
5. Endless plains and jagged chasms are on Mars.

See Lesson 10.3, pages 452–460.

Using Computers

Use a search engine to find an expository article in an online magazine. In one or two paragraphs, identify the thesis statement and summarize the article. Explain which of the five types of expository writing listed in the chart on page 230 are used in the article, and how they are appropriate to the purpose of the article. Be as critical as any good magazine editor would be!

LESSON 5.2

Going into Detail

Supporting details are essential elements in expository writing. Note how a science writer uses statistics and specific examples to explain the relationship between scents and human behavior.

Literature Model

"We have already developed a system to control the environment by fragrance," says Junichi Yagi, vice president of S. Technology Center-America, a subsidiary of Shimizu, Japan's largest architectural, engineering, and construction firm.... Experiments in Japan with thirteen keypunch operators, monitored eight hours a day for thirty days, showed that the average number of errors per hour dropped by 21 percent when office air was scented with lavender (it reduces stress) and by 33 percent when laced with jasmine (it induces relaxation); a stimulating lemon scent reduced errors by 54 percent....

Shimizu researchers also find that orange, peppermint, eucalyptus, chamomile, and Japanese cypress are soothing, while scarlet sage and rosemary are stimulating. (I would add Play-Doh and Rockin' Roger's Bar-B-Q Sauce to the stimulating list.)

Judith Stone, *Light Elements*

Here Judith Stone provides statistics to illustrate her point.

Stone adds two scents to the list. Which smells might you add?

Kinds of Supporting Details

Supporting details give expository writing its strength. Note the types of supporting details listed in the chart below.

Supporting Details for Expository Writing	
Kinds	**Example of Use in Exposition**
Facts	Alligators live largely in freshwater, while crocodiles live mostly in saltwater or in at least slightly salty water.
Statistics	The world's largest tree is a giant sequoia called the General Sherman tree. It measures 101.5 feet at the base, is 272.4 feet tall, and weighs about 12,334,000 pounds.
Examples/ Incidents	The chimpanzee is an example of an animal that makes and uses tools. Chimpanzees cut pieces of grass to specific lengths for fishing termites out of termite mounds.
Sensory details	The aurora borealis appears as a glimmering curtain of light flashing in the night sky.
Reasons	One reason some people think penguins are mammals rather than birds is that their feathers are short and fluffy and, from a distance, resemble hair.

> **Prewriting Tip**
>
> To help come up with supporting details, you can brainstorm with other students. To learn more about brainstorming, see Lesson 2.2, p. 62.

How to Select Supporting Details

Common sense will help you select supporting details. For example, if you are explaining a process, you will want to present all the steps. The following factors are the most important for selecting types of supporting details for a particular exposition:

- the type of exposition you are writing
- your purpose for writing, especially your secondary purpose (see examples of secondary purpose in the chart on page 234)
- the level of knowledge or expertise of your audience

Journal Writing

Read a magazine or newspaper article. Next, without reviewing the article, list in your journal the supporting details you recall. What makes these details memorable? Write your ideas.

5.2 Going into Detail

The chart below shows how to analyze key factors in selecting appropriate supporting details for two kinds of exposition.

Using Supporting Details		
Factor	**Situation #1**	**Situation #2**
Main purpose and type of your exposition	To explain the cause and effects of a natural phenomenon	To compare two theories about a natural phenomenon
Your secondary purpose	To interest your audience in the topic	To show your knowledge of different scientific theories
Level of knowledge of your audience	Audience unfamiliar with the topic	Specialized audience (scientists) familiar with the topic
Kinds of supporting details you might rely on most heavily	Incidents and interesting sensory details	Facts and statistics that provide convincing support

How to Organize Supporting Details

How you organize your supporting details depends in part on the type of exposition you are writing. For example, if you are writing about a cause and its effects, you might present the least important effect first and the most important effect last, as illustrated in the model below.

Model

Urban gardens—plots overflowing with juicy red tomatoes, shiny green cukes, crisp beans, and myriad flowers—have been popping up in greater numbers all over our neighborhood since spring. You've probably seen them in backyards, empty lots, even on rooftops. Rising vegetable prices, up 35 percent from last year, are surely one reason behind the spread of these garden plots. Even more important reasons include the desire for healthful, pesticide-free vegetables and for the better taste of the home-grown vegetables. Delia Jackson exemplifies this trend. She even took a course called City Gardens at the local community center. Soon after the class ended, she began a roof garden atop the high-rise where she lives. "My friends joked about it at first," she says, "but now the same ones are coming over for my vine-ripened tomatoes."

In what order does the writer list supporting details?

The writer concludes with a prime example of one urban gardener.

5.2 Writing Activities

Write a Background Information Article

Use the following details to write an explanation of the term *hurricane*. Your writing will be a background information piece for your community newspaper.

1. In 1992 one hurricane caused $20 billion in damage and killed at least 38 people.
2. Hurricanes develop over warm tropical ocean waters.
3. The winds and rain produce massive waves, called a storm surge, which bring floods.
4. A hurricane is a powerful, swirling storm with winds over 75 miles per hour.
5. The most destructive part of the hurricane (where winds may reach 150 miles per hour) is the area of wall clouds surrounding the eye, an area of calm about 20 miles in diameter.
6. A hurricane may cover an area of 200 to 300 miles in diameter.

PURPOSE To explain what a hurricane is and to describe its destructive power
AUDIENCE Newspaper readers
LENGTH 2–3 paragraphs

WRITING RUBRICS To write an effective background information article, you should
- choose memorable statistics and sensory details to get your readers' attention
- define new terms for a general audience
- order your details for their best effect

Viewing and Representing

Use an article from a print or an electronic source to create a poster illustrating the use of effective detail. Label the details that support the main and secondary purposes of the article and those that most forcefully or vividly convey the message.

Cross-Curricular Activity

SCIENCE Explain a natural process, such as soil erosion, for a science room reference notebook. In a small group, make a list of the supporting details that you will use to explain the process, and then write a draft of your explanation. Your audience will be students who need help to understand a process.

Grammar Link

Use commas correctly in a series.

Rewrite the following sentences, adding commas to separate three or more words or phrases.

1. Peppermint orange jasmine and chamomile are scents commonly used in teas.
2. Popular dessert coffees include those flavored with hazelnut Dutch chocolate or Swiss mocha.
3. She ground the coffee beans scooped them into the filter added four cups of water and turned on the coffeemaker.
4. Coffee is a tree or shrub native to tropical Africa Asia and Central and South America.
5. Coffee trees grow about fifteen feet tall have long leaves and produce white or cream flowers.

See Lesson 21.6, page 738.

LESSON 5.3

Explaining How To...

A "how to" paper, a common form of expository writing, is used to teach a skill or just to share knowledge. Usually the writer presents the instructions as a series of steps. What process is Patrick McManus explaining in the model below?

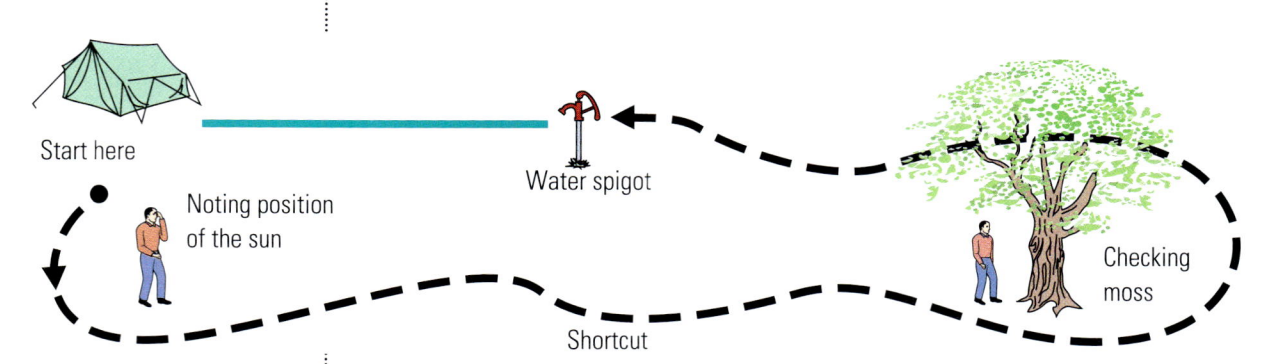

Literature Model

> Now how should you go about getting lost? ... If you are camped in a public campground, simply say that you are going to take a shortcut to the communal spigot [water faucet] to fill the water bucket.... Shortcuts rank number one among ways to get lost quickly and thoroughly.... Before starting your shortcut, take careful note of the position of the sun. This will give the impression that you know what you're doing.... [Also,] always study on which side of the trees the moss is growing. Guides and other experienced woodsmen are fond of giving this advice, because looking at moss helps even them to get lost.
>
> Patrick McManus, *Rubber Legs and White Tail-Hairs*

In his introductory sentence, McManus identifies the process he will be explaining.

McManus gives tips to help a camper get lost. Have you gotten lost anywhere besides in the woods? What tips would you give to get lost where you did?

How do you steer a canoe? How do bees make honey? Any process can be explained clearly, step by step.

Think About Your Purpose

Sometimes you explain a process in order to teach a skill, such as how to feed a pet snake.

Sometimes you may explain a process just to share knowledge, such as how fireflies make their flashing lights.

Suppose you wanted to explain how to bathe a dog. During prewriting, list all the steps in a chart similar to the one below.

Planning a "How To" Paper

1. Choose topic: how to bathe a dog.
2. Define audience: first-time dog owners.
3. Gather information: read manuals, interview, observe.
4. List steps of the process in chronological order.
   a. Set up safe bathing area—rubber mat in the tub, nonskid rug on floor.
   b. Gather shampoo, sponge, bucket or shower head, towels, comb or brush, and other equipment you need.
   c. If you don't have a hand-held shower head, fill tub half-full with lukewarm water.
   d. Plug dog's ears with cotton to prevent water from entering. (Remember to take cotton out after bath.)
   e. Wet dog all over with lukewarm water.
   f. Shampoo dog, using your fingers to scrub.
   g. Rinse dog with water, using bucket or shower head.
   h. Wash dog's face with sponge dipped in clear water.
   i. Let dog shake off excess water.
   j. Rub dog dry with towels, or use hair dryer.
   k. Comb dog when coat is dry.
5. Note any special instructions.
6. Tell result of process: clean, happy dog.

> **Grammar Tip**
>
> Some transitions useful in process writing are *after, always, as soon as, before, first, following, in order to, now, soon, so that, then, until.* To learn when to punctuate these transitions, see Lessons 21.5, page 735, and 21.6, page 738.

Journal Writing

In your journal, list five possible topics for a process explanation. Then write a brief statement explaining whether the purpose of each would be to teach a skill or simply to share knowledge.

5.3 Explaining How To...

Write About a Process

You can use the chart you made during the prewriting stage to help you write the first draft of your explanation. First, make sure the steps in the process are clear. You may need to combine steps for simplicity, as illustrated in the diagram below. Next, show the relationships between these steps with appropriate transitional words and phrases. The diagram indicates some transitions you might use to create a smooth chronological flow.

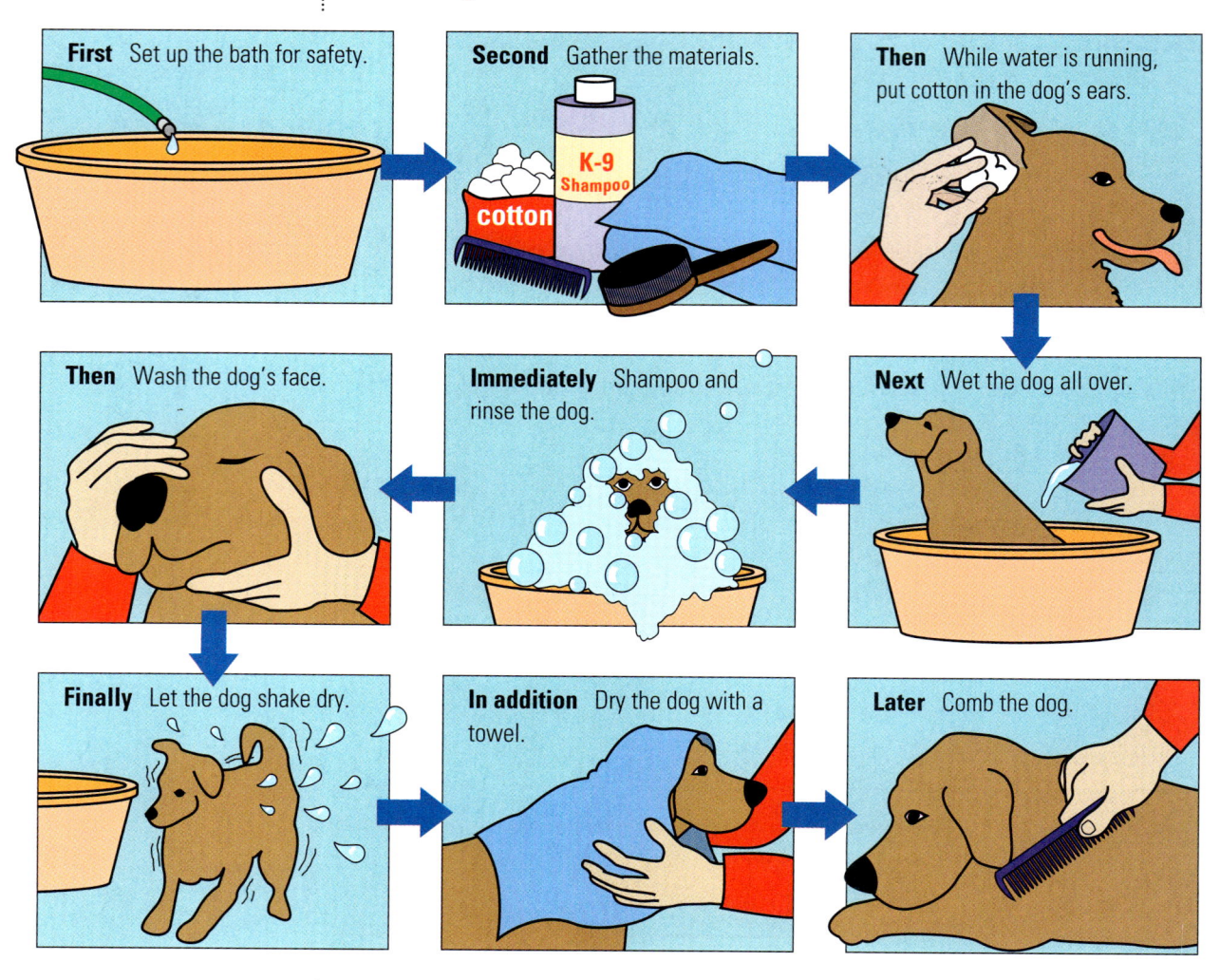

First Set up the bath for safety.

Second Gather the materials.

Then While water is running, put cotton in the dog's ears.

Then Wash the dog's face.

Immediately Shampoo and rinse the dog.

Next Wet the dog all over.

Finally Let the dog shake dry.

In addition Dry the dog with a towel.

Later Comb the dog.

In your **introduction** state the process you are explaining and the relevance of the process. This will help capture your reader's interest. Also, you can often use humor to engage your readers. In your **conclusion** emphasize the importance of the process you have explained, identifying its benefits to your audience. This will help leave your reader with a strong impression.

5.3 Writing Activities

Write a "How To" Paper

Think of something you know how to make or do that you could demonstrate to the class. Write a short paper about the process. Be prepared to give the demonstration in class.

PURPOSE To explain a process that involves a demonstration
AUDIENCE Your teacher and classmates
LENGTH 1–2 paragraphs

WRITING RUBRICS To write an effective "how to" paper, you should

- list all the materials you'll need
- list all the steps in order
- include an introduction and a conclusion
- use transitional words and phrases

Cross-Curricular Activity

HEALTH Think of a process you have learned about in your health class. Write an explanation of the process as you would for an essay test. Use transitions to show your teacher that you understand the steps in the process and the order in which they occur. If you wish, include a diagram or other illustration to help explain the process. Proofread carefully.

Listening and Speaking

Ask an adult who is an expert at something to explain a process to you. You might ask an electrician how to install a light switch or a librarian how to catalogue a book. Make notes of the steps in the process; then repeat the explanation back to your expert. Discuss how a speaker's knowledge of a procedure might affect an explanation: Can too much knowledge make the explanation too technical? Can too little make it too vague?

Grammar Link

Do not shift verb tenses unnecessarily.

Rewrite the following steps, using consistent verb tenses throughout the instructions.

How to Start Up the Computer

1. Found the ON and OFF power switch. This switch was somewhere on the monitor—at the bottom front, on one side, or in the back.
2. Move the power switch to the ON position.
3. After a few seconds the monitor screen will brighten.
4. Adjust the brightness control, usually located at the side or the bottom of the monitor, if it was not set at a level you preferred.
5. From the main menu or desktop, select the software program in which you wished to work.
6. If you are inserting a diskette, make sure that you inserted the diskette with the metal end first and the side with the arrow facing up.
7. If you experienced problems starting up, ask yourself the following questions:
8. Was the computer plugged into an electrical outlet?
9. Is the ON/OFF power switch turned to the ON position?
10. Had the brightness control been properly adjusted?

See Lesson 15.6, page 594.

Expository Writing

5.3 Explaining How To... **239**

LESSON 5.4

Explaining Cause and Effect

Cause-and-effect writing helps a reader understand the relationships between events or facts. In the model below, two science writers explain the surprising effects of gravity.

Literature Model

> The Earth and the other planets tend to be almost perfect spheres because, as Newton showed, gravity is a central force—it pulls everything equally toward the center of the world, itself held together by the force of gravity. The mountains sticking up above the spherical surface of the Earth represent less of a deviation from a perfect sphere than does the layer of paint or enamel on the surface of a typical globe that represents the Earth. If you were able to pile a sizable mountain on top of Mount Everest, it would not just sit there, poking in solitary magnificence into the stratosphere. The additional weight you had added would crush the base of Everest, and the new composite mountain would collapse until it was no larger than Everest is today. The Earth's gravity severely limits how much deviation from a perfect sphere our planet is permitted.
>
> Carl Sagan and Ann Druyan, *Comet*

- Sagan and Druyan describe a general effect and explain its cause in the first sentence.

- Sagan and Druyan use this simple comparison to help make their point.

- Do you think Sagan and Druyan's hypothetical example of Mount Everest is effective? Explain why or why not.

The explanation in the model focuses mainly on effects. As the chart on the next page shows, cause-and-effect writing may also focus on the causes.

Earthquake: Cause and Effects

Cause
Massive plates that make up the earth's surface move, putting great pressure on the rocks at the plates' edges. Sometimes the pressure becomes too great for the rocks to bear.

Effects
Rocks along the edges break and shift when pressure becomes too great, creating an earthquake.
▼
The earthquake releases energy in the form of waves, or vibrations.
▼
The waves shake the earth's surface, buildings, and bridges, sometimes causing great damage.

Link Cause and Effect

Cause-and-effect writing explains how one event causes another. Note how each effect listed in the chart above serves as the cause for the next effect. While some cause-and-effect writing is based on a complex series of causes and effects, some deals with only one cause and only one effect, giving a clear, detailed explanation of the relationship.

Beware of false cause-and-effect relationships. If one event follows another, the second wasn't necessarily caused by the first. Consider the sentence "The moon eclipsed the sun; then clouds covered the sky." This sentence does not show cause and effect, only sequential events. The eclipse did not cause the clouds to cover the sky.

An important way to make a true cause-and-effect relationship clear is with a thesis statement—a clear statement of your main idea—presented in a topic sentence. A thesis statement for an essay on earthquakes might be the following: "Great pressure along the edges of the earth's moving plates causes rocks to break and shift, creating an earthquake that can bring its destructive shock waves to the earth's surface."

Grammar Tip

When writing a cause-and-effect explanation of a recurring event or a natural phenomenon such as an earthquake, use the present tense. For information on other times present tense should be used, see Lesson 15.3, page 586.

Journal Writing

If you can use the word *because* to show the relationship between events or facts, the relation is causal, not just sequential. In your journal, write possible causal relationships, such as effects caused by watching television or causes for earning good grades, and try the "*because* test" on them.

Revising Tip

As you revise your cause-and-effect piece, decide whether you are placing proper emphasis on the causes, the effects, or both to achieve your purpose.

Organize Causes and Effects

Once you have a thesis statement, you can begin organizing your draft. You can follow either a cause-to-effect pattern or an effect-to-cause pattern. For example, you might organize a piece about the greenhouse effect by listing and explaining the many causes and concluding with the possible effects. A piece on the tides might first describe tides and the changes they bring to coastlines and then discuss their cause.

Whichever form of organization you use, you will need to connect your events, facts, and ideas with effective **transitions.** The chart below shows two types of transitions you may need to use.

Some Transitions for Cause-and-Effect Writing

CAUSE AND EFFECT	as a result	due to	so
	because	if, then	therefore
	consequently	since	thus
DEGREES OF CERTAINTY	certainly	necessarily	undoubtedly
	likely	possibly	unquestionably
	maybe	probably	of course

Your cause-and-effect piece will also need an **introduction** and a **conclusion**. In your introduction you should catch the reader's attention and give your purpose. Your thesis statement can serve as the introduction. Then you can conclude by summarizing the cause-and-effect relationship or extending the information you have presented. Note the introduction, transitions, and conclusion in the selection below by Eric Koszyk.

Eric begins with a topic sentence that clearly states the causal relationship he plans to explain.

What are some words in addition to "believe" that Eric uses to stress the uncertainty of the theory?

In his conclusion, Eric restates his cause-and-effect relationship but again stresses its uncertainty.

Student Model

An ice age usually occurs every couple of million years or so, but some scientists now believe that the current warming of the earth is likely to speed up this process. They believe that the warming of the planet will melt the polar ice caps. This, then, will change the level of water in the planet's oceans, which, therefore, will change the salt composition of the oceans. This altered salt composition would bring about a change in the jet stream winds that circle the earth. And this change in the jet stream would bring about the cooling trend that could well speed up the coming of the next ice age. Some scientists disagree, but a large number of other scientists and environmentalists believe in this theory.

Eric Koszyk
Quartz Hill High School, Quartz Hill, California

5.4 Writing Activities

Write a Cause-and-Effect Paragraph

Plan and write a cause-and-effect paragraph on the relationship between hours of study and good grades, or on another cause-and-effect topic of your choice.

PURPOSE To explain a cause-and-effect relationship
AUDIENCE Your teacher and classmates
LENGTH 1 paragraph

WRITING RUBRICS To write an effective cause-and-effect paragraph, you should

- decide whether to focus on causes or effects
- write a clear thesis statement
- include an introduction and a conclusion
- use appropriate transitions

Viewing and Representing

COOPERATIVE LEARNING Working in groups of three or four, find a painting or photograph in which an event has occurred (a triumphant athlete or the aftermath of a storm, for example). Write a brief cause-and-effect paragraph explaining what has occurred in the scene, presenting at least two causes and two effects. Take turns presenting your paragraphs orally to your group, to compare and contrast your interpretations of the event.

Grammar Link

Make subjects and verbs agree.

Subjects must agree with verbs no matter how many words come between them.

Rewrite the sentences below to make subjects and verbs agree.

1. According to environmentalists, current temperature changes of the earth signals the coming of the next ice age.
2. Thousands of years ago, many parts of the earth's surface was covered by ice sheets.
3. The movement of glaciers cause erosion.
4. Rocks buried in the ice scrapes and digs at the land.
5. Scientists at the local university is preparing reports on climate changes.

See 16.1, pages 609–610.

Cross-Curricular Activity

SPELLING Check the spelling in your paragraph by exchanging papers with a partner. Discuss the errors you found on one another's papers. What words are you misspelling? What do they have in common? Develop a strategy for learning to spell these words. Share it with your partner.

LESSON 5.5

Classifying a Subject

When you classify, you group items into categories based on common attributes, or qualities. Notice how loon calls are classified in the passage below.

> **Literature Model**
>
> In recent years, loon calls have been studied by researchers and it is now generally accepted that there are at least four basic calls in the loon's vocabulary, with gradations and combinations and shading to refine the meanings. Within a family, loons call to one another with a soft hoot. The wail, the cry with which the nightly chorus commences, is used when one loon is trying to establish contact with other loons. The tremolo calls that are supposed to sound like a madman's laughter are alarm calls.... The yodel is the song of the male loon, a complex series of rising notes followed by an undulation [pulsating tone]; it is gorgeous to human ears but a loon uses it to define and defend his territory. Very recently, researchers have discovered that male loons' yodels are distinctive, each from the other, and can be used as aural tags to study and follow individuals.
>
> Sue Hubbell, "For the Love of Loons," *Smithsonian*

Sidebar questions:
- What does Hubbell tell the reader in her first sentence?
- Hubbell describes the hoot, the wail, the tremolo, and the yodel as the four basic types of loon calls.
- What do you learn from Hubbell's conclusion?

Why Do You Classify?

Classification is an effective way to organize ideas. In the diagram below, one writer has classified clouds according to their general shapes. She has done so to help organize her ideas about clouds. With that type of classification, she will be able to provide a clear overview of the topic, make information accessible, and better inform or instruct her audience.

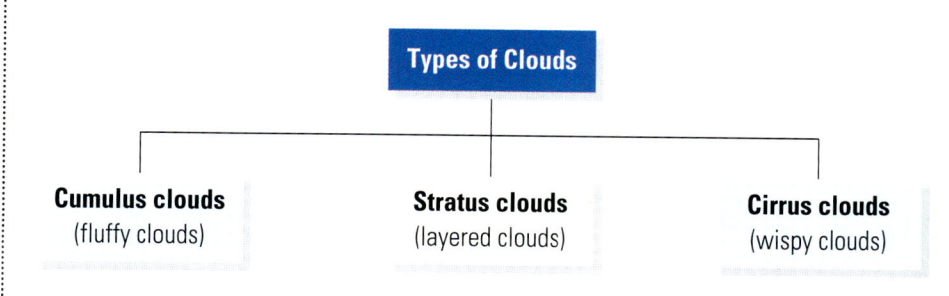

Types of Clouds
- **Cumulus clouds** (fluffy clouds)
- **Stratus clouds** (layered clouds)
- **Cirrus clouds** (wispy clouds)

Unit 5 Expository Writing

How Do You Plan a Classification?

Your most important task in planning a classification is to create meaningful categories appropriate for your purpose and audience. The chart below shows how different purposes and audiences may affect the way items are classified. Look at the common feature that ties together each category of trees in the chart.

Three Ways of Classifying Trees

AUDIENCE	CLASSIFICATION	COMMON FEATURE
SCIENTISTS	• Cone-bearing trees • Seed-bearing trees • Spore-bearing trees	Methods of reproduction
LANDSCAPE ARCHITECTS	• Shade trees • Trees for windbreaks • Ornamental trees	Usefulness
WILD-FOOD COLLECTORS	• Trees that bear edible nuts • Trees that bear edible fruits • Trees that have edible sap	Source of food

> **Vocabulary Tip**
>
> When drafting your classification, you may want to use some of the following terms: *categories, classes, groups, kinds, types, varieties, divisions, branches,* and *subclasses.*

Journal Writing

Think of a subject for which you will plan a classification, such as types of writing in your journal or types of music. In your journal create a diagram like the one at the top of this page in which you classify your subject. Make sure your categories are mutually exclusive and based on a common feature.

How Do You Write a Classification?

As you draft your classification, follow the organization shown in the diagram on page 246. Study the organization of the student model that follows.

5.5 Classifying a Subject **245**

Revising Tip

As you revise your classification, make sure your thesis statement is clear. For advice on writing thesis statements, see Lesson 7.2, pages 330–333.

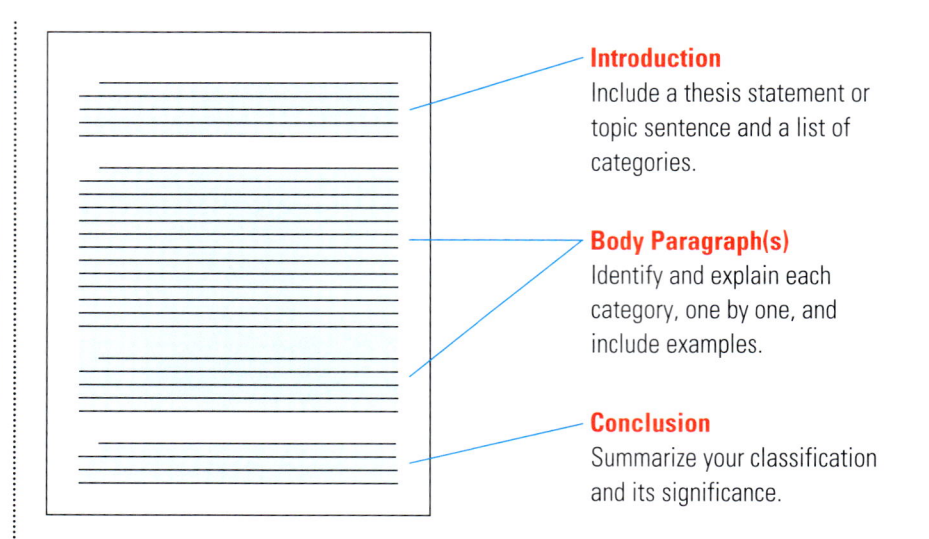

Introduction
Include a thesis statement or topic sentence and a list of categories.

Body Paragraph(s)
Identify and explain each category, one by one, and include examples.

Conclusion
Summarize your classification and its significance.

Student Model

On what feature does Arnold base the categories she introduces in her first sentence?

Wildflowers, admired for their beauty and magnificence, include flowers from woodlands, mountains, prairies, deserts, and swamps.

Body paragraph includes images such as "beardtongues clothe the prairie."

Woodland flowers rely on humus, the product of decaying leaves and wood, for food. Unable to grow in bright sunlight, they favor early spring for growth. Typical woodland flowers include rhododendron and violets. Mountain flowers flourish on any high mountaintop, but grow only after the ice and snow melt. Examples are alpine roses and saxifrages. Prairie flowers are voluptuous and plentiful; their bright colors represent the stereotypical wildflower. Masses of globemallows, sunflowers, and beardtongues clothe the prairie. The beauty of desert flowers is only temporary, as they quickly grow and flower after infrequent rains, then wither in the blinding sun. They have thorny branches, no leaves or very few, and thick, fleshy, water-holding stems. Desert plants include ocotillos and cacti. Finally, swamp flowers, such as lizard's-tails and willows, love wet meadows and ponds. Others, including pitcher plants and spider lilies, thrive in marshes.

From reading her conclusion, how would you explain Arnold's own attraction to this topic?

Their simple dignity and elegance make wildflowers an unequaled natural phenomenon and a worthy topic of study.

Alli Arnold,
Henry Clay High School, Lexington, Kentucky

5.5 Writing Activities

Write a Classification

Choose a group of items to classify. Select any group that interests you or one of the following topics: rocks and minerals; friends; movies; popular music groups; precipitation. Write a paragraph classifying the items.

PURPOSE To classify items
AUDIENCE Your classmates; an audience of your choice
LENGTH 1 paragraph

WRITING RUBRICS To develop an effective paragraph describing your classification scheme, you should

- classify the items in a way that fits your purpose and your audience
- include an introduction and a conclusion
- use complete sentences that state your classifications clearly

Viewing and Representing

COOPERATIVE LEARNING In a small group discuss the painting on this page. Have each group member then choose a different way to classify the items in the painting. Together, make a chart showing your classifications.

Using Computers

Using presentation software, create a presentation of your classification scheme. Devote one slide to an introduction, one slide to each of the classifications, and one to a conclusion. Write text for each slide that fits the purpose and audience. Present your project to the class.

Grammar Link

Use specific concrete nouns.

Alli Arnold uses precise concrete nouns such as "woodlands, mountains, prairies, deserts, and swamps" in her classification of wildflowers on page 246.

In the sentences below, replace the underlined words with specific concrete nouns.

1. As I hiked, I heard some strange <u>sounds</u>.
2. <u>Beautiful flowers</u> grew wild along the trail.
3. During the storm, <u>a few pieces of camping gear</u> were damaged.
4. <u>Many things</u> in my backpack were ruined.
5. Next year, I plan to visit <u>tourist attractions</u> in Washington, D.C.

See Lesson 10.1, page 439.

Pablita Velarde, *Old Father Storyteller*, 1960

5.5 Classifying a Subject

LESSON 5.6
Comparing and Contrasting

Comparing involves discussing similarities between two or more related things. Contrasting involves discussing differences between such items. In the model below, a nature writer uses comparison and contrast to present information about two extinct birds.

Literature Model

The Dodo was not the only pigeon to suffer extinction on Mauritius. There was also the striking crested Pigeon Hollandaise, which is commonly called the Mauritius Blue Pigeon (*Alectroenas nitidisima*). Like the Common Dodo, it was endemic [native only] to Mauritius. This exotic Blue Pigeon did not suffer from the Dodo's inability to fly, nor did it nest on the ground. It was a graceful forest bird that fed on fruit, berries and seeds. It lived in large flocks and nested communally in trees. Again, unlike the Dodo, this bird was delicious to eat. "Shooting parties" were often organized by the resident Europeans for sport and food.

David Day, *The Doomsday Book of Animals*

> In the first sentence the writer introduces the main idea—that two related birds suffered a similar fate on Mauritius.

> How were the birds alike? How were they different?

How might you compare and contrast two creatures with which you are familiar? How are a dog and a cat alike and different? What features do a goldfish and a shark have in common? How are they different?

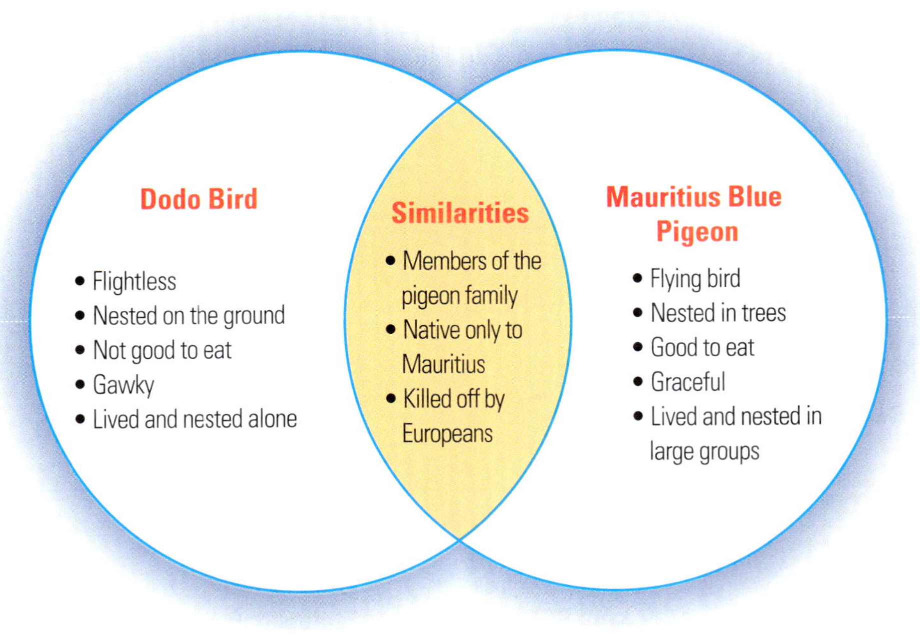

Dodo Bird
- Flightless
- Nested on the ground
- Not good to eat
- Gawky
- Lived and nested alone

Similarities
- Members of the pigeon family
- Native only to Mauritius
- Killed off by Europeans

Mauritius Blue Pigeon
- Flying bird
- Nested in trees
- Good to eat
- Graceful
- Lived and nested in large groups

Think About Similarities and Differences

One technique you can use to explore similarities and differences between two subjects is a Venn diagram. The Venn diagram above shows the similarities and differences between the two extinct birds described in the model on page 248. To set up a Venn diagram, follow these steps:

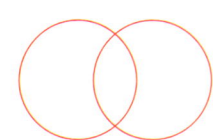

1. Draw two intersecting circles.
2. Title the circles with the subjects to be compared.
3. List unique features of each subject.
4. List the similarities of the two subjects in the space where the circles intersect.

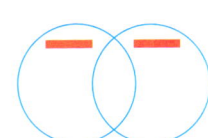

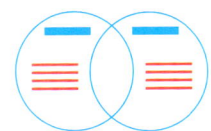

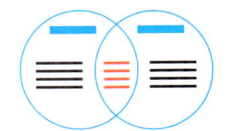

Vocabulary Tip

Transitions like the following help you organize a comparison-contrast paper: *but, however, in the same way, like, unlike, similarly.*

Journal Writing

What are some other tools you could use to explore similarities and differences between two subjects, such as you and your best friend? In your journal, try creating a chart or other tool to help you compare two subjects of your choosing.

5.6 Comparing and Contrasting **249**

Organize a Comparison-Contrast Paper

Once you have explored similarities and differences between two subjects, you can organize your comparison-contrast paper. The chart below shows two methods of organization: (1) by subject and (2) by feature. Notice how the writer organized the essay in the model that follows.

Grammar Tip

When you edit your comparison-contrast paper, make sure that your comparisons are complete. See Lesson 18.4, page 665.

Comparison-Contrast: Elephants and Hippos

By Subject

Subject 1: Elephants	Subject 2: Hippos
Feature A: Anatomy	Feature A: Anatomy
Feature B: Size	Feature B: Size
Feature C: Habitat	Feature C: Habitat
Feature D: Endangered	Feature D: Endangered

By Feature

Feature A: Anatomy
Subject 1: Elephants
Subject 2: Hippos

Feature B: Size
Subject 1: Elephants
Subject 2: Hippos

Feature C: Habitat
Subject 1: Elephants
Subject 2: Hippos

Feature D: Endangered
Subject 1: Elephants
Subject 2: Hippos

Model

Does the writer's use of organization by subject successfully create a vivid comparison between elephants and hippos? Explain.

Two of the world's most wondrous and enormous animals, the elephant and the hippopotamus, may one day disappear. Just think of the majestic elephant, the largest land-dwelling animal. A typical African bull, or male, measures eleven feet tall at the shoulders and weighs about four tons. African cows, or females, and Asiatic elephants are only slightly smaller. And, as you picture an elephant, you probably think of its thick gray skin, long trunk, fan-shaped ears, and great ivory tusks. The valuable ivory of the tusks presents the greatest danger for elephants, as ivory-seeking hunters kill thousands each year.

Note the writer's use of visual details in this comparison-contrast.

Not quite as massive as the elephant, the hippo is the third largest land animal, just behind the rhino. A typical hippo weighs about 2,500 to 3,000 pounds and is about five feet tall at the shoulders. Besides its huge body, among the hippo's most recognizable features are its bulging eyes, allowing it to submerge most of its head yet still keep its eyes above water. Farmers and hunters kill many hippos each year to protect farmlands and to sell the animals' meat, hide, and tusklike ivory canine teeth.

5.6 Writing Activities

Write a Comparison-Contrast Paper

Choose a pair of places or items to compare, such as big cities and small towns, board games and video games, or another pair of your choice. Write a brief paper comparing and contrasting the items.

PURPOSE To compare and contrast two items
AUDIENCE Your teacher and classmates
LENGTH 2 paragraphs

WRITING RUBRICS To write an effective comparison-contrast paper, you should
- choose related items
- use a Venn diagram to clarify similarities and differences
- organize your paper by comparing subjects or by comparing features
- use appropriate transitions

Cross-Curricular Activity

ART AND SCIENCE Study the painting below and think about how an art critic and a scientist might respond to it. With a partner, draw a Venn diagram that compares and contrasts the ways in which two such viewers might describe the painting. Share your diagram with the class.

Katsushika Hokusai, *The Great Wave off Kanagawa*, c. 1830

Grammar Link

Make compound subjects and verbs agree.

When compound subjects are joined by *either . . . or* or *neither . . . nor,* the verb always agrees with the subject nearer the verb.

Rewrite each sentence below so that the compound subjects and verbs agree.

1. Neither the dodo bird nor the blue pigeon were safe from European hunters.
2. Either Mauritius or other islands in the Indian Ocean was home to the dodo.
3. Either farmers or hunters has killed the hippos for their hides and teeth.
4. Either the African bull or the Asiatic elephant weigh about four tons.
5. Neither Kenya nor other African nations protects these animals adequately.

See Lesson 16.5, page 616.

Listening and Speaking

Interview a number of people in your school about a topic that invites comparison (for example, the similarities and differences in skiing and snowboarding). Take notes on the similarities and differences each person mentions. Then give a brief talk on the topic, using the similarities and differences you recorded. Ask classmates to evaluate the clarity and completeness of your talk.

LESSON 5.7

Writing with Graphics

Sometimes words alone can't convey enough information about a topic. Notice how the map and text work together in this magazine feature, a piece of exposition.

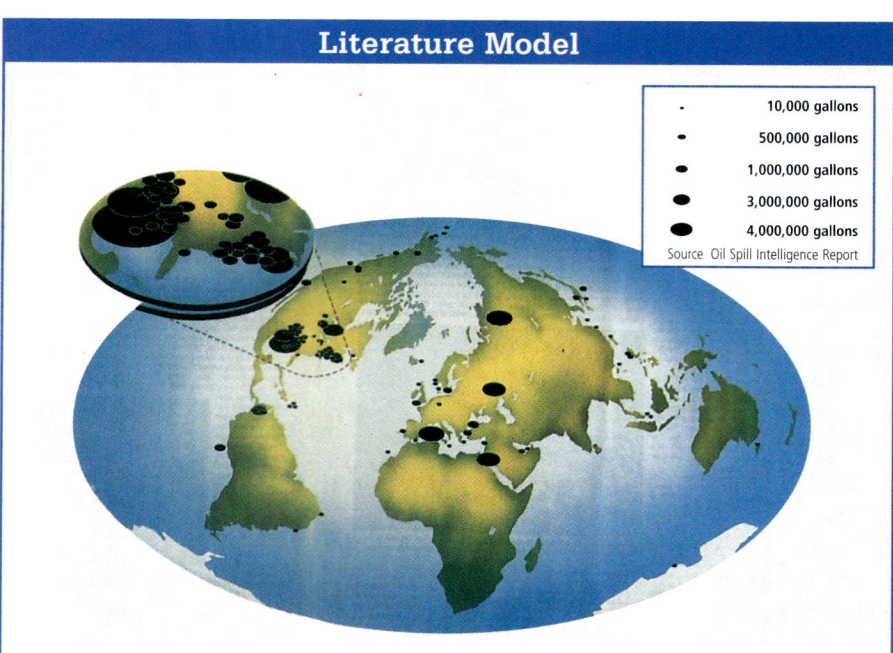

Literature Model

·	10,000 gallons
•	500,000 gallons
●	1,000,000 gallons
●	3,000,000 gallons
●	4,000,000 gallons

Source Oil Spill Intelligence Report

In March 1989 the world watched in horror as the *Exxon Valdez* disgorged 10.8 million gallons of North Slope crude [oil] into the pristine waters of Prince William Sound. It was the largest spill ever off the United States. But whatever lessons may have been learned about preventing spills were not effectively applied in 1990. Hardly a week passed without news of yet another disturbing spill. The first ten months of the year saw an estimated 28 million gallons of oil discharged around the world, which makes 1990 a typical year. . . . On our oil-soaked map you'll see the spills that reached at least 10,000 gallons, whether from tanker accidents caused by human error . . . or storage tanks struck by lightning.

"Another Crude Year," *Discover,* January 1991

Why do you think the writer uses the term "oil-soaked map"?

Here the writer explains to the reader what the map shows.

Know Your Basic Options

Graphics come in four main forms: maps, diagrams, tables, and graphs. Each type can help illustrate your expository writing.

Maps A map is a graphic most commonly showing all or part of the earth's surface. Maps often show what might take many paragraphs to describe. Whenever you use a map, be sure to include its legend, which explains the map's symbols.

Diagrams Diagrams use pictures to clarify the relationship among parts of a whole or to show how something works. The diagram at the right shows how the water cycle works. Such a diagram can help your reader visualize a process.

Tables By examining the information in the rows and columns of a table, you can see how a subject changes under different conditions, such as time or location. The table on page 254, for example, compares temperature range and precipitation among four of the world's biological zones, or biomes (regions divided according to climate and soil conditions).

Graphs Often the best way to convey numerical information will be a graph. Graphs can reveal patterns of information, showing relationships among different facts or statistics. They can thus be a useful tool in comparison-contrast writing: a bar graph, for example, may compare the wealth of three nations. Graphs can also show how something develops over time. The line graph at the right shows the change in sunspot activity over 36 years.

> **Editing Tip**
>
> Make sure you label all parts of any graphic clearly and accurately. Labels help the reader recognize and understand information.

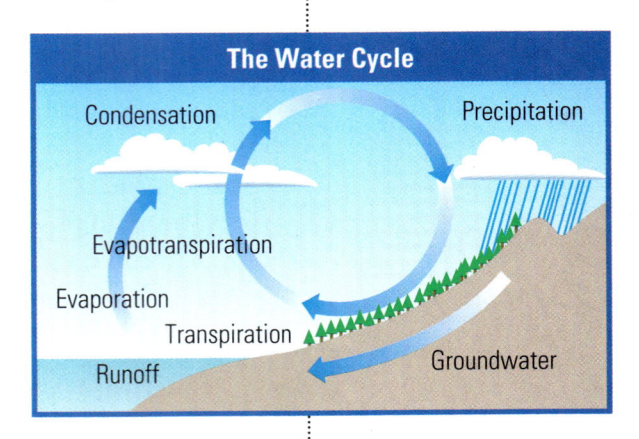

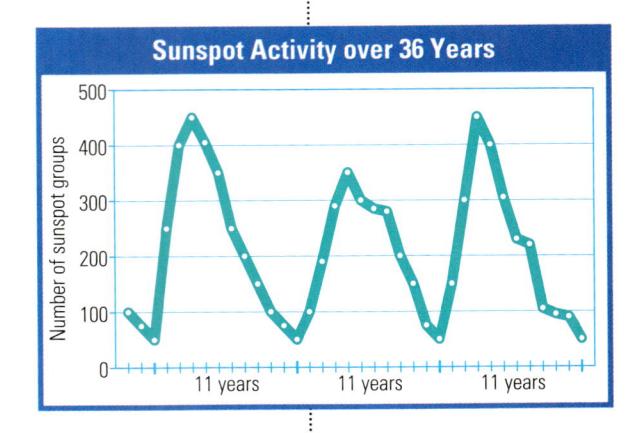

Journal Writing

Try using a graphic to explain something about yourself, for example, your study habits, eating habits, or how your tastes have changed. Place your graphic in your journal.

5.7 Writing with Graphics **253**

> **Revising Tip**
>
> As you read your first draft, check all references to graphics to be sure that they are helpful to the reader—that is, that they really add to the explanation.

Use Graphics for Greatest Impact

Whenever you use graphics in your writing, place them and refer to them so that they make the greatest impact on the reader.

Positioning Graphics Where you place a graphic depends on the function of the graphic and your purpose for using it. For example, to capture the reader's attention and establish a basic framework, you could put a graphic at the beginning of your piece. Imagine you're writing an explanation of cells. You might use a diagram of a basic cell, with all its parts labeled, as part of the opening paragraph.

In the middle of the essay, you might include graphics that convey a great amount of information in a concise way, reinforce information, or serve as a handy reference for the reader. In the example of an essay on cells, a table showing the variation in sizes of different types of cells might appear in the middle.

At the end of your explanation, you will probably want to summarize your main points. For example, in the conclusion of an essay on cells, you could include a table comparing and contrasting plant and animal cells. Wherever and however you use graphics, you need to let the reader know why they are there and when to look at them.

Referring to Graphics In referring to a graphic, you might simply tell the reader to look at it when the graphic helps illustrate a point you are making. For example, with a table of cell sizes, you might write, "Different kinds of cells vary in size, as shown in the table." You can also instruct the reader to use the information from a graphic in a specific way. If you were using the table below in a piece of exposition about biomes, you might tell the reader to use the table to compare the different levels of precipitation in *each biome.*

Whatever your purpose, title graphics clearly when you present more than one. In that way you will be sure that the reader is not confused and can refer to the appropriate graphic easily.

Four Biomes: Temperature and Precipitation		
Biome	**Avg. Yearly Temperature**	**Avg. Yearly Precipitation**
Deciduous forest	6° C to 28° C	75 to 125 cm
Grassland	0° C to 25° C	25 to 75 cm
Desert	24° C to 34° C	less than 25 cm
Tropical rain forest	25° C to 27° C	200 to 400 cm

5.7 Writing Activities

Write a Paragraph with a Graphic

Think of something you have learned about recently. How could the information be shown in a graphic? Create a graphic to show the information.

PURPOSE To use a graphic to show a concept
AUDIENCE Your classmates
LENGTH 1 page

WRITING RUBRICS To write an effective paragraph with a graphic, you should

- make a map, diagram, table, or graph
- write a paragraph about your subject, and in your paragraph refer to your graphic
- make sure your paragraph makes clear references to the graphic

Using Computers

Some graphics can be created using your computer's word processing program. You might also be able to use illustration software to create graphics. Experiment with different arrangements and styles to see which presents your information most clearly.

Viewing and Representing

Use a simple set of statistical data such as the number of male and female students in each grade in your school to create at least three different visual representations of the information. Your graphics could include a table, a graph, and a pie chart. Write a paragraph explaining which type of graphic best represents your data and why.

Grammar Link

Avoid using run-on sentences.

Run-on sentences occur when two or more complete sentences are written without proper punctuation between them.

Rewrite the run-on sentences below to make them grammatically correct.

1. Graphics come in four basic forms each type can enhance a piece of exposition.
2. Information in a table is organized in a concise, systematic way, it is presented in rows and columns.
3. Be sure to label all parts of your graphic clearly labels help the reader recognize and understand data.
4. Diagrams clarify relationships among parts of a whole and graphs reveal patterns of information.
5. There are many kinds of graphs, line, bar, and pictographs are among them.
6. A map needs a legend and it may need a scale, too.
7. Check all references to graphs in your writing they really add to the exposition.
8. The data in the table was easy to understand, the diagram was confusing.
9. He positioned the map in the middle of the essay and he used a table in his conclusion.
10. The water cycle is shown in the diagram you can find it on page 253.

See Lesson 13.10, pages 555–557.

LESSON 5.8

Writing a Feature Article

A feature story in a newspaper or magazine often presents in-depth information on a topic related to a current issue or event. The feature story may include photographs, such as the ones below, that focus on the setting and the subject of the story.

Usually longer than a news article, the feature story may try to capture a mood or a moment, or it may highlight a person, experience, or other topic of general human interest. Because feature writers use description, narration, and exposition, their stories tend to be both entertaining and informative. The literature models in this lesson are excerpts from a feature story, "Searching for Medicinal Wealth in Amazonia," published in *Smithsonian* magazine. Note how the writer, Donald Dale Jackson, opens his story with a detailed description of the rain forest and a scientist.

256 Unit 5 Expository Writing

Literature Model

An hour and a half had passed since we had seen any human scratches on the great green kingdom below us, the rain forest of southern Suriname at the northern fringes of Amazonia. Since then our Cessna six-seater had droned over an unforgiving landscape of jungle dotted with cloud-shadow puddles and tree-choked arroyos [stream beds] streaked by brown rivers. Even at 4,000 feet I could feel the oppressive heat, and we were beginning to descend. The lumpy carpet of rain forest gradually metamorphosed into a canopy of high trees that hid the ground.

Mark Plotkin leaned forward and squinted. Three plumes of smoke stained the horizon ahead. A few seconds later a clearing suddenly materialized, dun-colored and impossibly puny amid the green sea. Now I saw a village of about 80 thatched huts clustered beside a chocolate river. . . . Plotkin grinned. "Welcome to Kwamalasamutu," he said. "The first time I came here I thought I'd found paradise. I still think it's as close as we're apt to get."

Plotkin—New Orleans born, Harvard trained and Washington based—was coming home, in a sense, to this tiny settlement in Amazonia. . . . Plotkin has assigned himself the task of collecting and documenting the plants the Tiriós [Amazonian Indians] use before the mixed blessings of creeping civilization supplant the tribal medicine men and their wisdom. . . .

As a field ethnobotanist . . . Plotkin is the most visible exponent of a discipline that has only recently come into its own. Where ethnobotany was once mainly concerned with plant identification, it is viewed today as a potential lifesaver. The chemical components of plants that medicine men use in healing rites could conceivably be building blocks for new drugs or even cures for such scourges as cancer and AIDS.

Donald Dale Jackson
"Searching for Medicinal Wealth in Amazonia"
Smithsonian magazine

What do you learn from the opening sentence of Jackson's feature article?

The writer's direct quotes and sensory details give the reader an intimate view of people and places.

How would you define "ethnobotany" and explain its importance, based on Jackson's fourth paragraph?

Journal Writing

Look through a newspaper for an interesting feature story. In your journal, note what types of writing are used.

Plan a Feature Article

Feature writers face two basic challenges. First, they must identify current topics that will interest their readers. Then they must gather the information and uncover the details to bring that topic to life and give readers important background to the news.

Find a Topic Feature articles can be on just about anything. Many, but not all, feature articles focus on current news stories, casting them in new light with important background or interesting approaches. Feature writers may also provide information not related to the news. For example, they might tell of intriguing people or share personal experiences.

Coming up with a good topic for your own feature article requires insight into your audience. You need to know their general age, their interests, what they might hope to learn, and what it might take to capture their imaginations.

The best way to find an interesting topic is to think about things in the news or in your own life that are of special interest to you. What are you curious about? If an idea seems intriguing to you, it may also fascinate your audience. The following tips may help you think of fresh feature ideas.

Prewriting Tip

When you interview, double-check the correct spelling of the person's name and his or her exact title or position. If you plan to use a statement from the interview or from printed material as a direct quotation, be sure you have permission. For more tips on interviewing, see Lessons 2.4, pages 72–75, and 29.4, page 892.

Some Ways to Get Ideas for Your Feature Story

- Take a different route to school. What new things do you see?
- Go someplace you don't usually go. Listen to conversations. Watch what people do. What questions do these people spark?
- Sit in a familiar spot and note anything that seems out of the ordinary about the people or the place. What did you see that you didn't expect to see?
- Put yourself in the place of someone in the news, a character in a book, a person you see on the street. What ideas do you get from looking at the world through his or her eyes?
- Leaf through a type of book or magazine you don't generally read. What new topics spark your interest?

Gather Information Once you have settled on an idea for a feature story, you need to gather information. Reading will give you background. Visiting places related to your topic may help you write descriptions with greater detail and authority and even re-create a mood. The first chart on the next page will provide the most valuable information for your feature story. It presents some questions a writer might ask when interviewing a scientist such as Mark Plotkin about the rain forest.

Some Questions for a Rain Forest Scientist

- How did you first become interested in rain forests?
- How would you summarize the importance of your work in the rain forest?
- In what parts of the world do you think the rain forest is most likely to survive? Why?
- What is the most surprising thing you have seen on all your trips to the rain forest?

Draft a Feature Article

After you have gathered information for your feature, you can begin writing a draft of your article. Construct an outline to organize your ideas. Then use the following advice to create a lively article.

Begin with a Lead That Pulls Journalists use the term *lead* to describe the opening of a story. An effective lead sets the story in motion and draws the reader into the writing. The chart below lists some ways to create a successful lead.

A Lead for Your Feature Story

- a surprising detail
- an anecdote that gets at the story's essence
- a revealing image that indicates the direction of the story
- a vivid description of the place
- a summary of the central conflict
- a portrait of one of the main people
- a lively quote
- an event that kicks off the story

Revising Tip
When you revise, have a friend look for places where your story lacks supporting details (see Lesson 5.2, pages 232–235) or doesn't flow smoothly.

Editing Tip
Make sure your quotes are accurate and you have been fair to everyone. You might phone the people involved in the story to read them the final version.

Presenting Tip
When your feature story is complete, present it in a form and a place that will reach the appropriate audience. Choose illustrations for the feature that will add useful information to the story as well as catch the attention of the intended audience.

Journal Writing

Look through newspapers and magazines for feature stories. Clip some leads that catch your attention. Tape these clippings into your journal.

Grammar Tip

When editing your article, make sure that your quotations are punctuated correctly. For tips on when and how to use quotation marks, see Lesson 21.9, pages 752–756.

Add Lively Details The details you include in your feature will make or break your story. Pick details that make your main points vivid and memorable. Include anecdotes that create empathy for your subject. Include quotes that let the reader hear your subject speaking in his or her own voice. Craft explanations that give your audience a clear understanding of the history, significance, or inner workings of a topic. Notice the details Jackson includes in this excerpt from his article.

Literature Model

The Indians mobbed him [Plotkin] as he climbed out of the plane. Boys tugged at his arms and grabbed his luggage. Speaking Sranan tongo, the trading language of Suriname, Plotkin had a smile or joke for each of them. "We thought you forgot us," one boy said—he hadn't been there for two years. "We were crying." Here in this exotic outpost light-years removed from his own culture, in a remote corner of a country that few Americans can identify or pronounce, the kid from New Orleans was among friends. "It feels terrific," he said.

> Jackson uses sensory details to make this scene come to life.

> What do you learn about the people in this article from the quotations Jackson presents?

Use an Effective Ending The ending of your feature should be as fresh and vigorous as the lead. It should tie the feature together and, if possible, leave the reader with a new thought to ponder.

Some of the best ways to begin a feature are also good ways to end it. Quotes, humorous anecdotes, close-up portraits, lively details, and vivid scenes work as well at the end of a story as at the beginning. Why do you suppose Jackson concludes his article with an image of the rain forest as seen from the airborne Cessna?

Literature Model

The Cessna finally appeared in the northeast sky and touched down five minutes later. Thirty tense minutes ensued before the pilot could get the engine started for the return trip. The plane's cabin felt like a broiler. . . .

A few minutes later we were airborne. The dust-brown clearing that was Kwamalasamutu became smaller and smaller until it was a tiny brown speck lost in the great green, and then it was gone and there was only the green, the endless, timeless, pitiless, life-giving, suffocating green of the rain forest.

> Jackson uses strong sensory details to help bring his ending to life.

> Note Jackson's use of adjectives to tell his story, especially the string of adjectives in the concluding sentence.

5.8 Writing Activities

Write a Feature Story

Choose a topic that interests you and write a feature story for publication in your school paper or a community newspaper. The chart on page 258 can help you select a topic. Use illustrations with your feature if you wish.

PURPOSE To create a feature story
AUDIENCE Students or adults
LENGTH 5–8 paragraphs

WRITING RUBRICS To write an effective feature story, you should

- create a strong lead
- use vivid details
- include at least one quotation
- proofread to insure accurate spelling and punctuation

Viewing and Representing

COOPERATIVE LEARNING In a small group, discuss your individual impressions of the 53-foot-high sculpture shown below. Generate ten quotations about the work. Then have each member write a feature story that uses a quotation about how viewers react to the sculpture, which stands in the Federal Center Plaza in Chicago, Illinois.

Alexander Calder, *Flamingo*, 1974

Grammar Link

Use commas to set off nonessential appositives and adjective clauses.

Feature writers often use appositives and adjective clauses to add informative details. Appositives and adjective clauses that are not essential to the meaning of the sentence should be set off by commas.

Rewrite the sentences below, adding commas where they are needed.

1. The Amazon Basin a region two-thirds the size of the United States is home to thousands of plant species.
2. Field ethnobotanist Mark Plotkin lives and works among the Tiriós.
3. Plotkin who is Harvard trained and Washington based is also a speaker about conservation.
4. Ethnobotany is a complex field that I do not understand.
5. Ethnobotany which was once mainly concerned with plant identification is today viewed as a potential lifesaver.

See Lesson 21.6, pages 738–748.

Using Computers

Add depth to your feature story by gathering related information from the Internet. Use government sites to add statistics to your story. Check newspaper and other media sites for anecdotes and other human interest features.

LESSON 5.9

Answering an Essay Question

When you take an essay test, plan your time carefully, and write answers that demonstrate your knowledge. In the model below, columnist Cecil Adams's response to "Why Do Cats Purr?" gives you an idea of what it takes to answer an essay question successfully.

Literature Model

Cats don't purr just when they're feeling chipper—they also purr when they're frightened or badly hurt. Purring doesn't have any specific emotional connotation; rather it seems to be a kind of homing device. Cats learn the signal in the first few days of kittenhood, when they can't see, hear, or smell very well. The mother cat purrs to call the kittens to nurse—unable to hear the sound, the kitten can feel the vibrations.

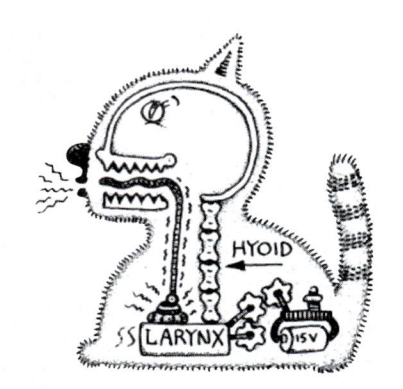

There are two schools of thought on exactly *how* a cat purrs. One theory traces the vibrations to a set of "false vocal chords," a bundle of membranes that lies above the genuine vocal chords and seems to have no other clear function. The other opinion locates the purr in the vibrations of the hyoid apparatus, a series of small bones connecting the skull and the larynx that nominally serves to support the tongue. Since it's very difficult to induce a cat to purr while you are examining his hyoid apparatus, the truth may never be known.

Cecil Adams, *The Straight Dope*

Adams begins his answer by explaining one thing he knows for sure about cats' purring: when they do it.

What does Adams mean when he says purring "seems to be a kind of homing device"? Does this hypothesis make sense to you?

Adams concludes with a theory that highlights what we don't know about cats' purring.

Look for Key Words in the Question

Answers to essay questions follow a basic format—the format of the essay. The **introduction** contains a **thesis statement,** a one-sentence summary of the thrust of your answer. The **body** of the answer supports the thesis statement with facts, examples, details, and reasons. The **conclusion** summarizes or gives the implications of your answer. The essay question itself often gives strong clues as to how the answer should be structured. The chart below can help you decipher the clues.

What Essay Questions Tell You

Clue Verb	Action to Take
Describe	Paint word pictures by providing precise details of an event, a process, or a person.
Explain	Tell why or how by using facts, examples, or reasons, and emphasize cause-and-effect relationships or step-by-step processes.
Compare	Show how two or more subjects are alike.
Contrast	Highlight the differences between two or more subjects.
Classify	Group and label the important features of a subject, and discuss the different categories into which you have grouped them.
Analyze	Break something down into the parts that compose it, show the relationship between the parts and the whole, and tell the function or significance of each of the parts.

Grammar Tip

Restate the essay question as the beginning of your thesis statement. "What were the causes of the Civil War?" becomes "The Civil War was caused by . . ." For information on using active and passive voices of verbs, see Lesson 15.7, page 596.

Journal Writing

For each clue verb in the chart above, identify one or more prewriting tools, such as a Venn diagram, that could help you answer that particular kind of essay question efficiently. List each tool in your journal next to the corresponding clue verb.

5.9 Answering an Essay Question **263**

Focus Your Answer

By taking time to identify and organize your information, you can avoid the common mistake of writing down everything you know about a subject in a haphazard, disjointed fashion.

Organize Your Information The following diagram details the process you might use to answer a "take home" essay question.

Answering an Essay Question

Question
Describe hail, and explain how and when hailstones form.

Underline clue verbs and other key words.
<u>Describe</u> hail, and <u>explain</u> <u>how</u> and <u>when</u> hailstones form.

▼

List notes.
- Hail: form of precipitation made up of lumps of ice
- Begins as tiny ice crystal in thundercloud
- Strong winds in cloud toss crystal up and down; water condenses around crystal and freezes, forming layers of ice on the crystal, thus creating a hailstone and making it grow larger and heavier.
- Hailstone becomes too heavy to remain aloft, so falls to ground.
- Size of stone depends on strength of wind, length of time in cloud.
- Most hailstones smaller than one inch in diameter, but some larger than a baseball.
- Large hailstones smash windows, dent cars, destroy crops.
- Hailstorms usually occur in summer, when thunderstorms are more frequent, violent.

▼

Develop thesis statement.
Hail is a form of precipitation made up of lumps of ice that form within thunderclouds.

▼

Outline answer and develop conclusion.
Organize your answer into main points and supporting details. The conclusion might summarize the answer.

Hail: What is it and how and when does it form?

What?
- A form of precipitation made up of lumps of ice

How?
- Begins as crystal in thundercloud
- Strong winds toss it up and down
- Water condenses around crystal, freezing into layer of ice
- Layers of ice build up around crystal, creating a hailstone, which continues to get larger and heavier
- Hailstone becomes too heavy to stay aloft, so falls to ground

When?
- Usually forms in summer, when thunderstorms are more frequent and violent

Write Your Answer If you follow a process like the one just laid out, writing an answer to an essay question will become a much easier task. Your plan for your answer will help you focus your ideas, write quickly, and avoid including unnecessary information. Follow the steps below when writing your answer to an essay question.

Writing Your Essay Answer

1. Express your thesis in the opening sentence to show that you understand the question. Writing your thesis at the beginning will also help you focus your answer.
2. Use your notes, thesis statement, and organizational plan to develop your major points and supporting details. You can draw additional supporting details from your notes.
3. Include transitions between each major point.
4. Do not stray from your plan unless you realize some point is incorrect or unworkable. Do not add information that does not support your thesis.
5. Provide an ending that reflects the basic answer you have written.

Prewriting Tip

Before working on one question in a test, read the directions and all the questions to find out what the essay exam involves. Budget time by the number of points each question is worth.

Journal Writing

In your journal, copy two essay questions from your science textbook, or make up two sample questions. For each question do some research to list enough notes to form an answer, and then write a thesis statement to help focus your answer.

Editing Tip

When you edit your essay answer, omit unnecessary details simply by crossing them out. Proofread to check your grammar and spelling. Make all corrections neatly, so that your answer is legible.

Revise and Edit Your Answer Leave time to read over your answer once you have finished. Make sure that your thesis statement is clear and that you have covered all important points. Correct any content errors first. Add details by inserting sentences where necessary. You can clarify a relationship between ideas by adding or changing a transitional word.

Now look at Jason Larmore's essay answer to the questions "Into what three general classes do astronomers group stars? What are the characteristics of each class of stars?"

Student Model

Astronomers group stars into three general classes: the main-sequence, the giant and supergiant, and the white dwarf. Each class has its own characteristics; size, brightness, and color all help determine a star's group. Of these three factors, size is the most important because size differences between classes are dramatically obvious.

Main-sequence stars are the most common. The yellowish main-sequences form an average between the white dwarves and the "red" giants, but because of the giant's immensity, everything seems microscopic in comparison.

The enormousness of the giant-class stars can be shown by comparing them to our own solar system. A single supergiant, placed where our sun is, would engulf all of the inner planets and some of the outer planets. Because the giant stars are so massive, they sometimes are unable to burn gases at a normal temperature. A decrease in this temperature causes them to have a reddish color, common to many giants. There are, however, exceptions to the "red" giant pattern. Deneb is a giant that shines with a blue light. This indicates an extremely high temperature. These exceptions comprise the brightest stars in the night sky.

The final class of stars is the white dwarf. These stars are the result of giant stars that collapsed because they couldn't maintain their mass. The white dwarves are very dense and shine white. These stars are much smaller than our sun, yet they outweigh it exponentially. The fact that white dwarves come from giant stars shows that even though stars are divided into classes, they are in some ways related.

Jason Larmore, Henry Clay High School, Lexington, Kentucky

- How does Larmore's first paragraph demonstrate that he understands the question?

- What supporting details does Larmore use to point out the characteristics of the stars in each of the three groups?

- In his conclusion, Larmore stresses the relationship among the different classes of stars.

5.9 Writing Activities

Write an Essay Answer

Find an end-of-chapter question in your history or science book that could be answered in a short essay. Review the chapter and then write your essay.

PURPOSE To write an essay answering a history or science question
AUDIENCE Your teacher
LENGTH 1–2 paragraphs

WRITING RUBRICS To write an effective answer to an essay question, you should

- decide exactly what the question is asking
- recast the question as a thesis statement
- make notes and organize them
- revise and edit your answer

Cross Curricular Activity

SCIENCE Work together in a small group, and brainstorm your own list of "imponderables," questions about the natural world like those Cecil Adams might answer in his column. (See the model on page 262.) What parts of the natural world puzzle or mystify you? Here's your chance to have someone else find the answers for you. Exchange lists with another group. Select one question from their list for your group to research and answer. Each group member should research and write an answer individually, using print and electronic sources to gather information.

Grammar Link

Make pronouns and their antecedents agree.

In this passage from Jason Larmore's essay answer, note how the indefinite pronoun and the antecedent agree: "Astronomers group stars into three general classes . . . *each* . . . has *its* own characteristics."

Use each indefinite pronoun below and an antecedent in a sentence.

Sample *several*
Answer *Several* of the astronomers explained their theories.

1. everything
2. everyone
3. both
4. few
5. each
6. no one
7. many
8. one
9. either
10. neither

See Lesson 16.7, pages 619–621, and Lesson 17.5, pages 640–644.

Listening and Speaking

COOPERATIVE LEARNING After students have done their individual research and writing, the original groups should reassemble and blend their work into one coherent answer. Each group should then present its answer to the whole class, which may grade the group's effort based on how well it responded to the question.

LESSON 5.10

WRITING ABOUT LITERATURE
Comparing and Contrasting Two Myths

A myth is an ancient story that offers an explanation about some aspect of the natural world. Notice the similarities in the Sioux and Zulu creation myths.

According to a myth of the Sioux, Native Americans of the Plains, the first man sprang from the soil of the Great Plains. As he emerged, he saw only the sun. After freeing himself from the clinging soil, he began to take halting steps. The sun shone on his body, toughening his skin and making him strong. The Sioux descended from this man.

A myth of the Zulu people of Africa describes how the sky god created the first people. After his marriage to the earth goddess, the sky god walked through a swamp. He broke off reeds of different colors and fashioned a man and a woman from each different colored reed. A different tribe descended from each pair of reed people.

Student Mathew Isaac read these ancient stories and pondered their similarities and differences. Here's what he came up with.

Student Model

The Sioux and Zulu myths attempt to explain the creation of mankind. The setting and the characters in the myths reveal a great deal about these groups. Both deeply revered their soil, for their pastoral life-styles revolved around it. This reverence may be inferred from the fertile land, the setting for both myths. The Sioux man emerged from the soil, while the Zulu were created from reeds in a swamp. The Zulu people recognized a god as their creator. The Sioux did not, at least according to this myth, although their myth notes the importance of the sun for continued life.

The beliefs and values of the Sioux and Zulu, some of which were shared, are visible in their creation myths.

Mathew Isaac, Rich East High School, Park Forest, Illinois

> Isaac finds a central point of comparison between the two myths—the fertile soil.

> What central difference does Isaac find between the two myths?

268 Unit 5 Expository Writing

Explain a Myth

Myths sometimes offer explanations for why things happen as they do. Science provides one kind of explanation, but myths offer alternative views. The ancient Romans explained the seeming movement of the sun across the sky as the work of a heavenly charioteer circling the earth daily. The ancient Japanese explained the creation of their islands with a myth about the spear of a god named Izanagi. In fact, there are probably as many distinctly different mythologies as there are different cultures.

Find Similarities and Differences

The chart below shows the common elements of literature, which all myths share. You can cite these elements to compare myths from different cultures.

> **Drafting Tip**
>
> In a comparison of two stories, use a feature-by-feature comparison. This form will help you weave together your points of comparison. See Lesson 5.6, page 248.

Common Elements of Literature

Element	Definition
Setting	The place and time in which the action of the story occurs. The location can be real or imaginary. In a myth, the time is usually the past.
Characters	The people, animals, or gods that participate in the action of the story
Conflict	The struggle that is central to the story. It can be a struggle between characters or forces.
Plot	The story's sequence of events. A plot revolves around a conflict and builds to a climax that is later resolved.
Theme	The message or main idea of the story. The theme may or may not be stated directly.

Journal Writing

Think about a myth with which you are familiar. In your journal, write a brief summary of the myth, and then, in a short list, identify each of the literary elements in that myth.

5.10 Comparing and Contrasting Two Myths   **269**

Use a Comparison Frame

How did the sun and the moon get into the sky? Here are two answers in the form of myths, one ancient Mexican and one ancient Nigerian.

According to the Mexican myth, the gods were arguing about who among them should light the earth by day and who by night. After four days of arguing, two gods volunteered. One was rich and strong, and the other was poor and feeble. The gods then built a huge bonfire, and the two volunteers stepped toward it. The rich god was afraid of the flames and drew back from the fire. The poor god jumped right into the fire and was catapulted high into the sky. He became the sun. The bonfire began to die. The rich god still wanted a share of the glory. He leaped into the embers, sailed into the sky, and became the moon.

According to the Nigerian myth, before there were people, the sun and the moon were married and lived on earth. The sun was good friends with the water and one day invited him to his village to meet his wife. The water flowed into the village, with the fish, the crabs, the whales, and all the other living things swimming in the seas. Soon the sun and the moon had to climb on top of the village huts because of all the water. But the water kept coming and began lapping the rooftops. The sun and the moon had to flee to safety. They each took a bounding leap into the sky, and there they remain.

The comparison frame below will help you compare and contrast the two myths.

> **Grammar Tip**
>
> When explaining a myth or describing past events, be consistent in your choice of verb tense. For more information on consistent tenses, see Lesson 15.6, page 594.

Comparison of Two Myths

Element	Mexican Myth	Nigerian Myth
Setting	A long time ago on earth	A long time ago on earth
Characters	The Mexican gods	The sun and moon, a married couple, and the water
Conflict	Which of the gods will get to be the sun and which the moon?	Water threatens to drown the sun and moon during a visit.
Plot	The gods argue. Two gods volunteer, one rich and strong, the other poor and feeble....	The sun invites water to his village. Water flows into the village, rising up to the rooftops....
Theme	Bravery, not wealth, brings great glory.	Some guests can't be accommodated in one's home.

5.10 Writing Activities

Write a Comparison-Contrast Essay

Imagine that you are writing a paper entitled "Some Common Themes in World Mythology" for your literature class. Write a comparison-contrast of the two myths below.

Iroquois myth: Four animals, bound on leashes by a giant, are responsible for the winds. A strong, fierce bear brings on the north winds of winter. A gentle fawn brings on the south winds of summer. An angry panther brings on the west winds that accompany storms and whirlwinds. A moose brings on the east winds with their chilling mists. The giant unleashes these animals to match his moods, but he tries to unleash each wind in its proper season.

Italian myth: The north wind is a woman who had wanted to marry the south wind. But the south wind told the north wind he couldn't marry her without a dowry. The north wind blew for three days and nights, covering the land with silver snow. This she presented as her dowry. The south wind, not wanting to marry, blew for three days and nights and melted all the snow. The north wind decided that she no longer wanted to marry someone who had frittered away her entire dowry in only three days.

PURPOSE To compare two myths
AUDIENCE Your high school literature teacher
LENGTH 1–2 paragraphs

WRITING RUBRICS To write an effective comparison-contrast essay, you should

- compare and contrast the literary elements of the two myths
- use a feature-by-feature treatment to weave together your points of comparison

Grammar Link

Make clear comparisons.

Rewrite each sentence below to correct the incomplete or unclear comparison.

1. There are more myths about creation than about any subject.
2. The Zulu myth is more religious in tone than the Sioux.
3. Did the ancient Greeks worship more gods than anyone?
4. The cleverness of the gods was always greater than the people.
5. Myths explaining the natural world are more ingenious than scientists.

See Lesson 18.4, page 665.

Listening and Speaking

COOPERATIVE LEARNING With a small group, find a brief myth. Produce a videotaped reading using sound effects and props. Practice your reading several times before taping it so that it is fluid and dramatic.

Using Computers

Use the copy feature of your word processing program to save the first draft of your comparison-contrast essay. Save your first draft, either as a new file or as a new page in the existing file. Continue to work on your essay, saving each successive draft to record your earlier ideas and the changes you've made.

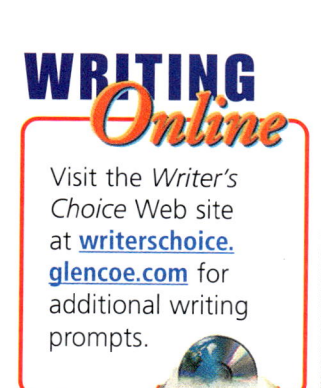

UNIT 5
Writing Process in Action

Expository Writing

In preceding lessons you learned about the different types of expository writing, the purpose of each, and ways to make expository writing informative and appealing. You have written cause-and-effect explanations, comparison-contrasts, and essays. Now it is time to apply what you have learned. In this lesson you are invited to write about an insect or other animal that repels most people, presenting information in a way that will help your reader better understand and empathize with the creature.

Assignment

Context

A science teacher has a problem: this year most of his sixth-grade students seem to be afraid of or disgusted by the creatures about which he wants to teach them. He wants your class to write brief articles about the insects and other animals. The articles should help his students appreciate these creatures.

Purpose

To write a brief article about a creature people often label "bad" to help children experience and appreciate this animal in its own right

Audience

Sixth-grade science students

Length

1–2 pages

The guidelines on the following pages can help you plan and write your article. Read through them, and then refer to them as you complete this assignment. Don't be tied down by the guidelines, however. Remember, you're in charge of your own writing process.

WRITING Online

Visit the *Writer's Choice* Web site at **writerschoice.glencoe.com** for additional writing prompts.

Writing Process in Action

Prewriting

What would you like to write about—wolves, sharks, spiders, bats? Any of these creatures are fair game, but see what other ideas you can come up with. Brainstorm with classmates to generate a list of "vicious," "disgusting," or just misunderstood creatures. From this list select a subject that both interests you and is likely to repel or intrigue your audience.

Once you have identified your subject, freewrite or brainstorm to create an inventory of what you already know about this creature. The Prewriting Questions will help you get started.

Next, do research to find the facts. Start by checking encyclopedias, magazines, and videotapes to determine the accuracy of each characteristic you listed in your initial inventory. Expand your inventory by interviewing authorities on this creature. These experts might include zookeepers, animal trainers and breeders, pet store owners, farmers, or rangers. Record your findings on note cards or in a journal.

Once you have gathered your data, look over your notes to determine how you can best organize your information. The notes themselves may suggest a particular kind of organization. However, if they don't, look for a main idea or focus, and consider weeding out all details not related to that focus. Select the most interesting details to use in your lead, or introduction, and then try to determine what would most logically flow from that.

Prewriting Questions

- If you experienced the creature close up, what would you see, hear, smell, and feel?
- How does the animal perceive the world?
- How does it interact with others of its species?
- How does it find a mate?
- How does it obtain its food?

Drafting

For this assignment, you need to grab and hold your readers' attention. You might want to start with a fact or myth that is likely to intrigue young readers.

As you write the body of your paper, be sure to support the points you want to make with specific details. Try also to bring your subject to life with facts, analogies, and other evidence. Read the passage on page 274 to see how natural history writer Barry Holstun Lopez brings to life the relationship between the wolf and his habitat.

TIME

For more information about the writing process, see **TIME Facing the Blank Page**, pp. 121-131.

Writing Process in Action

Drafting Tip

For suggestions about how to find an effective lead for your story, see Lesson 5.8, page 256.

When you've accomplished the purpose of your feature, conclude your article. If you chose to present one animal's life from birth to death, your conclusion might focus on the death. If you wrote your feature as a flashback, your conclusion would bring readers back to the present. Your conclusion should give your feature a sense of closure or completeness.

Literature Model

The wolf is tied by subtle threads to the woods he moves through. His fur carries seeds that will fall off, effectively dispersed, along the trail some miles from where they first caught in his fur. And miles distant is a raven perched on the ribs of a caribou the wolf helped kill ten days ago, pecking like a chicken at the decaying scraps of meat. A smart snowshoe hare that eluded the wolf and left him exhausted when he was a pup has been dead a year now, food for an owl. The den in which he was born one April evening was home to porcupines last winter.

Barry Holstun Lopez, *Of Wolves and Men*

Revising Tip

For examples of vivid supporting details, see Lesson 5.2, page 232, and Lesson 5.8, page 256.

Revising

To begin revising, read over your draft to make sure that what you've written fits your purpose and audience. Then have a **writing conference.** Read your draft to a partner or small group. Use your audience's reactions to help you evaluate your work.

Revising Checklist

- Does the reader gain an understanding of the creature and its habitat?
- Is the lead engaging, the conclusion effective?
- Is the information well organized?
- Do supporting details bring the subject to life?

Writing Process in Action

Editing/Proofreading

When you have revised your article for basic content and organization, **proofread** it carefully for errors in grammar, usage, mechanics, and spelling. Think again about your audience. You may find that you will need to simplify or shorten some of your sentences and make your tone more informal. Use the questions at the right as a guide.

Editing Questions
- Do my subjects and verbs agree?
- Are there any run-on sentences?
- Have I used commas where they are needed?
- Are my comparisons complete and clearly stated?
- Have I checked carefully for misspellings?

Self-Evaluation

Make sure your article—

✔ focuses on a creature likely to repel young students
✔ uses vocabulary and a writing style appropriate for your audience
✔ develops in a logical, natural way
✔ supports points with specific details
✔ follows correct grammar, usage, mechanics, and spelling

Publishing/Presenting

Think about how you can make your essay easy for sixth graders to read and understand. Would a map help you explain your animal's habitat? Would a graph help you present statistical information about your subject?

Proofreading Tip
For proofreading symbols, see page 411.

Presenting Tip
For information about how to enhance your paper with graphics, see Lesson 5.7, pages 252–255.

Journal Writing

Reflect on your writing process experience. Answer these questions in your journal: What do you like best about your article? What was the hardest part of writing it? What did you learn from talking to others about it? What new things have you learned as a writer?

UNIT 5
Literature Model

from

Of Wolves and Men

by Barry Holstun Lopez

Barry Holstun Lopez writes about natural history and the environment in short fiction, articles, essays, and books. Among his many books is Of Wolves and Men, *which grew out of a 1974 article he wrote for* Smithsonian *magazine. As you read, notice how Lopez's explanations help his reader "see" the wolf in its own right and its own world. Then try the activities in Linking Writing and Literature on page 280.*

Imagine a wolf moving through the northern woods. The movement, over a trail he has traversed many times before, is distinctive, unlike that of a cougar or a bear, yet he appears, if you are watching, sometimes catlike or bearlike. It is purposeful, deliberate movement. Occasionally the rhythm is broken by the wolf's pause to inspect a scent mark, or a move off the trail to paw among stones where a year before he had cached[1] meat.

The movement down the trail would seem relentless if it did not appear so effortless. The wolf's body, from neck to hips, appears to float over the long, almost

---

1 cached (kashd) stored up

Literature Model

spindly legs and the flicker of wrists, a bicycling drift through the trees, reminiscent of the movement of water or of shadows.

The wolf is three years old. A male. He is of the subspecies *occidentalis,* and the trees he is moving among are spruce and subalpine fir on the eastern slope of the Rockies in northern Canada. He is light gray; that is, there are more blond and white hairs mixed with gray in the saddle of fur that covers his shoulders and extends down his spine than there are black and brown. But there are silver and even red hairs mixed in, too.

It is early September, an easy time of year, and he has not seen the other wolves in his pack for three or four days. He has heard no howls, but he knows the others are about, in ones and twos like himself. It is not a time of year for much howling. It is an easy time. The weather is pleasant. Moose are fat. Suddenly the wolf stops in midstride. A moment, then his feet slowly come alongside each other. He is staring into the grass. His ears are rammed forward, stiff. His back arches and he rears up and pounces like a cat. A deer mouse is pinned between his forepaws. Eaten. The wolf drifts on. He approaches a trail crossing, an undistinguished crossroads. His movement is now slower and he sniffs the air as though aware of a possibility for scents. He sniffs a scent post, a scrawny blueberry bush in use for years, and goes on.

The wolf weighs ninety-four pounds and stands thirty inches at the shoulder. His feet are enormous, leaving prints in the mud along a creek (where he pauses to hunt crayfish but not with much interest) more than five inches long by just over four wide. He has two fractured ribs, broken by a moose a year before. They are healed now, but a sharp eye would notice the irregularity. The skin on his right hip is scarred, from a fight with another wolf in a neighboring pack when he was a yearling. He has not had anything but a few mice and a piece of arctic char[2] in three days, but he is not

Nancy Schutt, *Encroachment,* 1987

---

2 char (chär) a kind of trout

Literature Model

hungry. He is traveling. The char was a day old, left on rocks along the river by bears.

The wolf is tied by subtle threads to the woods he moves through. His fur carries seeds that will fall off, effectively dispersed, along the trail some miles from where they first caught in his fur. And miles distant is a raven perched on the ribs of a caribou the wolf helped kill ten days ago, pecking like a chicken at the decaying scraps of meat. A smart snowshoe hare that eluded the wolf and left him exhausted when he was a pup has been dead a year now, food for an owl. The den in which he was born one April evening was home to porcupines last winter.

It is now late in the afternoon. The wolf has stopped traveling, has lain down to sleep on cool earth beneath a rock outcropping. Mosquitoes rest on his ears. His ears flicker. He begins to waken. He rolls on his back and lies motionless with his front legs pointed toward the sky but folded like wilted flowers, his back legs splayed,[3] and his nose and tail curved toward each other on one side of his body. After a few moments he flops on his side, rises, stretches, and moves a few feet to inspect—minutely, delicately—a crevice in the rock outcropping and finds or doesn't find what draws him there. And then he ascends the rock face, bounding and balancing momentarily before bounding again, appearing slightly unsure of the process—but committed. A few minutes later he bolts suddenly into the woods, achieving full speed, almost forty miles per hour, for forty or fifty yards before he begins to skid, to lunge at a lodgepole pine cone. He trots away with it, his head erect, tail erect, his hips slightly to one side and out of line with his shoulders, as though hindquarters were impatient with forequarters, the cone inert in his mouth. He carries it for a hundred feet before dropping it by the trail. He sniffs it. He goes on.

The underfur next to his skin has begun to thicken with the coming of fall. In the months to follow it will become so dense between his shoulders it will be almost impossible to work a finger down to his skin. In seven months he will weigh less: eighty-nine pounds. He will have tried unsuccessfully to mate with another wolf in the pack. He will have helped kill four moose and thirteen caribou. He will have fallen through ice into a creek at twenty-two below zero but not frozen. He will have fought with other wolves.

He moves along now at the edge of a clearing. The wind coming down-valley surrounds him with a river of odors, as if he were a migrating salmon. He can smell ptarmigan[4] and deer droppings. He can smell willow and spruce and the fading sweetness of fireweed. Above, he sees a hawk circling, and farther south, lower on the horizon, a flock of sharp-tailed sparrows going east. He senses through his pads with each step the dryness of the moss beneath his feet, and the ridges of old tracks, some his own. He hears the sound his feet make. He hears the occasional movement of deer mice and voles.[5] Summer food.

---

3 splayed (splād) spread out
4 ptarmigan (tärʹ mi gən) a kind of northern or alpine bird
5 voles (vōlz) field mice

Makah wolf mask, late nineteenth century

Toward dusk he is standing by a creek, lapping the cool water, when a wolf howls—a long wail that quickly reaches pitch and then tapers, with several harmonics,[6] long moments to a tremolo.[7] He recognizes his sister. He waits a few moments, then, throwing his head back and closing his eyes, he howls. The howl is shorter and it changes pitch twice in the beginning, very quickly. There is no answer.

The female is a mile away and she trots off obliquely through the trees. The other wolf stands listening, laps water again, then he too departs, moving quickly, quietly through the trees, away from the trail he had been on. In a few minutes the two wolves meet. They approach each other briskly, almost formally, tails erect and moving somewhat as deer move. When they come together they make high squeaking noises and encircle each other, rubbing and pushing, poking their noses into each other's neck fur, backing away to stretch, chasing each other for a few steps, then standing quietly together, one putting a head over the other's back. And then they are gone, down a vague trail, the female first. After a few hundred yards they begin, simultaneously, to wag their tails.

In the days to follow, they will meet another wolf from the pack, a second female, younger by a year, and the three of them will kill a caribou. They will travel together ten or twenty miles a day, through the country where they live, eating and sleeping, birthing, playing with sticks, chasing ravens, growing old, barking at bears, scent-marking trails, killing moose, and staring at the way water in a creek breaks around their legs and flows on.

6 **harmonics** (här män′ iks) overtones
7 **tremolo** (trem′ ə lō′) a pulsating tone

Literature Model   279

Literature Model

Linking Writing and Literature

Readers Respond to the Model

What techniques does Barry Holstun Lopez use to convey in-depth information in a lively and appealing way?

Explore Barry Holstun Lopez's exposition by answering these questions. Then read what other students like about Lopez's writing.

1. Lopez uses third-person omniscient point of view. How does this point of view affect his writing?
2. What types of supporting details does Lopez use to bring his subject to life?
3. How well do you feel you got to know the wolf from this exposition? Explain.

What Students Say

"What I liked best about this selection from *Of Wolves and Men* was all the details the author used. Lopez's words made me realize exactly what the wolf was feeling. The mood was calm, but as a reader I still felt a sense of danger. The writer created that mood by carefully detailing the wolf's life— the danger that he had been through and that was yet to come.

I think Lopez's choice of third person was appropriate because it makes the reader an observer, watching the wolf and his movements rather than seeing the scene from the wolf's point of view. I would recommend this selection to a friend because it teaches you in an interesting way about the life of a wolf."

Claire Monty

"The writer chose third-person point of view for an unbiased examination of the wolf's actions. The dominant mood of the selection was one of solemnity, which the writer created by always making the episode serene, not bringing out action."

Chris Fickes

UNIT 5 Review

Reflecting on the Unit

Summarize what you learned in this unit by answering the following questions.

1. What are the important characteristics of effective expository writing?
2. What are the purposes of these types of expository writing: process explanation; cause-and-effect; classification; comparison-contrast? How does the writer organize each type?
3. How do graphics enhance expository writing?
4. What are the important steps in preparing a feature article?
5. What strategies are helpful for answering an essay question?

Adding to Your Portfolio

CHOOSE A SELECTION FOR YOUR PORTFOLIO Look over the expository writing you have done in this unit. Select a favorite piece to put into your portfolio. The piece you choose should show some or all of the following:

- a clear expository purpose
- a well-formulated thesis statement
- supporting details appropriate for its purpose and audience
- in-depth information presented appealingly
- an interesting introduction and a conclusion that gives a sense of closure.

REFLECT ON YOUR CHOICE Attach a note to the piece you chose, explaining briefly why you chose it and what you learned from writing it.

SET GOALS How can you improve your writing? What skill will you focus on the next time you write?

Writing Across the Curriculum

MAKE A SOCIAL STUDIES CONNECTION Choose a recent event that has affected the environment in some way. The event can be a natural disaster, an accident such as an oil spill, or the passage of an environmental protection law. Then write a cause-and-effect paragraph explaining the event. Try to identify at least two causes of the event and two possible consequences. Include a suggestion for one or more graphics that will strengthen your writing. Don't forget to use vivid details.

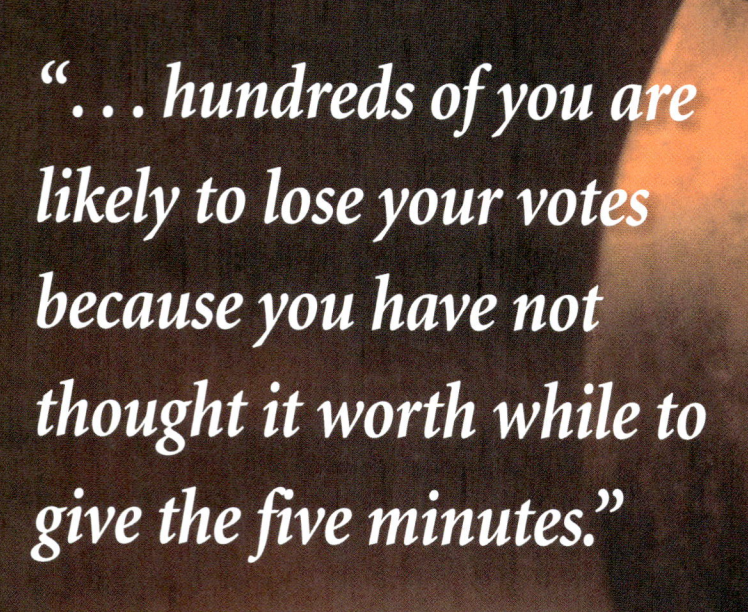

> "... hundreds of you are likely to lose your votes because you have not thought it worth while to give the five minutes."

—the *Democrat and Chronicle,* quoted in "The United States *vs.* Susan B. Anthony" by Margaret Truman

UNIT 6
Persuasive Writing

Writing in the Real World: *Melanie McFarland* — 284

Lesson **6.1** Writing Persuasively — 288

Lesson **6.2** Using Evidence Effectively — 292

Lesson **6.3** Checking Reasoning — 296

Lesson **6.4** Using Language to Advantage — 300

Lesson **6.5** Writing an Editorial — 304

Lesson **6.6** Writing About Literature: Writing a Movie Review — 308

Writing Process in Action — 312

Literature Model: "Skeletons in the Attic" by Clara Spotted Elk — 316

Unit 6 Review — 321

Writing in the Real World

Persuasive writing relies on facts, examples, logic, and strong feelings to sway a reader's opinion. Below is a persuasive article written by Melanie McFarland when she was a high school senior at Morgan Park Academy in Chicago, Illinois. Her movie reviews appeared in a monthly teen newspaper called *New Expression.* Today McFarland reviews movies for the *Seattle Times.*

Petrie's "Toy Soldiers" Has Glitches

by Melanie McFarland

People probably don't know Daniel Petrie, Jr. by name, but they probably know the screenplays he has written or co-written. . . . I had high expectations for his newest film, which was his directing debut: "Toy Soldiers."

It wasn't exactly what I expected.

"Toy Soldiers" is a film about a prep school called the Regis School (aka The Rejects School). Many students are discipline cases who were kicked out of other schools, and are also the sons of powerful families.

So it's not exactly surprising that one day, a group of Colombian terrorists led by Luis Cali, the son of the powerful drug lord Enrique Cali, take over the school. Luis Cali demands his father's release, or else he will kill off one hostage per day. Sounds grim, huh? Not exactly. Class prankster Billy Tepper and his entourage decide they are going to fight back and free their school.

Daniel Petrie, Jr. has great potential as a director. The cinematography was excellent, and the casting was right on. The executions of the scenes were great.

Sean Astin is excellent as Billy Tepper. The part seemed to come very naturally to him.

Wil Wheaton, however, really surprised me. Best known as the ingenious Wesley Crusher in "Star Trek: The Next Generation," he is usually cast as the shy youth. In "Toy Soldiers" he plays Joey Trotta, the son of a powerful mafia figure, who is tough as nails and full of rage. He certainly broke his mold.

In fact, all of the actors were wonderful. But their acting does not save them from a lackluster script. Billy Tepper, though he does have his share of pranks, does nothing spectacular. Other characters could have been more developed as well, such as Joey Trotta. The only thing we know about Joey is that he hates his mafia father.

The dialogue also lacked Petrie's usual spark. The villain, Luis Cali (Andrew Divoff) looked like a cartoon character, thanks to the script. . . .

Writing in the Real World

What's really exciting about a villain in an action film is that he or she seems invincible, but the audience and the hero have to find the villain's Achilles' heel. Cali and his boys weren't ruthless or cunning enough, but I guess that's why a bunch of teenaged mouthwash swigging boys were able to overpower them.

Finally, the score did not fit. The music was the critical, yet playful kind used in films like "Bambi."

The bottom line is this: the actors deserved a better script, the director deserved a better storyline. "Toy Soldiers" had all the makings of a great action film, but just missed its target.

A Writer's Process

Prewriting
Reading, Watching, and Listening

Before McFarland ever sets foot in a movie theater, she does her "research." In part, that means gleaning information from the press kit that film companies send to reviewers and critics.

The press kit is a thick, glossy notebook-sized folder filled with background information, including biographies of the actors, writers, producer, and director. "I read the biographies of the actors so I can see what other work they've done," McFarland explained. "If I'm not familiar with [their work], I'll go out and rent some films."

Watching movies that constitute an actor's body of work is crucial for reviewers. By knowing an actor's skill and range, reviewers can spot new achievements or the lack of them in an actor's current work.

Reviewers begin their real work as they walk into the movie theater. During the film, they look for original writing. "The lines should be imaginative," McFarland said. "They should make the actors glow." Reviewers also watch for strong directing and acting that's natural, not contrived. In a comedy, McFarland notes how much of the audience is laughing—"the entire audience, not just the [person] in front of you." In a drama or action film, she considers the "grip factor"—how much the film grabs your emotions.

Like every good persuasive writer, McFarland tries to understand a differing point of view. She makes a point of taking a friend to the movies "to get another opinion of the film," she said.

After the film, McFarland jots down notes about key scenes, dialogue, and acting, plus her insights and reactions. These prewriting notes

Melanie McFarland

Writing in the Real World

will help McFarland to focus her ideas when she sits down to write.

Drafting
Writing for a Specific Audience

Before McFarland writes her review, she mulls over her reactions for a day. She jots down any important insights and reviews her background information and press kits.

When she's ready to write, McFarland imagines her audience—a few teenagers who want an intelligent opinion of the film she's seen. "I imagine what I would say to an audience right in front of me," McFarland said. "And then I write it down."

Revising
Polishing the Draft

Like professional critics and reviewers, McFarland puts extra time and effort into writing a strong lead that will grab readers. "I tend to set up scenarios in the opening paragraphs that lead into the actual critique."

While revising, she pays special attention to her tone. "Never gush" is a key rule for strong persuasive writing. McFarland realizes that proof of her viewpoints—quoted dialogue, colorful descriptions—gets readers to listen.

Editing
Working with Editors

Once McFarland finishes her review, she checks spelling, grammar, and punctuation. Then she gives the review to one of her peer editors or supervising editors. In addition to proofreading, the peer editor checks the review for completeness, logic, and style. The supervising editor usually makes minor copyediting changes and, if there are major revisions needed, returns the manuscript to McFarland.

Publishing
Going to Press

After McFarland finishes her final draft, the copy is imported from one computer system to another, and dummy electronic pages are created. McFarland is always curious to see the layout and often returns to the office for one last check. A common error, she says, occurs when the copy is imported; text can "disappear" during the process, and she wants one last chance to proofread before press time.

Examining Writing in the Real World

Analyzing the Media Connection

Discuss these questions about the movie review on pages 284–285.

1. How does the first paragraph draw readers into the article and encourage them to read further?
2. What does the reviewer consider the major weakness in the film? What evidence or reasons does she offer to support her opinion?
3. What does the reviewer consider the strengths of the film? What evidence or reasons does she offer to support her opinion?
4. What does the reviewer assume her audience will know?
5. Would this review inspire you to see the film? Why or why not?

Analyzing a Writer's Process

Discuss these questions about Melanie McFarland's writing process.

1. How does McFarland prepare to see a movie?
2. What elements does McFarland look for when she goes to a movie?
3. How does audience reaction influence McFarland's reviews?
4. How might using a strong lead in a review help McFarland persuade her readers to accept her opinion?
5. How do editors help McFarland with her reviews?

Grammar Link

Use the correct word of a confusing pair.

Some confusing pairs of words are *homophones*—words like *their* and *there* that sound alike but have different meanings and spellings. Other words, such as *accept* and *except*, are easily confused simply because they sound similar.

Rewrite each sentence below, completing it with the correct word in parentheses. If you are in doubt, use your dictionary.

1. The theater reviewer was (formally, formerly) a movie critic.
2. Her opinion had no (affect, effect) on my decision.
3. Do you like horror movies better (then, than) comedies?
4. The scene was set in the lobby of the state (capital, capitol).
5. The group went to the movies (altogether, all together).

See Lesson 26.2, page 833.

LESSON 6.1

Writing Persuasively

Persuasive writing is writing that tries to influence a reader to accept an idea, adopt a point of view, or perform an action. Effective persuasive writing uses strong, relevant evidence to support its claims.

Use Persuasive Writing

Newspaper and magazine advertisements, as well as posters announcing events such as the concert pictured, are examples of persuasive writing. You might use persuasive writing to do any or all of the tasks in the following list:

- convince your principal to relax the school's dress code
- persuade others to see a movie or play
- advertise lawn-care services you can provide
- apply for a summer job

Construct a Logical Argument

An argument contains the body of evidence used to support a point of view. The purpose of the argument is to persuade readers to accept your point of view. When you present your evidence logically, you take your readers step by step through your argument.

The chief stages in the construction of a logical argument are detailed on pages 289–290.

Identify Your Purpose Before you begin constructing your argument, decide what you want your persuasive piece to accomplish. For instance, if you want to write a letter to your principal about the lack of sports opportunities for girls at your school, your purpose might be to ask the principal to help develop a girls' soccer team.

State Your Central Claim A claim is a statement that asserts something. In persuasive writing, your central claim usually clarifies your main purpose for writing, and this claim will often begin your argument. For example, the letter requesting increased sports opportunities for girls might begin, "Our school should organize a girls' soccer team." Identifying your claim at the beginning will help focus your argument.

Identify Supporting Evidence One way to start identifying evidence to support your claim is to ask yourself questions that begin, "What evidence do I have that . . . ?" Then look for answers to your questions.

For example, to support the claim that her school should organize a girls' soccer team, one writer asked herself, What evidence do I have that

- enough girls are interested in joining a soccer team?
- the team would benefit the girls and the school?
- there is a need for additional sports activities for girls?
- the school can provide the necessary staff?

To answer these questions, the writer then conducted a survey of the girls at her school. As a result, she discovered overwhelming interest in a soccer team. She also talked to the coach of the girls' soccer team at a nearby high school and some of the gym teachers at her own school. As authorities on the subject, these people supplied the writer with expert testimony to support her claim. By using these kinds of sound evidence in her persuasive writing piece, the writer will improve her chances of persuading her audience.

> **Drafting Tip**
>
> As you draft, use transitions to show relationships between ideas and to lead your readers step by step through your evidence.

Journal Writing

Identify a situation in which you were persuaded to do something. In your journal, note the evidence and tactics that were most effective in persuading you to take action. Then explain why these tactics may have been so effective.

Explain How the Evidence Supports Your Claim If the link between your claim and the evidence you use to support it is obvious, you don't need to state it. If, however, the connection is not clear, you must explain how the evidence supports your claim and why the reader should accept your evidence.

Read the following model in which the writer presents her case for a girls' soccer team in a letter to her high school principal. Notice how the evidence supports her claim.

Model

Dear Mr. Lopez,

I strongly believe that our school should organize a girls' soccer team, and I am not alone in this belief. After conducting a survey among the junior and senior girls at our school, I found that fifty girls would be interested in trying out for a soccer team.

> The link between the survey results and the claim for a soccer team is obvious. The connection does not need to be stated.

To discover how similar teams have worked out at other schools, I talked to Ms. Young, the girls' soccer coach at Fairfax High. When I asked her how the team has benefited the girls and the school, she said: "The girls on my team have become close friends. They help each other with everything—homework, personal problems." She added, "Their grades have improved—they've become all-around better students—and that's always good for a school."

A soccer team would be of equal benefit to the girls at our school. Just like the girls at Fairfax, many of the girls here would enjoy making close friends. A soccer team might enrich their lives at school.

> What is the logical link between the girls at Fairfax High and the writer's claim?

Moreover, it would be simple to start a team. I've already talked to my gym teacher, Ms. Jordan. She's willing to take on the responsibility of coaching the team. The question of where to practice isn't a problem either, since the playing field isn't used after three o'clock on Tuesdays and Thursdays. All we need now is your support.

Reaffirm Your Claim Conclude your argument by reaffirming your claim. You might suggest that, given the evidence you have presented, your claim is the logical conclusion. You might also explain how your claim could be put into action. In the model above, for example, the writer explains where and when the soccer team could meet and identifies a teacher who is willing to coach it.

6.1 Writing Activities

Write a Letter to the Editor

Write a letter to the editor of your school newspaper about some aspect of school life that you would like to see changed. Be sure to construct a logical argument.

PURPOSE To make a case for change in some aspect of school life
AUDIENCE Teachers and other students
LENGTH 1–2 paragraphs

WRITING RUBRICS To write an effective letter to the editor, you should

- identify your purpose
- state your central claim clearly
- present evidence in a logical sequence
- explain how your evidence supports your claim
- conclude by reaffirming your claim

Bronze plaque from Benin

Grammar Link

Double negatives, such as *can't...no*, cancel each other out. Avoid them.

Rewrite the sentences below, eliminating the double negatives.

[1]There isn't no reason why the school can't sponsor a computer club. [2]We don't have none now, but we could easily organize one. [3]People who don't have no computer games could share them. [4]People who don't know nothing about using a computer could get help. [5]Since we don't need no more computers, we aren't going to need no new printers either.

See Lesson 18.6, page 668.

Cross-Curricular Activity

ART In a small group, discuss whether the plaque at left should be shown in a school exhibit for students to view. Consider the subject and design of the work, as well as how students might react to it. Then write a paragraph stating why the work should or should not be exhibited in the school.

Listening and Speaking

In a small group, choose three letters to the editor from a recent edition of your local newspaper. Analyze the letters for effective persuasive writing by identifying each letter's purpose, central claim, and supporting evidence. Discuss which of the three letters is the most persuasive and give reasons for your choice.

6.1 Writing Persuasively **291**

LESSON 6.2

Using Evidence Effectively

Just as an attorney must present sound evidence in a courtroom, you must use strong, reliable, and relevant evidence to prove your claim in a piece of writing.

Identify the Evidence

The most common kinds of evidence used in persuasive writing include the following: facts, statistics, examples or incidents, opinions, and reasons. To collect these kinds of evidence, try freewriting, clustering, or making a list about your issue. You can also gather evidence by reading about your issue and by interviewing people. The more kinds of evidence you use to support your claim, the stronger your argument will be.

Evidence Used in Persuasive Writing

Kind	Definition	Example
Fact	Something that is known to be true	Prehistoric dancers pictured on rock surfaces in Africa and southern Europe prove that dancing is one of the oldest forms of human expression.
Statistic	A fact that is expressed in numbers	When the musical *A Chorus Line* finally closed on Broadway in 1990, it had achieved a record of 6,137 performances.
Example or Incident	A particular case or event	In some societies, dancing plays a role in courtship. For example, in the U.S., many high school students get to know one another at school dances.
Opinion	A personal judgment based on what the person believes or feels to be true	A famous dancer once claimed, "The dance is a poem of which each movement is a word."
Reason	A logical argument	Many ballet dancers protest the use of toe shoes because the shoes cause permanent damage to the wearer's feet.

Assess the Accuracy of the Evidence

To assess the accuracy of your evidence, verify it in up-to-date sources. Check facts and statistics by consulting current encyclopedias, atlases, and other reference sources. Consult an expert on your subject to clarify something you don't understand or to obtain information that printed sources cannot provide. If you cannot verify a statement, or if the only source available to you is out of date, you may want to omit the statement from your argument. Your position will be greatly weakened if your readers spot inaccuracies in your argument.

Journal Writing

What do you think are the most reliable kinds of evidence you can use to support a claim? Why do you think this may be so? Write down your ideas in your journal.

Grammar Tip

If you use statistics or number amounts in your evidence, be sure to check the subject-verb agreement. See Lesson 16.4, page 614.

Be sure that the people whose opinions you include are authorities on your subject. Resist using the opinions of well-known persons who have no connection to your subject. So-called testimonials do not have the validity of opinions supplied by authorities.

Evaluate the Relevance of the Evidence

To assess the relevance of your evidence, examine each detail and ask yourself if it helps to develop the point you want to make. If not, you should probably discard the detail as irrelevant to your argument. For example, if you were writing to convince your audience that Spike Lee is a great movie director, you probably wouldn't include a statement naming his favorite restaurant. The statement has nothing to do with Lee's ability as a director and would only distract your readers from your central point.

Now read the following selection by editorial columnist Anthony Lewis. Notice that Lewis uses sound, relevant evidence to support his claim that the nicotine in cigarettes is as addictive as heroin or cocaine.

Literature Model

Lewis cites facts and statistics from a highly respected source, the U.S. Surgeon General, to support his claim.

In what way is each point Lewis uses in his argument relevant to his claim?

Dr. C. Everett Koop, the Surgeon General, was only spelling out in scientific terms what we all have observed about cigarette smoking. Users become dependent on the habit, and breaking it can be extremely difficult.

Of those who try to give up smoking, 80 percent have relapsed by the end of a year. Heroin users who try to give up their addiction have the same rate of failure.

"The pharmacologic and behavioral processes that determine tobacco addiction," the Koop report concluded, "are similar to those that determine addiction to drugs such as heroin and cocaine."

There is one profound difference between heroin and nicotine addiction. Tobacco kills 80 times as many people in this country. About 320,000 Americans die every year as a result of using tobacco products, while 4,000 die from the effects of heroin and related drugs.

Anthony Lewis, "Merchants of Death," *New York Times*

6.2 Writing Activities

Evaluate an Editorial

Find an editorial in a local or school paper and evaluate the evidence it uses to make its case. Write a brief review explaining why you think the editorial is or is not effective. Give clear reasons to support your opinion of the editorial's argument.

PURPOSE To evaluate the evidence in an editorial
AUDIENCE Your teacher and classmates
LENGTH 1–2 paragraphs

WRITING RUBRICS To write an evaluation of an editorial, you should
- summarize the opinion expressed
- identify the evidence
- explain whether the evidence is accurate
- decide whether the evidence is relevant

Using Computers

Using a search engine, find several Web sites that contain editorials about a topic currently in the news. Evaluate the editorials for their use of evidence, effectiveness, and overall appearance. In one or two paragraphs, explain what factors contribute to the persuasiveness of a good online editorial.

Viewing and Representing

COOPERATIVE LEARNING In a small group, watch and discuss three television shows that feature teenagers. Identify ways you think each show could be improved. Then have each group member choose one show and write a letter to its producers in which he or she proposes ideas for change. Finally, take turns presenting each letter to the rest of the group, who will act as the show's producers and assess the relevance of the evidence.

Grammar Link

Use verb forms correctly.

Past forms of verbs, such as *went*, should not be used with helping verbs; past participle forms like *done* should not be used alone.

Write the correct verb form to complete each sentence below.

1. The trial (began, begun) six weeks ago.
2. The judge had (gave, given) very clear instructions.
3. The lawyers had (chose, chosen) a jury in about three weeks.
4. They had (took, taken) their time because this trial was so important.
5. Both lawyers (did, done) their best to persuade the jury.
6. The defendant has (wrote, written) notes to her lawyer during the trial.
7. The newspapers said that the trial has (gone, went) on too long.
8. The courtroom (was, been) filled with spectators every day.
9. Has the foreman (spoke, spoken) for a unanimous jury?
10. The defense has (win, won) an acquittal.

See Lessons 15.1 and 15.2, pages 581–585.

LESSON 6.3

Checking Reasoning

Learning to recognize the logical flaws in an argument can help you eliminate these flaws from your own writing. There are several types of faulty logic that you should be able to recognize.

Eliminate Faulty Logic

Once you've chosen the evidence to support an argument, you need to make sure that the conclusions you draw from that evidence are logical or follow sound reasoning. Suppose, for example, that you try to persuade your parents to buy you an outfit because it's on sale and they could save by buying it now. Their logical response to this argument could be that they'd save even more money if they didn't buy it at all. If your conclusions are illogical, or include logical fallacies, your readers may reject your entire argument—no matter how compelling your evidence or how well written your argument. As you write, watch out for three of the most common errors in reasoning: red herrings, either/or thinking, and cause-and-effect errors.

Red Herrings The term *red herring* derives from the practice of dragging a strong-smelling fish across a trail to confuse hunting dogs and throw them off the scent. In writing, a red herring is a topic or statement that distracts the reader's attention from the central issue or that hides a weak argument.

Read over your argument to check for red herrings. Make sure that each of your points is directly related to your claim. Anything that sends your reader in a different direction may be a red herring.

Either/Or Thinking Either/or thinking results from oversimplifying your argument by assuming that the issue has only two sides. For example, a writer might make the following claim: "Schools should eliminate computer instruction and return to teaching students the basics—reading, writing, and arithmetic." This position, however, fails to take into account the possibility that computers may aid in teaching these basic subjects.

To make sure that you have not used either/or thinking in your writing, look for other reasonable positions between the two sides you have presented in the argument. If you find them, you are probably oversimplifying the issue.

Cause-and-Effect Errors The fact that one event precedes another in time does not necessarily mean that the first event is the cause of the second. To make sure that you have identified true cause-and-effect relationships, plot your evidence on a cause-and-effect diagram. Check to be sure that each effect is the direct result of the cause you have listed.

In the cause-and-effect diagram shown below, one writer plots some evidence supporting the argument that the demand for ivory jewelry has endangered African elephants. Is each effect the direct result of its preceding cause? Remember that one way to check an argument for cause-and-effect errors is to use the "*because* test": if you can use the word *because* to show the relationship between events or facts, the relation is causal, not just sequential.

> **Grammar Tip**
>
> If you decide to present your argument orally, be sure it does not contain sentences with dangling modifiers, which will distract your audience. See Lesson 18.7, pages 670–675.

Consumers want ivory carvings and jewelry.

Hunters kill elephants to supply ivory.

Because old elephants with larger tusks have been killed, younger ones are hunted.

Younger elephants have smaller tusks, so more are killed to meet demand for ivory.

The killing of elephants accelerates, leading to possible extinction.

Journal Writing

Select an argument you have begun to write. In your journal, plot its evidence on a cause-and-effect diagram like the one shown above. Then ask yourself if each effect you have listed is the direct result of the preceding cause. If it is not, correct your argument.

Analyze Your Opponent's Logic

Often you can strengthen your position in an argument by pointing out flaws in the opposing argument. To find the logical flaws in an argument, evaluate the information presented, point by point. Look for and identify any red herrings, oversimplifications, or faulty cause-and-effect relationships.

If, upon close examination, you find points in the opposing argument that are difficult to disprove, you may need to concede their worth or admit that those points are valid. Frequently, making reasonable concessions can strengthen your position and give readers the impression that they are reading a well-researched, unbiased argument.

In the following selection, Yona Zeldis McDonough points out some logical flaws in the argument against wearing fur coats. However, she also concedes some points to the opposition. Is her argument strengthened by the concessions she makes?

Literature Model

As I walked along 57th Street in Manhattan, a woman hissed, "A lot of animals were tortured to make that coat!" I was surprised, not by her sentiment, which I understood and even respected, but by her need to express it, unsolicited, in public. In the following weeks, I discovered that my outspoken critic was not alone. . . . Like it or not, I realized I was going to have to defend my coat against detractors.

I understand the arguments against wearing fur and have decided to wear one anyway. Not only does fur solve, more efficiently than any other substance known to man, the need for warmth, it has also been with us for hundreds if not thousands of years.

Notice that McDonough points out a key flaw in the opposing view.

Since I eat meat, I find the distinction between wearing and eating arbitrary. Animals don't care whether their flesh is consumed or their skins are worn; the point is, they have died and we have killed them. This may sound cruel, but it is honest.

What point does McDonough concede? How does she use it to expose weaknesses in her opponents' argument?

I would like to ask those women who keep shouting at me just how consistent they are: What about wearing leather and suede? Animals must be killed for those skins, too. Do all these women wear only sneakers and carry canvas bags?

Yona Zeldis McDonough, "Sisters Under the Skin,"
The *New York Times*

6.3 Writing Activities

Write a Persuasive Argument

Write a brief report arguing to accept or reject each of these statements about relaxing a school's dress code. Evaluate each statement using sound logic.

1. The way students dress is one of the few things teenagers can control, and that independence shouldn't be restricted.
2. After the dress code at a nearby school was relaxed, the students' grade averages rose.
3. The dress code should be stricter because too many students concentrate on their looks rather than on their schoolwork.
4. Some students' dress expresses their ethnic and cultural diversity.
5. In addition to determining the dress code, students should also have a voice in choosing the books they read in class.

PURPOSE To write a persuasive argument evaluating the logic of certain statements
AUDIENCE A panel composed of teachers and school administrators
LENGTH 1 page

WRITING RUBRICS To write a persuasive argument, you should

- identify the kind of error or logical fallacy in each faulty statement
- explain how each faulty statement weakens the argument

Viewing and Representing

Review a popular television commercial and analyze the reasoning presented. Is the reasoning sound, or are red herrings, either/or thinking, cause-and-effect errors, or other logical fallacies presented? Write a paragraph explaining your findings, and share it with the class.

Using Computers

Some software programs can search writing for errors in grammar, usage, and mechanics. You might want to use such a program as you write. The program can aid the revising process, but you are still responsible for finding and correcting errors in reasoning.

Grammar Link

Use commas to set off parenthetical expressions and long introductory elements in sentences.

Rewrite the following sentences, adding commas where needed.

1. As you watch popular television programs you may ask yourself if they include too much violence.
2. During the course of the past few weeks a group has been monitoring programs to count the violent incidents.
3. The group's report shows that for the most part violence is depicted during prime time.
4. Although viewing violence may have no negative effects on older people constant exposure to violence may have a negative effect on young children.
5. Many parents as a matter of fact are convinced that they see evidence of violent behavior in their children.

See Lesson 21.6, pages 738–748.

LESSON 6.4

Using Language to Advantage

You can make your writing more precise by using limiting words, by replacing general words with specific ones, and by understanding the connotations of the words you use.

You can't always persuade an audience to accept your argument. Empty adjectives and wild promises such as those in the cartoon fool no one. However, using words that precisely express your meaning will give you a better chance of persuading your readers.

Use Limiting Words

Limiting words are words that allow you to account for exceptions when you state your point of view. Use limiting words to avoid glittering generalities, oversimplifications, or gross exaggerations of the facts. For example, if you said, "Today's rock singers depend on sophisticated sound equipment to make up for their lack of musical talent," many of your readers would recognize that your point of view is a gross overstatement. On the other hand, if you said, "Some of today's rock singers depend on sophisticated sound equipment to make up for a lack of musical talent," you'd narrow your statement and allow for exceptions to it. *Some* is a limiting word. The chart below lists some common limiting words that you can use to avoid making overgeneralizations.

Limiting Words		
almost never	in most cases	occasionally
a minority of	less than half	often
as a rule	many	rarely
certain	more than half	seldom
few	most	several
frequently	mostly	some
half	nearly all	sometimes
hardly ever	nearly always	the majority of
in general	not all	usually

Use Specific Words

Make your persuasive writing more precise by replacing general words with specific ones whenever you can. For example, compare the following two sentences:

"Certain types of television programs have really bad effects on young children."
"Violent television shows cause violent behavior and nightmares in young children."

Because the second sentence provides more definite information and brings more vivid thoughts and images to mind, it is more likely to hold the reader's attention. You'll never convince your readers of anything if you can't hold their attention.

Revising Tip

During revising, try using a thesaurus to help you find precise words that express your meaning exactly. See Lesson 24.2, page 816.

Journal Writing

What strategies might you use to help identify glittering generalities, oversimplifications, or gross exaggerations of the facts? What strategies might you use to help you identify general words that could be replaced with more specific ones? Write your ideas in your journal.

Consider Connotations

Choose words that not only express your specific meaning but also have the right connotation. *Connotation* refers to an emotion or an underlying value that accompanies a word's dictionary meaning. Suppose, for instance, that you describe the famous smile in Leonardo da Vinci's painting, the *Mona Lisa*, as "weird." The word *weird* implies that there is something negative—not just unusual—about the smile. If, on the other hand, you refer to Mona Lisa's smile as "mysterious," you suggest that it is interesting and attractive.

Words with highly emotional connotations cause strong negative or positive responses. Consider the words *bold* and *reckless*. Although they have similar meanings, these words prompt very different emotional responses. *Bold* excites positive feelings because it suggests a daring, confident spirit. *Reckless* stirs up negative feelings because it implies irresponsibility.

Leonardo da Vinci, *Mona Lisa*, 1503–1505

In the following model, the writer uses the connotations of words to praise the candidate he supports and to establish arguments against the opposition.

Model

I heartily encourage you to vote for Don "Bud" Edwards for mayor. He is a man of action and notable accomplishments. As a former alderman, Bud battled tirelessly against the bureaucrats on the city council to guarantee inexpensive housing for the underprivileged. Furthermore, his heroic efforts on behalf of the elderly have been chronicled by prominent journalists across the country.

In contrast to Bud, his opponent, Gus Badenough, is notorious for his waffling stands on the issues and for his vicious opposition to Bud. In fact, he has attempted to obstruct Bud's valiant work for the homeless more than once. Now Gus has begun to make petty allegations, which our candidate will not lower himself to address.

Are we going to allow these smear tactics to succeed? I hope not. On election day, I believe that there will still be enough upstanding citizens to vote for a true gentleman and statesman, Bud Edwards.

- Words such as "heroic" imply that Edwards nobly defends lost causes.
- How would the tone of the piece be affected if you substituted the phrase "level charges" for "make petty allegations"?
- What other words used in the model convey particular notions about Edwards and the candidate opposing him?

6.4 Writing Activities

Write a Positive Description

Write a paragraph describing the painting below, Pablo Picasso's *Two Acrobats with a Dog*, for your museum's newsletter. Try to inspire museum visitors to come to see the painting.

PURPOSE To write an appealing and intriguing description of a painting
AUDIENCE Potential art museum visitors
LENGTH 1 paragraph

WRITING RUBRICS To write a positive description, you should

- use limiting words to prevent over-generalizations
- choose precise words
- choose words with positive connotations

Cross-Curricular Activity

MUSIC Write a brief review of a song you have heard recently. Use connotative words to evoke either a positive or negative reaction in your readers and to persuade them to accept your opinion of the song.

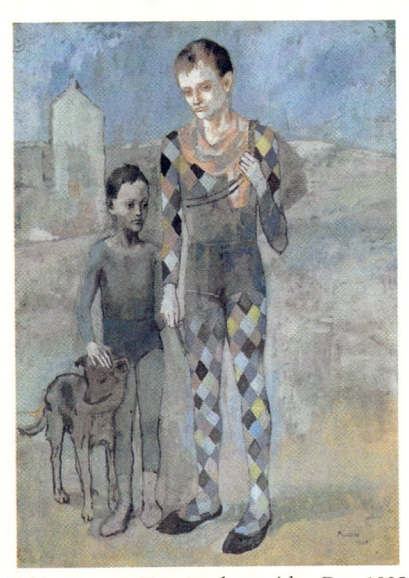

Pablo Picasso, *Two Acrobats with a Dog*, 1905

Grammar Link

Use specific nouns and modifiers.

The sentences below describe a new cereal. Rewrite the sentences using specific nouns and vivid modifiers that will persuade readers to try this product. Consider the connotations of the words you substitute. Each sentence can be revised in more than one way.

1. You should buy this brand of breakfast cereal because it tastes good.
2. This cereal contains many things that are good for you.
3. The shapes of the flakes are interesting.
4. The flakes have a nice texture.
5. The cereal is more nutritious when served with different kinds of fruits.

See Lesson 10.1, page 439, and Lesson 10.4, page 461.

Using Computers

Word Choice and Spelling Compile a list of ten general terms of description. Using the thesaurus function on your computer, find at least three richer, more specific words for each general term. Create an accurately spelled list of the richer terms and keep it posted near your computer, in your journal, or wherever you do your writing.

Persuasive Writing

6.4 Using Language to Advantage **303**

LESSON 6.5

Writing an Editorial

In an editorial, such as the one below, a writer expresses an opinion about a current news event or issue. An effective editorial is direct and absorbing and can move its readers to take action or to believe something. Do you think the argument in the model is effective?

Literature Model

Yesterday's announcement of a plan for U.S. and Soviet Olympic committees to test athletes for drugs is welcome news. It's also overdue. Sports organizations are fighting a losing battle against anabolic steroids, and the reason is that most don't have their hearts in the struggle. Only a handful of competitors, including Ben Johnson, the Canadian sprinter, were expelled from the Seoul Olympics for using the forbidden drugs. Yet, according to *The Times*'s recent series on drug use, probably half or more of the 9,000 athletes at Seoul had used steroids or similar drugs during training.

Steroid use has long been rampant, yet sports bodies from Olympic committees downward have been failing in their responsibility to deter it. Drug-using athletes set a dispiriting example to a society trying to fight drug abuse, especially to young people who are at grave risk of injury from the drugs. "The system is saying, do whatever it takes to win," says Bill Curry, football coach at Alabama.

. . . [D]iet and exercise are accepted ways of enhancing physical ability; drugs are not. Many athletes apparently take steroids not because they want to but from peer pressure or fear of losing to others who do. . . . Once the message is out that sports organizations are really serious about steroids, most athletes will probably abandon them with relief.

"Winking at Steroids in Sports," November 22, 1988,
The *New York Times*

> The writer uses comments such as "It's also overdue" to express an opinion on the use of steroids.

> What pieces of evidence does the writer use to support his opinion?

The New Television Season: Another Winning Lineup

What's Right with Rap

Fair Fare for Films

Whatever it is, it isn't art

Why do dancers always have to be on their toes?

Captive Audiences

Support your local drama club

Choose an Issue

Choose one issue about which you feel strongly and state it in the form of a question. If you don't have an issue in mind, get a sense of controversial topics in your community by reading local newspapers, talking to people, and listening to local talk shows on radio or television. Then brainstorm to generate evidence that supports your viewpoint. In the following example, two writers with opposing viewpoints answered this question: "Are rock musicians who lip-sync at live concerts cheating their fans?"

> **Prewriting Tip**
>
> If you are having trouble coming up with evidence to support your argument, try to imagine a conversation on the subject with someone who holds an opposing view.

Yes, because...	Fans who pay high prices for concert tickets deserve to hear live music. People go to live concerts to hear live music. It's not as exciting for the fans; they might as well listen to a record.
No, because...	Today's concerts offer more than just singing. It's exciting just to be there at a live performance. The audience gets more for its money because shows are so extravagant.

Journal Writing

In your journal, generate a list of currently controversial issues that interest you, and choose one that could be the topic of an editorial you might write. Then brainstorm to generate evidence that you could use to support your viewpoint.

6.5 Writing an Editorial

Appeal to Your Audience

Select evidence that will persuade your audience to take your stand. Keep in mind that a striking image can often speak more powerfully than a list of facts and statistics. For example, rather than saying "Thousands of people thronged the concert," you might say, "So many people attended the concert that the crowd that night formed the third largest city in the state."

You might also consider injecting some humor into your editorial. When you make your readers laugh, they may feel that they share common ground with you and, therefore, be more disposed to agree with what you're saying.

Draw a Conclusion

A good conclusion sums up the argument and spurs the reader to action. In the editorial below, Eugene Weresow makes his strongest point at the end.

Student Model

Hanging on my classroom wall is a long list of books that have been banned from certain schools. As I scanned the list, I recognized several that were among the best I've ever read, including *Catcher in the Rye, 1984,* and *Brave New World.* Although these books contain controversial language and situations, I believe it would be a mistake to ban them.

Admittedly, some of the characters in *Catcher in the Rye* use words that would be inappropriate in the classroom. But real people often swear and use slang expressions; the author is just trying to make his book realistic. Similarly, *1984* and *Brave New World* portray situations that some may consider unacceptable for political or social reasons. But the authors mean to convey a message with these works; the extreme situations they use make a more lasting impression upon the reader than would more acceptable situations.

I don't believe it is dangerous to expose students to the controversial material in these books. On the contrary, I believe the books should be valued for the ideas they express. Rather than protect impressionable students, those who ban these books do us a disservice: they deny us access to ideas.

Eugene Weresow, Edison High School, Edison, New Jersey

> Weresow makes concessions to his opponents but counters their objections by discussing the intentions of the authors.

> What is Weresow's strongest point?

6.5 Writing Activities

Write an Editorial for a TV Program

You have been asked to deliver a written editorial on *Teen Say*, a television program for teenagers, on the issue "Should the academic year be extended through July?"

PURPOSE To persuade your audience to accept your views on extending the school year
AUDIENCE Teenage TV viewers
LENGTH 2–3 paragraphs

WRITING RUBRICS To write an effective editorial, you should

- establish your position on the issue
- select evidence to persuade your audience
- summarize your argument with a strong conclusion

Using Computers

Suppose you want to send copies of your television editorial to several different teen magazines. Instead of typing multiple copies of your piece, use the Mail Merge feature of your word-processing program. Just type a list of the addresses to which you want to send the editorial. Then use Mail Merge to print as many copies as you want, each to a different address. Be sure you check your editorial for correct spelling and grammar before sending your copies.

Grammar Link

Make verbs agree with indefinite pronoun subjects.

A verb must agree with an indefinite pronoun subject, such as *each* or *several*:

Each (singular) **was** satisfactory.
Several (plural) **were** tested.

Rewrite each sentence, choosing the correct form of the verb in parentheses.

1. I inquired about certain books and was told that some (was, were) not available in the school library.
2. All (is, are) literary classics and (has been, have been) in print for a long time.
3. No one in the library (has, have) time to help me use the computer catalog to locate other books by that author.
4. Most (is, are) in different editions and (has been, have been) reprinted several times.
5. Though there are two copies, neither (is, are) on the shelf.

See Lesson 16.7, page 619.

Listening and Speaking

COOPERATIVE LEARNING In a small group, take turns reading aloud your editorials. After each person has presented his or her views, evaluate the editorial. Which part of the argument was the most persuasive? The least persuasive? What might have made the argument stronger? After you have read and discussed all of the editorials, decide what characteristics strong editorials have in common.

LESSON 6.6

Writing About Literature
Writing a Movie Review

A movie review is one person's evaluation of a film. Although critics may differ in their opinions, most critics go through a similar process in writing their reviews.

Scene from *Dances with Wolves*

Provide Background Information

Most critics begin a movie review by stating an opinion about a film. A reviewer, then, may provide background information on the film by briefly summarizing the plot and identifying the characters, actors, director, and scriptwriter. When you review a film, determine how much background information to include. Ask yourself what your audience already knows about the film and what they need to know to understand your review.

Examine the Movie's Elements

Reviewers often evaluate certain elements of the film and measure the film's success by specific criteria. These criteria differ somewhat for different types of films. For example, a comedy can be judged according to how funny it is; an action film can be judged by how exciting it is. However, some criteria are useful for judging most movies. These are outlined in the chart below.

The Elements of a Movie	
Plot — What happens in the film	Does it hold your interest? Does it seem plausible or contrived?
Theme — The main idea or message that the film conveys.	Is the movie's theme significant? Does the film develop the theme, or does it oversimplify a complex subject?
Characterization — The way the characters are developed by the scriptwriter and the director	Do the characters seem real? Believable? Are their motivations and actions true to their backgrounds and personalities?
Acting — The way the actors portray their characters	Do the actors create believable characters? Do they evoke the intended responses in the audience—laughter, fear, sorrow?
Special Effects — Techniques used to create illusions	Do special effects create the desired illusions? Do they enhance or overpower the story?
Sound Track — The music that accompanies the visuals	Is the music appropriate to the scene in which it is used? What is the quality of the music? Is the sound track well recorded? Clear?

Journal Writing

Choose a movie that you have seen recently. Use the questions in the chart above to deconstruct, or analyze, the movie's elements and help you generate details that you could use in a movie review. Record the details in your journal.

Evaluate the Movie Critically

Although you can approach a movie review in many ways, using the questions in the chart below may help you develop your own perspective to evaluate a movie. Read the checklist, then study student Lina Chern's review.

> **Editing Tip**
> When you edit your review, set off the movie title by underlining it. If you use a computer, input the title in italic type. Capitalize the movie title correctly. Refer to Lesson 20.2, page 713, to review capitalization rules.

A Critic's Checklist

1. Can I compare or contrast this film with another that explores the same theme?
2. Is this film adapted from a written work, such as a novel or a play? If so, can I compare the film to the original work?
3. Can I compare my reactions with those of the audience?
4. Can I critique the film from a particular social or political perspective? Am I well informed enough to do so?

Student Model

I must admit that I was not expecting terrific results from *Terminator 2: Judgment Day,* the most eagerly awaited sequel of the summer. After all, its predecessor was one of the most thoughtful, understated action movies ever made, while *T2* was promising to be a typical overblown summer blockbuster. I was only half-correct—the story has lost some thought and subtlety and gained a great deal of special effects, but is still interesting and definitely entertaining.

Arnold Schwarzenegger (too marketable now to play the bad guy) stars as a reprogrammed Terminator cyborg that is ordered to go back in time to protect the still-adolescent John Connor (Edward Furlong); the boy is to become a key figure in the future war between humans and machines. After John and the Terminator rescue John's mother, Sarah (Linda Hamilton)—now a tough, hell-bent warrior—from a mental hospital, the three set out to prevent the coming nuclear holocaust, or Judgment Day. Meanwhile, they have to deal with another, more advanced Terminator that has been sent back to kill John.

In general, *Terminator 2* is engaging and creative, but in a more conventional way than the original. It is a clean, slick moneymaker, which should not deter anyone from seeing it.

Lina Chern, Maine East High School, Chicago, Illinois

> What elements of *T2* does Chern examine in her review?

> What is Chern's opinion of the movie? Why do you think she compares *T2* with the original *Terminator* to express her opinion?

6.6 Writing Activities

Write a Movie Review

Select a film known for its special effects and review it for the readers of your school newspaper. Base your review on an evaluation of the movie's use of special effects.

PURPOSE To write a movie review
AUDIENCE Readers of your school newspaper
LENGTH 1–2 paragraphs

WRITING RUBRICS To write an effective movie review, you should

- provide background information
- discuss whether special effects enhance or overpower the movie
- explain whether the special effects create the desired illusions
- compare the special effects to those in another movie
- explain the audience's response to the movie

Cross-Curricular Activity

LITERATURE Choose one of the films listed below or another you have seen that is based on a work of literature. Then prepare a written review of the film in which you compare it with the original work of literature. If you like, submit the review for publication in your school's literary journal or newspaper.

- Wuthering Heights
- Howards End
- A Raisin in the Sun
- Out of Africa
- The Grapes of Wrath
- Elmer Gantry
- Great Expectations
- A Passage to India
- The Age of Innocence
- The Color Purple
- Beauty and the Beast
- Mansfield Park

Grammar Link

Use comparative and superlative forms of modifiers correctly.

more conventional, one of the most thoughtful

Rewrite the following sentences. Use the correct degree of comparison of the modifiers in parentheses.

1. *The Nightmare Before Christmas* is one of the _____ films I have ever seen. (good)
2. It is _____ than other animated films. (thought provoking)
3. My little brother thought that the creatures in this movie sang _____. (beautifully)
4. The special effects in *Nightmare* are _____ than those in *E.T.* (imaginative)
5. The words of the songs are the _____ I have ever heard. (witty)

See Lesson 18.1, pages 659–660.

Using Computers

Analyze the way an online movie reviewer and a movie critic for a print newspaper or magazine evaluate the same film. What do the two reviews have in common? What differences do you notice? How do you account for those differences? Write a one-page essay comparing and contrasting the reviews. Share your essay with a partner.

UNIT 6
Writing Process in Action

Persuasive Writing

In this unit you've learned about writing to persuade and about the logical considerations that contribute to presenting a strong and well-supported argument. You've learned how to write reviews, articles, and editorials. Now it's time to apply what you've learned. In this lesson you will select a problem in your school or community and take a stand in favor of whatever corrective action you think is appropriate.

Assignment

Context

You are an editor of *Student Voices,* a monthly newsletter with a broad circulation in your school and community. You have been asked to write an editorial about a problem situation or an injustice you want to see changed. This is your opportunity to reach people who make policies and decisions that affect your life, but who might not listen to you otherwise.

Purpose

To write an editorial that exposes a problem or injustice and encourages readers to take corrective action

Audience

Teenagers, teachers, school administrators, and community members

Length

2 paragraphs

The following pages can help you plan and write your editorial. Read through them and then refer to them as you need to. But remember, you're in charge of your own writing process.

WRITING Online

Visit the *Writer's Choice* Web site at **writerschoice.glencoe.com** for additional writing prompts.

312 Unit 6 Persuasive Writing

Writing Process in Action

Prewriting

What problems or injustices are on your mind? The suggestions in Prewriting Options may help you explore your thoughts.

Choose two or three problems that you have identified. Using lists or questions, explore the problems you've identified (see Lesson 2.2, page 62). Write down everything you can think of related to each problem. Think about your purpose and the best way to influence your audience. Read what you have written about each problem. Then ask yourself the following questions, and use the answers to narrow your choices to one topic:

- What problem do I care about the most?
- What claim do I feel the most confidence in making?
- About which topic are my readers most likely to share my concern?

Once you've narrowed your choice down to one topic, review your purposes—to persuade your readers that your claim is valid and to rouse them to take corrective action. Then take some time to think about your audience. Are your readers likely to agree or disagree with you? Do they already care about the issue, or must you persuade them to care? Persuading readers to act upon your argument may require meeting their needs and addressing or changing their attitudes.

Finally, begin to gather and evaluate statistics, opinions, examples, and other evidence that will help you back up your central claim.

Drafting

When you write persuasively, you want to present information in a way that will have a strong impact on your readers. To achieve this goal, use language that is forceful and direct. Choose specific words with strong connotations, as Clara Spotted Elk does in the excerpt on page 314.

Prewriting Options

- Review your journal writing.
- Check school and community newspapers.
- Freewrite; complete the sentence "It bothers me that . . ."
- Brainstorm to list and classify problems and injustices.

TIME

For more about the writing process, see **TIME Facing the Blank Page**, pp. 121-131.

Drafting Tip

For help in writing an editorial, see Lesson 6.5, pages 304–307.

Writing Process in Action **313**

Writing Process in Action

Literature Model

We are outraged that our religious views are not accepted by the scientific community and that the graves of our ancestors are desecrated. Many tribes are willing to accommodate some degree of study for a limited period of time—provided that it would help Indian people or mankind in general. But how many "specimens" are needed? We will not accept grave robbing and the continued hoarding of our ancestors' remains.

Clara Spotted Elk, "Skeletons in the Attic"

You might choose to state your claim forcefully at the start, then present the evidence and reinforce it with a strong conclusion. Alternatively, you can build up to your central claim, which you state last. As you present your evidence, address opposing arguments. Prove the arguments to be false, or concede them in some way.

Once you've built your case, write a conclusion that will leave a strong impression. Summarize your main points, state or restate your central claim, and urge readers to take action.

Revising Tip

For suggestions on checking the logic of your arguments, see Lesson 6.3, pages 296–299.

Revising

To begin revising, read over your draft to make sure that what you've written fits your purpose and audience. Then have a writing conference. Read your draft to a partner or small group. Use your audience's reactions to help you evaluate your work.

Revising Checklist

- Have I presented my central claim clearly?
- Is my evidence accurate and relevant?
- Is my reasoning sound?
- Have I presented my case in a way that will appeal to my audience?

Writing Process in Action

Editing/Proofreading

At this stage, look closely at your writing, paying special attention to your use of language. As you **proofread,** check for errors in grammar, spelling, usage, and mechanics. Use the questions in the checklist as a guide. Then use the self-evaluation list below to make sure that your editorial satisfies your purpose and communicates your message exactly as you want it to.

Editing/Proofreading Checklist

- Have I chosen the correct word of a confusing pair?
- Have I used commas to separate introductory and parenthetical elements from the rest of a sentence?
- Have I used specific nouns and modifiers with appropriate connotations?
- Have I checked the spelling of any unfamiliar words?

Self-Evaluation
Make sure your editorial—

- ✔ focuses on a school or community injustice
- ✔ contains a central claim and identifies a main purpose for writing
- ✔ supports the central claim with accurate and relevant evidence
- ✔ uses sound reasoning and addresses counter-arguments
- ✔ uses limiting words, specific words, and connotations to advantage
- ✔ uses correct grammar, spelling, usage, and mechanics

Publishing/Presenting

You can submit your editorial to the student newspaper, or you might consider using your article as the starting point for a campaign in support of your position. You can rework your editorial into a petition or a leaflet, or even present it as a speech.

Proofreading Tip

For proofreading symbols, see page 411. You can use a computerized spelling or grammar checker to help you edit and proofread your work.

Journal Writing

Reflect on your writing process experience. What do you like best about your editorial? What was the hardest part of writing it? What did you learn in your writing conference? What new things have you learned as a writer? Write your answers in your journal.

UNIT 6
Literature Model

Persuasive Writing

SKELETONS IN THE ATTIC

by Clara Spotted Elk

Clara Spotted Elk has worked to help her fellow Native Americans regain the skeletal remains of their ancestors from museums, collectors, and federal agencies. In September of 1989, thanks in part to persuasive efforts such as hers, the Smithsonian Institution began returning some of these remains to their Native American descendants. As you read the following article, note how Spotted Elk expresses her point of view on this cultural issue. Then try the activities in Linking Writing and Literature on page 320.

Literature Model

Millions of American Indians lived in this country when Columbus first landed on our shores. After the western expansion, only about 250,000 Indians survived. What happened to the remains of those people who were decimated by the advance of the white man? Many are gathering dust in American museums.

In 1985, I and some Northern Cheyenne chiefs visited the attic of the Smithsonian's[1] Natural History Museum in Washington, D.C., to review the inventory of their Cheyenne collection. After a chance inquiry, a curator[2] pulled out a drawer in one of the scores of cabinets that line the attic. There were the jumbled bones of an Indian. "A Kiowa,"[3] he said.

Subsequently, we found that 18,500 Indian remains—some consisting of a handful of bones, but mostly full skeletons—are unceremoniously stored in the Smithsonian's nooks and crannies. Other museums, individuals, and federal agencies such as the National Park Service also collect the bones of Indian warriors, women, and children. Some are on display as roadside tourist attractions. It is estimated that another 600,000 Indian remains are secreted away in locations across the country.

The museum community and forensic[4] scientists vigorously defend these grisly[5] collections. With few exceptions, they refuse to return remains to the tribes that wish to rebury them, even when grave robbing has been documented. They want to maintain adequate numbers of "specimens" for analysis and say they are dedicated to "the permanent curation of Indian skeletal remains."

Indian people are tired of being "specimens." The Northern Cheyenne word for ourselves is "tsistsistas"—human beings. Like people the world over, one of our greatest responsibilities is the proper care of the dead.

We are outraged that our religious views are not accepted by the scientific community and that the graves of our ancestors are desecrated.[6] Many tribes are willing to accommodate some degree of study for a limited period of time—provided that it would help Indian people or mankind in general. But how many "specimens" are needed? We will not accept grave robbing and the continued hoarding of our ancestors' remains.

> *Other museums, individuals, and federal agencies . . . also collect the bones of Indian warriors, women, and children. . . . It is estimated that another 600,000 Indian remains are secreted away in locations across the country.*

---

[1] **Smithsonian** the Smithsonian Institution, a research organization administered by the United States government
[2] **curator** (kyoo´rā tər) a person in charge of a museum
[3] **Kiowa** (kī´ ə wä) a Plains people formerly of what is now Colorado, Oklahoma, Kansas, New Mexico, and Texas
[4] **forensic** (fə ren(t)´ sik or fə ren´ zik) able to apply medical knowledge to legal matters
[5] **grisly** (griz´ lē) horrible; ghastly
[6] **desecrate** (de´ si krāt´) to treat something considered holy in an inappropriate manner

Literature Model

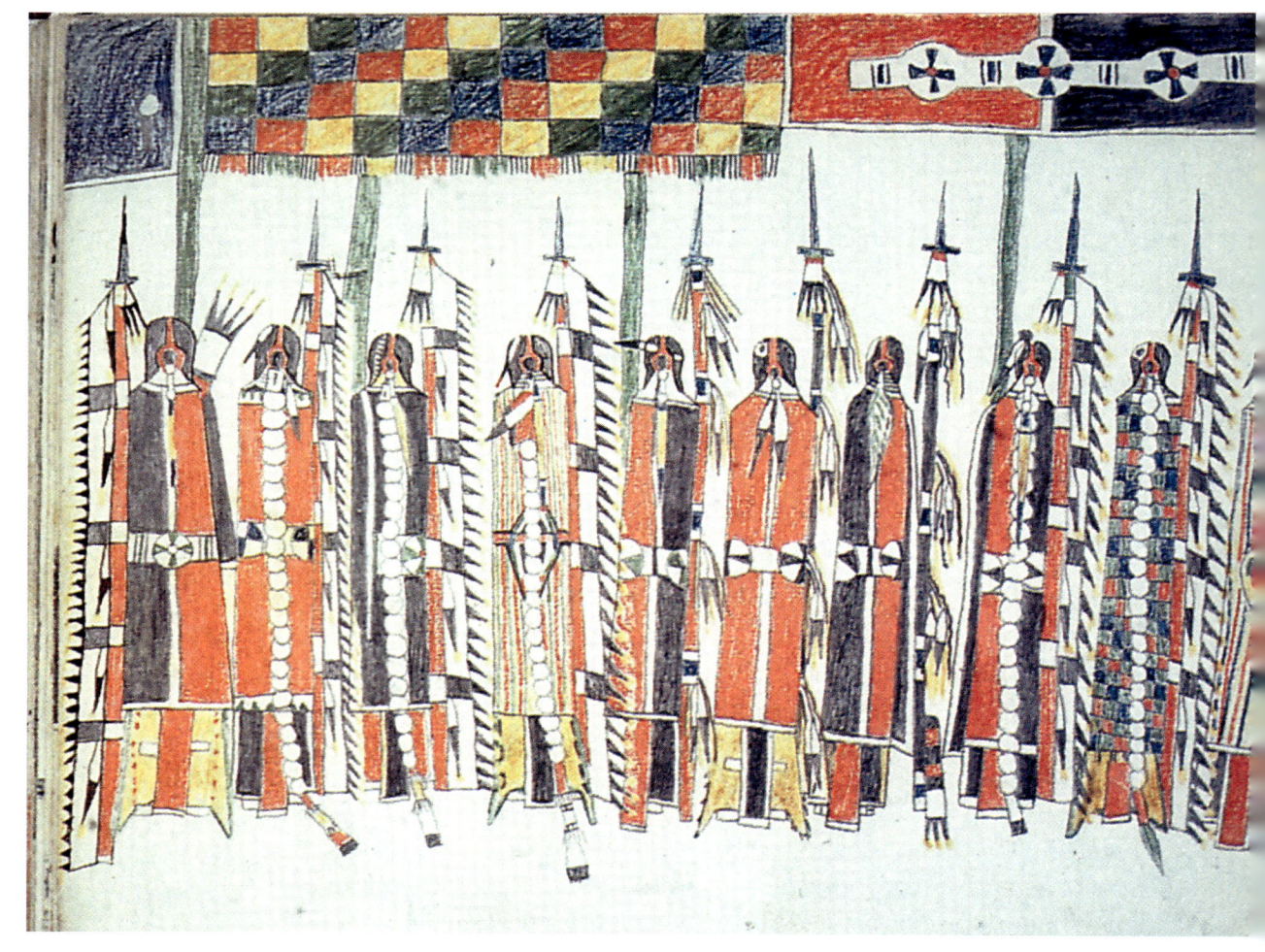

Howling Wolf, Untitled drawing, 1874

Would this be tolerated if it were discovered that it affected other ethnic groups? (Incidentally, the Smithsonian also collects skeletons of blacks.) What would happen if the Smithsonian had 18,500 Holocaust victims in the attic? There would be a tremendous outcry in this country. Why is there no outcry about the Indian collections?

Indians are not exotic creatures for study. We are human beings who practice living religions. Our religion should be placed not only on a par with science when it comes to determining the disposition of our ancestors, but on a par with every other religion practiced in this country.

To that end, Sen. Daniel K. Inouye (D.-HI)[7] will soon reintroduce the "Bones Bill" to aid Indians in retrieving the remains of their ancestors from museums. As in

---

[7] **(D.-HI)** Democrat, Hawaii

Literature Model

the past, the "Bones Bill" will most likely be staunchly resisted by the collectors of Indian skeletons—armed with slick lobbyists,[8] lots of money, and the mystique[9] of science.

Scientists have attempted to defuse this issue by characterizing their opponents as radical Indians, out of touch with their culture and with little appreciation of science. Armed only with a moral obligation to our ancestors, the Indians who support the bill have few resources and little money.

But, in my view, the issue should concern all Americans, for it raises very disturbing questions. American Indians want only to reclaim and rebury their dead. Is this too much to ask?

> *Indians are not exotic creatures for study. We are human beings who practice living religions.*

---

8 lobbyists (lä′ bē ists) people who work to influence laws and government decisions in favor of one special-interest group
9 mystique (mi stēk′) a set of mysterious feelings and attitudes surrounding a person, group, or activity

Literature Model **319**

Literature Model

Linking Writing and Literature

Readers Respond to the Model

What evidence makes Spotted Elk's argument effective?

Explore Clara Spotted Elk's point of view by answering these questions. Then read how other students reacted to Spotted Elk's argument.

1. How does Spotted Elk's choice of words affect the tone of the article? What effect does the tone have on your reading of the article?
2. What is Spotted Elk's principal argument? What "evidence" does she provide to support her view?
3. How did you react to the description of those who Spotted Elk thinks will oppose the "Bones Bill"? What words or phrases triggered your reaction?
4. How does Spotted Elk use limiting words to prevent presenting an either/or situation? Give examples to support your answer.

What Students Say

"This selection was about how one American Indian feels about scientists using her ancestors' bones for research. The article had an angry tone, which the author created simply by telling what the scientists are doing. I don't like the fact that scientists think they have a right to use Indian bones for research. They seem to have no respect for the dead. Because I am part Indian, this selection held my attention. I would definitely recommend it to a friend."

Maurice Phifer

"The writer kept my attention by giving statistics of the wrong that was being done to her people. The dominant tone of this article was sympathetic. Clara Spotted Elk made us sympathize with and feel sorry for her people. She showed us what was happening and opened our eyes to the facts. I would recommend this article because it is important for everyone to be aware of what has happened to the Indians."

Yahna Awazu

UNIT 6 Review

Reflecting on the Unit

Summarize what you learned in this unit by answering the following questions.

1. What are the most important elements of persuasive writing?
2. What are some steps to take in constructing a logical argument?
3. What are some criteria for selecting, evaluating, and using evidence?
4. How can choice of words make an argument more persuasive?
5. What are the purpose and the elements of an editorial?
6. What criteria might you use to judge and review a movie?

Adding to Your Portfolio

CHOOSE A SELECTION FOR YOUR PORTFOLIO Look over the persuasive writing you have done during this unit. Select a completed piece to put into your portfolio. The piece you choose should show some or all of the following:

- logical, accurate, relevant evidence to support a claim
- limiting words, specific words, and words with appropriate connotations
- strong evidence, a striking image, or humor to appeal to an audience

REFLECT ON YOUR CHOICE Attach a note to the piece you chose, explaining briefly why you chose it and what you learned from it.

SET GOALS How can you improve your writing? What skill will you focus on the next time you write?

Writing Across the Curriculum

MAKE A CIVICS CONNECTION How do you feel about the large percentage of the population that does not vote in elections? Is voting a citizen's responsibility that should be encouraged? Is not voting a positive way to express dissatisfaction with the candidates? Develop an argument in which you define your position on this topic. Be sure to identify your purpose, state your central claim, and support it with relevant and logical evidence.

"When you start on your journey to Ithaca,
then pray that the road is long,
full of adventure, full of knowledge."

—C.P. Cavafy, "Ithaca"

UNIT 7 Research Paper Writing

Lesson 7.1	Prewriting: Planning and Researching	324
Lesson 7.2	Prewriting: Outlining	330
Lesson 7.3	Drafting	334
Lesson 7.4	Citing Sources	338
Lesson 7.5	Revising	344
Lesson 7.6	Editing and Presenting: A Model Paper	348

Unit 7 Review 357

LESSON 7.1 Prewriting: Planning and Researching

George W. G. Ferris, the man who dreamed up the Ferris wheel, had a great challenge ahead of him: he had to turn his idea into a solid, working structure. After quite a bit of sketching and planning and a step-by-step approach, Ferris finally created this fantastic new contraption, the likes of which the world had never seen before. In much the same way—with careful planning and a step-by-step approach—you can create a successful and engaging research paper.

Evaluation Rubric

By the time you complete Lesson 7.1, you will have

- chosen a research paper topic that interests you and that is neither too broad nor too narrow
- identified a central idea for your paper and written research questions that will help focus your information search
- identified appropriate authoritative sources of information
- created complete and accurate source cards
- taken notes from your sources in a way that will help you avoid plagiarism

What Is a Research Paper?

The research paper differs from many other kinds of writing because it includes factual information from a variety of sources. These sources may be **primary** (records of the people who took part in the event or period you are studying, such as journals, documents, or photos) or **secondary** (books and articles written about the event or period). Whatever the sources, you can write one of four basic kinds of research paper.

Four Types of Research Paper	
Summary	The writer explores a topic by summing up the opinions of other writers and researchers.
Evaluative	The writer states an opinion and backs it up with evidence found in primary and/or secondary resources.
Original	The writer does original research on a topic and reports on his or her findings.
Combination	The writer combines approaches in one paper, such as summarizing opinions, then conducts original research.

324 Unit 7 Research Paper Writing

Choose a Good Topic

One of your first decisions is what to write about. Try to find a topic that interests you, one that you really want to learn about. If your teacher assigns a subject area, go to the library and skim some general articles covering that area in an encyclopedia. Look for any aspects of the subject that relate to your own interests and activities, or any personalities or events that sound intriguing and exciting. These can become topics to explore in the paper.

Also, keep in mind how much information will be manageable given the length of your research paper. If the topic is very broad, you'll have too much information and too many ideas to cover. On the other hand, if the topic is very narrow, you won't be able to uncover enough material. If you write about such a topic, your paper will probably lack substance (unless you do original research). If you can only find one or two articles on the topic, for example, and if the encyclopedia doesn't cover it, you will almost certainly not have enough to write about.

Do some preliminary reading on your topic to help you find an appropriate focus for your paper. Keep an open mind as you review encyclopedia articles or books and articles on your topic. Depending on your findings—and the amount and type of information you're able to uncover—your preliminary research may lead you to change or refine your topic.

Britta Waller, who wrote the model paper in Lesson 7.6, on pages 350–356, was instructed to write about technology in history. She wanted to avoid run-of-the-mill topics but had to choose a subject on which there was enough information to write an adequate paper. After some brainstorming and a trip to the library, she decided to write about the construction of the first Ferris wheel. It seemed an appropriate topic, since authors have devoted sections of books to it, and since she found articles on different aspects of the topic.

Prewriting Tip

You may wish to discuss your topic ideas with a classmate to get some feedback about the size and scope of your plans. Also, be sure to ask your teacher to approve your final topic.

Too narrow: The gear mechanisms of a Ferris wheel

Appropriate: The history of the Ferris wheel

Too broad: Amusement parks and carnivals

7.1 Prewriting: Planning and Researching   **325**

Prewriting Tip

For information on library resources, see Unit 23, pages 798–810.

Find Information on Your Topic

Once you have a topic, you need to decide on your paper's central idea—the idea that will guide your thinking and your selection of research questions. In your learning log, write three to seven research questions, each question focusing on one aspect of the topic. Ask the *why's, what's,* and *how's* about your topic (for example, "Why was it considered important? What effect did it have? How did it come into being?"). As you find answers, you'll have new questions. Feel free to modify your central idea as you learn more about the topic.

The chart below lists and describes various sources of information that can help you answer your research questions in the area of science and technology. Note that most of the examples listed have their own Web sites, and you may conduct research on the Internet.

Basic Sources of Science and Technology Information		
Type	**Description**	**Examples**
Periodicals	Newspapers, magazines, journals, and other sources that are published on a regular basis, either for general readers or for more specialized audiences	*Washington Post* *Scientific American* *National Geographic* *Science Digest* *Discover*
Government Agencies	Branches of federal, state, and local governments that publish reports, statistics, and other information on scientific topics	National Aeronautics and Space Administration U.S. Fish and Wildlife Service State and local departments of health
Nonprofit Organizations	Private groups that study certain scientific areas or topics and publish reports and statistics	World Wildlife Fund American Cancer Society American Dental Association Sierra Club
Computer Databases	General science information available through computer linkup for a fee	*Applied Science and Technology Index* *General Science Index* *Magazine Index*

TIME

For more information about prewriting, see **TIME Facing the Blank Page,** pp. 124-125.

Create Source Cards or a Computer File for Your Working Bibliography For each suitable source of information you find, record the publication information in a computer file or on a three-by-five-inch index card. Be sure to assign a number to each source, as shown in the upper left corner of the model cards on page 327. You will refer to the information as you complete the process of writing a research paper. For example, when you take notes, you'll jot down the number of the source in which you found each piece of information.

You'll also refer to your source cards or computer file when preparing your works-cited list at the end of your paper.

Different sources require that you record different information, as the samples below illustrate. Look for publication information on the title and copyright pages of books and magazines, and use the works-cited entries on pages 341 and 342 to help you see what information to include for a wider variety of source types.

Prewriting Tip

Be sure that all words, names, and titles are legible and spelled correctly on your source cards or in your electronic file. Follow the conventions of punctuation shown in the chart on page 341 and in the model works-cited list on page 342.

Sample Source Cards

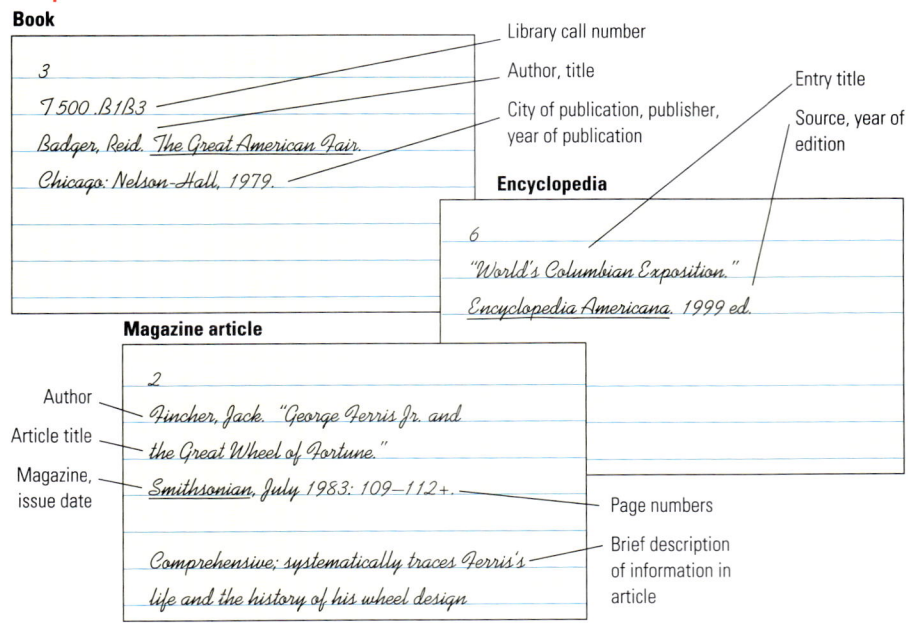

Book

- Library call number
- Author, title
- City of publication, publisher, year of publication

3
T 500 .B1B3
Badger, Reid. *The Great American Fair.*
Chicago: Nelson-Hall, 1979.

Encyclopedia

- Entry title
- Source, year of edition

6
"World's Columbian Exposition."
Encyclopedia Americana. 1999 ed.

Magazine article

- Author
- Article title
- Magazine, issue date

2
Fincher, Jack. "George Ferris Jr. and the Great Wheel of Fortune."
Smithsonian, July 1983: 109–112+.

Comprehensive; systematically traces Ferris's life and the history of his wheel design

- Page numbers
- Brief description of information in article

Take Notes

Taking notes is a good way to help you clarify and remember information, and is one of the most important steps in writing a good research paper. You will probably take many more notes than you will end up using, but don't worry—so do professional writers and researchers.

Prepare Note Cards Read your sources for information that relates to your paper's central idea. As you find answers to your research questions, take notes on four-by-six-inch index cards, with one piece of information per card, and record the corresponding number of the source card. On a separate page, jot down new questions that arise as you learn more about your topic. When taking notes, you can paraphrase, summarize, or quote the source directly. Note the differences in note-taking strategies as you study the sample cards on page 328.

Source

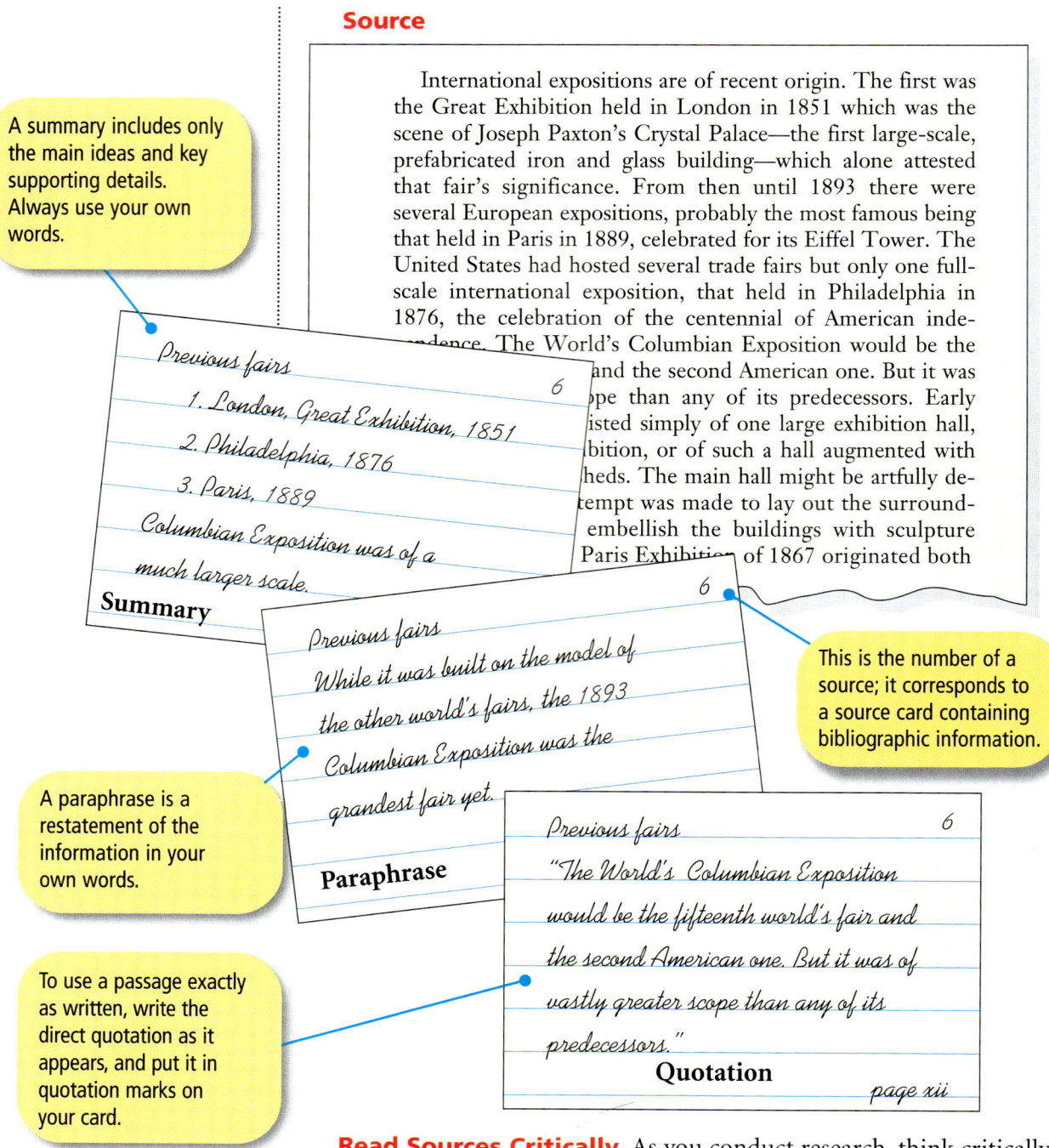

International expositions are of recent origin. The first was the Great Exhibition held in London in 1851 which was the scene of Joseph Paxton's Crystal Palace—the first large-scale, prefabricated iron and glass building—which alone attested that fair's significance. From then until 1893 there were several European expositions, probably the most famous being that held in Paris in 1889, celebrated for its Eiffel Tower. The United States had hosted several trade fairs but only one full-scale international exposition, that held in Philadelphia in 1876, the celebration of the centennial of American independence. The World's Columbian Exposition would be the ... and the second American one. But it was ... pe than any of its predecessors. Early ... isted simply of one large exhibition hall, ... bition, or of such a hall augmented with ... heds. The main hall might be artfully de... tempt was made to lay out the surround- ... embellish the buildings with sculpture ... Paris Exhibition of 1867 originated both

> A summary includes only the main ideas and key supporting details. Always use your own words.

Summary

Previous fairs   6
1. London, Great Exhibition, 1851
2. Philadelphia, 1876
3. Paris, 1889
Columbian Exposition was of a much larger scale.

> A paraphrase is a restatement of the information in your own words.

Paraphrase

Previous fairs   6
While it was built on the model of the other world's fairs, the 1893 Columbian Exposition was the grandest fair yet.

> This is the number of a source; it corresponds to a source card containing bibliographic information.

> To use a passage exactly as written, write the direct quotation as it appears, and put it in quotation marks on your card.

Quotation

Previous fairs   6
"The World's Columbian Exposition would be the fifteenth world's fair and the second American one. But it was of vastly greater scope than any of its predecessors."
                                      page xii

Read Sources Critically As you conduct research, think critically about your sources. Make sure that they are authoritative, reliable, and up-to-date, reflecting the most current thinking on your topic. Newspaper tabloids, for example, are not considered appropriate sources for reliable information. If your topic is scientific or technical in nature, you'll want to be especially sure that your data has been recently published because the field changes so rapidly. Also watch for author bias. Ask yourself whether the author might have a hidden purpose in presenting his or her point of view. Is the author a qualified expert?

Does the author fail to give evidence for certain claims? Is the author reliable on some points but not others? These are questions to consider as you read and evaluate your sources.

Avoid Plagiarism Presenting someone else's ideas or expressions as your own is plagiarism, a form of cheating. Therefore, you must always acknowledge the source of any information you use in your paper. There are two exceptions to this rule, however. You do not need to credit your own ideas, and you do not need to credit information that is considered common knowledge or that can be found in many sources.

The first step in avoiding plagiarism is to indicate on each note card whether an idea is your own or common knowledge or whether it is a paraphrase, summary, or quotation that comes from one of your sources. Notice how Britta Waller labeled her note cards on page 328. When she uses these cards during the drafting process, she will know to give credit to source number 6. See Lesson 7.4 for information about how to cite your sources properly in your research paper.

> **Vocabulary Tip**
>
> On your note cards, write the definition of any technical or unfamiliar terms. When you draft your paper, include the definition the first time you use one of these terms.

7.1 Writing Activities

Skills Practice

1. Write a brief explanation of why each topic below is too broad, too narrow, or about right for a five-page research paper:
   - effects of the car on the United States
   - 3-D movies—invention and refinement
   - building the Great Pyramid at Giza

2. If you were writing a paper about the development of high-definition television (HDTV), which of the following sources would you turn to for information, and which would you avoid? Explain.
   - *Newsweek* magazine
   - *Encyclopaedia Britannica*, 1965
   - *TV Guide*
   - *Scientific American*
   - *The Great Old Movies on TV*
   - *Video Technology Review*, this year's annual edition

Your Research Paper

Begin the process of writing a research paper by following the directions below:

- Select a research paper topic that interests you, and do some preliminary reading so that you can narrow the topic appropriately.

- Write at least five research questions.

- Conduct library research and prepare source cards, using the *MLA Handbook for Writers of Research Papers* and the examples on pages 327 and 342 as a guide to recording publication information accurately.

- Take legible notes from the sources you've gathered, and make sure to give proper attribution for each idea that is not your own.

LESSON 7.2

Prewriting: Outlining

WHAT PURE CHAOS! might be your thought, facing your mounds of research notes. But your notes are probably not any more impossible to sort out than is the pile of hardware shown here. All you need to bring order to the chaos is an organizing principle. For example, if you examine the hardware with the idea of function in mind, you might see that you could place all the items that hold things together in one pile, all the items that prevent leaks in another, and so on. Not only can an organizing principle help you bring order to your notes, it can help you develop an outline, which is a particularly useful tool for writing a research paper.

Evaluation Rubric

By the time you complete Lesson 7.2, you will have

- made a formal outline or graphic organizer that reveals an appropriate method of organization for your paper
- drafted a thesis statement and revised it until it provides a clear focus for your writing

You may also find that you need to return to the stages covered in Lesson 7.1.

Create an Outline

A working outline—one that you continue to write and revise as you conduct your research—helps you think about your topic critically and makes your research efficient. The following tips will help you create such an outline.

Tips on Outlining

1. Look for similarities among notes: group together note cards on similar topics. Use each group as a main topic in your outline.

2. Within groups cluster similar note cards into subgroups that elaborate on the larger and more general main topic. Use these subgroups as the subtopics in your outline.

3. Arrange main topics to build on your central idea. And, under each main topic, arrange subtopics so they elaborate on the main topic in a logical way.

4. As you continue your research and learn more, revise and elaborate in your outline. Subdivide information in subtopics into outline entries as well.

5. Set aside note cards that don't fit under any heading.

6. Before you begin your first draft, prepare a final outline.

```
                    Title of Paper
    I. Main Topic
        A. Subtopic
            1. Division of a subtopic
                a. Subdivision of a subtopic
                b. Subdivision of a subtopic
            2. Division of a subtopic
                a. Subdivision of a subtopic
                b. Subdivision of a subtopic
        B. Subtopic
    II. Main Topic
```

Number main topics with Roman numerals.

Notice the lettering, numbering, and indentation systems for subtopics and their divisions and subdivisions.

A subtopic doesn't have to have any subdivisions. But if you list any at all, you must list at least two.

Try creating your outline on a computer so you can easily add information and rearrange details as you continue researching. But what is the best way to arrange the ideas in your notes? Because ideas can be divided up many different ways, you have a number of options, depending on the nature of your information. In a history paper you might arrange ideas chronologically. In a science paper you might arrange ideas in causal order to show how one idea or event directly determines another. Britta Waller, writing on a topic that combines history and technology, creates an outline that proceeds from general to specific.

```
                George W. G. Ferris
          The Man Who Reinvented the Wheel

    I.  Background of 1893 Columbian Exposition
        A. Continued tradition of big fairs
            1. Previous world's fairs
                a. London and the Crystal Palace,
                   1851
                b. Philadelphia, 1876
                c. Paris and the Eiffel Tower, 1889
            2. Chicago fair to be larger than
               earlier fairs
        B. Emphasized cultural achievements
            1. Planners D. H. Burnham and
               F. L. Olmsted
            2. Nation's top artists, inventors,
               industrialists
        C. Reflected values of the era
    II. Background of George W. G. Ferris
```

Waller provides a chronological account of the years leading up to the 1893 fair.

In what order does Waller present her topics? Is this a good way to arrange this paper?

> **Drafting Tip**
>
> Thesis statements are often compound sentences. To review how to create compound sentences, see Lesson 13.3, pages 541–542.

Develop a Thesis Statement

So far, you have guided your research and outline according to your central idea, or the basic questions you've been exploring. You've probably rethought this idea as you have learned about the topic. Now, as you get ready to begin your first draft, it's time to turn that central idea into a thesis statement—that is, a concise idea that you try to prove, expand on, or illustrate in your writing. This statement gives your writing a focus from start to finish.

To create a thesis statement, look at your central idea critically. Is it as clear as it can be? Does it include all important aspects of your topic? Does it include historical background or new developments if these are relevant? Does it make the significance of your topic clear?

After asking these and other similar sorts of questions, write the idea again as a single sentence that describes your topic more precisely. This time include a mention of your approach to the topic. Are you comparing one topic with another, exploring a single topic in depth, or trying to prove or disprove any common notions?

The chart below progresses from central idea to thesis statement. The chart on page 333 gives four basic kinds of thesis statements.

Example of a central idea:
The Ferris wheel was a unique engineering feat when it was constructed.

▼

Examples of revising a central idea:
1. The Ferris wheel, a unique engineering feat in its day, came on the scene in time to help assert American superiority over Europe and became the most popular attraction at the Columbian Exposition.
2. The Ferris wheel, a unique engineering feat, was conceived at a time when America needed to show its superiority over Europe, and the wheel became the most popular attraction at the Columbian Exposition, overshadowing the many cultural exhibits.

▼

Example of a thesis statement:
The unique engineering feat of the Ferris wheel was one of many assertions of American pride at the World's Columbian Exposition, and its huge popularity overshadowed the fair's cultural attractions.

Four Types of Thesis Statements

Type	Description	Example
Original	Describes the background and results of original research to be presented in the paper	My survey of students and teachers at Lincoln High School has uncovered a desire for more and better computers and more instruction in computer science.
Evaluative	Identifies an issue and evaluates opinions on the issue that the writer will convey through the paper	Solar power provides our best option for future energy needs, taking into account both economic and environmental concerns.
Summary	Introduces the different perspectives on a topic for a paper that primarily summarizes the work of others	High-speed trains, traveling at speeds greater than 125 miles per hour, have revolutionized intercity travel in both France and Japan.
Combination	Combines any two or all three of the above approaches	Interviews with music-store salespeople and compact disc owners lead me to believe that the CD has replaced the record once and for all.

7.2 Writing Activities

Skills Practice

1. Organize the following pieces of information into outline form. Write headings and subheadings as necessary.

- Laser stands for *l*ight *a*mplification by *s*timulated *e*mission of *r*adiation.
- Lasers can be used in surgery.
- Compact discs are "read" by lasers.
- A laser creates a narrow beam of monochromatic and coherent light.
- Holograms rely on laser technology.
- Stores use lasers to ring up purchases.
- Laser light is the result of a chain reaction of atoms discharging photons.
- Manufacturing industries use lasers to inspect the quality of their products.

2. Rewrite the following into a concise, single-sentence thesis statement:

The race to put an astronaut on the moon had numerous motivations. Many people thought it was a waste of money. Yet the space program has resulted in many inventions that improve our lives.

Your Research Paper

Continue working on your research paper. Complete the following steps:

- Arrange your note cards in groups according to subject.
- Identify main ideas and use those as the main headings in a formal outline or graphic organizer.
- Complete your outline or graphic, adding subheadings and details.
- Write a thesis statement that reveals the main idea you will develop in your paper.

LESSON 7.3 Drafting

Think of the simple light bulb—something we take for granted. Yet the light bulb was once just an idea in the mind of Thomas Edison. To turn his idea into a reality, Edison had to do research, examine the research of others, make some original observations, and then refine his work. A research paper requires much the same effort. Even as you turn your outline and notes into a draft, you still need to experiment, ask new questions, and refine your ideas.

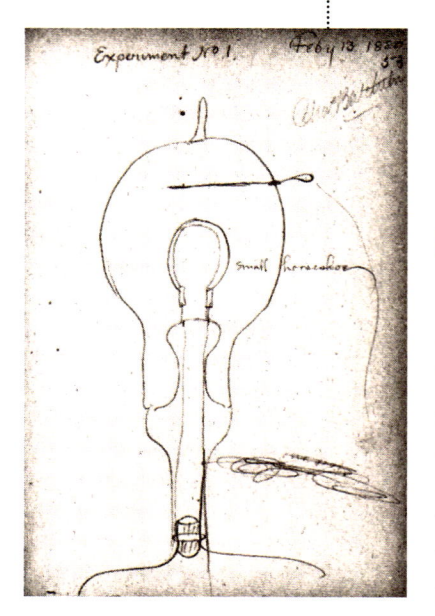

Use Your Outline and Notes

Look at your outline again to be sure you're satisfied with the flow of ideas from one to the next. Then, using your outline and your note cards, begin drafting. If your keyboarding skills are good, you may want to type your paper directly into a computer file. Keep in mind that even though you are writing a formal research paper, your goal at this point is to get down on paper your ideas and information. You can make adjustments to your voice and style when you revise your draft. The drafting tips in the chart on the next page may help you get started.

Sources

Fincher, Jack. "George Ferris Jr. and the Great Wheel of Fortune." Smithsonian July 1983: 109–118.

Anderson, Norman D., and Walter R. Brown. Ferris Wheels. New York: Pantheon, 1983.

Valenti, Michael. "100 Years and Still Going Around in Circles." Mechanical Engineering June 1993: 70+. ProQuest Direct. Chicago Public Lib., Chicago. 29 Nov. 1999 <http://proquest.umi.com>.

Notes

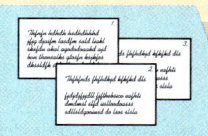

Admission 50 cents, the same as admission to fair. Still, 1.5 million rode it.
—Fincher, p. 114

Twenty-minute ride for 50 cents; two revolutions, six stops each time around; ran 8 A.M.–11 P.M.
—Anderson and Brown, p. 24

Lit by 3,000 electric bulbs at night, powered by generator in boiler house
—Valenti

Some Tips on Drafting

1. Set aside a couple of hours to begin writing. Find a quiet place where you won't be distracted.
2. Try to draft smoothly and quickly without getting stalled on details. Don't worry about finding the "perfect" word or phrase; you can revise later.
3. Write at least one paragraph for each heading in your outline. Each paragraph should have a topic sentence and supporting details.
4. Write the number of each note card as you use it. Later you will replace the numbers with information about your sources.

You don't have to include information from every note card in your draft. In fact, as the diagram below shows, you are likely to develop the ideas from several note cards into one or two outline entries, and likewise into one or two ideas in your paper. As you put these ideas into your paper, identify the source of every borrowed idea, and try to use your own words wherever possible.

As you draft, use your outline as a "map" to help guide you in your writing. The outline should remind you of what comes before or after a particular idea. Furthermore, the outline should suggest the links, or transitions, you might use in your writing. After all, you have already begun linking ideas in your outline; now simply carry on that process, as the diagram below illustrates.

Evaluation Rubric

By the time you complete Lesson 7.3, you will have

- drafted your research paper, making sure that your ideas logically progress from one to the next
- written an interesting introduction that includes your thesis
- created a conclusion that brings your paper to a satisfying close

Outline

III. Specifics of Ferris Wheel
    A. Dimensions
    B. Built on principle of bicycle wheel
    C. Riding
        1. Admission
        2. Hours
        3. Huge number of people riding
        4. Enthusiastic public response
IV. Early Criticism

Paragraph

    A twenty-minute ride, or two revolutions with six stops each time around, cost 50 cents (Anderson and Brown 24). The wheel ran from 8 A.M. to 11 P.M. At night, the wheel was lit by 3,000 electric light bulbs powered by a generator in the boiler house of the wheel (Valenti). One-and-one-half million people had ridden the wheel by Fair's end—a good number, considering that the 50-cent fee was equal to admission to the entire Exposition (Fincher 114).

> **Vocabulary Tip**
>
> For examples of transitions to link paragraphs, see Lesson 2.8, pages 88–91.

Prepare the First Draft

Now that you're ready to write your first draft, read the chart below for solutions to some common drafting problems.

Solving Drafting Problems	
Problem	**Solution**
How can I overcome "writer's block" on my first draft?	Just begin writing and get the ideas down. Try writing for five minutes on whatever comes into your mind. Then, you'll be looser and ready to write your draft.
Do I have to write the first part of the paper first, the second part second, and so on?	Write any way that is easiest for you. If you write out of sequence, pay close attention to the transitions between sections as you revise.
What can I do with all these notes I have?	Set aside any note that duplicates another, or is irrelevant to the main headings or subdivisions in your outline. Sort the others into groups according to topic.
I have many notes on some aspects of my topic but few on others. What should I do?	Do more research, or look at your outline to see if you can write a good paper with the notes you now have. If so, revise your outline.
How can I avoid running out of time before I get very far into my writing?	Set aside at least three hours just for writing your paper. Eliminate distractions by going to a quiet place.
How can I best create transitions between my paragraphs?	Identify one major similarity or difference between the paragraphs. Try linking the paragraphs with a short phrase or sentence describing how they are similar or different.
What can I do to avoid being bogged down correcting spelling and grammar?	Ignore these problems until you are ready to revise.

336 Unit 7 Research Paper Writing

Write the Introduction and Conclusion

A good introduction should present your topic and approach, along with your thesis statement. It should grab the attention of your readers and make them want to read on. Britta Waller begins her paper on the Ferris wheel with an intriguing quotation.

Your conclusion should alert the reader that you are wrapping up. You might summarize your main points or mention any new questions your paper raises. Waller concludes by recounting the "true achievement" of Ferris's magnificent wheel.

7.3 Writing Activities

Skills Practice

Write a few paragraphs about the elimination of yellow fever, using the outline and the notes that follow. Your audience is a high school history class.

Outline

I. Eradication of yellow fever
   A. Walter Reed sent to Cuba
      1. Knows about Carlos Finlay's theories
      2. Sets up experiments
   B. William Gorgas establishes mosquito control measures around Havana.

Notes

- 1881: Cuban physician Carlos Finlay suggested that a certain breed of mosquito carried the yellow fever disease.
- 1900: U.S. Army surgeon Walter Reed was sent to Cuba to investigate an epidemic of yellow fever among the U.S. troops there.
- Reed's fellow doctors and a number of soldiers volunteered for rather unconventional experiments:
  – Each was injected with yellow fever so Reed could study how the disease proceeds through the body.
  – All those intentionally injected contracted the disease but survived.
  – Two people who were infected accidentally came down with the disease and died.
- Reed's experiments proved that the disease was transmitted by the mosquito rather than by casual contact.
- 1905: William Gorgas developed and implemented measures to control mosquitoes, eliminating the disease as a major threat in Havana, Cuba.

Your Research Paper

Draft your research paper, completing the following steps:

- Begin by writing the section with which you feel most comfortable.
- Use the main and subordinate headings in your outline as a guide. Pull information from your note cards, providing strong transitions from one idea to the next.
- Craft an introduction that captures readers' attention and includes a thesis statement that reveals the direction your paper will take.
- Write a conclusion that reinforces your thesis and the paper's main points.

LESSON 7.4

Citing Sources

While Ferris developed his wheel, others worked on some of the earliest automobiles. Yet unlike the Ferris wheel, the automobile has gone through amazing changes. The photo below and to the left shows Henry Ford's early Model T, while the one below and to the right shows a "car of the future."

Evaluation Rubric

By the time you complete Lesson 7.4, you will have

- learned what information in your paper does and does not need to be documented
- chosen an appropriate method for citing your sources
- correctly cited your sources in the body of your paper

Suppose you're writing a research paper about cars and you read that Ford was one of the auto's early developers. You don't have to cite such common knowledge in your paper. But if you read about features planned for future cars, and you include that information in your paper, then you need to document the source.

Document Information

In a research paper, you don't need to document your own original ideas or common knowledge. You do need to document the source of data gleaned from tables, charts, or other graphs, as well as quotations, paraphrases, or summaries that you include in your paper. Such sources include books, magazines, newspapers, encyclopedias, online sources, CD-ROMs, interviews, TV programs, letters, and song lyrics. Proper documentation enables readers to find the source if they want to learn more about your topic; it also enables you to avoid plagiarism, as discussed in Lesson 7.1, page 329.

What to document? You should document your information whenever you use someone's exact words, or whenever you paraphrase or summarize a particular idea or series of ideas. The chart on page 339 offers tips on when to document your information. The rest of this lesson shows you *how* to document, or cite, your sources.

338 Unit 7 Research Paper Writing

Documenting Your Information

INFORMATION	CITATION?	EXPLANATION
"No single enterprise on the Midway or the grounds proper approached it either in patronage or in wonderment."	Yes	Direct quotations reflect an author's opinion. Readers may want to check the source for bias.
The fair signified economic ambition, the rise of the city, and rapid change.	Yes	This is a paraphrase of another author's opinion or research.
Ironically, there was a focus on cultural enlightenment and achievement.	No	This is a paraphrase of general information found in many sources.
The Ferris wheel cost about $400,000 to build and turned a total profit of $733,086.	Yes	Specific cost and profitability of Ferris's wheel are not common knowledge.
The Columbian Exposition commemorated the four hundredth anniversary of Columbus's first historic voyage.	No	This is common knowledge that would appear in most sources on the fair.
Ferris's name was forever matched with later machines.	No	Most people are aware that such rides are referred to as Ferris wheels.

Format Citations Properly

Documenting your sources will be easy as long as you accurately completed and numbered your source cards and note cards during the prewriting stage. All the information you need should be right at your fingertips. (If it isn't, you'll need to return to the library to find your sources again!)

You can cite your sources in one of three ways: footnotes, endnotes, or parenthetical documentation, which is recommended by the Modern Language Association of America (or MLA). Because parenthetical documentation is generally preferred, the instruction and models in this unit conform to the MLA guidelines. Check with your teacher, however, and use the method that he or she prefers.

Parenthetical Documentation with a Works-Cited List

A works-cited list is an alphabetized list of sources that you used in writing your research paper. In your paper, after each quotation, summary, or paraphrase of information from a source, you must include within parentheses a reference to a source and a page number, when appropriate. This citation points readers to the corresponding entry in your works-cited list.

When you drafted your paper, taking information from your note cards, you jotted down the corresponding number of the source from which you took the information. Now it's time to replace those numbers with proper parenthetical documentation. Place the citation as close as possible to the borrowed information. Generally, the parenthetical reference should be positioned where a pause would naturally occur, such as after a comma or at the end of a sentence (but before the final period):

Ferris sold stock to wealthy Chicago businessmen (Fincher 112).

The examples that follow and Britta Waller's final draft of her research paper on pages 350–356 provide guidance and models for how to reference sources in text, giving credit in parentheses.

Parenthetical Documentation Guidelines

1. **(Fincher 110)** Put the author's last name and the page reference in parentheses. If you're using two or more works by different authors with the same last name, include the author's first name or initial.

2. **(Anderson and Brown 18)** For a work by two or three authors, put the authors' last names and the page reference in parentheses. If a work has more than three authors, use the last name of the first author, followed by *et al.*, and the page reference: (Davis et al. 21).

3. **(Dream City)** When a source does not have an author, use a shortened form of the title in parentheses. Provide a page reference if possible.

4. **(Holliday, "Big Wheels" 229)** If you use more than one source by the same author, include the author's last name followed by a comma, the source title or a shortened form of it, and a page reference.

5. **(Badger 157; Burg 224)** If you use a piece of information that you found in more than one source, cite each work as you normally would, inserting a semicolon between the entries.

6. **(25)** If you use the author's name in the sentence that includes the information you need to document, you need only provide a page reference in parentheses, as shown in this example: *Howells accused the wheel of being a mere money-making contrivance—an exploitation of the visitors (25).*

7. **("Circus")** If you use a nonprint source, such as a videocassette, interview, film, or an article published online (the example above is for an article published by *Britannica Online*), name the work in running text or, in parentheses, give readers the information they need to find the complete citation in the works-cited list.

Format Your List of Works Cited

Whether you cite your sources with parenthetical documentation, footnotes, or endnotes, your paper should include a complete list of the sources you used. This is your list of works cited, and, unlike your working bibliography, it contains only those sources that you use in your final paper. While you may have consulted many additional sources for background and other general information, these sources shouldn't be included on this final list unless you use and cite ideas or data from the sources in your paper.

From your source cards, record the publishing information, following the formats shown here and in Britta Waller's works-cited list on page 356. If you use a source that is not modeled in this unit, consult your teacher or the *MLA Handbook for Writers of Research Papers*. Be sure to take note of the side-column explanations on pages 342 and 356.

When you prepare your final works-cited list, alphabetize each source by the last name of the author or editor (use the first name listed on the title page, if there is more than one). If you use more than one work by the same author, you need not repeat the author's name for each entry; use three hyphens followed by a period instead. If the source has no author or editor, alphabetize it by the title of the book or article. The chart below shows the proper style for various sources.

> **Editing Tip**
>
> Remember to underline or italicize titles of books, periodicals, and pamphlets. For more information see Lesson 21.10, pages 757–758.

Formats for Work-Cited Entries

SOURCE	ENTRY
Book with Single Author	Badger, Reid. *The Great American Fair*. Chicago: Nelson-Hall, 1979.
Book with Multiple Authors	Anderson, Norman D., and Walter R. Brown. *Ferris Wheels*. New York: Pantheon, 1983.
Book with No Author Named	*The Dream City: A Portfolio of Photographic Views*. St. Louis: Thompson, 1893. N. pag.
Magazine Article	Fincher, Jack. "George Ferris Jr. and the Great Wheel of Fortune." *Smithsonian* July 1983: 109–118.
Encyclopedia Article	"World's Columbian Exposition." *Encyclopedia Americana*. 1999 ed.
Newspaper Article	"The Rays Take in the Columbian Exposition." *Chicago Tribune* 26 July 1984, sec. 5: 2.
Online Encyclopedia	"World's Columbian Exposition." *Britannica Online*. Vers. 99.1 1994–1999. Encyclopaedia Britannica. 8 Nov. 1999 <http://www.britannica.com/bcom/eb/article/2/0,5716,79582+1,00.html>.
CD-ROM	Wilmeth, Don B. "Ferris Wheel." *The World Book Multimedia Encyclopedia*. Vers. 1.0 CD-ROM. Disc 1. Chicago: World Book, 1999.
A Professional or Personal Web Site	Rose, Julie K. *The World's Columbian Exposition: Idea, Experience, Aftermath*. 8 Nov. 1999 <http://xroads.virginia.edu/~ma96/wce/title.html>.

7.4 Citing Sources   **341**

How to Format a Works-Cited List The following works-cited excerpt shows proper format, indentation, and punctuation. Notice that all entries are alphabetized by author's name or by title, excluding words such as *A* and *The* at the beginning of a title.

Begin your works-cited list on its own page following the last text page of your research paper. Place your name and the page number in the top right corner, as on all other pages. Center the title, *Works Cited*, one inch from the top of the page, and double-space to begin the first entry. Double-space all entries and between the entries as well.

As you examine the works-cited model, take note of the explanations in the margin. Also notice that proper formats are used for a variety of sources not shown in the chart on page 341.

Model

Your name & the page number

Works Cited

Anderson, Norman D., and Walter R. Brown. <u>Ferris Wheels</u>. New York: Pantheon, 1983.

Badger, Reid. <u>The Great American Fair</u>. Chicago: Nelson-Hall, 1979.

"From Ferris Wheels to Virtual Reality." <u>U.S. News & World Report</u> 26 July 1993: 19.

Gomez, Maria. Personal interview. 12 Oct. 1999.

Holliday, Kate. "Big Wheels of the Fun Business." <u>Popular Mechanics</u> Mar. 1969: 144–146+.

Miller, Donald. "Professor Donald Miller Speaks about the History of the Opening of the World's Columbian Exposition." Interview with Neal Conan. <u>Weekend Edition</u>. Natl. Public Radio. 1 May 1993. 4 Nov. 1999 <http://www.elibrary.com>.

"World's Columbian Exposition." <u>Encyclopedia Americana</u>. 1999 ed.

Margin notes:

- For works with more than one author, reverse the first and last names of the first author only.
- No author was given for this weekly magazine article.
- Use this format for a face-to-face interview, citing the date on which the interview took place. You may also specify *Telephone interview* or *Online interview*, depending on which method you use.
- This is the proper format for a transcribed radio interview that was found online.
- Include the edition of the encyclopedia.

7.4 Writing Activities

Skills Practice

1. For each of the following pieces of information, tell whether you think source documentation is necessary and explain why.

- Many more calls can be handled by cellular mobile phone service than were handled by earlier systems.
- The first licenses to build and operate mobile telephone systems were granted in 1982.
- Many advances in telephone technology have taken place since Alexander Graham Bell invented the receiver in 1876.
- One author laments, "Cellular phone technology eliminates one more place—inside your own car—where you can be free from interruptions."
- Most Americans probably cannot conceive of life without the telephone.
- As a car equipped with a phone travels from cell to cell, the call is transferred via computer from one transmitter and receiver to another without interrupting the call.

2. Write proper entries for a list of works cited for the following sources:

- an article from the 1990 edition of the *World Book Encyclopedia* called "Jet Propulsion Engines"
- an article entitled "The Concorde Tests the Skies," written by Janet Feldman, which appeared on page 30 of *Newsweek* on August 14, 1975
- an article by John Simons entitled "Breakthroughs in Jet Technology," which appeared on pages 70–84 of the book *Aviation and Space,* edited by M. W. Wister and published in New York by Little, Brown in 1982
- a book written by Richard Samson entitled *Jet Engine Basics,* published by MIT Press in Boston in 1975

Your Research Paper

Continue working on your research paper by successfully completing the following steps.

- Insert proper documentation within the body of your paper. If you're using parenthetical documentation, replace the note card numbers that correspond to your source cards with a proper citation in parentheses.
- Create a draft of your works-cited page.
- Ensure the accuracy of your documentation and of your works-cited list by following the formats outlined in this lesson and in the *MLA Handbook for Writers of Research Papers.*

LESSON 7.5 Revising

"Mr. Watson, come here. I want you!" said Alexander Graham Bell—the first sentence ever uttered over his new invention, the telephone. Bell continued to work on his invention and refine it so that it would communicate even better. Likewise, the first draft of your research paper will also "communicate" even better after you revise it.

Improve Your Paper

When you revise your first draft, work on improving your choice of words, your transitions, and your presentation of ideas. Remember that in a formal research paper, you should write in a voice and style that is appropriate to your audience and purpose. The chart below describes problems you may face at this point—and offers possible solutions to them.

Evaluation Rubric

By the time you complete Lesson 7.5, you will have

- evaluated your research paper draft for both content and mechanics
- reviewed the paper's organization and reorganized the content to ensure coherence, logical progression, and support for ideas
- refined your writing style to suit the requirements of the research paper and to meet the needs of your audience

Solving Revision Problems

PROBLEM	SOLUTION
How can I give my first draft a clearer focus?	Review your thesis statement; delete or rewrite anything in the paper that doesn't support it.
How can I make my argument easier to follow?	Add transitions, rearrange sentences, and include new ideas to make the paper more coherent. Delete irrelevant information.
How can I make my paragraphs flow smoothly from one to another?	Add or change transitions between paragraphs; rearrange paragraphs in a more logical order.
What if my introduction doesn't connect well with the rest of the paper?	Add transitions or rewrite introduction to conform with the purpose and main idea.
What can I do if my sentences sound repetitive?	Vary sentence structure. Use precise, lively language. Find synonyms for repeated words.

Take a look at some samples of the kind of revising you might need to do on your own research paper. First, look at the model below, which shows the revision of two paragraphs. Consider the reasons for each revision. Next, on page 346, follow the stages in the smaller-scale revision of one particular passage from another part of the same paper.

> The Ferris wheel's popularity ~~was very popular.~~ ~~This~~ was due to the ~~popularity of the Midway.~~ The Midway provided escape both from ~~the pressure and pains of~~ real life and from the overwhelming culture ~~that was so overwhelming in~~ of the rest of the Fair. Couples rushed ~~went~~ to be married at the top of the wheel, but the closest they got was the superintendent's office. ~~Rumors were started in the~~ newspapers on the ground below started rumors of the wheel losing parts that then hurtled to the ground below; ~~Other rumors~~ or they told of the mechanism locking in place, trapping ~~with~~ the wheel's passengers ~~trapped~~ up in the air with no help. As ~~This~~ never happened. Such publicity made the gigantic toy ~~wheel~~ only more popular (Howells 25). ~~"No single enterprise on the Midway or the grounds proper approached it either in patronage or in wonderment" (Fincher 114).~~
>
> The wheel did have its critics. Howells accused the wheel of being a mere money-making contrivance--an

Change redundant sentence structures to make the paragraph more concise.

Does this change improve the paper? Why or why not?

Combine sentences that have the same subjects.

Why move this quotation?

A transition helps shift the tone between the two paragraphs.

Draft sentence contains a basic fact, but the specific topic isn't clear.

> In an era hoping for a better world, grand engineering projects concentrated on building things other than weapons.

First revision sets off the topic sentence and explains the era, with the modern reader in mind. Supporting details add color and connect sentence ideas to the paper's topic.

> The 1890s and early 1900s were marked by a general wish for a better world. Engineering projects focused on new marvels of iron and steel, such as the Ferris wheel, instead of weapons.

How does the choice of words and quotations improve this passage? What does revising the organization accomplish?

> The 1890s and early 1900s were marked by a universal wish for a better world, and most of all, "a world without war" (Fincher 109). Steel and iron were shaped into engineering marvels, such as the Ferris wheel, rather than weapons.

Revise Your Paper

When you write a research paper on a scientific subject, you need to pay particularly close attention to certain questions. Presenting scientific data requires precision, so double-check any data you cite. Make certain that you use the most up-to-date information possible. Look for journal, magazine, and newspaper articles for late-breaking developments on your topic. Be sure you use specialized terms precisely and copy direct quotations from sources very carefully.

If you are using the research of others to draw your own conclusions on a topic, you have to be sure that the research is valid. Look closely at your sources to be sure that they are free from possible bias and that they have made logical, convincing arguments. Also, look at your own argument to be sure it is logical and complete. Think about ways your information could be misinterpreted, and revise to make your meaning clearer.

If you wish, exchange papers with a partner to get another perspective on your work and to provide your partner with feedback. Be sure to review the points in the checklist on the next page as you revise your paper.

Revising Tip

If you drafted your paper on a word processor, experiment with organization by cutting and pasting sections of your draft. Save each new version under a new name so that you can track your progress and go back to earlier versions if you wish.

> **Checklist for Revising a Research Paper**
>
> 1. How can you strengthen your thesis statement so that it provides a clear focus for the paper?
> 2. How can your main ideas be better organized to ensure coherence and logical progression? What irrelevant or repetitious ideas can you delete?
> 3. Which points could be better supported with information from sources?
> 4. How can you strengthen transitions between ideas and paragraphs?
> 5. Have you written in a voice and style that is consistent throughout—and is appropriate, given your audience and purpose?
> 6. Have you varied your sentence structures and used lively verbs so that your paper isn't dull and boring to read?
> 7. What technical terms still need to be defined?
> 8. Which frequently used words can be replaced with appropriate synonyms?
> 9. Have you cited your sources correctly in the body of your paper?
> 10. Is your works-cited list accurate, complete, and properly formatted?

7.5 Writing Activities

Skills Practice

Revise the following passage for clarity, coherence, and readability.

Compact discs are made of plastic coated with aluminum so that the signals can be read by a laser. Then they are coated in more plastic to protect the pits. Music is recorded on a compact disc in a series of minute pits of varying depths in an outward spiral. In the CD player a low-intensity laser is directed at the pits in their track. As the laser is alternately reflected or scattered off the pits, an optical sensor picks up these signals and converts the signals into sound impulses. The laser never touches the CD, so the CD doesn't wear down or scratch. Also, dust and fingerprints do not distort the laser beam. This results in almost no distortion in the playback. Not surprisingly, CD recordings have become more popular than vinyl records.

Your Research Paper

Revise your research paper. Complete these steps, and use the Checklist for Revising a Research Paper above to guide you.

- Clarify your thesis if necessary, making sure that it adequately sets a purpose and direction for the paper.
- Evaluate the organization of your draft and decide how you can improve the flow of ideas.
- Conduct additional research if necessary to bolster your data in one or more sections of your paper.
- Strengthen your transitions to ensure that your paper is coherent.

LESSON 7.6

Editing and Presenting: A Model Paper

George W. G. Ferris's marvelous wheel was at last a reality. After much planning and research, construction and testing, Ferris put the finishing touches on his wheel and opened it to the public. And his efforts truly paid off—the Ferris wheel became a symbol of nineteenth-century technological ingenuity and the world-renowned centerpiece of Chicago's 1893 Columbian Exposition.

In the same way, after much planning, research, and writing, you are about to put the finishing touches on your paper. With these final touches you should have a complete and clean research paper, one that is free of errors and ready for presentation to your teacher and classmates.

Prepare the Final Copy

After revising your draft, type or print a new copy of it with your corrections included. Then you can give your paper one final proofreading, checking citations, grammar, spelling, punctuation, and word use. The checklist below can help you catch any remaining problems or errors.

Evaluation Rubric

By the time you complete Lesson 7.6, you will have

- proofread your paper, identifying and correcting errors in grammar, punctuation, and spelling
- confirmed that every summary, paraphrase, or quotation was properly credited to a source and checked that every source you used is listed in a properly formatted works-cited list
- created a clean final copy that is free of errors and ready to present to your audience

Editing Tip

For additional editing tips, refer to Lesson 2.10, pages 96–99, and Unit 9, pages 388–411.

Final Copy Checklist

1. Have I organized my ideas clearly?
2. Have I explained or defined any words that may be unfamiliar to the reader?
3. Have I discussed my topic completely and fairly?
4. Have I corrected all grammar and spelling mistakes?
5. Have I documented my sources properly?
6. Have I considered the proper meaning(s) of the words I've used?
7. Have I spelled and capitalized everything correctly?
8. Have I prepared a neat and easy-to-read final copy?

Present the Complete Paper

You may want to create a cover for your paper or enclose it in a special folder. If you have a separate title page, it should include the title of your paper, your name, your teacher's name, the course name, and the date on which you submit the paper to your teacher. If you don't have a separate title page, put this information on the first page of your paper, as shown here. The last page of your paper is always the list of works cited.

Give some thought to whether your paper would be enhanced by the use of any visuals, such as copies of photographs or works of art, diagrams, time lines, or charts. These materials may be attached to the end of your paper, before the works-cited list.

Keep in mind that your teacher may ask you to submit other materials along with your final paper. For example, you may be asked to submit your note cards, your final outline (which should not include your introduction and conclusion), or a summary statement. Make sure that you know what's expected of you well in advance of the due date! You don't want any last-minute surprises.

7.6 Writing Activities

Skills Practice

1. Identify the grammatical mistakes in each of the following sentences, and correct them.

- Scientists should be sure that experiments do not merely reinforce his preconceived ideas.
- Henry Ford is aware of the European experiments in creating a "horseless carriage." He knew about them for many years before he began his work.
- People are often unaware of the scientific advance that take place in the era they live in.

2. Edit the following entries for a final list of works cited. You may need to refer to Lesson 7.4, pages 338–343, to review the proper forms of different types of entries.

- Encyclopaedia Britannica, 1999 ed., Cardiovascular System Diseases and Disorders.
- Cooke, Alistair. Alistair Cooke's America. Alfred A. Knopf, New York: 1973
- John Molinari, Hurricane Prediction: Catching the Waves, Science News, 21 October 1989, p. 262

3. Read the research paper by Britta Waller on pages 350–355. Then write a summary statement, about two sentences long, explaining the topic and purpose of her paper.

Your Research Paper

Use what you have learned in this lesson to complete and present the final version of your own research paper.

Student Model

George W. G. Ferris: The Man Who Reinvented the Wheel
Britta C. Waller

> "Ferris is a crackpot. He has wheels in his head."
> (McGuire)

Even officials of the famous World's Columbian Exhibition of 1893, such as the one quoted above, seemed to think that George Washington Gale Ferris's idea for an industrial monument to rival the Eiffel Tower was far-fetched, if not downright insane. Yet, when it was finally finished, Ferris's colossal wheel embodied the "can-do optimism" of the Exhibition (Fincher 109), America's industrial dominance, the American dream, and the flexibility of a capitalistic society. This paper will discuss turn-of-the-century America, how these times inspired the World's Columbian Exposition, and the birth, demise, and significance of the great Ferris wheel.

The 1890s and early 1900s were marked by a universal wish for a better world, and most of all, "a world without war" (Fincher 109). Steel and iron were shaped into engineering marvels, such as the Ferris wheel, rather than weapons. Chicago's World's Columbian Exposition of 1893 commemorated the 400th anniversary of Columbus's historic voyage and was the largest, most elaborate, and most magnificent World's Fair ever (Rose). The first international exposition was London's Great Exhibition of 1851, boasting Joseph Paxton's Crystal Palace—the first large scale iron and glass building and the ancestor of the modern skyscraper. The first American exposition was held in Philadelphia in 1876 to celebrate the country's centennial. However, it was the Paris Exhibition of 1889 that inspired the World's Columbian Exhibition (Burg xii). Paris had produced the world-famous Eiffel Tower. America couldn't let Europe have all the limelight. In fact, this national rivalry was one of the prime moving forces behind the Fair. In addition, the Fair signified economic ambition, the rise of the city, and rapid progressive change (Badger 10). Ironically, there was a focus on cultural enlightenment and achievement. Buildings were in the "Greco-Roman-Oriental" style (Fincher 110). Under the direction of Chicago architect Daniel H. Burnham and landscape architect Frederick Law Olmsted, the nation's best sculptors, architects, painters, writers, and musicians joined with industrialists and inventors to put their best work into the Exposition. Its achievement in the arts far surpassed its historical significance: "We have put aside individual taste and have united in an effort to carry out the several parts of a design which . . . was dominated by one idea," wrote Professor Halsey C. Ives, the Chief of the Department of Fine Arts (Dream City). The dual nature—industry and culture combined—of the Fair was a direct reflection of the era. Henry Steele Commager called the decade of the 1890s a watershed in American history:

> On the one side lies an America predominantly agricultural; concerned with domestic problems; conforming, intellectually, at least, to the political, economic, and moral principles inherited from the 17th and 18th centuries. . . . On the other side lies the modern America, predominantly urban and industrial; inextricably involved in world economy and politics . . . experiencing profound changes in population, social institutions, economy, and technology; and trying to accommodate its traditional institutions and habits of thought to conditions new and in part alien (Burg xiii).

The cultural idealism of the Fair was embodied in its alternate title—"The White City," so named because of a substance called "staff" which covered many of the buildings. Composed of plaster of Paris and jute fibers, staff closely resembled white marble ("World's Columbian Exposition" 533). Author William Dean Howells praised the Fair as "the perfect embodiment of human ingenuity and Christian brotherhood—the ideal of Grecian democracy in industrial America" (vii–viii). Howells saw the Fair as a glimpse of the future of America, and as a departure from the "Age of Accumulation"—a term he used to denounce the period before World War I (xii).

However, Howells's altruistic ideals were pushed aside in favor of the Midway Plaisance, and its Queen—the Ferris wheel.

Early in 1892, Ferris sat quietly at Burnham's planning session for the fabulous Exposition. A tunnel and trestle engineer

(continued)

and bridge builder from Pittsburgh, Ferris was 33 years old, tall, slim, and pale, with a bushy black moustache and a "resolute face" (Fincher 110). Born the eighth child of a Nevada farmer, Ferris attended military school in Oakland, California, at age 16 and attended college at Rensselaer Polytechnic Institute (RPI) in Troy, New York. Graduating in 1881, Ferris was said to have a great ability to meet a challenge. Burnham told those who assembled at the planning session: "Mere bigness is not what is wanted. . . . something novel, original, daring and unique must be designed and built if American engineers are to retain their prestige and standing" (Fincher 110). An evening soon after, Ferris sketched the design for his famous amusement ride on a scrap of paper at a Chicago restaurant. He determined all aspects of the wheel—size, number of passengers, price of admission—in his original sketch. He had "re-invented the wheel . . . big" (Fincher 110).

Ferris's wheel was 264 feet high and supported by two 140-foot pyramid-shaped steel towers (Burg 224). The wheel was 26 stories high, taller than any building on the grounds. It weighed, fully loaded, approximately 1,200 tons, or as much as three Boeing 747s (Fincher 111–112). Thirty-six passenger cars were suspended between two steel rims. Made of wood and iron, paneled with plate glass windows, and furnished with swivel chairs, the cars were approximately the size of train passenger cars (Burg 224). The wheel had a total capacity of 2,160 people (Valenti).

The wheel was built on two 20-foot square, 35-foot deep concrete blocks. Plans were approved by the end of 1892. The thousands of parts needed for the steam-powered wheel were built by five different steel companies. In late March of 1893, five trains, each thirty cars long, brought all these parts to Chicago (Anderson and Brown 18). The most crucial was the huge axle—45½ feet long, 33 inches in diameter, weighing 46½ tons. Made by Bethlehem Iron Works of Bethlehem, Pennsylvania, the axle was the largest single piece of steel ever forged in the United States (Valenti; Anderson and Brown 18).

Ferris based his ride on the principle of the bicycle wheel. Heavy steel rods acted as the spokes and pulled toward the axle to keep the wheel's shape. By using tension, Ferris was able to build a lighter, stronger, and vastly larger structure than was ever before possible (Anderson and Brown 17).

A twenty-minute ride, or two revolutions with six stops each time around, cost 50 cents. The wheel ran from 8 A.M. to 11 P.M. At night, the wheel was lit by 3,000 electric light bulbs powered by a generator in the boiler house of the wheel (Valenti). One-and-one-half-million people had ridden the wheel by Fair's end—a good number considering that the 50-cent fee was equal to admission to the entire Exposition (Fincher 114). One North Dakota farmboy wrote in a letter home: "Do whatever you have to do—even sell the kitchen stove—come to Chicago and ride the Ferris wheel!" (Anderson and Brown 26). A ride on the wheel, it was said, "may truly be called a round trip" (Lee).

Though an engineering milestone when completed, the wheel was not so well accepted in the early stages of its development. Burnham said it was not strong enough to withstand Lake Michigan winds, and even if it could, the public would be afraid to ride such a "rickety-looking contraption" (Fincher 112). Others doubted the wheel, too, but Ferris was finally allowed to build it if he could finance it. The Exposition had no better match for the Eiffel Tower. Ferris sold stock to wealthy Chicago businessmen (Fincher 112). The wheel cost about $400,000 to build and turned a total profit of $733,086 (Holliday 229).

The Exposition was opened on May 1, 1893, by President Grover Cleveland, but the wheel was not completed. Work was done around the clock, but safety was still ensured. The wheel was powered by two 1,000-horsepower steam engines, one being held as a back-up (Anderson and Brown 21). It also had a huge air brake worked by two 10-foot steel bands that would tighten to stop the wheel in case it began to spin free (Fincher 111). With these features, the wheel was tested extensively. Wrote Ferris's partner and fellow RPI graduate William F. Gronau: "So perfect is the machinery that we did not feel the wheel move" (Fincher 114).

The Ferris wheel had its grand opening on Wednesday, June 21, 1893. Among the invited first riders were Mr. and Mrs. Ferris, the mayor of Chicago, and a 40-piece band, squeezed into one car (Anderson and Brown 23).

The Ferris wheel, and the Midway Plaisance where it was located, were both immediate successes. The Midway was a grand street of international displays and buildings meant

(continued)

> **What does this quotation contribute to the paragraph?**

> **Presenting Tip**
> Graphics, such as a labeled diagram of the Ferris wheel, will enhance a reader's understanding of a technical topic.

to show the everyday life and oddities of all countries (Rose). The Midway was designed to "popularize" the Exposition, which it did very well, because many visitors enjoyed its atmosphere much more than the cultural attractions (Badger 109). Ironically, Jackson Park, the location of the Midway, not the cultural Court of Honor, became the entrance to the University of Chicago, or the "Grey City," as it was known at the time (Badger 90). One anonymous limerick showed the true, educational value of the Fair to the University:

> Oh, there were more Profs than students,
> but then we didn't care;
> They spent their days in research work,
> their evenings at the Fair.
> and life upon the Campus
> was one continual swing,
> We watched the Ferris wheel go round
> and didn't do a thing.
> (Badger 157)

The Ferris wheel's popularity was due to the escape the Midway provided, both from real life and the overwhelming culture of the rest of the Fair. "No single enterprise on the Midway or the grounds proper approached it either in patronage or in wonderment" (Badger 108). Couples rushed to be married at the top of the wheel, but the closest they got was the superintendent's office on the ground below. Newspapers started rumors of the wheel losing parts that then supposedly hurtled to the ground below; or they told of the mechanism locking in place, trapping the wheel's passengers up in the air with no help. As this never happened, such publicity made the gigantic toy only more popular (Fincher 114).

The wheel did have its critics. Howells accused the wheel of being a mere money-making contrivance—an exploitation of the visitors (25). Others said Ferris had plagiarized the idea for the wheel, and that American, Asian, and European history was filled with similar, if less complex, models. This is true, but it was the design that made Ferris's creation unique (Anderson and Brown 37–38).

Though not the first to build such rides, Ferris was forever associated with later machines. British engineer W. B. Basset sought to outdo Ferris's wheel in size and scope. American William Sullivan was also among those inspired by Ferris.

Sullivan started the Eli Bridge Company in 1906 in Jacksonville, Illinois, the largest current manufacturer of Ferris wheels. Sullivan, after riding the great wheel at the Exposition as many times as possible, capitalized on the commercial possibilities of the wheel. He made smaller, portable versions of about 45 feet in diameter which could be built in quantity (Anderson and Brown 41). George and Mary Tilyou wanted to buy Ferris's wheel and take it to their newly built Brooklyn amusement park—Coney Island, which was modeled after the Midway. The Tilyous couldn't afford the ride and instead built a 125-foot diameter "Wonder Wheel," which still stands. Though it wasn't the first or largest, as the signs claimed, Coney Island's Wonder Wheel established Ferris wheels and their many variations as a permanent fixture in modern American amusement parks (Fincher 117).

The criticism over the wheel's originality began the wheel's decline. Ferris's assets collapsed over lawsuits with the Exposition about the wheel's profits. During the winter of 1893–94, the wheel was left deserted. With a brief appearance at the North Clark Street Fair beginning in early 1895, the wheel regained some of its original standing, but it had simply lost its novelty. Neighbors in Clark Street campaigned to remove the wheel, ironically, complaining of its "undesirable industrialism" (Fincher 117). The wheel then appeared at the Louisiana Purchase Exposition of 1904 in Saint Louis and was still running perfectly. However, it remained unsuccessful. In 1906, following the Louisiana Exposition, the great wheel was brought tumbling down with 100 pounds of dynamite. The *Chicago Tribune* reported, "Within a few minutes, it was a tangled mass of steel and iron forty feet high" (Fincher 118). However, Ferris was not there to see its end. In November 1896, George W. G. Ferris had died unexpectedly in a Pittsburgh hospital at the age of 37. The cause was diagnosed as several different ailments, but mostly Ferris's death was due to depression over his potential bankruptcy and loss of hope (Fincher 118).

The true achievement of the Ferris wheel lay not in how long it stood, but in its combination of pleasurable enjoyment and industrial achievement. It symbolized the ideals of the World's Columbian Exposition. Moreover, the Ferris wheel signified the industrial advancement of the times and provided an escape in the peaceful period before World War I.

(continued)

Works Cited

Anderson, Norman D., and Walter R. Brown. <u>Ferris Wheels</u>. New York: Pantheon, 1983.

Badger, Reid. <u>The Great American Fair</u>. Chicago: Nelson-Hall, 1979.

Burg, David F. <u>Chicago's White City of 1893</u>. Lexington: UP of Kentucky, 1976.

<u>The Dream City: A Portfolio of Photographic Views</u>. St. Louis: Thompson, 1893. N. pag.

Fincher, Jack. "George Ferris Jr. and the Great Wheel of Fortune." <u>Smithsonian</u> July 1983: 109–118.

Holliday, Kate. "Big Wheels of the Fun Business." <u>Popular Mechanics</u> Mar. 1969: 144–146+.

Howells, William Dean. <u>Letters of an Altrurian Traveller</u> (1893–1894). Gainesville: Scholars' Facsimiles and Reprints, 1961.

Lee, William H. <u>Beautiful Scenes of the White City: A Portfolio of Original Copper-plate Half-tone Engravings of the World's Fair</u>. Chicago: Laird and Lee, 1894. N. pag.

McGuire, John M. "Ferris Invented His Big Wheel for Chicago's 1893 Exposition." <u>St. Louis Post-Dispatch</u> 3 May, 1999. ProQuest Direct. Chicago Public Lib. Chicago. 9 Nov. 1999 <http://proquest.umi.com>.

Rose, Julie K. <u>The World's Columbian Exposition: Idea, Experience, Aftermath</u>. 8 Nov. 1999 <http://xroads.virginia.edu/~ma96/wce/title.html>.

Valenti, Michael. "100 Years and Still Going Around in Circles." <u>Mechanical Engineering</u> June 1993: 70+. ProQuest Direct. Chicago Public Lib. Chicago. 9 Nov. 1999 <http://proquest.umi.com>.

UNIT 7 Review

Reflecting on the Unit
Key concepts in writing a research paper include the following:

- Prewriting for a research paper involves finding a topic, getting information, developing a working bibliography, taking notes, preparing a working outline, and formulating a thesis statement.
- Drafting means using your outline and notes as you write an introduction, body, and conclusion.
- Proper documentation includes citations for specific ideas from sources as well as a list of works cited.
- Careful revision and proofreading prepare a research paper for its audience.

Adding to Your Portfolio

CHOOSE A SELECTION FOR YOUR PORTFOLIO Look over the research paper you prepared during this unit, and put it into your portfolio. Your research paper should show the following:

- a topic that interests you and is neither too broad nor too narrow
- a strong thesis statement and a logical outline
- an introduction that presents a topic and approach
- a conclusion that wraps it all up
- proper citations for all sources
- careful revision and proofreading

REFLECT ON YOUR CHOICE Attach a note to your research paper, explaining what you learned from writing it.

SET GOALS How can you improve your writing? What skill will you focus on the next time you write?

Writing Across the Curriculum

MAKE A SOCIAL STUDIES CONNECTION One type of research paper is a summary. Look through a newspaper or weekly news magazine. Choose a controversial issue that interests you. Look for different people's opinions on the topic. You can start with the editorial page. Then write a one-page report stating the issue, your position, and evidence supporting your position. Include a thesis statement and an effective conclusion, and be sure to cite your sources correctly.

"Fetch our buggy. Help me find my hat."

—Truman Capote, "A Christmas Memory"

UNIT 8
Sentence Combining

Style Through Sentence Combining 360

Lesson 8.1 **Description** 365

Lesson 8.2 **Narration** 369

Lesson 8.3 **Exposition** 373

Lesson 8.4 **Persuasion** 377

Lesson 8.5 **Literature Exercises** 381

UNIT 8

Style Through Sentence Combining

Skillful writing is partly a matter of habit, just like skillful shooting on the basketball court. Both require practice. You can practice some aspects of sentence writing so that they become habit. The ability to write sentences smoothly frees your mind for other important tasks—like getting your ideas right.

Practice in Sentence Combining

This unit focuses on combining short sentences into longer, more complex ones. Remember that the goal is clear writing, not merely long sentences. Practice in sentence combining reveals your stylistic options, the choices you can make as you write. Long sentences are not always the best option.

Regular practice in sentence combining enables you to find clear ways to express your ideas. To write effectively, you must form good sentences consistently. Sentence combining can help you achieve that goal. By making you aware of writing choices, sentence combining also develops your writing style. As you try new types of sentence structures, your personal style will emerge naturally.

Develop Your Style

One way to develop a personal style, as you already know, is by writing regularly in a journal. Such writing helps you unlock your ideas and find your own voice as a writer. Sentence combining is a second approach that has worked for millions of students.

Sentence combining presents you with clusters of short sentences and invites you to express their meanings in more interesting ways. Here's an example of a cluster:

> Writing is a game.
> It is full of challenges.
> It requires regular practice.
> It leads to personal rewards.

Scanning those four simple sentences, you can probably see different ways of combining them into a longer, more complex statement. Basically, there are four strategies for combining:

- deleting repeated words
- using connecting words
- rearranging words
- changing the form of words

The example below shows one way of combining these sentences.

Example

Writing is a game. [*that*]
~~It is full of~~ (challenges). [=ing]
~~It~~ requires regular practice. [*and*]
~~It~~ leads to personal rewards.

Rearranging words; changing the form of words

Using connecting words

Deleting repeated words

Notice that this editing example produces sentence 1 below. Try reading it and the other variations aloud, listening to differences in style.

1. Writing is a challenging game that requires regular practice and leads to personal rewards.
2. Writing, a game full of challenges, leads to personal rewards through regular practice.
3. Requiring regular practice, the challenging game of writing leads to personal rewards.
4. The challenges of the writing game require regular practice but lead to personal rewards.
5. Writing is a game that leads to personal rewards; overcoming its challenges, however, requires regular practice.

All of these sentences say basically the same thing, but they do so in different ways. In other words, each has a different emphasis. As a skilled writer, you choose the stylistic emphasis that best expresses your aims in the context of an emerging paragraph.

Style Through Sentence Combining   **361**

Sentence-Combining Hints

Sentence combining is easy and fun. Here are some basic suggestions you might try as you explore style.

1. **Whisper sentences to yourself.** As you work with clusters of sentences, try combining them aloud. This process is faster than writing and helps you decide on a "best sentence" to write down.
2. **Work with a partner.** By trying out sentences on a partner—and hearing your partner's ideas—you often discover new, interesting ways to solve specific challenges. Don't be afraid to borrow ideas.
3. **Use context when choosing sentences.** Each paragraph has an emerging context—the sentences you have already combined. Reading this context aloud helps you decide on the best sentence option.
4. **Compare your sentences with those of other students.** Seeing how others have solved combining tasks broadens your awareness of sentence options. Keep asking: Which do I prefer?
5. **Look for stylistic patterns in your writing.** Calculate your average words per sentence, study your sentence openers, and listen to rhythms in your style. Try new patterns to stretch yourself.
6. **Take risks.** Learning to make clear, effective sentences also means taking risks and making mistakes. So, strange as it may sound, it actually makes sense to accept mistakes—even *welcome* them—as you combine sentences. After all, mistakes provide feedback for your language learning. As you learn from them, you develop an expressive style, a voice of personal authority. You come to know yourself as a writer.

As you can see, sentence combining involves skills of talking to yourself, making judgments, and holding what you say in short-term memory so that you can transcribe it. These are oral skills as much as writing skills. Good writers trust an "inner voice."

A Workshop on Style

Looking ahead in this unit, you will find two kinds of sentence combining. The exercises in Lessons 8.1 through 8.4 present clusters of short sentences, with spaces between the clusters. The exercises in Lesson 8.5, drawn from literature selections in this book, are set up in an unclustered format.

Lessons 8.1 to 8.4 give you practice in writing descriptive, narrative, expository, and persuasive paragraphs. You can combine each cluster into a single sentence, leave a cluster partially combined, or combine clusters together. The idea, always, is to take risks and create the best sentences you can. Exercises on facing pages deal with the same topic or situation. Think of these exercises as "bookends" for the writing you will do. After you have combined sentences, your task is to connect the paragraphs into a longer essay or story. Doing so will help you transfer sentence-combining skills to your own writing.

Lesson 8.5 invites you to test your skills against those of a professional writer. As you do these unclustered exercises, you will need to figure out the ideas that logically belong together. After you have done the sentence combining, you can check your version against the author's original. By studying similarities and differences between the two passages, you will learn a great deal about your own style. Sometimes you will prefer the professional writer's sentences. Why, specifically, are they "better" than yours? But sometimes you will prefer your own style. Can you build on this writing skill, trying it out in your own stories and essays? Either way, you learn to write better.

Explore Your Own Style

The whole point of sentence-combining practice is to improve your revising and editing skills—to help you see that sentences are flexible instruments of thought, not rigid structures cast in concrete. The simple fact that you feel confident in moving sentence parts around increases your control of the writing process. To acquire this sense of self-confidence in combining and revising sentences, you can try strategies like those shown below.

1. **Vary the length of your sentences.** Work for a rhythmic, interesting balance of long and short sentences, remembering that brevity often has dramatic force.
2. **Vary the structure of your sentences.** By using different kinds of introductory clauses—and by sometimes tucking information into the middle of a sentence—you can create stylistic variety.

Example

```
Children, were curled in balls,
The balls were (little).
Children slept on the straw.
The straw was scattered on wagon beds.
```

- Tuck a participial phrase in the middle of the sentence by deleting the verb *were*.
- Rearrange the position of the adjective.
- Delete repeated words.
- End the sentence with a participial phrase describing the straw.

Author's Original Version:
Children, curled in little balls, slept on the straw scattered on wagon beds.

from *Winesburg, Ohio* by Sherwood Anderson

3. **Use parallelism for emphasis.** Experiment with repeating items in a series—words, phrases, and clauses—to help you understand how structural patterns work and how you can use them to your advantage.

Example

We shall pay any price,
~~We shall~~ bear any burden,
~~We shall~~ meet any hardship,
~~We shall~~ support any friend,
~~We shall~~ oppose any foe.
~~This will~~ *to* assure the survival and success of liberty.

Author's Original Version:
We shall pay any price, bear any burden, meet any hardship, support any friend, oppose any foe to assure the survival and success of liberty.

from "First Inaugural Address" by President John F. Kennedy

- Delete repeated words.

- Use **parallelism,** or similar grammatical structure, in the remaining phrases. Note how the repeated use of the pattern *(verb) + any + (noun)* creates a consistent, distinctive rhythm.

- Use commas to separate phrases in a series.

- Delete *This will* and place *to* before the verb *assure* to form an infinitive phrase.

4. **Use interruption for emphasis.** Colons, semicolons, dashes, commas, parentheses—all of these are useful tools in your stylistic tool kit; knowing how to use them well is important.

5. **Use unusual patterns for emphasis.** Reversing normal sentence patterns may never have occurred to you, but such a strategy can work—if you know how to use it.

LESSON 8.1 Description

Exercise A — First Date

Directions Combine each cluster of numbered items into one or more sentences. Combine clusters, if you wish.

1.1 Tony sat on the edge of a sofa.
1.2 The sofa was plush.
1.3 The sofa was mauve.
1.4 He waited for his date to appear.

2.1 The room felt like a funeral parlor.
2.2 The room looked like a funeral parlor.
2.3 This seemed only fitting.
2.4 Her father was a mortician.

3.1 A gas log burned in the fireplace.
3.2 Its burning was cheerless.
3.3 It bathed the room with warmth.
3.4 The warmth was antiseptic.

4.1 Next to it stood a TV console.
4.2 Its screen reflected the firelight.
4.3 The firelight was flickering.

5.1 Gold draperies extended along one wall.
5.2 The draperies were heavy.
5.3 They were like a dark shroud.
5.4 A painting depicted fading sunlight.
5.5 The sunlight was over an ocean shore.

6.1 The quietness of the room seemed eerie.
6.2 Its suggestions of death seemed eerie.
6.3 Its suggestions of dying seemed eerie.

7.1 In front of him was a marble table.
7.2 It had networks of veins.
7.3 It had networks of capillaries.
7.4 The networks were polished.

8.1 He traced its lines with his eye.
8.2 He listened to a mantle clock.

Continue the Story Whom does Tony meet—Mom, Dad, or the family pet? Writing further description will help you link "First Date" to "Ready to Party."

> **Revising Tip**
>
> In cluster 4, try changing *reflected* to *reflecting* as you combine. A connector such as *with* may be useful in cluster 6.

Exercise B   **Ready to Party**

Directions Combine each cluster of numbered items into one or more sentences. Combine clusters, if you wish.

1.1 At school she was pretty.
1.2 Tonight she looked gorgeous.
1.3 Tonight she wore her hair pulled back.

2.1 She had olive skin.
2.2 She had facial features.
2.3 Her features were finely chiseled.

3.1 Her hair was combed past her ears.
3.2 Her hair was shoulder-length.
3.3 Her hair was black and lustrous.
3.4 Her eyes sparkled with laughter.
3.5 Her eyes were dark.

4.1 She wore earrings.
4.2 The earrings were gold loops.
4.3 She wore a denim jacket.
4.4 The jacket was over a red blouse.
4.5 She wore blue jeans.
4.6 The jeans were faded.

5.1 Even her boots looked ready for dancing.
5.2 The boots had pointed toes.
5.3 The dancing would be serious.

6.1 At school her image was low-key.
6.2 At school her image was conservative.
6.3 Tonight's outfit showed a personality.
6.4 The personality was outgoing.
6.5 The personality was fun-loving.

7.1 Tony felt awkward in his white shirt.
7.2 The white shirt was stiff.
7.3 He felt awkward in his sport coat.
7.4 He felt awkward in his slacks.
7.5 The slacks were carefully pressed.

Continue the Story Describe the scene that you see happening *after* this scene. Then share your text—"First Date" plus "Ready to Party"—with a writing partner.

> **Revising Tip**
>
> In clusters 1 and 6, try different connectors—*but*, *yet*, *however*, *while*, *although*—before settling on one; then check punctuation.

Exercise C — Student Teacher

Directions Combine each cluster of numbered items into one or more sentences. Combine clusters, if you wish.

1.1 The day was only half over.
1.2 The student teacher was frustrated.
1.3 She was completely discouraged.

2.1 Morning classes had not cooperated.
2.2 This was despite her best efforts.
2.3 This was despite her planning.
2.4 Her planning was careful.

3.1 Now her mouth was tense.
3.2 It sagged with fatigue.

4.1 Her desk looked like a disaster.
4.2 It was cluttered with announcements.
4.3 It was cluttered with office notes.
4.4 It was cluttered with tardy slips.
4.5 It was cluttered with late papers.
4.6 The disaster was educational.

5.1 A buzzer echoed in the hallway.
5.2 It signaled a class change.
5.3 She still had not found the planner.
5.4 It contained her lecture notes.

6.1 She wore a badge of resignation.
6.2 The resignation was weary.
6.3 She watched the room fill with students.
6.4 They wanted lunchtime to continue.

7.1 The clock's second hand swept toward twelve.
7.2 She searched for a friendly face.
7.3 The face might help her through the period.

8.1 It was there near the back of the room.
8.2 This was much to her surprise.
8.3 This was much to her relief.

Continue the Story Describe yourself as the person who saves the student teacher's day. Link this description to "Thunderstorm."

> **Revising Tip**
>
> In cluster 4, try *cluttered* at the beginning, in the middle, and toward the end of the sentence. Which approach does *not* work?

Exercise D — Thunderstorm

Directions Combine each cluster of numbered items into one or more sentences. Combine clusters, if you wish.

1.1 The class moved to the windows.
1.2 The windows were half open.
1.3 The class waited for the show to begin.

2.1 Dust had turned the sky beige.
2.2 The dust was wind-blown.
2.3 The dust swirled up from the west.

3.1 Above the hills were shades of gray.
3.2 The gray was the color of gunmetal.
3.3 The gray darkened to purple.
3.4 The purple was ominous.

4.1 Lightning splintered the horizon.
4.2 The horizon was turbulent.
4.3 Its flash was followed by a boom.
4.4 The boom was heavy.
4.5 The boom rumbled.
4.6 The boom was like boxcars.
4.7 The boxcars were in the train yard.

5.1 Then the wind came up.
5.2 The atmosphere seemed luminous.
5.3 Its luminescence was strange.

6.1 Trees swayed like dancers.
6.2 Trees jerked like dancers.
6.3 The dancers were frantic.
6.4 Rain began to fall in drops.
6.5 The drops were fat.

7.1 They splattered the concrete.
7.2 They punched craters in the earth.
7.3 The craters were tiny.
7.4 The earth was thirsty.
7.5 They washed the air clean.

Continue the Story Describe what happens next in this classroom scene. Share the text—"Student Teacher" plus "Thunderstorm"—with a writing partner.

LESSON 8.2 Narration

Exercise A — Waking Up

Directions Combine each cluster of numbered items into one or more sentences. Combine clusters, if you wish.

1.1 The alarm rang at 6:30 A.M.
1.2 It brought Gary out of bed.
1.3 He had slept only a few hours.

2.1 He had thrashed about.
2.2 He had been unable to sleep.
2.3 He was worried about an interview.
2.4 The interview was for employment.

3.1 Now he blinked heavily.
3.2 He leaned against squares of tile.
3.3 The squares were smooth.
3.4 The tile was in the shower.
3.5 He tried to wake himself.

4.1 Warm spray stung his back.
4.2 It prickled his shoulders.
4.3 He only wanted to close his eyes.
4.4 He only wanted to go back to bed.

5.1 His brain had become sludge.
5.2 The sludge was thick.
5.3 The sludge was viscous.

6.1 He worked shampoo into his hair.
6.2 He turned under the shower head.
6.3 The shower head was hissing.
6.4 He hoped to revive himself.

7.1 He finally shut off the shower.
7.2 Cold drops spattered his back.
7.3 The drain sucked at his feet.

8.1 Then he pulled a towel from the rack.
8.2 He wrapped it around his waist.
8.3 He stumbled forward to meet the day.

Continue the Story What happens next? Narrate a transition from "Waking Up" to "Job Interview," perhaps using humor to build interest and tension.

> **Revising Tip**
>
> In cluster 1, use a *who* connector, making sure that sentence 1.3 follows *Gary*. Use a pair of commas for this relative clause.

Exercise B   **Job Interview**

Directions Combine each cluster of numbered items into one or more sentences. Combine clusters, if you wish.

1.1 The waiting area was noisy.
1.2 The waiting area was cramped.
1.3 The waiting area was poorly lit.
1.4 It looked like a large broom closet.

2.1 Gary sat with two other applicants.
2.2 He tried to relax.
2.3 His insides felt tense.

3.1 He touched his fingers to his face.
3.2 He noticed they were ice cold.
3.3 This was a sure sign of nervousness.

4.1 His plan was to sell himself.
4.2 The selling would be straightforward.
4.3 It would be without arrogance.

5.1 He would emphasize his adaptability.
5.2 He would emphasize his friendliness.
5.3 He would emphasize his work habits.
5.4 His work habits were responsible.

6.1 The secretary called his number.
6.2 He wiped his palms dry.
6.3 He adjusted his new tie.
6.4 He arranged his face into a smile.
6.5 The smile was upbeat.

7.1 He strode into the interview room.
7.2 He told himself he had nothing to lose.

8.1 He shook hands with the interviewer.
8.2 He settled into an armchair.
8.3 He noticed his mismatched shoes.
8.4 One was light brown.
8.5 The other was black.

Continue the Story Narrate an interesting conclusion for this story. Then share your text—"Waking Up" plus "Job Interview"—with a writing partner.

> **Revising Tip**
>
> In cluster 1, use *which* to create an adjective clause for sentence 1.4. For more on punctuating adjective clauses, see Lesson 21.6, page 741.

Exercise C — Breakup

Directions Combine each cluster of numbered items into one or more sentences. Combine clusters, if you wish.

1.1 Sabrina lay on a blanket.
1.2 The blanket was in the backyard.
1.3 Her jacket was off.
1.4 Her sunglasses were on.

2.1 She had tried to study for an exam.
2.2 Last night's breakup was on her mind.
2.3 The breakup was sudden.

3.1 She had been sharing a pizza.
3.2 The pizza was after school.
3.3 She was with her boyfriend.
3.4 They had begun to argue.

4.1 Their voices grew louder.
4.2 Their voices grew more angry.
4.3 He had clenched a fist.
4.4 He had slammed it on the table.
4.5 This caused a stir in the restaurant.

5.1 He had leaned forward.
5.2 He had tried to hold her hand.
5.3 She had turned away.

6.1 Her rejection had been unexpected.
6.2 It had been a sharp blow.
6.3 The blow was to his pride.
6.4 His pride was masculine.

7.1 She had said he was immature.
7.2 He was unable to control his temper.

8.1 She had made her decision.
8.2 Her decision was not to see him again.
8.3 His apologies had been weak.
8.4 His apologies had been pathetic.

Continue the Story Narrate what you imagine Sabrina to be thinking about. Is she having second thoughts? Use your narration as a link from "Breakup" to "The Spider."

Exercise D   **The Spider**

Directions Combine each cluster of numbered items into one or more sentences. Combine clusters, if you wish.

1.1 Spears cushioned her notebook.
1.2 The spears were grassy.
1.3 A spider moved up a page.
1.4 The spider was long-legged.

2.1 The spider hesitated.
2.2 It then changed direction.
2.3 It was threatened by a pencil.

3.1 Its legs scurried for safety.
3.2 Its legs were delicate.
3.3 Sabrina grabbed one.
3.4 She picked up the spider.
3.5 The spider was thrashing.

4.1 She was amused by its dance.
4.2 The dance was frantic.
4.3 She made a two-fingered vise.
4.4 She moved in for the kill.

5.1 Death hung merciless.
5.2 Death hung poised.
5.3 It was above the spider's scream.
5.4 The scream was silent.

6.1 The afternoon was breathless.
6.2 The afternoon was warm.
6.3 She thought about her boyfriend.
6.4 She considered her own impulsiveness.

7.1 Sabrina felt the sun's warmth.
7.2 It was on her back.
7.3 It was on her arms.
7.4 Sabrina rolled over on her side.
7.5 She smiled to herself.
7.6 She let the spider go.

Continue the Story Narrate a conclusion to this story. Then share your text—"Breakup" plus "The Spider"—with a writing partner.

Revising Tip

In clusters 4 and 7, try participial phrases to open the sentences. For more on participles, see Lesson 12.3, pages 523–524.

LESSON 8.3 Exposition

Exercise A — Dealing with Acne

Directions Combine each cluster of numbered items into one or more sentences. Combine clusters, if you wish.

1.1 Acne is a common skin condition.
1.2 It affects mostly teenagers and young adults.
1.3 Both males and females can be affected.
1.4 It may last from five to ten years.

2.1 You may have acne or fear getting it.
2.2 Gaining knowledge should be your first line of defense.
2.3 You should learn about its causes.
2.4 You should learn about its possible cures.

3.1 Information about acne is available.
3.2 You can learn from a physician or dermatologist.
3.3 You can learn from books on the topic.
3.4 You can learn from numerous Internet sites.

4.1 Simple steps can help you deal with acne.
4.2 They are mostly a matter of common sense.

5.1 Wash daily with soap and water.
5.2 Don't waste money on cleansers.
5.3 The cleansers are medicated.
5.4 Don't waste money on granular scrubs.

6.1 Use a drying lotion or cream.
6.2 This should contain benzoyl peroxide.

7.1 Wear your hair off your face.
7.2 This keeps it free of scalp oils.
7.3 Avoid hair dressings.
7.4 Hair dressings are greasy.

8.1 Don't pick at your face.
8.2 This increases inflammation.
8.3 This heightens your risk of pitting.
8.4 This heightens your risk of scarring.

Introduce the Article Introduce the hygiene advice in "Dealing with Acne" by explaining why people need to understand this skin condition.

> **Revising Tip**
>
> In cluster 2, try starting the sentence with the word *if*. In that same cluster, try using a semicolon to divide your sentence into two main parts.

Exercise B — Protecting Your Skin

Directions Combine each cluster of numbered items into one or more sentences. Combine clusters, if you wish.

1.1 Suntans may suggest good health.
1.2 They seriously damage your skin.
1.3 They destroy its elastic fibers.

2.1 Their consequence is premature aging.
2.2 No one wishes for the consequence.
2.3 This leaves skin dry and wrinkled.

3.1 Even less desirable are the health risks.
3.2 The risks include basal cell carcinoma.
3.3 The risks include malignant melanoma.

4.1 These skin cancers develop cumulatively.
4.2 These skin cancers develop irreversibly.
4.3 They are a result of sun exposure.

5.1 Early suntans can result in cancers.
5.2 Early sunburns can result in cancers.
5.3 The cancers are during adult years.

6.1 Many suntan salons promise safe tans.
6.2 They promise tans without burns.
6.3 They actually pose real health hazards.

7.1 Tanning booths use ultraviolet radiation.
7.2 This penetrates the skin deeply.
7.3 This causes premature aging.
7.4 This increases susceptibility to cancers.

8.1 Protecting your skin requires something.
8.2 You reduce direct exposure to sunlight.
8.3 Use sunscreens rated at SPF 15 or higher.
8.4 Wear protective clothing in the sun.

9.1 Avoiding suntan salons is common sense.
9.2 It also saves you money.

Continue the Article Create a transition paragraph after "Dealing with Acne" that links to "Protecting Your Skin." Share your text with a writing partner.

Revising Tip

In clusters 2, 3, 4, 7, and 8, you can practice writing adjective clauses. For help on punctuating adjective clauses, see Lesson 21.6, page 741.

Exercise C — Taking Notes

Directions Combine each cluster of numbered items into one or more sentences. Combine clusters, if you wish.

1.1 There are many systems for note taking.
1.2 Two have proved popular with students.
1.3 The students dislike traditional plans.

2.1 One system develops a spiderweb of words.
2.2 The system is sometimes called "webbing."
2.3 The system is sometimes called "mapping."
2.4 The words are from the reading.

3.1 Responses to reading trigger words.
3.2 The responses are personal.
3.3 Words are jotted down as "webs of meaning."

4.1 These webs may not make sense to someone else.
4.2 The webs speak clearly to us.
4.3 We are their authors.
4.4 We know what they are trying to say.

5.1 A second system also uses personal meaning.
5.2 The system is popular.
5.3 It is called the "dialogue journal."

6.1 The journal consists of two facing pages.
6.2 One page is for notes in outline form.
6.3 The other is for thoughts about the notes.

7.1 The notes record information objectively.
7.2 The facing page processes the information.
7.3 It provides emotional reactions.
7.4 It makes summaries.
7.5 It gives examples.
7.6 It asks questions.

8.1 A basic principle underlies both systems.
8.2 We bring unique experiences to reading.
8.3 We take away personal meanings.

Introduce the Article Develop a character sketch or dramatic incident that involves a student with poor study habits; use this sketch to introduce "Taking Notes."

Exercise D — Study Strategy

Directions Combine each cluster of numbered items into one or more sentences. Combine clusters, if you wish.

1.1 Many students have trouble studying.
1.2 They have not discovered certain principles.
1.3 The principles make it easy and fun.
1.4 They therefore get discouraged.

2.1 One approach is to get an overview.
2.2 The approach works for many students.
2.3 This is done by flipping through a text.
2.4 This is done by skimming major headings.
2.5 This is done by reading the chapter summary.

3.1 This overview is like a road map.
3.2 This overview provides "the big picture."
3.3 This overview triggers personal knowledge.
3.4 This overview leads to questions.

4.1 A person turns headings into questions.
4.2 Questions arouse a sense of curiosity.
4.3 Questions provide a focus for reading.
4.4 Reading will follow in a few moments.

5.1 Questions engage one's thinking processes.
5.2 They are a tool for preparing the mind.
5.3 The tool is indispensable.
5.4 The preparation is to remember ideas.

6.1 Many students take notes as they read.
6.2 The students are highly successful.
6.3 They jot down answers to questions.
6.4 They challenge the author.

7.1 These students are active readers.
7.2 The readers recite key points to themselves.
7.3 The readers discuss ideas with others.
7.4 The readers review their notes.
7.5 They cannot help but learn the material.

Continue the Article Write a conclusion for "Taking Notes" and "Study Strategy." Then share your text with a writing partner.

> **Revising Tip**
>
> In cluster 5, try *because* as a sentence opener; then try an appositive, with dashes, after the word *questions*. Choose the sentence you prefer.

LESSON 8.4 Persuasion

Exercise A — Diet Myths

Directions Combine each cluster of numbered items into one or more sentences. Combine clusters, if you wish.

1.1 Most Americans worry about their weight.
1.2 Our society says that "thin is in."
1.3 Advertisers sell us images of bodies.
1.4 The bodies are lean and handsome.

2.1 Forty percent of us are on diets.
2.2 This is at any given moment.
2.3 We are trying to shed excess pounds.

3.1 Helping people to lose weight is a major industry.
3.2 Promoters make a variety of claims.
3.3 The promoters seek quick profits.
3.4 The claims are given wide circulation.

4.1 One such myth centers on grapefruit.
4.2 It contains enzymes.
4.3 The enzymes are supposed to burn fats away.

5.1 No scientific evidence supports these claims.
5.2 Dozens of diets are based on this myth.

6.1 A second myth centers on diet pills.
6.2 The pills are touted as "sure cures."
6.3 The cures are for weight loss.

7.1 Pills sometimes have short-term effects.
7.2 No evidence supports long-term weight loss.

8.1 A third myth centers on electric stimulators.
8.2 These claim to provide "passive exercise."
8.3 These claim to trim fat in specific areas.

9.1 Scientific studies show something.
9.2 Such devices provide no change in body weight.
9.3 Such devices provide no change in body fat.
9.4 Such devices do not improve muscle tone.

Introduce the Article To introduce "Diet Myths," find an actual advertisement (from a Sunday supplement magazine, perhaps) and make it part of your paragraph.

> **Revising Tip**
>
> In cluster 1, try rearranging sentences to achieve emphasis; in cluster 9, delete *something* and use *that* as a connector.

Sentence Combining

Exercise B **More Diet Myths**

Directions Combine each cluster of numbered items into one or more sentences. Combine clusters, if you wish.

1.1 Some diet myths result from promotion.
1.2 Others seem to grow out of our folklore.
1.3 They are passed on by word of mouth.

2.1 There is a widely believed myth.
2.2 The stomach shrinks when you eat less.
2.3 This is simply untrue.
2.4 Your stomach cannot shrink.

3.1 Another myth is also quite common.
3.2 Potatoes are a fattening food.

4.1 A baked potato contains only 130 calories.
4.2 The potato is without butter.
4.3 The potato is without gravy.
4.4 The potato is without melted cheese.

5.1 Potatoes are a high-carbohydrate food.
5.2 The food has no fat or cholesterol.
5.3 The food has fewer calories than brown rice.

6.1 Yet another myth surrounds toast.
6.2 It is listed in many diets.
6.3 It may seem less fattening than untoasted bread.

7.1 Toasting bread removes only moisture.
7.2 It does not remove any calories.
7.3 This is contrary to popular belief.

8.1 A fourth myth concerns celery.
8.2 Some say it has "negative calories."
8.3 It takes so much work to chew celery.

9.1 Celery is a high-fiber vegetable.
9.2 It has only about six calories per stalk.
9.3 Chewing it does not use up extra calories.

Continue the Article Draw conclusions from "Diet Myths" and "More Diet Myths" that will persuade your reader. Then share your text with a writing partner.

Revising Tip

In either cluster 3 or cluster 4, try dashes to achieve additional emphasis.

Exercise C — Destroying History

Directions Combine each cluster of numbered items into one or more sentences. Combine clusters, if you wish.

1.1 Homolovi is an ancestral home.
1.2 Homolovi means "Place of the Mounds."
1.3 The home is for many Hopi people.
1.4 The Hopi live in the American Southwest.

2.1 This area has been plundered by looters.
2.2 The area covers 10,000 acres in Arizona.
2.3 The area is protected by federal and state laws.
2.4 The looters are in search of pottery.
2.5 The pottery is Native American.

3.1 The "pot hunters" use backhoes.
3.2 The "pot hunters" use other machinery.
3.3 The "pot hunters" leave a wake of destruction.

4.1 Hundreds of craters now scar the landscape.
4.2 Many buildings once stood there.
4.3 Two thousand people once lived there.
4.4 Two thousand people once worked there.
4.5 This was about 700 years ago.

5.1 The "pot hunters" rip the land.
5.2 The "pot hunters" gouge the land.
5.3 They destroy historical evidence.
5.4 The destruction is thoughtless.

6.1 Wealthy collectors support a black market.
6.2 The collectors are mainly from the United States.
6.3 The collectors are mainly from Japan.
6.4 The collectors are mainly from Germany.
6.5 The black market is flourishing.

7.1 Looters do the dirty work.
7.2 Private collectors are equally guilty.
7.3 They underwrite historical destruction.
7.4 They violate the heritage of Native Americans.

Continue the Article Should every culture have the right to record and document its own heritage? Make your case in a follow-up paragraph.

> **Revising Tip**
>
> In clusters 2 and 4, try *which* and *where as* connectors; in cluster 6, try a pair of dashes for stylistic emphasis.

Exercise D — Black Market

Directions Combine each cluster of numbered items into one or more sentences. Combine clusters, if you wish.

1.1 Many Native Americans believe in spirits.
1.2 They deeply value ancient burial sites.
1.3 They deeply value ancestral dwellings.

2.1 They see the continuity in life.
2.2 They regard themselves as caretakers.
2.3 The caretakers have sacred duties.

3.1 Pots have significance to them.
3.2 Beads have significance to them.
3.3 Baskets have significance to them.
3.4 Projectile points have significance to them.
3.5 These objects help spirits find eternal peace.

4.1 Alaskan totem poles are cut up.
4.2 Alaskan totem poles are shipped overseas.
4.3 Native Americans shudder in disgust.

5.1 Someone tries to sell a Native American infant.
5.2 The Native American infant is mummified.
5.3 The price is $30,000.
5.4 Native Americans' jaws clench tight.

6.1 Anasazi pots bring nearly $100,000.
6.2 Anasazi baskets bring over $150,000.
6.3 Native Americans' shake their heads sadly.

7.1 The black market in relics angers Native Americans.
7.2 The black market desecrates their past.
7.3 The black market insults their values.
7.4 Their anger is understandable.

8.1 They look forward to a happier time.
8.2 Their heritage is accorded respect.
8.3 The black market collapses.
8.4 The black market is now supported by looting.

Continue the Article Imagine finding an arrowhead while hiking. Does it go into your pocket? Write about the personal reasons behind your decision.

Revising Tip

Try using *when* as an opener in clusters 4, 5, and 6. This effect is called *parallelism*.

LESSON 8.5 Literature Exercises

Exercise A

Directions Some of the sentences below come directly from *The Crystal Cave* by Mary Stewart. The numbered sentences are adapted from Stewart's original. Combine the numbered sentences. Then compare your sentences with the Literature Model on page 165.

Next moment I stopped short, brought up by a shock which spilled the excitement through my bowels like water. Something had moved in the murk, just to my right.

1. I froze still.
2. I strained my eyes to see.
3. There was no movement.
4. I held my breath.
5. I listened.
6. There was no sound.
7. I flared my nostrils.
8. I tested the air round me.
9. My testing was cautious.
10. There was no animal or human smell.
11. I thought something.
12. The cave smelt of smoke.
13. The cave smelt of damp rock.
14. The cave smelt of the earth itself.
15. The cave had a scent.
16. The scent was musty.
17. The scent was queer.
18. I could not identify it.

I knew, without putting it into words, that had there been any other creature near me the air would have felt different, less empty. There was no one there.

19. I tried a word in Welsh.
20. My try was soft.
21. The word was "Greetings."
22. The whisper came back at me in an echo.
23. The whisper came back so quickly.
24. I knew I was very near the wall of the cave.
25. Then it lost itself.
26. It was hissing in the roof.

> **Revising Tip**
> Whisper possible combinations aloud to try them out as you revise.

Exercise B

Directions Scan the sentences below. Some come directly from *Of Wolves and Men* by Barry Lopez. The numbered sentences are adapted from Lopez's original. Decide which of the numbered sentences belong together, and combine them in your own way. Then compare your sentences with the Literature Model on pages 277–278.

1. It is now late in the afternoon.
2. The wolf has stopped traveling.
3. He has lain down to sleep on cool earth.
4. The earth is beneath a rock outcropping.
5. Mosquitoes rest on his ears.
6. His ears flicker.
7. He begins to waken.
8. He rolls on his back.
9. He lies motionless.
10. His front legs are pointed toward the sky.
11. They are folded like wilted flowers.
12. His back legs are splayed.
13. His nose and tail are curved toward each other.
14. They are on one side of his body.

After a few moments he flops on his side, rises, stretches, and moves a few feet to inspect—minutely, delicately—a crevice in the rock outcropping and finds or doesn't find what draws him there. And then he ascends the rock face, bounding and balancing momentarily before bounding again, appearing slightly unsure of the process—but committed.

15. A few minutes pass.
16. He bolts suddenly into the woods.
17. He achieves full speed.
18. This is almost forty miles per hour.
19. This is for forty or fifty yards.
20. He begins to skid.
21. He begins to lunge at a lodgepole pine cone.
22. He trots away with it.
23. His head is erect.
24. His tail is erect.
25. His hips are slightly to one side.
26. They are out of line with his shoulders.
27. It's as if hindquarters were impatient with forequarters.
28. The cone is inert in his mouth.

Exercise C

Directions Scan the sentences below. Some come directly from *How the García Girls Lost Their Accents* by Julia Alvarez. The numbered sentences are adapted from Alvarez's original. Decide which of the numbered sentences belong together, and combine them in your own way. Then compare your sentences with the Literature Model on pages 217–218.

"Go away," Yoyo wailed, but they both knew she was glad her mother was there, and needed only a moment's protest to save face.

1. Together they concocted a speech.
2. There were two brief pages of compliments.
3. The compliments were stale.
4. There were two brief pages of commonplaces.
5. The commonplaces were polite.
6. The commonplaces were on teachers.
7. It was a speech wrought by necessity.
8. It was a speech without much invention.
9. It was wrought by mother and daughter.
10. It was wrought late into the night.
11. It was wrought on one of the pads of paper.
12. Laura had once used the pads for her own inventions.
13. The speech was drafted.
14. Laura typed it up.
15. Yoyo stood by.
16. She corrected her mother's misnomers and mis-sayings.

Finally, her mother came up and pleaded with Yoyo to go down and reconcile with him [her father].

17. Yoyo found her father downstairs.
18. He was setting up a brand new typewriter.
19. The typewriter was on the kitchen table.
20. The typewriter was electric.
21. It was even better than her mother's.
22. He had outdone himself with all the extra features.
23. There was a plastic carrying case.
24. Yoyo's initials were decaled below the handle.
25. There was a brace to lift the paper upright while she typed.
26. There was an erase cartridge.
27. There was an automatic margin tab.
28. There was a plastic hood like a toaster cover.
29. The hood was to keep the dust away.

Exercise D

Directions Scan the sentences below. Some come directly from *I Know Why the Caged Bird Sings* by Maya Angelou. The numbered sentences are adapted from Angelou's original. Decide which of the numbered sentences belong together, and combine them in your own way. Then compare your sentences with the Literature Model on page 46.

She took the bags from me and disappeared through the kitchen door. I looked around the room that I had never in my wildest fantasies imagined I would see.

1. Photographs leered from the walls.
2. Photographs threatened from the walls.
3. The photographs were browned.
4. The curtains pushed against themselves.
5. The curtains pushed against the wind.
6. The curtains were white.
7. The curtains were freshly done.
8. I wanted to gobble up the room entirely.
9. I wanted to take it to Bailey.
10. He would help me analyze it.
11. He would help me enjoy it.

"Have a seat, Marguerite. Over there by the table." She carried a platter covered with a tea towel. Although she warned that she hadn't tried her hand at baking sweets for some time, I was certain that like everything else about her the cookies would be perfect.

12. They were wafers.
13. The wafers were flat.
14. The wafers were round.
15. They were slightly browned on the edges.
16. They were butter-yellow in the center.
17. They came with the cold lemonade.
18. They were sufficient for childhood's lifelong diet.
19. I remembered my manners.
20. I took nice little bites.
21. The bites were lady-like.
22. The bites were off the edges.
23. She said something.
24. She had made them expressly for me.
25. She had a few in the kitchen.
26. I could take them home to my brother.

Exercise E

Directions Scan the sentences below. Some come directly from "Skeletons in the Attic" by Clara Spotted Elk. The numbered sentences are adapted from Spotted Elk's original. Decide which of the numbered sentences belong together, and combine them in your own way. Then compare your sentences with the Literature Model on page 317.

After a chance inquiry, a curator pulled out a drawer in one of the scores of cabinets that line the attic. There were the jumbled bones of an Indian. "A Kiowa," he said.

1. We subsequently found 18,500 Indian remains.
2. Some consisted of a handful of bones.
3. Most were full skeletons.
4. They were stored in the Smithsonian's nooks.
5. They were stored in the Smithsonian's crannies.
6. Their storage was unceremonious.
7. Other museums also collect the bones.
8. Other individuals also collect the bones.
9. Other federal agencies also collect the bones.
10. The agencies include the National Park Service.
11. The bones are of Indian warriors.
12. The bones are of Indian women.
13. The bones are of Indian children.
14. Some are on display as attractions.
15. The attractions are for tourists.
16. The attractions are by the roadside.

It is estimated that another 600,000 Indian remains are secreted away in locations across the country.

17. The museum community defends these collections.
18. Forensic scientists defend these collections.
19. Their defense is vigorous.
20. The collections are grisly.
21. There are few exceptions.
22. They refuse to return remains to the tribes.
23. The tribes wish to rebury them.
24. This is even when grave robbing has been documented.

They want to maintain adequate numbers of "specimens" for analysis and say they are dedicated to "the permanent curation of Indian skeletal remains."

"... the things we worry about are never the things that happen."

—Naomi Shihab Nye, "Field Trip"

UNIT 9 Troubleshooter

*U*se Troubleshooter to help you correct common errors in your writing.

Lesson 9.1	Sentence Fragment	388
Lesson 9.2	Run-on Sentence	390
Lesson 9.3	Lack of Subject-Verb Agreement	392
Lesson 9.4	Lack of Pronoun-Antecedent Agreement	396
Lesson 9.5	Lack of Clear Pronoun Reference	398
Lesson 9.6	Shift in Pronoun	400
Lesson 9.7	Shift in Verb Tense	401
Lesson 9.8	Incorrect Verb Tense or Form	402
Lesson 9.9	Misplaced or Dangling Modifier	404
Lesson 9.10	Missing or Misplaced Possessive Apostrophe	406
Lesson 9.11	Missing Commas with Nonessential Element	408
Lesson 9.12	Missing Commas in a Series	410

9.1 Sentence Fragment

Problem 1

Fragment that lacks a subject

frag Sal put his best effort into his painting. ~~Hoped it would win a prize.~~

SOLUTION Add a subject to the fragment to make it a complete sentence.

Sal put his best effort into his painting. He hoped it would win a prize.

Problem 2

Fragment that lacks a complete verb

frag We heard a loud noise. ~~The fire alarm across the street.~~

frag The reviews are enthusiastic. ~~The critics encouraging us to put on future shows.~~

SOLUTION A Add a complete verb or a helping verb to make the sentence complete.

We heard a loud noise. The fire alarm across the street was wailing.

The reviews are enthusiastic. The critics are encouraging us to put on future shows.

SOLUTION B Combine the fragment with another sentence.

We heard a loud noise—the fire alarm across the street.

The reviews are enthusiastic, with the critics encouraging us to put on future shows.

Problem 3

Fragment that is a subordinate clause

> *frag* Maria was relieved. ~~Because she found her notebook.~~
> *frag* The restaurant is out of melon. ~~Which I wanted for dessert.~~

SOLUTION A Combine the fragment with another sentence.

Maria was relieved because she found her notebook.
The restaurant is out of melon, which I wanted for dessert.

SOLUTION B Rewrite the fragment as a complete sentence, eliminating the subordinating conjunction or the relative pronoun and adding a subject or other words necessary to make a complete thought.

Maria was relieved. She found her notebook.
The restaurant is out of melon. I wanted it for dessert.

Problem 4

Fragment that lacks both a subject and a verb

> *frag* Paul finally finished his homework. ~~At ten o'clock.~~

SOLUTION Combine the fragment with another sentence.
Paul finally finished his homework at ten o'clock.

If you need more help in avoiding sentence fragments, turn to Lesson 13.9, pages 553–554.

9.1 Sentence Fragment **389**

9.2 Run-on Sentence

Problem 1

Comma splice—two main clauses separated only by a comma

run-on On vacation Luisa enjoys hiking in the mountains, Leon prefers swimming at the beach.

SOLUTION A Replace the comma with an end mark of punctuation, such as a period or a question mark, and begin the new sentence with a capital letter.

On vacation Luisa enjoys hiking in the mountains. Leon prefers swimming at the beach.

SOLUTION B Place a semicolon between the two main clauses.

On vacation Luisa enjoys hiking in the mountains; Leon prefers swimming at the beach.

SOLUTION C Add a coordinating conjunction after the comma.

On vacation Luisa enjoys hiking in the mountains, but Leon prefers swimming at the beach.

Problem 2

Two main clauses with no punctuation between them

run-on Kim plays the guitar she writes music too.

SOLUTION A Separate the main clauses with an end mark of punctuation, such as a period or a question mark, and begin the second sentence with a capital letter.

Kim plays the guitar. She writes music too.

SOLUTION B Separate the main clauses with a semicolon.

Kim plays the guitar; she writes music too.

SOLUTION C Add a comma and a coordinating conjunction between the main clauses.

Kim plays the guitar, and she writes music too.

Problem 3
Two main clauses with no comma before the coordinating conjunction

run-on Carla is planning to visit Yellowstone National Park next summer and her sister may join her.

run-on The main course was boring but the dessert was magnificent.

SOLUTION Add a comma before the coordinating conjunction to separate the two main clauses.

Carla is planning to visit Yellowstone National Park next summer, and her sister may join her.

The main course was boring, but the dessert was magnificent.

If you need more help in avoiding run-on sentences, turn to Lesson 13.10, pages 555–557.

9.3 Lack of Subject-Verb Agreement

Problem 1

A subject that is separated from the verb by an intervening prepositional phrase

agr The sound of the nightingales (fill) the air.
agr The storms in winter (seems) severe.

SOLUTION Ignore a prepositional phrase that comes between a subject and a verb. Make the verb agree with the subject, which is never the object of a preposition.

The sound of the nightingales fills the air.
The storms in winter seem severe.

Problem 2

A predicate nominative that differs in number from the subject

agr Bicycle races (was) his passion.

SOLUTION Ignore the predicate nominative, and make the verb agree with the subject of the sentence.

Bicycle races were his passion.

Problem 3

A subject that follows the verb

agr Off the reef (lies) three sunken ships.
agr Here (comes) the first three volunteers.

392 Unit 9 Troubleshooter

SOLUTION In an inverted sentence look for the subject *after* the verb. Then make sure the verb agrees with the subject.

Off the reef lie three sunken ships.
Here come the first three volunteers.

Problem 4

A collective noun as the subject

agr The chorus ⟨sing⟩ splendidly.
agr The jury ⟨disagrees⟩ among themselves.

SOLUTION A If the collective noun refers to a group as a whole, use a singular verb.

The chorus sings splendidly.

SOLUTION B If the collective noun refers to each member of a group individually, use a plural verb.

The jury disagree among themselves.

Problem 5

A noun of amount as the subject

agr Ten months ⟨are⟩ the usual school year.
agr Ten dimes ⟨makes⟩ a dollar.

SOLUTION Determine whether the noun of amount refers to one unit and is therefore singular or whether it refers to a number of individual units and is therefore plural.

Ten months is the usual school year.
Ten dimes make a dollar.

9.3 Lack of Subject-Verb Agreement   **393**

Problem 6

A compound subject that is joined by *and*

agr   *Oxygen and hydrogen (is) essential to life.*
agr   *Oil and vinegar (are) my favorite salad dressing.*

SOLUTION A If the parts of the compound subject do not belong to one unit or if they refer to different people or things, use a plural verb.

Oxygen and hydrogen are essential to life.

SOLUTION B If the parts of the compound subject belong to one unit or if both parts refer to the same person or thing, use a singular verb.

Oil and vinegar is my favorite salad dressing.

Problem 7

A compound subject that is joined by *or* or *nor*

agr   *Neither hardships nor danger (deter) him.*
agr   *Either soup or sandwiches (makes) a good lunch.*

SOLUTION Make the verb agree with the subject that is closer to it.

Neither hardships nor danger deters him.
Either soup or sandwiches make a good lunch.

Problem 8

A compound subject that is preceded by *many a, every,* or *each*

agr   *Every nook and cranny (were) searched.*

394   Unit 9 Troubleshooter

SOLUTION Use a singular verb when *many a, each,* or *every* precedes a compound subject.

Every nook and cranny was searched.

Problem 9

A subject that is separated from the verb by an intervening expression

agr   Carlos, as well as Dana, love baseball.

Certain expressions, such as *as well as, in addition to,* and *together with* do not change the number of the subject.

SOLUTION Ignore an intervening expression between a subject and its verb. Make the verb agree with the subject.

Carlos, as well as Dana, loves baseball.

Problem 10

An indefinite pronoun as the subject

agr   Each of the climbers carry a rope.

Some indefinite pronouns are singular, some are plural, and some can be either singular or plural, depending upon the noun to which they refer. (See page 451 for a list of indefinite pronouns.)

SOLUTION Determine whether the indefinite pronoun is singular or plural, and make the verb agree.

Each of the climbers carries a rope.

If you need more help with subject-verb agreement, turn to Lessons 16.1 through 16.7, pages 609–621.

9.4 Lack of Pronoun-Antecedent Agreement

Problem 1

A singular antecedent that can be either male or female

ant A good athlete must practice **his** routine daily.
ant A parent and **his** child form a special bond.

Traditionally a masculine pronoun was used to refer to an antecedent that might be either male or female. This usage ignores or excludes females.

SOLUTION A Reword the sentence to use *he or she, him or her,* and so on.

A good athlete must practice his or her routine daily.
A parent and his or her child form a special bond.

SOLUTION B Reword the sentence so that both the antecedent and the pronoun are plural.

Good athletes must practice their routines daily.
Parents and their children form special bonds.

SOLUTION C Reword the sentence to eliminate the pronoun.

Good athletes must practice routines daily.
A parent and child form a special bond.

Problem 2

A second-person pronoun that refers to a third-person antecedent

ant Carlos and Jane love hiking because **you** benefit from vigorous exercise in peaceful, natural surroundings.

396 Unit 9 Troubleshooter

Be sure not to refer to an antecedent in the third person using the second-person pronoun *you*.

SOLUTION A Use the appropriate third-person pronoun.

Carlos and Jane love hiking because they benefit from vigorous exercise in peaceful, natural surroundings.

SOLUTION B Use an appropriate noun instead of a pronoun.

Carlos and Jane love hiking because hikers benefit from vigorous exercise in peaceful, natural surroundings.

Problem 3

A singular indefinite pronoun as an antecedent

ant Each of the women had (their) own goal.
ant Neither of the men showed (their) surprise at the vote.

Each, everyone, either, neither, and *one* are singular and therefore require singular personal pronouns.

SOLUTION Don't be fooled by a prepositional phrase that contains a plural noun. Determine whether the indefinite pronoun antecedent is singular or plural, and make the noun agree.

Each of the women had her own goal.
Neither of the men showed his surprise at the vote.

If you need more help with pronoun-antecedent agreement, turn to Lesson 16.7, pages 619–621, and Lesson 17.5, pages 640–644.

9.5 Lack of Clear Pronoun Reference

Problem 1

A pronoun reference that is weak or vague

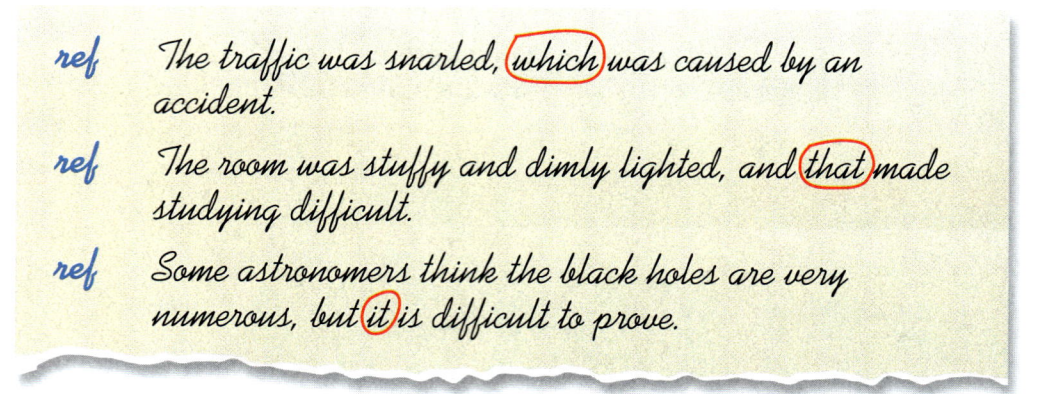

ref The traffic was snarled, (which) was caused by an accident.

ref The room was stuffy and dimly lighted, and (that) made studying difficult.

ref Some astronomers think the black holes are very numerous, but (it) is difficult to prove.

Be sure that *this*, *that*, *which*, and *it* have clear antecedents.

SOLUTION A Rewrite the sentence, adding a clear antecedent for the pronoun.

The traffic was snarled in a massive tie-up, which was caused by an accident.

SOLUTION B Rewrite the sentence, substituting a noun for the pronoun.

The room was stuffy and dimly lighted, and those conditions made studying difficult.

Some astronomers think that black holes are numerous, but that theory is difficult to prove.

Problem 2

A pronoun that could refer to more than one antecedent

ref *My sister always beats Susan at chess, but (she) still enjoys the game.*

ref *When the dancers performed for the children, (they) were pleased.*

SOLUTION A Rewrite the sentence, substituting a noun for the pronoun.

My sister always beats Susan at chess, but Susan still enjoys the game.

SOLUTION B Rewrite the sentence, eliminating the pronoun.

The children were pleased when the dancers performed.

Problem 3

The indefinite use of *you* or *they*

ref *In Japan (you) go to school on Saturday mornings.*
ref *In that school (they) have a fine music program.*

SOLUTION A Rewrite the sentence, substituting a noun for the pronoun.

In Japan students go to school on Saturday mornings.

SOLUTION B Rewrite the sentence, eliminating the pronoun entirely.

That school has a fine music program.

If you need more help in making clear pronoun references, turn to Lesson 17.6, pages 645–647.

9.5 Lack of Clear Pronoun Reference **399**

9.6 Shift in Pronoun

Problem

An incorrect shift in person between two pronouns

> *pro* They are going to the international fair, where ~~you~~ can sample foods from many nations.
>
> *pro* I think life was easier when ~~you~~ had fewer possessions.
>
> *pro* After one runs a marathon, ~~you are~~ exhausted yet exhilarated.

Incorrect pronoun shifts occur when a writer or speaker uses a pronoun in one person and then illogically shifts to a pronoun in another person.

SOLUTION A Replace the incorrect pronoun with a pronoun that agrees with its antecedent.

They are going to the international fair, where they can sample foods from many nations.

I think life was easier when I had fewer possessions.

After one runs a marathon, one is exhausted yet exhilarated.

SOLUTION B Replace the incorrect pronoun with an appropriate noun.

They are going to the international fair, where people can sample foods from many nations.

I think life was easier when people had fewer possessions.

If you need more help in eliminating incorrect pronoun shifts, turn to Lesson 17.5, pages 640–644.

9.7 Shift in Verb Tense

Problem 1
An unnecessary shift in tense

shift t Victor reads the newspaper and ~~noted~~ the sports scores.

shift t Nan arrived just as the play ~~begins~~.

When two or more events occur at the same time, be sure to use the same verb tense to describe both events.

SOLUTION Use the same tense for both verbs.

Victor reads the newspaper and notes the sports scores.
Nan arrived just as the play began.

Problem 2
A lack of correct shift in tenses to show that one event precedes or follows another

shift t By the time the fire broke out, we ~~were~~ asleep for hours.

When events being described have occurred at different times, shift tenses to show that one event precedes or follows another.

SOLUTION Shift from the past tense to the past perfect tense to indicate that one action began and ended before another past action began. Use the past perfect tense for the earlier of the two actions.

By the time the fire broke out, we had been asleep for hours.

If you need more help with shifts in verb tenses, turn to Lesson 15.4, pages 589–591, and Lesson 15.6, pages 594–595.

9.8 Incorrect Verb Tense or Form

Problem 1

An incorrect or missing verb ending

tense Yesterday I ~~walk~~ four miles in the morning.
tense Have you ever ~~watch~~ a soccer match?

SOLUTION Add *-ed* to a regular verb to form the past tense and the past participle.

Yesterday I walked four miles in the morning.

Have you ever watched a soccer match?

Problem 2

An improperly formed irregular verb

tense Mike ~~teared~~ his pants on a nail.
tense Angela has ~~sweeped~~ every room.

Irregular verbs form their past tense and past participle in some way other than by adding *-ed*. Memorize these forms, or look them up.

SOLUTION Use the correct past or past participle form of an irregular verb.

Mike tore his pants on a nail.

Angela has swept every room.

Problem 3

Confusion between the past form and the past participle

tense Mr. Yei has often ~~spoke~~ about life in China.

402 Unit 9 Troubleshooter

SOLUTION Use the past participle form of an irregular verb, not the past form, when you use the auxiliary verb *have*.

Mr. Yei has often spoken about life in China.

Problem 4

Improper use of the past participle

tense We **rung** the doorbell several times.
tense Jolene **swum** faster than anyone else on the team.
tense We **begun** the trip without much advance planning.

The past participle of an irregular verb cannot stand alone as a verb. It must be used with the auxiliary verb *have*.

SOLUTION A Add the auxiliary verb *have* to the past participle to form a complete verb.

We have rung the doorbell several times.
Jolene has swum faster than anyone else on the team.
We have begun the trip without much advance planning.

SOLUTION B Replace the past participle with the past form of the verb.

We rang the doorbell several times.
Jolene swam faster than anyone else on the team.
We began the trip without much advance planning.

If you need more help with correct verb forms, turn to Lessons 15.1 and 15.2, pages 581–585.

9.9 Misplaced or Dangling Modifier

Problem 1

A misplaced modifier

mod I got fine pictures of the puppies *with my new camera.*
mod *Dented and scratched,* Marta found her bicycle.
mod We took a backpack on the train *stuffed with sandwiches and fruit.*

Modifiers that modify the wrong word or seem to modify more than one word in a sentence are called misplaced modifiers.

SOLUTION Move the misplaced phrase as close as possible to the word or words it modifies.

With my new camera, I got fine pictures of the puppies.

Marta found her bicycle dented and scratched.

We took a backpack stuffed with sandwiches and fruit on the train.

Problem 2

The adverb *only* misplaced

mod Carlos *only* eats spaghetti with clam sauce.

The meaning of your sentence may be unclear if *only* is misplaced.

SOLUTION

Only Carlos eats spaghetti with clam sauce.

Carlos eats only spaghetti with clam sauce.

Carlos eats spaghetti only with clam sauce.

Place the adverb *only* immediately before the word or group of words it modifies. Note that each time *only* is moved in the sentence, the meaning of the sentence changes.

Problem 3
A dangling modifier

> mod ~~After working feverishly for days,~~ the science project was completed.
>
> mod ~~Watching television,~~ the screen suddenly went blank.
>
> mod ~~Hoping for a break from the heat,~~ a Canadian cold front brought relief.

Dangling modifiers do not logically seem to modify any word in the sentence.

SOLUTION Rewrite the sentence, adding a noun to which the dangling phrase clearly refers. Often you will have to add other words to complete the meaning of the sentence.

After working feverishly for days, Jan completed her science project.

Watching television, Yoshiko saw the screen suddenly go blank.

Hoping for a break from the heat, we were relieved when a Canadian cold front moved in.

If you need more help with misplaced or dangling modifiers, turn to Lesson 18.7, pages 670–675.

9.10 Missing or Misplaced Possessive Apostrophe

Problem 1
Singular nouns

poss The ⟨waitress⟩ wallet held that ⟨days⟩ tips.

SOLUTION Use an apostrophe and an *-s* to form the possessive of a singular noun, even one that ends in *-s*.

The waitress's wallet held that day's tips.

Problem 2
Plural nouns ending in *-s*

poss The ⟨soldiers⟩ tents dotted the field.

SOLUTION Use an apostrophe alone to form the possessive of a plural noun that ends in *-s*.

The soldiers' tents dotted the field.

Problem 3
Plural nouns not ending in *-s*

poss The ⟨childrens⟩ bookstore is on Broadway.

SOLUTION Use an apostrophe and an *-s* to form the possessive of a plural noun that does not end in *-s*.

The children's bookstore is on Broadway.

Problem 4

Pronouns

poss I found ~~somebodys~~ watch.
poss The best idea was ~~her's.~~

SOLUTION A Use an apostrophe and an *-s* to form the possessive of a singular indefinite pronoun.

I found somebody's watch.

SOLUTION B Do not use an apostrophe with any of the possessive personal pronouns.

The best idea was hers.

Problem 5

Confusion between *its* and *it's*

poss The boat has slipped ~~it's~~ mooring.
poss ~~Its~~ a great day for a picnic.

The possessive of *it* is *its*. *It's* is the contraction of *it is*.

SOLUTION Do not use an apostrophe to form the possessive of *it*. Use an apostrophe to form the contraction of *it is*.

The boat has slipped its mooring.
It's a great day for a picnic.

If you need more help with apostrophes and possessives, turn to Lesson 17.1, pages 633–634, and Lesson 21.11, pages 759–761.

9.11 Missing Commas with Nonessential Element

Problem 1

Missing commas with nonessential participles, infinitives, and their phrases

com Claude watched delighted as Cheryl accepted the award.

com Marla finishing her work set out for a late afternoon jog.

com To repeat the bus will leave promptly at five.

SOLUTION Determine whether the participle, infinitive, or phrase is truly not essential to the meaning of the sentence. If it is not essential, set off the phrase with commas.

Claude watched, delighted, as Cheryl accepted the award.
Marla, finishing her work, set out for a late afternoon jog.
To repeat, the bus will leave promptly at five.

Problem 2

Missing commas with nonessential adjective clauses

com César who is also a licensed pilot is a certified scuba diver.

SOLUTION Determine whether the clause is truly not essential to the meaning of the sentence. If it is not essential, set off the clause with commas.

César, who is also a licensed pilot, is a certified scuba diver.

Problem 3
Missing commas with nonessential appositives

com Margaret Donelly our letter carrier is on vacation.

SOLUTION Determine whether the appositive is truly not essential to the meaning of the sentence. If it is not essential, set off the appositive with commas.

Margaret Donelly, our letter carrier, is on vacation.

Problem 4
Missing commas with interjections and parenthetical expressions

com Gosh I enjoyed that game.
com You know of course that the office is closed on Saturdays.

SOLUTION Set off the interjection or parenthetical expression with commas.

Gosh, I enjoyed that game.
You know, of course, that the office is closed on Saturdays.

If you need more help with commas and nonessential elements, turn to Lesson 21.6, pages 738–748.

9.12 Missing Commas in a Series

Problem 1
Missing comma in a series of words, phrases, or clauses

com The garden was a riot of zinnias○hollyhocks○ marigolds○and lilies.

com Reggie stopped○bent down○and picked up the quarter he had dropped.

com Yuki ran down the street○around the corner○and into the Murphys' garage.

com We watched the kites soaring into the sky○ swooping back and forth○and gliding to earth.

com Angela plays the guitar○Bill sings○and José accompanies them on the drums.

SOLUTION When there are three or more items in a series, use a comma after each item that precedes the conjunction.

The garden was a riot of zinnias, hollyhocks, marigolds, and lilies.

Reggie stopped, bent down, and picked up the quarter he had dropped.

Yuki ran down the street, around the corner, and into the Murphys' garage.

We watched the kites soaring into the sky, swooping back and forth, and gliding to earth.

Angela plays the guitar, Bill sings, and José accompanies them on the drums.

If you need more help with commas in a series, turn to Lesson 21.6, pages 738–748.

410 Unit 9 Troubleshooter

Use the proofreading symbols below to mark corrections in your writing.

Proofreading Symbols

Symbol	Example	Meaning
⊙	Lieut⊙ Brown	Insert a period.
∧	No one came ⁀to the party.	Insert a letter or a word.
⩘	The bell rang⩘the students left for home.	Insert a semicolon.
≡	I enjoyed paris.	Capitalize a letter.
/	The Class ran a bake sale.	Make a capital letter lowercase.
⌒	The campers are home ⌒sick.	Close up a space.
ⓢⓟ	They visited (N.Y.) ⓢⓟ	Spell out.
∧	Sue please help.	Insert a comma.
∽	He enjoyed feild day.	Transpose the position of letters or words.
#	al#together	Insert a space.
ꝺ	We went tꝺo to Boston.	Delete letters or words.
ᵛᵛ	She asked, "Who's coming?"	Insert quotation marks.
/=/	mid⹀January	Insert a hyphen.
¶	"Where?" asked Karl.¶ "Over there," said Ray.	Begin a new paragraph.
ᵛ	She liked Sarahᵛs glasses.	Insert an apostrophe.

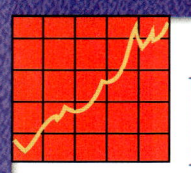

Business and Technical Writing

Contents

Business Letters	*413*
Memos, E-mail, and Applications	*421*
Using the Computer as a Writing Tool	*425*
Technical Writing	*431*
Collaborative Writing in the Business World	*434*

Business Letters

Why Write Business Letters?

Knowing how to write a business letter is a valuable skill—one that you will use while you are in school and throughout your life. Business letters are written not only by people of every age who are engaged in the business world but also by those who want to request help or information and to express their opinions.

Business writing is a special form of expository writing. The most important thing to know about business writing is that it must be efficient communication. The reader should be able to grasp the meaning of a business letter quickly with a minimum of effort. A long, complicated letter simply will not be read. A brief, clearly written letter is more likely to result in a positive response.

The impression a business letter makes on its reader will certainly influence the nature of his or her response. Correct grammar, spelling, and punctuation are musts. While a business letter should employ formal language, its tone may be conversational.

A business letter is usually single-spaced and written on only one side of a page. However, you may double-space a very short business letter so that it fills up more of the page. If the letter is longer than one page, begin each page after the first with the name of the recipient, the date, and the page number, each on its own line flush with the left margin, as shown in the sample below.

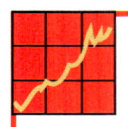

Activity

Bring a copy of a business letter to class. It may be a letter from a charity asking for a donation, a bank explaining a change in policy, your parents asking for information about a coming event, or a civic group seeking support for its policies. Work in small groups to analyze the letters. What do the letters have in common? For what purposes were they written? Share your observations with the rest of the class.

```
R. Garcia
10/23/01
page 2
```

Business Letters

Styles of Business Letters

The two main styles of business letters are block style and modified block style.

Block Style The use of conventional styles in business writing lets readers know exactly what to expect and where to look for relevant information. The block style is the most commonly used style today. In this style, all parts of the letter are aligned with the left margin. Paragraphs are not indented. They are separated by a line space.

The letter shown below uses block style. Notice that the letter is brief, clear, and carefully organized. The writer asks for what he wants in the first sentence and provides his reader with more detail in the sentences that follow.

---

224 W. Beale St.
Bowling Green, OH 43402
November 22, 2001

Ms. Jo Brown, Director
U.S. Space Camp
One Tranquility Base
Huntsville, AL 55555

Dear Ms. Brown:

I am writing to request information about the U.S. Space Camp. I read about your program on your Web site and am eager to learn more. Please send me information on the camp, including dates, costs, and transportation options.

I would also be interested to know whether there are scholarships available.

Sincerely,

Joe Bello

Joe Bello

- The heading is flush with the left margin. If you're using letterhead stationery, the return address is not necessary; begin with the date.
- The inside address is also flush left.
- A colon follows the salutation.
- Paragraphs are not indented.
- Paragraphs are separated by a line space.

414 Business and Technical Writing

Business Letters

Modified Block Style In the modified block style modeled below, the heading, the closing, the signature, and the typed name begin about three to four inches to the right. Paragraphs are indented and do not have a line space between them.

Parts of a Business Letter

A business letter has six parts.

Heading The heading contains three lines:
- your street address
- your city, state, and ZIP code
- the date

Inside Address The inside address has four or more lines:
- the name and title of the person to whom you are writing
- the name of the business or organization
- the address of the business or organization
- the city, state, and ZIP code

Salutation The salutation begins with the word *Dear* and is followed by a courtesy title (such as *Ms., Mr.,* or *Dr.*) and the last name of the person to whom you are writing. If you don't know the person's name and title, call the company and request that information. Be sure to ask for the correct spelling. If you cannot learn the person's name but know his or her title, you can use the title in the salutation, as in "Dear Manager," or you can use "To whom it may concern." Place a colon after the salutation.

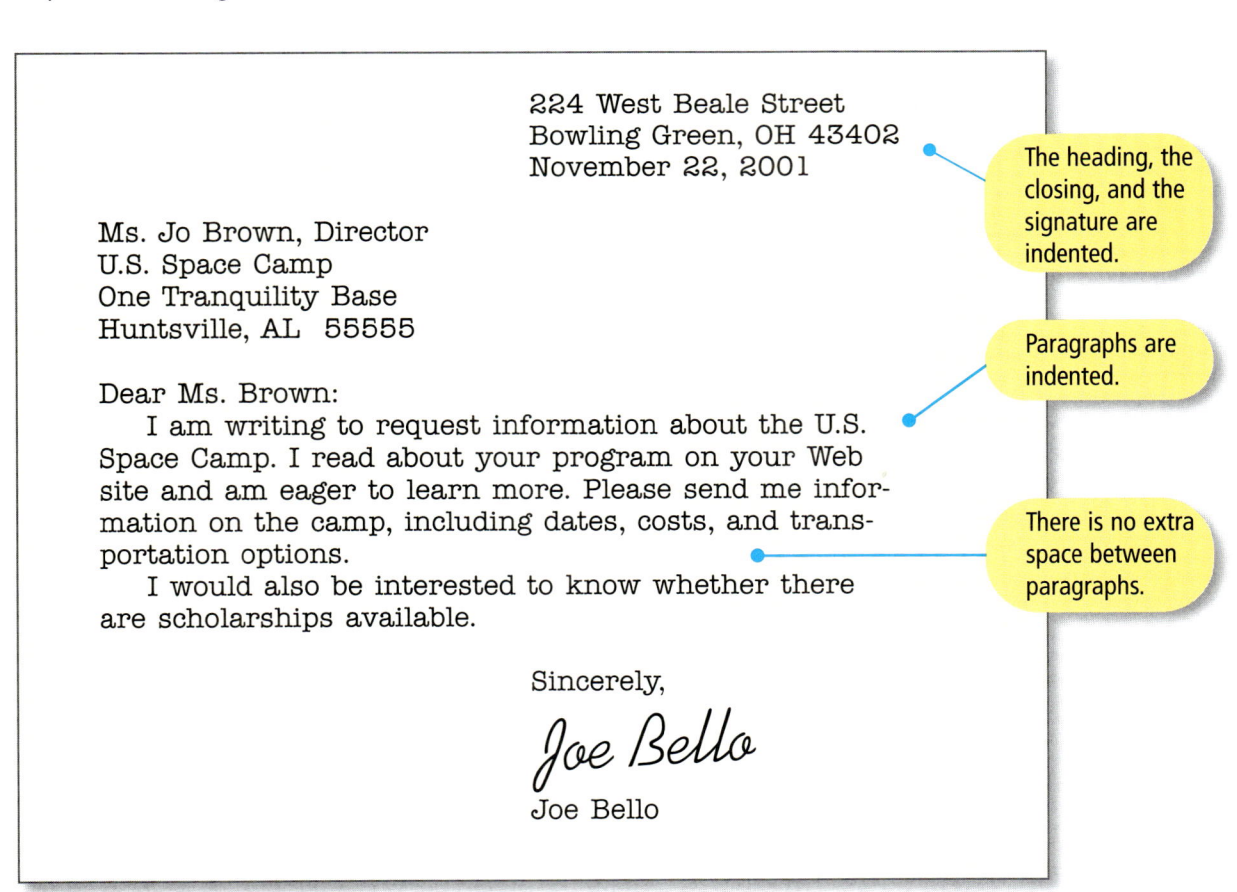

---

224 West Beale Street
Bowling Green, OH 43402
November 22, 2001

Ms. Jo Brown, Director
U.S. Space Camp
One Tranquility Base
Huntsville, AL 55555

Dear Ms. Brown:

    I am writing to request information about the U.S. Space Camp. I read about your program on your Web site and am eager to learn more. Please send me information on the camp, including dates, costs, and transportation options.
    I would also be interested to know whether there are scholarships available.

                          Sincerely,

                           Joe Bello

                           Joe Bello

- The heading, the closing, and the signature are indented.
- Paragraphs are indented.
- There is no extra space between paragraphs.

Business Letters

Body The body contains your message. Be sure to put the most important information in the first paragraph of your letter or as close to the beginning as possible. Tell your reader clearly and simply what you want. Because you want your letter to be easy to read, break a long message into several short paragraphs and leave as much white space as possible.

Closing The closing is a final word or phrase, such as *Yours truly*, *Sincerely*, *Sincerely yours*, *Best regards*, or *Respectfully*. The second word of a closing is not capitalized. The closing is followed by a comma.

Signature and Name Type your name four lines below the closing. Sign your name in the space between the closing and your typed name. If your first name could belong to either a male or a female, include *Miss*, *Mrs.*, *Ms.*, or *Mr.* in parentheses before your typed name and your signature.

Personal Letter

A business letter is usually written to a stranger. A personal letter is written to someone you know personally, such as a friend or a relative. Its language is less formal than that in a business letter. It differs from a business letter also in its use of indentation, spacing, and punctuation following the salutation. Following is an example of a personal letter written for business purposes.

---

224 West Beale Street
Bowling Green, OH 43402
November 22, 2001

Bart Hopkins
2150 Richmond Rd.
Toledo, OH 43605

Dear Uncle Bart,

    It was great to see you last week. I really enjoyed our conversation. As you suggested, I am looking into several specialty camps for this summer. One of the programs requires that I submit the names of two references. One of those can be a relative. Would you be willing to serve as a reference for me?

    I'll call you next week to find out your decision. Thanks so much.

Love,

Joe

The heading, the closing, and the signature are indented to the right.

A comma follows the salutation.

The language is less formal than that used in a business letter.

The writer's name is not repeated following the signature.

416   Business and Technical Writing

Business Letters

Types of Business Letters

There are several types of business letters. For example, you can use a business letter to request information or assistance, to make a complaint, to apologize for an error, to express an opinion, or to apply for a job. Although their basic form is always the same, the bodies of the various types of business letters differ in organization, structure, and style, depending on their purpose.

Request The key to writing an effective letter of request is to ask for what you want in the first paragraph. Then, in the paragraphs that follow, point out how you wish the recipient to respond. If you are requesting several items, indicate in a bulleted list what you want, as modeled in the first box below.

```
Please send the following items:
• two 20 pound bags of dog food
• one 5 pound bag of dog treats
• one 6 foot leash, black
```

A request for assistance requires an approach that is different from placing an order or asking for information. The tone of the letter should be respectful but not pleading or demanding. To write a request for assistance, use this approach:

1. Acquaint the reader with the basics of the situation.
2. Provide details.
3. Make it easy for the reader to do as you ask.

```
    I am writing to ask a favor of you. Would you lend
me your video camera for one month so that I can com-
plete a project I am working on at school?
    I will be extremely careful with the equipment and
will make sure that no one else has access to it.
```

Business and Technical Writing

Business Letters

Complaint When writing to complain about a product or service, first decide what you want the company to do. Do you want an apology, a replacement, or a refund, or would you like the company to change a product or service it provides?

In the first paragraph, explain the problem and ask for exactly what you want. When your tone is polite but firm, you are more likely to get a positive response. The formality of your letter conveys the idea that your complaint is to be taken seriously. Note the writer's approach in the sample letter of complaint shown below.

> Recently I ordered the enclosed sweatshirt from your catalogue. When the sweatshirt was washed according to the directions on the label, the logo dyed the whole shirt pink. I would like a full refund.

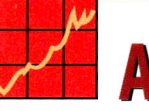

Activity

Use the Internet and the library to find information on summer-camp experiences for teenagers. Choose one camp that you think you might like to attend and write a business letter to request information about its activities, fees, requirements, and dates of operation. Use either block or modified block format.

PURPOSE To write a business letter requesting information
AUDIENCE Camp director
LENGTH 1 page

WRITING RUBRICS When writing a letter of request, you should
- write clearly and succinctly
- state your request in the first paragraph of the letter
- use polite but conversational language
- proofread your letter for errors in grammar, spelling, and mechanics
- use correct spacing and alignment

Business Letters

Apology There are two keys to writing an effective apology. First, be sure not to trivialize the concern of the person who made the complaint. Too often people who write apologies say things such as "I'm very sorry for any inconvenience you experienced." To the person who bothered to complain, *inconvenience* is probably much too weak a word to describe the experience.

Second, do not make excuses. The person who complained does not want to hear about how "the computer was down" or how "we were really busy." Apologize simply and directly. Note that the writer of the sample below takes the complaint seriously and doesn't offer excuses for the error.

> Thank you for alerting us to the fact that the dye used on the logo of your sweatshirt was not colorfast. We are enclosing a check for the full price of the shirt and are returning our entire stock of the item to the manufacturer. We can assure you that this will not happen again. Please bring the enclosed gift certificate with you the next time you come in, and we'll be happy to take $5.00 off your next purchase.

Business Letters

Opinion When you write to state your opinion, you are doing so in the hope of persuading others to adopt your point of view. Begin by expressing what you believe. If you are disagreeing with another point of view, state the opposing position clearly and correctly. This strategy avoids giving the impression that you are attacking a point of view you do not appreciate or understand. In the sample below, note the effort the writer makes to show an understanding of the other point of view.

Whenever you express an opinion, be sure that your facts are correct and your writing is error free. Your credibility as a writer is important, and mistakes in your letter will negatively affect the impact of your letter.

> I believe we should adopt block scheduling at Witmore High. Block schedules permit more in-depth study of a subject, and lengthened class times permit more discussion and participation than in standard class schedules. Although the traditional schedule has the advantage of providing a full year's worth of exposure, I believe the more concentrated effort required in a block schedule will eventually result in greater learning and improved retention.

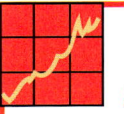

Activity

Select an issue that concerns you and write a letter to the editor of your local or school newspaper expressing your opinion on that issue. Before you write, take time to investigate and understand the other position or positions on the issue. Be sure to find out the publisher's guidelines for the length of your letter. Use either the block or the modified block format.

PURPOSE	To write a letter to the editor
AUDIENCE	Readers of your local or school newspaper
LENGTH	1 page

WRITING RUBRICS To write an effective letter of opinion, you should

- state your opinion clearly in a reasonable tone
- provide evidence or reasons to support your opinion
- give a fair picture of the opposing points of view
- make sure your statements are accurate

Memos, E-mail, and Applications

For most workers, memos and e-mail messages are far more common in their business life than letters. Applications are a form of communication almost everyone will come across sooner or later.

Memos

A memo (short for *memorandum*) is a letter that is written and distributed within a school, a business, or an organization. It shares many of the characteristics of the business letter but is less formal.

The memo is designed for maximum efficiency. Typically, it is one page or less in length, and all text aligns flush with the left margin. The heading is double-spaced and indicates to whom the memo was sent, who wrote it, the date it was sent, and what it is about. The body of the memo is single-spaced with a line space between paragraphs. The content is direct and to the point. Because the writer has already been identified in the heading, there is no closing or signature.

One of the advantages of the memo format is that the recipient can write a response on the memo itself before returning it. If you choose, you can end the memo with the word *Response:* or *Comment:* to make clear that you expect only a quick, handwritten reply.

To: All French Club Members

From: Beth Jones *BJ*

Date: November 10, 2000

Re: French Club meetings

The French Club has decided to change the date of its regular meeting from the first Tuesday of every month to the first Wednesday. Many members had scheduling conflicts on Tuesdays. Our meeting location will not change.

Thanks.

Memos may be sent to an individual or to a group.

Because the memo begins with a subject line, there is no need to repeat the subject at the beginning of the letter. You can deliver your message immediately and directly.

There is no closing or signature, but the writer can initial his or her name in writing on the From: *line.*

Business and Technical Writing   **421**

Memos, E-mail, and Applications

E-mail

Of all the forms of business communication, e-mail is by far the most informal. E-mail often reads like the transcript of a conversation.

Writers of e-mail need to analyze their audiences. Sentence fragments, colloquial language, and abbreviations may be fine in notes to friends, but they are not appropriate for many business exchanges.

For anyone other than a close friend, an e-mail message should be similar to a memo in format and style. The subject line is very important, because many readers use it to decide whether to open the message immediately.

When answering an e-mail, repeat enough of the original message to remind its writer of the context so that he or she doesn't have to guess what you are replying to. For example, answering "Sure, anytime" to an e-mail may be more puzzling than helpful.

Because you cannot always format an e-mail message as you can a letter, communications that must be somewhat formal should be written in a word processing program and e-mailed as attachments. Sending an attachment in most e-mail programs requires that you click on the Attachment button, type in the path and file name, and click on OK.

Activity

Imagine that as a member of the drama club, you have been asked to write a memo to all students requesting the donation of items to be used as props in plays. Mention the kinds of items you need and where and when they can be dropped off.

PURPOSE To write a memo

AUDIENCE All students in the school

LENGTH 1 or 2 paragraphs and a list

WRITING RUBRICS To write an effective memo, you should

- use the correct format
- convey the message clearly and concisely
- include all necessary information
- proofread for errors in spelling, grammar, and information that includes dates, times, or addresses

Memos, E-mail, and Applications

Applications

In your lifetime, you will complete many application forms. You may apply for library cards, credit, a driver's license, a marriage license, bank accounts, a social security card, memberships in organizations, and various jobs. There may also be forms to fill out for attending camps, colleges, and trade schools and for renting or buying a place to live.

It is important that an application form be completed accurately and neatly. A form that is incomplete or that contains incorrect information can cause problems and delays. In the hiring process, many employers use the application form as an indicator of a person's aptitude for a job. If the application form is incomplete or looks sloppy, the person may not be considered for the position. It is a good idea to ask for more than one copy of any application form that you are going to complete. You can fill out one copy in pencil, making changes until you are sure all the information is correct and in the right place. Then you can transfer the information in ink onto the copy that you will submit.

There are four important things to remember when filling out an application form:

1. Read the instructions, if any, and the entire form carefully before writing anything.
2. Use your best printing or handwriting. Neatness counts.
3. Fill in all the blanks. If the information asked for does not apply to you, write *n/a* (not applicable) in the blank. Leaving the blank empty suggests that you have something to hide or that you did not read the form carefully.
4. Complete the form in ink, preferably blue or black.

Study the sample application shown on page 424.

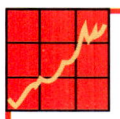

Activity

Obtain an application form for one of the following: organization membership, library card, apartment rental, credit card, savings account, loan, driver's license, volunteer work. Print two copies of the form. Complete a practice copy in pencil. Then complete a final copy in ink. Work with a partner to evaluate each other's work.

PURPOSE To complete a sample application

AUDIENCE Your classmates

LENGTH 1 or 2 pages

WRITING RUBRICS To prepare an application form properly, you should

- read the instructions and the entire form before you begin writing
- use a duplicate form as your draft version
- answer every question; leave no blanks
- place information on the form correctly
- print (preferably) or write neatly and legibly
- proofread for spelling and punctuation errors
- transfer the revised information in blue or black ink to the final form

Memos, E-mail, and Applications

Sample Application

Volunteer Application Form

Thank you for considering volunteer work at the Beckwith Library.

Name: _Quinn Peterson_   Date _January 20, 2001_
Address: _3532 11th Avenue North_
City: _Grand Forks_   State: _ND_   Zip: _58203_
Phone: _701-555-1212_   Fax: _701-555-5510_
DOB: _11/29/87_   SSN: _123-45-6789_
Best times to reach you: _After 3:30 p.m. weekdays_
Education (*circle highest level completed*):
    7   **(8)**   9   10   11   12
Is this experience for school credit?   Yes   **(No)**
School name and address: _Lake Agassiz School_
Why do you want to volunteer?

I have good organization skills and I know I would be an asset to the library staff. In addition, I am already very familiar with the layout of the library because I spend a lot of time there. I enjoy reading aloud to my little brother; I would especially like to be a volunteer reader during the story hour.

Describe previous volunteer experience.
    n/a

Signature: *Quinn Peterson*

- Note that the form is filled out neatly in blue ink.
- Abbreviations commonly used on applications include DOB (date of birth) and SSN or SS# (social security number).
- Include hyphens in your social security number.
- If the information asked for does not apply to you, write *n/a* in the blank.

Business and Technical Writing

Using the Computer as a Writing Tool

A computer is useful in researching information, creating and formatting documents, and presenting data graphically. Instructions that are given in this section for these functions are quite general. Every word processing, desktop publishing, or spreadsheet program works somewhat differently. To learn to use the capabilities of your computer software, read the instruction manual that comes with it or use the Help menu.

Making Tables and Graphs

You can use your word processing program to display information and data in tables or graphs. Keep in mind that in many software programs, tables and graphs are referred to as charts.

Tables Tables organize information into columns and rows. Columns are the vertical elements in a table, and rows are the horizontal elements. Cells are the individual boxes that contain data.

To make a table in most word processing programs, use the Table pull-down menu and then select the number of rows and columns you need. After you have created the table, you can insert or delete rows and columns as often as you wish. The table below was created with fifteen rows and five columns.

Many options allow you to customize a table. You can change the width of columns and the height of rows, add or alter borders, add color to the table, and change the way you align numbers within cells. Some table menus have a Quick Sum function that allows you to calculate sums by placing your cursor in the box where you want the sum to appear and clicking on the Quick Sum key.

Data entered in a table can be aligned right or left, centered in a cell, or aligned on a decimal point (as shown below). As you enter data, use the Tab key to move from cell to cell. By hitting the Enter key, you can create an additional row for data.

Income for Year

Month	Lawn Mowing	Snow Shoveling	Paper Route	Total for Month
January	$0.00	$37.75	$26.55	$64.30
February	$0.00	$42.50	$29.90	$72.40
March	$0.00	$22.00	$27.75	$49.75
April	$30.75	$0.00	$23.00	$53.75
May	$75.00	$0.00	$27.00	$102.00
June	$70.00	$0.00	$28.95	$98.95
July	$65.75	$0.00	$28.55	$94.30
August	$60.00	$0.00	$29.00	$89.00
September	$55.00	$0.00	$27.00	$82.00
October	$0.00	$0.00	$22.00	$22.00
November	$0.00	$0.00	$27.00	$27.00
December	$0.00	$34.75	$29.50	$64.25
Total	$356.50	$137.00	$326.20	$819.70

Using the Computer as a Writing Tool

Graphs While a table helps readers find, compare, and contrast data quickly, a graph highlights a comparison or contrast by showing it pictorially. Use the following information to help you choose the appropriate format in which to display data.

A **bar graph** usually shows numbers or quantities and is used to showcase comparisons or contrasts. It plots data along a vertical line called the y-axis and a horizontal line called the x-axis. The vertical or y-axis includes a scale showing the numbers involved. Both axes should be labeled.

The bar graph below compares the numbers of a school's freshmen, sophomores, juniors, and seniors on the honor roll at the end of a school year. Note that the bar graph does not provide information about the total number of students in the school. Therefore, comparisons should be made with caution.

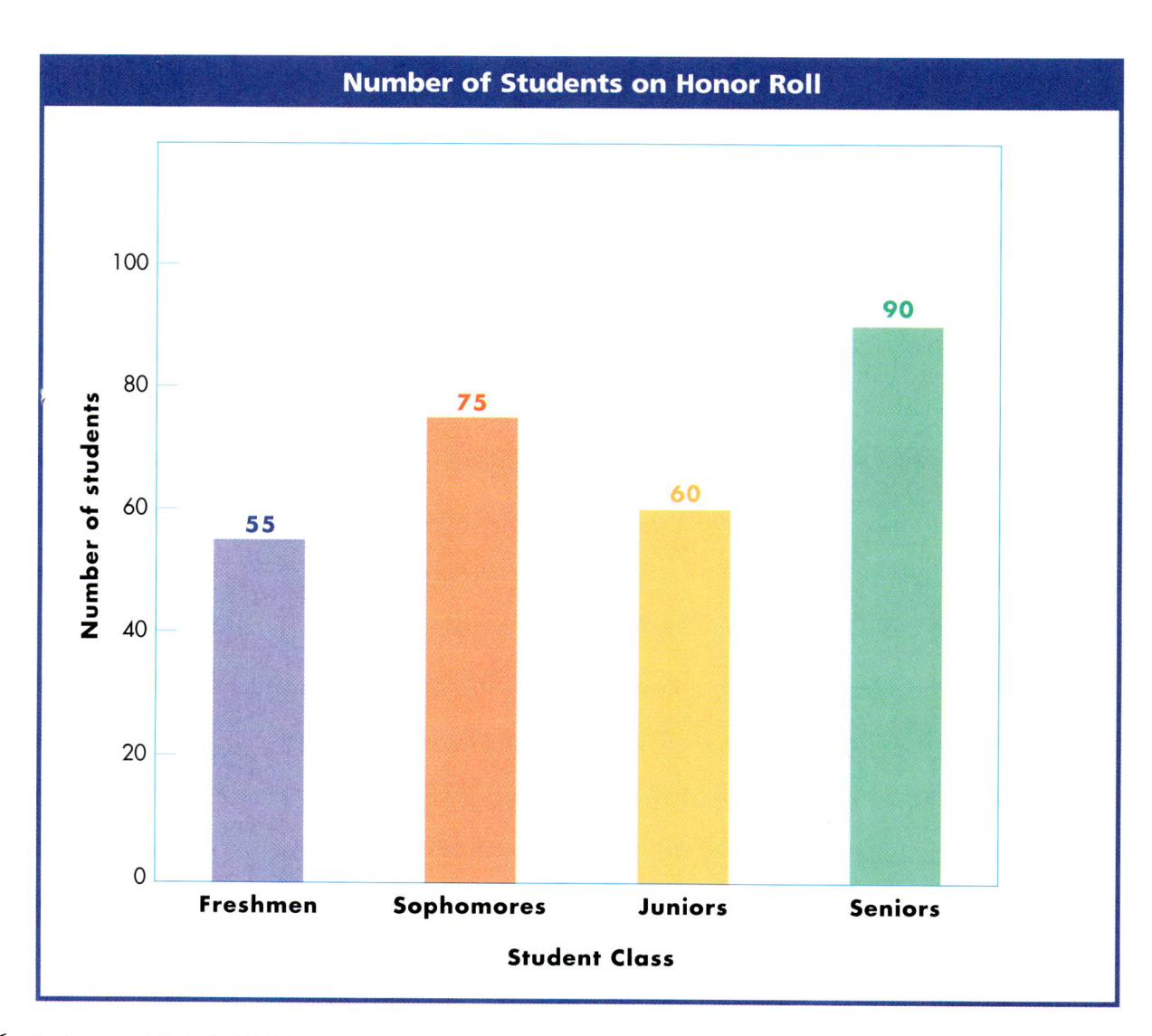

Number of Students on Honor Roll

Student Class	Number of students
Freshmen	55
Sophomores	75
Juniors	60
Seniors	90

Business & Technical Writing

Using the Computer as a Writing Tool

A **circle graph** or **pie chart** shows the relationship of parts to a whole. Each part can be expressed as a number or a percentage. The whole is always 100 percent. The circle graph below shows the distribution of elements within Earth's crust.

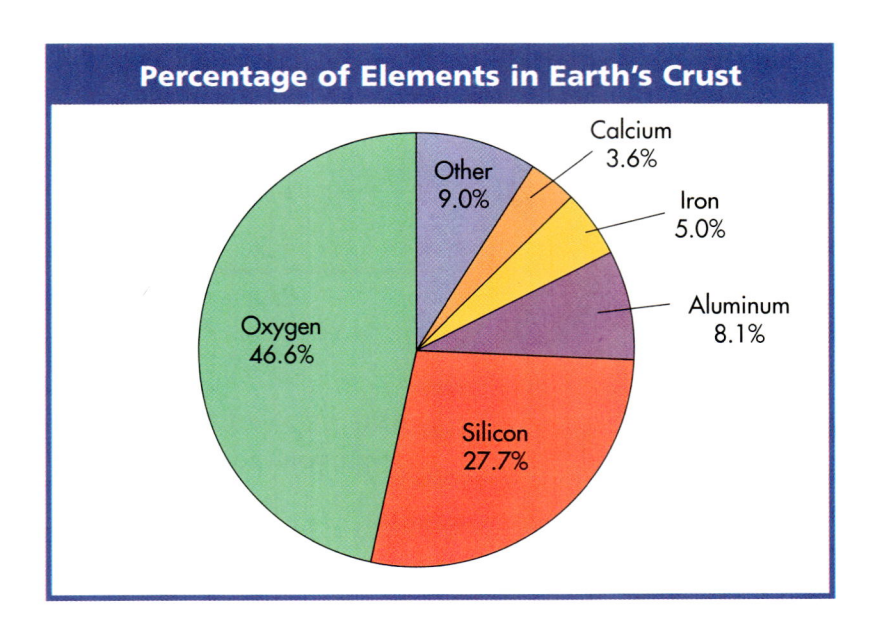

Percentage of Elements in Earth's Crust

- Oxygen 46.6%
- Silicon 27.7%
- Aluminum 8.1%
- Iron 5.0%
- Calcium 3.6%
- Other 9.0%

A **line graph** is used to show changes in numbers or quantities over time. The line graph below shows how waste in the United States was disposed of over a thirty-year period.

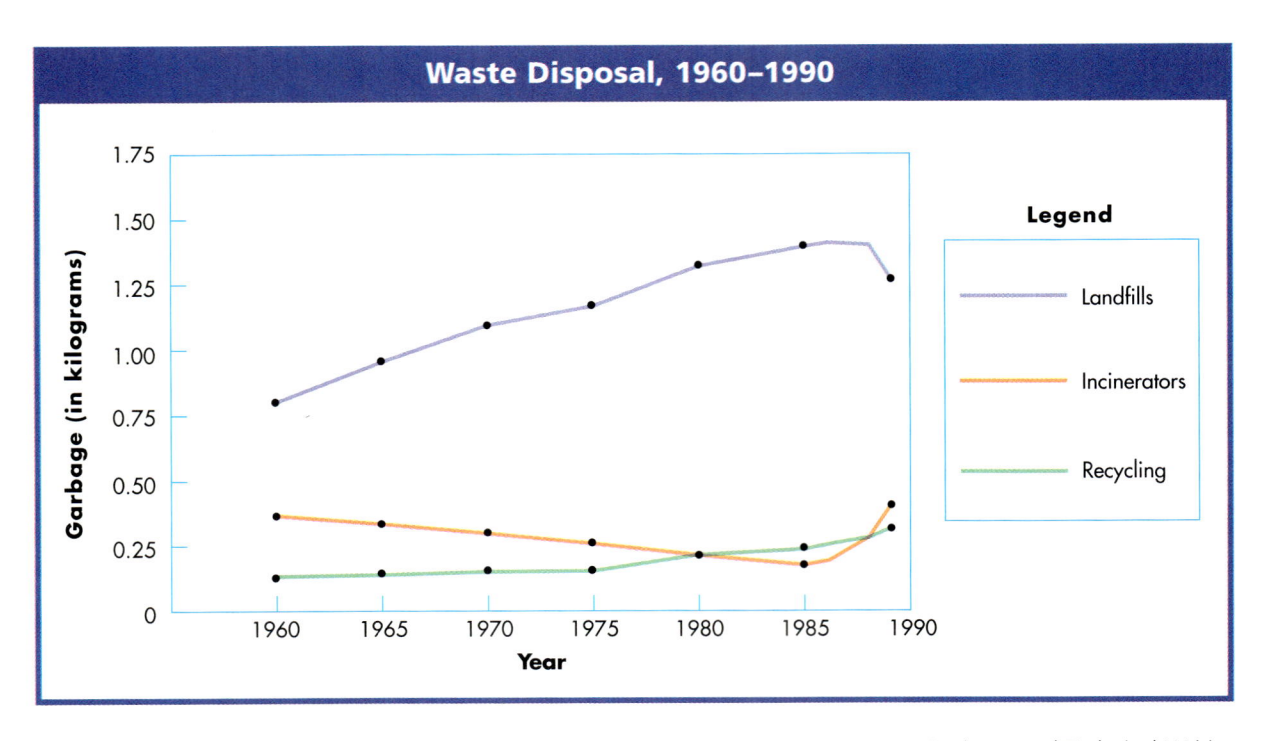

Waste Disposal, 1960–1990

Legend:
- Landfills
- Incinerators
- Recycling

Garbage (in kilograms) vs. Year (1960–1990)

Business and Technical Writing

Using the Computer as a Writing Tool

To create a graph in a word processing program that includes a graphing feature, you enter data directly into a table (called a worksheet) designed to work with the graphing function. Once the data has been entered, choose the kind of graph you want, enter titles, labels, and a legend, and click on OK. The word processor will create the graph for you and insert it into your document. If you discover an error in your graph after it has been inserted into the document, simply double click on the graph to return to the editing function. In some programs, you can switch between one kind of graph and another once the data has been entered to see which best conveys your information.

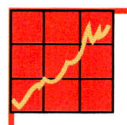

Activity

Gather statistical data about a school topic of interest to you. You might investigate how often tacos are served for lunch in a given month, how many people in each of your classes are absent on a given day, or how often the football team has won in each year of the last five years. Once you have collected the data, use your word processing program to convert it into a graph. Select the format that you think best showcases your information, insert the data, and print the graph. Present your graph to the class and explain why you chose that format.

PURPOSE To gather and present data in a graph
AUDIENCE Classmates
LENGTH 1 page

WRITING RUBRICS To prepare an effective graph, you should

- choose data that can be presented pictorially
- select a format that is appropriate for the audience
- present the data, using the most effective format for conveying your message
- include a descriptive title, labels, and (if needed) a legend
- proofread for accuracy

Using the Computer as a Writing Tool

Creating Organization Charts

Many word processing programs have an Organization Chart function under the Draw menu. An **organization chart** shows the relative standings or rankings of individuals or positions in an organization. Check your Help menu to see if your program has an Organization Chart function. Even if your program does not come with a template for creating organization charts, you may be able to use the drawing tools to create them.

To make an organization chart, click on the appropriate icon and then select the type you want. You can choose a vertical or a horizontal orientation. You can use the ready-made chart structure or alter it by changing the placement of boxes or modifying the branching structure. Once you have designed the structure, simply type in the names, titles, steps, or other information you need. The example below shows the basic organization of the federal government.

The Government of the United States

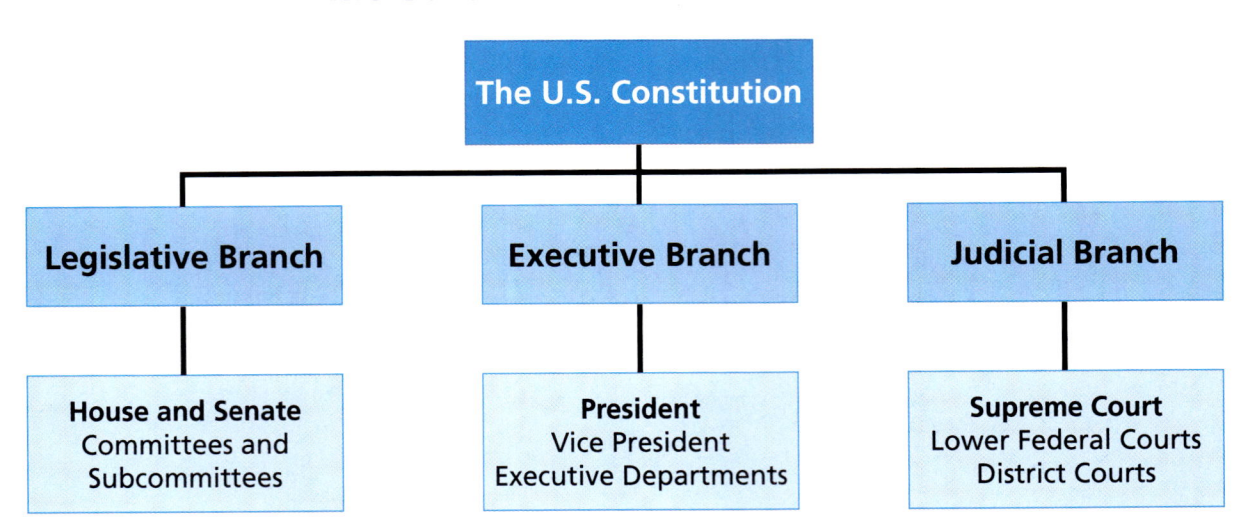

- **The U.S. Constitution**
  - **Legislative Branch**
    - House and Senate
    - Committees and Subcommittees
  - **Executive Branch**
    - President
    - Vice President
    - Executive Departments
  - **Judicial Branch**
    - Supreme Court
    - Lower Federal Courts
    - District Courts

Business and Technical Writing

Using the Computer as a Writing Tool

Creating Flowcharts

A **flowchart** highlights a different kind of relationship—the steps in a process. The flowchart example below shows the steps in making an investment decision. Remember always to include a descriptive title for any table, chart, or graph you create.

Making an Investment Decision

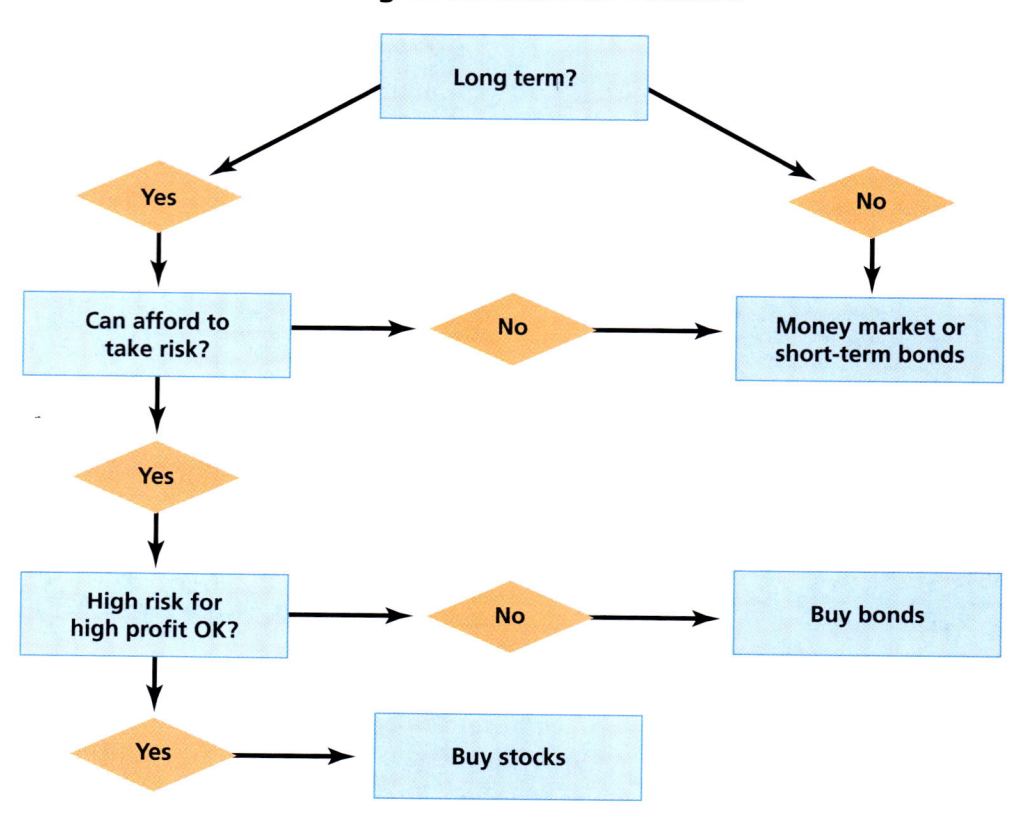

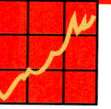

```
                    Long term?
                   /          \
                 Yes           No
                  |             |
          Can afford to  ──No──▶ Money market or
          take risk?             short-term bonds
                  |
                 Yes
                  |
          High risk for  ──No──▶ Buy bonds
          high profit OK?
                  |
                 Yes ──▶ Buy stocks
```

Activity

Use your computer to create a flowchart that outlines the steps in a process. Select a simple process with several steps. For example, it might be how to install software on a hard drive, change a tire, or study for a test.

PURPOSE To create a flowchart
AUDIENCE Your teachers and classmates
LENGTH 1 page

WRITING RUBRICS To create an effective flowchart, you should
- identify each step and its place in the process
- write a title for the chart
- be consistent in labeling
- check for accuracy

Business and Technical Writing

Technical Writing

Technical writing translates technical and scientific information into language that is easy to read and understand. The style of technical writing is simple and direct.

Elements of Technical Writing

Accuracy, consistency, clarity, and brevity are the most important elements of technical writing.

Accuracy Although errors in any kind of writing are undesirable, errors in technical writing must be avoided at all costs. For example, consider that merely substituting the word *left* for the word *right* in directions for the assembly of parts can lead to disaster if the item being assembled is an airplane or an industrial boiler.

Consistency Technical writers and copyeditors use a uniform style in their final drafts. Most companies that issue technical documents and reports use a manual of style to help establish consistency in the use of such matters as capitalization, abbreviations, and punctuation. For your purposes, you can use a standard style guide such as *The Chicago Manual of Style*.

Clarity In technical writing, the goal is to translate scientific or technical information into language that is easy to read and understand. Thus, a technical writer must be aware of his or her audience. Language appropriate for an audience of engineers may baffle nontechnical readers. On the other hand, if a document is intended for engineers, translating its technical terms into everyday language may complicate the writing unnecessarily.

Brevity Readers should not be hindered by long, convoluted sentences and poor organization. Therefore, a technical writer should use short sentences, bulleted lists, and brief paragraphs to convey information. Long reports should include a table of contents, and the text should be divided into chapters or sections. Presenting information in graphs, tables, or other pictorial forms is another way to communicate complex data in an easy-to-understand format.

A technical report or paper often begins with an abstract that summarizes the document in one tightly written paragraph. Many readers rely on the abstract to help them decide whether the document is one they need to read in its entirety. At the end of a technical report, there is often an appendix that contains details that are too cumbersome to include in the body of the report.

Technical Writing

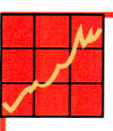

Activity

Read an article from *Discover*, *National Geographic*, *Psychology Today*, or *Nature*. Write an abstract of no more than 250 words that provides a summary of the article. Attach a copy of the original article to the abstract. Exchange abstracts with a partner and critique each other's work. Evaluate how well you summarized the articles.

PURPOSE To write an abstract of an article
AUDIENCE A partner
LENGTH 250 words or less

WRITING RUBRICS To write an effective abstract, you should

- summarize the major points of the original article
- write simply and succinctly
- state the conclusion clearly

Writing Instructions

Giving directions is a form of technical writing. To write meaningful instructions, you must thoroughly understand the process you are describing. Then you must recall what it was like not to understand it, so that you can explain it fully to others. You must reacquaint yourself with those steps in the process that have become automatic. For example, when parents teach their children to drive, they often have to stop to think about exactly how they execute a particular maneuver that has become automatic over time.

When writing instructions, remember to list all the tools and equipment needed to perform a task first, just as you would list the ingredients for a recipe before the instructions for putting them together. You do not want to send the reader to the basement or to the store in the middle of a project because you forgot to mention that it requires a socket wrench or a staple gun. Divide the process for which you are writing instructions into clearly defined steps. Then put those steps in the correct order so that a person who performs the process does not have to repeat steps or backtrack. It is important to define terms in the instructions that may be unfamiliar to some people. For example, someone who has never used a computer may not know what a cursor is.

Technical Writing

Include Visuals Use drawings and illustrations to supplement your text and to help a reader picture particularly complicated steps. A flowchart can help the reader visualize the process.

As you write instructions, remember that people approach tasks in different ways. Some will read the directions thoroughly; others will look only at illustrations; and still others will take a more experimental approach, resorting to directions and illustrations when all else fails. The best instructions are flexible and can be used easily no matter how a person approaches a task.

Hints for Technical Writing

Technical writers of instruction manuals recommend the following:
- Show or describe the finished product so that the reader knows the goal.
- List all required parts and tools at the outset.
- Label each step clearly: *Step One—Open the box.*
- Use imperative sentences: *Sort the parts by color.*
- Spell out even those steps that seem obvious: *Open the hood of the car.*
- Check for any errors or omissions. Try to follow the directions exactly as they are written and then ask someone else to follow them. This will help you to identify instructions that are confusing or difficult to understand.

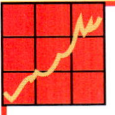

Activity

Select a task that can be performed in the classroom with readily available materials. It can be something as simple as sharpening a pencil or opening a window, as long as it has at least five steps. Write step-by-step instructions for performing the task. Assume that the person who will be following the directions has never performed the task. When your instructions are complete, ask a classmate to use them to perform the task. Have the classmate follow your instructions to the letter and then evaluate them for clarity and precision.

PURPOSE To write a set of clear instructions
AUDIENCE Your teacher and your classmates
LENGTH 1 page

WRITING RUBRICS To write effective instructions, you should
- list the tools and equipment needed
- identify the steps in the process
- put the steps in chronological order
- label each step
- write with clarity
- use helpful visuals
- consider the level of knowledge of the audience
- proofread for spelling and grammatical errors and vague language
- test for omissions

Business and Technical Writing

Collaborative Writing in the Business World

Today, most organizations stress collaboration and teamwork. People analyze and solve problems in groups, evaluate one another's performances, and report to management, customers, or clients as a team. Many businesses rely on the team approach because a group generates more and better ideas than its members do individually, and creativity is enhanced when people share ideas in open discussion.

Collaborating on a project can be frustrating and time consuming unless those involved know how to work together effectively. When people work in a group, there is always a risk that the more outgoing members may make it difficult for those who are more reserved to contribute. Some group members may be reluctant to challenge ideas and will go along with the majority even when they disagree. In fact, sometimes an entire group will follow a course of action that few individuals in the group actually think is a good idea.

On the other hand, there are few experiences more satisfying than a team experience in which everyone participates to create a first-class product. The key to working effectively in a group is active listening. To listen actively, you should

- make sure that everyone's point of view is not only heard but also understood
- pay attention to what others say and paraphrase their ideas to be sure that you have understood them
- avoid interrupting and try not to disagree with someone before he or she has fully expressed a point of view
- ask open-ended questions

Collaborative Writing in the Business World

Members of a group that is assigned a project should use the following approach. Begin by discussing the project and coming to an agreement on its purpose and its audience. Be as concrete and specific as possible: *The purpose of this report is to convince the administration of Central High to restore senior privileges for the coming year.* Do not assume that every member of the group understands or agrees on the purpose or the audience. Discuss both thoroughly and record the statements with which everyone is in agreement.

Don't try to create the project as a group. Assign sections of the document to individuals in the group. Then have the entire group evaluate each section, suggest revisions, and proofread the final document. In making the assignments, use the strengths of group members. One person may be especially good at research on the Internet; another may be more knowledgeable about library reference sources; still another may be able to create professional-looking graphics.

Be aware of potential interpersonal problems. If someone is not pulling his or her weight or is refusing to participate, meet as a group to discuss the problem. Use active listening skills. Don't accuse. Don't interrupt. Do try to find a mutually agreeable solution.

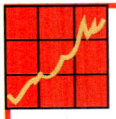

Activity

Work in a small group to create a new game—a board game, a computer game, or any other type of game. You can even base it on an existing game, as long as it is sufficiently changed to constitute something new. Work together to create game parts and packaging, a rules booklet for the game, a print advertisement (newspaper, magazine, poster, billboard), and a radio or TV commercial.

PURPOSE To create a new game as a group
AUDIENCE Game players
LENGTH As needed

PROJECT RUBRIC To complete the group game project, you should
- work effectively as a group
- create an original game
- write effective rules for playing the game
- create game parts and packaging
- create advertising for both print and electronic media

"As usual, in the towns of Ghana, the streets were filled with vendors selling their wares."

Maya Angelou

PART 2
Grammar, Usage and Mechanics

Unit 10	Parts of Speech	438
Unit 11	Parts of the Sentence	494
Unit 12	Phrases	518
Unit 13	Clauses and Sentence Structure	538
Unit 14	Diagramming Sentences	570
Unit 15	Verb Tenses and Voice	580
Unit 16	Subject-Verb Agreement	608
Unit 17	Using Pronouns Correctly	632
Unit 18	Using Modifiers Correctly	658
Unit 19	Usage Glossary	686
Unit 20	Capitalization	710
Unit 21	Punctuation, Abbreviations and Numbers	730

Ghanaian water jugs

UNIT 10 Parts of Speech

Lesson 10.1 **Nouns**	*439*
Lesson 10.2 **Pronouns**	*446*
Lesson 10.3 **Verbs**	*452*
Lesson 10.4 **Adjectives**	*461*
Lesson 10.5 **Adverbs**	*467*
Lesson 10.6 **Prepositions**	*473*
Lesson 10.7 **Conjunctions**	*475*
Lesson 10.8 **Interjections**	*481*
Grammar Review	482
Writing Application	493

10.1 Nouns

■ A **noun** is a word that names a person, a place, a thing, or an idea.

PERSON	teacher, uncle, niece, sister-in-law
PLACE	garage, city, park, school
THING	paw, giraffe, bicycle, ice cream, doorknob
IDEA	democracy, fame, love, disappointment

Exercise 1   Identifying Nouns

On your paper, list the twenty-five nouns that appear in the following literary passage.

Literature: In a New Country

Hanging from a cord attached to the middle of the ceiling there was an electric bulb, low enough for an adult to reach and turn the black switch. I realized that this was our own electric light for us to turn on and off as we pleased. I pushed a chair under it and after some instruction from my mother proceeded to create lightning in the room by turning the switch as fast as I could.

Next I discovered the bedsprings. When I sat on the bed it sank deliciously. Jumping on it in my stocking feet, I held my balance dangerously as I made the bed creak and the mattress bounce. The head and foot of the bed were made of iron scrollwork in loops and rosettes painted white.

From *Barrio Boy* by Ernesto Galarza

Exercise 2   Completing Sentences with Nouns

On your paper, write nouns to complete the following sentences. Be sure that your completed sentences make sense.

1. The _____ galloped by on her _____.
2. Ten of her _____ waved their blue _____.
3. The other _____ of her _____ cheered.
4. Her yellow _____ blew off her _____.
5. The _____ made her _____ fly wildly.
6. Three miniature _____ sat on the _____.
7. Their _____ were brushing their _____.
8. The _____ and her _____ approached the _____.
9. They walked their _____ and held their _____.
10. Everyone gathered around the tiny _____.

10.1 Nouns   **439**

Singular and Plural Nouns

- **Nouns** can be singular or plural, depending upon whether they name *one* person, place, thing, or idea or *more than one.*

To form the plural of most nouns, add *-s.* Other plural nouns are formed in different ways. For nouns ending in *-s, -ch, -sh, -x,* or *-zz,* add *-es* to form the plural. For nouns ending in *-y* preceded by a consonant, change the *-y* to *-i* and add *-es.* For most nouns ending in *-f* or *-fe,* change *-f* to *-v* and add *-es.* Other nouns have irregular plurals (e.g., *woman, women*). Some nouns do not change form from singular to plural (e.g., *sheep, sheep*).

SINGULAR boy, body, watch, wife, ox
PLURAL boys, bodies, watches, wives, oxen

Exercise 3 Forming the Plurals of Nouns

Write the plural form of each noun below on your paper. Consult a dictionary if you need help.

1. victory
2. moose
3. lunch
4. box
5. mouse
6. video
7. man
8. half
9. goose
10. valley
11. business
12. batch
13. galaxy
14. radio
15. lens
16. chief
17. foot
18. deer
19. child
20. person

Exercise 4 Completing Sentences with Singular and Plural Nouns

On your paper, write singular or plural nouns to complete the following sentences. Be sure that your completed sentences make sense.

Heidelberg

1. The _____ of Heidelberg, Germany, is neither very large nor strategically important.
2. However, the _____ who live there boast of its beautiful _____.
3. Among the city's _____ are textiles, leather goods, and precision instruments.
4. A wide _____ flows through the _____.
5. Even the gabled _____ are an impressive _____.
6. The _____ is blessed with fertile _____ and a mild _____.
7. In the nineteenth century, the _____ of Heidelberg tripled.
8. Many modern _____ were constructed next to historic _____.
9. New _____ and _____ dotted the _____.
10. Nevertheless, the _____ remain committed to preserving their _____.

Possessive Nouns

The possessive form of a noun can show possession, ownership, or the general relationship between two nouns. Add an apostrophe and -s to form the possessive of a singular noun, even one that already ends in -s. Use an apostrophe alone to form the possessive of a plural noun that ends in -s.

SINGULAR POSSESSIVE	PLURAL POSSESSIVE
the **car's** hood	the **cars'** hoods
a **baby's** bottle	the **babies'** bottles
the **dish's** pattern	the **dishes'** patterns
a **valley's** towns	the **valleys'** towns
the **calf's** mother	the **calves'** mother
the **business's** payroll	the **businesses'** payrolls

Add an apostrophe and -s to form the possessive of a plural noun that does not end in -s.

the **women's** decision

the **children's** toys

the **sheep's** wool

Exercise 5 Forming Possessive Nouns

Rewrite each phrase below, using the possessive form of the italicized noun.

1. the *cat* food
2. the *wagons* wheels
3. the *mice* cage
4. the *parents* advice
5. the *child* toy
6. the *oxen* horns
7. the *book* cover
8. the *family* car
9. the *trolleys* whistles
10. the *boys* homework
11. the *cities* facilities
12. the *states* rights
13. the *mattress* springs
14. the *people* choice
15. the *wives* party
16. the *churches* steeples
17. the *deer* food
18. the *region* climate
19. the *fox* den
20. the *factories* smokestacks

Exercise 6 Completing Sentences with Possessive Nouns

On your paper, write singular or plural possessive nouns to complete the following sentences. Be sure that your completed sentences make sense.

1. The _____ hearts began to pound as the chair lift brought them to the top of the _____ highest peak.
2. In the group behind them, their _____ face had a nervous look.
3. Only the young _____ voices sounded excited.
4. It had been the _____ idea to ski the _____ most challenging moguls.
5. Judy, the _____ most experienced skier, talked about the previous _____ trips.

10.1 Nouns **441**

Concrete and Abstract Nouns

- A **concrete noun** names an object that occupies space or that can be recognized by any of the senses.

    petal   smoke   cough   orange   nook

- An **abstract noun** names an idea, a quality, or a characteristic.

    motion   humor   quantity   tact   rudeness

Exercise 7   Identifying Nouns as Concrete or Abstract

On your paper, identify each noun as *concrete* or *abstract*.

1. wisdom
2. sunshine
3. book
4. bravery
5. attitude
6. library
7. music
8. guitar
9. happiness
10. electricity

Exercise 8   Using Abstract and Concrete Nouns

For each concrete noun in items 1–10, write an abstract noun that names an idea associated with the concrete noun. For each abstract noun in items 11–20, write a concrete noun that has the quality of the abstract noun.

SAMPLE ANSWERS   rocket—power   taste—salt

1. bicycle
2. laughter
3. itch
4. home run
5. snow
6. summer
7. apple
8. in-line skates
9. applause
10. sundowns
11. haste
12. warmth
13. poverty
14. insight
15. sadness
16. joy
17. gratitude
18. distraction
19. eagerness
20. softness

Exercise 9   Writing Sentences with Abstract Nouns

On your paper, write five sentences about what you think is important in life. In each sentence, use at least one abstract noun to identify a goal, idea, or personal trait you admire. Underline each abstract noun.

Proper and Common Nouns

■ A **proper noun** is the name of a particular person, place, thing, or idea.

Proper Nouns	
Person	Sean Connery, Uncle Peter, Emily Dickinson
Place	Mexico, Lake George, Grand Canyon
Thing	Statue of Liberty, *Great Expectations*, Thanksgiving
Idea	Romanticism, Baroque Age, Judaism

■ A **common noun** is the general—not the particular—name of a person, place, thing, or idea

Common Nouns	
Person	actor, uncle, poet
Place	country, lake, canyon
Thing	statue, book, holiday
Idea	movement, era, religion

Proper nouns are capitalized; common nouns are usually not capitalized.

Exercise 10   Matching Proper Nouns with Common Nouns

On your paper, match each proper noun on the left with the corresponding common noun on the right.

1. Middle Ages
2. *Romeo and Juliet*
3. Cuba
4. *The Wizard of Oz*
5. Renoir
6. Rocky Mountains
7. Chicago Cubs
8. San Francisco
9. Nile River
10. Houston Space Center

a. city
b. mountains
c. building complex
d. team
e. painter
f. play
g. river
h. country
i. era
j. motion picture

Exercise 11   Naming Proper Nouns

On your paper, add one more proper noun to each category that follows.

1. Wisconsin, North Dakota, New York, Georgia, _____
2. Atlantic, Antarctic, Indian, Arctic, _____

10.1 Nouns

3. Michael, Pedro, Gregory, Joel, _____
4. *Chicago Tribune, New York Times, Milwaukee Journal, Trumptown Herald,* _____
5. France, Ghana, Malaysia, Argentina, _____

Collective Nouns

■ A **collective noun** names a group.

family	(the) senate
(the) public	(a) gaggle (of geese)
team	(an) audience
(the) press	(the) board (of directors)

A collective noun is sometimes considered singular and sometimes considered plural. You consider a collective noun singular when you talk about a group as a whole. You consider a collective noun plural when you talk about the individual members of a group.

SINGULAR The audience shouts its approval.
PLURAL The audience have arrived in small groups.

Exercise 12 Identifying Collective Nouns

On your paper, list five collective nouns from each of the following paragraphs.

Porgy and Bess

¹The Metropolitan Opera's 1985 production of George Gershwin's *Porgy and Bess* had a chorus of seventy voices. ²The cast included such noted stars as Grace Bumbry and Simon Estes. ³The orchestra was conducted by James Levine. ⁴The audience had bought their tickets well in advance for all sixteen performances. ⁵The huge stage was filled with people representing the population of Catfish Row.

Animal Life in Africa

¹In Africa a team of zoologists can observe many kinds of wild animals. ²In a western forest might be seen a family of chimpanzees. ³In the eastern grasslands, quiet watchers might spy a herd of roaming zebras. ⁴In the northern desert, a flock of ostriches is not an uncommon sight. ⁵The African continent has an extraordinary collection of animal life.

The Power of the Press

¹The press plays an important and powerful role in contemporary life. ²Television news programs, newspapers, and periodicals reach a large and eager audience. ³As a result, journalists have a strong influence on society. ⁴Sometimes a team of reporters can make or break a candidate's campaign for office. ⁵To make an informed choice, the public must separate fact from opinion.

Exercise 13   **Identifying Nouns**

On your paper, identify each underlined noun as *common, proper,* or *collective,* depending upon how the noun is used in the sentence. Some nouns may belong in more than one category.

The Trail of Tears

In 1838 sixteen thousand Cherokee were forced from their [1]homes in the [2]Old South. Under armed guard, the [3]mass of Native Americans was pushed west across the [4]Mississippi River to Oklahoma's [5]Indian Territory. Other [6]cultures, including the Creek, Choctaw, and Chickasaw nations, were included in the removal [7]program. Many historians refer to this [8]journey west as the [9]Trail of Tears. They estimate that as many as a quarter of the [10]group may have died during the long and arduous migration.

Some [11]Native Americans rebelled against the removal program, while others fled to Canada or [12]Mexico. The Cherokee led the most organized [13]resistance. They had their own written language; their own [14]newspaper, the [15]*Cherokee Phoenix*; tax-supported schools; and a written [16]constitution. The Cherokee [17]nation also had the sympathy of some members of [18]Congress and of other government [19]officials. Although the Cherokee took legal action, they never were able to regain their [20]homelands.

Exercise 14   **Creating Sentences with Nouns**

On your paper, write five sentences about a shop in your town or neighborhood. Use concrete nouns to convey a vivid picture of the place.

Exercise 15   **Completing Sentences with Nouns**

On your paper, complete the paragraphs below by filling in each of the twenty blanks with the kind of noun specified in *italic* typeface. Be sure that your completed sentences make sense.

Thanksgiving Day

The festive [1]*abstract* of the Thanksgiving [2]*concrete* filled our [3]*concrete*. [4]*proper and concrete* told us the [5]*common* of the [6]*proper* who prepared the first Thanksgiving feast. All of the young [7]*common* listened. The table, set with our best [8]*concrete*, held steaming platters of [9]*concrete* and [10]*concrete*. For [11]*common* each of us had a generous [12]*common* of [13]*concrete*.

After dinner we sat by the blazing [14]*concrete*, and [15]*proper and concrete* told us that it was President Lincoln who declared Thanksgiving an official holiday. Then we turned on the [16]*concrete* and watched [17]*proper and concrete*. Later that [18]*common*, we agreed that we had had so much good [19]*abstract* we wished that [20]*proper* came more than once a year.

10.1 Nouns   **445**

10.2 Pronouns

■ A **pronoun** is a word that takes the place of a noun, a group of words acting as a noun, or another pronoun. The word or group of words to which a pronoun refers is called its **antecedent**. A pronoun must agree in number and gender with its antecedent.

> When James Baldwin was fourteen years old, **he** became a preacher. [The pronoun *he* takes the place of its proper noun antecedent, *James Baldwin*.]
>
> When Georgia O'Keeffe and Alfred Stieglitz were married in 1924, **both** were famous artists. [The pronoun *both* takes the place of the nouns *Georgia O'Keeffe* and *Alfred Stieglitz*.]
>
> Although Georgia O'Keeffe **herself** was a painter, **her** husband was a photographer. [The pronouns *herself* and *her* take the place of the noun *Georgia O'Keeffe*.]

English pronouns fall into these categories: personal and possessive pronouns, reflexive and intensive pronouns, demonstrative pronouns, interrogative pronouns, relative pronouns, and indefinite pronouns.

Personal and Possessive Pronouns

■ A personal pronoun refers to a specific person or thing by indicating the person speaking (the first person), the person being addressed (the second person), or any other person or thing being discussed (the third person).

Personal pronouns also express number; they are either singular or plural.

Personal Pronouns		
	Singular	**Plural**
First Person	I, me	we, us
Second Person	you	you
Third Person	he, him, she, her, it	they, them

FIRST PERSON **I** kept the dog. [*I* refers to the person speaking.]
SECOND PERSON The dog was afraid of **you**. [*You* refers to the person being addressed.]
THIRD PERSON **It** ran away. [*It* refers to the dog mentioned in the previous sentence.]

Third-person pronouns also express **gender**. *He* and *him* are masculine; *she* and *her* are feminine; *it* is neuter (neither masculine nor feminine).

The personal pronouns include several forms that indicate possession or ownership.

- A **possessive pronoun** takes the place of the possessive form of a noun.

Possessive Pronouns	Singular	Plural
First Person	my, mine	our, ours
Second Person	your, yours	your, yours
Third Person	his, her, hers, its	their, theirs

Some possessive forms are used before nouns. Other possessive forms can be used by themselves. Notice that possessive pronouns do not contain an apostrophe.

USED BEFORE A NOUN Take **your** bathing suit.
USED ALONE That bathing suit is **yours**.

Exercise 16 Using Personal and Possessive Pronouns

Improve the following paragraph by replacing the underlined words or groups of words with personal or possessive pronouns. Write your answers on your paper.

Isamu Noguchi, Sculptor

Isamu Noguchi is famous for [1]Noguchi's striking abstract sculptures. [2]These sculptures can be seen in museums everywhere. Noguchi's father was a Japanese poet, and [3]Noguchi's mother was an American writer. As a young man in Paris, Noguchi studied with the sculptor Constantin Brancusi, who encouraged [4]Noguchi to work in abstract forms. In the 1930s, Noguchi settled in New York. Soon, [5]Noguchi's spare and elegant sculptures were being exhibited, and many people went to see [6]the sculptures. One admirer, Martha Graham, invited [7]Noguchi to create sets for [8]Martha Graham's dance company. [9]Noguchi also designed sculpture gardens, as well as furniture and lamps. Noguchi's later interest in architectural forms and design is reflected in the monumental *Red Cube* (1968). [10]*Red Cube* stands outside the Marine Midland Building in New York.

Exercise 17 Creating Sentences with Personal and Possessive Pronouns

On your paper, write five sentences about someone or something that is special to you. Be sure to describe what you consider to be important or unique about the person or item. Use at least five personal or possessive pronouns. Then underline all the personal and possessive pronouns in your sentences.

Reflexive and Intensive Pronouns

Reflexive and intensive pronouns are formed by adding *-self* or *-selves* to certain personal and possessive pronouns.

Reflexive and Intensive Pronouns		
	Singular	**Plural**
First Person	myself	ourselves
Second Person	yourself	yourselves
Third Person	himself, herself, itself	themselves

- A **reflexive pronoun** refers, or reflects back, to a noun or pronoun earlier in the sentence.

    A reflexive pronoun always adds information to a sentence.

    You outdid **yourself** when you wrote that song.

    Cathy always timed **herself** when jogging.

    In dancing class we watch **ourselves** in the mirror.

    The basketball players prepared **themselves** for the game.

- An **intensive pronoun** adds emphasis to another noun or pronoun in the same sentence.

    I **myself** ate the pizza.

    The team **itself** chose the captain.

    Maria **herself** opened the door.

    George and Pedro planned the party **themselves.**

An intensive pronoun does not add information to a sentence. If the intensive pronoun is left out, the sentence still has the same meaning. An intensive pronoun usually comes immediately after its antecedent.

Demonstrative Pronouns

■ A **demonstrative pronoun** points out specific persons, places, things, or ideas.

Demonstrative Pronouns		
Singular	this	that
Plural	these	those

This is your homeroom.

These are your classmates.

That will be your seat.

Carla's desk is cleaner than **those.** [*Those* refers to other desks.]

A demonstrative pronoun can come before or after its antecedent. Sometimes the antecedent is understood.

Exercise 18   Using Reflexive, Intensive, and Demonstrative Pronouns

Supply the appropriate reflexive, intensive, or demonstrative pronoun for each blank. Write your answers on your paper.

An Orchestra Performance

1. He reminded _____ to watch the conductor's baton.
2. The string, woodwind, brass, and percussion sections had prepared _____ during rehearsals.
3. Even the conductor _____ seemed nervous.
4. The air _____ seemed motionless in expectation.
5. We positioned _____ for the opening note.
6. Soon we found _____ listening anxiously for our cues.
7. _____ is a very moving piece of music.
8. We were so inspired by the occasion that our instruments seemed to play _____.
9. Afterward we all felt very proud of _____.
10. "Take _____," the concert manager said, handing several bouquets to the conductor.

Interrogative and Relative Pronouns

■ An **interrogative pronoun** is used to form questions.

who?   whom?   whose?   what?   which?

Who will lead the way?   **What** makes a good leader?
Whom would you choose?   **Which** of these paths is easiest?
Whose is the lightest pack?

The interrogative pronouns include the forms *whoever, whomever, whichever,* and *whatever.*

Whoever could have made such a mistake?

■ A **relative pronoun** is used to begin a special subject-verb word group called a subordinate clause (see Unit 13).

who	whoever	which	that
whom	whomever	whichever	what
whose	whosoever	whatever	

The people **who** invented Monopoly were surprised by its success. [The relative pronoun *who* begins the subordinate clause *who invented Monopoly.*]

Dominoes is a game **that** many Texans play. [The relative pronoun *that* begins the subordinate clause *that many Texans play.*]

Exercise 19 Distinguishing Between Interrogative and Relative Pronouns

On your paper, list the relative and interrogative pronouns that appear in the following sentences, and label each pronoun as *relative* or *interrogative*.

Harriet Tubman, a Courageous Woman

1. Harriet Tubman, who was born an enslaved person in 1820, became a leader of the antislavery movement.
2. Who would have anticipated her development into one of the most powerful speakers in the United States?
3. Tubman, whose maiden name was Greene, married John Tubman.
4. She led hundreds of fugitive slaves along the Underground Railroad, a secret route that led from the South to Canada.
5. Which of her many talents did she use during the Civil War?
6. She did many jobs for the Union army, which fought to abolish slavery.
7. What did her fellow abolitionists call her?
8. Whatever she did, she lived up to her nickname, General Tubman.
9. Whom did she look after in the years following the Civil War?
10. She looked after orphans and old people, whom she loved dearly.

Indefinite Pronouns

■ An **indefinite pronoun** refers to persons, places, or things in a more general way than a noun does.

Everyone needs food. [The indefinite pronoun *everyone* refers to people in general.]

Did you get **enough** to eat? [The indefinite pronoun *enough* refers to a general, not a specific, amount.]

After two hamburgers he did not want **another.** [The indefinite pronoun *another* has the antecedent *hamburger*.]

Some Indefinite Pronouns

all	each	many	nothing	somebody
another	either	most	one	someone
any	enough	much	other	something
anybody	everybody	neither	others	
anyone	everyone	nobody	plenty	
anything	everything	none	several	
both	few	no one	some	

Exercise 20   Creating Sentences with Indefinite Pronouns

On your paper, write ten sentences with indefinite pronouns. Use at least eight different indefinite pronouns; refer to the chart if you need help. Underline the indefinite pronouns in your sentences.

Exercise 21   Identifying Pronouns

(a) On your paper, list in order the twenty-five pronouns that appear in the following paragraph. (b) Identify each pronoun as *personal, possessive, reflexive, intensive, demonstrative, interrogative, relative,* or *indefinite.*

A Great Magician

[1]Harry Houdini, a great magician who was born Erik Weisz, used a stage name borrowed from an earlier French magician called Houdin. [2]Whereas many of Houdin's illusions were optical ones, those that made Harry Houdini famous were daring escapes from complex traps—most of them designed by Houdini himself. [3]The most famous escape of all was the water-torture trick, in which Houdini, whose hands and feet were bound, was locked in a water-filled tank, only to emerge safe and free a moment later. [4]Audiences would ask themselves, What does Houdini do to free himself? [5]Wouldn't you wonder about this yourself? [6]Actually, Houdini created much of his magic by practicing yoga techniques, learning to survive on less oxygen than most of us need. [7]Whose name is synonymous with magic? [8]That is a question everyone can answer: it is Houdini's.

10.3 Verbs

■ A **verb** is a word that expresses action or a state of being and is necessary to make a statement.

The violinists **begin**.   Rehearsals **are** important.
A flutist **entered** late.   The conductor **seems** enthusiastic.

The primary characteristic of a verb is its ability to express time—present, past, and future. Verbs express time by means of *tense* forms.

PRESENT TENSE   They **walk** home together.
PAST TENSE   They **walked** home together.
FUTURE TENSE   They **will walk** home together.

Exercise 22   Identifying Verbs in Sentences

On your paper, write the verbs that appear in each of the following sentences.

1. National parks in the American Southwest include Bryce Canyon, Zion, Mesa Verde, and Grand Canyon.
2. Over the centuries, water and wind erosion change the land dramatically.
3. Each park's natural features attract people of all ages.
4. An information center at the entrance to the park offers exhibits, maps, and publications.
5. Park rangers provide little-known facts about the history of the park.

Exercise 23   Completing Sentences with Verbs

On your paper, write a verb to complete each of the following sentences.

The American Southwest

1. The Southwest _____ some of the most spectacular scenery in the country.
2. Deep canyons and tall mesas _____ the landscape.
3. Several Native American nations, including the Navajo and Hopi, _____ in the Southwest.
4. Many Native Americans still _____ the customs of their ancestors.
5. Some communities _____ in houses made of adobe (sun-dried earth and straw).
6. Even today, many people in the Southwest _____ their own adobe homes.
7. Navajo women still _____ rugs on handmade looms.
8. The Hopi people still _____ ancient rain dances.
9. The Native Americans of the Southwest _____ proud of their heritage.
10. Despite modern intrusions, many of their traditions _____ unchanged.

Action Verbs

- An **action verb** tells what someone or something does.

    Some action verbs express physical action; others express mental action.

    PHYSICAL ACTION The catcher often **signals** to the pitcher.
    MENTAL ACTION A good catcher **understands** the batter's technique.

- A **transitive verb** is an action verb that is followed by a word or words that answer the question *what?* or *whom?*

    Cats **see** their prey in the dark. [The action verb *see* is followed by the noun *prey,* which answers the question *see what?*]

- An **intransitive verb** is an action verb that is not followed by a word that answers the question *what?* or *whom?*

    Cats **see** well in the dark. [The action verb may be followed by words that tell *how* and *where* or by no words at all.]

Exercise 24   Identifying Action Verbs

On your, paper write the action verbs that appear in the following sentences. Indicate whether each action verb is used as a *transitive* or an *intransitive verb.*

Sacajawea, an Intrepid Woman

1. After President Thomas Jefferson bought the Louisiana Territory from France, he arranged for its exploration.
2. In 1804 Meriwether Lewis and William Clark launched a search for an overland route to the Pacific Ocean.
3. Lewis and Clark hired a French Canadian fur trapper, Toussaint Charbonneau, as guide and interpreter.
4. Charbonneau's wife, Sacajawea, a Shoshone, also joined the expedition.
5. With her linguistic skills, Sacajawea helped Lewis and Clark's communication with Native American tribes.
6. Four years earlier, hostile Native Americans had abducted Sacajawea and later had sold her to Charbonneau.
7. In 1805 Lewis and Clark encountered a group of Shoshone, among them Sacajawea's brother, a chief.
8. He gave Lewis and Clark the horses they needed.
9. Sacajawea, her husband, and their infant son stayed with the expedition until Lewis and Clark had explored the Pacific Coast and returned to Wyoming.
10. Sacajawea and Charbonneau later returned to the Dakota Territory, where, some historians believe, Sacajawea died in 1812.

Exercise 25 — Completing Sentences with Action Verbs

On your paper, write an action verb to complete each of the sentences below.

Stephen Crane

1. Stephen Crane _____ his first novel under the pen name Johnston Smith.
2. He _____ Syracuse University for a brief time, where he distinguished himself as a baseball player.
3. Crane's popular novel *The Red Badge of Courage* _____ the story of a young soldier during the Civil War.
4. The novel was widely acclaimed, and syndicated newspapers _____ Crane as a war correspondent.
5. The steamer on which Crane was traveling to Cuba, *The Commodore,* _____ off the coast of Florida.
6. He _____ his nearly fatal experience in "The Open Boat."
7. Crane's natural writing style _____ an understanding of the realities of combat.
8. Crane _____ his varied life experiences in his writings.
9. Critics often _____ Crane's portrayal of war as realistic and powerful.
10. English writer Joseph Conrad _____ Crane when he moved to England in 1897.

Exercise 26 — Distinguishing Between Transitive and Intransitive Verbs

On your paper, complete the following sentences using the action verb in *italics*. In one sentence, use it as a transitive verb. In the other sentence, use it as an intransitive verb. Add any other words that are necessary.

1. *hears*
   When hiking through the forest, Alicia _____. (transitive)
   When she pulls her hat over her head, she _____. (intransitive)
2. *studies*
   In the afternoon, the class _____. (transitive)
   In order to do well in school, Paul _____. (intransitive)
3. *eats*
   For breakfast the baby _____. (transitive)
   When the baby is sick, she _____. (intransitive)
4. *practices*
   Before the concert, Susan _____. (transitive)
   Because she wants to be in the band, she _____. (intransitive)
5. *play*
   In the afternoon, the children _____ (transitive)
   Despite their age difference, the children _____. (intransitive)

Linking Verbs

■ A **linking verb** links, or joins, the subject of a sentence (often a noun or pronoun) with a word or expression that identifies or describes the subject.

Be in all its forms—*am, is, are, was, were*—is the most commonly used linking verb.

| I **am** an athlete. | The players **are** fast. |
| Squash **is** an indoor sport. | They **were** hockey fans. |

Several other verbs besides the forms of *be* can act as linking verbs.

Other Linking Verbs

look	remain	seem	become
stay	grow	appear	sound
taste	smell	feel	

Exercise 27 Completing Sentences with Linking Verbs

On your paper, write a linking verb to complete each of the following sentences. Try to use as many different verbs as you can.

Georgia

1. The air at higher altitudes in Georgia _____ cool in the summer.
2. Georgia _____ one of the southern states.
3. Azaleas and other colorful plants _____ good in the summer.
4. The saws of the lumber mills in the mountains _____ loud and screechy.
5. The Okefenokee National Wildlife Refuge and Stone Mountain Park _____ two popular attractions.
6. The Civil War _____ a topic of great interest, especially in Atlanta.
7. Fishing, hunting, and golfing _____ popular with many Georgians.
8. The population of Georgia _____ more diverse every year.
9. With its many different industries and attractions, Georgia _____ ready for a bright future.
10. Atlanta _____ the site of the 1996 Summer Olympics.

Exercise 28 Writing Sentences with Linking Verbs

On your paper, write five sentences about yourself, your family, or your day at school. Use a different form of the verb *be* in each sentence.

Exercise 29 — Identifying Action and Linking Verbs

On your paper, make a list of the nineteen verbs that appear in the following paragraphs. Identify each verb as either *action* or *linking*.

The Statue of Liberty

[1]In 1884 France presented the United States with a gift as a dramatic gesture of friendship. [2]This spectacular gift was a huge copper statue. [3]Its official name is *Liberty Enlightening the World*. [4]Most people, however, know it simply as the Statue of Liberty. [5]The gift commemorated the hundredth anniversary of the American Revolution. [6]It also celebrated the alliance of France with the colonists during their fight for independence from England. [7]The immense figure of Liberty holds a torch in her right hand. [8]The inscription on the cover of her book reads "July 4, 1776."

[9]Artist Frédéric Auguste Bartholdi first made a nine-foot model of the statue. [10]Gustave Eiffel, a pioneer in the use of metal as an architectural material, created the iron framework for the full-size statue. [11]The completed statue was too large for delivery in one piece. [12]Workers in France dismantled it. [13]The pieces of the statue arrived in the United States in 214 cases.

[14]The French people donated the money for the construction of the statue. [15]Grateful, the people of the United States collected the funds for the massive granite and concrete pedestal. [16]This impressive monument found a permanent home on Liberty Island in New York Harbor. [17]The dedication of the statue by President Grover Cleveland on October 28, 1886, was a great ceremonial occasion.

[18]At 151 feet and 1 inch high, the Statue of Liberty remains one of the largest statues in the world. [19]The monumental lady with the torch quickly became a symbol of American democracy.

Exercise 30 — Completing Sentences with Action and Linking Verbs

On your paper, write a verb to complete each of the sentences below. Identify each verb as an *action* or a *linking* verb.

Those Amazing Hummingbirds

1. Hummingbirds _____ the smallest birds in the world.
2. About nineteen different kinds of hummingbirds _____ in the United States.
3. The ruby-throated hummingbird _____ approximately 3 1/2 inches in length.
4. The hummingbird _____ its wings between fifty and seventy times per second.
5. The rapid wing beating _____ soft and low, like the whirring of a distant motorboat.
6. The bird's wings _____ a blur to the human eye.
7. This rapid wing beating _____ the hummingbird hover in midair.
8. While hovering, the hummingbird _____ its long, slender bill into a flower.
9. The bird _____ the flower's nectar through its long, tubelike tongue.
10. Hummingbirds also _____ insects and may even steal them away from spider webs.

Verb Phrases

■ The verb in a sentence may consist of more than one word. The words that accompany the main verb are called **auxiliary,** or helping, **verbs.**

Auxiliary Verbs	
Forms of *Be*	am, is, are, was, were, being, been
Forms of *Have*	has, have, had
Other Auxiliaries	can, could may, might must do, does, did shall, should will, would

■ A **verb phrase** consists of a main verb and all its auxiliary, or helping, verbs.

The most common auxiliary verbs are the forms of *be* and *have*. They help the main verb express the various tenses.

> We **are working** in the yard.
> We **have worked** for the past two weeks.
> We **had been working** for an hour before the storm.

The other auxiliary verbs are not used primarily to express time. They are often used to emphasize meaning.

> I **should be leaving.**
> **Could** he **have finished?**
> Luisa **may** already **be waiting.**

Exercise 31   Using Auxiliary Verbs

On your paper, write two revisions of each sentence below by changing the italicized verb phrase. Remember that you will probably have to change the main verb as well as the auxiliary verb. Underline the verb phrase in each sentence you write.

SAMPLE   I *am going*.
ANSWER   I <u>have gone</u>.   I <u>might go</u>.

1. Jerry and Sue *will eat* dinner.
2. The rest of the family *has left*.
3. When *did* the Murrays *call*?
4. Janice *has been* waiting.
5. Who *should set* the table?

10.3 Verbs   **457**

Exercise 32 — Identifying Verb Phrases

On your paper, write each verb phrase that appears in the following sentences. (Some sentences have more than one verb phrase.) Put parentheses around the auxiliary verbs in each phrase. (A word or words that interrupt a verb phrase are not considered part of the verb phrase.)

Fats Waller, a Great Jazz Pianist

1. Fats Waller has been called one of the greatest jazz musicians of the twentieth century.
2. A versatile musician, he could compose, sing, and play several instruments with equal skill.
3. Fortunately, most of his music has been recorded.
4. Waller was already playing the piano at the age of six.
5. He had been taught by his mother, a musician herself.
6. Waller's father, a church deacon, had felt that his son should follow in his footsteps.
7. Nevertheless, young Waller had decided that his life would be dedicated to music.
8. By the age of sixteen, he was earning $23 a week as a theater organist and had already written his first instrumental composition, "Boston Blues."
9. People must have appreciated Waller's talents.
10. Can you believe that Waller's first song, "Squeeze Me," became a jazz classic?
11. A recording of the song by Louis Armstrong and Earl Hines had already become popular by 1928.
12. By the beginning of the 1930s, Waller had become known not only as a major composer, bandleader, and jazz vocalist but also as the greatest jazz organist of his time.
13. By 1932 he had already composed the song that would become his most famous work, "Ain't Misbehavin'."
14. An earlier Waller song, "Honeysuckle Rose" (1928), has remained a favorite ever since the time it was written.
15. It may not be widely recalled today that Waller had performed for several years on radio before becoming a recording artist.
16. By the mid-1930s, Waller had become famous as a recording star for RCA Victor.
17. At that time, people were buying more records by Waller than by any other African American musician.
18. *Ain't Misbehavin'*, a Broadway show with many of Waller's songs, was declared a hit in 1978, more than three decades after Waller's death.
19. Those people who have seen *Ain't Misbehavin'* will surely never forget the experience.
20. Waller will always have a special place in the history of American jazz.
21. Today we can still enjoy his exuberant style of piano playing.
22. Few musicians have been able to imitate Waller's humorous vocal renditions.
23. Fans should know that Fats's real name was Thomas.
24. Waller's lasting popularity has benefited from new recording technologies.
25. Our musical heritage has been greatly enriched by Fats Waller's talents, despite his death at an early age.

Exercise 33 Creating Verb Phrases

On your paper, write auxiliary verbs to create a verb phrase for each sentence. Be sure that your completed sentences make sense.

Satellites

1. Satellites _____ defined as artificial objects that orbit celestial bodies.
2. The first satellite, *Sputnik I*, _____ launched in 1957 by the Soviet Union.
3. Satellites _____ study solar radiation, magnetic fields, and atmospheric temperature.
4. Crewed satellites _____ include food, air, and life-support systems for astronauts.
5. One of the earliest crewed satellites _____ named *Skylab*.
6. Astronauts _____ performed experiments in space to find out more about the materials we use on Earth.
7. The Hubble Telescope _____ enabled astronomers to learn more about our universe.
8. Many scientists and engineers _____ work long hours to prepare the next satellite for its mission into space.
9. More advanced satellites _____ help meteorologists predict the weather more accurately.
10. Telecommunications companies _____ financing future experiments in space.

Exercise 34 Completing Sentences with Verb Phrases

On your paper, write a verb phrase to complete each of the following sentences. Be sure that your completed sentences make sense.

James Herriot, Veterinarian and Author

1. Many children and adults _____ a friend in James Herriot.
2. A country veterinarian in Yorkshire, England, Herriot decided after his fiftieth birthday that he _____ books.
3. His first book _____ *If Only They Could Talk*.
4. Herriot had hoped that someone would publish his book and a few people _____ it.
5. It soon became apparent that his book _____ a bestseller.
6. His first two books _____ in the United States in 1972 as one volume entitled *All Creatures Great and Small*.
7. By the time Herriot died in February 1995, his fifteen books _____ more than fifty million copies in twenty countries.
8. Critics _____ Herriot's stories as "fresh, clear, pure, and good."
9. Each of his stories features animals that _____ by the country veterinarian himself.
10. *James Herriot's Treasury for Children* _____ a wonderful gift for readers of all ages.

| Exercise 35 | Using Vivid Verbs |

Write five sentences about one of your favorite sports. Choose very specific action verbs and verb phrases to convey a vivid sense of the sport.

| Exercise 36 | Completing Sentences with Verbs and Verb Phrases |

On your paper, complete each of the following sentences as indicated in italic typeface. Be sure that your completed sentences make sense.

New York's World Trade Center

The massive World Trade Center in New York City [1]*linking verb* a city within a city. About fifty thousand people [2]*action verb* in its stores and offices, and another eighty thousand or so [3]*action verb* in and out each day. The center [4]*action verb* 110 stories in each of its twin towers, and another 6 levels [5]*action verb* underground. Its dozens of stores, from flower stores to drugstores, [6]*linking verb* attractive and busy. The stores often [7]*action verb* special services to their customers. Clients of the cleaners, for example, [8]*action verb* their clothes in large bags for protection on the subway. The enormous kitchens of the center [9]*action verb* as many as thirty thousand people each day. More than twenty restaurants [10]*action verb* inside the buildings. The vast complex even [11]*action verb* its own police station, with a force of thirty-nine officers. The manager's office [12]*linking verb* busy all the time. In fact, it [13]*action verb* over two hundred calls for assistance each day. Some people [14]*linking verb* too hot and [15]*action verb* a lower temperature. Others [16]*action verb* themselves out of their offices and [17]*action verb* spare keys. An ambulance [18]*action verb* outside the complex at all times in case of an emergency, and paramedics, with the latest in life-support equipment, [19]*action verb* the life of a seriously ill or injured person. With its impressive population and variety of services, the World Trade Center [20]*linking verb* a small city in the middle of New York City.

| Exercise 37 | Identifying Action Verbs, Linking Verbs, and Verb Phrases |

On your paper, identify the verb in each of the following sentences as an *action verb* or a *linking verb*. If the verb is a verb phrase, write *verb phrase* as well. Then use the information in the sentence to write a new sentence, using the italicized verb form in parentheses.

SAMPLE The pangolin and the lizard look similar. (*action verb phrase*)

ANSWER look; linking verb The pangolin and the lizard do have similar qualities.

The Pangolin

1. The pangolin has some of the characteristics of a lizard. (*linking verb*)
2. Overlapping scales instead of hair cover the back of this insect-eating mammal. (*linking verb*)
3. These scales feel sharp, similar to a razor in the mouth of a predator. (*action verb phrase*)
4. The pangolin curls itself into a tight ball for protection. (*action verb phrase*)
5. This toothless anteater lives in Asia and Africa. (*linking verb*)

10.4 Adjectives

■ An **adjective** is a word that modifies a noun or pronoun by limiting its meaning. An adjective tells *what kind, which one, how many,* or *how much.*

round window	**six** oranges	**that** hat	**adult** cat
romantic story	**many** ideas	**these** books	**Scottish** wool
interesting book	**enough** cups	**third** time	**no** reason

Nouns can also be used as adjectives. They tell *what kind* or *which one* about the noun modified.

afternoon class **music** lesson **football** practice

Possessive pronouns, such as *our* and *his,* can be considered adjectives because they modify nouns in addition to their usual function as pronouns.

our book **his** watch **their** house **my** hands

Similarly, possessive nouns can be considered adjectives.

Julia's dream the **knight's** castle the **Bowers'** car

Adjectives may be used in various positions in relation to the words they modify.

How **obedient** the poodle is!

That **obedient** poodle belongs to her.

The poodle is **obedient.**

The judges considered the poodle **obedient.**

The poodle, always **obedient,** waited by the door.

Many adjectives have different forms to indicate degree of comparison.

POSITIVE	COMPARATIVE	SUPERLATIVE
light	lighter	lightest
heavy	heavier	heaviest
funny	funnier	funniest
sad	sadder	saddest
practical	more practical	most practical
good	better	best
much	more	most
bad	worse	worst

Exercise 38 Identifying Adjectives

On your paper, list the twenty adjectives that appear in the following fictional passage, which describes a scene on a British heath during the last century. Count possessive pronouns as adjectives, but do not count the words *a, an,* and *the.*

Literature: A Long Road

Before him stretched the long, laborious road, dry, empty, and white. It was quite open to the heath on each side, and bisected that vast, dark surface. . . . The old man frequently stretched his eyes ahead to gaze over the tract that he had yet to traverse. At length he discerned, a long distance in front of him, a moving spot. . . . Its rate of advance was slow. . . . When he drew nearer he perceived it to be a . . . van, ordinary in shape, but singular in color. . . . The driver walked beside it; and, like his van, he was completely red.

From *The Return of the Native* by Thomas Hardy

Exercise 39 Completing Sentences with Adjectives

On your paper, write an adjective to complete each of the following sentences. Be sure that your completed sentences make sense.

1. The sheepdog trial was held on a _____ field.
2. It was near the edge of a _____ river.
3. The dogs, always _____, waited for the trial to begin.
4. Wearing _____ jackets, the trainers leaned on their long crooks.
5. Soon the judge waved his _____ handkerchief to begin the trial.

Exercise 40 Discovering How Adjectives Are Formed

Use your dictionary to discover the adjective form that is most closely related to each of the following nouns.

1. literature
2. grammar
3. declaration
4. residence
5. parent
6. science
7. intention
8. might
9. idealism
10. noise

Exercise 41 Using Forms of Adjectives

On your paper, complete the sentences in each group by writing the correct positive, comparative, and superlative forms of the given adjective.

sample **tall**
answers The basketball player is **tall**.
Other players are **taller** than he is.
The captain of the team is the **tallest** player of all.

bright
1. The male mandrill is a type of baboon that has a very ____ face.
2. Scientists think that the colors become even ____ when the baboon gets angry.
3. During a fight between mandrills, the male with the ____ color usually wins.

good
4. Most people agree that milk is ____ for you.
5. Others argue that water is even ____ for you than milk.
6. Personally, I think fruit juices are the ____.
7. I like orange juice ____ than grapefruit juice.

tasty
8. Last night's dinner was ____.
9. It was ____ than any other meal he has served this week.
10. Thanksgiving dinner is my candidate for our family's ____ meal.
11. Is Jack's cooking ____ than Minna's?

large
12. Compared to Mercury, Earth is a fairly ____ planet.
13. Saturn is much ____ than Earth.
14. Jupiter, however, is the ____ planet.
15. Which is ____, Neptune or Mars?

slow
16. The tortoise was very ____.
17. It was much ____ than the hare.
18. In fact, the tortoise was the ____ animal around.

curious
19. The detective is ____ about the case.
20. Her assistant is even ____.
21. The police captain is the ____ of all.

many
22. Jack won ____ awards at the sports banquet.
23. Did he win the ____ awards?
24. He won ____ awards than he did last year.
25. The team was surprised that Jack won ____ awards than the quarterback.

10.4 Adjectives

Articles

- Articles are the adjectives *a, an* and *the*. *A* and *an* are called indefinite articles. They can refer to any one of a kind of person, place, or thing. *A* is used before consonant sounds and *an* is used before vowel sounds. *The* is called a definite article. It refers to a specific person, place, or thing.

INDEFINITE	She found **a** ring.	They spotted **an** iceberg.
	I bought **a** used mask.	He was **an** honorable choice.
DEFINITE	She found **the** ring.	They spotted **the** iceberg.
	I bought **the** used mask.	He was **the** honorable choice.

Exercise 42   Completing Sentences with Articles

On your paper, write an article to complete each of the following sentences. Then identify each article as *indefinite* or *definite*.

Coral Reefs

1. Coral reefs are land features formed in _____ ocean.
2. _____ fringing reef extends from the shore of an island or mainland.
3. No body of water comes between _____ fringing reef and land.
4. _____ channel or lagoon comes between a barrier reef and shore.
5. Charles Darwin first explained _____ formation of coral reefs.
6. Darwin's theory is _____ one accepted by modern geologists.
7. Many coral reefs are in _____ Atlantic, Pacific, and Indian oceans.
8. _____ most famous barrier reef is in Australia.
9. The Bikini Atoll was the site of _____ underwater atomic explosion in 1946.
10. The coral that forms _____ atoll can be more than one thousand feet thick.

Exercise 43   Writing with Different Kinds of Adjectives

On your paper, write an adjective to complete each sentence. The kind of modifier to use in each case is indicated in italics. Be sure that your completed sentences make sense.

The African Elephant

The African elephant is [1]*article* largest of all land animals. [2]*article* mature elephant eats about three hundred pounds of plants every day. Some of [3]*possessive pronoun* favorite foods include grass, leaves, roots, bark, and fruit. The [4]*possessive noun* long trunk is actually a nose that serves as a hand. With [5]*possessive pronoun* trunk, the elephant can pick up a small berry or a heavy log. Most African elephants are dark gray with a little pink on the edges of [6]*possessive pronoun* ears. The [7]*possessive noun* big ears brush away flies and other pesty insects. [8]*article* African elephant also has two long, ivory tusks. Elephants use [9]*possessive pronoun* tusks to dig for food, fight, and carry heavy loads. Wild African elephants are found in areas south of [10]*article* Sahara.

Proper Adjectives

■ A **proper adjective** is formed from a proper noun and begins with a capital letter.

Rembrandt was a **Dutch** painter.
The **Berlin** Wall came down in 1989.

The following suffixes are often used to create proper adjectives: *-an*, *-ian*, *-n*, *-ese*, and *-ish*. Sometimes there are other changes as well. In some cases, the noun and adjective forms are the same.

PROPER NOUNS	PROPER ADJECTIVES
Alaska	Alaskan
Queen Victoria	Victorian
Vietnam	Vietnamese
Denmark	Danish
Navajo	Navajo

Exercise 44 — Identifying Proper Adjectives

On your paper, list the ten proper adjectives that appear in the following passage.

The Early Colonization of the Americas

[1]The Spanish colonization of the Americas began in the late 1400s after Christopher Columbus, an Italian explorer, sailed westward from Europe until he reached some Caribbean islands. [2]The great Columbian drama unfolded as hundreds of Native American cultures, including the Aztec and Incan civilizations, collided violently with conquistadors and colonists. [3]A century later, England and France joined in the quest for a North American empire. [4]Some Europeans hoped to acquire great wealth, while others hoped to spread the Christian faith. [5]Still others sought freedom from oppressive European laws and customs.

Exercise 45 — Forming Proper Adjectives from Proper Nouns

On your paper, write a proper adjective formed from each of the following proper nouns. Consult a dictionary if you need help.

1. Africa
2. China
3. Mexico
4. Thomas Jefferson
5. William Shakespeare
6. Dakota
7. Spain
8. Confucius
9. Hawaii
10. Senegal

Exercise 46   Identifying Adjectives

On your paper, write the twenty adjectives, including articles, that appear in the following paragraph.

Mayan Culture

¹Recent discoveries have revealed new facts about the ancient Maya, who formed one of the oldest societies in Central America. ²By A.D. 1000, they had already made impressive and original advancements in art and science. ³Recently, at a site in northern Belize, fortunate archaeologists unearthed the unmistakable remains of an early civilization. ⁴This discovery was remarkable and significant, for it pushed back the origins of Mayan culture to 2400 B.C.

Exercise 47   Creating Sentences with Adjectives

On your paper, write five sentences about someone you know and can picture clearly. In your description, include details about the person's appearance, voice, behavior, and personality. Choose adjectives that are especially descriptive to convey a vivid image of the person.

Exercise 48   Using Adjectives in Writing

On your paper, complete the paragraphs below by replacing each blank with an adjective, including definite and indefinite articles. Be sure that your completed sentences make sense.

Corn

Corn is an important ¹_____ crop in the United States. The country's annual ²_____ production is more than six billion bushels, accounting for almost half the total world production. Illinois is a(n) ³_____ producer, along with several other ⁴_____ states. Most of the corn grown in the United States is used as feed for ⁵_____ animals such as hogs, cattle, and chickens. Although corn is a(n) ⁶_____ source of energy, it is low in protein.

Each corn plant has a(n) ⁷_____ stem, averaging eight feet in height. The ear of corn is protected by ⁸_____ husk. The ⁹_____ tassels at the tip of the ear of corn contain pollen.

There are ¹⁰_____ different types of corn, and all of them have a specific use. Sweet corn is often served as a(n) ¹¹_____ dish at meals. Popcorn is a(n) ¹²_____ snack throughout the United States. During the fall, many people use pod corn as a(n) ¹³_____ decoration. Even the other parts of the corn plant have ¹⁴_____ uses. For example, corncobs are ground to make abrasives for cleaning ¹⁵_____ engines.

No one knows where or when ¹⁶_____ plants were first farmed, but corn was ¹⁷_____ important staple in the diet of Native Americans by the 1600s. When the ¹⁸_____ colonists arrived in the Massachusetts Bay Colony, Squanto taught them how to grow and harvest corn. Without his ¹⁹_____ help, the ²⁰_____ colony might not have survived.

10.5 Adverbs

■ An **adverb** is a word that modifies a verb, an adjective, or another adverb by making its meaning more specific.

The following sentences illustrate the use of adverbs to modify verbs, adjectives, and adverbs.

She **always** waited **patiently.**
verb

The waiting room was **very** noisy and **overly** crowded.
adjective   adjective

Rather oddly, we have **almost** never visited his farm.
adverb   adverb

Adverbs modify by answering the questions *when? where? how?* and *to what degree?*

I will call **tomorrow.**

His phone rings **often**.

The speaker will stand **here.**

Kim **carefully** polished the car.

We were **truly** sorry.

When an adverb modifies a verb, it may be placed in various positions in relation to the verb. When an adverb modifies an adjective or another adverb, it usually comes directly before the modified word.

MODIFYING A VERB   **Finally** the storm is ending.

The storm **finally** is ending.

The storm is **finally** ending.

The storm is ending **finally.**

MODIFYING AN ADJECTIVE   The snow was **quite** heavy.

Driving was **very** hazardous.

MODIFYING AN ADVERB   It **almost** never snows this heavily.

I **hardly** ever need to wear my boots.

Negative Words as Adverbs

The word *not* and the contraction *n't* are considered adverbs. Other negative words can function as adverbs of time and place.

The plane has **not** landed.   They have **hardly** boarded.
The plane is **nowhere** in sight.   I have **never** flown.

Exercise 49   Identifying Words Modified by Adverbs

On your paper, write the word or words that are being modified by the adverb in italics in each sentence.

The Cleaner Wrasse

1. The eel *instinctively* opened its mouth to let the small fish enter.
2. Surprisingly, the eel did *not* intend to eat the small fry.
3. The cleaner wrasse, a tropical fish, is *almost* always welcome to inspect the eel's teeth.
4. Some wrasses, such as blueheads, *thoroughly* clean the teeth of larger fish.
5. They eat the *extremely* tiny creatures and pieces of dead skin that cling to the bigger fish's teeth.
6. *Sometimes* snappers and groupers also go to the "cleaners."
7. One cleaner wrasse is *often* visited by as many as three hundred fish in a period of six hours.
8. Finding customers is *never* difficult for the bluehead wrasse.
9. Its *especially* bright neon color acts as a kind of undersea advertising.
10. Its dancelike swimming motion attracts customers *also*.

Exercise 50   Identifying Adverbs

On your paper, write all the adverb(s) that appear in each sentence below. Then write the word or words each adverb modifies.

A Great Blues Singer

1. Bessie Smith is often considered a great blues singer.
2. She was born into an extremely poor family in Chattanooga, Tennessee.
3. Hardly fourteen, she was already touring with Ma Rainey and her Rabbit Foot Minstrels.
4. Others have sung songs more matter-of-factly than she.
5. Jazz writers have called her style rhythmically adventurous.
6. In 1923 Smith began to make commercially successful records.
7. Louis Armstrong was one very famous jazz musician with whom she sang.
8. Her greatest fame probably came in the years from 1923 to 1928.
9. Her record *Nobody's Blues but Mine,* which covers the period from 1925 to 1927, remains popular today.
10. Bessie Smith did not survive a tragic car accident in 1937.

Adverbs That Compare

Like adjectives, some adverbs have different forms to indicate degree of comparison. The comparative form of an adverb compares two actions. The superlative form of an adverb compares more than two actions. For adverbs of only one syllable, add *-er* to make the comparative form and *-est* to make the superlative form.

POSITIVE	COMPARATIVE	SUPERLATIVE
runs **fast**	runs **faster**	runs **fastest**
arrived **late**	arrived **later**	arrived **latest**
works **hard**	works **harder**	works **hardest**

When an adverb ends in *-ly* or has more than one syllable, use the word *more* to form the comparative and *most* to form the superlative.

POSITIVE	COMPARATIVE	SUPERLATIVE
walks **quickly**	walks **more quickly**	walks **most quickly**
reads **carefully**	reads **more carefully**	reads **most carefully**
calls **often**	calls **more often**	calls **most often**

Some adverbs do not form the comparative and superlative in the regular manner.

POSITIVE	COMPARATIVE	SUPERLATIVE
feels **well**	feels **better**	feels **best**
behaves **badly**	behaves **worse**	behaves **worst**
cares **little**	cares **less**	cares **least**
throws **far**	throws **farther**	throws **farthest**

Exercise 51 — Forming Comparative and Superlative Adverbs

On your paper, write the comparative and superlative forms of each of the following adverbs. Consult a dictionary if you need help.

1. high
2. bravely
3. early
4. surprisingly
5. thoroughly
6. easily
7. low
8. far
9. happily
10. foolishly
11. near
12. softly
13. poorly
14. little
15. close
16. eagerly
17. well
18. fearfully
19. strangely
20. speedily

10.5 Adverbs **469**

Exercise 52   Using Adverbs That Compare

On your paper, write the form of the adverb specified in parentheses.

Balloons

1. The highest recorded plastic balloon flight _____ reached an altitude of more than 150,000 feet. (positive form of *easily*)
2. Seven years later, a rubber balloon went 18,000 feet _____. (comparative form of *high*)
3. The longest superpressured balloon flight on record lasted _____ than three hundred days. (comparative form of *long*)
4. The _____ the pilot computes the atmospheric pressures, the better is the chance of a successful flight. (comparative form of *carefully*)
5. A balloon can travel so _____ into the atmosphere because its skin can stretch. (positive form of *far*)
6. The balloon that rises _____ is the one that is the lightest. (superlative form of *fast*)
7. In general, a hot-air balloon will rise _____ if the air in it is heated to a higher temperature. (comparative form of *fast*)
8. Some of the earliest balloons were _____ tethered to the earth. (positive form of *carefully*)
9. Scientists are now working even _____ to improve balloon technology. (comparative form of *hard*)
10. Helium is used _____ than hydrogen because it is safer. (comparative form of *often*)

Exercise 53   Completing Sentences with Adverbs

On your paper, write an adverb to complete each sentence below.

The United States Capitol

1. The hill where the United States Capitol has stood since 1800 is _____ called Capitol Hill.
2. After many delays in construction, some feared that the Capitol would _____ be completed.
3. During the War of 1812, the inside of the Capitol was _____ destroyed by British troops.
4. The dome is _____ impressive, reaching a height of 188 feet.
5. A statue symbolizing freedom stands _____ on top of the Capitol dome.
6. Tourists consider the Capitol a _____ important sight in Washington, D.C.
7. Tourists _____ visit the Library of Congress and the Supreme Court, which are within walking distance of the Capitol.
8. They also see members of Congress, who _____ walk through the corridors on their way to one of the legislative chambers.
9. Statuary Hall _____ contains statues of some famous Americans.
10. Every four years, a new president is _____ sworn in at the Capitol.

Exercise 54 — Completing Sentences with Adverbs

On your paper, rewrite each sentence, adding the adverb in parentheses. Be sure that you place each adverb in an appropriate position.

Historically Speaking

1. The Greek writer Herodotus is considered to be the first historian. (generally)
2. A practical-minded individual, Herodotus did not worry about the purposes or goals of history. (much)
3. He wondered about the past. (simply)
4. He also asked some intriguing questions about past events. (very)
5. Then he recorded what he had discovered. (carefully)
6. Some people study history for its own sake. (still)
7. They are interested in the past. (truly)
8. Many historians find it challenging to make history relevant to others. (extremely)
9. Students of history learn when they are given the chance to draw their own conclusions about past events. (best)
10. Public officials use the lessons of the past to help find solutions to contemporary problems. (sometimes)

Exercise 55 — Positioning Adverbs

On your paper, rewrite each sentence adding an appropriate verb-modifying adverb. Then rewrite the sentence again, placing the adverb in a different position.

SAMPLE Track-and-field star Florence Griffith-Joyner accepted her gold medal.
ANSWER (a) Track-and-field star Florence Griffith-Joyner proudly accepted her gold medal.
(b) Proudly track-and-field star Florence Griffith-Joyner accepted her gold medal.

An Olympic Race

1. Another group of Olympic runners waited for the signal.
2. The starting shot rang out.
3. All eight racers leaped from their starting blocks.
4. The runner from Kenya began to lag.
5. The French contestant was pulling ahead of her.
6. The Kenyan runner exerted her last ounce of strength.
7. The two women were running neck and neck.
8. The Kenyan spectators jumped to their feet as their favorite crossed the finish line.
9. To the strains of her national anthem, the Kenyan runner accepted the gold medal.
10. The French runner shook her opponent's hand.

Exercise 56 Following Models

A Tom Swifty is a sentence in which an adverb comments in a humorous way on an action or object mentioned in a quotation. Note the relationship between each adverb and quotation in the following examples:

"Will you hang up these wet clothes?" asked Ben dryly.

"I've never seen such flat land," said the farmer plainly.

(a) For items 1–5, write each Tom Swifty on your paper, completing it with an adverb that comments in a humorous way on the quotation. (b) For items 6–10, write a Tom Swifty of your own, using the adverb provided. Consult a dictionary if you need help.

1. "Please turn on the light," requested Sara _____.
2. "I need the sandpaper," said the carpenter _____.
3. "The temperature is rising," said the weather forecaster _____.
4. "Be careful with that knife!" warned Hiroshi _____.
5. "My arm is aching," complained the pitcher _____.
6. coldly
7. heavily
8. sourly
9. snappily
10. idly

Exercise 57 Identifying Adjectives and Adverbs

On your paper, write each of the twenty adjectives and twenty adverbs that appear in the following paragraph. (Do not include *a, an,* and *the.*)

Hurricanes

[1]Hurricanes are severe storms with extremely strong winds. [2]Storms with this name are always limited to the northern Atlantic Ocean. [3]The same storm in the western Pacific Ocean is not called a hurricane; it is a typhoon. [4]In the Indian Ocean, such storms generally are known as cyclones. [5]A hurricane is defined officially as a storm with winds of seventy-five miles an hour. [6]Such storms usually start in the North Atlantic and move westward. [7]Sometimes they progress northeastward from the Mexican coast. [8]They move at approximately ten miles an hour in the beginning and gradually gain speed. [9]A fully mature hurricane is almost circular. [10]Air pressure in its center, or eye, can be extremely low. [11]In the eye the air barely moves, the atmosphere seems strangely calm, and the sky often looks blue. [12]Clouds that swirl rapidly outside quickly bring violent winds and torrential rains.

10.6 Prepositions

- A **preposition** is a word that shows the relationship of a noun or pronoun to some other word in a sentence.
- Prepositions begin phrases that end with a noun or pronoun that is called the **object of the preposition.**

> The silverware is **inside** the cabinet. [*Inside* shows the spatial relationship of the silverware and the object of the preposition, *cabinet*.]
>
> All the guests arrived **before** dinner. [*Before* tells the time relationship between the guests' arrival and the object of the preposition, *dinner*.]
>
> He brought a gift **for** the host. [*For* relates *gift* to the object of the preposition, *host*.]

Commonly Used Prepositions

aboard	beneath	in	regarding
about	beside	inside	since
above	besides	into	through
across	between	like	throughout
after	beyond	near	to
against	but*	of	toward
along	by	off	under
amid	concerning	on	underneath
among	despite	onto	until
around	down	opposite	unto
as	during	out	up
at	except	outside	upon
before	excepting	over	with
behind	for	past	within
below	from	pending	without

*meaning "except"

- A **compound preposition** is made up of more than one word.

Compound Prepositions

according to	aside from	in addition to	next to
ahead of	as to	in front of	on top of
along with	because of	in spite of	out of
apart from	by means of	instead of	owing to

Exercise 58 — Identifying Prepositional Phrases

On your paper, list the prepositional phrases that appear in each of the following sentences. Remember that some prepositions are made up of more than one word. (The numeral in parentheses at the end of each item indicates the number of prepositional phrases in that sentence.)

Sonny Rollins, a Great Jazz Saxophonist

1. The great jazz musician Sonny Rollins was born in New York in 1920 to musical parents. (3)
2. Instead of the usual piano, Rollins chose the tenor saxophone for his instrument. (2)
3. Like many jazz musicians, he often improvised on themes within the music. (3)
4. His exceptional album *Moving Out* put him at the top of his profession. (2)
5. During the late fifties and into the sixties, his work became notable for its energy. (3)
6. Rollins took music out of its usual locations and went beyond the usual limits of the saxophone. (3)
7. Sometimes he would play his saxophone outdoors instead of indoors. (1)
8. Another of his experiments involved making the sound from his saxophone bounce off walls. (3)
9. Rollins continued experiments with music throughout his long career. (2)
10. In addition to his experimental work, Rollins played the music for the movie *Alfie*. (2)

Exercise 59 — Identifying and Replacing Prepositions in Phrases

On your paper, write the preposition that appears in each sentence below. Then rewrite each sentence using a different preposition. You may also need to change the object of the preposition.

1. The basketball game started after seven o'clock.
2. The players eagerly ran onto the court.
3. In spite of the snowstorm, attendance was high.
4. The pep band played loudly during halftime.
5. Aside from a few minor injuries, the game went well.
6. My brother is a cheerleader for the team.
7. He and the other cheerleaders perform during the game.
8. They have attended games throughout the year.
9. They will attend the state tournament with the team members.
10. In addition to cheering, they also like winning.

10.7 Conjunctions

- A **conjunction** is a word that joins single words or groups of words.

Coordinating Conjunctions

- A **coordinating conjunction** joins words or groups of words that have equal grammatical weight in a sentence.

Coordinating Conjunctions						
and	but	or	so	nor	for	yet

Two **and** two are four.
She is good at algebra **but** not at arithmetic.
We must leave now, **or** we will be late.
The bell rang, **yet** everyone remained seated.
He could not sleep, **nor** would he eat.

When used as a coordinating conjunction, **for** means "for the reason that" or "because."

The children were tired, **for** they had run a long distance.

Exercise 60 Identifying Coordinating Conjunctions

On your paper, write the coordinating conjunctions that appear in the following sentences.

A Monument to Civil Rights

[1]The civil rights leaders of the 1960s strove to win greater respect, dignity, and political freedom for African Americans. [2]Martin Luther King Jr. was the most famous civil rights leader, but he was not the only person to participate in the struggle. [3]Ordinary citizens, such as Rosa Parks, who refused to sit at the back of a segregated bus, contributed to the fight for justice and equality. [4]Taunts did not deter the civil rights demonstrators, nor did physical abuse.

[5]A new monument in Alabama commemorates the famous heroes of the movement, yet it does not ignore its anonymous heroes. [6]The monument is in the city of Montgomery, for it was there that many famous civil rights demonstrations took place. [7]Made of smooth black granite, the monument is simple, yet it is remarkably powerful. [8]Water flows gently over the flat surface of the stone and collects in a pool. [9]The names of civil rights leaders and the dates of famous events in the struggle are engraved on the stone. [10]The monument was designed by the Chinese American architect Maya Lin, who is famous for her bold and austere monument to the veterans of the Vietnam War.

Correlative Conjunctions

■ **Correlative conjunctions** work in pairs to join words and groups of words of equal weight in a sentence.

Correlative Conjunctions		
both . . . and	just as . . . so	not only . . . but (also)
either . . . or	neither . . . nor	whether . . . or

Correlative conjunctions make the relationship between words or groups of words a little clearer than do coordinating conjunctions.

COORDINATING CONJUNCTIONS	CORRELATIVE CONJUNCTIONS
She **and** I were there.	**Both** she **and** I were there.
She **or** I can go.	**Either** she **or** I can go.
	Neither she **nor** I can go.
I met Jean **and** Ed.	I met **not only** Jean **but also** Ed.

Exercise 61   Identifying Correlative Conjunctions

On your paper, write both parts of the correlative conjunctions that appear in the following sentences.

Weather Forecasting

1. Just as people are interested in the weather forecast today, so people thousands of years ago tried to predict weather conditions.
2. Methods of predicting the weather have grown not only more complicated but also more accurate.
3. Both modern and ancient cultures have looked to the sky for signs of change in the weather.
4. The predictions of the ancients, whether correct or incorrect, were based on very different methods from those of today.
5. Neither the seemingly essential thermometer nor the equally useful barometer was invented until a few hundred years ago.
6. Both the modern telegraph and the even more recent satellite have made it possible to exchange weather information more rapidly.
7. Satellites are used for early spotting not only of hurricanes but also of tornadoes.
8. Neither high-speed computers nor other advanced technological breakthroughs have revealed all we need to know to predict the weather accurately.
9. The National Oceanic and Atmospheric Administration is responsible for both studying the weather and forecasting it.
10. Weather forecasting is an activity not only of government agencies but also of private companies.

Subordinating Conjunctions

■ A **subordinating conjunction** joins two clauses, or ideas, in such a way as to make one grammatically dependent upon the other.

The idea, or clause, that a subordinating conjunction introduces is said to be "subordinate," or dependent, because it cannot stand by itself as a complete sentence.

>We raked the leaves **because** so many had fallen.
>We raked the leaves **before** we had lunch.
>**When** more leaves fall, we will rake again.

Common Subordinating Conjunctions				
after	as soon as	inasmuch as	than	where
although	as though	in order that	though	whereas
as	because	provided (that)	unless	wherever
as far as	before	since	until	while
as if	considering (that)	so long as	when	
as long as	if	so that	whenever	

Exercise 62   Identifying Subordinating Conjunctions

On your paper, write the subordinating conjunction that appears in each sentence below. Remember that some subordinating conjunctions are made up of more than one word.

The Art of Mural Painting

1. Although they are found in many cultures around the world, murals have always been a particularly important art form in Mexico.
2. Some of the murals painted by Mayan artists in ancient Mexico still survive, though many are in poor condition.
3. Before the Mexican painter Diego Rivera came on the scene, twentieth-century Mexican murals were relatively unknown.
4. Rivera designed extraordinary murals before he died in 1957.
5. Many of Rivera's murals depict scenes from Mexican history because Rivera believed that Mexicans are defined by their past.
6. After Rivera died, many Mexican American muralists took up his style and themes.
7. Some Mexican American artists in Los Angeles paint murals wherever they can find space.
8. They paint on public buildings so that their work can be enjoyed by many people.
9. So that the murals can be easily seen, the muralists use bright colors and bold, eye-catching designs.
10. As long as Hispanic culture continues to thrive in the United States, we will surely have many colorful and exciting murals to enjoy.

Exercise 63 — Completing Sentences with Subordinating Conjunctions

On your paper, write a subordinating conjunction to complete each of the following sentences. Be sure that your completed sentences make sense.

Early Painters

1. We can't name the earliest painters _____ they did not sign their work.
2. The art of painting began as early as the Paleolithic Age, _____ prehistoric hunters decorated the walls of their caves.
3. _____ some ancient Greek painters are known, their works have not survived.
4. _____ images covered walls, gates, palaces, and temples, it seems likely that professional painters lived in Sumeria and ancient Egypt.
5. Decorations on Greek pottery were baked permanently into the surface _____ they could be preserved.
6. _____ they cannot be baked, many paintings on wood or walls have been lost.
7. Roman painters used a heating process _____ their paintings might be preserved.
8. They discovered that paints weathered better _____ they were mixed with boiling wax, resin, and vegetable oils.
9. _____ wealthy Roman citizens admired art, fresco paintings covered the walls of their houses.
10. _____ Roman painters were very skillful, few of their works have endured.

Exercise 64 — Adding Conjunctions to Make Sentences

On your paper, revise the sentences below. Use a coordinating conjunction, correlative conjunction, or subordinating conjunction to join the two sentences in each item. Try to use a variety of conjunctions. Make sure your completed sentences make sense.

SAMPLE It was such a hot day. I rested in the shade.

ANSWER *Because* it was such a hot day, I rested in the shade.

SAMPLE Whales are interesting. They are mysterious creatures.

ANSWER Whales are interesting *and* mysterious creatures.

Whale Watching

1. In the winter, young humpback whales sometimes feed off the coast of Virginia. They also feed off the coast of North Carolina.
2. The whale is a warm-blooded animal. It looks like a fish.
3. The whale needs oxygen to breathe. It will drown if submerged too long.
4. Porpoises are considered whales. Dolphins are considered whales.
5. Most whales dive for an average of three to ten minutes. Some of the toothed whales can remain submerged for more than thirty minutes.
6. The rib cage of a whale is very flexible. It can withstand great pressure.
7. No one has seen whales mate. Scientists think whales mate once a year.
8. Blue whales are the largest whales. Blue whales are the fastest whales.
9. Blue whales are rare. They can be found in all oceans of the world.
10. Finback whales are a valuable catch. They are the mainstay of the whaling industry.

Conjunctive Adverbs

- A **conjunctive adverb** is used to clarify the relationship between clauses of equal weight in a sentence.

Conjunctive adverbs are usually stronger, more precise, and more formal than coordinating conjunctions.

COORDINATING CONJUNCTION	Most people think of deserts as very hot places, **but** desert nights can be quite cool.
CONJUNCTIVE ADVERB	Most people think of deserts as very hot places; **however,** desert nights can be quite cool.

There are many conjunctive adverbs, and they have several uses, as the following examples show:

TO REPLACE *AND*	also, besides, furthermore, moreover
TO REPLACE *BUT*	however, nevertheless, still, though
TO STATE A RESULT	consequently, therefore, so, thus
TO STATE EQUALITY	equally, likewise, similarly

Exercise 65   **Identifying Conjunctive Adverbs**

On your paper, write the conjunctive adverb in each sentence.

Toltec Civilization

1. The Toltec civilization of ancient Mexico was advanced in arts and architecture; moreover, it produced impressive stonework.
2. Toltec religion centered on Quetzalcoatl; consequently, he appeared in many images.
3. Quetzalcoatl was the name of a deity; furthermore, it was the name of a legendary ruler.
4. Quetzalcoatl was identified with the planet Venus; likewise, he was linked with the wind.
5. Usually he was depicted as a plumed serpent; however, he was often shown as a wind god.
6. The people wished to please Quetzalcoatl; therefore, they built circular temples that presented no sharp obstacles to the wind.
7. There were many different religious ceremonies and rituals; moreover, people played a sacred ball game called *tlatchi* that resembled basketball.
8. The Toltec civilization expanded southward during the tenth century; therefore, the Toltecs dominated the Mayas of the Yucatan.
9. Other nomadic Mexican groups conquered the Toltecs; thus, their civilization declined.
10. The Aztecs soon built their own empire; consequently, art continued to flourish.

Exercise 66 — Identifying Kinds of Conjunctions

On your paper, write the conjunction that appears in each sentence below. Indicate whether the conjunction is a *coordinating, correlative,* or *subordinating* conjunction.

The Galápagos Tortoise

1. After they have mated, adult female Galápagos tortoises lay their eggs on the beach.
2. Each tortoise finds a spot of bare soil where she digs a foot-wide pit.
3. She lays fifteen to twenty eggs inside the pit and covers them with soil.
4. Neither the male nor the female tortoises watch over the eggs.
5. Baby tortoises are on their own after birth because they are able to find their own food.

Exercise 67 — Creating Sentences with Conjunctions

Think of a day in which several interesting and varied events happened to you. On your paper, write five sentences about that day, using as many conjunctions as possible.

Exercise 68 — Completing Sentences with Conjunctions

On your paper, replace each blank in the following sentences with a conjunction that makes sense. The kind of conjunction to use is stated in parentheses at the end of each sentence.

Modern Tunnel Construction

1. Modern tunnel building is a complicated process; _____, it is a very costly process, involving millions of dollars. (conjunctive adverb)
2. _____ it costs considerably more than a bridge, a tunnel under a river may have certain advantages. (subordinating conjunction)
3. _____ does it allow the unhindered passage of ships, _____ it is less vulnerable. (a pair of correlative conjunctions)
4. A tunnel is a marvelous construction, _____ building one is extremely hazardous. (coordinating conjunction)
5. There are basically three ways to build a tunnel; _____, tunnels may be divided into three types. (conjunctive adverb)
6. A "true" tunnel is dug horizontally through earth _____ rock. (coordinating conjunction)
7. For the cut-and-cover tunnel, a large ditch is dug, a tube is built in the ditch, _____ the tube is covered over. (coordinating conjunction)
8. _____ the first subway in the world, in London, _____ the first on the European continent, in Budapest, were built in this way. (a pair of correlative conjunctions)
9. The trench tunnel involves a kind of cut-and-cover method used _____ the tunnel is dug underwater. (subordinating conjunction)
10. _____ a route is chosen for any tunnel, a careful geologic study is made of the type of earth and rock along the way. (subordinating conjunction)

10.8 Interjections

■ An **interjection** is a word or phrase that expresses emotion or exclamation. An interjection has no grammatical connection to other words.

Oh, I didn't know that.　　**Whew,** it's hot.
Ouch! That hurts!　　**Why,** children!

Exercise 69 Identifying Interjections

On your paper, write the interjection that appears in each item.

1. Dear me! Whatever shall we do?
2. Oh, don't ask me.
3. Alas! The ship was doomed.
4. This box is heavy. Ugh!
5. Yuck! What a disgusting thought!
6. Phooey! I give up.
7. Wow, it's really snowing out there.
8. Whee! We're sliding all over.
9. Well! This is a surprise.
10. Hey, what's that noise?

Exercise 70 Using Interjections

On your paper, replace each blank below with an appropriate interjection from the following list. Remember to add punctuation.

| Wow | Oops | Ssh | Ah | Whew |
| Well | Psst | Yipes | Alas | Ouch |

1. _____ That was an amazing catch!
2. _____ I dropped the plate.
3. _____ you are here at last.
4. _____ The stove is hot!
5. _____ the concert is beginning.
6. _____ That was pretty close!
7. _____ it is finally over.
8. _____ come here a second, but do not let anyone see you.
9. _____ That is the wildest thing I have ever heard!
10. _____ It is pouring, and I forgot to shut the windows.

10.8 Interjections **481**

UNIT 10 Grammar Review

Parts of Speech

This passage from Marilynne Robinson's novel *Housekeeping* has been annotated to show some of the parts of speech covered in this unit. Read the passage and do the exercises that follow.

Literature Model

from Housekeeping
by Marilynne Robinson

It was a hard winter, too. The **snow** crested, finally, far above our heads. It drifted up our eaves on one side of the house. Some houses in **Fingerbone** simply fell from the weight of snow on their roofs, a source of grave and perpetual **anxiety** to my great-aunts, who were accustomed to a brick building, and to living below ground. Sometimes the sun would be warm enough to send a **thick** sheet of **snow** sliding off the roof, and sometimes the fir trees would shrug, and the snow would fall with surprisingly loud and earthy thuds, which would terrify my great-aunts. . . .

For some reason the lake was a source of particular pleasure to Fingerbone that year. It **was** frozen solid early and long. Several acres of it were swept, for people brought brooms to tend and expand it, till the cleared ice spread far across the lake. Sledders heaped snow on the shore into a precipitous chute **that** sent them sailing far across the ice. There were barrels on the shore for fires to be built in, **and** people brought boxes to sit on and planks and burlap bags to stand on around the barrels, and frankfurters to roast, and clothespins to clip frozen mittens to the lips of barrels. A number of dogs began to spend most of their time at the ice. **They** were young, leggy dogs, affable and proprietary, and exhilarated by the weather. They liked to play at retrieving bits of ice which sped fantastically fast and far across the lake. The dogs made a gallant and youthful joke of their own strength and speed,

Annotations (Parts of Speech):
- Common noun
- Proper noun
- Abstract noun
- Adjective
- Concrete noun
- Linking verb
- Relative pronoun
- Coordinating conjunction
- Personal pronoun

Grammar Review

and *flaunted* an utter indifference to the safety of their limbs. Lucille and I took our skates to school, *so that* we could go to the lake directly and stay there through the twilight. Usually we would skate *along* the edge of the swept ice, tracing its shape, and coming finally to *its* farthest edge, we would sit on the snow and look back at Fingerbone.

We felt giddily far from shore, though the lake was so solid that winter that it would *certainly* have supported the weight of the entire population of Fingerbone, past, present, and to come. Nevertheless, only we and the ice sweepers went out so far, and only we stayed.

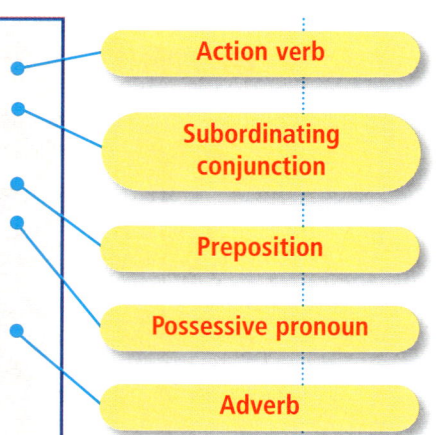

- Action verb
- Subordinating conjunction
- Preposition
- Possessive pronoun
- Adverb

Review: Exercise 1   Identifying Nouns

The following sentences elaborate on ideas from *Housekeeping*. On your paper, write each of the nouns in these sentences. After each noun, write *common*, *proper*, or *collective*, depending upon how the noun is used in the sentence.

SAMPLE   *Housekeeping* is about two sisters and their family.
ANSWER   *Housekeeping* (proper), sisters (common), family (common, collective)

1. The village of Fingerbone, Idaho, endured severe winters.
2. During a particularly bad winter, Fingerbone was nearly buried by a fierce storm.
3. The snowfall was heavy, and temperatures were low.
4. Half of the roof was covered with snow.
5. According to Aunt Lily and Aunt Nona, the house might collapse from the weight.
6. The idea that the house could fall made the aunts nervous.
7. Lily and Nona were even startled by the noise made by huge clumps of falling snow.
8. A crowd of local residents gathered daily at Fingerbone Lake.
9. The lake froze early, well before Thanksgiving Day.
10. A team of sweepers cleared the snow from the icy surface.
11. People packed the snow into a steep chute for sledders to use.
12. The public enjoyed many activities on the ice.
13. One crowd of merrymakers roasted wieners.
14. Another group rode sleds down a snowy hill.
15. Gleefully, a pack of dogs scampered among the throng.
16. Ruth and Lucille were among the throng of townspeople at the festivities.
17. After school the pair of girls went straight to the lake.
18. The sisters skated to the boundary of the swept ice.
19. Later, the two skaters rested on a snowbank and looked at the village.
20. Ruth and her sister returned to their home after hours of fun.

Grammar Review

Review: Exercise 2 — Using Pronouns Effectively

The paragraph below elaborates on ideas suggested by a passage from *Housekeeping* that is not reprinted in this textbook. On your paper, write each sentence in the paragraph, substituting pronouns for nouns when a pronoun would make good sense. Do not substitute a pronoun for a noun if the pronoun would make the sentence unclear.

¹Ruth and Ruth's sister, Lucille, lived in the small town of Fingerbone, Idaho. ²Ruth's and Lucille's grandfather was originally from the Midwest, but the grandfather had come to Idaho years ago and built the grandfather's home there. ³Ruth did not remember the grandfather, since the grandfather had died before Ruth was born. ⁴Ruth had been raised by Ruth's grandmother until the grandmother died. ⁵Then Ruth's great-aunts came to Fingerbone to take care of the two girls. ⁶The great-aunts were unfamiliar with rural life and did not really enjoy rural life. ⁷The great-aunts felt isolated in Fingerbone because of Fingerbone's small population. ⁸The heavy snowfall troubled the great-aunts, and the great-aunts also worried about the great-aunts' nieces. ⁹Ruth did not mind the harsh winter, since Ruth had lived in Fingerbone all Ruth's life. ¹⁰Ruth often took Ruth's ice skates with Ruth to school and afterward went to Fingerbone Lake to skate on Fingerbone Lake's frozen waters.

Review: Exercise 3 — Completing Sentences with Pronouns

The following sentences elaborate on ideas suggested by a passage from *Housekeeping* that is not reprinted in this textbook. On your paper, write the type of pronoun specified in italics for each sentence. Be sure that your completed sentences make sense.

1. *Indefinite* of the winters in Fingerbone, Idaho, were severe.
2. During a particularly harsh winter, the people found simple ways to amuse *reflexive*.
3. *Indefinite* seemed to enjoy sledding down snowy hills and skating on Fingerbone Lake.
4. Ruth and *possessive* sister enjoyed skating on the frozen lake after school.
5. *Personal* were certain that the frozen ice was solid enough to hold them.
6. *Indefinite* seemed to stop the girls from enjoying the great outdoors.
7. Of course, the girls' great-aunts needlessly worried *reflexive* about the weather.
8. The great-aunts also worried about *possessive* nieces.
9. *Interrogative* could blame them?
10. The aunts were not accustomed to rural living, and *demonstrative* was an especially severe winter.

484 Unit 10 Parts of Speech

Grammar Review

Review: Exercise 4 — Identifying Verbs and Verb Phrases

The following sentences are adapted from the passage. Write on your paper any verbs and verb phrases that appear in the sentences, and label them accordingly.

SAMPLE Ruth's great-aunts had lived in brick houses all their lives.
ANSWER had lived—verb phrase

1. The snow had been falling for days.
2. It piled into drifts and covered the eaves of the house.
3. Finally the sun returned to the sky.
4. Sometimes the fir trees would shudder under a heavy load of snow.
5. A dense layer of snow often slid to the ground with an earthy thud.
6. Many weeks of cold weather had frozen the waters of Fingerbone Lake to its very depths.
7. There must have been a dozen children among the skaters.
8. Townspeople had cleared several acres of ice with their brooms.
9. After school Lucille and Ruth skated until twilight, and they would have stayed even later.
10. They would venture farther out than anyone else onto the frozen surface of the lake.

Review: Exercise 5 — Identifying Transitive and Intransitive Verbs

The following sentences contain verbs that appear in the passage from *Housekeeping*. For each item, write *transitive* or *intransitive* on your paper, depending upon the way the italicized verb is used in the sentence.

SAMPLE Mounds of snow *crested* as high as the windows.
ANSWER intransitive

SAMPLE The skaters *brought* extra mittens.
ANSWER transitive

1. Snow *drifted* against the fence.
2. A child *fell* in the deep snow.
3. The howling blizzard *terrified* the small children.
4. Some neighbors *brought* snowshoes with them.
5. Children *heaped* snow into small hills to build igloos.
6. An expert skier *sped* through the countryside.
7. Ice skaters *flaunted* their skills before crowds.
8. They *skated* around the lake at dizzying speeds.
9. Toddlers *traced* patterns with their feet in the cold, sparkling snow.
10. The frozen lake *supported* hundreds of skaters.

Grammar Review

Review: Exercise 6 — Identifying Adjectives

The following sentences are about Idaho. On your paper, write the adjectives that appear in each sentence. Include pronouns and proper adjectives, but not the words *a, an,* and *the*. After each adjective, write the word that the adjective modifies.

SAMPLE Idaho is an unusual setting for a novel about ordinary life.
ANSWER unusual—setting; ordinary—life

1. Few aspects of life in the state are unremarkable.
2. The lofty Rocky Mountains provide spectacular sights.
3. A large portion of Idaho remains a remote wilderness.
4. Its icy streams provide a suitable habitat for many varieties of trout.
5. The early Native American peoples of the region were expert hunters of the mighty buffalo.
6. After the discovery of gold in the 1860s, many European settlers came to make their homes in Idaho.
7. Hardy miners were prominent among these hard-working settlers in northern sections of Idaho.
8. Because of the hostile landscape, life was difficult for most people.
9. Primitive conditions fostered a generous spirit of cooperation, however.
10. Today, farming is a major industry in this large state.

Review: Exercise 7 — Expanding Sentences with Adjectives

The following sentences elaborate on the passage from *Housekeeping*. On your paper, write adjectives that would make sense in the places indicated by carets. Although there are no specific correct answers, base your choices on the passage.

SAMPLE Temperatures were ∧, and a ∧ layer of snow blanketed the town.
ANSWER low, thick

1. In the ∧ village the air was frosty and ∧ .
2. The town of Fingerbone looked for a few days like a ∧ and ∧ wonderland.
3. When the ∧ sun returned, ∧ neighbors dug paths from their homes.
4. Ruth's ∧ aunts worried about the ∧ roof.
5. Fingerbone Lake became a ∧ sheet of ice, ∧ for skating.
6. The ∧ townspeople took ∧ pleasure in the lake.
7. ∧ sledders built a ∧ chute of snow.
8. ∧ dogs raced across the ice at ∧ speeds.
9. Ruth and Lucille skated on the ∧ ice and looked back at the ∧ town.
10. Tired but ∧, the girls trudged home in the ∧ twilight.

Grammar Review

Review: Exercise 8   **Identifying Adverbs**

The following sentences are about ice skating. On your paper, write each adverb that appears in these sentences and the word that the adverb modifies.

SAMPLE   Skilled ice skaters twirl quite gracefully.
ANSWER   quite—gracefully; gracefully—twirl

1. Experienced skaters move rather rapidly on the ice.
2. Frequently they form special patterns, or figures.
3. In cold climates they often skate outside.
4. Sometimes they glide on frozen lakes and ponds.
5. Safety is very important for all skaters.
6. Wise skaters never skate alone.
7. Professional figure skaters generally perform indoors.
8. Special equipment creates the ice mechanically.
9. Have you ever seen a professional ice show?
10. The skaters dress beautifully and usually perform to music.

Review: Exercise 9   **Using Adverbs**

Each of the following sentences is based on the information in the passage from *Housekeeping*. On your paper, write an appropriate adverb to take the place of the prepositional phrase in italics. The adverb should express the same idea as the prepositional phrase.

SAMPLE   That year winter descended with much harshness on Fingerbone.
ANSWER   harshly

1. The snow fell *in heavy masses* for many days.
2. *In a sudden motion* a heavy slab of snow slid from a tree.
3. Ruth's great-aunts looked *with anxiety* at their own snow-laden roof.
4. *To everyone's amazement* the dilapidated roof held up under the weight of the snow.
5. The villagers walked *with eagerness* to the frozen lake.
6. Some sledded *in a reckless way* down a steep chute of snow.
7. The dogs chased pieces of ice that slid *in a quick manner* across the frozen lake.
8. Dogs scampered *in an exuberant fashion* across the ice.
9. For hours Ruth and Lucille skated *with swiftness* on the frozen lake.
10. After twilight the girls returned home *in a weary manner*.

Grammar Review   **487**

Grammar Review

Review: Exercise 10   **Identifying Prepositions**

The following sentences are based on passages from *Housekeeping* not reprinted in this book. On your paper, list the prepositions that appear in each sentence. Remember that some prepositions are made up of more than one word. (The numeral in parentheses at the end of each item indicates the number of prepositions the sentence contains.)

1. *Housekeeping* is about two orphaned sisters in Idaho. (2)
2. The novel is narrated by Ruth, one of the sisters. (2)
3. Ruth's grandmother brought order to the household through her insistence on strict attention to chores. (4)
4. After the death of Ruth's grandmother, Ruth's great-aunts came to Idaho and cared for the girls. (4)
5. The great-aunts came from Spokane, Washington, and were unfamiliar with life in a small town like Fingerbone. (4)
6. They moved to Fingerbone in spite of their preference for city life. (3)
7. During crises the aunts took refuge in the repetition of familiar chores. (3)
8. The normal needs of adolescents in the home caused too many changes in routine for the aunts' liking. (4)
9. They fled to the safety of a hotel and left Aunt Sylvie in charge as the girls' guardian. (4)
10. According to Sylvie, life is about change and surprises, not housekeeping. (2)

Review: Exercise 11   **Using Prepositions**

Each of the sentences below elaborates on the passage from *Housekeeping*. On your paper, write a preposition that completes the word or phrase in italics and makes sense in the sentence. More than one preposition may make sense.

SAMPLE   The cold spell lasted _____ *weeks*.
ANSWER   for

1. Because temperatures had remained _____ *the freezing point*, Fingerbone Lake had turned to solid ice.
2. Townspeople _____ *brooms* steadily swept the snow from acres of ice.
3. They dumped snow from sleds into huge mounds _____ *the shore*.
4. Some villagers skated _____ *the frozen surface* almost to the far shore.
5. Sledders raced _____ *a steep hill* of snow.
6. People roasted meat _____ *barrels* on shore.
7. Frozen mittens were clipped _____ *clothespins* to the rims of the barrels.
8. Some of the townsfolk brought boxes to use _____ *chairs*.
9. Dogs scampered playfully _____ *the crowd*.
10. The lake assumed the aspect _____ *an impromptu festival*.

488   Unit 10   Parts of Speech

Grammar Review

Review: Exercise 12 — Using Conjunctions

The following sentences tell more about Idaho, the setting for *Housekeeping*. On your paper, complete each sentence by writing an appropriate conjunction according to the direction in parentheses. Choose your conjunctions from the list below, which has more conjunctions than you will need.

CONJUNCTIONS

and	or	but	yet
neither . . . nor	not only . . . but also		
although	because	before	if	when	wherever

SAMPLE Idaho is located in the Rocky Mountains, _____ it is very beautiful. (Add a coordinating conjunction.)

ANSWER and

1. _____ you go in Idaho, you are likely to find spectacular scenery. (Add a subordinating conjunction.)
2. _____ you visit the Snake River Canyon, be sure to see Shoshone Falls. (Add a subordinating conjunction.)
3. You might fish in one of Idaho's two thousand lakes in the summer _____ visit the state during the skiing season. (Add a coordinating conjunction.)
4. _____ Idaho is far from the coast, it has the cold winters typical of the North American interior. (Add a subordinating conjunction.)
5. Winter temperatures often dip below freezing, _____ several feet of snow fall each year. (Add a coordinating conjunction.)
6. _____ Idaho is the thirteenth largest state in area, it is sparsely populated. (Add a subordinating conjunction.)
7. _____ Boise, Idaho's capital city, _____ the even smaller city of Twin Falls has a population of over 150,000. (Add a pair of correlative conjunctions.)
8. Native American communities had inhabited Idaho for centuries _____ the first European explorers arrived in 1805. (Add a subordinating conjunction.)
9. _____ gold was discovered in Idaho in the 1860s, thousands of prospectors flocked to the state. (Add a subordinating conjunction.)
10. Today Idaho is famous for its potatoes, _____ few people know that it also has the largest silver mine in the nation. (Add a coordinating conjunction.)

Grammar Review

Review: Exercise 13 **Using Interjections**

Each of the sentences below relates to the theme of the passage from *Housekeeping*. On your paper, replace each blank below with an appropriate interjection from the following list. Remember to add punctuation.

Yikes	Wow	Boy	Well	Ssh
Ah	Whee	Alas	Oops	Uh-oh

1. _____ That was a hard winter.
2. _____ the snow finally crested.
3. _____ Some houses fell from the weight of snow on their roofs!
4. _____ The clumps of falling snow almost hit me!
5. _____ the great-aunts are very nervous.
6. _____ I slipped on some ice!
7. _____ Skating is so much fun!
8. _____ We are really far from shore!
9. _____ Can you hear the snow falling?
10. _____ what a winter wonderland!

Review: Exercise 14

Proofreading

The following passage describes the artist Grandma Moses, whose painting appears on the opposite page. Rewrite the passage, correcting the errors in spelling, capitalization, usage, and grammar. Add any missing punctuation. There are twenty-five errors.

Grandma Moses

¹Anna Mary Robertson Moses (1860–1961) who was known as Grandma Moses, was born in Greenwich, New York, to a family of Scottish and irish desent. ²She begun painting at the age of seventy-seven. ³During the last two decades of her life, Moses painted hundreds of scenes of rural farm life, she became perhaps the most famous folk painter in America.

⁴Encouraged by her father Moses developed her talent for drawing; she, however, had little time to pursue hers interest in art. ⁵She married a farmer, Thomas Salmon Moses and bore ten children. ⁶She spent much of her life on a dairy farm in the tiny community of Eagle Bridge in upstate new york. ⁷She begun to paint seriously only after her arthritis became so crippling that she could no longer work on the farm. ⁸A few of her paintings on display at a Eagle Bridge drugstore was discovered by an art collector who happened to pass

490 Unit 10 Parts of Speech

Grammar Review

Anna Mary Robertson ("Grandma") Moses, *Early Skating*, 1951

through town. ⁹Somewhat taken aback by her sudden fame, Moses was scandalized when both dealers or tourists began to offer large sums for paintings that she thought were worth only a few dollars'.

¹⁰Moses paintings are remarkable for their harmony and detail. ¹¹Although she had no formel training, Moses had a strong intuitive grasp of color, pattern, and design. ¹²Recorded the landscapes and customs of her rural countryside with the sensitivity of a poet. ¹³Every detail is careful observed: the gray cast of the sky on a snowy morning the steam rising from a locomotive, and the straining muscles of a horse pulling a sleigh. ¹⁴Moses's *Early Skating*, like the passage from Marilynne Robinson's novel *Housekeeping*, capture the atmosphere of a small community on a winter day. ¹⁵Although the painting depict New York, whereas the novel is set in Idaho, the mood are the same. ¹⁶There are a playfulness about the two scenes of children cavorting on the ice. ¹⁷There is also a feeling of isolation, as if these two small towns were seperated from the outside world by time and winters snowy blanket.

Grammar Review

Review: Exercise 15

The following biography of Marilynne Robinson is followed by ten sentences. On your paper, write an appropriate word to complete each sentence. Use the directions in parentheses as a guide. You will need to consult the biography in order to fill in some of the blanks properly.

Marilynne Robinson

Born in 1944, Marilynne Robinson is one of contemporary America's promising new writers. Her first novel, *Housekeeping* (published in 1981), was widely acclaimed for its poetic language, its vivid characterizations, and its keen understanding of human nature. Set in an isolated Rocky Mountain community in Idaho, *Housekeeping* describes two orphaned sisters who are cared for by a number of different guardians, each with her own ideas about what is important in life. This touching story about small-town life earned Robinson the 1982 Ernest Hemingway Foundation Award for Best First Novel. The book was the basis of a critically acclaimed motion picture. Robinson is also the author of a nonfiction book called *Mother Country*. In addition, she has contributed several stories and articles to *Harper's* and other major magazines.

1. The _____ author Marilynne Robinson was born in 1944. (Add a proper adjective.)
2. Robinson _____ her novel *Housekeeping* in 1981. (Add an action verb.)
3. _____ *Housekeeping* was only a first novel, it received much critical attention. (Add a subordinating conjunction.)
4. *Housekeeping* takes place in a remote community in the _____ of Idaho. (Add a proper noun.)
5. The novel was praised for its _____ language and keen understanding of human nature. (Add an adjective.)
6. Critics also _____ applauded its finely drawn and well-developed characters. (Add an adverb.)
7. *Housekeeping* _____ a winner of the Ernest Hemingway Foundation Award for Best First Novel. (Add a linking verb.)
8. The _____ based on the novel was also critically acclaimed. (Add a common noun.)
9. Robinson has not yet published a second novel _____ has written a nonfiction work titled *Mother Country*. (Add a coordinating conjunction.)
10. Some of Robinson's short stories have appeared _____ *Harper's*, the noted literary magazine, as well as other major publications in the United States. (Add a preposition.)

Writing Application

Nouns in Writing

Amy Tan uses nouns in this passage from *The Joy Luck Club* to convey the bustle and confusion a California girl feels traveling in a foreign country for the first time. Examine the passage, focusing especially on the italicized nouns.

> Before the *train* even comes to a *stop, people* are bringing down their *belongings* from above their *seats*. For a *moment* there is a dangerous *shower* of heavy *suitcases* laden with *gifts* to *relatives,* half-broken *boxes* wrapped in *miles* of *string* to keep the *contents* from spilling out, plastic *bags* filled with *yarn* and *vegetables* and *packages* of dried *mushrooms,* and camera *cases.* And then we are caught in a *stream* of *people* rushing, shoving, pushing us along, until we find ourselves in one of a dozen *lines* waiting to go through *customs.* I feel as if I were getting on the number 30 Stockton *bus* in *San Francisco.* I am in *China,* I remind myself. And somehow the *crowds* don't bother me. It feels right. I start pushing, too.

Techniques with Nouns

Try to apply some of Amy Tan's writing techniques when you write and revise your own work.

❶ Whenever possible, replace general words with precise concrete nouns. Compare the following:

GENERAL WORDS bags filled with *things*

TAN'S VERSION plastic bags filled with *yarn* and *vegetables* and *packages* of dried *mushrooms*, and camera *cases*

❷ Use proper nouns to help make your writing more specific.

GENERAL WORDS I am in a foreign *country.* . . . a crowded bus in a *city.* . . .

TAN'S VERSION I am in *China.* . . . the number 30 Stockton bus in *San Francisco.* . . .

❸ Expand single nouns into longer groups of specific words when you wish to provide more details.

SINGLE NOUN suitcases

TAN'S VERSION heavy suitcases laden with gifts to relatives

TIME

For more about the writing process, see **TIME Facing the Blank Page**, pp. 121-131.

Parts of Speech

Practice Practice these techniques by revising the following passage, using a separate sheet of paper. Pay particular attention to the underlined words.

By seven o'clock on that snowy morning, the <u>park</u> was a scene of great activity. A <u>group</u> of <u>dogs</u> was racing across the <u>area</u>, putting <u>birds</u> to flight. Frantic owners followed, shouting the names of their dogs. Squirrels flicked their tails and scampered to safety. Along the pathway, the <u>dog</u> <u>owners</u> stamped their feet in the snow and chatted about <u>things</u>. Others fed birds that chirped and hopped nervously on the path. Before long, <u>children</u> came running through the park, dragging their <u>toys</u> behind them. Their <u>voices</u> blended with all the other <u>sounds</u>. In a moment, the usually serene park had become quite a hectic place.

Writing Application **493**

UNIT 11 Parts of the Sentence

Lesson 11.1	Simple Subjects and Simple Predicates	495
Lesson 11.2	Complete Subjects and Complete Predicates	496
Lesson 11.3	Compound Subjects and Compound Predicates	498
Lesson 11.4	Order of Subject and Predicate	501
Lesson 11.5	Complements	504
Grammar Review		510
Writing Application		517

11.1 Simple Subjects and Simple Predicates

- A **sentence** is a group of words expressing a complete thought.

  Every sentence has two basic parts, a *subject* and a *predicate*.

- The **subject** is the part of the sentence about which something is being said.

- The **predicate** is the part that says something about the subject.

- The **simple subject** is the key noun or pronoun (or word or group of words acting as a noun) that tells what a sentence is about.

  The simple subject may be a compound noun consisting of more than one word.

- The **simple predicate** is the verb or verb phrase that expresses the essential thought about the subject of the sentence.

  A simple predicate that is a verb phrase consists of the verb and any helping verbs.

SIMPLE SUBJECT	SIMPLE PREDICATE
Dionne Warwick	will perform.
Owls	were hooting.
José Canseco	ran.
Things	change.

The simple subject is found by asking *who?* or *what?* about the verb.

Exercise 1   Identifying Simple Subjects and Predicates

Write each simple subject and each simple predicate. Underline the simple predicates.

The Yo-Yo

1. Donald Duncan was an American inventor.
2. He founded a toy company in the 1920s.
3. A popular Duncan toy was the yo-yo.
4. The yo-yo is a double disc with a string between the discs.
5. The yo-yo moves up and down the string.
6. Duncan used a yo-yo from the Philippines as a model.
7. Prehistoric Philippine hunters used yo-yos as weapons.
8. *Yo-yo* means "to return" in Pilipino.
9. The ancient Philippine people had made their yo-yos of stone.
10. Since the 1950s, Duncan has been making yo-yos out of plastic.

11.2 Complete Subjects and Complete Predicates

Whoooooo

...was hooting in the night?

In most sentences the meaning of the simple subject and the simple predicate is expanded or modified by the addition of other words and phrases.

■ The **complete subject** consists of the simple subject and all the words that modify it.

■ The **complete predicate** consists of the simple predicate, or verb, and all the words that modify it or complete its meaning.

COMPLETE SUBJECT	COMPLETE PREDICATE
Talented Dionne Warwick	will perform her biggest hits.
Large owls with bright eyes	were hooting loudly in the dark forest.
The speedy José Canseco	ran all the way home from first base on a double.
Many things	change daily.

Exercise 2   Identifying Complete Subjects and Predicates

Write the following sentences on your paper. Underline each complete subject once and each complete predicate twice.

Virginia State Parks

1. The state of Virginia has a fine park system.
2. Virginia state parks offer access to lakes, rivers, and the Chesapeake Bay.
3. Virginia's lakes contain largemouth bass, trout, and bream.
4. Boats can be rented only in the summer months.
5. Canoes are available in many places.
6. Frequent visitors can purchase season tickets for state parks.
7. The variety of trails gives hikers access to many different kinds of terrain.
8. Hilly and flat areas can be reached on the various trails.
9. Some trails lead to the Appalachian Trail.
10. Many families explore the Virginia countryside by horseback.
11. Certain parks have facilities for horse rental.
12. The Virginia state park system provides numerous camping facilities.
13. Campgrounds are located in many different settings.
14. Some parks have on-site exhibits about Virginia's rich history.
15. Parents enjoy these exhibits with their children.

Exercise 3 — Identifying Complete and Simple Subjects and Predicates

Copy each of the following sentences, and draw a vertical line between the complete subject and the complete predicate. Then underline the simple subject once and the simple predicate twice.

SAMPLE An important <u>event</u> | <u>sparked</u> the civil rights

ANSWER movement in the United States.

Rosa Lee Parks, a Woman of Courage

[1]Rosa Lee Parks made history in Montgomery, Alabama, in 1955. [2]She boarded a bus there late one December day. [3]Parks took a seat at the front of the bus. [4]This action was illegal for an African American person in Alabama at the time. [5]The angry driver ordered Parks to the back of the bus. [6]She ignored his orders courageously. [7]The police arrested Parks for her action. [8]The African American community of Montgomery conducted a year-long boycott of the city buses in protest. [9]A Supreme Court decision in November 1956 made segregation on all public transportation illegal. [10]Many people consider Parks the catalyst of the modern civil rights movement.

Exercise 4 — Expanding Subjects and Predicates

Expand each of the following sentences by adding words and phrases to both the simple subject and the simple predicate. Write your sentence. Then underline the simple predicate in each sentence.

SAMPLE Sky darkened.

ANSWER The blue sky <u>darkened</u> slowly to indigo.

1. The sun set.
2. Night fell.
3. Darkness descended.
4. Frogs croaked.
5. Stars shone.
6. Moon rose.
7. Owls hooted.
8. Possums skulked.
9. People slept.
10. Wind howled.
11. Leaves rustled.
12. Curtains fluttered.
13. The train rattled.
14. Baby cried.
15. Sky lightened.
16. Rooster crowed.
17. The dog barked.
18. Workers left.
19. Cars honked.
20. Day began.

11.3 Compound Subjects and Compound Predicates

A sentence may have more than one simple subject or more than one simple predicate.

Compound Subjects

■ A **compound subject** is made up of two or more simple subjects that are joined by a conjunction and have the same verb.

The conjunctions most commonly used to join the subjects in a compound subject are *and* and *or*.

Tomatoes and **carrots** are colorful vegetables.

Tomatoes or **carrots** are my favorite vegetable.

Correlative conjunctions may be used to join compound subjects.

Neither the **tomato** nor the **pepper** grows underground.

Both the **tomato** and the **pepper** are rich in vitamin C.

When more than two words are included in the compound subject, the conjunction is usually used only between the last two words, and the words are separated by commas.

Tomatoes, carrots, and **peppers** are healthful.

Exercise 5   Identifying Compound Subjects

Write the compound subject in each of the following sentences.

The Planets in Our Solar System

1. Jupiter and Saturn are the largest planets.
2. Mercury, Venus, and Earth are the warmest planets in our solar system.
3. Mars or one of Jupiter's moons could harbor life forms.
4. Both Jupiter and Saturn have many moons.
5. Neither Mercury nor Venus has moons.

Exercise 6   Expanding Subjects

(a) Write five sentences. In each one use a simple subject and a simple predicate.
(b) Expand each sentence by making the subject compound.

SAMPLE ANSWER
a. John Hancock signed the Declaration of Independence.
b. John Hancock and John Adams signed the Declaration of Independence.

498   Unit 11 Parts of the Sentence

Compound Predicates

■ A **compound predicate** (or **compound verb**) is made up of two or more verbs or verb phrases that are joined by a conjunction and have the same subject.

> Horses **gallop** and **charge**.
> Nina **inserted** the film, **looked** through the viewfinder, and **snapped** the first photograph.

In compound verbs that contain verb phrases, the helping verb may or may not be repeated before the second verb.

> Sea gulls **will glide** or **swoop** down to the ocean.

A sentence may have both a compound subject and a compound predicate.

```
         S              S        P     P
```
Butterflies and **hummingbirds dart** and **dip** in the air.

Exercise 7   Identifying Compound Predicates

Write the compound predicate in each of the following sentences.

Dogs and Water

1. Some dogs swim and play in the water as a recreational activity.
2. Other dogs jump into water but then immediately return to shore.
3. Fearful dogs may scratch or whine.
4. Confident dogs can sit quietly in a canoe and enjoy the scenery.
5. I have swum and played in the water with many dogs.
6. Retrievers jump into the water readily and fetch objects for their owners.
7. Some dogs climb up ladders, dive off docks, or rescue people from the water.
8. Water play relaxes dogs and offers them excellent exercise.
9. Exercise increases energy and improves the dog's health.
10. Many dogs may not recognize polluted water and, unfortunately, may drink it.

Exercise 8   Expanding Predicates

(a) Write five sentences. In each one use a simple subject and a simple predicate.
(b) Expand each sentence by making the predicate compound.

SAMPLE ANSWER
  a. A businessperson bought the Nettlehurst Company.
  b. A businessperson bought and sold the Nettlehurst Company.

11.3 Compound Subjects and Compound Predicates

Exercise 9 — Identifying Subjects and Predicates

Copy each of the following sentences on your paper. For each sentence, underline the simple subject(s) once and the simple predicate(s) twice. Note that some subjects and predicates are compound.

Chief Joseph

1. The Nez Percé lived and flourished for centuries in the Northwest.
2. The federal government ordered them away from their lands in 1877 and assigned them to a reservation in Oregon.
3. The government wanted land for many new white settlers and their families.
4. The leader of the Nez Percé at the time was Chief Joseph, a wise and compassionate man.
5. Chief Joseph and the Nez Percé men, women, and children packed their belongings and left their homes.
6. A small group of Nez Percé encountered and killed several white settlers during their journey.
7. Chief Joseph and his advisers foresaw a long and bloody battle with the United States Army as a result of this incident.
8. Chief Joseph therefore sought freedom for the Nez Percé in Canada.
9. He and his outnumbered people fought courageously but finally surrendered to the United States Army just forty miles from the Canadian border.
10. The Nez Percé accepted land from the United States government on a reservation in Oklahoma and settled there in 1878.

Exercise 10 — Writing Compound Subjects and Predicates

On your paper, expand each of the following sentences by making both the subject and the predicate compound. (You may need to make other changes, too.)

SAMPLE Birds fly.
ANSWER Birds and bats fly and eat insects.

School Subjects

1. American history is taught in schools.
2. Children in kindergarten practice simple mathematical concepts.
3. Young children play word games.
4. The school lunch period never lasts long enough.
5. Coaches will teach players useful strategies.
6. Basic algebra is introduced in middle school.
7. Special projects improve students' research skills.
8. Computers will be used more frequently in the future.
9. Geography teaches about other cultures.
10. A longer school year remains a controversial topic.

11.4 Order of Subject and Predicate

In most sentences in English, the subject comes before the predicate. There are exceptions, however, to this usual word order.

Commands

In commands and requests, the subject is usually not stated. The predicate is the entire sentence. The pronoun *you* is understood to be the subject.

[You] **Run**!   [You] **Give** it to me.   [You] Please **be** careful.

Questions

Questions frequently begin with a verb or helping verb or the words *who, whom, what, when, where, why* or *how.*

Was she right?
Have you **read** Gary Soto's stories?
Whom did he invite?

In both of these cases, the subject generally follows the verb or helping verb. To find the subject of a question, rearrange the words to form a statement.

SUBJECT	PREDICATE
She	was right.
You	have read Gary Soto's stories.
He	did invite whom.

Exercise 11   Identifying Subjects and Predicates in Questions and Commands

Write the simple subject and the simple predicate of each of the following sentences. (Remember that the simple predicate may include one or more helping verbs.) If the sentence is a command, write (*You*) as the subject.

Drivers' Licenses

1. Where are drivers' licenses issued?
2. Go to the Department of Motor Vehicles.
3. What kind of preparations should I make?
4. Study the manual carefully.
5. Practice good driving skills every day for about four months before taking the test.

Inverted Order

At times a sentence is written in **inverted order**—that is, with the predicate before the subject. This reversal of the usual order can add emphasis to the subject.

PREDICATE	SUBJECT
Across the field **galloped**	the three **horses.**
In the distance **ran**	a **river.**

Remember, a word in a prepositional phrase is never the subject.

When the word *there* or *here* begins a sentence and is followed by a form of the verb *be,* the subject follows the verb. The words *there* and *here* are almost never the subject of a sentence.

PREDICATE	SUBJECT
There **is**	a **chill** in the air.
Here **are**	my **thoughts** on the subject.

To find a subject in an inverted sentence, ask "Who?" or "What?"

What galloped across the field? The three horses galloped.
What is in the air? A chill is in the air.

Exercise 12 Reordering Inverted Sentences

On your paper, rewrite each of the following sentences so that the complete subject comes before the predicate. Then underline the simple subject once and the simple predicate twice. (Remember that both subjects and predicates may be compound.)

Poisonous Snakes of the United States

1. From under a rock crawled the coral snake.
2. Around the bend swam a water moccasin.
3. In the stream wiggled six small water snakes.
4. There were a dozen hiding along the shore.
5. In the United States live only two types of poisonous snakes.
6. Included in the poisonous category are coral snakes and pit vipers.
7. On the low-lying plains of the American Southeast lives the deadly coral snake.
8. There are circular bands of different colors on the coral snake's body.
9. On some nonpoisonous snakes are similar but incomplete color bands.
10. Among the pit vipers in the United States is the notorious rattlesnake.

Exercise 13 — Recognizing the Order of Subject and Predicate

Copy each of the following sentences. For each sentence, draw a vertical line between the complete subject and the complete predicate, and label each.

SAMPLE ANSWERS

| Look at that painting. (P)

On the opposite wall is | another work of art. (P | S)

There is | the loveliest statue in the museum. (P | S)

An African Art Exhibit

1. A visit to an African art exhibit can be a fine educational experience.
2. Many museums offer temporary shows in addition to their permanent collections.
3. Call ahead for information about special displays of African art.
4. Where are the best examples of beadwork, basketry, woodwork, leatherwork, and metalwork?
5. In some museums are beautiful displays of African textiles.
6. Excellent craftsmanship is found in decorative ornaments and ceremonial objects.
7. Here is a Nigerian bronze sculpture of a priest-king.
8. This ancient civilization used sculptures of former kings in memorial rites for the dead.
9. Look at this elaborately carved ceremonial mask.
10. Dancers wore such masks as these at coronations and royal funerals.
11. There are still more African artifacts of great complexity.
12. On the shelf to the left sits a seventeenth-century ivory bracelet from the kingdom of Benin.
13. Notice the intricate carvings of kings on the antique bracelet.
14. From the workshops of Benin came some of Africa's finest bronze figures.
15. Among the most ancient African art objects are masks and ancestor figures.
16. Terra-cotta is a kind of earthenware.
17. Superb bronze and terra-cotta heads were made in Nigeria from the tenth to the fifteenth centuries.
18. In the museum's exhibit there are even older examples of African art.
19. Prehistoric cave paintings were discovered in the Tassili Plateau in the Sahara.
20. African people of today still create many such exquisite art objects.

Exercise 14 — Writing Sentences

Write five sentences about a topic of your choice. Make at least one sentence a question, one a command, one a statement beginning with *here* or *there*, and one a statement in which a prepositional phrase and the verb precede the subject.

11.4 Order of Subject and Predicate

11.5 Complements

■ A **complement** is a word or group of words that completes the meaning of a verb.

There are four kinds of complements: *direct objects, indirect objects, object complements,* and *subject complements.*

Direct Objects

■ A **direct object** answers the question *what?* or *whom?* after an action verb.

The subject of a sentence usually performs the action indicated by the verb. That action may be directed toward or received by someone or something—the direct object. Nouns, pronouns, or words acting as nouns may serve as direct objects. Only transitive verbs have direct objects.

Carlos served **dinner**. [Carlos served *what?*]

Marie admires **him** deeply. [Marie admires *whom?*]

Carlos served a Mexican **dinner** and a fabulous **dessert**.
[Carlos served *what?*]

Exercise 15   Identifying Direct Objects

Write the action verb in each sentence. Then write any direct objects and underline them.

U.S. Cowboys

1. U.S. cowboys copied the style of Mexican cowboys.
2. Historians see the Mexican vaqueros as the first real cowboys.
3. At all times of the year, the vaquero wore a floppy sombrero.
4. This large hat kept snow, rain, or sun off his face.
5. The U.S. cowboy modeled his own hat on the Mexican sombrero.
6. During branding season the vaqueros roped cows with a sturdy riata.
7. Cowboys in the United States lassoed cows with a lariat (from the Spanish word *la riata*).
8. Mexican cowboys protected their shins and thighs with leather chaparejos.
9. In a similar fashion, U.S. cowboys put leather chaps over their pants.
10. Cowboys also roam the grassy plains, or *pampas,* of Argentina and Uruguay.
11. These plains provide excellent food for cattle or sheep.
12. The cowboys, or *gauchos,* of these areas share many qualities with U.S. cowboys.
13. For example, *gauchos* wear hats and chaps for protection against the elements.
14. Cowboys in any country do the same sorts of jobs.
15. Cowboys from North and South America would probably tell very similar tales.

Indirect Objects

■ An **indirect object** answers the question *to whom? for whom? to what?* or *for what?* after an action verb.

In most cases, a sentence may have an indirect object only if it has a direct object. The indirect object will always come between the verb and the direct object.

Tyrone served his **sisters** dinner. [Tyrone served dinner *to whom?*]

Greta saved **him** a seat. [Greta saved a seat *for whom?*]

Kim saved **Rosa** and **José** seats. [Kim saved seats *for whom?*]

The children gave the worthy **charity** all their savings. [The children gave all their savings *to what?*]

Marsha gave the **game** her best effort. [Marsha gave her best effort *for what?*]

Kim saved Rosa a seat.

Kim saved Rosa.

Exercise 16 Identifying Indirect Objects

For each sentence, write the direct object, and list any indirect object(s). (Not all sentences have an indirect object.) Label the objects *DO* and *IO* for *direct object* and *indirect object*.

Careers in Sports

1. Professional sports offer many careers.
2. Television or radio sportscasters broadcast sports events.
3. A good sports announcer gives fans play-by-play descriptions of the game.
4. The announcer tells them anecdotes.
5. Newspaper writers and photographers also cover athletic competitions.
6. Newspapers give their readers sports coverage.
7. Teaching may give a person satisfaction.
8. Managers, coaches, and trainers all bring teams success.
9. Sports also give referees, umpires, and doctors jobs.
10. Athletic events even give hot-dog and peanut vendors work.
11. Some boys and girls contemplate sports careers at a very young age.
12. They give famous basketball stars attention.
13. They show their coaches their dedication to their sports.
14. They tell their friends endless stories about their skill on the court or field.
15. Unfortunately, few young athletes will achieve success as professionals.

Object Complements

■ An **object complement** answers the question *what?* after a direct object. That is, it *completes* the meaning of the direct object by identifying or describing it.

Object complements occur only in sentences with direct objects *and* only in those sentences with action verbs that have the general meaning of "make" or "consider," such as the following:

| appoint | elect | render | consider | name |
| declare | make | call | find | think |

An object complement usually follows a direct object. It may be an adjective, a noun, or a pronoun.

Residents find the park **peaceful.** [adjective]
Katie appointed me **treasurer** and **cook.** [nouns]
My grandmother considers the property **hers.** [pronoun]

Exercise 17 — Identifying Object Complements

Write the object complement(s) that appear in the following sentences. (Not every sentence has an object complement.)

Musical Tastes

1. The Music Club has appointed Felipe president.
2. He finds that honor extraordinary.
3. One member, Maya, thinks Mozart the best composer.
4. Another member, Diane, considers Bach stupendous.
5. Felipe, Maya, and Diane make music a priority.
6. Diane calls Verdi a great composer and a musical genius.
7. Felipe likes chamber music better than opera.
8. Maya thinks opera sublime.
9. Diane names the basso singer Justino Díaz her favorite.
10. Maya finds the voice of Kiri Te Kanawa exquisite.

Exercise 18 — Using Object Complements

On your paper, complete the following sentences by writing object complements. Then write the letter *A, N,* or *P* to identify the object complement as an *adjective, noun,* or *pronoun.*

1. The fearful swimmers found the ocean _____.
2. Generations of fishers consider the ocean _____.
3. Sailors make the ocean _____.
4. Early explorers thought the ocean _____.
5. Surfers call the ocean _____.

Subject Complements

- A **subject complement** follows a subject and a linking verb and identifies or describes the subject.

There are two kinds of subject complements: *predicate nominatives* and *predicate adjectives*.

- A **predicate nominative** is a noun or pronoun that follows a linking verb and points back to the subject to rename it or to identify it further.

   Sopranos are **singers.**

   Clearly the star of the opera was **she.**

   Many current opera stars are **Italians** or **Spaniards.**

Predicate nominatives are usually found in sentences that contain forms of the linking verb *be*. A few other linking verbs (for example, *become* and *remain*) can be followed by a predicate nominative.

   Julia became both a **musician** and an **actress.**
   That experience remains a cherished **memory** for me.

- A **predicate adjective** follows a linking verb and points back to the subject and further describes it.

   Ballerinas are **graceful.**

   Ballerinas must be extremely **dedicated.**

   Most ballerinas seem **intense** and **hard-working.**

Predicate adjectives may follow any linking verb.

   I felt very **carefree.**
   Only a few marathoners appear **fresh** even now.
   The water tasted **delicious.**
   I grew increasingly **tired.**
   My sister appeared **weary.**
   My friend Tanya looked **exhausted** but **happy.**
   The musty room smelled **bad.**
   The band sounded **loud.**
   The noise became **louder** as we approached the finish line.

Exercise 19 — Identifying Predicate Nominatives

On your paper, write the predicate nominatives that appear in the following sentences. (Not all sentences contain predicate nominatives.)

Dwight D. Eisenhower

1. Dwight Eisenhower was one of seven sons.
2. Eisenhower was a student at West Point.
3. He graduated from the academy with the class of 1915.
4. During World War II, he rose to the rank of Supreme Allied Commander in Europe.
5. After that, Eisenhower's name became a household word.
6. He was the Republican presidential candidate in 1952.
7. His election was the first presidential victory for the GOP in twenty-four years.
8. Eisenhower was a proponent of "Modern Republicanism."
9. He remained an advocate of reducing the federal government's power.
10. He also was a supporter of higher minimum wages.

Exercise 20 — Identifying Predicate Adjectives

On your paper, write each simple subject and each predicate adjective. Underline the predicate adjectives.

Dinner Is Served

1. The gym was ready for the class banquet.
2. The tables looked beautiful in the soft candlelight.
3. On the walls, portraits of the class members appeared almost alive.
4. Their unwavering gazes seemed lifelike.
5. The music of the combo sounded romantic.
6. All of the students felt ravenous.
7. The onion soup smelled especially good.
8. The food tasted excellent to all of the elegantly dressed diners.
9. The students remained unusually talkative throughout the meal.
10. The chaperones, however, grew sleepy rather early.

Exercise 21 — Using Subject Complements

On your paper, complete the following sentences with nouns, pronouns, or adjectives. Write *PN* or *PA* to indicate if the complement you wrote is a *predicate nominative* or a *predicate adjective*.

1. The most popular sport, in my opinion, is _____.
2. The lifestyles of many prominent players seem _____.
3. Very few athletes become _____.
4. The great majority of athletes are _____.
5. Their lives remain _____.

Exercise 22 — Identifying Subject Complements

On your paper, write all the subject complements that appear in the following sentences. Write *predicate nominative* or *predicate adjective* to identify each. (Five sentences have more than one predicate nominative or predicate adjective.)

Japanese Flower Arrangements

¹Flower arrangement is an ancient Japanese art. ²This tradition grew popular in the sixth century. ³Early flower arrangements were decorations for Buddhist temple altars. ⁴Over the centuries the art of flower arrangement became increasingly specific. ⁵Important materials in Japanese floral arrangement are leaves, stems, and branches. ⁶The lines of the branches should be graceful and sleek. ⁷In Western countries blossoms are generally the only important features. ⁸The best Japanese floral arrangements look natural and colorful. ⁹A Japanese florist must be a designer and an artist. ¹⁰The art of Japanese flower arrangement is both simple and complex.

Exercise 23 — Identifying Complements

On your paper, write the complements that appear in the following sentences. Next to each complement, write the kind of complement it is: *direct object, indirect object, object complement, predicate nominative,* or *predicate adjective.*

A Jazz Musician

1. Davenport, Iowa, was the hometown of Leon Bix Beiderbecke.
2. Mississippi riverboats passing by Davenport gave Bix Beiderbecke a taste for jazz.
3. Bix Beiderbecke played the cornet and the piano.
4. The cornet's sound is mellow and rich.
5. Bix Beiderbecke carried his cornet with him.
6. Beiderbecke's music attracted attention and praise.
7. Louis Armstrong called Beiderbecke's "In a Mist" immortal.
8. No one gave Bix any financial assistance for his musical career.
9. Beiderbecke's reputation is still great in music circles today.
10. In fact, many musicians consider him a true classic of American jazz.

Exercise 24 — Writing Sentences with Complements

Write five sentences about a natural phenomenon, such as an eclipse, a thunderstorm, or a sunset. In each sentence, use at least one of the four kinds of complements: direct object, indirect object, object complement, or subject complement. Label the complements for each sentence that you write.

UNIT 11 Grammar Review

PARTS OF THE SENTENCE

A member of the Ibo tribe of eastern Nigeria, Chinua Achebe writes about his people in *Things Fall Apart*. Set in the Ibo village of Umuofia around the turn of the century, the novel chronicles the life of a proud young wrestler named Okonkwo. In this passage Okonkwo is just about to go to bed when he hears the town crier, who beats his metal drum and summons the men of the village to a meeting. The passage has been annotated to show some of the parts of sentences covered in this unit.

Literature Model

from *Things Fall Apart*
by Chinua Achebe

Okonkwo had just blown out the palm-oil lamp and stretched **himself** on his bamboo bed when he heard the *ogene* of the town crier piercing the still night air. *Gome, gome, gome, gome,* boomed the hollow metal. Then the crier **gave** his message, and at the end of it **beat** his instrument again. And this was the **message.** Every man of Umuofia was asked to gather at the market place tomorrow morning. Okonkwo wondered what was amiss, for he knew certainly that something was amiss. He had discerned a clear overtone of tragedy in the crier's voice, and even now he could still hear it as it grew dimmer and dimmer in the distance.

The night was very **quiet.** It was always quiet except on moonlight nights. Darkness **held a vague terror for these people, even the bravest among them.** Children were warned not to whistle at night for fear of evil spirits. Dangerous **animals** became even more sinister and uncanny in the dark. A snake was never called by its name at night, because it would hear. It was called a string. And so on this particular night as the crier's voice was gradually swallowed up in the distance, silence **returned** to the world, a vibrant silence made more intense by the universal trill of a million forest insects.

Annotations (Parts of a Sentence):
- Direct object
- Compound predicate
- Subject complement (predicate nominative)
- Subject complement (predicate adjective)
- Complete predicate
- Simple subject
- Simple predicate

Grammar Review

> On a moonlight night it would be different. **The happy voices of children playing in open fields** would then be heard. And perhaps those not so young would be playing in pairs in less open places, and old **men and women** would remember their *youth*. As the Ibo say: "When the moon is shining the cripple becomes hungry for a walk."

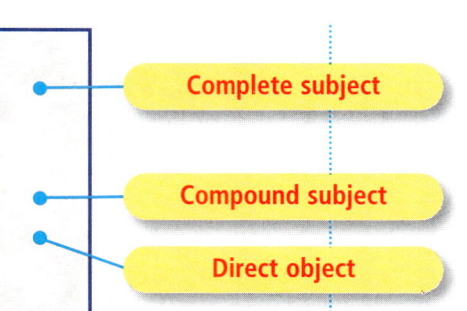

- Complete subject
- Compound subject
- Direct object

Review: Exercise 1 — Identifying Complete Subjects and Complete Predicates

Copy each of these sentences, which are based on the content of *Things Fall Apart*. Draw a line between the complete subject and complete predicate.

1. Okonkwo was going to bed for the night.
2. His palm-oil lamp had been blown out.
3. The comfort of his bamboo bed beckoned him.
4. The hollow metal sound of the town crier's drum aroused everyone from sleep.
5. His message of a morning meeting surprised Okonkwo.
6. A clear note of tragedy in the crier's voice made Okonkwo fearful.
7. Nights without moonlight, such as this one, were always very quiet and sinister.
8. The vibration from the crier's voice could be sensed long after his departure.
9. Children were always silenced on dark, moonless nights.
10. The absence of moonlight changed the outlook of the community completely.

Review: Exercise 2 — Writing Sentences with Complete Subjects and Complete Predicates

These sentences draw on ideas from *Things Fall Apart*. On your paper, write a complete subject or a complete predicate, without repeating the novel's exact words.

SAMPLE   The town crier _____.
ANSWER   The town crier beat his metal drum.

1. The voice of the crier _____.
2. _____ listened in the darkness.
3. The dark, moonless night _____.
4. Even the bravest villagers _____.
5. _____ roamed the jungle on dark nights.
6. A string _____.
7. _____ trilled in the darkness.
8. Moonlight _____.
9. _____ went outside in the moonlight.
10. Even the older people _____.

Parts of a Sentence

Grammar Review   **511**

Grammar Review

Review: Exercise 3   **Writing Sentences with Compound Subjects and Predicates**

Write on your paper a complete sentence answering each of these questions about *Things Fall Apart*. Begin your sentence with the subject, and follow the directions in parentheses. Then underline and label the simple or compound subject and the simple or compound predicate.

SAMPLE   What two kinds of nights had opposite effects on the people of Umuofia? (Use a compound subject.)

ANSWER   Dark nights and moonlit nights [COMPOUND SUBJECT] had opposite effects on the people of Umuofia. [SIMPLE PREDICATE]

1. What did Okonkwo do to prepare for sleep? (Use a compound predicate.)
2. What sounds broke the silence of the night? (Use a compound subject.)
3. What did Okonkwo do as the crier gave his message? (Use a compound predicate.)
4. What qualities of the night made the crier's message all the more ominous to the villagers? (Use a compound subject.)
5. What things were troublesome on a dark night? (Use a compound subject.)
6. What did the villagers never do in the dark? (Use a compound predicate.)
7. What happened to the sound of the crier's voice? (Use a compound predicate.)
8. What did the villagers do on moonlit nights? (Use a compound predicate.)
9. What groups of villagers would go outside on a moonlit night? (Use a compound subject with three different nouns.)
10. Who would reminisce about the past? (Use a compound subject.)

Review: Exercise 4   **Writing Inverted Sentences**

The following sentences develop an image or idea suggested by the passage from *Things Fall Apart*. On your paper, rewrite each sentence in inverted order, following the instructions in parentheses and making any needed changes.

SAMPLE   A fear of darkness was in the hearts of the villagers. (Begin the sentence with *There was*.)

ANSWER   There was a fear of darkness in the hearts of the villagers.

1. Okonkwo lay on the bamboo bed. (Begin the sentence with *On the bamboo bed*.)
2. The town crier came down the road. (Begin the sentence with *Down the road*.)
3. Tragic overtones were in the crier's voice. (Begin the sentence with *There were*.)
4. Many a scary creature was out and about. (Begin the sentence with *There was*.)
5. Dangerous animals lurked in the darkness. (Begin the sentence with *In the darkness*.)
6. A snake might hide within any shadow. (Begin the sentence with *Within any shadow*.)
7. The drum faded into the distance. (Begin the sentence with *Into the distance*.)

Grammar Review

8. Millions of insects were in the dark jungle. (Begin the sentence with *There were.*)
9. No children were outside on this moonless night. (Begin the sentence with *There were.*)
10. People of all ages appeared on a moonlit night. (Begin the sentence with *On a moonlit night.*)

Review: Exercise 5 — Writing Sentences with Predicate Nominatives and Predicate Adjectives

The pairs of words that follow are derived from the passage from *Things Fall Apart*. For each pair, write a sentence that uses the first word as the subject and the second word as a predicate adjective or a predicate nominative. Do not use Achebe's exact words, and add more than just a verb to the pair of words. After you have written the sentence, indicate whether the second word from the pair is acting as a *predicate adjective* or a *predicate nominative*.

SAMPLE Umuofia, village
ANSWER Umuofia was Okonkwo's village in Africa. predicate nominative

1. *Things Fall Apart,* novel
2. Nigeria, country
3. villagers, members
4. Okonkwo, wrestler
5. *ogene,* drum
6. sound, loud
7. message, worrisome
8. morning, time
9. overtone, tragic
10. night, silent
11. people, fearful
12. darkness, time
13. animals, danger
14. string, name
15. trill, persistent
16. silence, extreme
17. villagers, lively
18. children, happy
19. fields, playgrounds
20. elderly, thoughtful

Review: Exercise 6 — Identifying Direct Objects and Object Complements

The sentences below are based on the content of *Things Fall Apart*. On your paper, write the direct object and object complement from each sentence. Write *direct object* and *object complement* to identify each.

1. The town crier's message made Okonkwo fearful.
2. He considered the crier's tone of voice ominous.
3. The people of his village thought moonless nights menacing.
4. In contrast, the people found moonlit nights comfortable and friendly.
5. The light made their worst fears more bearable.

Grammar Review

Review: Exercise 7 **Writing Sentences with Direct and Indirect Objects**

The following groups of words describe incidents related to the passage from *Things Fall Apart.* Each word is labeled *S* (for *subject*), *DO* (for *direct object*), or *IO* (for *indirect object*). On your paper, write a sentence using these words as those parts of the sentence, but do not use the exact wording from the novel. Try to add modifiers or prepositional phrases.

SAMPLE lamp (S), Okonkwo (IO), light (DO)
ANSWER A palm-oil lamp gave Okonkwo light at night.

1. town crier (S), drum (IO), thump (DO)
2. Okonkwo (S), sound (DO)
3. crier (S), instrument (DO)
4. crier (S), villagers (IO), message (DO)
5. Okonkwo (S), tragedy (DO)
6. darkness (S), townspeople (IO), feelings (DO)
7. whistle (S), trouble (DO)
8. distance (S), voice (DO)
9. trill (S), silence (DO)
10. moonlight (S), villagers (IO), courage (DO)

Review: Exercise 8

Proofreading

The following passage describes the people and the art of Nigeria. (An example of Nigerian sculpture appears on the opposite page.) Rewrite the passage, correcting the errors in spelling, grammar, and usage. Add any missing punctuation. There are twenty-five errors.

The Art of Nigeria

[1]The country of Nigeria are the most populous nation in West Africa it is more than twice the size of California. [2]Perhaps four hundred native tribes inhabits modren Nigeria. [3]The largest tribes are the Hausa and the Fulani who live mainly in the north; the Yoruba, in the southwest; the Ibo, in the southeast; and the Ijo, on the southern coast. [4]Each of the tribal groups have their own language but the common language of all the groups are English, reflecting Nigeria's century-long domination by Great Britain. [5]Nigeria finally acheived it's independence from Great Britain in 1960.

[6]Nigerian cultures have produced some of Africas' most impressive art. [7]The Yoruba fashioned magnificent bronze sculptures and the people of

Grammar Review

western Nigeria produced fine ivory figures. ⁸Many of these sculptures and figures was used during the religious ceremonies of the people.

⁹The Ijo who live in the warm and humid region of the Niger River delta, are closely related to their neighbors, the Ibo, who live nearby. ¹⁰The Ijo traditionally venerated many gods, each god was thought to control a particular aspect of everyday life. ¹¹Some of the Ijo people continues to practice the religion of their ancestors.

¹²On this page are pictured a shrine that is typical of the sacred objects of the Ijo culture. ¹³It is made of highly polished wood and showed a figure—possibly a tribal ancestor—sitting on a throne. ¹⁴Generally, such an image was not displayed every day, it was probably created for a special ritual, such as a marriage or a funeral.

¹⁵In recent years many Nigerians have abandoned their native villages and migrate to large cities. ¹⁶Those who remain in the country still lives close to nature. ¹⁷The Ibo villagers described by Chinua Achebe in *Things Fall Apart* is aware of every sound heard on a moonless night. ¹⁸They attribute some of those sounds to animals and insects; they attributes others to the supernatural. ¹⁹Such sacred objects as this shrine may have symbolized a bridge between the natural and the supernatural world's.

Artist unknown, Ijo shrine, Nigeria

Grammar Review

Review: Exercise 9

Mixed Review

The following sentences describe the life of Chinua Achebe. Rewrite each sentence on your paper according to the instructions that appear after each item.

Chinua Achebe

1. According to many critics, Chinua Achebe's works are insightful.
   (Add *and educational* to create a second predicate adjective.)
2. A member of the Ibo tribe of Nigeria, Achebe grew up in the village of Ogidi. (Add *and graduated from the University College at Ibadan* to expand the complete predicate.)
3. He spoke the Ibo language first.
   (Add *but learned English as a child* to expand the complete predicate.)
4. A member of a large family, Achebe was always a reader.
   (Add *eager* as a modifier of the subject complement.)
5. Achebe's mother insisted on the best education possible for the family's children.
   (Add *and father* to create a compound subject.)
6. From his experiences with African life have come Achebe's powerful themes.
   (Rewrite the sentence so that it begins with the complete subject.)
7. Many of his books give a sense of the effects of colonialism on African culture.
   (Add *readers* to the complete predicate so that it functions as an indirect object.)
8. Numerous examples of problems caused by colonial rule are in Achebe's works.
   (Rewrite the sentence so that it begins with *There are.*)
9. Over the years the popular Nigerian author has received many awards.
   (Add *and honorary doctorates* to the direct object.)
10. Chinua Achebe has become an important spokesperson for African people.
    (Add *and has been praised for his eloquent writings* to expand the complete predicate.)
11. Achebe's writings describe African life. (Add *rural* to modify the direct object.)
12. In the southeast section of Nigeria had lived the Ibo for hundreds of years. (Rewrite the sentence so that the complete subject comes before the complete predicate.)
13. English helped the unification of Nigeria. (Add *and provided a language for communication with the West* to expand the predicate.)
14. Achebe provides detailed pictures. (Add *his audience* to serve as an indirect object.)
15. Achebe's works present vivid images of life in Nigeria during colonial times.
    (Add words to create a compound predicate.)
16. Many of Achebe's themes were provided by the long presence of the British government in Nigeria. (Rewrite the declarative sentence as a question.)
17. Many stories about religion are in Achebe's work.
    (Rewrite the sentence as an inverted sentence that begins with *There are.*)
18. His readers and followers consider Achebe a rare voice in Nigerian literature.
    (Add *and important* to the object complement.)
19. Achebe is an important figure in twentieth-century African history.
    (Add *literary* to the predicate nominative.)
20. Achebe's works speak to people everywhere. (Add *of all ages* to the predicate.)

516 Unit 11 Parts of the Sentence

Writing Application

Sentence Elements in Writing

Jack London uses a variety of sentence elements and patterns in this passage from *The Call of the Wild* to create a lively, engaging prose rhythm. As you read the passage, focus especially on the italicized words.

> Buck's first day on the Dyea beach was like a nightmare. Every hour was filled with shock and surprise. He *had been* suddenly *jerked* from the heart of civilization and *flung* into the heart of things primordial. *No lazy, sun-kissed life was this,* with nothing to do but loaf and be bored. Here was neither peace, nor rest, nor a moment's safety. All was confusion and action, and every moment life and limb were in peril. There was imperative need to be constantly alert; for *these dogs and men were not town dogs and men.* They were savages, all of them, who knew no law but the law of club and fang.

Techniques with Sentence Elements

Try to use various sentence elements and patterns, as London does, when you write and revise your work.

❶ Vary sentence length and rhythm by using compound subjects and predicates. Compare the following:

BORING PATTERN He *had been* suddenly *jerked* from the heart of civilization. *He had* been *flung* into the heart of things primordial.

LONDON'S PATTERN He *had been* suddenly *jerked* from the heart of civilization and *flung* into the heart of things primordial.

❷ Occasionally use repetition for effect in sentences with predicate nominatives.

BORING PATTERN These dogs and men weren't from towns.

LONDON'S PATTERN These dogs and men were not town dogs and men.

❸ Achieve sentence variety by sometimes using inverted word order.

USUAL ORDER This was no lazy, sun-kissed life . . .

LONDON'S ORDER No lazy, sun-kissed life was this . . .

> **TIME**
> For more about the writing process, see TIME **Facing the Blank Page**, pp. 121-131.

Parts of a Sentence

Practice   Practice these techniques by revising the following passage, adapted from *The Call of the Wild*, combining ideas to expand the basic sentence patterns. Try to write one sentence in inverted order.

Then an old wolf, gaunt and battle-scarred, came forward. Buck writhed his lips into the preliminary of a snarl. He sniffed noses with him. Whereupon the old wolf sat down. He pointed his nose at the moon. He broke out the long wolf howl. The others sat down, too. They howled. Then the call came to Buck in unmistakable accents. He, too, sat down. He howled. . . . And the story of Buck may well end here.

UNIT 12 Phrases

Lesson **12.1** **Prepositional Phrases**   519

Lesson **12.2** **Appositives and Appositive Phrases**   521

Lesson **12.3** **Verbals and Verbal Phrases**   523

Grammar Review   528

Writing Application   537

12.1 Prepositional Phrases

- A **prepositional phrase** is a group of words that begins with a preposition and ends with a noun or a pronoun called **the object of the preposition.**

  The stairs lead **to the attic.** [*Attic* is the object of the preposition *to.*]

  The staircase is too steep **for her.** [*Her* is the object of the preposition *for.*]

  They laid carpeting **on the stairs.** [*Stairs* is the object of the preposition *on.*]

For lists of common prepositions, see page 473.

Adjectives and other modifiers may be placed between the preposition and its object. A preposition may have more than one object.

  The staircase leads **to the crowded, dusty attic.** [adjectives added]

  The staircase leads **to the attic and the roof.** [two objects]

A prepositional phrase acts in the same way an adjective or an adverb does. Used as an adjective, a prepositional phrase modifies a noun or a pronoun. Used as an adverb, it modifies a verb, an adjective, or an adverb.

  They used the staircase **on the left.** [adjective phrase modifying the noun *staircase*]

  Which **of the staircases** leads downstairs? [adjective phrase modifying the pronoun *which*]

  At midnight you can come downstairs **to the kitchen.** [adverb phrases modifying the verb phrase *can come*]

  My grandfather explained that a daily walk is healthful **for him.** [adverb phrase modifying the adjective *healthful*]

  She walks very quickly **for a young baby.** [adverb phrase modifying the adverb *quickly*]

12.1 Prepositional Phrases **519**

Exercise 1 Identifying Prepositional Phrases

On your paper, write each prepositional phrase that appears in the following sentences. (You will find a total of twenty-five prepositional phrases.)

Crispus Attucks

[1]Crispus Attucks, a former enslaved person, is a hero of the American Revolution. [2]He was one of five men who died in 1770 during the historic Boston Massacre. [3]At the time, British troops were stationed in Boston. [4]Approximately four hundred inhabitants of Boston gathered around a small group of British soldiers. [5]They shouted insults and threw snowballs at the British. [6]Suddenly the soldiers fired into the unruly crowd. [7]Attucks was hit instantly by a bullet and died beside two other men. [8]Later two more men, who were also shot by the British during the attack, died from their wounds. [9]Bostonians throughout the city expressed shock and outrage over the incident. [10]At a trial, however, only two soldiers were found guilty, and for punishment they were branded on their thumbs. [11]A monument in Boston honors the memory of Crispus Attucks and the others who perished with him in the Boston Massacre.

Exercise 2 Identifying Adjective and Adverb Phrases

On your paper, write the word or words each prepositional phrase in Exercise 1 modifies. Then indicate whether each phrase is acting as an adjective or an adverb in the sentence.

Exercise 3 Expanding Sentences with Prepositional Phrases

Copy and expand the following sentences by adding at least one adjective phrase and one adverb phrase to each.

SAMPLE   The new equipment arrived.
ANSWER   The new equipment for the office arrived by truck.

1. The candle flame flickers.
2. Someone should have asked me.
3. The comedian performed.
4. The gardener pulled the weeds.
5. The children brought flowers.
6. The classroom emptied quickly.
7. I have used a shovel many times.
8. The woman was buying cat food.
9. The farmers drove their tractors.
10. Her cousin will send a letter.

Exercise 4 Writing with Prepositional Phrases

Write five sentences that include two or more prepositional phrases. Then underline each prepositional phrase and tell whether it is being used as an *adjective* or an *adverb*.

SAMPLE ANSWER   Most students in my grade watch television on weekends. (adjective; adverb)

12.2 Appositives and Appositive Phrases

■ An **appositive** is a noun or pronoun that is placed next to another noun or pronoun to identify or give additional information about it.

> My friend **Paulo** sends me long letters from Brazil. [The appositive *Paulo* identifies the noun *friend*.]

■ An **appositive phrase** is an appositive plus any words that modify the appositive.

> He is living and working in Brasília, **the capital city.** [The appositive phrase, in bold type, identifies *Brasília*.]

Use commas to set off any appositive or appositive phrase that is not essential to the meaning of a sentence.

> Paulo's brother **Ernesto** also lives there. [The appositive **Ernesto** is essential because Paulo has more than one brother.]
>
> Dora, **Paulo's only sister,** lives in New York. [The appositive phrase is not necessary to identify Dora.]

Usually an appositive or appositive phrase follows the noun or pronoun it identifies or explains. Occasionally an appositive phrase precedes the noun or pronoun.

> **A skilled mechanic,** Paulo could probably find work anywhere.

Exercise 5   Identifying Appositives and Appositive Phrases

Write the appositives and appositive phrases in the sentences below.

1. Our neighbor Katie Rosenfeld organized the dance.
2. The most tickets were sold by Mia and Vanessa, two tenth graders.
3. After a long search, Greg finally found and booked the band, a fantastic group.
4. A clever class president, Juan Lopez talked his cousin into performing one of the opening comedy acts.
5. Two of Mr. Swanson's art classes, the third and the fifth periods, began work on the decorations a month in advance.

Exercise 6 — Identifying Appositives and Appositive Phrases

Write the appositive or the appositive phrase that appears in each sentence. Then write the noun or pronoun that is identified or explained by the appositive.

Stars of American Culture

1. Alvin Ailey, an innovative choreographer, founded a lively modern dance company.
2. *The Heart Is a Lonely Hunter* is a novel by the acclaimed twentieth-century author Carson McCullers.
3. The great contralto Marian Anderson was the first African American singer to perform leading roles at the Metropolitan Opera in New York City.
4. Midori, one of the most brilliant violinists of her generation, launched her career as a very young girl.
5. The Pulitzer Prize was awarded to Gwendolyn Brooks for *Annie Allen,* a collection of poems.
6. The Guggenheim Museum in New York was one of the last projects of Frank Lloyd Wright, the famous modern American architect.
7. Georgia O'Keeffe, one of the most influential twentieth-century American painters, lived in New Mexico from 1949 to 1986.
8. Fans admired the jazz vocalist Billie Holiday for the emotionally charged quality of her singing.
9. Rita Hayworth, the daughter of a Spanish dancer, starred in many American films in the 1940s.
10. *Nobody Knows My Name* is a collection of personal essays by the author James Baldwin.

Exercise 7 — Expanding Sentences with Appositive Phrases

On your paper, expand the following sentences by adding an appositive phrase to each sentence. Be sure to use commas where necessary.

SAMPLE Vitus Bering was the first European to chart the Alaskan coast.
ANSWER Vitus Bering, a Danish explorer, was the first European to chart the Alaskan coast.

1. The film was nominated for an Academy Award.
2. The local newspaper printed my letter on its editorial page.
3. Robert Frost wrote the poem.
4. Alaska entered the Union in 1959.
5. Every year New Orleans celebrates Mardi Gras.
6. The novel is my favorite.
7. In Washington are many cherry trees.
8. My favorite singer will be appearing here in concert in July.
9. Our team won.
10. The principal of the school has resigned.

12.3 Verbals and Verbal Phrases

- A **verbal** is a verb form that functions in a sentence as a noun, an adjective, or an adverb.
- A **verbal phrase** is a verbal plus any complements and modifiers.

There are three kinds of verbals: *participles, gerunds,* and *infinitives.* All three types can be expanded into phrases.

Participles and Participial Phrases

- A **participle** is a verb form that can function as an adjective.
- A **present participle** is made up of the base form of the verb plus *-ing: falling.* A past participle is usually made up of the base form plus *-ed: burned.* Some past participles are irregularly formed.

Participles are often used as adjectives.

No one would eat the **burned** toast.

We were warned to watch out for **falling** rocks.

The **fallen** tree blocked the **winding** road.

A participle may also be used as part of a verb phrase. When a participle is part of a verb phrase, it is not acting as an adjective.

PARTICIPLE AS ADJECTIVE   The **growing** child was curious.
PARTICIPLE IN VERB PHRASE   They saw that he **was growing** stronger.

- A **participial phrase** contains a participle plus any complements and modifiers.

Participial phrases can be placed in various positions in a sentence.

We watched the best teams **playing baseball.**

The **badly defeated** team accepted its fate with grace.

The victors, **elated by the victory,** shook hands with the losers.

Throwing their hats into the air, the fans of the victorious team let out a great roar.

A participial phrase at the beginning of a sentence is usually followed by a comma.

Exercise 8 — Identifying Participles in Sentences

Write the participle that functions as an adjective in each of the following sentences.

1. The blowing trees were etched against the sky.
2. A broken branch scratched against the window.
3. The closed barn doors rattled in the strong wind.
4. Everywhere was evidence of the gathering storm.
5. Shivering, the young boy returned to his chair near the fireplace.

Exercise 9 — Identifying Participles and Participial Phrases

Write the participial phrase that acts as an adjective in each of the following sentences. Then identify the word each phrase modifies.

Early Native Americans of the Northwest

1. The northwestern coast of North America, extending from southern Alaska to northern California, was the home of many Native American groups.
2. The dense forests inhabited by these groups have a temperate climate and plentiful rainfall.
3. Salmon caught in streams was an important source of food.
4. Knowing the woodlands well, the groups gathered wild fruit.
5. Northwest Native Americans ordinarily lived in houses built of wood.
6. Prepared for battle, they carried shields made of copper.
7. Some of the groups had totem poles decorated with carvings.
8. Displaying great artistic skill, the Northwest Native Americans produced baskets, rattles, masks, and other artifacts.
9. Native Americans of the Northwest had distinctive cultures established over hundreds of years.
10. Determined to find furs and other natural resources, Europeans came into the area in the late 1700s.

Exercise 10 — Writing Sentences with Participial Phrases

Write five sentences with participial phrases. Then underline each phrase and write what noun or pronoun the phrase modifies.

SAMPLE ANSWER   <u>Determined to be the next class president</u>, Kevin began his campaign the first day of school.   Kevin

Gerunds and Gerund Phrases

- A **gerund** is a verb form that ends in *–ing* and is used in the same way a noun is used.

    Eating is something I enjoy. [gerund as subject]
    My grandfather likes s**trolling.** [gerund as direct object]
    Tony gives **baking** his best effort. [gerund as indirect object]
    How much enthusiasm do you feel for **bowling?** [gerund as object of preposition]
    Rachel's favorite pastime is **painting.** [gerund as predicate nominative]
    My hobbies, **writing** and **reading,** are quiet activities. [gerunds as appositives]

- A **gerund phrase** is a gerund plus any complements and modifiers.

    Dancing the tango is not as easy as it looks.
    Fred Astaire's marvelous dancing will always be considered superb.

The difference between a present participle and a gerund is that a present participle is used as a verb or an adjective and a gerund is used as a noun.

Running around the track, Yuki felt exhilarated. [present participle]
Running gives Yuki a sense of well-being. [gerund]

Exercise 11 — Identifying Gerunds and Gerund Phrases

List on your paper the gerunds and gerund phrases that appear in the following sentences. The number of gerunds or gerund phrases in each sentence is given in parentheses.

A Spanish Conqueror

1. Conquering was the goal of the ruthless Spanish adventurer Hernando Cortés. (1)
2. His greatest accomplishment was claiming for Spain land in central and southern Mexico. (1)
3. Capturing territory was a challenging experience, Cortés found. (1)
4. The famous Spaniard enjoyed discovering and exploring new places. (2)
5. Cortés was adept at gaining the trust of some Native Americans. (1)
6. The result was his winning the Aztec capital, Tenochtitlán, through the overthrow of Emperor Montezuma. (1)
7. By 1521 several of Cortés's goals—finding gold, claiming Mexican lands, and conquering native groups—were fulfilled. (3)
8. For several years, Cortés was famous for controlling much of present-day Mexico. (1)
9. His trip to Spain in 1528 resulted in his receiving the title of *marquis*. (1)
10. Cortés sailed back to Mexico in 1530 and began building his palace and exploring the Pacific region. (2)

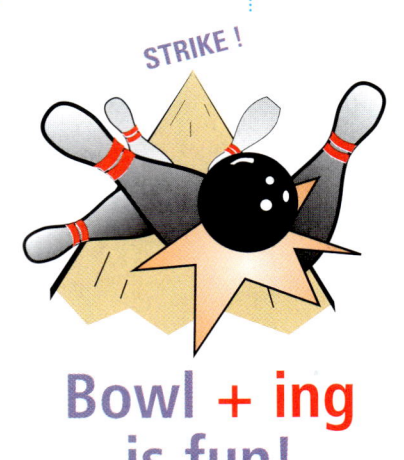

Infinitives and Infinitive Phrases

■ An **infinitive** is a verb form that is usually preceded by the word *to* and is used as a noun, an adjective, or an adverb.

When you use the word *to* before the base form of a verb, *to* is not a preposition but part of the infinitive form of the verb.

To stand can be uncomfortable. [infinitive as subject]
Infants first learn **to crawl.** [infinitive as direct object]
Her aim is **to walk.** [infinitive as predicate nominative]
Birds have an instinct **to fly**. [infinitive as adjective]
I am happy **to run.** [infinitive as adverb]

■ An **infinitive phrase** contains an infinitive plus any complements and modifiers.

We decided **to sail across the lake.**
They wanted **to drive slowly around the park.**
To run in a marathon someday is my secret ambition.
A triathlon requires athletes **to train diligently.**
To complete a triathlon is a success in itself.

Exercise 12   Identifying Infinitives and Infinitive Phrases

Write the infinitive phrase that appears in each of the following sentences.

Mary Cassatt

1. Mary Cassatt was one of the foremost American artists to paint in the Impressionist style.
2. Cassatt spent much of her childhood in Europe but decided to study at the Pennsylvania Academy of Fine Arts.
3. In 1866 she went to live in France.
4. The great French painter Edgar Degas began to influence her work.
5. Degas helped Cassatt to master her drawing techniques.
6. Cassatt often chose to paint portraits of mothers and children.
7. Degas invited Cassatt to exhibit paintings with other Impressionists.
8. Cassatt encouraged her American relatives and friends to purchase the paintings of the French Impressionists.
9. In so doing, Cassatt helped to influence a growing American interest in contemporary art.
10. Today art lovers are able to appreciate Cassatt's work for its own remarkable qualities.

Exercise 13   Identifying Verbal Phrases

On your paper, write each of the verbal phrases that appears in the following sentences. Write whether each phrase is a *participial phrase, a gerund phrase,* or an *infinitive phrase.*

Elephants

1. Elephants have the distinction of being the largest land mammals.
2. Living in the tropical regions of Asia and Africa, they may reach a height of 13 feet.
3. Their tusks, weighing as much as 200 pounds each, can be more than 10 feet long.
4. The distinctive ears of the African elephant are huge, measuring up to 4 feet in width.
5. Elephants use their fingerlike trunks to pick up objects.
6. Elephants browse all day, feeding on a variety of plants.
7. Elephants can learn to carry logs and to perform in circuses.
8. Training young elephants takes great skill.
9. Handling the elephants may be difficult for the trainers.
10. Hunted for ivory and often deprived of their natural surroundings, elephants now must struggle for their survival.
11. An adult elephant needs to eat about 300 pounds of food a day.
12. The elephant needs to search almost constantly for food.
13. Weighing over 200 pounds, a newborn elephant stands about 3 feet tall.
14. The adults form a circle around their offspring to protect them from predators.
15. Young elephants amuse themselves by playing with each other.
16. Traveling to water holes each day, elephants spend a lot of time in and around water.
17. Splashing themselves with muddy water keeps elephants cool.
18. Elephants love to bathe in fresh water and are excellent swimmers.
19. Most wild Asian elephants, protected by regional governments, live on preserves.
20. Large predators avoid attacking adult elephants because of their size.

Exercise 14   Using Verbal Phrases

On your paper, use each of the following verbal phrases in an original sentence. Write whether each phrase is a *participial phrase, a gerund phrase,* or an *infinitive phrase.*

1. blaming us for the loud music
2. to test the speakers
3. playing the drums
4. to annoy the neighbors
5. turning down the speakers
6. listening at the door
7. to play more softly
8. upset by all the commotion
9. to make everyone happy
10. putting pads on the floor

UNIT 12 Grammar Review

PHRASES

The passage below is taken from a novel by the Japanese American writer Yoshiko Uchida. The novel tells of a young Japanese woman who arrives in San Francisco in 1917 to marry a man whom she has never met. In this passage, she contemplates her fate. The passage has been annotated to show many of the kinds of phrases covered in this unit.

Literature Model

from *Picture Bride*
by Yoshiko Uchida

Hana Omiya stood at the railing of the small ship that shuddered toward America in a turbulent November sea. She shivered as she pulled the folds *of her silk kimono* close to her throat and tightened the wool shawl *about her shoulders.*

She was thin and small, her dark eyes shadowed in her pale face, her black hair piled high in a pompadour that seemed too heavy for so slight a woman. She clung to the moist rail and breathed the damp salt air deep into her lungs. Her body seemed leaden and lifeless, as though it were simply the vehicle transporting her soul to a strange new life, and she longed with childlike intensity *to be home again in Oka Village.*

She longed to see the bright persimmon *dotting the barren trees beside the thatched roof,* to see the fields of golden rice stretching to the mountains where only last fall she had gathered plump white mushrooms, and to see once more the maple trees lacing their flaming colors through the green pine. If only she could see a familiar face, eat a meal without retching, walk on solid ground and stretch out at night on a *tatami* mat instead of in a hard narrow bunk. She thought now of *seeking the warm shelter of her bunk* but could not bear to face the relentless smell of fish that penetrated the lower decks.

Annotations (left margin):
- Prepositional phrase (adjective phrase) → *of her silk kimono*
- Prepositional phrase (adverb phrase) → *about her shoulders*
- Infinitive Phrase → *to be home again in Oka Village*
- Participial phrase (adjective phrase) → *dotting the barren trees beside the thatched roof*
- Gerund phrase (object of preposition) → *seeking the warm shelter of her bunk*

528 Unit 12 Phrases

Grammar Review

> Why did I ever leave Japan, she wondered bitterly. Why did I ever listen to my uncle? And yet she knew it was she herself who had begun the chain of events that placed her on this heaving ship. It was she who had first planted in her uncle's mind the thought that she would make a good wife for Taro Takeda, **the lonely man who had gone to America to make his fortune in Oakland, California.**

Appositive phrase

Review: Exercise 1 Expanding Sentences with Prepositional Phrases

The following sentences describe an imaginary journey on a boat. Read through the sentences quickly to get an idea of the scene. Then rewrite each sentence, adding at least one prepositional phrase—either an adjective phrase or an adverb phrase—to the sentence. You can imagine any scene that you wish.

1. The ship rocked violently.
2. The boy watched the dark waves.
3. His hair was tossed.
4. He wore a long scarf.
5. The breeze flushed his cheeks.
6. He carried a small suitcase.
7. He was taking a long trip.
8. The previous night he had slept poorly.
9. The boy ate little.
10. Memories flooded his mind.
11. He felt intense longing.
12. He had left his family.
13. All his friends had stayed behind.
14. The ship was crowded.
15. Many people were traveling.
16. Some men sang songs.
17. Small children played games.
18. Young women chatted.
19. Sailors came and went.
20. The captain appeared only once.
21. The boy sat quietly.
22. He had a faraway look.
23. The ship arrived late.
24. A man greeted the boy.
25. The boy's new life had begun.

Grammar Review

Review: Exercise 2 **Expanding Sentences with Appositives and Appositive Phrases**

The following sentences describe Hana Omiya, the main character of *Picture Bride*. Each sentence is followed by a group of words in parentheses. Rewrite each sentence, incorporating the words in parentheses as an appositive or appositive phrase. Use a comma or commas to set off the appositive or appositive phrase from the rest of the sentence.

SAMPLE The ship sailed toward San Francisco. (a small steamer)
ANSWER The ship, a small steamer, sailed toward San Francisco.

1. A solitary figure stood on the open deck. (a small woman with a shawl)
2. The woman was traveling to America. (Hana Omiya)
3. She had left her home and was traveling to meet her future husband. (a small village in Japan)
4. Her father had died, leaving four daughters and a wife behind. (a prosperous landowner)
5. Of the four sisters, Hana was the only one without a husband. (the youngest)
6. Hana's mother was determined to find a match for her. (a practical woman)
7. The idea that Hana should go to America was suggested by another relative. (Uncle Oji)
8. Oji knew a Japanese man who had gone to California to seek his fortune. (Taro Takeda)
9. Taro Takeda had opened a small shop in Oakland. (the son of a friend of Oji's)
10. Oji said that Taro would make a good husband. (a hardworking and honest man)
11. Hana's dark eyes were fixed on the horizon. (a barely perceptible line of blue)
12. The bracing scene contrasted with her mood. (a heavy feeling of dread)
13. Familiar faces filled her mind. (now only distant memories)
14. She yearned to see not the ocean but the graceful persimmons and maples. (the trees of home)
15. The discomforts of the trip were becoming unbearable. (seasickness and unpleasant odors)
16. Even more unbearable was her fear. (a constant companion on the voyage)
17. Another land was to be her new home. (a country with strange people and an unfamiliar language)
18. A man totally unknown to her was to be her husband. (her companion for the rest of her life)
19. His picture offered few clues to his character. (a faded photograph)
20. She was overwhelmed by bitterness. (an emotion unfamiliar to her)
21. She longed for familiar customs. (the simple ceremonies of her homeland)
22. She longed as well for the familiar landmarks of her village. (the carefully cultivated gardens and flaming maple trees)
23. Yet she was being hurled toward America. (an unknown wilderness)
24. Would she ever again see her old home? (Oka Village)
25. Tears streamed from her brimming eyes. (drops of sorrow)

Grammar Review

Review: Exercise 3 **Expanding Sentences with Participial Phrases**

The following sentences relate to Hana Omiya and her life. Each sentence is followed by another sentence in parentheses. Combine the sentences, changing the sentence in parentheses into a participial phrase. Be sure to place the participial phrase near the word that it modifies. Note that some of the sentences may be expanded in more than one way.

SAMPLE Hana stood on the deck of the ship. (She was shivering in her thin clothes.)
ANSWER Shivering in her thin clothes, Hana stood on the deck of the ship.

1. The woolen shawl offered little warmth. (The shawl was draped over her shoulders.)
2. Her silk kimono made her look like a bird. (Her kimono was fluttering in the wind.)
3. The sea air was damp and cheerless. (The air was rushing past her face.)
4. Hana recalled the warm colors of her village. (She was gazing absently at the sea.)
5. The memory of familiar faces haunted her. (The faces were filled with goodwill.)
6. She recalled the rice fields. (The rice fields were rustling in the breeze.)
7. She longed to see the orange persimmons. (The persimmons were hanging from the bare trees.)
8. Why was she going to America to marry a man? (The man was unknown to her.)
9. Her uncle had described Taro as decent and hardworking. (Her uncle was speaking eagerly.)
10. Hana had decided to leave Japan. (Hana had been longing for a different kind of life.)
11. Her sisters lived in big cities. (Her sisters were married to merchants.)
12. Their lives were monotonous. (Their lives were filled with routine.)
13. Hana did not want to be a bored wife. (A bored wife is trapped in a dull marriage.)
14. At first Hana had looked forward to a new life. (Her life would be filled with excitement.)
15. She dreaded the future now. (She was plagued with uncertainty.)
16. She had reluctantly boarded the ship. (She was leaving her family behind.)
17. Many passengers had stayed in their quarters. (They were exhausted by the trip.)
18. Hana remained on the deck. (She was not accompanied by even a single friend.)
19. She listened to some Russian travelers. (The Russians were singing of home.)
20. The loneliness was as endless as the sea. (The loneliness was stretching before her.)
21. Family members would have made the journey less terrifying. (They would have provided companionship.)
22. Hana would be alone in America too. (She would be isolated by language.)
23. She listened to the cries of sea gulls. (The gulls followed the ship.)
24. The cries tore at her heart. (The cries reminded her of abandoned infants.)
25. Hana cried. (She lowered her head.)

Grammar Review

Review: Exercise 4   **Writing Sentences with Gerund Phrases**

The exercise that follows focuses on the lives of immigrants who came from Japan to the United States. Each item consists of a question followed by a phrase in parentheses that answers the question. For each item, write a sentence that answers the question, using the words in parentheses as a gerund phrase.

SAMPLE   What is painful? (leaving one's homeland)
ANSWER   Leaving one's homeland is painful.

1. In the late nineteenth century, what was difficult in Japan? (earning a living)
2. What seemed like a good idea? (moving to the United States)
3. What was a first step for many poor immigrants? (signing a work contract)
4. What was impossible for early Japanese immigrants? (becoming an American citizen)
5. What did many Japanese immigrants find practical? (living in California)
6. What was a common job for Japanese families who moved to California? (picking grapes)
7. What did many Japanese immigrants have to accept? (working for low wages)
8. What was a goal for many of them? (owning property)
9. How did many Japanese immigrants survive? (applying skills learned in their native land)
10. What did one Japanese immigrant begin doing? (growing rice on wasteland)
11. What is now an important industry in California? (cultivating rice)
12. How did other Japanese immigrants earn a living? (fishing for abalone, tuna, and sardines)
13. What enterprise did some Japanese families in California develop? (extracting salt from sea water)
14. How did many Japanese businesspeople survive? (banding together in associations)
15. What was one goal of the associations? (lending money to members)
16. As more Japanese families arrived, what became a part of their lives? (maintaining a sense of their cultural heritage)
17. What became prevalent in many parts of the West? (segregating Japanese schools and communities)
18. What helped keep their heritage alive? (wearing traditional dress for special occasions)
19. What was one particularly important tradition? (practicing the ancient tea ceremony)
20. What was another means of preserving cultural ties? (singing traditional songs)
21. What was the only way to cross the ocean before the invention of the airplane? (traveling by boat)
22. What provided the Japanese with a healthy supply of protein? (fishing the ocean waters)
23. What enabled Japanese immigrants to continue to enjoy seaweed, a Japanese staple? (living near an ocean)
24. Over what issue did some Japanese young people in the United States begin to disagree with their elders? (keeping to the traditional ways)
25. What is one value that has enabled many Japanese Americans to succeed? (working hard)

Grammar Review

Review: Exercise 5   **Writing Sentences with Infinitive Phrases**

The exercise that follows describes some cultural characteristics and practices of Japanese immigrants to the United States early in the twentieth century. Each of the items consists of a question followed by a phrase in parentheses that answers the question. For each item, write a sentence that answers the question, using the words in parentheses as an infinitive phrase.

SAMPLE   What did many Japanese immigrants to the United States hope to do? (to start a new life in the new land)

ANSWER   Many Japanese immigrants to the United States hoped to start a new life in the new land.

1. What did many Japanese men want to do? (to get married)
2. What was difficult in the United States? (to find a Japanese bride)
3. What did some men return to Japan to do? (to seek a wife)
4. What did other men ask their parents in Japan to do? (to send them a suitable woman for a wife)
5. What did a friend usually agree to do? (to arrange the marriage)
6. What was the young wife forced to do? (to face her frightening and uncertain future with courage)
7. What did the wife need to do? (to travel to America alone)
8. What was wrenching for the picture brides? (to leave their families and their familiar villages behind)
9. What did most wives expect to do in the United States? (to work hard)
10. What did most wives hope to do? (to find economic security)
11. What were Japanese taught as small children? (to control their feelings)
12. What was considered to be proper public conduct for Japanese women? (to be shy and retiring)
13. How was a Japanese wife supposed to act toward her husband? (to act quiet and obedient)
14. What was considered to be a fate worse than death? (to be disgraced)
15. What did Japanese farmers expect their children to do? (to work in the fields)
16. What was the purpose of the large bowl-like hats worn by Japanese fishers? (to protect the head from the sun and the ocean spray)
17. What was the reason behind the Japanese custom of removing shoes upon entering the home? (to avoid damaging the floor mats)
18. What did the large windows in Japanese living rooms allow the members of the family to do? (to view the garden outside)
19. What was one thing that Japanese girls liked to do on holidays? (to wear brightly colored kimonos)
20. What was the purpose of cultivating the silkworm in Japan? (to make silk fabric)

Grammar Review

Review: Exercise 6   **Writing Sentences with Verbal Phrases**

Use each phrase below in an original sentence about the excerpt from *Picture Bride*. Forms ending with *-ing* may be used in either participial or gerund phrases.

1. standing at the ship's railing
2. to protect herself from the cold sea winds
3. transported to a new country
4. wishing desperately for her home
5. remembering the beauty of the trees and fields
6. to see the face of someone she knew
7. smelling the strong fish odors
8. anguished about her decision to leave
9. influenced by her uncle's words
10. to meet her husband-to-be

Review: Exercise 7

Proofreading

The following passage describes the artist Andō Hiroshige, whose work appears on the opposite page. Rewrite the passage, correcting the errors in spelling, grammar, and usage. Add any missing punctuation. There are twenty-five errors.

Andō Hiroshige

¹Andō (or Ichiyu-sai) Hiroshige (1797–1858) the son of a fire warden, was born in Edo, a city later called Tokyo and he plans to follow in his fathers footsteps. ²However, he soon begun to study painting with the famous painter Utagawa Toyohiro.

³At first Hiroshige followed another painters practice of using human subjects, but he was soon recognized as a landscape artist. ⁴Trying a number of pictorial themes Hiroshige finally settled on landscapes birds, and flowers. ⁵Abandoning portraiture and historical subjects he focused on nature themes throughout his life.

⁶Making steady artistic progress Hiroshige experimented with printmaking. ⁷Began to make wood-block prints in a style called *ukiyo-e,* which, literally translated, means "floating world." ⁸These prints was inexpensively mass-produced for popular consumption. ⁹Following an artists instructions craftspeople made the prints.

¹⁰The subject matter of the *ukiyo-e* prints were historical events portraits, and landscapes. ¹¹Sometimes the prints was even used to teach people, mainly

Grammar Review

Andō Hiroshige, *The Compound of the Tenjin Shrine at Kameido*, 1856

children about some of the elements of Japanese culture. ¹²Enabling the populace to have art in their homes printmakers produced countless numbers of such prints. ¹³These prints popular and inexpensive works at the time, today are quite valuable.

¹⁴The artwork on this page, a typical wood-block print is made in the *ukiyo-e* style. ¹⁵Applied with a separate wood block each color is clear and vivid. ¹⁶Hiroshige combined plants, birds, water, and figures crossing a bridge to form a subtly poetic atmosphere in an everyday seen.

¹⁷To Hana Omiya, the character in Uchida's *Picture Bride* such an image would undoubtedly recall many fond images of Japan and of all things Japanese. ¹⁸Its delicate desine, decorative colors, hanging leaves, and arched bridge would remind her of the world she had left behind.

Grammar Review

Review: Exercise 8

Mixed Review

Read the brief biography of Yoshiko Uchida. Then use the facts in the biography and the guidelines in parentheses to expand the sentences.

Yoshiko Uchida

Yoshiko Uchida was born in California, in 1921. Her parents, seeking a better life, had moved to the United States several years before Uchida was born. Her mother, who was an amateur poet, taught Uchida to love words. As a child, Uchida witnessed the struggles of many Japanese Americans. Many of them spoke little English but ran their own businesses and earned a reputation as hard workers.

When Uchida was about to begin her final college exams, Japan attacked Pearl Harbor, and the United States entered World War II. Soon afterward the Uchidas, along with thousands of other Japanese Americans, were moved to relocation camps. At the camp at the Tanforan Race Track in California, Uchida's family lived in a horse stall for five months. Uchida spent three years in the grim, dusty camps.

After the war, Uchida studied education and taught in a Philadelphia school. She later left her teaching job and traveled to Japan, where she collected folktales and visited her ancestors' tombs. After learning a great deal about Japanese culture, she returned to California and dedicated herself to writing fiction. Uchida has written mostly for children; *Picture Bride* is her first novel for adults. It appeared in 1987.

1. Yoshiko Uchida was born in 1921. (Add an appositive phrase.)
2. Her parents came to America. (Add an infinitive phrase.)
3. Uchida's mother taught her to love words. (Add an appositive phrase.)
4. As a child, Uchida observed many Japanese immigrants. (Add a participial phrase.)
5. Most of them knew few words. (Add an adjective phrase.)
6. Many of the immigrants earned a living. (Add a participial phrase.)
7. The immigrants earned a reputation. (Add the preposition *for* and a gerund phrase.)
8. The United States entered World War II. (Add an adverb phrase.)
9. When Pearl Harbor was attacked, Uchida was studying. (Add an adverb phrase.)
10. The Uchidas were sent to the Tanforan Race Track. (Add an appositive phrase.)
11. Thousands were sent to the camps. (Add an adjective phrase.)
12. Uchida's entire family lived in a stall. (Add an adjective phrase.)
13. Uchida lived in the camps. (Add an adverb phrase.)
14. After the war Uchida studied. (Add an infinitive phrase.)
15. She taught school. (Add an adverb phrase.)
16. Later she decided to stop and travel to Japan. (Add a gerund or a gerund phrase.)
17. She went to Japan. (Add an infinitive phrase.)
18. After she returned, she made a decision. (Add an infinitive phrase.)
19. Most is written for children. (Add an adjective phrase.)
20. *Picture Bride* was published in 1987. (Add an appositive phrase.)

Writing Application

Phrases in Writing

Note how Mary Stewart uses appositives, participles, and prepositional phrases to enliven this passage from *The Crystal Cave*. As you read, pay particular attention to the italicized words.

> *Behind me* the flow of bats had ceased, and the cave was still. *Reassured*, I stayed where I was, *studying myself with interest in the mirror*. My mother had had one once, *an antique from Egypt*, but then, *deeming such things to be vanity*, she had locked it away. Of course I had often seen my face *reflected in water*, but never my body mirrored, till now. I saw a dark boy, wary, all eyes *with curiosity*, nerves, and excitement. *In that light* my eyes looked quite black; my hair was black, too. . . .

Techniques with Phrases

Try to apply some of Mary Stewart's techniques as you write and revise your own work.

❶ Use prepositional phrases to pinpoint location as well as to add specific detail to your sentences. Compare the following:

IMPRECISE VERSIONS The flow of bats had ceased. My eyes looked quite black.

STEWART'S VERSIONS *Behind me* the flow of bats had ceased. . . . *In that light* my eyes looked quite black. . . .

❷ Use appositives to combine short, choppy sentences.

CHOPPY VERSION My mother had had one once. It was an antique from Egypt.

STEWART'S VERSION My mother had had one once, *an antique from Egypt* . . .

❸ Use participles and participial phrases to connect ideas and show the relationships between them.

UNCLEAR VERSION I was reassured. I stayed where I was. I studied myself with interest.

STEWART'S VERSION *Reassured*, I stayed where I was, *studying myself with interest* . . .

> # TIME
> For more about the writing process, see **TIME Facing the Blank Page**, pp. 121–131.

Phrases

Practice Revise the following passage by adding prepositional phrases to show location and by combining choppy sentences with appositives and participles.

Vinland, or Wineland, is an area of North America. It is believed to have been along the coast. The Vikings probably explored this part before other Europeans did. The Vikings were courageous and skillful. The Vikings began to send ships in about the year 1000. They established no settlements. Leif Eriksson was probably sailing from Norway to Greenland. His ship was blown off course. He came to a land. It had first been sighted a few years earlier by another Viking.

Writing Application **537**

UNIT 13 Clauses and Sentence Structure

Lesson 13.1	Main Clauses	539
Lesson 13.2	Subordinate Clauses	540
Lesson 13.3	Simple and Compound Sentences	541
Lesson 13.4	Complex and Compound-Complex Sentences	543
Lesson 13.5	Adjective Clauses	545
Lesson 13.6	Adverb Clauses	548
Lesson 13.7	Noun Clauses	550
Lesson 13.8	Four Kinds of Sentences	552
Lesson 13.9	Sentence Fragments	553
Lesson 13.10	Run-on Sentences	555

Grammar Review 558

Writing Application 569

13.2 Subordinate Clauses

■ **A subordinate, or dependent, clause has a subject and a predicate, but it cannot stand alone as a sentence.**

A subordinate clause must be attached to a main clause in order for it to make sense. Subordinate clauses frequently begin with subordinating conjunctions or relative pronouns. When the subordinate clause comes first, a comma separates it from the main clause.

SUBORDINATE CLAUSE	MAIN CLAUSE
When the audience applauded,	the cast bowed.
S V	S V

MAIN CLAUSE
SUBORDINATE CLAUSE

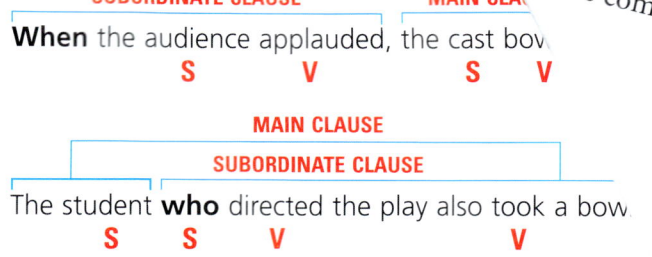

The student **who** directed the play also took a bow.
S   S   V   V

In the first example, the subordinating conjunction *when* plus *the audience applauded* creates a word group—*when the audience applauded*—that cannot stand alone as a main clause. Although the clause has a subject and a predicate, it does not express a complete thought.

In the second example, the relative pronoun *who* begins a subordinate clause that comes between the subject and the verb of the main clause. *Who* also serves as the subject of the subordinate clause.

Exercise 2 Identifying Main and Subordinate Clauses

In each of the following sentences, the first clause appears in italics. On your paper, write *main clause* or *subordinate clause* to identify the first clause. (Remember that a subordinate clause cannot stand alone as a sentence.)

Romana Bañuelos, a United States Treasurer

[1]*Romana Acosta Bañuelos was treasurer of the United States from 1971 to 1974,* while Richard Nixon was President. [2]*Though many others have held this position,* Bañuelos was the first Mexican American woman in such a high government post. [3]*Her signature became a familiar sight,* since the treasurer's name is printed on all paper currency. [4]*Because the job of treasurer involves a number of diverse tasks,* the job is a challenging one. [5]*When Bañuelos was in office,* she wrote checks for all government agencies. [6]*Whenever currency became worn out,* she oversaw the destruction and replacement of the bills.

[7]*Although Bañuelos grew up in Mexico,* she was born in Arizona. [8]*After she invested in a small tortilla stand in 1949,* the business grew into a 5-million-dollar food company. [9]*Because her tortilla company had become such a success,* Bañuelos undertook another challenge. [10]*In 1964 she founded the Pan-American National Bank of East Los Angeles,* which was the first bank in the United States run by a Mexican American.

13.3 Simple and Compound Sentences

■ A **simple sentence** has only one main clause and no subordinate clauses.

A simple sentence may have a compound subject or a compound predicate or both. The simple subject and the simple predicate may also be expanded in many other ways. Adjectives, adverbs, prepositional phrases, appositives, and verbal phrases may make some simple sentences seem anything but simple. Nevertheless, as long as the sentence has only one main clause and no subordinate clauses, it remains a simple sentence.

> Bobcats stalk. [simple sentence]
>
> Bobcats and lynxes stalk. [simple sentence with compound subject]
>
> Bobcats stalk and pounce. [simple sentence with compound predicate]
>
> Bobcats and lynxes stalk and pounce. [simple sentence with compound subject and compound predicate]
>
> Bobcats silently stalk their prey during the night. [simple sentence expanded with modifiers]

■ A **compound sentence** has two or more main clauses and no subordinate clauses.

As the following examples show, each main clause of a compound sentence has its own subject and predicate. Notice that the main clauses of a compound sentence are usually joined by a comma and a coordinating conjunction, such as *and, but, or, nor, yet, so,* or *for.*

> **MAIN CLAUSE 1**   **MAIN CLAUSE 2**
> Bobcats stalk, and lynxes pursue.
>   S   V   S   V
>
> **MAIN CLAUSE 1**   **MAIN CLAUSE 2**   **MAIN CLAUSE 3**
> Bobcats stalk, and lynxes pursue, but house cats slink.
>   S   V   S   V   S   V

Two main clauses may also be joined by a semicolon to form a compound sentence.

> **MAIN CLAUSE 1**   **MAIN CLAUSE 2**
> The frightened rabbit ran swiftly; the lynx followed at a close pace.

Exercise 3   Identifying Simple and Compound Sentences

Write *simple* or *compound* to identify each sentence.

Climbing Mount Everest

1. Sir Edmund Hillary and Tenzing Norgay, his Sherpa guide, were the first conquerors of Mount Everest.
2. Norgay was already a well-known mountaineer, but Hillary's experience had been limited to climbing in ice and snow in New Zealand.
3. Norgay was tall and strong, and Hillary liked the Sherpa's friendly attitude.
4. Hillary, Norgay, and all the other members of the expedition looked for the easiest and safest route to the top of Mount Everest.
5. Today climbers look for greater challenges and choose the more difficult routes.
6. Hillary once had traveled overland to the South Pole and also had followed the Ganges River to its source.
7. The public and the media had shown considerable interest in Hillary.
8. Fame came with Hillary's successful ascent of Mount Everest, and afterward he raised money for the Sherpa people of Nepal.
9. They had helped Hillary, and in return he generously helped them.
10. Hillary gave lectures and raised funds for schools, hospitals, clinics, bridges, water pipelines, and airstrips in Nepal.

Exercise 4   Writing Simple Sentences

Combine each pair of ideas below into a simple sentence. Remember that each sentence must have only one main clause, although it may have a compound subject and/or a compound predicate.

SAMPLE   Arctic explorers are brave. They must receive special training.
ANSWER   Arctic explorers are brave but must receive special training.

1. Robert E. Peary was a brave man. He explored arctic regions.
2. He made his first expedition to Greenland in 1886. Later he made several other trips there.
3. Peary planned a trip to the North Pole. He announced his plans in 1898.
4. He made the trip with his assistant, Matthew Henson. Peary's team also included four Inuit.
5. Peary succeeded in reaching his goal. He arrived at the North Pole on April 6, 1909.

Exercise 5   Writing Compound Sentences

Use the information in each item from Exercise 4 to write a compound sentence. Remember that each sentence must have two or more main clauses joined by a comma and a coordinating conjunction or by a semicolon.

SAMPLE   Arctic explorers are brave. They must receive special training.
ANSWER   Arctic explorers are brave, but they must receive special training.

13.4 Complex and Compound-Complex Sentences

- A **complex sentence** has one main clause and one or more subordinate clauses.

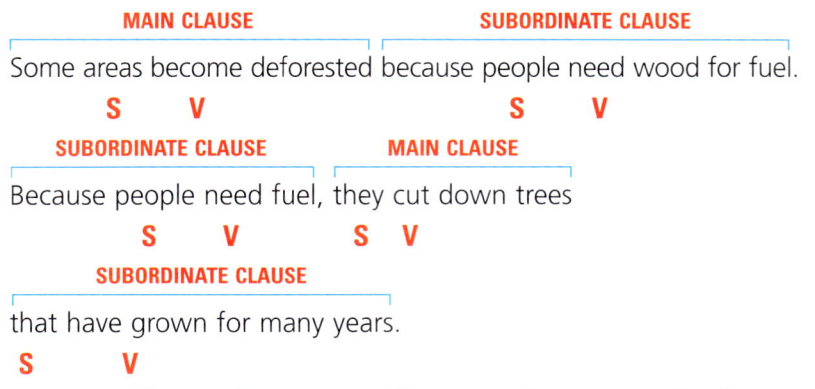

    MAIN CLAUSE | SUBORDINATE CLAUSE
    Some areas become deforested because people need wood for fuel.
    S   V   S   V

    SUBORDINATE CLAUSE | MAIN CLAUSE
    Because people need fuel, they cut down trees
         S   V   S   V
    SUBORDINATE CLAUSE
    that have grown for many years.
     S   V

- A **compound-complex sentence** has more than one main clause and at least one subordinate clause.

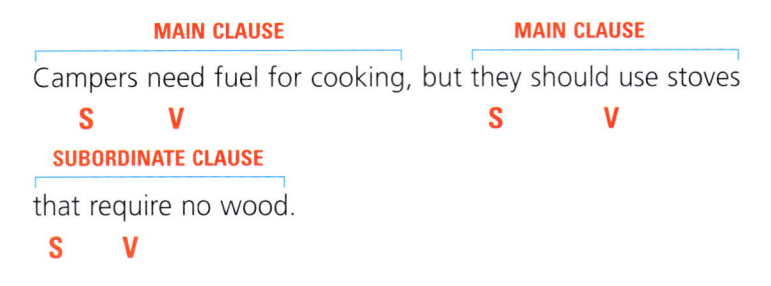

    MAIN CLAUSE | MAIN CLAUSE
    Campers need fuel for cooking, but they should use stoves
      S   V   S   V
    SUBORDINATE CLAUSE
    that require no wood.
     S   V

Exercise 6   Identifying Subordinate Clauses

Write the subordinate clause in each of the following sentences. If a sentence has no subordinate clause, write *none*.

1. Since the world's supply of wood is limited, environmentalists encourage conservation of timber resources.
2. The United States government controls large areas of national forest and sets the policy for use of the timber.
3. Many states have set aside land for state forests, which may also be used for recreation.
4. People's ideas about forest conservation differ, and opposing groups present arguments that deserve serious consideration.
5. Because opinions on the subject are so different, no simple solution exists.

Exercise 7 — Identifying Complex and Compound-Complex Sentences

Write the subordinate clause that appears in each of the following sentences. Then write *complex* or *compound-complex* to identify each sentence.

Conservation

1. Energy conservation has become extremely important because millions of energy-consuming devices are in use every day.
2. When builders construct new homes, they should install solar panels and other passive solar devices and as many energy-saving appliances as possible.
3. Although energy-efficient appliances cost more, their use results in long-term savings for the owner, and the environment benefits, too.
4. Because legislators have enacted certain laws, all new cars must be energy efficient.
5. When cars use less gas, the air is cleaner, and people may have less trouble breathing.
6. Though sulfur pollution is a threat to human health, it also damages lakes, wildlife, and buildings.
7. Although water power can generate electricity, hydroelectric dams may cause floods on farmland, in forests, and in wildlife areas.
8. We must always find ways of producing more goods, but at the same time we must reduce the amount of energy that we consume in producing those goods.
9. Conservation and solar power are the keys to a safe future, so we must cautiously use the devices that cool, heat, and transport us.
10. Because our natural resources clearly cannot last forever, we must find better ways of conserving them.

Exercise 8 — Writing Four Kinds of Sentences

Use your own knowledge and the information below to create four different kinds of sentences about electrical power. Write *simple, compound, complex,* or *compound-complex* to identify each sentence you write.

An electric motor is a source of power.
It is convenient.
It is clean.
It is silent.
It starts instantly.
It stops instantly.
It can be built in almost any size.
It can power a speeding train.
It can run a tiny watch.
Power can come through a wire from an outside source.
Power can come from a battery.
An electric car does not pollute.
It is expensive to manufacture.
It needs frequent recharging.

Exercise 9 — Creating Sentences with Various Structures

Write a simple sentence. Then rework it, making it into a compound sentence. Now go back to the simple sentence, and rework it to make it part of a complex sentence. Finally, rework your compound sentence into a compound-complex sentence. Label each sentence.

13.5 Adjective Clauses

■ An **adjective clause** is a subordinate clause that modifies a noun or a pronoun.

An adjective clause normally follows the word it modifies.

> The hikers **who reached the peak** were overjoyed.
>
> The trail, **which was rarely used,** had been a difficult one.
>
> I forgot about the blisters **that covered my feet.**
>
> The hiker **whom we appreciated most** carried the food.

Both relative pronouns (*who, whom, whose, that,* and *which*) and the words *where* and *when* may begin adjective clauses.

> I will always remember the time **when I hiked to Pike's Peak.**
>
> That is the spot **where we set up camp.**

Sometimes the relative pronoun is dropped at the beginning of an adjective clause.

> Our camp was the place **every hiker loved the most.**
> [The relative pronoun *that* has been omitted.]

An adjective clause is sometimes essential to a sentence; that is, it is needed to make the meaning of the sentence clear. This kind of adjective clause is called an *essential clause,* or a *restrictive clause.*

> One characteristic **that many Native Americans had in common** was a love of dancing. [essential clause]

An adjective clause that is not needed to make the meaning of a sentence clear is called a *nonessential clause,* or a *nonrestrictive clause.* It adds information to a sentence, but the sentence would be perfectly logical without it. (Note that a nonessential clause must be set off with commas.)

> The Iroquois people of the East, **who were farmers,** thanked the spirits for the gift of food. [nonessential clause]
>
> In the Southwest, **where water is scarce,** the Pueblo people performed rain dances. [nonessential clause]

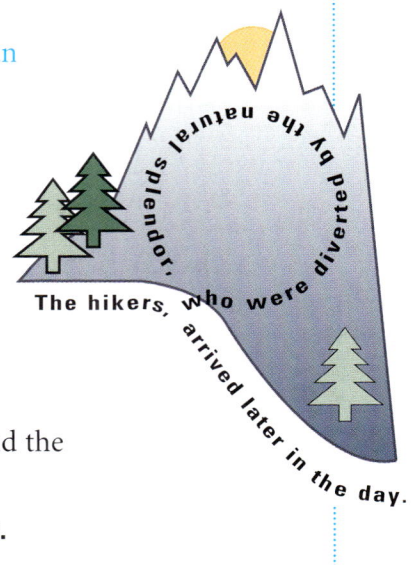

The hikers, who were diverted by the natural splendor, arrived later in the day.

When choosing between *that* and *which,* use *that* to introduce an essential clause and *which* to begin a nonessential clause.

The Cheyenne hunted buffalo, **which supplied them with meat and skins for clothing and shelter.** [nonessential clause]

The animal **that was most important to the Cheyenne** was the buffalo. [essential clause]

Exercise 10   Identifying Adjective Clauses and the Words They Modify

On your paper write the adjective clause from each sentence. Then write the word the clause modifies. (In one sentence the relative pronoun has been dropped.)

International Dances

1. The Pueblo rain dancers use dance steps that are deceptively simple.
2. In the eagle dance, the dancers' movements are like those of the eagle, which swoops and dives for its food.
3. Chinese schoolchildren learn dances that require difficult body movements.
4. The Chinese ribbon dance, which has been performed for thousands of years, is often performed by Chinese folk-dance companies.
5. Japanese dancers may wear several layers of kimonos, each of which represents a different character.
6. A lively dance that is very popular is the square dance.
7. Probably the best-known early American dance is the Virginia reel, which became popular in George Washington's time.
8. Flamenco is a dance form the Gypsies in Spain invented.
9. A flamenco dancer, who is accompanied by a guitarist, typically wears bright and colorful clothing.
10. Folk dances often require steps that are difficult to learn.

Exercise 11   Adding Adjective Clauses to Sentences

On your paper complete each sentence below by adding a noun. Then write an adjective clause to modify the noun.

1. My favorite meal is _____.
2. I will always remember _____.
3. Did you see the _____?
4. I really don't like the _____.
5. I had forgotten all about the _____.
6. Where did you get the _____?
7. Tomorrow I will pick up the _____.
8. This is the _____.
9. Last week I visited _____.
10. We laughed about the _____.

Exercise 12 Identifying Essential and Nonessential Clauses

For each sentence in the following pairs, write the adjective clause, and then write *essential* or *nonessential* to identify it.

Maya Lin, Architect

1. a. Maya Lin, who was born and raised in Athens, Ohio, designed the Vietnam Veterans Memorial.
   b. The person who designed the Vietnam Veterans Memorial was Maya Lin.
2. a. Lin was an architecture student who submitted the once-controversial design.
   b. Lin, who submitted the once-controversial design, was an architecture student at Yale University.
3. a. Her simple design consisted of two gleaming black walls that were inscribed with the names of the dead and missing.
   b. The memorial, which has attracted numerous visitors since its unveiling, contains the names of the war's dead and the missing.
4. a. In 1988, Maya Lin designed the Civil Rights Memorial, which is in Montgomery, Alabama.
   b. In 1988, Maya Lin designed a memorial that commemorates the Civil Rights Movement.
5. a. Maya Lin's parents, who were college professors, emigrated from China in the 1940s.
   b. The college professors who were Lin's parents emigrated from China in the 1940s.

Exercise 13 Identifying Adjective Clauses

Rewrite the sentences below. Underline each adjective clause. If a clause is nonessential, set it off with commas.

1. In most cultures around the world, people have dances that they use to tell stories.
2. Often the dancers who may wear colorful costumes are accompanied by singing, chanting, or playing of special instruments.
3. Many immigrants who moved to the United States from Europe, Africa, Asia, and South America brought their dances with them.
4. The dances that came from England, Ireland, and Scotland became the basis for American square dancing.
5. Native Americans who are descendants of the earliest inhabitants of this continent still perform colorful ceremonial dances of their own.

13.6 Adverb Clauses

■ An **adverb** clause is a subordinate clause that modifies a verb, an adjective, or an adverb. It tells *when, where, how, why, to what extent,* or *under what conditions.*

Whenever it rains, the river rises. [The adverb clause modifies the verb *rises*. It tells *when.*]

This canoe can take us **wherever we want to go.** [The adverb clause modifies the verb phrase *can take*. It tells *where.*]

The canoe will be safe **as long as everyone remains seated.** [The adverb clause modifies the adjective *safe*. It tells *under what conditions.*]

You are paddling harder **than I am paddling.** [The adverb clause modifies the adverb *harder*. It tells *to what extent.*]

Subordinating conjunctions, such as those listed on page 439, introduce adverb clauses. Being familiar with those conjunctions will help you recognize adverb clauses.

An adverb clause may come either before or after the main clause. Notice how the comma is used when the adverb clause begins the sentence.

The canoe capsized **when the river got rough.**
When the river got rough, the canoe capsized.

Occasionally words may be left out of an adverb clause. The omitted words can easily be supplied because they are understood, or implied. Such adverb clauses are described as *elliptical.*

You are paddling harder **than I am [paddling].**
Paddling made me more tired **than [it made] him [tired].**

Exercise 14 — Identifying Adverb Clauses

Write the adverb clauses that appear in the following sentences. (Three sentences have more than one adverb clause.)

Yo-Yo Ma, an Outstanding Cellist

1. Yo-Yo Ma played the cello at Carnegie Hall, when he was only nine years old.
2. Because he had such talent, young Ma already played better than most adults do.
3. When Ma was only four, his father gave him cello lessons.
4. Since Ma's father was a musicologist, he nurtured his son's talent.
5. When he was big enough, Ma switched to a regular cello.
6. After his family moved from Paris to New York, Ma studied at the Juilliard School of Music.
7. Wherever he played, Ma dazzled audiences with his deftness.
8. Ma continued on the cello while he worked on a degree from Harvard.
9. A highlight in his career came in 1978, when Ma received the Avery Fisher Prize for his musical talent.
10. Whenever Ma performs, fans can hardly imagine a cellist more talented than he.
11. When Ma played with the Chicago Symphony recently, I saw him in person.
12. The tickets were more expensive than I had expected.
13. Many people attended that evening because Ma's performance earlier that week had received rave reviews.
14. Before Ma appeared on stage, everyone waited impatiently as the orchestra tuned up their instruments.
15. When the great performer finally made his entrance, the audience jumped to their feet and applauded.

Exercise 15 — Using Adverb Clauses in Sentences

Use each of the following adverb clauses in an original sentence. Vary the positions of the clauses in your sentences.

1. whenever the first members of the audience arrive
2. as long as I can hear from the back of the auditorium
3. unless something happens at the last minute
4. although she still used her father's old stereo system
5. because the traffic was so heavy that night
6. although no one was given information beforehand
7. until everyone finds a place to sit down
8. before the master of ceremonies could say a single word
9. since I had decided earlier not to go with them
10. wherever people get together to hear fine music

13.6 Adverb Clauses

13.7 Noun Clauses

■ A **noun clause** is a subordinate clause used as a noun.

You can use a noun clause as a subject, a direct object, an indirect object, an object of a preposition, a predicate nominative, or an object complement.

        NOUN
Campers enjoy the outdoors.
   S

      NOUN CLAUSE
Whoever camps enjoys the outdoors.
   S

             NOUN
Footgear affects hikers.
             DO

                NOUN CLAUSE
Footgear affects whoever walks often.
                DO

In the preceding examples, notice that each noun clause is an inseparable part of the sentence's main clause; the main clause is the entire sentence.

Here are some of the words that can be used to introduce noun clauses:

how	when	who, whom
that	where	whoever
what	which	whose
whatever	whichever	why

Here are additional examples of noun clauses.

I do not know **where my hiking boots are.** [direct object]

That is **why I did not join the others.** [predicate nominative]

We will make do with **whatever camping equipment we can borrow.** [object of a preposition]

Sometimes the introductory word may be dropped at the beginning of a noun clause.

I believe **we can have a great time outdoors.** [The introductory word *that* is omitted.]

550   Unit 13 Clauses and Sentence Structure

Exercise 16   **Identifying Noun Clauses**

Write the noun clauses that appear in each of the following sentences. (Three of the sentences have two noun clauses each. In one sentence the relative pronoun introducing the noun clause has been dropped.)

The Importance of Police Dogs

1. Everyone knows that dogs have a keen sense of smell.
2. What makes their sense of smell valuable is that people can train dogs to sniff out explosives.
3. Specially trained dogs search for whatever explosive device they can find.
4. What the dog finds may save whoever is in danger.
5. Do you believe that police dogs are valuable?
6. Whoever works with a police dog is trained along with the dog.
7. Many police officers say that police dogs make good partners.
8. Whoever says police dogs are vicious animals is misinformed.
9. That these dogs become aggressive upon command is true.
10. Police officers are grateful for whatever help these dogs provide.
11. Most people realize that police dogs will not attack them without cause.
12. They will pay little attention to whoever leaves them alone.
13. The laws of some communities state that police dogs should be muzzled.
14. Another regulation is that they should usually be on leashes.
15. Can you see why their appearance frightens some people?

Exercise 17   **Identifying Subordinate Clauses**

On your paper write the subordinate clause that appears in each sentence. Then write *adverb clause, adjective clause,* or *noun clause* to identify what kind of clause it is.

Sojourner Truth, a Crusader for Justice

[1]Sojourner Truth was an enslaved person who was born in New York in the late eighteenth century. [2]Isabella is what she was called as a child. [3]Whoever has studied her life understands the importance of her work. [4]She fought against slavery wherever she went. [5]An antislavery law was passed in New York in 1817, which led to Isabella's freedom in 1827. [6]In 1843, after she took the name Sojourner Truth, she began a series of lecture tours throughout New England and the Midwest. [7]Her speeches expressed her strong belief that all people are equal. [8]One source of income was the proceeds from her biography, which was published in 1850. [9]Sojourner Truth campaigned for land where former enslaved persons could establish homes. [10]Sojourner Truth was a woman whom everyone admired.

Exercise 18   **Writing Subordinate Clauses in Sentences**

Write four original sentences. In the first, use an adverb clause. In the second, use an adjective clause. In the third, use a noun clause as a subject. In the fourth, use a noun clause as a direct object. Label the clauses.

13.8 Four Kinds of Sentences

- A **declarative sentence** makes a statement.

    An owl is hooting.
    I cannot see it.

A declarative sentence normally ends with a period. It is the type of sentence used most frequently in speaking and writing.

- An **imperative sentence** gives a command or makes a request.

    Look at that bird.
    Please tell me what it is.

An imperative sentence usually ends with a period. The subject "you" is understood.

- An **interrogative sentence** asks a question.

    What kind of bird is that?
    Is the hawk hunting for prey?

An interrogative sentence ends with a question mark.

- An **exclamatory sentence** expresses strong emotion.

    Watch out for that hawk's sudden dive!
    What a powerful hunter the hawk is!

An exclamatory sentence ends with an exclamation point.

Exercise 19   Identifying and Punctuating Four Kinds of Sentences

On your paper write *declarative, imperative, interrogative,* or *exclamatory* to identify each sentence below. Then give the correct ending punctuation.

1. Have you ever been to Niagara Falls
2. What an awesome sight they are
3. The falls are on the Niagara River between New York State and Ontario, Canada
4. When you go, I hope that you plan to visit both the American and the Canadian sides
5. Don't miss the boat ride on the *Maid of the Mist*

Exercise 20   Writing Four Kinds of Sentences

Write four sentences about a recent school event. Use one declarative, one imperative, one interrogative, and one exclamatory sentence. Remember to punctuate each sentence correctly.

13.9 Sentence Fragments

■ A **sentence fragment** is an error that occurs when an incomplete sentence is punctuated as though it were a complete sentence. In general, avoid sentence fragments in your writing.

When you check your work for sentence fragments, look for three things. First, be alert for a group of words that lacks a subject. Then, look for a group of words that lacks a verb, especially a group that contains a verbal form rather than a complete verb. Finally, be careful that you have not punctuated a subordinate clause as a complete sentence.

Often you can correct a sentence fragment by joining it to an idea that comes before or after the fragment. Sometimes, however, you may need to add missing words to form a complete sentence.

FRAGMENT	Toshiko and Kenji are happy together. **Seem to be in love.** [lacks subject]
COMPLETE SENTENCE	Toshiko and Kenji are happy together, and they seem to be in love.
FRAGMENT	The two will marry. **Their new life together.** [lacks verb]
COMPLETE SENTENCE	The two will marry, and their new life together will begin.
FRAGMENT	They are planning an out-of-town wedding. **Many of their gifts arriving in the mail.** [lacks complete verb]
COMPLETE SENTENCE	They are planning an out-of-town wedding. Many of their gifts have been arriving in the mail.
FRAGMENT	On their honeymoon they will be traveling to Italy. **Which they both love.** [has subordinate clause only]
COMPLETE SENTENCE	On their honeymoon they will be traveling to Italy, which they both love.

Artist Unknown, *Nike of Samothrace*, 200–190 B.C.

Professional writers sometimes use sentence fragments to create a special effect—to add emphasis to what they are saying or to convey realistic dialogue. Remember that professionals use sentence fragments *carefully* and *intentionally*. In most of the writing you do, however, including your writing for school, you should avoid sentence fragments.

Exercise 21   Identifying Sentence Fragments

Write on your paper *complete sentence* or *sentence fragment* to identify each of the items below.

The Piñata Game

[1]Children in Mexico often celebrate festivals and birthdays with parties. [2]By breaking a colorful piñata. [3]An earthenware or papier-mâché container covered with crepe-paper streamers. [4]A piñata is often shaped like an animal or a person. [5]Filled with nuts, candy, and small toys, it is hung by a rope from the ceiling. [6]Or—if the party is outdoors—from a tree limb. [7]The blindfolded children take turns hitting the piñata with a stick. [8]Not always easy, because an adult raises and lowers the piñata with a rope. [9]Finally, after many attempts, the break. [10]Children rush to collect the treats scattered about.

Exercise 22   Correcting Sentence Fragments

Revise the preceding paragraph by correcting each fragment. Whenever possible, combine the fragments with other sentences in the paragraph.

Exercise 23   Identifying and Correcting Sentence Fragments

Add your own words and phrases to rewrite each item that is not a sentence as a complete sentence. Change wording if you need to. For any item that is already a sentence, write *sentence*.

1. Jack and Kera help with the cooking for the family.
2. After they get home from school or on the weekends.
3. Soup, pasta, and grilled cheese sandwiches.
4. Which they like the best.
5. Planning the menu or the grocery shopping.
6. The oven and the stove being broken.
7. To fix cold foods and use the toaster and microwave.
8. Because he was too impatient to wait for the electrician.
9. Juice, pancakes, waffles, and muffins, the favorites for Sunday breakfast.
10. Enjoys fixing special dishes for birthdays and holidays.
11. They both enjoy cooking together.
12. Especially like to make dinner for their parents
13. When their parents let them prepare the whole meal.
14. Whenever they have a chance to help make the refreshments for a party.
15. The twins are especially happy after cleaning up.

13.10 Run-on Sentences

■ Avoid run-on sentences in your writing. A **run-on sentence** is two or more complete sentences written as though they were one sentence.

There are three basic kinds of run-on sentence.

1. A **comma splice,** probably the most common type of run-on sentence, occurs when two main clauses are separated by a comma rather than a period or a semicolon. To correct this type of run-on, replace the comma with a period (or other end mark of punctuation), and start the new sentence with a capital letter. You can also correct this error by changing the comma to a semicolon or by inserting a coordinating conjunction after the comma.

    RUN-ON Luis and Fredericka are going to Washington, D.C., with their school, they are very excited.

    CORRECT Luis and Fredericka are going to Washington, D.C., with their school. They are very excited.

    CORRECT Luis and Fredericka are going to Washington, D.C., with their school, **and** they are very excited.

2. Another kind of run-on sentence occurs when two main clauses are written with *no* punctuation between them. To correct this type of run-on, separate the main clauses with a semicolon, or insert an end mark of punctuation after the first clause and begin the second one with a capital letter. Still another way to correct the error is to insert a comma and a coordinating conjunction between the main clauses.

    RUN-ON They hope to see many famous sights the Lincoln Memorial will surely be among them.

    CORRECT They hope to see many famous sights; the Lincoln Memorial will surely be among them.

    CORRECT They hope to see many famous sights, **and** the Lincoln Memorial will surely be among them.

3. Still another kind of run-on sentence occurs when the comma is omitted before a coordinating conjunction joining two main clauses. To correct this error, simply add the comma before the coordinating conjunction.

    RUN-ON Fredericka and Luis will need to take notes for a written report on their Washington trip but they plan to have fun anyway.

    CORRECT Fredericka and Luis will need to take notes for a written report on their Washington trip, but they plan to have fun anyway.

Exercise 24 — Distinguishing Between Run-ons and Correct Sentences

On your paper write *correct* or *run-on* to identify each sentence below.

The Amazon River and the Nile River

1. The Amazon River is 3,900 miles (6,280 km) long it is the second longest river in the world.
2. The river flows generally eastward across northern South America and into the Atlantic Ocean through a wide delta in northern Brazil.
3. The Amazon is formed by the junction of two rivers in Peru, the Ucayali and the Marañón.
4. The Amazon has more than 500 tributaries and its river system drains half of South America.
5. Ships can travel almost the entire length of the river, it has no rapids or waterfalls to obstruct traffic.
6. The Nile is the world's longest river; it flows about 4,145 miles (6,905 km) from its headwaters in Burundi to the Mediterranean Sea.
7. The main part of the river is formed by the joining of two rivers, the Blue Nile and the White Nile.
8. The Blue Nile begins at Lake Tana it flows 1,000 miles to Khartoum.
9. The White Nile is 1,600 miles long, and its source is Lake Victoria.
10. The Blue and the White Nile converge at the city of Khartoum, which is the capital of Sudan.
11. Khartoum was founded as a camp for the Egyptian army in 1821 and developed into a major trading center.
12. Above Khartoum the Nile makes a huge S-curve and then it flows north through Egypt.
13. The Nile valley in Egypt was the location of a great ancient civilization, the tombs of kings and many other historic monuments are preserved there.
14. Dams on the Nile in Egypt have created a water supply for irrigating crops; the dams also produce hydroelectric power for the region.
15. Beyond Cairo the river forms an enormous triangular delta, here the river slows and drops much of its load of sediment before it flows into the sea.

Exercise 25 — Correcting Run-on Sentences by Adding Commas

Correct each run-on sentence below by adding a comma before the coordinating conjunction.

1. Wilbur Wright was born in Dayton, Ohio, in 1867 and his brother Orville was born in 1871.
2. They ran a weekly newspaper together and then they started a bicycle manufacturing business.
3. The brothers read about aeronautics and they experimented with gliders.
4. Kitty Hawk, North Carolina, had long expanses of rolling sand dunes and the winds there were quite steady and dependable.
5. The Wright brothers tested their gliders on the dunes of Kitty Hawk and in 1903 they made the first powered flight.

Exercise 26 Correcting Run-on Sentences with a Period or a Semicolon

Correct each run-on sentence below by adding a period or a semicolon.

1. Benjamin Franklin was an important political figure during the period of the American Revolution, he was a man of many other talents as well.
2. He lived in Boston as a young man, there he learned the printing trade.
3. Franklin published an almanac he also experimented with electricity.
4. Franklin started a university, in Philadelphia he also started a lending library.
5. Franklin helped draft the Declaration of Independence he was also one of the signers of the peace treaty that in 1783 formally ended the American Revolution.

Exercise 27 Correcting Run-on Sentences

Rewrite the following paragraph, correcting the run-on sentences.

Animal Care in Zoos

¹The earliest known zoo was the Park of Intelligence in the province of Hunan it was started by a Chinese ruler about 1150 B.C. ²Today zoo facilities are limited and zookeepers cannot keep every animal on display year-round. ³In the winter in colder climates, most birds must be brought indoors but zookeepers cannot always keep each bird on view for the public. ⁴Many visitors are surprised to see that some animals remain outside all year, penguins, polar bears, and timber wolves are happy outdoors in wintertime. ⁵Some animals are always indoors in northern areas, reptiles and small desert animals always have indoor displays. ⁶Zookeepers must provide indoor shelters for large animals such as elephants how large those shelters must be! ⁷Today zoologists understand much more about animal behavior and zoos are being designed that are similar to the animals' natural habitats. ⁸Viewers can closely observe animals at animal parks, animals roam free. ⁹Zoo kitchens keep a wide variety of foods and these are used to prepare meals that meet each animal's nutritional needs. ¹⁰Zoos contribute to wildlife conservation, they nurture species that are in danger of becoming extinct.

Exercise 28 Correcting Sentence Fragments and Run-on Sentences

Rewrite this paragraph, correcting all sentence fragments and run-on sentences.

Chinese New Year

¹The biggest and most popular of all Chinese festivals. ²The Chinese New Year, an exciting and colorful holiday. ³Falling anywhere between January 21 and February 19. ⁴The New Year is celebrated by Chinese people all over the world, they parade through the streets and set off fireworks. ⁵People pay visits to friends they wish them luck and prosperity with a greeting that means "happy greetings, and may you gather wealth." ⁶On the final day of the year, preparations are made for a great New Year's Eve supper. ⁷All doors are sealed with paper strips and no one may leave or enter until the next morning. ⁸Businesses are closed. ⁹For days after the new year begins. ¹⁰Children receive presents of money in red envelopes no wonder they look forward to this festival.

UNIT 13 Grammar Review

CLAUSES AND SENTENCE STRUCTURE

As Eudora Welty's novel *Delta Wedding* begins, young Laura McRaven is on her way from her home in Jackson, Mississippi, to Shellmound, the plantation where her cousin Dabney is to be married. It is Laura's first trip alone, and she savors every minute of it. The passage has been annotated to show the types of sentences and clauses covered in this unit.

Literature Model

from *Delta Wedding*
by Eudora Welty

The nickname of the train was the Yellow Dog. Its real name was the Yazoo-Delta. It was a mixed train. The day was the 10th of September, 1923—afternoon. **Laura McRaven, who was nine years old, was on her first journey alone.** She was going up from Jackson to visit her mother's people, the Fairchilds, at their plantation named Shellmound, at Fairchilds, Mississippi. . . .

In the passenger car every window was propped open with a stick of kindling wood. A breeze blew through, hot and then cool, fragrant of the woods and yellow flowers and of the train. **The yellow butterflies flew in at any window, out at any other, and outdoors one of them could keep up with the train, which then seemed to be racing with a butterfly.** Overhead a black lamp in which a circle of flowers had been cut out swung round and round on a chain **as the car rocked from side to side,** sending down dainty drifts of kerosene smell. The Dog was almost sure to reach Fairchilds before the lamp would be lighted by Mr. Terry Black, the conductor, **who had promised her father to watch out for her. Laura had the seat facing the stove, but of course no fire was burning in it now.** She sat leaning at the window, the light and the sooty air trying to make her close her eyes. Her ticket to Fairchilds was stuck up in her Madge Evans straw hat, in imitation of the

Annotations:
- Simple sentence
- Complex sentence
- Compound-complex sentence
- Adverb clause
- Adjective clause
- Compound sentence

Grammar Review

drummer [salesman] across the aisle. Once the Dog stopped in the open fields and Laura saw the engineer, Mr. Doolittle, go out and pick some specially fine goldenrod there—for whom, she could not know. Then the long September cry rang from the thousand unseen locusts, urgent at the open windows of the train. . . .

From the warm window sill the endless fields glowed like a hearth in firelight, and Laura, looking out, leaning on her elbows with her head between her hands, felt **what an arriver in a land feels**—that slow hard pounding in the breast.

Noun clause

Review: Exercise 1 Identifying Main and Subordinate Clauses

The following sentences are based on the passage from *Delta Wedding*. Each sentence contains a clause that appears in italics. On your paper write *main clause* or *subordinate clause* to identify the italicized clauses.

1. *Although she was only nine years old*, Laura was traveling alone.
2. The conductor, *who was watching out for Laura*, would soon light the lamp.
3. *The ticket* that was stuck in Laura's hat *would take her to Fairchilds, Mississippi*.
4. Laura was traveling to Fairchilds *so that she could attend her cousin's wedding*.
5. *She would stay at her cousin's plantation*, which was named Shellmound.
6. *The train was called the Yellow Dog*, although its name was really the Yazoo-Delta.
7. *While the train moved along*, Laura sat quietly in her seat.
8. *The car had a faint smell of kerosene*, which came from the swinging lamp overhead.
9. As the car rocked from side to side, *the lamp swung in a big circle*.
10. Laura could see the unlighted stove just opposite *where she sat*.
11. *Even though it was September*, the weather in the delta was still summery.
12. Because it was a warm day, *all the windows of the train were open*.
13. *Since the windows would not stay open by themselves*, they were propped up with sticks.
14. In the car were yellow butterflies, *which had flown in through the open windows*.
15. While the train was stopped, *Laura could hear the loud sounds made by locusts in the fields*.
16. Laura saw a field of goldenrod *as she looked out the window*.
17. Where the sun shone on them, *the broad fields glowed like a lighted fireplace*.
18. *After the engineer had picked some goldenrod*, the train started up again.
19. Laura could feel the warmth of the windowsill beneath her elbows *as she sat with her head between her hands*.
20. *Because the sun was bright*, Laura's eyes wanted to close.

Grammar Review

Review: Exercise 2   **Identifying Simple, Compound, Complex, and Compound-Complex Sentences**

The following sentences elaborate on ideas in the passage from *Delta Wedding* and tell something about its author. On your paper write whether each sentence is *simple, compound, complex,* or *compound-complex*.

1. The train's name was the Yazoo-Delta, but people called it the Yellow Dog.
2. It was September 10, 1923, and Laura McRaven was traveling by train to Fairchilds, Mississippi, where her cousin was getting married.
3. Nine-year-old Laura watched the countryside as it passed by.
4. Laura was enjoying the trip, for she was traveling alone for the first time.
5. The car rocked gently as the train hurried along, and the overhead lamp swung round and round.
6. The windows, which were held open with sticks of wood, let breezes into the cars.
7. The train had been traveling for a long time, yet the conductor had still not collected the tickets from Laura and the salesperson across the aisle.
8. Because the day was warm, no fire burned in the stove.
9. Laura watched while the engineer picked some goldenrod, and she noticed that the flowers were especially fine.
10. Though she sat quietly, Laura could feel her heart pounding.
11. While she sat alone on the train, Laura noticed many details inside the railroad car, and she observed the passing landscape as well.
12. Because she was traveling alone for the first time, she was unusually aware of her surroundings.
13. She compared what she was seeing with her hometown.
14. The author of *Delta Wedding*, Eudora Welty, was born in Jackson, Mississippi, in 1909.
15. When she created the character of Laura McRaven in *Delta Wedding*, Welty created a girl whose life was similar to hers.
16. Welty has lived in the Mississippi Delta for most of her life, and the delta landscape is familiar to her.
17. Eudora Welty, like Laura, probably traveled by train through the delta as a young girl.
18. Welty says that she has always been aware of words and of the way people speak.
19. As a young girl, she paid attention to the ordinary sights, sounds, and objects of daily life, and they formed vivid sensory images that remained with her.
20. When Welty grew up and became a writer, her store of early impressions and memories provided a wealth of convincing details for her books and stories.

Grammar Review

Review: Exercise 3 **Writing Sentences with Adjective Clauses**

Use the passage from *Delta Wedding* to rewrite the sentences below. To each sentence add an adjective clause that answers the question in parentheses. Your clause must begin with one of the relative pronouns below. It must contain a verb, and it must be correctly punctuated. There may be more than one correct answer.

RELATIVE PRONOUNS   who   whom   whose   which   that

SAMPLE   The train was heading toward Fairchilds, Mississippi. (What was the name of the train?)
ANSWER   The train, whose name was the Yazoo-Delta, was heading toward Fairchilds, Mississippi.

1. Laura was traveling alone for the first time in her life. (How old was she?)
2. Laura's father had taken her to the train. (How did her father feel about her trip?)
3. Laura was traveling from Jackson, Mississippi. (What was Jackson to Laura?)
4. She was going to visit her mother's family. (Where did Laura's mother's family live?)
5. Laura's journey was taking place on a September afternoon. (What was the weather like?)
6. Laura felt very dressed up for her ride on the train. (What hat was she wearing?)
7. A breeze blew through the open windows. (What did the breeze smell like?)
8. Laura watched the yellow butterflies. (What were the butterflies doing?)
9. One butterfly seemed to be having a race with the train. (Where was the butterfly?)
10. A black lamp swung to the rhythm of the rocking car. (How was the lamp decorated?)
11. The lamp would probably not be lighted during the journey. (What odor did the lamp give off?)
12. The conductor would light the lamp later. (What was the conductor's name?)
13. Mr. Black had not yet collected the tickets. (What promise had he made?)
14. Laura sat in her seat. (Where was her seat?)
15. The stove provided heat for the car in cold weather. (Was the stove being used on this day?)
16. The air made her want to close her eyes. (What was the air like?)
17. Laura imitated the drummer, or traveling salesperson. (Where was his ticket?)
18. Many drummers traveled by train to call on customers. (Where were the customers?)
19. Mr. Doolittle stopped the train. (What was Mr. Doolittle's job?)
20. The engineer picked some goldenrod. (What was the goldenrod like?)
21. Laura wondered to whom Mr. Doolittle would give the goldenrod. (Why did she want to know?)
22. Through the train's open windows Laura heard a cry. (From what did the cry come?)
23. Laura heard locusts. (Where were they?)
24. Laura gazed at the fields. (What did the fields look like?)
25. Laura wanted her journey to end. (How did she feel?)

Grammar Review

Review: Exercise 4 **Writing Sentences with Adverb Clauses**

Use the passage from *Delta Wedding* to rewrite each sentence, adding an adverb clause that answers the question in parentheses. Your clause must begin with one of the subordinating conjunctions listed below, and it must contain a subject and a verb. There may be more than one correct answer for each item.

SUBORDINATING CONJUNCTIONS

after	as if	if	so that	when	wherever
as	because	since	than	whenever	while

SAMPLE   Laura McRaven was traveling to Shellmound. (Why?)

ANSWER   Laura McRaven was traveling to Shellmound because her cousin Dabney was getting married.

1. It was an exciting day for Laura. (Why?)
2. Laura sat looking out the window. (When?)
3. Laura felt excited. (Why?)
4. Laura had a ticket to Fairchilds, Mississippi. (Why?)
5. Laura carefully observed everything that went on around her. (Why?)
6. The passenger car swayed back and forth. (When?)
7. Pieces of kindling were being used at the windows of the passenger car. (Why?)
8. There were butterflies inside the car. (Why?)
9. Butterflies flew into the train. (Where?)
10. One butterfly flew alongside the train. (In what manner?)
11. The black lamp over Laura's head swung in circles on its chain. (Why?)
12. The conductor would finally light the lamp. (When?)
13. Laura's father had asked the conductor to look after her. (When?)
14. A fire would be lighted in the stove opposite Laura. (Under what condition?)
15. Laura almost had to close her eyes. (Why?)
16. Laura put her ticket in her hat. (Why?)
17. The passengers would give the conductor their tickets. (When?)
18. The engineer stopped the train. (Why?)
19. The engineer picked goldenrod. (Where?)
20. Laura found the engineer's actions somewhat mysterious. (Why?)
21. Laura heard the locusts. (Why?)
22. The fields glowed in the daylight. (How?)
23. Laura could feel the warmth of the windowsill. (Why?)
24. Laura's heart pounded. (When?)
25. Laura would see her mother's family. (When?)

Grammar Review

Review: Exercise 5   **Identifying Noun Clauses**

The following sentences describe the Mississippi Delta area, to which Laura McRaven was traveling. On your paper write the noun clauses that appear in the sentences. Two of the sentences have two noun clauses each. In one sentence the relative pronoun before the noun clause has been dropped.

1. Does this book explain what the Mississippi Delta is?
2. Whoever has visited Mississippi is probably familiar with the area.
3. That the Mississippi River periodically floods its banks is the reason for the delta's existence.
4. What we now call the Mississippi Delta was formed by whatever deposits of silt the receding Mississippi River floodwaters left behind.
5. You can easily understand why many farmers live in the delta.
6. What attracts many farmers to the delta is that the soil is so fertile.
7. Do you know what makes the delta so famous?
8. One reason for its fame is that the area produces large crops of cotton.
9. You may also have read that large crops of soybeans are grown in the delta.
10. I know that visitors are also attracted by the area's many beautiful plantations.

Review: Exercise 6   **Identifying Adjective, Adverb, and Noun Clauses**

The following sentences give information about the author of *Delta Wedding*, Eudora Welty. Write the adjective clauses, adverb clauses, and noun clauses that appear in the sentences. Then write *adjective clause, adverb clause,* or *noun clause* to identify each clause. One sentence has more than one clause.

1. Author Eudora Welty, who was born in Jackson, Mississippi, is well known for her entertaining and insightful novels and short stories.
2. Because everyone in her family loved to read, there were always many books around Welty's home.
3. After Welty attended Mississippi State College for Women in 1926 and 1927, she was graduated from the University of Wisconsin.
4. Later Welty studied at Columbia University, which is in New York City.
5. Welty's reason for returning to Jackson in 1931 was that her father died.
6. While Welty has traveled in the United States and Europe, most of her work focuses on southern rural life.
7. Welty's stories of human relationships often tell about people who live in small towns.
8. *Delta Wedding*, which was Welty's first full-length novel, was published in 1946.
9. The novel describes a comfortable southern world that would soon change forever.
10. Whoever reads Welty's stories realizes that she believes in the importance of change and love in human life.

Grammar Review

Review: Exercise 7   **Writing Four Kinds of Sentences**

On your paper write *declarative, imperative, interrogative,* or *exclamatory* to identify each of the following sentences. Then rewrite each sentence in the form noted in parentheses.

SAMPLE ANSWER   The engineer stopped the train. (Rewrite as an imperative sentence.)
declarative
Engineer, please stop the train.

1. Was the train's official name the Yazoo-Delta? (Rewrite as a declarative sentence.)
2. We call the train the Yellow Dog. (Rewrite as an imperative sentence.)
3. The date was September 10, 1923. (Rewrite as an interrogative sentence.)
4. It was very warm that September day. (Rewrite as an exclamatory sentence.)
5. Were all the train windows open? (Rewrite as a declarative sentence.)
6. Will you open all the train windows? (Rewrite as an imperative sentence.)
7. How delicate the butterflies were! (Rewrite as an interrogative sentence.)
8. Was Laura sitting across the aisle from the drummer? (Rewrite as an imperative sentence.)
9. Laura, put the ticket in your hat. (Rewrite as a declarative sentence.)
10. Laura liked the smell of the kerosene from the lamp. (Rewrite as an interrogative sentence.)
11. Cool breezes came from the woods nearby. (Rewrite as an interrogative sentence.)
12. How beautiful the goldenrod was! (Rewrite as a declarative sentence.)
13. Mr. Doolittle, please give her some goldenrod. (Rewrite as a declarative sentence.)
14. Mr. Doolittle stopped the train in order to pick some goldenrod. (Rewrite as an interrogative sentence.)
15. How loud the cries of the locusts were! (Rewrite as a declarative sentence.)
16. Did Laura look forward to seeing her cousins? (Rewrite as a declarative sentence.)
17. Laura's heart was pounding. (Rewrite as an exclamatory sentence.)
18. Mr. Black promised to look after Laura. (Rewrite as an imperative sentence.)
19. Laura's cousins were going to meet her train. (Rewrite as an interrogative sentence.)
20. Laura had a wonderful time. (Rewrite as an exclamatory sentence.)

Review: Exercise 8   **Creating Four Kinds of Sentences**

For each topic below, write two different kinds of sentences: declarative, imperative, interrogative, or exclamatory. Within the exercise, use each type of sentence at least twice. Use correct punctuation. Label each sentence *declarative, imperative, interrogative,* or *exclamatory.*

1. things you see in the classroom
2. your trip to school this morning
3. a visit to a new place
4. a person you have talked to today
5. a meal with your friends or family

564   Unit 13   Clauses and Sentence Structure

Grammar Review

Review: Exercise 9   Correcting Sentence Fragments

The following paragraph describes Uncle Battle, another character from *Delta Wedding*. Revise the paragraph, correcting any sentence fragments. The fragments may be corrected by combining sentences, by adding words (such as a subject or a verb), or by changing the form of a verb.

SAMPLE   Laura arrived. Her cousins rushing out to meet her.
ANSWER   When Laura arrived, her cousins rushed out to meet her.

¹At Shellmound, Laura so happy to see Uncle Battle again. ²A big man, her mother's brother. ³Always called all the children Skeeta. ⁴All of his children exactly like him. ⁵Wore tall boots that creaked when he stood up. ⁶His hair always combed back over his brow. ⁷At mealtime Uncle Battle always carving and serving the turkey. ⁸Likely to drive off at any time of the day or night, without a moment's notice. ⁹Because he needed to check to see that the plantation work was getting done. ¹⁰Also to protect the plantation's workers from the sheriff.

Review: Exercise 10   Correcting Run-on Sentences

The following sentences elaborate on ideas suggested by the passage from *Delta Wedding*. On your paper revise each sentence, correcting any run-ons. Remember that run-on sentences may be corrected in more than one way. For the sentences that do not contain run-ons, write *correct*.

SAMPLE   It was September 10, 1923, Laura McRaven was on her way to Fairchilds.
ANSWER   It was September 10, 1923. Laura McRaven was on her way to Fairchilds.
ANSWER   It was September 10, 1923, and Laura McRaven was on her way to Fairchilds.

1. Laura was only nine years old, nevertheless, she was traveling alone.
2. Laura's cousins lived at Fairchilds Laura was going to visit them.
3. The day was warm and butterflies flew in and out of the open windows.
4. The breeze kept changing, it would be hot for a while and then it would be cool.
5. Laura wanted to catch every detail of the countryside; however, the sooty air from the train's engine kept making her want to close her eyes.
6. Mr. Black was the conductor, Laura's father had asked him to watch out for Laura.
7. Laura wore a straw hat, she had stuck her ticket in it.
8. The train came to a halt and Mr. Doolittle went into the open fields.
9. Laura couldn't wait to get to Fairchilds she was anxious to see her mother's people.
10. Laura tried to stay calm, but her heart kept pounding.

Grammar Review

Review: Exercise 11   **Correcting Sentence Structure**

The following paragraphs tell about the state of Mississippi. Revise the paragraphs, correcting sentence fragments or run-on sentences. Some sentences are correct, but you may wish to combine them with other sentences. Try to vary your sentence structure, and use correct punctuation.

¹Mississippi is bordered on the east by Alabama, its southern border is the Gulf of Mexico. ²On the north by Tennessee, on the west by Arkansas and Louisiana. ³The Mississippi River actually forms most of the state's western boundary. ⁴Jackson, the capital of Mississippi and its largest city. ⁵The Yazoo-Mississippi Delta, in western Mississippi, a broad, flat plain with rich, dark soil.

⁶Mississippi has a warm climate and long growing season, its main crops are cotton and soybeans. ⁷Much of the southern part of the state covered by pine forest. ⁸The Delta National Forest northwest of Jackson. ⁹Covers 60,000 acres, has facilities for camping, fishing, and picnicking. ¹⁰The Yazoo River borders the forest and flows into the Mississippi River just above Vicksburg.

Review: Exercise 12

Proofreading

The following passage describes the artist Robert Duncan, whose painting appears on the opposite page. Rewrite the passage, correcting the errors in spelling, grammar, and usage. Add any missing punctuation. There are twenty-five errors.

Robert Duncan

¹Robert Duncan was borned in Salt Lake City, Utah, in 1952. ²He spent his summers on his grandfathers' ranch in Wyoming. ³His grandmother, beleiving in Duncan's talent gave the eleven-year-old boy a set of oil paints and arranged for him to take art lessons ⁴Duncan continues to paint in high school. ⁵Duncan, however, is largely self-taught he has been painting full-time since 1972. ⁶He, his wife, and their six children lives in Midway, Utah. ⁷Utahs citizens and rugged landscapes are frequent subjects in his paintings.

⁸Duncan who has visited many museums in Europe and the United States, derived his style from his study of traditional figurative and landscape art. ⁹He was particlarly influenced by the work of painters from the turn of the century, such as John Singer Sargent. ¹⁰When Sargent was young he had been influenced by the Impressionists. ¹¹Who created their paintings with rapid strokes of pure color. ¹²Duncan, who uses naturalistic settings and loose

Grammar Review

Robert Duncan, *Mandy's Sunhat*, 1988

brushwork displays his debt to such Realists as Sargent and, indirectly, to the Impressionists. [13]Although his style is at odds with many currents in modren art it has won him modest acclaim.

[14]Duncan portrays many aspects of rural life his goal is to show that all people are fundamentally the same. [15]Often paints outdoors to capture the natural light. [16]He depicts farms gardens, and country people; children are among his favorite subjects [17]Duncan's style, which is romantic and somewhat sentimental is evident in all his paintings.

[18]*Mandy's Sunhat* shows Duncans facility for depicting atmosphere and light. [19]Anyone who has read Eudora Welty's *Delta Wedding* could easily believe that the girl in the painting are Laura McRaven. [20]The youngster in Welty's novel. [21]Can you imagine her stepping off the train and into the open fields

Grammar Review

Review: Exercise 13

Mixed Review

The items that follow describe the writing career of Eudora Welty. Revise each item in the manner indicated in parentheses; there may be more than one correct answer.

SAMPLE Eudora Welty was born in Jackson, Mississippi, in 1909. She is well-known for her entertaining and insightful novels and short stories. (Rewrite as a complex sentence.)

ANSWER Eudora Welty, who is well-known for her entertaining and insightful novels and short stories, was born in Jackson, Mississippi, in 1909.

Eudora Welty's Published Work

1. Welty's first book of short stories, *A Curtain of Green*, was published in 1941. (Rewrite as an interrogative sentence.)
2. Her novella *The Robber Bridegroom* was published in 1946. It contains all the virtues of a good fairy tale.
(Combine the sentences by turning the second sentence into an adjective clause beginning with *which*.)
3. Did Welty publish two collections of short stories between 1949 and 1955? (Write as a declarative sentence.)
4. *The Golden Apples* (1949), her next book after *Delta Wedding*, contained seven related stories about a group of families. The lives of these families were intertwined. (Combine the sentences by turning the second sentence into an adjective clause beginning with *whose*.)
5. Like *The Robber Bridegroom*, Welty's novel *The Ponder Heart* (1954) does not follow Welty's initial pattern. *The Ponder Heart* has been called Welty's comic masterpiece. (Rewrite as a complex sentence.)
6. Welty published almost nothing between 1955 and 1970, but 1970 brought the publication of her novel *Losing Battles*. The novel deals with humorous characters and situations. (Rewrite as a compound-complex sentence.)
7. Welty won the Pulitzer Prize in 1972 for her novel *The Optimist's Daughter*, this event further increased her popularity.
(Eliminate the run-on by writing a compound sentence.)
8. One reason for Welty's success is clear. Her fiction is often very humorous. (Combine the sentences by turning the second sentence into a noun clause beginning with *that*.)
9. Besides novels and short stories, Welty has written several works of nonfiction. Including a collection of essays and an autobiography.
(Eliminate the fragment by writing a complex sentence.)
10. Many readers pay special attention to Welty's gift for vivid detail and to her wry insights into human nature. (Rewrite as an imperative sentence.)

Unit 13 Clauses and Sentence Structure

Writing Application

Clauses and Sentence Structure in Writing

In the following paragraph from "A Day's Pleasure," Hamlin Garland uses a variety of sentence types to capture the reader's interest and to develop a pleasing rhythm and an appropriate mood of relaxation. Notice how the structure of each of Garland's four sentences varies: compound-complex, simple, complex, compound-complex.

> They went into the little sitting room, so dainty and lovely to the farmer's wife, and as she sank into the easy chair she was faint and drowsy with the pleasure of it. She submitted to being brushed. She gave the baby into the hands of the Swedish girl, who washed its face and hands and sang it to sleep, while its mother sipped some tea. Through it all she lay back in her easy chair, not speaking a word, while the ache passed out of her back, and her hot, swollen head ceased to throb.

Techniques with Clauses and Sentence Structure

Try to apply some of Garland's techniques when you write and revise your own work.

1 Avoid using the same sentence structure repeatedly.

MONOTONOUS STRUCTURE She lay back in her chair. She did not speak. The ache passed out of her back.

GARLAND'S VERSION . . . she lay back in her easy chair, not speaking a word, while the ache passed out of her back. . . .

2 Use subordination to call attention to some ideas and downplay others.

EQUAL ATTENTION TO EACH IDEA She sank into a chair. She was faint and drowsy. She sipped her tea.

GARLAND'S VERSION . . . as she sank into the easy chair, she was faint and drowsy . . . The Swedish girl . . . sang it to sleep, while its mother sipped some tea.

TIME For more about the writing process, see **TIME Facing the Blank Page**, pp. 121-131.

Practice

Practice these techniques by revising the following series of simple sentences, using a separate sheet of paper. Decide which ideas should be subordinated, and try to use a variety of sentence structures.

The day grew warmer. A strong wind rose, blowing from the south. They were all thirsty. They had only half a barrel of water left. They knew the next watering place was several hours ahead. The sun rose higher. Dust settled on their hair and clothing. It coated the children's bare feet. The woman sat holding the reins. The deep ruts in the trail jolted the wagon. Her back and neck ached. She shaded her eyes against the glare. Nowhere on the wide horizon could she see a tree or a building. In fact, they had seen no other people for two days. Her husband remained confident. Today, though, even he seemed tired.

UNIT 14 Diagraming Sentences

Lesson 14.1	Diagraming Simple Sentences	571
Lesson 14.2	Diagraming Simple Sentences with Phrases	574
Lesson 14.3	Diagraming Sentences with Clauses	577

14.1 Diagraming Simple Sentences

■ **Diagraming is a method of showing how the various words and parts of a sentence function and relate to the sentence as a whole.**

You begin to diagram a sentence by finding the simple subject. (Keep in mind that a sentence may have a compound subject.) After you have found the subject, find the action or linking verb that goes with it. Write the subject and the verb on a horizontal line, called a baseline. Separate the subject and the verb with a vertical line that bisects the baseline. This line indicates the division between the complete subject and the complete predicate.

Athletes train.

subject	action verb

Athletes	train

Adjectives and Adverbs

To diagram a simple sentence with adjectives and adverbs, follow the model diagram below.

A very good athlete must train extremely hard.

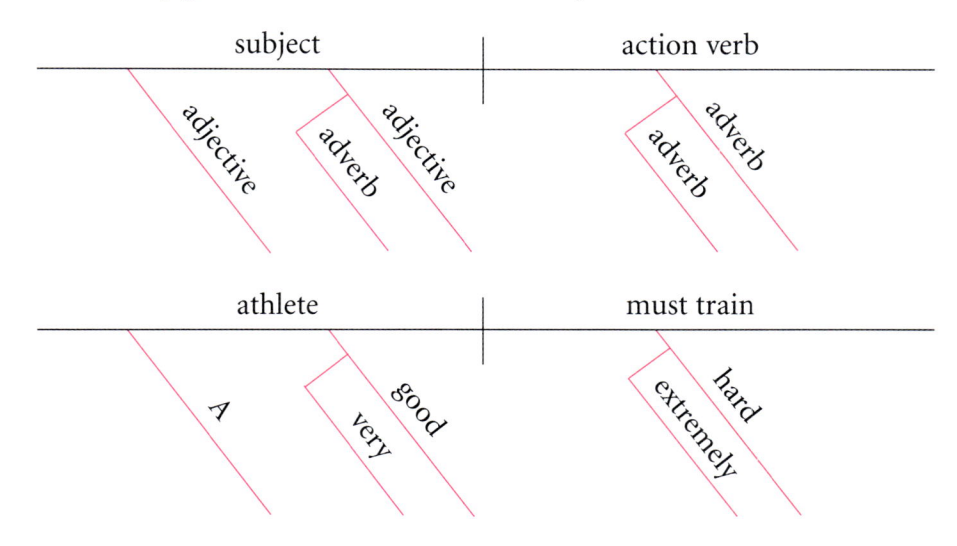

14.1 Diagraming Simple Sentences **571**

Direct Objects and Indirect Objects

To diagram a simple sentence with an indirect object and a direct object, follow the model diagram below.

Coaches give players guidance.

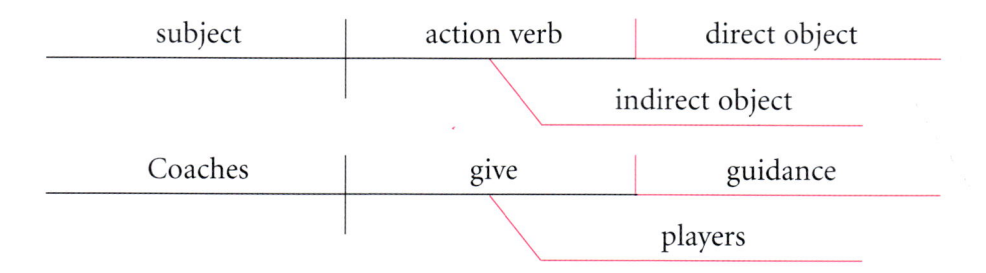

Object Complements

To diagram a simple sentence with a compound subject, a direct object, and an object complement, follow the model diagram below. If the parts of a compound subject are connected by a conjunction, place the conjunction on a dotted vertical line between them. If the parts are connected by a correlative conjunction, such as *both . . . and* or *either . . . or*, place the introductory conjunction on one side of the line and the second conjunction on the other side.

Coaches and players consider practice essential.

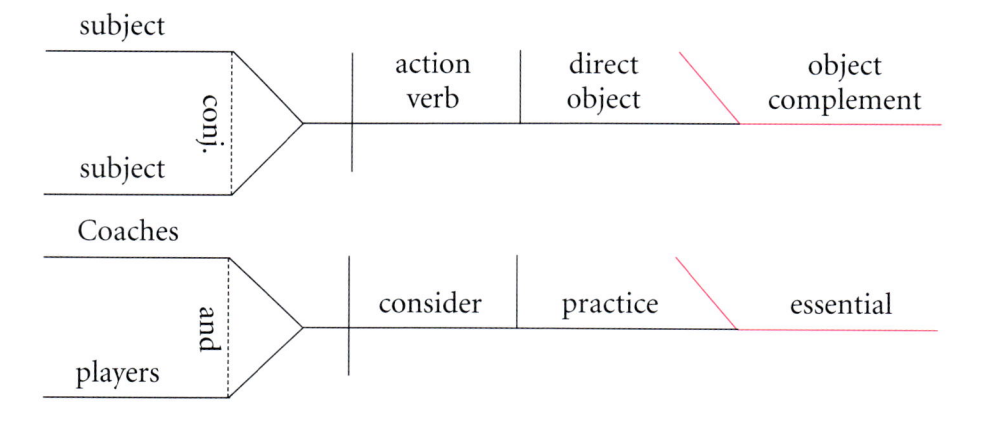

Subject Complements

To diagram a simple sentence with a subject complement (a predicate nominative or a predicate adjective), follow the model diagrams below.

Swimmers are athletes.

| subject | linking verb \ predicate nominative |

| Swimmers | are \ athletes |

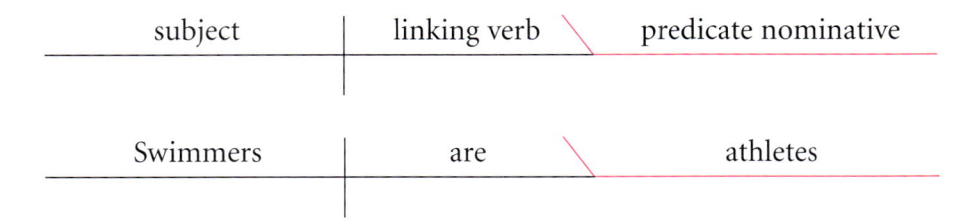

Gymnasts are strong and must be coordinated.

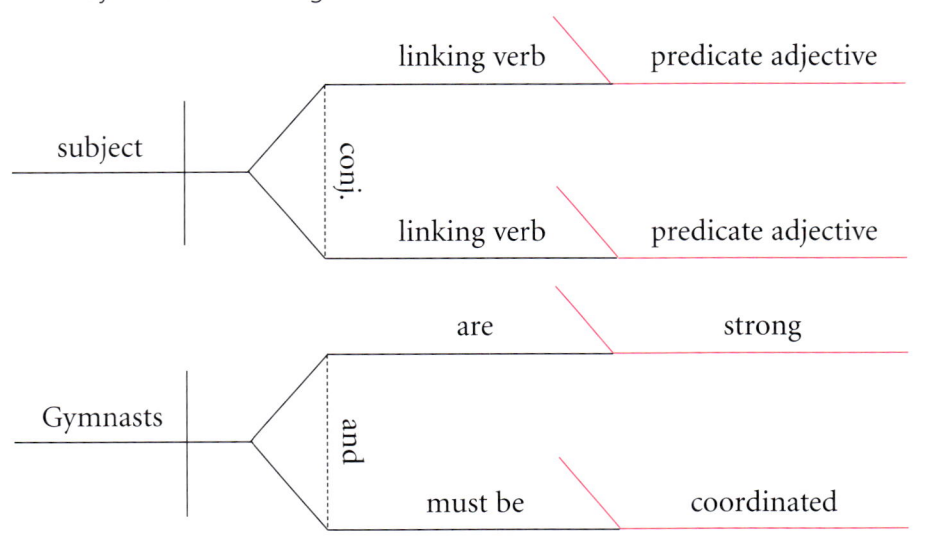

[Diagram showing "Gymnasts" as subject connected via "and" conjunction to two linking verb phrases: "are \ strong" and "must be \ coordinated"]

Exercise 1   Diagraming Simple Sentences

Using the preceding models as a guide, diagram the following sentences.

1. The muddy field was drying slowly.
2. A coach gave the players instructions.
3. The players and the coach considered the game critical.
4. It was the championship game.
5. The players were ready but felt nervous.
6. They looked calm but felt uneasy.
7. The coach encouraged them.
8. She gave the players a pep talk.
9. The players paid attention and listened silently.
10. They were ready.

14.2 Diagraming Simple Sentences with Phrases

Prepositional Phrases

Place the preposition on a diagonal line that descends from the word the prepositional phrase modifies. Place the object of the preposition on a horizontal line that joins the diagonal. The diagonal line on which the preposition is placed should extend somewhat beyond the horizontal on which the object of the preposition is placed, forming a "tail."

Athletes of today set new records at every opportunity during a season.

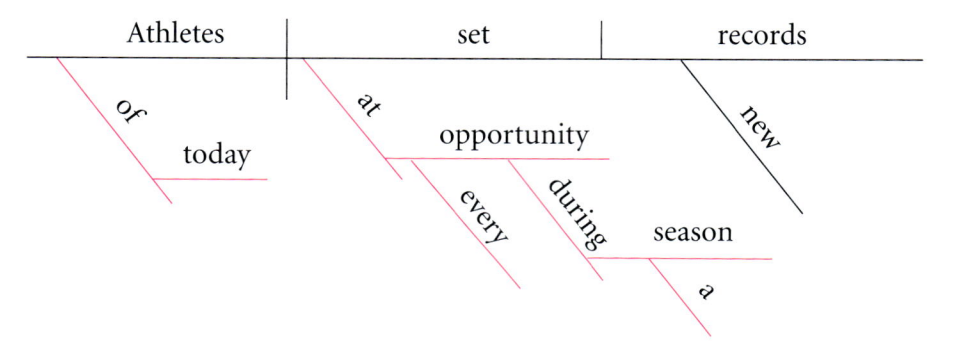

Appositives and Appositive Phrases

Place an appositive in parentheses after the noun or pronoun it identifies. Beneath it add any words that modify the appositive. Any words that modify the noun or pronoun itself, and not the appositive, should be placed directly beneath the noun or pronoun.

The coach, a graduate of the school, preaches team spirit, an important ideal.

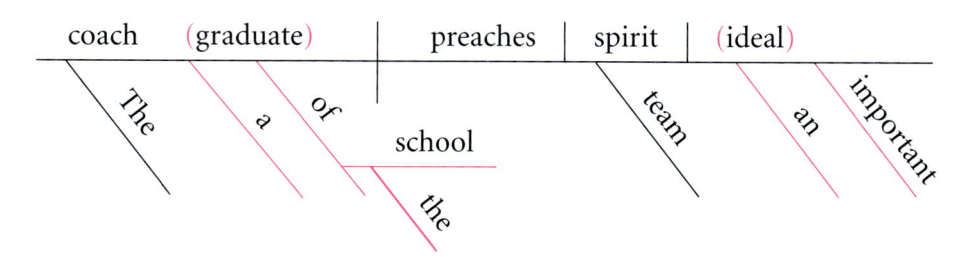

Participles and Participial Phrases

The line on which the participle is placed descends diagonally from the word the participle modifies and then extends to the right horizontally. The participle is written on the curve, as shown below. Add any modifiers and complements to the horizontal line in the same way that you would show the modifiers and complements of an action verb.

Stumbling, the quarterback fell, gracefully completing the pass in midair.

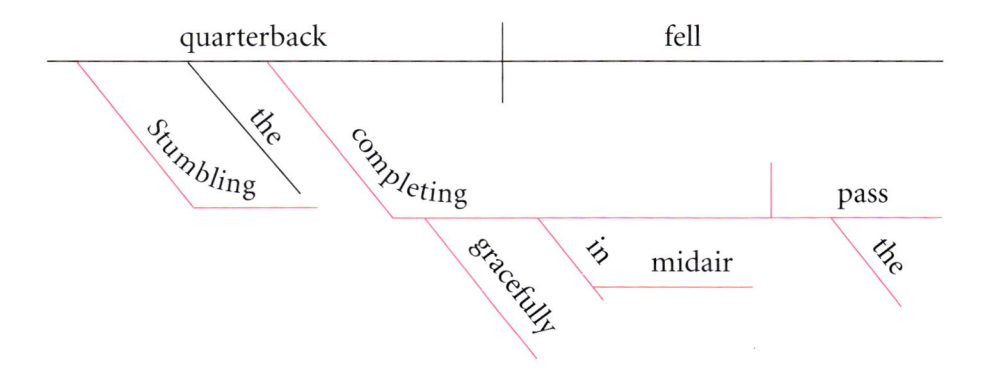

Gerunds and Gerund Phrases

Place a gerund on a "step," adding complements and modifiers in the usual way. Then set the gerund or the gerund phrase on a "stilt" and position the stilt according to the role of the gerund in the sentence. (Remember that a gerund can be a subject, a direct object, an indirect object, a predicate nominative, an object of a preposition, or an appositive.)

Winning is one way of gaining confidence.

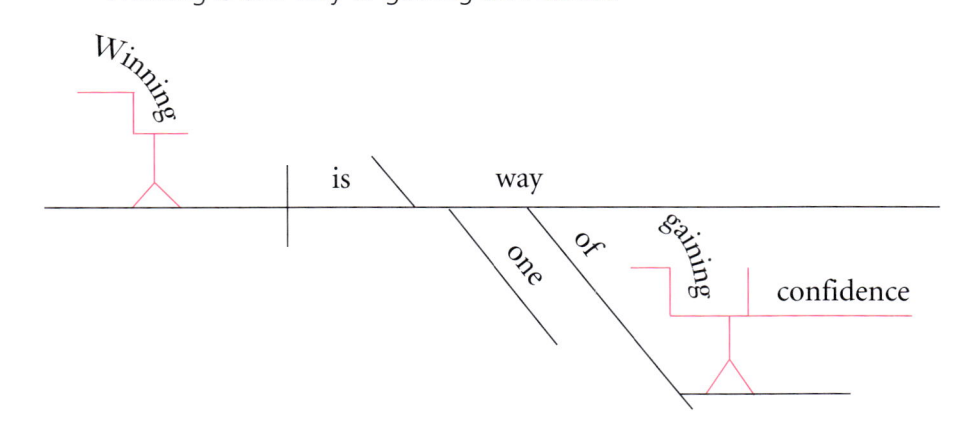

14.2 Diagraming Simple Sentences with Phrases

Infinitives and Infinitive Phrases as Adjectives or Adverbs

When an infinitive or an infinitive phrase is used as an adjective or an adverb, it is diagramed as a prepositional phrase is.

Teams have a need to travel frequently.

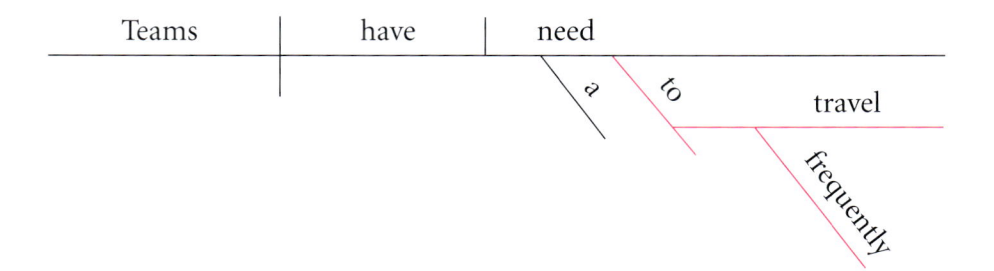

Infinitives and Infinitive Phrases as Nouns

When an infinitive or an infinitive phrase is used as a noun, it is diagramed as a prepositional phrase is and then placed on a "stilt" in the subject, direct object, or predicate nominative position.

To triumph is to taste glory.

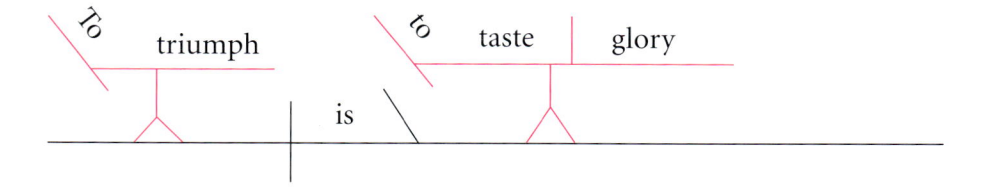

Exercise 2 Diagraming Simple Sentences with Phrases

Using the preceding models as a guide, diagram the following sentences.

1. People of that time knew nothing about the rest of the world.
2. My cousin Janet got her wish, a part in the play.
3. Thousands of leaves, falling gently, covered the damp sidewalk.
4. Watching television is one way of relaxing.
5. To write well means to think clearly.
6. My grandmother wants to learn about everything.
7. Roaring, the rapidly widening river raced to cover waiting farmland.
8. Eating well is the best revenge.
9. Pedestrians, shadows in the fog, hurried to reach home.
10. Blinking in bewilderment, I stared at the scene before me.

14.3 Diagraming Sentences with Clauses

Compound Sentences

Diagram each main clause separately. If the clauses are connected by a semicolon, use a vertical dotted line to connect the verbs of each main clause. If the main clauses are connected by a conjunction, place the conjunction on a solid horizontal line and connect it to the verbs of each main clause by vertical dotted lines.

Athletes like to win, but they must also learn to lose.

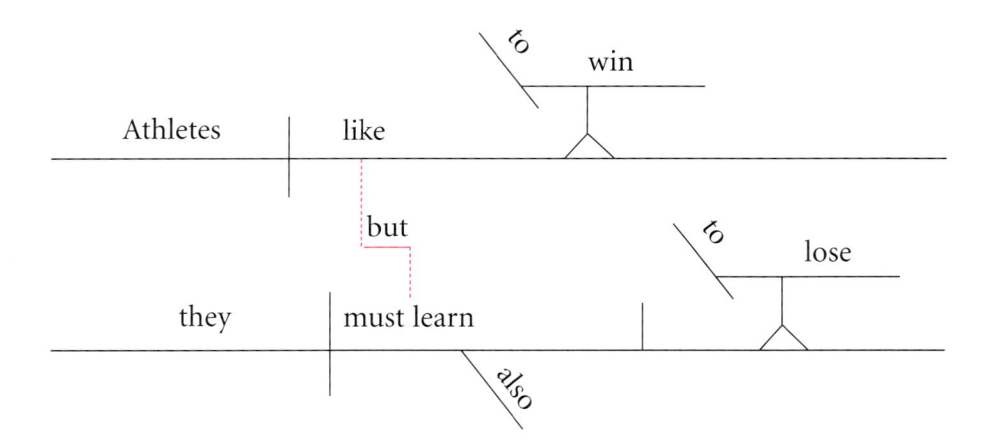

Complex Sentences with Adjective Clauses

Place the main clause in one diagram and the adjective clause beneath it in another diagram. Use a dotted line to connect the relative pronoun or other introductory word in the adjective clause to the modified noun or pronoun in the main clause.

The player whom you like won games that were close.

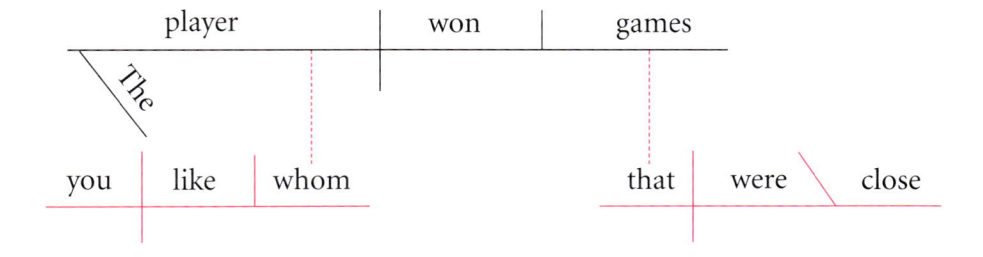

14.3 Diagraming Sentences with Clauses 577

Complex Sentences with Adverb Clauses

Place the main clause in one diagram and the adverb clause beneath it in another diagram. Place the subordinating conjunction on a diagonal dotted line, connecting the verb in the adverb clause to the modified verb, adjective, or adverb in the main clause.

Before a game begins, the coach gives encouragement.

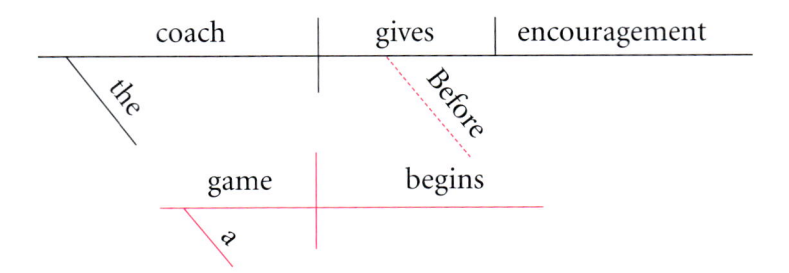

Complex Sentences with Noun Clauses

First decide what role the noun clause plays within the main clause. Is it the subject, direct object, predicate nominative, or object of a preposition? Then diagram the main clause, placing the noun clause on a "stilt" in the appropriate position. Place the introductory word of the clause in the position of subject, object, or predicate nominative within the noun clause itself. If the introductory word merely begins the noun clause, place it on a line of its own above the verb in the noun clause, connecting it to the verb with a dotted vertical line.

NOUN CLAUSE AS SUBJECT

What the coach says is extremely important.

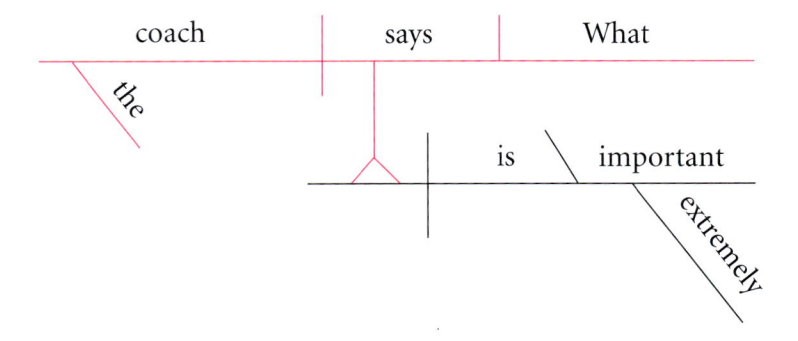

NOUN CLAUSE AS DIRECT OBJECT

The coach knows that the rival may win.

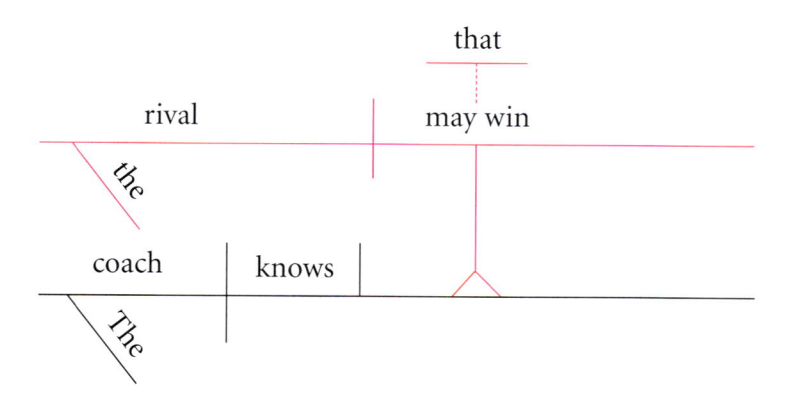

NOUN CLAUSE AS OBJECT OF A PREPOSITION

The coach assigns more practice to whoever needs it.

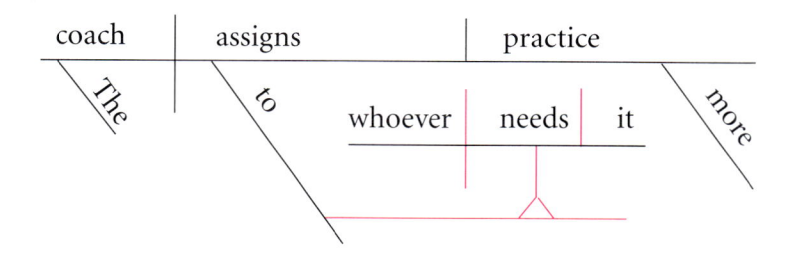

Exercise 3   Diagraming Sentences with Clauses

Using the preceding models as a guide, diagram the following sentences.

1. John is the oldest child, and Rebecca is the youngest.
2. The pilot who won last year's competition has sold his airplane.
3. Whenever Manolo remembers, he buys an extra newspaper for Juanito.
4. Whoever wins this game chooses the next one.
5. Everybody knows that Hefflemeyer is the greatest player.
6. After Bettina scored on a jump shot, the score was tied.
7. I liked watching the movie, but the book was better.
8. The team that is better prepared will probably win.
9. Whoever goes first will have the advantage.
10. I want to learn more about what you said.

UNIT 15: Verb Tenses and Voice

Lesson 15.1	**Principal Parts of Verbs**	581
Lesson 15.2	**Regular and Irregular Verbs**	582
Lesson 15.3	**Tenses of Verbs**	586
Lesson 15.4	**Perfect Tenses**	589
Lesson 15.5	**Progressive and Emphatic Forms**	592
Lesson 15.6	**Compatibility of Tenses**	594
Lesson 15.7	**Voice of Verbs**	596

Grammar Review   598

Writing Application   607

15.1 Principal Parts of Verbs

■ All verbs have four **principal parts:** a *base form,* a *present participle,* a *simple past form,* and a *past participle.* All the verb tenses are formed from these principal parts.

Principal Parts of Verbs			
BASE FORM	**PRESENT PARTICIPLE**	**PAST FORM**	**PAST PARTICIPLE**
nail	nailing	nailed	nailed
carry	carrying	carried	carried
ring	ringing	rang	rung
be	being	was, were	been
sit	sitting	sat	sat

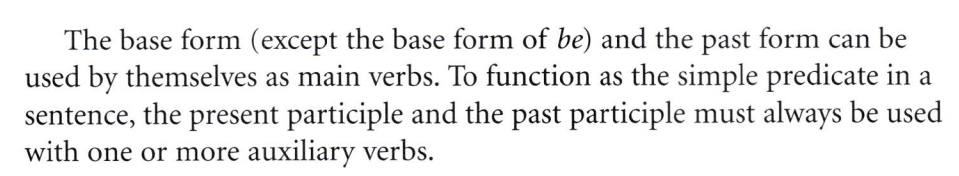

The base form (except the base form of *be*) and the past form can be used by themselves as main verbs. To function as the simple predicate in a sentence, the present participle and the past participle must always be used with one or more auxiliary verbs.

Lions **roar.** [base or present form]

Lions **roared.** [past form]

Lions **are roaring.** [present participle with the auxiliary verb *are*]

Lions **have roared.** [past participle with the auxiliary verb *have*]

Exercise 1 Using Principal Parts of Verbs

Write the correct form of the principal part of the verb indicated in parentheses.

1. They ____ for an auto dealership. (base form of *work*)
2. They are ____ up sales of minivans and jeeps. (present participle of *ring*)
3. Last month, he ____ ten people into buying minivans. (past form of *talk*)
4. She is ____ harder than any other salesperson. (present participle of *work*)
5. They have both ____ a bonus and an award. (past participle of *receive*)
6. They are ____ to other salespeople at the award dinner. (present participle of *talk*)
7. They have often ____ techniques with their colleagues. (past participle of *discuss*)
8. Now they ____ a wider audience. (base form of *need*)
9. Their supervisor ____ very proud when they were selected. (past form of *be*)
10. He was actually ____ around in his office. (present participle of *dance*)

15.2 Regular and Irregular Verbs

■ A **regular verb** forms its past and past participle by adding *-ed* to the base form.

Regular Verbs		
BASE FORM	**PAST FORM**	**PAST PARTICIPLE**
roar	roared	roared
talk	talked	talked
learn	learned	learned

Some regular verbs undergo spelling changes when a suffix beginning with a vowel is added.

ruffle + **-ed** = ruffl**ed**   spy + **-ed** = spi**ed**   flop + **-ed** = flop**ped**

argue + **-ed** = argu**ed**   tie + **-ed** = ti**ed**   refer + **-ed** = refer**red**

■ An **irregular verb** forms its past and past participle in some way other than by adding *-ed* to the base form.

Irregular Verbs		
BASE FORM	**PAST FORM**	**PAST PARTICIPLE**
be	was, were	been
beat	beat	beaten *or* beat
become	became	become
begin	began	begun
bite	bit	bitten or bit
blow	blew	blown
break	broke	broken
bring	brought	brought
buy	bought	bought
catch	caught	caught
choose	chose	chosen
come	came	come
do	did	done
draw	drew	drawn
drink	drank	drunk
drive	drove	driven
eat	ate	eaten
fall	fell	fallen
feel	felt	felt
find	found	found

Irregular Verbs

BASE FORM	PAST FORM	PAST PARTICIPLE
fly	flew	flown
freeze	froze	frozen
get	got	got *or* gotten
give	gave	given
go	went	gone
grow	grew	grown
hang	hung *or* hanged	hung *or* hanged
have	had	had
keep	kept	kept
know	knew	known
lay*	laid	laid
lead	led	led
leave	left	left
lend	lent	lent
lie*	lay	lain
lose	lost	lost
make	made	made
put	put	put
ride	rode	ridden
ring	rang	rung
rise*	rose	risen
run	ran	run
say	said	said
see	saw	seen
seek	sought	sought
sell	sold	sold
set*	set	set
shrink	shrank *or* shrunk	shrunk *or* shrunken
sing	sang	sung
sink	sank *or* sunk	sunk
sit*	sat	sat
sleep	slept	slept
speak	spoke	spoken
spring	sprang *or* sprung	sprung
steal	stole	stolen
swim	swam	swum
swing	swung	swung
take	took	taken
teach	taught	taught
tear	tore	torn
tell	told	told
think	thought	thought
throw	threw	thrown
wear	wore	worn
win	won	won
write	wrote	written

*For more detailed instruction on *lay* versus *lie* and *raise* versus *rise*, see Unit 19.

*For more detailed instruction on *sit* versus *set*, see Unit 19.

Verb Tenses and Voice

15.2 Regular and Irregular Verbs

Exercise 2 — Writing Principal Parts of Verbs

Copy and complete the chart. Make sure that you have spelled each form correctly.

BASE FORM	PAST FORM	PAST PARTICIPLE
1. start		
2. think		
3. climb		
4. stop		
5. hit		
6. occur		
7. grow		
8. skip		
9. fly		
10. deter		
11. murmur		
12. pray		
13. cry		
14. go		
15. swim		
16. flip		
17. insure		
18. steal		
19. wear		
20. submit		
21. write		
22. run		
23. deny		
24. lend		
25. know		

Exercise 3 — Using Principal Parts of Irregular Verbs

Write the correct form of the principal part of the verb indicated in parentheses.

1. I ____ breakfast for my family every Sunday. (base form of *make*)
2. Last Sunday I ____ late. (past form of *rise*)
3. I was still ____ in bed when a wonderful aroma hit me. (present participle of *lie*)
4. I almost ____ out of bed with excitement. (past form of *fall*)
5. My brother had ____ to give me a present. (past participle of *choose*)
6. I ____ out of bed and sprinted down the stairs. (past form of *spring*)
7. His choice couldn't have ____ a better one. (past participle of *be*)
8. How could he have ____ what I really wanted? (past participle of *know*)
9. I sat and ____ my teeth into my favorite breakfast. (past form of *sink*)
10. I have never ____ better pancakes. (past participle of *eat*)

Exercise 4 Using Principal Parts of Verbs

Write the principal part of the verb indicated in parentheses.

Arthur Ashe, a Tennis Pioneer

1. The name Arthur Ashe has ___ to symbolize athletic brilliance and outstanding achievement. (past participle of *come*)
2. Over the past two decades, the name has also ___ personal integrity and grace. (past participle of *signify*)
3. Ashe ___ playing tennis in elementary school. (past form of *begin*)
4. His athletic talent ___ the attention of a local physician, Dr. Robert "Whirlwind" Johnson. (past form of *catch*)
5. Dr. Johnson ___ talented African American youngsters to play for the U.S. Tennis Association. (past form of *teach*)
6. Dr. Johnson had ___ tennis lessons to Althea Gibson. (past participle of *give*)
7. Althea Gibson ___ the first African American to win a championship at Wimbledon, a famous tennis tournament in England. (past form of *be*)
8. By the age of 18, Arthur Ashe had ___ to national prominence. (past participle of *rise*)
9. In 1960 and again in 1961, he ___ the Junior Indoor Singles Championship. (past form of *win*)
10. While he ___ at the University of California in Los Angeles, Ashe was coached by Pancho Gonzales, a tennis champion. (past form of *study*)
11. In 1963 Ashe was ___ for the Davis Cup team. (past participle of *choose*)
12. In 1966 he ___ himself the winner of both the singles and doubles titles in the National Collegiate Athletic Association Championship. (past form of *find*)
13. In 1968 Ashe's dream of winning at the highest levels of American tennis finally ___ true. (past form of *come*)
14. He ___ first place at the U.S. National Men's Singles Championship. (past form of *take*)
15. By the end of 1968, Ashe had ___ all opponents in the men's singles competition of the first U.S. Open tournament. (past participle of *beat*)
16. Unfortunately, his tournament career ended when he ___ heart surgery. (past form of *undergo*)
17. As a result of a blood transfusion, Ashe ___ HIV. (past form of *contract*)
18. Years later, he ___ a news conference and discussed his illness publicly for the first time. (past form of *hold*)
19. Arthur Ashe ___ in 1993, five months before his fiftieth birthday. (past form of *die*)
20. Friends who ___ at his memorial service praised Ashe for his professional and humanitarian achievements. (past form of *speak*)

15.3 Tenses of Verbs

- **Tense** is the time of the action expressed by a verb.
- There are six tenses in English: *present, past, future, present perfect, past perfect,* and *future perfect.*

Present Tense

The present-tense form of a verb (excluding the third-person singular, which adds an *-s* or *-es*) is the same as the verb's base form. The one exception is the verb *be*.

THE VERB *STAY*	SINGULAR	PLURAL
FIRST PERSON	I **stay**.	We **stay**.
SECOND PERSON	You **stay**.	You **stay**.
THIRD PERSON	She, he, or it **stays**.	They **stay**.
	Jesse **stays**.	The children **stay**.

THE VERB *BE*	SINGULAR	PLURAL
FIRST PERSON	I **am** sad.	We **are** sad.
SECOND PERSON	You **are** sad.	You **are** sad.
THIRD PERSON	She, he, or it **is** sad.	They **are** sad.
	Sheila **is** sad.	The players **are** sad.

- The **present tense** expresses a constant, repeated, or habitual action or condition. It can also express a general truth.

    My garden **grows** well in the summer. [not just this summer but every summer: a repeated action]

    Helena **bakes** bread well. [always: a habitual action]

    Gold **is** valuable. [a condition that is generally true]

- The **present tense** can also express an action or condition that exists only now.

    Jenny **feels** happy. [not always but just now]

    I **see** a fly on the ceiling. [at this very moment]

- The **present tense** is sometimes used in historical writing to express past events and, more often, in poetry, fiction, and reporting (especially in sports) to convey to the reader a sense of "being there."

    Washington and his troops **spend** the winter at Valley Forge.

    The exhausted runner **seems** to stumble, but in a final spurt he **rushes** over the finish line and **wins**.

Past Tense

■ Use the **past tense** to express an action or condition that began and ended in the past.

> The orchestra **performed** well.
> The musicians **seemed** pleased.
> The soloist **sang** beautifully.
> The conductor **praised** the musicians.

Nearly all regular and irregular verbs—except *be*—have just one past-tense form, such as *soared* or *began*. The word *be* has two past-tense forms: *was* and *were*.

	SINGULAR	**PLURAL**
FIRST PERSON	I **was** sad.	We **were** sad.
SECOND PERSON	You **were** sad.	You **were** sad.
THIRD PERSON	She, he, or it **was** sad.	They **were** sad.

Exercise 5   Using the Present Tense

Write a sentence using each of the following present-tense verbs. The content of your sentence should express the kind of present time indicated in parentheses.

SAMPLE   does (a repeated action)
ANSWER   He does his housecleaning on Saturday.

1. sleeps (a habitual action)
2. feel (just now)
3. is (generally true)
4. hopes (at this moment)
5. takes (constant action)
6. opens (at this moment)
7. am (not always, but just now)
8. practices (a repeated action)
9. need (a condition that is generally true)
10. signs (an event in history)

Exercise 6   Using the Past Tense

Write two paragraphs, one using the past tense of verbs 1 through 5 and one using the past tense of verbs 6 through 10.

1. feel
2. catch
3. freeze
4. eat
5. write
6. be
7. give
8. take
9. wear
10. drink

Future Tense

■ Use the **future tense** to express an action or condition that will occur in the future.

You form the future tense of any verb by using *shall* or *will* with the base form: *I shall study; you will go.*

Roberta **will send** the telegram.

I **shall practice** the piano tonight.

The following are other ways to express future time besides using *shall* or *will*:

1. Use the present tense of *be* with *going to* and the base form of a verb.
   Roberta **is *going to* send** the telegram.
2. Use the present tense of *be* with *about to* and the base form of the verb.
   Roberta **is *about to* send** the telegram.
3. Use the present tense of a verb with an adverb or an adverb phrase that shows future time.
   Roberta **leaves** *tomorrow.*
   Roberta **arrives** *in the middle of next week.*

Exercise 7   Using Expressions of Future Time

Rewrite each of the following sentences so that the verb is in the future tense. Try to use at least two other ways of expressing future time in addition to *shall* and *will*.

Japan's Classical Theater

[1]Two classmates and I presented a cooperative report on the history of Japanese theater for our literature class. [2]There were three parts to the presentation. [3]First, Kate spoke about the form of medieval theater called No. [4]She described the formality and beauty of No plays. [5]Then Miguel covered the history of Japan's Joruri puppet theater. [6]He focused on the extraordinary realism of the colorful and expressive Joruri puppets. [7]I was responsible for information on Kabuki theater. [8]I began with a description of the typical Kabuki stage with its trapdoors and revolving platforms. [9]I explained the stylized and exaggerated movements of Kabuki actors. [10]The report concluded with a demonstration of Kabuki dance.

Exercise 8   Expressing Future Time in Sentences

Write five statements or predictions about the future. Your sentences may be as realistic or as unrealistic as you wish. Remember to vary the ways in which you express future time.

SAMPLE ANSWER   Household robots are going to become a reality.

15.4 Perfect Tenses

Present Perfect Tense

■ Use the **present perfect tense** to express an action that took place or a condition that existed at some *indefinite time* in the past.

Form the present perfect tense by using *has* or *have* with the past participle of a verb: *has stopped, have waited.**

> She **has caught** the flu.
> They **have brought** a present for us.

The present perfect can refer to completed action in past time only in an indefinite way. Adverbs such as *yesterday* cannot be added to make the time more specific.

> Sophia **has completed** her project.
> Jack **has wanted** to visit Mexico.

* Do not be confused by the term *present perfect*; this tense expresses past time. *Present* refers to the tense of the auxiliary verb *has* or *have*.

To be specific about completed past time, you would normally use the simple past tense.

> Sophia **completed** her project yesterday.
> Jack **wanted** to visit Mexico last summer.

The present perfect can also be used to communicate the idea that an action or a condition *began* in the past and *continues* into the present. This use is normally accompanied by an adverb of time or an adverb phrase beginning with *for* or *since*.

> The museum **has displayed** the exhibit for months.
> We **have kept** the dogs indoors since Sunday.

Exercise 9 — Using the Present Perfect Tense

(a) Rewrite each of the following sentences, changing the tense of the verb from past to present perfect. (b) Add adverbs or adverb phrases to each new sentence to communicate the idea that an action or condition began in the past and continues into the present.

SAMPLE We wanted to go to Paris.
ANSWER a. We have wanted to go to Paris.
b. We have wanted to go to Paris for two years.

1. Lila gave piano lessons.
2. My parents owned two dogs.
3. The trees were in bloom.
4. My friend wrote poetry.
5. The team played with determination.

Past Perfect Tense

■ Use the **past perfect tense** to indicate that one past action or condition began *and* ended before another past action or condition started.

You form the past perfect tense by using *had* with the past participle of a verb: *had loved, had written.*

PAST PERFECT   **PAST**

She **had been** the captain of the team before I **became** captain. [She was captain; she stopped being captain; I became captain.]

PAST   **PAST PERFECT**

Before I **slipped,** many other pedestrians **had slipped** in the same place. [They slipped; they finished slipping; I slipped.]

PAST PERFECT   **PAST**

He **had** already **dried** the dishes by the time I **arrived**. [He dried the dishes; he finished drying the dishes; I arrived.]

Future Perfect Tense

■ Use the **future perfect tense** to express one future action or condition that will begin *and* end before another future event starts.

You form the future perfect tense by using *shall have* or *will have* with the past participle of a verb: *shall have walked, will have walked.*

By summertime I **will have lived** here four months. [The four months will be over by the time another future event, the coming of summertime, occurs.]

By the time the astronauts reach the moon, they **will have practiced** the maneuver many times.

Exercise 10   Writing the Past Perfect and Future Perfect Tenses

Write the verb in parentheses in the tense indicated in brackets.

1. When the president resigned, he (hold) office for three years. [past perfect]
2. My father projects that forty years from now the majority of people (become) comfortable with voting by computer. [future perfect]
3. Before she realized it, Janice (throw) away the newspaper with the candidates' statements. [past perfect]
4. Peter learned that he (drive) to the wrong polling place. [past perfect]
5. By the time the candidate makes a speech, she (rehearse) it for weeks. [future perfect]

Exercise 11 — Review: Identifying the Verb Tenses

On your paper, write the tense of each italicized verb. Identify the tense as *present, past, future, present perfect, past perfect,* or *future perfect.*

Reggae Music

1. Perhaps you *listen* to a style of music known as reggae.
2. This intensely rhythmic music *has been* popular in Jamaica for some time.
3. Jamaican and African folk music and American rhythm and blues *had influenced* the reggae star Bob Marley before he *began* to play music himself.
4. Bands *had performed* reggae in Jamaica for twenty years before it was heard in either the United States or Europe.
5. It *has been* popular in the United States since the 1970s.
6. Before the musical style *took* the name reggae, fans *had called* it by various names—including rudie blues, ska, blue beat, and rock steady.
7. Reggae music *gained* international fame as a result of two groups, Bob Marley and the Wailers and Toots and the Maytals.
8. By the time it *became* popular outside Jamaica, reggae *had influenced* such rock musicians as Eric Clapton, John Lennon, and the Police.
9. Reggae *will remain* popular because reggae musicians *tour* frequently.
10. By the time he *completes* his latest tour, Bob Marley's son Ziggy, for example, *will have performed* in dozens of American cities.

Exercise 12 — Review: Using Verb Tenses

For each sentence, write the tense of the verb indicated in parentheses.

A Legendary Concert

1. The Woodstock Music and Art Fair ____ to symbolize the hippie culture of the 1960s. (present perfect tense of *come*)
2. By the time Jimi Hendrix played the "Star Spangled Banner," an estimated 500,000 young people ____ in Saugerties, New York, for a weekend of rock and roll. (past perfect tense of *arrive*)
3. At the event, Richie Havens ____ for over two hours. (past tense of *sing*)
4. For years a rumor ____ that Joni Mitchell, known for her rendition of the song "Woodstock," was never at Woodstock. (present perfect tense of *persist*)
5. In August 1994, what some had called the "Reunion at Yasgur's Farm" ____ place on the actual site of Woodstock '69. (past tense of *take*)
6. Rock elders such as Joe Cocker and Bob Dylan, who ____ favor with young audiences, performed at the anniversary concert. (past perfect tense of *gain*)
7. I ____ happy that I had the opportunity to attend. (present tense of *be*)
8. By the fortieth anniversary of Woodstock, many of the "flower children" of the 1960s ____ their sixties. (future perfect tense of *reach*)
9. Do you think they ____ Janis Joplin, Jimi Hendrix, and the other legendary musicians who performed at Woodstock? (future perfect tense of *forget*)
10. I think they ____ still ____ (future tense of *remember*)

15.4 Perfect Tenses **591**

15.5 Progressive and Emphatic Forms

■ Each of the six tenses has a **progressive** form that expresses a continuing action.

Make the progressive forms by using the appropriate tense of the verb *be* with the present participle of the main verb:

PRESENT PROGRESSIVE	They *are* reading.
PAST PROGRESSIVE	They *were* reading.
FUTURE PROGRESSIVE	They *will be* reading.
PRESENT PERFECT PROGRESSIVE	They *have been* reading.
PAST PERFECT PROGRESSIVE	They *had been* reading.
FUTURE PERFECT PROGRESSIVE	They *will have been* reading.

■ The present and past tenses have **emphatic forms,** which add special force, or emphasis, to the verb.

Make the emphatic forms by using *do, does,* or *did* with the base form of the verb.

PRESENT EMPHATIC	I *do* read the newspaper every day.
	Tony *does* read it occasionally.
PAST EMPHATIC	Inez *did* read the newspaper yesterday.

Exercise 13 Using the Progressive and Emphatic Forms

For each of the following sentences, write the progressive or the emphatic form of the verb in parentheses that makes sense in the sentence.

The Modern Bicycle

1. Today more than seventy-five million Americans (ride) bicycles.
2. Over the years, bicycling (gain) popularity as a form of both exercise and recreation.
3. Even before bicycles began to be widely used for transportation and exercise, numerous organizations already (work) to promote long-distance trips for experienced riders.
4. Today the bicycle (provide) efficient transportation to and from work for many people.
5. Despite the dangers, many people (ride) bicycles in metropolitan areas.
6. Because of accidents involving bicyclists, safety rules (grow) increasingly important.
7. There is no doubt that bicyclists (find) it difficult to ride on busy streets.
8. We can predict that if environmental conditions don't improve, legislators (try) to pass laws to protect bicyclists.
9. Before the recession, many cities (plan) to create bikeways, special lanes for bicyclists.
10. To ensure safety for all, new traffic laws (require) bicyclists to ride more carefully.

Exercise 14   **Identifying Verb Tenses and Their Uses**

Explain the difference in meaning between the sentences in each of the pairs below. Name the tenses and forms used in each sentence.

SAMPLE   a. Why was Gloria so secretive?
           b. Why has Gloria been so secretive?

ANSWER   In sentence *a*, the action occurred and ended (past). In sentence *b*, the action occurred in the past and is still continuing (present perfect).

1. a. Do you think Anna is writing a birthday poem for the twins' twenty-first birthday?
   b. Do you think Anna has been writing a birthday poem for the twins' twenty-first birthday?
2. a. Anna had finished the poem by the twins' birthday.
   b. Anna did finish the poem by the twins' birthday.
3. a. Michael had been painting a picture for the twins before he left town on a business trip to Salt Lake City.
   b. Michael had painted a picture for the twins before he left town on a business trip to Salt Lake City.
4. a. The twins had been telling everyone not to make a fuss.
   b. The twins told everyone not to make a fuss.
5. a. Nonetheless, the twins' friends planned a surprise party.
   b. Nonetheless, the twins' friends were planning a surprise party.
6. a. Last year, they forgot to celebrate the twins' birthday.
   b. Last year, they did forget to celebrate the twins' birthday.
7. a. I have been shopping for the perfect gift for weeks.
   b. I had been shopping for the perfect gift for weeks.
8. a. Marc and Lydia had been arguing before the twins arrived.
   b. Marc and Lydia were arguing when the twins arrived.
9. a. The twins looked happy.
   b. The twins were looking happy.
10. a. By this time next week, the twins will have begun their thank-you notes.
    b. By this time next week, the twins will begin their thank-you notes.

Exercise 15   **Expressing Past Time in a Paragraph**

Write a paragraph of at least eight sentences about an important event in your past. Underline five verbs or verb phrases that you have used. Use some progressive and emphatic forms if possible. (Remember that the perfect tenses, as well as the past tense, can be used to express past action.)

15.6 Compatibility of Tenses

- Do not shift, or change, tenses when two or more events occur at the same time.

  INCORRECT During the concert the pianist **forgot** the notes, and she **stops** in the middle of the piece. [The tense needlessly shifts from the past to the present.]

  CORRECT During the concert the pianist **forgot** the notes, and she **stopped** in the middle of the piece. [Now it is clear that both events happened at nearly the same time in the past.]

  INCORRECT The maestro **leaves** the podium. The audience **gave** him a standing ovation. [The tense needlessly shifts from the present to the past.]

  CORRECT The maestro **leaves** the podium. The audience **gives** him a standing ovation. [It is clear that both events are happening at about the same time.]

- Shift tenses to show that one event precedes or follows another.

  INCORRECT By the time we **arrived,** they **ate** dinner. [The two past-tense verbs give the mistaken impression that both events happened at the same time.]

  CORRECT By the time we **arrived,** they **had eaten** dinner. [The shift from the past tense *(arrived)* to the past perfect tense *(had eaten)* clearly indicates that they ate the dinner before we arrived.]

- Keep a statement of universal truth in the present tense even if the main verb is in the past tense.

  Columbus proved that the earth is round.

Exercise 16 Choosing Compatible Tenses

Determine which action or condition preceded the other one. Then write the compatible tense of the verb in parentheses.

1. Kim Mason was saving her earnings to buy a CD player she (saw, had seen) in the window of Music World.
2. It had been almost a year since she (opens, opened) her savings account.
3. By the time she saved enough money to buy the CD player, it (had gone, went) on sale.
4. She purchased the CD player and also (buys, bought) some CDs.
5. Kim learned that saving (is, was) a good way to get what you want.

Exercise 17 **Making Tenses Compatible**

First find the two verbs that appear in each of the following sentences. Then rewrite each sentence, making the second verb compatible with the first verb.

Maxine Hong Kingston: A Writer's Heritage

1. Maxine Hong Kingston was born in Stockton, California, in 1940 and was speaking Cantonese as a child.
2. After she had received several scholarships, she attends college at the University of California at Berkeley.
3. Before she switched to English, Kingston studies engineering.
4. Kingston found out in college that she is not a reporter.
5. While she wrote her first book, Kingston supports herself with a full-time job.
6. When *The Woman Warrior: Memoirs of a Girlhood Among Ghosts* was published in 1976, reviewers praise its combination of autobiography, fiction, and history.
7. By the time I finished *The Woman Warrior,* I learned a great deal about Kingston's childhood.
8. Kingston published *China Men* four years after she was writing *The Woman Warrior.*
9. In *China Men,* Kingston described her grandfather, who works on the transcontinental railroad in the early 1900s.
10. After I had completed *The Woman Warrior,* I had decided to read *China Men* as well.
11. *The Woman Warrior* won the National Book Critics Circle Award for nonfiction in 1976; and four years later, *China Men* had received the National Book Award.
12. Kingston made her debut as a novelist when she has written *Tripmaster Monkey: His Fake Book.*
13. This novel tells the story of Wittman Ah Sing, who had been a graduate of Berkeley and a Chinese American hippie.
14. Kingston sets the story in San Francisco in the 1960s and has made Sing a kind of rebel with a cause.
15. The story follows Sing as he will pursue his dream of writing and staging a huge Chinese saga.
16. The novel has been described as surreal and will have been called a bitter and funny tale.
17. In the course of the story, Sing falls in love and also searched for his grandmother in Reno, Nevada.
18. Maxine Hong Kingston is married to Earll Kingston, the actor, and they had had a son, Joseph.
19. Unlike his mother, Joseph Kingston is not a writer; instead, he had been a musician.
20. Maxine Hong Kingston makes her home in Oakland, California, where she continued to write.

15.6 Compatibility of Tenses

15.7 Voice of Verbs

- An action verb is in the **active voice** when the subject of the sentence performs the action.

  The student **submitted** her report.

- An action verb is in the **passive voice** when the action is performed on the subject.

  The report **was submitted** by the student.

Generally, the active voice is stronger, but at times the passive voice is preferred or, in fact, necessary. If you do not want to call attention to the performer or do not know who the performer is, use the passive voice.

  The dinner **was ruined.** [You may not want to identify the culprit.]
  The manuscript **was stolen.** [You may not know who the culprit is.]

Form the passive voice by using a form of the auxiliary verb *be* with the past participle of the verb. The tense of a passive verb is determined by the tense of the auxiliary verb.

  The child **is pleased** with the dog. [present tense, passive voice]
  The child **was pleased** with the dog. [past tense, passive voice]
  The child **will be pleased** with the dog. [future tense, passive voice]

Exercise 18 Identifying Active and Passive Voice

Write the verb in each sentence, and tell whether it is *active* or *passive*.

Denver International Airport

1. In 1995 the largest airport in North America opened for business.
2. Denver International Airport has been labeled by its supporters as the airport for the twenty-first century.
3. The airport was built on fifty-three square miles of prairie land northeast of the city.
4. Mismanagement and technological mishaps pushed the final cost to almost $5 billion, $3 billion over budget.
5. Three parallel runways are designed to handle ninety-nine aircraft every hour.
6. The control tower, 327 feet tall, will operate even in severe weather.
7. An automated underground transit system and a superhighway of moving sidewalks transport passengers to their gates.
8. Some of the glitches in the $232-million automated baggage system have been corrected.
9. Baggage is no longer shredded by the state-of-the-art system.
10. The baggage system winds for twenty miles beneath the terminal.

Exercise 19 — Changing the Voice of Verbs

Rewrite the following sentences, changing active verbs to passive and passive verbs to active. When using passive verbs, drop the performers of the action if they do not need to be identified. Make other wording changes as needed.

SAMPLE Long-distance health care *was made* possible by new technology.
ANSWER New technology *has made* long-distance health care possible.

Explorer Robots

1. The explorer robot has been brought to us by new technology.
2. Human beings operate some of these robots.
3. Areas dangerous to people have been explored by these robots.
4. NASA has tested some explorer robots.
5. Marine biologists expect explorer robots to do underwater research.
6. Endurance superior to that of humans is offered by these robots.
7. Therefore, explorer robots can maintain underwater equipment.
8. Pictures of Mars were relayed to Earth by planetary explorer robots.
9. Engineers have designed some explorer robots to help the physically challenged.
10. Scientists predict a great future for explorer robots.
11. A robotic arm has been constructed by engineers at NASA's Jet Propulsion Laboratory.
12. The device can imitate any action of a surgeon's electronic pointer.
13. The arm provides surgeons access to remote regions of the spine and brain.
14. The robotic arm will be tested on humans by medical researchers.
15. Engineers at MIT are developing a surgical robot for fulfilling a surgeon's commands.
16. Two small cameras have been placed inside the robot's head by engineers.
17. The cameras can continually transmit magnified images back to a video console.
18. A surgeon can direct the robot's movements by manipulating surgical tools mounted on the console.
19. For the next century, long-distance operating rooms with fiber-optic cable connectors are envisioned by researchers.
20. However, many obstacles must first be overcome by medical researchers and electronic engineers.

Exercise 20 — Writing Sentences with Active and Passive Voice

Write a paragraph of ten sentences describing a process with which you are familiar. Use a combination of active and passive verbs in your paragraph.

UNIT 15 Grammar Review

VERB TENSES AND VOICE

The following literary passage is taken from *Black Boy,* Richard Wright's autobiography. Born in Natchez, Mississippi, in 1908, Wright grew up poor, neglected, and hungry. In this passage, he describes a happy memory: the abundant meals that his Aunt Maggie served at her home in Arkansas. The passage has been annotated to show some of the kinds of verbs covered in this unit.

Literature Model

from Black Boy: A Record of Childhood and Youth
by Richard Wright

... At mealtime Aunt Maggie's table **was** so **loaded** with food that I could scarcely believe it was real. It **took** me some time to get used to the idea of there being enough to eat; I felt that if I **ate** enough there would not be anything left for another time. When I first sat down at Aunt Maggie's table, I could not eat until I had asked:

"Can I eat all I want?"

"Eat as much as you like," Uncle Hoskins said.

I did not believe him. I ate until my stomach hurt, but even then I did not want to get up from the table.

"Your eyes **are** bigger than your stomach," my mother said.

"Let him eat all he wants to and get used to food," Uncle Hoskins said.

When supper was over I saw that there were many biscuits piled high upon the bread platter, an astonishing and unbelievable sight to me. Though the biscuits were right before my eyes, and though there was more flour in the kitchen, I was apprehensive lest there be no bread for breakfast in the morning. I was afraid that somehow the biscuits might disappear during the night, while I **was sleeping.** I did not want to wake up in the morning, as I had so often in the past, feeling hun-

Annotations:
- Passive voice
- Active voice
- Past tense of an irregular verb
- Present tense of an irregular verb
- Past progressive form

598 Unit 15 Verb Tenses and Voice

Grammar Review

> gry and knowing that there was no food in the house. So, surreptitiously, I took some of the biscuits from the platter and slipped them into my pocket, not to eat, but to keep as a bulwark against any possible attack of hunger. Even after I **had got used** to seeing the table loaded with food at each meal, I still stole bread and put it into my pockets. In washing my clothes my mother found the gummy wads and **scolded** me to break me of the habit; I stopped hiding the bread in my pockets and hid it about the house, in corners, behind dressers. I did not break the habit of stealing and hoarding bread until my faith that food would be forthcoming at each meal had been somewhat established.

Past perfect tense

Past tense of a regular verb

Review: Exercise 1 Identifying Principal Parts of Verbs

The following sentences elaborate on ideas suggested by the passage from *Black Boy*. Each sentence contains an italicized verb in one of four forms: (a) the base form, (b) the past form, (c) the present participle, or (d) the past participle. At the end of the sentence is a second verb in parentheses. First, identify the form of the verb in italics. Then write the verb in parentheses in the same form as the original verb.

SAMPLE The family *dined* at Aunt Maggie's. (eat)
ANSWER past form; ate

1. At home in Mississippi, food had often *seemed* scarce. (be)
2. Young Wright *had* the acute, daily ache of hunger. (feel)
3. His stomach frequently was *churning* with discomfort. (growl)
4. Then Wright and his mother *traveled* to his aunt's home in Arkansas. (come)
5. They are *visiting* Wright's Aunt Maggie and Uncle Hoskins today. (see)
6. The kindly pair *welcome* them into their home. (take)
7. Wright *wondered* at the amount of food in the kitchen. (marvel)
8. Later, Wright was *devouring* an abundant dinner. (eat)
9. He had *consumed* the food until his stomach ached. (eat)
10. Aunt Maggie *carried* a lavish platter of hot biscuits to the table. (bring)
11. Wright had *grown* fearful that the biscuits would disappear before breakfast. (become)
12. He was even *concealing* extra food in his pocket. (hide)
13. His mother had *found* gummy wads of bread in his pocket. (discover)
14. For many days, he *feared* that every full meal might be his last. (think)
15. This fear of hunger *remained* with him for months. (stay)

Grammar Review

Review: Exercise 2 Using the Present, Past, and Future Tenses

The following sentences are based on passages from *Black Boy* that are not reprinted in this textbook. On your paper, write each italicized verb so that it matches the tense in parentheses. Use only the present, past, and future tenses; with the exception of *will* to express the future tense, do not use any helping verbs.

SAMPLE Wright's mother *will bring* her son to Arkansas. (present tense)
ANSWER brings

1. On the train to Elaine, Arkansas, Wright *will become* aware of racism and segregation. (present tense)
2. In those days, African Americans and whites *ride* in separate sections of the train. (past tense)
3. The naive youngster *wanted* a peek at the whites' part of the train. (present tense)
4. His mother *says,* "Quit talking foolishness!" (past tense)
5. The travelers *went* to Aunt Maggie and Uncle Hoskins's home to live. (future tense)
6. Uncle Hoskins *owned* a prosperous business in town. (present tense)
7. Aunt Maggie *will have* plenty of food on the dinner table. (past tense)
8. Soon a major calamity *will break* Wright's mood of contentment. (present tense)
9. Some white people in town, envious of Uncle Hoskins's success, *murder* him one night. (past tense)
10. Aunt Maggie, Wright, and Wright's mother *flee* to safety in another town. (future tense)
11. Wright's four years at Jim Hill Public School *were* his only opportunity for formal study. (present tense)
12. At first the principal *puts* him in the fifth grade. (past tense)
13. After studying day and night, Wright *passes* to the sixth grade. (future tense)
14. Flushed with success, Wright *thinks* about studying medicine. (past tense)
15. In school he *will try* to deter questions about his home and his life. (present tense)
16. At noon he *went* to the sandwich shop with some of his classmates. (future tense)
17. One of the boys *sensed* Wright's dilemma. (present tense)
18. Later, he *suggests* that Wright earn some money by selling newspapers published in Chicago. (future tense)
19. Slowly, Wright *collects* customers in the African American neighborhoods. (past tense)
20. Later, he *found* out that the newspapers preach the Ku Klux Klan doctrine. (present tense)

Grammar Review

Review: Exercise 3   **Using the Perfect Tenses**

Each of the following sentences is based on events in Richard Wright's *Black Boy*. On your paper, write the form of the italicized verb that belongs in the place indicated by the caret. Follow the directions in parentheses, using the past participle of the main verb and the appropriate form of the helping verb *have*.

1. By the time he became a teenager, Wright ∧ in several southern states. (past perfect tense of *live*)
2. Wright ∧ the age of four before he moved from his grandparents' home near Natchez, Mississippi. (past perfect tense of *reach*)
3. When Richard's grandmother ∧ ill for some time, a fire nearly destroyed the Wright home. (past perfect tense of *be*)
4. The fire ∧ through several rooms by the time Wright could flee to safety. (past perfect tense of *tear*)
5. When the adults at last put out the blaze, nearly half the house ∧ down. (past perfect tense of *burn*)
6. Wright ∧ to Arkansas to live with his aunt and uncle. (present perfect tense of *come*)
7. Wright ∧ in Memphis, Tennessee, but he had never lived in Arkansas before. (past perfect form of *live*)
8. For most of her life before she decided to leave Memphis, his mother ∧ against exhaustion and despair. (past perfect tense of *struggle*)
9. Her meager wages ∧ her almost no money for food. (present perfect tense of *leave*)
10. Now that his mother ∧ Wright to his aunt's home, he is finally getting enough to eat. (present perfect tense of *bring*)
11. Because he ∧ constant hunger, at first he eats until his stomach hurts. (present perfect tense of *know*)
12. After he ∧ a meal, he hides bread in his pockets. (present perfect tense of *finish*)
13. His mother often finds gummy wads of bread in the clothes that she ∧ . (present perfect tense of *wash*)
14. She realizes what he ∧ and scolds him. (present perfect tense of *do*)
15. In spite of her criticism, she understands why he ∧ the bread. (present perfect tense of *steal*)
16. During his short life, he already ∧ great hardship. (present perfect tense of *endure*)
17. In a month or so, Wright ∧ the habit. (future perfect tense of *break*)
18. By then he ∧ more confident that food will always be available. (future perfect tense of *become*)
19. Violence tears the family apart when they learn that envious whites ∧ Uncle Hoskins. (present perfect tense of *murder*)
20. By the following morning, mother and son ∧ safety in a nearby town. (future perfect tense of *reach*)

Grammar Review

Review: Exercise 4   **Using the Progressive and Emphatic Forms**

Each of the following sentences is based on events in Richard Wright's *Black Boy*. On your paper, write the form of the italicized verb that belongs in the place indicated by the caret. Follow the directions in parentheses, using the present participle of the main verb and the appropriate tense of *be*, or the base form of the main verb and the appropriate form of *do*.

SAMPLE   The writer ∧ about the meaning of his life. (present progressive form of *think*)
ANSWER   is thinking

1. A train trip to Arkansas in 1917 ∧ Wright about the realities of the Jim Crow laws that limited the rights of African Americans. (past emphatic form of *teach*)
2. He wonders why whites and African Americans ∧ in separate sections of the train. (present progressive form of *sit*)
3. During the train ride to Arkansas, Wright ∧ about his grandmother's life as a slave before the Civil War. (present progressive form of *ask*)
4. Tonight young Wright ∧ in the home of his Uncle Hoskins. (future progressive form of *sleep*)
5. Although startled at first by all the food served by his aunt, eventually Wright ∧ to Hoskins's home. (past emphatic form of *adjust*)
6. Envious men in town ∧ Uncle Hoskins's life. (past progressive form of *threaten*)
7. One night, Aunt Maggie ∧ for Uncle Hoskins's return when a tall boy knocked on the door. (past progressive form of *wait*)
8. The threat ∧ a reality: Uncle Hoskins was murdered. (past emphatic form of *become*)
9. Weeks later, a regiment of African American soldiers ∧ with rifles on their shoulders. (future progressive form of *parade*)
10. Soon these troops ∧ in World War I. (future progressive form of *fight*)

Review: Exercise 5   **Identifying and Using Voice of Verbs**

The following sentences are about Richard Wright and *Black Boy*. First, identify each sentence as being in either the *passive voice* or the *active voice*. Then rewrite each sentence, changing the active voice to the passive or the passive voice to the active.

SAMPLE   *Black Boy* was written by Richard Wright.
ANSWER   passive voice; Richard Wright wrote *Black Boy*.

1. The events in *Black Boy* are recounted by the author with fury and eloquence.
2. The Civil War ended slavery in the United States.
3. Little was done by society about the plight of African Americans.
4. *Black Boy* was written by Richard Wright as a story of protest.
5. Wright's forceful voice has inspired generations of Americans.

Grammar Review

Review: Exercise 6 **Making Tenses Compatible**

The following sentences elaborate on events in the passage from *Black Boy*. On your paper, correct the tense of the italicized verb so that the tenses are compatible.

SAMPLE Before Wright came to his aunt's home in Arkansas, he *lived* in Memphis, Tennessee.
ANSWER had lived

1. Aunt Maggie was married to Uncle Hoskins, who *runs* a thriving business near their home in Arkansas.
2. In Memphis Wright *is eating* poorly, but at Aunt Maggie's he ate well.
3. He *sits* shyly at the table when Aunt Maggie brought out the first meal.
4. Aunt Maggie was a fine cook, and she *sets* a variety of savory foods on the table.
5. As Wright *bites* into a biscuit, he recalled his many hungry times.
6. The others had not yet finished their first portion when Wright *takes* a second helping of the food.
7. After his meals, Wright *puts* some extra food into a pocket or hid it in the house.
8. Wright's mother *finds* wads of bread when she washed his clothes.
9. Wright controlled his urge to hoard food only after he *becomes* certain of the source of his next meal.
10. In his years in Memphis, Wright *is failing* to gain weight, but in Arkansas, at Aunt Maggie's table, he never went hungry.
11. Wright is hired by a white family who *will want* someone to milk cows, feed chickens, and serve meals.
12. The woman teaches him how to milk and *had shown* him how to gather eggs.
13. When he came into the house, Wright noticed that the dining table *will have been set* for five people.
14. He was appalled that the family habitually *had cursed* each other.
15. When the time came for him to return to school, he *will be* physically tired and emotionally spent.
16. He *clings* to the job, however, because the family never measured how much food he ate.
17. Back home, when he described his meals, his family *feels* envious.
18. In class Wright *will fall* behind with his academic work because he had drifted off to sleep so many times.
19. To keep himself awake and alert, he goes to the water fountain and *ran* cold water over his wrists.
20. Now that he is earning money, he *has bought* sandwiches for lunch.

Grammar Review

Review: Exercise 7 **Using Verb Tenses in Writing**

Choose a story you have read recently or seen at the movies or on television. Write ten sentences about the story and the characters. In each sentence, use at least two verbs that are compatible in tense. Write the verbs and label the tenses. Use all six verb tenses in your sentences: present, past, future, present perfect, past perfect, and future perfect.

SAMPLE ANSWER I recently read a story that I had wanted to read for some time. read–past tense; had wanted–past perfect tense

Review: Exercise 8

Proofreading

The following passage describes the artist William H. Johnson, whose painting appears on the opposite page. Rewrite the passage, correcting the errors in spelling, grammar, and usage. Add any missing punctuation. There are twenty-five errors.

William H. Johnson

¹William H. Johnson (1901–1970), one of the most innovative artists of the Harlem Renaissance is born in Florence, South Carolina. ²One day, one of his elementary school teachers founded on Johnson's desk a piece of paper with a remarkable likeness of herself. ³His teachers and his family, recognizing his talent encourage Johnson to develop his skill as a painter.

⁴When he was seventeen, Johnson moved to Harlem a neighborhood in New York City. ⁵Three years later, he accepted into the prestigious National Academy of Design, where he won several awards. ⁶He gone to Paris in 1926. ⁷He was spending twelve years altogether in Europe, nine of them in Scandinavia. ⁸There he studied art and met the Danish woman who become his wife. ⁹His painting was influenced by the highly expressive works of Vincent van Gogh the famous Dutch Postimpressionist.

¹⁰Johnson once describes himself as primitive and cultured at the same time. ¹¹When he come back to the United States, he had refined his hybrid style. ¹²Using vivid colors and a delibreatly primitive technique, he painted scenes of contemporary African American life. ¹³Poor farm workers city dwellers, soldiers, convicts, musicians, and preachers appear often in his work. ¹⁴The heightened colors and the strong emotional tone of his paintings shows the influence of the European school of painting known as Expressionism.

Grammar Review

William H. Johnson, *Jim*, 1930

[15]Soon after World War II ended, Johnson hospitalized for a nervous disorder. [16]Tragically, his last years was spent in mental institutions. [17]His works has continued to be exhibited and praised despite his career's premature end.

[18]*Jim*, a relatively early portrait is painted in a style that Johnson later abandoned. [19]The vivid colors and loose brush strokes is reminiscent of Expressionist techniques. [20]It is not hard to imagine the young Richard Wright as the boy in Johnsons painting. [21]The gaze in Jim's eyes suggest an inner turmoil that seems akin to the physical and spiritual hunger that Wright feeled as a boy.

Grammar Review

Review: Exercise 9

Mixed Review

The following sentences describe the life and literary achievements of the author Richard Wright. Rewrite each sentence, following the directions in parentheses.

SAMPLE Richard Wright portrayed his childhood and also writes about urban life. (Change the second verb to make the tenses compatible.)

ANSWER Richard Wright portrayed his childhood and also wrote about urban life.

Richard Wright

1. Richard Wright was born in a rural region of Mississippi, where his grandparents were enslaved before the Civil War. (Change the second verb to the past perfect tense.)
2. Wright lived in Memphis when his father abandoned the family to a life of poverty. (Change the first verb to the past progressive form.)
3. After he had spent time with relatives in Arkansas and Mississippi, Wright had returned to Memphis. (Change the second verb to the past tense.)
4. In Memphis Wright worked as a postal clerk when he decided to become a writer. (Change the first verb to the past progressive form.)
5. He reads several books that stimulated his interest in becoming a writer. (Change the first verb to make the tenses compatible.)
6. The American author H. L. Mencken wrote one of those books. (Rewrite the sentence in the passive voice.)
7. Financial aid was given to the budding author by the Federal Writers' Project, a government assistance program. (Rewrite the sentence in the active voice.)
8. Before he moved to New York City in 1937, Wright lived for a time in Chicago. (Change the second verb to the past perfect tense.)
9. Wright first wins attention with *Uncle Tom's Children,* a collection of short works of fiction that appeared in 1938. (Correct the error caused by the use of the present tense.)
10. Two years later he published his popular novel *Native Son.* (Rewrite the sentence in the passive voice.)
11. *Native Son* was adapted for the Broadway stage by the noted director Orson Welles. (Rewrite the sentence in the active voice.)
12. Eventually, Hollywood turned *Native Son* into a film drama. (Change the verb to the past emphatic form.)
13. When an Argentine film version of *Native Son* appeared in 1951, Wright himself plays the main character, Bigger Thomas. (Correct the error caused by the use of the present tense.)
14. An American studio recently released a film adaptation of *Native Son.* (Change the verb to the present perfect tense.)
15. In fact, the video store in my neighborhood stocks the 1986 version of *Native Son.* (Change the verb to the present emphatic form.)

Writing Application

Verbs in Writing

In this passage from her autobiography *I Know Why the Caged Bird Sings*, Maya Angelou describes the relationship between her grandmother and the aristocratic Mrs. Flowers. As you read, concentrate on Angelou's use of verbs, especially the italicized ones.

> Mrs. Flowers didn't belong to our church, nor *was* she Momma's familiar. Why on earth *did* she *insist* on calling her Sister Flowers? Shame made me want to hide my face. Mrs. Flowers deserved better than to be called Sister. Then, Momma left out the verb. Why not ask "How *are* you, Mrs. Flowers?" With the unbalanced passion of the young, I hated her for showing her ignorance to Mrs. Flowers. It didn't occur to me for many years that they were as alike as sisters, separated only by formal education.

Techniques with Verbs

When you write and revise your own work, try to use verbs as Angelou does.

❶ Do not shift tenses when referring to events in the same time frame.

INCORRECT VERSION Mrs. Flowers doesn't belong to our church, nor was she Momma's familiar.

ANGELOU'S CORRECT VERSION Mrs. Flowers didn't belong to our church, nor was she Momma's familiar.

❷ Use the emphatic form and the active voice to make a point.

UNEMPHATIC PASSIVE VERSION Why was Mrs. Flowers called Sister Flowers by her?

ANGELOU'S VERSION Why on earth did she insist on calling her Sister Flowers?

TIME

For more about the writing process, see **TIME Facing the Blank Page**, pp. 121-131.

Verb Tenses and Voice

Practice   Revise the following passage on a separate sheet of paper. Keep verb tenses consistent and use active voice as much as possible.

> Maya Angelou has enriched American culture with the many books and poems she had written. Perhaps best known for her multivolume autobiography, she also will have been remembered for the poem she wrote to commemorate the inauguration of President William Jefferson Clinton. She completed the poem several days before Clinton was inaugurated.
>
> Interestingly, an experience was shared by President Clinton and this gifted African American writer: They both spent their childhood in Arkansas and were cared for by grandmothers whom they will remember with great affection.

UNIT 16 Subject-Verb Agreement

Lesson 16.1	Intervening Prepositional Phrases	609
Lesson 16.2	Agreement with Linking Verbs	611
Lesson 16.3	Agreement in Inverted Sentences	612
Lesson 16.4	Agreement with Special Subjects	614
Lesson 16.5	Agreement with Compound Subjects	616
Lesson 16.6	Intervening Expressions	618
Lesson 16.7	Indefinite Pronouns as Subjects	619

Grammar Review 622

Writing Application 631

16.1 Intervening Prepositional Phrases

■ A verb must agree with its subject in number and person.

Number can be singular or plural. Singular words indicate one; plural words indicate more than one. A singular subject takes a singular verb. A plural subject takes a plural verb.

With most verbs, the only change in form to indicate agreement in person occurs in the present tense. An -s (or -es) is added to the base form of the verb when its subject is third-person singular.

SINGULAR	PLURAL
She **speaks**.	They **speak**.
He **exercises**.	They **exercise**.
She **pitches**.	They **pitch**.

The linking verb *be* changes in both the present and the past tense.

SINGULAR	PLURAL
He **is** there.	They **are** there.
It **was** sweet.	They **were** sweet.

In verb phrases, the auxiliary verbs *be*, *have*, and *do* change in form to show agreement with third-person subjects.

SINGULAR	PLURAL
He **is going**.	They **are going**.
She **is reading**.	They **are reading**.
She **has seen** a movie.	They **have seen** a movie.
Does he **stay** here?	**Do** they **stay** here?

■ Do not mistake a word in a prepositional phrase for the subject of a sentence.

The simple subject is never within a prepositional phrase. Make sure the verb agrees with the actual subject and not with the object of a preposition.

> The **taste** of the cherries **surprises** us. [The subject, *taste*, is singular; *of the cherries* is a prepositional phrase; therefore, the verb, *surprises*, is singular.]

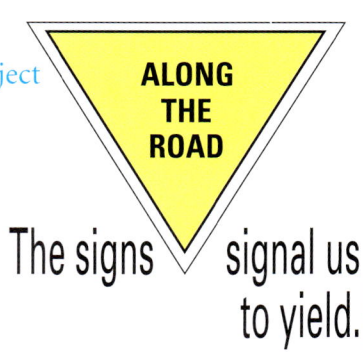

ALONG THE ROAD

The signs signal us to yield.

Exercise 1   Making Subjects and Verbs Agree

Write on your paper the form of the verb indicated in parentheses that agrees with the subject of each sentence.

A Class Field Trip

1. Don (is/are) looking forward to the field trip.
2. Carol (wants/want) to take the bus.
3. The teacher (tells/tell) the class about the park.
4. They (is/are) going to the zoo after lunch.
5. The bus driver (waits/wait) for the students to return.

Exercise 2   Making Subjects and Verbs Agree When Prepositional Phrases Intervene

Find the simple subject in each of the following sentences. Then write on your paper the form of the verb indicated in parentheses that agrees with the subject of each sentence.

Barbara Jordan: A Prominent Texan

1. Barbara Jordan's years in the U.S. Congress (has/have) given her a unique perspective on American politics.
2. Over thirty years ago, this distinguished graduate of two universities (was/were) first attracted to politics.
3. Jordan, despite many setbacks and difficulties, (has/have) achieved many of her goals.
4. A public speaker with Jordan's exceptional talents (is/are) rare.
5. Politicians from many states (was/were) impressed with Barbara Jordan's address at the 1976 Democratic National Convention.
6. Perhaps Jordan's extraordinary abilities in public speaking (was/were) encouraged by her father, a Baptist minister.
7. African American women, in Jordan's opinion, (needs/need) to make their voices heard in government.
8. Jordan's reputation in political circles (was/were) enhanced by her strong role in the congressional hearings about the impeachment of President Richard Nixon.
9. Jordan, in spite of her popularity among Texas voters, (was/were) prepared to leave politics by 1978 for a teaching career.
10. Barbara Jordan's place in history books clearly (seems/seem) secure.

16.2 Agreement with Linking Verbs

- Do not be confused by a predicate nominative that is different in number from the subject. Only the subject affects the number of the linking verb.

    The lightest **crate is** two tons. [The singular verb, *is*, agrees with the singular subject, *crate*, not with the predicate nominative, *tons*.]

    Recent **studies** on the behavior of wild animals **are** his topic for the day. [The plural verb, *are*, agrees with the plural subject, *studies*, not with the predicate nominative, *topic*.]

Exercise 3   Making Linking Verbs Agree with Their Subjects

Find the simple subject or subjects in each of the following sentences. Then write on your paper the form of the verb in parentheses that agrees with the subject of each sentence.

Our Endangered Forests and Wildlife

1. The growing threat to America's wild animals (is/are) a national problem.
2. Another problem (is/are) the many acres of forest land we lose each year.
3. Wildlife (remains/remain) a rich and vital part of our national heritage.
4. Animals (is/are) also an important part of our world.
5. Research on plant and animal life (is/are) the means of much scientific discovery.
6. Our forests (is/are) also a wonderful resource for recreation.
7. Once our forest land (was/were) millions of acres more extensive.
8. Growing cities (is/are) part of the problem.
9. By the 1990s, one result of deforestation (was/were) high numbers of endangered species.
10. Adequate food (is/are) a necessity for animals.
11. The cost of deforestation (is/are) years of floods and damaging soil erosion.
12. Harmful effects on the wild animals that depend on the forest (is/are) a result of deforestation.
13. The long-term effects of excessive hunting and fishing (is/are) another problem.
14. State governments (is/are) important agencies in protecting our endangered forests.
15. The destructive results (is/are) a disturbance in the balance of nature.
16. Our land (is/are) our home, our heritage, and our gift to the future.
17. Protected lands (seem/seems) the only hope for wildlife.
18. Our forests (remains/remain) an important part of their survival.
19. Efforts by government and private citizens (seems/seem) the solution.
20. We (is/are) all part of the solution.

16.3 Agreement in Inverted Sentences

■ In an **inverted sentence**—a sentence in which the subject follows the verb—take care in locating the simple subject and make sure that the verb agrees with the subject.

Inverted sentences often begin with prepositional phrases. Do not mistake the object of the preposition for the subject.

	V **S**
SINGULAR	In the jungle **roars** the *lion*.
	V **S**
PLURAL	In the jungle **roar** the *lions*.
	V **S**
SINGULAR	In a large cage at the zoo **rests** a noble *lion*.
	V **S**
PLURAL	In a large cage at the zoo **rest** two noble *lions*.

In inverted sentences beginning with *there* or *here*, look for the subject after the verb. The word *there* or *here* is almost never the subject of a sentence.

	V **S**
SINGULAR	There **is** a *lion* in the jungle.
	V **S**
	Here **goes** the *ambulance*.
	V **S**
PLURAL	There **are** *lions* in the jungle.
	V **S**
	Here **go** the two *ambulances*.

In questions, an auxiliary verb may come before the subject. Look for the subject between the auxiliary verb and the main verb.

	V **S** **V**
SINGULAR	**Does** that *lion* **live** in the jungle?
	V **S** **V**
PLURAL	**Do** those *jungles* **contain** lions?

Exercise 4   **Making Subjects and Verbs Agree in Inverted Sentences**

Find the simple subject in each of the following sentences. Then write on your paper the form of the verb in parentheses that agrees with the subject of each sentence.

Dining Out

1. There (is/are) three excellent and unusual restaurants in my neighborhood.
2. In the window of one of the restaurants (hangs/hang) an interesting menu.
3. Over the door of another (swings/swing) an old and elaborate sign.
4. Outside the third (stands/stand) two statues representing servers.
5. (Does/Do) the restaurant owners ever cook and bake?
6. (Is/Are) expert chefs brought in to create mouth-watering specialties to please the demanding clientele?
7. There (is/are) a pleasant decor in all three of these restaurants.
8. Into the restaurants (crowds/crowd) the hungry customers.
9. Here (comes/come) the people who want to eat before they go to the theater.
10. There (gathers/gather) the people waiting to be seated.
11. On one menu (is/are) a picture of an unusual animal.
12. On the sign there (is/are) three pictures of the food served.
13. In the lap of one statue in a corner of the restaurant (rests/rest) a knife.
14. How (does/do) the owner find all the foods for the menus?
15. There (is/are) special menus for children in each restaurant.
16. On each table (is/are) a vase of flowers.
17. On a table in the center of the restaurant (is/are) dishes from other countries.
18. There (is/are) a line of three young men outside the door.
19. (Does/Do) the three men have reservations?
20. Here (comes/come) the third delivery of food for today.

Exercise 5   **Writing Inverted Sentences**

On your paper, write the following sentences as inverted sentences. Make sure each verb agrees with its subject.

Team Trophies

1. The prize trophy rests in the office.
2. The members of the team are sitting in the hall.
3. Ten other trophies won by other teams are also in the case.
4. The principal hopes to keep the trophies in the new case. (Write as a question.)
5. The trophy for the basketball tournament is here.

16.4 Agreement with Special Subjects

Collective Nouns

■ A **collective noun** names a group. Consider a collective noun singular when it refers to a group as a whole. Consider a collective noun plural when it refers to each member of a group individually.

SINGULAR His *family* arrives.
PLURAL His *family* are well.

SINGULAR The *committee* decides.
PLURAL The *committee* sign their names.

Special Nouns

■ Certain nouns that end in *-s*, such as *mumps, measles,* and *mathematics,* take singular verbs.

SINGULAR **Mumps is** a disease.

■ Certain other nouns that end in *-s*, such as *scissors, pants, binoculars,* and *eyeglasses,* take plural verbs.

PLURAL The **scissors were** sharp.
Your **eyeglasses need** cleaning.

■ Many nouns that end in *-ics* may be singular or plural, depending upon their meaning.

SINGULAR **Statistics is** an interesting subject. [one subject of interest]
PLURAL **Statistics show** that women live longer than men. [more than one application of this particular field of study]

Exercise 6 — Using Special Subjects in Sentences

Write 10 sentences. In each sentence, use one of the following nouns as the subject. Make sure each subject agrees with a present-tense verb.

SAMPLE measles
ANSWER Measles is a common childhood disease.

1. club
2. politics
3. family
4. fleet
5. audience
6. stairs
7. mathematics
8. news
9. analysis
10. group

Nouns of Amount

- When a noun of amount refers to a total that is considered as one unit, the noun is singular. When it refers to a number of individual units, the noun is plural.

    SINGULAR   Three **dollars is** not too much for that book. [one amount]
    PLURAL   Three **dollars are** on the table. [three individual bills]
    SINGULAR   Ten **years is** a decade. [one unit of time]
    PLURAL   Ten **years have** passed. [ten individual periods of time]

Five players is a team.

Titles

- A title is always singular, even if a noun within the title is plural.

    SINGULAR   ***Great Expectations* is** one of the best-loved novels in English literature.

Five players are on the court.

Exercise 7   Making Verbs Agree with Special Subjects

Find the subject in each sentence. Then write on your paper the form of the verb in parentheses that agrees with the subject.

Roberto Clemente, a Baseball Hero

1. The first baseball team to hire Roberto Clemente (was/were) the Santurce Cangrejeros of Puerto Rico.
2. When Clemente joined the Pittsburgh Pirates in 1954, fifty thousand dollars (was/were) considered a princely salary.
3. Clemente's family (was/were) eager to show its pride in him.
4. Roberto Clemente's impressive offensive and defensive statistics (shows/show) that he was a versatile player.
5. Professional athletics (is/are) a demanding field.
6. Clemente's eighteen years in major-league baseball (is/are) considered a long career.
7. Five hours (is/are) a long time for a professional baseball game to last.
8. On December 31, 1972, his team (was/were) all very much shocked to hear that Clemente had died in a plane crash while taking supplies to earthquake victims in Nicaragua.
9. Sometimes a professional athlete's second family (is/are) his or her teammates.
10. Our class agrees that *The Great One* (is/are) an appropriate title for a biography of Roberto Clemente.

16.5 Agreement with Compound Subjects

Compound Subjects Joined by *And*

■ A compound subject that is joined by *and* or *both . . . and* is plural unless its parts belong to one unit or the parts both refer to the same person or thing.

PLURAL   The **lion** and the **tiger** are roaring.

Both **skiing** and **skating** are fun.

SINGULAR   **Peanut butter** and **jelly** is a favorite combination.
[Compound subject is one unit.]

His **friend** and **companion** accompanies him.
[One person is both friend and companion.]

Compound Subjects Joined by *Or* or *Nor*

■ With compound subjects joined by *or* or *nor* (or by *either . . . or* or *neither . . . nor*), the verb always agrees with the subject nearer the verb.

PLURAL   Neither the **lion** nor the **tigers** are roaring.
SINGULAR   Either the **lion** or the **tiger** is roaring.

Neither the **lions** nor the **tiger** roars.

Exercise 8   Writing Sentences with Compound Subjects

Write five sentences. In each sentence, use one of the following items as the compound subject. Make the compound subject agree with a present-tense verb.

1. bread and butter
2. neither the players nor the coach
3. both the climate and the geography of the South
4. Aunt Susan or Uncle Harold
5. either a cat or a dog

Many a, Every, and Each with Compound Subjects

■ When *many a, every,* or *each* precedes a compound subject, the subject is considered singular.

SINGULAR *Many a* **giraffe** and **elephant lives** in the nature preserve.

Every **chair, bench,** and **table was taken.**

Each **lion** and **tiger is roaring.**

Exercise 9 Making Verbs Agree with Their Subjects

On your paper, write the appropriate form of each verb in parentheses.

Leontyne Price, Opera Star

1. The opera expert and the casual listener (agrees/agree) that Leontyne Price is one of the greatest living sopranos.
2. Many people in Price's life (was/were) influential in her decision to pursue a career in music.
3. When Price undertook four demanding years of formal training in New York, neither her talents nor her ambition (was/were) lacking.
4. Before Price became a star, producers Robert Breen and Blevins Davis (was/were) impressed by Price's singing.
5. Price's longtime friend and adviser, vocal coach Florence Page Kimball, probably (feels/feel) that Price's finest role was that of Bess in Gershwin's *Porgy and Bess.*
6. Neither Price's performance in *The Magic Flute* nor her triumphs in Verdi's operas (has/have) given me as much pleasure as her singing in *Madame Butterfly.*
7. Fortunately, neither serious illnesses nor stage fright (has/have) interrupted Price's long career.
8. To be a successful singer like Price, talent and perseverance (is/are) required.
9. Every note, gesture, and facial expression (is/are) crucial to the success of a performance.
10. Many a performer and audience member (feels/feel) excited when the lights in a theater dim.

16.6 Intervening Expressions

Certain expressions, such as *accompanied by, as well as, in addition to, plus,* and *together with,* introduce phrases that modify the subject but do not change its number. Although their meaning is similar to that of *and*, these expressions do not create compound subjects.

- If a singular subject is linked to another noun by an intervening expression, such as *accompanied by,* the subject is still considered singular.

SINGULAR **Margaret,** *accompanied by* her date, **was** the first girl to dance.

The **pianist,** *as well as* the guitarist, the saxophonist, and the lead singer, **is** late.

Her **course load,** *plus* her extracurricular activities, **was** a lot to handle.

Sleet, *in addition to* snow, **is expected** tomorrow.

Sports, *together with* band, **is** the most popular extracurricular activity.

Exercise 10   Making Verbs Agree with Intervening Expressions

On your paper, write the appropriate form of each verb in parentheses.

Becoming a Singer

1. A voice teacher, as well as friends and relatives, (is/are) helpful in encouraging a young singer.
2. Talent, together with perseverance and practice, (makes/make) a successful career possible.
3. The student, accompanied by a pianist, (sings/sing) for the first time tonight.
4. Members of the orchestra, plus the soloist and the teacher, (prepares/prepare) for the evening's performance.
5. The teacher, together with family and friends, (applauds/applaud) the students.
6. The students, in addition to the teacher, (is/are) relieved that the performance went so well.
7. The performers, as well as the audience, (departs/depart) satisfied with the evening.
8. Lessons, in addition to practice, (has/have) proven valuable.
9. Every student, plus the students' parents, (realizes/realize) the importance of rehearsing.
10. The class, together with the teacher, excitedly (discusses/discuss) the performance.

16.7 Indefinite Pronouns as Subjects

■ A verb must agree in number with an indefinite pronoun subject.

Indefinite pronouns can be divided into three groups, as shown in the following chart:

Indefinite Pronouns					
ALWAYS SINGULAR	each either neither one	everyone everybody everything no one	nobody nothing anyone anybody	anything someone somebody something	
ALWAYS PLURAL	several	few	both	many	
SINGULAR OR PLURAL	some	all	any	most	none

Plural indefinite pronouns take plural verbs. Singular indefinite pronouns take singular verbs.

SINGULAR   ***Everybody* is** going to the rodeo.
                 No one in the audience **looks** upset.
                 Something in the kitchen **smells** good.

PLURAL   ***Both*** of the children **are** in school this morning.
                 Many of the books **were** donated to the library.

A pronoun from the group labeled singular or plural can be either singular or plural, depending upon the noun to which it refers.

SINGULAR   ***Some*** of the dessert **is** left. [*Some* refers to *dessert*, a singular noun.]

PLURAL   ***Some*** of the commuters **were caught** in the rainstorm. [*Some* refers to *commuters*, a plural noun.]

Exercise 11   Making Verbs Agree with Indefinite Pronoun Subjects

Find the pronoun subject in each sentence and the noun to which it refers. On your paper, write the form of the verb in parentheses that agrees with the subject.

A Night at the Opera

1. All of the performers of the opera (knows/know) their parts.
2. Few of the soloists (was/were) needed for this particular work.
3. Any of the audience who came late (was/were) handed a program by the usher.
4. Each of the programs left after the performance (was/were) recycled.
5. Most of the audience members (was/were) pleased by the performance.

16.7 Indefinite Pronouns as Subjects   **619**

Exercise 12 — Writing Sentences with Indefinite Pronoun Subjects

Write 10 sentences. In each sentence, use one of the following indefinite pronouns as the subject. Make each subject agree with a present-tense verb.

SAMPLE one
ANSWER One of my friends owns a racing bike.

1. each
2. many
3. few
4. both
5. neither
6. nobody
7. nothing
8. everything
9. one
10. several

Exercise 13 — Writing Sentences with Indefinite Pronoun Subjects

For each indefinite pronoun listed below, write two sentences, using the pronoun as the subject of both sentences. In the first sentence of each pair, use a singular present-tense verb. In the second sentence, use a plural present-tense verb.

SAMPLE some
ANSWER Some of the work is not finished.
Some of the books are on the shelf.

1. none
2. any
3. most
4. all
5. some

Exercise 14 — Making Verbs Agree with Their Subjects

On your paper, write the appropriate form of the verb in parentheses.

Butterflies

1. Almost all of these insects (has/have) some means of protection from enemies.
2. Many of them (excels/excel) at the art of imitation.
3. Some insects, like the walking stick, (looks/look) like inanimate objects when they rest on a plant stem.
4. Some butterflies, like this one, (has/have) special coloration to startle would-be predators.
5. Some of the members of one group (has/have) subdued colors and fly at night.
6. Both of these (is/are) true butterflies.
7. Protective coloration, as well as spiny larvae, (is/are) characteristic of many butterflies.
8. The monarch butterfly, along with its caterpillar, (has/have) a bitter taste.
9. Neither of these insects (makes/make) a tempting meal for a hungry bird.
10. Many of these birds (avoids/avoid) some butterflies.

Exercise 15 **Correcting Subject-Verb Agreement**

The following paragraph contains ten errors in subject-verb agreement. Locate the sentences with errors and rewrite those sentences, using the verb form that agrees with the subject. (Not every sentence contains an error.)

Popular Music

¹Many people in the cities of Los Angeles, Miami, and New York enjoys several kinds of popular music. ²While a family in Brooklyn listen to reggae music together, a family in Miami enjoy merengue. ³Many a music lover, whether young or old, like jazz and blues. ⁴Many Americans, as well as people from around the world, dances to the brassy music known as salsa. ⁵The syncopated rhythms of calypso music is popular among people who like the steel drum. ⁶Very popular in some communities is Mexican folk songs called *rancheras*. ⁷From the recording studios come one new popular hit after another. ⁸Usually thousands of dollars are the sum needed to record a new song. ⁹In many American cities, neither the Motown tunes of the 1960s nor rock-and-roll have gone out of style. ¹⁰Ask whether your family or friends enjoy a special kind of music.

Exercise 16 **Making Verbs Agree with Their Subjects**

On a separate sheet of paper, rewrite the following paragraphs, replacing each blank with a verb in the present tense.

The boy with black eyes _____ over the rim of the canyon into the valley below. Everything _____ pale, as if the hot midday sun has bleached the colors from the landscape. The boy stands with arms upraised and _____ a stone over the cliff. "One, two, three," _____ the boy as the stone falls, and on "four" he hears it clatter on the rocks. Then he remembers that in one of his pockets _____ the carving of the bird he finished the night before. As polished as river rocks _____ his bird, and as white as sunlight. Quickly, without thinking, the boy from Wide Ruins _____ the bird and _____ it over the cliff. There _____ a brief flash of white, and the bird is gone. Nobody, not even the boy, _____ whether it hits the ground.

The boy listens. No sounds from the valley far below _____ his ears. The silence of his surroundings _____ absolute. Suddenly, faint flutterings _____ a signal to turn his gaze downward. Far below him in the shade of the canyon _____ the valley floor. The boy peers intently, adjusting his gaze from the brightness of sun to the darkness of shadow. In the dimness there _____ a flash of white. _____ his eyes deceive him? Again _____ the white, and then it is gone. Both the valley and the air _____ again still. The boy waits another moment, but there _____ nothing. His family _____ . He turns away from the canyon.

UNIT 16 Grammar Review

SUBJECT-VERB AGREEMENT

Simin Daneshvar is from Iran, and her novel *Savushun* describes the fortunes of an Iranian family at the time of the Second World War. The chief characters of the novel are a sensitive young woman named Zari and her husband, Yusof. In this passage, Zari spends a quiet afternoon in her garden with her twin daughters. The passage has been annotated to show some examples of subject-verb agreement covered in this unit.

Literature Model

from Savushun
by Simin Daneshvar
translated from the Persian
by M. R. Ghanoonparvar

Ten days had passed since Yusof had left for the winter pastures, and the weather in the garden wasn't much better than where he was. Summer always hurried in like this, chasing away spring. It was afternoon and Gholam was sprinkling water on the patio in front of the house. Zari, carrying gardening clippers, was looking for flowers to pick. But there were none worth picking in the garden. Mina and Marjan, chirping like birds, followed their mother from one bush to another. By the stream around the patio there were some cockscombs so wilted and dusty that not even an old hen would have looked at them twice. By another stream, the faces and heads of the snapdragons were all covered with dust. Some more humble plants were straining to close their eyes and sleep as the sun set. The only hope was for the tuberoses, which Gholam claimed would "blossom when there is a full moon." The orange-blossom petals had dried up completely and, under the trees, looked like dried and shriveled brown stars. How one missed winter, when the narcissuses opened at the edge of the streams, and gave their reflections to the passing water as a memento. The water flowed

---

Annotations:
- Agreement between a singular pronoun subject and a singular past form of *be* → It was
- An inverted sentence with agreement between an indefinite pronoun subject (referring to the plural noun *flowers*) and the plural past form of *be* → were none
- An inverted sentence with agreement between a plural noun subject and the plural past form of *be* → were ... cockscombs
- Agreement between a compound noun subject and the plural past form of *be* → faces and heads ... were
- Agreement between a singular noun subject and a singular past form of *be* → hope was

622 Unit 16 Subject-Verb Agreement

Grammar Review

> on, losing the reflections, pouring into the pool without a witness. One could only hear its current. And when spring came, the white and purple violets gracefully greeted the passing water without promise or memento.

Review: Exercise 1   **Making Subjects and Verbs Agree When Prepositional Phrases Intervene**

Each of the following sentences describes characteristics of the Persian garden. On your paper, rewrite each sentence, following the directions in parentheses. In some cases, you will need to change the form of the verb to make the sentence correct; in other cases, the verb will remain the same.

SAMPLE   For Persians, an image of paradise is created by gardens. (Change *an image* to *images*.)

ANSWER   For Persians, images of paradise are created by gardens.

1. The scene on ancient Persian pottery often depicts garden images. (Change *scene* to *scenes*.)
2. A pool of water usually plays a role in these scenes. (Change *A pool* to *Pools*.)
3. Often, too, the patterns on Persian rugs suggest a garden. (Change *Persian rugs* to *a Persian rug*.)
4. Persian gardens throughout the years have been laid out in four sections. (Change *the years* to *time*.)
5. Pavilions of cypress trees were often built at the center of the garden. (Change *Pavilions* to *A pavilion*.)
6. In Iran some gardens still follow this plan. (Move the prepositional phrase so that it comes directly after the subject.)
7. The pool in such a garden is still an important feature. (Change *such a garden* to *these gardens*.)
8. Sometimes streams from nearby areas supply the water for these pools. (Change *nearby areas* to *a nearby area*.)
9. In some seasons, water is provided by sloping tunnels called *qanat* lines. (Move the first prepositional phrase so that it comes directly after the subject.)
10. The length of the *qanat* line varies considerably. (Change *line* to *lines*.)
11. Beneath the surface, *qanat* lines connect the valleys to the snow-capped mountains. (Move the first prepositional phrase so that it comes directly after the subject.)
12. Owners of gardens rent the channel for a certain length of time. (Change *gardens* to *a garden*.)
13. From the mountains, melting snow thus becomes a source of water. (Move the first prepositional phrase so that it comes directly after the subject.)

Grammar Review   **623**

Grammar Review

14. Varieties of roses dominate Persian gardens. (Change *Varieties* to *A variety.*)
15. A rose with deep aroma has been used in many ways. (Change *A rose* to *Roses.*)
16. Gardeners of certain roses press petals to make fragrant rosewater. (Change *Gardeners* to *A gardener.*)
17. A flavoring from the rose is used in a variety of desserts. (Change *the rose* to *roses.*)
18. The song of a nightingale makes a garden even more delightful. (Change *song* to *songs.*)
19. A common sight in Persian gardens is brightly colored tulips. (Change *A common sight* to *Common sights.*)
20. A plane tree of huge proportions often provides shade for the garden. (Change *A plane tree* to *Plane trees.*)

Review: Exercise 2 — Writing Sentences with Intervening Prepositional Phrases

The following sentences describe an imaginary garden. Rewrite each sentence, adding an appropriate prepositional phrase in the place indicated by the caret and choosing the correct form of the verb in parentheses.

SAMPLE The flower garden ∧ (is/are) beautiful.
ANSWER The flower garden behind my grandmother's house is beautiful.

1. Flowers ∧ (offers/offer) a spectacle of color throughout the growing season.
2. Some kinds of flowers ∧ (provides/provide) food and nectar for insects.
3. Fresh flowers ∧ (makes/make) the whole house smell good.
4. Flowers ∧ (adds/add) pleasure to your world.
5. Fragrant roses ∧ (delights/delight) all who behold them.
6. Lilacs ∧ (is/are) a charming sight.
7. The first crocuses ∧ (announces/announce) the coming of spring.
8. A small garden ∧ (needs/need) to be planned carefully.
9. Weeding ∧ (is/are) an important part of caring for a garden.
10. Bulbs ∧ (is/are) planted long before they are expected to bloom.
11. The rich soil ∧ (nourishes/nourish) the flowers.
12. People passing ∧ (enjoys/enjoy) the flowers' beauty and fragrance.
13. A birdbath ∧ (attracts/attract) robins and sparrows.
14. A vegetable garden ∧ (is/are) practical but not necessarily beautiful.
15. Vegetables ∧ (enhances/enhance) one's diet.
16. Fresh vegetables ∧ often (tastes/taste) better than vegetables bought in a store.
17. Surplus crops ∧ (is/are) frozen, dried, or canned.
18. A small herb garden ∧ (provides/provide) fresh seasonings for cooking.
19. Herb gardens ∧ (is/are) easy to take care of.
20. Daily watering ∧ (is/are) a must when rainfall is scarce.

Grammar Review

Review: Exercise 3   **Making Linking Verbs Agree with Their Subjects**

Each of the following sentences describes the scene from the passage from *Savushun*. On your paper, rewrite each sentence, following the directions in parentheses. If necessary, change the number of the linking verb.

1. Usually Zari's garden is a beautiful sight. (Change *garden* to *flowers*.)
2. Today, however, the main feature of the garden is a cluster of wilted flowers. (Change *a cluster* to *clusters*.)
3. An orange-blossom petal has become a shriveled jumble. (Change *An orange-blossom petal* to *Orange-blossom petals*.)
4. The streams are mirrors for the drooping blossoms. (Change *mirrors* to *a mirror*.)
5. The garden tool is a useless device on such a day. (Change *tool* to *clippers*.)
6. The only animals in the garden are birds. (Change *animals* to *surprising sight*.)
7. In winter a flowering plant is a welcome sight. (Change *a flowering plant* to *flowering plants*.)
8. In spring one image of loveliness is the violet. (Change *the violet* to *violets*.)
9. Water is the key to survival for these fragile plants. (Change *key to* to *means of*.)
10. Irrigation systems are the best solution for dry areas. (Change *Irrigation systems* to *An irrigation system*.)

Review: Exercise 4   **Making Subjects and Verbs Agree in Inverted Sentences**

Each of the following sentences elaborates on an idea suggested in *Savushun*. First write each sentence on your paper, choosing the correct form of the verb in parentheses. Then rewrite each sentence in inverted order, using the correct verb form.

SAMPLE   The hot sun (beats/beat) upon the dry plants.
ANSWER   The hot sun beats upon the dry plants.
                Upon the dry plants beats the hot sun.

1. The clippers (is/are) in Zari's hand.
2. The gardener (stands/stand) among some bushes.
3. A gently curving stream (flows/flow) between the towering trees.
4. Some wilted cockscombs (droops/droop) by the side of the stream.
5. Crumbling orange-blossom petals (lies/lie) in the dry dust.
6. The colorful snapdragons (blooms/bloom) near another stream.
7. The limp blossoms (bends/bend) toward the parched earth.
8. The refreshing water (flows/flow) onto the thirsty plants.
9. New growth (comes/come) with frequent waterings.
10. The white tuberose (appears/appear) on cool moonlit nights.

Grammar Review

Review: Exercise 5   **Making Verbs Agree with Special Subjects**

The following sentences are about a panel discussion on the occupation of Iran during the Second World War by Great Britain and the Soviet Union. First write the subject of each sentence and then write the form of the verb in parentheses that agrees with the subject.

SAMPLE   A panel of experts (prepares/prepare) for discussions of various aspects of the occupation of Iran.

ANSWER   panel prepares

1. Because mumps (is/are) spreading throughout the community, some students will miss the discussion.
2. Binoculars (helps/help) those in the back of the large auditorium to see the speakers.
3. *The Effects of Allied Occupation on Iran* (is/are) a book recommended by one of the speakers.
4. First the audience (learns/learn) about the German influence in Iran at the beginning of World War II.
5. The panel then (discusses/discuss) among themselves the British and Soviet control of Iran in the early 1940s.
6. The group at the podium (disagrees/disagree) about whether that occupation was necessary.
7. Five years (was/were) the length of the Allied occupation of Iran.
8. Our class next (hears/hear) about the economic and social problems in Iran at the time.
9. One panel member claims that thirty thousand (was/were) the approximate number of troops provided by the United States when it joined the occupation in 1942.
10. Statistics (shows/show) that the years of occupation were difficult for Iran.
11. The Committee on International Affairs (sponsors/sponsor) the discussion.
12. The committee (discusses/discuss) the issues thoroughly.
13. Nobody (arrives/arrive) late for the discussion.
14. Six months (has/have) passed since the last panel discussion.
15. A brief synopsis of the events leading to the occupation (is/are) given.
16. The ethics of the occupation (is/are) also discussed.
17. *World War II Military Occupations* (is/are) a book referred to by a speaker.
18. The faculty (is/are) represented by several teachers.
19. The hours spent at the panel discussion (is/are) very productive.
20. Afterwards, our class (is/are) divided on the need for the occupation.

Grammar Review

Review: Exercise 6   **Making Verbs Agree with Compound Subjects**

Each of the following sentences elaborates on an idea suggested by the passage from *Savushun*. On your paper, rewrite each sentence, following the directions in parentheses and making any necessary adjustments to the form of the verb.

SAMPLE   Every flower needs water. (Add *and shrub* to the complete subject.)
ANSWER   Every flower and shrub needs water.

1. Mina scampers from bush to bush. (Add *and her sister* to the complete subject.)
2. Zari and the girls look for flowers. (Delete *and the girls* from the complete subject.)
3. Every cockscomb droops. (Add *and orange blossom* to the complete subject.)
4. Many a violet has faded. (Add *and narcissus* to the complete subject.)
5. Each stem withers. (Add *and blossom* to the complete subject.)
6. Zari and Gholam tend the garden. (Delete *and Gholam* from the complete subject.)
7. The stream and the pond supply water for the garden. (Delete *and the pond* from the complete subject.)
8. Many a dried leaf floats on the still water. (Add *and petal* to the complete subject.)
9. The spring and the winter bring fresh foliage. (Delete *and the winter* from the complete subject.)
10. Now Zari and her children want only the safe return of Yusof. (Delete *and her children* from the complete subject.)

Review: Exercise 7   **Making Subjects and Verbs Agree When Expressions Intervene**

The following sentences describe the situation and characters in *Savushun*. Rewrite each sentence, correcting any errors in subject-verb agreement. If the sentence contains no errors, write *correct*.

1. In the novel *Savushun,* the British army, as well as Soviet troops, occupy Iran.
2. The troops, plus a poor harvest, causes a food shortage.
3. Yusof, as well as Zari, is sympathetic to the hungry nomads and peasants.
4. A tribal leader, accompanied by his brother, bring Yusof news of the peasants' hardships.
5. The peasant population, plus its sheep, is starving.
6. Yusof, accompanied by servants, have gone to his pastures.
7. Yusof, in addition to his foreman, visits the shepherds.
8. Zari, together with Yusof's sister, give food to the poor.
9. Bread, as well as dates, are taken by Zari to hospitals.
10. Famine, together with disease, cause death everywhere.

Grammar Review   **627**

Grammar Review

Review: Exercise 8 **Making Verbs Agree with Indefinite Pronoun Subjects**

The following sentences describe gardens around the city of Shiraz, the setting of *Savushun*. Rewrite each sentence, replacing the indefinite pronoun in italics with the pronoun in parentheses. If necessary, change the number of the verb.

SAMPLE   *Many* of Iran's historic sites are near Shiraz. (One)
ANSWER   One of Iran's historic sites is near Shiraz.

1. *Most* of the sites, such as the tombs of the ancient poets Hafiz and Sadi, feature gardens. (A few)
2. *Both* of these poets are revered in Muslim cultures. (Each)
3. *Either* of their tombs attracts numerous visitors. (Both)
4. *Most* in Iran are familiar with the poems of Hafiz. (Everyone)
5. *Many* enjoy reading his verse in a nearby garden. (Anybody)
6. *Several* of the older gardens have vanished entirely. (Some)
7. *Each* of the area's palaces was decorated with mirrored tile. (Many)
8. *All* are able to imagine the beauty of the palaces. (Someone)
9. *Few* of the ancient gardens have been fully restored. (Several)
10. *Some* of the renovation of the Rose Garden is complete. (Most)

Review: Exercise 9

Proofreading

The following passage describes manuscript illumination; an example by a Persian artist appears on the opposite page. Rewrite the passage, correcting any errors in spelling, usage, and grammar. Add any missing punctuation. There are twenty-five errors.

Persian Illuminated Manuscripts

¹Illustrated, or illuminated, books was one of the highest art forms in the Islamic world. ²From the tenth through the sixteenth centuries, manuscript painting was highly cherished for it celebrated the beauty and the power of the writen word. ³Because in Islam books were considered to be the embodiment of devine revelation, they was treated with reverence. ⁴Moreover, written Arabic lend itself to exquisite calligraphy a type of stylized handwriting.

⁵In Persia and in other Middle Eastern countries, the teachings of the sixth-century prophet Mohammed was often illustrated. ⁶Similarly, many literary manuscripts was illustrated in the sixteenth century. ⁷The illustration above

Grammar Review

Habib Allah, from *Mantiq at-Tayr (Language of the Birds)*, c. 1600

date from that time. ⁸It is taken from a book entitled *Mantiq at-Tayr (Language of the Birds)* which was written by Farid-Al-Din 'Attar. ⁹The image of the birds in the garden are quite small intricate, and carfully painted. ¹⁰Parts of the painting is covered with gold leaf, which was used to brighten the scene. ¹¹The rich brocade imaje represents the idealized realm of the birds. ¹²The birds themselves represents creatures of the heavens.

¹³At the upper right of the picture are the figure of a man. ¹⁴This figure can be interpreted in two ways—as a guardian of the birds sanctuary or as a representation of the human threat to that world. ¹⁵The painting, however, mirror the content of the book in reflecting an ideal world rather than an actual world. ¹⁶Therefore, peace and harmony predominates.

¹⁷Garden-related themes appears in many Persian literary classics. ¹⁸The richly varied colors and textures of nature is found not only in Persia's art but in it's architecture and in the many complex decorative designs that pervade Persian culture. ¹⁹In the illumination at the top of this page, the colors and sounds of the garden calls up visions of natural beauty.

Grammar Review

Review: Exercise 10

Mixed Review

The following sentences describe the life and achievements of Simin Daneshvar [sē mēn´ dä´nesh vär´]. For each sentence, write the appropriate form of the verb in parentheses.

Simin Daneshvar

1. Simin Daneshvar, as well as her husband, (figures/figure) prominently among contemporary Iranian writers.
2. Daneshvar, along with other Iranian writers, (criticizes/criticize) the lack of justice in her homeland.
3. Studies at Tehran University (was/were) the foundation for her doctorate in Persian literature.
4. Daneshvar's lectures at Tehran University (has/have) exposed many scholars to her ideas.
5. All of Iran's social classes (is/are) represented in her fiction.
6. Among the greatest influences on her works (was/were) the famous American author O. Henry.
7. *The Quenched Fire* (1948) and *A City as Paradise* (1961) (deals/deal) with women's roles in society.
8. None of the stories in *The Quenched Fire* (has/have) been reprinted because the author was dissatisfied with the work.
9. In Daneshvar's most widely read novel, *Savushun* (1969), the descriptions of suffering (composes/compose) a portrait of the effects of war on common people.
10. Daneshvar's works (is/are) a realistic depiction of social problems in her country.
11. Politics in Iran (does/do) not generally encourage artistic freedom.
12. In Iran a woman who receives a doctorate, especially in Persian studies, (is/are) unusual.
13. There (is/are) many things Daneshvar wants to do to help her country.
14. One of her concerns (is/are) the needs of the people of Iran.
15. All of Iranian society (is/are) the subject of her work.
16. One of Daneshvar's objectives (has/have) been to help women.
17. Daneshvar (is/are) an author and storyteller who takes pride in her work.
18. Both her clear language and her graceful style (gives/give) a compelling picture of life in Iran.
19. I, as well as my best friend, (has/have) a better understanding of life in Iran after reading her books.
20. Persian, the language of Daneshvar's books, (is/are) an ancient language.

Writing Application

Subject-Verb Agreement

In this passage from *House Made of Dawn*, N. Scott Momaday demonstrates several examples of correct subject-verb agreement. Examine the passage, focusing on the italicized subjects and verbs.

My grandmother lived in a house near the place where Rainy Mountain Creek runs into the Washita River. Once there *was* a *lot* of sound in the house, a lot of coming and going, feasting and talk. The *summers* there *were* full of excitement and reunion. The Kiowas are a summer people; they abide the cold and keep to themselves, but when the season turns and the land becomes warm and vital they cannot hold still; an old *love* of going *returns* upon them. The old people have a fine sense of pageantry and a wonderful notion of decorum. The aged *visitors* who came to my grandmother's house when I was a child *were* men of immense character, full of wisdom and disdain.

Techniques with Subject-Verb Agreement

Use some of Momaday's techniques when you write and revise your own work.

❶ Be alert to prepositional phrases and other expressions that fall between a subject and its verb. Mentally block them out when you check for agreement.

INCORRECT USE *visitors* who came to my house when I was a child *was*

MOMADAY'S CORRECT USE *visitors* who came to my house when I was a child *were*

❷ When you check for agreement in inverted sentences, remember that the subject follows the verb. In inverted sentences beginning with *there* or *here*, remember that *there* or *here* is almost never the subject.

INCORRECT USE there *were* a *lot* of sound in the house

MOMADAY'S CORRECT USE there *was* a *lot* of sound in the house

> **TIME** For more about the writing process, see **TIME** *Facing the Blank Page*, pp. 121-131.

Practice

Practice these techniques by revising the following passage, using a separate sheet of paper. Rewrite the paragraphs, replacing each blank with a verb in the present tense.

At the tip of a high point overlooking the waves far below _____ the town. The handsome houses of the village _____ me of beautifully bound books on a high shelf. The wide windows facing the sea _____ the curve of book spines.

There, stretching into the distance on three sides, _____ the sea. The light glancing off the waves _____ me squint. The screech of gulls _____ the air. A sloop with billowing sails _____ toward the horizon. A fishing boat laden with crabs _____ toward the safety of harbor. The whole scene—cliff, sea, and houses— _____ so picturesque that it _____ like a watercolor.

UNIT 17 Using Pronouns Correctly

Lesson **17.1**	**Case of Personal Pronouns**	*633*
Lesson **17.2**	**Pronouns with and as Appositives**	*635*
Lesson **17.3**	**Pronouns After *Than* and *As***	*637*
Lesson **17.4**	***Who* and *Whom* in Questions and Subordinate Clauses**	*638*
Lesson **17.5**	**Pronoun-Antecedent Agreement**	*640*
Lesson **17.6**	**Clear Pronoun Reference**	*645*
Grammar Review		*648*
Writing Application		*657*

17.1 Case of Personal Pronouns

- Pronouns that are used to refer to persons or things are called **personal pronouns**.
- Personal pronouns have three **cases,** or forms, called **nominative, objective,** and **possessive.** The case of a personal pronoun depends upon the pronoun's function in a sentence (whether it is a subject, a complement, an object of a preposition, or a replacement for a possessive noun).

Personal Pronouns

CASE	SINGULAR PRONOUNS	PLURAL PRONOUNS	FUNCTION IN SENTENCE
NOMINATIVE	I, you, she, he, it	we, you, they	subject or predicate nominative
OBJECTIVE	me, you, her, him, it	us, you, them	direct object, indirect object, or object of preposition
POSSESSIVE	my, mine, your, yours, her, hers, his, its	our, ours, your, yours, their, theirs	replacement for possessive noun(s)

Exercise 1 — Identifying Pronoun Case and Function

On your paper, write each personal pronoun in the sentences below. Then write what case each is, and how the pronoun functions in the sentence. One pronoun is used in a contraction.

SAMPLE I first met him at our neighbor's party.
ANSWER I—nominative, subject; him—objective, direct object; our—possessive, replacement for possessive noun

1. His parents had just moved into the vacant house next to ours.
2. My mother and father had just been introduced to his mother and father.
3. Maybe they should meet him, too, I thought.
4. We walked up to my mother, and I introduced him to her.
5. She extended her hand and said, "It's certainly a great pleasure to meet any friend of our son's."

Use these rules to avoid errors with the case of personal pronouns.

1. Use the nominative case for a personal pronoun in a compound subject.

   Paul and **I** play the guitar.   **She** and **I** sing duets.

2. Use the objective case for a personal pronoun in a compound object.

   Al's sister visited Al and **her**.   This is between you and **me**.

Hint: In a sentence with a compound subject or object, listen for correctness by saying the sentence aloud without the conjunction and the other subject or object.

3. Use the nominative case of a personal pronoun after a form of the linking verb *be*.

   The best guitar player is **he**.   The best singer was **she**.

This rule is changing. In informal speech, people often use the objective case after a form of the linking verb *be*; they say, *It's me* or *It was her*. Some authorities even recommend using the objective case in informal writing to avoid sounding pretentious. In formal writing, however, use the nominative case after a form of the linking verb *be*.

4. Do not spell possessive pronouns with apostrophes.

   This sheet music is **hers**.   The instruments are **theirs**.

It's is a contraction for *it is*. Do not confuse *it's* with the possessive pronoun *its*.

   It's a great day for a walk. Bring me the guitar and **its** case.

5. Use possessive pronouns before gerunds (*-ing* verb forms used as nouns).

   Your dancing bothers me. He wasn't pleased with **my** singing.

Exercise 2   Choosing the Correct Case Form

On your paper, write the correct personal pronoun from each pair in parentheses.

Phillis Wheatley, Poet

1. When you and (I/me) think of African American poets, we often forget Phillis Wheatley.
2. Susannah Wheatley, wife of slaveholder John Wheatley, took great interest in Phillis's education, and it was (she/her) who taught Phillis how to read and write English.
3. John Wheatley encouraged Susannah and (she/her) in their studies.
4. (Its/It's) sad that Phillis's health was not good.
5. My knowledge of Phillis Wheatley has increased by (me/my) reading about her.

17.2 Pronouns with and as Appositives

- Use the nominative case for a pronoun that is in apposition to a subject or a predicate nominative.

   The judges, **she** and **Mrs. Chiu,** will have a difficult task. [*Judges* is the subject of the sentence.]

   The winners were the pianists, **Linda** and **he.** [*Pianists* is the predicate nominative.]

- Use the objective case for a pronoun that is in apposition to a direct object, an indirect object, or an object of a preposition.

   The audience cheered their favorite performers, **Darnell** and **her.** [*Performers* is the direct object.]

   The director gave the stage crew, **Lee** and **him,** special thanks. [*Crew* is the indirect object.]

   The judges explained the rules to both groups, **them** and **us.** [*Groups* is the object of the preposition *to*.]

- When a pronoun is followed by an appositive, choose the case of the pronoun that would be correct if the appositive were omitted.

   We violinists hope one day to play in a concert hall. [*We* is the correct form because *we* is the subject of the sentence.]

   The music teacher handed the scores to **us musicians.** [*Us* is the correct form because *us* is the object of the preposition *to*.]

Exercise 3   Using Pronouns with and as Appositives

For each sentence in the following paragraph, write on your paper the correct pronoun from the pair in parentheses.

Making a Movie

[1]The writers, Lawrence Kasdan and (she/her), were willing to revise the script. [2]The director worked well with the leads, Harrison Ford and (she/her). [3]The two cinematographers, Gordon Willis and (him/he), were both efficient and creative. [4](We/Us) young actors were lucky to work with such a fine team. [5]There is no question that working on this film had a positive effect on (we/us) beginners.

Exercise 4 — Using Pronouns with and as Appositives

For each of the following sentences, write on your paper the correct personal pronoun from the pair in parentheses.

The Game of Golf

1. The first lecturers, Anna and (I/me), explained to the class that golf was popularized by King James IV of Scotland and his granddaughter, Mary.
2. The two of them, James IV and (she/her), helped to introduce the game to sports enthusiasts in England and France.
3. We then mentioned that (we/us) Americans often do well in professional tournaments.
4. Julie Inkster and (he/him), two very successful contemporary golfers, earn top salaries.
5. Tiger Woods and (she/her), two golf masters, were two recent winners of major golf tournaments.
6. Then the class asked golf experts Anna and (I, me) some questions about the game.
7. Two students, (he/him) and Larry, wanted to know how many Americans actually play the game.
8. (She, Her) and I, the experts, mentioned that the game is enjoyable for all age groups, both older people and (we/us) youngsters, because it emphasizes skill rather than strength.
9. We gave two students, Gayle and (he/him), a putter and a ball.
10. Both of us, Anna and (I, me), felt that our lecture to the class had gone very well.

Exercise 5 — Using Pronouns in Sentences

On your paper, complete the following sentences by replacing each blank with a personal pronoun that makes sense.

Impressionism

1. We art lovers, Claire and _____, have learned to appreciate the contribution made by Auguste Renoir to the art style known as Impressionism.
2. Two leaders in Impressionism were Monet and _____ .
3. The first Impressionist exhibit showcased Degas, Cézanne, and _____ .
4. Viewers were highly critical of the work by Renoir and _____ .
5. Critics were not pleased by _____ using mauve shadows.
6. The painters were derisively called Impressionists because of *Impression, Sunrise,* by Monet, which later became one of _____ more famous paintings.
7. The artists, Renoir and _____, were undaunted by the negative criticism.
8. Although Edouard Manet was never part of the group, he was a good friend of _____.
9. Renoir and _____ sometimes painted together.
10. The Impressionists have left a valuable legacy for _____ art lovers.

17.3 Pronouns After *Than* and *As*

■ In elliptical adverb clauses using *than* and *as*, choose the case of the pronoun that you would use if the missing words were fully expressed.

> You use a brush more skillfully than **I**. [The nominative pronoun *I* is the subject of the complete adverb clause *than I use a brush.*]
>
> The logic of the problem puzzled Jennifer as much as **me**. [The objective pronoun *me* is the direct object of the complete adverb clause *as much as it puzzled me.*]

Some sentences can be completed with either a nominative or an objective pronoun, depending on the meaning intended.

> Art liked Pat more than **I** [liked Pat].
>
> Art liked Pat more than [he liked] **me**.

In informal speech, people often use the objective rather than the nominative form in sentences such as *He is several years older than me.* In your writing, however, you should be careful to use the correct case.

Exercise 6 — Using the Correct Pronoun After *Than* and *As*

Each sentence contains an italicized word or group of words. On your paper, rewrite each sentence, substituting the correct pronoun for the words in italics.

Rembrandt van Rijn, Dutch Painter

1. Nobody enjoys Rembrandt's paintings as much as *my family and I*.
2. Few Dutch artists in the seventeenth century could paint as well as *Rembrandt*.
3. Although Rembrandt's father had hoped his son would be a clergyman, few people supported the artist more than *Mr. van Rijn*.
4. It seems Rembrandt's artistic talent astonished his father as much as *his art teachers*.
5. Critics seemed to agree that nobody in Holland could paint better than *Rembrandt*.
6. Rembrandt's rise to fame must have pleased the artist even more than *the leaders of Amsterdam*.
7. As a portrait artist, Rembrandt was sought after much more than *other painters*.
8. Few models seemed as beautiful to Rembrandt as *a girl named Saskia*.
9. On the day of their wedding, it seemed nobody could have been happier than *Rembrandt and Saskia*.
10. Rembrandt's paintings seem to amaze people today even more than *the people of Rembrandt's century*.

17.4 *Who* and *Whom* in Questions and Subordinate Clauses

■ Use the nominative pronoun *who* for subjects.

Who won the contest? [*Who* is the subject of the verb *won.*]

Tell me **who** is in your class. [*Who* is the subject of the noun clause *who is in your class.*]

In questions with an interrupting expression, such as *did you say* or *do you think,* it is often helpful to drop the interrupting phrase to determine whether to use *who* or *whom.*

Who do you think will emcee the show? [Think: *Who* will emcee the show? *Who* is the subject of the verb *will emcee.*]

■ Use the objective pronoun *whom* for the direct or indirect object of a verb or verbal or for the object of a preposition.

Whom are you introducing first? [*Whom* is the direct object of the verb *are introducing.*]

Whom did you say Maria invited to the party? [*Whom* is the direct object of the verb *invited.*]

They told him **whom** he could invite to the show. [*Whom* is the direct object of the verb *could invite* in the noun clause *whom he could invite to the show.*]

Theodore Roosevelt is a president about **whom** I have read quite a bit. [*Whom* is the object of the preposition *about* in the adjective clause *about whom I have read quite a bit.*]

In informal speech, people generally use *who* in place of *whom* in sentences like *Who did you tell?* In writing and in formal speaking situations, however, make the distinction between *who* and *whom.*

direct object

Maria invited *them* to the party.
Maria invited *whom* to the party?

Exercise 7   Choosing *Who* or *When*

For each sentence, write on your paper the correct pronoun from the pair in parentheses.

Learning About Holography

1. (Who/Whom) did you say gave you the passes to the Museum of Holography?
2. Setsuko Ishii is the holographic artist about (who/whom) I've been reading.
3. Setsuko Ishii, (who/whom) many consider one of Japan's top holographic artists, has put together an exhibit at the museum.
4. The museum director, (who/whom) our teacher knows, will show us a twenty-minute film.
5. The director mentioned several artists (who/whom) he said will exhibit in the future.

Exercise 8   Choosing *Who* or *Whom*

For each of the following sentences, write on your paper the correct pronoun from the pair in parentheses.

George Washington Carver, Scientist

1. (Who/Whom) would you say changed forever the way we look at the lowly peanut?
2. George Washington Carver, (who/whom) many consider one of the best scientists of his day, developed hundreds of products from peanuts.
3. Carver, (who/whom) many still admire today, was born on a Missouri plantation in 1861 and left home when he was ten years old.
4. He was accepted by a college in Kansas, but he was barred from attending by faculty members (who/whom) were prejudiced.
5. Carver was later admitted to Simpson College in Iowa and paid his way by ironing laundry for students (who/whom) were attending the college.
6. Carver, (who/whom) every student of agriculture has studied, made several important discoveries about plants.
7. Booker T. Washington, a scientist (who/whom) Carver greatly respected, invited Carver to work at the Tuskegee Institute in Alabama.
8. Carver, (who/whom) Washington believed to be hard working and imaginative, eventually came up with more than three hundred products derived from peanuts, including peanut butter, ink, shampoo, vinegar, and a coffee substitute.
9. For (who/whom) did Carver develop these products?
10. Carver developed them for poor southern farmers, about (who/whom) he was greatly concerned.

Exercise 9   Using *Who* or *Whom* in Sentences

On your paper, complete the following paragraph by replacing each blank with *who* or *whom*.

Mary Cassatt, an American Painter

[1]Mary Cassatt, _____ many students of art admire, was a successful nineteenth-century American painter who spent much of her time in France. [2]Her friends, _____ included Edgar Degas, were some of the great French Impressionists. [3]Degas, _____ we know primarily for his paintings of ballerinas, greatly influenced Cassatt. [4]Cassatt also encouraged American collectors to purchase the art of the Impressionists, _____ she considered very important. [5]_____ are some other American artists influenced by the European Impressionists?

Exercise 10   Using *Who* or *Whom* in Writing

Write ten sentences. In five, use the nominative pronoun *who*. In the other five, use the objective pronoun *whom*.

17.5 Pronoun-Antecedent Agreement

■ An **antecedent** is the word or group of words to which a pronoun refers or that a pronoun replaces. All pronouns must agree with their antecedents in number, gender, and person.

Agreement in Number and Gender

■ A pronoun must agree with its antecedent in number (singular or plural) and gender (masculine, feminine, or neuter).

A pronoun's antecedent may be a noun, another pronoun, or a phrase or clause acting as a noun. In the following examples, the pronouns appear in bold type and their antecedents in bold italic type. Note how they agree in both number and gender:

> ***Helen Keller*** did not let an inability to see and hear prevent **her** from graduating *cum laude* from Radcliffe College. [singular feminine pronoun]
>
> ***Helen Keller*** and ***Robert Smithdas*** overcame many challenges to earn **their** college degrees. [plural pronoun]
>
> ***Octavio Paz*** is one of the greatest poets of **his** era. [singular masculine pronoun]
>
> ***Walt Whitman*** and ***Emily Dickinson*** are also famous for **their** poetry. [plural pronoun]
>
> The ***horseshoe crab,*** despite **its** name, is not a true crab but is related to the spider. [singular neuter pronoun]
>
> ***Oysters*** and ***clams*** are becoming endangered because of oil spills near **their** breeding grounds. [plural pronoun]

Traditionally a masculine pronoun has been used when the gender of the antecedent is not known or may be either masculine or feminine.

> An ***author*** must capture **his** readers' interest.

This usage has changed, however. Many people now prefer to use gender-neutral wording. If you do not wish to use a masculine pronoun when the antecedent may be feminine, you can frequently reword the sentence in one of three ways: (1) by using *he or she, his or her,* and so forth, (2) by using a plural pronoun, or (3) by eliminating the pronoun.

> An ***author*** must capture **his or her** readers' interest.
>
> ***Authors*** must capture **their** readers' interest.
>
> ***Authors*** must capture readers' interest. [no pronoun]

640   Unit 17   Using Pronouns Correctly

Agreement in Person

■ A pronoun must agree in person with its antecedent.

Many problems with agreement in person arise when the second-person pronoun *you* is used incorrectly to refer to an antecedent in the third person. Either change *you* to an appropriate third-person pronoun, or replace it with a suitable noun.

POOR	Suki and James are going to visit the Everglades, where ~~you~~ can see storks and alligators.
BETTER	Suki and James are going to visit the Everglades, where **they** can see storks and alligators.
BETTER	Suki and James are going to visit the Everglades, where **tourists** can see storks and alligators.

When the antecedent of a pronoun is another pronoun, be sure that the two pronouns agree in person. Avoid unnecessary shifts from *they* to *you*, *I* to *you*, or *one* to *you*.

POOR	**They** often visit New Orleans, where ~~you~~ can enjoy French cooking.
BETTER	**They** often visit New Orleans, where **they** can enjoy French cooking.
POOR	**I** hiked on trails that amazed ~~you~~ with their beauty.
BETTER	**I** hiked on trails that amazed **me** with their beauty.
POOR	When **one** travels, ~~you~~ can learn a lot.
BETTER	When **one** travels, **one** can learn a lot.
BETTER	When **you** travel, **you** can learn a lot.

Exercise 11   Making Pronouns and Antecedents Agree

Complete the following sentences by writing an appropriate possessive pronoun in each blank. Then write the antecedent for each pronoun that you supply.

Sarah Winnemucca, a Piute Spokeswoman

[1]Sarah Winnemucca, the daughter of a Piute chief, was taken by _____ grandfather to California in 1850. [2]Some years later, after she had learned English and Spanish, she moved to Nevada and worked for a stagecoach agent and _____ wife and family. [3]When several bands of Piutes were forced off their ancestral land in the 1860s, Winnemucca served as _____ interpreter. [4]After lecturing in the East about the plight of her people, she moved to the town of Vancouver and taught in one of _____ schools for Native Americans. [5]Winnemucca's book *Life Among the Piutes* was a great success, and it has added to _____ understanding as Americans of an important chapter in Native American history.

Exercise 12 Making Pronouns and Antecedents Agree

In each of the following sentences, find the personal pronoun and its antecedent. If there is an error in agreement, rewrite the sentence in one or more ways to correct the problem. If there is no error, write *correct*.

Ethnic Cuisines

1. A cook who likes unusual food is in luck these days, for they can find plenty of ethnic recipes and special ingredients.
2. A lover of Japanese food can prepare their own shrimp or vegetable tempura.
3. Even an amateur chef can make their own pasta at home, using an electric or hand-cranked machine.
4. A person who is partial to Mexican food can concoct their own hot sauce with tomatoes, onions, and hot green peppers.
5. Shoppers can visit ethnic grocery shops, where they can purchase many hard-to-get ingredients, such as dried Chinese mushrooms, tortilla mix, collard greens, juniper berries, pine nuts, and litchi nuts.
6. People who crave a North African dish can purchase your own couscous and add morsels of meat or fish.
7. A seafood lover might want to try his luck at paella, a delicious Spanish dish that includes shrimp, clams, rice, and vegetables.
8. While sipping bouillabaisse, a fish stew, an American can imagine that they are sitting at a French café.
9. Food lovers can take cooking classes, where you will learn how to prepare lefse and other Norwegian foods.
10. Connoisseurs of ethnic foods know that they can distinguish an Italian meatball from a Swedish one by their different seasonings.

Exercise 13 Making Pronouns and Antecedents Agree in Person

On your paper, rewrite each of the following items, eliminating the inappropriate use of *you* by substituting a third-person pronoun or a suitable noun.

José Feliciano: A Success Story

1. Visually impaired people face more obstacles than the sighted, for you must be unusually self-reliant and persevering.
2. José Feliciano is a highly respected visually impaired musician. He grew up in Puerto Rico, where you had to struggle hard to get ahead.
3. When Feliciano was five, he and his family moved to New York, where you hoped to find better opportunities.
4. From his idol, Ray Charles, Feliciano learned that visually impaired people can succeed in the music business. You must learn to expect setbacks and disappointment, however.
5. Feliciano's fans praise his skillful guitar playing. They say that you can expect nothing less than the best from this disciplined musician.

Agreement with Indefinite Pronoun Antecedents

■ In general, use a singular personal pronoun when the antecedent is a singular indefinite pronoun, and use a plural personal pronoun when the antecedent is a plural indefinite pronoun.

Indefinite Pronouns				
ALWAYS SINGULAR	each	everyone	nobody	anything
	either	everybody	nothing	someone
	neither	everything	anyone	somebody
	one	no one	anybody	something
ALWAYS PLURAL	several	few	both	many
	others			
SINGULAR OR PLURAL	some	all	any	most
	none			

Each of the boys must buy **his** own uniform.
One of the women has **her** own diving equipment.
Many of the students bring **their** lunch to school.

Note that the plural nouns in the prepositional phrases—*of the boys, of the women*—do not affect the number of the personal pronouns. *His* and *her* are singular because *each* and *one,* their antecedents, are singular. In speaking, however, people often use the plural pronoun *their.*

| **INFORMAL** | **Neither** of the boys bought **their** own uniforms. |
| **FORMAL** | **Neither** of the boys bought **his** own uniform. |

When no gender is specified, use gender-neutral wording.

Everyone must buy **his or her** own uniform.

If you find the sentence above a bit awkward, you may want to reword the sentence. You might substitute a plural indefinite pronoun or a word such as *people* for the singular indefinite pronoun. Or you might eliminate the personal pronoun entirely.

All must buy **their** own uniforms.
People must buy **their** own uniforms.
Everyone must buy a uniform. [no pronoun]

Exercise 14 — Making Pronouns Agree with Indefinite Pronoun Antecedents

On your paper, indicate which of the following sentences are correct. Then revise each of the incorrect sentences to make it correct. In some cases, you will need to change a single word; in others you may wish to revise the entire sentence.

Native American Medicine

1. Many of the Native American nations relied on their shaman, or medicine man, to treat anyone who became ill.
2. All of the herbs in the shaman's collection had special curative powers of its own.
3. Many in the Dakota nation drank powdered skunk-cabbage roots to relieve his asthma.
4. Each of the women in the Cheyenne nation would gather their own stock of wild mint, which was used to treat nausea.
5. Everybody searched for natural remedies for their illnesses; the Cree people chewed the cones of the spruce tree to soothe sore throats.
6. Among the Kiowa, anybody with dandruff knew that their scalp should be washed with soaproot.
7. Some of the Utes treated his cuts and bruises with a salve made from the yarrow plant.
8. Many who lived on the frontier owed his life to natural cures.
9. Some of the pioneers ended their bouts with scurvy by eating wild garlic, a plant used by many Native American nations.
10. Today, few doctors question the curative powers of Native American medicines, and their respect for the shaman's remedies continues to grow.

Exercise 15 — Using Pronouns in Sentences

On your paper, complete each of the following sentences by writing a personal pronoun that agrees with its indefinite pronoun antecedent.

Early Native American Nations

1. Each of the Native American leaders spoke _____ own language.
2. Few of the Native Americans shared a language with _____ neighbors.
3. Each of the Inuit mothers dressed _____ children in fur parkas, while some children in more southern climates wore little clothing.
4. In some of the Native American nations, everybody carried _____ goods by canoe.
5. Many of the Great Plains groups hunted animals for _____ food.
6. Some of the other Plains nations developed _____ farming skills.
7. Everyone worked hard harvesting _____ crops.
8. Some of the Native Americans in the Southwest foraged for food, and acorns were a mainstay of _____ diet.
9. Many who lived in the Southwest made _____ homes of adobe.
10. In some nations, each of the men had to support _____ own family, while in other nations, resources were shared.

17.6 Clear Pronoun Reference

■ Make sure that the antecedent of a pronoun is clearly stated and that a pronoun cannot possibly refer to more than one antecedent.

Vague Pronoun Reference

Do not use the pronouns *this, that, which,* and *it* without a clearly stated antecedent.

VAGUE	She is an excellent singer, and **this** was evident in the performance last night. [What showed in the performance? Her talent showed, but the word *talent* is not specifically mentioned.]
CLEAR	She is an excellent singer, and **her talent** was evident in the performance last night.
VAGUE	The senator loved public speaking, and **that** greatly helped boost his popularity. [What helped boost his popularity? His speeches did, but the word *speeches* is not specifically mentioned.]
CLEAR	The senator loved public speaking, and **his speeches** greatly helped boost his popularity.
VAGUE	Last week our garage burned, **which** started from a kerosene heater. [What started from a kerosene heater? A fire started, but the word *fire* is not specifically mentioned.]
CLEAR	Last week a fire, **which** started from a kerosene heater, burned our garage.
VAGUE	The Supreme Court is deliberating on the question of the death penalty, and **it** will have a great impact on the nation. [What will have a great impact? The Supreme Court's decision will, but the word *decision* is not specifically mentioned.]
CLEAR	The Supreme Court is deliberating on the question of the death penalty, and the court's **decision** will have a great impact on the nation.

Using Pronouns Correctly

Ambiguous and Indefinite Pronoun Reference

If a pronoun seems to refer to more than one antecedent, either reword the sentence to make the antecedent clear or eliminate the pronoun.

UNCLEAR ANTECEDENT	When the tickets slipped between the reports, **they** were lost. [Which word is the antecedent of *they*? Were the tickets or the reports lost?]
CLEAR ANTECEDENT	The tickets were lost when **they** slipped between the reports.
NO PRONOUN	When the tickets slipped between the reports, **the tickets** were lost.

Avoid the indefinite use of the pronouns *you* and *they*.

INDEFINITE	In Japan **you** bow after saying hello.
CLEAR	In Japan **people** bow after saying hello.
INDEFINITE	In some countries **they** take a nap after lunch.
CLEAR	In some countries **people** take a nap after lunch.

Exercise 16 — Making Pronouns References Clear

For each sentence, determine whether the antecedent of the italicized pronoun is clear or unclear. If the antecedent is unclear, rewrite the sentence to make it clear. You may need to reword the sentence or eliminate the pronoun. If the antecedent is clear, write *clear*.

France

1. France is the largest country of western Europe, and *it* is quite beautiful and historic.
2. France has sunny beaches, *which* stretch along the Mediterranean Sea.
3. Their delicious food and wine are important to the French, and *they* are often considered the best in the world.
4. In France *they* really know how to enjoy life.
5. France also plays an important role in world politics, and *this* affects many other countries.
6. Paris is the capital of France, and *it* is also the country's largest city.
7. Paris has been home to many of the world's best artists, and *this* is reflected in the number of masterpieces that have been painted there.
8. When writers and artists arrive in Paris, *they* immediately fall in love with the city.
9. Paris is both cultured and beautiful, *which* impressed American writers Ernest Hemingway and Gertrude Stein.
10. Hemingway met the popular writer F. Scott Fitzgerald in Paris, and *he* helped *him* get his stories published.

Exercise 17 — Making Pronoun References Clear

On your paper, rewrite each of the following sentences, making sure that all pronoun references are clearly stated.

Politics

1. The governor told the mayor that she would win by a landslide.
2. When the mayor thanked the governor, she was happy.
3. People who wish to vote must get to the polling places before 7:00 P.M., for after that you are turned away.
4. A citizens' group charged that the elections had been fixed, and it angered the officials.
5. The newspaper's editors criticized the politicians, and they argued for full disclosure of the facts.
6. The activists said that some of the politicians in the city had accepted bribes; this was a scandal.
7. Eric's father was mayor of the city, which gave him considerable social status.
8. When several of the newspapers disclosed the mayor's actions, it caused a great decline in his prestige.
9. The city council member told the newspaper reporter that he had manipulated the coverage of the election.
10. The early election returns pleased the senator, which had been widely predicted.

Exercise 18 — Using Pronouns Correctly

On your paper, rewrite each of the following sentences by eliminating any mistakes in the use of pronouns. Each sentence has one error.

Sports Jargon

1. Sportscasters and us use sports jargon frequently.
2. A word that means one thing in ordinary conversation sometimes changes it's meaning when applied to sports.
3. Anyone who watches tennis knows that you call an unreturned serve an ace.
4. The same word is used in golf, which refers to a hole in one.
5. In baseball a bean ball is a pitch thrown so near a batter's head that you're in danger of being hit.
6. The batter must watch each ball carefully and determine it's speed and position.
7. We watched Roger Clemens pitch three shutouts in a row, and him pitching so well seemed almost miraculous to us.
8. The word *eagle* is familiar to my friends and I.
9. No one was more surprised than me to learn that in golf the word *eagle* means "two strokes under par."
10. I always thought I knew sports, but it was her who first made me especially aware of sports jargon.

17.6 Clear Pronoun Reference **647**

UNIT 17 Grammar Review

USING PRONOUNS CORRECTLY

In this passage from *The Old Man and the Sea*, an aging Cuban fisher named Santiago sets out for his day's work after eighty-four days without a catch. A young boy named Manolín has come to see him off. The passage has been annotated to show examples of the kinds of pronouns covered in this unit.

Literature Model

from *The Old Man and the Sea*
by Ernest Hemingway

The boy was back now with the sardines and the two baits wrapped in a newspaper and they went down the trail to the skiff, feeling the pebbled sand under *their* feet, and lifted the skiff and slid her into the water.

"Good luck old man."

"Good luck," the old man said. He fitted the rope lashings of the oars onto the thole pins and, leaning forward against the thrust of the blades in the water, he began to row out of the harbor in the dark. There were other boats from the other beaches going out to sea and the old man heard the dip and push of their oars even though he could not see *them* now the moon was below the hills.

Sometimes someone would speak in a boat. But most of the boats were silent except for the dip of the oars. *They* spread apart after they were out of the mouth of the harbor and each one headed for the part of the ocean where he hoped to find fish. The old man knew *he* was going far out and he left the smell of the land behind and rowed out into the clean early morning smell of the ocean. He saw the phosphorescence of the Gulf weed in the water as he rowed over the part of the ocean that the fishermen called the great well because there was a sudden deep of seven hundred fathoms where all sorts of fish congregated because of the swirl the current made

Annotations:
- **Pronoun in the possessive case**
- **The pronoun *them* in the objective case is used as a direct object. The pronoun agrees in number with its antecedent, *boats*.**
- **Pronoun in the nominative case used as a subject**
- **The pronoun in the nominative case used as a subject agrees in gender and number with its antecedent, *the old man*.**

648 Unit 17 Using Pronouns Correctly

Grammar Review

against the steep walls of the floor of the ocean. Here there were concentrations of shrimp and bait fish and sometimes schools of squid in the deepest holes and these rose close to the surface at night where all the wandering fish fed on *them.*

In the dark the old man could feel the morning coming and as he rowed he heard the trembling sound as flying fish left the water and the hissing that their stiff set wings made as they soared away in the darkness. He was very fond of flying fish as *they* were his principal friends on the ocean. He was sorry for the birds, especially the small delicate dark terns that were always flying and looking and almost never finding, and he thought, the birds have a harder life than we do except for the robber birds and the heavy strong ones. Why did they make birds so delicate and fine as those sea swallows when the ocean can be so cruel? She is kind and very beautiful. But she can be so cruel and it comes so suddenly and such birds that fly, dipping and hunting, with their small sad voices are made too delicately for the sea.

He always thought of the sea as *la mar* which is what people call her in Spanish when they love her. Sometimes those *who* love her say bad things of her but they are always said as though she were a woman.

Pronoun in the objective case used as the object of a preposition

The pronoun *they* in the nominative case is used as a subject. The pronoun agrees with its antecedent, the irregular plural *fish*.

The pronoun *who* in the nominative case is used as the subject of *love*.

Using Pronouns Correctly

Review: Exercise 1 — Choosing Nominative and Objective Pronouns

The following sentences give background information on the passage from *The Old Man and the Sea*. For each sentence, determine whether the italicized nominative or objective pronoun is used correctly. If it is not, on your paper write the pronoun as it should appear. If it is used properly, write *correct*.

1. The boy and Santiago had worked together for many years, but now Santiago and *him* would no longer be able to fish together.
2. The boy's parents had made it clear that *they* disapproved of his working with the unlucky old fisher.
3. It was *him* who had brought supper the previous night for the old man and himself to share.
4. Forgetting his parents, the boy had decided, "It is *us* who will eat supper together this evening."
5. Martin, the owner of a nearby restaurant, had kindly provided the supper for Santiago and *he*.

Grammar Review

Review: Exercise 2   **Choosing the Correct Pronoun Case**

The following sentences give background information on the passage from *The Old Man and the Sea*. Determine whether the italicized pronoun is used correctly. If it is not, write the correct pronoun on your paper. If it is used correctly, write *correct*.

1. Santiago stood by the boat with the other fishers as the fisher and *him* prepared to leave.
2. By *him* fitting the ropes onto the thole pins, the old man secured the boat's oars.
3. Other fishers were near, and Santiago could hear them rowing, although he could not see their boats or *them*.
4. It was *him* who would catch a fish so huge that it would astonish the other fishers.
5. The ocean suddenly became deep, and *it's* current made a deep swirl over the well in the ocean floor.
6. Santiago seemed to realize the ocean was beautiful, but the ocean was also cruel to wildlife and men like *he*.
7. The old man watched the terns and thought, "The gulls and terns have a harder life than *me*."
8. He also pitied the sea swallows, and the sad voices he heard were *their's*.
9. Santiago landed a huge marlin, but *it's* size was a challenge.
10. After sharks bit the marlin's head, Santiago thought the fish was now *theirs* and his.

Review: Exercise 3   **Using Pronouns Correctly with and as Appositives**

The following sentences are based on passages from *The Old Man and the Sea* not reprinted in this textbook. For each sentence, determine whether the italicized pronoun appears in the proper form. If it does not, write the correct pronoun on your paper. If it is used properly, write *correct*.

1. The restaurant owner sometimes fed the two fishers, the boy and *he*.
2. The two early risers, Santiago and *him*, quietly left the hut and went to the boat.
3. Joe DiMaggio was a great athlete; apparently Santiago's idols were two baseball players, Dick Sisler and *him*.
4. While at sea, Santiago caught a dolphin with two fish in its stomach; such catches, *they* and a tuna, were his only food.
5. Santiago loved the terns and often watched two groups of birds, *they* and the swallows.
6. Santiago hooked a marlin that attracted sharks; he had to contend with two powerful species, the marlin and *them*.
7. The other fishers, the boy and *them*, felt sad at the sight of Santiago's poor marlin.
8. The boy might have decided, "Now we will again be partners, Santiago and *me*."
9. He thought, "The villagers, the other fishers and *me*, have never seen such a fish."
10. Tourists showed interest in the fish, but no onlookers, not *them* or the fishers, could fully understand Santiago's experience.

Grammar Review

Review: Exercise 4   **Using Pronouns After *Than* and *As***

The following sentences are based on passages from *The Old Man and the Sea*. Each sentence contains an italicized word or group of words. On your paper, rewrite each sentence, substituting the correct pronoun for the word or words in italics.

1. Still, the other fishers caught more fish than *Santiago*.
2. They did not even go as far out as *the old man*.
3. The boy might have concluded, "Santiago is braver than *the other fishers*."
4. Not caring as much for the other fishers as he did for Santiago, the boy helped Santiago more than *the others*.
5. The old man rowed as steadily as *the younger fishers*.
6. Later Santiago would seem to vow to the marlin, "You are not as strong as *Santiago*."
7. Although the sea could be cruel to humans, Santiago reflected that it seemed more cruel to birds than to *his fellow human beings*.
8. The sea swallows searched as hard for food as *the terns*.
9. Watching the ocean's ceaseless waves, Santiago wondered whether anything was as cruel as *the ocean*.
10. Did he love anything else as much as *the ocean*?

Review: Exercise 5   **Making Pronouns and Antecedents Agree**

Each of the following sentences about terns contains an example of pronoun-antecedent agreement. On your paper, rewrite each sentence, replacing the word or words in italics with the word or words in parentheses and changing the pronouns if necessary. In some cases, you will also have to change the form of the verb and other words in the sentence.

1. *These sea birds* make tropical and semitropical islands their habitat. (This sea bird)
2. *The male tern* grooms the female's face as part of his courtship. (Male terns)
3. As *people* watch the terns, their wonder at the birds' behavior increases. (we)
4. Because *females* build no nest, their eggs may appear in odd, even unsuitable, places. (the female)
5. The *mother* often lays her egg on the edge of a roof or in the fork of a tree. (mothers)
6. *Both* of the parent birds take their turn tending the egg. (Each)
7. *Fairy tern eggs* hatch thirty-four days after they are laid. (A fairy tern egg)
8. *Many* of the parents leave their young untended for hours while they search for food. (Some)
9. *A flying fish* sometimes finds itself in the throat of a hungry tern. (Flying fish)
10. *Chicks* may fall while their parents are gone. (A chick)

Grammar Review   **651**

Grammar Review

Review: Exercise 6 **Choosing *Who* or *Whom***

On your paper, write the correct pronoun from the pair in parentheses.

1. When Columbus reached Cuba in 1492, he encountered the Taino, (who/whom) he discovered were farmers.
2. (Who/Whom) did the Spanish Crown appoint to conquer Cuba?
3. The mountains helped hide the natives, (who/whom) the Spanish treated harshly.
4. The Taino population, to (who/whom) European diseases proved deadly, became greatly reduced.
5. Enslaved Africans, (who/whom) the Spaniards wished to use for mining gold, were imported in 1524.
6. The enslaved people, (who/whom) the plantation owners bought, toiled long hours in sugarcane and coffee fields.
7. Hernán Cortés, (who/whom) we know conquered Mexico, used Cuba as a base for his expeditions.
8. (Who/Whom) did you say established Havana as an important port?
9. Ports like Havana offered recreation for sailors, (who/whom) the natives entertained with African drums and Spanish guitars.
10. At sea many dangers threatened these sailors, (who/whom) pirates attacked regularly for their ships' gold.
11. Tobacco growers, (who/whom) the Spanish government regulated, rebelled unsuccessfully as early as 1717.
12. (Who/Whom) did you say told you that the name *criollos* refers to people of Spanish descent?
13. In Haiti enslaved people, (who/whom) the American Revolution inspired, rebelled and set up a free republic.
14. Enslaved Cubans, (who/whom) the government freed in 1880, revolted several times between 1812 and 1840.
15. Chinese laborers, (who/whom) nervous landowners recruited, added a new ethnic group to the Cuban population.
16. Cubans, (who/whom) Indian, Spanish, African, and Chinese cultures have influenced, share a colorful heritage.
17. In 1895 revolutionary armies, (who/whom) were led by José Martí, demanded Cuba's independence from Spain.
18. American investors, for (who/whom) an independent Cuba would be profitable, rejoiced when America aided the revolutionaries.
19. Cuban independence in 1898 attracted the attention of American businesspeople, (who/whom) invested heavily in Cuba for nearly sixty years.
20. Nonetheless, peasant classes, to (who/whom) fishers like Santiago belonged, continued to live in poverty.

Grammar Review

Review: Exercise 7   **Making Pronouns and Antecedents Agree**

The following sentences are about Hemingway's characters. Each sentence contains an example of pronoun-antecedent agreement. Rewrite the sentences according to the directions in parentheses, changing the pronouns if necessary. In some cases, you will also have to change the verb and other words.

SAMPLE   Sports enthusiasts have compared their true experiences to Santiago's fictional one. (Change *Sports enthusiasts* to *A sports enthusiast*.)

ANSWER   A sports enthusiast has compared his or her true experiences to Santiago's fictional one.

1. Cuban fishers have described their own struggles with a large fish. (Change *Cuban fishers* to *A Cuban fisher*.)
2. In these stories, a marlin has fought as long as fifteen hours before it was caught. (Change *a marlin* to *a few marlins*.)
3. Two of Hemingway's skippers have stated their ideas about the true identity of Santiago. (Change *Two* to *Each*.)
4. Are some of the real people who found their way into Hemingway's fiction famous? (Change *some* to *any*.)
5. In fact, readers find themselves drawn to Hemingway's characters because they seem so real. (Change *readers* to *we*.)
6. Have all of Hemingway's wives seen reflections of themselves in his female characters? (Change *all* to *each*.)
7. Any veteran of war might recognize his or her own feelings in Hemingway's soldiers. (Change *Any veteran* to *Veterans*.)
8. All people must fight personal obstacles to maintain their self-respect. (Change *All people* to *Everyone*.)
9. Hemingway characters show their valor amidst violence. (Change *Hemingway characters* to *A Hemingway character*.)
10. The stories, with their familiar conflicts, help us understand real life. (Change *The stories* to *Each story*.)
11. Does any character in the Nick Adams stories take his likes and dislikes from Hemingway's own personality? (Change *any character* to *the characters*.)
12. Did Hemingway's friends in Europe live their lives as desperately as the characters in *The Sun Also Rises*? (Change *friends* to *best friend*.)
13. Did someone like Catherine in *A Farewell to Arms* actually exert her influence on Hemingway's life? (Change *someone* to *women*.)
14. Consider the narrator in *For Whom the Bell Tolls*—does his experience reflect Hemingway's own experiences? (Change *narrator* to *characters*.)
15. It is clear that Hemingway created vivid characters because he wrote about people and situations he knew. (Change *Hemingway* to *both Hemingway and Fitzgerald*.)

Using Pronouns Correctly

Grammar Review   **653**

Grammar Review

Review: Exercise 8   **Making Pronoun References Clear**

The following sentences give background information on the passage from *The Old Man and the Sea*. Each sentence contains an unclear pronoun reference. On your paper, rewrite each sentence to make the pronoun reference clear. In some cases, you will need to reword the sentence or eliminate the pronoun.

1. Santiago's wife had died years ago, and that must have been a source of almost unbearable pain.
2. Santiago removed his wife's picture from the wall, which made him sad.
3. The boy and the old fisher enjoyed spending time together, and he sometimes ignored his parents' objections.
4. One day while Santiago was talking with the boy, he spoke of his love of fishing.
5. Santiago finally got the huge marlin into his boat, but it had been severely damaged by sharks.

Review: Exercise 9

Proofreading

The following passage describes the artist Winslow Homer, whose painting appears on the opposite page. Rewrite the passage, correcting the errors in spelling, grammar, and usage. Add any missing punctuation. There are twenty-five errors.

Winslow Homer

¹Winslow Homer (1836–1910) were one of America's finest watercolorists. ²Born in Boston, Massachusetts, him, along with his family, moved to the town of Cambridge when he was six. ³Growing up with his two brothers in the country Homer learned to love the outdoors. ⁴This interest in nature preoccupied him for much of their life.

⁵For the first seventen years of his long career, Homer supported himself by doing illustrations for periodicals, including *Ballou's Pictorial* and *Harper's Weekly*. ⁶During the four years of the Civil War, it was him who *Harper's Weekly* sent to the front lines in Virginia, where he drawed many illustrations of battle scenes.

⁷Homer's training in illustration enables him to depict dramatic scenes naturally and unsentimentally. ⁸His masterful draftsmanship allowed him to create a clear and honest record of landscapes and people as he saw it.

⁹After the war was over, Homer begun to exhibit his paintings, and them were very well received. ¹⁰When he reached his late thirties, he begun making

Grammar Review

Winslow Homer, *Palm Trees, Nassau*, 1898

watercolors directly from nature. [11]His' watercolors are forceful, direct, and saturated with pure color. [12]It was later in life that she began to paint large and powerful canvases of the sea. [13]No American painter is more closely associated with scenes of the sea than him.

[14]*Palm Trees, Nassau* is charateristic of Homers' late watercolors. [15]The casual observer may see an apparently simple nature scene, but looking closer, you can see the tension between the calm setting and the coming storm. [16]The trees bend in the rising wind, clouds scud acros the sky, and a red flag (possibly signaling an oncoming hurricane) flutters near the lighthouse.

[17]*The Old Man and the Sea* is about an old Cuban fisher whom is confronted with the great power of nature. [18]In the passage from the novel reprinted in this textbook, Hemingway hinting at the seas ominous power. [19]He write, "She is kind and very beautiful. But she can be so cruel. . . ." [20]Homers watercolor also evokes this insight.

Grammar Review

Review: Exercise 10

Mixed Review

Each of the following sentences describes aspects of Hemingway's life and work. For each sentence, choose the proper pronoun from the pair in parentheses and write it on your paper.

Ernest Hemingway

1. Ernest Hemingway, (who/whom) we know was one of America's finest writers, was born in Oak Park, Illinois, in 1899.
2. Hemingway's numerous sports activities were balanced by (him/his) playing the cello and writing for his school newspaper.
3. His father was an outdoors enthusiast, and the two of them, (he/him) and Ernest, often took fishing trips to Michigan.
4. It was (he/him) who discouraged Hemingway from enlisting in the army when the United States entered World War I.
5. While driving an ambulance in the war, Hemingway received a wound that might have killed a man who was weaker than (he/him).
6. In Paris after the war, Hemingway met F. Scott Fitzgerald and Gertrude Stein, both of (who/whom) influenced him.
7. These young writers, Fitzgerald and (he/him), were part of what Stein called the Lost Generation.
8. A friendship also grew up between the writer Sherwood Anderson and (he/him).
9. The Lost Generation writers found the politics and morality of (its/their) society destroyed by war.
10. (Who/Whom) would you say is the most admirable character in *The Sun Also Rises*, Hemingway's first novel?
11. Several pieces of Hemingway's writing have found (its/their) way into movies.
12. Everybody has (his or her/their) favorite Hemingway novel.
13. Hemingway, (who/whom) many know was a journalist, wrote in a spare style.
14. He and his third wife bought a home in Cuba in 1940; the couple, Ernest and (she/her), entertained many celebrities.
15. Some of these celebrities remember adventures they had with Hemingway—for example, (their/them) watching bullfights in Spain and hunting in Africa.
16. This lifestyle appealed less to Hemingway's third wife than to (he/him), and the marriage failed.
17. His wartime experiences as an ambulance driver and as a news correspondent had (its/their) own profound effects on Hemingway's fiction.
18. Hemingway, (who/whom) Cuba fascinated, stayed in this tropical country even after Castro gained control in 1958.
19. *The Old Man and the Sea,* a best-seller in 1952, led to (his/him) winning the Pulitzer and Nobel prizes.
20. In the years following Hemingway's death in 1961, the novel has retained (its/it's) immense popularity.

Writing Application

Pronouns in Writing

In the following excerpt from *Great Expectations* by Charles Dickens, the narrator, Pip, is discussing two other characters, Mr. Jaggers and Mr. Pocket. Examine the passage closely, noting the many italicized masculine pronouns. Focus especially on how Dickens avoids unclear pronoun references.

My guardian took me into *his* room, and while *he* lunched, standing, from a sandwich-box and a pocket flask of sherry (*he* seemed to bully *his* very sandwich as *he* ate it), informed me what arrangements *he* had made for me. I was to go to "Barnard's Inn," to young Mr. Pocket's rooms, where a bed had been sent in for my accommodation; I was to remain with young Mr. Pocket until Monday; on Monday I was to go with *him* to *his* father's house on a visit, that I might try how I liked it.

Techniques with Pronouns

Try to apply some of Charles Dickens's writing techniques when you write and revise your own work.

① Avoid confusion by keeping pronoun references clear. Compare the following:

UNCLEAR REFERENCE I was to remain with *him* . . .

DICKENS'S VERSION I was to remain with *young Mr. Pocket* . . .

② When you revise sentences containing many pronouns, make sure that each pronoun has a clear antecedent.

UNCLEAR REFERENCE I was to go to "Barnard's Inn," to *his* rooms . . .

DICKENS'S VERSION I was to go to Barnard's Inn, to young *Mr. Pocket's* rooms . . .

> **TIME**
> For more about the writing process, see **TIME *Facing the Blank Page,*** pp. 121-131.

Practice Practice these techniques by revising the following passage, using a separate sheet of paper. Eliminate confusion by making the unclear pronoun references clear. Make sure each pronoun has a clear antecedent.

The young child sat cuddled on her grandmother's wide lap, as she rocked the old oak chair back and forth. She loved swaying with her. Wonderful scents wafted past her delicate little nose on the shifting breeze created by the rocking motion. She easily detected the pungent scent of garlic. Had she helped herself to a generous serving of her famous calzones? (Nobody could refuse her spicy creations, and especially not she, who succumbed easily to all cheesy, tomatoey foods.) Less obvious was the almost sterile scent of her heavily starched dress, which she was careful to iron each morning. Her grandmother had an awful impatience with anything less than perfection, a fact that the young girl on her lap knew only too well.

UNIT 18 Using Modifiers Correctly

Lesson 18.1	**The Three Degrees of Comparison**	*659*
Lesson 18.2	**Irregular Comparisons**	*661*
Lesson 18.3	**Double Comparisons**	*663*
Lesson 18.4	**Incomplete Comparisons**	*665*
Lesson 18.5	*Good* or *Well; Bad* or *Badly*	*666*
Lesson 18.6	**Double Negatives**	*668*
Lesson 18.7	**Misplaced and Dangling Modifiers**	*670*

Grammar Review *676*

Writing Application *685*

18.1 The Three Degrees of Comparison

Most adjectives and adverbs have three degrees: the positive, or base, form; the comparative form; and the superlative form.

- The **positive** form of a modifier cannot be used to make a comparison. (This form appears as the entry word in a dictionary.)
- The **comparative** form of a modifier shows two things being compared.
- The **superlative** form of a modifier shows three or more things being compared.

POSITIVE	My cousin is **tall**. The cat ran **swiftly**.
COMPARATIVE	My cousin is **taller** than I am. My dog ran **more swiftly** than the cat.
SUPERLATIVE	Of the three cousins, Paula is **tallest**. The rat ran **most swiftly** of all.

She ran **swiftly**.

She ran **more swiftly**.

She ran **most swiftly** of all.

The following rules will guide you in forming the comparative and superlative degrees of adjectives and adverbs:

In general, for one-syllable modifiers add *-er* to form the comparative and *-est* to form the superlative.

green, green**er**, green**est**
The neighbor's grass always looks **greener** than ours.

loud, loud**er**, loud**est**
That sonic boom is the **loudest** noise I've ever heard.

fast, fast**er**, fast**est**
Her hair grows **faster** than mine.

In some cases adding *-er* and *-est* requires spelling changes.

big, bi**gger**, bi**ggest**   true, tru**er**, tru**est**
hot, ho**tter**, ho**ttest**   dry, dr**ier**, dr**iest**

With some one-syllable modifiers, it may sound more natural to use *more* and *most*.

just, **more** just, **most** just
Of the three, that judge's ruling was the **most just** of all.

Using Modifiers Correctly

For most two-syllable adjectives, add *-er* to form the comparative and *-est* to form the superlative.

>ugly, ugl**ier,** ugl**iest**
>Your mask is **uglier** than mine.
>That is the **ugliest** mask I've ever seen.

If *-er* and *-est* sound awkward with a two-syllable adjective, use *more* and *most*.

>afraid, **more** afraid, **most** afraid
>No one is **more afraid** of spiders than I am.
>Of all of us, I was the **most afraid.**

For adverbs ending in *-ly*, always use *more* and *most* to form the comparative and superlative degrees.

>clearly, **more** clearly, **most** clearly
>Lewis gives directions **more clearly** than most people.
>This candidate explains his views **most clearly** of all.

For modifiers of three or more syllables, always use *more* and *most* to form the comparative and superlative degrees.

>attractive, **more** attractive, **most** attractive
>I think red looks **more attractive** on you than on me.
>That watercolor is the **most attractive** one in the exhibit.

Less and *least,* the opposite of *more* and *most,* can also be used with most modifiers to show comparison.

>Are prepared foods **less economical** than fresh foods?
>I think cabbage is the **least appetizing** of all vegetables.

Exercise 1 **Identifying Comparisons**

In the following sentences, identify the adjectives and adverbs, and write them on a separate sheet of paper. Then write *positive, comparative,* or *superlative* to indicate the degree of comparison.

The Blues

1. A talented blues band can play more softly than a hard-rock band.
2. The slow blues, to my way of thinking, sound the sweetest of all.
3. The sadder the lyrics, the more mellow the melody becomes.
4. The vocalist tells the tale of woe most clearly when the trumpet's tone becomes less strident.
5. Then the most emotional mood is created out of songs that describe the least fortunate circumstances.

18.2 Irregular Comparisons

A few modifiers form their comparative and superlative degrees irregularly. It is most helpful simply to memorize their forms.

Modifiers with Irregular Forms of Comparison

POSITIVE	COMPARATIVE	SUPERLATIVE
good	better	(the) best
well	better	(the) best
bad	worse	(the) worst
badly	worse	(the) worst
ill	worse	(the) worst
far (distance)	farther	(the) farthest
far (degree, time)	further	(the) furthest
little (amount)	less	(the) least
many	more	(the) most
much	more	(the) most

Exercise 2 Making Correct Comparisons

On another sheet of paper, complete the following sentences by writing the correct degree of comparison of the modifier in parentheses.

SAMPLE Which vegetable tastes the _____ of all? (good)
ANSWER best

Space and Space Exploration

1. Are there _____ planets in our solar system than the nine we know about? (many)
2. The distance between Venus and Earth is _____ than that between Mars and Earth. (little)
3. Mercury has the _____ mass of all the planets. (little)
4. The _____ planet from the sun is Pluto. (far)
5. *Voyager I* did a _____ job of photographing Jupiter than its predecessor. (good)
6. One of the _____ space catastrophes ever was the destruction of the *Challenger* spacecraft in 1986. (bad)
7. Of all the descriptions of the motion of the planets, that of the seventeenth-century astronomer Johannes Kepler is the _____. (good)
8. There are _____ celestial bodies in the Milky Way than just our solar system. (many)
9. Some asteroids have diameters of _____ than 120 miles. (much)
10. A comet, with its bright head and glowing tail, is one of the _____ astronomical sights you will ever see. (good)

Exercise 3 — Making Correct Comparisons

On another sheet of paper, complete the following sentences by writing the correct degree of comparison of the modifier in parentheses.

SAMPLE *The Joy Luck Club* is one of the _____ novels I have ever read. (interesting)
ANSWER most interesting

1. *The Joy Luck Club* is an entertaining book, and it is _____ to read than many other contemporary novels. (easy)
2. The novel is by Amy Tan, perhaps the _____ voice in contemporary Asian American fiction. (lively)
3. *The Joy Luck Club* is a _____ book than some that have recently been on the best-seller list. (long)
4. Maxine Wong is another talented Asian American writer, although Amy Tan is _____ than Wong. (famous)
5. In the book the members of the Joy Luck Club do many things, but their _____ activity is playing mah-jongg. (frequent)
6. Though she is _____ experienced than the other club members, June Woo is asked to join the mah-jongg game. (little)
7. Though mah-jongg resembles rummy, it is _____. (complicated)
8. In my opinion it relies _____ on strategy than rummy does. (much)
9. Most people believe, however, that chess is still the _____ of all board games. (challenging)
10. Even so, one can play chess _____ than mah-jongg. (quickly)
11. The club members, who are June's unofficial aunts, are _____ than June and observe traditional Chinese customs. (old)
12. At first June is _____ to be with friends her own age than she is to be playing games with her aging aunts. (happy)
13. The aunts are the _____ of all when they are reminiscing about their years in China. (content)
14. China seems even _____ away for June than it does for her aunts, for whom China is a distant memory. (far)
15. Eventually, though, June learns that the _____ decision of all would be to abandon her Chinese heritage completely. (bad)
16. From all the aspects of her Chinese heritage, it seems that June learns to accept only the _____. (good)
17. The ethnic roots of many Americans are _____ than June's. (remote)
18. Many of us would have to go much _____ back in time to recapture information about our ancestors. (far)
19. Researching, tracing, and studying one's genealogy has become a _____ pursuit than it once was. (popular)
20. There are some people who will travel to the _____ corners of the earth to trace their family histories. (far)

18.3 Double Comparisons

Do not make a double comparison by using both *-er* or *-est* and *more* or *most*.

INCORRECT A redwood grows more taller than an oak.
CORRECT A redwood grows taller than an oak.

INCORRECT Aunt Rosa is my most kindest aunt.
CORRECT Aunt Rosa is my kindest aunt.

INCORRECT He will visit us more oftener in the fall.
CORRECT He will visit us more often in the fall.

Exercise 4 Correcting Double Comparisons

Rewrite each of the following sentences, correcting the double comparison.

Thomas Edison, Inventor

1. Many people believe that Thomas Alva Edison was the world's most best inventor.
2. Some people consider him even more greater than Leonardo da Vinci.
3. The phonograph and the electric light are probably Edison's most usefulest creations.
4. Edison was most happiest with his phonograph.
5. He was most proudest of his work on the electric light.
6. Electric light is certainly more safer than candlelight.
7. Edison also took others' inventions, such as the telephone and the typewriter, and made them more better.
8. As a boy, Edison was more curiouser than other children.
9. He worked more harder and longer than his peers.
10. Historians agree that Edison was one of the most fruitfulest inventors of modern times.
11. After electric lights were invented, nights seemed more brighter.
12. People could read or do chores more longer after dark.
13. Before the phonograph was invented, hearing great music was more difficulter.
14. The phonograph and the electric light, though expensive at first, became more cheaper as time went by.
15. Edison was blessed with a more quicker mind than most boys his age.
16. After only a few months of formal schooling, he entered the more wider world of work.
17. An illness caused him to become more harder of hearing than he had been before.
18. One of his most earliest inventions was a stock ticker for printing stock-exchange quotations.
19. A more later invention, the movie projector, aided the development of motion pictures.
20. During his lifetime, Edison patented over 1,000 inventions, the most greatest number ever recorded for one person.

Exercise 5 — Correcting Irregular and Double Comparisons

Rewrite each of the following sentences, correcting the comparisons.

Twins

1. Mother says that raising twins has been the goodest experience of her life.
2. When they were born, Laura weighed littler than Lonnie, but she soon caught up.
3. All of us children had sunny dispositions, but Lonnie's was the most cheerfulest.
4. Lonnie was always serene, even though his health was worser than it should have been.
5. When he got sick, Mother used to go through some of the baddest days of her life.
6. The higher his temperature rose, the more upsetter she became.
7. The worser he felt, the more time she devoted to him.
8. "Sometimes," she told us, "I would like to go farrer back in history to an era when people had more time to spend with their children."
9. Being the oldest, I tried to be the most good, but I made a lot of mistakes.
10. I could have found more frequenter opportunities to lend a hand.
11. As toddlers, the twins tried to see which one could wander more farther from home.
12. Mother or the babysitter would chase them for the gooder part of the morning.
13. We would have appreciated a lesser adventurouser spirit on the twins' part.
14. Mucher peace and quiet was what we wanted.
15. The most happiest day of our lives was the twins' first day of school.

Exercise 6 — Writing Correct Comparisons

On your paper, complete the following sentences by writing the correct degree of comparison of the modifier in parentheses. In two sentences you will use *less* or *least*.

Ethnic Cuisine

1. (Many) Americans than ever before are enjoying the pleasures of ethnic cuisine.
2. Mexican dishes are usually (spicy) than those prepared north of the border.
3. Mexican chilies run the gamut in flavor and appearance, but the habañero is the (spicy) one of all.
4. French food, with its emphasis on sauces and careful methods of preparation, is for some people the (elegant) of all the world's cuisines.
5. French recipes often call for (rich) ingredients, such as real butter and whole cream, than do American recipes.
6. Strangely enough, in spite of their eating habits, the French appear to be no (healthy) than Americans.
7. Mediterranean cultures—Italian, Spanish, Greek, Turkish, Moroccan—rely (heavily) on foods low in cholesterol than do other cuisines.
8. For many years Chinese food was the (popular) ethnic cuisine in our town, but now Mexican and Tex-Mex foods have more fans.
9. Chinese delicacies such as dim sum and Peking duck are (common) taste treats than the more ordinary chop suey and chow mein.
10. A quick look at the restaurant listings in the yellow pages will convince you that the (good) words to describe America's food preferences are ethnic and diverse.

18.4 Incomplete Comparisons

Do not make an incomplete or unclear comparison by omitting *other* or *else* when you compare a person or thing with the group of which it is a part.

UNCLEAR Mercury is closer to the sun than any planet in our solar system. [*Any planet* includes Mercury.]

CLEAR Mercury is closer to the sun than any **other** planet in our solar system.

UNCLEAR My aunt has more pets than anyone. [*Anyone* includes the aunt.]

CLEAR My aunt has more pets than anyone **else.**

Be sure your comparisons are between like things.

UNCLEAR The grace of a basketball player is more obvious than a baseball player. [The grace of a basketball player is being compared illogically with everything about a baseball player.]

CLEAR The grace of a basketball player is more obvious than **that of a baseball player.**

CLEAR The grace of a basketball player is more obvious **than a baseball player's.**

UNCLEAR The claws of a lion are sharper than a cat. [The claws of a lion are being compared illogically with everything about a cat.]

CLEAR The claws of a lion are sharper than **those of a cat.**

CLEAR The claws of a lion are sharper than **a cat's.**

Exercise 7   Making Complete Comparisons

Rewrite the following sentences to correct the incomplete comparison in each.

Historical Native American Dwellings

¹Native American homes of the past were just as varied as today. ²The buffalo-skin dwellings of the Plains groups were more portable than the Wichita. ³The design of the tepees of the Plains peoples was perhaps more ingenious than any design. ⁴Women were responsible for erecting the tepees, and they could do this faster than anyone. ⁵Many people think that the tepee was more beautiful than any Native American dwelling. ⁶The lodges of the Pawnees were warmer and sturdier than the Plains groups. ⁷Because the Pawnees did not move frequently, their homes were less portable than Native American dwellings. ⁸The Pueblo groups of New Mexico were probably cooler than anyone, for they lived in well-insulated buildings made of adobe. ⁹Some Pueblo dwellings were several stories high, like many city dwellers today. ¹⁰If I could, I would rather live in a tepee than any place.

18.5 *Good* or *Well*; *Bad* or *Badly*

Always use *good* as an adjective. *Well* may be used as an adverb of manner telling how ably or adequately something is done. *Well* also may be used as an adjective meaning "in good health."

> Blue is a **good** color for you. [adjective]
>
> You look **good** in blue. [adjective after a linking verb]
>
> You dress **well**. [adverb of manner]
>
> Aren't you feeling **well**? [adjective meaning "in good health"]

Always use *bad* as an adjective. Therefore, *bad* is used after a linking verb. Use *badly* as an adverb. *Badly* almost always follows an action verb.

> That was a **bad** idea. [adjective]
>
> The milk tasted **bad**. [adjective following a linking verb]
>
> I feel **bad** about your moving to another state. [adjective following a linking verb]
>
> The faucet is leaking **badly**. [adverb following an action verb]

Exercise 8 Correcting Errors with *Good, Well, Bad,* and *Badly*

If a sentence contains an error with *good, well, bad,* or *badly,* on your paper write the form that should have been used. If a sentence is correct, write *correct*.

SAMPLE Marisa did bad on her algebra test.
ANSWER badly

1. "You'll do good on your tests if you will just remember to study," my mother always tells me.
2. "That's easy for you to say," I always answer. "You were always a good student."
3. I don't feel good enough to study because of this headache.
4. My mother feels badly that I am ill.
5. "Would a little chicken soup taste good to you today?" she inquires kindly.
6. "I'll eat whatever you think will make me well," I respond.
7. "But, really, my head hurts so bad that I don't know that soup will help much," I continue.
8. "I know, but your grandmother always believed that eating good could cure anything," Mom says.
9. "Let's give it a try, then. Maybe it will help me study well for the test, too," I say.
10. "That soup smells so well that I'm starting to feel cured already."

Exercise 9   **Using *Good*, *Bad*, *Well*, and *Badly***

On your paper complete the following sentences by writing *good*, *well*, *bad*, or *badly*.

Taking a Hike

1. No one can hike _____ without comfortable hiking shoes.
2. Improper equipment can make a hiker or camper feel _____ .
3. _____ planning is absolutely essential for a long and difficult hike.
4. A hike that is planned _____ will not be enjoyable and may be unpleasant.
5. Locating a _____ trail is one important aspect of planning a hike.
6. A hiker who is not feeling _____ can become a serious problem on the trail.
7. Hikers feel _____ if they cannot keep up with their companions.
8. If a hike begins _____, the hikers may become discouraged and decide to turn back.
9. The views along the Appalachian Trail look as _____ as the views that one sees in the Rocky Mountains.
10. Hikers should know their capabilities _____ before they start off on an ambitious hike.
11. I recently took an energetic walk with my friend Arnold, who could not hike _____.
12. Arnold tripped and hurt himself _____ after we had hiked only about a mile and a half.
13. Arnold said that his new hiking boots felt _____, but I thought they looked quite loose on his feet.
14. It also appeared that the soles were too thin to support his weight _____.
15. I felt _____ that he had hurt himself because I had really wanted our hike to go _____.
16. Arnold had been feeling _____ about his girlfriend, but then she suddenly broke up with him.
17. Needless to say, his confidence was _____ shaken.
18. He needed a _____ friend to spend time with him and make him forget his problems.
19. Ever since we were young children, we have gotten along with each other very _____.
20. I will be very disappointed if this misadventure hurts our friendship _____.

Exercise 10   **Writing Paragraphs with Modifiers**

Write two paragraphs, using each of the phrases below. You can use the phrases for each paragraph in any order.

SAMPLE   danced badly
SAMPLE SENTENCE   Ellie danced badly at her first audition.

Paragraph 1
1. feel well
2. stumbled badly
3. than any other basketball player
4. than those of Patrick Ewing
5. played well

Paragraph 2
6. feel good
7. drove well
8. than any other student
9. failed her driving test badly
10. looked bad

18.6 Double Negatives

In general, do not use a **double negative,** two negative words in the same clause. Use only one negative word to express a negative idea.

INCORRECT	I don't have no stereo equipment.
CORRECT	I do**n't** have **any** stereo equipment.
CORRECT	I have **no** stereo equipment.
INCORRECT	We haven't seen no concerts this year.
CORRECT	We have**n't** seen **any** concerts this year.
CORRECT	We have seen **no** concerts this year.
INCORRECT	My parrot never says nothing.
CORRECT	My parrot **never** says **anything.**
CORRECT	My parrot says **nothing.**

The words *hardly* and *scarcely* are also negatives. Do not use them with other negative words such as *not*.

INCORRECT	I haven't hardly finished.	He can't scarcely never be on time.
CORRECT	I have **hardly** finished.	He can **scarcely** ever be on time.

Exercise 11 Identifying Double Negatives

On your paper write each double negative in the following sentences. If a sentence is correct, write *correct*.

Working Out

1. I used to think there wasn't no reason for me to exercise.
2. I didn't want no new activity to distract me from my other interests.
3. I hadn't never explored the possibility of joining an aerobics class.
4. Eventually, my friend Ramón convinced me that my negative attitude was neither sensible nor smart.
5. I signed up for an aerobics class at the "Y," but at first I didn't want nobody to watch me make mistakes.
6. The other students never said nothing about my clumsy moves.
7. They didn't seem to have no interest in anything but stepping, jogging, and dancing to the high-energy music.
8. Soon I realized that exercising never gets no harder; it just gets easier.
9. Now I hardly never miss a session.
10. Not even bad weather can keep me from working out.

Exercise 12   **Correcting Double Negatives**

On your paper rewrite the following sentences, eliminating the double negative in each. (Most sentences can be corrected in more than one way.) If a sentence is correct, write *correct*.

Camping

1. When our family goes camping, we like to find a site where there isn't no one around.
2. Don't never pitch your tent on sloping ground, for you will be very uncomfortable.
3. Nobody should never forget to dig a trench around the tent, in case it rains during the night.
4. Can't none of them help us pitch our tent?
5. It's best never to leave no food in your tent, for animals may be attracted to it.
6. One time my sister and I discovered a raccoon in our tent, and after that we didn't leave nothing edible inside.
7. In some wilderness areas, campers aren't allowed to build no fires, and they must cook all their meals on a portable stove.
8. Some campers bring canned food along, but we don't bring none because it is too heavy to carry.
9. My parents always pack dried food because it is light and doesn't never spoil.
10. When it is time to break camp, no one should leave no trash on the ground, and all fires should be put out.
11. Our most memorable camping trip was one I don't never want to repeat.
12. One summer we decided to go to Crater Lake in southern Oregon because we hadn't never been to that site in the Cascade Range.
13. There isn't no more beautiful place in all the world.
14. The lake hasn't no inlet or outlet.
15. Nobody can't see it without being amazed by its sapphire-blue color.
16. However, we didn't have no idea about the area's changeable summer weather when we pitched our tent.
17. We hadn't no sooner gone to bed than it began to rain.
18. We didn't get hardly any sleep as the rain poured down, the wind blew, and the temperature dropped.
19. In the morning when we opened our tent flap, we realized we hadn't had no other camping experience like this before.
20. The rain had turned to snow, leaving not a patch of green grass or a brown tree trunk anywhere to be seen.
21. We had never seen nothing like it before in our lives.
22. We wanted something hot to drink, but we couldn't start no fire.
23. There wasn't scarcely any dry firewood around.
24. We decided that we didn't want to spend no more time there, even though the lake looked beautiful surrounded by the snow-covered trees.
25. We just hadn't no idea that it could snow in the Cascades in the middle of summer.

18.6 Double Negatives

18.7 Misplaced and Dangling Modifiers

Place modifiers as close as possible to the words they modify in order to make the meaning of the sentence clear.

- **Misplaced modifiers** modify the wrong word, or they seem to modify more than one word in a sentence. To correct a sentence with a misplaced modifier, move the modifier as close as possible to the word it modifies.

MISPLACED **Soaring over the edge of the cliff,** the photographer captured the eagle. [participial phrase incorrectly modifying *photographer*]

CLEAR The photographer captured the eagle **soaring over the edge of the cliff.** [participial phrase correctly modifying *eagle*]

MISPLACED He easily spotted the eagle **with his high-powered binoculars.** [prepositional phrase incorrectly modifying *eagle*]

CLEAR **With his high-powered binoculars,** he easily spotted the eagle. [prepositional phrase correctly modifying *he*]

Place the adverb *only* immediately before the word or group of words it modifies.

If *only* is not positioned correctly in a sentence, the meaning of the sentence may be unclear.

UNCLEAR Dan **only** has art on Monday. [Does Dan have only one class on Monday, or does he have no class on any day but Monday, or is Dan the only person (in a group) who has one class on Monday?]

CLEAR Dan has **only** art on Monday. [He has no other class.]

CLEAR Dan has art **only** on Monday. [He does not have art on any other day.]

CLEAR **Only** Dan has art on Monday. [No other person has art on Monday.]

Soaring over the edge of the cliff, the photographer captured the eagle.

Using Modifiers Correctly

670 Unit 18 Using Modifiers Correctly

Dangling modifiers seem logically to modify no word at all. To correct a sentence that has a dangling modifier, you must supply a word the dangling phrase can sensibly modify.

DANGLING	**Working all night long,** the fire was extinguished. [participial phrase logically modifying no word in the sentence]
CLEAR	**Working all night long,** firefighters extinguished the fire. [participial phrase modifying *firefighters*]
DANGLING	**After a valiant effort,** the blaze was still raging uncontrollably. [prepositional phrase logically modifying no word in the sentence]
CLEAR	**After a valiant effort,** the firefighters still faced a blaze that was raging uncontrollably. [prepositional phrase modifying *firefighters*]
DANGLING	**Sleeping soundly,** the raucous alarm startled me into consciousness. [participial phrase logically modifying no word in the sentence, since *me* is an object pronoun]
CLEAR	**Sleeping soundly,** I sprang into consciousness at the sound of the raucous alarm. [participial phrase modifying *I*]

Exercise 13   Identifying Misplaced and Dangling Modifiers

On your paper, write the misplaced or dangling modifier from each sentence. If a sentence is correct, write *correct*.

SAMPLE The police officer saw the tire explode in his binoculars.
ANSWER in his binoculars

1. Last night Darnell had a flat tire on the way to his job.
2. A motorcycle rider offered to fix the tire with a friendly grin.
3. Coming out from behind some parked cars, neither Darnell nor his helper could see the police officer.
4. Watching the motorcycle rider work, the tire was soon fixed.
5. "I only have trouble on this road," Darnell lamented.

Exercise 14 — Correcting Misplaced Modifiers

Rewrite each sentence, moving the misplaced modifier closer to the word it modifies.

SAMPLE I noticed the park walking home from school.
ANSWER Walking home from school, I noticed the park.

At the Park

1. The sign at the park entrance said, "Children should be with an adult under eight years of age."
2. A little boy was riding around on a bicycle with unmatched shoes.
3. Scampering around the top rung of the jungle gym, Marty noticed a baby squirrel.
4. Helen saw the sand castle her little sister had built on the way home from school.
5. The new paint set was under the porch that he had received for his birthday.

Exercise 15 — Identifying and Correcting Dangling Modifiers

Rewrite each sentence that needs correction, fixing the dangling modifier. If a sentence has no dangling modifier, write *correct*.

SAMPLE Waking to the screech of the alarm, the blankets were pulled up over Pete's head.
ANSWER Waking to the screech of the alarm, Pete pulled the blankets over his head.

Rise and Shine

1. Waking up in the dark, Pete's room seemed mysterious and gloomy.
2. After taking a shower, the sun finally came out.
3. Putting on a short-sleeved shirt, the temperature outside was warm.
4. Shouting from the kitchen downstairs, Pete's dad let him know that juice and cereal were on the table.
5. The school bus pulled up right on time after a hurried breakfast.

Exercise 16 — Using the Adverb *Only*

Rewrite each of the following sentences, adding the word *only*. Then explain what *only* means in your sentence.

SAMPLE I sleep late on Saturday.
ANSWER I sleep late only on Saturday. I don't sleep late on any day except Saturday.

Only on Saturday

1. I wake up early on Saturdays if there's an emergency.
2. The chore I have is mowing the grass.
3. I go to the movies on Saturday afternoons.
4. I eat pizza at my favorite pizzeria, Paul's Place.
5. I can appreciate how much my Saturdays mean to me.

Exercise 17   **Correcting Misplaced and Dangling Modifiers**

On your paper rewrite the following sentences, correcting any misplaced or dangling modifiers. (Some sentences can be corrected in more than one way.)

Going to the Circus

¹The Barnum and Bailey circus is a big event, for it comes only to our town once a year. ²Julio and I arrived early and took our seats inside the tent in high spirits. ³Dimming the lights, the elephants lumbered into the ring. ⁴Swinging their great trunks, the trainers marched the elephants in a circle. ⁵On a tightrope high above the ring, we watched the acrobat walk steadily and fearlessly. ⁶Three lions were released from a cage growling fiercely. ⁷The clown pretended that he had been attacked by the lions, but one girl in the audience only screamed. ⁸Galloping around the ring, a woman in a blue sequined dress waved to the crowd on horseback. ⁹Julio watched nervously as the trapeze artists leaped through the air clutching his chair. ¹⁰We watched her intently sitting on the bleachers and eating cotton candy.

¹¹Facing north, the second ring could be seen quite clearly. ¹²The snake charmer only charmed one snake, but it was a big one. ¹³A trainer commanded a bear with a chair. ¹⁴Watching the acrobats, the thrills never stopped. ¹⁵Barking furiously, the clowns chased little dogs around the tent. ¹⁶Julio enjoyed photographing the ringmaster with his miniature camera. ¹⁷Knowing what a bad photographer I was, the spectacle itself was enough. ¹⁸The band played a march dressed in star-spangled khaki. ¹⁹Taking their bows, the crowd applauded all the performers. ²⁰Under the stars our hearts were content as we walked home.

Exercise 18   **Review: Correcting Modifiers**

The following paragraph contains 10 errors in the use of modifiers. Rewrite the paragraph, correcting the errors.

Ted Williams, Home-Run Ace

¹Ted Williams is considered one of the most finest baseball players of all time. ²At the age of 17, a team in San Diego was the team he joined. ³By 1939 he was playing good enough to start with the Boston Red Sox. ⁴From that time until his retirement in 1960, Ted Williams only played baseball with the Red Sox; he never played for no other team. ⁵Williams was one of baseball's all-time most greatest hitters. ⁶His batting average was higher than most other players. ⁷He hit especially good in 1941, when he had a 0.406 batting average. ⁸Williams did not play so bad in 1942 either. ⁹In both 1941 and 1942, he hit more home runs than any player in the league.

Exercise 19 — Correcting Modifiers

On your paper rewrite the following sentences, correcting the misplaced, dangling, or other incorrect modifiers in each. (Some sentences can be corrected in more than one way.) If a sentence is correct, write *correct*.

SAMPLE Winston and Sabah only go out together once a week.
ANSWER Winston and Sabah go out together only once a week.

Winston and Sabah

1. Walking along the sidewalk, a stone made Winston trip and fall.
2. Winston hadn't hardly time to get to Sabah's house without being late.
3. In a great hurry, the buzzer rang as Sabah ran to the door.
4. Out for a walk, Winston and Sabah walked more farther than they usually did.
5. The yogurt sundaes they stopped to eat tasted well.
6. As they walked to the movies, they saw that a fire had destroyed a neighbor's house and the chimney was only left standing.
7. Sleeping too late the next morning, the school bus left Sabah behind.
8. Sabah felt worser than she had felt in a long time.
9. Walking to school, Sabah bought a stuffed bear from a vendor with fuzzy pink fur.
10. Because she was late, Sabah's teacher reprimanded her.
11. Sabah felt badly that she had overslept.
12. Sabah decided that English grammar was more easier than algebra.
13. She liked English class better than any class.
14. Winston and Sabah only had one class together.
15. Winston wrote an essay about his cat using a ballpoint pen.
16. Sabah wrote a paragraph about her dog concentrating deeply.
17. The teacher announced that both had done good.
18. Hoping to do well on the pop quiz, a silence fell over the classroom.
19. Having fallen asleep, Sabah threw her pencil at Winston.
20. Winston felt well that his friend was looking out for him.
21. Greeting each other enthusiastically, Winston and Sabah met after school.
22. Running in all directions, Sabah waved as their classmates left for home.
23. In the middle of the football field, Winston and Sabah watched the team practice.
24. The bestest player was not at the practice.
25. Starting for home, Winston and Sabah bid each other a fond farewell.

Exercise 20   **Correcting Modifiers**

On your paper rewrite any of the following sentences in which there are errors in the use of modifiers, correcting the errors in your revision. (Some sentences may be corrected in more than one way.) Write *correct* for each sentence that does not contain any errors.

Famous Comic Strips

1. In 1896 the first comic strip appeared in the New York *World,* called "The Yellow Kid."
2. The next comic strip to come along was "The Katzenjammer Kids," whose prankster stars, Hans and Fritz, usually behaved bad.
3. Hans and Fritz never gave the Captain and Mama no peace.
4. In "Mutt and Jeff," a strip that started in 1908, Mutt is more taller than Jeff.
5. "Mutt and Jeff" was one of the most early strips to appear in the newspaper.
6. All the comic strips in the early years depended upon slapstick more than any form of comedy.
7. Based on a typical family, the cartoonist of "The Gumps" drew popular characters.
8. The character Andy Gump had a mustache, but he didn't have no chin.
9. First appearing in 1919, Frank King sometimes drew innovative backgrounds for his "Gasoline Alley" strip.
10. People liked this strip very much, especially after the character Uncle Walt adopted little Skeezix.
11. Before "Gasoline Alley" there had been no comic strip in which the characters grew up and aged.
12. Although full of political content, "Little Orphan Annie" also told a good story.
13. The eyes of Little Orphan Annie are larger than most people.
14. For its first 10 years, the "Thimble Theatre" comic didn't have no Popeye in it.
15. "Blondie" was more widely circulated than any comic strip.
16. Dagwood, Blondie's husband, only made huge sandwiches when he raided the refrigerator; he never made an average-sized sandwich.
17. In his pursuit of such bizarre criminals as Flattop and Eighty-eight Keys, a yellow hat and square jaw were the trademarks of the cartoon detective Dick Tracy.
18. In "Peanuts," Pigpen is more dirtier than his friends Charlie Brown, Lucy, and Linus.
19. The comic-strip opossum, Pogo, makes philosophical comments on life.
20. In spite of its sometimes controversial political remarks, Garry Trudeau won a Pulitzer Prize for his "Doonesbury" strip.
21. The editorial page only runs political cartoons, not comic strips.
22. Solving one problem, another problem always faces the kindly heroine of "Mary Worth."
23. In the strip "Peanuts," Charlie Brown always feels badly after his baseball team loses.
24. Many people believe that "Calvin and Hobbes" is funnier than any comic strip.
25. The strip "Flash Gordon" is more older than most of the other strips in newspapers today.

UNIT 18 Grammar Review

USING MODIFIERS CORRECTLY

The passage in this workshop is taken from *An American Childhood*, a memoir by Annie Dillard. In it Dillard recalls her fascination with books that describe the pleasures and perils of rock collecting, one of her hobbies as a child. The passage has been annotated to show the kinds of modifiers covered in this unit.

Literature Model

from An American Childhood
by Annie Dillard

People who collected rocks called themselves "rockhounds." In the worst of cases, they called their children "pebble pups." Rockhounds seemed to be *wild* and obsessive amateurs, my kind of people, who had stepped aside from the rush of things to devote themselves to folly. . . .

Some rockhounds had *recently* taken up scuba diving. These people dove down into "brawling mountain streams" with tanks on their backs to look for crystals underwater, or to pan for gold. The gold panning was especially *good* under boulders in rapids.

One book included a photograph of a mild-looking hobbyist in his basement workshop: he sawed chunks of Utah wonderstone into wavy, landscapy-looking slabs suitable for wall hangings. Here was a photograph of rockhounds in the field: Two men *on a steep desert hillside* delightedly smash a flat rock to bits with two hammers. Far below stands a woman in a dress and sensible shoes, doing nothing. Here is their campsite: a sagging black pyramidal tent pitched on the desert floor. A Studebaker fender nudges the foreground. The very hazards of field collecting tempted me: "tramping for miles over rough country," facing cold, heat, rain, cactus, rough lava, insects, rattlesnakes, scorpions, and glaring alkali

- Positive form of the adjective *wild*
- Positive form of the adverb *recently*
- Correct use of *good*
- Correctly placed prepositional phrase modifying *men*

676 Unit 18 Using Modifiers Correctly

Grammar Review

flats. Collectors fell over boulders and damaged crystals. Their ballpoint pens ran out of ink. . . .

　　Getting back home alive *only* aggravated their problems. If you bring home five hundred pounds of rocks from an average collecting trip, what do you do with them? Splay them attractively about the garden, one book suggested lamely. Give them away. Hold yard sales. One collector left five tons of rough rock in his yard when he moved. . . .

　　On the other hand, rock collecting had unique rewards. For example, the *thinner* you sliced your specimens when you sawed them up, the more specimens you had. In this way you could multiply your collection without leaving home.

Correct placement of the adverb *only*

Comparative form of the adverb *thin*

Review: Exercise 1　Making Correct Comparisons

The following sentences are about rock collecting. For each sentence, write on your paper the proper comparative or superlative form of the modifier in parentheses.

SAMPLE　Rock collecting is _____ in some areas than in others. (easy)
ANSWER　easier

1. Rock hunting in areas where the ground is already broken, such as quarries and building sites, is _____ than hunting in areas with unbroken ground. (simple)
2. Some rock hunters gather rocks at a local site, whereas others travel _____ than that for specimens. (far)
3. One of the _____ practices to engage in while rock hunting is trespassing on private property. (bad)
4. One of the _____ and most dangerous things a rock hunter can do is to hunt alone on a steep rock wall. (silly)
5. Of the rock hunter's various tools, a rock hammer is the _____ implement for loosening solid rock. (good)
6. To loosen individual crystals, a chisel works _____ than a pocketknife. (good)
7. Museum specimens are often larger and _____ than those kept by amateur rock collectors. (impressive)
8. Minerals can be identified _____ than rocks because the atoms in minerals are arranged in a regular pattern, resulting in the formation of crystals. (quickly)
9. Rocks and minerals cannot always be identified simply by looking at them; _____ testing is often required. (far)
10. Of the various testing methods, the one that is probably used _____ is the streak test. (frequently)

Grammar Review

Review: Exercise 2 **Correcting Double Comparisons**

The following sentences are based on passages from *An American Childhood* that are not reprinted in this textbook. Rewrite the sentences, correcting any errors of double comparison. If a sentence contains no errors, write *correct*.

SAMPLE To outsiders no one seems more crazier than rockhounds.
ANSWER To outsiders no one seems crazier than rockhounds.

1. The young Annie Dillard liked nothing more better than the natural sciences.
2. She was more curiouser about rocks than she was about stamps or coins.
3. To Dillard, rock hunting seemed like the most liveliest of hobbies.
4. The books she read showed rockhounds hunting for specimens in the most wildest places imaginable.
5. Although Dillard obtained her own specimens by less ruggeder methods, she still found the rocks' secrets intriguing.
6. Some plain-looking rocks, when scratched on a rough surface, created streaks of color more brighter than greasepaint.
7. Even the dullest rocks, when cracked open, might reveal lovely crystals inside.
8. Of the rocks in Dillard's collection, the most prettiest was a red one called cinnabar.
9. Many minerals have strange names, but chalcopyrite (a brassy yellow mineral) was the most hardest for Dillard to pronounce.
10. Dillard longed to possess rocks with names even odder than that of chalcopyrite: sillimanite and agaty potch, for example.
11. Dillard was impressed with the fact that the earth is more older than any rock yet discovered.
12. Before she began to read about rocks, she thought they were the most drabbest things imaginable.
13. Only with more further exposure to the subject did she begin to find them fascinating.
14. Once she started her collection, she looked for the most fastest way to expand it.
15. With delight she learned that the more thinner she sliced her specimens, the bigger her collection became.
16. She realized that more sooner or later she would need a larger room for the collection.
17. With time and training, Dillard developed a more stronger descriptive prose than most other authors of her generation.
18. One of her most greatest gifts is her keen eye for detail.
19. All of her most latest books, including her fiction, continue to reflect her strong grounding in nature.
20. It's interesting to note that the seeds of her talent as an adult author were planted much more earlier in a youthful enthusiasm for rock collecting.

Grammar Review

Review: Exercise 3 **Correcting Incomplete Comparisons**

The following sentences are about minerals and gemstones. Rewrite the sentences, correcting any errors of incomplete comparison. Some of the sentences can be revised in more than one way. If a sentence contains no errors, write *correct*.

SAMPLE The value of a diamond is far greater than an amethyst.
ANSWER The value of a diamond is far greater than that of an amethyst.

1. On the Mohs scale, which lists minerals by their hardness, the mineral talc is softer than any mineral.
2. Quartz, a mineral that can cut glass, is much harder than talc.
3. Diamonds, among the world's most valuable minerals, are harder than anything in nature.
4. The facets, or flat surfaces, of a diamond are different from an amethyst.
5. Among the stones called beryls, which come in different colors, green is more valuable than any color.
6. Green beryls are called emeralds, and the value of some emeralds is higher than some diamonds.
7. The emeralds from Colombia are finer than those supplied by any South American country.
8. More fine rubies are found in Southeast Asia than anywhere.
9. The appearance of many synthetic rubies is very close to natural rubies.
10. Unlike most other gemstones, pearls are not minerals but an organic material.
11. A gemologist is more interested in the chemical structure of precious stones than any scientist.
12. Unlike other gemstones, such as lapis and malachite, diamonds are not only polished, but also facet-cut.
13. The aquamarine from Brazil is of better quality than Colombia.
14. In Thailand one can find finer sapphires than anywhere.
15. Unlike any rubies, star-rubies appear to contain six-rayed stars that can be seen in bright light.
16. In ancient China, jade was considered more precious than any gemstone.
17. Chinese collectors often valued a tiny piece of jade sculpture over any artifact.
18. The turquoise jewelry created by a Navajo is different from a Zuni.
19. Native American artisans create more exquisite turquoise jewelry than anyone.
20. Today there is a greater selection of gemstones available than at any time in history.

Using Modifiers Correctly

Grammar Review

Review: Exercise 4   **Choosing the Correct Modifier**

The following sentences are based on passages from *An American Childhood* not reprinted in this textbook. For each sentence choose the correct form of the modifier in parentheses, and write it on your paper. Then indicate whether the modifier you have chosen is being used as an *adjective* or an *adverb*.

SAMPLE   To the young Annie Dillard, few hobbies seemed as (good/well) as rock collecting.
ANSWER   good—adjective

1. Dillard obtained the first rocks in her collection from a newspaper boy whom she did not know very (good/well).
2. The newspaper boy had received the rocks as a gift from a (good/well) customer named Mr. Downey.
3. Mr. Downey, an avid rock hunter and collector, could no longer maintain his collection because his health was failing (bad/badly).
4. He had not been feeling (good/well) for several months and decided to give the collection to his newspaper boy, one of the few young people he knew.
5. The newspaper boy felt (bad/badly) because he did not have enough time to devote to the rock collection, and eventually he decided to give it to Dillard.
6. Dillard noticed right away that some of the rocks were attractive; others did not look too (good/well).
7. The fact that he could identify only two stalagmites made the newspaper boy feel (bad/badly) about his right to the collection.
8. Dillard herself was not (good/well) informed about the rocks and minerals when she first accepted the collection.
9. Had someone tested her on the names of Mr. Downey's rocks, Dillard would have done quite (bad/badly).
10. It was (good/well) that Dillard was able to borrow and read several books about rocks and minerals.
11. Dillard became more and more interested in rocks, quickly learning how to identify them (good, well).
12. She discovered that "rockhounds" were people that she got along with very (good, well).
13. She felt (good, well) about the amount of information and assistance some of these rockhounds could provide for her.
14. When she went on rock-finding expeditions, Dillard at first was (bad, badly) frustrated about not knowing what to do when she brought her findings home.
15. The rigors of actually looking for the rocks did not seem (bad, badly) by comparison.

Grammar Review

Review: Exercise 5   **Correcting Double Negatives**

The following sentences are about precious metals. Rewrite the sentences, eliminating any double negatives. Most sentences can be corrected in more than one way.

SAMPLE   Finding precious metals isn't no easy task.
ANSWER   Finding precious metals is no easy task.

1. Gold is a very malleable metal; if you hammer it, it won't never break.
2. Because there isn't no more malleable metal, people began using gold for jewelry thousands of years ago.
3. Nobody never has to worry that gold will tarnish, as many other metals do.
4. You can't make no jewelry out of pure gold, however, for it is too soft.
5. Pure gold is hardly never found; usually it is combined with another metal.
6. For centuries there wasn't nothing more valuable than gold.
7. Silver was also deemed valuable, but there wasn't no interest in platinum.
8. Medieval alchemists tried to create gold, but no one could make none.
9. Few early European explorers of the Americas hadn't never heard about the legend of El Dorado.
10. Most prospectors in nineteenth-century America never had no scientific training.

Review: Exercise 6   **Correcting Misplaced Modifiers**

The following sentences elaborate on ideas suggested by the passage from *An American Childhood*. Rewrite the sentences, correcting each misplaced modifier. If a sentence has no errors, write *correct*.

SAMPLES   Dillard identified rocks consulting books and visiting local museums.
ANSWER   Consulting books and visiting local museums, Dillard identified rocks.

1. Rockhounds seem eccentric to conventional people, having an unusual obsession.
2. Everyday activities seem unimportant to adventurous rockhounds with their dull routines.
3. Divers find some of the most interesting specimens in mountain streams using scuba-diving equipment.
4. Rockhounds often pan for gold in streams leaving no opportunity unexplored.
5. Some hobbyists might find enough gold to turn a tidy profit in the water.
6. Browsing through a book, Dillard noticed a strange photograph of a rockhound.
7. The picture showed a hobbyist sawing a chunk of wonderstone in his workshop destined for use as a wall hanging.
8. Lugging home huge quantities of rock, the question of practicality gnaws at the hobbyist.
9. The rockhound now begins to search for ideas about unloading his bounty in books.
10. One idea is to sell the specimens to friends occupying too much space.

Grammar Review   **681**

Grammar Review

Review: Exercise 7 — Correcting Dangling Modifiers

The following sentences elaborate on ideas suggested by the passage from *An American Childhood*. Rewrite the sentences, correcting each dangling modifier by adding appropriate information. Reword the sentence if necessary. Some sentences can be corrected in more than one way. If a sentence has no errors, write *correct*.

SAMPLE Finding rock collectors wildly impractical, their hobby was attractive.
ANSWER Finding rock collectors wildly impractical, Dillard was attracted to their hobby.

1. Calling themselves "rockhounds," rock collectors sometimes called their children "pebble pups."
2. Pausing to reflect, rock hunting began to seem like a wild obsession.
3. Strapping on their heavy tanks, the hunt for rock crystals in mountain streams began.
4. After studying the photographs and reading the anecdotes in books about rock collecting, Dillard decided the hobby was both artistic and adventurous.
5. Sawed into wavy slabs by one hobbyist, its suitability for wall hangings was achieved.
6. After climbing a steep hillside, the flat rock was smashed with two hammers.
7. Pitched in the desert, a tent served as the rockhounds' refuge from the elements.
8. Hunting for unusual rock specimens in wild and isolated places, minor problems like running out of ink arose.
9. After moving to a new home, five tons of rock remained in the rockhound's old yard.
10. Tramping for miles over rough country, their ballpoint pens ran out of ink.

Review: Exercise 8

Proofreading

The following passage describes the artist Georgia O'Keeffe, whose painting appears on the opposite page. Rewrite the passage, correcting the errors in spelling, grammar, and usage. Add any missing punctuation. There are twenty-five errors.

Georgia O'Keeffe

¹Born in 1887 in Sun Prairie, Wisconsin, art was an early love of Georgia O'Keeffe. ²She began studing art while still in her teens. ³She worked in Chicago as an advertising illustrator in 1909 but she resumed her art studies in 1912. ⁴First worked as a teacher for the public school system in Amarillo, Texas. ⁵She then taught art at the University of Virginia And more later, she returned to Texas to head the art department at West Texas State Normal College.

Grammar Review

Georgia O'Keeffe, *The White Place in Shadow*, 1940

⁶Although she had been painting good for some years, O'Keeffe did not produce no important works until 1915. ⁷They were large charcoal drawings based on elements in nature showing great promise. ⁸These works were seen by the photographer and gallery owner Alfred Stieglitz who admired them very much. ⁹O'Keeffe's first exhibition was in 1916 at one of Stieglitzs galleries in New York City. ¹⁰Eight years later O'Keeffe and Stieglitz was married. ¹¹Every year until her husband's death, it had an exhibit at one of Stieglitz's galleries.

¹²After visiting New Mexico in 1929, the dessert landscape became O'Keeffe's main subject. ¹³She was more happier painting there than anywhere. ¹⁴In the years after her husband's death, she made Abiquiu, New Mexico, her permanant home.

¹⁵O'Keeffe belonged to the first generation of American abstract artists and drew on her American roots (particularly the vastest landscape of the arid Southwest) more than many of her compatriots. ¹⁶She was not greatly influenced by no European art. ¹⁷O'Keeffe often used large, simplest forms that combined both soft and vivid colors. ¹⁸In many of her works, she exaggeratted the size of an object.

¹⁹O'Keeffe painted some of the more dramatic landscapes in all America. ²⁰In her painting *The White Place in Shadow,* she used subdued tones and massive shapes more than anything to capture the dry, sun-bleached cliffs of northern New Mexico. ²¹A setting such as this would perhaps be attractive to the rockhounds described by Annie Dillard than to most people.

Using Modifiers Correctly

Grammar Review

Review: Exercise 9

Mixed Review

Read the following biography of Annie Dillard. Then rewrite the sentences below it, correcting any errors in the use of modifiers. If you need additional information in order to complete any of your sentences, consult the biography.

Annie Dillard

Born and raised in Pittsburgh, Annie Dillard fell in love with nature when, at the age of 10, she discovered *The Field Book of Ponds and Streams* at a local library. Always a fine scholar, Dillard excelled in her studies at Hollins College. For her master's degree, she wrote a paper on Henry David Thoreau, the famous American nature writer to whom she is often compared. Dillard's journal of a year spent alone in rural Virginia became the basis for *Pilgrim at Tinker Creek,* which earned her the 1975 Pulitzer Prize. This vivid and introspective exploration of the natural world remains Dillard's best-known work. She has also published a volume of poetry and several more works of nonfiction, including her fine autobiography, *An American Childhood* (1987).

In 1992 Dillard published her first book of fiction, *The Living,* to great critical acclaim. In this novel she described the harsh life of the pioneers who came to the Pacific Northwest during the nineteenth century. In spite of her successes, Dillard claims to dislike writing because it takes her away from the great outdoors.

1. Writing vividly about the world of nature and her own experiences, Annie Dillard's books have enjoyed great popularity.
2. Some readers and critics consider her writings about nature as powerful as the classic American author Henry David Thoreau.
3. Born in Pittsburgh, her youth is described vividly in the book *An American Childhood,* an autobiography published in 1987.
4. As a child, Dillard was an avid reader and almost never had no trouble with her schoolwork.
5. She later did good at Hollins College in Virginia.
6. After spending a year in rural Virginia, her journal of that period was expanded into her acclaimed best-seller *Pilgrim at Tinker Creek.*
7. *Pilgrim at Tinker Creek* is probably more popular than any book by Dillard.
8. Although it was Dillard's first book, *Pilgrim at Tinker Creek* won her the 1975 Pulitzer Prize as the year's most finest work of nonfiction.
9. Dillard has only published a single volume of poetry.
10. Cooped up in her office, writing often keeps Dillard away from the natural world she loves.

684 Unit 18 Using Modifiers Correctly

Writing Application

Modifiers in Writing

Good writers are careful about the clear use and placement of modifiers. Notice, for example, the italicized modifiers in the following passage from Flannery O'Connor's *A View of the Woods*.

No one was particularly glad that Mary Fortune looked like her grandfather except the old man himself. He thought it added greatly to her attractiveness. He thought she was the *smartest* and the *prettiest* child he had ever seen and he let the rest of them know that if, IF that was, he left anything to anybody, it would be Mary Fortune he left it to. She was now nine, *short* and *broad* like himself, *with his very light blue eyes, his wide prominent forehead, his steady penetrating scowl, and his rich florid complexion;* but she was like him on the inside too. She had, to a singular degree, his intelligence, his strong will, and his push and drive.

Techniques with Modifiers

Try to apply some of O'Connor's techniques when you write and revise your own work.

1 Use comparative and superlative forms of modifiers when appropriate.

WEAK VERSION a smart and pretty child

O'CONNOR'S VERSION the *smartest* and the *prettiest* child

2 Place modifiers correctly to make your meaning clear.

CONFUSING PLACEMENT *With his very light blue eyes, his wide prominent forehead, his steady penetrating scowl, and his rich florid complexion,* she was now nine, *short* and *broad* like himself. . . .

O'CONNOR'S VERSION She was now nine, *short* and *broad* like himself, *with his very light blue eyes, his wide prominent forehead, his steady penetrating scowl, and his rich florid complexion.*

> **TIME**
> For more about the writing process, see **TIME Facing the Blank Page**, pp. 121-131.

Practice Practice using modifiers correctly by revising the following passage on a separate piece of paper.

Margaret watched her friend Linda windsurf sitting on the prow of the small boat. She wondered if she would ever be able to do it as effortlessly. There only was one way to find out. Taking a deep breath, her board was tossed into the water. Then she took another deep breath and plunged in after it. Climbing aboard, her feet were positioned just as Linda had taught her. She began to skim over the water as the wind became stronger. Feeling more freer than a seagull and more playful than a dolphin, suddenly the wind shifted, tossing her off the board. The sea was icy. It had not been icy near the shore. Struggling to the surface, a sobering thought occurred to her. She had a long way to go before she could windsurf in Linda's league.

UNIT 19 Usage Glossary

Usage Glossary *687*

Grammar Review *702*

Writing Application *709*

19 Usage Glossary

The glossary that follows presents some particularly troublesome matters of preferred usage. The glossary will give you guidance, for example, in choosing between two words that are often confused. It will also make you aware of certain words and expressions that you should avoid when speaking or writing for school or business.

a, an   Use the article *a* when the word that follows begins with a consonant sound, including a sounded *h*: *a poem, a house*. Use *an* when the word that follows begins with a vowel sound or an unsounded *h*: *an apple, an heirloom*. Use *a* before a word that begins with the "yew" sound: *a European, a unit*.

a lot, alot   This expression is always written as two words and means "a large amount." Some authorities suggest avoiding it altogether in formal English.

> **A lot** of snow fell last night.

a while, awhile   *A while* is made up of an article and a noun. *In* and *for* often come before *a while*, forming a prepositional phrase. *Awhile* is an adverb.

> We'll stop in **a while**.
>
> We'll stop for **a while**.
>
> We'll stop **awhile** before hiking to the top of the mountain.

accept, except   *Accept* is a verb that means "to receive" or "to agree to." *Except* is a preposition, a verb, or a conjunction. As a preposition, *except* means "but."

> Eric will **accept** the trophy for the team.
>
> Alanna will not **accept** defeat.
>
> Everyone will be at the ceremony **except** the captain. [preposition]

affect, effect   *Affect* is a verb that means "to cause a change in" or "to influence." *Effect* may be a noun or a verb. As a noun, it means "result." As a verb, it means "to bring about" or "to accomplish."

> The mayor's policies have **affected** every city agency.
>
> The mayor's policies have had a good **effect** on every agency. [noun meaning "result"]
>
> The mayor has been able to **effect** his goals in every city agency. [verb meaning "to bring about"]

ain't *Ain't* is unacceptable in speaking and writing unless you are quoting somebody's exact words. Instead of using *ain't*, use *I am not; she is not; he is not;* and so on.

all ready, already The two words *all ready* mean "completely ready." *Already* is an adverb that means "before" or "by this time."

> The band was **all ready** to play its last number, but the fans were **already** leaving the stadium.

all right, alright Always write this expression as two words. Although the expression is often seen in print as one word, most language authorities prefer *all right*.

> She was sick yesterday, but today she feels **all right.**

all the farther, all the faster These are regional expressions. Use *as far as* and *as fast as* in writing.

> We drove **as far as** we could during daylight hours.
> I'm pedaling this bike **as fast as** I can.

all together, altogether Use *all together* to mean "in a group." Use the adverb *altogether* to mean "completely" or "on the whole."

> For the holidays, our family will be **all together** at my grandmother's house.
> My grandmother is **altogether** delighted to have us with her.

amount, number *Amount* and *number* both refer to quantity. Use *amount* when referring to nouns that cannot be counted. Use *number* when referring to nouns that can be counted.

> Fort Knox contains a vast **amount** of gold.
> Fort Knox contains a large **number** of gold bars.

bad, badly See Unit 18.

being as, being that These expressions are sometimes used instead of *because* or *since* in informal conversation. In formal speaking and writing, always use *because* or *since*.

> **Because** their car broke down, they could not get here.
> **Since** they did not call, we assumed they were not coming.

beside, besides　　*Beside* means "at the side of." *Besides* usually means "in addition to."

> Katrina sat **beside** her mother at the table.
>
> **Besides** yogurt and fruit, they had homemade muffins.

between, among　　In general, use *between* to compare one person or thing with one other person or thing or with an entire group.

> What is the difference **between** Seattle and Portland? [Two cities are compared.]
>
> What was the difference **between** Pavlova and other ballet dancers? [One dancer is compared with an entire group of dancers.]

In general, use *among* to show a relationship in which more than two persons or things are considered as a group.

> The committee members were arguing **among** themselves.
>
> You are **among** friends.

Exercise 1　Making Usage Choices

For each of the following sentences, choose the correct word or expression from the pair in parentheses.

San Francisco

1. When gold was discovered in California in 1848, people seeking their fortune traveled there (all the faster/as fast as) they could.
2. Although most prospectors found no gold, some of them discovered that staying on in California as storekeepers or farmers was quite (all right/alright).
3. During the summer months, San Francisco has everything residents could want (except/accept) a hot, sunny climate, for the weather is often cool and foggy then.
4. In 1906 a terrible earthquake and fire destroyed much of San Francisco, but by 1915 the city had recovered and was (all ready/already) for the Panama-Pacific International Exposition.
5. There are (a lot/alot) of people of Chinese ancestry in San Francisco.
6. Many of them live in (a/an) area known as Chinatown.
7. The buildings in this district, many of which echo traditional Chinese architectural styles, create a picturesque (affect/effect).
8. Many visitors spend quite (a while/awhile) browsing in the shops on Grant Avenue, Chinatown's main thoroughfare.
9. There probably (ain't/is not) another Chinese community in the entire Western Hemisphere that is as large as San Francisco's Chinatown.
10. At first the Chinese families who immigrated to San Francisco lived (all together/altogether) in Chinatown, but now many of them have resettled in other parts of the city.

Usage Glossary

borrow, lend, loan *Borrow* and *lend* have opposite meanings. *Borrow* is a verb meaning "to take something with the understanding that it must be returned." *Lend* is a verb meaning "to give something with the understanding that it will be returned." *Loan* is a noun. It may be used as a verb, but most authorities prefer *lend*.

> May I **borrow** ten dollars till payday? [verb]
> Will you **lend** me some money? [verb]
> Did the bank give you a **loan?** [noun]

bring, take Use *bring* to mean "to carry from a distant place to a closer one." Use *take* to mean the opposite: "to carry from a nearby place to a more distant one."

> Will you **bring** me some perfume when you come back from Paris?
> Don't forget to **take** your passport when you go to Europe.

can, may *Can* indicates the ability to do something. *May* indicates permission to do something or the possibility of doing it.

> You **can** make hot chocolate by dissolving cocoa in warm milk.
> You **may** have a cup of hot chocolate before going to sleep.

can't hardly, can't scarcely These terms are considered double negatives because *hardly* and *scarcely* by themselves have a negative meaning. Therefore, avoid using *hardly* and *scarcely* with *not* or *-n't*.

> Eduardo **can hardly** tell the twins apart.
> The driver **can scarcely** see through the dense fog.

could of, might of, must of, should of, would of After the words *could, might, must, should,* or *would,* use the helping verb *have,* not the preposition *of.*

> Some historians say that the United States **could have** prevented the stock market crash of 1929.
> The country **might have** avoided the Great Depression that followed.
> The Great Depression **must have** been a difficult time to raise a family.

different from, different than The expression *different from* is generally preferred to *different than.*

> The sport of cross-country skiing is **different from** downhill skiing.

Exercise 2   Making Usage Choices

For each of the following sentences, choose the correct word or expression from the pair in parentheses.

Kansas City and Native American History

1. The Missouri River flows (between/among) Kansas City, Missouri, and Kansas City, Kansas.
2. Both cities are situated (beside/besides) the river.
3. If you look at a map, you (can/may) see that the Missouri River forms part of the boundary between Kansas and Missouri.
4. Until the Civil War, Kansas City's economy was based on supplying and outfitting the large (number/amount) of travelers headed west.
5. After the first railroads reached the city in the 1860s, (alot of/a lot of) things changed.
6. One major (affect/effect) was that the city became a busy cattle-trading center.
7. The city was (already/all ready) a railroad hub, and it soon became a great grain center.
8. A large (amount/number) of Native Americans once lived in the area that is now Kansas City.
9. Pioneers who settled in the area established trading posts (being as/because) the river facilitated travel and trade.
10. (Beside/Besides) the Osage nation, the Kansa, Delaware, and Wyandot nations lived in the area where Kansas City now stands.
11. Until the late nineteenth century, visitors to Kansas City (could of/could have) seen people of several Native American nations living around the town.
12. One (can scarcely/can't scarcely) exaggerate the importance of the role played by Native Americans in the history of Kansas City.
13. If you visit Kansas City, carry your camera or (borrow/loan) one from a friend.
14. Years ago Native Americans would (bring/take) furs to Fort Osage from far away to exchange for manufactured goods.
15. Many historians claim that the federal government's resettlement of many Native Americans to Indian Territory in Oklahoma was carried out (bad/badly).
16. (Being as/Because) most of the Native Americans who were resettled had not chosen to move, many people today feel that the mass movement was unjust.
17. The Cherokee, Chicksaw, Creek, Choctaw, and Seminole peoples each had traditions and customs that were quite (different than/different from) those of the others.
18. The history of all of these Native American nations (would of/would have) been quite different had they not been moved forcibly to Indian Territory.
19. Originally, Indian Territory also included a vast (number/amount) of land in Kansas and Nebraska.
20. When Oklahoma became a state in 1907, the last of the Indian Territory was dissolved, leaving Native Americans in Oklahoma to live (between/among) the general population.

Usage Glossary

doesn't, don't   *Doesn't* is a shortened form of *does not*, which is used with *he, she, it*, and all singular nouns. *Don't* is a shortened form of *do not*, which is used with *I, you, we, they*, and all plural nouns. Authorities usually discourage the use of contractions in formal writing.

> Our state **doesn't** allow people to drive before the age of seventeen.
>
> Some countries **don't** require their citizens to attend school.

emigrate, immigrate   Use *emigrate* to mean "to leave one country and go to another to live." Use *immigrate* to mean "to come to a country to settle there." Use *from* with *emigrate* and *to* or *into* with *immigrate*.

> Mr. Roh **emigrated** from South Korea.
>
> He **immigrated** to the United States.

farther, further   *Farther* should be used in reference to physical distance. *Further* should be used in reference to degree or time.

> San Antonio is **farther** south than Dallas.
>
> She did not question him **further**.

fewer, less   Use *fewer* when referring to nouns that can be counted. Use *less* when referring to nouns that cannot be counted. *Less* may also be used with figures that are seen as single amounts or single quantities.

> **Fewer** students have enrolled in physics this year than last year.
>
> This year there is **less** interest in physics among the students.
>
> We traveled to New York City in **less** than two hours. [*Two* is treated as a single period of time, not as individual hours.]
>
> It cost **less** than $20.00 to go by train. [The amount of money is treated as a single sum, not as individual dollars.]

good, well   See Unit 18.

had of   Do not use *of* between *had* and a past participle.

> I wish I **had received** this information earlier.

hanged, hung   Use *hanged* when you mean "put to death by hanging." Use *hung* in all other instances.

> Were any convicts in our state **hanged** during the twentieth century?
>
> The teacher **hung** the bulletin board above her desk.

in, into   Use *in* to mean "inside" or "within" and *into* to indicate movement or direction from the outside to a point within. The preposition *in* suggests a fixed location within a particular area or place. The preposition *into* suggests movement within or between locations.

> Jeanine was sitting outdoors **in** a lawn chair.
>
> When it got too hot, she went **into** the house.

irregardless, regardless   Use *regardless*. The prefix *ir-* and the suffix *-less* both have negative meanings. When used together, they produce a double negative, which is incorrect.

Regardless of what the critics said, I liked the movie.

Exercise 3   Making Usage Choices

For each of the following sentences, choose the correct word or expression from the pair in parentheses.

San Antonio

1. During its early history, San Antonio, Texas, was under the control of no (fewer/less) than three countries.
2. In 1731, fifteen families (emigrated/immigrated) from Spain's Canary Islands and settled in San Antonio.
3. The beautiful mission of San José still looks (good/well) after many years.
4. If you visit San Antonio, (don't/doesn't) miss seeing the Alamo.
5. To see the Alamo, the site of the famous 1836 battle between Texas and Mexico, you must go (in/into) the center of San Antonio.
6. If the Texas garrison (had/had of) been larger, would it have withstood the Mexican attack?
7. (Irregardless/Regardless) of their defeat at the Alamo, the Texans went on to win the war.
8. Do you suppose that officials (hanged/hung) the flag of the independent Republic of Texas in buildings in San Antonio?
9. During the 1800s, pioneers flocked to Texas, pushing the frontier (farther/further) west.
10. The modern city of San Antonio is quite different (from/than) the original Spanish settlement founded hundreds of years ago.
11. (In/Into) the modern city are a number of military bases.
12. The bases (affected/effected) population growth in the region.
13. Because of jobs on the bases, many people (emigrated/immigrated) to the area.
14. It's possible that the military has (less/fewer) economic importance for the region today.
15. The future of the defense industry in San Antonio is open to (farther/further) study.
16. San Antonio has (less/fewer) residents than Houston or Dallas.
17. At the time of the 1990 census, San Antonio's population was (less/fewer) than 1 million.
18. That population figure is (all ready/already) out of date.
19. It (doesn't/don't) take into account the many people who live in the surrounding metropolitan area.
20. Many people think that there (can/can't) hardly be a better place to live than San Antonio.

this kind, these kinds *Kind* is singular. Therefore, the singular form *this* or *that* modifies *kind*. *This* and *that* should also be used with *sort* and *type* (*this type, that type, this sort, that sort*). *Kinds* is plural. Therefore, the plural form *these* or *those* modifies *kinds*. Also use *these* and *those* with the plural nouns *sorts* and *types*.

This kind of bulb should be used in your lamp.

These kinds of lamps are very attractive.

This sort of food is found in many ethnic cuisines.

These sorts of foods are nutritious.

That type of exercise is my favorite.

Those types of exercises are considered good for your heart.

lay, lie *Lay* means "to put" or "to place"; it takes a direct object. *Lie* means "to recline" or "to be positioned"; it never takes an object.

Lay your coat on the bed.

I am going to **lie** in the sun now.

Problems arise particularly in using the principal parts of these verbs. Notice, for example, that the past tense of *lie* is *lay*. Learn all the principal parts of these verbs.

BASIC FORM	lay	lie
PRESENT PARTICIPLE	laying	lying
PAST FORM	laid	lay
PAST PARTICIPLE	laid	lain

She **laid** her coat on the bed.

I **lay** in the sun too long and got sunburned.

She had **laid** her coat on the bed before the party started.

I have **lain** in the sun longer without getting as sunburned.

learn, teach *Learn* means "to gain knowledge or understanding," and *teach* means "to give knowledge or instruction."

Jon **learned** to play the piano at the age of nine.

Mrs. Ramos **teaches** American history.

leave, let *Leave* means "to go away," and *let* means "to allow" or "to permit."

When you **leave** next week, I will miss you.

Please **let** me use your dictionary.

like, as *Like* is a preposition and introduces a prepositional phrase. *As* is a subordinating conjunction and introduces a subordinate clause. Many authorities say that it is incorrect to use *like* before a clause.

> Phil plays baseball **like** a professional.
>
> Teresa is confident, **as** I am, that everything will go well on the expedition.

loose, lose The adjective *loose* means "free," "not firmly attached," or "not fitting tightly." The verb *lose* means "to have no longer," "to misplace," or "to fail to win."

> That ring is so **loose** you are sure to **lose** it.
>
> Which team do you think will **lose** the game?

passed, past *Passed* is the past form and the past participle of the verb *to pass*. *Past* may be an adjective, a preposition, an adverb, or a noun.

> We **passed** your house on the way to school. [verb]
>
> Chris had a cold this **past** week. [adjective]
>
> We drove **past** your house last Sunday. [preposition]
>
> What time did you drive **past**? [adverb]
>
> Louise's grandmother always tells wonderful stories about her **past**. [noun]

precede, proceed *Precede* means "to go before" or "to come before." *Proceed* means "to continue" or "to move along."

> Our band **preceded** the homecoming float as the parade **proceeded** through town.

raise, rise The verb *raise* means "to cause to move upward"; it always takes an object. The verb *rise* means "to go up"; it is intransitive and does not take an object.

> **Raise** your hand if you know the answer.
>
> The rocket will **rise** from the launching pad at 9:01 A.M.

reason is, because *Because* means "for the reason that." Therefore, do not use *because* after *reason is*. Use *that* after *reason is* or use *because* alone.

> The **reason** I am tired is that I did not sleep last night.
>
> I am tired **because** I did not sleep last night.

Usage Glossary **695**

Exercise 4   **Making Usage Choices**

For each of the following sentences, choose the correct word or expression from the pair in parentheses.

New York City

1. New York City (lies/lays) near the mouth of the Hudson River in the southeast corner of New York State.
2. The reason New York is often called a melting pot is (because/that) many ethnic groups have settled there.
3. At the Ellis Island Immigration Museum, exhibits (teach/learn) visitors about the history of European immigration to the United States.
4. More than twelve million people (immigrated/emigrated) from their homelands and passed through the reception center on Ellis Island between 1892 and 1954.
5. The federal government now (lets/leaves) tourists visit Ellis Island.
6. If you wish to learn more about ethnic America, (like/as) our class did, you can visit the Hispanic Society of America, the Japan Society Gallery, the Museum of the American Indian, and the Jewish Museum.
7. You can admire works by African American artists at the Studio Museum in Harlem and then (precede/proceed) to the Schomburg Center for Research in Black Culture.
8. At the Metropolitan Museum of Art, visitors can stroll (past/passed) exhibits of art from around the world.
9. In Chinatown, near an apartment building that (rises/raises) high above the street, is a bronze statue of Confucius, the venerable Chinese philosopher.
10. Tourists and New Yorkers alike enjoy visiting (these kinds/this kind) of places to learn more about our country's multicultural heritage.
11. New York is still a city in which people of many races and ethnic backgrounds can live together and not (lose/loose) their cultural identity.
12. You can (teach/learn) much about New York City's history by visiting the Museum of the City of New York and the New York Historical Society.
13. The South Street Seaport Museum, which (lays/lies) near the East River, specializes in maritime history.
14. (Preceding/Proceeding) from Manhattan to the Bronx, maritime buffs can also visit the City Island Nautical Museum.
15. In 1998 New York City held many festivals to celebrate its (passed/past).
16. (As/Like) they did a century ago, traditional sailing ships moor in New York Harbor.
17. When the time arrives to depart, sailors (raise/rise) the ships' billowing white sails.
18. When the ships set sail, they (let/leave) many admirers gazing after them.
19. What is the reason (because/that) so many people are intrigued by the sea?
20. (This kind/These kinds) of question is hard to answer.

respectfully, respectively   *Respectfully* means "with respect." *Respectively* means "in the order named."

> The audience listened **respectfully** as the poet spoke.
>
> Phoenix and Phoenixville are, **respectively,** in Arizona and Pennsylvania.

says, said   *Says* is the third-person singular of the verb *say*. *Said* is the past tense of *say*. Be careful not to use *says* for *said*.

> At dinner last night, Nelson **said** that he wasn't hungry.
>
> He always **says** that, but he eats everything anyway.

sit, set   *Sit* means "to place oneself in a seated position." *Sit* rarely takes an object. *Set* means "to place" or "to put" and usually takes an object.

Set is also an intransitive verb when it is used with *sun* to mean "the sun is going down" or "the sun is sinking below the horizon." When *set* is used in this way, it does not take an object.

> Grandpa likes to **sit** on the porch.
>
> Lian **set** the pots on the stove after the sun **set.**

than, then   *Than* is a conjunction used to introduce the second element in a comparison; it also shows exception.

> Elsa is taller **than** Isabel.
>
> Our visitor was none other **than** Uncle Al!

Then is an adverb that means "at that time," "soon afterward," "the time mentioned," "at another time," "for that reason," or "in that case."

> My grandmother was a young girl **then.**
>
> Marguerite finished the book and **then** turned out the light.
>
> By **then** the party was almost over.
>
> If it rains, **then** we cannot go.

this here, that there   Avoid using *here* and *there* after *this* and *that*. Use *this* and *that* alone.

> All of us want to read **this** magazine.
>
> Have you heard **that** story?

where at   Do not use *at* after *where*.

> **Where** is Valley Forge?

who, whom   See Unit 17.

Usage Glossary   **697**

Exercise 5 — Making Usage Choices

For each of the following sentences, choose the correct word or expression from the pair in parentheses.

Santa Fe

1. Santa Fe, New Mexico, has more sites of historic interest (than/then) some other American cities.
2. Tourists in Santa Fe can explore the narrow, winding streets and (than/then) visit museums that display Native American crafts.
3. In summer, audiences (set/sit) in the open-air theater of the Santa Fe Opera.
4. (This/This here) opera house is one of the most famous in the world.
5. Audiences listen (respectfully/respectively) as some of the world's greatest opera singers perform.
6. Native Americans and Spanish colonists were, (respectfully/respectively), the first two groups to reside in the Santa Fe area.
7. Many of the early Spaniards (who/whom) we know about in this area came to search for fabulous riches.
8. These early Spaniards reported hearing of a man who (said/says) he had seen seven cities of gold in the area.
9. Santa Fe is the place (where/where at) the historic Santa Fe Trail ended.
10. (This/This here) trail was used by pioneers traveling west during the 1800s.

Exercise 6 — Making Usage Choices

For each of the following sentences, choose the correct word or expression from the pair in parentheses.

Washington, D.C.

1. (Where/Where at) is Washington, D.C., located?
2. The capital of the United States (sets/sits) at what may be considered the dividing line between the North and the South.
3. The city (lies/lays) along the banks of two rivers, the mighty Potomac and its tributary, the Anacostia.
4. When the location was first selected for the capital of the country, some people thought that the choice had been (bad/badly) made.
5. (Between/Among) the two rivers stretched a broad area of what many people considered swamp.
6. They did not believe that a graceful city would (raise/rise) where they saw only bog.
7. (Besides/Beside) the swampy ground, the hot summer climate was a problem.
8. (Like/As) other towns and cities of the time, Washington had streets that were little better than rutted dirt roads.
9. Planes, cars, and trains today (take/bring) about 20 million tourists a year to this beautiful city with a multicultural population.
10. In addition, people from many countries and states move to the capital and (teach/learn) to call it home.

Exercise 7   **Making Usage Choices**

For each of the following sentences, choose the correct word or expression from the pair in parentheses.

New Orleans

1. New Orleans, Louisiana, has (a/an) average annual rainfall of about fifty-five inches, and much of the city (lays/lies) below sea level.
2. (A lot/Alot) of levees were constructed along the banks of the Mississippi River to prevent flooding.
3. The Mississippi River flows through Baton Rouge and then (precedes/proceeds) southeasterly to New Orleans.
4. New Orleans (ain't/is not) only a shipping center.
5. (Being that/Because) New Orleans is picturesque, many people enjoy vacationing there.
6. The temperature in the winter months (doesn't/don't) drop below freezing very often.
7. French and Spanish settlers (preceded/proceeded) German and Irish immigrants to the city of New Orleans by more than one hundred years.
8. In addition, people from Italy (emigrated/immigrated) to New Orleans.
9. In some New Orleans restaurants, customers can choose (among/between) French and Creole cuisine.
10. Most visitors enjoy strolling through the streets of the historic French Quarter for quite (a while/awhile), taking in the beautiful architecture.
11. No skyscrapers (raise/rise) above the low skyline of the French Quarter.
12. Visitors need walk no (farther/further) than Bourbon Street to hear jazz.
13. A large (number/amount) of visitors attend concerts at music venues like the famous Preservation Hall.
14. Visitors crowd (in/into) this hall whenever jazz is being played.
15. In Preservation Hall, women (set/sit) their purses on their laps as they (set/sit) on the crowded wooden benches.
16. Here musicians play jazz (like/as) it was played in the early 1900s.
17. This style of jazz is quite (different from/different than) the style of modern jazz.
18. By February of each year, the citizens of New Orleans are (all ready/already) to hold their famous Mardi Gras festival.
19. During Mardi Gras, the city (can scarcely/can't scarcely) accommodate its many visitors.
20. During this celebration, it is (all right/alright) to dress in elaborate costumes and take part in carnivals and parades.
21. Although the heat and humidity of New Orleans may (affect/effect) some visitors, the local inhabitants seem to be used to it.
22. Similarly, they (accept/except) without serious complaint the amount of rainfall.
23. It seems the residents are (altogether/all together) used to the climate.
24. (Between/Among) the inhabitants of New Orleans are Creoles, descendants of early French and Spanish settlers, and Cajuns, descendants of French Canadian refugees from Nova Scotia.
25. They have all (taught/learned) to live together in harmony.

Exercise 8   Making Usage Choices

For each of the following sentences, choose the correct word or expression from the pair in parentheses.

Boston

1. Boston is an (all together/altogether) special place.
2. Do you think that if Boston had been more centrally located, it (might have/might of) become the nation's capital?
3. New York City and Philadelphia were, (respectively/respectfully), the first and second capitals of the United States.
4. In 1773 Bostonians who would not (accept/except) King George III's taxes dumped three shiploads of tea into Boston Harbor.
5. They wanted independence from England (bad/badly).
6. They (set/sit) several demands before the English king.
7. The government of the city of Boston has (hanged/hung) plaques at historic sites.
8. Some people say that Beacon Hill, more (than/then) any other area in Boston, is known for its beauty and historic importance.
9. Boston is a very accessible city. The reason is (because/that) it has an efficient transit system.
10. If you want to get from the suburbs to the city center, just go (in/into) the nearest station of the rapid transit system, and you'll be there in no time.
11. Be sure to (bring/take) a raincoat if you come to Boston in the fall, for the weather can be stormy.
12. A visitor can tour the Boston Museum of Fine Arts and (then/than) visit the Museum of Science.
13. Boston abounds in (this kind/these kinds) of museums.
14. After the Charles River has (passed/past) through the city, the river empties into Boston Harbor.
15. People can picnic in the parks (beside/besides) the river.
16. A visitor who likes to walk (can/may) follow the Freedom Trail to many of Boston's historic sites.
17. Along the one-and-a-half-mile-long trail are no (less/fewer) than 15 historic sites.
18. Guidebooks will (learn/teach) the visitor about places on the trail.
19. The visitor will not (lose/loose) the way because the trail is well marked.
20. Time spent in Boston (can't hardly/can hardly) be forgotten.
21. (Besides/Beside) being a historical treasure trove, Boston is a leader in education.
22. In 1636 Harvard College was founded in what was (than/then) Newtowne.
23. Harvard, the first university founded in the English colonies, had many (less/fewer) students in the 1600s than it does now.
24. (Among/Between) Boston's many institutions of higher learning are Tufts, Boston University, Northeastern University, and the Massachusetts Institute of Technology.
25. If you run, (like/as) I have, along the jogging trail that follows the Charles River, you can glimpse at least three of these universities.

Exercise 9 Making Usage Choices

For each of the following sentences, choose the correct word or expression from the pair in parentheses.

Seattle

1. Recently a report (said/says) that Seattle, Washington, is one of America's most attractive cities.
2. (Irregardless/Regardless) of whether or not people choose to live in Seattle, most agree it is a beautiful place.
3. Many tourists (who/whom) the Century 21 Exposition attracted in 1962 later returned to Seattle to live.
4. Seattle is known as the Emerald City, a name (borrowed/loaned) from *The Wizard of Oz.*
5. The city of Seattle (lays/lies) near the Pacific Ocean.
6. (This/This here) location made Seattle a gateway to the Far East.
7. Many Japanese were (between/among) Seattle's early settlers.
8. Other early settlers (emigrated/immigrated) from Scandinavia.
9. A glance at the beautiful Cascade Mountains east of Seattle can easily (raise/rise) one's spirits.
10. This is the mountain range (where/where at) Mount Saint Helens is located.

Exercise 10 Making Usage Choices

For each of the following sentences, choose the correct word or expression from the pair in parentheses.

Atlanta

1. (Leave/Let) us go to Atlanta, Georgia.
2. Atlanta is a larger city (than/then) Birmingham, Alabama.
3. Today's Atlanta is very (different from/different than) the city portrayed in *Gone with the Wind.*
4. Traces of the Old South (can't hardly/can hardly) be found in Atlanta.
5. A devastated city after the Civil War, Atlanta is more than (alright/all right) now.
6. Other cities seeking Atlanta's success have done (like/as) Atlanta has.
7. Because of its location, Atlanta is (all ready/already) well situated as a transportation crossroads.
8. By promoting itself (good/well), Atlanta has attracted national corporations and federal government offices.
9. Some visitors who (could have/could of) seen the *Cyclorama,* a depiction of the Battle of Atlanta and one of the three largest paintings in the world, (passed/past) up the opportunity.
10. Many of those who see the painting agree that its (affect/effect) is striking.

UNIT 19 Grammar Review

USAGE GLOSSARY

The following quotations, which relate to the themes of friendship and love, have been annotated to show usage items covered in this unit.

Literature Models

Quotations About Friendship and Love

- The relative pronoun *who* in the nominative case because it is the subject of a clause

He *who* has a thousand friends has not a friend to spare.
And he *who* has one enemy will meet him everywhere.

From Sentences *by Ali Ibn-Abi-Talib (seventh century), translated from the Arabic*

- *Can* used to suggest ability

To me, fair friend, you never *can* be old. . . .

From Sonnet 104 by William Shakespeare

- The preposition *into* used to suggest movement from one place to another

- The preposition *in* used to mean "inside"

I breathed a song *into* the air,
It fell to earth, I knew not where. . . .
And the song, from beginning to end,
I found again *in* the heart of a friend.

From "The Arrow and the Song" by Henry Wadsworth Longfellow

"Every man's his own friend."

- *Except* used as a conjunction meaning "but"

"*Except* sometimes some people are nobody's enemies but their own."

From Oliver Twist *by Charles Dickens*

- *Like,* a preposition, used to introduce a prepositional phrase

For there is no friend *like* a sister
In calm or stormy weather;
To cheer one on the tedious way,
To fetch one if one goes astray. . . .

From "Goblin Market" by Christina Rossetti

- *May* used to suggest possibility

The process of falling in love at first sight is as final as it is swift . . . , but the growth of true friendship *may* be a lifelong affair.

From The Country of the Pointed Firs *by Sarah Orne Jewett*

Grammar Review

Only solitary men know the full joys of friendship. Others have their family; but to **a** solitary and **an** exile his friends are everything.

From Shadows on the Rock *by Willa Cather*

> ***A*** before a consonant sound; ***an*** before a vowel sound

We have **fewer** friends than we imagine, but more than we know.

From The Book of Friends *by Hugo von Hofmannsthal, translated from the German by Mary Hottinger and Tania and James Stern*

> ***Fewer*** referring to a noun that can be counted

Among those **whom** I like or admire, I can find no common denominator, but among those **whom** I love, I can: all of them make me laugh.

From The Dyer's Hand *by W. H. Auden*

> The relative pronoun ***whom*** in the objective case because it is a direct object

"Love, Umi, means something very **different from** 'falling in love,'" Daddyji said. "It's not an act but a lifelong process. . . ."

From The Ledge Between the Streams *by Ved Mehta*

> ***Different from*** rather than ***different than***

Review: Exercise 1   Making Usage Choices

The following sentences describe friendships between famous artists. For each item, choose the correct word or expression in parentheses and write it on your paper.

1. Though they were very (different from/different than) each other in temperament, the Dutch painter Vincent van Gogh and the French painter Paul Gauguin were close friends.
2. The French artist Edgar Degas noted the similarities (between/among) his drawing style and that of his friend, the American artist Mary Cassatt.
3. (Beside/Besides) Degas, Cassatt was also friendly with several other Impressionist painters.
4. (Being as/Since) Berthe Morisot's close friend, fellow French painter Edouard Manet, so admired one of her paintings, she gave it to him as a gift.
5. The friendship may have influenced Morisot's work more (than/then) it influenced that of Manet.

Usage Glossary

Grammar Review

Review: Exercise 2 — Making Usage Choices

The following sentences describe more friendships between famous artists. For each item, choose the correct word or expression in parentheses and write it on your paper.

1. Spanish artist Pablo Picasso and French artist Georges Braque had a great (affect/effect) on each other's work.
2. They are known as the founders of Cubism, which was an (all together/altogether) new style of art for its time.
3. In the 1920s, the Russian artist Wassily Kandinsky and the Swiss artist Paul Klee were colleagues at the Bauhaus, a school of architecture and design in Berlin, (where they taught painting/where they taught painting at).
4. An artistic friendship between two Americans, the painter Georgia O'Keeffe and the photographer Alfred Stieglitz, (preceded/proceeded) their marriage.
5. Stieglitz (hanged/hung) O'Keeffe's paintings in his gallery.

Review: Exercise 3 — Making Usage Choices

The following sentences describe friendships between famous writers. For each item, choose the correct word or expression in parentheses and write it on your paper.

1. In Rome in the first century B.C., the poet Virgil was supported, (like/as) his friend and fellow poet Horace also was, by the patron Maecenas.
2. (This/This here) article says that the writers Edith Wharton and Henry James were friends.
3. The authors Gustave Flaubert and Ivan Turgenev exchanged letters faithfully for two decades; (this kind/these kinds) of long-term correspondence is now rare.
4. Flaubert and Turgenev had (all ready/already) published some of their most famous novels when they met in 1863.
5. *Madame Bovary* and *Fathers and Sons,* by Flaubert and Turgenev, (respectfully/respectively), remain classics.
6. Herman Melville befriended his fellow American writer Nathaniel Hawthorne, (who/whom) he greatly admired.
7. During these authors' lifetimes, Hawthorne's works were more widely read (than/then) Melville's.
8. The novelists Joseph Conrad and Ford Madox Ford thought it was (all right/alright) to collaborate on two novels.
9. In the course of their friendship, the American poets Elizabeth Bishop and Marianne Moore (must of/must have) enjoyed each other's lively wit and humor.
10. The poet Joseph Brodsky received much support from his fellow Russian poet Anna Akhmatova before he was forced to (immigrate/emigrate) to the United States.

Grammar Review

Review: Exercise 4 — Making Usage Choices

The following sentences describe famous fictional friendships and romances. For each item, choose the correct word or expression in parentheses and write it on your paper.

1. In Arthur Conan Doyle's works, Sherlock Holmes investigates a great (amount/number) of criminal cases with his friend Watson.
2. Horatio tells his dear friend Hamlet, one of Shakespeare's tragic heroes, that he has seen the ghost of Hamlet's father (raise/rise) from the dead.
3. Romeo and Juliet, Shakespeare's famous young lovers, (can't/can't hardly) bear to be apart from each other.
4. By the end of Jane Austen's novel *Pride and Prejudice,* Elizabeth Bennet thinks she (passed/past) judgment on Mr. Darcy much too quickly.
5. In Emily Brontë's *Wuthering Heights,* Cathy's brother, who feels (bad/badly) about her impending marriage, tries to prevent the match and causes a tragedy.
6. In Tolstoy's novel *War and Peace,* Prince Andrei and Pierre are devoted friends, (irregardless/regardless) of their opposing personalities.
7. Huckleberry Finn and Tom Sawyer have (a lot/alot) of adventures together in Mark Twain's novels.
8. At the outset of Herman Melville's *Moby Dick,* Ishmael is terrified to find that he is (laying/lying) beside the bizarre-looking Queequeg, but they later become close friends.
9. Unhappy at school, the orphan Jane Eyre, Charlotte Brontë's main character, finds comfort for (a while/awhile) in a friendship with the sweet but sickly Helen Burns.
10. Although Cervantes's character Don Quixote (looses/loses) touch with reality, his squire and friend, Sancho Panza, maintains common sense.

Review: Exercise 5 — Making Usage Choices

The following sentences describe relationships from mythology and folklore. For each item, choose the correct word or expression in parentheses and write it on your paper.

1. In Homer's *Iliad,* Achilles (borrows/lends/loans) his armor to his dear friend Patroclus, who lacks armor of his own, but Patroclus is nevertheless killed in battle.
2. Because Orpheus cannot (accept/except) the death of Eurydice, he enters the underworld to try to retrieve her.
3. In a tale told by Ovid, the parents of Pyramus and Thisbe tell the young lovers they (cannot/may not) marry.
4. The reason Pyramus stabs himself is (that/because) he believes a lioness has killed Thisbe.
5. Orestes, with his friend Pylades, goes (in/into) the palace of Clytemnestra to avenge Orestes' father's death.

Grammar Review

Review: Exercise 6   **Making Usage Choices**

The following sentences describe collaborations in science. For each item, choose the correct word or expression in parentheses and write it on your paper.

1. In 1903 the inventors Orville and Wilbur Wright altered aviation history with the first sustained flight; its distance was (fewer/less) than 150 feet.
2. The French chemist Marie Curie, working (beside/besides) her husband, Pierre Curie, discovered the element radium.
3. The Curies' work caused scientists to (raise/rise) their hopes about treating certain medical problems.
4. The Swiss psychologist Carl Jung and the Austrian founder of psychoanalysis, Sigmund Freud, worked (good/well) together for a brief time.
5. Jung (might of/might have) supported Freud's ideas initially, but he later disputed many of Freud's doctrines.
6. The discovery of the DNA double helix by James D. Watson and Francis H. C. Crick (farther/further) advanced our understanding of biology.
7. Their discovery, in turn, spurred a great (amount/number) of research into the role of DNA in the human body.
8. The anthropologists Louis and Mary Leakey and the team of Don Johanson and Tom Gray, working in Tanzania and Ethiopia (respectfully/respectively), made astounding archaeological discoveries.
9. The first lunar landing succeeded through cooperation (between/among) Neil Armstrong, Buzz Aldrin, and Michael Collins of the *Apollo 11* spaceflight.
10. (All together/Altogether) there were sixteen Apollo space missions.

Review: Exercise 7

Proofreading

The following passage describes the artist John Singer Sargent, whose painting is reproduced on the opposite page. Rewrite the passage, correcting any errors in spelling, grammar, and usage. Add any missing punctuation. There are twenty-five errors.

John Singer Sargent

[1]John Singer Sargent, a famous portrait and landscape painter of the passed century was born in Italy in 1856. [2]His father, a physician and his mother, a amateur painter, were wealthy New Englanders. [3]They spend alot more time in Europe then in America, however. [4]Sargent begun his studies in Florence at the age of fourteen. [5]And moved to Paris four years later. [6]He

Grammar Review

John Singer Sargent, *Carnation, Lily, Lily, Rose*, 1886

discovered in Paris that he preferred to paint directly on the canvass without making preliminary sketches.

⁷When he was still younger then twenty-one, Sargent made his first trip to the United States. ⁸He became instantly popular his portraits were in great demand in Boston and New York for awhile. ⁹He quickly made a name for himself in London and emigrated there permenently in 1884.

¹⁰While living in London, Sargent cultivated influential friends; between these were the painter Edwin Abbey and the writer Henry James. ¹¹Sargents taste for aristocratic life are reflected in his portraits of upper-class people. ¹²Although it may look as if Sargent painted all the faster he could, he actually labored over each piece until he achieved the affect he wanted. ¹³He never excepted anything but the best from himself.

¹⁴As the art world turned increasingly toward modernism and abstraction, Sargent's realistic style gradually fell out of fashion. ¹⁵His great talent as a painter however, was never challenged. ¹⁶The Sargent work above show Sargent's extraordinary technique. ¹⁷This here painting echoes the love and friendship expressed in the quotations that appear in this review.

Grammar Review

Review: Exercise 8

Mixed Review

The following sentences provide information about the authors of the quotations in this review. For each sentence, write the correct word or expression from parentheses.

1. Ali Ibn-Abi-Talib, (who/whom) was married to Mohammed's daughter, became a leader of Islam.
2. The division of Islam between Shia and Sunni (can/may) be traced back to events that occurred during the lifetime of Ali Ibn-Abi-Talib.
3. If you could (bring/take) only one writer's works to a desert island, the plays of William Shakespeare might suffice.
4. (Accept/Except) for *King Lear,* I prefer Shakespeare's comedies to his tragedies.
5. In narrative poems such as *Hiawatha* and *The Courtship of Miles Standish,* Henry Wadsworth Longfellow explored the events and folklore of the American (passed/past).
6. Longfellow combined the epic form of poetry with (a/an) simple and sentimental style that was his own.
7. It (can/may) be fair to say that Charles Dickens ranks among the most popular English writers of all time.
8. Most of Dickens's novels, (as/like) *Nicholas Nickleby,* first appeared in installments in periodicals.
9. Christina Rossetti, (like/as) her brother, Dante Gabriel Rossetti, was an English poet known for vivid imagery.
10. (Beside/Besides) writing lyrical religious poetry, Christina Rossetti specialized in writing verses for children.
11. The stories and novels of Sarah Orne Jewett give readers a sense of lingering (a while/awhile) in the countryside of the author's native Maine.
12. Christina Rossetti and Sarah Orne Jewett died in 1894 and 1909, (respectively/respectfully).
13. Her childhood in Nebraska had a great (affect/effect) on Willa Cather.
14. One reason Willa Cather was able to create strong characters who embody the pioneer spirit is (because/that) she knew many such people when she was growing up.
15. Hugo von Hofmannsthal, an Austrian writer, wrote (fewer/less) lyric poems as he grew older.
16. Von Hofmannsthal, a poet, dramatist, and essayist, wrote the text for some operas composed by Richard Strauss during the (passed/past) century.
17. The poet W. H. Auden (emigrated/immigrated) from England in 1939 and became an American citizen.
18. I listened (respectfully/respectively) when our teacher told us that Auden won the Pulitzer Prize in 1948 for *Age of Anxiety.*
19. Although the Indian-born author Ved Mehta had become completely blind by the age of three, he (preceded/proceeded) to excel in college and in his profession.
20. Ved Mehta owns a summer home on the island of Isleboro, which (sets/sits) in Penobscot Bay off the coast of Maine.

Writing Application

Usage of *Lie* in Writing

In this passage from *Of Wolves and Men*, Barry Holstun Lopez uses several forms of the intransitive verb *lie*. Read the passage, concentrating on the italicized verb forms.

    It is now late in the afternoon. The wolf has stopped traveling, has *lain* down to sleep on cool earth beneath a rock outcropping. Mosquitoes rest on his ears. His ears flicker. He begins to waken. He rolls on his back and *lies* motionless with his front legs pointed toward the sky but folded like wilted flowers, his back legs splayed, and his nose and tail curved toward each other on one side of his body.

Techniques with Usage of *Lie*

Try to use correct principal parts of the verb *lie* when you write and revise your own work.

❶ Learn the difference between *lie* and *lay*. Remember that *lie* means "to recline" or "to be positioned." *Lie* never takes an object. *Lay*, on the other hand, takes a direct object. *Lay* means "to put" or "to place."

INCORRECT USE He rolls on his back and *lays* motionless . . .
CORRECT USE He rolls on his back and *lies* motionless . . .

❷ Learn the principal parts of the verb *lie: lie, lying, lay, lain.*

INCORRECT USE The wolf has stopped traveling, has *laid* down . . .
CORRECT USE The wolf has stopped traveling, has *lain* down . . .

TIME
For more about the writing process, see **TIME Facing the Blank Page**, pp. 121–131.

Practice   Practice these techniques by revising the following passage on a separate sheet of paper. Replace each set of parentheses with the correct form of *lie* or *lay*.

    When I got home from school, I was exhausted. I ( ) down my backpack, which felt like a ton of bricks, and wanted nothing more than to ( ) down and lose some of my weariness. First, though, I had to ( ) out the ingredients my father would use to make his famous chicken stew. I trudged to the kitchen, where I found the cat ( ) in its own private patch of sunlight. It has probably ( ) there all day, I thought with resentment. I'd be ( ) there myself if I didn't have to go to school and to work and then home to do chores. "How long have you ( ) there, Hercules?" I demanded. A wheezy purr was its only response, so I picked up the hairy critter and ( ) it outside the kitchen door. Then I quickly ( ) out the food on the counter next to the stovetop before finally ( ) my own weary body to rest on my bed.

Writing Application   **709**

UNIT 20 Capitalization

Lesson 20.1 **Capitalization of Sentences**   711

Lesson 20.2 **Capitalization of Proper Nouns**   713

Lesson 20.3 **Capitalization of Proper Adjectives** 720

Grammar Review   724

Writing Application   729

20.1 Capitalization of Sentences

■ Capitalize the first word of every sentence, including the first word of a direct quotation that is a complete sentence.

> **O**ne of the first computers was large enough to fill a two-car garage.
>
> Henry Ford said, "**T**hinking is the hardest work there is, which is the probable reason why so few engage in it."

Do not capitalize the first word of a quotation unless the entire quotation can stand as a complete sentence or it is capitalized in the original text.

> Although astronauts must learn how to use computers, experts say most astronauts are "**c**omputer users, not computer wizards."

Do not capitalize an indirect quotation. An **indirect quotation** gives the meaning of an original statement without repeating it word for word. It is often introduced by the word *that*.

> This letter from a computer camp states that **s**wimming, hiking, and archery will be offered this summer.

Capitals form the top of Greek columns.

Exercise 1 Capitalizing Quotations

Rewrite any incorrect sentences that follow, correcting any errors in capitalization. If a sentence is correct, write *correct*.

Franklin's Wisdom

1. Writer and publisher Benjamin Franklin observed, "nothing should be expressed in two words that can be as well expressed in one."
2. He advised writers to choose words that were "Smooth, clear, and short, for the contrary qualities are displeasing."
3. Franklin believed that writers should rarely, if ever, use synonyms or words that have almost the same meaning as other words.
4. He said, "words should be the most expressive that the language affords."
5. He recommended that words be so placed "As to be agreeable to the ear in reading."

Capitalize the first word of a sentence in parentheses that stands by itself. Do not capitalize a sentence within parentheses that is contained within another sentence.

> Games can be tools for learning about computers. (**M**any programmers think that programming itself is the best game of all.)
>
> They were looking for software (**t**hey hoped to buy no more than three or four programs) that they could use in writing reports.

Exercise 2 Capitalizing Within Parentheses

Rewrite each item that is incorrect, correcting the capitalization. If an item is correct, write *correct*.

1. He went in through the back door. (he hoped no one would notice him.)
2. He expected to be nervous facing a huge crowd (ironically, no one was even in the room).
3. When he heard the noise (Someone was sneaking up behind him), he turned quickly.
4. Eventually the audience filled with young adults (no children were allowed).
5. His speech was very well received. (his wife always knew that it would be.)

Exercise 3 Capitalizing Sentences

Rewrite correctly any of the following sentences that have errors in capitalization. Write *correct* if a sentence has no errors.

Words to Ponder

1. the great Indian leader Mohandas Gandhi said, "civilization is the encouragement of differences."
2. The Chinese American novelist Maxine Hong Kingston remarked, "you can be a writer at any time. you don't have to worry about talent."
3. Eleanor Roosevelt wrote, "No one can make you feel inferior without your consent."
4. the civil rights leader Dr. Martin Luther King Jr. wrote that nonviolence is a powerful weapon. (he described nonviolence as a "sword that heals.")
5. The Russian-born sculptor Louise Nevelson said, "I never liked the middle ground—the most boring place in the world."
6. the Spanish philosopher and statesman José Ortega y Gasset wrote, "living is a constant process of deciding what we are going to do."
7. The Native American poet Simon J. Ortiz answered the question "why do you write?" by saying, "Your children will not survive unless you tell them something about them."
8. Albert Einstein wrote that imagination is more important than knowledge.
9. The American abolitionist Frederick Douglass wrote, "if there is no struggle, there is no progress."
10. Margaret Mead (She was an anthropologist) wrote, "today's children are the first generation to grow up in a world that has the power to destroy itself."

20.2 Capitalization of Proper Nouns

- Capitalize a proper noun.

Proper nouns name particular persons, places, things, or ideas. In proper nouns composed of several words, capitalize only the important words. Do not capitalize articles, coordinating conjunctions, and prepositions of fewer than five letters.

1. Names of individuals

Seiji **O**zawa	**S**equoya
Sally **R**ide	**S**erena **W**illiams
Mark **T**wain	**J**esse **J**ackson
Charles de **G**aulle	**C**atherine the **G**reat

2. Titles of individuals

- Capitalize titles used before a proper name and titles used in direct address.

Dr. Henry Ramirez	**C**hief Sitting Bull
Princess Caroline	**P**rime **M**inister Tony Blair
General Robert E. Lee	**S**ecretary of **S**tate Jefferson
Mother **T**eresa	**M**s. **J**ones
Pope John Paul II	**S**enator Durbin
Congresswoman Schroeder	Aye, aye, **C**aptain. [direct address]

- In general, do not capitalize titles that follow a proper name or are used alone.

Lawton Chiles, the **g**overnor of Florida, met with the **p**resident last evening at the White House.

- In general, capitalize a title that describes a family relationship when it is used with or in place of a proper name.

Have you met **A**unt Flora?	but	Have you met my **a**unt?
Please ask **G**randfather.		Please ask your **g**randfather.
What did you say, **M**other?		What did my **m**other say?
After a moment, **M**other spoke.		After a moment, my **m**other spoke.

3. Names of ethnic groups, national groups, and languages

Native **A**mericans	**I**talian
Laotians	**S**wahili
Mexicans	**J**apanese
Scots	**L**atin

4. Names of organizations, institutions, political parties and their members, and firms

Food and **D**rug **A**dministration
Girl **S**couts of **A**merica
Utah **S**tate **U**niversity
the **C**ongress
the **D**emocratic party
a **R**epublican
Bank of **A**merica
General **E**lectric

The word *party* is not capitalized. Do not capitalize common nouns such as *court* or *university* unless they are part of a proper noun.

She was appointed judge of the **F**irst **D**istrict **C**ourt.
Mr. Tavares was a witness in **t**raffic **c**ourt.
He became interested in science at the **u**niversity.

Exercise 4 Capitalizing Names and Titles

Rewrite the following items if they are incorrect, adding capital letters as necessary. If an item is correct, write *correct*.

1. george allen, the governor of Virginia
2. senator barbara boxer
3. aunt luisa and her mother
4. the progressive party
5. mount vernon college
6. our secretary of the interior
7. attorney general janet reno
8. securities and exchange commission
9. Sign here, general.
10. small claims court
11. general motors corporation
12. chief justice john marshall
13. scotch irish
14. hernando de soto
15. bishop john walker
16. What did you mean, grandfather?
17. 4-h club
18. Please respond, mr. secretary.
19. arabic
20. vietnamese americans
21. commodore matthew c. perry
22. mothers against drunk driving
23. We saw your uncle last night.
24. secretary of state albright
25. the university

5. **Names of monuments, buildings, bridges, and other structures**

   the **E**iffel **T**ower
   Vietnam **V**eterans **M**emorial
   World **T**rade **C**enter
   Golden **G**ate **B**ridge
   the **P**arthenon
   Sears **T**ower
   Lincoln **T**unnel
   Hoover **D**am
   Shea **S**tadium
   the **W**hite **H**ouse

6. **Trade names**

Chevrolet	**C**heerios
Kleenex	**F**riskies cat food
Xerox	**L**ifesavers

7. **Names of documents, awards, and laws**

the **C**onstitution	**P**ulitzer **P**rize
Fifth **A**mendment	a **G**rammy
Emancipation **P**roclamation	**B**ill of **R**ights
Treaty of **P**aris	**E**nvironmental **P**rotection **A**ct

   Do not capitalize short prepositions that appear as part of the name.

8. **Geographical terms**

   ■ Capitalize the names of continents, countries, states, counties, and cities, as well as the names of specific bodies of water, topographical features, regions, and streets.

Asia	**L**ake **H**uron
Africa	**B**iscayne **B**ay
Mexico	**G**rand **C**anyon
Virginia	**B**lue **R**idge **M**ountains
Oregon	**C**ape **C**od
Dade **C**ounty	the **S**ahara
Dallas	**M**iddle **E**ast
Atlantic **O**cean	**S**outhern **H**emisphere
Mississippi **R**iver	**M**ain **S**treet
Great **P**lains	**P**rince **E**dward **I**sland

The World Trade Center is a center of commerce.

9. Names of planets and other celestial bodies

Pluto	the constellation **S**corpio	the **S**un
Mars	**N**orth **S**tar	the **M**oon
the **B**ig **D**ipper	the **M**ilky **W**ay	

Earth is capitalized only when the word refers to the planet, but in that case, do not use the definite article, *the*.

Venus and **M**ars are **E**arth's closest planetary neighbors.
The archaeologists dug deep into the hard, sandy **e**arth.

10. Compass points

■ Capitalize the words *north, east, south,* and *west* when they refer to a specific area of the country or the world or when they are part of a proper name. Do not capitalize them when they merely indicate direction.

the **N**orth	*but*	**n**orth of 42nd Street
the **W**est **C**oast		the **w**est **c**oast of Africa
South **P**acific		**s**outh of Bangor
East **L**ansing		**e**ast of the school

11. Names of ships, planes, trains, and spacecraft

U.S.S. **C**onstitution	*S*pirit of *S*t. *L*ouis
Challenger	*Y*ankee *C*lipper

12. Names of most historical events, eras, and calendar items

Reconstruction	**W**ashington's **B**irthday
Middle **A**ges	**L**abor **D**ay
Ming **D**ynasty	**W**orld **W**ar **II**
the **C**rusades	**B**attle of **H**astings

Do not capitalize a historical period when it refers to a general span of time.

the **t**wenties
the **t**enth **c**entury

■ Capitalize the days of the week and the months of the year, but do not capitalize the names of the seasons *(spring, summer, autumn, fall, winter)*.

We met on a **M**onday in **M**arch; it was the first day of **s**pring.

13. Religious terms

■ Capitalize names of deities, religions and their denominations and adherents, words referring to a supreme deity, and religious books and events.

God	**M**uslims
Allah	**Q**ur'an
Christianity	**N**ew **T**estament
Russian **O**rthodox	the **A**lmighty
Protestants	**H**anukkah
Jews	the **S**econd **C**oming
Buddhism	**F**our **N**oble **T**ruths

14. Names of school courses

■ Capitalize only those school courses that are the name of a language or the title of a specific course. Do not capitalize the name of a subject.

Advanced **A**lgebra	*but*	**a**lgebra
Spanish		**g**eography
Music 101		**m**usic
World **C**ultures II		**w**orld **h**istory

15. Titles of works

the *Odyssey*	[epic poem]
"The Gift of the Magi"	[story]
the *Los Angeles Times*	[newspaper]
"Home on the Range"	[song]
Information Please Almanac	[reference book]

Always capitalize the first and last words of a title or subtitle. Do not capitalize articles, coordinating conjunctions, or prepositions of fewer than five letters unless they appear as the first word of the title itself.

■ Capitalize articles (*a, an,* and *the*) at the beginning of a title only when they are part of the title itself. It is common practice not to capitalize (or italicize) articles preceding the title of a newspaper or a periodical. Do not capitalize (or italicize) the word *magazine* unless it is part of the title of a periodical.

"The Fifty-first Dragon"	the *Christian Science Monitor*
"A Marriage Proposal"	a *Newsweek* magazine

20.2 Capitalization of Proper Nouns

Exercise 5 — Capitalizing Proper Nouns

Write the following items, adding capital letters where necessary.

SAMPLE jefferson memorial
ANSWER Jefferson Memorial

1. antioch college
2. jacqueline kennedy onassis
3. library of congress
4. the *wall street journal* and *time* magazine
5. portuguese, spanish, and latin
6. the capitol
7. aunt lydia and uncle ted
8. the speaker of the house, denny hastert
9. the magna carta
10. national urban league
11. amy tan's *the kitchen god's wife*
12. the oscars
13. sunday, march 5
14. the eastern hemisphere
15. hispanics
16. pikes peak
17. aunt vanessa
18. venus, pluto, mars, and earth
19. my favorite classes are calculus II and my history class.
20. *the world book encyclopedia*
21. "the legend of sleepy hollow"
22. ivory soap
23. fourth of july
24. the uss *maine*
25. fifth avenue in new york city

Exercise 6 — Identifying Reasons for Capitalization

On your paper, explain why you capitalized or did not capitalize each of the items in Exercise 5.

SAMPLE Jefferson Memorial
ANSWER name of a monument

Exercise 7   **Capitalizing Proper Nouns**

For each sentence below, find the words with capitalization errors and write them correctly.

Early Settlers in America

1. Early in the Seventeenth Century, king james I of England gave a trading company the right to send settlers to live in what would become north america.
2. The settlers, among them captain John Smith, set sail in the Company's ships, the *godspeed,* the *discovery,* and the *susan constant.*
3. After crossing the atlantic ocean, the Settlers founded jamestown, Virginia, the first permanent British settlement in north america.
4. In 1619 a ship owned by holland brought the first africans to the colonies in america.
5. The pilgrims, a group of English puritans, landed a good distance North of Virginia, in present-day massachusetts, in december of 1620.
6. Squanto, a native american, helped the pilgrims survive their first harsh Winter in the Settlement named plymouth.
7. Wall street in New York city is named after a wall built in 1653 by colonists from holland who feared an attack by the British.
8. In 1681 william penn, the english quaker leader, together with a group of quakers, founded the City of Philadelphia on the Delaware river.
9. In philadelphia members of all religious groups were allowed to worship god and interpret the bible in their own way.
10. In 1704 the first issue of a successful colonial newspaper, the *boston newsletter,* was printed.
11. Samuel de Champlain, who built the first french settlement in north America at quebec, established friendly ties with the powerful algonquian nation.
12. Among the hundreds of french explorers who explored the area around the great lakes was father marquette, a Priest.
13. La salle claimed the entire valley of the mississippi River for France and named the area louisiana in honor of king Louis XIV.
14. The southern section of the carolinas, South Carolina, attracted scots, germans, and emigrants from the west Indies.
15. In the winter of 1634, some 200 settlers, many of them catholics, sailed into the chesapeake bay and established the colony of maryland.
16. In 1649 lord baltimore secured the passage of the toleration act, guaranteeing freedom of worship for all Christians.
17. In 1636 the first colonial college, harvard, was founded in massachusetts.
18. Two of the early Presidents of the college were the reverend increase mather and his son cotton.
19. Among the required subjects were greek, latin, and theology.
20. In the north, schoolchildren were taught not only to read but also to write about god from the *new england primer.*

20.3 Capitalization of Proper Adjectives

■ Capitalize proper adjectives (adjectives formed from proper nouns).

Most proper adjectives fit into the following categories:

1. Adjectives formed from names of people

Napoleonic era	**J**acksonian ideals
Victorian customs	**M**arxist revolutionary
Georgian architecture	**D**ickensian character

2. Adjectives formed from place names and names of national, ethnic, and religious groups

Chinese acupuncture	**H**ispanic studies
Saharan winds	**I**sraeli dances
Midwestern accent	**N**orwegian accent
European languages	**B**uddhist temple

Many proper nouns do not undergo a change in form when they are used as adjectives.

United **N**ations calendar	**T**hanksgiving dinner
New **O**rleans cooking	**P**assover meal
Beethoven sonata	**M**onday night
Kodak camera	**R**epublican victory

Exercise 8 Using Proper Adjectives

Form a proper adjective from each of the proper nouns listed below.

SAMPLE Queen Elizabeth I
ANSWER Elizabethan

1. Thomas Jefferson
2. Guatemala
3. Pablo Picasso
4. South America
5. Alaska
6. Japan
7. Islam
8. Greece
9. Easter
10. Navajo
11. William Shakespeare
12. Australia
13. Michigan
14. Paris
15. Hanukkah
16. Middle East
17. Malaysia
18. Joseph Stalin
19. African American
20. Pacific Ocean

Exercise 9   Capitalizing Proper Adjectives and Proper Nouns

For each sentence below, find the words with capitalization errors and write them correctly.

The Triumph of Kathleen Battle

1. Kathleen Battle, a talented contemporary american Opera singer, is celebrated for the purity of her voice.
2. Born in the City of Cleveland, Ohio, she studied at the College Conservatory of music at the university of Cincinnati.
3. In addition to being one of the favorite Sopranos at the Metropolitan Opera House in New York city, she has won ovations in many european Opera Houses.
4. Battle is best known for her roles in mozart operas, including *the magic flute.*
5. She has worked closely in many Concerts and on many Musical Recordings with James Levine, a well-known Conductor.
6. In 1988 Battle sang in New York's central park with the italian star luciano Pavarotti.
7. Later that year, she traveled to the far east and sang in Tokyo with the spanish opera star Placido Domingo.
8. One of her greatest triumphs was her role in *antony and cleopatra,* an opera based on a shakespearean play.
9. The Opera recounts the story of Mark Antony, a Roman Consul, who is bewitched by the charms of queen Cleopatra of Egypt.
10. Although they often appeared in broadway musicals, few african American singers won major roles in opera.
11. In recent years, however, Kathleen Battle, Leontyne price, and Jessye norman have reversed that trend.
12. Battle may perform at the tallest opera house, a 42-story building on wacker drive in Chicago, illinois.
13. She may sing excerpts from italian operas written during the Nineteenth Century.
14. It is unlikely that she will sing one of the long Arias from a wagnerian opera.
15. My Aunt Julia is taking her Mother to the concert as a mother's day present.
16. It is believed that the first opera was *dafne,* written by jacopo Peri and introduced in florence, italy, in 1597.
17. One Winter, Battle's outstanding recording of spirituals was nominated for a grammy.
18. Battle may one day follow in the steps of the Contralto marian anderson and sing at the Lincoln memorial.
19. Do you think the daughters of the american revolution will invite her to perform at constitution hall in Washington, d.c.?
20. I would like Battle to be invited to sing when the democratic party meets to nominate its next Candidate for President.

The chart below reviews which words should be capitalized.

Summary of Capitalization Rules

CAPITALIZE	DO NOT CAPITALIZE
She gave us thirty pages of reading for homework. (**S**he said we needed to do it.)	For homework (**s**he said we needed to catch up) she gave us thirty pages of reading.
He said, "**L**et me drive."	He said that **h**e would drive.
Then **F**ather smiled at me.	My **f**ather wants to retire.
Captain **A**hab	The **c**aptain paced the deck.
Texas **S**tate **U**niversity	a **u**niversity in Texas
Lawrence **H**all of **S**cience	the **s**cience **m**useum in town
Prell shampoo; **I**vory soap	Bring **s**oap and **s**hampoo.
Bill of **R**ights	an animal **b**ill of **r**ights
Pacific **O**cean; **G**hirardelli **S**quare; **S**anta **C**lara **A**venue	the **s**quare where the two **a**venues meet near the **o**cean
Neptune; **M**ercury; **E**arth	**p**lanets; the **e**arth
the **K**orean **W**ar	the **w**ar in the former Yugoslavia
the **B**ible; **H**alloween	**s**acred **b**ook; **h**olidays
Russian; **E**nglish **L**iterature I	**f**oreign **l**anguage; **l**iterature
Third **D**istrict **C**ourt	**s**mall **c**laims court
the **F**ar **E**ast	the **f**ar **e**astern tip of **K**orea
the **I**ce **A**ge	the **t**wentieth **c**entury
"**T**he **F**all of the **H**ouse of **U**sher"	the **s**tory
the *Dayton Daily News*	the **b**ook, **n**ewspaper, or **m**agazine
Tuesday; **J**uly	**s**pring; **f**all

Exercise 10   Using Correct Capitalization in a Dialogue

Write several sentences of dialogue between you and a friend about a country you would like to visit and the sights you would like to see. Use a variety of proper nouns and proper adjectives. Capitalize all sentences, quotations, proper nouns, and proper adjectives correctly.

Exercise 11   **Identifying Correct Capitalization**

Write the letter of the one item that is correctly capitalized in each of the following pairs.

1. **a.** James Baldwin wrote, "one cannot deny the humanity of another without diminishing one's own."
   b. James Baldwin wrote, "One cannot deny the humanity of another without diminishing one's own."
2. **a.** university of California
   b. University of California
3. **a.** General George Patton
   b. general George Patton
4. **a.** The English stage actress Rachel Kempson is the mother of Vanessa and Lynn Redgrave.
   b. The English stage actress Rachel Kempson is the Mother of Vanessa and Lynn Redgrave.
5. **a.** Georgia O'Keeffe's painting *New York night* is done mostly in dark colors.
   b. Georgia O'Keeffe's painting *New York Night* is done mostly in dark colors.
6. **a.** *A Raisin In The Sun*
   b. *A Raisin in the Sun*
7. **a.** European History I and physics
   b. European History I and Physics
8. **a.** a Buddhist temple on Homan Avenue
   b. a buddhist temple on Homan avenue
9. **a.** I wished that summer would not fade so quickly.
   b. I wished that Summer would not fade so quickly.
10. **a.** West of the Colorado River
    b. west of the Colorado River

Georgia O'Keeffe's
New York Night

New York at night

20.3 Capitalization of Proper Adjectives   **723**

UNIT 20 Grammar Review

CAPITALIZATION

Immortalized in Garrison Keillor's radio show *A Prairie Home Companion* is the fictional town of Lake Wobegon. Keillor's book *Lake Wobegon Days* grew out of the radio show. This passage from the book has been annotated to show some of the rules of capitalization covered in this unit.

Literature Model

from Lake Wobegon Days
by Garrison Keillor

The town of Lake Wobegon, Minnesota, lies on the shore against Adams Hill, looking east across the blue-green water to the dark woods. From the south, the highway aims for the lake, bends hard left by the magnificent concrete Grecian grain silos, and eases over a leg of the hill past the SLOW CHILDREN sign, bringing the traveler in on Main Street toward the town's one traffic light, which is almost always green. A few surviving elms shade the street. Along the ragged dirt path between the asphalt and the grass, a child slowly walks to Ralph's Grocery, kicking an asphalt chunk ahead of him. It is a chunk that after four blocks he is now mesmerized by, to which he is completely dedicated. At Bunsen Motors the sidewalk begins.... The boy kicks the chunk at the curb, once, twice, then lofts it over the curb and sidewalk across the concrete to the island of Pure Oil pumps. He jumps three times on the Bunsen bell hose, making three dings back in the dark garage. The mayor of Lake Wobegon, Clint Bunsen, peers out from the grease pit, under a black Ford pickup.

Incorporated under the laws of Minnesota but omitted from the map due to the incompetence of surveyors, first named "New Albion" by New Englanders who thought it would become the Boston of the west, taking its ultimate name from an Indian phrase that means either "Here we are!"

Annotations:
- Place names
- Compass point, not capitalized
- Proper adjective
- First word of a sentence
- Name of a firm
- Title not capitalized because not followed directly by an individual's name
- Trade name
- First word of a full sentence in quotation marks

Grammar Review

or "We sat all day in the rain waiting for [you]," Lake Wobegon is the seat of tiny Mist County, the "phantom county in the heart of the heartland" (Dibbley, *My Minnesota*), founded by Unitarian missionaries and Yankee promoters, then found by Norwegian Lutherans who straggled in from the west, having headed first to Lake Agassiz in what is now North Dakota, a lake that turned out to be prehistoric, and by German Catholics, who, bound for Clay County, had stopped a little short, having misread their map, but refused to admit it.

A town with few scenic wonders such as towering pines or high mountains but with some fine people of whom some are over six feet tall, its highest point is the gold ball on the flagpole atop the Norge Co-op grain elevator south of town on the Great Northern spur, from which Mr. Tollefson can see all of Mist County when he climbs up to raise the flag on national holidays, including Norwegian Independence Day, when the blue cross of Norway is flown. (No flag of Germany has appeared in public since 1917.) Next highest is the water tower, then the boulder on the hill, followed by the cross on the spire of Our Lady, then the spire of Lake Wobegon Lutheran (Christian Synod), the Central Building (three stories), the high school flagpole, . . . etc.

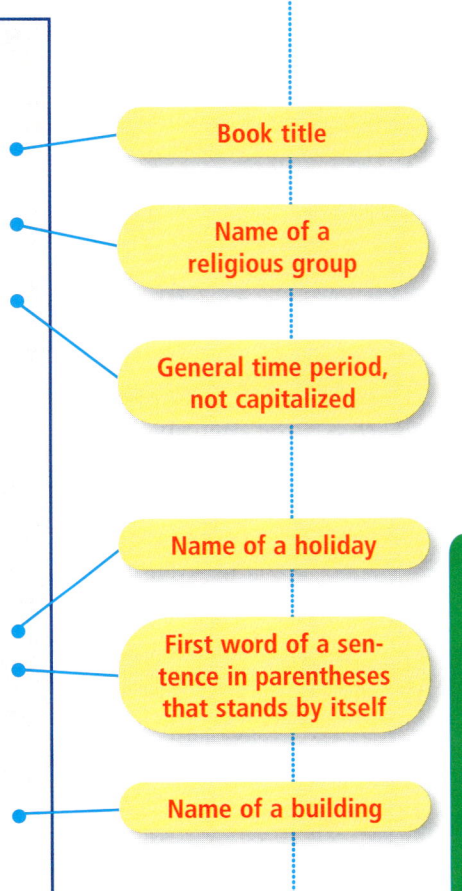

- Book title
- Name of a religious group
- General time period, not capitalized
- Name of a holiday
- First word of a sentence in parentheses that stands by itself
- Name of a building

Capitalization

Review: Exercise 1 — Capitalizing Sentences

For each sentence below, find the words with capitalization errors and write them correctly. If a sentence has no errors, write *correct*.

1. Lake Wobegon has been called "The little town that time forgot."
2. Keillor claims the town is not on any map because of surveying errors. (it is supposedly in central Minnesota.)
3. One explorer thought Lake Wobegon was the headwaters of the Mississippi River.
4. A statue of an unknown Norwegian Settler is a major landmark.
5. There is also a stone carved with Viking runes. (runes are old alphabetical symbols.)
6. A settler from Boston said that no civilized society could find comfort in the town.
7. later she said, "Providence has led us here."
8. The young woman (She had come west as a missionary) married a French trapper.
9. In his broadcasts, Keillor said, "that's the news from Lake Wobegon, where all the women are strong, all the men are good-looking, and all the children above average."
10. he also described the residents of Lake Wobegon as "Skeptical of progress."

Grammar Review

Review: Exercise 2   **Capitalizing Proper Adjectives and Proper Nouns**

For each of the following sentences, find the words that contain errors in capitalization and write them correctly. If a sentence has no errors, write *correct*.

1. Though lake wobegon characters seem ordinary, many famous americans, both real and imaginary, have minnesota roots.
2. Sinclair Lewis, a nobel prize winner, set his novel *babbitt* in a town that resembled his birthplace, sauk Centre.
3. Charles Lindbergh, a minnesota native of swedish descent, made the first solo flight across the atlantic ocean.
4. The Mayo Clinic founders, Drs. Charles and William Mayo, established their famous hospital in Minnesota.
5. The Minnesota-born actress and singer Judy Garland won worldwide popularity as Dorothy in *The Wizard of Oz.*
6. Ole Rölvaag, a Minnesotan of scandinavian ancestry, wrote novels about pioneers in the dakotas.
7. Eugene McCarthy, who was a united states senator from Minnesota, sought the democratic party's nomination for President in 1968.
8. John S. Pillsbury, a founder of pillsbury, a food-products company, served as a republican Governor of Minnesota for three terms.
9. The minnesota-born author F. Scott Fitzgerald depicted the decaying morality of society in the years following world war I.
10. The paul bunyan and hiawatha legends, both based on fictional heroes, are set in the minnesota frontier.

Review: Exercise 3

Proofreading

The following passage describes the artist Grant Wood, whose painting appears on the opposite page. Rewrite the passage, correcting the errors in spelling, capitalization, grammar, and usage. Add any missing punctuation. There are twenty-five errors.

Grant Wood

¹Grant Wood (1892–1941) was born on a farm outside the small town of anamosa, Iowa. ²He studied at the Handicraft Guild in Minneapolis and at the Art institute of Chicago. ³Before he began militery service in 1918, he worked as a schoolteacher, an interior decorator and a metalworker. ⁴After World war I ended, he returned to Iowa to teach Art.

Grammar Review

Grant Wood, *Stone City, Iowa*, 1930

⁵Wood made several trips to Europe over the next decade, and he studied at a parisian art school. ⁶His European travels reflected his discontent with american art, and his early works recall those of the french painters of the late nineteenth century. ⁷Wood later had a change of hart and began to concentrate on American subjects. ⁸Eventually, he, along with thomas Hart Benton, was ranked as one of America's great regional painters.

⁹Wood is best known for his portrayals of the land and the people of the midwest. ¹⁰His pictures are finely detailed his landscapes are reduced to round shapes, and his people are witty caricatures. ¹¹His technique was influenced by the lush and detailed paintings of the flemish masters. ¹²He was also influenced strangely enough, by the stylized pattern on his Mother's dishes. ¹³His best-known work, *American gothic,* is typical of his mature style. ¹⁴The painting, which was completed in the 1930s, show a man holding a pitchfork and standing with his wife in front of a farmhouse.

¹⁵Wood, who painted very slowly produced relatively few major works during his lifetime. ¹⁶In *Stone City, Iowa,* the painting on this page, neither his skill as an Artist nor his reverence for the rural countryside are missing. ¹⁷Woods gently ironic realism is like that of Garrison Keillor. ¹⁸Each poke fun at the obsevise orderliness—both physical and moral—of the people who live in the small towns of the Midwest. ¹⁹Do so with respect and tenderness.

Grammar Review

Review: Exercise 4

Mixed Review

For each of the following sentences, find the words that contain errors in capitalization and write the words correctly. If a sentence has no errors, write *correct*.

Garrison Keillor

1. Garrison Keillor was born in 1942 in Anoka county, Minnesota, to parents of scottish descent.
2. After finishing High School, he entered the University of Minnesota. (he earned a degree in english in 1966.)
3. Keillor had written earlier for the *Anoka herald,* and he became Editor of the literary magazine at the University.
4. Hoping to work as a journalist, Keillor went East to New York after college, but he soon returned to minnesota.
5. in 1974 he sold a story about the Grand ole Opry to the *New Yorker* for $6,000 (More money than he had ever seen).
6. In the Spring of 1974, Keillor and his Wife and son traveled by train through the Northern rockies.
7. In idaho the Keillor family boarded an old bus heading for Washington. (the train they had been traveling on had derailed.)
8. From portland they took the southbound train, the *coast starlight,* to San Francisco.
9. On the trip, Keillor started a story titled "the lake wobegon memoir," but it was stolen from his briefcase in the Train Station.
10. Years later, in the Eighties, Keillor would write *Lake Wobegon Days,* a book that he insists Is not as fine as his lost story.
11. The book has been described as an unforgettable portrait of why we "are what we are" and why being smart "doesn't count for much."
12. In july 1974, Keillor began hosting a *Prairie Home Companion,* a radio show on Public Radio in Minnesota.
13. Keillor has said that one of his Great-Uncles, Uncle Lew (his Grandmother's brother), inspired some of the show's homespun characters.
14. The imaginary sponsors for the humorous show were Raw bits Cereal and a pet shop called Bertha's kitty boutique.
15. On the show, Keillor talked about the unitarian missionaries who started the town and the arrival of the first settlers, norwegian lutherans and german catholics.
16. He described albion college and its crazed founder, the reverend watt.
17. Students at the college studied latin, poetry, penmanship, and moral psychology I.
18. On Groundhog Day, the Sons of Knute sponsored an ice melt contest.
19. The radio show was a recipient of the peabody award.
20. At times Garrison Keillor has lived in Wisconsin and in new york city.

Writing Application

Capitalization in Writing

In "Skeletons in the Attic," Clara Spotted Elk describes how Native Americans regained the skeletal remains of their ancestors. As you read the passage below, pay special attention to the use of capitalization.

> Millions of American Indians lived in this country when Columbus first landed on our shores. After the western expansion, only 250,000 Indians survived. What happened to the remains of these people who were decimated by the advance of the white man? Many are gathering dust in American museums.
>
> In 1985, I and some Northern Cheyenne chiefs visited the attic of the Smithsonian's Natural History Museum in Washington, D.C., to review the inventory of their Cheyenne collection. After a chance inquiry, a curator pulled out a drawer in one of the scores of cabinets that line the attic. There were the jumbled bones of an Indian. "A Kiowa," he said.

Techniques with Capitalization

Like Clara Spotted Elk, you should apply the rules of capitalization when you write and revise your own work.

❶ Capitalize proper nouns that name monuments, bridges, buildings, and other structures. Do not capitalize common nouns unless they are part of a proper noun.

PROPER NOUN the attic of the Smithsonian's Natural History Museum
COMMON NOUN the attic of the museum

❷ Capitalize adjectives formed from proper nouns but not those formed from common nouns.

PROPER ADJECTIVE Cheyenne collection
COMMON ADJECTIVE chance inquiry

> **TIME**
> For more about the writing process, see **TIME Facing the Blank Page**, pp. 121-131.

Practice Practice the rules of capitalization by revising the following paragraph on a separate sheet of paper. (You will need to capitalize twenty-five additional words.)

The explorer christopher columbus landed on what is now the island of san salvador in the late fifteenth century. Although he thought he had landed in india (because he thought so, he mistakenly called the people he found indians), he really landed in the bahamas, a chain of islands, cays, and reefs lying southeast of florida. At the time, the continent of north america was home for a wide array of independent cultural groups. since that time, archaeologists have discovered artifacts left by these pre-Columbian (that is, "before columbus") societies. Some of these artifacts are displayed in natural history museums such as the museum of natural history in new york city. Federal agencies such as the national park service in the department of the interior also house native american collections.

UNIT 21 Punctuation, Abbreviations, and Numbers

Lesson 21.1	The Period	731
Lesson 21.2	The Exclamation Point	732
Lesson 21.3	The Question Mark	732
Lesson 21.4	The Colon	733
Lesson 21.5	The Semicolon	735
Lesson 21.6	The Comma	738
Lesson 21.7	The Dash	749
Lesson 21.8	Parentheses	750
Lesson 21.9	Quotation Marks	752
Lesson 21.10	Italics (Underlining)	757
Lesson 21.11	The Apostrophe	759
Lesson 21.12	The Hyphen	762
Lesson 21.13	Abbreviations	765
Lesson 21.14	Numbers and Numerals	768

Grammar Review 772

Writing Application 779

21.1 The Period

- There are three punctuation marks used at the ends of sentences: the period, the exclamation point, and the question mark.
- Use a period at the end of a declarative sentence and at the end of an imperative sentence that is a polite command or request.

DECLARATIVE SENTENCE Track practice is held twice a week.
IMPERATIVE SENTENCE Please sign up for two track events.

Exercise 1 Identifying Use of the Period

Identify each of the following sentences that should end with a period by writing *declarative* or *imperative* on your paper. If a sentence is neither a declarative sentence nor a polite command, write *no period*.

The Swim Team

1. Our swim team will hold its first meeting next Tuesday
2. The first big swim meet will take place in one month
3. Please sign up in the gym
4. My specialty is the backstroke
5. Do you want to become a winner
6. We won three gold medals at the last swim meet
7. Be sure to wear your goggles
8. To remain on the team, you must maintain good grades
9. We have a lot of fun during practice
10. After practice we often get together at the restaurant across the street
11. Have you heard us sitting there talking about swimming
12. If you learn something about the sport, our conversations will be livelier
13. The ancient Greeks trained their soldiers to swim so they could cross rivers
14. In medieval times, swimming was unpopular because people feared the water might be unhealthful
15. In the nineteenth century, the British discovered that Native Americans used a swimming method similar to the modern crawl
16. Development of the flutter kick inspired the Australian crawl, the most common stroke today
17. Tell me how swimming became part of the modern Olympic games
18. There are four basic categories of Olympic swimming events: freestyle, backstroke, breaststroke, and butterfly
19. Have you heard that some Olympic swimmers have become movie stars
20. John Weissmuller, who won five Olympic gold medals in the 1920s, played Tarzan in the movies in the 1940s

21.2 The Exclamation Point

■ **Use an exclamation point to show strong feeling and indicate a forceful command.**

| Oh, no! | Look out! | What lovely weather! |
| Hurrah! | Wake up! | Get going! |

21.3 The Question Mark

■ **Use a question mark to indicate a direct question.**

Who would like a part-time job?

Which call should I answer first?

■ **Do not place a question mark after an indirect question (one that has been reworded so that it is part of a declarative sentence).**

He asked whether I needed a work permit.

I wondered why such a document was needed.

Exercise 2 Using End Punctuation

On your paper, rewrite the following sentences, adding periods, exclamation points, and question marks where necessary. You will add 20 marks in all.

First Aid

1. Don't you think that everyone should learn about first aid I think it's crucial
2. First aid is the immediate medical care given to an ill or injured person First aid can save lives
3. Oh, if only people realized the importance of first aid So many people could be helped
4. An instruction manual by John S. Kelly, published by the U.S. Bureau of Mines, has useful information about first aid Will you get the book from the library
5. The primary goals of first aid are to treat serious injuries, prevent infection, and make the injured or ill person as comfortable as possible Other problems are less important
6. If you come upon an injured person, try to send for medical help right away Don't panic
7. Are you the person best qualified to take charge If two of you know first aid, the one with more experience and training should take charge, and the other one can assist
8. If people are crowding the injured person, make them stand at a distance Be firm
9. Once you have sent for help and the patient is lying still, ask yourself which injuries require immediate attention Which are less critical
10. Because of possible broken bones or internal injuries, move an injured person only if it is absolutely necessary How vital this is

21.4 The Colon

Colons to Introduce

1. **Lists**
■ Use a colon to introduce a list, especially after a statement that uses such words as *these*, *the following*, or *as follows*.

> The science test on Friday will cover **these** areas**:** the circulatory system, the digestive system, and the nervous system.
>
> He requested **the following:** a hammer, a screwdriver, four nails, and a level.

Do not use a colon to introduce a list if the list immediately follows a verb or a preposition.

> The best nonanimal sources of protein **are** soybeans, wheat germ, brewer's yeast, nuts, seeds, and whole grains. [The list follows the verb *are*.]
>
> My sister likes to top her hamburger **with** lettuce, tomato, mustard, ketchup, and relish. [The list follows the preposition *with*.]

2. **Illustrations or restatements**
■ Use a colon to introduce material that illustrates, explains, or restates the preceding material. A complete sentence following a colon is capitalized.

> I often wish that my parents had had more than one child**:** They worry too much about me.

3. **Quotations**
■ Use a colon to introduce a long or formal quotation. A formal quotation is often preceded by such words as *this*, *these*, *the following*, or *as follows*.

> Mrs. Hopkins asked us to write an essay on **the following** African saying**:** "It is the rainy season that gives wealth."

Poetry quotations of more than one line and prose quotations of more than four or five lines are generally written below the introductory statement and indented on the page.

> In his long poem *The Other Pioneers*, Roberto Félix Salazar describes some of this nation's early settlers**:**
>
> > Now I must write
> > Of those of mine who rode these plains
> > Long years before the Saxon and the Irish came.

Other Uses of Colons

■ Use a colon between the hour and the minute of the precise time, between the chapter and the verse in biblical references, and after the salutation of a business letter.

| 12**:**30 A.M. | Genesis 7**:**20–24 | Sir**:** |
| 4**:**00 P.M. | Ruth 1**:**16–18 | Dear Ms. Snow**:** |

Exercise 3 — Using the Colon

For the items below, write each word or number that should be followed by a colon. Then write the colon itself. For any sentence that does not need a colon, write *correct*.

SAMPLE Any of these will work as substitutes ketchup, chili sauce, or salsa.
ANSWER substitutes:

The Game of Chess

1. Many people enjoy playing these board games chess, checkers, and pachisi.
2. Chess may have spread from place to place in the following order India, Persia, and Spain.
3. There are several board games that resemble chess checkers, the Japanese game *go* and Chinese checkers.
4. In chess each player has the following playing pieces one king, one queen, two bishops, two knights, two rooks, and eight pawns.
5. The qualities essential to a good chess player are a good memory, a quick mind, and foresight.
6. In some ways, chess is like war it pits two "armies" against each other.
7. The *Encyclopaedia Britannica* notes that chess players use strategies of attack and defense aimed at the surrender of the opponent's king. The encyclopedia continues as follows "Nevertheless, the game is only a rather limited simulation of war or, in Freudian terms, a sublimation of that aggressive impulse."
8. The Old Testament has the following to say about war

    They shall beat their swords into plowshares
    and their spears into pruning-hooks;
    nation shall not lift up sword against nation,
    neither shall they learn war anymore.
    —Isaiah 2 4

9. A regional chess tournament typically takes place on a three-day weekend, with two rounds each day at the following times round 1 occurs from 1100 A.M. to 100 P.M. and round 2 from 500 P.M. to 730 P.M.
10. In addition to the type of chess that most people play, other types include blindfold chess, lightning chess, postal chess, and computer chess.

21.5 The Semicolon

Semicolons to Separate Main Clauses

■ Use a semicolon to separate main clauses that are not joined by a coordinating conjunction (*and, but, or, nor, yet,* and *for*).

> Paul Robeson was an excellent singer and actor**;** he was also a talented football player.
>
> Paul Robeson was an excellent singer and actor, **and** he was also a talented football player.

■ Use a semicolon to separate main clauses joined by a conjunctive adverb (such as *however, therefore, nevertheless, moreover, furthermore,* and *subsequently*) or by an expression such as *for example* or *that is.*

In general, a conjunctive adverb or an expression such as *for example* is followed by a comma.

> Robeson appeared in many plays and musicals**;** for example, he starred in *Othello* and *Porgy and Bess.*
>
> Robeson appeared in *Show Boat* in 1926**;** subsequently, he acted in the films *Jericho* and *Song of Freedom.*

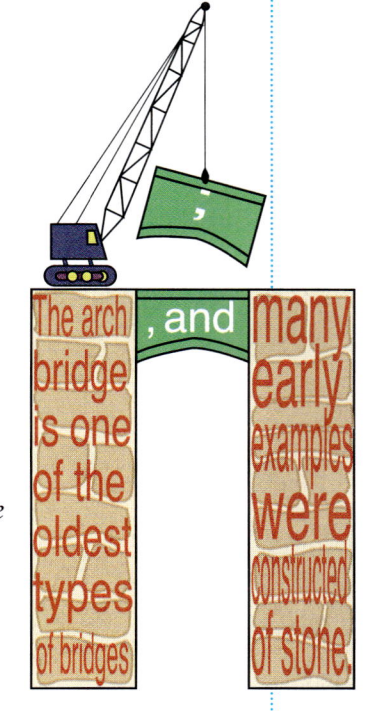

Exercise 4 — Using Semicolons and Commas in Clauses

On your paper, rewrite the following sentences, adding semicolons and commas where necessary.

Ancient Bridges

1. An early type of bridge was a tree trunk thrown across a stream another type was a primitive suspension span of twisted bamboo.
2. In 500 B.C., the Persian king Xerxes created a "bridge" of boats over the Bosporus Strait his purpose was to rapidly deploy ground troops into ancient Greece.
3. The finest ancient bridges were built by the Romans nearly 2,000 years ago for example the semicircular arch bridge over the Tagus River in Spain is still standing.
4. In the Middle Ages, Europeans began to build bridges with pointed arches however these features had been invented by Persian and Muslim engineers many years earlier.
5. In 1973 the Bosporus Bridge created the first road link between Europe and Asia since King Xerxes's bridge of boats more recently, a second bridge was built across that same waterway.

Semicolons and Commas

■ **Use a semicolon to separate the items in a series when the items contain commas.**

> Some of the powerful African kingdoms that flourished before the sixteenth century were Kush, which dominated the eastern Sudan; Karanga, which was located around Zimbabwe in southern Africa; Ghana, Mali, and Songhai, which successively controlled the Niger River in West Africa; and Benin, which had its center in what is now Nigeria.

■ **Use a semicolon to separate two main clauses joined by a coordinating conjunction when the clauses already contain several commas.**

> The rule of Mansa Musa, the Moslem emperor of the African kingdom of Mali from 1312 to 1337, is remembered for military success, trade expansion, and Moslem scholarship; but this period is probably most noteworthy as a golden age of peace and prosperity.

Exercise 5 Using Semicolons with Items Containing Commas

For the following sentences, write each word that should be followed by a semicolon and add the semicolon.

Ancient Kush

1. The heroes of the ancient kingdom of Kush were King Kashta, Prince Piankhi, and Piankhi's brother, Shabako, and they and their Kushite successors ruled Egypt for almost 100 years.
2. The Kushites, like the ancient Egyptians they conquered, worshipped Ra, the god of sky and sun, Isis, the great mother goddess, Osiris, the god of the underworld, and Horus, the son of Isis and Osiris.
3. In early times, Kush was famous for its ebony, ivory, gold, silver, incense, wood, and precious gems, but later its most precious resource became iron.
4. The gifts of the Nile River included rich soil for farming, water for irrigation, and a route for trading, and Kush was one of many societies that benefited from these gifts.
5. On its way to the Mediterranean Sea, the Nile River passes Khartoum, Sudan, Merowe, Sudan, Aswan, Egypt, Luxor, Egypt, and Cairo, Egypt.

Exercise 6   Using Semicolons

For the sentences below, write each word that should be followed by a semicolon and add the semicolon.

Louise Nevelson, Sculptor

1. The sculptor Louise Nevelson lived in a number of places in Europe and the United States, including Kiev, Ukraine, Rockland, Maine, Munich, Germany, and New York City.
2. At the age of five, Nevelson moved to Rockland with her family she lived there for fifteen years.
3. Nevelson's family name was Berliawsky at the age of twenty she married Charles Nevelson and moved to New York.
4. Nevelson studied art under Hans Hofmann, the abstract painter who used primary colors in explosive contrasts she also studied with the muralist Diego Rivera.
5. Many artists are not willing to struggle however, Louise Nevelson worked for years without money or fame.
6. Nevelson's first one-woman sculpture show was in 1940 after that she became world renowned.
7. Nevelson made sculptures with found objects her artworks were large and intricate.
8. Nevelson used many materials in her sculptures nevertheless, her wooden assemblages in black and white are the best known.
9. A pioneer in environmental art, Nevelson created walls of framed sculptures her large-scale works sometimes take up an entire room.
10. Nevelson's art was influenced by multimedia sculpture as well as Cubism and Surrealism in addition, the art of Africa and pre-Columbian America affected her work.
11. Her life spanned most of the twentieth century she was born in 1900 and died in 1988.
12. She collected old parts of furniture subsequently, she used such objects in her famous black-box sculptures.
13. The black boxes are arranged like shelves along a wall however, their effect is almost musical, with changes in tone and rhythm.
14. Nevelson's decorated walls reached the height of their development in the 1950s nevertheless, she continued to explore new artistic avenues.
15. In some of her later works, she employed aluminum, steel, and Plexiglas she became interested in working with these materials as time passed.
16. From an early emphasis on somber blacks and whites, she turned to brighter materials for example, she gave a white and gold finish to the sculpture known as Transparent Sculpture VI.
17. At first the untrained eye may find Nevelson's art difficult to understand however, close attention increases the viewer's appreciation for her imagination.
18. Nevelson's works can be seen in the Whitney Museum in New York City she also created an all-white chapel in Saint Peter's Lutheran Church in New York City.
19. There are several books that describe Nevelson's life and art one is a biography by John Gordon.
20. Other noted twentieth-century sculptors include Henry Moore, Alberto Giacometti, Alexander Calder, and Claes Oldenburg their styles are all fairly distinct from each other.

21.6 The Comma

As you study the rules for comma usage, keep in mind that to *separate* elements means to place a comma between two equal elements. To *set off* an element means to put commas before and after it.

Commas and Compound Sentences

■ Use commas between the main clauses in a compound sentence.

Place a comma before a coordinating conjunction *(and, but, or, nor, yet,* or *for)* that joins two main clauses.

> I am not going to the concert**,** for I am too busy.
>
> Many of the prospectors searched for years**,** but others struck gold immediately.

You may omit the comma between very short main clauses that are connected by a coordinating conjunction unless the comma is needed to avoid confusion.

> Mara washed the dishes and Jim dried them. [clear]
>
> We visited Miami and the Everglades are next. [confusing]
>
> We visited Miami**,** and the Everglades are next. [clear]

Exercise 7   Using Commas in Compound Sentences

For each sentence below, write the word that should be followed by a comma and add the comma.

The Everglades

1. We wanted to visit the Everglades National Park and we tried to learn as much as possible about the area before taking our trip.
2. These large marshlands are located in southern Florida but they once extended all the way to the Gulf of Mexico.
3. The northern part of the Everglades has been drained to provide more dry land and this area is now used for farming.
4. A hundred years of dredging, draining, and land clearing have taken their toll yet the Everglades have managed to survive.
5. We must work diligently to protect the Everglades or we will lose a unique ecological system.

Commas in a Series

■ Use commas to separate three or more words, phrases, or clauses in a series.

> A chair, a table, and a sofa were the room's only furnishings.
> The cat ran out of the house, across the lawn, and down the street.
> I rounded third, headed for home, and slid in safely.
> Read carefully, take good notes, and outline the chapter.

No commas are necessary when all of the items are connected by conjunctions.

> It was a sunny and hot and humid day in July.

Nouns that are used in pairs (*thunder and lightning, table and chairs, bread and butter*) are usually considered single units and should not be separated by commas. If such pairs appear with other nouns or groups of nouns in a series, they must be set off from the other items in the series.

> My favorite breakfast is bacon and eggs, toast, and milk.

Exercise 8   Using Commas in Series

For each sentence below, write the words that should be followed by commas and add the commas.

Our Scottish Terrier

1. We decided to get a Scottish Terrier to be our family's companion watchdog and friend.
2. Terriers were originally used to dig for small furry game engage their quarry underground and drive it out of the hole.
3. Today terriers are prized for their curiosity high spirits and friendliness.
4. Monty likes to take long walks ride in the car and eat all kinds of food.
5. We enrolled Monty in an obedience school where he learned to sit to stay and to heel.
6. The instructor told us that the secret to successful dog training is praise patience and persistence.
7. Sometimes Monty runs across the street sits in the neighbors' yard and watches their cat.
8. When he refuses to come, we try to entice him with a treat toy or ride in the car.
9. Monty's favorite toys are a squeaky soccer ball a rubber hamburger and a rope bone.
10. Everyone in our family agrees that Monty is a good friend valued family member and loving pet.

Commas and Coordinate Adjectives

■ **Place a comma between coordinate adjectives that precede a noun.**

Coordinate adjectives modify a noun equally. To determine whether adjectives are coordinate, try to reverse their order or put the word *and* between them. If the sentence still sounds natural, the adjectives are coordinate.

> Pepper is a good**,** obedient**,** gentle dog.

Do not use a comma between adjectives preceding a noun if they sound unnatural with their order reversed or with *and* between them. In general, adjectives that describe size, shape, age, and material do not need commas between them.

> Jelani grew up in a small white frame house.

Commas may be needed between some of the adjectives in a series but not between others.

> I like to read in our bright**,** cozy family room.

In the preceding sentence *and* would sound natural between *bright* and *cozy*, but it would not sound natural between *cozy* and *family*.

Exercise 9   Using Commas in Sentences

On your paper, rewrite the following sentences, adding commas between coordinate adjectives, items in a series, and main clauses. If a sentence needs no comma, write *correct*.

Arthur Schomburg, Collector

1. Arthur Schomburg led a long active productive life.
2. He grew up in Puerto Rico studied in the Virgin Islands and came to the United States in 1891.
3. Schomburg was an author and historian but he is best known as a collector of literature about African American culture.
4. Schomburg was also an important figure in the literary artistic and musical movement known as the Harlem Renaissance.
5. His collection included over 10,000 books and manuscripts and pamphlets.
6. The Carnegie Corporation bought the collection donated it to the New York Public Library and named it in Schomburg's honor.
7. The Schomburg Collection has a wide reputation because it has more books on African American history and literature than any other library in North America.
8. The collection is housed in a tall modern brick building in the Harlem neighborhood.
9. Users of the collection study African American history literature art or music.
10. You may find that your own local library has a collection of books about African American culture or that a nearby historical society has some information about local African American families.

Commas and Nonessential Elements

1. Participles, infinitives, and their phrases
■ Use commas to set off participles, infinitives, and their phrases if they are not essential to the meaning of the sentence.

> She watched, puzzled, as the man in the yellow hat drove away.
> A customer, complaining loudly, stepped up to the counter.
> I have no idea, to be honest, what you would like for a graduation present.

Do not set off participles, infinitives, and their phrases if they are essential to the meaning of the sentence.

> The man standing by the door is my father. [The participial phrase tells *which* man.]
> My mother's car is the one parked in the driveway. [The participial phrase identifies the car.]
> She went to medical school to become a doctor. [The infinitive phrase tells *why*.]
> To become a doctor had been her goal for years. [The infinitive phrase is used as the subject of the sentence.]
> I wanted to go home. [The infinitive phrase is used as the direct object.]

2. Adjective clauses
■ Use commas to set off a nonessential adjective clause.

A nonessential (nonrestrictive) clause can be considered an extra clause because it gives additional information about a noun. Because an extra clause adds to the basic meaning of a sentence, it is set off by commas.

> Atlanta, which is the capital of Georgia, is the transportation center of the Southeast. [*Which is the capital of Georgia* is a nonessential clause.]

Do not set off an essential adjective clause. Because an essential (restrictive) clause gives necessary information about a noun, it is needed to convey the exact meaning of the sentence.

> People who are afraid of heights do not like to look down from balconies or terraces. [*Who are afraid of heights* is an essential clause.]

3. Appositives
■ Use commas to set off an appositive if it is not essential to the meaning of a sentence.

A nonessential (nonrestrictive) appositive can be considered an extra appositive; it calls for commas.

> Nelson Mandela, the president of South Africa, was freed from a South African prison in 1990.
>
> My mother lives in Escondido, a town near San Diego in southern California.

A nonessential (nonrestrictive) appositive is sometimes placed before the noun or pronoun to which it refers.

> An insurance executive, Charles Ives wrote music in his spare time. [The appositive, *An insurance executive*, precedes the subject of the sentence, *Charles Ives*.]

An essential (restrictive) appositive gives necessary information about a noun and is not set off.

> The word *fiesta* came into English from Spanish. [The appositive, *fiesta*, is needed to identify *word*.]

Exercise 10   Using Commas with Nonessential Elements

On your paper, rewrite the following sentences that need commas, adding commas as necessary. If a sentence needs no commas, write *correct*.

The Great Red Ape

1. Junior the oldest male orangutan in the National Zoo in Washington, D.C., is a favorite of visitors.
2. The orangutan whose formal name is Atjeh is a great red ape.
3. He is a member of a species created by zookeepers who crossbred two subspecies of orangutans.
4. Many scientists have lately been surprised to learn that Sumatran and Bornean orangutans are more genetically different from each other than lions are from tigers.
5. Being so different from each other they probably would not interbreed in nature.
6. The organization overseeing zoo programs in the United States has called a halt to the interbreeding of Sumatran and Bornean orangutans.
7. The hybrids that are now in zoos will not reproduce.
8. Critics of the policy disagreeing vocally claim that the hybrids are being treated as second-class apes.
9. These critics' argument that the existence of the great red ape does not endanger the zoos' mission to emphasize conservation represents a controversial viewpoint.
10. A long-lived animal the orangutan can survive as long as sixty years.

Commas with Interjections, Parenthetical Expressions, Conjunctive Adverbs, and Antithetical Phrases

■ Use commas to set off interjections (such as *oh* and *well*), parenthetical expressions (such as *on the contrary, on the other hand, in fact, by the way, to be exact,* and *after all*), and conjunctive adverbs (such as *however, moreover,* and *consequently*).

>Well, we'd better be going home.
>Oh, I don't know.
>We have to leave, unfortunately.
>Last night, on the other hand, we could have stayed longer.
>We said we'd be home early; consequently, we must leave now.
>You might want to come with us, however.

■ Use commas to set off an antithetical phrase.

An **antithetical phrase** uses a word such as *not* or *unlike* to qualify what precedes it.

>You, not I, deserve this honor.
>Bicycles, unlike cars, cause no pollution.

Exercise 11   Using Commas

On your paper, rewrite the following sentences, adding commas where they are needed. If a sentence needs no commas, write *correct*.

Sequoya and the Cherokee Language

1. Most Native American languages unlike European ones were not written down before the eighteenth century; consequently it was difficult for people to learn them.
2. The Cherokees thought that writing was the privilege of certain people.
3. Like many other Native American groups in fact the Cherokees used smoke and drum signals to communicate with people some distance away.
4. Sequoya for example saw the need for a way of writing down his language.
5. Having considered the idea for some time he realized how valuable a written language would be.
6. He had been hurt in a hunting accident; therefore he had the leisure to think about a writing system.
7. Specifically he began to draw marks on twigs and stones.
8. People at first laughed at Sequoya's dream; however they soon began to change their minds about him.
9. Sequoya produced the first Cherokee alphabet making it possible for his people to write messages and record its history.
10. Sequoya who became successful despite the doubts of others was sent to Washington, D.C., in 1828 to represent the Cherokees.

Commas with Other Phrases and Clauses

1. Introductory prepositional phrases

■ Although a comma after a short introductory prepositional phrase is not incorrect, it is necessary only if the sentence would be misread without the comma.

> To those outside, the house appeared deserted. [comma needed to prevent misreading]
>
> At the last moment we decided not to go. [comma not needed]

■ Use a comma after a long prepositional phrase or after the final phrase in a succession of phrases.

> On the extremely steep and rocky cliff, the mountain climbers carefully found their footholds.
>
> On the afternoon of the day of the game, we made a banner.

Do not use a comma if the phrase is immediately followed by a verb.

> On the stone above the front door of the building was the date.

2. Introductory participles and participial phrases

■ Use commas to set off introductory participles and participial phrases.

> Purring, the kitten curled up in my lap.
>
> Sitting in a tree, my little sister called down to us.

3. Adverb clauses

■ Use commas to set off all introductory adverb clauses.

> Although I like country music, I did not want to hear his entire collection.
>
> Until she arrived, I thought that no one was coming.

■ Also use commas to set off internal adverb clauses that interrupt the flow of a sentence.

> Evan, after he thought about it awhile, agreed with our idea.

In general, do not set off an adverb clause at the end of a sentence unless the clause is parenthetical or the sentence would be misread without the comma.

Exercise 12 Using Commas with Phrases and Clauses

On your paper, rewrite the sentences that need commas, adding commas as necessary. If a sentence needs no additional commas, write *correct*.

I. M. Pei

1. To most people the name I. M. Pei means good taste and quality of design.
2. Among contemporary architects throughout the world Pei's name is unquestionably one of the best known and most respected.
3. Because his firm has frequently combined a beautiful and practical design with an affordable budget Pei is considered a gifted architect.
4. Among Pei's most successful designs are the East Building of the National Gallery of Art in Washington, D.C., and the pyramidal entrance to the Louvre in Paris.
5. Architects unlike artists must seek to harmonize appearance with purpose.
6. After a series of problems with the John Hancock Tower in Boston Pei's firm lost some business.
7. Pei and his staff gradually regained their hands-on reputation after the problems with the John Hancock Tower were resolved.
8. For a resort hotel in mainland China Pei created a design that pleased everyone.
9. Having been born in China Pei was happy to design a structure for his native land.
10. Although Pei has become highly successful as an architect he continues to welcome new challenges.

Exercise 13 Using Commas with Phrases and Clauses

Rewrite the sentences that need commas adding commas as necessary. If a sentence needs no commas, write *correct*.

Corn in the Americas

1. When it was recently determined that corn was first cultivated in the Americas only 4,700 years ago many scientists were puzzled.
2. Before this discovery they had thought that people in central Mexico started farming corn about 7,000 years ago.
3. Perplexed the scientists are trying to figure out if an earlier example of cultivated corn could have existed.
4. About 9,000 years ago in the Middle East around the Jordan River valley both plants and animals were domesticated.
5. If they do not locate an earlier sample scientists may have to rethink the chronology of civilization in the Western Hemisphere.
6. One famous botanist after he studied the matter cautioned his fellow scientists not to be too hasty.
7. In other parts of Mexico still older corn may be found.
8. Growing wild a plant that is similar to domesticated corn still exists in Mexico.
9. Scientists believe that ancient people once they discovered the wild corn plant began to cultivate it.
10. After it was discovered by the rest of the world corn became very popular.

Additional Uses of Commas

1. Titles of people
■ Use commas to set off titles when they follow a person's name.

> Alan Wong, M.D.   Maureen O'Connor, mayor of San Diego
> Jorge Gonzalez, Ph.D., will speak on Thursday.

2. Addresses, geographical terms, and dates
■ Use commas to separate the various parts of an address, a geographical term, or a date.

> Anaheim, California, is the home of Disneyland.
> Her address is 9 Lee Road, Nome, AK 99762.
> Friday, March 15, 1995, was the day I got my driver's license.

Use the following forms for letter writing.

> 90 Sherwick Road
> New Bedford, MA 02745
> July 7, 1997

Do not use commas if only the month and the day or only the month and the year are given.

> October 31   September 1996

3. References
■ Use commas to set off the parts of a reference that direct the reader to the exact source.

> Odysseus becomes reunited with his son Telemachus in the *Odyssey*, Book 16, lines 177–219.

4. Direct Address
■ Use commas to set off words or names used in direct address.

> Nathaniel, do you know where Kathleen is?
> I can order the book for you, sir, if you like.

5. Tag Questions
■ Use commas to set off a tag question.

A tag question (such as *shouldn't I?* or *have you?*) emphasizes an implied answer to the statement preceding it.

> You've already seen this film, haven't you?

6. Letter Writing

■ Place a comma after the salutation of an informal letter and after the closing of all letters.

Dear Dolores,   Very truly yours,

Misuse of Commas

In general, do not use a comma before a conjunction that connects a compound predicate or compound subject.

INCORRECT	She started the car, and drove down the hill. [compound predicate]
CORRECT	She started the car and drove down the hill.
INCORRECT	The adults playing softball, and the children playing soccer argued in the field. [compound subject]
CORRECT	The adults playing softball and the children playing soccer argued in the field.

Do not use only a comma to join two main clauses that are not part of a series. Use a coordinating conjunction with the comma, or use a semicolon.

INCORRECT	John Wayne worked in Hollywood for almost 50 years, he made more than 200 films.
CORRECT	John Wayne worked in Hollywood for almost 50 years, and he made more than 200 films.

Do not use a comma between a subject and its verb or between a verb and its complement.

INCORRECT	What you do with your money, is your business.
CORRECT	What you do with your money is your business.
INCORRECT	For the overnight camping trip, you will need, a sleeping bag, a towel, soap, and a toothbrush.
CORRECT	For the overnight camping trip, you will need a sleeping bag, a towel, soap, and a toothbrush.

Exercise 14 — Using Commas with Various Elements

On your paper, rewrite the following letter, adding twenty commas.

1516 Evergreen Road
Bonita CA 92002
October 5 1997

Dear Belinda

Your mom told me that you want advice about a good diet. She said you want to lose twenty pounds. I hope that she has misunderstood your goal Belinda because you would be quite thin if you lost that much weight wouldn't you?

I have enclosed a copy of an article about diet and weight loss that was published in the May 6 1996 issue of *News in America* page 22. Ruth Smith M.D. the author is a specialist in nutrition. In November 1990 I heard Dr. Smith speak at a conference in Washington D.C. and I have a great deal of respect for her knowledge. You will read this article carefully won't you?

I am looking forward to visiting your family at Thanksgiving. I haven't seen any of you since I was in San Diego on May 14 1989 for a convention. When I visit this year I hope we'll be able to spend some time together Belinda.

Love
Aunt Miriam

Exercise 15 — Using End Marks, Colons, Semicolons, and Commas

On your paper, rewrite the following sentences, adding all necessary punctuation.

The Movies

1. In the 1939 movie *The Wizard of Oz* a cyclone sweeps Dorothy out of rural Kansas and deposits her in the wild wonderful land of the Munchkins
2. You've surely seen and enjoyed *The Lion King* haven't you
3. As my grandmother remembers Shirley Temple a famous adorable and talented child star of the 1930s appeared in dozens of films
4. Movies such as these from the 1930s and 1940s have stood the test of time *Gone with the Wind It's a Wonderful Life* and *Treasure of the Sierra Madre*
5. To be honest most of Hollywood's films about cowboys and pioneers and Native Americans don't reflect the cold cruel facts of history
6. Quite a few movies by the way have been inspired by comic strip characters *Batman* and *Superman* are two outstanding examples
7. Robert Redford best known for his acting directed *A River Runs Through It*
8. According to my great-grandfather who will soon be eighty-five the comedy *The Gold Rush* starring Charlie Chaplin opened in May 1925
9. Because of their acting in *The Miracle Worker* both Anne Bancroft who played Annie Sullivan and Patty Duke who played Helen Keller won Academy Awards
10. Stars who perform their own stunts take unnecessary foolish childish chances

21.7 The Dash

When using a typewriter, indicate the dash with two hyphens (--). Do not place a comma, semicolon, colon, or period before or after a dash.

If you use a computer, you may make a dash with a certain combination of keystrokes. Refer to the manual of your word-processing program for instructions.

1. Dashes to Signal Change

■ Use a dash to indicate an abrupt break or change in thought within a sentence.

> A small stand sells sugar loaves—the gift to bring when invited to dinner—sugar for the mint tea and for the sweet pastry, so flaky and light, that they bake.
>
> Anaïs Nin

2. Dashes to Emphasize

■ Use a dash to set off and emphasize supplemental information or parenthetical comments.

> It was a shiny new car—the first he had ever owned.
>
> A shiny new car—the first he had ever owned—was his most prized possession.

Do not overuse dashes in your writing.

Exercise 16   Using Dashes

For each sentence below, write the phrase that should be set off with dashes and add the dash or dashes.

SAMPLE   He waxed and polished the old car a waste of time before he tried to sell it.
ANSWER   —a waste of time—

1. Uncle Raymond by the way, he's my mother's brother-in-law was the proud owner of a new foreign car.
2. He had purchased the sedan at the start of a driving tour of Europe his first visit to the place he called the Old Country.
3. When he brought the car back to the United States, he realized it had a few drawbacks especially the cost of maintenance.
4. Ironically, this car from northern Europe a region of frigid, snowbound winters performed poorly on icy roads in the upper Midwest.
5. The car proved its worth, however, after Uncle Raymond was involved in a major accident a highway pileup on Route 1 that totaled some of the other vehicles but left his car undamaged.

21.8 Parentheses

Parentheses with Supplemental Material

■ Use parentheses to set off supplemental material.

Commas and dashes as well as parentheses can be used to set off supplemental material; the difference between the three marks of punctuation is one of degree. Use commas to set off supplemental material that is closely related to the rest of the sentence. Use parentheses to set off supplemental material that is not important enough to be considered part of the main statement. Use dashes to set off and emphasize material that interrupts the main statement.

> Many contemporary women's fashions **(**business suits and low heels**)** show the influence of Gabrielle "Coco" Chanel.

A complete sentence within parentheses is not capitalized and needs no period if it is contained within another sentence. If a sentence in parentheses is not contained within another sentence (if it stands by itself), both a capital letter and a period are needed.

> The unisex trend **(i**t still seems to be popular**)** was started by Chanel, who wore a man's trench coat.

> Chanel introduced the world's most famous perfume, Chanel No. 5. **(T**his scent is still in great demand.**)**

Exercise 17 Using Parentheses

Rewrite the following sentences, adding parentheses where needed.

New Mexico

1. Albuquerque this fast-growing city is headquarters for a large computer chip manufacturer has a hot-air balloon fiesta every October.
2. The "sky city" of Acoma in this cliff-top site Native Americans have lived for hundreds of years is a place to view handsome geometric pottery.
3. The altitude of Santa Fe and Taos 5,000 to 7,000 feet helps to explain the cold winters that these two cities frequently get.
4. Bandelier National Monument contains fascinating cliff dwellings carved out of the volcanic rock by the Anasazi people. The Anasazi mysteriously disappeared from the pueblo long before the Spanish arrived.
5. Los Alamos named after the Spanish word for poplar trees is where the atomic bomb was developed in the 1940s.

Parentheses with Other Marks of Punctuation

1. With a comma, semicolon, or colon
- Place a comma, semicolon, or colon *after* the closing parenthesis.

> Despite the simple clothes that Chanel designed and wore (the little black dress became her uniform), she became wealthy.
>
> In the early 1950s, women wore long skirts with cinched waists and high heels (the Dior look); Chanel helped change that.

2. With a question mark or an exclamation point
- Place a question mark or an exclamation point *inside* the parentheses if it is part of the parenthetical expression.

> Chanel believed that simplicity and practicality were more important than obviously expensive, complicated-looking clothes (who would not agree today?).
>
> Chanel exerted little influence on fashion during World War II (1939–1945), but she reopened her fashion house in 1954 (when she was seventy!).

- Place a question mark or an exclamation point *outside* the parentheses if it is part of the entire sentence.

> Did you know that Chanel introduced many of today's fashion classics (sweaters, costume jewelry, sling-back shoes)?
>
> How amazed I was to find out that it was Chanel who made a suntan fashionable (in the 1930s)!

Exercise 18 — Using Parentheses

Rewrite the following sentences correctly, adding parentheses where they are needed.

1. Roger he lived next door to us for years had a great love for baseball.
2. Amarillo from the Spanish word for "yellow" is a town in the Texas Panhandle.
3. It was a December night the first winterlike night of the month, and snow was falling.
4. That song is it by Handel or Mozart? always reminds me of Paula, for she used to play it constantly when we were in college together.
5. He was aggressive, overbearing, mean, and who would have thought it possible! completely devoted to his dachshund.
6. Anorexia can have serious even tragic consequences if not treated properly.
7. Some people I am not one of them think that Elvis Presley was devastatingly handsome.
8. Do you believe in love at first sight forgive the cliché?
9. It was an extraordinary feat: she threw the javelin 245 feet about 75 meters!
10. Otis was an Air Force pilot during the Persian Gulf War the war against Iraq.

21.9 Quotation Marks

Quotation Marks for Direct Quotations

■ Use quotation marks to enclose a direct quotation.

Place quotation marks around the quotation only, not around purely introductory or explanatory remarks. Generally, separate such remarks from the actual quotation with a comma. (For the use of colons to introduce quotations, see page 733.)

A famous poster asks**,** **"**What if they gave a war and nobody came?**"**

A Pawnee poem reminds us of **"**the sacredness of things.**"**

Do not use a comma after a quotation that ends with an exclamation point or a question mark.

"What is the question**?"** Gertrude Stein asked.

■ When a quotation is interrupted by explanatory words such as *he said* or *she wrote,* use two sets of quotation marks.

Separate each part of the quotation from the interrupting phrase with marks of punctuation before and after the phrase. If the second part of the quotation is a complete sentence, begin it with a capital letter.

"A thing of beauty**,"** wrote John Keats**, "**is a joy forever.**"**

"It wasn't just that Babe Ruth hit more home runs than anybody else**,"** said Red Smith**. "**He hit them better, higher, and farther.**"**

Do not use quotation marks in an indirect quotation (a quotation that does not repeat a person's exact words).

ORIGINAL QUOTATION   **"**Dance is life at its most glorious moment**,"** said Pearl Lang.

INDIRECT QUOTATION   Pearl Lang said that dance is life's most glorious moment.

■ Use single quotation marks around a quotation within a quotation.

President John F. Kennedy said, "I am one person who can truthfully say, **'**I got my job through the *New York Times.***'**"

■ In writing dialogue, begin a new paragraph and use a new set of quotation marks every time the speaker changes.

He looked at me proudly. **"**Was it so hard to do, Daughter?**"**

"Not so hard as I thought.**"** I pinned the brooch on my dress. **"**I'll wear it always,**"** I said. **"**I'll keep it forever.**"**

—Kathryn Forbes

Exercise 19   Writing Dialogue Correctly

Copy the following sentences, setting them up correctly as a dialogue.

¹"I need help," Robert said. ²"What happened?" I asked. ³"I just locked the car keys in the trunk," he responded. ⁴"How did you ever happen to do such a thing?" I demanded. ⁵"I set them down there while I was looking for my house keys, which are missing too."

Exercise 20   Using Quotation Marks with Direct Quotes

Rewrite the following sentences, adding quotation marks where they are needed. For sentences that need no changes, write *correct*.

1. My method for remembering the numbers of days in all twelve months was given by my first-grade teacher, who said, Thirty days hath September, April, June, and November. All the rest have thirty-one, excepting February, and that has twenty-eight.
2. These are the times that try men's souls, warned eighteenth-century American pamphleteer and patriot Tom Paine.
3. Poet Bliss Carman writes, There is something in the autumn that is native to my blood / Touch of manner, hint of mood.
4. According to poet Bliss Carman, there is something about the autumn that is native to her blood—a touch of manner and a hint of mood.
5. Describing the false sense of good days ahead that Indian summer frequently inspires, poet Emily Dickinson writes, These are the days when skies put on the old, old sophistries.
6. If you were coming in the fall, writes Dickinson in another poem, I'd brush the summer by / With half a smile.
7. Poet T. S. Eliot tells us that for him April is the cruelest month.
8. April is the cruelest month, writes Eliot, breeding lilacs out of the dead land, mixing memory and desire.
9. Shall I compare thee to a summer's day? wrote Shakespeare. Thou art more lovely and more temperate.
10. At her sixtieth birthday party, the guest of honor said, This occasion inspires me to repeat the words of that old song, Though it's a long, long time from May to December, the days grow short when you reach September.

21.9 Quotation Marks

Quotation Marks with Titles and Unusual Expressions

- Use quotation marks to enclose titles of short works, such as short stories, short poems, essays, newspaper and magazine articles, book chapters, songs, and single episodes of a television series.

> "The Legend of Sleepy Hollow" [short story]
> "The Raven" [poem]
> "On the Duty of Civil Disobedience" [essay]
> "Steven Spielberg's Newest Film" [newspaper article]
> "The 1980s in America" [chapter]
> "If I Had a Hammer" [song]
> "Division of the Spoils" [episode in a television series]

(For the use of italics with titles of longer works, see page 757.)

- Use quotation marks to enclose unfamiliar slang and other unusual or original expressions.

> My cousin uses the expression "the cat's meow" to describe something she likes.
> The 1920s were known as the "roaring twenties."

- Be careful not to overuse quotation marks with expressions like these. Generally, use quotation marks only the first time you use the expression in a piece of writing.

Exercise 21 Using Quotation Marks with Titles and Expressions

Rewrite the following sentences, adding quotation marks where they are needed.

1. Before they began to write their essay, Sara and Miguel read the short story The Gift of the Magi.
2. Sara decided the title Giving to the Other Person would be good.
3. Miguel suggested adding his poem Time for Others at the end.
4. The teacher asked Miguel to explain the term the giving tree in the first paragraph.
5. Stephanie remarked, Your essay is going to be so good that I really think you ought to submit it to the school paper.

Quotation Marks with Other Marks of Punctuation

1. **With a comma or a period**
■ Always place a comma or a period *inside* closing quotation marks.

> "The frog does not drink up the pond in which it lives**,"** states a Native American proverb.
>
> Henry David Thoreau humorously advises, "Beware of all enterprises that require new clothes**."**

2. **With a semicolon or a colon**
■ Always place a semicolon or a colon *outside* closing quotation marks.

> Her father said, "We cannot go**";** her mother said, "Perhaps we can go next year**";** her elder brother just shrugged his shoulders.
>
> This is what I think of Lady Ōtomo's poem "My Heart, Thinking**":** it is romantic and powerful.

3. **With a question mark or an exclamation point**
■ Place the question mark or the exclamation point *inside* the closing quotation marks when it is part of the quotation.

> A famous sonnet by Shakespeare begins with these words: "Shall I compare thee to a summer's day**?"**
>
> She said, "I never want to hear from you again**!"**

■ Place the question mark or the exclamation point *outside* the closing quotation marks when it is part of the entire sentence.

> I've finally memorized all of "Paul Revere's Ride**"!**
>
> Why do you keep saying, "I'm sorry**"?**

If both the sentence and the quotation at the end of the sentence need a question mark (or an exclamation point), use only one punctuation mark, and place it *inside* the quotation marks.

> When did he ask, "Would you like to go to the movies**?"**

21.9 Quotation Marks **755**

Exercise 22 — Using Quotation Marks

Rewrite the following sentences, adding quotation marks where they are needed. For the sentences that need no changes, write *correct*.

Gabriela Mistral and Pablo Neruda

1. When Chilean poet Gabriela Mistral received the Nobel Prize for literature in 1945, the Swedish Academy said that Mistral had almost become a legend.
2. The poem Close to Me, which appears in Gabriela Mistral's first book, *Despair,* is a lullaby that is sung by a mother to a young child.
3. The refrain sleep close to me! appears at the end of each verse of the poem.
4. In his introduction to a collection of Mistral's poems, the African American poet Langston Hughes implies that her language is simple and direct.
5. Even when she sings the commonplace in life, writes critic A. Ortiz-Vargas, there is always a restraint, a dignity in her tone.
6. Ortiz-Vargas goes on to say, Sometimes her song soars high as on eagle wings, but more often it is rooted in the fertile region of her own heart.
7. Ortiz-Vargas writes, There is never any gaiety in her poetry—nor lightness—for her emotions are always ardently passionate; many other critics agree with his view.
8. The phrase a cry from the heart could be used to describe many of Mistral's verses.
9. Do you know Mistral's powerful poem about motherhood, Song of Virgo?
10. In his introduction to *Selected Poems of Gabriela Mistral,* Langston Hughes writes: Mildred Adams wrote, Gabriela's clarity and precision, her passion and that characteristic which can only be called her nobility of soul are accepted as ideals.
11. Another Chilean poet, Pablo Neruda, has been described by Luis Monguió in this way: a son of the New World, surging, creating, and coming to be, in quest of his destiny.
12. Neruda, also a Nobel Prize winner, says of his work, It is a poetry impure as the clothing we wear, or our bodies, soup stained, soiled with our shameful behavior.
13. In his poem You Flame-Foot! Neruda writes, Those feet of yours—pint-sized, no bigger than bees, how they eat up the shoe leather!
14. In his introduction to Neruda's *Selected Poems,* Monguió writes this about the critic Montesinos, Montesinos has said of the old Spanish baroque, It is the art of denying oneself nothing.
15. Poetry, to quote Neruda, is useful and usable; true and virtuous.
16. Have you read Neruda's famous poem Walking Around?
17. In it the poet compares Monday morning to an oil slick.
18. In Ode with a Lament, Neruda mourns, Only with waves at my back can I love you.
19. Juan Jiménez has said of Neruda, He is a great poet; a great, bad poet.
20. Neruda, in Monguió's view, seeks his salvation not in fantasy but in realism.

21.10 Italics (Underlining)

Italic type is a special slanted type that is used in printing. (*This is printed in italics.*) Indicate italics on a typewriter or with handwriting by underlining. (This is underlined.) When using a computer, find out the special keystrokes or icon needed for italics by referring to the manual for the software you are using.

1. **Italics with Titles**

- Italicize (underline) titles of books, lengthy poems, plays, films and television series, paintings and sculptures, and long musical compositions. Also italicize the names of newspapers and magazines, ships, airplanes, and spacecraft.

Great Expectations [book]	*Gone with the Wind* [film]
Romeo and Juliet [play]	*Starry Night* [painting]
Nova [television series]	*Grand Canyon Suite* [musical work]
The Thinker [sculpture]	the *Oakland Tribune* [newspaper]
Sports Illustrated [magazine]	*Spirit of St. Louis* [airplane]
USS *Enterprise** [ship]	*Columbia* [spacecraft]
Snow-Bound [long poem]	

    *Do not italicize abbreviations such as USS that precede the name of a ship.

- Italicize (underline) and capitalize articles (*a, an, the*) written at the beginning of a title only when they are part of the title itself. It is common practice not to italicize (underline) the article preceding the title of a newspaper or a magazine. Do not italicize the word *magazine* unless it is part of the title of a periodical.

A Light in the Attic	but	a *National Geographic* magazine
The Red Badge of Courage		the *Chicago Tribune*

2. **Italics with Foreign Words**

- Italicize (underline) foreign words and expressions that are not used frequently in English.

    The motto of the U.S. Marine Corps is **semper fidelis** ("always faithful").

Do not italicize a foreign word or expression that is commonly used in English.

I eat **croissants** for breakfast.

3. Italics with Words and Other Items Used to Represent Themselves
■ Italicize (underline) words, letters, and numerals used to represent themselves.

Do not start a sentence with **and** or **but.**

She was too superstitious to say the number aloud, so she handed the elevator operator a piece of paper on which she had written **13.**

Replace all of the number signs (**#**'s) with the word **number.**

Exercise 23 Using Italics

Write the words in each sentence below that should be italicized. Underline the words.

Women in the Olympics

1. In the book Golden Girls by Carli Laklan, you will find information about the many women who have won Olympic medals.
2. The ancient Greeks based the first Olympics on the concept of arete, which means "excellence in every area of life—physical, moral, and intellectual."
3. The author of Golden Girls notes that the earliest games featured just one event, the stade, a 200-yard footrace; the English word stadium comes from the Greek word stade.
4. The word Olympics comes from Olympia, the name of the Greek city where the first Olympic games were held in 776 b.c.
5. Sonja Henie, who won three gold medals in figure skating at three successive Olympic games, gained recognition as a movie star with her first film, One in a Million.
6. Peggy Fleming won a gold medal in figure skating at the 1968 Grenoble Olympics; she skated to Tchaikovsky's Pathétique.
7. With the financial backing of the publishers of the Chicago Tribune, Gertrude Ederle, who had won the gold medal for swimming in 1924, became the first woman to swim the English Channel in 1926; the French tug the Alsace followed her with a jazz band on board "to keep up her spirits."
8. Wilma Rudolph, who overcame serious illnesses in childhood, was the first American woman to win three gold medals in track and field; she later became a commentator for the radio series Olympic Odyssey.
9. After the 1984 Olympics, gold-medal winners Florence Griffith-Joyner and Jackie Joyner-Kersee were featured in Time, Life, Newsweek, the New York Times, and Sports Illustrated.
10. Many of the Olympic gold medalists have been on television series ranging from Saturday Night Live to 20/20.

21.11 The Apostrophe

Apostrophes with Possessives

1. Pronouns
■ Use an apostrophe and -s for the possessive of a singular indefinite pronoun.

Do not use an apostrophe with other possessive pronouns.

everybody's problem	*but*	**its** owner
each other's parents		**whose** talents
one's beliefs		The bikes are **theirs**.

2. Singular nouns
■ Use an apostrophe and -s to form the possessive of a singular noun, even one that ends in -s

the woman's team	San Francisco's earthquake
the class's election	Robert Burns's poetry
the princess's career	Cape Hatteras's beauty
the box's lettering	Groucho Marx's biography

There are some exceptions to this rule, however. To form the possessive of ancient proper nouns that end in -es or -is, and the names *Jesus* and *Moses*, just add an apostrophe.

Euripides' plays	Jesus' teachings
Acropolis' structure	Moses' laws
Hercules' feats	

3. Plural nouns ending in -s
■ Use an apostrophe alone to form the possessive of a plural noun that ends in -s.

| the countries' treaty | the Joneses' picnic |
| the trees' leaves | the Greens' barbecue |

4. Plural nouns not ending in -s
■ Use an apostrophe and -s to form the possessive of a plural noun that does not end in -s.

| women's clubs | Women's Bar Association |
| oxen's harness | mice's squeaks |

5. Compound nouns
- Put only the last word of a compound noun in the possessive form.

    my sister-in-law**'s** office
    the court-martial**'s** effect
    attorney general**'s** job
    the chief of staff**'s** order

6. Joint possession versus individual possession
- If two or more persons (or partners in a company) possess something jointly, use the possessive form for the last person named.

    Claude and Louise**'s** children
    Johnson and Johnson**'s** baby-care products
    Abbott and Costello**'s** antics

- If two or more persons (or companies) possess an item (or items) individually, put each one's name in the possessive form.

    Tina Turner**'s** and the Rolling Stones**'** songs
    Chrysler**'s** and the American Motor Company**'s** cars

7. Expressions of time and money
- Use a possessive form to express amounts of money or time that modify a noun.

The modifier can also be expressed as a hyphenated adjective. In that case, no possessive form is used.

    one dollar**'s** increase   *but*   a one-dollar increase
    five minutes**'** drive   a five-minute drive
    ten days**'** wait   a ten-day wait

Exercise 24   Using Apostrophes with Possessives

Copy the phrases below, adding apostrophes and whatever else is needed to make the italicized parts possessive. If a phrase is correct, write *correct*.

1. the *Smiths* car
2. a book of *hers*
3. one *lawyer* opinion
4. the *children* playground
5. *Johnson and Goldberg* main office
6. *Orestes* father
7. *somebody* mistake
8. two *weeks* worth of laundry
9. the *editor in chief* orders
10. *Larry and Joel* bicycles

Apostrophes with Special Plurals

■ Use an apostrophe and *-s* to form the plural of letters, numerals, symbols, and words used to represent themselves.

Italicize (underline) the letter, numeral, symbol, or word but not the apostrophe and the *-s*.

Your *q*'s look like *g*'s, and your *5*'s look like *S*'s.
She told me to replace the *henceforth*'s with *therefore*'s.

Apostrophes in Contractions

■ Use an apostrophe in place of letters omitted in contractions.

A **contraction** is a single word made up of two words that have been combined by omitting letters. Common contractions combine a subject and a verb or a verb and an adverb.

you'd	*formed from*	you had, you would
you're		you are
who's		who is, who has
it's		it is, it has
won't		will not

■ Use an apostrophe in place of the omitted numerals of a year.

the class of '94   the '92 campaign

Exercise 25 — Using Apostrophes

Write the words from the following sentences that require an apostrophe or an apostrophe *-s*. Mark them as needed.

Women and Literature

[1]Imagine that you were making a list of writers names for a new encyclopedia about female authors. [2]Under the *a*s youd include Louisa May Alcott, whos best known for *Little Women,* and Isabel Allende, author of *The House of the Spirits.* [3]Maya Angelou, who wrote *I Know Why the Caged Bird Sings,* would surely be on everyones list. [4]The *b*s would include the names of Toni Cade Bambara and Gwendolyn Brooks. [5]Both Bambaras novels and Brooks poems focus on the lives of African Americans and on womens issues. [6]Nikki Giovanni is a poet whod be listed under the *g*s; her books include *Black Feeling* and *My House.* [7]At least five twentieth-century authors names would be listed under the *m*s: Carson McCullers, Edna St. Vincent Millay, Margaret Mitchell, Marianne Moore, and Toni Morrison. [8]Millays and Moores names would be found on anyones list of talented poets; McCullers and Morrisons names are familiar to lovers of prose. [9]Most people don't know that Margaret Mitchells *Gone with the Wind* took ten years labor to write; it was finally published in 36. [10]In the entry about the novelist Katherine Anne Porter, youd want to mention Porters great-great-grandfathers name: Daniel Boone.

21.12 The Hyphen

Hyphens with Prefixes

A hyphen is not ordinarily used to join a prefix to a word. There are a few exceptions, however. If you are in doubt about using a hyphen, consult a dictionary. You should also keep in mind the following guidelines:

- Use a hyphen after any prefix joined to a proper noun or a proper adjective. Use a hyphen after the prefixes *all-, ex-* (meaning "former"), and *self-* joined to any noun or adjective.

    mid-Atlantic   pre-Renaissance
    all-city   trans-Pacific
    ex-coach   all-American
    self-confidence   post-Elizabethan

- Use a hyphen after the prefix *anti-* when it joins a word beginning with *i-*. Also use a hyphen after the prefix *vice-*, except in *vice president*.

    anti-intellectual
    vice-mayor
    vice president

- Use a hyphen to avoid confusion between words beginning with *re-* that look alike but are different in meaning and pronunciation.

    re-cover the couch   *but*   recover the ball
    re-store those cans   restore your confidence
    re-lease the car   release the brake

The offensive end recovered the ball.

Exercise 26 Using Hyphens with Prefixes

On your paper, write each word in the following sentences that needs a hyphen and add the hyphen.

Colonial America

1. In the preRevolutionary War era, there was a slow growth of antiBritish sentiment.
2. The average individual living in the midAtlantic colonies, for example, was beginning to feel more selfconfident about taking control of the government.
3. America was a land of opportunity where an exindentured servant could become a property owner, although the transformation sometimes required an allout effort.
4. After the Boston Tea Party, the colonists would have been doubly resentful had the British resent tea shipments into Boston Harbor.
5. The main place in the colonies where antiindependence feelings remained surprisingly strong was New York.

762 Unit 21 Punctuation, Abbreviations, and Numbers

Hyphens with Compounds and Numbers

1. Compound adjectives

■ Use a hyphen in a compound adjective that precedes a noun.

In general, a compound adjective that follows a noun is not hyphenated.

dark-green eyes	*but*	Her eyes are dark green.
a fifteen-year-old aunt		His aunt is fifteen years old.
a well-liked reporter		That reporter is well liked.

An expression made up of an adverb ending in *-ly* and an adjective is not hyphenated.

a nicely behaved dog	a fairly close race
a slightly rusted exterior	a hastily written report

2. Compound numbers

■ Hyphenate any spelled-out cardinal or ordinal compound number up to ninety-nine or ninety-ninth.

sixty-four	sixty-fourth
eighty-two	eighty-second

3. Fractions used as adjectives

■ Hyphenate a fraction used as an adjective (but not one used as a noun).

one-eighth teaspoon	*but*	one eighth of a teaspoon
one-quarter cup		one quarter of a cup
one-half pound		one half of a pound

4. Connected numerals

■ Hyphenate two numerals to indicate a span.

pages 30-56	1986-1990

Hyphens to Divide Words at the End of a Line

Words are generally divided between syllables or pronounceable parts. Because it is frequently difficult to determine where a word should be divided, check your dictionary.

■ **In general, if a word contains two consonants occurring between two vowels or if it contains a double consonant, divide the word between the two consonants.**

foun-tain	struc-ture
lin-ger	sup-per
profes-sor	tomor-row

■ **If a suffix has been added to a complete word that ends in two consonants, divide the word after the two consonants.**

| pull-ing | point-less |
| meaning-ful | strong-est |

Exercise 27 Using Hyphens

Hyphens must be added to five of the following sentences. On your paper, rewrite those sentences, adding the hyphens where they are needed. Then make a list of all the italicized words, showing where each would be divided if it had to be broken at the end of a line.

Sally Ride, Astronaut

1. Sally Ride was thirty one in 1983 when she became the first American woman to *orbit* the earth.
2. She was also the *youngest* American astronaut to go into orbit.
3. At Swarthmore College, where she did her undergraduate work, Sally Ride won a national tennis tournament for *college* students.
4. Astronaut Ride received her *doctorate* from Stanford University.
5. Dr. Ride said that one third of the *scientists* at NASA are women.
6. A thirty four year old Russian woman, Svetlana Savitskaya, *orbited* the earth about eight months before Dr. Ride.
7. Astronauts are *resourceful,* self confident, healthy, highly educated, and experienced in their special fields of study.
8. By the year 2010, space flight may become *common;* within your lifetime, thousands may be taking trips into space every year.
9. Well known ex astronauts such as John Glenn and Neil Armstrong were viewed as all American heroes for years after their space *missions.*
10. Astronaut trainees must learn to live in an almost *weightless,* low gravity environment.

21.13 Abbreviations

Abbreviations are shortened forms of words. Abbreviations save space and time and prevent unnecessary wordiness. For instance, *M.D.* is more concise and easier to write than *Medical Doctor*. Most abbreviations take periods. If you are unsure of how to write an abbreviation, consult a dictionary.

- Use only one period if an abbreviation occurs at the end of a sentence that would ordinarily take a period of its own.

- If an abbreviation occurs at the end of a sentence that ends with a question mark or an exclamation point, use the period and the second mark of punctuation.

> Gerry left at 8:00 **A.M.**   Did she leave at 8:00 **A.M.?**

Capitalizing Abbreviations

1. Abbreviations of proper nouns
- Capitalize abbreviations of proper nouns.

> 109-46 Queens **Blvd.**   **Rev.** Martin Luther King Jr.
> **N.** Michigan **Ave.**   **U.S.** Congress

2. Abbreviations formed from initial letters

Abbreviations of organizations and government agencies are often formed from the initial letters of the complete name. Such abbreviations, whether pronounced letter by letter or as words, omit periods and are written with capital letters.

> YWCA   NAACP   IRS
> NASA   UNICEF   CBS

3. Abbreviations related to dates and times

Capitalize the following abbreviations related to dates and times:

A.D. (*anno Domini*), "in the year of the Lord" (since the birth of Christ); place before the date: **A.D.** 5

B.C. (before Christ); place after the date: 1000 **B.C.**

C.E. (common era; equivalent to *A.D.*); place after the date: 66 **C.E.**

B.C.E. (before the common era; equivalent to *B.C.*); place after the date: 164 **B.C.E.**

A.M. (*ante meridiem*), "before noon"; place after exact times: 7:45 **A.M.**

P.M. (*post meridiem*), "after noon"; place after exact times: 2:30 **P.M.**

21.13 Abbreviations   **765**

Postal Abbreviations

In ordinary prose spell out state names. On envelopes, however, abbreviate state names as shown in the following list.

Alabama	**AL**	Montana	**MT**
Alaska	**AK**	Nebraska	**NE**
Arizona	**AZ**	Nevada	**NV**
Arkansas	**AR**	New Hampshire	**NH**
California	**CA**	New Jersey	**NJ**
Colorado	**CO**	New Mexico	**NM**
Connecticut	**CT**	New York	**NY**
Delaware	**DE**	North Carolina	**NC**
Florida	**FL**	North Dakota	**ND**
Georgia	**GA**	Ohio	**OH**
Hawaii	**HI**	Oklahoma	**OK**
Idaho	**ID**	Oregon	**OR**
Illinois	**IL**	Pennsylvania	**PA**
Indiana	**IN**	Rhode Island	**RI**
Iowa	**IA**	South Carolina	**SC**
Kansas	**KS**	South Dakota	**SD**
Kentucky	**KY**	Tennessee	**TN**
Louisiana	**LA**	Texas	**TX**
Maine	**ME**	Utah	**UT**
Maryland	**MD**	Vermont	**VT**
Massachusetts	**MA**	Virginia	**VA**
Michigan	**MI**	Washington	**WA**
Minnesota	**MN**	West Virginia	**WV**
Mississippi	**MS**	Wisconsin	**WI**
Missouri	**MO**	Wyoming	**WY**

The postal abbreviation for the District of Columbia is **DC.** In ordinary prose, however, use periods to write **Washington, D.C.**

Exercise 28 Using Abbreviations with Capital Letters

On your paper, write the abbreviations for the italicized words or phrases in the following sentences. If the terms should not be abbreviated, write *correct*.

1. My aunt lives near Washington, *District of Columbia.*
2. The *Internal Revenue Service* is responsible for collecting federal taxes.
3. The House of Representatives will be in session today from 10:00 *ante meridiem* to 4:00 *post meridiem.*
4. President Franklin Delano Roosevelt took office in *anno Domini* 1933.
5. The senior senators from *Illinois, California,* and *South Carolina* are having lunch together this week.

Using Abbreviations

■ Use abbreviations for some personal titles.

Titles such as *Mrs., Mr., Ms., Sr.,* and *Jr.* and those indicating professions and academic degrees (*Dr., Ph.D., M.A., B.S.*) are almost always abbreviated. Titles of government and military officials and members of the clergy are frequently abbreviated when used before a full name.

Mrs. Roosevelt	**Sen.** Dianne Feinstein
Harry Connick **Jr.**	**Gen.** Colin Powell
Rosalyn Ying, **Ph.D.**	Myron Greene, **D.D.S.**

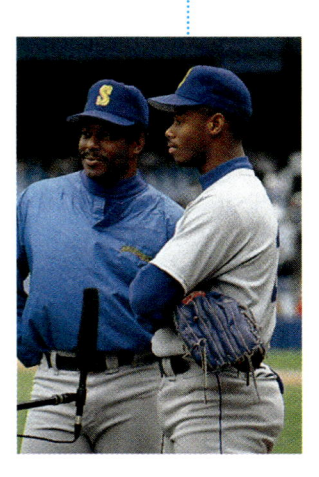

Ken Griffey **Sr.** and Ken Griffey **Jr.**

■ Abbreviate units of measure used with numerals in technical or scientific writing. Do not abbreviate them in ordinary prose.

The abbreviations that follow stand for both plural and singular units:

ENGLISH SYSTEM

ft.	foot	**mi.**	mile	**tbsp.**	tablespoon
gal.	gallon	**oz.**	ounce	**tsp.**	teaspoon
in.	inch	**pt.**	pint	**yd.**	yard
lb.	pound	**qt.**	quart		

METRIC SYSTEM

cg	centigram	**l**	liter
cl	centiliter	**m**	meter
cm	centimeter	**mg**	milligram
g	gram	**ml**	milliliter
kg	kilogram	**mm**	millimeter
km	kilometer		

Exercise 29   Using Abbreviations of Titles and Measurement Units

On your paper, write the abbreviations for the italicized words or phrases in the following sentences. If the terms should not be abbreviated, write *correct*.

1. *Senator* John F. Kennedy was elected president in 1960.
2. *Doctor* C. Everett Koop was surgeon general during the administration of President George Bush.
3. Harvey J. McCarthy *Junior* will testify before a Senate subcommittee during the first week of February.
4. I believe that the Washington Monument stands *555 feet* 5 1/8 *inches* high.
5. Bethesda, Maryland, a suburb of Washington, is located 8 *miles* (14.8 *kilometers*) from the Capitol.

21.13 Abbreviations   **767**

21.14 Numbers and Numerals

In nontechnical writing, some numbers are spelled out, and some are expressed in figures. Numbers expressed in figures are called *numerals*.

Regular Uses of Numbers and Numerals

- In general, spell out cardinal and ordinal numbers that can be written in one or two words.

    New Hampshire is one of the original **thirteen** states.
    There are **twenty-seven** students in the class.
    Alaska was the **forty-ninth** state to join the Union.

- Spell out any number that occurs at the beginning of a sentence.

    Sixteen hundred fifteen delegates attended.
    Eleven thousand people live in that town.

- In general, use numerals to express numbers that would be written in more than two words.

    Mount Mitchell, the highest mountain in the eastern United States, is **6,684** feet tall.
    In 1790 the total population of the United States (according to the first census) was **3,929,214.**
    In 1984 Joe W. Kittinger covered **3,535** miles in eighty-three hours and fifty-three minutes, setting a new record for balloon flight.

Very large numbers are often written as a numeral followed by the word *million* or *billion*.

    The surface area of the earth is close to **197 million** square miles.

- If related numbers appear in the same sentence and some can be written out while others should appear as numerals, use all numerals.

    Edgar ranked **5th** in the class; his brother ranked **119th.**
    They ordered **38** doll houses and **112** toy robots.

Special Uses of Numbers and Numerals

1. Money, decimals, and percentages

■ Use numerals to express amounts of money, decimals, and percentages.

>**$897** million **1.2** kilograms **5** percent

Amounts of money that can be expressed in one or two words, however, should be spelled out.

>**forty-five** cents **two thousand** dollars

2. Dates and time

■ Use numerals to express the year and day in a date and to express the precise time with the abbreviations A.M. and P.M.

> The U.S.S.R. launched *Sputnik I* on October **4, 1957.**
> She went to the meeting at **4:15 P.M.**

■ Spell out expressions of time that do not use A.M. or P.M.

> She set her alarm clock for **five** o'clock.

■ To express a century when the word *century* is used, spell out the number. Likewise, to express a decade when the century is clear from the context, spell out the number.

> The **twentieth** century saw great technological advances.
> The Great Depression of the **thirties** was an economic crisis.

■ When a century or a decade is expressed as a single unit, use numerals followed by an *-s*.

> **1930s** **1400s**

3. Addresses

■ Use numerals for numbered streets and avenues over ten and for all house, apartment, and room numbers. Spell out numbered streets and avenues of ten or under.

> **1654** West **66th** Street **4** North Main Street
> Apartment **8C** **20 Second** Avenue

4. References

■ Use numerals for page, line, act, and scene numbers and the like.

> Look on pages **20** and **59** for information about Pablo Casals.
> Read lines **1–80** in Book **I** of the *Iliad*.
> We rehearsed act **2,** scenes **3** and **4,** of the play.

21.14 Numbers and Numerals

Exercise 30   Using Numbers and Numerals

On your paper, rewrite each sentence below, correcting the errors with numbers or numerals. If a sentence has no errors, write *correct*.

1. Please come to our meeting on October 4 at eight thirty P.M.
2. It will be held at 153 3rd Street.
3. Our speaker will discuss everyday life in the 16th century.
4. Then two group members will read act One, scenes 1 and 2, from *Hamlet*.
5. The admission charge for tonight only will be $3.50.

Exercise 31   Using Numbers and Numerals

For each sentence below, write correctly any number or numeral that should be changed to a different form.

Althea Gibson, Tennis Star

1. In 1957, the year Althea Gibson turned 30, she became the 1st African American tennis player to win the championship in the annual tennis tournament at Wimbledon in England.
2. Gibson traveled three thousand five hundred miles from her home in New York City to Wimbledon, but the distance that she traveled from being a 13-year-old high school dropout to a renowned tennis champion was even greater.
3. Gibson was born on a farm in South Carolina on August twenty-fifth, 1927; she was the oldest of 5 children.
4. For many years, she lived with her family at 135 West One hundred forty-third Street in Harlem, and she spent her free time playing basketball at the Boys Club.
5. When she was a lanky girl of fifteen (she would eventually be five feet eleven inches tall), she started taking tennis lessons from a 1-armed coach named Fred Johnson.
6. In 1947, when Gibson was 19, she played in 9 tennis tournaments and won the singles title in every single one.
7. Through the late 40s and into the early 50s, Gibson concentrated on both her tennis and her education.
8. She went back to high school, finishing 10th in her class, and then went to college, graduating in 1953 at the age of twenty-five.
9. 49 minutes was all the time it took Gibson to win the championship at Wimbledon in 1957.
10. After Wimbledon she won a one-hundred-thousand-dollar contract to play exhibition tennis matches and, in 1960, the women's professional singles title; she later became a professional golfer.

Exercise 32 **Using Punctuation, Abbreviations, and Numbers**

On your paper, rewrite the following sentences, correcting the errors in punctuation, abbreviations, and numbers. There may be several errors in each sentence.

1. In the travel section of Campbells Bookshop, I looked at books about Kenya Switzerland and Mexico.
2. The travel sections most informative book about Mexico I should know because I visited there last year had lavish colorful realistic photographs of people landscapes and architecture
3. Before I took it off the shelf my eyes were drawn to a book titled America bc written by Harvard professor Barry Fell phd.
4. Skimming through it I realized it had been misplaced for its subject was actually archaeology not one of my interests instead of travel.
5. My sights in case you are interested are focused on the people and places of the world as it looks in the 20th century not some mud covered artifacts from over 2,000 years ago.
6. While I looked at travel books Jane and Rafael wandered into other sections.
7. Jane went to the literature section for she wanted a copy of Wuthering Heights.
8. On her way, Jane spied a book of quotations with an attractive bright red cover.
9. Picking it up she thumbed through the thick white pages.
10. Then her eye fell on a familiar saying Ask me no questions and Ill tell you no lies.
11. Oh she said to herself. I didn't know that Oliver Goldsmith first wrote that line in his play She Stoops to Conquer.
12. Rafael in the meantime hurried to the compact disc videotape and audiocassette section.
13. A music student he was hoping to find a videotape of Mozarts Magic Flute.
14. May I help you? inquired Mrs Kato a sales clerk.
15. Rafael who wanted to browse first thanked her and then headed for the neatly arranged video packages.
16. Mozarts opera was not on the shelf but Rafael found twenty one copies of a new release, James Galway Plays Mostly Mozart.
17. With all out enthusiasm he grabbed a copy paid for the tape and came looking for me.
18. Having found the travel books I wanted I had moved to the humor section to find a birthday present for my brother.
19. I thought I might give him a book of cartoons perhaps Gary Larsons The Far Side, but Rafael nixed that idea.
20. Rafael suggested James Thurbers Fables for Our Time.
21. I especially like The Unicorn in the Garden he said referring to his favorite fable. Then he added Your brother will like it.
22. Jane arrived next, having bought Wuthering Heights and the book of quotations.
23. I have no self restraint she explained. I wish I could buy out the whole store.
24. Laughing I admitted that I had found approximately thirty five books I would have liked to buy.
25. With our arms laden with the purchases we had made we left the bookstore and headed for the post office where I mailed the Thurber book to my brother.

UNIT 21 Grammar Review

PUNCTUATION, ABBREVIATIONS, AND NUMBERS

In *Arctic Dreams,* Barry Lopez describes the landscapes of the North and the people and animals who live there. In the following passages, which have been annotated to show some of the rules of punctuation covered in this unit, he describes the Arctic's most magnificent creature: the polar bear.

Literature Model

from Arctic Dreams
by Barry Lopez

The polar bear is a creature of arctic edges: he hunts the ice margins, the surface of the water, and the continental shore. The ice bear, he is called. His world forms beneath him in the days of shortening light, and then falls away in the spring.

Polar bears vary in size, and their weights can change dramatically during the year. (Very large polar bears may stand 12 feet on their hind legs and weigh 2000 pounds. The number of 12- and 13-foot bears weighing 2200 or 2400 pounds that have been reported, however, says more about unadjusted scales, stretched hides, and wishful exaggeration than about polar bears.) Bears eat prodigiously in the spring, lightly in late summer, and lightly or not at all (in the case of denning females) during the winter. An adult male might weigh between 550 and 1700 pounds and measure 75 to 100 inches from tip of nose to tip of tail.

The Polar Eskimos of northwest Greenland call the polar bear *pisugtooq,* the great wanderer. On the basis of mark-and-recapture studies and radio-tracking information, scientists have determined that individual bears wander largely within a local area; but some, indeed, are long-distance travelers. A polar bear tagged in Svalbard, for example, showed up a year

Annotations:
- Colon to introduce a sentence that explains the preceding material
- Commas to separate elements in a series
- Comma to separate two main clauses joined by a coordinating conjunction
- Parentheses to set off supplemental material
- Hyphen in a compound adjective preceding a noun
- Semicolon to separate two main clauses

Grammar Review

later near Nanortalik, Greenland, 2000 miles to the southwest. Another bear, a female, traveled a straight-line distance of 205 miles in two days. Polar bears have also been found far afield in unlikely places, at the crest of Mount Newton in Svalbard, for example, 6600 feet above sea level, or 30 miles inland on the Greenland ice cap. An American crew on the ice island Alpha saw a female and her cub at 84°N in December 1957.

Thor Larsen, a biologist who has observed polar bears in Svalbard for more than fifteen years, when I asked him about their hunting behavior, said, "Cats. They are like big cats." Fast? "It is absolutely unbelievable how fast they are—oh, do they come fast." Shrewd? "Yes. They are making judgments at every point about what to do. And they are patient."

- Period at the end of a declarative sentence
- Commas to set off a nonrestrictive appositive
- Quotation marks for dialogue
- Dash to mark an abrupt break
- Question mark to indicate a direct question

Review: Exercise 1 — Using End Punctuation

Rewrite each sentence, correcting any errors in end punctuation. If a sentence contains no errors, write *correct*.

1. How is the arctic region commonly defined.
2. Geographers describe it as the region around the North Pole lying north of the Arctic Circle.
3. The Arctic can also be defined as the area north of the tree line, which is the area where trees cannot grow.
4. How the Arctic has always fascinated people?
5. People wonder who first reached the North Pole?
6. Robert E. Peary attained this goal on April 6, 1909.
7. Can you imagine a blizzard that, in Peary's words, "surpasses in fury the sandstorms of the Sahara."
8. Imagine an immense, ice-covered ocean?
9. Water temperatures in the Arctic remain near the freezing point of salt water—about 29 degrees Fahrenheit or minus 1.7 degrees Celsius?
10. "On this great frozen Sahara of the North," wrote Peary, "the wind never ceases to blow."
11. Did you realize that many adventurers besides Peary have explored the Arctic.
12. As recently as 1995, a group began an expedition!
13. Their goal was to traverse the Arctic by going "over the top of the world".
14. They set out from the European side of the Arctic during the winter months.
15. How surprising many people found that departure date?

Grammar Review

Review: Exercise 2 — Using Colons and Semicolons

Rewrite each sentence, correcting any errors in the use of colons and semicolons. If a sentence contains no errors, write *correct*.

SAMPLE Arctic winters are cold and long: summers are cool and short.
ANSWER Arctic winters are cold and long; summers are cool and short.

1. The Arctic includes parts of the following regions; Greenland, Canada, Alaska, Russia, Finland, Sweden, and Norway.
2. Some geographers include Iceland in the Arctic: others, however, exclude it from the region.
3. These are the minerals that have been discovered in the Arctic; gold, tin, nickel, copper, and coal.
4. The climate is harsh: nevertheless, the Arctic is home to a variety of animals and plants.
5. Two features of the area are permafrost and lack of rainfall.

Review: Exercise 3 — Using the Comma

Rewrite each sentence, adding the material in parentheses in the place indicated by the caret. If the material in parentheses is *not* essential to the meaning of the sentence, add commas. If it is essential, do not add commas.

SAMPLE The Arctic ∧ is home to many animals. (a region of extreme cold)
ANSWER The Arctic, a region of extreme cold, is home to many animals.

1. Caribou ∧ migrate in huge herds. (similar to reindeer)
2. ∧ the caribou might not seem threatened. (No)
3. ∧ this animal has, however, been overhunted. (As a prime resource for the peoples of the Arctic)
4. Caribou are prized for their meat ∧. (which is extremely nutritious)
5. Another arctic animal ∧ is the musk ox. (that lives on the tundra)
6. ∧ musk oxen can easily withstand the bitter chill of the Arctic. (Wrapped in their dense wool)
7. Snowshoe hares ∧ seek the protection of the taiga, the forests of the Arctic North. (unlike musk oxen)
8. The taiga is also the habitat of the hare's archenemy ∧. (the lynx)
9. In 1986 ∧ Fred Buemmer estimated that fifteen thousand polar bears remained in the Arctic. (the writer)
10. A remarkable sight along the shoreline is polar bears hunting their favorite prey ∧. (the harp seal)

Grammar Review

Review: Exercise 4 — Using the Comma

Rewrite each sentence, adding or deleting commas where necessary.

1. In general, arctic animals have only two major defenses against the harsh pervasive cold.
2. Voracious eating helps animals to stay warm and insulation minimizes heat loss.
3. A seventy-pound sea otter for example frequently will eat fifteen pounds of food in an average day.
4. An otter's typical diet includes sea urchins mollusks and fish.
5. Life is feast or famine for wolves; consequently a single meal may be 25 percent of a wolf's body weight.
6. Fur, and fat, and feathers are all insulation devices that shield arctic animals from the intense cold.
7. The musk ox's long, glossy skirt of coarse, guard hair is undeniably its most striking feature.
8. Musk oxen will in fact seek shelter during severely cold weather, but their thick fur provides such excellent insulation that they routinely endure extremes of minus forty degrees Fahrenheit in the open air for prolonged periods.
9. Nature insulates many animals, but leaves humans unprotected.
10. For warmth the Inuit dress in animal skins; indeed they have long copied the animals' survival strategies.

Review: Exercise 5 — Using the Dash and Parentheses

Rewrite each sentence, adding dashes or parentheses where necessary. Use the marks of punctuation indicated in parentheses at the end of each sentence.

SAMPLE Eric the Red he was a Norse chieftain explored Greenland in the tenth century. (parentheses)
ANSWER Eric the Red (he was a Norse chieftain) explored Greenland in the tenth century.

1. The Dutch navigator Willem Barents a sea is named for him led a mission of exploration in 1597. (dashes)
2. Barents's arctic expedition the first in recorded history set out to survive a winter in the Far North. (dashes)
3. The Dutch were looking for a Northeast Passage a northern route from Europe to the Pacific. (dash)
4. Vitus Bering the strait between Asia and North America bears his name was a Dane in service to Russia during the eighteenth century. (parentheses)
5. The strait usually frozen from October to June is a mere fifty-five miles wide. (parentheses)

Grammar Review 775

Grammar Review

Review: Exercise 6 — Using Quotation Marks and Italics

Rewrite each sentence, adding quotation marks or italics (underlining) where necessary. For the sentences that contain no errors, write *correct*.

1. In his book Arctic Dreams, Barry Lopez describes his first encounter with a narwhal.
2. According to the chapter of the book entitled Lancaster Sound, narwhals are very mysterious.
3. "We know more about the rings of Saturn, Lopez writes, than we know about the narwhal.
4. The scientific name of this whale consists of two Greek words: Monodon monoceros.
5. The first part of this name literally means "one tooth, and the second part means one horn."

Review: Exercise 7

Rewrite each sentence, adding or deleting apostrophes where necessary. If a sentence has no errors, write *correct*.

1. Another of Barry Lopezs major books is entitled *Of Wolves and Men*.
2. In this widely acclaimed work, Lopez studies wolve's behavior.
3. Minnesota's and Canada's wolves have drastically declined in number, Lopez reports.
4. Wolves are so shy that some people havent spotted one even after a three-month stay in the woods where wolves live.
5. Its surprising how many myths feature wolves as major characters.

Review: Exercise 8

Proofreading

The following passage describes the artist Rockwell Kent, whose painting appears on the opposite page. Rewrite the passage, correcting the errors in spelling, usage, and grammar. Add any missing punctuation. There are twenty-five errors.

Rockwell Kent

[1]Rockwell Kent (1882–1971) was born in Tarrytown Heights a small town on the Hudson River north of New York City. [2]He was strongly influenced by these 3 teachers William Chase, Robert Henri and Abbott Thayer. [3]These men, all prominent artists portrayed American life with a clear and unsentimental eye.

[4]When Kent was in his early twenties. [5]He developed a strong interest in the landscape people, and culture of the Arctic and the Antarctic. [6]Like many other

Grammar Review

Rockwell Kent, *The Trapper*, 1921

young men of his time Kent had become interested in Alaska and the Yukon after reading the novels of Jack London. ⁷Kent, like London, lived an adventurous life, spending much of his time in the harsh cold climates that he loves. ⁸He trap lobsters in Maine, sailed through treacherous waters off the tip of South America and lived in the hinterlands of Alaska, Newfoundland, and Greenland.

⁹Kent were also a gifted writer. ¹⁰He wrote and illustrated several books, including *Wilderness* (1920), which describes his travels through Alaska and *Voyaging Southward from the Strait of Magellan* (1924), which tells of his seafaring adventures in South America. ¹¹Kent received wide praise for the powerful evocative wood engravings that appeared in the books he illustrated during the 1920's and 1930s. ¹²Developed a boldly graphic style that used strong but simple patterns and decorative designs. ¹³His interest in simplicity and stylized forms is apparent in *The Trapper* which depicts a solitary man trudging through a bleak landscape.

¹⁴Kent would have been the ideal illustrater for Barry Lopez' *Arctic Dreams*. ¹⁵The book was published in 1986, 15 years after Kents death). ¹⁶Both men felt a deep affinity for the harsh landscape of the Arctic and the struggles endured by your inhabitants. ¹⁷Lopez writes in *Arctic Dreams,* "I came to believe that people's desires and aspirations were as much a part of the land as the wind, solitary animals, and the bright fields of stone and tundra.

Grammar Review

Review: Exercise 9

Mixed Review

The following sentences are about Barry Lopez. Rewrite each sentence, correcting all errors in punctuation. For a sentence that contains no errors, write *correct*.

Barry Lopez

1. Barry Lopez one of Americas' foremost writers on nature was born in 1945.
2. He grew up in the postwar world of the 1950's an optimistic era in American history.
3. A precocious child Lopez began to demonstrate a gift for keen observation careful thought and precise writing even during grade school.
4. Lopez attended a prestigious privately-funded midwestern university.
5. Soon after his graduation from the University of Notre Dame (in 1966), Lopez became a full time writer.
6. However most writers (even those with great talent, find they must hold another job in order to pay for these daily necessities food shelter and clothing.
7. Isnt it ironic that Lopez said, "I never thought I would be able to make a living as a writer?"
8. "Arctic Dreams" a celebration of animals and people in the frozen Arctic was published in 1986, it earned the Francis Fuller Victor Award in nonfiction from the Oregon Institute of Literary Arts, in 1987.
9. A literary award is not simply a great honor, it also helps persuade a publisher to accept future manuscripts from a struggling young author.
10. Among the animals, Lopez describes are these; polar bears, narwhals, musk ox, and caribou.
11. Most Americans you should realize, have never seen these animals in their natural habitat and they enjoy observing them vicariously through "armchair travels
12. Arctic Dreams—the work won a National Book Award explores human being's relationship with the landscape.
13. Like the nature writer, Peter Matthiessen, with whom he has been compared), Lopez of course has traveled widely in search of material for his books.
14. Other writers—William Least Heat Moon springs to mind, describe in great detail the ordinary landscapes, that are closer to home.
15. Nature which most of us take for granted is frequently the springboard that an author uses to exercise the imagination.

Writing Application

Commas and Parentheses in Writing

In the following passage from *Of Wolves and Men*, Barry Lopez gives the reader a palpable sense of the wolf's reality by his attention to detail. His careful use of commas and parentheses clarifies his message and contributes to the effect. Examine the passage, focusing on the commas and the italicized words.

> The wolf weighs ninety-four pounds and stands thirty inches at the shoulder. His feet are enormous, leaving prints in the mud along a creek (*where he pauses to hunt crayfish but not with much interest*) more than five inches long by just over four wide. He has two fractured ribs, broken by a moose a year before. They are healed now, but a sharp eye would notice the irregularity. The skin on his right hip is scarred, from a fight with another wolf in a neighboring pack when he was a yearling.

Techniques with Commas and Parentheses

Try to apply some of Barry Lopez's techniques when you write and revise your own work.

1 Use commas to set off material not essential to the meaning of a sentence.

CARELESS STYLE He has two fractured ribs broken by a moose a year before.
LOPEZ'S STYLE He has two fractured ribs, broken by a moose a year before.

2 Use parentheses to set off material that is purely incidental to the meaning.

CONFUSING STYLE His feet are enormous, leaving prints . . . along a creek, *where he pauses to hunt crayfish but not with much interest*, more than five inches long . . .
LOPEZ'S STYLE His feet are enormous, leaving prints . . . along a creek (*where he pauses to hunt crayfish but not with much interest*) more than five inches long . . .

TIME For more about the writing process, see **TIME Facing the Blank Page**, pp. 121-131.

Practice

On your paper, practice these techniques by revising the following passage, adding commas, capitalization, parentheses, and other forms of punctuation where appropriate.

The West Highland white terrier commonly known as the Westie is an imaginative hunter of badgers otters, rabbits and rats. It is a "small game" dog weighing twenty pounds or less. Its fur should be double-coated, with the outer coat consisting of straight hard hair about two inches long. The ideal Westie should measure about eleven inches around the withers withers is a term borrowed from horse breeding that refers to the ridge between the shoulder bones. The ears should be small and terminate in a sharp point. Be sure to keep them free of fringes. The tail ideally measuring about six inches in length is the Westie's pride and joy and should be carried gaily.

"The ants that built miniature volcanoes on the vacant lot left piles of tiny stones with telltale markings of black on white."

Gerald Haslam

PART 3

Resources and Skills

Unit 22	**Sources of English Words**	*782*
Unit 23	**Library Resources**	*798*
Unit 24	**Using Dictionaries**	*811*
Unit 25	**Vocabulary**	*818*
Unit 26	**Spelling**	*827*
Unit 27	**Study Skills**	*836*
Unit 28	**Taking Tests**	*847*
Unit 29	**Listening and Speaking**	*884*
Unit 30	**Viewing and Representing**	*893*
Unit 31	**Electronic Resources**	*905*

Paul Klee, *Ad Parnassum*, 1923

UNIT 22: Sources of English Words

Lesson 22.1 English in Our Time   783

Lesson 22.2 Conquest and Conversion   786

Lesson 22.3 A Conqueror from France   789

Lesson 22.4 Commerce, Culture, and Settlement   792

Lesson 22.5 New Technology and Ideas   795

22.1 English in Our Time

Twenty years ago, the following news item probably wouldn't have made much sense to most Americans. Can you imagine why?

> A cyberspace traffic jam as never before—that's what many called the situation on the Internet this Sunday evening between 6 P.M. and midnight. So many people logged on that popular Web sites reported twice the normal number of hits for a Sunday evening. Eventually some e-mail carriers crashed for much of the evening. Many users who tried to go online were furious, calling tech support numbers at record rates.

Most Americans of the 1980s would have been baffled by the above news item. Words like *cyberspace, Internet,* and *e-mail* would have been largely unknown at that time. Yet by 2000, these words were routinely used in conversation and in broadcast, print, and online news. How did these words find their way into English?

A Living Language

Like all living languages, English is continually changing. The creation of new words to describe developments in science and technology is not a new phenomenon. Just think about it; the word *telephone* was once a brand-new word in our language, as were *airplane, automobile,* and *television.*

So when the Internet rose to such great popularity during the latter part of the twentieth century, people simply created the words needed to describe the new technology. The more often such words were used, the less "technological" they sounded, and they came to be used routinely in speech and writing.

As fresh ideas evolve and innovative technologies are developed, new English words are created to describe them. These words may be words borrowed from other languages, existing words taking on new meanings, acronyms, blends, compounds, or newly coined words, as the following examples and the chart on the next page show.

Kwanza	borrowing from Swahili: seven-day African American cultural festival
rap	old word, meaning "to knock quickly," taking on a new meaning: a form of music
AIDS	acronym for Acquired Immune Deficiency Syndrome
cineplex	blend of existing words *cinema* + *complex*
download	compound of existing words
cellulite	new word for fatty deposits on the hips and thighs, coined in 1971

In the next four lessons, you'll be introduced to some of the history and mechanisms that continue to shape the language we use. No matter where the words we speak originated, they illustrate a vital feature of English—adaptability. English is alive.

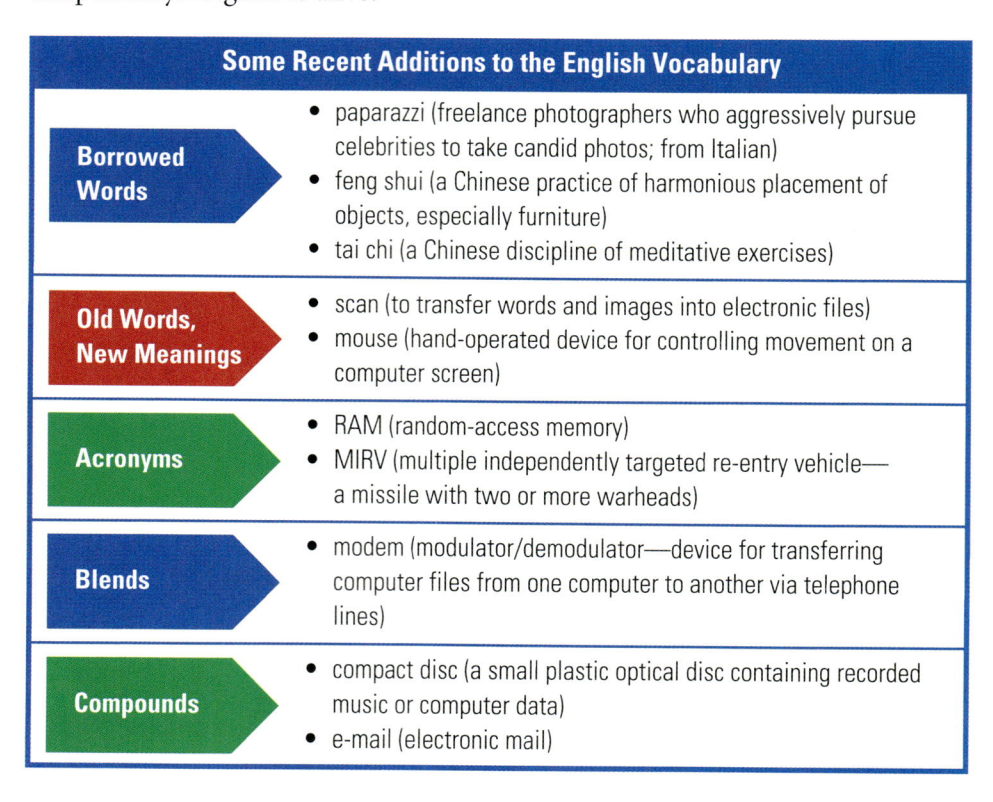

Some Recent Additions to the English Vocabulary

Borrowed Words
- paparazzi (freelance photographers who aggressively pursue celebrities to take candid photos; from Italian)
- feng shui (a Chinese practice of harmonious placement of objects, especially furniture)
- tai chi (a Chinese discipline of meditative exercises)

Old Words, New Meanings
- scan (to transfer words and images into electronic files)
- mouse (hand-operated device for controlling movement on a computer screen)

Acronyms
- RAM (random-access memory)
- MIRV (multiple independently targeted re-entry vehicle—a missile with two or more warheads)

Blends
- modem (modulator/demodulator—device for transferring computer files from one computer to another via telephone lines)

Compounds
- compact disc (a small plastic optical disc containing recorded music or computer data)
- e-mail (electronic mail)

Exercise 1

Skim the contents of several popular magazines, looking for words that you think are in the process of being assimilated into English. These might be words from foreign languages (often italicized) or words that have been created, or adapted from existing words, to name new ideas, technologies, events, consumer goods, and so on. Make a list of the words you find and define each word. In a brief oral report, share your findings with the class.

Wordworks

EPONYMS

Making History

Have you ever wondered why men, boys, and sometimes whole groups of people are called *guys*? Well, here's the story. Guy Fawkes was an English traitor who plotted to murder the king. Fawkes was hanged for his treason in 1606, but each year on November 5 (Guy Fawkes Day), the British burn a straw figure of Guy Fawkes in effigy. Originally, any ragged or odd-looking men—men who resembled Fawkes's straw effigy—were called guys. Today the word refers to men, boys, or people in general.

Guy Fawkes is an eponym. An eponym is a person whose name is the source for the name of someone or something. William Penn, for example, is the eponym for Pennsylvania. Madame de Pompadour (pictured at the right) gave her name to a hairstyle.

Some people have become eponyms because of their inventions or achievements. The Ferris wheel is named for George W. G. Ferris, who invented this popular ride. Louis Pasteur gave his name to pasteurization—the process of sterilizing milk and other bacteria-rich liquids.

Other people have become eponyms because their names were associated with a certain thing. Jules Léotard, for example, was a nineteenth-century French circus performer whose costume included a form-fitting body stocking—what we today call a leotard. Similarly, Samuel Maverick was a Texas cattle rancher who, unlike his fellow ranchers, refused to brand his cattle. These unbranded cattle became known as *mavericks,* and the word *maverick* has now come to mean anyone who refuses to go along with the group.

François Boucher, *Madame de Pompadour* (detail), 1756

ACTIVITY

Eponymous Explorations

Look at the list of definitions on the left and match them with their eponyms on the right. If necessary, use a dictionary.

1. a wind instrument
2. a type of car engine
3. a temperature scale
4. a railroad sleeping car
5. a unit of power

A. Rudolf Diesel
B. Adolphe Sax
C. George Pullman
D. James Watt
E. Gabriel Fahrenheit

Sources of English Words

22.2 Conquest and Conversion

The year is A.D. 449, and throughout the British Isles the apprehensive mood of the Celtic people is reflected in the low gray clouds of the winter sky. The Roman legions that have enforced the rule of law in this distant outpost of the empire have now withdrawn to Rome in what will prove to be a futile effort to repel invading barbarians from the north. The once-invincible empire is collapsing.

Meanwhile, poised for attack just across the English Channel are three fierce Germanic tribes—the Angles, the Saxons, and the Jutes. (The Celts had enlisted the aid of these tribes to fight off the Picts and Scots, who had been attacking the Celts from the west and the north—the areas we now know as Ireland and Scotland.) The Germanic warriors have routed the Picts and Scots but now will turn on their Celtic hosts, driving the Celts into the mountains of what are today Wales and Scotland. A new culture will take root on the island of Britain, and its principal language will be Anglo-Saxon, or Old English.

Emissaries from the Pope

Almost as soon as Old English was established, it began to change. Many of the language changes were due to foreign influences. Both Celtic and Anglo-Saxon already had been influenced by Latin because of the dominance of the Roman Empire. That influence increased during the sixth century when Pope Gregory, the spiritual leader of the Roman Catholic Church, sent missionaries to Britain to convert the Anglo-Saxons to Christianity.

The monks opened schools where they taught Latin to the Anglo-Saxon people. In addition, religious services were routinely conducted in Latin, and most texts were written in Latin. As you might expect, many Latin words, especially those pertaining to school and religion, became part of the Anglo-Saxon vocabulary.

Latin into English

LATIN	OLD ENGLISH	MODERN ENGLISH
schola	scōl	school
magister	magister	master
altare	altar	altar
candela	candel	candle
vinum	wīn	wine
cuppa	cuppe	cup
templum	tempel	temple

Invaders from the North

Starting around 800, the conquering Anglo-Saxons were given a taste of their own military medicine. Vikings from the Scandinavian countries to the north began raiding Engla Land (Land of the Angles) much as the Angles, Saxons, and Jutes had invaded Britain four hundred years earlier. This sporadic warfare continued for more than two hundred years. By the eleventh century, many Norse had settled in Engla Land, and again English underwent change with the addition of Scandinavian words.

Significantly, the Scandinavians contributed three Danish words: the personal pronouns *they*, *their*, and *them*. One language borrowing pronouns from another language is unusual. Generally, pronouns are firmly entrenched in a language, and the native forms are not readily displaced.

Scandinavian into English

OLD NORSE	MIDDLE ENGLISH	MODERN ENGLISH
kalla	callen	call
sæti	sete	seat
skinn	skin	skin
skȳ	sky	sky
bāthir	bothe	both
deyja	dien	die
fēlagi	felawe	fellow

Exercise 2

Each of the following words from modern English was originally borrowed from either Latin or a Scandinavian language. Use a dictionary to research the origin of each word. Give its Latin or Scandinavian form as well as its Old or Middle English form.

1. discipline
2. low
3. skull
4. priest
5. Sabbath
6. take

Wordworks

SPOONERISMS

Time Wounds All Heels

Have you ever made some unintentionally humorous or embarrassing slip of the tongue, such as telling someone to "ship up or shape out" when you meant to say "shape up or ship out"? Well, if that's the case, you're in good company.

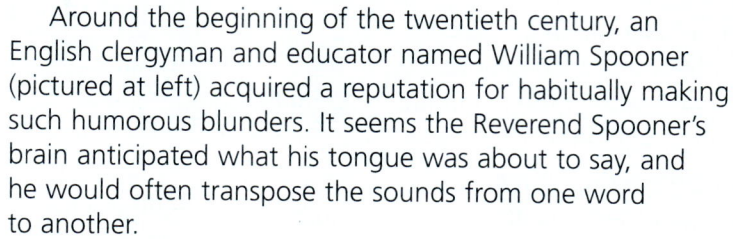

Around the beginning of the twentieth century, an English clergyman and educator named William Spooner (pictured at left) acquired a reputation for habitually making such humorous blunders. It seems the Reverend Spooner's brain anticipated what his tongue was about to say, and he would often transpose the sounds from one word to another.

For example, when steering a prominent member of his congregation away from a reserved pew, he supposedly offered this assistance: "Let me sew you to another sheet." Another time, to the amusement of his congregation, when Spooner was delivering a sermon about half-formed wishes, he announced, "We all know what it is to have a half-warmed fish within us." The Reverend Spooner became so notorious for these linguistic bungles that people began calling them spoonerisms.

Everyone makes such slips now and then. The technical term for this normal process is *metathesis*. Other practitioners of the art besides Spooner include the meteorologist who forecast "rain and slow, followed by sneet" and the radio announcer who, while describing the audience at a world championship bout at Madison Square Garden, informed his listeners, "I see the beautiful Mrs. DePuyster Van Courtland looking gorgeous in her stunning white gownless evening strap."

ACTIVITY — Scrambled Sayings

With a partner, unscramble the following spoonerisms.

1. Is the bean dizzy?
2. a blushing crow
3. You have tasted a whole worm.
4. Someone is occupewing my pie.
5. a well-boiled icicle

Sources of English Words

788   Unit 22 Sources of English Words

22.3 A Conqueror from France

The English weren't the only people to be harassed by Scandinavian warriors. Coastal areas of France were also attacked and settled. The French called the invaders Normans, the Old French word for "Northmen." The region of France settled by the Normans became known as Normandy.

In 1066 the seventh Duke of Normandy, William the Conqueror (pictured at right), was embroiled in a dispute for succession to the English throne. The dispute ended when William defeated King Harold II at the Battle of Hastings. William became king, and the Norman Conquest, as William's victory came to be called, altered the English language.

Parlez-vous Français?

Because the conquering Normans were from France, French became the language of the aristocracy in England. The working classes still spoke English, but after several decades of French rule, English was borrowing liberally from the French language. Words relating to religion, the arts and sciences, military affairs, social life, clothing, manners, and food were taken from French.

The vocabulary of food provides an interesting example of how social class influenced the development of English. Farmers and herders were

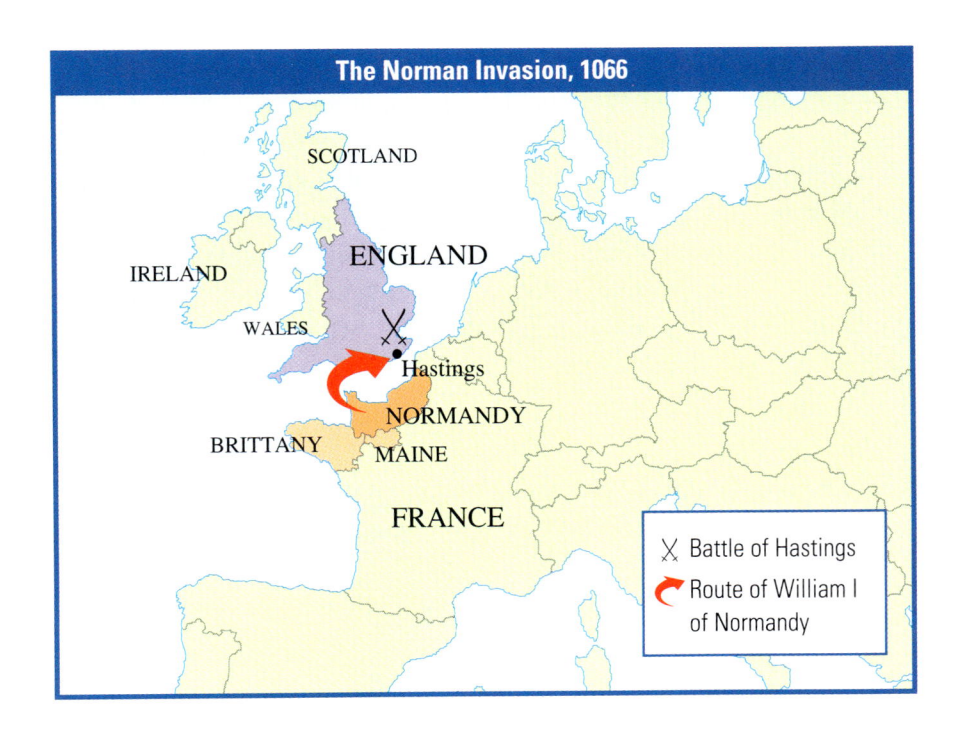

The Norman Invasion, 1066

- X Battle of Hastings
- Route of William I of Normandy

part of the working class, so the names of the animals they tended are from Old and Middle English: *cou (cow), cealf (calf), sceap (sheep), deor (deer),* and *swin (swine).* When these animals were prepared as elaborate dishes for the nobility, their names shifted from English to Old and Middle French: *buef (beef), veel (veal), moton (mutton), veneison (venison),* and *porc (pork).*

English Borrowings from French	
Social Life	peasant (paisant), court (court)
Food	roast (rostir), sausage (saussiche)
Government	authority (auctorité), constable (conestable)
Housing	palace (palais), tower (tor)
Religion	chaplain (chapelain), saint (saint)
Arts and Sciences	music (musique), medicine (medicine)
Military	charge (chargier), powder (poudre)

Plague and War

During the fourteenth century, a terrible plague known as the Black Death swept across Europe and Asia. Some historians think that nearly one-fourth of the European and Asian population died from the plague during this period.

In England the plague left businesses in the towns without enough workers. Eventually, jobs were filled by peasants, who spoke only English, because no proper aristocrat was about to become a tradesperson. In addition, the Hundred Years' War between England and France, which began in 1337, caused French culture to decline in favor. Soon French became a language studied only in school. English, with significant French influence, was again the principal language of England.

Exercise 3

Look up these words in a dictionary. Create a chart showing the Old or Middle French word from which each of the following English words was derived.

1. bacon
2. porch
3. castle
4. boil
5. prayer
6. judge
7. gentle
8. courage
9. lieutenant

Wordworks

PUNS AND TOM SWIFTIES

Ever Seen a Horse Fly?

Remember when you were a kid and loved to tell silly riddles like "What's black and white and red (read) all over?" (Answer: a newspaper) This riddle is an example of a pun, or a play on words.

Shakespeare loved puns. So did Lewis Carroll, author of *Alice in Wonderland*. Here's how the Mock Turtle describes his education to Alice:

> "I only took the regular course."
> "What was that?" enquired Alice.
> "Reeling and Writhing, of course, to begin with," the Mock Turtle replied; "and then the different branches of Arithmetic—Ambition, Distraction, Uglification, and Derision."

The puns in this passage are double-sound puns—words that sound very similar to other words. Homophone puns are based on different words that sound the same, such as *red* and *read*. Homograph puns are based on words that are spelled and pronounced the same but have different meanings. Benjamin Franklin used this type of pun when, after signing the Declaration of Independence, he told the gathering of revolutionaries, "We must all hang together or, most assuredly, we shall all hang separately!"

Some of the funniest puns are "Tom Swifties." In the Tom Swift stories, created by Edward Stratemeyer, Tom and his cronies never just plain said anything—they said it *happily* or *hurriedly* or *speedily* or in some other adverbial way. The humor in Tom Swifties occurs when the adverb describing how something is said forms a pun on what the speaker is saying, for example: "I love pancakes," said Tom flippantly.

ACTIVITY

"Try This Game," Said Tom Playfully

Work with a partner to match each quotation with a punning adverb below.

1. "These cherries aren't quite ripe," said Tom _____.
2. "This tire needs repair," said Tom _____.
3. "My dog just had puppies," said Tom _____.
4. "Come in out of the rain," said Tom _____.
5. "We studied the body's circulatory system," said Tom ___

A. literally **B.** tartly **C.** dryly **D.** vainly **E.** flatly

22.4 Commerce, Culture, and Settlement

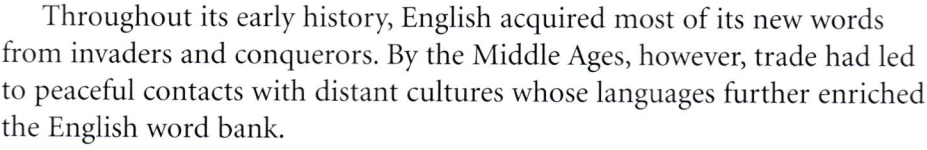

اَلْجَبْر
algebra

جَفَر
cipher

سكر
sugar

Throughout its early history, English acquired most of its new words from invaders and conquerors. By the Middle Ages, however, trade had led to peaceful contacts with distant cultures whose languages further enriched the English word bank.

When traders came back from the Middle East, their cargoes of exotic imports included sugar. In Middle English, sugar was called *sucre,* originally from the Arabic *sukkar.* Arabic was also the source of the name for the mathematical discipline of algebra, *al-jabr,* and for the numeral cipher, from the Arabic *sifr.* Later, commercial contacts with Spain added *vanilla (vainilla), brocade (brocado),* and *embargo (embargar)* to the English vocabulary.

Cultural Exchange

The exchange of goods between nations led inevitably to an exchange of culture. For example, William Shakespeare's *The Merchant of Venice* (1597) was based on a story written by the Italian author Giovanni Fiorentino. In contrast, Shakespeare's *Othello* (1604), adapted from an Italian story by Cinthio, was itself adapted in 1887 by Italian composer Giuseppe Verdi for his opera *Otello.* Such cultural exchanges, particularly in the field of music, led to cultural word borrowings in English. From Italian, English borrowed *stanza (stanza), studio (studio),* and *violin (violino).* Other English borrowed words are shown in the chart below.

Some English Borrowed Words

Language	Word	Date into English
French	shanty (chantier)	1822
	depot (dépôt)	1795
Dutch	cookie (koekje)	1786
	snoop (snoepen)	1832
German	quartz (quarz)	1631
	nix (nichts)	1789
Yiddish	bagel (beygel)	1932
	klutz (klotz)	1960
Italian	ravioli (ravioli)	1611
	piano (pianoforte)	1803
Spanish	alligator (el legarto)	1568
	cannibal (canibal)	1553

Settling North America

As English-speaking people settled North America, contact with Native Americans soon added new words to the settlers' vocabularies. From both the Natick and Narraganset languages came *squash (askootasquash)* and from the Natick came *moccasin (mokussin)*. The chart below shows additional borrowings from Native American languages.

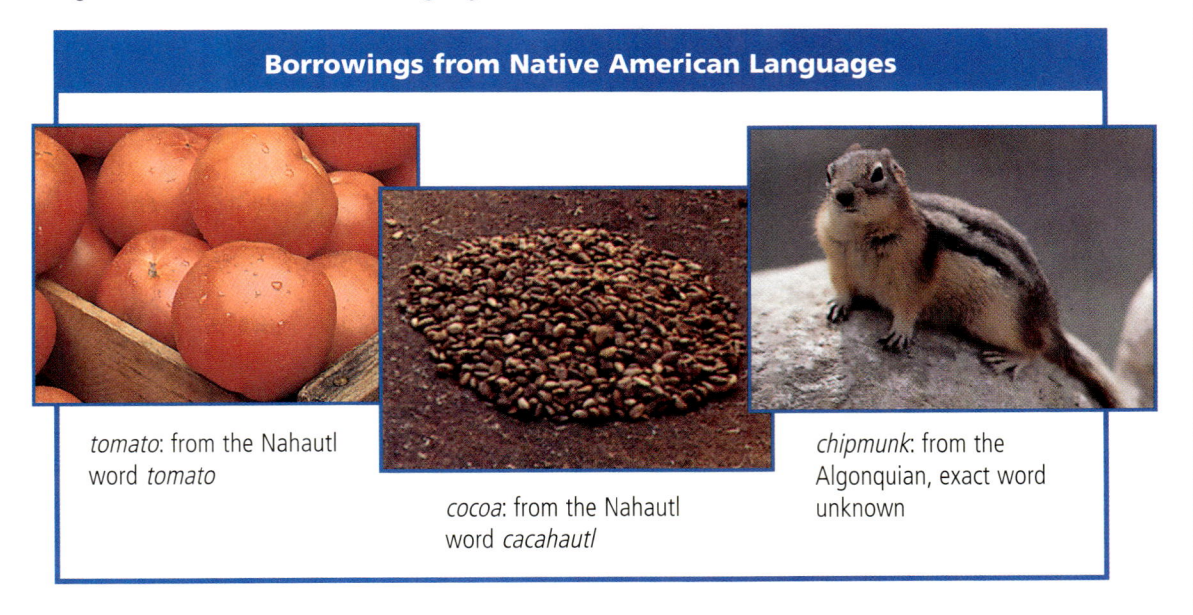

Borrowings from Native American Languages

tomato: from the Nahautl word *tomato*

cocoa: from the Nahautl word *cacahautl*

chipmunk: from the Algonquian, exact word unknown

Native American languages were just one influence on the English settlers' speech. The Spanish who settled in what is now the southwestern United States added *corral (corral)* and *rodeo (rodear)*. The Dutch contributed *bakery (bakkerij)* and *sleigh (slee)*. Enslaved Africans brought to America added *gumbo* (from the Bantu *gombo*) and *banjo* (akin to Kimbundu *mbanza*).

Exercise 4

Look up the following words in a dictionary. From what language was each word borrowed?

1. coleslaw
2. afghan
3. delicatessen
4. lariat
5. moose
6. tycoon

Wordworks

EUPHEMISMS

Burt's Gone West

"Well," said the young man with a sigh, "Burt bought the farm this morning. Who would have thought the old guy would cash in his chips so soon? His wife's been checking out a few resting places in the memorial park. We'll all be pushing up daisies soon enough."

No, this young man isn't talking about real-estate transactions, a poker game, or gardening. He's talking about death, an unpleasant subject that most people would just as soon avoid mentioning. When people talk about it, they often employ euphemisms to soften this unpleasant fact of life.

A euphemism is an agreeable or neutral word or phrase used in place of another word or phrase that is considered harsh, insensitive, or offensive. People have created euphemisms to cover a wide variety of subjects, especially anything having to do with the human body. The concern to avoid mention of the human body was taken to absurd lengths during the Victorian era.

The Victorian era, named for Queen Victoria of England, was characterized by extreme modesty and propriety. For example, not only was it considered indecent to display one's legs, it was even thought improper to say the word *leg*. Instead, Victorians said *limb*. *Belly* was another Victorian no-no. Much preferred were *tummy* and *breadbasket*.

At the dinner table, no proper Victorian, eyeing the roast chicken, would dream of shocking the other diners by requesting a breast or a thigh. *White meat* and *dark meat* became the accepted euphemisms.

ACTIVITY

Euphemistically Speaking

Try to match the words on the left with their euphemisms on the right.

1. fire
2. dirty
3. retreat
4. spying
5. poor

A. intelligence gathering
B. terminate
C. underprivileged
D. strategic withdrawal
E. unhygienic

22.5 New Technology and Ideas

Do you know what a *CAT scan* is? How about a *hantavirus*, a *velociraptor*, or *nanotechnology*? All of these words or phrases are fairly recent additions to the English vocabulary, made necessary by the advance of science and technology and the need to name and describe new things, ideas, and concepts.

As the world changes, so does English. New words are invented to name and describe space exploration, computers, medical science, social movements—any new aspect of any people's culture. The chart on page 796 shows some new words added to the English language.

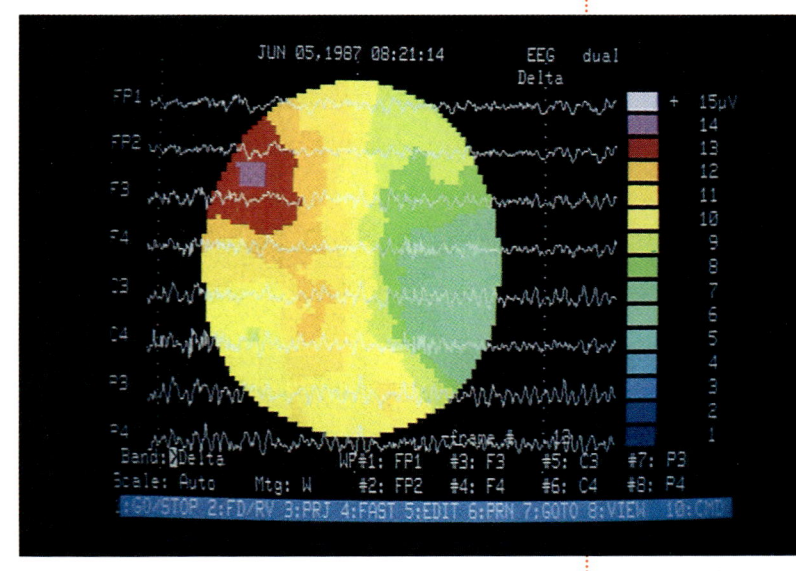

Compounds and Blends

These new words arise through a variety of methods. Some are compounds, such as *meltdown*, which describes the uncontrollable burning of the fuel rods in a malfunctioning nuclear reactor. Another new compound is *cross-training*, a physical workout that combines several different types of exercise, such as running, swimming, weight lifting, and rowing.

Blending, another way new words are formed, occurs when parts of two or more words are blended into one. *Simulcast*, the process of broadcasting a program simultaneously on radio and television, is a blend of *simultaneous* and *broadcast*. *Jazzercise*, a popular form of aerobic dance, is a blend of *jazz* and *exercise*.

CAT scan of human brain

Acronyms

Acronyms are yet another way new words enter English. *CD*, for example, stands for *c*ompact *d*isc, a thin, round, silver-colored disk that contains laser-etched, digitally coded music and information. In 1963, when the U.S. Postal Service wanted to speed up delivery, the service urged that all mail include a ZIP code, for *z*one *i*mprovement *p*lan.

Existing Words with New Meanings

Around the time of World War II, military scientists working with radar discovered short radio waves that travel in straight lines. They called this particular type of radio wave a microwave. Today, however, say *microwave* and most people assume you mean "a small oven that cooks food quickly using microwave radiation." The word has taken on a new meaning.

Launder is another such example. It has always meant "to wash in water." Today it also means "to 'cleanse' money obtained from illegal or disreputable sources." Similarly, *rap* once meant "to knock." Today, rap is a style of music based on rhymed verses spoken to a particular beat.

Words Added to English

	Word	Date	Source
Compounds and Blends	netiquette	1988	net (Internet) + etiquette
	three-peat	1988	three + repeat
	screen saver	1990s	screen + saver
Acronyms	RAM	1957	*r*andom *a*ccess *m*emory
	CD-ROM	1983	compact *d*isk *r*ead-*o*nly *m*emory
Existing Words, New Meanings	aerobics	1967	physical exercise designed to increase oxygen intake
	net	1990s	shortened form of *Internet,* often capitalized

Exercise 5

Make a list of new words you and your friends use in casual conversation. Most, if not all, of these words will be slang, but chances are they have their roots in other words. Which are completely new creations? Compounds or blends? Are any acronyms? Are any existing words with new meanings?

Wordworks

SLANG

Awesome, Daddy-O!

The scene: Lou's Short Orders Deluxe on a rainy Sunday in 1952. A woman walks in and seats herself at the counter. After a quick glance at the menu, she tells the waitress that she'd like two scrambled eggs on toast and some coffee. The waitress turns to the kitchen and yells, "Adam and Eve on a raft—wreck 'em—and a cup of jamoch!"

A young man who's already ordered toast and orange juice decides he'd like a couple of eggs as well. The waitress sighs and shouts to the cook, "Make that toast cackle!" A mother orders a hamburger for her daughter—"Hitch old Dobbin to a bun!" the waitress calls out.

Such colorful and inventive language was once part of the atmosphere in every American diner. The words and phrases are slang, popular, informal, faddish, and nonstandard speech. The use of slang is probably as old as language itself, but early examples of slang are difficult to document because most slang has a very brief life span. What is popular today is often long forgotten by tomorrow.

Consider a case in point. When you're leaving a party today, you might say "Catch you later" or "I'm outta here." In the 1960s, you would have said "Let's split"; in the 1940s, "Let's amscray" (pig Latin for "scram"); and in the Roaring Twenties, the popular expression was "Twenty-three skiddoo!" A few years from now, the expression will change again. That's the nature of slang.

Slang

1920
the cat's meow
anything desirable

1940
mess around
to kill time, hang out

1950
dig
to understand

1960
groovy
wonderful

1970
far out
great, wonderful

1980
excellent
first-rate

1990
dis, or *diss*
to treat with disrespect or to criticize

Today
?

ACTIVITY

Generations of Slang

How have slang expressions changed over the years? You can find out by conducting a slang survey. First, make a list of popular slang expressions that you and your friends use. Assign each word to a category—such as "used when leaving," "means up-to-the-minute," and so on. Ask adults you know of different ages about comparable expressions from their youth. In a brief report, share your findings with the class.

UNIT 23 Library Resources

Lesson 23.1	Library Arrangement	799
Lesson 23.2	Locating Books and Other Resources	801
Lesson 23.3	How to Search for Periodicals	806
Lesson 23.4	Using Reference Sources	808

23.1 Library Arrangement

Modern libraries offer many resources. You can borrow a book to read for pleasure, or you can research a topic. You can take out videos, CDs, computer software, and audiocassettes. Public libraries also provide Internet access. Many libraries offer services such as community information, reading programs, and evening classes. While each library is unique, the graphic below shows a typical library organization.

Stacks The stacks, or shelves, hold fiction and nonfiction books. Nonfiction books, which are based on fact, are written about subjects such as history, religion, technology, or literature. Fiction books are works of the imagination. They include novels and short story collections.

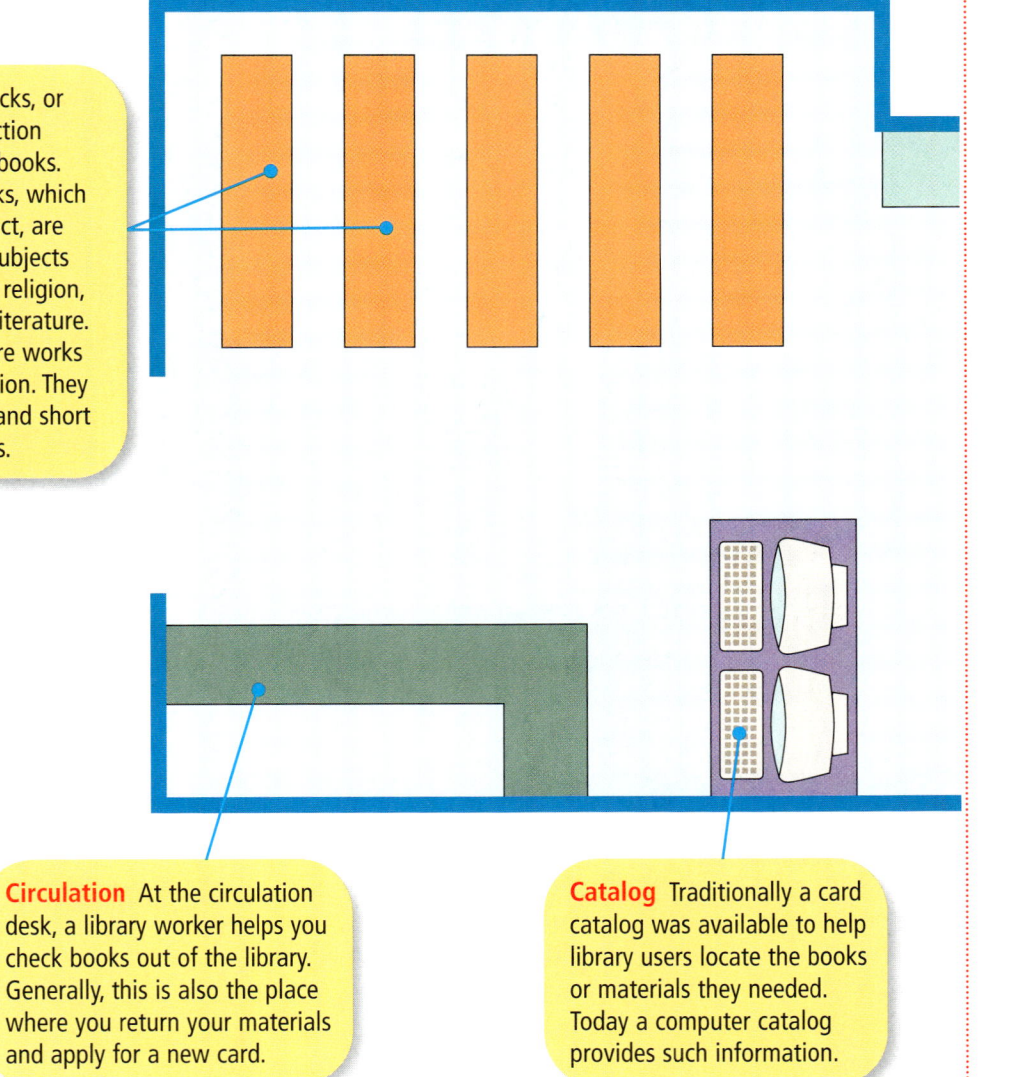

Circulation At the circulation desk, a library worker helps you check books out of the library. Generally, this is also the place where you return your materials and apply for a new card.

Catalog Traditionally a card catalog was available to help library users locate the books or materials they needed. Today a computer catalog provides such information.

Young Adult and Children's Sections These sections contain books, magazines, and other materials which should appeal to young children and to teenagers.

Audio-Visual Materials The library's audiovisual collection includes videos, compact discs, audiocassettes, and even computer software. Many audiovisual departments also have listening rooms.

Reference The reference section holds atlases, encyclopedias, dictionaries, almanacs, and other reference materials. Many of these resources are also available online. Most reference materials cannot be checked out. Reference librarians will answer your questions and help locate materials. They will also teach you how to use the print and online sources.

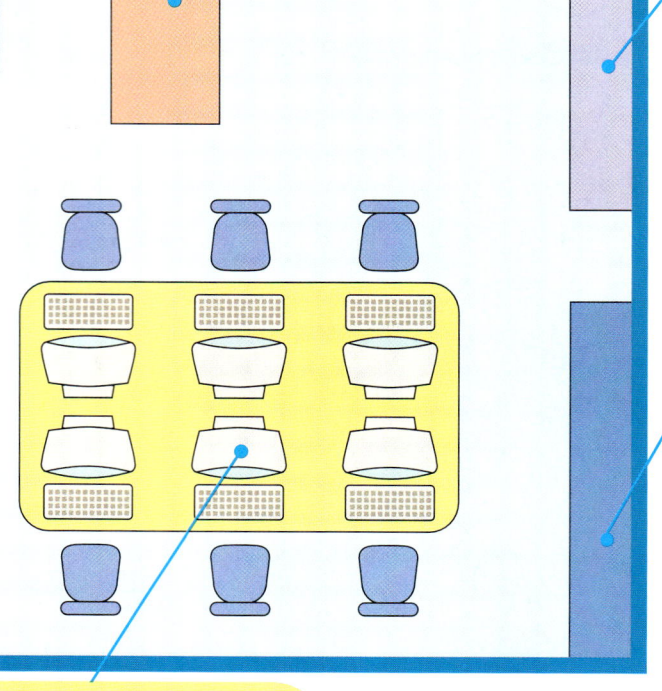

Periodicals Until the early 1990s, the periodicals section was the primary place in the library in which you could find periodicals—journals, newspapers, and magazines. Now many periodicals can be retrieved electronically. In the periodicals section, you will find current magazines and newspapers, as well as microfilm copies of older magazines and newspapers. Your library may offer computer indexes and electronic databases in this section as well as in the reference section.

Computers Today most libraries provide computers that offer access to electronic databases and indexes, as well as to the Internet.

Exercise 1

In which section or sections of the library might you find these items?

1. *Les Miserables* (an audiocassette of the musical)
2. *Statistical Abstract of the United States*
3. *Newsweek,* an issue from 1969
4. *Ragtime* (a novel)
5. *Wilson Readers' Guide to Periodical Literature* (a database)
6. *Cricket* (magazine), an issue from 1999

23.2 Locating Books and Other Resources

When searching for materials in the library, first identify what subject area you would like to research. Unit 7, Research Paper Writing, includes information on choosing an appropriate topic (see page 324). When doing library research, be as specific as possible. Instead of choosing the terms *History* and *War*, choose terms that are more specific to your research, such as *Vietnam War*, for example. Then decide on the best source to use to begin your research. For a general overview of a subject, choose an encyclopedia. For items currently in the news or for newsgroups on a topic, try the Internet first. The Internet often has the most up-to-date material, including daily newspapers, TV and radio transcripts, and current issues of many magazines.

If you have only a vague idea of your topic, try typing several keywords into the library catalog and then carefully read through the records that your search pulls up. When you find a likely book, locate its subject headings. (These will be displayed on the record.) Then search under that term to find more books on that topic.

Using the Computer Catalog

Library catalogs allow you to search by author, title, subject, and keyword, among other options. If you know the title, start with that first for the most direct search. However, several books can have the same title. In libraries the word *subject* refers to a specific set of words selected by the Library of Congress. If you type *Texas Cooking* for a subject, you will find nothing because the heading actually should read *Cookery—Texas*. Whenever you come up with no results, try that same term in a keyword search. The keyword search will find many books on your topic; in fact, the keyword search will list all books that use the phrase in a title or a section. The main problem with keyword searches is that they often find too much, and some of what they find is not on target. Scan your results list for something similar to what you want; then open that record and find its Library of Congress subject heading. Now go back and search under that subject. Your results list should now be exactly what you want.

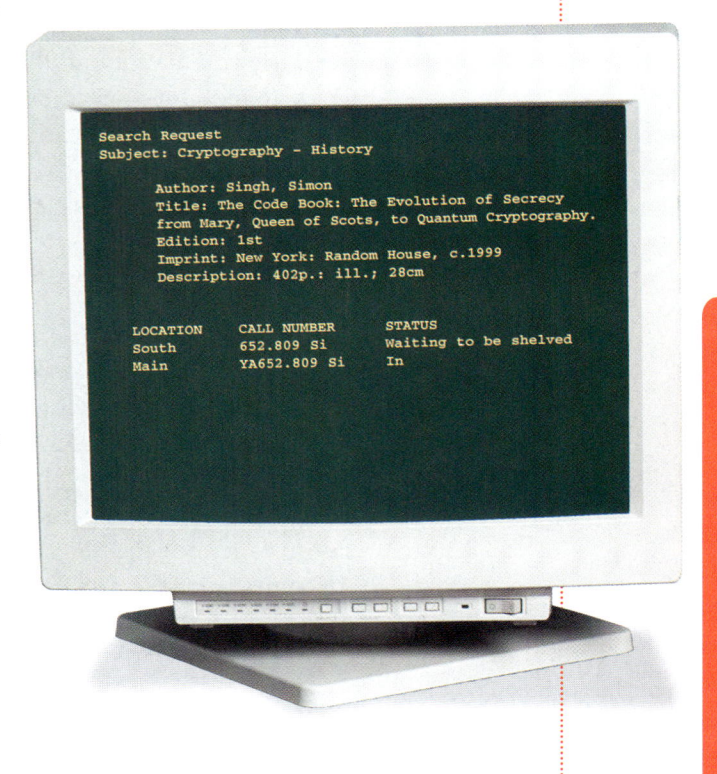

Hints for a Good Search

1. Make sure that you are spelling the words correctly.
2. If you want only recent books, set your computer to search for books published in the last year or two years only. This is called limiting your search. You can also limit by format; that is, you can choose only books or only videos.
3. Try synonyms for your words.
4. Print out the call number for each record you have found. That way you won't forget the call number by the time you reach the stacks.

The catalog record gives a lot of information in a small space. Besides author, title, and publisher, you are also given the copyright date and the number of pages. The term *ill.* stands for illustrations. If you are searching for photos or drawings on a subject, make sure the book you choose has the symbol *ill.,* for illustrations, in its record. The listing *YA* or *YA Collection* means that the book will be found in the young adult section rather than the regular nonfiction shelf.

The online catalog also lists books in other branches of your library system. These books can probably be delivered for you. If the catalog says that a book is waiting to be shelved, ask a librarian to help you find it. If the book is checked out, you can place a *hold* on it. Then, when the book comes back, a library worker will save it for you.

Understanding Classification Systems

Once you have found the information you need in the catalog, you are ready to look for a specific book in a particular section of the library, often in the stacks. All libraries use a system to categorize their collections and physically organize their materials. Most libraries use either the Dewey decimal system or the Library of Congress classification.

Dewey Decimal System

In 1876 librarian Melvil Dewey created a system that groups books into ten broad categories based on general areas of thought and study. In a library using the Dewey decimal system, books are shelved according to the categories listed in the chart on page 803.

Books are shelved by their Dewey Decimal call number and then by author. In the case of anthologies, the letters after the number will come from the title. For instance, for the book *Latino Voices,* the call number will be 860.8 La. The *La* comes from the first two letters of the title because this book has many authors instead of one.

Dewey Decimal System

CALL NUMBERS	CATEGORY	EXAMPLES OF SUBCATEGORIES	SAMPLE TITLES
000–099	General Works	encyclopedias, computer books, journalism	*Outstanding Books for the College Bound* *Doing Documentary Work*
100–199	Philosophy	ethics, psychology	*Enduring Issues in Psychology* *The Enigma of Personality*
200–299	Religion	theology, mythology	*Greek Myths* *Tao Te Ching*
300–399	Social Sciences	sociology, economics, education	*The Rise and Fall of the American Teenager* *Investing for Women*
400–499	Language	dictionaries, foreign languages	*American Sign Language* *French Lessons* *Dictionary of Slang*
500–599	Sciences	biology, math, physics	*Chasing Monarchs* *The Night Sky*
600–699	Technology	medicine, engineering, cooking	*The Cake Bible* *Countdown: A History of Space Flight*
700–799	Arts	painting, photography, dance, recreation, sports	*From Satchmo to Miles* *Backcountry Snowboarding* *Star Trek Encyclopedia and Reference Guide*
800–899	Literature	poetry, plays, essays	*Latino Voices* *The Writer on Her Work*
900–999	History and Geography	ancient history, biography, travel	*Green Alaska* *The History of Mexico*

Some books will share the same call number. When they do, they will be filed next to each other, alphabetically by the author's last name. For instance, two books about African American Society will both be filed in the 301.45 section, but a book by W. E. B. DuBois would appear before a book by Henry Louis Gates.

Public libraries usually do not use call numbers for fiction books. Instead, they are shelved alphabetically by the author's last name. When the author has more than one book, the titles are shelved alphabetically. Some libraries have special sections for mystery, science fiction, and westerns. If you're not sure what collection the book belongs to, ask a librarian.

23.2 Locating Books and Other Resources

Library of Congress Classification

Very large libraries that have many books on a specific topic use a different classification scheme. If they did not, they would have hundreds or even thousands of books with the same call number. University libraries use the Library of Congress classification, or LC classification. This system divides books into twenty-one general categories. Each category is assigned a letter, as shown in the chart below.

Like the Dewey decimal system, the LC classification has subcategories, identified by additional letters and numbers. Look at the LC call number for the book *Planets* by Carl Sagan.

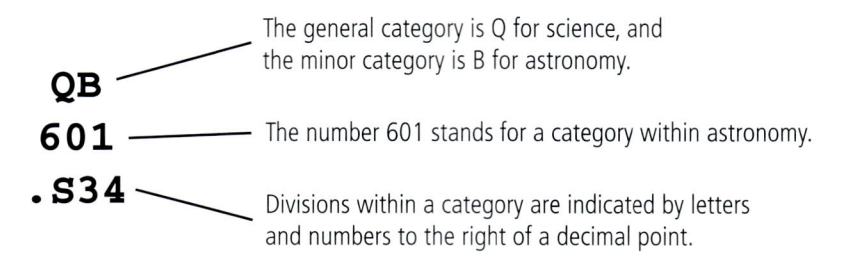

QB — The general category is Q for science, and the minor category is B for astronomy.

601 — The number 601 stands for a category within astronomy.

.S34 — Divisions within a category are indicated by letters and numbers to the right of a decimal point.

Library of Congress Classification System

CATEGORY LETTER	MAJOR CATEGORY	CATEGORY LETTER	MAJOR CATEGORY
A	General works	N	Fine arts
B	Philosophy, psychology, religion	P	Language and literature
C–F	History	Q	Science
G	Geology, anthropology, recreation	R	Medicine
H	Social sciences	S	Agriculture
J	Political science	T	Technology
K	Law	U	Military science
L	Education	V	Naval science
M	Music	Z	Bibliography and library science

Special Sections

Libraries often have special sections for books. The symbols *R* or *REF* stand for reference. Reference books will be found in the reference section. Biographies are shelved in the B's, mysteries in the D's, and science fiction books in the SF section. Many libraries shelf new books in a special section; so if the record says *new* for its location, make sure that you find the stacks for new books and search there.

Exercise 2

Use the computer catalog to find a book for each of the following topics. List the author, title, call number, and publication date of the books you find.

1. How to create your own Web page
2. Black holes
3. Comedy writing
4. Indonesia
5. Ebola virus
6. A book by Gabriel García Márquez
7. An autobiography of Langston Hughes
8. Robots
9. A history of the Vietnam War
10. A book about haiku
11. Speeches by American presidents
12. A science fiction novel by Ursula LeGuin
13. Korean folktales
14. A book of herbal remedies
15. A car repair book
16. A book on pre-algebra
17. A collection of letters
18. A book on how to use the Internet
19. A memoir by a Chinese American
20. A collection of short stories by Edgar Allan Poe

23.3 How to Search for Periodicals

Recent issues of newspapers, magazines, and journals are kept in the periodicals section. Most libraries keep a few years of back issues either bound or stored in folders. Older issues may be kept on microfilm. A microfilm, which looks like a long roll of photographic negatives, can store complete copies of a magazine or newspaper. To read microfilm, you need a special microfilm reader. If you are doing a report on an event that happened fifteen or more years ago, the library's microfilm sources may provide excellent background material. An article in an old magazine will have many details of the time and help you imagine what life was like in that period. Remember that older magazine articles will not be available online. To research older issues, you will need to use a printed index called *The Readers' Guide to Periodical Literature.*

Often you will search for periodicals online. Most libraries provide two different types of electronic databases: general periodical databases and databases specific to a subject. *The Electric Library,* which searches newspapers, general magazines, maps, and TV and radio transcripts, is an example of a general periodical database. *Literature Resource Center* is an example of a database that is focused on only one subject.

Although databases differ, they share common features. Most offer a basic search or a more advanced search. Each one will have a query screen where you need to type in your search term(s)—either one word or a search phrase. Sometimes you can search by subject or by keyword, sometimes only by keyword. Other databases allow you to use *natural language;* in other words, you can ask the question the way you would if talking to another person. Most online indexes will allow you to limit by date. This is very helpful when you are searching for only recent articles. Some databases will let you limit your search to *full-text* articles only. *Full text* means that the entire text of the article is available on the computer. Other databases will let you limit your search to one format only, such as maps.

The results of your search will be displayed either in chronological order or in order of *relevancy. Relevancy* means that the returns that have the closest relationship to your topic will be listed first. Look over your display results carefully. The display screen will tell you many things about the article, including the title, a brief summary of the article, the source, the date of the article, the length of the article, and the availability of photos or graphics.

Example of a Periodical Search

Look at the following sample. This search was done on a database called *MasterFILE Premier,* which searches many magazines and newspapers.

Screen 1

Type in the topic you are researching. On the sample search shown here, the researcher is interested in the role of women in the field of rap music.

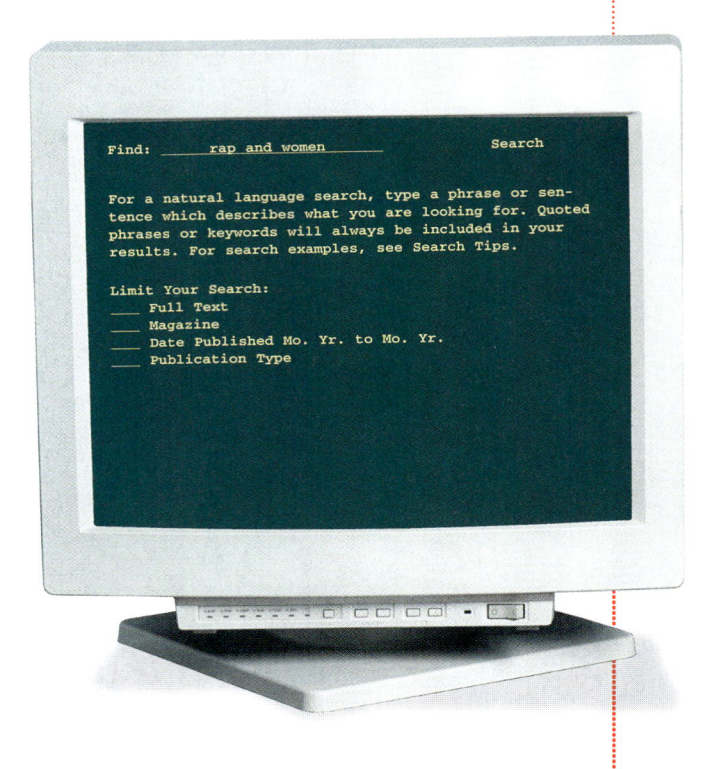

```
Find:      rap and women            Search

For a natural language search, type a phrase or sen-
tence which describes what you are looking for. Quoted
phrases or keywords will always be included in your
results. For search examples, see Search Tips.

Limit Your Search:
___ Full Text
___ Magazine
___ Date Published Mo. Yr. to Mo. Yr.
___ Publication Type
```

Screen 2

Here is part of the first screen of displayed results.

The page number for the article is always listed immediately after the date. The term *0p* means less than one page. A number followed by either *c* or *bw* tells you that color or black and white illustrations or photographs are available.

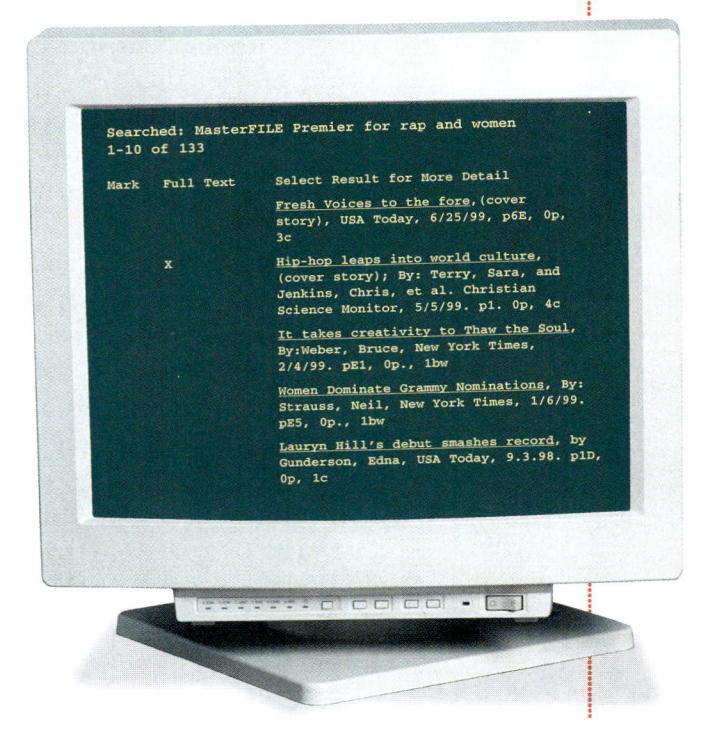

```
Searched: MasterFILE Premier for rap and women
1-10 of 133

Mark   Full Text    Select Result for More Detail
                    Fresh Voices to the fore,(cover
                    story), USA Today, 6/25/99, p6E, 0p,
                    3c
         x          Hip-hop leaps into world culture,
                    (cover story); By: Terry, Sara, and
                    Jenkins, Chris, et al. Christian
                    Science Monitor, 5/5/99. p1. 0p, 4c
                    It takes creativity to Thaw the Soul,
                    By:Weber, Bruce, New York Times,
                    2/4/99. pE1, 0p., 1bw
                    Women Dominate Grammy Nominations, By:
                    Strauss, Neil, New York Times, 1/6/99.
                    pE5, 0p., 1bw
                    Lauryn Hill's debut smashes record, by
                    Gunderson, Edna, USA Today, 9.3.98. p1D,
                    0p, 1c
```

Other Computerized Indexes

Other specialized databases allow you to search for materials on specific subjects, such as biography, sociology, art, science, or literature. *Social Issues Resources* allows you to search for a topic from a sociological perspective, such as single parenting, drug abuse, or pollution. *Literature Resource Center* allows you to research authors, literary themes, and information about specific literary works.

Exercise 3

Look at the display results from the search on *rap and women* to answer the following questions:

1. Did the searcher use a natural language query in this search? Give an example of a natural language search you would use for a topic of your choice.
2. How many articles have full text? List the article or articles that have full text.
3. What articles are less than a page long?
4. What article contains the most color photographs? How many does it contain?
5. What article or articles are cover stories?

23.4 Using Reference Sources

General reference works, such as encyclopedias and almanacs, can answer many of your reference questions easily and quickly. Almanacs are good for simple reference questions, such as "Who was the fifteenth president of the United States?" or "How much does it cost to mail a letter to China?" Almanacs also provide good information about events that occurred in the past year. Encyclopedias give a thorough overview of a topic. They also provide bibliographies. A bibliography is a list of books or materials on a specific topic. Online versions of encyclopedias are available at most libraries. In addition to text, online encyclopedias provide film clips, photos, and audio clips. Since online encyclopedias are updated frequently, they provide information that is more current than the print versions.

Internet reference sites also can answer many reference questions. One advantage of these sites is that they are available twenty-four hours a day. You can connect from home if you have access to a computer and a modem. One disadvantage of these sites is that there are no librarians available to help you find the information you need quickly. Examples of excellent online reference sites include *The Internet Public Library*, sponsored by the School of Information at the University of Michigan, and *Thor: The Virtual Reference Desk +*, the online resource site of Purdue University Library.

The chart on page 809 gives examples of some widely used reference resources, many of which can be found both in print and online.

Using General Reference Works to Answer Questions		
QUESTION	**WHERE TO LOOK FOR AN ANSWER**	**EXAMPLES OF SOURCES TO CHECK**
Were any Civil War battles fought in Indiana?	**Encyclopedias** include general information on a variety of topics.	• *Grolier Encyclopedia* • *World Book Encyclopedia* • *Encyclopaedia Britannica*
Who were the recipients of Pulitzer Prizes in letters for fiction and for general nonfiction in 1989?	**Almanacs** and **yearbooks** provide statistics, lists, and detailed information on recent issues.	• *Information Please Almanac* • *Guinness Book of World Records*
What is the coldest month of the year in Lima, Peru?	**Atlases** are collections of maps. They often include special maps on climate, land use, history, and other features.	• *Hammond Contemporary World Atlas* • *Times Atlas of World History* • *Cambridge Atlas of Astronomy*
Where was Ernest Hemingway born?	**Biographical reference works** include short life histories of noteworthy individuals, both living and deceased.	• *Webster's New Biographical Dictionary* • *Current Biography* • *Dictionary of American Biography*

Specialized Reference Sources

Other reference sources target more specific subject areas. *The Concise Encyclopedia of Science and Technology*, available in both print and online, is one source for scientific information. *Granger's Index to Poetry*, available both in print and online, will help you find a specific poem. *Statistical Abstract of the United States* will give you statistics on various topics.

The Internet

The Internet is a valuable resource for doing research. Not only does the Internet provide the most current news, but it also supplies the full text of speeches and laws and excerpts of many books. On the Internet, you can search for the title of a new book. You can also search the catalogs of world-class libraries, such as the Library of Congress and the New York Public Library. You can visit the National Gallery in Washington, D.C., and see portraits of all the presidents.

However, when researching the Internet, you must be very careful to check for accuracy. Information on the Internet may be unreliable. Whenever you are surveying a Web site for information, always evaluate what you see. Ask yourself the following questions:

1. Is the material authoritative? Who sponsors this site? Is the sponsor a government agency, a business promoting its own products, a nonprofit organization, or a private individual? The most reliable sites are sponsored by government agencies, universities, libraries, and similar organizations.
2. How current is the information? A site that has not been updated for three years may be too old for your purposes.

3. Look over the screens. Are there many errors, misspellings, typos? If so, the person may have been careless with the accuracy of the information as well.
4. Is the site easy to navigate? Or are you lost in a sea of words and images?
5. Are there links to other helpful sites? Although this isn't absolutely necessary, the linking feature is an important and useful addition.

Online Search Terms

ABSTRACT	A summary of an article or information source.
DATABASE	A collection of information resources that can be searched electronically. Some databases, such as Biography Index, only search a specific subject; others, such as Nexus/Lexus or the Electric Library, search all subjects.
DISCUSSION GROUPS	An online location where you can ask questions or discuss problems and current events. Discussion groups exist on almost every topic, such as the environment, pets, music, and sports.
HIT	The term for a successful result after you have searched online.
FULL TEXT	Indication that the entire article is present online. However, sometimes full-text articles do not include charts and graphics.
INTERNET	A computer network that is composed of many smaller computer networks. The Internet is the largest computer network in the world.
RELEVANCY	In computer searching, how closely your search results answer your search query. Many databases and search engines display results in a hierarchy from the most relevant to the least. These relevancy relationships are usually given in percentages.
SEARCH ENGINE	Computer software that browses the Internet for places where your words appear. Examples are Yahoo, Goober, Lycos, and Ask Jeeves.
URL	Acronym for Universal Resource Locator. An address for a Web site that contains the computer name, directory name, and Web page name.
WORLD WIDE WEB	The part of the Internet that provides information in various formats, including print, sound, photos, graphics, and video. Links allow you to move within a Web site or from Web site to Web site.

Exercise 4

Use the Internet or a print resource in your school library to answer five of the following questions.

1. Who won the Academy Award for best actress in 1999?
2. Were the historical figures Herod and Herod Antipas (from Roman times) the same person? Explain.
3. Where is Mount Kilimanjaro?
4. What are Guatemala's chief crops?
5. Who wrote the poem "The Waste Land"?
6. Who was the first person on record to run one mile in less than four minutes?
7. Which planet was the most recently discovered?
8. When did Hank Aaron retire as a baseball player?
9. Where are the nations of Yugoslavia, Slovenia, and Macedonia?
10. What was the population of the United States in 1999?

UNIT 24 Using Dictionaries

| Lesson 24.1 | **General Dictionaries** | *812* |
| Lesson 24.2 | **Thesauruses** | *816* |

24.1 General Dictionaries

Through its alphabetical listing of words with their definitions, called entries, dictionaries can tell you about almost everything. Most dictionaries fall into one of the categories below.

Unabridged Dictionaries
250,000 or more entries

Characteristics
- Extensive word histories
- Detailed definitions
- May be in several volumes
- Found mostly in libraries

Examples
- *Random House Dictionary of the English Language*
- *Webster's Third New International Dictionary*

College Dictionaries
About 150,000 entries

Characteristics
- Detailed enough to answer most questions on spelling or definitions
- Widely used in schools, homes, and businesses

Examples
- *Random House Webster's College Dictionary*
- *American Heritage Dictionary of the English Language*
- *Webster's New World Dictionary*

School Dictionaries
90,000 or fewer entries

Characteristics
- Definitions based on students' backgrounds
- Emphasis on common words

Examples
- *Macmillan Dictionary*
- *Webster's School Dictionary*

The Organization of Entries

With many entries to search through, how do you find the one you want? Guide words, the first and last words listed on the page, can help you locate entries much more quickly than if you simply browse. The sample dictionary page on page 813 shows the organization of word entries and how to use guide words and the pronunciation key.

812 Unit 24 Using Dictionaries

Guide words indicate the first and last entry on the page: **plagiarism/planetoid**.

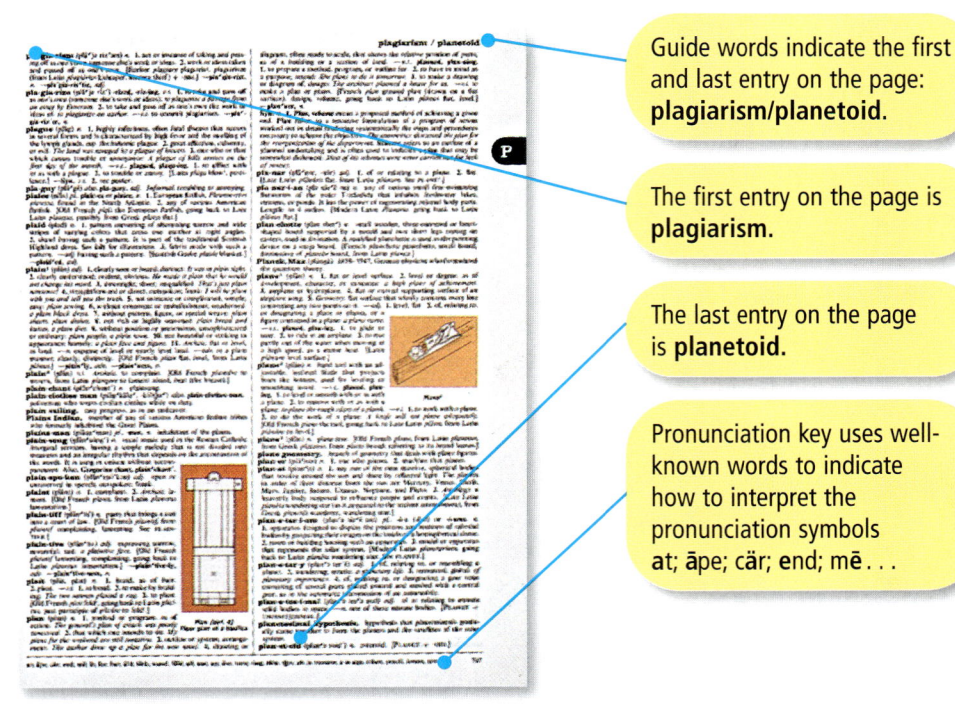

The first entry on the page is **plagiarism**.

The last entry on the page is **planetoid**.

Pronunciation key uses well-known words to indicate how to interpret the pronunciation symbols **at; āpe; cär; end; mē . . .**

If you do not know how to spell a word, you can usually find it in a dictionary if you try to sound it out. You may also want to look at the tips for improving your spelling presented in Unit 26. The following tips suggest other ways of finding unfamiliar words.

Tips on Finding Unfamiliar Words

1. Consider whether the word contains silent consonants. They might appear at or near the beginning of a word, such as *k* in *knife* and *h* in *rhyme.* Silent consonants may also appear in the middle of a word, such as *b* in *debt* and *gh* in *night.*

2. Consider alternative spellings of consonants. For example, the *sh* sound can be spelled several ways, as in these words: *ocean, tissue, election, chandelier, special, conscious,* and *sugar.*

3. Consider alternative spellings of vowels. Some vowel sounds are formed by combinations of vowels, such as the ā sound in *paid, suede, eight, obey,* and *break.*

4. Check a larger dictionary. Even if you have the right spelling in mind, a school dictionary may not contain the word you need. If you can't find the word in a college or unabridged dictionary, try the above tips again.

The Main Entries

The main part of a dictionary consists of word entries and their definitions. Other information is given as well. The entry for *forbid* on the next page shows some of the main information in an entry.

24.1 General Dictionaries **813**

The entry word is listed first.

The pronunciation is indicated by symbols.

Inflected forms, such as past tense and past participle for a verb, are sometimes listed.

The part or parts of speech that the word takes are indicated.

The etymology explains the history of a word.

> **for·bid** (fər bid′, fôr-) **-bade** (-bad′, -bād′) or **-bad** (-bad′), **bid·den** or (*archaic*) **-bid**, **-bid·ding**, *v.t.* **1.a.** to command (someone) not to do something; refuse to allow: *I forbid you to go out.* **b.** to prohibit (something); ban: *to forbid the wearing of makeup.* **2.** to command to keep away from; bar or exclude from: *I forbid you the car.* **3.** to stand in the way of or make impossible; hinder; prevent: *The snowstorm forbids air travel.* [Old English *forbēodan* to prohibit, restrain.]
> **Syn. 1. Forbid, prohibit** mean to order that something not be done. **Forbid** suggests a direct command from an authority who expects to be obeyed: *The airline forbids smoking on takeoff and landing.* **Prohibit** implies a legal order, as by statute, or a less arbitrary command: *The law prohibits smoking on the subways.*

Syllabication The entry word indicates how to divide, or hyphenate, a word of more than one syllable. Notice how *for·bid* is divided by the dot. A word entry may also indicate when a word is a solid compound, such as *folklore*; a hyphenated compound, such as *follow-up* when used as a noun or an adjective; or two words, such as *folk song*.

Synonyms When an entry includes synonyms, words with similar meanings, it often also includes examples to help you distinguish between the meanings. Compare the synonyms *forbid* and *prohibit* in the example above.

Homographs Words that are spelled the same but have different meanings and histories are called homographs. They are listed separately and identified by small, raised numerals after the word. If pronunciation varies between different homographs, these pronunciations are noted in the entry. Two separate entries are listed below for *meal*.

Some homographs, like meal¹ and meal², have the same pronunciations.

Notice the different etymologies for these homographs.

> **meal¹** (mēl), *n.* **1.** the food served and eaten at one time or occasion. **2.** one such regular time or occasion for eating. [bef. 900; ME *mel*, OE *mǣl* measure, fixed time, occasion, meal, c. OFris *mel* (meal)time, OHG *māl*, ON *māl*. Go *mēl* time, hour] —**meal′·less**, *adj.*
> **meal²** (mēl), *n.* **1.** a coarse, unsifted powder ground from the edible seeds of any grain: *barley meal.* **2.** any ground or powdery substance, as of nuts or seeds. [bef. 900; ME *mele*, OE *melu*, c. OFris *mele*, OS, OHG *melo*, ON *mjǫl*; akin to Go *malan*, L *molere* to grind; cf. MILL¹] —**meal′·less**, *adj.*

Cross-references The entry for *depreciate* lists a cross-reference to *deprecate*. The usage information for *deprecate* shows you that *depreciate* and *deprecate* sometimes have the same meaning; however, *deprecate* has almost totally replaced *depreciate* in certain situations.

> **de·pre·ci·ate** (di prē′ shē āt′), v., **-at·ed, -at·ing.** —v.t. **1.** to reduce the purchasing value of (money). **2.** to lessen the value or price of. **3.** to claim depreciation on (a property) for tax purposes. **4.** to represent as of little value or merit; belittle. —v.i. **5.** to decline in value. [1640–50; < LL *dēprētiātus* undervalued, ptp. of *dēpretiāre* (in ML sp. *dēpreciāre*) = L *dē-* DE- + *-pretiāre*, der. of *pretium* PRICE + *-ātus* -ATE¹] —**de·pre′ci·at′ing·ly,** *adv.* —**de·pre′ci·a′tor,** *n.* —**Usage.** See DEPRECATE.

Cross-references direct you to other main entries for information that may help you understand a word's meaning and when to use it.

> **dep·re·cate** (dep′ ri kāt′), v.t., **-cat·ed, -cat·ing.** . . . —**Usage.** The most current sense of DEPRECATE is "to express disapproval of." In a sense development still occasionally criticized. DEPRECATE has come to be synonymous with the similar but etymologically unrelated word DEPRECIATE in the sense "belittle": *The author deprecated the importance of his work.* In *self-* compounds, DEPRECATE has almost totally replaced DEPRECIATE in modern usage: *She charmed the audience with a self-deprecating account of her career.*

Usage information explains the differences between the uses of certain words.

Usage Information Some definitions may be preceded by usage labels. These labels indicate when to use a particular definition of a word. For example, the label "baseball" appears before a definition of the term *hit-and-run*. The label tells you that the definition that follows is used only when describing a baseball play. The following chart describes different kinds of usage information.

Usage Information in Dictionary Entries

TYPE OF INFORMATION	DESCRIPTION	EXAMPLE
Capitalization	Indicates when a word or a particular meaning of a word needs to be capitalized	**southeast** . . . **3. the Southeast.** southeastern part of the United States.
Out-of-date usage	Labels words as obsolete—no longer used—or archaic—once used commonly but now used only in special contexts	**quick** . . . **1.** *Archaic.* living; alive.
Special field usage	Indicates with subject labels a definition that is restricted to a particular study or area of reference	**fly²** . . . **8.** *Baseball.* to hit a fly ball.
Regional usage	Indicates how a word is used in a certain geographical area	**tonic** . . . **5.** *Chiefly Eastern New Eng.* soda pop.
Usage note	Provides general guides for using (or not using) words in particular situations	**scorcher** . . . **2.** *Informal.* an extremely hot day.

24.1 General Dictionaries

Other Information in Dictionaries

In addition to a greater number of word entries, some larger dictionaries include separate biography and geography sections. A biography section alphabetically lists names of important people and provides brief details about them. Names of cities, countries, and other geographical areas and information about them are alphabetically listed in the geography section. These sections usually appear at the back of the dictionary, after the main entries.

Accessing Dictionaries on Computers

You can obtain CD-ROM versions of many major dictionaries. You can also access numerous dictionaries on the Internet. Using an online dictionary, you simply enter a search word to find its definition. Often, even an illustration is provided. Online dictionaries also offer features such as help with spelling your search word, word games, language tips, and amusing facts about words. Some online dictionary services allow access to numerous general and specialized dictionaries in one search.

Exercise 1

Use a school or college dictionary to answer the following questions.

1. What is the plural of *hero?*
2. What are the guide words for the page on which *hakim* is listed?
3. What does *try* mean in the game of rugby?
4. What are the origins of the two homographs of *fair?*
5. Is *Draconian* always capitalized? Explain your answer.

24.2 Thesauruses

One special type of dictionary is a collection of synonyms, also known as a thesaurus. Such a book can help a writer choose just the right word in a given context. Even though a thesaurus is a type of dictionary, it is used in the opposite way from most dictionaries. You usually refer to a dictionary to find the meaning of a certain word. You refer to a thesaurus when you know the meaning you want to convey but need a specific word to express that meaning.

You can also access thesauruses on CD-ROMs, on the Internet, and even on some word processing software.

Thesaurus Formats

The best-known thesaurus was first developed by British doctor Peter Mark Roget, in 1852. Roget's *Thesaurus of English Words and Phrases* organized large lists of words into broad categories, such as *color* and *honor*. He then developed an index to the categories. This original thesaurus format is still used. To use this type of thesaurus, first check the index. Then refer to one of the lists of possible synonyms given in the index.

Dictionary-style Entries

A dictionary-style thesaurus, which organizes words alphabetically, is also widely used. In the dictionary format, each word entry is followed by several synonyms and cross-references to related major categories. A major category includes words that are all related to one main idea. Thus, if you can't find an appropriate synonym under the regular entry, try one of the major categories, which appear in parentheses in the regular entry. Most major category entries also include cross-references to antonyms. The following entry for the major category *generality* shows the main parts of a thesaurus entry.

GENERALITY

Nouns—**1,** generality, generalization; universality, broadness, collectivity; average; catholicity, catholicism; miscellany, miscellaneousness; prevalence; DISPERSION.
2, everyone, everybody [and his brother]; all hands, all the world and his wife; anybody. *Colloq.*, whole kit and caboodle. *Slang*, the works.
Verbs— be general, prevail, be going about; generalize, render general.
Adjectives—general, generic, collective; broad, comprehensive, sweeping; encyclopedic, widespread, dispersed; universal, catholic, common, all-inclusive, worldwide; ecumenical; transcendental; prevalent, prevailing, rife, epidemic, besetting; all over, covered with; every, all; unspecified, impersonal; customary (see HABIT).
Adverbs—generally, in general, generally speaking; always, for better or worse; for the most part, in the long run; whatever, whatsoever; to a man, one and all, all told.

Antonym, see SPECIALITY.

- Major categories appear in boldface, capital letters.
- In this thesaurus, synonyms are listed by part of speech.
- Cross-references to other major categories appear in capital letters.
- Antonyms can be located by referring to the cross-reference at the end of an entry.

Exercise 2

Use a thesaurus to find one synonym and one antonym for each word listed below. Then write an original sentence to illustrate the meaning of either the synonym or the antonym for each word listed. You may wish to check the exact meaning of each word in a dictionary before you use it in a sentence.

1. ability (noun)
2. defeat (verb)
3. modesty (noun)
4. move (verb)
5. strong (adjective)
6. fear (noun)
7. courtesy (noun)
8. difficult (adjective)
9. growth (noun)
10. talk (verb)

UNIT 25 Vocabulary

Lesson 25.1 **Building Vocabulary** *819*

Lesson 25.2 **Recognizing Parts of a Word** *823*

25.1 Building Vocabulary

With Marcie's helpful tips whispered in her ear, Peppermint Patty might yet develop a stronger vocabulary. As with any student, the better she understands words and their meanings, the better equipped she will be to communicate with others.

Developing Your Vocabulary

You hear and read unfamiliar words and phrases every day. Even words you know in one context or subject area can have new meanings when used in a different subject area. For example, technology has given new meaning to the word *mouse*. You can develop strategies for learning and remembering the new words and phrases you encounter. The following steps suggest ways to strengthen your vocabulary.

> **Steps for Learning and Remembering a New Word**
>
> 1. **Notice** new words and phrases while reading or listening. You might want to keep a vocabulary journal in which you record unfamiliar words and their meanings as well as familiar words with unusual meanings in specific contexts.
> 2. **Understand** the meaning of a new word by studying the context—the surrounding words and sentences that provide clues to the meaning.
> 3. **Verify** your understanding of a word with someone else. Use a dictionary or ask a teacher or a friend whether you correctly understand the meaning of the word.
> 4. **Use** the new word or phrase in your speaking and writing. You might want to double-check the meaning to be sure you're using the word appropriately.

You may also want to study vocabulary with someone—a friend or a small group of classmates. Then you can share your journals, agree to use new words in conversation, and help each other figure out vocabulary meanings. The chart below suggests a few ways to increase your vocabulary, both on your own and with other people.

> **Tips on Discovering New Words**
>
> **1.** Read extensively in a variety of areas. The more time you spend reading high-quality material, the more new words and phrases you are certain to encounter.
>
> **2.** Use a thesaurus. Especially when you write, challenge yourself to use new vocabulary. Try to replace "worn out" verbs, such as forms of the verb *to be*, with vivid verbs.
>
> **3.** Play word games. There are many word games on the market that can be challenging and fun. You might also enjoy inventing a game of your own.

Learning from Context

An unfamiliar word nearly always appears among other words that are familiar to you. These surrounding words provide the context for the new word. Thinking about the meaning of the rest of the phrase, sentence, paragraph, or passage, and analyzing how the unknown word fits into that meaning help you figure out the meaning of the new word.

Analyzing Specific Clues Writers often supply clues that help you figure out the meanings of unfamiliar words. Notice how the sentence structure provides clues to the meaning of *mélange*.

Our last talent show featured a *mélange* of acts: classical vocalists, jugglers, gymnasts, tap dancers, and performance artists.

The colon tells you that examples of the acts follow. Because the examples are diverse, you might guess that *mélange* means "a mixture." In the following sentence, clue words can help you determine the meaning of *impediment*:

The Postal Service allows no *impediment*, such as bad weather, to prevent the delivery of mail.

The clue phrase is *such as*. Bad weather is an example of an impediment. You can figure out that the Postal Service does not let any obstacle, such as bad weather, get in its way. *Impediment* means "obstacle."

The chart on the next page describes different types of context clues and the specific clue words that help you interpret them. In the Example column, the clue words are in **boldface** type. The unfamiliar words and the context that will help you interpret them are in *italic* type.

Interpreting Clue Words

TYPE OF CONTEXT CLUE	CLUE WORDS	EXAMPLE
Definition: The meaning of the unfamiliar word is stated in the sentence.	that is in other words or also known as which means	The lecturer was *verbose*; **in other words,** he was *long-winded*.
Example: The meaning of the unfamiliar word is explained through one familiar case.	like for example such as for instance including	The paramedic quickly checked Amy's *vital signs*, **including** her *pulse rate* and *body temperature*.
Comparison: The unfamiliar word is similar to a familiar word or phrase.	also likewise similarly resembling identical	Joan's friend testified to her *veracity*; **likewise,** her teacher said that Joan's *honesty* was evident to all who knew her.
Contrast: The unfamiliar word is the opposite of a familiar word or phrase.	but on the other hand on the contrary unlike however	Rachel is always *punctual*, **unlike** Brendan, who is usually *late*.
Cause and effect: The unfamiliar word describes a cause in a sentence for which the effects are understood.	because since therefore as a result consequently	Maria felt the stranger was being *intrusive* **because** he *asked too many personal questions*.

Analyzing the General Context What if the context of an unfamiliar word has no specific clue words? You can still interpret unfamiliar words when the context clues are more general. After figuring out the part of speech of the unfamiliar word, you can try to figure out the idea of the word from supporting and contrasting details, as shown in the following examples.

Because your friend Jesse was reading a book about the field of *ornithology*, she went to the library to view some of John James Audubon's famous drawings of birds.

How can you figure out the meaning of *ornithology*? You know from the passage that ornithology is a field of study. You also know that Jesse wanted to look at drawings of birds while she was reading about that subject. Therefore, you might deduce that *ornithology* is the study of birds.

The satellite was 670 miles from Earth at its *apogee* but only 260 miles away at its *perigee.*

What are the meanings of *apogee* and *perigee?* You know these two words are nouns because they are both objects of a preposition in a prepositional phrase. The particular measurements cited must be significant. You might guess that the *apogee* is the farthest point away from Earth in the satellite's orbit, while the *perigee* is the closest point.

You can see that being a good word detective helps you figure out unfamiliar words. Paying attention to all of the surrounding details and to the general tone of a passage can help you learn new vocabulary. Once you begin to notice and interpret new vocabulary, each consecutive experience with those words or phrases will expand and deepen your understanding of them. If you pay attention to context as you read, you can often wait until a more convenient time to consult a dictionary or another reliable source.

Exercise 1

Each of the following passages contains an italicized word that may be unfamiliar to you. Determine the meaning by examining the context, looking for the different types of context clues described in the chart on page 821. Write the italicized word and its meaning. Then indicate the strategy you used in each case by writing *definition, example, comparison, contrast,* or *cause and effect.* Afterwards, check your work in a dictionary to see how close you came to figuring out the word meanings.

1. Gayle frequently performed *gratis;* for example, last year she accepted no payment for singing the lead in the new community musical.
2. Copper is highly *malleable*, that is, easily shaped.
3. The first day of winter was downright *balmy*, and the days that followed were similarly mild.
4. Because this room is so small, you don't need a *stentorian* voice to be heard.
5. The village was *enshrouded*, or enveloped, in a thick fog.
6. Although Eduardo is an *immaculate* housekeeper, his twin sister, Mercedes, is an untidy person.
7. Michael's *acrophobia* was intense; his father also had an overwhelming fear of heights.
8. *Contiguous* countries, such as the United States and Canada, usually have border patrols.
9. Before the accident, my car bumper was perfectly *symmetrical*; however, it is now uneven.
10. Teresa joined a *philately* club because she enjoyed looking at stamps from different countries.

25.2 Recognizing Parts of a Word

Another way to understand words is by analyzing their parts. The main part of a word is its **root.** When it is a complete word, the root is called a **base word.** A root can be thought of as the "spine" of the word: it gives the word its backbone of meaning. It is often combined with a **prefix** (a part inserted at the beginning), a **suffix** (a part attached to the end), or another root. Prefixes and suffixes often change the direction of a word's meaning. Look at the following example.

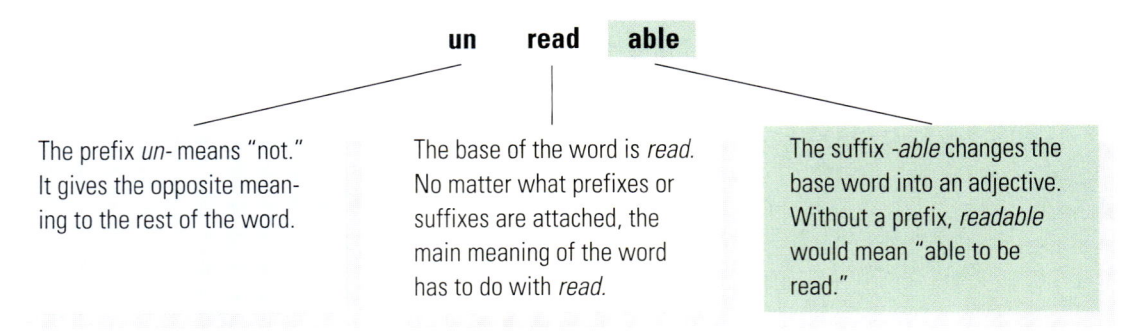

un   read   able

The prefix *un-* means "not." It gives the opposite meaning to the rest of the word.

The base of the word is *read.* No matter what prefixes or suffixes are attached, the main meaning of the word has to do with *read.*

The suffix *-able* changes the base word into an adjective. Without a prefix, *readable* would mean "able to be read."

Analyzing its parts, you can see that the word *unreadable* means "not possible to read."

Word Roots

Although prefixes and suffixes can change a word's meaning, remember that the root gives the word its central meaning. The following words have the same root.

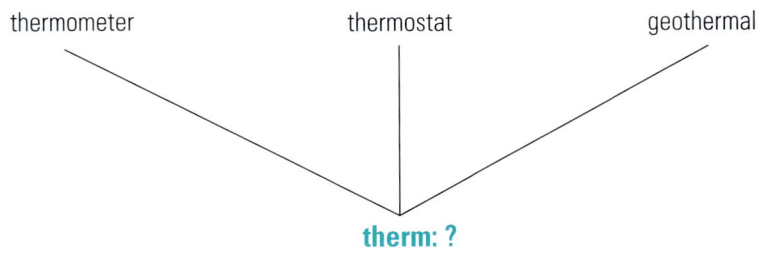

thermometer   thermostat   geothermal

therm: ?

You may know that a meter is a unit of measure and that a thermometer measures temperature. You may also know that *static* can mean "motionless" and that a thermostat is a device that keeps the temperature steady. Finally, you may know that *geo* means "earth" and that *geothermal* means "related to heat produced by the earth." Because all three words in the graphic concern temperature or heat and contain the root *therm,* you can infer that *therm* has a similar meaning. If you didn't know the meaning of one of the words above, you could begin to figure it out by using what you know about *therm.* The table on page 824 shows some words that share roots.

Analyzing Word Roots

WORDS	MEANINGS	ROOTS
animate	having life	*anima* means "mind" or "life"
unanimous	being of one mind	
anarchy	without government	*arch* means "rule" or "govern"
archives	government records	
beneficial	good, helpful	*bene* means "good"
benevolent	inclined to do good	
recede	go back, yield again	*ced* means "go"
proceed	go forward	
contradict	to say the opposite of	*dict* and *dic* mean "say" or "speak"
dedicate	to set apart for recognition	
facsimile	a copy or an item similar to	*fac* and *fact* mean "make"
factory	a place where goods are made	
general	affecting a whole class	*gen* means "class" or "origin"
generate	to start or create	
hydrant	a large pipe or water main	*hydr* means "water"
dehydrate	to remove water from	
manuscript	a document written by hand	*man* means "hand"
manual	done by hand	
portable	possible to carry	*port* means "carry"
porter	one who carries	
science	knowledge about the natural world	*sci* means "know"
omniscient	knowing everything	
stringent	binding, severe	*string* and *strict* mean "bind"
unrestricted	not bound, free	
traction	friction that occurs when a load is pulled across a surface	*trac* means "draw" or "pull"
extract	to pull out	
vivacious	full of life, lively	*viv* means "live" or "alive"
revive	to bring back to life	

Prefixes

Prefixes are inserted before a root to alter or enhance its meaning. Although the English language does not contain as many prefixes as suffixes, prefixes are still important tools for understanding and learning new words.

A prefix can sometimes completely change the meaning of a word. For example, the prefix *un-* gives the opposite meaning to any word before which it is inserted. The following chart shows other valuable prefixes and their meanings. Notice that some prefixes have more than one meaning and that sometimes different prefixes can convey the same meaning.

Analyzing Prefixes

WORDS	MEANINGS	PREFIXES
circumstance	surrounding conditions	*circum-* means "around" or "about"
circumference	distance around a circle	
circumvent	to avoid by going around	
demote	to move down in rank	*de-* means "down" or "from"
deduction	conclusion drawn from reasoning	
disapprove	not to approve	*dis-* means "not"
disassociate	not to associate	
hypersensitive	overly sensitive	*hyper-* means "excessive"
hyperbole	great exaggeration	
illegal	not legal	*il-, im-, in-,* and *ir-* mean "not"
immortal	not mortal	
insignificant	not significant	
irresponsible	not responsible	
misspell	to spell badly	*mis-* means "do badly" or "hate"
misogamy	hatred of marriage	
precede	to go before	*pre-* means "before"
premonition	advance warning	
submarine	beneath the ocean	*sub-* means "beneath" or "less than"
subhuman	less than human	

Suffixes

Suffixes can be added to the ends of base words to create new words with new meanings. Besides having specific meanings, however, suffixes also have grammatical functions. For example, the suffix *-ness* means "state of," "act of," or "quality of." In addition to creating a new meaning, this suffix also turns the base word *deaf*, which is an adjective, into an abstract noun. The word *deafness* is a noun meaning "the state, act, or quality of being deaf." As you study the following chart, notice that the spelling of the root may change when a suffix is added.

Analyzing Suffixes

WORDS	MEANINGS	SUFFIXES	PART OF SPEECH FORMED
movable peaceable visible	capable of being moved inclined to promote peace able to be seen	*-able* and *-ible* mean "capable of," "inclined to," or "able to be"	Adjective
occupant dependent	one who occupies a place one who depends on another for support	*-ant* and *-ent* mean "one who performs an action"	Concrete noun
quicken moisten deepen	make quick or alive make moist make deep	*-en* means "to become"	Verb
parenthood childhood	state of being a parent state of being a child	*-hood* means "condition" or "state"	Abstract noun
dentist scientist	one who repairs teeth one who is knowledgeable about science	*-ist* means "one who works at"	Concrete noun
evenly closely slowly	in an even manner in a close manner in a slow way	*-ly* means "in the manner or way mentioned"	Adverb
joyous courageous	full of joy full of courage	*-ous* means "full of"	Adjective
suspension civilization	state of being suspended process of becoming civilized	*-sion* and *-tion* mean "the state of" or "process of"	Abstract noun

Exercise 2

Copy the words below onto a separate sheet of paper. Then draw one line under the prefix in each of the words. Circle the root or the base word. Draw two lines under the suffix. Then write the meaning of the original word.

1. unfriendly
2. procession
3. dissatisfy
4. incredible
5. transmission
6. circumnavigation
7. incorruptible
8. omnivorous
9. repentance
10. intermediation

UNIT 26 Spelling

Lesson 26.1 **Improving Your Spelling** *828*

Lesson 26.2 **Spelling Difficult Words** *833*

26.1 Improving Your Spelling

One of your goals as a writer is to communicate your ideas clearly to your audience. If your writing is filled with misspelled words, your ideas may be lost. One of the best ways to become a good speller is to be an avid reader.

You can do a number of things to improve your spelling and help others understand what you write. First, you can learn some basic spelling rules. Second, by noticing how words have spelling patterns, you can learn to guess accurately when attempting to spell a new word. Third, you can learn to check your spelling with an authoritative source.

Basic Spelling Rules

The following rules, examples, and exceptions will help you master the spellings of many words.

Spelling *ie* and *ei* Many writers find the rules for certain combinations of letters, such as *ie* and *ei*, difficult to remember. One helpful learning strategy is to develop a rhyme to remember a rule, such as the following rhyme for the *ie* and *ei* rule.

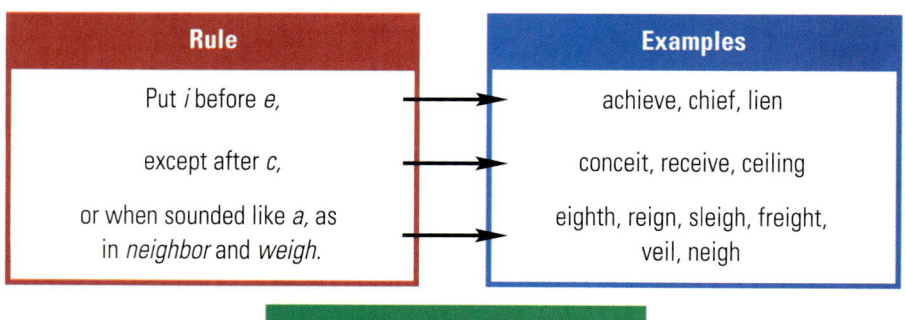

Rule	Examples
Put *i* before *e*,	achieve, chief, lien
except after *c*,	conceit, receive, ceiling
or when sounded like *a*, as in *neighbor* and *weigh*.	eighth, reign, sleigh, freight, veil, neigh

Exceptions
seize, leisure, weird, height, either, forfeit, protein

Spelling -*cede*, -*ceed*, and -*sede* Because various letters in the English spelling system are sometimes pronounced the same way, it is often easy to make slight spelling errors. The similarity of pronunciation between *c* and *s* accounts for the confusion in spelling words ending in -*cede*, -*ceed*, and -*sede*. Because there are only four exceptions, however, you should be able to memorize them.

Rule	Examples
Spell the *sēd* sound as *cede*. →	concede, recede, intercede

Exceptions
Three words use *-ceed* to spell the *sēd* sound: *proceed, exceed, succeed*.
One word uses *-sede* to spell the *sēd* sound: *supersede*.

Spelling Unstressed Vowels Notice the vowel sound in the second syllable of the word *or-i-gin*. This is the unstressed vowel sound, and it can be spelled several ways. Dictionary respellings use the schwa symbol (ə) to represent it. To help spell words with unstressed vowels correctly, try thinking of a related word in which the syllable containing the vowel sound is stressed. The following chart shows examples of this process.

Spelling Unstressed Vowels		
UNKNOWN SPELLING	**RELATED WORD**	**SPELLED CORRECTLY**
leg_l	le**gal**ity	legal
fant_sy	fan**tas**tic	fantasy
host_le	hos**til**ity	hostile
opp_site	op**pose**	opposite

Adding Prefixes When adding a prefix to a word, keep the original spelling of the word. If the prefix results in a double letter, keep both letters.

    dis- + appear = disappear   ir- + regular = irregular
    mis- + direct = misdirect   co- + operate = cooperate

Suffixes and the Silent e Many English words end in a silent letter *e*. Sometimes the *e* is dropped when a suffix is added. The following chart shows when to keep and when to drop the *e*.

Adding Suffixes to Words with Silent e	
RULE	**EXAMPLES**
When adding a suffix that begins with a consonant to a word that ends in silent *e*, keep the *e*. **Common exceptions**	*place* + *-ment* = *placement* *rare* + *-ly* = *rarely* *awe* + *-ful* = *awful* *judge* + *-ment* = *judgment* *(continued)*

Adding Suffixes to Words with Silent e

RULE	EXAMPLES
When adding a suffix that begins with a vowel or *y* to a word that ends in silent *e*, usually drop the *e*.	excite + -able = excitable shine + -y = shiny
Common exceptions	*mile + -age = mileage*
When adding a suffix that begins with *a* or *o* to a word that ends in *ce* or *ge*, keep the *e* so the word will retain the soft *c* or *g* sound.	trace + -able = traceable courage + -ous = courageous
When adding a suffix that begins with a vowel to a word that ends in *ee* or *oe*, keep the *e*.	agree + -able = agreeable canoe + -ing = canoeing

Suffixes and the Final *y* When adding a suffix to a word that ends in a consonant + *y*, change the *y* to *i*. Do not change the *y* to *i* when the suffix begins with *i*.

    try + -ed = tried   copy + -ing = copying

When adding a suffix to a word that ends in a vowel + *y*, keep the *y*.

    joy + -ous = joyous   convey + -ed = conveyed

Doubling the Final Consonant When adding a suffix to a word, you sometimes need to double the final consonant before adding the suffix. You double the consonant when adding a suffix that begins with a vowel to a word that ends in a single consonant preceded by a single vowel, if the original word

- is a one-syllable word
  dip + -ing = dipping   stop + -age = stoppage
- has an accent on the last syllable and the accent remains there after the suffix is added
  occur + -ence = occurrence   repel + -ing = repelling
- is a prefixed word based on a one-syllable word
  reset + -ing = resetting

On the basis of the preceding rule, you would not double the final consonant when

- the accent is not on the last syllable
  develop + -ing = developing
- the accent shifts when the suffix is added
  refer + -ence = reference
- the final consonant is preceded by two vowels
  train + -ing = training

- the final consonant is preceded by another consonant
  remind + -er = reminder
- the word ends in a consonant and the suffix begins with a consonant
  reck + -less = reckless

Adding -ly When adding -ly to a word that ends in a single l, keep the l. When the word ends in a double l, drop one l. When the word ends in a consonant + le, drop the le.

    real + -ly = really   dull + -ly = dully   terrible + -ly = terribly

Adding -ness When adding -ness to a word that ends in n, keep the n.

    sullen + -ness = sullenness   keen + -ness = keenness

Forming Compound Words When joining a word that ends in a consonant to a word that begins with a consonant, keep both consonants.

    after + noon = afternoon   key + board = keyboard

Forming Plurals English nouns form plurals in many ways. Most nouns simply add -s. The following chart shows other ways of forming plural nouns and some common exceptions to the patterns.

General Rules for Plurals

IF THE NOUN ENDS IN	THEN GENERALLY	EXAMPLE
ch, s, sh, x, or z	add -es	crutch → crutches wish → wishes
a consonant + y	change y to i and add -es	baby → babies
a vowel + y	add -s	day → days
a vowel + o	add -s	studio → studios
a consonant + o	generally add -es	potato → potatoes cargo → cargoes
Common exceptions	but sometimes add -s	silo → silos
f or ff	add -s	reef → reefs cuff → cuffs
Common exceptions lf	change f to v and add -es change f to v and add -es	leaf → leaves half → halves wolf → wolves
fe	change f to v and add -s	life → lives

    A few plurals are exceptions to the rules listed previously (or they present some other special problem) but are easy to remember. The following chart lists these plurals and some examples.

Special Rules for Plurals

SPECIAL CASES	EXAMPLES
To form the plural of proper names, add either -s or -es.	D'Amico → D'Amicos Sanchez → Sanchezes
To form the plural of one-word compound nouns, follow the general rules for plurals.	penknife → penknives blackberry → blackberries
To form the plural of hyphenated compound nouns or compound nouns of more than one word, generally make the most important word plural.	father-in-law → fathers-in-law attorney general → attorneys general
Some nouns have irregular forms. These nouns do not follow any rules.	man → men ox → oxen
Some nouns have the same singular and plural form.	series → series deer → deer

Learning to Spell New Words

As you read, note unfamiliar words as well as words that you recognize but that look hard to spell. As you write, pay attention to any words that you have difficulty spelling. Then try the following simple process to learn to spell those words.

1. Say It
Look at the printed word, and say it out loud. Then say it again, pronouncing each syllable.

▶

2. Visualize It
Without looking at the printed word, imagine seeing the word printed or written. Try to picture the word spelled correctly.

▶

3. Write It
Look at the printed word, and write it. Then write it again without looking at the printed word.

▶

4. Check It
Check what you have written against the printed word. Did you spell the word correctly? If not, try the process again.

Remember that the dictionary can help you find the correct spelling of words. You may ask, How can I look up a word if I don't know how to spell it? Many times you will be able to spell enough of the beginning of a word to find it in the dictionary. If you don't find a word in the first place you look, think of other probable spellings, based on sound patterns you know. Once you have located the correct spelling of a word, use the four-step process shown above to help you learn the word.

Exercise 1

In each group of words, find the one word that is misspelled. Write the word correctly. Cite the rule that applies to the spelling of the word. If the word is an exception to a rule, note that as well.

1. biege, conceit, thief
2. exceed, supercede, accede
3. definite, editor, abdumen
4. enjoiment, daily, carriage
5. truly, arguement, brownness

26.2 Spelling Difficult Words

Clearly, some words are more difficult to spell than others. As you have learned, not all words follow basic spelling rules, but you can learn to spell even the most difficult words.

One very useful strategy for learning difficult words is to develop a personal word list. What words are especially difficult for you? What words do you frequently misspell? Include those words in your personal word list. Study the words, using the four-step process you learned in Lesson 26.1, page 832.

Another helpful strategy for learning to spell difficult words involves developing memory devices. For example, if you have trouble remembering whether the word is spelled *cemetery* or *cemetary*, you might think of how we get there with *e*'s (ease). Puns, like this one, can help you remember how to spell difficult words.

Frequently Misspelled Words

Following is a list of words that many people misspell. Which words on the list do you have difficulty spelling?

Words Often Misspelled			
absence	buffet	concede	environment
accidentally	bureau	conscientious	exceed
accommodate	business	convenient	familiarize
adviser	cafeteria	definite	fascinating
allot	canceled	deodorant	foreign
answer	catastrophe	descend	forty
arctic	choir	discipline	genius
attendant	colonel	efficiency	government
ballet	commercial	eligible	guarantee
beautiful	complexion	embarrass	height

(continued)

26.2 Spelling Difficult Words

Words Often Misspelled			
hippopotamus	necessary	pneumonia	supersede
humorous	neighborhood	precede	technique
hygiene	niece	proceed	technology
incidentally	occasion	receipt	theory
jewelry	pageant	recommend	traffic
laboratory	pamphlet	restaurant	truly
leisure	parallel	rhythm	unanimous
license	pastime	schedule	usually
mischievous	permanent	separate	vacuum
misspell	pharmacy	sincerely	variety
molasses	physical	succeed	versatile
muscle	physician	sufficient	Wednesday

Easily Confused Words

Some words are easily confused with others because they contain similar sounds. Other words are confused because they are homophones, words that have the same pronunciation but different meanings and spellings. Study the following list of easily confused words. Are there any words on the list that you find confusing?

Words Often Confused	
Affect	to influence; to act upon: *A sad movie will affect her mood.*
Effect	a result: *What effect did the punishment have on him?*
Altogether	entirely: *Mom is altogether pleased with my report.*
All together	everyone in one place: *We waited all together at the bus stop.*
Capital	a city that is the seat of government: *Jefferson City is the capital of Missouri.*
Capital	wealth: *The company invested its capital.*
Capitol	a building in which a legislature meets: *In the capitol we observed the Senate in session.*
Formally	politely; officially; according to custom or rule: *Because our visitor was so important, we addressed him formally.*
Formerly	previously: *The principal was formerly a teacher.*
Holy	sacred: *Religious travelers make pilgrimages to holy places.*
Holey	having holes: *You should probably stop wearing that holey jacket.*
Wholly	completely; fully: *I am wholly satisfied with your story.*

(continued)

\textbf{Words Often Confused}	
Its	possessive pronoun: *The United States celebrated its bicentennial in 1976.*
It's	contraction of *it is*: *It's not about winning; it's about fair play.*
Lose	to misplace; to drop: *Did you lose your assignment on the way to school?*
Loose	free; not confined; not tight: *My clothes are loose since I lost ten pounds.*
Passed	moved through; elapsed; completed satisfactorily: *I passed you in the hall several times today.*
Past	the time before the present; gone by; ended; over: *You can't change the past.*
Stationary	fixed; unmoving: *For a moment the plane appeared stationary in the sky.*
Stationery	writing paper and envelopes: *Rhonda wrote me a letter on hot pink stationery.*
Than	in comparison with: *You studied harder today than I have ever seen you study.*
Then	at that time; next: *He did his chores, and then he played a computer game.*

Exercise 2

For each sentence below, determine which word in parentheses correctly completes the sentence.

1. The ambulance (passed, past) us.
2. Our teacher was (formerly, formally) a stockbroker.
3. (Its, It's) beginning to snow.
4. (Then, Than,) what do you do?
5. I always seem to (loose, lose) my keys.

26.2 Spelling Difficult Words **835**

UNIT 27 Study Skills

Lesson 27.1	Taking Notes in Class	*837*
Lesson 27.2	Studying Outside of Class	*838*
Lesson 27.3	Learning from Graphics	*843*

27.1 Taking Notes in Class

Taking notes from classroom lectures can help you review important ideas later on. Jotting down a teacher's directions also can save time and prevent you from making careless mistakes. Whenever you take good notes, you help yourself do the following:

- organize ideas
- recognize relationships among different topics
- remember and evaluate information
- identify points you find confusing

Many students take notes in the form of an outline. For information on outline form, see Lesson 7.2 in Composition, pages 330–333. The following chart lists other suggestions on how to take class notes.

Tips on Taking Notes

1. Write down only key words and phrases. Focusing on main points allows you to continue to listen while you write.
2. Underline or star main ideas. Highlighting the most important points makes reviewing easier.
3. Revise your notes after class. Clarifying your organization and adding details makes your notes more complete.
4. Keep your notes in a folder or notebook. Having a separate folder for each class helps you keep your notes organized.

Life in an ecosystem   Sept. 28 Biology

  Ecosystem: plants, animals, and physical environment of a community

  Types of biomes

    1. rain forest—Amazon   4. tundra—Arctic
    2. desert—Sahara, Gobi   5. deciduous forest—Europe
    3. grassland—U.S. Plains   6. taiga—northern Asia

> Organize your notes by topic, date, and class for easy reference.

> To save time, use symbols, numerals, and abbreviations.

Exercise 1

Watch a television program or listen to a radio broadcast in order to practice taking two-column notes. Divide a piece of paper in half vertically. On the left-hand side, take notes on what you see and hear. On the right-hand side, record comments and questions for later classroom discussion. Two-column notes allow for your own responses to topics and result in better comprehension of materials you study.

Exercise 2

In a small group, have one volunteer read aloud from an encyclopedia article for five minutes. Other students in the group should take notes as the volunteer reads. After the reading, the students taking notes should compare what they have written. What can you learn from your classmates about how to take good notes?

27.2 Studying Outside of Class

Your teacher usually determines what learning activities take place in class. Outside class, though, you're responsible for allocating your study time and learning material. The first step in studying efficiently is to learn how to manage your study time.

Using Study Time Wisely

Proper preparation and organization can help you make the most effective use of your study time. The following suggestions may help you study more efficiently.

- Divide large assignments into smaller tasks. Reading four pages of a textbook each night is easier than trying to read twenty pages every fifth night.

- Gather necessary materials. If possible, leave study supplies such as pencils and a dictionary at your study place.

- Select a place to study. By using the same place for studying each day, you will begin to associate that place with studying.

- Make a monthly assignment calendar. By writing down due dates, test dates, and notes about tasks to complete, you can see at a glance what work you need to do and when.

When you sit down to study, follow the tips on page 839 to help you make the best use of your study time.

Tips on Studying Effectively

1. Focus on one assignment at a time. Try to stay on task until you accomplish your goal.
2. Take short breaks after reaching a goal. Stretching, walking, or having a light snack can help keep you alert.
3. Write down questions about any material you are studying. This gives you a written record of what to ask during classroom discussions or when speaking with your teacher.
4. Review each major section of material you have studied. Even a short review can greatly increase the amount of information you remember.

Reading Efficiently

To be an efficient reader, you must pay close attention to how well you understand what you are reading. You literally must think about your thinking. Efficient readers have ongoing conversations with themselves as they work through a selection. They also adjust their reading speed with the demands of the task. Can you summarize what you have read? Is anything unclear? What questions do you have about the selection so far? What information do you think will come next? Use appropriate reading strategies for each reading purpose. Look at the three strategies in the chart below.

Hints for Using Three Reading Strategies

STRATEGY	DESCRIPTION	PURPOSE
SKIMMING	Glancing over the text to identify main ideas by reading chapter and lesson titles, words in bold or italic type, and topic sentences	• To preview material and get a general overview of the topic • To determine main ideas and the author's purpose • To decide whether a book covers a subject you are interested in
SCANNING	Glancing over the text to find specific information by looking for key terms	• To review key terms • To look for details to support an opinion • To search for specific information
IN-DEPTH READING	Reading the text carefully to absorb new ideas and facts	• To analyze new concepts or gather new information • To evaluate the information presented • To prepare to explain the information to someone else

When you prepare to study, follow the tips on page 839 to help you make the best use of your time.

■ Skimming
— Scanning
— In-depth reading

The Quran According to a Muslim tradition, the angel Gabriel revealed divine messages to Muhammad over a twenty-two-year period. Faithful Muslims wrote down or memorized these messages, but they were not compiled into one written collection until after Muhammad died. Then his successor, Abu Bakr, ordered Muslims to retrieve these messages from wherever they could be found, from the ribs of palm-leaves and tablets of white stone and from the breasts of men. It took twenty years before the messages were compiled into the holy book of Islam, the Quran, whose name means recital. For all Muslims, the Quran is the final authority in matters of faith and practice.

Written in Arabic, the Quran is believed to contain God's message as revealed to Muhammad. This message is expressed in stories, legends, and poems. Some of the stories—such as Noah's ark and Jonah in the belly of the whale—are variations of those found in the Bible.

Using the SQ3R Method

One way to increase your efficiency when studying material for the first time is to follow a five-step process known as the SQ3R method. The steps are described below.

1. Survey	2. Question	3. Read	4. Record	5. Review
Skim the material first. Read heads, highlighted terms, and the first sentence of each paragraph. Look at all pictures and graphs.	Ask questions about the material. Your questions might begin with *who, what, when, where, why,* and *how.*	Read the selection carefully. Identify the main idea of each section. Take notes, and add questions to your list.	Write answers to your questions without looking at the text. Make brief notes about additional main ideas or facts.	Check answers in the text. Continue to study the text until you can answer all questions correctly.

840 Unit 27 Study Skills

You can apply the SQ3R method to studying any subject. If you use the method regularly, it will become a habit. You may find that this habit brings several benefits, including the following:

- You remember more of what you read.
- You develop specific questions about information that is unclear.
- You are better prepared for class discussions and lectures.

Evaluating What You Read

The more you think about what you read, the better you will remember it. Therefore, if you get in the habit of evaluating material as you read it, you will find that you learn it better.

Identifying Facts and Opinions Most of what you read includes both facts and opinions. A fact is a statement that can be verified or proved to be true. How do you prove that something is true? One way is through direct experience—something you see or experience for yourself. If someone says that it is raining outside, you can step outside and see for yourself.

Proof also might come from an authoritative source, such as a reference book or an expert on the subject. Did the Inca emperor Pachacuti come to power in 1438? You can check the date in an encyclopedia.

An opinion is a personal judgment. Because opinions are expressions of someone's beliefs or feelings, they cannot be proved true or false. A valid opinion, however, is one that is based on accurate information. Opinions are most convincing when supported by evidence.

The following chart shows examples of facts and opinions. Learning how to distinguish between them will help you evaluate what you read.

Distinguishing Between Facts and Opinions

STATEMENT	FACT OR OPINION
1. Computers now do much of the assembly-line work that formerly was performed by factory workers.	**Fact:** Examining factories over the last twenty years would verify this statement.
2. Computerized manufacturing is bad because it causes people to lose their jobs.	**Opinion:** Computerized manufacturing may actually cause some unemployment, but whether it is good or bad is a value judgment.
3. Many kinds of vegetation and wildlife live in areas known as wetlands.	**Fact:** You could check this statement by reading studies done by biologists or by visiting a wetland yourself.
4. The federal government should do more to protect wetlands from pollution.	**Opinion:** Facts could be used to support or oppose this statement, but the statement is an opinion. People often disagree on the role of the federal government in protecting the environment.

Using Figurative Language Writers use figurative language to make their texts more interesting and to express their ideas more clearly. Figurative language is a word or phrase used in an imaginative way rather than in a literal sense. Similes, metaphors, and idioms are examples of figurative language. The example below includes several examples of figurative language. Do they work to help convey the writer's message?

> The dancers, clad in silks of green and blue, took their positions as the curtain rose. The music floated softly upward from somewhere below the stage and gathered like mist about their feet. As the melody swelled, their frozen forms melted into a celebration of movement. They swept across the floor, colorful rivers seeking their own paths along the barren landscape of the stage.

- The dancers were not cold enough to be actually "frozen." Rather, they were as motionless as if they were frozen.
- The description of how the dancers "melt" into "rivers" suggests their graceful, fluid movements.

Exercise 3

Read a newspaper article, a magazine article, or an editorial. In the piece you have chosen, identify ten statements as being either fact or opinion. If any of the statements are opinions, decide which ones are supported by accurate information. Share your comments with your class.

Exercise 4

Select a short passage from a novel or short story that uses figurative language. Rewrite the passage, changing the figurative language to literal language. How does the passage change? What is the overall effect?

Exercise 5

Find a three- or four-paragraph passage in a history or science textbook. Rewrite the passage, expressing the same information with figurative language. Evaluate the results.

27.3 Learning from Graphics

Read the following sentence quickly: "In 1990 the percentages of women in the U.S. labor force were 63 percent among women aged 16–24, 74 percent among women aged 25–54, 45 percent among women aged 55–64, and 8 percent among women aged 65 and older." Did you grasp all of that? Probably not. The mass of numbers in the sentence makes the information difficult to comprehend at a glance. To present numbers and other facts that are difficult to communicate clearly in sentences, writers often use tables, graphs, flow charts, cluster diagrams, and maps. The rest of this lesson will give you tips on how to interpret each of these types of graphics.

Tables

Tables separate information into categories so that you can compare specific items easily. The following table shows the percentage of women in the labor force for several countries during 1990. Notice how much more easily you can pick out information from the chart than from the example above.

Percentage of Women in the Labor Force, 1990

NATION	16–24 YEARS OLD	25–54 YEARS OLD	55–64 YEARS OLD	65+ YEARS OLD
UNITED STATES	63	74	45	8
CANADA	66	76	36	4
FRANCE	34	73	31	2
ITALY	41	49	10	2
JAPAN	45	64	47	16
SWEDEN	68	91	66	5
UNITED KINGDOM	73	73	37	3

Across the top row and down the left-hand column are the categories of information in the chart.

Compare information across columns. Among which age group were the fewest women in the labor force in France?

Compare information between rows. In which country was the percentage of women workers aged 55–64 highest in 1990?

To find out what percentage of Japanese women aged 25–54 were in the labor force in 1990, you would first read down the left-hand column in the table to find *Japan*. Then you would read across the top row of the table until you find the age group *25–54*. Moving down the column of numbers to the row even with *Japan*, you would see that 64 percent of Japanese women between the ages of 25 and 54 were in the labor force in 1990.

Bar Graphs

In bar graphs, each quantity is shown as a bar. The height of the bar reflects the amount. Because the bars are separate and distinct, writers often use bar graphs to compare quantities.

The bar graph shown here compares the consumption of vegetable protein in different world regions. The horizontal axis identifies the five world regions studied, while the vertical axis shows the amount of protein actually consumed (measured in grams per person per day).

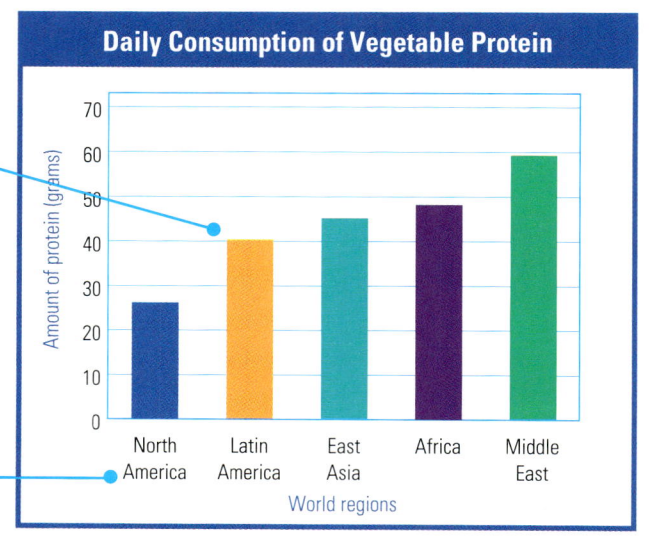

Daily Consumption of Vegetable Protein

- The height of the bar represents the amount of vegetable protein consumed.
- Each bar represents a different region.

The bars provide a quick way to see which regions consume the most and the least vegetable protein.

In the bar graph shown here, the bars run vertically. In other bar graphs the bars run horizontally. When bars run horizontally, the vertical axis indicates the categories being compared, and the horizontal axis indicates the quantities being compared.

Flow Charts

Flow charts show relationships among items, ideas, and events. Often they show the steps in a process. Arrows connect the ideas or steps to show how one flows into the next. For example, a flow chart might show the steps a bill goes through in becoming a law or the stages in the life of a frog. The flow chart below shows the selection process for a Supreme Court justice.

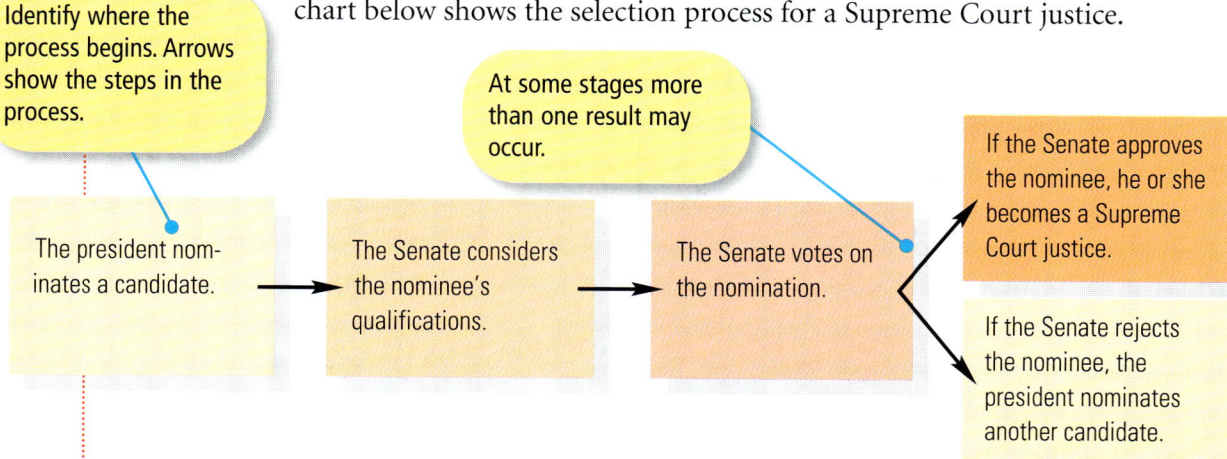

- Identify where the process begins. Arrows show the steps in the process.
- At some stages more than one result may occur.

The president nominates a candidate. → The Senate considers the nominee's qualifications. → The Senate votes on the nomination. →

- If the Senate approves the nominee, he or she becomes a Supreme Court justice.
- If the Senate rejects the nominee, the president nominates another candidate.

Cluster Diagrams

Another way to show the relationships among ideas is through a cluster diagram. Start by writing a topic or main idea inside a circle in the center of a piece of paper. As you think of ideas related to your topic, add those in circles arranged around the central one. Connect new ideas with related ideas.

Cluster diagrams connect the ideas you learn in class. The example below shows a cluster diagram about South American rain forests. Notice how the diagram shows the relationships among ideas.

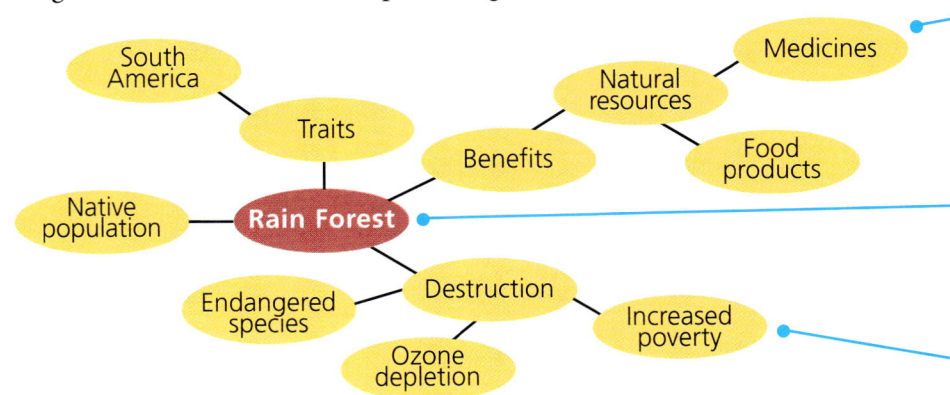

- Each new idea creates the possibility of another cluster.
- The main idea is listed in the center of the diagram.
- If you expanded the diagram, what ideas might you add?

Maps

Maps are a representation of a section of the earth. Political maps show features that are created by people or reflect their cultures, such as countries, cities, or roads. Physical maps show the natural features of the earth, such as mountains, rivers, and plains. The map at right shows both political and physical features.

- A blue line on a landmass indicates a river.
- Using the color key, you can determine that the Greeks occupied most of southern Italy.
- Why would you use a map such as this one?

27.3 Learning from Graphics **845**

Political maps and physical maps usually show large land areas: the world, a country, a state, a city. Maps can also show smaller areas: the houses in a neighborhood, the buildings on a college campus, or the location of rooms in a building. Architects use one type of map, a floor plan, to help them visualize their ideas. Below is an example of a floor plan that you might see in a history book. The floor plan shows the layout of a palace built in Morocco about one thousand years ago.

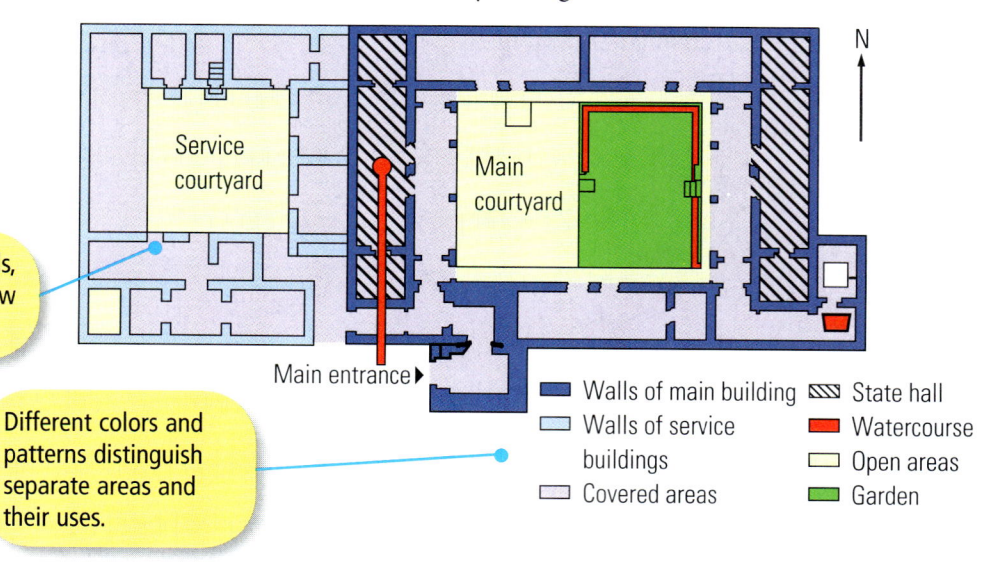

Solid lines represent walls, while breaks in lines show doors or windows.

Different colors and patterns distinguish separate areas and their uses.

- Walls of main building
- Walls of service buildings
- Covered areas
- State hall
- Watercourse
- Open areas
- Garden

Exercise 6

Assume that you found the following information in an encyclopedia. Create a table that shows the increase in the number of female scientists between 1970 and 1986.

In 1970 about 23 percent of social scientists were women. About 17 percent of mathematical scientists and about 14 percent of natural scientists were women. Among physicians, 10 percent were women. Only 2 percent of engineers were women. By 1986, women constituted 46 percent of social scientists, 36 percent of mathematical scientists, 23 percent of natural scientists, 18 percent of physicians, and 6 percent of engineers.

Exercise 7

In a group of four to six students, develop a cluster diagram. Decide on a broad concept or idea for your center circle. Members of the group should take turns adding related ideas to the diagram. Once you have filled the page, analyze the connections and discuss their meanings.

UNIT 28 Taking Tests

Lesson 28.1 **Classroom Tests** *848*

Lesson 28.2 **Standardized Tests** *853*

Lesson 28.3 **Standardized Test Practice** *859*

28.1 Classroom Tests

Careful attention to daily classroom work is the most important step you can take to prepare for a test. In addition, though, you can get ready for an exam by learning how to answer the types of questions your teachers will ask.

This lesson will show you some strategies for answering different types of objective test items. An objective test item is one that asks for very specific information about material that you have studied.

Multiple-Choice Items

A multiple-choice test item includes an incomplete sentence, or a question and a number of responses. You are to pick the response that best completes the sentence or answers the question. Consider the following tips.

> **Tips on Answering Multiple-Choice Items**
> 1. Read the item carefully. You need to know what information you are looking for.
> 2. Read all the responses. Even if the first one seems right, another response may be better.
> 3. Eliminate any responses that are clearly incorrect. Eliminating incorrect responses helps you focus your attention on the responses that may be correct.
> 4. Be cautious about responses that contain absolute words—*always, never, all,* or *none.* Because many statements have exceptions, absolute statements are often incorrect.

Here is an example of a multiple-choice test item. In this case, you are given a statement with a missing word. You are to choose the response that, when placed in the blank, will make the statement correct.

> In *The Thousand and One Nights,* _____ prevents her execution by telling tales of high adventure to her husband.
>
> a. an Arab writer   c. Scheherazade
> b. Sinbad   d. an unnamed man

Though the stories were written by Arab writers, choice a *does not complete the sentence correctly.*

The sentence structure indicates that the answer is a female, so choices b *and* d *are incorrect. The correct answer is choice* c.

848 Unit 28 Taking Tests

Here is another multiple-choice item. This one is phrased as a question. You are to select the best answer to the question.

> Which of the following statements concerning the book *Native Son* is accurate?
> a. It was written by Richard Wright.
> b. It takes place in the North.
> c. It is a work of fiction.
> d. all of the above.

Though choice a sounds correct, read all of the responses before answering.

Select this response only if you are sure that at least two of the responses are correct. In this case, choice d is correct.

True-False Items

A true-false item asks you to decide whether a statement is true or not. Many true-false items include some information that is true and some that is false. If any part of a statement is false, the entire statement is considered false. For the answer to be true, the entire statement must be true. Look at the statement on word usage below. Why is it false?

> The word *affect* is usually a verb meaning "to influence," and the word *effect* is always a noun meaning "the result."

The first part of this sentence is true, but the second is not because effect can also be a verb meaning "to cause." The correct answer is false.

Short-Answer Items

Short-answer items ask for specific information. Therefore, they are usually best answered with precisely phrased complete sentences. Also, since these items may ask you to supply several pieces of information, your answers to these items may be worth more than answers to other questions. For example, look at the following question, which might appear on an earth-science test.

> Why is soil erosion viewed as both helpful and harmful to people?

The preceding question asks for more than a list of the effects of soil erosion. In your answer, you should clearly distinguish between effects of soil erosion that are viewed as helpful and those that are viewed as harmful. Soil erosion is seen as helpful because it breaks up rocks and earth, moving rich soil to valleys and the mouths of rivers. Erosion is seen as harmful because it often strips farmland of valuable topsoil and threatens crop production.

28.1 Classroom Tests **849**

Fill-in Items

Fill-in items usually consist of a sentence with one or more blanks for you to fill in. The number of blank spaces provided often indicates the number of words needed in the response. Your answer should make the statement true and also grammatically correct. Consequently, rereading the statement with your answer included will help you check whether your choice is correct. Try to answer the fill-in question below.

> In our solar system, the first three planets in order from the sun are _____, _____, and _____.

Notice that the order of planets is important. The only correct answer is Mercury, Venus, *and* Earth.

On some tests, you may be given a list of words from which to choose your answers. If so, complete the ones you're sure of first. If answers from the list can be used only once, cross them off as you use them. As you reduce the number of possible answers, you increase your chances of finding the correct answers to the harder items. For example, assume that you can answer the first two items below but not the third.

> 1. Astronomers believe that the sun is a star in the _____ galaxy.
> 2. The _____ revolves around the earth about once per month.
> 3. The second closest star to the earth is _____.
>
> Milky Way   moon
> Andromeda   Alpha Centauri
> quasar

After answering *Milky Way* for the first item and *moon* for the second, only three possible responses remain. Because the structure of the sentence suggests that the correct answer is the name of a star, and star names are capitalized, you can eliminate *quasar*. Choosing between only two answers improves your chances of choosing correctly. What is the correct answer? *Alpha Centauri*.

850   Unit 28 Taking Tests

Matching Items

In matching items, you have two sets or lists of items, and you must match those in the first column or group to those in the second. Reading the directions carefully helps you know what type of match you should make. Some common matches are

- terms and their definitions
- events and the dates they occurred
- causes and their effects
- chemical elements and their symbols

Whatever the subject, compare the lists. Do they include the same number of items? Will every item be used exactly once? If so, you can cross out each one as it is used. Just as you used the process of elimination to help you with fill-ins, you can use the same approach again here. In the following example, match each country with its capital. Each city is used only once.

```
1. _____ Japan           a. New Delhi
2. _____ Uruguay         b. London
3. _____ India           c. Montevideo
4. _____ Great Britain   d. Cairo
5. _____ Egypt           e. Tokyo
```

As with other test items, answer the ones you're sure of first. Note, however, that if each response is used only once, you'll have to make two changes if you change an answer.

Time Management

Tests usually last no more than one class period. Because time is limited, you need to use it efficiently. The chart that follows gives a few suggestions for using your time wisely.

Tips for Allocating Time During a Test

1. Spend the first few minutes preparing. Reading the directions carefully will help you answer items appropriately.
2. Answer the items you are sure of first. Skipping difficult items will allow you to respond to all of the items you know.
3. Return to the difficult items. Using the strategies learned in this lesson, give the best answers you can.
4. Spend the last few minutes reviewing your answers. Taking time to check your answers will help prevent simple mistakes.

Exercise 1

Read the passage below and use the test-taking strategies in this lesson to help you complete the items that follow.

  Over the centuries, Japanese kabuki theater has grown and flourished. Continuing a tradition that historians have traced back to the 1600s, kabuki plays are still performed in Japan to large audiences. Kabuki theater seems to have originated as a new form of drama to satisfy the lavish and melodramatic tastes of a new social class in Tokugawa, Japan.
  When the lower and middle classes of society began to increase in the urban centers, they sought new forms of entertainment. The name *kabuki* means "to lean in the direction of fashion," reflecting kabuki theater's popular origins.
  Kabuki dramatizes subjects ranging from historical events to daily life. With elaborate costumes, exaggerated movements, and amazing special effects (including snowstorms and fires), kabuki theater is a spectacular event. Sometimes the stories make fun of political figures. During the 1600s, government officials banned some performances they felt were too controversial. If anything, this censorship seems to have made kabuki all the more popular.

1. Which of the following is true of kabuki theater?
    a. It is an old art form.
    b. It can be controversial.
    c. It is still performed today.
    d. all of the above
2. True or False: Kabuki has a name appropriate to its origins.
3. Like many popular films today, kabuki theater makes spectacular use of elaborate staging and _____ _____, such as snowstorms and fires.
4. How did the government's ban on certain political plays affect public opinion of kabuki?
5. For each effect in the following list, choose the cause from which that effect most directly resulted.
    a. bans on kabuki by the government
    b. increase in the popularity of kabuki
    c. desire for a new form of drama

    ___ rise of a new social class
    ___ ridicule of political figures
    ___ censorship of performances

28.2 Standardized Tests

To compare large numbers of students, schools often give standardized tests, or examinations that have been given to similar groups of students around the country. By studying these test results, experts develop standards of performance. Most standardized tests fall into one of three categories:

- Ability tests evaluate general learning skills, such as how well you can read, write, or use logic.
- Achievement tests evaluate knowledge in specific content areas, such as how much you know about biology or world history.
- Aptitude tests evaluate individual talents and interests, such as whether you prefer working in groups or alone.

Standardized tests contain several types of items. Becoming familiar with the kinds of test items most often used on standardized tests will improve your chances of scoring well.

Reading-Comprehension Items

How well you understand what you read is measured by reading-comprehension items. These items usually include a long passage about a literature, social studies, or science topic, and several questions about the passage. You should be able to answer all of the questions on the basis of the information in the passage. These questions often require you to

- identify main ideas
- recognize details supporting main ideas
- figure out what is not stated in the passage

The last type of item, also known as an inference item, requires coming to a conclusion that is based on the information in the passage but is not explicitly expressed. As you read the following passage and the items that follow it, notice the suggestions for how to respond to the items.

> Siddhartha Gautama, the founder of Buddhism, began his life as a Kshatriya prince. Born the son of a prince in northern India around 566 B.C., Gautama was raised in luxury. As a young man he continued to live a sheltered life, shielded from sickness and poverty. Tradition states that one day Gautama's charioteer drove him around his estates, and for the first time Gautama saw sickness, old age, and death. Shocked at these scenes of misery, Gautama decided to find out why people suffered and how suffering could be ended. At the age of 29, he left his wife and newborn son and wandered throughout India in what is known as the Great Renunciation.

> Although each sentence is true, choice *d* states the most important point, so it is correct.

1. Which sentence best summarizes the most important information in this passage?
   a. Gautama was raised in luxury in India.
   b. Gautama was born around 566 B.C.
   c. Gautama left home at the age of 29.
   d. Gautama wanted to know why people suffered.

> This item requires you to infer the correct response, which is choice *b*.

2. Based on this passage, Gautama seemed to be
   a. proud of his achievements
   b. concerned about others
   c. angry about his family's situation
   d. eager to meet other people

Vocabulary Items

Standardized tests often evaluate vocabulary knowledge through varieties of multiple-choice items. Sometimes you may be asked to complete a sentence by filling in the meaning of a word, as in the item that follows.

A preliminary step is taken _____.
   a. before any other step in a process
   b. during the most important steps of a process
   c. after all other steps in a process are completed
   d. only when necessary to complete a process
   e. only if the first step of a process fails

One tip for completing vocabulary items is to analyze the parts of an unknown word. See Unit 25, pages 818–826, for more information on how to build vocabulary. Notice that the word *preliminary* begins with the letters *pre-*. If you recall other words that begin with these letters, such as *precede*, *preface*, and *prepare*, you may realize that *pre-* often means "in front of" or "before." Using this knowledge, you may correctly determine that the answer is choice *a*.

A different type of vocabulary item, an analogy, tests the ability to analyze the relationships between words, not just an understanding of the meanings of words. Consider the words *healthy* and *robust*. What is the relationship between them? They are synonyms, words that have the same or nearly the same meaning. Now examine the pairs of words at the top of page 855. Which pair has the same relationship as *healthy* and *robust*?

Healthy is to robust as
   a. sociable is to disagreeable
   b. haughty is to arrogant
   c. mumbled is to audible
   d. scholastic is to readable
   e. loving is to polite

> *Sociable* is the opposite of *disagreeable*. *Haughty* and *arrogant* are synonyms. *Mumbled* speech is very different from speech that is *audible*. *Scholastic* and *readable* do not have similar meanings, and a *loving* person is not the same as a *polite* person.

None of the choices listed has anything to do with being healthy. However, the relationship you're looking for is one in which the pairs are synonyms. Only in choice *b* are the word meanings nearly the same. Therefore, choice *b* is the correct answer.

Some analogy items are shown in a different format. Each pair of words is separated by a colon, with a double colon used after the first pair. However, this format still requires you to choose the pair of words with the same relationship as the first. What is the relationship below?

carpenter : hammer : :
   a. swimmer : athlete
   b. hospital : doctor
   c. waiter : tray
   d. letter : post office
   e. bottle : beverage

One strategy for answering analogy items is to create a simple sentence in your mind that states the relationship between the first pair of words—for example, *A carpenter uses a hammer*. Then try each pair of words, using that particular sentence format. For choice *a* you would come up with the statement *A swimmer uses an athlete*. Since this sentence makes no sense, you could conclude that the relationship between *swimmer* and *athlete* is not the same as the relationship between *carpenter* and *hammer*. After trying each pair of words in the sentence, you would find that choice *c* makes the most sense.

Grammar, Usage, and Mechanics Items

Standardized tests often include sections that evaluate the ability to recognize and use standard English. Items may ask you to find grammatical errors in sentences, point out misused words, or choose the best way to correct an awkward or incorrect sentence.

English-usage items often show a sentence with several underlined and lettered sections. As you read the sentence, decide whether one of the underlined parts contains an error, and then mark the corresponding letter on your answer sheet. If the sentence contains no error, mark that choice; it usually follows the sentence. Examine the following item.

> The competition between Michelle and I became more intense
>   a   b   c
> as the school year progressed.   no error
>   d   e

The error is in b. "I" should be "me."

Some usage questions test the knowledge of homonyms, or words that sound alike but have different spellings and meanings. Given a list of phrases that contain homonyms, you might be asked to find the one item with a word used incorrectly or the one item with no errors. In the following example, find the response in which all words are used correctly.

> a. a heard of cattle
> b. a jury of your peers
> c. a steal beam
> d. to much sun

The only phrase in which all words are used correctly is choice b.

Correction items ask you to correct a mistake as well as to recognize it. Usually in such items, only one part of the given sentence is underlined. Each response is a possible correction. You have to choose the response that best corrects the error in the sentence. Often one of the choices will look identical to the underlined section. Choose it if you feel the sentence contains no error. Here is an example of a sentence-correction item.

> Ms. Hasan is the best of the two candidates running for mayor.
> a. is the best of
> b. is the more better of
> c. is the very best of
> d. is the better of

As you read the sentence, decide if the underlined words are incorrect.

"Best" should be used only in discussing three or more items, so choices a and c are incorrect. "More better" is incorrect usage. The best response is choice d.

Test-taking Strategies

Certain test-taking strategies will help you as you take a test. The chart that follows lists some strategies you might use.

Tips for Taking Standardized Tests

1. Skip difficult items at first. Because standardized tests are usually timed, focus on answering items you know. You can return to skipped items later.
2. Mark only your answers on the answer sheet. Because the test is machine-graded, stray marks may be read as wrong answers.
3. Frequently compare the item numbers on your test and answer sheet. This helps you avoid putting your answers in the wrong spaces.
4. If you have time, check your answers. If the test does not penalize you for wrong answers, guess the answers for all items you did not have time to complete.

Exercise 2

Use the test-taking strategies described in this lesson to help you complete the following items.

1. Choose the phrase that best completes this sentence:

    A transatlantic message is one that _____.
    - **a.** travels under a body of water
    - **b.** is sent across the ocean
    - **c.** is sent by passengers on a ship
    - **d.** is always about navigation

2. Find the pair of words with the same relationship as the given pair.

    player : team : :
    - **a.** conductor : baton
    - **b.** engineer : bridge
    - **c.** United States : country
    - **d.** soldier : army
    - **e.** cat : pet

3. Where is the error in the following sentence?

    Our teacher <u>was pleased</u> that <u>all of us</u> <u>have passed</u> the exam,
                        a   b   c
    and <u>we were happy</u> that the test was over. <u>no error</u>
         d   e

4. Which item includes a word that is used incorrectly?
    - **a.** a strong ally
    - **b.** gives good advice
    - **c.** the capital building
    - **d.** the bare facts

5. Correct the underlined section in the following sentence.

    I wanted to remind her that the party starts at seven o'clock, but she <u>had already went</u> out the door.
    - **a.** had already went
    - **b.** had went already
    - **c.** had went
    - **d.** had already gone

28.2 Standardized Tests

Exercise 3

Read the following passage. Then read each question below and choose the best answer. Mark the letter for that answer on your paper.

Dear Neighbor,

I am the Chairman of Troop 597's October Charity Drive. The proceeds of our activities will benefit the Willimet Community Center on Dodd Street. To raise money, we are holding a recycling drive, and you can help!

As you know, state laws require a 5-cent deposit on all aluminum cans sold. When a can is emptied, it may be redeemed at the recycling center for the nickel deposit. However, many people throw their "empties" out with the trash or litter them along our highways and in our parks.

Help us to help the environment and our Community Center at the same time. Troop 597 will set up a collection stall in the Community Center parking lot from October 1st–31st. Please stop by to drop off any empty cans you would like to donate. In addition, Troop 597 will lead volunteer clean-up crews to key sites across town to collect discarded recyclables. If you would like to join us, the crews will meet in the Community Center parking lot every Saturday in October at 9:00 A.M.

On behalf of Troop 597, I'd like to thank you in advance for whatever efforts you can make on behalf of this worthy campaign.

Yours,
David Hafner, Troop 597

1. David's purpose for writing this letter is primarily to —
   a. ask the community for its support in the scout troop's recycling drive
   b. explain why members of his scout troop will take up space in the Community Center parking lot during the month of October
   c. try to get more boys to join the scout troop
   d. request that people not park in the Community Center parking lot on Saturday

2. Which of the following is a concerned member of the community most likely to do after reading David's letter?
   a. Buy fewer cans at local stores
   b. Discard more cans in local parks and along highways
   c. Drop off empty cans at the Community Center parking lot
   d. Go to the library to find out more about fund-raising drives

3. David probably thinks that people who throw their empty cans in the parks are —
   a. helpful and concerned
   b. careless and wasteful
   c. uninformed about state laws
   d. likely to volunteer for a clean-up crew

4. David attempts to show that this year's October Charity Drive will not only raise money for the Community Center but also —
   a. allow the scouts to earn a merit badge
   b. help restore and maintain buildings on Dodd Street
   c. convince the local government to increase the deposit on aluminum cans
   d. help clean up local highways and parks

28.3 Standardized Test Practice

Introduction

The following pages of exercises have been designed to familiarize you with the standardized writing tests that you may take during the school year. These exercises are very similar to the actual tests in how they look and what they ask you to do. Completing these exercises will not only provide you with practice but also will make you aware of areas you might need to work on.

These writing exercises—just like the actual standardized writing tests—are divided into three sections.

Sentence Structure In this section, pages 860 to 867, you will be given a short passage in which some of the sentences are underlined. Each underlined sentence is numbered. After you finish reading the passage, you will be asked questions about the underlined sections. The underlined sections will be either incomplete sentences, run-on sentences, correctly written sentences that should be combined, or correctly written sentences that do not need to be rewritten. You will need to select which is best from the four choices provided.

Usage In this section, pages 868 to 875, you will also be asked to read a short passage. However, in these exercises, a word or words in the passage will be omitted and a numbered blank space will be in their place. After reading the passage, you will need to determine which of the four provided words or groups of words best belongs in each numbered space.

Mechanics Finally, in the third section, pages 876 to 883, the short passages will have parts that are underlined. You will need to determine if, in the underlined sections, there is a spelling error, capitalization error, punctuation error, or no error at all.

Writing well is a skill that you will use the rest of your life. You will be able to write more accurate letters to your friends and family, better papers in school, and more interesting stories. You will be able to express yourself and your ideas more clearly and in a way that is interesting and engaging. These exercises should help to improve your writing and to make you comfortable with the format and types of questions you will see on standardized writing tests.

Standardized Test Practice

Read each passage. Some sections are underlined. The underlined sections may be one of the following:

- Incomplete sentences
- Run-on sentences
- Correctly written sentences that should be combined
- Correctly written sentences that do not need to be rewritten

Choose the best way to write each underlined section and mark the letter for your answer.
If the underlined section needs no change, mark the choice "Correct as is" on your paper.

Angelina and Sarah Grimké, sisters born in South Carolina, are known for their contributions to the abolitionist movement. <u>Not having the tolerance for slavery that their friends and family had. The two sisters moved to Philadelphia, and ultimately settled in New York in the early 1830s.</u> (1) The American Anti-Slavery Society sponsored the Grimkés' early public speeches. <u>These lectures were very successful, they drew large audiences.</u> (2)

In 1838, after a lecture tour of New England, Angelina gave testimony to the Massachusetts legislature. <u>She was the first American woman to address a legislative body. She presented thousands of anti-slavery petitions.</u> (3) Since women did not normally speak like this in public, the sisters faced criticism, even from fellow abolitionists; yet they continued with their crusade.

---

1 A Not having the tolerance for slavery that their friends and family had, the two sisters moved to Philadelphia and ultimately settled in New York in the early 1830s.
  B The two sisters did not have the tolerance for slavery that their friends and family had. Moving to Philadelphia, and ultimately settled in New York in the early 1830s.
  C The two sisters did not have the tolerance for slavery that their friends and family had, they moved to Philadelphia, and ultimately settled in New York in the early 1830s.
  D Correct as is

2 F These lectures were very successful and drawing large audiences.
  G These lectures were very successful. Drawing large audiences.
  H These lectures were very successful, drawing large audiences.
  J Correct as is

3 A She was the first American woman to address a legislative body, which presented thousands of anti-slavery petitions.
  B Presenting thousands of anti-slavery petitions, she was the first American woman to address a legislative body.
  C Since she was the first American woman to address a legislative body, she presented thousands of anti-slavery petitions.
  D After she presented thousands of anti-slavery petitions, she was the first American woman to address a legislative body.

Standardized Test Practice

Victor's parents sighed as the players walked off the field. The baseball game had been cancelled at the last minute after thunder had rumbled through the sky. <u>Victor had been looking forward to playing his first game of the season, his mom and dad knew that this was a disappointment for him.</u>(1) The team had been practicing hard and were ready to win. <u>But now, with a big storm coming, they would have to wait until next week.</u>(2)

Victor's parents tried to go to every one of Victor's games. They were always the most enthusiastic fans in the bleachers. <u>The first game of the year was usually very crowded. They had arrived early and managed to get a good seat.</u>(3) Now everyone was running to their cars as the rain started. <u>Thoughts of attending the next game. This would help Victor's parents to get through the week!</u>(4)

1. **A** Victor had been looking forward to playing his first game of the season. His mom and dad knowing that this was a disappointment for him.
   B Victor had been looking forward to playing his first game of the season, and his mom and dad knew that this was a disappointment for him.
   C Victor looking forward to playing his first game of the season. And his mom and dad knew that this was a disappointment for him.
   D Correct as is

2. **F** But now, with a big storm coming. They would have to wait until next week.
   G But now, with a big storm coming, they would have to wait. Until next week.
   H But now, with a big storm coming, they would have to wait, until next week.
   J Correct as is

3. **A** The first game of the year was usually very crowded, and they had arrived early, and they had managed to get a good seat.
   B The first game of the year, which was usually very crowded, had arrived early and managed to get a good seat.
   C The first game of the year was usually very crowded, but they had arrived early and managed to get a good seat.
   D The first game of the year, which had arrived early, was usually very crowded and they managed to get a good seat.

4. **F** Thoughts of attending the next game helping Victor's parents to get through the week!
   G Thoughts of attending the next game would help Victor's parents. To get through the week!
   H Thoughts of attending the next game would help Victor's parents to get through the week!
   J Correct as is

STOP

28.3 Standardized Test Practice **861**

Standardized Test Practice

Read each passage. Some sections are underlined. The underlined sections may be one of the following:

- Incomplete sentences
- Run-on sentences
- Correctly written sentences that should be combined
- Correctly written sentences that do not need to be rewritten

Choose the best way to write each underlined section and mark the letter for your answer.
If the underlined section needs no change, mark the choice "Correct as is" on your paper.

The hike to this point had been difficult. <u>Alberto could see the peaks of nearby mountains, he could see the treetops for miles around.</u> (1) The view was spectacular. Alberto reached into his backpack and removed the camera that his grandfather had given him. <u>When the sun came out from behind the clouds. He snapped the perfect photo.</u> (2) A great picture, while no substitute for the real thing, would help Alberto describe the hike to his family. He was looking forward to putting together an album. <u>He had already taken some photographs of the lake. It was far below at the foot of the mountain.</u> (3)

<u>Alberto knew it was time to go even before the troop leader gathered everyone together.</u> (4) The sun would be setting soon, and the hike back down to camp was still ahead. Nevertheless, the view had made the entire trip worthwhile.

---

1 **A** Alberto could see the peaks of nearby mountains, and he could see. The treetops for miles around.
  B Alberto could see the peaks of nearby mountains and the treetops for miles around.
  C Alberto could see the peaks of nearby mountains. And the treetops for miles around.
  D Correct as is

2 **F** When the sun came out from behind the clouds, he snapped the perfect photo.
  G The sun came out from behind the clouds, because he snapped the perfect photo.
  H The sun. It came out from behind the clouds and he snapped the perfect photo.
  J Correct as is

3 **A** He had already taken some photographs of the lake that was far below at the foot of the mountain.
  B Far below at the foot of the mountain, he had taken some photographs of the lake, already.
  C He had already taken some photographs. Of the lake that was far below at the foot of the mountain.
  D He had already taken some photographs of the lake when it was far below at the foot of the mountain.

4 **F** Alberto knew it was time to go. Even before the troop leader gathered everyone together.
  G Alberto knowing it was time to go even before the troop leader gathered everyone together.
  H Time to go. Alberto knew it even before the troop leader gathered everyone together.
  J Correct as is

862 Unit 28 Taking Tests

Standardized Test Practice

The high school Young Astronomers club was hoping to see a rare comet tonight. <u>The comet was only visible in February. That's why the group was standing out in the cold waiting for it.</u>(1) Patrick silently thanked his parents for reminding him to bring an extra sweater.

Patrick set up the telescope and gathered the group around. <u>It was hard to believe that what they were about to see only became visible every few years.</u>(2) Everyone looked through the telescope at the comet, which appeared as a bright streak in the sky. Patrick felt proud. <u>The comet had been discovered by his uncle. A former member of the Young Astronomers, who was now a well-known astronomer.</u>(3) The comet would still be visible for the next few nights. <u>Patrick was delighted after seeing it once, they had seen something beautiful.</u>(4)

1.
   A The group was standing out in the cold waiting for the comet because it was only visible in February.
   B The comet was only visible in February since the group was standing out in the cold waiting for the comet.
   C The comet was only visible in February, the group was standing out in the cold waiting for it.
   D The group was standing out in the cold waiting for the comet, who was only visible in February.

2.
   F It was hard to believe. That what they were about to see only became visible every few years.
   G It was hard to believe that what they were about to see becoming visible every few years.
   H It was hard to believe that what they were about to see. It only became visible every few years.
   J Correct as is

3.
   A The comet had been discovered by his uncle, he was a former member of the Young Astronomers, who was now a well-known astronomer.
   B The comet had been discovered by his uncle, a former member of the Young Astronomers. Who was now a well-known astronomer.
   C The comet had been discovered by his uncle, a former member of the Young Astronomers, who was now a well-known astronomer.
   D Correct as is

4.
   F Patrick was delighted after seeing it once. Because they had seen something beautiful.
   G After seeing it once, Patrick was delighted that they had seen something beautiful.
   H After seeing it once, Patrick was delighted. That they had seen something beautiful.
   J Correct as is

Standardized Test Practice

Read each passage. Some sections are underlined. The underlined sections may be one of the following:

- Incomplete sentences
- Run-on sentences
- Correctly written sentences that should be combined
- Correctly written sentences that do not need to be rewritten

Choose the best way to write each underlined section and mark the letter for your answer.
If the underlined section needs no change, mark the choice "Correct as is" on your paper.

Today it is simple to get a national newspaper at your local newsstand. <u>However, obtaining a newspaper was very difficult in colonial America. Publishers faced many obstacles.</u> (1) Their equipment was primitive compared to today's equipment. <u>Printing presses had to be operated by hand. They were extremely slow.</u> (2) Distribution was also a problem. <u>Since all the newspapers were delivered on horseback. Subscribers usually lived in the same town where the paper was published.</u> (3) Circulation was low. The largest newspapers published weekly and only printed a few hundred copies. <u>But now, with better printing technology and larger distribution, newspapers can be found on almost any corner in America.</u> (4)

---

1 **A** However, obtaining a newspaper and publishers facing many obstacles was very difficult in colonial America.
B However, since publishers faced many obstacles, obtaining a newspaper was very difficult in colonial America.
C However, since obtaining a newspaper was very difficult in colonial America, publishers faced many obstacles.
D However, publishers faced many obstacles because obtaining a newspaper was very difficult in colonial America.

2 **F** Printing presses had to be operated by hand when they were extremely slow.
G Printing presses having to be operated by hand, they were extremely slow.
H Printing presses had to be operated by hand and they were extremely slow.
J Printing presses had to be operated by hand, and these printing presses were extremely slow.

3 **A** Since all the newspapers were delivered on horseback, subscribers usually lived in the same town where the paper was published.
B All the newspapers were delivered on horseback, so subscribers usually lived in the same town. Where the paper was published.
C All the newspapers were delivered on horseback, subscribers usually lived in the same town where the paper was published.
D Correct as is

4 **F** But now, with better printing technology and larger distribution. Newspapers can be found on almost any corner in America.
G But now, to have better printing technology and larger distribution, newspapers can be found on almost any corner in America.
H Newspapers can be found with better printing technology and larger distribution on any corner in America.
J Correct as is

864 Unit 28 Taking Tests

Standardized Test Practice

In the first century, the city of Pompeii was destroyed when Mount Vesuvius, a nearby volcano, erupted. <u>Scientists have studied similar phenomena for centuries. Scientists have created a number of different categories to classify volcanoes.</u> (1) Composite volcanoes are tall and pointy, and are composed of thick lava and ash. <u>Shield volcanoes, such as Kilauea in Hawaii, are made up of sloping layers of rock formed by small eruptions of lava.</u> (2) A third type of volcano is called a cinder cone. This kind of volcano has very steep sides made up of small chunks of solid lava.

<u>When a volcano erupts. Molten rock is forced to the surface by pressure deep inside the earth.</u> (3) The intensity of an eruption varies, but sometimes it can result in a massive explosion. <u>Scientists can learn not only about nature's fury from volcanoes. But also about the materials that can be found under the surface of our planet.</u> (4)

1
- **A** Scientists have studied similar phenomena for centuries but have created a number of different categories to classify volcanoes.
- **B** Scientists have studied similar phenomena for centuries, have created a number of different categories to classify volcanoes.
- **C** Scientists have studied similar phenomena for centuries, creating a number of different categories to classify volcanoes.
- **D** Studying similar phenomena for centuries, scientists have studied a number of different categories to classify volcanoes.

2
- **F** Shield volcanoes, such as Kilauea in Hawaii, are made up of sloping layers of rock. Which are formed by small eruptions of lava.
- **G** Shield volcanoes, such as Kilauea in Hawaii. Are made up of sloping layers of rock formed by small eruptions of lava.
- **H** Shield volcanoes, such as Kilauea in Hawaii, making sloping layers of rock formed by small eruptions of lava.
- **J** Correct as is.

3
- **A** When a volcano erupts, molten rock is forced to the surface by pressure deep inside the earth.
- **B** When a volcano erupts, then molten rock is forced to the surface by pressure deep inside the earth.
- **C** When a volcano. Erupting molten rock is forced to the surface by pressure deep inside the earth.
- **D** Correct as is

4
- **F** Scientists can learn not only about nature's fury. From volcanoes but also about the materials that can be found under the surface of our planet.
- **G** Scientists can learn not only about nature's fury, but also about the materials surfacing under our planet from volcanoes.
- **H** Scientists can learn not only about nature's fury from volcanoes, but also about the materials that can be found under the surface of our planet.
- **J** Correct as is

STOP

Standardized Test Practice

Read each passage. Some sections are underlined. The underlined sections may be one of the following:

- Incomplete sentences
- Run-on sentences
- Correctly written sentences that should be combined
- Correctly written sentences that do not need to be rewritten

Choose the best way to write each underlined section and mark the letter for your answer.
If the underlined section needs no change, mark the choice "Correct as is" on your paper.

<u>A visit to New York City may feel overwhelming. To someone who has never been there before.</u> The
(1)
buildings appear to go on for miles. In fact, Manhattan is only a little more than 22 square miles in area.

<u>Running beneath New York's surface, the subway system is a vast transportation network. This network
(2)
contains 772 miles of active track.</u> It is the largest underground transportation system in the world. <u>The first
(3)
subway was constructed in 1870 by Alfred Ely Beach, who was also the inventor of the typewriter.</u> Of
course, there are many different ways to get around town in New York. <u>The subway, however, is often the
(4)
fastest option, it gets you where you need to go without the worry of traffic.</u>

---

1 **A** A visit to New York City overwhelming to someone who has never been there before.
  B A visit to New York City may feel overwhelming to someone. Who has never been there before.
  C A visit to New York City may feel overwhelming to someone who has never been there before.
  D Correct as is

2 **F** Running beneath New York's surface, the subway system is a vast transportation network that contains 772 miles of active track.
  G Running beneath New York's surface, the subway system and a vast transportation network contain 772 miles of active track.
  H Running beneath New York's surface, the subway system is a vast transportation network, and this transportation network contains 772 miles of active track.
  J Running beneath New York's surface, the subway system is a vast transportation network, and the subway system also containing 772 miles of active track.

3 **A** The first subway was constructed in 1870 by Alfred Ely Beach, he was also the inventor of the typewriter.
  B The first subway was constructed in 1870 by Alfred Ely Beach. Who was also the inventor of the typewriter.
  C The first subway constructing in 1870 by Alfred Ely Beach, who also the inventor of the typewriter.
  D Correct as is

4 **F** The subway, however, is often the fastest option. Getting you where you need to go without the worry of traffic.
  G The subway, however, is often the fastest option, getting you where you need to go without the worry of traffic.
  H The subway, however, is often the fastest option getting you where you need to go. Without the worry of traffic.
  J Correct as is

Standardized Test Practice

On October 2, 1800, Nat Turner was born as an enslaved person, it was in Virginia. Thirty-one years later, he would be known as one of the bravest enslaved people in history when he led the Southampton Slave Revolt.

Nat Turner had grown increasingly angry with the way that his people were treated in the South. It was an early morning in August of 1831. Nat Turner decided to rebel against slavery in his community. He recruited seventy fellow enslaved men and, together, they marched through the streets of Southampton. The revolt lasted two days. Before the Virginia Militia finally put an end to it. Nat Turner escaped, but was captured two months later. Although Nat Turner was not able to put an end to slavery with his revolt, he did make an important contribution toward freedom for enslaved peoples.

1. A On October 2, 1800, Nat Turner was born an enslaved person. In Virginia.
   B On October 2, 1800, Nat Turner was born an enslaved person in Virginia.
   C On October 2, 1800. Nat Turner was born an enslaved person in Virginia.
   D Correct as is

2. F It was an early morning in August of 1831 if Nat Turner decided to rebel against slavery in his community.
   G Nat Turner decided to in 1831 to rebel on an early August morning against slavery in his community.
   H It was an early morning in August of 1831 when Nat Turner decided to rebel against slavery in his community.
   J Early morning 1831 when Nat Turner in August decided to rebel against slavery in his community.

3. A The revolt lasted two days before the Virginia Militia finally put an end to it.
   B The revolt lasted. Two days before the Virginia Militia finally put an end to it.
   C The revolt lasted two days before. The Virginia Militia finally put an end to it.
   D Correct as is

4. F Although Nat Turner. Was not able to put an end to slavery with his revolt, he did make an important contribution toward freedom for enslaved peoples.
   G He did make an important contribution toward freedom for enslaved peoples, then Nat Turner was not able to put an end to slavery with his revolt.
   H Although Nat Turner was not able to put an end to slavery with his revolt. He did make an important contribution toward freedom for enslaved peoples.
   J Correct as is

28.3 Standardized Test Practice

Standardized Test Practice

Read each passage and choose the word or group of words that belongs in each space. Mark the letter for your answer on your paper.

> There are two types of sound recordings: digital recording and analog recording. __(1)__ are both acceptable ways to record effects and music.
>
> Analog tape is made of thin, sturdy plastic. This material __(2)__ with an oxide powder, which is magnetized when exposed to a magnetic field. The record head of a tape recorder is a very small electromagnet. When an audio signal passes through __(3)__, the oxide is magnetized and imprinted with sound. A digital recorder picks up sound at rapid intervals and __(4)__ it into numbers. A compact disc may store as many as 44,000 bits of sound per second. One of the __(5)__ advantages digital technology has over analog technology is that digital recordings do not degrade over time.

1. **A** it
   B they
   C we
   D you

2. **F** will be coated
   G was coated
   H is coated
   J had been coated

3. **A** you
   B it
   C them
   D us

4. **F** converts
   G is converting
   H has converted
   J convert

5. **A** significantly
   B significantest
   C more significantly
   D most significant

868 Unit 28 Taking Tests

Standardized Test Practice

Millions of people across the globe are nearsighted. The __(1)__ way to correct this problem is with the use of eyeglasses or contact lenses.

The inner layer of the eye is called the retina. This light-sensitive membrane __(2)__ to the brain by the optic nerve. When someone is nearsighted, or myopic, the light that enters the eye is focused in front of the retina rather than directly on it. This causes distant objects to appear blurred.

Wearing glasses or contact lenses helps to focus incoming light waves directly onto the retina. This is how corrective lenses allow people who suffer from myopia to see __(3)__. So if you should discover that you have blurred vision, at least you know that you can correct __(4)__ without difficulty.

1. A easier
   B more easy
   C easiest
   D most easiest

2. F was connected
   G is connected
   H will be connected
   J had been connected

3. A more clearly
   B more clearer
   C more clear
   D more clearest

4. F they
   G it
   H we
   J you

Standardized Test Practice

Read each passage and choose the word or group of words that belongs in each space. Mark the letter for your answer on your paper.

> The rash that most people get from poison ivy can be itchy and uncomfortable. This rash __(1)__ by a chemical called urushiol.
>
> Urushiol is found in the sap of the poison ivy plant. When your skin is exposed to poison ivy, an allergic reaction does not occur immediately. The urushiol must penetrate the outer layer of skin before your body's immune system reacts. If you have been exposed to poison ivy, washing your skin immediately is the __(2)__ way to prevent a rash.
>
> Urushiol will rub off onto anything that comes into contact with __(3)__ . That means if you walk through a patch of poison ivy, you can get a rash later by touching your shoes or clothes. Anything that touches the plant will help the urushiol to spread __(4)__ .

1 A will be caused
   B is caused
   C was caused
   D had been caused

2 F most effective
   G effectivest
   H more effective
   J effective

3 A you
   B we
   C it
   D them

4 F more wider
   G more wide
   H more widest
   J more widely

870 Unit 28 Taking Tests

Standardized Test Practice

Zoos, with __(1)__ diverse array of wildlife, are now a popular destination in cities across America. This was not always the case. Centuries ago, traveling __(2)__ with only one wild animal on display were normal. The first wild animal exhibited in America was a lion, but perhaps the __(3)__ of these early attractions was an elephant. In 1797 an elephant was displayed in Boston's Market Square. Visitors __(4)__ an admission of 25 cents to see the giant animal. At the time, viewing any type of exotic wildlife was a rare treat. Elephants continued to be a popular tourist attraction well into the 1800s.

1 A its
   B your
   C their
   D our

2 F exhibits
   G exhibitor
   H exhibiting
   J exhibited

3 A successest
   B successful
   C most successful
   D more successfully

4 F have paid
   G will pay
   H pay
   J paid

Standardized Test Practice

Read each passage and choose the word or group of words that belongs in each space. Mark the letter for your answer on your paper.

> Investigative journalists in America research news stories and try to uncover buried pieces of information. At the turn of the century, President Theodore Roosevelt __(1)__ to investigative journalists as "muckrakers." This name was derived from a character in a John Bunyan novel who always looked down and raked the dirt, or "muck." Muckrakers were writers and reporters who __(2)__ on society's problems. Some of __(3)__ subjects included political corruption in city government and racial discrimination in the South. Today, they __(4)__ as journalists who alerted the public to controversial issues and called for social change.

1 A refers
   B refer
   C referred
   D will refer

2 F focused
   G have been focusing
   H had focused
   I will focus

3 A us
   B our
   C your
   D their

4 F have been remembered
   G has been remembered
   H is remembered
   J are remembered

Standardized Test Practice

In 1848, the U.S. Army __(1)__ creating a cavalry of soldiers mounted on camels. In 1856, thirty-four camels arrived from various Mediterranean countries. They __(2)__ at Camp Verde in Texas, which some people called "Little Egypt." Camels had a number of advantages over horses. First of all, camels could travel great distances without water, making difficult journeys __(3)__ . Camels were not afraid of gunfire, and the sight of an oncoming camel herd would cause enemy horses to turn and flee. Unfortunately, some soldiers were not able to sit securely on the camels for long periods of time. Ultimately, this project __(4)__ , but not before a few camels had the opportunity to experience military service.

1. **A** consider
   B considered
   C are considering
   D will consider

2. **F** stationed
   G is stationed
   H was stationed
   J were stationed

3. **A** more easiest
   B most easiest
   C easier
   D more easy

4. **F** have been abandoned
   G has been abandoned
   H is abandoned
   J was abandoned

Standardized Test Practice

Read each passage and choose the word or group of words that belongs in each space. Mark the letter for your answer on your paper.

Have you ever carried a big pile of magazines to the recycling box? The next time you do, think twice. Those magazines, and the images on __(1)__ pages, can be transformed into a work of art. Even if you don't consider yourself to be an artist, cutting and pasting pictures together from different magazines is a fun way for __(2)__ to create a collage. Advertisements, illustrations, and photographs are just a few of the __(3)__ used images in this type of collage.

If you __(4)__ to be really creative, you can also attach cloth, wood or other materials to your picture. Then you can hang the magazines on your wall instead of putting them in the recycling box.

1 **A** our
    B its
    C their
    D your

2 **F** begin
    G beginner
    H began
    J beginners

3 **A** most common
    B most commonly
    C common
    D commonest

4 **F** want
    G wanted
    H will want
    J had wanted

Standardized Test Practice

Many Native Americans of the American Southwest were among the first apartment dwellers. Hundreds of years ago, these __(1)__ people lived in multistory communities not unlike the apartment houses of today. Instead of staircases, the inhabitants moved from floor to floor by using ladders. They __(2)__ these homes out of stone or adobe, which is a type of clay used for construction. They fashioned bricks, reinforced them with straw, and dried them in the sun.

The builders were also skilled craftsmen and known for their pottery and basketwork. Although not aggressive, the people did not hesitate to rise in __(3)__ of their homes when attacked. The Apache and Navaho were legendary enemies of the pueblo dwellers. Today, the unique buildings can still be seen in the Southwest, where they __(4)__ for centuries.

1 A invention
   B inventions
   C inventive
   D invent

2 F built
   G will build
   H build
   J are building

3 A defend
   B defends
   C defender
   D defense

4 F stand
   G is standing
   H have been standing
   J has been standing

Standardized Test Practice

Read each passage and decide which type of error, if any, appears in each underlined section. Mark the letter for your answer on your paper.

In today's cinema, it seems that almost any visual trick can be accomplished through the use of special effects. This kind of movie <u>magic, while commonplace today, may not have been possible without the films of french director Georges Méliès.</u> (1) As early as 1896, Méliès was using trick photography in his work. His films <u>featured monsters spaceships, and women vanishing into thin air</u> (2). While any of these things might be found in a modern science-fiction blockbuster, Méliès was one of the first to develop them for the screen. For <u>example, if Méliès wanted to suggest an underwater scene, he placed</u> (3) a fish tank in front of the camera. His effects may seem crude by today's <u>standards, but without his inovative first attempts at cinematic illusion,</u> (4) the films we see today might not have been made.

1. A Spelling error
   B Capitalization error
   C Punctuation error
   D No error

2. F Spelling error
   G Capitalization error
   H Punctuation error
   J No error

3. A Spelling error
   B Capitalization error
   C Punctuation error
   D No error

4. F Spelling error
   G Capitalization error
   H Punctuation error
   J No error

Standardized Test Practice

It was the first friday in May and it was simply beautiful outside. Mrs. Major thought she would try
(1)
something new. She decided to hold her English class on the field in front of the school.

All of the students sat in a circle, with Mrs. Major in the center. She began by reciting an elizabethan
(2)
sonnet. The gorgeous weather only added to the sonnets beauty. The sweet smell in the air complemented
(3)
the words perfectly. When she was finished reading, Mrs. Major initiated a discusion with a few questions
(4)
about the poem. The conversation was lively and stimulating. Mrs. Major was very happy with the results of
her experiment. For the rest of the spring, she hoped to conduct at least one more class outdoors.
(5)

1. A Spelling error
   B Capitalization error
   C Punctuation error
   D No error

2. F Spelling error
   G Capitalization error
   H Punctuation error
   J No error

3. A Spelling error
   B Capitalization error
   C Punctuation error
   D No error

4. F Spelling error
   G Capitalization error
   H Punctuation error
   J No error

5. A Spelling error
   B Capitalization error
   C Punctuation error
   D No error

Standardized Test Practice

Read each passage and decide which type of error, if any, appears in each underlined section. Mark the letter for your answer on your paper.

Mark and Julio wanted to see a movie. <u>Julio's mother promised to take them to the theater and pick them up after the show.</u> (1) The only problem was, they couldn't decide which movie to see.

Mark loved movies with elaborate mystery plots. He wanted <u>to see the movie about an investigator in the himalayan mountains.</u> (2) Julio's main interest was science fiction. He wanted to see the movie about a space alien who lands in Los Angeles, California.

<u>Attempting to convince his friend to pick the movie he liked Julio said "Remember</u> (3) that movie we saw together about the extraterrestrial creature?"

<u>Mark noded his head. "I remember."</u> (4)

"Well, <u>you loved that movie! Julio exclaimed.</u> (5)

Mark thought for a moment. His friend had a point.

"Why don't we see the movie you want this time and the movie I want next time?"

<u>Julio thanked his friend for being so fare. "Your generosity will be returned!"</u> (6)

1.   A Spelling error
    B Capitalization error
    C Punctuation error
    D No error

2.   F Spelling error
    G Capitalization error
    H Punctuation error
    J No error

3.   A Spelling error
    B Capitalization error
    C Punctuation error
    D No error

4.   F Spelling error
    G Capitalization error
    H Punctuation error
    J No error

5.   A Spelling error
    B Capitalization error
    C Punctuation error
    D No error

6.   F Spelling error
    G Capitalization error
    H Punctuation error
    J No error

Standardized Test Practice

The Inuit, sometimes called Eskimos, are known for building igloos to provide warmth in sub-zero temperatures. Contrary to popular belief, these dome-shaped shelters are <u>rarely permmanent homes. For the most part, the Inuit</u> (1) use igloos only when they are hunting or traveling. Snow provides remarkable protection from the cold. <u>For instance a candle burning inside an igloo can sometimes</u> (2) raise the <u>Interior temperature 40 degrees.</u> (3) Igloos can be <u>made of snow, Earth, sod, or stone. These materials</u> (4) are formed into rectangular <u>blocks. A hole is left at the top of the igloo for ventilation.</u> (5)

1.
   A Spelling error
   B Capitalization error
   C Punctuation error
   D No error

2.
   F Spelling error
   G Capitalization error
   H Punctuation error
   J No error

3.
   A Spelling error
   B Capitalization error
   C Punctuation error
   D No error

4.
   F Spelling error
   G Capitalization error
   H Punctuation error
   J No error

5.
   A Spelling error
   B Capitalization error
   C Punctuation error
   D No error

Standardized Test Practice

Read each passage and decide which type of error, if any, appears in each underlined section. Mark the letter for your answer on your paper.

<u>When United States soldiers were deployed to Europe and the pacific during World War II, our country</u>
(1)
faced a shortage of defense workers. During this time, 5 million women entered the U.S. workforce. They accepted jobs that were traditionally reserved for men.

To aid in the war effort, <u>women worked on production lines in factories in steel mills, and on the docks.</u>
(2)
The government offered incentives to encourage women to work. <u>For example, government-sponsored day care centers allowed women</u> with children to leave home and go to their jobs. Although women's wages were
(3)
very low <u>at the start of the war, over time their wages became more competative.</u> These working women and
(4)
<u>their contributions to our Country helped change the American perception</u> of a woman's position in the
(5)
workforce.

1. A Spelling error
   B Capitalization error
   C Punctuation error
   D No error

2. F Spelling error
   G Capitalization error
   H Punctuation error
   J No error

3. A Spelling error
   B Capitalization error
   C Punctuation error
   D No error

4. F Spelling error
   G Capitalization error
   H Punctuation error
   J No error

5. A Spelling error
   B Capitalization error
   C Punctuation error
   D No error

Standardized Test Practice

Howard was in the highest math class. He had always been good at math. <u>Before a mid-term math test</u>
<u>Howard noticed that several</u> of his peers were having trouble studying for the exam. Howard decided that it
(1)
might <u>be a good idea to offer his services as a tutor. He would</u> post a sign in the school cafeteria.
(2)
<u>Howards sign read: "Howard Goldstein: Available</u> to help with math."
(3)
About a week later, <u>a girl from Howard's homeroom aproached him in the gym.</u>
(4)
The girl explained <u>that she wanted to start a buisness tutoring students</u> in various subjects. <u>"Would you</u>
(5)
<u>like to be my partner? she asked.</u>
(6)
"That's a great idea!" Howard remarked. "We can help each other find students and devise the best ways
to explain things."

1. **A** Spelling error
   B Capitalization error
   C Punctuation error
   D No error

2. **F** Spelling error
   G Capitalization error
   H Punctuation error
   J No error

3. **A** Spelling error
   B Capitalization error
   C Punctuation error
   D No error

4. **F** Spelling error
   G Capitalization error
   H Punctuation error
   J No error

5. **A** Spelling error
   B Capitalization error
   C Punctuation error
   D No error

6. **F** Spelling error
   G Capitalization error
   H Punctuation error
   J No error

Standardized Test Practice

Read each passage and decide which type of error, if any, appears in each underlined section. Mark the letter for your answer on your paper.

There are a few different kinds of thermometers but the bulb thermometer is the most common. This
(1)
type of thermometer contains a liquid, which is usually mercury. Bulb thermometers work because as the
(2)
temprature rises, the volume of a liquid increases. All liquids, including water oil and milk, take up more
(3)
space when they are heated. This change is not generally visible to the Naked Eye. The mercury inside a
(4)
bulb thermometer is encased in a thin glass tube. When it is hot, the mercury expands and rises. When it is
cold, the mercury takes up less space, and the thermometer indicates that it is cooler.
(5)

1. A Spelling error
   B Capitalization error
   C Punctuation error
   D No error

2. F Spelling error
   G Capitalization error
   H Punctuation error
   J No error

3. A Spelling error
   B Capitalization error
   C Punctuation error
   D No error

4. F Spelling error
   G Capitalization error
   H Punctuation error
   J No error

5. A Spelling error
   B Capitalization error
   C Punctuation error
   D No error

Standardized Test Practice

Mail delivery was slow and unreliable during the <u>expansion of the american western territories.</u> (1) <u>This prompted the creation</u> of the Pony Express in 1860, which was established to organize a faster mail service between Missouri and California. The 1,600 mile route took mail carriers through a number of <u>states, including the following, Kansas, Nebraska, Wyoming</u> and Nevada. <u>Pony Express employees, riding</u> (2) (3) <u>on horseback, were expected</u> to travel thirty to seventy miles a day. The journey could take weeks. Close to two hundred <u>relay stations were built along the route, where exausted riders could hand their mail</u> (4) pouches over to the next available courier. In 1861, a telegraph line was completed that <u>connected the</u> (5) <u>East to the west. After only nineteen months of operation,</u> the Pony Express was shut down. It still stands as a reminder of American ingenuity.

1. A Spelling error
   B Capitalization error
   C Punctuation error
   D No error

2. F Spelling error
   G Capitalization error
   H Punctuation error
   J No error

3. A Spelling error
   B Capitalization error
   C Punctuation error
   D No error

4. F Spelling error
   G Capitalization error
   H Punctuation error
   J No error

5. A Spelling error
   B Capitalization error
   C Punctuation error
   D No error

UNIT 29 Listening and Speaking

Lesson 29.1	**Listening Effectively**	885
Lesson 29.2	**Speaking Effectively**	888
Lesson 29.3	**Participating in Groups**	891
Lesson 29.4	**Conducting Interviews**	892

29.1 Listening Effectively

How well you listen can affect your success in school, sports, jobs, and personal relationships. If you're like most people, however, you understand about half of what you hear and remember only about half of that. In this lesson, you'll learn how to improve your listening comprehension.

Active Listening

Whether you're listening to a friend, a coach, or a teacher, you need to do more than just hear what the person says. Only by listening actively will you be able to understand, interpret, and respond to what you hear. The chart below presents strategies for active listening.

Strategies for Active Listening

PREPARE TO LISTEN
- **Eliminate physical distractions.** Set aside other work and make yourself comfortable.
- **Clear your mind of other thoughts.** Don't think about your schedule for the day or what you're going to do over the weekend.
- **Adopt a positive attitude and keep an open mind.** Be willing to listen to what the speaker has to say, and don't jump to conclusions before the speaker is finished.

LISTEN TO THE MESSAGE
- **Focus your attention on what the speaker is saying.** Don't jump ahead and think about what the speaker may say next.
- **Maintain your concentration by finding something of interest in the message.** Don't doodle, daydream, constantly look around, or become impatient for the speaker to finish.
- **Take notes if the situation calls for it.** Note taking is often useful for classroom presentations, speeches, and interviews.

INTERPRET THE MESSAGE
- **Summarize the message.** Identify the purpose of the message and the main ideas or themes presented.
- **Reflect on what you hear.** Ask yourself: Does this information sound reasonable? Does it conflict with anything else I know?

RESPOND TO THE MESSAGE
- **Ask questions.** Request clarification of ideas and terms you don't understand, and ask questions that relate to the topic.
- **Discuss the message.** Compare your interpretations with those of others.
- **Assess the message.** What significance or consequences does the message have for you or for others?

Evaluating What You Hear

In all listening situations, you can use the strategies for active listening to help you absorb, understand, and interpret the messages you hear; but, in certain situations, you'll want to do even more with the information you hear. Some situations—such as responding to persuasive messages and performances of poems, short stories, plays, and other literary works—require you to evaluate and to analyze critically what you hear.

Persuasive Messages

Each day you hear many persuasive messages—from your friends, teachers, parents, radio commercials, and other sources. Some of these messages are reasonable and worth following or acting on; others are not. How do you decide when a persuasive message is convincing and worthwhile? You can use the questions in the chart below to help you analyze and evaluate persuasive messages.

Questions for Evaluating Persuasive Messages

- **Purpose:** What is the purpose of the message? In other words, what is the speaker trying to sell or convince people to do?
- **Audience:** To what audience is the message targeted?
- **Facts/opinions:** What are the facts and what are the opinions in the message? Do the facts support the opinions or claims? What facts or opinions are missing?
- **Errors in reasoning:** Does the message contain errors in reasoning, such as overgeneralizations and either/or arguments?
- **Persuasive techniques:** What kinds of persuasive techniques—such as bandwagon appeal, loaded language, celebrity testimonial, and exaggeration—are used in the message? How does the message appeal to people's emotions?
- **Values and biases:** What values or biases does the message reflect? Do these values match yours?
- **Your opinion:** After analyzing the message, what is your opinion of it? Do you agree, disagree, or need more information to make a decision?

Literary Performances

Some literary works, such as poems and plays, are intended to be read aloud or performed. However, even short stories and essays, which are intended for silent reading, can seem to come to life in a performance. You can use the questions in the chart below both to assess literary performances and to improve your own performance of literary works.

> ### Questions for Evaluating Literary Performances
>
> - **Voice qualities:** Does the performer effectively use voice qualities such as volume, stress, tone, and pronunciation to present the work?
> - **Body language:** Does the performer use body language—including posture, eye contact, facial expressions, gestures, and movements—to engage the audience and bring the work to life?
> - **Literary elements:** What element of the literary work (e.g., character development, plot, imagery, rhyme, or figurative language) does the performance emphasize? What is the effect of this element?
> - **Your rating:** How would you rate the performer's interpretation of the literary work? Why?

Exercise 1

Work in a small group to practice the Strategies for Active Listening presented on page 885. Brainstorm a list of topics on which each member of the group could give a brief, informative speech. Take turns presenting one- or two-minute impromptu speeches on some of these topics. Listen actively to each speech. Then, as a group, follow the steps outlined in the chart under the headings Interpret the Message and Respond to the Message.

Exercise 2

Listen to a persuasive message on radio or television (such as a commercial or a news editorial), or obtain a videotape or audiotape of a historic persuasive speech. Use the Questions for Evaluating Persuasive Messages presented on page 886 to write an analysis and evaluation of the speech. Then present your analysis and evaluation orally to the class. Be sure to provide concrete support for the points in your analysis.

Exercise 3

Attend a poetry reading or a play in your community or watch the performance of a drama on television. Listen actively to the performance, keeping in mind the Questions for Evaluating Literary Performances presented in the chart above. Use the questions to write an evaluation of the performance.

Exercise 4

Schedule an artistic-performance week in your class. Working alone, with a partner, or in a small group, select and perform a poem or scene from a play. Use the Questions for Evaluating Literary Performances above both as you practice your own performance and as you listen to the performances of others. After your performance, ask for the audience's evaluation. Use their comments to help you write your own performance evaluation, including goals for future presentations.

29.2 Speaking Effectively

The way you speak can influence your relationships with other people and your success in groups. In this lesson, you'll gain important advice on how to speak effectively in both informal and formal situations.

Speaking Informally

Most of the speaking you do is informal. You talk with friends, family, teachers, and others. You speak on the phone, introduce people to others, give directions. Keep in mind, though, that even in such casual situations it is important to communicate effectively.

In all informal speaking, be sure to communicate clearly and in a lively tone. Don't mumble or talk too loudly or too softly. Be careful about "filler" words that have no real meaning, such as *like* ("He was, like, studying"), *um,* and *you know.* Finally, always be polite to your audience.

In most instances of informal speaking, common sense and consideration are the best guides to effective communication. For example, when you are on the telephone, identify yourself and explain your reason for calling. Be sure to call people at times that are convenient for them, and keep the call to a reasonable length.

When giving directions or instructions, present your points as a series of logical steps. Speak slowly and be sure the listener understands. Encourage the listener to ask questions. You might even ask questions yourself to help your listener understand.

Making Formal Speeches

Unlike informal speaking, formal speeches are prepared, rehearsed, and then delivered at a prearranged place and time. Preparing a formal speech is similar to writing a research paper or a persuasive essay, but involves more steps.

Consider Purpose and Audience Once you have a topic, focus on your purpose for making the speech. Do you want to inform, persuade, or entertain your audience? You may end up doing all three—an audience that is entertained is more likely to listen attentively, and an audience that hears solid evidence is more likely to be persuaded. But as you start out, write a clear statement of your main purpose, such as *I want to persuade my audience to donate money to disaster relief efforts that help flood victims in North Carolina.*

After clearly defining the purpose of the speech, identify your audience. Is it made up of urban high school students with diverse backgrounds? Suburban middle-class parents? Evaluate what your audience already knows about your topic, even interviewing some of them if possible. What concerns or biases do they have? What misinformation might you need to correct? Then think about the level of language that is suitable for your audience. For a formal speech, you'll use standard English, but you may need to tailor your vocabulary to your audience and explain any technical terms you use.

Research the Topic Gather facts, examples, and experts' opinions on your topic by conducting library and Internet research—even polls and interviews, if appropriate. After studying the information you gather, write a clear statement of your thesis. Then select accurate, relevant evidence and examples from reliable sources to support your thesis.

Create an Outline Choose a pattern of organization that fits your information and your purpose. Outline your information, using your thesis as the controlling idea. At this point, consider whether visual aids might be useful in presenting your topic.

Draft and Revise Use your outline as a guide to drafting your speech, following the standard structure of an introduction, a body, and a conclusion. If you are preparing a persuasive speech, you may want to review Unit 6, Persuasive Writing, pages 282–321.

In your introduction, think of a way to attract your audience's attention. Consider one of the methods listed in the following chart.

Getting Your Audience's Attention

STRATEGY	EXAMPLE
Tell a story	When my family's home was washed away in a flood three years ago, I felt as though my whole past had been swept away.
Ask a question	Why should you care about the possible extinction of gorillas?
Use a quotation	Mark Twain wrote, "Civilizations proceed from the heart rather than from the head."
State an amazing fact or statistic	A bolt of lightning is five times hotter than the surface of the sun.

For your conclusion, you might refer to the method you used in your introduction and provide a twist that sums up your speech. For example, if you began with a question, you might pose it again and then give the answer. Whatever method you use, strive for a strong finish that drives home your message. Your last words are the ones your audience will be most likely to remember.

Revise your speech, just as you would any other work of informative or persuasive writing. Then read your speech out loud and make further changes so that it flows smoothly. You have to be able to say what you write.

29.2 Speaking Effectively **889**

If your sentences are too long, shorten them. If you stumble over a group of words, change them.

Prepare Materials Unless you choose to memorize your speech, you'll need to prepare materials to use during your delivery. Some speakers read from manuscript pages; others speak from an outline or note cards. If you are not required to use a particular method, choose the method that works best for you and your situation. If you read your speech, prepare a double- or triple-spaced manuscript with wide margins. If you choose to speak from an outline or note cards, use your written speech to prepare these materials. Underline topic sentences, number supporting points, and transfer the ideas to an outline or note cards. Be sure to number your manuscript pages, outline pages, or note cards at the top.

Practice and Deliver Your Speech Practice your speech a few times in front of a mirror. Then ask a friend or relative to listen to your speech or to videotape it. As you rehearse, pay attention to the points listed in the chart below. Even if you read your speech, be sure to look up often and make eye contact with your audience, especially at the beginning and the end of sentences.

Techniques for Giving a Speech

VERBAL TECHNIQUES
- **Volume:** Speak loudly enough so that everyone in the audience can hear you.
- **Pronunciation:** Speak clearly, pronouncing all the words.
- **Pace:** Speak at a moderate speed, but vary the rate; use pauses to convey your meaning.
- **Tone:** Speak in a lively tone.
- **Emphasis:** Stress important words and ideas.

NONVERBAL TECHNIQUES
- **Posture:** Stand up tall with your head straight.
- **Eye contact:** Make eye contact with people throughout your audience.
- **Facial expressions and gestures:** Vary your facial expressions to reflect what you are saying, and use natural gestures to reinforce your ideas.
- **Visual aids:** If appropriate for your topic, use charts, diagrams, graphs, or video clips to enhance your speech and to convey important information.

Audience questions and comments At the end of your speech, allow your audience to respond by asking for any questions or comments. Answer your listeners' questions honestly and respectfully. Use this question-and-answer period to correct misunderstandings, to repeat points that your listeners may have missed, and to learn what you may need to make clearer in your speech.

Exercise 5

Follow the process described in this lesson to prepare, practice, and present a ten-minute informative or persuasive speech. Choose from the following topics, or come up with a topic of your own:

- safety and security measures at your school
- censorship of books in public schools
- high school students' working at part-time jobs
- sports programs at your school

As you listen to the speeches of your classmates, apply the Strategies for Active Listening presented on page 885. Use the Questions for Evaluating Persuasive Messages on page 886 as you offer comments on the persuasive speeches to the presenters.

29.3 Participating in Groups

Throughout your life, you'll participate in many groups—families, classes, study groups, teams, clubs or organizations, and work groups. To be an active member who contributes in positive ways to any of these groups, you need good listening and speaking skills as well as an understanding of how to function in, and contribute to, a group.

In a typical study or discussion group, the members have roles such as group leader, recorder, and participants. The group leader guides the discussion and keeps the group focused on the topic or task. The recorder takes notes on ideas and records final decisions. The participants contribute ideas, respond to the ideas of others, and vote on decisions. A study group operates most effectively if all members follow the guidelines listed in the chart below.

Guidelines for Participating in a Study Group

- **Be prepared:** Complete any assigned reading or research before the group meets.
- **Focus on the issue:** Don't bring up unrelated topics.
- **Listen actively:** Make an effort to understand each person's viewpoint. Don't interrupt when anyone is speaking. Make a note of any word you might not understand. Try to define the word in context. Later, you can look up any word or, if possible, ask the speaker to define the word.
- **Show respect:** Recognize that each person has something worthwhile to contribute. An effective group draws upon the different strengths of its members.
- **State your ideas clearly and concisely:** Don't talk on and on so that others have little chance to speak.
- **Respond constructively to the ideas of others:** Explain why you agree or disagree with someone's idea, providing reasons or evidence for your position.
- **Encourage everyone to participate:** If someone has not spoken, ask for his or her opinion.

Exercise 6

In a group of five or six students, discuss the following question: What is the most crucial problem facing high school students today? Choose a group leader and a recorder. In addition, select an observer, a person to keep track of how well the group is functioning. The observer should note whether all group members participate, stay focused, listen actively, and respond constructively. After the discussion concludes, the observer should give an evaluation of how well the group functioned, providing specific examples of each observation.

29.4 Conducting Interviews

Good listening and speaking skills are also useful in conducting interviews, a valuable way of gathering information for reports and projects. The following guidelines will help you conduct an effective interview.

Guidelines for Conducting Interviews	
Prepare for the interview	• Research the subject and learn a little about the person you will interview. • Prepare a list of five or more *who, what, where, when, why,* and *how* questions. Avoid questions that require just a yes or no answer. For example, instead of *Do you enjoy your work?* ask *What do you enjoy most about your work?* • If you plan to tape the interview, make sure your tape recorder works. If you plan to take notes, make sure you bring along two pens that work and a pad of paper as well as your list of interview questions.
Listen actively during the interview.	• Take notes or tape-record the interview. Ask for the correct spelling of the person's name and of any unfamiliar places or terms the person uses. If necessary, ask the person to explain or repeat statements you do not understand. • Ask intelligent follow-up questions. • At the end of the interview, be sure to thank the person.
Follow up after the interview.	• As soon as possible after the interview, write a full account of everything you remember, referring to your notes or your tape. • If necessary, ask the person interviewed to clarify any points of confusion. • Write the person a thank-you letter.

Exercise 7

With a partner, take turns conducting an interview about each other's favorite interests and activities, following the guidelines in this lesson. Check each other's written accounts of the interview for accuracy and completeness. Then offer each other observations on how well the interview was conducted.

UNIT 30 Viewing and Representing

Lesson 30.1 **Examining Visual Messages** *894*

Lesson 30.2 **Evaluating Media Messages** *899*

Lesson 30.3 **Producing Media Messages** *902*

30.1 Examining Visual Messages

Television and the other mass media have an immense influence on your life. They keep you informed and entertained; in many cases, what you see and hear in mass media presentations will attempt to persuade you in one way or another. Whether you are aware of it or not, media presentations help shape your attitudes, values, and behavior. Media presentations not only reflect your culture, they help create it. Developing *media literacy*—the ability to understand, interpret, analyze, and critique media messages, as well as the ability to create your own media messages—will help you recognize the ways media messages might influence your thinking and your life. The goal of this unit is to help you gain such media literacy.

Except for radio, all mass media send visual messages. Being aware of the techniques used in developing visual messages will help you to interpret the messages you see and to understand and analyze the ideas being presented.

Interpreting Visual Design

To understand the design of a visual image such as a photograph or illustration, you examine its *composition*, or arrangement of elements. The following chart lists some basic elements in the composition of a photograph or illustration and describes effects that can be achieved by manipulating these elements. The actual effect of an element depends on the overall context of the picture, however.

Elements of Visual Design

ELEMENT	EXAMPLE	POSSIBLE EFFECTS
SHAPE	Circle	Suggests wholeness, lovableness
	Square	Suggests firmness, stability
	Triangle	Suggests unity, balance; tension
LINE Lines can be real or implied. An example of a real line is the edge of a building; a person's gaze can create an implied line.	Straight lines Curved lines Vertical lines Horizontal lines Diagonal lines	Direct the eye to something Suggest motion, warmth Suggest dignity, status, power Suggest peace, stillness Suggest tension, action, energy

(continued)

Elements of Visual Design

ELEMENT	EXAMPLE	POSSIBLE EFFECTS
COLOR OR TONE	Cool colors (blue, green, gray)	Convey calm, emotional distance
	Warm colors (red, yellow, orange)	Convey energy, vibrancy, warmth
	Bright colors	Convey joy, action, excitement
	Subdued or pastel colors	Suggest innocence, softness, serenity
	Light tones	Create a happy, playful mood
	Dark tones	Convey sadness, mystery, dullness
TEXTURE	Smooth, flat	Suggests emptiness; something modern, streamlined
	Rough, woven	Conveys wholesomeness, naturalness, homeliness
	Silky, shiny	Creates sense of luxury
POSITIONING OF SUBJECTS The positions of figures grouped together can show how the artist views the relationships to one another.	Top of frame Center of frame Bottom of frame	Conveys importance, power Conveys stability Conveys inferiority, weakness
LIGHT A viewer's eye naturally travels to the most lighted area.	Bright light Dim light or shadows	Draws the eye to a specific area; creates a cheerful mood Creates a sense of mystery, doom
SPACE	Large space around subject Little space around subject	Draws attention to the subject; isolates details; creates a sense of openness, emptiness, loneliness. Makes the subject seem dominating, overwhelming

To understand how elements of visual design work together in a photograph, study this picture of a section of an ocean shoreline. The curving lines and rounded shapes of the mountains, hills, and ocean waves create a soothing, warm mood. The pale color of the ocean water and mist fills most of the frame, giving the picture a soft look. The hazy light adds to the soft, wispy feel of the picture. All these elements combine to convey a warm, soothing portrait of the meeting of water and land.

30.1 Examining Visual Messages 895

The photograph on page 895 presents one view of an ocean shoreline at a particular place and time and from a particular perspective. If this were the only picture of a shoreline that you had ever seen, you would probably develop a single impression of coastlines. However, many other photographs could be taken of the same location under varying conditions and from varying perspectives to create radically different impressions. Similarly, different photographs of a foreign environment would probably give you different impressions of its culture. Every photograph presents just one view of a subject from a particular perspective.

Exercise 1

Use the Elements of Visual Design chart to describe the effects of at least three elements in this photograph of rock climbers in the Central Asian country of Kyrgyzstan. Summarize the ideas that the photograph conveys about the relationship between the people and the landscape.

Interpreting Film Techniques

The basic elements of visual design apply to the media of motion pictures and videos as well as to photographs and illustrations. Motion picture and television directors also use a wide variety of film techniques to tell stories and to convey messages. The chart on page 897 describes some of these techniques and the effects they can have.

Basic Film Techniques

TECHNIQUE	EXAMPLE	POSSIBLE EFFECTS
CAMERA ANGLE	High (looking down)	Minimizes importance or status of subject
	Straight on (eye level)	Puts viewer on equal level with subject; promotes identification with subject
	Low (looking up)	Emphasizes importance or power of subject
CAMERA SHOTS	Close-up (magnified view)	Promotes identification with subject
	Long shot (wide view)	Establishes relationship between characters and a setting
	Reaction shot	Shows effect of one character on another, or of an event on a character
LIGHTING	High key (bright, even)	Creates cheerful, optimistic mood
	Low key (producing shadows)	Creates gloomy, eerie mood
	Light from above	Allows subject to glow with significance
	Light from below	May raise audience apprehension
MOVEMENT	Slow motion	Emphasizes movement and heightens drama
	Blurred motion	Suggests speed, confusion, or dreamlike state
EDITING (selection and arrangement of scenes)	Sequence of short shots	Builds tension; creates a rushed mood
	Sequence of long shots	Conveys a feeling of stability
SPECIAL EFFECTS	Artwork and miniature models	Appear real when filmed
	Computer enhancement	Creates composite images; distorts qualities of a character or scene
BACKGROUND MUSIC		Evokes audience's emotional response, sets mood, reinforces theme

Examine the elements of visual design and the film techniques used in the still on page 898 from the movie *Star Wars: Episode 1—The Phantom Menace* (1999). In the scene, the Sith Lords, Darth Sidious and Darth Maul, are making a report to the trade federation leaders after the invasion of Naboo. The

30.1 Examining Visual Messages

diagonal lines of the table draw the viewer's gaze into the picture to focus on Darth Sidious and Darth Maul. The outline of the body of each character forms a triangle, conveying tension. Dark colors dominate the picture, suggesting evil and menace. The viewer's sense of fear is heightened when Darth Maul seems to be looking down upon him or her. This scene was created with special effects. Darth Sidious and Darth Maul appear as holographic images, which are produced with lasers. This technique makes them seem even more menacing and otherworldly. All the elements in this scene reinforce the idea that these characters represent evil and are dangerous.

Exercise 2

Study the still below from the movie *Star Wars: Episode 1—The Phantom Menace* (1999). Use the Elements of Visual Design and Basic Film Techniques charts to help you identify at least three elements or techniques used in the scene and to analyze their effects. Share your analysis in a brief oral report to the class.

30.2 Evaluating Media Messages

Many photographs, movies, and television programs seem to capture realistic, believable scenes from life. Media messages are constructed for a purpose, which is typically to inform, entertain, or persuade. As a result, the presentation may show only one particular view of life.

Think about a music video that has been designed to entertain teen viewers. The creators of the video might feature clothing, hair styles, or music that appeal to a very specific portion of teen culture. However, the styles and music do not necessarily represent the tastes of all teenagers in the country. Even in a documentary that you would consider to be strictly factual, a director may have made many decisions about how to shoot scenes, what information to include and exclude, and what effects to strive for to achieve his or her purpose. The purpose or goal may or may not be worthwhile—that is for you to decide. To make an informed decision, you need to be able to **deconstruct,** or analyze, media messages. This lesson will help you develop that skill.

Recognizing Media Genres

Media messages reach you in a wide variety of forms. These forms, or genres, can be grouped into four main types: print, broadcast, film, and the Internet. *Print media* include newspapers, magazines, billboards, books, product packaging, and other materials that convey messages through printed words and images. In *Broadcast media,* consisting of radio and television, sounds alone or both sounds and moving images are transmitted to a wide public audience. *Film media,* including movies and videotapes, also consist of sounds and moving images. The *Internet* contains a wide variety of Web sites that consist of some combination of printed words, still and moving images, and sounds.

The form of a media message can affect its meaning or your interpretation of or response to the message. For information on a specific topic, you might choose between several types of presentations, depending on the kind and amount of information you need. For example, for a quick rundown of a current news story, such as a recent earthquake, you might read a newspaper or a newsmagazine. However, you could gain a fuller appreciation of the effects of an earthquake from watching a live television newscast. The sounds and moving images on television have a strong impact and often arouse a stronger emotional response than print does. To learn more about earthquakes in general, you could refer to a book, an in-depth magazine article, or you might view a film documentary. Imagine learning from the newspaper that the United States was involved in aiding earthquake victims in a foreign country. How might your view of events and your reactions be different than if you watched the television news coverage?

Exercise 3

List four kinds of media presentations that provide information on current events, and identify the unique properties of each genre. Then watch a television newscast for coverage of an important news event and take notes on what you learn. Follow the coverage of the same event in one of the other kinds of presentations on your list. Create a Venn diagram comparing and contrasting the coverage in the two media, the impressions you gain from each, and the impact that each has on you.

Examining Media Messages

Before you form an opinion about a media message—whether it's a television commercial, an informational Web site, or a popular movie—you need to think about how and why the message was created. The following chart describes how to deconstruct a media message.

How to Analyze a Media Message

IDENTIFY	BY ASKING YOURSELF	EXAMPLE
SOURCE	Who made this? How does the source affect the message?	A television commercial says, "Our athletic shoes are the best ever made." The source of the ad is the shoe manufacturer. This company would want viewers to think their shoes are the best because they want people to buy them.
PURPOSE	Why was the message made? Is it meant to inform, entertain, or persuade?	The commercial seems made to inform people about the benefits of these particular shoes. But really, it is meant to persuade viewers to buy the shoes.
TARGET AUDIENCE	For whom is the message intended? How has the content been shaped to appeal to the intended audience?	The message is intended for preteens in middle school. The commercial shows groups of attractive, stylish eleven- and twelve-year-olds winning a foot race and a basketball game as well as walking around a mall.
MAIN IDEA OR THEME	What is the intended message?	The intended message is that buying the shoes will make you a winner and will also make you popular and stylish.
DESIGN ELEMENTS AND/OR FILM TECHNIQUES	How are design elements or film techniques used to communicate a message or manipulate a viewer's response?	Bright lighting, vivid colors, and sleek, popular styles all suggest energy and success. Actors moving diagonally across the screen convey a sense of energy and action. The eye-level camera angle helps viewers identify with the children in the commercial.

(continued)

How to Analyze a Media Message		
IDENTIFY	**BY ASKING YOURSELF**	**EXAMPLE**
ELEMENTS THAT REFLECT A SPECIFIC CULTURE	What cultural values and assumptions are reflected in this presentation?	The presentation suggests that athletic ability and winning are important; preteens are portrayed as carefree, energetic, and stylish, with plenty of time for fun.
PERSUASIVE TECHNIQUES		
• glittering generalities	Does the message make sweeping claims that are impossible to support?	Yes, because the message suggests that the winner of the race will *always* be the one wearing our shoes.
• logical fallacies	Are the statements in the message logical, or are there errors in logic?	The message is illogical because it suggests that all you need to be a winner is to buy the shoes.
• symbols	Does the message use symbols that stand for popular ideas or values?	The company logo, a bird in flight, appears on all the sports gear that the actors use. The bird symbolizes independence and freedom.
• celebrity testimonial	Do admired celebrities add to the message or endorse the product?	A famous soccer player, wearing the company's shoes, is seen jogging with a group of young people.

Exercise 4

Select a television advertisement targeted to teenagers and analyze it by answering the questions in the How to Analyze a Media Message chart. Then create a billboard advertisement, promoting the same product or service but using techniques that are different from the ones in the advertisement you found. Write an explanation of the techniques used in your ad.

Exercise 5

Write a short editorial stating your opinion on how media shape the perceptions and habits of people in your age group. Consider, for example, how magazines, television, and movies influence your buying habits and the style of clothes you wear. Share your editorial with other members of your class, and then conduct a poll to find out which of your classmates allow the media to influence the purchases they make.

30.3 Producing Media Messages

Another way to increase your understanding of media messages and the decisions that go into their creation is to produce your own media presentation. This lesson provides guidelines for producing two forms of media messages: videos and Web pages.

Making a Video

The creation of a video requires the skills and cooperation of a group of people. Each group member should take on one or more of the following roles, based on his or her skills and interests. For example, creating a video documentary that features interviews with people might include these roles:

- **Director:** coordinates the activities of the group members and supervises the filming of the video
- **Researcher:** finds background information on the topic and the interviewees
- **Scriptwriter:** writes and revises the script
- **Storyboard designer:** prepares a series of simple sketches of each video scene to go along with the dialogue or narration
- **Interviewer:** prepares questions to ask the interviewees and conducts the interviews
- **Narrator:** reads the script during the filming
- **Camera operator:** films the interviews and other shots

Depending on the size of the group, some members may take on two or more roles. For example, the scriptwriter might also function as the researcher and narrator. Making a video provides an opportunity to try out different roles and learn new skills.

As you plan and produce your video, consider the elements of visual design and the film techniques described in the first section of this unit. Be sure you can clearly summarize the focus of your video in a paragraph. The following chart provides guidelines for completing a video project.

Tips on Producing a Video

1. **Begin by brainstorming.** In your group, discuss these questions: Who are the intended viewers? What do they already know or think about the subject? What is the purpose of the video? What information do we need to find out? Who will we interview? What scenes will we shoot? You may want to have a group member write down these questions and the answers that come up in the discussion.

2. **Plan your video by creating a storyboard.** A storyboard provides a blueprint for shooting your video. It consists of simple sketches of the sequence of scenes you will shoot, with the dialogue or narration for each scene. You want your video to tell a story—so create a beginning, a middle, and an end. Include scenes that set the stage, show the location, or provide details that enrich the story.

(continued)

> **Tips on Producing a Video**
>
> 3. **When you shoot, vary your scenes.** Mix long shots that show a location with closer shots that focus on a single subject. Shoot from different angles and heights to achieve different effects. Vary the length of the shots you take as well.
>
> 4. **Pay attention to lighting.** Shoot in strong light—outside during daylight or inside near windows and with all the lights on. Set up your own lights if necessary.
>
> 5. **Shoot to edit.** To make it easier to edit scenes later, leave a little room before and after each scene by letting the camera run. Reshoot scenes that don't turn out well.
>
> 6. **Edit to create a polished final product.** At the editing stage, you can eliminate bad footage, add music and sound effects, and insert titles. You also can mix short cuts and long cuts to achieve the pacing you want.
>
> 7. **Ask for viewer feedback.** After you present your video, ask the audience to fill out a questionnaire or to participate in a discussion to give you feedback. Ask viewers to state the main idea of your video and to comment on how effectively the main idea was conveyed. In addition, elicit viewers' comments on the pacing, the camera techniques, and the audio and visual quality.

Exercise 6

Working in a small group, choose one of the following video projects to undertake:

- a three-minute documentary on training for a sport
- a public-service advertisement on the importance of staying in school
- a demonstration of designing a cereal box targeted to teenagers

Decide on a topic and agree on roles for each group member. Then work together to plan, write, shoot, and edit your video. After presenting the video to the class, hold a discussion to gather feedback from your audience.

Developing a Web Page

Using a software program or hypertext mark-up language (HTML), you can create a Web page, like the one shown on page 904, that incorporates photographs, graphics, text, and even sound. A good Web page is attractive, informative, and easy to follow. The following guidelines will help you design a Web page that has all of these qualities.

> **Guidelines for Developing a Web Page**
>
> 1. **Begin with a clear purpose.** Identify your intended audience and make sure that you have something useful to share. Create a title that tells visitors what your page is about.
>
> 2. **Plan your page before you build it.** View other pages on your topic, or on similar topics, for ideas about what to include and how to make the presentation. Design a layout for the page that is logical, easy to follow, and attractive.
>
> *(continued)*

Guidelines for Developing a Web Page

3. **Keep the design simple.** Pick a few colors and fonts (or styles of type) for your page. Avoid a busy background that detracts attention from your message.

4. **Be sure the page is quick to download.** Viewers avoid pages that take too long to download. Keep the images small in size and few in number so that your page downloads quickly.

5. **Consider including links.** Links enable visitors to reach related sites.

6. **Keep the text short and easy to read.** Use a font that is easy to read and a background color that provides enough contrast for your text. Carefully proofread and correct all text.

7. **Test your page and revise it.** Ask your friends or classmates to visit your page and test how well it works. Make an evaluation form and ask them to complete it.

Exercise 7

Work with a partner to design a Web page that analyzes how teenage culture is portrayed in a particular medium, such as a teen magazine, a television sitcom, or a movie. Ask classmates to visit your page and complete an evaluation form. Study the responses you receive, and then revise and improve your page as necessary.

UNIT 31
Electronic Resources

Lesson 31.1	Word Processing and the Writing Process	906
Lesson 31.2	Learning with Technology	909
Lesson 31.3	Communicating Visually	912
Lesson 31.4	Producing in Multimedia	915

31.1 Word Processing and the Writing Process

Almost anything you can write on paper with a pen or pencil can be done more efficiently on a computer with word processing software. When you work on a computer, you don't have to copy something over and over again from one sheet to another as you write and revise. You can cut and paste words, sentences, or an entire draft from one file to a new file in a few seconds. If you prefer, you can simply keep your work on the same file—adding, deleting, correcting, and revising until you're satisfied with what you've written.

Prewriting

You might begin a writing project by freewriting or by brainstorming for ideas or topics—either alone or in collaboration with one or more other students. Brainstorming may start with a list of random thoughts on a sheet of paper. Try listing your ideas on an electronic file instead. You might find starting a special file for your writing ideas to be useful. You can add to the file whenever you get a new idea, or look through the file when you're searching for something to write about.

At the prewriting stage, you should also consider your purpose and your audience. Thinking about purpose and audience will help define the kinds of ideas you hope to generate. For example, if your purpose is to entertain and your audience is your fellow students, you will brainstorm for ideas that will meet that purpose and appeal to those readers.

Finding Information

Once you have a topic, you may need to find out more about it. This, too, can be done with your computer, especially if the computer is connected to the Internet. Almost any writing topic you can think of has probably generated at least a few Web sites, if not hundreds of them. Newspapers, magazines, and standard references like dictionaries and encyclopedias are also available on the Web. Information from Internet sources can be downloaded to your hard drive or printed out directly from the source to your printer.

Planning and Organizing

As you begin planning and organizing a piece of writing, word processing comes into its own. You can easily take your prewriting ideas or pieces of information and reorganize them into an outline. You might start by looking for your main ideas. For a brief essay, for example, identify three or four main ideas. Then look through the remaining information. Drag and drop each detail under the main idea it relates to. As you work, you may think of other details you can add. If a piece of information doesn't fit, you can either drop it or revise your main ideas so that the information does fit under one of the main ideas.

Your word processing program probably allows you to use an outline format. After you've identified the main ideas and the details that support each idea, you can add the headings *Introduction* and *Conclusion* above and below the main ideas and the supporting details that will make up the body of your essay.

At this point, your outline should be set in the following format:

    I. Introduction
    II. Body
        A. [First main idea]
          1. [Detail]
          2. [Detail]
        B. [Second main idea]
        . . . .
    III. Conclusion

You can then think about what you might want to do in your introduction and conclusion. Will you start by simply stating a thesis and end by restating it? Or is there an attention-catching anecdote or example that would make a better introduction? The computer frees you to play with different ideas.

Drafting

When you're satisfied with your outline, you can begin drafting your essay by simply expanding the outline. Try turning each main idea and supporting detail into a sentence (or more, if necessary). Then keep expanding as needed. Each main idea might be expanded into a paragraph. Anything that doesn't work can be easily replaced or revised. You can also save any part of your work-in-progress, duplicate it on another file, and try a new version. In fact, you can save as many versions as you like, so that all of your thoughts remain available as you continue drafting and revising your work.

Revising and Editing

Your word processing program probably has tools that will help you in the revising and editing stages. The most common tool is a spelling checker. In a few seconds, this tool will check the spelling of every word in a file. Be careful, however. A computer spelling checker can only identify words that are in its memory as correctly spelled words. Proper names and foreign words may be questioned by the program even though they're correctly spelled. The program cannot distinguish between homonyms, so if you type *their* when you should have typed *they're*, the word will not be identified as misspelled. Always proofread your writing carefully in addition to using a computer spelling check.

A grammar checker may also be available on your word processor. This function checks for problems like sentence fragments, capitalization, and the overuse of passive voice. Usually you can choose which grammar and usage items you want checked. A word processor's grammar checker can be time-consuming and frustrating if you ask it to check everything, so use it sparingly. Don't depend on it to discover every problem in your writing. The programs are not foolproof. Read your work carefully yourself for grammar and usage problems even if you use a computer grammar checker.

Exercise 1

Check out the word processing program on your computer at home or at school. Find out what writing tools the program includes and what each item does. Look at the menu bar, tool bar(s), and rules.

Technology Tip

Specialized software programs are available to help you produce different writing projects. Some CD-ROM programs, such as Glencoe's *Writer's Assistant*, will take you step-by-step through various specific writing projects from prewriting through the publishing stage. These programs may include such features as writing models and help in revising and editing a project.

Publishing

Word processing programs offer you many options for publishing your writing projects. You can experiment with different fonts, make type **bold** or *italic* or ***bold and italic,*** change the size of the type, adjust spacing, and set different types of margins. In fact, you can make your printed work look every bit as good as something published professionally. Most programs also allow you to add illustrations—such as photos, artwork, graphs, and maps—to your work.

Your word processing program may include some of the features of more-complex desktop publishing programs. These features will allow you to design professional-looking newsletters, brochures, and booklets. They may include pre-designed templates with attractive layouts you can use or adapt as you see fit. Working with classmates, you can collaborate to put together an attractive collection of writings, including full-color illustrations.

Exercise 2

Think of a topic that is currently in the news. Use a computer to learn more about the topic from Internet sources. (For more about researching topics on the Internet, see pages 909–911.) Then, using word processing software, explore your own feelings about the topic and write a brief essay expressing your opinion.

31.2 Learning with Technology

In the not-so-distant past, if you needed information on a topic you had only one choice. You would have visited a library and searched through various books, encyclopedias, magazines, and newspapers to find out what you needed to know. You might have chosen to write a letter and send away for information. Libraries are still important resources, but the growth of the Internet means that you do not always have to leave your computer in order to find information.

The Internet

The Internet allows you to travel to distant places and communicate with people around the world. You can often get information directly from the source. For example, even if you are not able to visit Washington, D.C., you can tour the White House via the Internet. The Internet includes both sources of information and ways of communicating with people in other places.

Sources of Information There are millions of Web sites dealing with nearly any topic you can think of. The chart below lists a few sites you might use for help with your homework. These sites will not do your work for you, but they will lead you to Internet sources of information and help you find answers to your questions.

Helpful Internet Sites

SITE	URL (Uniform Resource Locator, or net address)
Answers.com	http://www.answers.com
Homework Central	http://www.homeworkheaven.com
Infoplease	http://www.infoplease.com
Kids Search Tools	http://www.rcls.org/ksearch.htm
Study Web	http://www.studyweb.com

E-mail Electronic mail, or e-mail, is a way of reaching out to people by way of the Internet. E-mail allows you to keep in touch with friends, write to pen pals in foreign countries, and ask questions of NASA scientists. E-mail is available twenty-four hours a day, seven days a week, and can be sent and received almost instantaneously. Many people use it more often than the telephone or regular mail. You can conduct interviews via e-mail as part of your research for a writing project. In addition, the information you get will often be the most up-to-date that you can find.

Chat Rooms Chat rooms are Internet links with people who have similar interests—such as astronomy, soccer, or science fiction. You can join these groups of people in real-time discussions in chat rooms. When you type comments or questions into your computer, chat room visitors anywhere in the world can respond via their computers. Visiting a chat room is similar to having a telephone conversation, except you use writing instead of speaking and can communicate with more than one person at a time.

Newsgroups Newsgroups are something like e-mail chat rooms. Like chat rooms, newsgroups bring together people interested in a particular topic, but they do so by way of e-mail. When you send an e-mail comment or question to the group, your message goes to all group members—and they, in turn, can respond to the entire group. Thus, everyone shares in the exchange of information.

Finding What You Want

In seeking information, the hardest part of using the Internet may be sorting through the possibilities. Often the best way is to start with a search engine or a subject directory. These are Internet sites that provide you with lists of Web pages on a particular topic. A search engine seeks out sites from keywords that you type into the engine. For example, typing in the keyword *armadillo* would send you to dozens of Web sites containing information about that animal. A subject directory presents a list of general topics that you use to gradually narrow your search. Following are some popular search engines and subject directories.

Useful Search Engines

SEARCH ENGINES	URL
Alta Vista	http://www.altavista.digital.com
Excite	http://www.excite.com
Infoseek	http://www.infoseek.com
Lycos	http://www.lycos.com
HotBot	http://www.hotbot.com

Sample Subject Directories

SUBJECT DIRECTORIES	URL
The Argus Clearinghouse	http://www.clearinghouse.net
Magellan	http://www.mckinley.com
The Mining Company	http://www.miningco.com
Yahoo!	http://www.yahoo.com

Tracking Web Sites

As you find different interesting sites, you will want to keep track of them. Internet browsers let you keep track of useful sites you might want to go back to again and again by creating a bookmark (in Netscape Navigator) or a favorite place (in Microsoft Explorer). Your collection of bookmarks or favorite places is a kind of Internet address book. As you come across a site of interest, you only need to pull down a menu on your browser and select the bookmark (or favorite place).

CD-ROMs and DVDs

While the Internet is filled with information, getting the information can sometimes be slow. Information can also be gathered from specific software packages on CD-ROMs (*c*ompact *d*isc *r*ead-*o*nly *m*emory). CD-ROMs, which you insert into the computer's CD drive, can hold large amounts of information, including video clips, animation, photos, and sound clips as well as text. Encyclopedias, atlases, dictionaries, and other useful references are available on CD-ROMs. You can't alter the information on a CD-ROM, but you can copy and paste information from the disks into your writing. After you do so, however, be sure to use quotation marks around it and note the source from which you've taken it. (For more about citing sources, see Lesson 7.4 on pages 338–343.)

DVDs (*d*igital *v*ideo *d*iscs) represent a more advanced storage technology. A DVD can hold far more information than a CD-ROM. A single DVD can hold an entire full-length, wide-screen motion picture that you can view on your computer monitor.

Technology Tip

Using Keywords to Search

When you use a search engine, think carefully about the keywords you use. For example, if you used *armadillo* as your only keyword, a search engine would list sites about that animal. However, it might also list sites for a real-estate office, a softball club, and a country-western band—all of which use the animal's name somewhere on their site. By adding a second keyword, such as *mammal* or *animal*, you would narrow your search and avoid some of those unusable sites. On most search engines, you can use the command AND between two keywords to tell the engine to find only sites that contain both words, or the command OR to find sites that include either keyword.

Exercise 3

Use an Internet source mentioned in this lesson to find the answer to at least one of the following questions, or a question of your own.

a. What is the difference between a band and an orchestra?
b. What happened on this day in history?
c. How many Mexican pesos will a dollar buy today?
d. What is today's weather forecast in Cape Town, South Africa?
e. What online English–language newspaper is published in Hong Kong, China?

Exercise 4

Think of a topic you want to research. Enter the most general keyword into your search engine and see how many sites come back. Then narrow or expand the search by using the commands AND or OR (for example, "armadillo AND mammal AND Texas"), and compare the quantity and quality of the information returned.

31.3 Communicating Visually

While words are the building blocks of most writing, design plays an important part as well. Everything from the size and style of the font, to the spacing between lines and the size of the margins contributes to the readability of a document.

Design Elements

As you already know, there are many different forms of writing, each with its own peculiarities of style. Essays and reports may include headings and sub-headings that help organize the ideas presented. A drama looks different on the page than a novel or a short story. A screenplay will include camera directions as well as directions for the actors. A science report may contain diagrams, graphs, and other pictorial elements, while a history paper may include maps, time lines, and photos. All these and other design elements help determine how your writing will look on the page.

Many design elements can be found on the pull-down menus of the menu bar and on the tool bars and ruler at the top of your word processing window. Some design elements are shown in the following picture of a typical tool bar. If you are not familiar with these features of your word processing program, experiment with them the next time you're at the computer. Find out what each one does and consider how it can help you format your own writing.

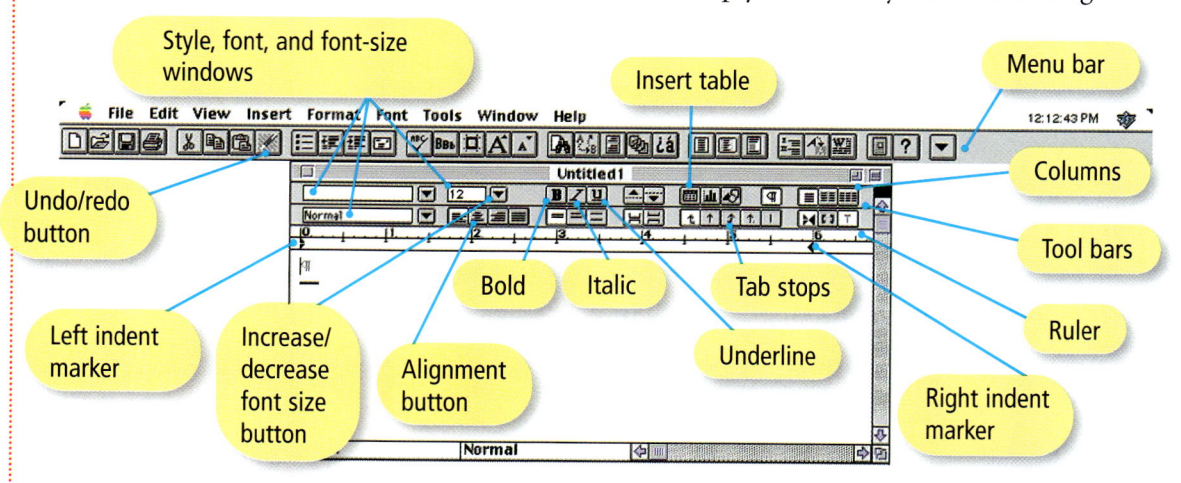

Each design element contributes to the document. By making a word **bold** or by underlining it, you indicate that it has extra importance. *Italics* are also used for emphasis as well as for other reasons—indicating book titles, for example. A list can be bulleted or numbered to make the list items stand out. You can use pictures, graphs, or other pictorial matter. Word processing software makes adding any of these elements to your writing as easy as pressing a button or pulling down a menu.

Graphics and Writing

As your writing becomes more sophisticated, you will want to become more skilled at presenting your work. Graphic images can help. You can write about how world population grew in the twentieth century, but a graph showing the growth pictorially can be more powerful. You can describe the devastation that a flood has caused, but a photo of a car floating down the street will add to the impact of your words. Describing a complicated route between two places is much better done on a map than in a wordy description. Visual images do not take the place of good writing, but they can enhance it.

The computer allows you to include all these elements. Just as you can cut and paste text, you can create and paste visual elements into your writing. Various graphing, drawing, photo editing, and publishing software programs are available. Your word processing software probably includes some of these features. All graphic programs have similar tools, with icons that help show what the tools do. A paint brush icon, for example, functions as a button that will allow you to add color to a line or group of lines. A paint bucket icon is a button that adds color to an enclosed area. Following is a typical drawing toolbar.

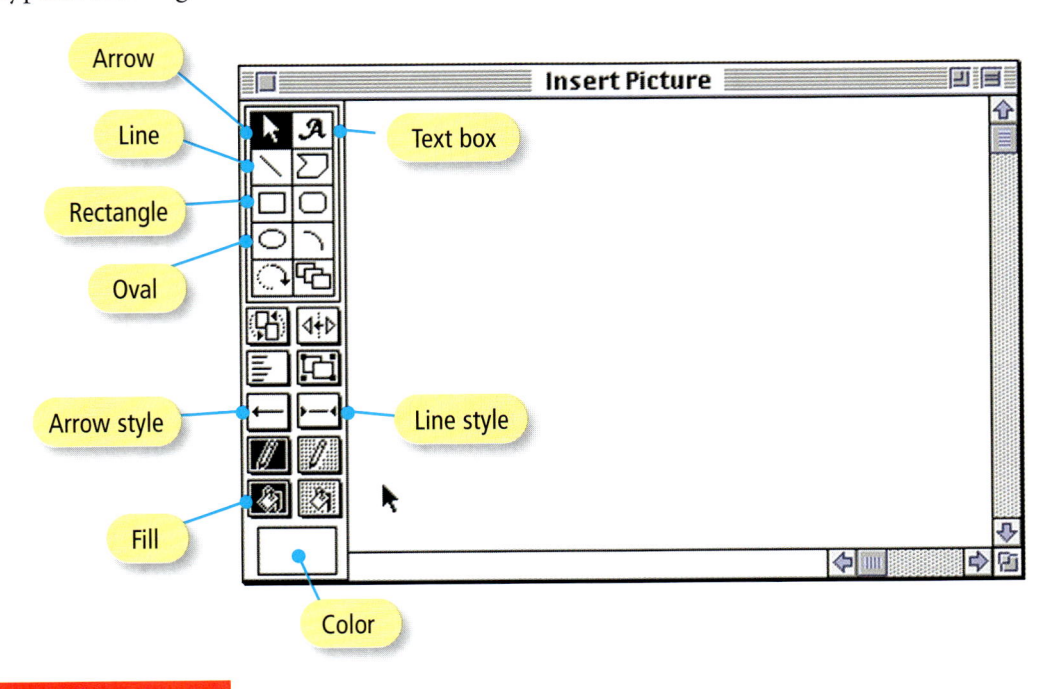

Exercise 5

Experiment with the drawing tools included with your word processing software (or with a separate drawing program if you have access to one). Learn to use the various drawing tools. Then discuss with a group how these tools could be used to enhance your writing assignments.

Graphic Explanations

Once you become comfortable with a graphing program, you can begin to experiment with different types of charts and graphs. The number of earthquakes that took place over a period of five years might be represented in a bar graph like the one on this page.

From this graph, you can tell at a glance that an overwhelming majority of the earthquakes were of low magnitude. You can also easily see that there was a dramatic increase in 4.0–4.9 earthquakes between 1994 and 1996, followed by moderate decreases over the next two years.

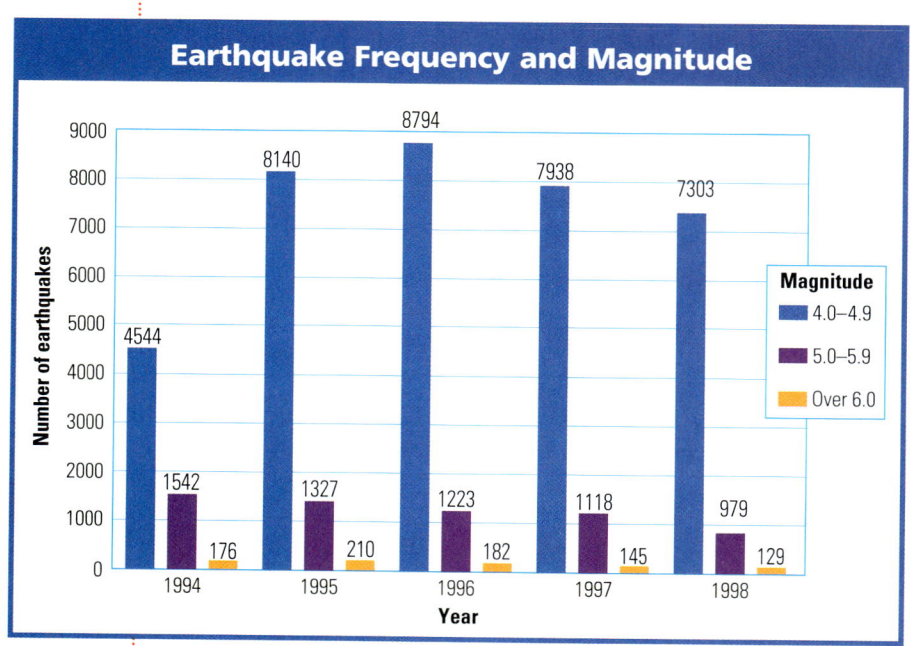

Earthquake Frequency and Magnitude

Year	4.0–4.9	5.0–5.9	Over 6.0
1994	4544	1542	176
1995	8140	1327	210
1996	8794	1223	182
1997	7938	1118	145
1998	7303	979	129

A graph allows you to present information in an easy-to-understand manner. The use of colors helps to distinguish among the different elements of the graph. The legend, or key, on the side tells what each color represents. A graphing program makes it easy to create and revise such illustrations.

Computer software allows a writer to construct or manipulate many forms of graphic representation—artwork, photographs, drawings, tables, and various kinds of graphs and charts. The best way to gain a better understanding of the power of graphics is to experiment with the software available to you.

Exercise 6

If you have access to graphing software (it may be included as a feature of your word processing program), try creating a few graphs of your own. Use either the data on the bar graph or find some data of your own. Use the same data to create two different kinds of graph—for example, a bar graph and a line graph. Consider which type of graph best suits your data, or your purpose, and explain why.

Exercise 7

Look through your portfolio for a piece of your writing that would benefit from the addition of graphics. Work with a partner or small group to revise your writings to make greater use of graphic representation.

31.4 Producing in Multimedia

It's hard to believe, but as recently as the 1980s, multimedia productions required very expensive equipment and expertise that few people had. Now almost anyone with a desktop computer and presentation software can create multimedia productions.

Types of Multimedia Productions

Multimedia is the merging of text (written words), sound (speech, music, sound effects) and images (photos, art, video clips, animation) into a single presentation. Multimedia can be as low-tech as a slide show with a tape recorder or as high-tech as your own Web page with video and audio clips. Some multimedia productions are created to be viewed in a linear fashion—that is, from beginning to end along a particular path as the author assembled it. Others productions include hyperlinks that allow users to choose the paths they want to follow.

The following chart shows three easy ways to create a multimedia production.

Technology Tip

Complex projects like Web site design with full-motion video require additional computer hardware and software. Images (photos and video clips) and audio clips take up an enormous amount of hard drive space. However, with enough computer memory, a reasonably fast processing speed, a digital camera, and the right software, you can use your computer to make a movie.

Creating Multimedia Productions

HARDWARE	SOFTWARE
Camera, slide or overhead projector, screen, and tape recorder (with speakers)	Use 35-mm slides and/or overhead transparencies for the visuals (text and images). Use a tape recorder for narration, music, or other sounds.
Computer with speakers, monitor, and a microphone Also useful: digital camera, video camera, scanner (to scan and digitalize images)	Use presentation software to create a computer-based "slide show" combining text, graphics, images, and sound.
Computer with speakers, monitor, and a microphone Also useful: digital camera, video camera, scanner (to scan and digitalize images)	Use a hypertext program to combine text, graphics, images, and sound to create a series of "cards" containing hyperlinks that can make different sequences possible.

Multimedia Techniques

The power of multimedia is its ability to provide you with additional tools with which to communicate. Describing in an essay your recent trip through a national park is great. But creating a multimedia project with pictures you took, postcards you bought, audio clips of remarks by park rangers, and perhaps a short film clip you downloaded from the Internet can make the experience much more alive.

In multimedia, as in writing, different subjects lend themselves to different forms. If you are demonstrating how to build a bicycle, you will want to start at point A and follow the instructions point-by-point to point Z. This is a linear progression that ensures that the bike will be put together properly and operate well when it is finished. The author is in charge of how the user navigates through the production.

However, if you are informing people about six favorite bike trails in your area, you may want to let them choose how they view these trails. You provide all the pieces and the hyperlinks, but the viewers are in control of their own experience. Part of the fun is letting viewers explore and discover what you have discovered before them. Both of these examples work well in a multimedia format; the experiences are richer when you add images and sound to the text.

Creating a Project

Perhaps the best way to start a multimedia project is by creating an outline or storyboard for what you want to do. A storyboard describes what is going to take place in each segment of the presentation. For example, if your project is a documentary on a neighborhood bakery, the storyboard might begin like the one below.

Storyboard: How Sweet It Is

Segment	Text	Sounds	Images
1	Title: How Sweet It Is A Multimedia Presentation by Olivia Sugar	Song: "If I Knew You Were Comin' I'd've Baked a Cake"	Beautiful cake
2	This bakery was first opened at the end of the nineteenth century.	None	Picture of bakery storefront
3	Hans and Gretchen Sacher came from Austria to the city's Lower West Side.	Kitchen noises—pots and pans clanging	Photo of old kitchen counter with equipment

Remember not to overload the production with extras (too much information, too many colors, too many different things happening in each segment) and thus lose the story. Have each segment make a single point, and support that point with sounds and images. You may want to use a spoken narration for your presentation. In that case, you may need little or no written text except for titles and credits. Similarly, if the images are particularly powerful, a segment may not need text. At the end of the presentation, include a segment to credit your sources.

Keep the audience in mind, as you would if you were writing an essay. If your audience is familiar with the topic, include more specifics and assume the audience knows the basics. If your audience is likely to know nothing about the topic, start with the basic ideas and explain everything carefully.

In creating your multimedia project, use some of the skills you learned in Unit 30: Viewing and Representing, found on pages 893–904 of this book. In addition, try to view other multimedia presentations, both amateur and professional, and note what you like or dislike. Look for techniques that you can adapt for your project. Mostly, though, have fun being creative and expressing yourself.

Evaluating a Project

You have spent many hours creating a multimedia project that you think is wonderful. How can you be sure? Following is a checklist to ensure that the project works.

> ✓ Turn the sound off. Do the written text and the images tell the story?
> ✓ Is the information easy to understand?
> ✓ Are the visual elements powerful and relevant?
> ✓ Are the look and tone appealing?
> ✓ Do the sounds and visuals work together, each supporting the other?
> ✓ Does the organization make sense?

Ask a friend to go through your presentation to see if it is understandable. Because a multimedia presentation is ultimately viewed by an audience, working with a friend is probably the best way to make sure that you have accomplished your goal. Often what an author thinks is obvious is not obvious to the viewer. You may have left out information or provided too much information. Ask a friend to help you revise the project until it is as good as it can be.

Exercise 8

Think about various forms of communication—writing, video, movie, multimedia—and consider how some ideas are better suited to one form than another. Make a list of other examples—like the bicycle and bike trails examples—where one presentation should be controlled by the multimedia author while the other should be controlled by the user/viewer.

Writing and Language Glossary

This glossary will help you quickly locate grammatical and other terms useful for writers.

A

Abstract noun. *See* Noun.

Active voice. A verb is in the **active voice** if the subject of the sentence performs the action.

Adjective. A word that modifies a noun or pronoun by limiting its meaning. An adjective may tell *what kind, which one, how many,* or *how much.*

> The **positive degree** is the simple form of the adjective.
> The **comparative degree** compares two persons, places, things, or ideas.
> The **superlative degree** compares more than two persons, places, things, or ideas.

Adjective clause. A dependent clause that modifies a noun or pronoun. *See also* Clause.

Adverb. A word that modifies a verb, an adjective, or another adverb by making its meaning more specific. Adverbs tell *how, when, where,* and *to what degree.*

> The **comparative** form of an adverb compares two actions. *(more quickly, better)*
> The **superlative** form compares three or more actions. *(most quickly, best)*

Adverb clause. A dependent clause that modifies a verb, an adjective, or an adverb. *See also* Clause.

Allusion. A reference in a composition to a well-known character, place, or situation from a work of literature, music, or art or from history.

Analysis. The act of breaking down a subject into its separate parts to determine its meaning.

Anecdote. A short story or incident, usually presented as part of a longer narrative.

Antecedent. *See* Pronoun.

Appositive. A noun or a pronoun placed next to another noun or pronoun to identify or give additional information about it. (My cousin *Lonnie* is going to Guatemala this summer.)

Argument. A statement, reason, or fact for or against a point; a composition intended to persuade.

Article. The adjectives *a, an,* and *the.* **Indefinite articles** (*a* and *an*) refer to one of a general group of persons, places, or things. The **definite article** (*the*) indicates that the noun is a specific person, place, or thing.

Audience. The person(s) who reads or listens to what the writer or speaker says.

Auxiliary verb. *See* Verb.

B

Bias. A tendency or inclination that prevents impartial consideration of an idea; a quality to consider when producing or evaluating persuasive writing.

Bibliography. A list of the books, articles, and other sources used as reference sources in a research paper.

918 Writing and Language Glossary

Body. The central part of a composition that communicates the main idea identified in the introduction.

Bookmarks/Favorites. The feature on many Web browsers that allows the user to save addresses of Internet sites so that the sites can be accessed quickly.

Brainstorming. A group activity in which people generate as many ideas as possible without stopping to judge them.

C

Case. The form of a noun or pronoun that is determined by its use in a sentence. A noun or pronoun is in the **nominative case** when it is used as a subject or after a linking verb, in the **objective case** when it is used as an object, and in the **possessive case** when it is used to show possession.

Cause-and-effect development. A kind of organization that involves examining the reasons for actions or events and the results of those actions.

Character. An individual involved in the plot of a work of fiction. **Round characters** have different traits, some of which may be contradictory. **Flat characters** are those which display one dominant trait. **Static characters** do not change. **Dynamic characters** show development in the course of a story.

Characterization. The techniques a writer uses to reveal character. Characterization may be **direct,** revealed through the description of the character and the character's own words and actions, or **indirect,** revealed through what other characters think and say about the character.

Chronological order. The arrangement of events in order of time.

Clarity. The quality of a piece of writing that makes it easy to understand.

Clause. A group of words that has a subject and a predicate and is used as part of a sentence. Clauses fall into two categories: **independent clauses,** which are also called **main clauses,** and **dependent clauses,** which are also called **subordinate clauses.**

> An **independent clause** has a subject and a predicate and can stand alone as a sentence.
> A **dependent clause** is one that cannot stand alone as a sentence. It may be restrictive or nonrestrictive.
> A **nonrestrictive clause,** also called a **nonessential clause,** is one that is not needed to make the meaning of a sentence clear. (Mae Jemison, *who comes from Chicago,* gained fame as an astronaut.)
> A **restrictive clause,** also called an **essential clause,** is essential to the meaning of a sentence. (A free doughnut will be given to everyone *who arrives before 9 A.M.*)

Cliché. An overused expression. *(quiet as a mouse)*

Climax. The point of greatest emotional intensity, interest, or suspense in the plot of a narrative.

Clustering. A technique for generating writing ideas, which involves writing a word, circling it, and surrounding it with other words and phrases.

Coherence. The quality of a paragraph or composition in which sentences are clearly and logically connected; also called cohesiveness.

Cohesive writing. A type of writing in which sentences and paragraphs are logically connected to one another.

Collaboration. The process of working with others on writing or other projects.

Collective noun. *See* Noun.

Writing and Language Glossary **919**

Colloquialism. A casual, colorful expression used in everyday conversation.

Common noun. *See* Noun.

Comparative degree. *See* Adjective; Adverb.

Compare-and-contrast development. A type of organization used in expository writing that examines similarities and differences in order to find relationships and draw conclusions.

Complement. A word or phrase that completes the meaning of a verb. The four basic kinds of complements are **direct objects, indirect objects, object complements,** and **subject complements.**

Conceptual map. A graphic device that develops a central concept by surrounding it with examples or related ideas in a weblike arrangement.

Conclusion. A restatement or summing up of the ideas in a composition that brings it to a definite close.

Conflict. The struggle between opposing forces that lies at the center of the plot in a story or drama.

Conjunction. A word that joins single words or groups of words.
  Coordinating conjunctions (*and, but, or, nor, for, yet*) join words or groups of words that are equal in grammatical importance.
  Correlative conjunctions work in pairs to join words and groups of words of equal importance.
  Subordinating conjunctions join a dependent idea or clause to a main clause.

Conjunctive adverb. An adverb used to clarify the relationship between clauses of a compound sentence. (The team lost the game last night; *consequently*, they will not play in the tournament.)

Connotation. The thoughts and feelings associated with a word, rather than its dictionary definition.

Constructive criticism. Comments on another person's writing made with the intention of helping the writer improve a particular draft.

Context. The words and sentences that come before and after a specific word and help to explain its meaning.

Coordinating conjunction. *See* Conjunction.

Correlative conjunction. *See* Conjunction.

Credibility. The quality of a speaker or writer that makes that person's words believable.

Critical analysis. The consideration of the elements of a literary work to examine, organize, evaluate, or draw conclusions about them.

D

Declarative sentence. A sentence that makes a statement.

Deconstructing. Breaking down into component parts, or analyzing.

Deductive reasoning. A way of thinking or explaining that begins with a general statement or principle and applies that principle to specific instances.

Definite article. *See* Article.

Denotation. The dictionary definition of a word.

Dependent clause. *See* Clause.

Descriptive writing. Writing that uses sensory details to convey a dominant impression of, for example, a setting, a person, an animal, and so on.

Desktop publishing. The use of computer programs to format and produce a document that may include written text, graphics, and/or images.

Dialect. A variation of a language spoken by a particular group of people. A dialect may be regional (based on location) or ethnic (based on cultural heritage).

Dialogue. The conversation between characters in a story, play, or novel.

Diction. A writer's choice of words and the arrangement of those words in phrases, sentences, or lines of a poem.

Documentation. Identification of the sources used in writing research or other informative papers, usually in the form of endnotes or footnotes, or using parenthetical documentation.

Drafting. One of the steps in the writing process; the transforming of thoughts, words, and phrases into sentences and paragraphs.

E

Editing. One of the steps in the writing process in which a revised draft is checked for standard usage, varied sentence structure, and appropriate word choice.

Editorial. An article in a newspaper or other form of media that expresses a personal opinion about a subject of current or general interest.

Either-or reasoning. A logical fallacy that limits possibilities to two opposite choices, ignoring other valid possibilities.

Elaboration. The support or development of a main idea with facts, statistics, sensory details, incidents, examples, or quotations.

Ellipsis. A mark of punctuation, consisting of three spaced periods, that indicates the omission of one or more words.

E-mail. Short for electronic mail; messages, usually text, sent from one person to another by way of computer.

Emphatic form. *See* Verb tense.

Essential clause. A subordinate clause that cannot be omitted without changing the intended meaning of a sentence.

Evaluation. Making a judgment about the strengths and weaknesses of a draft in content, organization, and style.

Evidence. Facts or examples from reliable sources that can be used to support statements made in speaking or writing.

Exclamatory sentence. A sentence that expresses strong or intense emotion.

Explanatory writing. *See* Expository writing.

Expository writing. A kind of writing that aims at explaining an idea or presenting a process; also called informative or explanatory writing.

Expressive writing. Writing that emphasizes and conveys the writer's feelings.

F

Fact. A piece of information that can be verified from direct experience or from an authoritative source.

Feedback. The response a listener or reader gives a speaker or writer about his or her work.

Fiction. Literature in which situations and characters are invented by the writer.

Figurative language. Words used for descriptive effect that express some truth beyond the literal level. Figures of speech such as similes, metaphors, or personification are examples of figurative language.

Foreshadowing. Clues that hint at events that will occur later in the plot.

Formal language. Language that uses correct grammar and omits slang expressions and contractions. It is especially common in nonfiction writing that is not personal.

Freewriting. Writing for a specific length of time without stopping or limiting the flow of ideas.

Future perfect tense. *See* Verb tense.

Future tense. *See* Verb tense.

G

Generalization. A statement that presents a conclusion about a subject without going into details or specifics.

Genre. A division of literature. The main literary genres are prose, poetry, and drama. Each of these is further divided into subgenres.

Gerund. A verb form that ends in *-ing* and is used as a noun.

Glittering generality. An attractive claim based on insufficient evidence.

Graphic organizer. A visual way of organizing information; types of graphic organizers include clustering, graphs, tables, time lines, and tree diagrams.

H

Home page. The location on a Web site by which a user normally enters the site. A typical home page may explain the site, summarize the content, and provide links to other sites.

Hyperlink. A highlighted or underlined phrase or word on a Web page that, when clicked, moves the user to another part of the page or to another Web page.

Hypertext. Links in some text that can be clicked with a mouse to take the user to another document or to a different section in the same document.

I

Idea map. *See* Cluster.

Idiom. A word or phrase that has a special meaning different from its standard or dictionary meaning. (*In the same boat* is an idiom that means "having the same problem.")

Imagery. Language that emphasizes sensory impressions that can help the reader of a literary work to see, hear, feel, smell, and taste the scenes described in the work.

Imperative sentence. A sentence that makes a request or gives a command.

Independent clause. *See* Clause.

Inductive reasoning. A way of thinking or explaining that arrives at a conclusion by examining a series of examples.

Infinitive. A verb form that usually begins with the word *to* and functions as a noun, adjective, or adverb in a sentence.

Informative writing. *See* Expository writing.

Intensifier. An adverb that emphasizes an adjective or another adverb. (*very* important, *quite* easily)

Interjection. A word or phrase that expresses emotion or exclamation. An interjection has no grammatical connection to other words.

Internet. A worldwide computer network that allows users to link to any computer on the network electronically for social, commercial, research, and other uses.

Interpretation. An explanation of the meaning of a piece of writing, a visual representation, or any other type of communication.

Interrogative sentence. A sentence that asks a question.

Interview. A question-and-answer dialogue that has the specific purpose of gathering up-to-date or expert information.

Intransitive verb. *See* Verb.

Introduction. The beginning part of a composition, in which a writer identifies the subject and gives a general idea of what the body of the composition will contain.

Inverted order. The placement of a predicate before the subject in a sentence. In most sentences in English, the subject comes before the predicate.

Irregular verb. *See* Verb tense.

J–L

Jargon. Special words and phrases used by a particular trade, profession, or other group of people.

Journal. A personal notebook for freewriting, collecting ideas, and recording thoughts and experiences.

Learning log. A journal for clarifying ideas about concepts covered in various classes.

Lexicon. A wordbook or dictionary.

Listing. A technique used in generating ideas for writing.

Literary analysis. The act of examining the different elements of a piece of literature in order to evaluate it.

Logical fallacy. An error in reasoning often found in advertising or other persuasive writing. *See* Glittering generalities; Either-or reasoning.

M

Main clause. *See* Clause.

Main idea. *See* Thesis statement.

Media. The forms of communication used to reach an audience; newspapers, radio, TV, and the Internet reach large audiences and so are known as mass media.

Memoir. A type of narrative nonfiction that presents an account of an event or period in history, emphasizing the narrator's personal experience.

Metaphor. A figure of speech that compares seemingly unlike things without using the word *like* or *as*. (The girl's aloof *manner* was her *armor* against snubs.)

Mood. The feeling or atmosphere that a writer creates.

Multimedia presentation. The presentation of a piece of writing accompanied by other media, such as music, video, and visual art.

N

Narrative writing. A type of writing that tells about events or actions as they change over a period of time and often includes story elements such as character, setting, and plot.

Nominative pronoun. *See* Pronoun case.

Nonessential clause. A clause that adds information but is not absolutely needed to express the meaning of the sentence.

Nonfiction. Prose writing about real people, places, and events.

Nonrestrictive clause. *See* Nonessential clause.

Noun. A word that names a person, a place, a thing, an idea, a quality, or a characteristic.
   An **abstract noun** names an idea, a quality, or a characteristic.

A **collective noun** names a group of people or things.

A **common noun** names a general type of person, place, thing, or idea, characteristic, or quality.

A **proper noun** names a particular, person, place, thing, or idea.

Noun clause. A dependent clause that functions as a noun.

Number. The form of a noun, pronoun, or verb that indicates whether it refers to one (**singular**) or to more than one (**plural**).

O

Objective pronoun. *See* Pronoun case.

Onomatopoeia. A word with a sound that suggests its meaning. *(buzz, clink, pop)*

Opinion. A belief or attitude that cannot be proven true or false. Readers and writers should clearly distinguish opinion from fact.

Oral tradition. Literature that passes by word of mouth from one generation to the next. Oral tradition often reflects the cultural values of a people.

Order of importance. A way of organizing details in a paragraph or composition from least to most or most to least important.

Organization. A system of ordering ideas.

Outline. A systematic arrangement of main and supporting ideas, using Roman numerals, letters, and numbers for a written or an oral presentation.

P

Paragraph. A unit of writing that consists of related sentences.

Parallelism. The use of a series of words, phrases, or sentences that have similar grammatical form.

Paraphrase. A restatement of an idea in different words that retains the meaning, tone, and general length of the original.

Parenthetical documentation. A specific reference to the source of a piece of information; it is placed in parenthesis directly after the information appears in a piece of writing.

Participle. A verb form that can function as an adjective. Present participles always end in *-ing*. Although past participles often end in *-ed,* they can take other forms as well.

Passive voice. The form of a verb used when the subject of the sentence receives the action of the verb.

Peer response. The suggestions and comments provided by peers, or classmates, about a piece of writing or another type of presentation.

Personal writing. Writing that expresses the writer's own thoughts and feelings.

Personification. A figure of speech that gives human qualities to an animal, object, or idea.

Perspective. *See* Point of view.

Persuasive writing. Writing that aims at influencing a reader's opinion and actions.

Phrase. A group of words that acts as a single part of speech in a sentence.

A **prepositional phrase** consists of a preposition, its object, and any modifiers of the object. A **verb phrase** consists of one or more auxiliary verbs followed by a main verb.

Plagiarism. The dishonest presentation of another's words or ideas as one's own.

Plot. The series of events that follow one another in a story, novel, or play.

924 Writing and Language Glossary

Poetry. A form of literary expression that emphasizes the line as the unit of composition. Traditional poetry contains emotional, imaginative language and a regular rhythm.

Point of view. The perspective, or angle, from which a story is told. Most writing is done from a first-person, third-person limited, or third-person omniscient point of view.

Portfolio. A collection of various pieces of writing, which may include finished pieces and works in progress.

Positive degree. *See* Adjective.

Possessive pronoun. *See* Pronoun case.

Predicate. The verb or verb phrase and any of its modifiers that make an essential statement about the subject of a sentence.

Preposition. A word that shows the relationship of a noun or pronoun to some other word in the sentence.

Presenting. The last step in the writing process, which involves sharing the final writing product with others.

Prewriting. The first step in the writing process, which includes deciding what to write about, collecting ideas and details, and making an outline or a plan. Prewriting strategies include brainstorming, clustering, word webs, and freewriting.

Prior knowledge. The facts, ideas, and experiences that a writer, reader, or viewer brings to a new activity.

Progressive form. *See* Verb tense.

Pronoun. A word that takes the place of a noun, a group of words acting as a noun, or another pronoun. The word or group of words that a pronoun refers to is called its **antecedent.**

Pronoun case. A personal pronoun refers to a specific person or thing. Personal pronouns have three **cases**—nominative, objective, and possessive. *See also* Case.

Proofreading. The last part of the editing process that involves checking work to discover typographical and spelling errors.

Propaganda. Information aimed at influencing thoughts and actions; it is usually of a political nature and may contain distortions of truth.

Prose. Writing that is similar to everyday speech and written language, as opposed to poetry and drama.

Publishing. The preparation of a finished piece of writing, often using available technology, so that it can be presented to a larger audience.

Purpose. The aim of writing, which may be to express, discover, record, develop, reflect on ideas, problem solve, entertain, influence, inform, or describe.

R

Regular verb. *See* Verb tense.

Representation. A way in which information or ideas are presented to an audience.

Research. Locating information on a topic from a variety of sources.

Restrictive clause. *See* Essential clause.

Review. An analysis and interpretation of a subject presented through the mass media.

Revising. The stage of the writing process in which a writer goes over a draft, making changes in content, organization, and style in order to improve it. Revision techniques include adding, elaborating, deleting, combining, and rearranging text.

Root. The part of a word that carries the main meaning.

Run-on sentence. Two or more sentences or clauses run together without appropriate punctuation.

S

Sensory details. Words that appeal to the senses—sight, hearing, taste, smell, and feeling; important element of descriptive writing, especially of poetry.

Sentence. A group of words expressing a complete thought. Every sentence has a **subject** and a **predicate.** Sentences can be classified by function or by structure.
> A **simple sentence** has only one main clause and no subordinate clauses.
> A **compound sentence** has two or more main clauses.
> A **complex sentence** has one main clause and one or more subordinate clauses.
> A **compound-complex sentence** has two or more main clauses and at least one subordinate clause. *See also* Declarative sentence; Exclamatory sentence; Imperative sentence; Interrogative sentence.

Sentence variety. The use of different types of sentences to add interest to writing.

Setting. The time and place in which the events of a story happen.

Simile. A figure of speech that compares two unlike things, using the word *like* or *as*. (The clouds looked *like* melted marshmallows.)

Spatial order. The arrangement of the details of a setting according to their location—for example, from left to right or from top to bottom.

Standard English. The most widely used and accepted form of the English language.

Style. The writer's choice and arrangement of words and sentences.

Subordinate clause. *See* Clause.

Subordinating conjunction. *See* Conjunction.

Summary. A brief statement of the main idea of a composition.

Superlative degree. *See* Adjective, Adverb.

Supporting evidence. *See* Evidence.

Suspense. A literary device that creates growing interest and excitement leading up to the climax or resolution of a story. A writer creates suspense by providing clues to the resolution without revealing too much information.

Symbol. An object, a person, a place, or an experience that represents something else, usually something abstract.

T

Tense. *See* Verb tense.

Theme. The main idea or message of a piece of writing.

Thesis statement. A one- or two-sentence statement of the main idea or purpose of a piece of writing.

Time line. A line, usually horizontal, divided into equal segments, each of which represents a specific interval of time; a helpful device for organizing events in chronological order.

Time order. The arrangement of details based on when they occurred.

Tone. A reflection of a writer's or speaker's attitude toward a subject.

Topic sentence. A sentence that expresses the main idea of a paragraph.

Transition. A connecting word or phrase that clarifies relationships between details, sentences, or paragraphs.

U–V

Unity. The quality of a composition in which all the sentences and paragraphs support one main idea.

URL. The standard form of an Internet address; stands for Uniform Resource Locator.

Venn diagram. A graphic organizer consisting of two or more overlapping circles; used to compare items that have both similar and different traits.

Verb. A word that expresses action or a state of being and is necessary to make a statement. An auxiliary verb, or helping verb, accompanies the main verb of a sentence. An intransitive verb does not take a direct object. (Horses *run* across the plains.)

Verbal. A verb form that functions in a sentence as a noun, an adjective, or an adverb. The three kinds of verbals are gerunds, infinitives, and participles. *See* Gerund; Infinitive; Participle.

Verb phrase. *See* Phrase.

Verb tense. The tense of a verb indicates when the action or state of being occurs. The **present tense** names an action that happens regularly. The **past tense** names an action that has happened, and the **future tense** names an action that will take place in the future.

All verb tenses are formed from the four principal parts of a verb: a base form *(swim)*, a present participle *(swimming)*, a simple past form *(swam)*, and a past participle *(swum)*. A **regular verb** forms its simple past and past participle by adding *-ed* to the base form. *(jump, jumped, jumped)* An **irregular verb** forms its past and past participle in some other way. *(drive, drove, driven; begin, began, begun)* In addition to present, past, and future tense, there are three perfect tenses: present perfect, past perfect, and future perfect. The **progressive form** of a verb expresses a continuing action with any of the six tenses. To make the progressive forms, use the appropriate tense of the verb *be* with the present participle of the main verb. The **emphatic form** adds special force, or emphasis, to the present or past tense of a verb. For the emphatic form, use *do, does,* or *did* with the base form.

Voice. The distinctive use of language that conveys the writer's or narrator's personality to the reader. Sentence structure, word choice, and tone are elements that communicate voice.

W

Web site. A location on the World Wide Web that can be reached through links or by accessing a Web address, or URL. *See* URL.

Word processing. The use of a computer for the writing and editing of written text.

World Wide Web. A global system that uses the Internet and allows users to create, link, and access fields of information. *See* Internet.

Writing process. The series of stages or steps that a writer goes through to develop ideas and to communicate them.

GLOSARIO
DE ESCRITURA Y LENGUAJE

Este glosario permite encontrar fácilmente definiciones de gramática inglesa y términos que usan los escritores.

A

Abstract noun/Nombre abstracto. *Ver Noun.*

Active voice/Voz activa. Forma verbal usada cuando el sujeto de la oración realiza la acción.

Adjective/Adjetivo. Palabra que modifica, o describe, un nombre (*noun*) o pronombre (*pronoun*), limitando su significado. Un adjetivo indica *qué tipo, cuál, cuántos* o *cuánto*. Los adjetivos aparecen en varias posiciones en la oración.

> **Positive degree/Grado positivo.** Forma simple del adjetivo.
>
> **Comparative degree/Grado comparativo.** Adjetivo que compara a dos personas, lugares, cosas o ideas.
>
> **Superlative degree/Grado superlativo.** Adjetivo que compara más de dos personas, lugares, cosas o ideas.

Adjective clause/Proposición adjetiva. Proposición dependiente que modifica un nombre o pronombre. *Ver también Clause.*

Adverb/Adverbio. Palabra que modifica a un verbo, adjetivo u otro adverbio, haciendo que su significado sea más específico. Los adverbios responden a las preguntas *cómo, cuándo, dónde, de qué manera* y *qué tan seguido* sucede algo.

> **Comparative/Comparativo.** Compara dos acciones (*more quickly, better*; en español: *más rápido, mejor*).
>
> **Superlative/Superlativo.** Compara tres o más acciones (*most quickly, best*; en español: *el más rápido, lo mejor*).

Adverb clause/Proposición adverbial. Proposición dependiente que modifica un verbo, un adjetivo o un adverbio. *Ver Clause.*

Allusion/Alusión. Referencia en un texto escrito a un personaje, lugar o situación muy conocidos de una obra literaria, musical, artística o histórica.

Analysis/Análisis. Acción de descomponer un tema o escrito en distintas partes para encontrar su significado.

Anecdote/Anécdota. Narración breve o incidente que se presenta como parte de una narrativa más larga.

Antecedent/Antecedente. *Ver Pronoun.*

Appositive/Apositivo. Nombre colocado junto a otro para identificarlo o agregar información sobre él. (Mi prima *Lupe* va a ir a Guatemala este verano.)

Argument/Argumento. Afirmación, razón o hecho en favor o en contra de algún comentario; texto escrito que trata de persuadir.

Article/Artículo. Nombre dado a las palabras *a, an* y *the* (en español: *un, uno/a, el, la*). *A* y *an* son artículos **indefinidos** (*indefinite articles*), que se refieren a cualquier cosa de un grupo. *The* es un artículo **definido** (*definite article*); indica que el nombre al que precede es una persona, lugar o cosa específicos.

Audience/Público. Persona (o personas) que lee o escucha lo que dicen un escritor o un hablante.

Auxiliary verb/Verbo auxiliar. *Ver Verb*.

B

Bias/Tendencia. Inclinación a pensar de cierta manera que impide la consideración imparcial de una idea; importante de considerar al producir o evaluar un texto persuasivo.

Bibliography/Bibliografía. Lista de los libros, artículos y otras fuentes que se utilizan como referencia en una investigación.

Body/Cuerpo. Parte central de una composición que comunica la idea principal identificada en la introducción.

Bookmarks/favorites/Marcadores/favoritos. Característica de muchos buscadores de red que permiten guardar direcciones de Internet para entrar a ellas rápidamente.

Brainstorming/Lluvia de ideas. Actividad de grupo por medio de la cual se generan ideas al hacer una lista de todo lo que se nos ocurre sin evaluarlo.

C

Case/Caso. Forma de un nombre o pronombre que se determina por su uso en la oración. El nombre o pronombre está en caso **nominativo** (*nominative case*) cuando se utiliza como sujeto o después de un verbo copulativo; en caso **acusativo** y **dativo** (*objective case*) cuando recibe la acción del verbo; y en caso **posesivo*** (*possessive case*) cuando se utiliza para indicar posesión o propiedad.

Cause and effect development/Desarrollo de causa y efecto. Técnica de organización que examina las razones y los resultados de las acciones.

Character/Personaje. Individuo presentado en la trama de una obra de ficción.
> **Round character/Personaje redondeado.** El que tiene una variedad de características, algunas de las cuales pueden ser contradictorias.
> **Flat character/Personaje plano.** El que tiene una característica dominante.
> **Static character/Personaje estático.** El que no cambia.
> **Dynamic character/Personaje dinámico.** El que se desarrolla a lo largo de la narración.

Characterization/Caracterización. Técnicas que utiliza un escritor para crear sus personajes. Puede ser **directa,** por medio de descripción y de las palabras del personaje, o **indirecta,** por medio de lo que dicen de él otros personajes.

Chronological order/Orden cronológico. Organización de detalles de acuerdo con el tiempo en que sucedieron los acontecimientos o acciones.

Clarity/Claridad. Cualidad de un escrito que lo hace fácil de entender.

Clause/Proposición. Grupo de palabras que consta de sujeto y predicado y que se usa como parte de una oración.
> **Independent clause/Proposición independiente.** También llamada **proposición principal** (*main clause*); tiene sujeto y predicado y hace sentido por sí misma.
> **Dependent clause/Proposición dependiente.** También llamada **proposición subordinada** (*subordinate clause*); tiene sujeto y predicado pero depende de la proposición principal. La proposición dependiente puede ser:

Writing and Language Glossary

Restrictive o **essential clause/Proposición restrictiva** o **esencial,** que es necesaria para el significado de la oración. **Nonessential** o **nonrestrictive clause/Proposición no esencial** o **no restrictiva,** que no es necesaria para entender el significado de la oración.

Cliché/Cliché. Expresión usada con demasiada frecuencia *(blanco como la nieve).*

Climax/Clímax. Momento donde ocurre la mayor intensidad emocional, interés o suspenso en la trama de una narración.

Clustering/Agrupamiento. Técnica para generar ideas que consiste en escribir una palabra, ponerla dentro de un círculo y rodearla con otras palabras y frases.

Coherence/Coherencia. Cualidad de un párrafo o composición en que las oraciones tienen una relación clara y lógica; también se llama cohesión.

Cohesive writing/Escritura coherente. Tipo de escritura en que las oraciones y párrafos están lógicamente relacionados entre sí.

Collaboration/Colaboración. Proceso de trabajar en equipo para escribir un texto o realizar un proyecto.

Collective noun/Nombre colectivo. *Ver Noun.*

Colloquialism/Expresión coloquial. Expresión informal y pintoresca que se utiliza en la conversación diaria.

Common noun/Nombre común. *Ver Noun.*

Comparative degree/Grado comparativo. *Ver Adjective; Adverb.*

Comparison-and-contrast development/Desarrollo por comparación y contraste. Técnica de organizar ideas, señalando sus similitudes y diferencias a fin de ver relaciones y sacar conclusiones.

Complement/Complemento. Palabra o frase que completa el significado de un verbo en una oración. En inglés hay cuatro clases básicas de complementos: **directo** (*direct object*), **indirecto** (*indirect object*), **de objeto** (*object complement*) y **predicativo** (**atributo**) (*subject complement*).

Conceptual map/Mapa conceptual. Recurso gráfico que desarrolla un concepto central rodeándolo con ejemplos o ideas relacionadas a manera de red.

Conclusion/Conclusión. Afirmación que resume las ideas de una composición, antes de ponerle punto final.

Conflict/Conflicto. Lucha entre dos fuerzas opuestas que constituye el elemento central de la trama en un cuento u obra de teatro.

Conjunction/Conjunción. Palabra que une dos palabras o grupos de palabras.
  Coordinating conjunction/Conjunción coordinante. Las palabras *and, but, or, nor, for, yet* (*y, pero, o, no, para, aun*) unen palabras o grupos de palabras que tienen igual importancia gramatical.
  Correlative conjunction/Conjunción correlativa*. Las palabras *both . . . and, just as . . . so, not only . . . but also, either . . . or, neither . . . nor* (*tanto . . . como, así como, no sólo . . . sino, o . . . o*) son palabras en pares que vinculan palabras o frases de igual importancia.
  Subordinate conjunction/Conjunción subordinante. Une una idea u proposición subordinada con la proposición principal.

Conjunctive adverb/Adverbio de coordinación. Adverbio para aclarar la relación entre las proposiciones de una oración compuesta. (El equipo perdió anoche; *por lo tanto,* no jugará en las finales.)

Connotation/Connotación. Pensamientos y sentimientos relacionados con una palabra, más que con su definición de diccionario.

930 Glosario de escritura y lenguaje

Constructive criticism/Crítica constructiva. Comentario sobre lo que escribe otra persona, con la intención de ayudar a que mejore el borrador.

Context/Contexto. Palabras y oraciones que vienen antes y después de una palabra y ayudan a explicar su significado.

Coordinating conjunction/Conjunción coordinante. *Ver Conjunction.*

Correlative conjunction/Conjunción correlativa*. *Ver Conjunction.*

Credibility/Credibilidad. Cualidad de un hablante o escritor que hace creer sus palabras.

Critical analysis/Análisis crítico. Consideración de los elementos de una obra literaria para examinarlos, organizarlos, evaluarlos o sacar conclusiones sobre ellos.

D

Declarative sentence/Oración afirmativa. Oración que declara algo.

Deconstructing/Desensamblar. Separar en componentes o analizar.

Deductive reasoning/Razonamiento deductivo. Pensamiento o explicación que parte de una afirmación o principio generales y los aplica a casos específicos.

Definite article/Artículo definido. *Ver Article.*

Denotation/Denotación. Definición de una palabra que da el diccionario.

Dependent clause/Proposición dependiente. *Ver Clause.*

Descriptive writing/Escritura descriptiva. Tipo de escritura que da detalles sensoriales para comunicar una impresión predominante de un escenario, persona, animal, etcétera.

Desktop publishing/Edición por computadora. Uso de programas de computadora para formar un documento con texto escrito, gráficas y/o imágenes.

Dialect/Dialecto. Variedad de lenguaje hablado que usa un grupo particular. Un dialecto puede ser regional (de un lugar) o étnico (de un grupo cultural).

Dialogue/Diálogo. Conversación entre personajes en un cuento, obra o novela.

Diction/Dicción. Palabras que escoge un escritor y cómo las utiliza en frases, oraciones o versos.

Documentation/Documentación. Identificación de las fuentes que se emplean para escribir un documento u otros textos informativos; generalmente se ponen como notas al pie, al final del texto o entre paréntesis.

Drafting/Borrador. Paso del proceso de escritura; transformación de ideas, palabras y frases a oraciones y párrafos.

E

Editing/Edición. Paso del proceso de escritura en que se revisa que el borrador corregido tenga un lenguaje estándar, una estructura sintáctica variada y la elección adecuada de palabras.

Editorial/Editorial. Artículo en un periódico u otro medio que expresa las ideas personales y la opinión del escritor.

Either-or reasoning/Razonamiento excluyente. Falacia lógica que limita las posibilidades a dos alternativas opuestas sin tomar en cuenta otras posibilidades válidas.

Elaboration/Elaboración. Sustento o desarrollo de una idea principal con hechos, estadísticas, detalles sensoriales, incidentes, anécdotas, ejemplos o citas.

Ellipsis/Puntos suspensivos. Signo de puntuación que consiste en dejar tres puntos con espacios iguales para indicar que se están suprimiendo una o varias palabras.

E-mail/Correo electrónico. Abreviatura de correo electrónico; mensajes, generalmente textos, que se envían por computadora.

Emphatic form/Forma enfática. *Ver Verb tense.*

Essential clause/Proposición esencial. Proposición subordinada que no puede omitirse sin cambiar el significado de una oración.

Evaluation/Evaluación. Juicio sobre las fallas y los aciertos de un texto en borrador en cuanto a contenido, organización y estilo.

Evidence/Evidencia. Datos o ejemplos de fuentes confiables que sirven para sustentar afirmaciones escritas o habladas.

Exclamatory sentence/Oración exclamativa. Oración que expresa una emoción fuerte o repentina.

Explanatory writing/Texto explicativo. *Ver Descriptive text.*

Expository writing/Texto descriptivo. Tipo de escritura que informa al público presentando información y explicando conceptos e ideas; también llamada escritura informativa o explicativa.

Expressive writing/Texto expresivo. Texto que realza y transmite los sentimientos del escritor.

F

Fact/Hecho. Información que puede comprobarse a partir de la experiencia directa o de una fuente reconocida.

Feedback/Retroalimentación. Respuesta del escucha o lector al mensaje de un hablante o escritor.

Fiction/Ficción. Literatura donde las situaciones y los personajes son inventados por el escritor.

Figurative language/Lenguaje figurado. Palabras usadas con un efecto descriptivo que expresa una verdad más allá del nivel literal. Los tropos, como el símil, la metáfora y la personificación, son ejemplos de lenguaje figurado.

Foreshadowing/Presagio. Pistas o claves que utiliza un autor para advertir a los lectores de los acontecimientos que ocurrirán más adelante en la narración.

Formal language/Lenguaje formal. Lenguaje que utiliza una gramática correcta y omite contracciones y expresiones coloquiales. Es adecuado para textos de no ficción, que no son de carácter personal.

Freewriting/Escritura libre. Búsqueda de ideas escribiendo durante un tiempo determinado, sin detenerse ni limitar el flujo de ideas.

Future tense/Tiempo futuro. *Ver Verb tense.*

G

Generalization/Generalización. Afirmación que presenta una conclusión acerca de un tema sin entrar en detalles específicos.

Genre/Género. Clasificación literaria o de otro medio. Los principales géneros literarios son la prosa, la poesía y el drama. Cada uno se divide en subgéneros.

Gerund/Gerundio. Verboide que termina en *-ing* y se usa como nombre (en inglés).

Glittering generality/Generalización deslumbrante. Afirmación atractiva sin pruebas suficientes.

Graphic organizer/Organizador gráfico. Manera visual de organizar la información, como el agrupamiento, las tablas, las gráficas, las redes y los árboles de ideas.

H

Home page/Página principal. Página por medio de la cual un usuario entra normalmente a un sitio de Web. Por lo general, explica el sitio, resume el contenido y proporciona vínculos con otros sitios.

Hyperlink/Hipervínculo. Oraciones o palabras sombreadas o subrayadas en una página en red que al activarse con un clic conectan al usuario con otra parte de la página o con otra página de la red.

Hypertext/Hipertexto. Vínculos en algunos textos que con el clic del ratón el usuario llega a otro documento o a una sección distinta del mismo documento.

I

Idea map/Mapa de ideas. *Ver Cluster.*

Idiom/Modismo. Palabra o frase cuyo significado es diferente del significado estándar o de diccionario. (*Hacer la vista gorda* es un modismo que significa "pasar por alto".)

Imagery/Imaginería. Lenguaje que describe impresiones sensoriales para que el lector de un texto literario pueda ver, oír, sentir, oler y gustar las escenas descritas.

Imperative sentence/Oración imperativa. Oración que exige u ordena algo.

Independent clause/Proposición independiente. *Ver Clause.*

Inductive reasoning/Razonamiento inductivo. Pensamiento o explicación que parte de varios ejemplos para llegar a una afirmación general.

Infinitive/Infinitivo. Verboide que comienza con la palabra *to* (en español termina en *-ar*, *-er* o *-ir*). En inglés se usa como sustantivo, adjetivo o adverbio en la oración.

Informative writing/Texto informativo. *Ver Descriptive text.*

Intensifier/Intensificador. Adverbio que refuerza un adjetivo u otro adverbio (*very* important, *quite* easily; *muy* importante, *bastante* fácil).

Interjection/Interjección. Palabra o frase que expresa emoción o exclamación. No tiene relación gramatical con las demás palabras.

Internet/Internet. Red mundial computarizada que permite comunicarse electrónicamente con cualquier computadora de la red para buscar información social, comercial, de investigación y de otro tipo.

Interpretation/Interpretación. Explicación del significado de un texto, de una representación visual o de cualquier otro tipo de comunicación.

Interrogative sentence/Oración interrogativa. Oración que hace una pregunta.

Interview/Entrevista. Diálogo a base de preguntas y respuestas cuyo propósito es obtener información actualizada o de expertos.

Intransitive verb/Verbo intransitivo. *Ver Verb.*

Introduction/Introducción. Sección inicial de un texto en la que el escritor identifica el tema y da la idea general de lo que contendrá el cuerpo del mismo.

Inverted order/Orden invertido. Colocación del predicado antes del sujeto. En la mayoría de las oraciones en inglés, el sujeto va antes del predicado.

Irregular verb/Verbo irregular. *Ver Verb tense.*

J-L

Jargon/Jerga. Terminología peculiar de una profesión, comercio u otro grupo de personas.

Journal/Diario. Libreta personal en la que con

toda libertad se anotan ideas, pensamientos y experiencias.

Learning log/Registro de aprendizaje. Diario para aclarar ideas sobre conceptos tratados en varias clases.

Lexicon/Léxico. Diccionario.

Listing/Lista. Técnica para generar ideas a partir de las cuales se escribe un texto.

Literary analysis/Análisis literario. Examen de las diferentes partes de una obra literaria a fin de evaluarla.

Logical fallacy/Falacia lógica. Error de razonamiento que se encuentra con frecuencia en publicidad o en escritos persuasivos. *Ver Glittering generality; Either or reasoning.*

M

Main clause/Proposición principal. *Ver Clause.*

Main idea/Idea principal. *Ver Thesis statement.*

Media/Medios. Formas de comunicación usadas para llegar a un público. Los periódicos, la radio, la televisión y la Internet llegan a públicos muy grandes, por lo que se conocen como medios de comunicación masiva.

Memoir/Memoria. Tipo de narrativa de no ficción que presenta el relato de un hecho o período de la historia, resaltando la experiencia personal del narrador.

Metaphor/Metáfora. Tropo que compara dos cosas aparentemente distintas sin usar las palabras *like* o *as* (*como*). (*Él es una roca.*)

Mood/Atmósfera. Sentimiento o ambiente de un texto escrito.

Multimedia presentation/Presentación multimedia. Uso de una variedad de medios como video, sonido, texto escrito y artes visuales para presentar ideas e información.

N

Narrative writing/Narrativa. Tipo de escritura que narra sucesos o acciones que cambian con el paso del tiempo; por lo general tiene personajes, escenario y trama.

Nominative pronoun/Pronombre nominativo. *Ver Pronoun case.*

Nonessential clause/Proposición no esencial. Proposición que agrega información pero que no es absolutamente necesaria para expresar el significado de la oración.

Nonfiction/No ficción. Literatura que trata sobre personas, sucesos y experiencias reales.

Nonrestrictive clause/Proposición no restrictiva. *Ver Nonessential clause.*

Noun/Nombre (o sustantivo). Palabra que nombra a una persona, lugar, cosa, o a una idea, cualidad o característica.

    Abstract noun/Nombre abstracto. Nombra una idea, una cualidad o una característica.

    Collective noun/Nombre colectivo. Nombra un grupo de personas o cosas.

    Common noun/Nombre común. Nombra a cualquier persona, lugar, cosa o idea.

    Proper noun/Nombre propio. Nombra a una persona, lugar, cosa o idea específica.

Noun clause/Proposición nominal Proposición dependiente que se usa como nombre.

Number/Número. Forma del nombre, pronombre o verbo que indica si se refiere a uno (**singular**) o a más de uno (**plural**).

O

Objective pronoun/Pronombre personal de complemento directo o indirecto. *Ver Pronoun case.*

Onomatopoeia/Onomatopeya. Palabra o frase que imita o sugiere el sonido que describe (*rattle, boom*; en español: *pum, zas*).

Opinion/Opinión. Creencia o actitud; no puede comprobarse si es falsa o verdadera.

Oral tradition/Tradición oral. Literatura que se transmite de boca en boca de una generación a otra. Puede representar los valores culturales de un pueblo.

Order of importance/Orden de importancia. Forma de acomodar los detalles en un párrafo o en otro texto escrito según su importancia.

Organization/Organización. Sistema para ordenar las ideas.

Outline/Esquema. Organización sistemática de ideas principales y secundarias con números romanos, letras y números arábigos para una presentación oral o escrita.

P

Paragraph/Párrafo. Una unidad de texto que consta de oraciones relacionadas.

Parallelism/Paralelismo. Uso de una serie de palabras, frases y oraciones que tienen una forma gramatical similar.

Paraphrase/Parafrasear. Reformulación de un pasaje en palabras diferentes que conservan el significado, el tono y la longitud general del original.

Parenthetical documentation/Documentación parentética. Referencia específica a la fuente de la información que se pone entre paréntesis directamente después de ésta.

Participle/Participio. Verboide que se usa como adjetivo. El participio presente siempre termina en *-ing* y el participio pasado por lo general termina en *-ed*.

Passive voice/Voz pasiva. Forma verbal usada cuando el sujeto de una oración recibe la acción del verbo.

Peer response/Respuesta de compañeros. Sugerencias y comentarios que dan los compañeros de clase sobre un texto escrito u otro tipo de presentación.

Personal writing/Escritura personal. Texto que expresa los pensamientos y sentimientos del autor.

Personification/Personificación. Tropo que da cualidades humanas a un animal, objeto o idea.

Perspective/Perspectiva. *Ver Point of view.*

Persuasive writing/Texto persuasivo. Tipo de escritura, generalmente de no ficción, encaminado a llevar al lector a aceptar el punto de vista del escritor mediante la lógica, la emoción, la súplica o la sugestión.

Phrase/Frase. Grupo de palabras que funcionan como unidad en una oración.

> **Prepositional phrase/ Frase preposicional.** Consta de una preposición, su objeto y cualquier modificador del objeto; puede funcionar como adjetivo o adverbio.
>
> **Verb phrase/ Frase verbal.** Consta de uno o más **verbos auxiliares** (*auxiliary verbs*) seguidos del verbo principal (*main verb*).

Plagiarism/Plagio. Presentación deshonesta de palabras o ideas ajenas como si fueran propias.

Plot/Trama. Serie de sucesos en secuencia en un cuento, novela u obra de teatro.

Poetry/Poesía. Forma de expresión literaria compuesta por versos. La poesía tradicional contiene un lenguaje emotivo e imaginativo y un ritmo regular.

Point of view/Punto de vista. Relación del narrador con la historia. La mayoría de las obras están escritas en primera persona, tercera persona, o tercera persona omnisciente.

Portfolio/Portafolio. Colección de obras creativas que representan el logro de un artista o escritor.

Positive degree/Grado positivo. *Ver Adjective.*

Possessive pronoun/Pronombre posesivo. *Ver Pronoun case.*

Predicate/Predicado. Verbo o frase verbal y sus modificadores que hacen una afirmación esencial sobre el sujeto de la oración.

Preposition/Preposición. Palabra que muestra la relación de un nombre o pronombre con otra palabra en la oración.

Presenting/Presentación. Último paso del proceso de escritura que implica compartir con otros lo que se ha escrito.

Prewriting/Preescritura. Primer paso del proceso de escritura: decidir sobre qué se va a escribir, reunir ideas y detalles, y elaborar un plan para presentar las ideas; usa estrategias como lluvia de ideas, organizadores gráficos, notas y registros.

Prior knowledge/Conocimiento previo. Hechos, ideas y experiencias que un escritor, lector u observador lleva a una nueva actividad.

Progressive form/Durativo. *Ver Verb tense.*

Pronoun/Pronombre. Palabra que va en lugar del nombre; grupo de palabras que funcionan como un nombre u otro pronombre. La palabra o grupo de palabras a que se refiere un pronombre se llama **antecedente** (*antecedent*).

Pronoun case/Caso del pronombre. Forma del pronombre que se determina por su uso en la oración. El pronombre está en caso **nominativo** (*nominative case*), en caso **acusativo** y **dativo** (*objective case*) y en caso **posesivo**★ (*possessive case*), dependiendo de su función en la oración. *Ver también Case.*

Proofreading/Corrección de pruebas. Último paso del proceso editorial en que se revisa el texto en busca de errores tipográficos y de otra naturaleza.

Propaganda/Propaganda. Información encaminada a influir en los pensamientos o acciones; en general es de naturaleza política y puede distorsionar la verdad.

Prose/Prosa. Escritura que se diferencia de la poesía por su similitud con la dicción y los ritmos del lenguaje común.

Publishing/Publicación. Presentación de una obra escrita terminada mediante el uso de la tecnología, para darla a conocer a un público amplio.

Purpose/Finalidad. Objetivo de la escritura: expresar, descubrir, registrar, desarrollar o reflexionar sobre ideas, resolver problemas, entretener, influir, informar o describir.

R

Regular verb/Verbo regular. *Ver Verb tense.*

Representation/Representación. Forma en que se presenta información o ideas al público.

Research/Investigación. Proceso de localizar información sobre un tema.

Restrictive clause/Proposición restrictiva. *Ver Essential clause.*

Review/Reseña. Análisis e interpretación de un tema presentado por lo general a través de los medios de comunicación masiva.

Revising/Revisión. Paso del proceso de escritura en que el autor repasa el borrador, cambia el contenido, la organización y el estilo para mejorar el texto. Las técnicas de revisión son agregar, elaborar, eliminar, combinar y reacomodar el texto.

Root/Raíz. Parte de una palabra que contiene el significado principal.

Run-on sentence/Oración mal puntuada. Dos o más oraciones o proposiciones seguidas, cuyo significado es confuso debido a su inadecuada puntuación.

S

Sensory details/Detalles sensoriales. Lenguaje que apela a los sentidos; los detalles sensoriales son elementos importantes de la escritura descriptiva, sobre todo en la poesía.

Sentence/Oración. Grupo de palabras que expresa un pensamiento completo. Cada oración tiene **sujeto** (*subject*) y **predicado** (*predicate*). Las oraciones se clasifican según su función o según su estructura:

    Simple sentence/Oración simple. Consta de una sola proposición principal y no tiene proposiciones subordinadas.
    Compound sentence/Oración compuesta. Tiene dos o más proposiciones principales.
    Complex sentence/Oración compleja. Formada por una proposición principal y una o más proposiciones subordinadas.
    Compound-complex sentence/Oración compuesta-compleja. Consta de dos o más proposiciones principales y por lo menos una proposición subordinada. *Ver también Declarative sentence; Exclamatory sentence; Imperative sentence; Interrogative sentence.*

Sentence variety/Variedad de oraciones. Uso de diferentes tipos de oraciones para agregar interés al texto.

Setting/Escenario. Tiempo y lugar en que ocurren los sucesos de un cuento, novela u obra de teatro.

Simile/Símil. Tropo que compara dos cosas esencialmente distintas, usando las palabras *like* o *as* (*como*).

Spatial order/Orden espacial. Forma de presentar los detalles de un escenario según su ubicación: de izquierda a derecha o de arriba hacia abajo.

Standard English/Inglés estándar. La forma más ampliamente usada y aceptada del idioma inglés.

Style/Estilo. Forma en que un escritor elige y organiza las palabras y oraciones.

Subordinate clause/Proposición subordinada. *Ver Clause.*

Subordinating conjunction/Conjunción subordinante. *Ver Conjunction.*

Summary/Resumen. Breve explicación de la idea principal de una composición.

Superlative degree/Grado superlativo. *Ver Adjective; Adverb.*

Supporting evidence/Sustento. *Ver Evidence.*

Suspense/Suspenso. Recurso literario que genera interés y emoción para llegar al clímax o desenlace de una historia. Un escritor crea suspenso al proporcionar pistas sobre el desenlace pero sin revelar demasiada información.

Symbol/Símbolo. Objeto, persona, lugar o experiencia que representa algo más, por lo general, abstracto.

T

Tense/Tiempo. *Ver Verb tense.*

Theme/Tema. Idea o mensaje principal de una obra escrita.

Thesis statement/Exposición de tesis. Exposición de la idea principal o finalidad de una obra en una o dos oraciones.

Time order/Orden temporal. Organización de detalles en un texto escrito según el momento en que ocurrieron.

Tone/Tono. Reflejo de la actitud del escritor o hablante hacia un sujeto.

Topic sentence/Oración temática. Oración que expresa la idea principal de un párrafo.

Transition/Transición. Palabra o frase de enlace que aclara las relaciones entre los detalles, oraciones o párrafos.

U-V

Unity/Unidad. Integridad de un párrafo o composición; coherencia entre todas las oraciones o párrafos para expresar o sustentar una idea principal.

URL/URL. Forma estándar de una dirección de Internet. (Son iniciales de *Uniform Resource Locator.*)

Venn diagram/Diagrama de Venn. Representación visual que consta de dos círculos que se traslapan, usado para comparar dos cosas con características comunes y diferentes.

Verb/Verbo. Palabra que expresa acción o estado y que es necesaria para hacer una afirmación.

Verbal/Verboide. Forma del verbo que funciona como nombre, adjetivo o adverbio en la oración. Los verboides son: participio (*participles*), gerundio (*gerunds*) e infinitivo (*infinitives*). Ver Gerund; Infinitive; Participle.

Verb phrase/Frase verbal. *Ver Phrase.*

Verb tense/Tiempo verbal. El tiempo de un verbo indica cuándo ocurre la acción.
    Present tense/Presente. Indica una acción que sucede regularmente.
    Past tense/Pasado. Indica una acción que ya sucedió.
    Future tense/Futuro. Indica una acción que va a suceder.

En inglés todos los tiempos verbales están formados por las cuatro partes principales del verbo: base derivativa (*base form*) (*swim, nadar*), participio presente (*present participle*) (*swimming, nadando*), pretérito simple (*simple past form*) (*swam, nadó*) y participio pasado (*past participle*) (*swum, nadado*).

Un **verbo regular** (*regular verb*) forma su pretérito simple y su participio pasado agregando la terminación -*ed* al infinitivo. Los verbos que forman su pretérito y participio pasado de otra forma se llaman **verbos irregulares** (*irregular verbs*). Además de los tiempos presente, pasado y futuro hay tres tiempos perfectos: presente perfecto (*present perfect*), pretérito perfecto (*past perfect*) y futuro perfecto (*future perfect*).

Cada uno de los seis tiempos tiene una forma **durativa** (*progressive form*) que expresa acción continua.

    Emphatic form/Forma enfática. Agrega fuerza especial, o énfasis, al tiempo presente o pasado de un verbo. Para la forma enfática se usa *do, does*, o *did* con el infinitivo.

Voice/Voz. Uso del lenguaje que transmite al lector la personalidad del escritor o narrador. La estructura de la oración, la elección de las palabras y el tono son elementos que comunican la voz.

W

Web site/Sitio Web. Sitio de World Wide Web que puede ser alcanzado mediante vínculos o una dirección Web o URL. *Ver también* URL; *World Wide Web.*

Word processing/Procesador de palabras. Programa de computadora para escribir y editar un texto.

World Wide Web/World Wide Web. Sistema global que usa Internet y permite a los usuarios crear, vincularse y entrar a campos de información. *Ver también Internet.*

Writing process/Proceso de escritura. Serie de pasos o etapas por los que atraviesa un escritor para desarrollar sus ideas y comunicarlas.

*Este término o explicación solamente se aplica a la gramática inglesa.

INDEX

A

A, an, 464, 687
A lot, alot, 687
Abbreviations, 356, 765–767
  addresses, 765
  capitalization of, 765
  organizations and
    companies, 356, 765
  punctuating, 765–767
  states, 766
  time of day, 765
  titles used with name, 767
  units of measure, 767
  years, 765
Abstract, 431–432
Abstract nouns, 442, 923
Accept, except, 687
Accuracy, 431
Acronyms, 784, 795, 796
Action verbs, 198, 453, 505
Active listening, 434, 885–887, 891
Active voice, of verbs, 596, 918
Addresses
  commas in, 746
  numerals in, 769
Adjective clauses, 545–547, 918
  commas with, 409, 741
  diagraming, 577
Adjectives, 461–466, 918
  articles as, 464
  commas in series, 740
  comparative form of, 461, 659–660, 918
  compound, 763
  coordinate, 740
  definition of, 461
  diagraming, 571
  fractions used as, 763
  infinitives as, 526, 576
  as object complement, 506
  participles as, 523
  position in sentence, 461
  possessive nouns as, 461
  predicate, 507, 573
  prepositional phrases as, 519
  proper, 465, 720
  using specific, 146, 147
  verbals as, 523, 576
Adverb clauses, 548, 918
  commas with, 741–743
  diagraming, 578
  elliptical, 637
Adverbs, 918
  commas with, 735, 743
  comparing, 469, 659–660, 918
  conjunctive, 479, 735, 743
  definition of, 467
  diagraming, 571
  infinitives, 526, 576
  negative words as, 468
  prepositional phrases as, 519
  using specific, 146, 147
  verbals as, 523, 526, 576
Affect, effect, 687, 834
Affixes. *See* Prefixes; Suffixes
Agreement. *See* Amount, nouns of;
  Collective nouns; Compound
    subject; Indefinite pronouns;
    Intervening expressions;
    Nouns, special; Number;
    Predicate nominatives;
    Pronoun-antecedent agreement; Subject-verb agreement; Titles of works; Verbs
Ain't, 688
All ready, already, 688
All right, alright, 688
All the farther, all the faster, 688
All together, altogether, 688, 834
Allusion, 918
Ambiguous pronoun reference, avoiding, 646
Among, between, 689
Amount, nouns of, 395, 615
Amount, number, 688
Analogies, 854–855
Analysis, 918
Analyzing messages, 886
And, in compounds, 394, 616–617
Anecdotes, 192–195, 918
  literature model for, 192
  in narrative writing, 194, 195
Antecedents, agreement with pronouns, 396–397, 640–647, 925
  and pronoun reference, 645–646
Antithetical phrases, 743
Antonyms, in thesaurus, 817
Apostrophes
  in contractions, 761
  correcting, 407–408
  with possessives, 759–760
  with special plurals, 761
Appendix, 431
Applications, 423–424
Appositives and Appositive
  phrases, 521–522, 918
  commas to set off nonessential, 410, 742
  diagraming, 574
  essential/nonessential, 410, 521, 742
  pronouns with and as, 635
Argument, logical, 288–291, 918
Art, list of works herein.
    See xxvii
Articles
  definite, 464, 918
  indefinite, 464, 918
  in titles of works, 717, 757
As, like, 695
As, pronouns after, 637
Audience, 918
  addressing in prewriting, 70, 234, 258
  considering needs of, 71, 90, 306, 313–314
  getting attention of, 889
  identifying, 68–71, 258, 306, 313–314, 435, 888
  of media message, 894–895, 899–901, 903–904
  reaching out to, 258, 306, 313–314
Audio-visual materials, 800
Autobiography, 20–23, 36–39
  definition of, 21
  developing outline for, 23
  drafting, 38
  editing, 39
  finding material for, 21, 37
  literature model for, 40–50
  presenting material in, 22, 39

prewriting, 21, 37
revising, 38
writing, 20, 23
See also Biography
Auxiliary verbs, 457, 927
Awards, capitalizing, 715

B

Bad, badly, 666
Bar graphs, 426, 844, 914
Base words, 581, 582
   See also Word roots
Be. See Linking verbs; Helping verbs; Passive voice
Being as, being that, 688
Beside, besides, 689
Between, among, 689
Bias, 328, 918
   and opposing arguments, 298
   overcoming attitudes, 313
   See also Sexist language
Bible
   capitalization, 722
   references to, 734
Bibliography, 918
   working, 326
   See also Works-cited list
Bibliography cards, 326–327
Biography, 32–35
   write a response to a, 35
   See also Autobiography
Biography section, in dictionary, 816
Blends, 784, 795, 796
Body, in writing, 230, 263, 919
Bookmarks, 911, 919
Borrow, lend, loan, 690
Borrowed words, 784, 786, 787, 790, 792
Brainstorming, 21, 25, 99, 105, 147, 149, 155, 187, 199, 202, 209, 233, 267, 272, 313, 902, 918
Bridges, capitalizing names of, 715
Bring, take, 690
Buildings, capitalizing, 715
Business letters, 413–420, 734
   block style, 414
   modified block style, 415
   of apology, 419
   of complaint, 418
   of opinion, 420
   of request, 417
   parts of, 415–416

C

Calendar items, capitalizing names of, 716
Call numbers, 803
Can, may, 690
Can't hardly, can't scarcely, 690
Capitalization
   of abbreviations, 765–767
   of articles in titles of works, 717
   of compass points, 716
   of direct quotations, 711
   of geographical names, 715
   of historical events and periods, 716
   names of family members, 713
   names of persons, 713
   names of school courses, 717
   names of ships, 716
   of nationalities, 714
   of proper adjectives, 465, 720–723
   of proper nouns, 179, 443, 713–719, 729
   of sentences, 711–712, 725
   summary of capitalization rules, 722
   titles of literary works, 717
   titles of persons, 713
   of trade names, 715
   in writing, 729
Card catalog, 799
Case, 919
   forms of personal pronouns. *See* Personal Pronouns
Cause-and-effect diagram, 241
Cause-and-effect writing, 240–243, 281
   as context clue, 821
   eliminating errors in, 297
   literature model in, 240
   organization, 84, 86, 234, 242, 919
   revising, 242–243
   thesis statement in, 241
   transitions for, 89, 242
CD-ROMs, 911
Characterization, 106, 152–159, 919
Characters, 106, 919
   in descriptive writing, 152–155, 156–159
   in expository writing, 259
   in narratives, 180, 183
Charts, 844, 914
Chat rooms, 909

Chicago Manual of Style, The, 431
Chronological order, 84, 182, 355, 919
Circle graph, 427
Circulation desk, 799
Citing sources. *See* Works-cited list
Civics, writing topics in, 51, 68, 103, 299
Clarity, 431, 919
Classification in expository writing, 244–247, 272
   definition of, 244–245
   drafting, 245, 246
   literature model in, 244
   prewriting, 245
   revising, 246
Classroom tests. *See* Tests
Clauses, 919
   adjective, 408, 545–547, 577, 741, 918
   adverb, 548–549, 578, 744, 918
   definition of, 539, 919
   dependent, 919
   diagraming, 577–579
   elliptical, 548, 637
   essential/nonessential, 409, 545, 741, 919
   independent, 919
   main, 539, 919
   noun, 550, 579
   punctuation of, 409, 545, 548, 741, 744
   subordinate, 540, 638–639, 919
Cliché, 919
Climax, 919
   in short story. *See* Narrative Writing, conflict in
Closing of letter. See Letter writing
Clustering, 14, 17, 51, 149, 919
Coherence, 919
   in paragraphs, 88–91, 94
Cohesive writing, 919
Collaboration, 908, 919
   writing, 122, 434–435
Collaborative learning. *See* Cooperative Learning
Collecting, in prewriting, 63
Collective nouns, 444, 924
   and subject-verb agreement, 393, 614–615
Colloquialism, 920
Colons
   in biblical references, 734

Index   **941**

in expressions of time, 734
to introduce, 733, 820
parentheses with, 751
quotation marks with, 733
before quotations, 733
after salutation of business letter, 414, 415, 734
Combining Sentences. *See* Sentence combining
Comma fault, 747
Comma splice, 390, 555, 747
Commands, 731
Commas
with addresses, 746
with adjective clauses, 409, 741
with adverb clauses, 548, 744
with antithetical phrases, 743
to avoid confusion, 738
in compound sentences, 390–391, 541, 738
with conjunctive adverbs, 743
and coordinate adjectives, 740
with coordinating conjunctions, 390–391, 541, 555, 747
with geographical terms, 746
with interjections, 410, 743
in letter writing, 416, 747
misuse of, 747
with nonessential appositives, 410, 741
with nonessential phrases, 409, 545, 741
parentheses with, 751
with parenthetical expressions, 410, 743
after participial phrases, 409, 744
with parts of reference, 746
with prepositional phrases, 744
quotation marks with, 755
and run-on sentences, 555
versus semicolons, 736
in series, 410, 739, 740
with states, 746
with tag questions, 746
with titles of people, 746
with words or names in direct address, 746
Common noun, 443, 924
Communication. *See* Speaking; Listening; Oral presentations; Creative writing; Business letters

Community forums, for presenting, 101
Comparative form of modifiers, 461, 469, 659–661, 918, 920
Compare-and-contrast development, 248–251, 920
Compare-and-contrast essay, 248–251, 281
drafting, 249, 269
editing, 250
literature model for, 248
for a movie review, 310
prewriting, 251, 310
transitions for, 89
of two myths, 268–271
Comparison
of adjectives, 461, 463, 659–660, 918
of adverbs, 469, 659–660, 918
as context clue, 821
double, 663
incomplete, 665
irregular, 661
Comparison frame, 270
in comparing movies, 310
in comparing myths, 270, 271
Compass points, capitalizing, 716
Complements, 504–509, 920
definition of, 504, 920
direct objects, 504, 572
indirect objects, 505, 572
object complements, 506, 572
subject complements, 507, 573
Complete predicate, 496
Complete subject, 496
Complex sentence, 543, 926
diagraming, 577–579
Compound adjectives, hyphens in, 763
Compound-complex sentence, 543, 926
Compound direct object, 504
Compound indirect object, 505
Compound nouns, forming possessive of, 760
Compound numbers, 763
Compound object, personal pronouns in, 633
Compound predicate, 498, 499, 541
Compound prepositions, 473
Compound sentences, 541, 926
commas in, 390, 391, 541, 555, 735, 738

coordinating conjunctions in, 390, 391, 475, 541, 735, 738, 747
diagraming, 577
semicolon to join, 735
Compound subject, 498, 541
diagraming, 572
personal pronoun as, 633
and subject-verb agreement, 394, 616–617
Compound verbs. *See* Compound predicate
Compounds, forming new words, 784, 795, 796
Computer catalog, 763, 799, 801–802
Computers, 906–917
bookmarks, 911
CD-ROMs, 911
chat rooms, 909
cut and paste, 913
design elements, 912
drawing, 913
DVDs, 911
e-mail, 909
favorites, 911
graphics, 913–914
hardware, 915
icons, 913
Internet, 909–911
keywords, 911
menus, 912
multimedia, 915–917
newsgroups, 910
search commands, 911
search engines, 910
software, 914, 915
subject directories, 910
tool bars, 912–913
Web sites, 909, 911
word processing software, 906–908, 912–914
See also Using Computers; Word processing
Conceptual map, 920
See also Graphic organizers
Conclusions, 920
in editorials, 306
in essay tests, 265
in expository writing, 230, 238, 242
in feature articles, 260
in research papers, 337, 355
writing, 337
Concrete nouns, 442
Conflict, 920

942 Index

external, 185
  in narrative writing, 180, 182, 184–187, 208–211, 221
  internal, 185
Conjugation of verbs. *See* Verbs: irregular, regular, tenses of
Conjunctions, 920
  coordinating, 390–391, 475, 541, 555, 735, 738, 921
  correlative, 476, 478, 572, 920
  definition of, 475, 920
  subordinating, 477, 540, 548, 920
Conjunctive adverbs, 479, 735, 920
  punctuation with, 735, 743
Connotations, of words, 144–147, 302, 303, 920
Consistency, 431
Constructive criticism, 920
Context, 920
Context clues
  cause-and-effect as, 821
  comparison as, 821
  contrast as, 821
  definition as, 821
  example as, 821
  in learning vocabulary, 820–822
Contractions, 408, 468, 692, 761
Contrast, as context clue, 821
Cooperative Learning, 35, 67, 71, 79, 99, 143, 147, 151, 183, 195, 199, 207, 243, 247, 261, 267, 271, 295, 307
Coordinate adjectives, 740
Coordinating conjunction, 390, 391, 475, 541, 555, 735, 747, 920
Correlative conjunctions, 476, 478, 920
  diagraming, 572
Could of, might of, must of, should of, would of, 690
Creative writing, 24–27, 152–155, 180–183, 196–199, 200–203
Credibility, 920
Critical analysis, 920
  in active listening, 886
  of biography, 32–35
  of character descriptions, 156–159
  characters in, 106
  comparing and contrasting myths in, 268–271
  explaining theme in, 104–107
  of movie, 284–287, 308–311
  plot in, 106
  in reader-response journal, 28–31
  sentence combining in, 380–384
  setting in, 106
Critical listening, 885–887
Critical thinking
  analyzing cause and effect, 240–241
  analyzing characters, 156–159
  analyzing and drawing conclusions about context clues, 820–822
  analyzing and drawing conclusions about words, 823–826
  classifying ideas, 244–245
  constructing a logical argument, 288–290, 305–306
  critical listening, 885–887
  evaluating a logical argument, 296–298
  evaluating evidence, 293–294
  organizing ideas, 76–77
  in writing a topic sentence/thesis statement, 76–77, 332–333
Cross-curricular writing topics.
  in art, 27, 87, 91, 107, 143, 187, 195, 231, 251, 291
  in broadcast journalism, 199
  in civics, 51, 321
  in geography, 173
  in government, 19
  in health, 239
  in history, 155, 191
  in literature, 221, 311
  in media studies, 203
  in music, 151, 303
  in science, 83, 235, 251, 267
  in social studies, 11, 15, 95, 120, 281
  in spelling, 35, 243
Cross-references, in dictionaries, 815
Culture. *See* Myths

D

Dangling modifiers, 405, 670
Dashes
  for emphasis, 749
  to signal change, 749
Dates
  abbreviations for, 765
  commas in, 746
  numerals for, 769
Declarative sentences, 552, 731, 920
Deconstructing, 920
  media, 899–901
Deductive reasoning, 920
Definite article, 464, 918
Definitions
  as context clues, 821
  in dictionary, 813–815
  in expository writing, 230, 233
Demonstrative pronouns, 449
  as adjectives, 461
Denotation, 920
Dependent clauses, 919
  See also subordinate clauses
Descriptive writing, 134–173, 920
  analysis of character descriptions, 156–159
  connotation of words in, 144–147, 173
  creating an overall impression in, 139–141, 173
  describing an imaginary person in, 152–155, 173
  describing an imaginary place in, 147, 148–150, 173
  descriptive language in, 144–147, 173
  drafting, 135, 143, 145, 161–162
  editing, 136, 154, 163
  explaining theme in, 104–107
  literature models, 138–139, 142, 144, 148, 153, 164–171
  mood in, 139
  portfolio in, 173
  presenting, 157, 163, 173
  prewriting, 135, 141, 149, 161
  revising, 136, 139–140, 146, 150, 158, 162
  sentence combining in, 364–365
  spatial organization in, 141
  topic sentence in, 140–141
  transitions in, 142
Design, elements of, 894–896, 912–914
Desktop publishing, 23, 425, 908, 912–914, 920
Details
  in a character description, 157
  checking for, in revising, 140, 150, 158
  creating mood with, 150
  in creating suspense, 202
  in expository writing, 226, 232–235

Index **943**

in a feature article, 260, 261
in a news story, 252
ordering, 78, 84–87, 235. *See also* Order of importance; Organization
in a personal essay, 18
in a screen play, 135
spatial organization, 85
supporting, 78, 140, 232–235
Dewey decimal system, 802–803
Diagraming sentences, 571–579
Diagrams
in planning classification, 244
See also Graphic organizers
Dialect, 921
Dialogue, 921
developing, 189–190
editing, 190
in narratives, 188–191, 219
prewriting, 190
punctuation of. *See* Quotation marks
uses of, 188
writing, 190, 191
Diction, 921
Dictionary
biography section in, 816
cross-references in, 815
geography section in, 816
guide words in, 812–813
homographs in, 814
main entries, 813–814
organization of entries in, 812–813
syllabication in, 814
synonyms in, 814
usage information in, 815
using, 812–816, 832
Different from, different than, 690
Direct address, commas to set off words or names in, 746
Direct characterization, 919
Direct objects, 504
diagraming, 572
noun clause as, 550, 579
Direct quotations, capitalization of. *See* Capitalization
punctuation. *See* Quotation marks
Documentation, 338–343, 921
finding, 327–329
parenthetical, 339, 350–355, 924
See also Works-cited list
Documents, capitalizing names of, 715

Doesn't, don't, 692
Double comparisons, 663
Double negatives, 668
Drafting, 58, 76–91, 921
in classification, 245
coherent paragraphs in, 88–90, 91
in descriptive writing, 135, 143, 145, 161–162
in expository writing, 226, 241, 244, 248, 262, 264, 269, 270, 273–274
in feature articles, 56, 259–260
in formal speeches, 889
in narrative writing, 178, 185, 191, 202, 209–210
ordering details in, 78, 84–87
in personal writing, 6, 38
in persuasive writing, 286, 287, 313–314
in a research paper, 332, 334–337
revising, 136
in suspense writing, 202
TIME Facing the Blank Page, 122, 126–127
topic sentence in, 78
turning prewriting into a paragraph, 76–78, 79
unified paragraphs in, 80–83
using word processing, 907
in the writing process, 56, 110
Drawing conclusions. *See* Critical thinking
DVDs, 911
Dynamic character, 919

E

Each, compound subjects joined by, 394–395, 617
Editing, 56, 59, 96–99, 111, 921
in comparison-contrast writing, 250
in descriptive writing, 136, 154, 163
dialogue, 189
in an essay answer, 266
in expository writing 226, 250, 253, 259, 260, 275
in feature articles, 56
labels for graphics, 253
marking draft in, 98
in narrative writing, 178, 189, 202, 205, 211
in personal writing, 6, 39, 50–51

in persuasive writing, 286, 294, 310, 315
in a research paper, 341, 348–356
for sense, 96–97, 99
in a sports narrative, 178
TIME Facing the Blank Page, 123, 130
using word processing, 907
See also Proofreading; Revising; Troubleshooter
Editorials, 304–307, 921
appealing to audience, 306
choosing an issue for, 305
literature model for, 304
summing up, 306
Effect, affect, 687, 834
Either/or thinking, 921
eliminating, 297
Elaboration, 921
Ellipsis, 351, 921
Elliptical adverb clause, 548, 637
E-mail, 422, 909, 921
Emigrate, immigrate, 692
Emphatic forms of verb, 592, 927
End marks
exclamation point, 732
period, 552, 731
question mark, 732
quotation marks and, 755
Endnotes, 339, 340
English language
acronyms in, 795, 796
borrowed words in, 784, 786, 787, 792
eponyms in, 785
euphemisms in, 794
formal versus informal, 70, 922
French words in, 789–790
history of, 783–784, 786–787, 789–790, 792–793, 795–796
Latin words in, 786
puns in, 791
Scandinavian words in, 787
slang in, 797
spoonerisms in, 788
Tom Swifties in, 791
Eponyms, 785
Eras, capitalizing names of, 716
Essay test question answers, 262–267
and clues in questions, 263
drafting, 263, 264–265
editing, 266
literature model for, 262

944 Index

organizing information for, 264
revising, 266
time management in, 265
Essays, 230. *See also* Critical analysis; Expository writing; Personal writing; Persuasive writing
Essential clauses, 545, 921
Ethnic groups, capitalizing names of, 714
Euphemisms, 794
Evaluating and Revising. *See also* Editing; Peer editing; Proofreading; Revising; Thesis statement
Evaluation, 921
Every, compound subjects joined by, 394–396, 617
Evidence, 921
assessing, in persuasive writing, 293–294
defining, in persuasive writing, 292
explaining, as claim support, 290
identifying supporting, 289
selecting, in persuasive writing, 295
Examples
as context clues, 821
as supporting details, 82
transitions for, 89
Except, accept, 687
Exclamation point, 732
to end exclamatory sentence, 732
parentheses with, 751
quotation marks with, 755
Exclamatory sentences, 732, 921
Expository writing, 224–280, 921
adding detail in, 226, 232–235
answering essay questions, 262–267
cause and effect in, 230, 234, 240–243, 281
classification in, 230, 244–247, 281
comparing and contrasting, 225, 230, 248–251, 281
comparing and contrasting myths in, 268–271
conclusion in, 238, 242, 337
definition in, 230
drafting, 226, 241, 245, 249, 263, 269, 270, 273–274, 334–337
editing, 226, 250, 253, 259, 260, 275
essay tests as, 262–267
explaining and informing in, 228–231
feature article, 256–261, 281
graphics in, 252–255, 425–429
identifying audience, 226
introduction in, 238, 242, 337
literature models in, 228, 232, 236, 240, 244, 248, 252, 257, 260, 262, 276–279
mixing strategies in, 225
nature of, 229
news articles as, 256–261
portfolio in, 281
presenting, 259, 260, 275, 348–349
prewriting, 225, 229, 233, 237, 258, 263, 264, 273, 324–333
process explanation in, 230–232, 236–239, 281
revising, 226, 229, 242, 246, 254, 259, 274, 344–347
sentence combining in, 372–375
technical writing, 431–433
varieties of, 230
Expressive writing, 921
See also Personal writing
External conflicts, 185
Eyewitness report. *See* Interview

F

Facts, 921
anecdotes based on, 192
distinguishing between opinions and, 841
getting, for news article, 72–75
as supporting details, 82
Fantasy writing, Case Study in, 134–137
Farther, further, 692
Faulty logic, eliminating, 296–297
Favorites, 911, 919
Feature articles, 256–261
Case Study in, 54–57
conclusion in, 260
details in, 260
drafting, 56, 259–260
lead in, 259, 261
literature model for, 257
prewriting, 258–259
presenting, 259
researching, 55, 258–259
revising, 56, 259
Feature-by-feature comparison, 250
in comparing and contrasting myths, 269
Feedback, 921
Fewer, less, 692
Fiction, 921
Figurative language, 921
interpreting, 25
metaphor, 25
personification, 25
simile, 25
Fill-in items on tests, 850
Film techniques, 897–898, 900
Fine art, list of works herein, *See* xxvii
Firms, capitalizing names of, 714
First-person narrator, 204, 205
First person pronouns, 446
Flashbacks, in personal essay, 22
Flat character, 919
Flow charts, 429–430, 844
Fonts, 908, 912
Footnotes, 339, 340
Foreign languages
capitalizing names of, 714
Foreign words, italics with, 757
See also Borrowed words
Foreshadowing, in suspense writing, 200, 922
Formal English. *See* English language
Formal language, 413, 922
Formal speaking, 888–890, *See also* Speaking
Formally, formerly, 834
Fractions, 763
Fragments, sentence, 388–389, 553–554
Free verse, 24–25
Freewriting, 10, 11, 13, 15, 17, 21, 27, 51, 62, 63, 67, 76, 83, 105, 107, 118, 120, 149, 181, 183, 186, 187, 189, 191, 202, 313, 922
French, words from, 789–790
Further, farther, 692
Future tense, 588, 927

Index **945**

G

Gender, pronoun-antecedent agreement in, 640, 642
Generalization, 922
Genre, 922
Geographical terms
 capitalizing, 715
 commas in, 746
Geography section, in dictionary, 816
Gerunds and Gerund phrases, 525, 527, 922
 diagraming, 575
Glittering generality, 300, 901, 922
Glossary
 of usage terms, 687–708
Goals
 in Descriptive writing, 173
 in Expository writing, 281
 in Narrative writing, 221
 in Personal writing, 51
 in Persuasive writing, 321
 in Research Paper writing, 357
 in the Writing Process, 120
Good, well, 666
Government agencies, abbreviations of, 765
Grammar, 399–779. *See also* specific topics
Grammar checker, 299, 908
Grammar items on standardized tests, 855–856
Grammar Link, 7, 11, 15, 19, 23, 27, 31, 35, 57, 61, 67, 71, 75, 79, 83, 87, 91, 95, 99, 103, 107, 137, 143, 147, 151, 155, 159, 179, 183, 187, 191, 195, 199, 203, 207, 227, 231, 235, 239, 243, 247, 251, 255, 261, 267, 271, 287, 291, 295, 299, 303, 307, 311
Graphic organizers, 82, 252–255, 844, 922
 bar graphs, 426, 844, 914
 cluster diagrams, 14, 17, 51, 845
 diagrams, 101, 245, 249, 250, 253, 264, 845
 editing labels for, 253
 flow charts, 430, 844
 graphs, 253, 425
 guidelines for making, 249
 idea map, 66, 920
 life map, 21
 maps, 253, 845-846
 positioning, 254

 revising, 254
 tables, 253, 425, 843
 text references to, 254
 time line, 82, 926
 using word processing software, 425–430
 Venn diagrams, 249, 251, 927
Graphics, producing, 913–914
Groups, working in
 procedures, 891–892
 roles, 891
Guide words, in dictionaries, 812–813

H

Had of, 692
Haiku, 26
Hanged, hung, 692
Hardware, computer, 915
Heavenly bodies, capitalizing names of, 716
Helping verbs, 457
Here, and subject-verb agreement, 612
Historical events, capitalizing names of, 716
Historical writing, present tense in, 586
Holey/holy/wholly, 834
Home page, 922
Homographs
 in dictionaries, 814
How-to writing. *See* Process explanation
Hung, hanged, 692
Hyperlink, 915, 922
Hypertext, 903, 922
Hyphens
 in compounds, 763
 to divide words at the end of a line, 764
 in numbers, 763
 with prefixes, 762

I

Icons, 913
Idea map, 66, 920
 See also Graphic organizers
Idiom, 922
Illustrations, colons to introduce, 733
Imagery, 138–139, 922
Immigrate, emigrate, 692
Imperative sentences, 552, 731, 922

Importance, order of, 84, 86
 transitions to show, 89
Impression, creation of, with description, 139
In, into, 692
Incidents, adding to paragraph, 82
Incomplete comparisons, 665
Indefinite articles, 464, 918
Indefinite pronouns, 451
 pronoun agreement with, 398, 643, 646
 and subject-verb agreement, 395, 601, 603
Independent clauses, 919
 See also Main clauses
In-depth reading, 839
Index, 810
Indirect characterization, 919
Indirect objects, 505
 diagraming, 572
Indirect quotations, 711–712, 752
Individuals, capitalizing names of, 713
Inductive reasoning, 922
Infinitive, 922
Infinitive phrases, 526
 as adjectives, 576
 as adverbs, 526, 576
 diagraming, 576
 distinguished from prepositional phrases, 526
 as nouns, 526, 576
Informal English. *See* English language
Information
 gathering, 72–75, 326
 recording, 328
 withholding, in creating suspense, 200
Information sources
 crediting, in research paper, 338–343
 reading critically, 328
Informational interviews, 73, 892
Informative writing. *See* Expository writing
Institutions, capitalizing names of, 714
Instructions, writing, 432–433
Intensifiers, 922
Intensive pronouns, 448
Interjections, 481, 922
 commas with, 409, 743
Internal conflict, 185
Internet, 418, 809–810, 899, 906, 909–911, 922

946 Index

Interpretation, 922
Interpreting messages, 885
Interrogative pronouns, 450
Interrogative sentences, 552, 732, 923
Intervening expressions, and subject-verb agreement, 392, 395, 609, 618
Interview, 892, 923
   conducting, as prewriting stage, 73–74, 892
   and sports reporting, 176–177
   structuring autobiography as, 22
   of subject of biography, 34
Intransitive verbs, 453
Introduction, 923
   in expository writing, 230, 238, 242, 246
   writing, 337
Invented anecdotes, 193
Invention. *See* Prewriting
Inverted word order, 923
   and subject-verb agreement, 392–393, 612
Irregardless, regardless, 693
Irregular comparison of modifiers, 661–662
Irregular verb, 582–584, 927
Italics
   with foreign words, 757
   with titles of works, 757
   for words, letters or numbers used to represent themselves, 758
Its, it's, 407, 761, 835

J

Jargon, 923
Journal, 12, 923
Journal Writing, 9, 12–15, 17, 21, 25, 28–31, 33, 39, 59, 63, 65, 69, 73, 77, 81, 85, 89, 93, 97, 101, 105, 111, 141, 145, 153, 157, 164, 180, 185, 189, 193, 197, 201, 205, 211, 229, 233, 237, 241, 245, 249, 253, 257, 259, 263, 265, 269, 275, 289, 293, 301, 305, 309, 315
   cause-and-effect diagram in, 297
   reader-response, 28–31
   reasons for, 12–13
   tips for writing in, 14

K

Keywords, 911

L

Languages, capitalizing names of, 714
Latin, words from, 786
Laws, capitalizing names of, 715
Lay, lie, 694
Leads
   for feature article, 259, 261
   writing effective, 259
Learn, teach, 694
Learning log, 923
Leave, let, 694
Lend, loan, borrow, 690
Less, fewer, 692
Let, leave, 694
Letter writing
   business, 413–420, 734
   colons in, 414, 415, 734
   commas in, 416, 747
   personal, 416
   persuasive, 291
Letters
   abbreviations formed from initials, 765
   apostrophe to form plural of, 761
Lexicon, 923
Library
   arrangement of, 799–800
   call number, 802
   card catalog, 799
   checking the shelves in, 805
   classification systems in, 802–805
   computer catalog, 799, 801–802
   computerized indexes, 808
   Dewey decimal system, 802–803
   general reference works in, 808–810
   Internet, 809
   locating books and other resources in, 801–805
   locating periodicals and newspapers in, 806–808
   online searching, 810
   Readers' Guide to Periodical Literature in, 806
   searching, 802
   specialized reference works in, 809
   using, 72

Library of Congress classification, 804
Lie, lay, 694
Life map, 21
Like, as, 695
Limerick, 26
Limiting words, 300–301
Line graphs, 253, 427
Linking verbs, 455
   nominative case after, 634
   subject-verb agreement with, 611
Listening, 434, 885–887, 891
   See also Active listening; Speaking
Listening and Speaking, 15, 27, 35, 67, 71, 75, 79, 87, 95, 151, 155, 183, 195, 199, 203, 239, 251, 267, 271, 291, 307
Listing, 64, 77, 139, 149, 237, 923
Lists, colon to introduce, 733
Literary analysis, 30, 104–107, 923
   author reflections on, 4–6, 134
   biography, responding to, 32–35
   comparison of literature to other endeavors, 61
   and connotations of words, 144–146
   and dialogue, value of, 190
   elements of literature, 269
   essay questions, analysis of, 262–266
   expository writing, discussion of, 227
   expository writing, varieties of, 230
   movies, analysis of, 308–310
   plagiarism, avoiding, 329
   and poetry, 24–27
   point of view, identifying, 204–206
   reader-response journal, 28–31
   and self-discovery, 8–11, 20–22
   themes, identifying, 104–105
   See also Writing about Literature
Literary performances, evaluating, 887
Literature. For a complete list of works herein, see p. xxv
Literature, responding to, 50, 119, 172, 220, 280, 320
   See also Writing about Literature

Literature, writing topics in, 137, 179, 207, 227, 287, 311
  in reader-response journal, 28–31
  about biography, 32–35
  See also Critical analysis
Loan, borrow, lend, 690
Logic
  analyzing opponent's, 298
  eliminating faulty, 296–297
Logical argument, constructing, 288–292
Logical fallacy, 296–297, 901, 923
Logical organization, 331, 346, 352
Loose, lose, 695, 835
Lose, loose, 695, 835

M

Magazine articles
  capitalization of titles, 717
  punctuation, 754
  researching in and citing, 326–327, 341–342, 356
Magazine writing, 122–131
Magazines
  and presenting, 101–102
Main clauses, 539, 919
Main idea, 926. *See also* Thesis statement; Topic sentence
  to develop, 93
  implied, 81
  of media message, 900
  in paragraph, 77
  supporting evidence, 81–82
  and unity, 80–82
Main verb, 457
Many a, compound subjects joined by, 394–395, 617
Maps, to explain and describe, 253, 845–846
Matching tests, 851
May, can, 690
Measure, abbreviations of units of, 767
Mechanics, on standardized tests, 855–856
  See also Capitalization; Punctuation
Media Connections, 4–5, 54–55, 134, 176–177, 224–225, 284–285
Media genres, 899, 909–911
Media literacy, 894
Media messages, 894
  analyzing, 899

evaluating, 899–901
producing, 902–904
Menus, computer, 912
Metaphor, 923
  in poetry, 25
Metric system, 767
Might of, must of, should of, would of, could of, 690
Misplaced modifiers, 404, 670–671
MLA Handbook for Writers of Research Papers, 329, 341, 343
Modern Language Association, 339
Modifiers
  dangling, 405, 406, 670
  irregular comparison of, 661–662
  misplaced, 404–406, 670–671
  See also Adjectives; Adverbs
Money expression, forming possessive of, 760
Money, numerals for, 769
Monuments, capitalizing names of, 715
Mood, 139, 923
  and setting, 135–136, 138, 148, 150, 203
Movie reviews
  drafting, 286
  evaluating a movie in, 310
  examining elements in, 309
  prewriting, 285
  providing background information, 308
  revising, 286
  writing, 311
Multimedia presentation, 915–917, 923
Multiple-choice items, on tests, 848–849
Music, writing in, 151, 303
Must of, should of, would of, could of, might of, 690
Myths
  comparing and contrasting two, 268–271
  definition of, 268, 269

N

Narrative writing, 174–221, 923
  analyzing point of view in, 204–207
  anecdotes in, 192–195, 221

basics of, understanding, 180–182
building on ideas in, 182
characters in, 180, 220
conflict in, 180, 182, 184–187, 208–211, 220
dialogue in, 188–191, 220
drafting, 178, 180–183, 185, 192, 202, 209–210, 218–219
editing, 178, 189, 202, 205, 211
generating ideas for, 181
literature model, 180, 186, 192, 198, 201, 205, 206, 212–219
plot in, 180, 182, 221
portfolio in, 221
presenting in, 178, 193, 211, 221
prewriting in, 177, 181–183, 185, 209
revising, 178, 210
sentence combining in, 369–372
setting in, 180
on sports, 176–179, 196–199, 221
suspense writing in, 200–203
telling stories in, 180
Narrator
  first-person, 204, 205, 207
  third-person limited, 204–207
  third-person omniscient, 204, 206, 207
National groups, capitalizing names of, 714
Nature writing, Case Study in, 224–227
Negative words, as adverb, 468
Negatives, double, 668
Network tree, 66
Newsgroups, 910
Newspapers
  capitalization of titles, 717
  as forums for presenting, 100–102
  locating, in library, 800, 806–808
  researching in and citing, 326–327, 341–342, 356

Nominative case, 919
   for personal pronoun, 633, 925
Nominatives, predicate, 507
Nonessential appositives, commas with, 409, 742
Nonessential clauses, 545–547
   commas with, 408, 545, 741, 919, 923
Nonessential elements, commas with, 741
Nonessential phrases, commas with, 408, 521, 523, 741
Nonfiction, 923
Nonrestrictive clauses, 545, 919
Nonverbal communication, 887, 890–891
Nor, compound subjects joined by, 394, 616
Note taking, 327–329, 837–838
   research paper, 326–329
   See also Study skills
Noun clauses, 550, 924
   diagraming, 578–579
   as object of preposition, 579
Nouns, 923
   abstract, 442
   amount, nouns of, 615
   collective, 393, 444, 614, 924
   common, 443, 482, 924
   compound, 760
   concrete, 442
   definition of, 439
   in direct address, 746
   as direct object, 504
   gerund as, 525
   infinitives and infinitive phrases as, 576
   as object complement, 506
   possessive, 441
   as predicate nominative, 507
   proper, 443, 713–719, 766, 924
   singular and plural, 440
   special, and subject-verb agreement, 614
   using precise, 145, 147, 442
   verbals as, 523–527
Nouns of amount, and subject-verb agreement, 392–393, 614–630
Number, amount, 688
Number, of nouns, pronouns, verbs, 924
Number, pronoun-antecedent agreement in, 640–644

Numbers
   apostrophe to form plural of, 761
   hyphens in, 763
   spelling out, 768
Numerals, 768–771

O

Object complements, 506
   diagraming, 572
Object of the preposition, 473
   noun clause as, 579
Objective case, 919, 925
   for personal pronouns, 633–636
   See also Objects
Objective tests, 848–852
Objects
   direct, 504, 572, 579
   indirect, 505, 572, 920
Observing
   and letter writing, 5
   and literature, 30
   with poetry, 24–27
   public speaking, audience reaction, 890
   See also Critical Thinking; Point of view
Omniscient point of view. *See* Point of view
Onomatopoeia, 924
Open-market forums, 102
Opinion, letters of, 420
Opinions, distinguishing between facts and, 293, 841, 924
Or, compound subjects joined by, 394, 616
Oral histories, 74
   See also Myths
Oral presentations, 102, 889–890
Oral tradition, 924
   See also Myths
Order of importance, 924
   in cause-and-effect, 240–242
   in descriptive writing, 138–142
   in persuasive writing, 292–294
   in research writing, 324–336
   in writing process, 84–90
   See also Organization
Organization, 924
   cause-and-effect, 84, 86, 234, 235, 242
   charts, 429–430
   chronological, 84, 182
   effect-to-cause pattern, 235

   importance, 84, 86
   logical, 253, 346
   spatial, 84, 85, 141, 143
Organizations
   abbreviations of, 356, 765
   capitalizing names of, 714
Outline, 330–331, 924
   correct form for, tips on, 330
   for autobiographical sketch, 21
   for class notes, 837
   for essay test, 264
   for formal speech, 889
   for research paper, 330–331, 334–335
   using word processing, 906
   in writing process, 77
Overgeneralizations, avoiding, 300–301

P

Paragraphs, 924
   adding examples or incidents to, 82
   adding facts and statistics to, 82
   definition of, 76
   pronouns in, 90
   repetitions in, 90
   revising, 92–95
   structure of, 76–78
   supporting details in, 80–81
   synonyms in, 90
   topic sentence in, 80–81
   transitions in, 89
   writing coherent, 88–91
   in writing process, 77–78
Parallelism, 94, 364, 924
Paraphrase, 327–328, 924
Parentheses
   capitalization of first word of sentence in, 712
   with other marks of punctuation, 751
   to set off supplemental material, 750
Parenthetical documentation, 339, 350–355, 924
Parenthetical expressions, commas with, 410, 743
Participial phrases, 523, 527
   commas to set off, 523, 744
   diagraming, 575
Participles, 523, 924
   as adjectives, 523
   commas to set off, 744
   diagraming, 575

Index **949**

past, 523
present, 523
Parts of speech
   adjectives, 461
   adverbs, 467
   conjunctions, 475
   interjections, 481
   nouns, 439
   prepositions, 473
   verbs, 452
Passed, past, 695, 835
Passive voice, of verb, 596, 924
Past participles, 523
   confusion between past form and, 403
   improper use of, 404
Past, passed, 695, 835
Past perfect tense, 590
Past tense, 452, 587
Peer editing, 98, 235, 255, 289, 924
Peer response. *See* Peer editing
Periodicals indexes, using, 806–807
Periodicals, locating, in library, 800, 806–808
Periods
   with abbreviations, 765
   to end declarative sentence, 552, 731
   to end imperative sentence, 552, 731
   quotation marks with, 755
Person, pronoun-antecedent agreement in, 640–644
Personal letters, 4–6, 416
Personal pronouns, 446
   nominative case for, 633–634, 635
   objective case for, 633–634, 635
   possessive case for, 633–634
Personal response to literature, 50, 119, 172, 220, 280, 320
   See also Literary analysis
Personal writing, 924
   adding details to, 18
   autobiography, 19–23, 51
   about biography, 32–35
   definition of, 17
   distinguishing fact from opinion, 296–298
   drafting, 6, 38
   editing, 6, 39
   literature models, 8, 12, 16, 22, 24, 25, 26, 37, 40–49
   personal essay in, 16–19

poetry, 24–27
portfolio for, 51
presenting, 51
prewriting, 5, 37
process of, 8–39
reader-response journal in, 28–31, 33
recognizing bias. *See* Bias
revising, 6, 38
selecting topic for, 17–18
self-portraits in, 8–11
sources for, 9
thesis statement for, 18
word choice in, 18
Personification, 924
   in poetry, 25
Persuasive message, 886
Persuasive techniques, 901
Persuasive writing, 924
   checking reasoning in, 296–299, 321
   connotations in, 302
   constructing logical argument in, 288–291
   drafting, 286, 288, 313–314
   editing, 286, 294, 310, 315
   editorials in, 304–307, 321
   effective use of evidence in, 296–299
   letter-writing, 291
   limiting words in, 300–301
   literature models in, 294, 298, 304, 314, 316–319
   movie reviews in, 284–287, 308–311, 321
   portfolio in, 321
   presenting, 315, 321
   prewriting, 285, 296–313
   revising, 301, 314
   selecting evidence in, 294–295
   sentence combining in, 377–380
   specific words in, 301
   using language to advantage in, 300–303
Phrases, 924
   adjective, 519
   adverb, 519
   appositive, 635
   definition of, 521, 523, 924
   gerund, 525, 527
   infinitive, 526, 576
   participial, 523, 744
   prepositional, 519, 529, 744, 924
   verb, 457–460, 523, 924

Pie chart. *See* Circle graph
Plagiarism, avoiding, 329, 338, 924
Planets, capitalizing names of, 716
Plot, 106, 924
   in literature, 261
   in narrative, 180, 183, 221
Plurals, 440–441
   apostrophe and, 759–761
   collective nouns, 444
   compound nouns, 760
   numbers, dates, 768–769
Poetry, 24–27, 925
   experimenting with, 26
   poetic devices in, 25
   self-expression in, 24
   sensory details in, 25
   traditional versus free verse in, 24–25
   writing, 27
Point of view, 925
   analyzing, in narrative, 204–207
   drafting, 205
   examining effect of, 205–206
   first-person, 204, 205
   identifying, 204
   limited. *see* third-person *below*
   literature model for, 204–205
   omniscient. *see* third-person *below*
   prewriting, 205
   third-person limited, 204–207
   third-person omniscient, 204, 206
Political parties, capitalizing names of, 714
Portfolios, 51, 120, 173, 221, 281, 321, 357, 925
Positive form, of comparison, 461, 469, 659–660, 918
Possessive case, nouns in, 441, 759–761, 919
Possessive pronouns, 447, 633, 925
   as adjectives, 461, 919
Possessives, apostrophes with, 759–760
Precede, proceed, 695
Predicate adjectives, 507
   diagraming, 573
Predicate nominatives, 507
   diagraming, 573
   noun clauses as, 550
   and subject-verb agreement, 392
Predicates, 925
   complete, 496, 510

950   Index

compound, 499, 512, 517
predicate nouns. *See* predicate nominatives
predicate pronouns. *See* predicate nominatives
position of, in sentence, 501–503, 512
simple, 495, 512
word order of, 501–503, 512
See also Verbs
Prefixes, 824–825
hyphens with, 762
Prepositional phrases, 519, 924
as adjective phrases, 519
as adverb phrases, 519
commas with, 744
diagraming, 574
intervening, and subject-verb agreement, 609–610
Prepositions, 925
compound, 473
definition of, 473
list of common, 473
object of the, 473, 488
Present participles, 523
Present perfect tense, 589
Present tense, 586
Presenting, 59, 100–103, 925
autobiography, 22, 39
community forums for, 101
contests for, 101
in descriptive writing, 136, 163, 173
in expository writing, 256, 259, 275, 281
in narrative writing, 111, 178, 193, 211, 221
open market forum for, 102
oral, 102, 889–890
in personal writing, 39, 51
in persuasive writing, 297, 315, 321
school forums for, 101
sharing writing, 100–103
in sports narratives, 178
TIME Facing the Blank Page, 123, 131
Prewriting, 55, 58, 62–74, 906, 925
addressing audience, 70
in autobiography, 21, 37
in biography, 33
brainstorming, 15, 21, 105, 147, 149, 155, 187, 199, 202, 205, 209, 233, 267, 273, 313
charts in, 33, 237, 238, 269, 309

choosing topic, 325–326
clustering, 14, 17, 51, 149
collecting, 63
comparison frame in, 249, 270, 271, 310
in descriptive writing, 135, 141, 149, 161
determining purpose, 68–69
diagrams in, 101, 245, 253, 263
in expository writing, 225, 229, 233, 236–238, 258, 264, 265, 273
in feature articles, 258–259
freewriting, 10, 11, 13, 15, 17, 21, 27, 51, 62, 63, 67, 76, 105, 119, 120, 149, 181, 183, 186, 189, 202, 313
gathering information in, 72–75, 326
idea map in, 66, 920
identifying audience and purpose, 68–71
interviewing, 73–74, 261
life map in, 21
listing, 64, 77, 139, 149, 237
in narrative writing, 177, 180–181, 185, 190, 194, 198, 209
narrowing focus in, 66
network tree in, 66
note taking in, 75, 327–329
outlining in, 330–333
in personal writing, 5, 37
in persuasive writing, 285, 305–313
questioning, 9, 65, 75, 182
in research paper, 75, 324–333
spider map in, 17, 51
in sports narrative, 177
talking in, 181
TIME Facing the Blank Page, 122, 124–125
turning into paragraph, 76
using word processing, 906
Venn diagram in, 249, 251
word maps in, 253
Primary source, 324, 342
Principle parts of verbs, 581
Prior knowledge, 925
Proceed, precede, 695
Process explanation, 236–239
conclusion in, 238
drafting, 237
introduction in, 238

literature model for, 236
prewriting for, 237
transitions in, 237, 238
Progressive forms of verb, 592, 927
Prompts. *See* Writing prompts
Pronoun-antecedent agreement, 640–647
with indefinite pronoun antecedent, 643, 646
in number and gender, 640
in person, 641
Troubleshooter for, 396–397
Pronoun case. *See* Case.
Pronoun reference. *See* Pronouns, antecedent for, avoiding unclear reference in
Pronouns, 446, 925
antecedent for, 640–647
with and as appositives, 635
after *as,* 637
avoiding shifts in, 400
avoiding unclear reference in, 645–646
definition of, 446
demonstrative, 449
as direct object, 504
indefinite, 451, 643
intensive, 448
interrogative, 450
as object complement, 506
in paragraph writing, 90
person, first, 446–448
person, second, 446–448
person, third, 446–448
personal, 446
possessive, 447, 634
as predicate nominative, 507
reflexive, 448
relative, 450
after *than,* 637
Proofreading, 39, 111, 163, 211, 275, 315, 925
of essay answer, 266
symbols for, 98, 411
TIME Facing the Blank Page, 123, 130
See also Editing; Revising; Troubleshooter
Propaganda, 925
Proper adjectives, 465
capitalization of, 720
Proper nouns, 443
abbreviations of, 765

capitalization of, 713–719
forming possessive of ancient, ending in *-es* or *-is,* 759
Prose, 925
Publishing, 925. *See also* Presenting
TIME Facing the Blank Page, 123, 131
using word processing, 908
Punctuation
apostrophes, 406–407, 759–761
colons, 733–734, 751
commas, 409–411, 738, 743–744, 746–747
dashes, 749
end marks, 731–732
hyphens, 762–764
italics (underlining), 757–758
parentheses, 712, 750–751
quotation marks, 752, 754–755
semicolons, 541, 615, 735–737, 743, 755
See also specific marks
Puns, 791
Purpose, 925
determining, in prewriting, 68–69
identifying audience, and, 70, 434, 888
identifying, in persuasive writing, 289
Purpose for writing
to analyze/explain, 240–243, 324–356
to describe, 132–163
to develop main idea, 93
to express/discover oneself, 2–39
to inform, 223–275
to persuade, 282–315
to tell a story, 174–211

Q

Question mark, 732
to end interrogative sentence, 732
parentheses with, 751
quotation marks with, 755
Questions
answering, in narrative writing, 182
in prewriting, 65, 75, 182
who, whom in, 638
See also Interrogative sentences
Quotation marks

and comma, 190
with dialogue, 190
for direct quotations, 752
with other marks of punctuation, 755
with titles of short works, 754
with unusual expressions, 754
Quotations
adding, to news stories, 258–259
capitalization of first word of, 711–712
checking for accuracy, 259
colons before, 733
direct, 752
ellipses in, 351
indirect, 752
in research papers, 327–329, 350–355

R

Raise, rise, 695
Reader-response journal, 28–31, 33, 50. *See also* Journal writing
Readers' Guide to Periodical Literature, 806
Reading
evaluation of material in, 841–842
styles of, 839–840
Reading comprehension, on standardized tests, 853–854
Reason is because, 695
Reasoning, checking, in persuasive writing, 296–299
Red herrings, eliminating, 296
Reference materials
almanacs, atlases, yearbooks, 808–810
bibliographies, 72, 326, 810
books, 341–342
dictionary, 812–816
encyclopedia, 341–342, 808–810
libraries, 72, 801–805
magazines, 326–327, 338–341
newspapers, 326–327, 338–341
periodical index, 326–327, 806–807
thesauruses, 816–817
References
commas to set off parts of, 746
numerals in, 769

Reflecting, 51, 120, 173, 221, 281, 321, 357
Reflexive pronoun, 448
Regardless, irregardless, 693
Regular verb, 927
Relative pronoun, 450
Religious terms, capitalizing, 717
Repetitions, in paragraph writing, 90
Report. *See* Reference materials; Research paper
Representation, 893–904, 925. *See also* Viewing and Representing
Research paper
avoiding plagiarism in, 329, 338
bibliographies, 72, 326, 810
citing sources in, 338–343, 357
conclusion in, 337, 355
drafting, 334–337, 357
endnotes in, 339, 340
footnotes in, 339, 340
format, 348–349
introduction in, 337
note cards, 328
outlining, 330–331, 334–335
parenthetical documentation in, 339, 350–355
portfolio in, 357
preparing final copy, 348
presenting completed paper, 356
prewriting, 324–333, 357
proofreading, 348, 357
quotations, 327–329, 350–355
researching, 324–329
revising, 344–347, 357
source materials. *See* Reference materials
student model, 350–356
summary statement in, 337, 333
taking notes for, 326–329
thesis statement in, 332–333, 350
titles, 348
types of, 324
using word processing, 906
working bibliography for, 326
works-cited list, 339–343, 356
Researching, 925
for feature story, 55, 254–261
for formal speech topic, 889
for nature story, 225
for research paper, 326–329
for sports narrative, 177
using word processing, 906

Respectfully, respectively, 697
Responses from readers, 50, 119, 172, 220, 280, 320
Restatement, colon to introduce, 733
Restrictive clauses, 545. *See also* Adjective clauses; Essential clauses
Review, 925
Revising, 59, 110, 925
   in cause-and-effect writing, 242
   in character descriptions, 158
   checking details in, 140, 150, 158
   checking for coherence in, 94, 95
   checking for meaning in, 93
   checking for unity in, 94
   in classification, 246
   in descriptive writing, 136, 139, 140, 146, 158, 162
   essay answers, 266
   expository writing, 227, 229, 232, 246, 254, 259, 274
   in feature story, 56, 259
   formal speeches, 889
   graphic referrals in text, 254
   improving paragraphs in, 92–94, 95
   for incorrect verb tense, 402–403
   for misplaced or dangling modifiers, 405–406
   for missing commas, 409–411
   for missing or misplaced possessive apostrophe, 406–407
   in narrative writing, 178, 182, 198, 210
   in nature story, 226
   personal writing, 6, 38
   in persuasive writing, 301, 314
   for pronoun-antecedent agreement, 396–397
   for pronoun reference, 399–400
   for pronoun shift, 401
   in research paper, 344–347
   for run-on sentences, 390–391
   for sentence fragments, 388–389
   for shift in verb tense, 404
   for subject-verb agreement, 392–396
   TIME Facing the Blank Page, 123, 128–129
   using limiting words in, 297, 300–301
   using thesaurus in, 301
   using transitions in, 94
   using word processing, 907
   See also Editing; Proofreading
Rise, raise, 695
Roget's Thesaurus, 816
Role-playing, 34
Root, 925
Round character, 919
Rubrics. *See* Writing rubrics
Run-on sentences, 555, 747, 926
   correcting, 390–391

S

Said, says, 697
Says, said, 697
Scandinavian words, 787
Scanning, 839
School courses, capitalizing, 717
Science, writing topics in, 83, 235
Screenplay, 134–137
Search commands, 911
Search engines, 910
Secondary source, 324
   See also Reference materials
Self-editing, 97
Semicolons
   versus commas, 735–736
   in compound sentences, 390–391, 541, 555, 735
   parentheses with, 751
   quotation marks with, 755
   to separate main clauses, 735
Sensory details, 926
   in narrative writing, 198
   in poetry, 25
   in suspense writing, 202
   in writing process, 81
Sentence combining, 360–385
   in description, 369–372
   in exposition, 372–375
   literature-based activities, 380–385
   in narration, 369–372
   in persuasion, 377–380
Sentence fragments, 388–389, 553
   correcting, 553
   use of, by professional writers, 553
Sentence variety, 358–385, 926
Sentence writing exercises, 365–385, 442, 445, 447, 455, 460, 466, 480, 498, 503, 509, 513, 520, 524, 542, 544, 551, 552, 588, 593, 597, 616, 620, 639, 664, 667, 773
Sentences, 495, 926
   capitalization of, 711–712
   complete predicate in, 496
   complete subject in, 496
   complex, 543, 926
   compound, 541, 926
   compound-complex, 543, 926
   compound predicate in, 498
   compound subject in, 498, 500
   declarative, 552, 731, 920
   definition of, 495
   diagraming, 571–579
   exclamatory, 552, 732
   fragments, 553
   imperative, 552, 731, 922
   interrogative, 552, 732, 923
   inverted, and subject-verb agreement, 612–613
   parts of, 495
   run-on, 390–391, 555, 747, 926
   simple, 541, 926
   simple predicate in, 495
   simple subject in, 495
   subject of, 495
   topic. *See* topic sentence
   varying, 552
   word order in, 501–503
Sequence of events, Plot and writing process, 60, 238
   See also Organization
Series
   commas in, 410, 739
   semicolons in, 736
Set, sit, 697
Setting, 106, 926
   in expository writing, 260
   in narratives, 180, 202
Sexist language, avoiding, 640
Ships, capitalizing names of, 716
Short-answer tests, 849
Short stories, 190, 194, 202, 205, 206, 209, 212–219
   See also Story writing
Should of, would of, could of, might of, must of, 690
Simile, 926
   in poetry, 25
Simple predicates, 495, 541
Simple sentences, 541, 926
Simple subjects, 495, 541
Sit, set, 697
Skimming, 839
Slang, 797
Social studies, writing topics in, 11, 15, 95, 120, 281, 357

Index **953**

Software, 906–908, 914, 915. *See also* Computers; Word processing
Sound effects, in poetry, 25
Source cards, 326–327
Spacecraft, capitalizing names of, 716
Spatial order, 84, 85, 141, 143, 926
　in descriptive writing, 141
Speaking
　answering audience questions, 890
　formal speeches, 888–890
　informally, 888
　nonverbal techniques, 890
　oral presentations, 102, 889–890
　practicing, 890
　preparing materials, 890
　verbal techniques, 890
　in writing conference, 38, 110, 162, 210, 274, 314
　See also Active listening
Special nouns, and subject-verb agreement, 614
Spelling, 35
　adding *ly*, 831
　adding *ness*, 831
　cede, ceed, sede, 828
　doubling final consonant, 830
　easily confused words, 155, 834
　editing for, 35
　forming compound words, 831
　forming plurals, 831
　learning to spell new words, 832
　list of frequently misspelled words, 833–834
　prefixes, adding, 829
　suffixes and silent *e*, 829
　suffixes and final *y*, 830
　unstressed vowels, 829
　See also Nouns, Plurals; Verbs
Spelling checker, 99, 207, 907
Spider map, 17, 845
Spoonerisms, 788
Sports narrative, 196–199
　Case Study in, 176–179
　editing, 178
　finding idea for, 177
　literature model, 198
　prewriting, 177, 197–199
　publishing, 178
　researching, 177
　writing, 178, 196–199
SQ3R study method, 840–841
Standard English, 926

Standardized tests, 853–858
　analogies on, 854–855
　grammar, usage, and mechanics items on, 855–856
　reading comprehension items on, 853–854
　test-taking strategies, 857–858
　types of, 853
　vocabulary items on, 854–855
States, abbreviations for, 766
Static character, 919
Stationary, stationery, 835
Statistics, adding to paragraph, 82
Story ideas, generate, 67
Story writing, 180–183. *See also* Narrative writing
Storyboard, 902, 916
Student models, 10, 13, 18, 20, 27, 28, 30, 32, 34, 63, 86, 146, 154, 156–157, 190, 194, 196, 202, 206, 229, 242, 246, 266, 268, 306, 350–356
Study skills
　analyzing graphics and illustrations, 425–430, 843–846
　classification of library systems, 802–805
　classification of subject, 244–247
　comparison frame, use of, 270
　evaluation of reading, 841–842
　evidence study of, 293
　graphics in, 253, 843–844
　logic, 296–298
　logical argument, 288–290
　outline for research paper, 330–331, 334–335
　reading efficiently, 839–840
　SQ3R study method in, 840–841
　taking class notes, 837–838
　time management in, 838–839
　See also Tests
Style, 926
　develop your own, 360–363, *and following exercises*
Subject, 926
　complete, 496
　compound, 498, 541
　noun clause as, 550, 578
　position of, in sentence, 501
　simple, 495
　word order of, 501–502
Subject-by-subject comparisons, 250
Subject complements, 507, 573

　predicate adjective, 507
　predicate nominative, 507
Subject directories, 910
Subject-verb agreement, 609–631
　and collective nouns, 393, 614
　and compound subjects, 394–396, 616–617
　diagraming, 571
　and indefinite pronouns, 399, 619
　with intervening expressions, 392, 395, 618
　in inverted sentences, 392–393, 612
　with linking verbs, 611
　and nouns of amount, 393, 615
　and predicate nominatives, 392
　with special nouns, 614
　with *there*, 612
　with titles of works, 615
Subordinate clauses, 540, 638, 919
　adjective, 545–546
　adverb, 548
　noun, 550
　and varying sentence structure, 569
　who, whom in, 638
Subordinating conjunctions, 477, 540, 548, 920
Suffixes, 825–826
　spelling words with 828, 829, 831
Summary, 327–329, 431
Summary statement, 926
　in research paper, 332–333, 337
Superlative form of modifiers, 461, 469, 659–661, 918
Supplemental materials, parentheses to set off, 750
Supporting details
　adding to expository writing, 232–235
　criteria for selecting, 233–234
　organizing, 234
Supporting your opinion. *See* Logical argument
Suspense writing, 200–203, 926
　drafting, 202
　foreshadowing in, 200
　literature model in, 201
　withholding information in, 200
Syllables, 814

954　Index

hyphens to indicate, 764
Symbols, 901
   apostrophe to form plural of, 761
Synonyms
   in dictionaries, 814
   in paragraph writing, 90
   See also Thesaurus

T

Tables, 253, 843
   using word processing software, 425, 914
Tag questions, commas to set off, 746
Take, bring, 690
Teach, learn, 694
Technical writing, 431–433
Technology, impact of, on language, 795–796
   learning with, 909–911
Technology Tip, 908, 911, 915
Tense of verbs. *See* Verbs
Tests. *See also* Study skills
   essay, 262–266
   fill-in items, 850
   multiple-choice items on, 848–849
   objective, 848–851
   preparing for, 848, 853
   for short-answer items, 849
   standardized tests, 853–854
   strategies for taking, 857–858
   time management in, 265, 851
   for true-false items, 849
Than, pronouns after, 637
Than, then, 697, 835
That there, this here, 697
Theme, 926
   in literature
      explaining, 104–107
      identifying, 105
      writing about, 106
Then/than, 697, 835
There, and subject-verb agreement, 612
Thesaurus, 146, 301, 816
   dictionary-style entries in, 817
   formats in, 816
These kinds, this kind, 694
Thesis statement, 230, 926
   for cause-and-effect writing, 241

for essay test, 263
   for personal essay, 18
   for research paper, 332–333, 350
   See also Topic sentence
They, indefinite use of, 400
Thinking skills. *See* Critical Thinking Skills
Third-person limited narrator, 204–207
Third-person pronoun. *See* Pronouns
Third-person omniscient narrator, 204, 206
This here, that there, 697
This kind, these kinds, 694
Time
   abbreviations for, 765
   colon in expressions of, 734
   forming possessive of, in expressions, 760
   numerals for, 768–769
   using transitions to show, 89
TIME Facing the Blank Page, 122–131
Time lines, 926
   to organize facts and statistics, 82
Time management
   for study skills, 838–839
   for tests, 265, 851
Time order, 926
Titles of persons, 415
   abbreviations of, 767
   capitalizing, 713
   commas with, 746
Titles of works
   articles in, 757
   capitalizing, 717
   italics with, 757
   quotation marks with short, 754
   and subject-verb agreement, 615
Tom Swifties, 791
Tone, 926
Tool bars, computer, 912–913
Topic, finding a, 17, 258, 325
Topic sentence, 76, 78, 138, 335, 926
   in descriptive paragraph, 140
   stating main idea in, 80–81
   See also Thesis statement
Trade names, capitalizing, 715
Trains, capitalizing names of, 716
Transitions, 354, 926

in descriptive writing, 142, 143
   in paragraph writing, 89
   in persuasive writing, 290
   in process writing, 237, 238
   in research papers, 336, 344–347, 354
Transitive verbs, 453
Troubleshooter, 386–411
True-false tests, 849

U

Underlining. *See* Italics
Understood subject, 501
Unity, 927
   checking for, 92, 94
Unusual expressions, quotation marks with, 754
URL, 909, 927
Usage
   on standardized tests, 855–856
   subject-verb agreement, 609–622
   verb tenses and voice, 586–597
Usage information, in dictionaries, 815
Using Computers
   copy feature on, 271
   creating visual aids on, 61, 247, 255
   desktop publishing on, 23
   distinguishing main idea from supporting details on, 79
   e-mail, 71
   entering and retrieving reader-response entries, 31
   gathering information on, 75
   generating topics on, 67
   grammar program on, 299
   mail-merge feature on, 307
   note-taking options on, 327
   organizing details on, 159
   outlining feature on, 183
   page layout program on, 255
   refining your topic on, 71
   searching the Internet on, 67, 231, 261, 295, 311
   spelling checker on, 99, 207, 907
   storing information on, 75
   thesaurus on, 303
   visually distinguishing copy on, 103

V

Vague pronoun references, avoiding, 645–646
Venn diagrams, 249, 251, 927
Verb phrases, 457, 523, 927
   definition of, 523
   gerunds, 525
   infinitives, 526
   participles, 523
Verbals, 927
   definition of, 523
   gerunds, 525
   infinitives, 526
   participles, 523
Verbs, 927
   action, 198, 453
   active voice of, 596
   agreement with subject, 609–630
   auxiliary, 457, 927
   commands, 501
   compatibility of tenses, 594
   definition of, 452
   emphatic forms of, 592, 927
   future perfect tense of, 927
   future tense of, 588, 927
   helping, 457
   incorrect tense in, 402–403
   intransitive, 453
   irregular, 582–583, 927
   linking, 455, 611
   passive voice of, 596
   past tense of, 587, 927
   present perfect tense of, 589
   present tense of, 586, 927
   principal parts of, 581
   progressive forms of, 592, 927
   regular, 582, 927
   shifts in, 594
   tenses of, 452, 586–607, 927
   transitive, 453
   Troubleshooter for, 402–404
   unnecessary shift in tense, 401
   voice of, 596–597
Video production, 902–903, 915–917
Viewing and Representing, 11, 19, 23, 31, 61, 83, 91, 99, 103, 107, 143, 147, 159, 187, 191, 207, 235, 243, 247, 255, 261, 295, 299, 894–904
Viewpoint. *See* Point of view
Visual design, 894–896, 912–914
Visual learning. *Writer's Choice* contains numerous instructional visuals. 14, 77, 86, 88, 94, 197, 230, 236, 238, 252, 253, 297, 325, 567
Visual messages, 894–898, 912–914, 915–917
Visuals, 427–430, 433, 890
Vocabulary
   developing, 819–820
   eponym, 785
   learning from context, 820–822
   prefixes, 824
   recognizing parts of a word, 823–826
   roots of words, 823
   on standardized tests, 854–855
   suffixes, 825
   See also Words
Vocal clues, interpreting, in listening, 885
Voice, 135, 334, 927

W

Web sites, 103, 927
   development of, 903–904
   as sources of information, 909
   tracking, 911
Webbing. *See* Clustering
Well, good, 666
Where at, 697
Who, in questions and subordinate clauses, 638
Who, whom, 638
Wholly/holey/holy, 834
Whom, in questions and subordinate clauses, 638
Whom, who, 638
Word roots, 823–824
Word processing, 927
   to display information, 425–430
   drafting, 907
   editing, 907
   outlining, 907
   prewriting, 906
   publishing, 908
   researching, 906
   revising, 907
   software, 906–908, 912–914
   and writing process, 906–908
   See also Computers
Words
   acronyms, 795
   apostrophe to form plural of, 761
   blending, 795
   compounds, 795
   connotations of, 144–145
   prefixes, 824–825
   roots of, 823–824
   suffixes, 825–826
   See also Vocabulary
Works-cited list, 339–343, 356
   format for, 342, 356
   formats for entries, 340–343, 356
   parenthetical documentation for, 339
World Wide Web, 927
Would of, could of, might of, must of, should of, 690
Writer's Assistant, 908
Writer's Portfolio, 51, 120, 173, 221, 281, 321, 357
Writing about art, 27, 67, 79, 81, 85, 87, 91, 107, 142, 143, 147, 195, 231, 251, 261, 291, 302, 491, 515, 535, 567, 629, 655, 707
Writing about literature
   analyzing character descriptions, 156–159
   analyzing point of view in a narrative, 204–207
   analyzing setting, 203
   comparing and contrasting two myths, 268–271
   explaining theme, 104–107
   writing about biography, 32–35
   writing a movie review, 308–311
   See also Literature, responding to
Writing across the curriculum. *See* Cross-curricular writing
   in art, 27, 87, 91, 107, 143, 187, 195, 231, 251, 291
   in broadcast journalism, 199
   in civics, 51, 321
   in geography, 173
   in government, 19
   in health, 239
   in history, 155, 191
   in literature, 221, 311
   in media studies, 203
   in music, 151, 303
   in science, 83, 235, 251, 267
   in social studies, 11, 15, 95, 120, 281, 357
Writing application, 493, 517, 537, 569, 607, 631, 657, 685, 709, 729, 779
Writing instructions, 432–433

Writing process, 52–120, 927
  drafting, 38, 110, 122, 126–127, 161–162, 209–210, 273–274, 313–314, 334–337
  editing, 39, 111, 123, 130, 163, 211, 275, 315
  presenting, 39, 111, 123, 131, 163, 211, 275, 315, 348–349
  prewriting, 37, 109, 122, 124–125, 161, 209, 273, 313, 324–333
  proofreading, 123, 130
  publishing, 123, 131
  revising, 38, 110, 123, 128–129, 161, 210, 274, 314, 344–347
  and word processing, 906–908
Writing prompts, 11, 15, 19, 23, 27, 31, 35, 61, 67, 71, 75, 79, 83, 87, 91, 95, 99, 103, 107, 143, 147, 151, 155, 159, 183, 187, 191, 195, 199, 203, 207, 231, 235, 239, 243, 247, 251, 255, 261, 267, 291, 295, 299, 303, 307, 311, 329, 333, 337, 343, 347, 356
Writing rubrics, 11, 15, 19, 23, 27, 31, 35, 61, 67, 71, 75, 79, 83, 87, 91, 95, 99, 103, 107, 143, 147, 151, 155, 159, 183, 187, 191, 195, 199, 203, 207, 231, 235, 239, 243, 247, 251, 255, 261, 267, 271, 291, 295, 299, 303, 307, 311
Writing skills and strategies, 122–131

Y

You, indefinite use of, 400, 641
Your, you're, 446, 761

Index 957

ACKNOWLEDGMENTS

Text

UNIT ONE Letter to Gwendolyn Brooks by Sandra Cisnero, reprinted by permission of Susan Bergholz Literary Services, New York. All rights reserved.

From *Selected Poems* by Langston Hughes. Copyright 1926 by Alfred A. Knopf, Inc., and renewed 1954 by Langston Hughes. Reprinted by permission of Random House, Inc.

"Reflection" from *A Light in the Attic* by Shel Silverstein. Copyright © 1981 by Shel Silverstein. Reprinted by permission of HarperCollins Publishers.

From *I Know Why the Caged Bird Sings* by Maya Angelou. Copyright © 1969 and renewed 1997 by Maya Angelou. Reprinted by permission of Random House, Inc.

UNIT TWO "The Quest for Hispanic Roots" by Lorenzo Chavez. Reprinted by permission of the author.

From *The Kitchen God's Wife* by Amy Tan. Copyright © 1991 by Amy Tan. Used by permission of Amy Tan and the Sandra Dijkstra Literary Agency.

UNIT THREE From *The Crystal Cave* by Mary Stewart. Copyright © 1970 by Mary Stewart. Reprinted by permission of HarperCollins Publishers, Inc.

UNIT FOUR Reprinted courtesy of *Sports Illustrated*: "Salute to an Amazing Ironman" by Lisa Twyman Bessone, July 2, 1990. Copyright © 1990, Time Inc. All rights reserved.

From *How the Garcia Girls Lost Their Accents*, by Julia Alvarez. Copyright © 1991 by Julia Alvarez. Published by Plume, an imprint of Dutton Signet, a division of Penguin USA, Inc., and originally in hardcover by Algonquin Books of Chapel Hill. Reprinted by permission of Susan Bergholz Literary Services, New York. All rights reserved.

UNIT FIVE From "Counting Cacti" by Suzanne Winckler. *Audubon*, November 1985. Reprinted by permission.

From *Of Wolves and Men* by Barry Lopez. Copyright © 1978 by Barry Holstun Lopez. Reprinted by permission of Sterling Lord Literistic, Inc.

UNIT SIX "Petrie's 'Toy Soldiers' Has Glitches" by Melanie McFarland. *New Expression*, May 1991. Reprinted by permission of the author.

UNIT SEVEN From *The Concord Review*, Copyright 1991 by The Concord Review, P.O. Box 661, Concord, Massachusetts 01742. Reprinted by permission.

Photo

Cover KS Studios; **vi** The Estate of John Lennon, 1989; **vii** Courtesy Bernice Steinbaum Gallery, New York; **viii** *The Starry Night*, (1889). Vincent Van Gogh. Oil on Canvas, 29 x 36 1/4". Collection, The Museum of Modern Art, NY. Acquired through the Lillie P. Bliss Bequest.; **ix** Iran, late 12th-/early 13th-century. Ceramic 3 3/8 x 8 1/2". The Brooklyn Museum 86.227.61. Gift of the Ernest Erickson Foundation.; **x** Courtesy the Chapingo Chapel of the National School of Agriculture and the Instituto Nacional de Bellas Artes, Mexico; **xi** file photo; **xii** PhotoDisc, Inc; **xiii** P. and G. Bowater/The Image Bank; **xiv** © 1985, The Estate of Keith Haring; **xv** (t)file photo, (b)The Telegraph Colour Library/ FPG; **xvi** Kent Fleming/Lifestyles; **xvii** (t)file photo; **xx** © 1990 Thames & Hudson, Ltd., London. Photo by David Lavender; **xxi** (t)Courtesy of the Lilly Library, Indiana University, Bloomington, Indiana, (b)PhotoDisc, Inc; **xxii** © 1986 Courtesy of Collier, Macmillan Publishers, London. Photo by Ralph J. Brunke; **xxiii** Scala/Art Resource, NY; **xxiv** PhotoDisc, Inc; **xxv** Stella, Frank. *Kastura*. (1979) Oil on epoxy on aluminum, wire mesh, 9' x 7'8" x 30" (292.1 x 233.7 x 76.2 cm). Collection, The Museum of Modern Art, New York. Acquired through Mr. And Mrs. Victor Ganz; **xxxi-1** Edward Owens/Art Resource, NY; **2-3** Steve Niedorf/The Image Bank/PictureQuest; **4** (t)John Dyer, (b)David Muench; **5** Ralph J. Brunke; **6** John Dyer; **8** The Estate of John Lennon; **14** Ralph J. Brunke; **19** Boston Athenaeum; **24** D. Taylor/H. Armstrong Roberts; **27** Courtesy Fundación Rufino Tamayo/Art Resource, NY; **29** (t)*Lord of the Flies* courtesy of Castlerock Entertainment/Columbia Pictures, (b)Eric Futran; **32** Bettmann/CORBIS; **41** Bequest of Maxim Karolik. Courtesy, Museum of Fine Arts, Boston; **43** Courtesy Bernice Steinbaum Gallery, New York; **45** Courtesy of the Evans-Tibbs Collection, Washington, DC; **47** Courtesy of the collection of the B. R. Brazeal Family, Atlanta, Georgia; **51** Steve Niedorf/The Image Bank/ PictureQuest; **52-53** Alan & Linda Detrick/Photo Researchers; **55** Manuel Chavez/The Houston Post; **58** Nippon Television Network, Japan; **62** Matthew Naythons/Stock Boston; **70** Eric Futran; **72** Private Collection; **74** Dorothy Gallagher/The Estate of Hannah Lambertson Nesbitt; **78** The Metropolitan Museum of Art, Gift of Frederic H. Hatch, 1926; **79** Collection of the Chase Manhattan Bank, N.A.; **81** The Bridgeman Art Library Ltd./Art Resource, NY; **85** SCALA/Art Resource, NY; **87** Iran, late 12th-early 13th-century. Ceramic 3 3/8 x 8 1/2". The Brooklyn Museum 86.227.61. Gift of the Erenest Erickson Foundation; **91** Carl Van Vechten Gallery of Fine Arts, Fisk University, Nashville, Tennessee; **92** The Far Side © 1990 Universal Press Syndicate. Reprinted with permission; **100** The Peninsula Outlook; **102** Bob Daemmrich/The Image Works; **106** Paramount Pictures Corporation. All Rights Reserved; **114** Tomie Arai; **117** Courtesy Bluett and Sons, London/ Bridgeman Art Library, London; **120** Alan & Linda Detrick/Photo Researchers; **132-133** Shaun Egan/Tony Stone Images; **134** John Dougan; **135** Eric Futran; **136** Photofest; **138** Frank Siteman/Stock Boston; **141** (l, c)Budd Symes, (r)SuperStock; **142** Nancy Thill; **144** Collection Grimaldi, Monaco/SuperStock; **147** Marc Chagall. *Paris Through the Window*. 1913. Oil on Canvas, 53 1/2 x 55 3/4". Solomon R. Guggenheim Museum, NY. Gift, Solomon Guggenheim, 1937. Photo: David Heald. Copyright Solomon R. Guggenheim Foundation; **150** Masahiro Sano/The Stock Market; **152** Courtesy Holly Solomon Gallery, New York; **156** David Wenzel; **167** The Academy of Natural Science/CORBIS; **170** Francis G. Mayer/ CORBIS; **173** Shaun Egan/Tony Stone Images; **174-175** O. Alamany & E. Vicens/CORBIS; **176** Eric Futran; **177** Tracy Frankel; **178** Eric Futran; **181** Bob Daemmrich/Stock Boston; **184** Photofest; **187** Courtesy of the artist and J. Cacciola Gallery; **188** Calvin and Hobbes © 1985 Universal Press Syndicate. Reprinted with permission; **195** Courtesy Frumkin/Adams Gallery, New York. Private collection; **196** Nicholas Foster/The Image Bank; **200** Grant Wood, *Death on Ridge Road*, 1935 oil on masonite, 32 x 39" Collection Williams College Museum of Art, Williamstown, Massachusetts. Gift of Cole

..3; **201** Eric Futran; **204** Sherry Rayn Barnett/Michael ...rchives; **215** Courtesy the Chapingo Chapel of the National ...ool of Agriculture and the Instituto Nacional de Bellas Artes, ...exico; **218** Thames and Hudson, Ltd., London. Photo by David Lavendar; **221** O. Alamany & E. Vicens/CORBIS; **222-223** Arnold Zann/Black Star; **225** David Smart; **226** (l)David Smart, (r)Art Wolfe; **228** Ralph J. Brunke; **232** Obremski/The Image Bank; **240** NASA; **241** Scott Anger/Liaison International; **247** Reprinted with permission from Clear Light Publishers from Old Father Story Teller by Pablita Velarde; **251** Spaulding Collection. Courtesy, Museum of Fine Arts, Boston; **252** Andrew Christie/© Discover Magazine; **256** Mike Mazzaschi/Stock Boston; **261** Jake Rajs/The Image Bank; **262** Slug Signorino; **276** file photo; **277** Nancy Schutt; **279** Courtesy of the Thomas Burke Memorial Washington State Museum, Catalog Number 2.5E 1543. Photo by Eduardo Calderon; **281** Arnold Zann/Black Star; **282-283** CORBIS; **285** Scott Raffe; **286** Ralph J. Brunke; **287** Morray Alcosser/The Image Bank; **288** Camera Five; **291** Field Museum of Natural History, Chicago, Neg # A 108764 c, Cat. #8258; **292** Julie Houck/Stock Boston; **296** L. Roberts/H. Armstrong Roberts; **300** *For Better or Worse* © 1990 Lynn Johnston. Reprinted with permission of Universal Press Syndicate; **302** SCALA/Art Resource, NY; **303** Pablo Picasso, *Two Acrobats with a Dog*. Paris, spring 1905. Gouache on cardboard, 41 1/2 x 29 1/2". Collection, The Museum of Modern Art, New York, Gift of Mr. And Mrs. William A.M. Burden; **308** Photofest; **318** Collection New York State Museum. Photo by Peter T. Furst; **321** CORBIS; **322-323** Richard Hamilton Smith/CORBIS; **324** Chicago Historical Society. ICHi-1893; **325** P. and G. Bowater/The Image Bank; **330** Stephen Kennedy; **334** Courtesy of the U.S. Department of the Interior, National Park Service, Edison National Historic Site, West Orange, New Jersey; **338** (l)Photoworld/FPG International, (r)Courtesy of General Motors Corp; **344** Bettman/CORBIS; **356** Mark J. Plotkin/Conservation International; **357 358-359 385** Richard Hamilton Smith/CORBIS; **386-387** Henry Diltz/CORBIS; **436–437** Dave G. Houser/CORBIS; **461** The Telegraph Colour Library/FPG International; **477** Steve Woit/Stock Boston; **491** Anna Mary Robertson Moses (Grandma Moses) 1860—1961 *Early Skating*. (1951) tempera or oil on masonite 17 7/8 x 24" The Brooklyn Museum 83.122.1. Bequest of R. Thorton Wilson; **505** (t)Shawn Weiner/Lifestyles, (b)Kent Fleming 1991/Lifestyles; **515** The Metropolitan Museum of Art, The Michael C. Rockefeller Memorial Collection, Gift of the Matthew T. Mellon Foundation, 1960; **535** The Metropolitan Museum of Art, Rogers Fund, 1936 (JP 2517); **553** Giraudon/Art Resource, NY; **567** Robert Duncan; **586** The Estate of Harold Edgerton. Courtesy of Palm Press, Inc; **596** Don Smetzer/Tony Stone Images; **605** National Museum of American Art, Washington, D.C./Art Resource, NY; **615** Jerry Wachter/Focus on Sports; **629** The Metropolitan Museum of Art, Fletcher Fund, 1963 (63.210.11); **655** The Metropolitan Museum of Art, Amelia B. Lazarus Fund, 1910; **659** (t)Benn Mitchell/The Image Bank, (c) David Brownell/The Image Bank, (b)Janeart Ltd./The Image Bank; **683** Courtesy of The Phillips Collection, Washington, DC; **707** Tate Gallery, London/Art Resource, NY; **715** Steve Elmore/Tony Stone Images; **723** (l)NAA-Thomas C. Woods Memorial Collection, Sheldon Memorial Art Gallery, University of Nebraska–Lincoln, (r)Joseph Pobereskin/Tony Stone Images; **727** Joslyn Art Museum, Omaha, Nebraska; **752** Gino Beghe Encore Art Prints, New York; **762** Elyse Lewin/The Image Bank; **767** Chuck Solomon/Focus on Sports; **777** Rockwell Kent, *The Trapper*, 1921. Oil on canvas, 34 x 44", Collection of Whitney Museum of American Art. Purchase 31.258; **780–781** Kunsthalle, Bern/Bridgeman Art Library, London/SuperStock; **785** (inset)The Bridgeman Art Library Ltd./Art Resource, NY, **785 through 797** (gears) VCG/FPG International; **787** Bettman/CORBIS; **788** The Hulton Deutsch Collection, London; **789** Bettman/CORBIS; **791** Courtesy of The Lilly Library, Indiana University, Bloomington, Indiana; **793** (l)Jon Feingersch/Stock Boston, (c)Robert Frerck/Odyssey Productions, (r)Andre Gallant/The Image Bank; **794** By permission of Johnny Hart and Creators Syndicate, Inc; **795** Jay Freis/The Image Bank; **796** Bill Horsman/Stock Boston; **812** Ralph J. Brunke; **813** File Photo; **819** PEANUTS reprinted by permission of UFS, Inc; **838** Stephen Kennedy; **845** Courtesy of Collier, Macmillan Publishers, London. Photo by Ralph J. Brunke; **895** Terry Donnelly/Tony Stone Images; **896** Panos; **898** Digital work by Industrial Light & Magic. © Lucasfilm Ltd. & tm. All Rights Reserved. Used Under Authorization; **904** File Photo.